Clarke's Offshore Tax Planning

1st edition 1986	8th edition 2001	17th edition 2010
2nd edition 1990	9th edition 2002	18th edition 2011
3rd edition 1994	10th edition 2003	19th edition 2012
Reprinted 1995	11th edition 2004	20th edition 2013
4th edition 1996	12th edition 2005	21st edition 2014
Special edition 1997	13th edition 2006	22nd edition 2015
5th edition 1998	14th edition 2007	23rd edition 2016
6th edition 1999	15th edition 2008	
7th edition 2000	16th edition 2009	

Clarke's Offshore Tax Planning

Giles Clarke
MA (Cantab), PhD, FTII

Dominic Lawrance
BA (Dunelm), MA (Sussex), CPE, Solicitor

Twenty-third Edition

Members of the LexisNexis Group worldwide

United Kingdom	RELX (UK) Limited trading as LexisNexis, 1–3 Strand, London WC2N 5JR and 9–10 St Andrew Square, Edinburgh EH2 2AF
Australia	Reed International Books Australia Pty Ltd trading as LexisNexis Butterworths, Chatswood, New South Wales
Austria	LexisNexis Verlag ARD Orac GmbH & Co KG, Vienna
Benelux	LexisNexis Benelux, Amsterdam
Canada	LexisNexis Canada, Markham, Ontario
Chile	LexisNexis Chile Ltda, Santiago
China	LexisNexis China, Beijing and Shanghai
France	LexisNexis SA, Paris
Germany	LexisNexis GmbH, Dusseldorf
Hong Kong	LexisNexis Hong Kong, Hong Kong
India	LexisNexis India, New Delhi
Italy	Giuffrè Editore, Milan
Japan	LexisNexis Japan, Tokyo
Malaysia	Malayan Law Journal Sdn Bhd, Kuala Lumpur
New Zealand	LexisNexis New Zealand Ltd, Wellington
Singapore	LexisNexis Singapore, Singapore
South Africa	LexisNexis, Durban
USA	LexisNexis, Dayton, Ohio

© 2016 RELX (UK) Limited

Published by LexisNexis

ISBN for this volume: 9781405799911

Printed and bound by CPI Group (UK) Ltd, Croydon, CR0 4YY

Visit LexisNexis at: www.lexisnexis.co.uk

Preface

In this, the twenty-third edition of *Offshore Tax Planning*, I am once again joined in authorship by Dominic Lawrance. As in previous years, we have also had valuable contributions from a number of Dominic's colleagues at Charles Russell Speechlys LLP. To all I am grateful.

The closing date for this edition is 31 August 2016, but one or two developments thereafter are included.

Giles Clarke

30 September 2016

Author Biographies

Giles Clarke

Giles Clarke has been the author of *Offshore Tax Planning* since it was first published in 1986. He is also the General Editor of *Spitz & Clarke: Offshore Service* (*LexisNexis* looseleaf), which carries commentary, legislation and cases relevant to offshore jurisdictions. He now works for his own Jersey-based consultancy company, Giles Clarke International Ltd.

Dominic Lawrance

Dominic is a partner in Charles Russell Speechlys LLP. He has been working in the field of private client law for about 14 years. He specialises in advising internationally mobile high net worth clients, especially RNDs. He also has an interest in philanthropy by international individuals and families, and cross-border giving.

Other contributors from Charles Russell Speechlys LLP:

Alice Wilne
Lisa-Jane Dupernex
Sangna Chauhan
Robert Birchall
Helen Coward
Catrin Harrison

Contents

Contents

PART B   THE DOMESTIC LEGAL FRAMEWORK

Section I: Characterisation

Section II: The Territorial Limits of UK Taxation

Section III: Residence and Domicile

Section IV: The Remittance Basis

Section V: The Meaning of Remittance

Contents

Contents

PART D   INTERNATIONAL AGREEMENTS

Section I: Double taxation treaties

Section II: EU Law

Table of Statutes

Table of Statutes

Table of Statutes

Other Jurisdictions

Canada

Table of Statutory Instruments

Table of Cases

A

Table of Cases

B

C

Table of Cases

Table of Cases

G

Table of Cases

H

I

Table of Cases

J

M

N

O

Table of Cases

R

S

T

U

V

W

X

Decisions of the European Court of Justice are listed below numerically. These decisions are also included in the preceding alphabetical list.

Table of Cases

Part A

PLANNING

PLANNING

Section I

UK Resident and Domiciled Individuals: use of Offshore Structures as Tax Shelters

Chapter 1
OFFSHORE TRUSTS

INTRODUCTION

1.1 The offshore trust is the vehicle of choice in offshore tax planning. By offshore trust is meant simply a trust where all the trustees are non-UK resident, with the result that the trust itself is non-UK resident (see CHAPTER 42).

This chapter evaluates whether and if so to what extent a UK domiciliary can secure tax advantages by creating a new offshore trust now. In making this evaluation two distinct issues have to be kept in mind. One is the tax planning opportunities afforded by any trust, whether offshore or UK resident. The second is the difference in tax treatment which may be secured by the trust being offshore.

As this chapter explains, anti-avoidance legislation now makes it difficult, in practice, for an offshore trust to be used by a UK domiciled settlor as a tax shelter. However, in particular situations, opportunities remain.

ALL TRUSTS

1.2 Any trust, whether offshore or UK resident, can confer inheritance tax advantages. These advantages are achieved so long as the terms of the trust prevent the settlor from benefiting and he does not in fact benefit. Provided that condition is satisfied, the trust property is outside the settlor's estate for IHT purposes.

A trust does not, of course, deliver complete freedom from IHT. Under the relevant property regime described in CHAPTER 60, the trust suffers a 6% charge every ten years, and pro rata charges on distribution. These charges, over time, can when aggregated equal or even exceed the death rate but, being regular and at modest level, are more manageable.

In some cases, reliefs such as business property relief may eliminate or reduce the relevant property charges. Business property relief is discussed later in this chapter. But it is not an argument in favour of trusts as distinct from personal ownership, for personally held assets attract the relief as well.

As indicated above it is essential that the settlor is excluded and does not benefit. This is required by the gift with reservation rules (see CHAPTER 83). Should those rules be infringed, the trust is pointless for effectively the settled property is treated as remaining in the settlor's estate for IHT purposes. Indeed, the IHT position is worse than if the trust had not been made at all, for the 6% charges under the relevant property regime remain levied as well.

INCOME SHELTERING

1.3 The prime difference between an offshore trust and a UK resident trust is that an offshore trust shelters income. In order to do this, the trust must be discretionary in form for, where the trust gives a beneficiary entitlement to income, the income is treated as that of the beneficiary (see para **8.3**). So too, the settlor must be excluded and not receive any benefit. This is the same requirement as is applicable to IHT, but is occasioned by different legislation, namely the income tax settlement code described in CHAPTER 75. In contrast to IHT, the exclusion must extend to the settlor's spouse as well as to the settlor personally (see para **75.2**).

Income sheltered

1.4 In general it is only foreign source income that can be sheltered, for the UK source income of non-residents is subject to UK tax (see CHAPTER 64). The exception for UK dividends and interest described in CHAPTER 64 does not apply to trusts with UK beneficiaries (see para **64.8**).

There is a means whereby an offshore trust can shelter UK dividends, namely holding the investments through an offshore holding company, for then the relief for non-resident recipients of dividends is fully in point (see para **64.5**). But holding companies have a number of drawbacks, reviewed in CHAPTER 6, and should not be put in place without careful consideration of all the implications. For portfolio investment a better means of securing exposure to UK equities is through offshore mutual funds (as to which see further CHAPTER 3).

Deferral

1.5 Strictly the sheltering of income is merely a deferral, for UK tax liabilities are likely to be incurred if income or capital is distributed to UK resident beneficiaries. As is described in CHAPTERS 8 and 9, income distributions are taxed as a new source, and capital distributions are subject to the non-transferor benefits charge under the transfer of assets code, ITA 2007, ss 731–735. This charge is made to the extent that income has been or is retained in the structure. In contrast to CGT (see below), the tax on capital distributions is not inflated by notional interest to reflect the element of deferment. But to some extent this is counterbalanced by the fact that tax under ss 731–735 does not give credit for any tax suffered by the trustees when the income matched with the benefit arose (see para **71.11**). Nor does tax under ss 731–735 reflect the dividend rates which would have been available had the trust income been dividend income receivable by the beneficiary directly.

In some cases, however, deferral can turn out to be a complete shelter. Such follows if capital is distributed to a beneficiary who is non-UK resident in the tax year of the distribution, for then no tax is chargeable under ss 731–735 (see para **70.14**). There is at present no requirement for him to be non-resident for more than five tax years, as ss 731–735 are not one of the provisions caught by the temporary non-residence rule (see paras **41.38** to **41.43**).

Equally cogently, there may come a time when beneficiaries who have remained in the UK look for not the accumulated capital but merely current income. Such is taxable as income when distributed, but the income available is enhanced, like a pension fund, by the prior gross accumulation of income within the trust. Moreover, the rate of tax on such distributions may be reduced either by spreading them around low income beneficiaries (see further para **10.11**) or by appointing life interests to one or more beneficiaries. As explained in CHAPTERS **60** and **61**, such appointments are now without IHT consequences and they enable the income to attract the dividend rates in the hands of the beneficiaries (see para **8.6**). It should however be noted that if a strategy of distribution is adopted, the recipients cannot include minor children of the settlor, as any distributions to them are taxable as his income (para **75.8**).

CAPITAL GAINS TAX

1.6 An offshore trust can also serve as a shelter of capital gains. In two respects sheltering of capital gains is easier than with income. The first is that all forms of non-resident trust are separate entities for CGT purposes, so the potential to shelter gains from tax is not limited to trusts which are discretionary (see para **37.5**). The second point is that the gains which may be sheltered include both those on non-UK assets and those on UK assets (see para **37.6**), albeit that one class of UK asset is excepted, namely UK residential property (see CHAPTER **65**).

But in reality the use of an offshore trust to shelter gains is more challenging than its use for income. The reason is that if the settlor is both UK resident and domiciled, all the net gains are assessed as his in the tax year in which they arise if what is called a defined person is an actual or potential beneficiary or receives a benefit. The term 'defined person' means not only merely the settlor and his spouse, but also his children and grandchildren and their respective spouses, and companies controlled by all or any of these individuals. These rules are laid down by TCGA 1992, s 86 and Sch 5, and are considered in detail in CHAPTER **76**.

The extended definition of 'defined person' means TCGA 1992, s 86 is the most far-reaching anti-avoidance legislation directed at trusts, whether resident or non-resident. All other anti-avoidance legislation applies only if the settlor or his spouse can or do benefit. The result of s 86 is that gains in an offshore settlement can be attributed to the settlor in many cases where the income is not so attributable. But the difficulties posed by s 86 should not be overstated. There are a number of methods by which its impact can be avoided or, if not avoided, managed.

Dead settlor

1.7 It is self-evident that the rules attributing income and gains to the settlor cannot apply if he is dead. Indeed, gains realised at any time in the tax year of death cannot be attributed to him either (TCGA 1992, Sch 5 para 3).

TCGA 1992, s 86 is therefore inapplicable to an inter vivos settlement whose settlor has died and also to any testamentary settlement. To be an effective shelter a testamentary settlement needs to have been constituted by the deceased's will rather than by any variation made by the beneficiaries because, for CGT purposes, the settlor of a trust established by deed of variation is the individual who was entitled under the will, rather than the deceased (TCGA 1992, s 68C). The same applies to income tax (ITA 2007, s 472).

Non-resident settlor

1.8 Although this chapter presupposes that the settlor is currently UK resident, he may at some stage become non-resident. Should he do so, the attribution of gains to him is precluded provided that he remains non-resident for more than five years (see paras **29.6**, **29.7** and **76.19**).

Planning on the basis of eventual non-residence may be appropriate where the settlor is now working in the UK but envisages eventual retirement abroad. In such cases, an investment strategy of gain deferral may be adopted. One such strategy is investment through mutual funds, whether domestic or offshore. The advantage of such investment is that gain recognition is deferred until the participation in the fund is realised, as gains on investments within the fund are not attributed to investors (see further paras **3.12** and **3.13**).

Trusts with all defined persons excluded

1.9 Settlements where defined persons are all excluded are difficult to achieve given that the term includes both children and grandchildren. But settlements are sometimes made by remote relations or friends of the beneficiaries, and these operate as a shelter of gains as well as income.

An important context in which such a settlement may be considered is to hold shares in newly formed private companies. The sum required for the settlement may be modest and the promoter of the company may be able to persuade a friend or distant relative to contribute the necessary funds for the trustees to invest into the company.

Where the friend or relative genuinely makes the settlement out of his own resources, he should be the sole settlor for CGT purposes. However, it should be stressed that where this is not so, the promoter will normally fall to be treated as a settlor. Thus a person is deemed to be a settlor under the settlement code if he made or entered into the settlement directly or indirectly, if he directly or indirectly provided funds, or if he made reciprocal arrangements for another person to make the settlement (ITTOIA 2005, s 620; see further para **75.18**).

A difficulty is often that the promoter is working for the company and building it up and it is feared that this makes him settlor, as happened in *Butler v Wildin* [1989] STC 22. However, there will be good arguments that the promoter is not a settlor if he is remunerated on a proper commercial basis and the risk and cost of financing the business is borne by the company or the trustees (cf paras **75.17** and **75.22**). It is to be noted that in *IRC v Mills* [1974] STC 130, Viscount Dilhorne said it is not the provision of services but of funds which makes a person settlor. So too in *Jones v Garnett* [2007] STC 1536, it was the expectation that the husband would receive uncommercial remuneration which brought the arrangement within the settlement code.

Investment selection

1.10 Perhaps the simplest method of managing the s 86 charge is minimising the returns that are taxed as capital gain. It is possible to construct a portfolio which satisfies all normal investment aspirations where none of the return is taxed as capital gain. The vehicle for achieving this is the non-reporting offshore fund, for here the return on redemption is treated as an offshore income gain under the offshore fund legislation (see CHAPTER **95**). This means it is deemed to be income regardless of the fund's underlying investments and it is only taxed on the settlor if he is within the transferor charge under the transfer of assets legislation (see CHAPTER **82**). In broad terms this legislation is in point in the same circumstances as the income tax settlement code, ie if he is a beneficiary under the settlement or has or does benefit (see CHAPTER **70**).

Many investment houses offer or indeed encourage clients to invest through in-house mutual funds and such can frequently result in a saving of costs, most notably by ensuring the trust holds a single asset, namely the interest in the fund, rather than a multiplicity of assets, namely all the securities in an investment portfolio. In many respects, investment through non-reporting funds can make commercial sense as well as tax sense.

Deferral or shelter

1.11 As with income, the strategies outlined above are strictly only a deferral. The capital payment rules in TCGA 1992, s 87 treat capital distributions or benefits as gains of the beneficiaries to the extent of trust gains (see CHAPTER **77**) and similar rules, described in CHAPTER **82**, match offshore income gains to capital distributions or benefits. Assuming the recipient beneficiary is UK resident, income tax is the result if the distribution is matched with offshore income gains, and otherwise the tax charged is CGT. Further, and in contrast to income tax, where the tax in issue is CGT the element of deferral is countered by supplemental tax which represents notional interest at 10% for up to six years. At its highest the ensuing rate of CGT is 32% (see paras **77.48** to **77.50**).

These charges are not, however, in point if the recipient beneficiary is non-resident when the capital distribution or benefit is matched with the trust gains (see para **10.2**). As with income, therefore, the deferral can be converted to a complete shelter. But such conversion is in one respect more difficult than with income, for neither the income charge on offshore income gains nor the CGT charge on ordinary gains is avoided unless the recipient is non-UK resident for more than five years (see paras **29.6** and **41.40** to **41.42**).

Assuming the beneficiaries remain UK resident, distributions can sometimes be made in a tax-efficient manner if spread among multiple beneficiaries as described in CHAPTER **10**. Otherwise if the strategy is in due course the pension-type strategy described above in relation to income, the fund generating the income will have been enhanced by the prior gross capital gains as well as by the prior gross income.

CREATING NEW SETTLEMENTS

1.12 The discussion above has shown that an offshore trust from which the settlor and his spouse are excluded can represent good tax planning. The difficulty, however, is passing the value into the settlement in the first place. Here the principal tax which has to be faced is IHT, where the position is the same as applies on the creation of a UK settlement.

The key point is that a gift into trust cannot be a potentially exempt transfer and so is immediately chargeable (see para **60.2**). As a result of the changes made to IHT by FA 2006, this is so regardless of the form the trust takes. The result is that once the settlor's nil-rate band (currently £325,000) is exceeded tax at 20% is charged. The rate of 20% rises to 40% if the settlor dies within three years of the transfer, to 32% if he dies in the fourth year after the transfer, and 24% if he dies in the fifth year.

Tax at this level is a deterrent. This is particularly so as outright gifts to individuals qualify as potentially exempt transfers. In other words, no tax is payable provided the donor survives seven years (IHTA 1984, s 3A). Given this, IHT may be thought to be a powerful argument against trusts, whether offshore on onshore, outweighing any advantages of the kind described earlier in this chapter. However, there are several scenarios under which the entry charge is not made.

Nil-rate band trusts

1.13 One such scenario is if the amount settled is within the settlor's nil-rate band. Provided that a putative settlor has made no chargeable transfers in the previous seven years, he can give an amount equal to the nil-rate band into a trust without charge to IHT. If he then waits a further seven years without making any other chargeable transfers, he can repeat the exercise, up to whatever limit the nil-rate band then stands at.

The values thus able to be settled may not be great, but they can be enhanced by two factors. The first is that, in a marriage, the spouses each enjoy a nil-rate band, thereby enabling the tax-free amount to be doubled up. Second, and much more importantly, once value is settled into a trust, any growth in value is in the trust and outside the settlor's estate. Thus if growth assets are acquired by the trust, the value in the trust after a few years may be much greater than the nil-rate band. This is particularly in point where the trust assets are shares in young or newly formed private companies.

Normal expenditure out of income

1.14 The second scenario in which the entry charge is not made is if the gift into settlement qualifies as normal expenditure out of income. Under IHTA 1984, s 21, a transfer is exempt if it is part of the donor's normal expenditure and is made out of his income, leaving him with sufficient income to maintain his normal standard of living. It is necessary to establish a pattern of regular annual transfers, either retrospectively by what has happened over a number of years, or by prior commitment (see *Bennett v IRC* [1995] STC 54). But once these conditions are met, the gifts are free of IHT and this is so whether the donee is an individual or a trust. These days some wealthy individuals have incomes which greatly exceed what is needed to maintain a normal standard of living. With careful planning the surplus can be passed into trust.

Business property relief

1.15 A third relief from the entry charge is business property relief (IHTA 1984, ss 103–114). This important relief was first introduced in 1976 and originally was partial in that it reduced the value transferred by only 50%. Now however the principal relief, for unquoted shares, is 100% with the result that the transfer of such assets to a settlement is free of IHT (IHTA 1984, ss 104 and 105(1)(a) and (bb)).

The conditions for relief are complicated and must be considered with care before effecting any tax planning in reliance on them. The two most important points are first that the settlor must have owned the shares for at least two years (IHTA 1984, s 106) and second that the business of the company must not consist, wholly or mainly, in the making or holding of investments (IHTA 1984, s 105(3)). There are special rules for holding companies, the broad effect of which requires the group as a whole to be non-investment (IHTA 1984, s 105(4)(b)). Further even if a company as a whole escapes the investment restriction, the relief can be partially disapplied if the value of the company reflects excepted assets, ie assets not used or required for use in its business (IHTA 1984, s 112).

Another point to keep in mind is that the additional tax payable on a gift into settlement should the settlor die within seven years may apply, notwithstanding the availability of the relief when the property was transferred to the trust. This is the case if, at the time of his death, the trust has sold the unquoted shares or they otherwise no longer qualify for relief (IHTA 1984, s 113A(2)). In such a case the 20% entry charge is not clawed back, but the additional tax payable by reason of early death is charged.

CGT difficulties

1.16 Although IHT is the principal tax that has to be faced on the creation of a non-UK resident settlement, CGT has to be considered as well since the transfer of the assets to the settlement is a disposal for CGT purposes. As the settlor is treated as connected with the settlement, the disposal takes place at the market value of the assets concerned (TCGA 1992, ss 18 and 286). This means that if the assets are standing at a gain, a liability to CGT results.

The practical result of this is that the assets settled should normally be cash or individual assets not pregnant with gain or a portfolio of assets not showing an overall net gain. This may be easy to achieve with a nil-rate band settlement or where what is settled is normal expenditure out of income. But the CGT occasioned by the creation of the settlement can be a real issue with the one category of asset where substantial value can be settled without occasioning IHT, namely assets eligible for BPR. By their nature shares in successful companies are often pregnant with gain and, under UK domestic law at least, no form of hold-over relief is available as the recipient trustees are non-UK resident (TCGA 1992, ss 166 and 261).

There are two approaches which may be taken to this CGT issue. The first is in point where any non-UK resident settlement created to own the assets would be within s 86, as it will be in the normal case where the beneficiaries include the settlor's children or grandchildren. In such circumstances, the better course may be to create a UK resident trust, where the gain can normally be held over and business property relief used to avoid the IHT entry charge (TCGA 1992, s 165). If in due course the business is sold, CGT is paid on the full gain. While the trust asset is still cash, the trust can emigrate as described in Chapter 30 without further CGT consequences and thereafter be managed in accordance with the suggestions made in this chapter. The important point is that the value then in the trust will have got there without incurring the IHT entry charge.

The second approach may be more appropriate if, were an offshore trust created, the s 86 charge would not be in point by the time the business asset is sold. Such could be the position if the settlor is proposing to emigrate or the trust is one of those from which all defined persons can be excluded. Here, if the latent gain is modest, it may be appropriate to accept a CGT charge on the creation of the settlement, particularly as until any sale the tax can be paid by instalments, albeit interest-bearing (TCGA 1992, s 281). Business property relief means the value will enter the trust without IHT entry charge and the post settlement gain will be sheltered from tax on an arising basis provided TCGA 1992, s 86 is then inapplicable.

FOUNDATIONS

1.17 Foundations are now much better understood in the UK, and as a result a UK domiciliary minded to form a trust might consider a foundation as an alternative. In general such a course of action is not to be recommended. The main reason is that the very point which makes a foundation appropriate for non-domiciliaries does not apply, namely familiarity with foundations and unfamiliarity with trusts (see para **18.1**). But perhaps equally compelling is the point that although a foundation can equate to a trust it is not in fact a trust and may therefore not replicate the desired form of trust in any detail. Some of the issues this raises are discussed in paras **18.8** to **18.12** in relation to non-domiciliaries and they apply equally in the present context.

COMPLIANCE

1.18 It is fundamental to all legitimate planning using offshore trusts that the settlor and beneficiaries disclose all relevant liabilities on their tax returns and that information reasonably requested by HMRC is supplied. It should not be forgotten that HMRC have wide information gathering powers, notably ITA 2007, s 748 (where liability under the transfer of assets code is suspected) and TCGA 1992, s 98 (which relates to TCGA 1992, s 87), as well as the more general powers to obtain information in FA 2008, Sch 36.

Compliance obligations arise when an offshore trust is set up. Thus a person making a non-resident settlement must, if he is resident and domiciled in the UK, make a return to HMRC within three months giving details of the trustees and the date on which the settlement was made (TCGA 1992, Sch 5A para 3). If assets are settled, a CGT disposal may have to be notified. An account has to be delivered to the Capital Taxes Office unless the value of the gift into settlement is less than 80% of the nil-rate band or, in the case of cash and securities, 100%. In applying these limits account is taken of chargeable transfers within the previous seven years and business property relief is ignored (Inheritance Tax (Delivery of Accounts) (Excepted Transfers and Excepted Terminations) Regulations 2008 (SI 2008/605)).

A duty often overlooked is that imposed on professionals by IHTA 1984, s 218. Section 218 applies to any person who in the course of a trade or profession is concerned with the making of a settlement. He must within three months make a return to HMRC if he believes the trust is non-resident and the settlor is domiciled in the UK or deemed to be domiciled in the UK under IHTA 1984, s 267 (see CHAPTER 45). Non-compliance carries a penalty of up to £300 (IHTA 1984, s 245A(1)). Section 218 is not breached if the settlor has returned the settlement to HMRC, or some other person has made a s 218 return. Section 218 is normally thought of as applying to UK lawyers and other professionals and it does certainly apply where such persons advise or prepare documents. In connection with offshore trusts created by UK domiciliaries HMRC argue that s 218 catches the offshore trustees themselves. It may be doubted whether s 218 is extra-territorial in this way as it is a reasonable inference that its purpose was to secure information from UK professionals which would not readily be forthcoming from foreign trustees. But there is little to be gained by not making s 218 returns and offshore trust providers should do so whenever the settlor is known to or believed to have an actual or deemed UK domicile.

1.19 In recent years, the regime of penalties for non-compliance has become more onerous, and even inadvertent careless omissions can attract substantial penalties if left uncorrected. As is explained in CHAPTER 97, penalties are more severe if triggered by offshore structures set up in non-transparent jurisdictions and legislation are being brought into force to target the so-called enablers of offshore evasion as well as the taxpayers themselves. For all these reasons it is not only essential to ensure any offshore trust is tax compliant when created but also equally important to monitor its continuing tax compliance thereafter.

Chapter 2
OFFSHORE COMPANIES

INTRODUCTION

2.1 This chapter explains the extent to which an offshore company can be used in tax planning. Its subject is offshore companies in the direct ownership of UK resident and domiciled individuals as distinct from companies owned by offshore trusts. The use of companies owned by offshore trusts is analysed in detail in CHAPTER 6.

Perhaps the greatest use of offshore companies in the direct ownership of UK residents is as a shelter of business profits. This is a topic in its own right and is covered in CHAPTER 24. This chapter, by contrast, deals with companies used for holding investments or other assets – in other words passive investment holding companies.

ANTI-AVOIDANCE LEGISLATION

2.2 As a general rule, passive investment companies cannot serve as a shelter of income and gains. Their use is countered by two codes, the transfer of assets code directed at income and TCGA 1992, s 13 directed at gains.

Transfer of assets

2.3 The transfer of assets code attributes the income of an offshore company to its UK resident shareholder if he has power to enjoy its income and falls within the definition of the term transferor (ITA 2007, s 720). This charge is described in detail in CHAPTER 69. A shareholder or even a loan creditor inevitably has power to enjoy a company's income, for one head of power to enjoy is that the income increases the value of assets held by the taxpayer (see para **69.13**). The shareholder or loan creditor is a transferor if he caused the company to be set up and/or subscribed for shares or otherwise transferred assets to it (see para **69.48**).

It will be apparent from this that a UK resident and domiciled individual who sets up an offshore investment holding company to hold some or all of his investments is within the transferor charge. As such the company's income is taxed as his, with the result the company brings no income tax advantage.

There are certain defences which preclude liability under the code, most notably a motive defence and an EU defence, described in CHAPTERS 73 and 74 respectively. These defences, however, are most unlikely to be in point in the contexts now being considered given that the company is being set up for tax planning reasons and is likely to be formed in an offshore jurisdiction. Certainly it is most unwise to use them as the basis for planning. There used to be an argument that the transferor charge was precluded by double tax treaties insofar as the company was resident in a treaty jurisdiction and the treaty gave the treaty partner sole taxing rights over the income in question. But changes made in 2013 preclude this (see para **69.37**).

Section 13

2.4 TCGA 1992, s 13 is analysed in Chapter **88**. It attributes the gains of non-UK resident close companies to participators who own more than 25% of the company. It thus precisely counters sheltering of the kind envisaged here. Indeed even if a given participator owns less than 25% of the company, apportionment is possible if he, with connected persons, own more than 25% of the company.

Like the transfer of assets code, s 13 is subject to a motive defence. This is explained in paras **88.4** and **88.37** and its effect is that s 13 only applies if the acquisition holding or disposal of the company's assets formed part of arrangements whose purposes included the avoidance of CGT or corporation tax. Although the contrary can be argued, the prudent view is that the arrangements that have to be looked at include the formation and capitalisation of the company. On this basis, the motive defence is not in point where, as is postulated here, the company is envisaged as a CGT shelter.

Where the position with s 13 is better than with the transfer of assets code is that what is apportioned to participators is not the full amount of the company's gains. Thus indexation is allowed, and currency and other loan relationship gains are excluded (see paras **88.7** and **88.8**). But these advantages, if such they be, are countered by a harsh rule for losses: in contrast to the individual's personal losses the company's losses cannot be carried forward or set against the individual's personal gains (see para **88.19**).

It is generally accepted that a double tax treaty can preclude s 13 if the company is resident in a treaty country and the treaty gives the treaty partner sole taxing rights over the gain. But in the present context this is rarely of advantage, for treaty countries tend to impose their own CGT. In any event few offshore jurisdictions are treaty countries and modern treaties tend to prevent the disapplication of s 13.

THE POSITION IN PRACTICE

2.5 The result of the transfer of assets code and s 13 is that directly owned offshore investment companies rarely operate as a shelter of income and gains. The principal exception to this arises where the company is bought or inherited. Here the transferor charge under the transfer of assets code is precluded precisely because on this scenario the shareholder is *not* the transferor.

In principal such a company does indeed operate as an income shelter. However the inheritance or purchase must be genuine: if in reality the taxpayer procured or was associated with the formation or capitalisation of the company HMRC would have grounds for arguing he was a quasi transferor (see para **69.50**).

The issue of whether a company acquired by purchase or inheritance also shelters gains is of some complexity. The better view is that it does if its formation and operation, before it was acquired by the UK resident shareholder, was untainted by any CGT avoidance purpose. But this result would not follow if the acquisition could be seen as part of the arrangements under which the company's assets are acquired or disposed of and CGT avoidance was on the facts one of the purposes behind that acquisition (see further CHAPTER 88).

COMPANY RESIDENCE

2.6 Even assuming the transfer of assets code and s 13 are circumvented, an offshore company cannot operate as a shelter of income or gains unless it is non-UK resident under the central management and control test described in CHAPTER 43. Should it not be UK resident under this test, its profits are exposed to corporation tax.

At one time the House of Lords decision in *Unit Construction v Bullock* [1960] AC 351 meant there was great uncertainty as to whether, and if so how, an offshore company owned by UK residents could be certain of being non-resident. Indeed the risks in this area were not just financial. In *R v Allen* [2001] UKHL 45, [2001] STC 1537 and *R v Dimsey* [2001] UKHL 46, [2001] STC 1520, HMRC brought criminal prosecutions inter alia on the basis that certain individuals had cheated the Crown of tax on the profits of directly-owned companies. The defendants considered the companies were non-resident and in accordance with that view the companies had not made returns for corporation tax. HMRC took a different view and persuaded the jury that the companies were centrally controlled and managed in the UK. The defendants were convicted and sentenced to terms of imprisonment.

More recently the case of *Wood v Holden* [2006] EWCA Civ 26, [2006] STC 443 brought helpful clarification. That case, and others approved in it, concerned facts recognisable to any offshore practitioner and, perhaps more importantly, entailed the High Court and then the Court of Appeal overturning the decision of the Special Commissioners. HMRC sought permission to appeal further to the House of Lords, but were refused.

What *Wood v Holden* establishes beyond peradventure is that an offshore company is resident where its board meet if the board meets regularly and gives genuine and properly informed consideration to whatever business the company transacts. Provided these conditions are met it does not matter if most if not all of what the company does is pursuant to requests from its controlling shareholder(s). *Wood v Holden* indicates that residence is not jeopardised even if the directors have insufficient understanding to properly discharge their duties as a matter of company law. But relying on the decision in that respect is unwise, both because of the company law implications and because of the importance, in a tax context, of avoiding risk.

Accordingly the upshot of the case is that, provided the board meets and properly discharges its duties under the applicable company law, the company resides where the board meets. The risks referred to above still remain if those conditions are not met, but proper corporate disciplines ensure they are avoided. It goes without saying that proper minutes and record keeping are essential, so that if HMRC require evidence of where the company resides, they can be given it.

A point sometimes raised is whether the UK resident owner can be on the board. In theory his membership of the board should not jeopardise the company's non-resident status if all the disciplines referred to above are followed. But involvement in the company's affairs from the UK may be difficult to avoid in practice and on that basis there could be an argument the company is dual resident (see para 43.8). In general the risks and uncertainties render board membership unwise.

OTHER ISSUES

2.7 If a directly owned offshore company is being considered other tax implications also need to be kept in mind.

Inheritance tax

2.8 As the postulated shareholder is UK resident and domiciled, holding assets through an offshore company brings no IHT advantage. It should also be remembered that gratuitous dispositions by the company are treated as transfers of value and apportioned to the participators (IHTA 1984, s 94). In contrast to most lifetime gifts, PET treatment is not available (IHTA 1984, s 3A(1A)(C)). The result is an immediate charge at 20% insofar as participator's nil-rate band and other applicable reliefs are not available. One exception to the charge is where the recipient of the bounteous disposition is the shareholder himself (s 94(1)).

Realisation

2.9 Even if an offshore company is used and in fact serves to shelter income or gains, the tax implications of distribution or realisation should be kept in mind.

Dividends from an offshore company of the kind postulated here attract the dividend rates as, in the circumstances envisaged in this chapter, the shareholder is UK domiciled (ITA 2007, s 13). A sale or liquidation attracts CGT on any gain. Such tax is avoided if the owner has emigrated and is non-UK resident throughout the tax year of realisation. But in both cases he has to be non-UK resident for more than five years (see further paras **29.6** and **41.40** to **41.42**).

2.10 Assuming CGT is payable on a liquidation, the rate is 20%. CGT may also have to be considered in relation to the company's assets if s 13 is not precluded by the motive defence, but here any s 13 tax is a credit against the CGT payable in respect of the shares (s 13(5A); see para **88.22**).

On any liquidation the transactions in securities legislation described in CHAPTER **89** has to be considered, as does the legislation aimed at 'phoenix' type liquidations, also described in CHAPTER **89**. Should either apply income tax rather than CGT is chargeable. The transactions in securities legislation used to be precluded on simple liquidations, but this ceased to be so in 2016. Neither code is likely to be in point if the liquidation is effected for genuine commercial reasons and neither results in tax if the shareholder is non-resident for more than five years, for then any dividend the legislation might substitute would not be taxable in any event.

Overseas tax

2.11 It should always be checked whether, even if the company does operate as a shelter of income and gains from UK tax, the income and gains suffer foreign tax. Such foreign tax may be levied on the company by reason of residence unless it is resident in an offshore jurisdiction which does not impose corporate tax. Or it may be source country taxation charged where the income arises. In either event a judgement is needed whether the company saves overall tax, given that if the individual owned the assets directly the foreign tax would be a credit against UK tax.

CONCLUSION

2.12 The overall result of the points made in this chapter is that a directly owned offshore investment company is not a structure to be recommended. Indeed, if a corporate ownership vehicle is desired, a UK resident company may make more sense, for this secures the lower, corporate tax rates. Further dividends received by the company may be entirely exempt from UK tax. This is the position if the paying company is UK resident or resident in a treaty jurisdiction and the payment of the dividend is untainted by tax avoidance purposes (CTA 2009, s 931B). The UK is increasingly attractive as a holding company jurisdiction and as such any advantage that might be obtained by using an offshore company is much eroded.

Chapter 3

OFFSHORE FUNDS

INTRODUCTION

3.1 This chapter explores the extent to which investment in offshore funds serves as a tax shelter for individuals resident and domiciled in the UK. The anti-avoidance legislation targeted at offshore funds is contained in TIOPA 2010, ss 354–363 and the Offshore Funds (Tax) Regulations 2009 (SI 2009/3001). It is explained in Chapter 95.

3.2 For tax purposes, the term offshore fund has a specific definition (TIOPA 2010, s 355). The salient feature is that it must be a mutual fund in which investors buy and redeem units or shares for consideration based on the net asset value of the fund's investments. In legal form it can be a company, a unit trust, or a contractual arrangement creating rights in the nature of co-ownership. A partnership, however, cannot be a mutual fund. The definition is considered in more detail in Chapter 95.

CHARACTERISATION

Companies

3.3 If an offshore fund is corporate in form, it is regarded as a company for all UK tax purposes.

Unit trusts

3.4 Offshore unit trusts are by definition not authorised and so are not deemed to be companies for income tax purposes (CTA 2010, s 617). So too CTA 2010, s 621 does not deem the unit trust to be a separate fiscal entity as that section applies only to UK resident unit trusts. The result is that the income tax treatment of unit trusts has to be inferred from general principles. The matter is discussed in para **40.16** and the conclusion is that an offshore unit trust may be transparent or opaque for income tax purposes, depending on whether or not the unit-holders are entitled to have the income after expenses paid out to them. The Offshore Funds (Tax) Regulations themselves recognise that some offshore unit trusts are transparent (see especially Regs 11 and 16).

For CGT purposes the position is simpler, in that any non-resident unit trust is deemed to be a company and the units shares (TCGA 1992, s 99(1)).

As regards IHT, the issue is whether, for the purposes of that tax, the investor's asset is the unit or an aliquot share in the underlying assets. This issue is discussed in para **38.13** and the conclusion is that offshore unit trusts should, in general, be treated as opaque.

Many advisers are of the view that if it is desired to have certainty as to the IHT and income tax treatment, an offshore fund in corporate form is preferable. This is particularly so where it is important not to receive UK source income or to avoid holding UK assets directly. Fortunately, the majority of offshore funds are, in fact, corporate.

Other arrangements

3.5 In civil law jurisdictions, non-corporate mutual funds can be contractual in form. It is unclear how such arrangements should be characterised for the purposes of income tax or IHT. Such arrangements should therefore be avoided if clarity as to source or situs is required.

For CGT purposes, funds which are neither in corporate nor unit trust form are deemed to be companies (TCGA 1992, s 103A). This treatment has applied to investors in such funds who are within the charge to corporation tax since 1 April 2010 to investors who are within the charge to CGT since 1 December 2009 (see FA 2009, Sch 22 para 12, SI 2010/670, and HMRC Notice 15 March 2010 (reproduced [2010] SWTI p 776).

CATEGORISATION

3.6 The Offshore Funds (Tax) Regulations divide offshore funds into two categories, namely reporting funds and non-reporting funds. A non-reporting fund is any fund which does not have reporting status (Reg 4).

The requirements which have to be satisfied for a fund to have reporting status are explained in para **95.10**. The key obligations are to prepare accounts in accordance with international accounting standards and give information as to distributed and undistributed income to the investors and to HMRC. Reporting status is only available if applied for and granted by HMRC.

The practical effect is that funds with mostly non-UK investors are unlikely to have reporting status. If UK investors are not an important constituency to the fund, the compliance implicit in reporting is an unnecessary expense.

Non-reporting funds: tax treatment

3.7 Gains realised by investors on disposals of interests in non-reporting funds are designated offshore income gains and so taxed as income. The computational rules are broadly those of CGT and are explained in paras **95.13** to **95.18**. Losses realised by investors on a non-reporting fund may be set against ordinary capital gains but not against offshore income gains.

Reporting funds: tax treatment

3.8 The key tax feature of reporting funds is that any undistributed income is treated as if it had been distributed. The fund is thus viewed in the same way as an authorised UK fund. When the investor realises his interest in the fund he does not realise an offshore income gain and is subject only to CGT. Any undistributed income on which he has been taxed is treated as allowable expenditure in the computation of the chargeable gain. Losses realised by investors on a reporting fund may be set against ordinary capital gains but not against offshore income gains.

DISTRIBUTIONS

3.9 The general rule is that distributions by corporate offshore funds are taxed as dividends at the dividend rates. This follows as a matter of general principle and is confirmed by the Offshore Funds (Tax) Regulations, which inter alia provide that the undistributed income of corporate funds is treated as if it were dividend (Reg 95).

There is one exception to dividend treatment, namely where the fund fails what is called the qualifying investments test (ITTOIA 2005, s 378A). This is discussed in para **95.8**. It is failed if more than 60% of the fund's investments comprise cash, loan stock or other similar fixed interest assets (CTA 2009, s 494). The practical result is that unless the offshore fund's cash and fixed interest-assets are below 60%, the advantages of dividend treatment are lost.

Distributions from non-corporate funds are, assuming the fund is opaque, taxed either as annual payments or as miscellaneous income (ITTOIA 2005, ss 683 and 687). This treatment follows as a matter of general principle, and is confirmed by the Offshore Fund (Tax) Regulations, which provide that undistributed income is taxed as miscellaneous income (Reg 96).

The result is that unless the fund fails the qualifying investments test, distributions from corporate funds are more favourably taxed than those from non-corporate funds. This provides an additional tax reason to prefer funds in corporate form.

ANTI-AVOIDANCE LEGISLATION

3.10 Certain general anti-avoidance legislation requires consideration in connection with offshore funds.

Transfer of assets code

3.11 Most investments in offshore funds are made by subscription rather than purchase from pre-existing investors. The element of subscription raises the question of whether investors can be taxed under the transfer of assets code on a proportion of the income of the fund (see ITA 2007, s 720 and CHAPTER 69). The answer generally given is no, on the basis that a Commissioner's case prior to the original introduction of the offshore fund legislation is generally understood to have decided to the contrary, principally on the grounds that the motive defence described in CHAPTER 73 applies.

There is no doubt that in the normal case of an investment in an offshore fund the motive defence does apply, for offshore funds are investment products bought for commercial reasons. Further the offshore fund legislation itself provides a comprehensive code for taxing non-reporting funds. As such it may be equated with the chargeable event code, the existence of which was one of the factors in securing the motive defence in *IRC v Willoughby* [1997] STC 955 (see para **73.22**).

But if the matter is closely examined, the motive defence is not a complete answer. The following points may be made:

(1)   As explained in para **73.9**, the key issue in applying the motive defence is what, subjectively, is the purpose of the transferor. In theory at least, an investor in an offshore fund who has the subjective purpose of avoiding tax is not protected.

(2)   To secure the motive defence, both the transfer and any associated operation must be untainted by a tax avoidance purpose. The defence could therefore be lost if activity by the fund itself has a tax avoidance purpose.

(3)   Investment in an offshore fund is frequently an operation associated with a prior transfer, most notably where the investor is a trust or company. If that trust or company was formed for tax avoidance reasons, the defence is not available.

(4)   As explained in para **73.31** it is HMRC's view that taxpayers relying on the motive defence should so disclose in their tax return. Investors in offshore funds seldom, if ever, do this.

These points suggest it is not the motive defence which disapplies the transfer of assets code. The correct analysis, it may be suggested, is that the code only comes into play if there is a relevant transfer – ie if the income becoming payable to the person abroad is so payable as a result of the transfer and/or associated operations. With a widely held offshore fund, there is simply not the requisite connection between a given investor's subscription, and the generation of income in the fund.

To date the transfer of assets code has not been invoked in relation to widely held offshore funds, albeit that some fund prospectuses do highlight the code as a possible risk factor. In their response to representations made by professional bodies as regards the changes to the motive defence made by FA 2006, HMRC said they did not intend to apply what is now ss 720–726 to offshore funds. However, they reserved the right to do so should the regime be abused beyond the apparent intention of Parliament.

CGT

3.12 As is explained in CHAPTER 88, TCGA 1992, s 13 can require gains realised by non-UK resident close companies to be apportioned to participators. Offshore funds in corporate form are companies, and so capable of coming within s 13. But in practice s 13 is rarely in point, since conventional offshore funds are widely held and, even allowing for the wide definition of close company (see CHAPTER 87), are therefore unlikely to be close. Further, even if close, s 13 is precluded by a generous de minimis threshold in that apportionment to a participator is not possible unless he and connected persons hold more than 25% of the fund (see para **88.14**).

If for any reason these two points did not avail, a further defence to s 13 would fall to be considered, namely the motive defence. As explained in para **88.4**, that defence would focus on assets held by the fund and disapplies s 13 unless the acquisition, holding, or disposal of any such asset forms part of a scheme, and one of the purposes of the scheme was avoidance of CGT or corporation tax. This is a much more generous motive defence than that applicable to the transfer of assets code, and it is difficult to see commercially run offshore funds falling foul of it.

The issue of whether s 13 could apply to a non-corporate fund is one of some difficulty as, for it to apply, the entity has not merely to be a company for CGT purposes but also close within the meaning of TA 1988, ss 415 and 416 (TCGA 1992, ss 13(1) and 288(1)). Although the contrary is arguable, the better view is that the deeming in TCGA 1992, ss 99 and 103A is wide enough to make a unit trust treated as a company close if it would be close were it in fact a company.

PLANNING

Reporting funds

3.13 As all the income of a reporting fund is treated as distributed, it might be thought that there is no advantage in investing in such funds. But in reality this is not so, and three points in particular may be made.

The first concerns funds in corporate form and arises from the fact that the dividend rates apply provided the fund does not fail the qualifying investments test. The dividend rates are lower than the rates applicable to non-dividend income, and the result is that distributing corporate funds represent an attractive income investment. It is of course true that other foreign dividends attract the same tax treatment. But with other foreign dividends there is a greater likelihood of significant underlying foreign tax than is the case with offshore funds.

The second point relates to capital gains. Assuming that s 13 does not apply, the capital gains of the fund are not attributed to investors as they arise. Accordingly the investor only becomes concerned with CGT when he redeems or otherwise disposes of his interest in the fund. At the very least a deferral is achieved and this may be converted into avoidance if at the time of realisation the investor is non-resident and his non-residence lasts for more than five years.

A third point is of particular interest to those seeking long-term exposure to foreign denominated fixed-interest investments. Such portfolios are, despite their nature, exposed to CGT as CGT is charged on the currency element on any bond gain as well as on the purely investment amount. In theory over time gains and losses ought to average each other out, but even if that is so the computation and compliance for direct investors can be tiresome and expensive. These difficulties are avoided, if exposure is secured through an offshore fund.

Having said this, onshore funds enjoy many of the same advantages as offshore funds. Thus gains realised by authorised unit trusts and investment trusts are exempt, as are those in open-ended investment companies (TCGA 1992, s 100; SI 2006/964 regs 98 and 100).

Investment in reporting funds contains at least two traps. One is that the fund can at any time choose to give up reporting status and may involuntarily be deprived of that status if it is in serious breach of its compliance obligations (Regs 114 and 116). Investors have no control over these processes and yet should reporting status be lost the investor may be faced with two unpalatable alternatives. One is to do nothing and suffer income tax on any gain realised when he disposes of his investment (unless he is then non-resident for more than five tax years). The other is to elect for a deemed disposal of his interest at the time the fund's status changes, paying CGT on any gain thereby recognised despite not having received any actual process of sale.

The second trap is that if the fund does not distribute all its income, the investor is still taxed as if it had. Here too there is a risk of a tax liability without any actual receipt and, as with reporting status, the investor has no control over whether or not the fund distributes.

Non-reporting funds

3.14 Investment in a non-reporting offshore fund brings three income tax advantages:

(1)   Assuming the fund is not transparent for income tax purposes (see para 3.4), there is a deferral in that the income in the fund is rolled up tax-free and is not charged on the investor unless and until he disposes of his interest.

(2)   The deferral may result in a tax reduction if and insofar as the rate of income tax payable by the individual when he sells his investment is lower than that applicable when the income accrues to the fund.

(3)   The deferral is converted into avoidance if by the time of realisation the individual has become non-resident. However, as with CGT, the investor must be non-resident when the gain is realised and he must also be non-resident for more than five years (Reg 23).

A non-reporting fund provides deferral of tax on gains realised within the underlying portfolio, in the same way as a reporting fund, thereby postponing any charge until realisation of the investment. But the deferral carries a price:

(a)   As the gain on realisation is taxed as income, the effect is that capital growth in the fund is turned into income in the investor's hands, thereby losing the benefit of the normally lower CGT rates. This is particularly unfortunate should the fund be a currency fund, for the effect is that gains resulting from the depreciation of sterling against the relevant currency become taxed as income.

(b)   On death there is a deemed disposal, but the gain then accruing is charged (The Offshore Funds (Tax) Regulations 2009, Reg 34). There is no tax-free rebasing.

The practical result is that if the growth in a non-reporting fund is capital rather than income, the tax treatment is unattractive, although it remains the case that tax on underlying capital gains is deferred, and that income tax on a disposal of the fund can be avoided by emigration for at more than five years (see Reg 23).

Offshore trusts

3.15 Non-reporting offshore funds can be a useful investment for offshore trusts. This is for two reasons. The first is that, as described in Chapter 1, the anti-avoidance legislation applicable to the income of offshore trusts is in certain respects less severe than that applicable to capital gains. The offshore fund legislation converts what would otherwise be capital gains into income even if the underlying growth in the fund is mainly capital. This takes them out of the ambit of the settlor charge in TCGA 1992, s 86 (see para **1.10**). The second reason is that provided the fund is not transparent, UK investments may be held without the additional income tax on dividends or interest payable by offshore trustees with UK beneficiaries (cf para **64.8**).

Private funds

3.16 The above discussion has focused on quoted funds. In practice small private funds are not uncommon. Provided the fund falls within the definition of offshore fund given above (para **3.2**), the tax treatment is generally as described in this chapter. However, TCGA 1992, s 13 is in point if it is close (unless the motive defence discussed above applies), and a unit trust which is privately held may more readily be characterised as transparent for IHT purposes (see para **38.13**). A further issue is that if the transfer of assets code is applicable to offshore funds at all, it is much more likely to be engaged by a small private fund.

COMPARISON WITH OFFSHORE TRUSTS

3.17 Non-reporting offshore funds offer the following advantages over a private offshore trust:

(a)   An offshore trust cannot achieve a tax-free roll-up of income and gains unless the settlor is wholly excluded. An individual can achieve a tax-free roll-up by investing in a fund and still be able to take the proceeds at the end.

(b)   As standard commercial investments, offshore funds may be less provocative to HMRC and carry lower compliance costs.

The drawbacks include the following:

(i)   A trust enables assets to be tied up for several generations. An interest in an offshore fund is simply an asset which has to be given away, bequeathed or otherwise dealt with.

(ii)   With an offshore fund, normally the only income and gains that can be sheltered are from portfolio investments. Private company shares, land, and other one-off assets cannot generally be so sheltered.

COMPARISON WITH AUTHORISED FUNDS

3.18 It is reasonably well recognised that one of the policy objectives behind the 2009 changes to the offshore fund rules was to create a level playing field as between offshore funds and UK authorised funds. This is particularly so as respects reporting funds and as a result any investor minded to buy into an offshore reporting fund should consider whether a UK authorised fund would serve his interests just as well.

Chapter 4

LIFE POLICIES

INTRODUCTION

4.1 This chapter deals with the sheltering possibilities offered by offshore life policies. The use of life policies in both onshore and offshore tax planning is widespread. This chapter focuses on the use of offshore life policies as a specifically offshore tax shelter.

GENERAL

4.2 An offshore policy is a policy issued by an offshore life insurance company which does not trade in the UK. Such policies can effectively be investment vehicles. The policy may be a 'with profits' policy or unit-linked, although, 'with profits' policies have in recent years fallen from favour. Where a policy is 'with profits', the policyholder shares in the profits of the life insurance company, usually in the form of bonuses credited to the policy annually. Where the policy is unit-linked, the sum payable on maturity or surrender is linked to the performance of an underlying fund. Units in the fund are allocated to the policy and the value of those units determines the amount payable.

In substance, unit-linked policies resemble a managed portfolio of investments, but whatever the apparent substance, the legal reality of insurance products is that the policyholder owns not a portfolio of investments but merely a right in contract against the life insurance company. Should the life insurance company become insolvent, the policyholder is an unsecured creditor.

The arrangement must, of course, be a life policy. But a life policy need have little or no mortality risk. Thus in *Fuji Finance Inc v Aetna Life Insurance Co Ltd* [1997] Ch 173, the sum payable on surrender was essentially the same as that which would have been payable had the life assured died at the time of the surrender. This, the Court of Appeal held, did not prevent the policy from being life assurance.

In England a life policy is only valid if the person effecting the policy has an insurable interest (Life Assurance Act 1774, ss 1 and 3). In broad terms this normally means the life which is assured has to be that of the person effecting the policy or his spouse. In other jurisdictions, and in particular in some offshore jurisdictions, there is no such restriction and accordingly it is possible to effect life assurance on one or more third party lives. This gives offshore life assurance considerably more flexibility than in England, although in practice a life insurance company would be unlikely to write a policy with significant mortality risk on the life of a stranger.

TAX TREATMENT

General principles

4.3 Since the life insurance company is offshore and does not trade in the UK, it is not subject to tax on the income and gains from the investments backing the policy, save insofar as tax is withheld in countries of source.

In the policyholder's hands, the policy is a capital asset. Thus in the absence of the chargeable event legislation described below, the proceeds on maturity or surrender would be free of income tax. The same is true of partial surrender. An attempt to characterise regular, annual, partial surrenders as income failed before a Special Commissioner (*Sugden v Kent* [2001] STC (SCD) 158).

Although capital, life policies are not chargeable assets for CGT purposes (TCGA 1992, s 210(2)). The only exception is where the policy has at any time been acquired for actual consideration (s 210(3)). Where for this reason the policy is chargeable, a disposal takes place both when the policy is assigned and on receipt of the sum assured (s 210(10)).

The chargeable event legislation

4.4 The legislation dealing with the taxation of chargeable events, which is contained in ITTOIA 2005, Part 4, Chapter 9 is analysed in Chapter 93. It was drafted principally with onshore policies in mind but, with modifications, it applies equally to offshore policies, including foreign capital redemption policies (see para **96.10**). It counters the tax sheltering potential of policies by treating the gain realised when the policy matures or is surrendered as income. This legislation differentiates between qualifying and non-qualifying policies, but offshore policies are by definition non-qualifying.

Other anti-avoidance legislation

4.5 It was held in *IRC v Willoughby* [1997] STC 995 that what is now ITA 2007, ss 720–726 do not apply to the income from funds backing a life policy (see para **73.22**). The CFC legislation cannot apply to an offshore life insurance company provided the bulk of its business is with unconnected persons. The life insurance company's gains could only be attributed to UK participators under TCGA 1992, s 13 if it were close (cf CHAPTER 88).

Personal portfolio bonds

4.6 It is possible for a policy to track the value of a fund which is managed by the policyholder or his investment adviser. Such policies are known as personal portfolio bonds.

HMRC consider that personal portfolio bonds, being personalised rather than forming part of a collective scheme of investment, should not benefit from what they regard as the favourable tax regime applicable to life assurance. Initially they took the case of *IRC v Willoughby* (supra) to the House of Lords, seeking to tax the income of a personal bond fund under what is now ITA 2007, ss 720–726. Then, having lost, they introduced punitive anti-avoidance legislation imposing an annual charge on the holder of such policies (ITTOIA 2005, ss 515–526; see para **96.30**).

Connected persons

4.7 A policyholder can be connected with a company held in a fund linked to his policy within the meaning of the income tax and CGT definitions (TCGA 1992, s 286; ITA 2007, s 993). This is the position where on the facts the policyholder and the life insurance company act together to secure or exercise control of the company. So too the settlor of a trust owning the policy is connected with the company if he and the life insurance company so act together (*Foulser v MacDougall* [2005] STC (SCD) 374, affirmed (on a different point) [2006] STC 311). One consequence of the policyholder/settlor and underlying company being connected persons is that transactions between them will not be regarded as being at arm's length, so that (for example) for CGT purposes market value may be substituted for the actual consideration changing hands.

TAX PLANNING

Deferral

4.8 At its most basic, an offshore policy secures a deferral of tax. Subject to withholding tax, investment income and gains accrue and are reinvested gross. Tax is not payable by the policyholder under the chargeable event legislation until the policy matures or is surrendered.

If the policy matures on the death of the policyholder, the gain charged is not the difference between the proceeds and the base cost, but the difference between the base cost and the surrender value immediately prior to death. Accordingly, if the surrender value is less than the maturity value, as it may be where there is a significant element of life cover, the mortality gain (the difference between the surrender value and the maturity value) is tax-free.

As is explained in para **96.14**, gains on a policy held in trust are taxed as the settlor's if he is alive and UK resident at or immediately before maturity or surrender. This applies regardless of the residence of the trust, and includes the scenario where the policy matures on the death of the settlor. But if the settlor is already dead or he is non-resident, the gain on a policy in trust is subject to tax at the rate for trusts if the trust is UK resident. If the trust is non-resident and the gain is not taxable on the settlor, the gain on maturity is not taxable as it arises. It is treated as relevant income for the purposes of ITA 2007, ss 731–735 which means tax liability is deferred until capital is distributed to a UK beneficiary (see CHAPTER 70).

An unattractive aspect of life policy taxation is that the gain on the policy is taxed as income, rather than gain, which may in practice result in economic gain being taxed at more than double the normal CGT rate. But it remains the case that there is no CGT on gains accruing to the life insurance company, so there is the benefit of a tax-free roll-up of gains until withdrawals are made or the policy is redeemed.

Non-residence

4.9 The deferral of the tax on the income and the gains reinvested in the policy fund becomes a complete shelter if the person liable to tax is an individual who becomes non-resident before the policy matures or is surrendered (ITTOIA 2005, s 465(1); see para **96.14**). For years of departure from 6 April 2013 onwards, the individual must be non-resident for more than five years in order to avoid a tax charge on return to the UK.

Partial withdrawals

4.10 A unique feature of the tax regime for life policies is that a partial surrender of up to 5% of the premium may be taken tax-free each year (see para **96.2**). However, the amount of any such surrender is included in computing the income gain when the policy matures or is sold or is fully surrendered (ITTOIA 2005, s 492(1)(b); see para **96.7**). Strictly therefore, it is only another form of deferral, and once the total of tax-free partial surrenders equals the premium, future partial surrenders are immediately chargeable to tax.

What is undoubtedly true, however, is that the right to tax-free 5% withdrawals enhances the scope for life policies to be used to achieve tax deferral. This enhanced deferral becomes a complete shelter if by the time of maturity or surrender the policyholder is non-resident (and will remain non-resident for more than five years). Such is also to a large extent achieved if by the time of maturity or surrender the policy is held in an offshore trust, and the person who transferred the policy to the trust is then dead. As noted above, the gain in that event is only chargeable insofar as distributions are made to UK beneficiaries.

There are proposals for reform of the rules on partial surrenders, which may conceivably result in a regime which is even more generous in terms of the ability for policyholders to defer tax on economic gains (see para **96.29**).

Personal portfolio bonds

4.11 As noted above, if a personal portfolio bond is caught by the anti-avoidance legislation directed at such policies, the tax consequences are severe. Policies with an element of self-selection (including those which permit self-selection, even where this right is not in fact exercised) should therefore be avoided, unless they fall within the exceptions to the legislation.

In fact those exceptions do give some flexibility. In particular, it may be possible to have an individual portfolio of quoted investments provided the selection is not by the policyholder but solely by an investment manager. The manager may be nominated by the policyholder provided his actual appointment is by the life insurance company (cf para **96.34**).

Self-selection by the policyholder himself is allowed if the investments which may be selected are confined to unit trusts, open-ended investment companies and other mutual funds, or property which the life insurance company has appropriated to an 'internal linked fund' (see para **96.32**). Now that so many mutual funds exist, this gives wide scope for a policyholder who is keen to self-select, although care is needed both over the wording of the contract and the actual selection of the investments to ensure they really do steer clear of the anti-avoidance legislation. The 'internal linked fund' exception offers an even wider investment offering (as discussed at para **96.33**), but typically the life insurance company will require a minimum level of investment to offer this, if it offers this option at all.

As discussed at para **13.7**, when an individual is contemplating becoming UK resident, it is particularly important to review the terms of any pre-existing single premium life insurance policies which he or she may hold, to check if such products are likely to be classified as personal portfolio bonds for UK tax purposes. If this is the case, it should be recommended that the individual either encashes the policy, or (if possible) enters into a variation of the policy to take it outside the personal portfolio bond regime, before the end of the insurance year which falls after the individual becomes UK resident (see para **96.35**).

COMPARISON WITH OFFSHORE TRUSTS

4.12 Offshore policies offer the following advantages as compared with offshore trusts:

(1)   The income and gains within the policy fund accrue gross even though the person providing original funds (the policyholder) can benefit. With a trust the person providing the funds (the settlor) has to be totally excluded, for the trust to operate as a tax shelter.

(2)   The 5% withdrawals do not attract tax when made. With a trust any distribution to a UK-domiciled resident is potentially taxable.

(3)   Even when the gain on the maturity or surrender of a life policy is taxed, there is no notional interest on the tax, as there is with CGT capital payments (cf paras **77.49** to **77.51**).

The drawbacks include the following:

(1)   A trust can protect assets for several generations and can act as a succession vehicle. A policy does not of itself do that.

(2)   A trust can hold all forms of assets, whereas there are practical and tax restrictions on the assets that can be 'held within' a life policy.

(3)   The charges made by life insurance companies are often opaque and may be high.

(4)   Life policies can be subject to aggressive selling, which may make it difficult to identify the real advantages for any particular individual.

(5)   As noted above, economic gains may end up being subject to income tax at double or more than double the normal CGT rate.

Section II

Existing Offshore Trusts established by UK Resident and Domiciled Individuals

Chapter 5
OVERVIEW

INTRODUCTION

5.1 This part addresses existing settlements created by UK domiciliaries. As is explained in CHAPTER 1, considerable practical difficulties attach to the creation of settlements by UK domiciliaries and as a result few are now being created. But many of the difficulties did not obtain in the past, and existing settlements may enjoy significant advantages. In relative terms settlements created by UK domiciliaries are few in number by comparison with those created by foreign domiciliaries who may have no UK connection at all. But those that remain continue, at least in some situations, to provide planning opportunities.

HISTORY

5.2 Prior to 1979, few individuals resident and domiciled in the UK created offshore settlements. The reason was the transferor charge under the transfer of assets code, now ITA 2007, ss 720 and 727 and then TA 1970, s 478. As explained in para **68.2**, the law, based on *Congreve v IRC* (1948) 30 TC 163 was that any UK resident who had power to enjoy offshore income was potentially taxable on the whole of it. This made offshore settlements hazardous in the extreme, only to be countenanced by the exceptionally brave or foolhardy.

Changes 1979–81

5.3 The misconstruction of s 478 ended in November 1979 (*Vestey v IRC* [1980] STC 10), and from then on what are now ss 720 and 727 were limited to transferors and quasi transferors (see para **69.48**). The way was thus open to family trusts in offshore jurisdictions.

Other developments encouraged this trend. One was the abolition of exchange controls, also in late 1979. A second was the recasting in 1981 of the CGT rules pertaining to non-resident settlements into what is now TCGA 1992, s 87 (see CHAPTER 77). These rules made it clear gains in non-resident trusts could not be taxed save insofar as capital was distributed to UK resident beneficiaries. The way was thus open for both income and capital gains to be sheltered.

Inheritance tax

5.4 Inheritance tax, or Capital Transfer Tax as it was then, remained a significant issue. Capital Transfer Tax, introduced in 1974, imposed a comprehensive tax on lifetime gifts, including gifts into trust. The one exception was trusts in which the settlor or his spouse took an initial life interest, for then, under what is now IHTA 1984, s 49 as originally enacted, the trust property was treated as his or, as the case may be, hers.

This IHT difficulty was removed in 1986 on what, with hindsight, was the final freeing up of the applicable tax rules. In 1986, Capital Transfer Tax turned into IHT, and gifts into interest in possession trusts became potentially exempt transfers, or PETs, and thus tax-free provided that the settlor survived seven years (IHTA 1984, s 3A(1) as originally enacted). The same applied to gifts to one form of discretionary trust, namely accumulation and maintenance trusts within IHTA 1984, s 71 as originally enacted. The prerequisite of these trusts was that beneficiaries had to take absolute interests or interests in possession in the trust capital on or before attaining 25 (see para **61.16**).

Trusts in the 1980s

5.5 Until 1991, perhaps the prime role of offshore trusts created by UK domiciliaries was to shelter capital gains. The key point was that gains were not assessable as they arose, the sole anti-avoidance rule being the s 87 regime. Further, even when capital was distributed to a UK resident, the tax payable under s 87 was not supplemented by notional interest (see para **77.48**). As a result of these advantages a standard tax planning technique of the 1980s was to hold growth assets in offshore trusts.

Under some of these trusts the settlor and his spouse were excluded but under others they were not. Where they were not excluded, it was accepted that the income was taxable as theirs. But often this drawback was more apparent than real as the assets were growth assets generating little or no income. A potentially more substantial problem in such cases was that the trust was in the settlor's estate for IHT purposes, either because he was the life tenant or under the gift with reservation rules introduced in 1986. But often little attention was given to this problem, if only because many settlors were relatively young.

The 1990s

5.6 There is no doubt that the hey-day of offshore trusts for UK domiciliaries was the decade up to 1991. That year saw the first curtailment of the advantages of such trusts, namely the enactment of the CGT settlor charge, now TCGA 1992, s 86 (see CHAPTER 76) and the imposition of supplemental tax on capital payments (see para **77.48**). The settlor charge, as first enacted, generally applied only to post-1991 trusts but in relation to such trusts it applied if either the settlor or his children or their respective spouses were beneficiaries.

The 1991 developments were followed in 1998 by the extension of the settlor charge to pre-1991 trusts and post-1998 grandchildren's trusts. Two years later, FA 2000 enacted the CGT trustee borrowing rules (see CHAPTERS 80 and 81).

IHT changes

5.7 A more fundamental change took place in 2006, when the IHT rules dealing with trusts were recast so as to prevent newly created interests in possession from being equated with the personal property of the holder of such interest (see para **61.3**). Finance Act 2006 also effectively abolished accumulation and maintenance trusts (see para **61.16**) and thus ended PET treatment on gifts into trust. The result was that it became much more difficult to create trusts, whether onshore or offshore, without an immediate IHT charge. Although as explained in paras **1.12** to **1.15** there are techniques for overcoming this problem, the combined effect of all the changes since 1991 is that the creation of offshore trusts is far less attractive than it once was for UK domiciliaries.

But as indicated above, this does not mean that existing settlements created under the more benign rules described above are redundant. They have a valuable and continuing role in tax planning and that is what this Part is about.

TYPES OF SETTLEMENT

5.8 The historical background described above means that the settlements which now exist have come about for many different reasons and take a variety of forms. For convenience of analysis they may be divided into four categories:

• Favoured settlements, ie settlements which shelter both income and gains.
• Settlements which shelter income but not gains.
• Settlements which shelter gains but not income.
• Settlements which shelter neither income nor gains.

It will be observed that the above list does not mention IHT. This is because settlements created by UK domiciliaries are fully exposed to that tax, offshore settlements being in this regard in the same position as UK resident settlements (see CHAPTER 62).

FAVOURED SETTLEMENTS

5.9 Existing settlements which shelter both income and gains are those where neither the income nor the gains are attributed to the settlor on an arising basis. As is explained in paras **1.7** to **1.9** in general this requires the settlor to be non-resident or dead. But this is not so if he, his children and grandchildren, and their respective spouses are all excluded and, should the settlement have been created before 17 March 1998, it is not necessary for grandchildren to be excluded provided the settlement is 'untainted' (see paras **7.8** and **76.5**).

An equally important requirement is that the settlement be discretionary so that the income can be accumulated. Should this condition not be met, and the settlement be one where one or more beneficiaries has an interest in possession, income sheltering is not achieved for then the income is taxed as that of the life tenant(s) (see para **8.3**).

It might be thought the number of existing favoured settlements is small, but in reality that is not so. Any existing settlement is likely to be 20 or 30 years old, which means it is inherently more likely to be one where the settlor is non-resident or dead.

Planning issues

5.10 Favoured settlements which now exist are in general worth retaining, for they permit the continuing sheltering of income and gains and, provided the settlor is dead or completely excluded, they are not in his or anybody else's estate for IHT purposes. Cases where the better course is to terminate the settlement are rare, and usually entail settlements of modest value, where the costs of administration and management are disproportionate.

Ongoing tax issues raised by favoured settlements are that they are within the IHT relevant property regime and distributions to UK residents are subject to income tax or CGT. The relevant property regime is explained in Chapter 60 and, at worst, entails a 6% charge every ten years. In most cases this is well able to be funded out of one or two years income and in some cases may be obviated by reliefs such as business property relief.

The income tax or CGT attaching to distributions is explained in Chapters 8 and 9. Strictly it means that the trust operates only as a deferral, and in the case of gains the deferral is countered by the supplemental tax levied on some capital payments (see para **77.48**). But in reality a number of planning techniques exist to reduce or even eliminate the charges on distributions, as explained in Chapter 10.

An issue often raised is whether, from a tax standpoint, the more tax efficient investment return is income or gains. The initial point to stress is that investment decisions should be driven by commercial factors, not tax. But that said, in tax terms capital gains are currently more attractive than income. Thus the highest rate of tax on a distribution taxed as income is the income tax top rate of 45%. This compares with the maximum rate of CGT plus supplemental tax of 32%.

INCOME SHELTERED

5.11 Settlements which shelter income but not gains are those where the settlor is alive and UK resident. He and his spouse are excluded from benefit, but his children are not, or, where they also are excluded, the grandchildren are beneficiaries and the settlement either post-dates 1998 or is an earlier tainted settlement.

A settlement of this sort may be described as a conventional family settlement, taxation of income on the settlor being precluded because he and his spouse are excluded (see para **1.13** and CHAPTER **75**). Gains, however, remain chargeable on him under TCGA 1992, s 86 (see CHAPTER **76**). As with the favoured settlements described above, the settlement has to be discretionary, for otherwise the income is treated as that of the life tenant. IHT is a continuing, albeit manageable issue, in that the charge of 6% every ten years applies unless some relief is in point.

Given that gains but not income are taxed on an arising basis, there is a clear tax case with these settlements for securing investment return taxed as income. As explained in para **1.10**, there is one simple means of achieving this, namely investment in non-reporting offshore funds. The tax rules applicable to such funds are explained in CHAPTER **95**, and the particular points applicable to non-UK resident trusts in CHAPTER **82**. For present purposes, the key point is that offshore income gains can normally only be taxed on the settlor if he has power to enjoy within the transfer of assets code. Power to enjoy is unlikely to be in point with settlements of the kind postulated here, given that the settlor is completely excluded (see CHAPTER **69**).

The potential for investing in non-distributor funds removes many of the disadvantages settlements of this kind considered here have as compared with the favoured settlements described above. Further factors pointing to the same conclusion are that sooner or later the settlor will become non-resident or die, possibilities of increasing relevance as these settlements mature. On any of these eventualities gains fall out of the s 86 charge. Neither possibility triggers a deemed disposal recognising latent but unrealised gains.

These various factors mean that the case for retaining these settlements is not significantly weaker than that pertaining to the favoured settlements described above. There is however one important practical issue, namely that if the trust does realise chargeable gains, the settlor bears the tax, assuming he is alive and UK resident. But the benefit of the gain accrues to the trust from which he is completely excluded. There is a statutory right of reimbursement (TCGA 1992, Sch 5 para 6) but this is a right conferred by UK statute and it is a matter for the proper law of the trust as to whether it is enforceable against the trustee in the trust's home jurisdiction.

This problem is discussed in para **76.18**. In the present era of much greater recognition of international tax obligations, it may be that offshore courts would be readier than in the past to enforce the English right of reimbursement. Other solutions include a court approved variation expressly authorising reimbursement or, somewhat unconventionally, changing the proper law of the trust to that of England. But there may be other implications in adopting English law, to which full consideration should be given.

GAINS SHELTERED

5.12 A non-UK resident trust can shelter only gains if it is subject to an interest in possession held by a UK resident, since as described above, the interest in possession means the income is that of the life tenant as it arises. But it is not all such trusts which shelter gains. For the reasons explained above in relation to favoured trusts, it is also necessary for the trust to be outside s 86. In most cases this requires the settlor to be either dead or non-UK resident but as indicated above, certain other trusts from which he and his close relatives are completely excluded perform this function as well.

Types of interest in possession

5.13 In tax terms, there are two types of interest in possession, namely qualifying and non-qualifying. As explained in para **61.2**, the term 'qualifying interest in possession' is an IHT concept and, in the main, it signifies an interest in possession which has subsisted since before 22 March 2006. Most interests in possession which came into existence after that date are non-qualifying.

The significance of the distinction is that settled property subject to a qualifying interest in possession is subject to the pre-2006 rules and so treated as being in the life tenant's estate for IHT purposes. This means that the settled property attracts tax at the IHT death rate of 40% should he die (see para **61.12**). Equally the settled property remains outside the relevant property regime of 10-yearly and exit charges. Non-qualifying interests in possession are treated entirely differently in that they are ignored for IHT purposes, the settled property being relevant property in the same way as discretionary trusts (see CHAPTER 60).

Non-qualifying interest in possession

5.14 In planning terms a settlement which is both outside s 86 and subject to non-qualifying interest in possession is in the same position as a favoured trust described above, for there is no adverse IHT consequence if the trustees simply revoke the interest and appoint discretionary trusts in its place. Indeed, the non-qualifying interest may itself have been an appointment under a discretionary trust, for, where beneficiaries under a discretionary trust have need of income, such is often best delivered by appointing a revocable interest in possession (see further para **10.13**).

Qualifying interest in possession

5.15 Matters are altogether different where the interest in possession is qualifying. Many settlements exist which are subject to a qualifying interest in possession, for, as explained above, until 2006 such interests were within the PET regime. This meant the gift into the settlement was a PET and so too was the replacement of one interest in possession with another. A further reason for the popularity of qualifying interests in possession is that many accumulation and maintenance trusts within the former IHTA 1984, s 71 had matured into interests in possession by the time the rules changed on 22 March 2006.

As indicated above, the existence of the qualifying interest in possession means that the trust does not operate as an income shelter. But the difficulties this poses may be more apparent than real. One reason for this is sheltering of income can be achieved if the investments are held through an underlying company and the income is retained and invested in the company. This is discussed further in the next chapter (para **6.12**). A second reason is in point should the trustees invest in non-reporting funds which do not distribute income. This avoids the potential income tax charge on the life tenant by ensuring the return is not income but capital. The gain when the trust's interest in the fund is redeemed is an offshore income gain, but, being capital, it does not belong to the life tenant and so is not taxed unless and until the trustees make a capital distribution (see CHAPTER 82).

As a result of these points, qualifying interest in possession trusts outside s 86 can be almost as attractive as the favoured trusts described above. And in one respect they may be better, for the qualifying interest in possession means there are no 10-yearly charges (see para 60.1).

The potential IHT charge

5.16 In a sense this freedom from 10-yearly charges comes at a price, for, being in the life tenant's estate, the settled property attracts IHT at the death rate should the life tenant die. But this price may be more apparent than real:

- If the life tenant is young or middle-aged death on average expectancy may be many years off, by which time the IHT rules could well be different.
- The risk of untimely death can be covered by term assurance.
- Should the life tenant be survived by his widow, qualifying interest in possession treatment can continue during her life provided that under the settlement she takes a successive life interest. Such successive life interest need not have been appointed before 2006, and, as well as securing continuing freedom from 10-yearly charges it also defers the death IHT to the spouse's death on account of the spouse exemption (IHTA 1984, s 18).

Despite these points, concern is sometimes expressed about the potential death charge, particularly where the life tenant is elderly and unmarried. In such a case what would have been done pre-2006 would have been to replace the existing life interest with one in favour of a younger member of the family and rely on the existing life tenant surviving seven years to avoid IHT. Unfortunately this does not now work: as explained above, any inter vivos termination is an immediately chargeable transfer for IHT purposes if the property remains settled. This means that IHT is chargeable at 20% insofar as the life tenant's nil-rate band is exceeded.

As the law now stands, there are two possible solutions. One is to ensure that at the time of termination the assets held in trust are business assets eligible for 100% relief from IHT. The other is to terminate the trust by outright distribution. As is explained in para 61.14, this is without IHT consequence if the recipient is the life tenant or his spouse and otherwise it qualifies for PET treatment. In other words IHT is avoided provided that the former life tenant survives seven years and avoids benefiting from the assets in such a way as would bring the gift with reservation rules into play.

Unfortunately, terminating the trust in this way cannot normally be recommended. The prime reason is that the distribution is a capital payment resulting in CGT on the recipient to the extent there are unmatched gains in the trust (see CHAPTER 9). Income tax may also be in issue to the extent that income has been accumulated in the past or the portfolio has generated offshore income gains. A secondary reason is that the distribution itself often compounds the CGT problem as it is a CGT disposal, thereby crystallising any hitherto unrealised gains, and thus increasing the total able to be allocated to the distribution.

The upshot is that termination is normally only a solution if there is little or no unmatched income or gains in the structure or if the intended recipient is non-UK resident and so outside the charges on distributions (see para **10.2**). In other cases the better strategy is to retain the settlement, perhaps converting to relevant property where business property relief or other reliefs so allow, and otherwise taking advantage of the freedom from 10-yearly charges.

There is a potential CGT bonus in such inaction for on the death of the holder of a qualifying interest in possession the assets subject to that interest are rebased (see para **77.6**). This prevents any latent gains as at the death from going into the pool matched to capital payments thereafter and, in cases where latent gains are substantial, may be reason in itself to keep a qualifying interest in possession on foot.

NEITHER INCOME NOR GAINS SHELTERED

5.17 There are two main categories of trust which shelter neither income nor gains. One is settlor-interested trusts, ie trusts where the settlor and his spouse are not excluded from benefit. The other is trusts subject to an interest in possession where the settlor and his spouse are both excluded but their children and (where appropriate) grandchildren are not. Such trusts do not operate as an income shelter on account of the interest in possession and do not operate as a gains shelter because TCGA 1992, s 86 attributes the gains to the settlor (see CHAPTER 76).

Settlor-interested trusts

5.18 The normal type of settlor-interested trust gave the settlor an initial life interest followed by a successive life interest to his spouse. As described at the beginning of this chapter, such settlements were often set up in the period prior to March 1991 as a CGT shelter. Settlements of this kind confer no tax advantage so long as the settlor remains UK resident as the income and gains are taxed as his and, for IHT purposes, his life interest is, by pre-dating 2006, a qualifying interest in possession, so resulting in a death charge in the event of his death.

It is often said that such settlements have little point and where possible should be terminated by distribution to the settlor. Unfortunately termination is not always easy for, while the distribution is free of IHT (see para **61.14**) there are likely to be CGT consequences. First, all assets distributed count as disposed of at market value, thereby crystallising a charge on the settlor under TCGA 1992, s 86 on any latent gain. Second, there may well be unmatched s 2(2) amounts dating back to before 1998, for the general rule was that until then, pre-1991 settlements were not within s 86 but within the capital payments regime in s 87 (see para **9.14**). If this is indeed the position, termination results also in a s 87 charge on the settlor.

In practical terms these factors may render termination unattractive, unless the settlor decides to emigrate. Should that not be the position, the strategies are essentially the same as described above for other types of qualifying interest in possession trust, namely managing the potential IHT charge on death by life assurance and/or a successive life interest to a surviving spouse. As with the trusts described above, retaining the life-interest until death secures the CGT rebasing.

Interest in possession held by another beneficiary

5.19 In practical terms, the trusts at issue here are those where a beneficiary other than the settlor holds a qualifying interest in possession and TCGA 1992, s 86 is in point because the settlor is alive and UK resident and the beneficiaries include his children or (in the case of tainted settlements or post-1998 settlements) his grandchildren. For the reasons given above, the pre-2006 IHT regime means such settlements are comparatively common.

The IHT planning issues and techniques for these settlements are essentially the same as those described in para **5.16** above. One difference is that any latent gain on termination of the settlement is taxed as the settlor's rather than on the beneficiary under s 87 rules.

The practical problems posed by s 86 are as much an issue with these settlements as with the settlements described in para **5.11** above. This factor may itself prompt termination, such termination being by distribution to the life tenant and so free of IHT. In a sense, the tax position following termination will be the same as that under the trust in that income and gains will be fully taxable and the assets will remain in the former life tenant's estate for IHT purposes. Indeed the position may be better, for the practical difficulties of indemnifying the settlor under s 86 will have gone and the former life tenant will be able to engage in conventional IHT mitigation by timely lifetime gifts.

In many cases these factors may render termination attractive, particularly where the trust is small and the costs charged by the trustees are high relative to value. But if the decision is to terminate two factors should be kept in mind.

The first is that the termination will be a CGT disposal and, as the trust is within s 86, tax on any latent gain is charged on the settlor, with the possible difficulties in recovery noted above. A holdover election is not normally valid, as the general relief under TCGA 1992, s 260 applies only where the disposal is an immediately chargeable transfer for IHT purposes.

The second point is that at some stage the settlor will die or (possibly) emigrate. On such scenario, termination now will mean the CGT advantages which then become available will have been lost.

A positive reason for keeping the settlement is that there are, in appropriate cases, means of ensuring it can operate as a tax shelter. One is to invest in non-reporting funds. As noted in para **5.15** above, these funds tend not to pay income such as would be taxable on the life tenant and instead the return is rolled up and realised only on sale (see CHAPTERS 3 and 95). Here it is taxed as income, but critically it is neither actual income taxed on the life tenant nor a gain within the settlor charge (see CHAPTER 82). Instead it is taxed only by reference to capital payments and benefits to beneficiaries.

A second technique is that also noted above, namely to hold the investments through a holding company. This removes income retained in the company from charge on the life tenant, and, because the settlor and his spouse are excluded, it cannot normally be charged on the settlor either. In most cases gains in such a company would still be taxed on the settlor as TCGA 1992, s 13 should attribute the gains to the trust and bring them within s 86 (see para 88.31). But in some cases the s 13 motive defence may preclude this and even if that is not in point, indexation can make s 13 treatment more favourable (see paras 88.4 and 88.7).

The upshot of these points is that a qualifying interest in possession trust within s 86 can be restructured to operate as a tax shelter, albeit that in some cases the restructuring may trigger realisation of existing latent gains with s 86 consequences then. These possibilities mean the decision to wind up such a trust should not lightly be taken.

CONCLUSION

5.20 The overall conclusion from the discussion above is that where a settlement established by a UK domiciliary now exists it should normally be retained. The one qualification is where the trust fund is modest, for here costs may outweigh any possible tax advantages.

Assuming the settlement is retained, the discussion needs to move to the planning of distributions and wider tax planning points. These topics form the subject of the remainder of this Part.

On the basis the settlement is retained, care must be taken to ensure the trustees and the beneficiaries comply with all relevant UK tax obligations. Even inadvertent mistakes can result in penalties if left uncorrected, as is described in CHAPTER 97. The prudent course for trustees is to ensure regular UK advice and review. This process of itself has a cost and, with small settlements, may be a factor tipping the balance towards winding up the trust.

Chapter 6
HOLDING COMPANIES

INTRODUCTION

6.1 Many trusts settled by UK domiciliaries hold their investments through non-UK resident holding companies and, as indicated in the previous chapter, there may on occasion be good reasons for trusts without a holding company to put one in place now. This chapter considers whether and if so in what circumstances holding companies are appropriate and how they impact on the planning described in the previous chapter.

FRAMEWORK

6.2 At the outset it is important to clarify advantages holding companies cannot deliver.

Inheritance tax

6.3 On the assumption the settlor is UK domiciled, use of a holding company does not reduce IHT exposure. All that happens is that the relevant asset for IHT purposes is the trust's shares in and loans to the company rather than the underlying investments. As the settlor was UK domiciled these assets are fully in charge to IHT (see CHAPTER 62). This is in contrast to settlements created by non-domiciliaries, where the shares and loans to the company are excluded property in a way that underlying UK assets are not if held at trust level (see CHAPTER 15).

Income tax anti-avoidance legislation

6.4 Use of a holding company does not in general alter the impact of anti-avoidance legislation on the income of the underlying investments. Should the trust be settlor-interested, the company's income is likely to be taxed as his under the transfer of assets code (see CHAPTER 69). In the more normal case where the settlor and his spouse are excluded, the company's income is relevant income for the purposes of the non-transferor charge in the same way that income at trust level is (see CHAPTER 71).

This income tax treatment is precluded where the transfer of assets motive defence applies (see CHAPTER 73). But the motive defence is rarely in point given the tax planning genesis of most existing settlements created by UK domiciliaries. Here too there is a contrast with settlements created by non-domiciliaries where the motive defence often requires consideration (see para **20.7**).

CGT anti-avoidance legislation

6.5 As with income, the general rule is that use of a holding company does not remove gains on the underlying investments from potential tax charges under anti-avoidance legislation. This is because TCGA 1992, s 13 attributes gains to non-resident trust participators in the same way as to UK resident participators (see para **88.31**). This means the gains are then taxed as the settlor's if the trust is within TCGA 1992, s 86 and otherwise go into the s 2(2) amount for the year in question.

But the position with gains is more nuanced than with income. In part this is because of the s 13 motive defence introduced in 2013 (as to which see para **88.4**). This protects gains at company level unless one of the purposes of the relevant arrangements was the avoidance of CGT or corporation tax. As is explained in para **88.37**, the precise scope of this exemption is unclear. But it should be available if neither the trust nor the company were put in place to avoid CGT.

Given the history of settlements created by UK domiciliaries it might be thought few such structures exist, and certainly a company put in place now to capture the motive defence would ipso facto fail the test. But this may not be true of some historic structures, for example children's trusts with underlying companies formed during 1998–2010, when CGT sheltering through such settlements was not possible and so could not have had a CGT avoidance purpose (see para **88.37**).

A second reason why the position with gains is more nuanced than with income is that the s 13 computational rules can be more favourable than those applicable to gains at trust level. The prime example is that gains within s 13 are computed with the benefit of indexation whereas gains at trust level are not (see para **88.7**).

DISADVANTAGES

6.6 There are certain undisputed drawbacks in holding investments through a company, some of which are well recognised.

Double counting

6.7 Doubling up of income and gains is the prime drawback. Doubling up focuses on an item of income or gain in the company. That item is taken into account under the anti-avoidance legislation described above when it enures to the company. But the value it represents cannot reach the trust unless the company pays a dividend or the trust liquidates the company or sells shares. In either event the ensuing receipt will engage the tax charges listed above for a second time.

In the case of income paid up in dividend this difficulty may be more apparent than real, for under both the transferor and the non transferor charge income should be counted only once (see paras **69.40** to **69.43** and **71.30**). But in almost all other situations the potential for the same economic value to be taken into account twice is difficult to avoid.

The point is particularly harsh with s 13, for the general rule with s 13 is that the distribution of a s 13 gain within three to four years of realisation allows the s 13 tax to be credited against tax on the distribution (see para **88.22**). But this rule is difficult to operate with s 13 gains accruing to offshore trusts, particularly where the charge at issue is the beneficiary charge under s 87 (see para **88.32**). The fact that s 13 gains may be computed on a more generous basis than trust gains does not alter the fundamental point that part at least of the same economic value can be taken into account twice.

Practical issues

6.8 The practicalities entailed in operating a company can be an equally powerful argument against having one. The key point is that the company's affairs must be so conducted as to ensure there is no basis for HMRC to argue it is UK resident. The applicable test is the central management and control test described in Chapter **43**. What is required is for the company's board to genuinely run and understand its business, and for there to be no suggestion of unauthorised control by the settlor or beneficiaries

In general most well-run fiduciary businesses understand what is needed to ensure a company in trust ownership is not at risk of residence in the UK. Indeed the requirements of the central and management and control test are less onerous than the fiduciary duties of directors under most systems of company law (see para **43.7**) and, in many instances, than is required by regulators.

But the implication of what is required is time and thus cost. A careful evaluation is needed as to whether the costs entailed in an offshore company outweigh any supposed advantage it might bring. In making this evaluation it needs to be kept in mind that the costs include not merely the costs of directors properly discharging their functions but the preparation of company accounts and appropriate record keeping. This kind of work is certainly duplicated where a structure involves a company as well as a trust.

Other CGT points

6.9 Doubling up is not the only CGT drawback in using a company. Four others may be noted.

The first is that if the company is indeed within s 13, its losses may be unrelieved, whether in computing the settlor's liability under TCGA 1992, s 86 or trust gains under s 87. This is because TCGA 1992, s 13 does not, in general, allow losses to be apportioned (see para **88.19**). All that is possible is that losses in the company may be set on a current-year basis against gains apportioned from the same company or from another company in which the trust concerned is also a participator. Losses cannot be carried forward in the company and, more importantly, losses in the company cannot be set against gains realised by the trustees.

The practical result is that in a trust and company structure there may be substantial unrelieved losses. This problem simply does not arise if the company or companies are dispensed with, for then all losses and gains arise at trust level.

The second point concerns trusts subject to a qualifying interest in possession (see para **61.2**). Here the assets at trust level will receive a tax-free updated base cost for CGT purposes on the death of the life-tenant (TCGA 1992, s 72). But should the investments be held through a holding company, the new base cost does not extend to the underlying investments. This again is material if the company is within s 13 and can be particularly unfortunate should the company vest in UK beneficiaries absolutely on the death of the life-tenant, for then they will potentially be subject to tax on the unrealised gains in the company under TCGA 1992, s 13 when it realises its assets.

A third point is that an underlying company can create traps under the trustee borrowing rules described in CHAPTER 80. This is because an upstream loan from the company to the trust is trustee borrowing. If the trustees do not apply the loan for normal trust purposes, any subsequent distribution or loan by the trustees triggers a complete or partial disposal of the trust's shares in the company and of any other asset held at trust level. A related risk arises if the trustees borrow money from another source and transfer it to the company. Here too there is a deemed disposal unless the transfer is structured as a subscription for shares or securities in the company (see para **80.15**).

The fourth and final point is highly technical. It is that a payment from the trustees to the company may count as a capital payment to UK resident individuals. The problem arises because a capital payment to a non-resident company counts as a capital payment to any UK resident individual who controls it (TCGA 1992, s 96). By concession, the problem does not arise if, as is normal, none of the shares in the company is owned by a UK individual (TCGA 1992, s 96(10); ESC D40). If, however, the settlor or a beneficiary owns some shares and the trust the rest, a non-arm's length payment from the trustees to the company does count as a capital payment to the settlor or beneficiary, for the trust holding is attributed to them in determining whether they control the company (TA 1988, s 417(3)(b), (c)) (see further para **78.18**).

Income tax points

6.10 Use of a company can also have specific income tax drawbacks over and above the general points referred above. Three in particular may be mentioned.

The first is that UK or foreign tax borne by the company cannot be credited against UK tax charged on distributions from the trust. Where the investments are held directly by the trustees, discretionary distributions of income by the trust may attract credit for UK tax borne by trust income (ESC B18; see para **8.11**). This point is particularly serious where the trust is subject to a life interest, for then, as explained in para **8.2**, the income is treated as that of the life-tenant from inception. This means he secures any credit for foreign withholding tax attached to the income. This advantage is lost if the assets are held in an underlying company, for foreign tax credits are not normally in point on dividends paid by offshore companies.

The second point is that use of a company means the benefit in kind legislation described in CHAPTER 93 has to be considered. The risks under this legislation arises if either the settlor or a beneficiary can be said to be a shadow director (see CHAPTER 93). It used to be thought there was little risk in this area, for the most they can do is make requests to the trustees, it being up to the trustees to communicate with the directors if they think fit. Unfortunately, as is described in CHAPTER 93, the definition of the term shadow director is wide and on one view at least a settlor or beneficiary could be caught if the actual directors regularly take account of his views and benefits are conferred on them.

It might be thought the impact of this legislation is not significant as most benefits are in any event taxable under the transfer of assets code or the CGT capital payments code. But this ignores the fact that national insurance contributions can attach to benefits in kind and also the fact that a benefit under the benefit in kind code is taxed even if there is no income or gain in the structure against which to match it.

The third point is that a company requires the transactions in securities legislation to be considered whenever a planning exercise is undertaken. This legislation is described in CHAPTER 89, and its application to the charges on settlors and beneficiaries is far from clear (see para 89.30). Further it applies only if HMRC initiate counteraction and there is a stringent purpose filter. But no planning exercise should ignore the legislation if the result of the exercise is a receipt in capital form, as on a liquidation or buy-back.

ADVANTAGES

6.11 In the light of all the drawbacks it may be wondered why any trust settled by a UK domiciliary should hold assets through an underlying company at all. In reality, however, there can be advantages, some of which have already been highlighted in CHAPTER 5.

Retention of income

6.12 One advantage arises where the trust is subject to a qualifying interest in possession. Here, as is explained in paras 5.15 and 5.19, the holding of the trust investments permits de facto accumulation as income can be retained in the company and invested. This defers any charge on the life-tenant until the income is paid out in dividend, and, provided the settlor and his spouse are completely excluded from the trust, taxation on the settlor under the transfer of assets code is avoided as well.

Use of a holding company in this context can certainly be attractive in some family situations but it may have trust law implications. The basic duty of trustees of fixed-interest trusts is to maintain a balance between the life-tenant and remaindermen, including providing the life-tenant with a reasonable income. Trustees can only permit income to be rolled-up in the company if they have given genuine consideration to the life-tenant's interests before doing so.

UK source income

6.13 A holding company is also of value where the underlying investments are in the UK. Here UK income arising to the trustees is taxed at the trust rates of 45%, or in the case of dividends, at the dividend trust rate (see para **64.8**). Use of a company reduces or eliminates this tax, in that UK dividends do not suffer tax at all and other income is taxed at 20% (see para **64.5**).

These advantages do not obtain if the trust is settlor-interested, for then the settlor is taxed on the income under the transfer of assets code. Nor are they relevant where the income is going to be paid out to UK beneficiaries, for then, as described above, ESC B18 means overall tax is normally less if the income arises at trust level, and this is certainly so if the trust is subject to an interest in possession.

Subject to these points, the advantages of a holding company are clear where the trustees wish commercially to hold shares in UK companies and accumulate the income. It is true that the same advantage can be achieved by investing in the UK through an offshore mutual fund (see para **3.15**) but there may be good commercial reasons why such is unattractive. This is the position where the trust investment is one or more large or controlling holdings or where it is designed to pick stock on a bespoke basis.

Holding companies are also widely used where the trustees wish to invest in UK commercial property. This is discussed further in CHAPTER 30.

Trustee borrowing

6.14 A third and final point to note on the plus side is that borrowing by a holding company does not count as trustee borrowing for the purposes of TCGA 1992, Sch 4B (see para **80.30**). This means all the risks entailed in that schedule are avoided. As a result where borrowing is needed to pay for an investment, borrowing and holding the investment through a company may be attractive.

CONCLUSION

6.15 Despite the points just made, the overall conclusion in most cases is that a holding company is unattractive where the settlement was created by a UK domiciliary. But with many trusts a holding company is already in place and the issue arises of whether it should be wound up and the assets transferred up to trust level.

Save where the points made in paras **6.12** to **6.14** are material, the general answer is yes. But in some cases two specific factors may point to a contrary conclusion. One is if either the trust's shares in the company, or the assets held in the company, are showing significant latent gains. Here crystallisation of the gains may be inadvisable, particularly where the settlement is within TCGA 1992, s 86, with the result the gains would be immediately chargeable on the settlor.

An equally cogent factor is if the company is or may be within the s 13 motive defence. Here the effect of that defence is to keep gains at company level out of charge. The consequence is both an avoidance of doubling up and deferral of the single CGT event until the company is sold or liquidated. In appropriate cases this could be a real advantage although inevitably the availability of the motive defence is not always clear. Some of the issues as to this are discussed in para **88.37**.

Should the decision be to liquidate the possible impact of the transactions in securities legislation described in CHAPTER **89** should be considered. In many cases the conclusion will be the practical risk of HMRC counteraction is remote.

Chapter 7

TRAPS AND PITFALLS

INTRODUCTION

7.1 CHAPTERS 1 and 5 have explained the difficult tax issues which confront offshore trusts created by UK domiciliaries. This chapter highlights some further areas of tax risk.

THE SETTLOR

7.2 As will be apparent from CHAPTERS 1 and 5, most of the offshore trusts being considered here are outside the settlor's estate for IHT purposes and operate as an effective income tax shelter. As is explained in those chapters, achievement of these goals requires there to be no possibility under the terms of the settlement that the settlor or his spouse can benefit. But what should not be forgotten is that these objectives can be frustrated even if the terms of the settlement are in the requisite form.

Benefits

7.3 The first point to make is that the focus has to be on what actually happens as well as on what is drafted. Thus a settlor who receives a benefit may find the settled property has ceased to be enjoyed to his exclusion for the purposes of the gift with reservation rules (see CHAPTER 83). So too the amount or value of the benefit may be subject to income tax under the transfer of assets code should the asset out of which the benefit is provided be derived from income (see para **69.39**).

Where the intention is for the settlor and trustees to deal on an arm's length basis, thought can be given to including an adjuster clause in the agreement between the parties, under which the consideration changing hands will be adjusted if it is alleged by HMRC or established by any court or tribunal that the original terms of the transaction involved an element of benefit to the settlor. SP 5/92 suggests that HMRC accept the effectiveness of adjuster clauses.

Power to enjoy

7.4 A second point is that the income of a non-resident trust is attributed to the settlor under the transfer of assets code if he has power to enjoy it (see CHAPTER 69). In most cases 'power to enjoy' covers the same ground as actual or potential benefit in the settlement code and where that is so, it is the settlement code which applies (see para **69.36**). But power to enjoy is defined in terms of five enjoyment conditions and, at least in theory, it is possible for a settlor who is excluded under the terms of the trust to fall within them. If so, the trust income is taxed as his.

A case where this happened was *IRC v Brackett* [1986] STC 521. As is described in paras **69.13** and **69.14**, the settlor here was completely excluded from the settlement, but transactions between him and an underlying company were held to be sufficient to engage two of the enjoyment conditions. The moral is that great care is needed in any dealings between the settlor and the trust.

Payments

7.5 Potentially the greatest traps for settlors are posed by ITA 2007, s 727 and ITTOIA 2005, s 633, described in paras **70.17** and **75.9** respectively. The precondition for the application of each of these sections is receipt by the settlor of a capital sum, a concept defined as any payment which is not income and for which full consideration is not given. More significantly, the settlor is treated as receiving a capital sum if the trustees lend money to him, or if they repay to him money he has previously lent them. Such loans and repayment are caught even if entirely commercial and thus proper transactions for trusts where the settlor is excluded.

Should s 633 be in point, the capital sum is taxed as the settlor's income to the extent of past income accumulated by the trustees. In the event the past income is insufficient the payment can be carried forward by up to ten years and taxed to the extent the trustees accumulate income within that time.

Section 727 is potentially more serious, because, in contrast to s 633, it does not restrict the tax charge to the capital sum. Rather, the way it operates is to deem all the current and future income of the trust and any underlying company to be the settlor's income, in the same way as would be the position if he had power to enjoy the income. Some doubt whether s 727 really does have this draconian effect, but as a matter of strict language it plainly does (see para **69.26**).

As explained in para **69.23**, there should be a defence to liability under s 727 if the payment of the capital sum is unconnected with the original transfer of assets and operations which may reasonably be regarded as associated. But such a possibility should not be relied on in planning.

Minor children

7.6 As a final point it should not be forgotten that income paid to minor children of the settlor is treated as his (ITTOIA 2005, s 629; see para **75.8**). Self-evidently this charge is not in issue if the settlor is dead but otherwise it needs to be kept in mind if he has children under the age of 18. The charge also extends to capital distributions to the settlor's minor children insofar as the trust has retained income (ITTOIA 2005, s 631).

TRUSTEE BORROWING

7.7 The rules relating to trustee borrowing are described in CHAPTER 80. These rules present real difficulties for offshore trustees. The best practical advice is that trustees should not borrow. If they do borrow any proposed course of action thereafter needs to be reviewed to check it is not a transfer of value within the meaning of TCGA 1992, Sch 4B or, if it is, that the borrowing has been applied for normal trust purposes.

A particular danger is where the trustees borrow from an underlying company. If thereafter they lend money down to another company, or distribute or lend it to a beneficiary, such is a transfer of value for the purposes of Sch 4B. A deemed disposal of the trust assets will thereby be triggered if the borrowing is still outstanding and has not been applied for normal trust purposes.

Should there be a Sch 4B transfer, not merely are the ensuing gains assessable on the settlor on an arising basis if the trust is within s 86, but the settlement's s 2(2) and OIG amounts are carried into Sch 4C pools. This has two disadvantages, namely that they cannot be washed out by distributions to non-residents and can be allocated in full to the beneficiaries of any other settlement to which the settlement transfers funds. Inter alia this last point means that s 2(2) amounts in excess of the value of the trust fund may still all be taxable. Sch 4C is discussed further in CHAPTER 81.

TAINTING

7.8 As explained in paras **5.9** and **76.7**, grandchildren's settlements created before 17 March 1998 can be outside the scope of TCGA 1992, s 86. This is the position if the settlor, his children, and their respective spouses and companies controlled by them, are all excluded from any possibility of benefit and do not in fact benefit. Being outside s 86 means gains in the trust and any underlying company are not assessable on the settlor as they arise should he be alive and UK resident.

This favourable treatment is lost should the settlement become 'tainted'. By 'tainting' is meant falling foul of one of the four conditions specified in TCGA 1992, Sch 5 para 2A (see para **76.7**). Much the most important of these is provision of property or income to the settlement, and this should therefore be avoided in relation to any settlement relying on the protection from s 86 afforded to pre-1998 grandchildren's settlements.

Until 1998 the issue of tainting was of much greater potential significance since in the absence of tainting any settlement created before 19 March 1991 was outside s 86. HMRC produced extensive guidance as to the tainting conditions in SP 5/92 and this should be consulted whenever issues as to tainting arise with grandchildren's settlements. It should also be kept in mind that a pre-1998 settlement not currently within the grandchildren exemption can be brought within it if it has remained untainted and the necessary exclusions are made (see para **76.5**).

UNEXPECTED S 13 GAINS

7.9 Gains in a close company can be apportioned under TCGA 1992, s 79B to trustee participators if the company is resident in a country with which the UK has concluded a double tax treaty and the gains are treaty protected. The same result follows if the trustees are participators in a UK company and that company is a participator in the company resident in the treaty jurisdiction. As with all gains so apportioned, the gains come within TCGA 1992, s 86 if that section applies to the settlement and otherwise they are included in the trust's s 2(2) amount.

Section 13, and thus s 79B, have since 6 April 2012 been subject to the motive defence described in para **88.4** and nor do they apply to gains on assets used for the purposes of non-UK trades or economically significant activities (see para **88.5**). These exceptions are certainly in point in relation to many companies established in treaty jurisdictions and to that extent s 79B is of restricted impact.

But where the exceptions are or may not be in point, the ambit of s 79B is potentially wide, for it extends to any trust participator with more than 25% of the company concerned and to participators with smaller percentage interests if they and connected persons together exceed the 25% threshold.

Many trustees hold shares in UK private companies and, until the first enactment of TCGA 1992, s 79B in 2000, were not concerned with what went on in foreign subsidiaries of such companies. Now, however, they should be, for s 79B means gains in the foreign subsidiaries may be apportionable to the trust. Because this applies only where the gain is treaty protected, the gains caught will tend to be those realised by foreign subsidiaries in high tax jurisdictions rather than by purely offshore subsidiaries. The latter are not treaty protected and so are outside s 79B.

UK REAL ESTATE

7.10 Offshore trustees holding UK land need to keep the anti-avoidance rules directed at land transactions in mind. These rules were recast in 2016 and are described in CHAPTER 90. In most cases any acquisition of UK real estate is through an offshore company and a corporation tax charge on the company is likely if the land is bought or developed with a view to sale at a profit. Potentially more serious for trustees is the risk of an income tax charge on the sale of the shares. This comes into issue if at the time of the sale over half the value of the shares is derived from UK real estate. The charge is made if an arrangement can be identified which entails dealing in or developing the land and then realising any profit by selling the shares. In practice such cases may be rare, but the legislation should be considered whenever trustees sell a company which owns UK land. Should the legislation be engaged the result is onerous, for the charge on the trustees, being income tax, is at the 45% trust rate rather than at the corporation tax rates applicable where the company sells the land.

Another sting lies in the provider charge. This requires the provider to be assessed instead of the person who actually realises the gain (see para **90.11**). It is clear this subsection applies where a person such as the settlor diverts the opportunity to make a profit to an offshore trust or company (*Yuill v Wilson* [1980] STC 460). The true ambit of the charge is unclear, particularly how far it applies to those who do no more than introduce a land development opportunity to an offshore entity. But what is clear is that it is unwise for the settlor or beneficiaries to be involved in any way in the buying or selling of land by the trust or any underlying company.

DISPOSALS OF BENEFICIAL INTERESTS

7.11 No UK resident beneficiary should effect a disposal of a beneficial interest in a non-UK resident trust. Should he do so, the transaction is subject to CGT, for the exemption for beneficial interests does not apply unless the trust is UK resident (TCGA 1992, s 85). A particular sting is that normally the beneficiary has a nil acquisition cost, for the creation of an interest under the terms of a settlement does not involve a corresponding disposal and so market value is not substituted (TCGA 1992, s 17(2)). An exception to this is where the trust has emigrated from the UK without previously having been non-resident, for then beneficial interests are rebased (TCGA 1992, s 85(3)).

A beneficiary disposes of his beneficial interest if he sells it, gives it away, or releases it. Save in the case of a sale, market value is substituted, for the transaction is not at arm's length (TCGA 1992, s 17(1)). In many instances where an interest is released, market value is nil, for the interest is either discretionary or subject to overriding powers. But save where this is clearly so, transactions in beneficial interests should be avoided.

Schemes to avoid the charge on beneficial interests have in the past involved repatriating the trust to the UK prior to the sale of the beneficial interest, or repatriating the trust and then emigrating it again. These schemes are now blocked, the former completely (TCGA 1992, s 76(1B)) and the latter wherever there are unallocated trust gains outstanding at the time of the emigration (TCGA 1992, s 85(10)).

TRANSFERS TO UK TRUSTS

7.12 The transfer of all or part of the trust fund from one trust to another transfers all or part of the transferor trust's outstanding s 2(2) and OIG amounts to the transferee trust (see para **77.29**). Should the transferee trust be a pre-existing UK settlement specific adverse consequences may follow. The exercise will render capital distributions from the UK settlement, hitherto tax-free, taxable by reference to s 2(2) amounts in the offshore settlement (see paras **77.36** and **81.14**). A similar analysis is likely to obtain as respects relevant income for the purposes of ITA 2007, ss 731–735 (see para 70.28). An additional consequence is that any disposals of beneficial interests under the UK settlement will become chargeable (TCGA 1992, s 76(1A)(b)).

A further issue is raised by the rules as to trustee borrowing. Should the transferor trust itself have a Sch 4C pool of gains, or have received funds from another trust which is a relevant settlement in relation to such a pool, the effect of the transfer is not to transfer gains between trusts but to render all the gains in the Sch 4C pool assessable on the beneficiaries of either the transferor or the transferee trust (see para 81.13). The practical result is that the trustees of the transferee trust need to review the Sch 4C position of the transferor trust before accepting the transfer. The same considerations apply if the transfer is itself a Sch 4B transfer, ie if the transferor trust then has outstanding trustee borrowing for in such circumstances the effect of the transfer is to convert the transferor's trusts s 2(2) amounts into a Sch 4C pool. All this is explained in CHAPTER 81.

SEPARATE FUNDS

7.13 A trust with separate funds can give rise to difficulties in that, unless a sub-fund election has been made, it has a single s 87 pool of gains. Accordingly gains realised in one fund can be allocated to capital payments from another. This issue and possible solutions is discussed in para 77.53. A similar problem can arise with relevant income for the purposes of ITA 2007, ss 731–735 (paras 71.32 to 71.34).

SAME-SEX RELATIONSHIPS

7.14 As explained in paras 69.53 and 75.3, a trap exists where the settlor of any settlement whose income is not currently assessed as his under ITA 2007, ss 720–730 or ITTOIA 2005, s 624 enters into civil partnership or same-sex marriage. In such case, the income becomes assessable as his unless the terms of the settlement, as well as excluding the settlor and any different-sex spouse, also exclude any civil partner or same-sex spouse. Where, therefore, a civil partnership or same-sex marriage of the settlor is in prospect, amendment to the trust deed should be made in advance of the ceremony.

As a matter of strict construction, there is scope for assessment of income on the settlor under ss 720–730 even where the settlor has no civil partner or same-sex spouse, if there is a possibility of benefits being received by a future civil partner or same-sex spouse – regardless of whether there is any likelihood of such a union being entered into (see para 69.52). The same point arises in relation to the attribution of trust gains (see para 76.11). For this reason any new settlement should expressly exclude civil partners and same-sex spouses in the same way as different-sex spouses.

As explained at para 76.11, HMRC have stated informally they would not take any point on the non-exclusion of civil partners in relation to settlements existing on 23 November 2005, when civil partnerships first became possible under English law. Presumably they would take the same line in relation to the non-exclusion of same-sex spouses from settlements existing on 13 March

2014, when the concept of same-sex marriage was introduced. But prudent trustees will undoubtedly wish to exercise powers of appointment or exclusion so as to put the matter beyond doubt.

COMPLIANCE AND PENALTIES

7.15 As explained in CHAPTERS 1 and 5, offshore trusts created by UK domiciliaries have always been subject to IHT. So too UK source income arising to the trustees is and always has been taxable at the trust rate unless, in the case of dividends and interest, there are no UK beneficiaries (see para **64.8**). In recent years the tax exposure of offshore trustees has increased, now including non-resident CGT (see CHAPTER 65). Underlying companies holding UK residential property may entail exposure to ATED and ATED-related CGT (see CHAPTER 66). As noted above (para **7.10**), the anti-avoidance code directed at land transactions also has to be kept in mind.

At one time offshore trustees could be cavalier about UK tax compliance obligations and HMRC tacitly accepted there was little they could do to enforce the tax liabilities of non-residents. This era, however, is long gone. Any well-regulated jurisdiction requires its trust service providers to be compliant and, perhaps more importantly, the UK has an increasingly stringent range of penalties for non-compliance. These are described in CHAPTER 97 and can be levied even for inadvertent error if the error is left uncorrected.

Regulatory and penalty considerations make it important for offshore trustees to keep their possible UK tax exposure under regular review, taking appropriate specialist advice. A particular incentive to do this comes from HMRC's Requirement to Correct Policy. This encourages taxpayers to come forward and correct any past errors by 30 September 2018 or face increased penalties for failure to do so (see further para **97.10**). The significance of 2018 is that HMRC believes it will receive a great deal of further information by virtue of automatic information exchange under the Common Reporting Standard. The Common Reporting Standard is outside the scope of this book, but the need for offshore trustees to be fully tax compliant is not and is increasingly important.

Chapter 8

INCOME DISTRIBUTIONS

INTRODUCTION

8.1 It is probably a fair generalisation to say that as offshore trusts mature, UK resident beneficiaries increasingly want to enjoy some benefit. Absent non-residence, enjoying benefit, whether in income or capital form, normally results in at least some UK tax. This chapter explains how income distributions to UK resident and domiciled beneficiaries are taxed and the next chapter deals with distributions of capital. Planning suggestions are offered in CHAPTER 10.

Both this chapter, and CHAPTERS 9 and 10, assume the settlor was resident and domiciled in the UK when he made the settlement. In this chapter it is further assumed that, if he is still alive, he and his spouse are excluded from benefit and so outside the income tax settlement code discussed in CHAPTER 75. It is also assumed that the income of the trust is not taxable as his under the transfer of assets code (see paras 7.4 and 7.5 and CHAPTER 69).

FIXED-INTEREST TRUSTS

8.2 As explained in CHAPTER 5, a significant proportion of offshore trusts settled by UK domiciliaries are subject to an interest in possession. This means the holder of that interest, or life tenant as he is known, is entitled as of right to the income.

The general rule

8.3 The general rule is that the life tenant is treated as directly entitled to the underlying income. Thus if the underlying assets are in the UK he has UK source income and if they are abroad he has foreign income. The principle of direct entitlement was established in the 1920s in the leading cases of *Singer v Williams* [1921] 1 AC 41 and *Baker v Archer-Shee* [1927] AC 844. It is generally known as the *Archer-Shee* rule or principle, and trusts where it is in point are sometimes referred to as *Baker* trusts.

The *Archer-Shee* principle has on occasion been criticised as incompatible with equitable principles but, resting as it does on the authority of the House of Lords, it is too well entrenched to be anything other than the law. Indeed, in *Revenue and Customs Comrs v Anson* [2015] UKSC 44, [2015] STC 1777, 17

ITLR 1007 the Supreme Court referred to the two cases without criticism (see further para **32.2**).

Exceptions to the general rule

8.4 A trust is only a *Baker* trust insofar as the proper law of the trust follows that of England and treats the life tenant as having a specific equitable interest in the income of the trust investments. Some other systems of law do not view the matter this way and consider that what the life tenant has is the right to have the trustee account to him for the balance of the income after expenses. If this is the position, the source of the life tenant's income is his right against the trustee and is a new source (*Archer-Shee v Garland* [1931] AC 212). Trusts of this kind are sometimes termed *Garland* trusts.

It is settled that trusts governed by the law of New York are *Garland* trusts (*Archer-Shee v Garland* (above)). So also are Scottish trusts (see ITA 2007, s 464 and the Inland Revenue Press Release '*Finance Bill – Scottish Trusts*' 9 July 1993). But as is well known, the trust law of most offshore jurisdictions follows English law, and so trusts governed by such laws are *Baker* trusts. But the point may perhaps be live with jurisdictions such as Liechtenstein where the local trust law has a purely statutory basis and draws on American as well as English ideas.

HMRC publish a list of territories in respect of which they have a view as to whether interest in possession trusts are *Baker* trusts, ie like English law, or *Garland* trusts (TSEM 10420 and 10423). All three Crown Dependencies are on the *Baker* list, but Liechtenstein is on the *Garland* list.

Trustee expenses

8.5 With either characterisation of the life tenant's interest, a deduction is made for the trustees' expenses and remuneration in computing the income which is payable to him (*IRC v Berrill* [1981] STC 784, 797). With *Baker* trusts, this is not consistent with the idea that the life tenant is entitled to the income from inception, but is based on old cases and well-established law (see for example *Macfarlane v IRC* (1929) 14 TC 532). The expenses which may be deducted are not merely those which are income expenses as a matter of general law but also capital expenses insofar as the trustees are empowered to and do charge them against income (ITA 2007, s 500, codifying the law as stated in *Carver v Duncan* [1984] STC 556, 565 per Oliver LJ).

Dividends

8.6 The *Archer-Shee* principle is of great practical importance where the trust income includes dividends. Provided the trust is a *Baker* trust, the effect of the principle is that the life tenant enjoys the dividend rates of income tax. These apply to both UK and foreign dividends.

The first £5,000 of an individual's dividend income is tax free, and then the dividend rates are 7.5% basic rate, 32.5% higher rate and 38.1% top rate.

Distributions from trust capital

8.7 A series of cases on English trusts has established that where trustees are required or empowered to top-up the life tenant's income out of capital, the payments thereby made are taxable as annual payments. The leading case is *Cunard's Trustees v IRC* (1945) 27 TC 122. Here if the income fell short, the trustees were empowered to apply such portion of the trust capital by way of addition to the income as they in their absolute and uncontrolled discretion saw fit. The Court of Appeal held that the purpose of the top-up payments out of capital was an income purpose and that as such they fell to be treated as the life tenant's income despite having been made out of capital.

This principle can apply equally in relation to foreign trusts. In applying it, the characterisation principles discussed in CHAPTER 32 apply, to the effect that the nature of the life tenant's interest has to be ascertained under the appropriate foreign law and then the question of whether a given receipt is income or capital is ascertained under English law. Thus in *Inchyra v Jennings* [1965] 2 All ER 714, the trustees were required to distribute 1% of the value of the trust fund annually to the life tenant. This was capital under the Canadian proper law of the trust, but under English law it fell to be characterised as income.

There has been no decided case where this principle has been applied otherwise than to regular payments explicitly made to top up income. Nor, in relation to fixed-interest trusts, has it applied otherwise than to payments to the life tenant, although in *Inchyra v Jennings* it is worth noting that the recipient of the capital was life tenant in just one quarter of the fund.

DISCRETIONARY TRUSTS

New source

8.8 The principle in *Baker v Archer-Shee* plainly has no application to discretionary trusts. Indeed it could be argued that a distribution from a discretionary trust is not subject to income tax at all on the grounds that it is a voluntary payment by the trustees or that it lacks recurrence. These arguments, however, were rejected in relation to distributions from a foreign discretionary trust in *Drummond v Collins* (1915) 6 TC 525, on the grounds that such payments were income arising from possessions out of the UK within the former Schedule D Case V. In relation to UK trusts, *Cunard's Trustees v IRC* (supra) established that discretionary income distributions from a UK resident trust are assessable as annual payments (*IRC v Berrill* [1981] STC 784, 797 per Vinelott J).

It is clear from the authorities that the discretionary trust is the source (see para 40.13) and thus that the distribution has a source separate from that of the underlying income in the trust. It is reasonably clear that distributions from a

UK discretionary trust are taxable under ITTOIA 2005, s 683 as annual payments not otherwise charged, and indeed ITTOIA 2005, ss 684(3) and 686(2) expressly assume this to be so. It may be on a strict reading of *Drummond v Collins* that income distributions from a foreign discretionary trust are income not otherwise charged within ITTOIA 2005, s 687, but even if so, there is little discernible difference between the two heads of charge.

Capital or income

8.9 *Drummond v Collins* did not address the issue of when distributions by discretionary trustees are income and when they are not. There is little direct authority on this in relation to non-resident trusts and somewhat confusing case law in relation to UK trusts.

In relation to UK trusts, the starting point is *Cunard's Trustees v IRC* (supra). Although this case concerned payments to a life tenant, the payments were, as just noted, discretionary in the sense that the trustees had a discretion as to whether to make them. Accordingly, the principle that can be extrapolated from the case is that in deciding whether a distribution from a discretionary trust is income, it is necessary to look at the purposes of the distribution.

Essentially these were the points taken by HMRC in what is now the leading case on the subject, *Stevenson v Wishart* [1987] STC 266. Here discretionary trustees had power to make either capital distributions or income distributions. An elderly beneficiary became ill, and over a three-year period the trustees made regular payments totalling in excess of £100,000 to meet terminal nursing-home fees. These payments were made out of trust capital in exercise of a power over capital.

HMRC argued that the payments had the character of income and should therefore be taxed as the beneficiary's income. The Court of Appeal rejected this, stating that terminal care is normally funded out of capital and that no issues as to income could possibly have arisen if a single capital sum had been appointed at the outset. The Court also stressed the fact that the power exercised had been a power to appoint capital. The mere fact of recurrence was not itself sufficient to make the payments income, *Cunard's Trustees* being distinguishable because the power exercised was not an express power to top up income.

HMRC consider that discretionary payments out of trust capital are not normally the income of the beneficiary (TSEM para 3781). An exception is made where under the terms of the trust payments out of capital are required to be made, or may be made, to supplement the beneficiary's income (TSEM para 3783). It may be suggested that this is a fair summary of the effect of the decided cases.

Accumulations

8.10 As will be apparent from the above, the nature of the power being exercised and the question of whether the funds distributed are capital or income is important. In this context, the issue of accumulations has to be considered. The effect of accumulation is to turn income into capital, most accumulation clauses directing that the accumulations be treated as trust capital for all purposes. Once accumulation has occurred, a subsequent distribution of the accumulated fund is a distribution of capital (*Stanley v IRC* [1944] 1 All ER 230). Accordingly, it is only income of the recipient if it can be made so under the principles described above.

Trusts differ in the detail of the provisions relating to income. In some cases there is a trust to accumulate with a power to distribute, and in others there is a long-stop trust to distribute with power to accumulate. Whichever the case it needs to be remembered that a power has to be exercised within a reasonable period – conventionally by the end of the year following that in which the income arises unless there are indications to the contrary (see for example *Re Allen-Meyrick's Will Trusts* [1966] 1 All ER 740).

If the trust is to accumulate and no distributions are in fact made, the income is plainly accumulated. But if the trust is to distribute there must be a positive decision to accumulate if accumulation is to be achieved. The decision can be inferred from slight evidence, for example the trust accounts. But if it is clear that the income has not been accumulated, the position remains that the income must be distributed. If there is a fixed default beneficiary the income is his and taxable as his, but otherwise, if there is a discretion, the discretion remains exercisable on the basis that all the income must be paid out (see *Re Locker's Settlement Trusts, Meachem v Sachs* [1978] 1 All ER 216). In such an event, what is distributed is still income and so taxable as such even though the trustees may be paying it later than they should have done.

ESC B18

8.11 The effect of the trust being the source of the beneficiary's income means that, in the absence of special provision, no credit is given to the beneficiary for tax borne by the trustees. Where the trustees are resident in the UK, there is special provision, in the form of ITA 2007, s 494, which requires the trustees to operate deduction at source in relation to income distributions and offset the tax due on the distributions against tax on their income as it arose. Section 494 does not cover the position where UK trustees have suffered foreign tax, but credit for the foreign tax is allowed to the beneficiary insofar as the foreign income arose in the tax year of the payment or the five previous years (TIOPA 2010, s 111).

Section 494 is limited to UK resident trusts (ITA 2007, s 493(1)(b)). It follows that in law distributions to UK beneficiaries by a non-resident discretionary trust are double-taxed insofar as the income at trust level is taxed. This is particularly noteworthy in relation to trusts with UK income, in that the trustees are taxable on that income at the trust rate (see para **64.8**) and the beneficiary then suffers further tax at his personal rate on the net sum distributed.

This anomaly is addressed by ESC B18, for that concession allows the beneficiary to take the same credit for the trust's UK tax as would have applied under s 494 if the trust had been UK resident. To obtain this treatment, the trustees must be fully compliant in that their self assessment returns must be up-to-date and all tax due on UK income paid. The UK tax credited can be that for the tax year of the distribution or the previous five tax years. The operation of the concession is in the hands of HMRC's Trusts and Estates office in Nottingham, to whom a claim must be made (TSEM para 3790). ESC B18 indicates that income is set against distributions on a last in first out basis, and that foreign and UK source income is treated as distributed rateably. As the trust rate is now equal to the highest rate of income tax, the ESC B18 credit eliminates tax at beneficiary level insofar as the trust income is UK source.

The reference in ESC B18 to trust tax for the previous five tax years being allowed is curious for normally, under the principles described above, retained income which is more than a year or two old will have been capitalised. This does not of itself mean a distribution of such capitalised income is per se capital in the hands of the beneficiary: as described above it could be income if distributed on a recurrent basis for an income purpose. But of their nature such cases are rare and the issue which therefore arises is whether ESC B18 implicitly allows a taxpayer to treat what would otherwise be a capital distribution as income and take the benefit of the concession. It is difficult to see how it can have this effect.

It is not wholly clear from the wording of ESC B18 whether it allows the beneficiary to take credit for foreign tax born by the trust as well as for UK tax. It is however a reasonable inference that it does, as the concession operating in respect of non-resident trusts is expressed to be similar to that applied to UK trusts. TSEM 3790 indicates HMRC so reads it. However the concession is, on its terms, limited to cases where treaty relief would have been applicable had the beneficiary received the income directly.

SETTLOR'S MINOR CHILDREN

8.12 The above discussion has assumed that the individual entitled to the income or, as the case may be, in receipt of discretionary distributions, is not a minor child of the settlor. Should this assumption be wrong the income or, as the case may be, the distribution is taxed as the income of the settlor, assuming he is still alive (ITTOIA 2005, s 629; see para 75.8). In general this point only arises with discretionary distributions, as the proper law of most trusts has provisions equivalent to Trustee Act 1931, s 31, which effectively imposes a default trust to accumulate where a minor is otherwise entitled to the income. But s 31 or its equivalent can be disapplied and in such a case the income would be that of the settlor if the minor beneficiary were his child.

The above points mean that, in general, distributions to a minor child of the settlor should be avoided as they defeat the income sheltering purpose of the trust.

NON-RESIDENT SETTLOR

8.13 In general the above analysis in this chapter applies in one scenario where the settlor is alive and not excluded, namely where he is non-UK resident. However in such a case one category of income remains taxed as his as it arises or if distributed to a minor child, namely UK source income arising at trust level. This point is explained in para **75.26**.

Chapter 9

CAPITAL DISTRIBUTIONS

INTRODUCTION

9.1 This chapter summarises the income tax and capital gains tax liabilities which arise when the trustees of an offshore trust distribute capital to a beneficiary resident and domiciled in the UK. It is assumed the trust was created by a settlor resident and domiciled in the UK and that it is not protected by the motive or EU defences in ITA 2007, ss 736–742A (see CHAPTERS 73 and 74).

The issue of whether a distribution is capital or income is addressed in the previous chapter. In this chapter, it is assumed that as a result of applying the principles there described, it has been established that the distribution is capital.

The rules described in this chapter also apply where a beneficiary resident and domiciled in the UK enjoys trust assets in specie. As is described in paras 70.19 and 78.14, such enjoyment equates to an annual capital distribution equal to the rent or interest foregone.

Capital distributions are rendered taxable by reference to available relevant income and capital gains. Potentially there are two types of capital gain, namely offshore income gains and ordinary capital gains. The computational rules applicable to these two types of gain are broadly the same, being explained in CHAPTERS 77 and 82. A further complication, discussed at the end of this chapter, arises where a deemed disposal occurs under the trustee borrowing rules. In this event both the ordinary gains and the offshore income gains as at the end of the tax year of the deemed disposal constitute Sch 4C pools (see CHAPTER 81 and para 82.10).

The basic rule is that a distribution of capital is taxed as income to the extent of available relevant income. Only if there is none, or it is insufficient, are the offshore income gains and the ordinary gains looked at, the former being taken before the latter. Should the distribution be taxed by reference to relevant income or offshore income gains, it is taxed as income. It is taxed as a capital gain insofar as matched with ordinary gains in a s 87 or a Sch 4C pool.

Should the distribution be to the settlor, it cannot be taxed by reference to relevant income. It can be taxed by reference to ordinary gains if such gains accrued before 17 March 1998 and the settlement was made before 19 March

1991. As is explained in CHAPTER 82, it may also be taxable by reference to offshore income gains.

AVAILABLE RELEVANT INCOME

9.2 It follows from the above that the first stage in determining the taxability of a capital distribution to a beneficiary other than the settlor, is to ascertain the available relevant income. The concept of relevant income is explained in CHAPTER 71. It has to be ascertained, in relation to any given benefit or distribution, what non-resident entities are capable of generating relevant income in relation to the recipient beneficiary and which (if any) have in fact generated such relevant income.

CHAPTER 71 explains that in answering these questions many technical issues arise, some of which, if advanced, would favour the taxpayer. Where the amounts at stake justify significant professional costs, it is worth investigating some or all of these points. There is nothing wrong in taking a reporting position in cases of uncertainty, provided that full disclosure is made of how liability under ITA 2007, ss 731–735 has been arrived at or, if as a result of these points there is nil liability, how that conclusion has been reached.

But in the generality of trust cases, the pragmatic approach is undoubtedly to treat the trust as having a notional pool of available relevant income or, where there is a holding company, treat the trust and company as together having a single combined pool. In normal cases, the pool will simply be the income of past years which has neither been used in expenses nor been distributed as income. In addition the pool is net both of income which has been taxed as the settlor's under the transfer of assets code or the settlement code and of income allocated under ss 731–735 to past capital distributions or benefits to UK resident beneficiaries (see paras **71.18**, **71.22**, and **71.25**).

If the trustees are well advised they will have maintained a computation of their available relevant income. If they have not, such will need to be prepared and, quite apart from ascertaining the tax treatment of any particular distribution, it should be prepared so as to facilitate future planning. The computation needs to go back to the inception of the trust or, if later, 10 March 1981. In most cases, trust or company accounts should in practice give the necessary information, the relevant income being income which has been accumulated or retained.

Trust advances

9.3 Even in a simple case there may be situations in which relevant income outside the trust/company structure has to be considered. One such is if the trust making the distribution has received an advance from another trust. Here income in that trust is relevant income in relation to the beneficiary receiving the distribution, unless the income arose after the advance or the beneficiary receiving the distribution is wholly excluded from the trust which made the advance (see para **71.33**). So too if the trust making the distribution has advanced capital to another trust, income arising in that trust may be relevant income if it is able to be used to benefit the recipient beneficiary.

Income excluded

9.4 Although, as indicated above, the pragmatic approach should in simple cases be to treat the trust as having a single pool of available relevant income, there are certain instances where this approach should not be taken.

One such case is if the income arose in a fund from which the beneficiary was excluded and could never be a beneficiary. In contrast to gains, strictly there is no single pool of relevant income and so if the recipient beneficiary could never in fact have benefited from income it should not be treated as relevant income in relation to him. The better view is that the same is true if the income has been segregated in banking terms and he has been excluded from it subsequently or it has been distributed to another beneficiary but this may not be accepted by HMRC (see para **71.15**).

A second instance of income being excluded is where there is a holding company and the company has paid retained income up to the trust. Here double counting should not be required (see para **71.30**).

Income included

9.5 There are also cases where items which are capital need to be included in the total of relevant income. One is where the trust or company holds fixed-interest securities sold between interest periods. Here the accrued interest scheme requires the accrued interest element received as part of the proceeds to count as relevant income (see para **71.9**). So too offshore income gains can be available relevant income if the trust has made a capital payment to a non-resident (see para **82.15**). Further examples are gains on life policies, which in certain circumstances are also deemed to be relevant income (see para **96.34**), and gains on the disposal of deeply discounted securities, a category of investment which encompasses many 'structured products' (see para **15.14**).

Dry trusts

9.6 It is common to encounter what are sometimes called 'dry' trusts. These are trusts which do not or are not thought to have any available relevant income. Such can be for one of three reasons:

(1)   No income has ever arisen as for example where the sole trust asset is a property which has never been let or shares in a UK company which has never paid dividends.
(2)   The trust is an interest in possession trust, which means by definition income cannot be retained.
(3)   All income which has ever arisen has been used in expenses or distributed to beneficiaries as income.

If a trust has hitherto been dry it is often felt prudent to keep it dry so as to avoid tiresome computations under ss 731–735 for the future. A trust will not of course be dry to the extent it owns shares in underlying, non-resident companies unless those companies too are dry. Nor will it be dry if it has received capital sums of the kind described in the previous paragraph.

9.7 *Capital distributions*

The charge to tax

9.7 Assuming there is relevant income, the distribution is taxed and should be returned as the income of the recipient beneficiary. In practice the uncertainties over ss 731–735 highlighted both here and in Chapters 70 and 71 render it desirable to explain the basis on which liability has been calculated. HMRC in any event expect to be advised of the entity to which the relevant income accrued.

In some cases, the trust's retained income may be relevant income in relation to more than one distribution. Here the rule is that the income is apportioned on a just and reasonable basis (see para **71.18**). Whatever basis is adopted should be explained in relevant tax returns. In general it may be suggested that allocation should be done on a year by year basis and, as between distributions, within each year should be on a pro rata basis. The difficult issues raised by allocation are discussed in paras **71.18** to **71.31**).

There is one scenario in which the distribution may be taxed as that of the settlor. This arises if the settlor is still alive and the recipient is a minor child of his. Here the distribution is taxed as the settlor's income rather than on the recipient beneficiary (ITTOIA 2005, s 631; see further para **70.16**).

If when all the required calculations have been done, the capital distribution is less than the available relevant income allocated to it, the distribution is fully taxable under ss 731–735 and the available relevant income is correspondingly reduced. But should the distribution exceed the available relevant income it is necessary to go to the next stage, which is to look at gains. It is always necessary to go to gains where the distribution is to the settlor.

OFFSHORE INCOME GAINS

9.8 As indicated at the beginning of this chapter offshore income gains are attributed before ordinary gains. The rules in force as from 1 December 2009 are described in Chapter 82 and they require the trust to have computed its offshore income gains for each year since inception or, if later, since 1 January 1984. The amount so computed for any given year is the OIG amount for that year.

Computing OIG amounts

9.9 The OIG amount of each year comprises offshore income gains, ie gains realised on the disposal of non-distributor or, after 1 December 2009, non-reporting offshore funds. Such gains are included if they were realised by the trust or by an underlying company in circumstances where apportionment is required under TCGA 1992, s 13 (see para **95.27**). The computational rules are mainly those applicable in computing capital gains and are described in paras **95.13** to **95.15** and **82.3**. In practice the most difficult issue in computing the pool is identifying which investments really are offshore funds and confirming they did not have distributor or reporting status.

The OIG amounts may be larger than might be thought, both because losses are not allowed (see para **95.18**) and because offshore income gains are not taxable on the settlor under TCGA 1992, s 86 (see para **82.1**).

Matching

9.10 In the first instance, the distribution, or such of it as is not taxed under ss 731–735, is matched with the current year OIG amount. Such of the distribution as is left after current year matching is matched against brought forward OIG amounts on the normal LIFO basis (see para **82.4**). Such brought forward OIG amounts are, of course, reduced insofar as already matched in prior years against distributions – distributions to both UK resident and non-UK resident beneficiaries being taken into account (see para **82.4**). There are no brought forward OIG amounts where the trust is settlor-interested and so within ss 720–730, for those sections treat OIGs as the settlor's income insofar as not matched with current year capital payments (see paras **82.13** and **82.14**).

Should the settlement have made more than one capital distribution in the tax year, all are matched with the OIG amounts. When under the LIFO process a given year's OIG amount is less than the available distributions, the latter are matched pro rata.

Trustee borrowing

9.11 Should there have been a deemed disposal under TCGA 1992, Sch 4B in 2008–09 or a later year, the OIG amounts for the year of the disposal and prior years are in a Sch 4C pool. The main practical result this has is that the OIG amounts of the year of the Sch 4B disposal and prior years are matched before the OIG amounts of later years (see para **82.10**). Further consequences of the Sch 4C pool are that the OIG amounts in it will not have been reduced by past distributions to non-residents but can be matched to distributions from other settlements which have directly or indirectly received funds from the subject settlement. This is by virtue of the rules as to relevant settlements, discussed in paras **82.10** and **81.13** to **81.22**.

The tax charge

9.12 The recipient beneficiary is treated as realising an offshore income gain to the extent that the capital distribution is matched with an OIG amount of the same or a prior tax year. As offshore income gains are income, the charge, like that under ss 731–735, is to income tax.

Insofar as the capital payment exceeds both the available relevant income and all OIG amounts, ordinary capital gains fall to be considered. Conversely, if the capital payment is fully absorbed by the OIG amounts, the offshore income charge concludes the taxation of the distribution(s). The remaining OIG amounts are then carried forward.

CAPITAL GAINS TAX

9.13 The distribution is taxed as capital gain insofar as (a) it is not taxed as income under the rules described above and (b) the settlement has s 2(2) amounts able to be matched with it.

As with offshore income gains the requirement is for the settlement to compute, for each tax year of its existence, the amount on which the trustees would have been charged to CGT if UK resident. The amount so computed for each year is the s 2(2) amount for that year. There is no s 2(2) amount for a year insofar as all the gains of the year are taxed as those of the settlor under TCGA 1992, s 86 (see para **77.13**).

Computing s 2(2) amounts

9.14 Well-advised trustees will have computed their gains for past tax years and will continue to do so in the future. But if they do not, a full computation is necessary. The relevant rules are explained in CHAPTER 77. Essentially what is required for each tax year is a computation of the net gains (after allowing for losses) on which the trustees would have been chargeable if UK resident. Gains in underlying companies apportionable under TCGA 1992, s 13 are included (see para **88.31**) and express rules deal with transfers between settlements (see para **77.29**).

The section 2(2) amounts of 2007–08 and prior include any applicable allowance under the former rules relating to indexation and taper (see para **77.26**). This is particularly valuable where business taper was in point, as for several years business taper had the effect of bringing only 25% of the gain into the s 2(2) amount. Gains apportioned from companies never attracted taper and have always been indexed.

It might be thought that as a result of TCGA 1992, s 86 few trusts of the kind being considered in this chapter have s 2(2) amounts. But in fact most settlements now within s 86 do have s 2(2) amounts, albeit of some age, for s 86 was not enacted until 1991, and did not generally apply to pre-1991 settlements until 17 March 1998 (see paras **5.6** and **76.13**). Accordingly, most long-standing offshore settlements have old s 2(2) amounts. Further gains inevitably constitute s 2(2) amounts once the settlor is dead, non-domiciled or non-resident.

Computing old s 2(2) amounts can be a more complex exercise than might be supposed. In the past foreign currency bank accounts counted as chargeable assets. As a result withdrawals from such accounts were disposals for CGT purposes. This was the position as respects accounts held at trust level until 5 April 2012 (see para **77.9**). The rule ceased to apply to bank accounts held by underlying companies from when the former taper relief was introduced in 1998 (see para **88.8**).

Matching

9.15 Matching is governed by the same rules as apply to OIGs, in that such of the capital distribution as is not taxed as income is matched first against the current year s 2(2) amount. It is then matched against prior year s 2(2) amounts on a LIFO basis (para **77.20**). Self evidently those prior year s 2(2) amounts are net of any capital payments previously matched with them, distributions to both UK and non-UK beneficiaries being taken into account.

Sch 4C pools

9.16 As with offshore income gains, a deemed disposal under TCGA 1992, Sch 4B means that the s 2(2) amounts of the year of the Sch 4B disposal and prior years become a pool under TCGA 1992, Sch 4C. The Sch 4C pool includes any gains triggered by the Sch 4B disposal itself, these being included in the s 2(2) amount of the year of the disposal (see para **81.4**).

In contrast to the offshore income gains rules, a Sch 4C pool can exist by virtue of a Sch 4B disposal before 6 April 2008. But such a pool is a single pool computed under the pre-6 April 2008 rules (see paras **81.28** to **81.31**). The pool cannot be added to by any Sch 4B transfer made in 2008–09 or post, any such transfer resulting in a separate Sch 4C pool governed by the post 5 April 2008 rules.

As with offshore income gains, ordinary gains in a Sch 4C pool are matched before s 2(2) amounts for tax years subsequent to the Sch 4B disposal. This has the effect of reversing LIFO, for by definition gains in the Sch 4C pool will have accrued before the s 2(2) amounts of subsequent years. LIFO does not apply within Sch 4C pools of 2007–08 and prior (para **81.31**) but it does apply within pools of 2008–09 post and, as indicated above LIFO is also respected in the rule that gains in a Sch 4C pool of 2008–09 and post are matched before those in any pool of 2007–08 and prior.

As with offshore income gains, ordinary gains in a Sch 4C pool are not reduced by distributions to non-residents, and those in a Sch 4C pool of 2007–08 are not reduced by distributions to non-domiciliaries either. Distributions from settlements which, directly or indirectly, have received funds from the subject settlement are taken into account, under the rules relating to relevant settlements (see paras **81.13** to **81.22**).

The charge to tax

9.17 The capital distribution is taxed as gain insofar as matched with s 2(2) amounts, whether in a Sch 4C pool or otherwise. Where the trust makes multiple distributions so treated in the same tax year, each distribution is so matched, the matching being pro rata insofar as the otherwise unmatched distributions exceed the s 2(2) amount (see para **77.21**).

Should the distribution or distributions not taxed as income be less than the available s 2(2) amounts, the part not taxed as income is taxed in full as capital gain in the tax year of the distribution and the taxation of the distribution is concluded. But should the distribution or distributions exceed the pool(s) and s 2(2) amounts, the excess is carried forward and dealt with under the rules described in para **9.19** below.

As already indicated the tax charged is CGT, the gains resulting from matching being taxed as personal gains (see paras **77.39** to **77.42**). But in contrast to the income tax charges described earlier in this chapter, tax may be inflated by notional interest, the maximum rate being 32%. The rules are described in paras **77.48** to **77.51**.

SCH 4C AND RELEVANT SETTLEMENTS

9.18 In most cases that should be the end of the matter as respects the tax liability of the beneficiary in the year of distribution. But there is one exception. This is where the distributing settlement is itself a relevant settlement in relation to the trustee borrowing rules – ie it has directly or indirectly received capital from another settlement which is itself already a relevant settlement under those rules (see paras **81.13** to **81.17**). Offshore income gains and capital gains in any Sch 4C pool of the settlement which effected the original Sch 4B transfer can be attributed to capital payments from any relevant settlement until exhausted. Accordingly, in the event that the distributing settlement is a relevant settlement in relation to the Sch 4C pool of another settlement, the OIG and s 2(2) amounts able to be allocated to the distribution include those in that Sch 4C pool.

SURPLUS DISTRIBUTION

9.19 Even after all the above calculations, a part of the capital distribution may be left. This will be so if it exceeds the available relevant income and all OIG and s 2(2) amounts and Sch 4C pools capable of being matched with it. In such case the surplus is tax-free if the distribution has terminated the settlement. But if the settlement continues, the excess distribution is carried forward and can be taxed by reference to the relevant income and OIG or s 2(2) amounts of the following tax year.

To the extent that income in that tax year is not distributed, the brought forward distribution and any further distributions made in that year are matched with that income under ss 731–735 and taxed accordingly. Should the brought-forward and current year distributions exceed the undistributed income, they are taxed as offshore income gains insofar as the settlement has OIG amounts for the year, pro rata if in excess of such offshore income gains. The surplus is taxed as capital gains to the extent of any s 2(2) amounts of the year, again pro rata if the brought-forward and current year distributions exceed the current year OIG and s 2(2) amounts. Insofar as there is such excess, the excess is carried forward to the next tax year and the process repeated. This goes on until either the settlement ends or all distributions have been matched with undistributed income or with s 2(2) or OIG amounts.

IHT

9.20 In many cases a capital distribution also occasions an IHT exit charge. This subject is covered in CHAPTER **60**.

Chapter 10

PLANNING POINTS IN RELATION TO CAPITAL DISTRIBUTIONS

INTRODUCTION

10.1 This chapter outlines some techniques for minimising the income tax and capital gains tax charged on capital distributions. As in the rest of this section, it is assumed the settlor is resident and domiciled in the UK or was so when he made the settlement.

DISTRIBUTIONS TO NON-RESIDENTS

Complete distribution

10.2 The only completely satisfactory means of conferring tax-free benefit on beneficiaries is to make distributions to non-residents. This avoids all the income tax and CGT liabilities described in the previous chapters as those liabilities arise only insofar as the recipient beneficiary is resident in the UK. This is so whether the distribution is income in trust accounting terms or capital. If the distribution is of the entire trust fund, the tax problems of the settlement are at an end.

In many cases, the intended object or objects of the trustees' discretion may all be UK resident. But if the fund is large enough and the desire to distribute is strong enough, emigration may be an acceptable price for the beneficiaries to pay for freedom from tax. As described in para **29.22**, sheltering trust distributions is a potential reason for tax-driven emigration.

But if this strategy is to be adopted, the following points must be remembered.

(1) To avoid the capital payment being taxed as a capital or an offshore income gain, the recipient should be non-resident for more than five years. Unless the individual avails himself of split year treatment (see paras **41.34** to **41.36**) the requirement that he be non-resident for more than five years means his period of non-residence has to be six complete tax years (see para **41.39**).

(2)   To avoid the capital payment being taxed as income under ss 731–735, no distribution should be made in the tax year of emigration or in that of return. This is so even if split year treatment is otherwise available (see para **70.14**)

(3)   Emigration should not be to a country which might tax the distribution. Many countries have penal regimes for the taxation of trust distributions, at least where the trust in question is non-resident.

A further point arises if the settlement is one where capital gains are assessable on the settlor on an arising basis (see CHAPTER **76**). In such a case any latent gains in the settlement when the trust fund is distributed will be charged on the settlor, for there is a deemed disposal when a beneficiary becomes absolutely entitled to the trust property (TCGA 1992, s 71). Complete distribution is normally, therefore, only attractive if there are no latent gains or the settlement is not one where the gains are assessable on the settlor.

Some resident beneficiaries

10.3 In practice, even if one or more of the beneficiaries is or is prepared to become non-resident, others will not be. In this event complete distribution to the non-residents will result in family inequality.

There are two possible solutions. One is to distribute the entire trust fund to the non-residents. It can then be left to them to compensate other members of the family. This is a risky strategy, for if there is an obligation on the non-residents to benefit the other members of the family, the exercise may fall to be taxed as a distribution to them (see paras **70.29** and **78.6**). If there is no such obligation, the UK residents may lose out.

The second solution has only limited application. It entails making a distribution to a non-resident beneficiary in one tax year equal to the aggregate s 2(2) amounts then in the settlement. In the following tax year the balance of the trust fund is distributed to resident beneficiaries. The idea is that this second distribution is tax-free as all gains have been washed out, free of tax, by the prior year distribution.

The main reason why this second solution has only limited application is that it is unlikely to work if the settlement has relevant income. This is because a distribution to a non-resident does not have relevant income allocated to it (see para **70.14**). An exception may exist if the income has at all times been segregated in banking terms, provided what is distributed to the non-resident in fact removes and is traceable to such income (see para **71.28**). But it is not clear that this exception really exists.

A second reason for the technique having limited application is that it is unlikely to work if the settlement has OIG amounts or unrealised offshore income gains. This is because the distribution to the non-resident will mean the gains are treated as relevant income (see para **82.15**).

A third reason is in point should the settlement have a Sch 4C pool. Here the effect of the pool is that s 2(2) amounts in the pool are not allocated to the distribution to the non-resident and so remain available for allocation to the residents (see CHAPTER 81). As explained in CHAPTER 81, this issue also arises should the settlement be relevant settlement in relation to another settlement with a Sch 4C pool.

If none of these reasons is in point the non-resident beneficiary will need to be or remain non-resident for more than five years to avoid tax on the distribution if or when he returns to the UK. A further point is that any latent gains need to be realised in the tax year of the distribution to him, so that they can be washed out by that distribution.

Partial distributions

10.4 In practice the only distribution made may be a distribution of part of the trust fund to non-residents, the balance of the trust fund being retained.

If this course is taken one point should be kept in mind. This is that if the distribution exceeds the aggregate OIG and s 2(2) amounts as at that time, the s 2(2) or OIG amounts of subsequent years will be allocated to it insofar as not covered by future distributions. If by then a non-resident recipient has become UK resident, a tax charge will result (see para **77.46**). A tax charge does not result, however, by reference to income accumulated in the retained fund, for ss 731–735 only apply if the recipient is resident at the time of receipt (see para **70.14**).

It may be that in the following tax year, a further partial distribution is made to the UK beneficiaries. As noted above, this will be free of tax provided the prior year's distribution washed out any s 2(2) amount to date and there is no relevant income, Sch 4C pool or pool of offshore income gains. It is also necessary to ensure there is no relevant income, OIG amount, or s 2(2) amount in the year of the further distribution. And even if that condition is met, the distribution may not remain free of tax, for income accumulated or gains realised in the future will result in a tax charge then.

This carry forward of unmatched capital payments may be avoided in relation to OIG and s 2(2) amounts if in the same tax year as the distribution to the non-residents, the part of the trust fund which is not going to be distributed is resettled on the trusts of a separate settlement. This works because a transfer to another trust carries with it OIG and s 2(2) amounts which are unmatched at the end of the tax year concerned, but not excess capital payments (see para **77.30**). However, a number of points need to be noted:

(1) The distribution to the non-resident beneficiaries has to be sufficient to wash out all the s 2(2) and OIG amounts in the transferor settlement, including any gains realised on the resettlement or subsequently in the same tax year.

(2) It must be clear the transferee settlement is a separate settlement.

It is unlikely that such a resettlement prevents income accumulated in the resettlement from being relevant income in relation to any distribution from the original settlement to UK beneficiaries. Save, perhaps, where the recipient of the distribution is unable to benefit under the resettlement (see para **71.34**), such accumulation would therefore still result in a tax charge on the UK beneficiaries.

A problem can arise with Sch 4C pools where a distribution has been made to a non-resident beneficiary who subsequently becomes resident. At the time a capital distribution is made to a non-resident beneficiary there is no matching of the distribution with any gains in the Sch 4C pool (TCGA 1992, Sch 4C para 8(3)(b)). But the capital distribution, to the extent it remains unmatched, is carried forward, and is available to be matched with any gains in the Sch 4C pool in the year the beneficiary becomes UK resident or any subsequent year of residence (FA 2008, Sch 7 para 154). This difficulty is avoided if the distribution is matched with s 2(2) or OIG amounts which post-date the Sch 4C pool but accrue in a year before the beneficiary becomes UK resident. Then there are no capital payments left to match with the gains in the Sch 4C pool when the beneficiary becomes UK resident.

Short-term non-residence

10.5 The temporary non-residence rule does not apply to income (other than offshore income gains). Accordingly, a trust with available relevant income but no gains pool can make a distribution to a beneficiary who is non-resident for only one complete tax year. This is tax-free provided that it is made in the complete year of non-residence (see paras **70.14** and **29.22**). However, this strategy is not without risk, for even if there is no pool of gains at the time of the distribution, gains realised by the trust in the future could cause the distribution to be taxed at that stage, assuming the beneficiary is then UK resident. This difficulty may be overcome by the resettlement technique described above, but only if the resettlement does not itself cause gains to be realised.

DISTRIBUTIONS TO NON-DOMICILIARIES

10.6 On occasion a settlement created by a UK resident and domiciled settlor may have one or more non-UK domiciled but UK resident beneficiaries. Most commonly this arises by reason of marriage.

Complete distribution of the trust fund

10.7 Should the entire trust fund be distributed to a non-domiciliary, any tax issues will be for him. Provided he is a remittance basis user tax will be avoided so long as none of what is distributed is remitted to the UK and there was no retained UK source income or remitted foreign income in the trust or any underlying company. Even if he is not a remittance basis user or some of the distributed proceeds are remitted, tax may still be avoided so long as there is no retained income in the trust structure and the various 2008 transitional reliefs available to non-domiciliaries are in point. These issues are discussed further in CHAPTERS 22 and 23. Essentially the tax exposure of a non-domiciled beneficiary is the same where the settlor is resident and domiciled in the UK as where the settlor is wholly unconnected with the UK.

Partial distribution

10.8 On a partial distribution of the trust fund to a non-domiciliary, the non-domiciliary's tax exposure is as just described. The continuing position of the trust is broadly the same as where a partial distribution is to a non-resident beneficiary but in certain respects it is better. This is for the following reasons:

(1)   By contrast with distributions to non-residents, distributions to non-domiciliaries are within ITA 2007, ss 731–735 and so do wash out relevant income. As indicated above, and as more fully explained in CHAPTER 72, tax is avoided provided the trust or underlying company income was all foreign source and neither the trust or company income nor the funds distributed are remitted.

(2)   Again by contrast with non-residents, OIG amounts matched to distributions to non-domiciled residents do not become available relevant income. This is explained further in para **82.15**.

(3)   In a third contrast with distributions to non-residents, gains in a Sch 4C pool are matched to distributions to non-domiciliaries provided the pool is a post 2008 pool (see para **81.27**).

In appropriate cases, these three points may render distribution of part of the trust fund to a non-domiciliary a convenient technique for 'cleaning up' the settlement and thereby permitting tax-free distributions to resident domiciliaries in a subsequent tax year. But if this strategy is adopted, the points made in para **10.4** about the impact of future income or gains should be kept in mind.

Changes on 6 April 2017

10.9 It should be kept in mind that after 6 April 2017, the various strategies described above will not work if the non-domiciliary is deemed UK domiciled under the rules coming into force then. But at the time of writing the indications are the 2008 transitional reliefs will remain available.

UK RESIDENT AND DOMICILED BENEFICIARIES

10.10 Many settlements of the kind considered in this chapter do not have non-resident or non-domiciled beneficiaries and emigration of beneficiaries is unlikely to be in prospect in the future. In these circumstances tax on distributions is difficult to avoid entirely, but a variety of strategies exist by which it may be mitigated.

Small distributions

10.11 A distribution to a non-taxpaying beneficiary is free of income tax to the extent of his personal allowance (£11,000 in 2016–2017). Should there be no available relevant income or offshore income gains in the trust, a distribution equal to the CGT basic annual exemption (£11,100 in 2016–2017) is free of CGT, assuming the beneficiary's annual exemption is otherwise available. If, however, the trust has no s 2(2) amounts or relevant income, the distribution is carried forward and taxed as and when the trustees do realise gains or accumulate income. Since in that year the beneficiary's personal allowance or annual exemption may have been used, it is better not to make small distributions unless, in the tax year concerned, there is relevant income or s 2(2) amounts to cover it.

In theory it is possible to use both a beneficiary's personal allowance and his annual exemption. But this is only possible if the relevant income is wholly absorbed by the personal allowance, for otherwise the distribution is taxed as income until the relevant income is exhausted. The better method for securing both the allowance and exemption is to ensure there is no available relevant income by distributing income as income, and then (assuming there are s 2(2) amounts) making modest capital distributions equal to the annual exemption.

Should the trust have multiple beneficiaries, quite a number may have available personal allowances and annual exemptions and if so significant amounts of income and gains may over time be decanted out without tax charge. It should be kept in mind that minor children are entitled to the personal allowance and the annual exemption, and that the distributed funds can be held by either the trustees or parents as nominees. Personal allowances are not available if the settlor is the child's parent, as the distribution is then treated as the parents' income (see para 75.8). But this ceases once the child is 18 and does not apply to the CGT annual exemption.

Dry trusts

10.12 It might be thought appropriate to keep a trust free of relevant income by ensuring that all income is distributed as income. It is generally accepted that if income is distributed as income it never becomes relevant income (see para 71.14). In the absence of relevant income, planning is simpler as only gains have to be looked at. As a general rule, however, this strategy is not to be recommended unless the recipient of the income is non-resident or a remittance basis user who does not remit. The reason is that the income tax rates applicable to income distributions are the same as those applicable under ITA 2007 ss 731–735. There is no supplemental tax such as applies to capital gains, and so, retaining income has the potential advantage of securing deferral. A further point is that distributing income as income may not remove all available relevant income for the latter includes certain types of deemed income (see paras 9.5 and 71.9).

But despite this there are certain scenarios under which income distributions to UK residents make sense. Most notably this arises where the distributions are relatively modest and the recipients either have available personal allowances or, if not that, utilised basic rate band. The latter caps the tax at 20%, which may be preferable to the higher rates inevitably in point if a later, large, capital distribution is matched with retained income under ITA 2007, ss 731–735.

Life interests

10.13 A settlement of the kind discussed here may be subject to a life interest. Even where the settlement is not so subject, a life interest can now be appointed without IHT costs, as under the 2006 changes, the trust remains within the relevant property regime for IHT (see para 60.8).

The issues raised by life interests are in a sense the same as those raised by a discretionary distribution of income. The advantage is that available relevant income is avoided or minimised, which means planning on distributions can focus on gains. The disadvantage is that the benefit of income tax deferral is lost.

In income tax terms, life interests do have one advantage over discretionary distributions of income, which is that the dividend rates are available insofar as the trust income takes the form of UK or foreign dividends (see para 8.6). The dividend rates are significantly less than the normal income tax rates such as are applicable where tax is charged on capital distributions under ITA 2007, ss 731–735. In appropriate cases, they render life interests attractive, particularly where regular distributions are desired in any event.

Role of dividends

10.14 In 2007–08 and prior, planning opportunities arose where the trust held its investments through an underlying company. In such a case procuring a dividend achieved two objectives. One was generating current income able to be distributed as income. The other was that such of the dividends as was not so distributed generated available relevant income, thereby increasing the amount of future capital distributions taxed as income. In both cases the objective was to increase distributions taxed as income and so reduce the amount which could be taxed at the potentially penal rate of 64% represented by CGT at the then rate of 40% plus supplemental tax.

At current rates, strategies of this sort are not normally attractive. Thus the higher rate tax on dividends is 32.5%, and the top rate 38.1%. This compares with the maximum rate of CGT plus supplemental tax, namely 32%.

Losses

10.15 Tax may be avoided on a distribution if it is, or is taxed as, income and the recipient beneficiary has trading or other income tax losses. In such a case the losses may be offset in the same way as against other income. The same applies if the capital distribution is taxed as an offshore income gain. With capital gains the position is normally otherwise as section 87 gains cannot be set against the recipient's capital losses (TCGA 1992, s 2(4)).

Somewhat curiously, the bar against setting s 87 gains against personal losses does not extend to Sch 4C gains (see para 81.26). As will be apparent from CHAPTER 80, it is relatively easy to generate a Sch 4B transfer such as transfers all existing s 2(2) amounts into a Sch 4C pool: all that is needed is borrowing by the trustees followed by a loan or distribution while the borrowed money remains uninvested. If therefore utilisation of personal losses is important, a Sch 4B transfer prior to the distribution may be considered, albeit with due regard to the potential drawbacks of such a course.

Free use of property

10.16 In *Billingham v Cooper* [2001] STC 1177, the Court of Appeal held that interest-free loans represent annual capital payments equal to the rent or interest foregone (para **78.12**). It must be assumed the same reasoning applies to the free use of property and to ss 731–735 (see para **70.19**).

Despite this, trustees may still be tempted to benefit beneficiaries by interest-free loans or the free use of property. Such has the merit of at least initially resulting in only a modest tax charge. But in the long-run it cannot be recommended, for effectively it results in tax charges both when the free use is allowed and then when the capital is distributed. The total tax bill is greater than if the capital is distributed at the outset. A different view may of course be taken if the trustees envisage the capital may eventually be distributed to non-residents.

Sometimes the potential tax charges may be avoided by requiring the beneficiary to pay interest or rent. If this is done, the interest or rent is both taxable as UK source income of the trustees and also goes to increase the relevant income in the trust. In addition the beneficiary has to withhold basic rate tax, although this is not required in the case of rent if the landlord is within the non-resident landlord scheme (cf para **64.15** and **64.20**).

CGT MINIMISATION TECHNIQUES

10.17 Many trusts exist where there is little or no available relevant income. Typical instances are trusts with a single asset such as a house or a UK company or trusts adopting the strategies discussed in paras **10.12** and **10.13** above. In such cases distribution planning focuses on gains alone, and here certain specific techniques may be in point, in addition to those discussed above.

Order of distributions

10.18 On the assumption there is neither available relevant income nor any OIG amount, the LIFO rules under TCGA 1992, s 87A mean that a capital distribution is matched first with the current year s 2(2) amount and then with the prior year s 2(2) amount and, insofar as so matched, cannot attract supplemental tax. The rate of tax is 20% and yet, because matching under s 87 has occurred, there is no risk of taxation by reference to future relevant income or offshore income gains.

In appropriate cases this is an argument for annual distributions equal to the current year s 2(2) amount, particularly where one or more annual CGT exemptions can also be utilised. But if such exercises are done regularly, care should be taken to ensure the distributions cannot be characterised as income. Risk here ought to be avoided provided the distribution is debited to capital and is expressed to be in exercise of a power over capital (cf para **8.9**). A point also to keep in mind is that this technique does not work if the trust is a relevant settlement in relation to another settlement's Sch 4C pool, for then s 2(2) amounts in that pool are matched first (see para **81.13**).

Distributions to charity

10.19 HMRC accept that a capital distribution to a UK charity is a capital payment for the purposes of s 87 (see para **78.10**) It is also accepted that the charity is not taxed on s 87 gains provided that the distribution is applied for charitable purposes, and therefore covered by the general exemption for gains accruing to UK charities (TCGA 1992, s 256).

If a distribution to a charity is made in one tax year and the balance of the trust fund is distributed in the following year, CGT on the latter distribution may be reduced or eliminated by the prior distribution due to the reduction in the s 87 pool. But if the subsequent distribution is not of the whole trust fund, it may occasion tax in a future tax year. This will happen if income is retained or gains are realised in the future (cf para **10.4** above).

HMRC's practice in relation to charities and s 87 was announced before the enactment of Sch 4C. However, it may be argued that it should also apply to Sch 4C gains (see para **81.12**).

Split the trust fund

10.20 This technique takes advantage of the fact that if part of the trust fund is transferred to a new settlement, the s 2(2) and OIG amounts as at the end of the tax year of the transfer are split pro rata between the two trusts (see para **77.29**). If the s 2(2) and OIG amounts equal half the value of the original trust fund a distribution by the trustees of that trust of half the trust fund will be fully taxable. But, if in a prior tax year half the trust fund has been transferred to another trust, a complete distribution from one or other trust is taxable as to only 50%.

This technique cannot be used if the trust has outstanding borrowing within the meaning of TCGA 1992, Sch 4B, for then the transfer will trigger a Sch 4B deemed disposal and carry the s 2(2) and OIG amounts into a Sch 4C pool (see CHAPTER 80). Nor can it be used if the settlement has an existing Sch 4C pool for such pools are not split pro rata (see CHAPTER 81).

This technique does not apply to available relevant income, and any such income remains able to be allocated in full to distributions form either trust (cf para **71.33**). As with similar exercises described in para **10.4** above, it must be ensured the two trusts are truly separate and that the transfer between the two trusts cannot be characterised as a capital distribution.

A sub-fund election within TCGA 1992, Sch 4ZA achieves the same result as splitting the trust fund in the manner described above. The ability to make such an election is not confined to UK trusts. But the restrictions in Sch 4ZA render it unlikely that sub-fund elections will be widely used in practice.

10.20 *Planning points in relation to capital distributions*

The tribunal decisions in *Herman* and *Bowring* called these techniques into question as they raised the possibility the distribution by the transferee trust could be treated as made by the transferor trust. But it is now clear this is only the position if on the facts the transferee trust is an intermediary (see *Bowring v HMRC* [2016] STC 816 and para 78.6).

Chapter 11

BRINGING THE TRUST ONSHORE

INTRODUCTION

11.1 This chapter reviews the tax consequences and possible planning opportunities which arise when an offshore trust becomes UK resident. The position in relation to underlying companies is also considered. The chapter assumes the settlor and beneficiaries are resident and domiciled in the UK.

HOW A TRUST BECOMES UK RESIDENT

11.2 A non-resident trust becomes UK resident if the non-resident trustees retire and UK trustees are appointed in their place. The tests of what renders a trust UK resident are explained in CHAPTER 42.

If the trust is governed by English law, there is no trust law obstacle to appointing English trustees (cf para **30.2**). Should the trust be governed by foreign law, that law determines whether the foreign trustees can validly resign in favour of UK trustees. But most trusts contain express powers to appoint trustees in any part of the world and in that event there is unlikely to be difficulty although the point should be checked with local lawyers.

A trust governed by foreign law retains the foreign law as its governing law notwithstanding the appointment of UK trustees. Most trusts contain power to change the governing law and consideration should be given as to whether this power should be exercised on immigration to replace the foreign law with English law.

INCOME TAX

Discretionary trusts

11.3 Once a discretionary or accumulation trust becomes UK resident, its worldwide income is assessable on the trustees. As a general rule the rate of tax is the trust rate, although the first slice of trust income enjoys basic rate tax (ITA 2007, s 491). The first slice is normally £1,000, but it is reduced if the settler has made other settlements (ITA 2007, ss 491–492). The trust rate is 38.1% for dividends and 45% for other income.

11.3 *Bringing the trust onshore*

The income tax position post-immigration contrasts with the position pre-immigration in that immigration brings the foreign income into charge to tax. The tax exposure on UK income is unaffected as UK tax payable by non-resident trustees is not restricted to tax withheld where the trust has UK beneficiaries (see para **64.8**).

Once the trust becomes UK resident, income distributions by the trustees fall within the provisions of ITA 2007, ss 493–498. This legislation requires tax at the trust rate to be withheld from any distribution and paid over to HMRC. The trustees are entitled to offset this tax against any tax paid by them while UK resident on the trust income as it arises (ITA 2007, s 496). The tax on income distributions cannot be offset by tax on UK-source income incurred while the trust was non-resident (ITA 2007, s 497(2); see also explanatory notes to ITA 2007, change 89).

Once the trust is UK-resident, TIOPA 2010, s 111 operates to allow a beneficiary in receipt of an income distribution the benefit of any double tax relief applicable when the income arose to the trustees. ESC B18 operates to like effect when the trust is non-resident as respects UK and, it is thought, foreign income (see further para **8.11**).

Fixed-interest trusts

11.4 As described in para **8.2**, the income of a fixed-interest trust is taxed as that of the life tenant. Accordingly, tax treatment is determined by his residence status, rather than that of the trustees, and immigration of the trust has little impact. However, once the trust is UK resident, the trustees are accountable for basic rate tax.

In one respect immigration does alter the tax treatment. Certain categories of foreign capital receipt are deemed to be income, for example offshore income gains (see CHAPTER **95**). These are not assessable on the trustees while non-resident but become chargeable at the rate applicable to trusts once the trust immigrates (ITA 2007, ss 481–482).

Settlor-interested trusts

11.5 Should the trust be settlor-interested all the trust income is taxed as the settlor's under ITTOIA 2005, s 624 if he is UK resident (see CHAPTER **75**). These rules apply regardless of the residence status of the trustees and so are unaffected by the immigration of the trust. Immigration does cause ITA 2007, ss 720–730 to cease to apply (cf CHAPTERS **68** and **69**), but this is normally not significant as the income of settlor-interested non-resident trusts is caught by s 624 rather than ss 720–730 (see para **69.30**).

Trust capital distributions

11.6 The general rule is that capital distributions by the trust once it is resident are free of income tax. This, however, is subject to the following exceptions:

(1)   If the recipient is a minor child of the settlor, liability may arise under ITTOIA 2005, s 629 (see para **75.8**). This applies equally whether the trust is resident or non-resident.

(2)   Outstanding OIG amounts on immigration are matched with distributions of capital when the trust is resident until exhausted (see para **82.6**).

(3)   Distributions of capital when the trust is resident may be taxed under ITA 2007, ss 731–735 insofar as the trust has outstanding available relevant income when it immigrates (see Chapters **70** and **71**).

(4)   Distributions of capital may also be taxed under ss 731–735 by reference to income in any underlying non-resident company owned by the trust. Income so taken into account includes both post as well as pre immigration income as, so long as the company is non-UK resident, it remains a person abroad for the purposes of the transfer of assets legislation.

CAPITAL GAINS TAX

Section 86 trusts

11.7 Should an immigrating trust be within TCGA 1992, s 86 while non-resident, its gains, while non-resident, are taxed as those of the settlor. Section 86 is explained in Chapter **76** and applies if the settlor, his children, or in some cases, his grandchildren, are beneficiaries. This normally results in a tax rate of 20%, but the tax may be nil if the settlor has personal losses and otherwise is 10% if he has unused basic rate band (TCGA 1992, s 4; see para **76.17**).

When such a trust immigrates, the gains are no longer taxed as the settlor's. But they are taxed as those of the trustees at the trust rate of 20% (TCGA 1992, s 4(3)). This applies from the beginning of the tax year in which the change of trustees occurs (see para **11.14** below).

Other trusts

11.8 Should the trust not be within s 86, the effect of immigration is to bring trust gains into charge to tax in the hands of the trustees at the rate of 20%. Again, this applies from the beginning of the relevant tax year. Such gains are not allocated to capital payments.

An exception to the rule that capital payments by the resident trustees are not taxable is made if, when the trust immigrates, it has outstanding s 2(2) amounts (TCGA 1992 s 89). As described in para **77.35** these may be allocated to capital payments after immigration. The same applies if the trust has a Sch

4C pool or has received, or while resident receives, capital from another trust which has such a pool (para **81.14**). Supplemental tax is applicable so the rate of tax may be as high as 32%.

UK residential property

11.9 Gains on UK residential property held by the trust are taxed at 28% both before and after immigration. Before immigration the charge is to non-resident CGT (see CHAPTER 65) and after immigration the gains are upper rate gains (TCGA 1992, s 4(3)). But in many cases gains realised pre-immigration will attract more favourable treatment, for NR CGT allows rebasing as at 5 April 2015 (see para **65.11**). The pre-2015 gain is dealt with under s 87 or (where appropriate) s 86. In the case of s 87, tax only results if a matched capital distribution is made.

Beneficial interests in trusts

11.10 The exemption for disposals of beneficial interests in trusts does not apply if the trust has previously been non-resident (TCGA 1992, s 76(1A)). Accordingly, the position in this regard remains the same as when the trust was non-resident (see further para **7.11**).

Trustee borrowing

11.11 The rules as to trustee borrowing in TCGA 1992, Sch 4B cease to apply once the trust is UK resident. But an exception is made if and so long as there are outstanding OIG or s 2(2) amounts from the non-resident period (see para **80.29**).

Rebasing on immigration

11.12 In contrast to some jurisdictions, the UK does not rebase the assets of immigrants. The result is that a gain realised on the disposal of an asset acquired prior to immigration includes the pre-immigration proportion of the gain.

Where the trust is not within TCGA 1992, s 86, thought should therefore be given to rebasing prior to immigration. Such could be achieved by selling and buying back assets, although if this is done, the possible impact of the *Ramsay* principle on the purchase and buy back should be considered. In the case of shares and securities more than 30 days must elapse between the two transactions (TCGA 1992, s 106A(5)). An alternate method of rebasing is to create a new settlement and transfer the assets to it.

The gains on rebasing will go into the trust's OIG or s 2(2) amount for the year of rebasing, and so rebasing is of little point if capital is likely to be distributed to UK resident and domiciled beneficiaries, or if capital has been distributed to such beneficiaries and is as yet unmatched with trust gains. As noted below, rebasing must be undertaken in the tax year prior to immigration rather than in the year of immigration itself.

Assets showing a loss should not be rebased. This is because the loss is allowable once the trust is UK resident.

Rebasing should not be undertaken without investigation of whether the ensuing gain will or might be taxed in another jurisdiction. Such tax could be that levied where the trust is previously resident, although this scenario is unlikely where the trust has been resident in an offshore jurisdiction. A greater risk may be taxation in the country in which assets of the trust are situated.

Emigration

11.13 Should the trust re-emigrate, then, in contrast to immigration, there is a deemed disposal of its assets at market value (TCGA 1992 s 80 and 185; see para 30.8). The practical result is that once the trust moves to the UK, its gains are locked into charge to UK tax. This is often cited as an argument against immigration.

Year of immigration

11.14 Trustees are liable to CGT in a tax year if they are resident in the UK during any part of the year (TCGA 1992, s 2(2)). In contrast to individuals, this has never been abrogated by any split-year treatment. As a result any gain realised in the tax year of immigration is chargeable even if realised prior to the appointment of UK resident trustees (subject to any available treaty relief). As just noted, this needs to be borne in mind if consideration is being given to pre-immigration rebasing.

INHERITANCE TAX

11.15 Immigration does not affect the IHT status of a trust. The matter remains governed by the domicile of the settlor when the settlement was made and the situs of the assets (see CHAPTER 62).

UNDERLYING COMPANIES

11.16 Should the trustees own one or more companies, the position of the companies should be separately considered. On certain scenarios immigration of a company may be considered even if the trust remains non-resident.

Becoming resident

11.17 As explained in CHAPTER 43, a company resides where the central management and control of its business is exercised. In the normal case such management and control is exercised by the board and the company resides where the board meets. Accordingly, moving the company to the UK is achieved if the foreign directors resign and a UK board which meets regularly in the UK is appointed in their place.

English company law does not allow the re-registration or re-domiciliation of foreign companies, and so the immigrating company has to remain subject to foreign law. Once the company has immigrated, advice on UK company law formalities for foreign registered companies should be taken.

Immigration of an underlying company should always be considered where the owning trust is itself immigrating. This is because ownership by a UK shareholder can in certain cases make it more difficult to establish that central management and control has remained with the board offshore.

Income

11.18 Once a foreign company becomes UK resident, its worldwide income comes into charge to corporation tax (CTA 2009, s 5). But provided it is not resident anywhere else, it ceases to be a person abroad for the purposes of the transfer of assets legislation (see para **68.16**). This means its income ceases to be taxable on the settlor even if the transferor charge would otherwise be in point. Nor, furthermore, can its post immigration income be taken into account under ITA 2007, ss 731–735 in taxing benefits conferred on non-transferors.

Once the company is UK resident any dividends it pays are taxed on the trust at the trust dividend rate (38.1%). This is so whether the trust is resident or non-resident. As noted above (para **11.3**) the trust is taxable on UK source dividends when non-resident as by definition it has UK beneficiaries (see para **64.8**).

Should the company remain non-resident after the trust immigrates, the dividend rate of 38.1% also applies to any dividend it pays to the trust.

The trust dividend rates do not apply if the trust is fixed interest, whether resident or non-resident. As noted above (para **11.4**), the dividend is then treated as the income of the life tenant. So too different rates may apply if the trust is settlor interested (para **11.5**).

Company gains

11.19 Once the company becomes UK resident, attribution of gains under TCGA 1992 s 13 (see Chapter **88**) ceases. Instead its gains are subject to corporation tax. The gains continue to be indexed rather than tapered.

In some cases immigration is unattractive from the standpoint of gains, specifically where the company is protected from s 13 by one of the defences to that section (see paras **88.4** and **88.5**). Here immigration causes gains which were previously tax free to become taxable at corporate rates.

Year of immigration

11.20 Corporation tax is charged by accounting periods. A new period starts when a company becomes UK resident (CTA 2009, s 9(1)(a)) and so from then its income and gains are fully subject to corporation tax.

Section III

Planning in relation to UK resident, non-UK domiciled individuals

Chapter 12

BASIC PLANNING

INTRODUCTION

12.1 A key area in offshore tax planning is understanding the generous reliefs afforded to non-UK domiciliaries and ensuring all proper advantage is taken of them. The technical details of the reliefs are given in Sections IV, V and VI of Part B. This section is devoted to the principal planning points which need to be kept in mind.

THE GENERAL PRINCIPLE

12.2 The general rule is that a non-UK domiciliary is not subject to UK tax on his foreign assets, or the income and gains they generate. But important preconditions have to be met, and there are also significant exceptions and limitations.

The general rule dates back to the inception of direct taxes, and for that reason the law is a mixture of case law and statute. Since 2008 statute has predominated, for in that year the then Labour government introduced significant codification to the rules applicable to income and gains (FA 2008, Sch 7). Further modifications occurred in 2012 (FA 2012, Sch 12).

DOMICILE

12.3 A point to emphasise is that in order to access the favourable rules, the individual must be non-UK domiciled under English common law principles, and must not be deemed domiciled in the UK. At the time of writing, the tax legislation includes deemed domicile rules that apply for the purposes of inheritance tax (IHT) only. However, such rules are due to be changed shortly, and extended so that they also apply to income tax and CGT.

The common law rules on domicile are explained in CHAPTER 44. An important point to keep in mind is that retention of non-UK domiciliary status is not inevitable. An individual coming to the UK and making his sole or main home there acquires a UK domicile on his arrival if his intention is to reside in the UK permanently or indefinitely. Strictly, the acquisition of a domicile within the UK is only avoided if there is a definite contingency on which the individual will cease living there. The individual retains his foreign domicile so long as such a definite contingency continues to subsist.

It is frequently possible to demonstrate the requisite contingency, for many foreigners living in the UK envisage leaving on retirement, on completion of their children's education, or when political stability returns to their country of origin. But should such a contingency come about and the individual not leave, HMRC may be in a position to claim he has acquired a UK domicile, not merely currently but perhaps in the past as well.

In practice, HMRC tend to be wary of challenging the claimed foreign domiciles of living taxpayers. However, they are much less reticent about challenging the domiciles of individuals who have died.

There is no procedure whereby HMRC can be required to agree an individual's foreign domicile. Instead the individual must tick the appropriate boxes in his tax return. There will only be engagement with HMRC on the domicile issue if HMRC choose to enquire into the return (see further paras **44.11** to **44.13**).

INHERITANCE TAX

12.4 In relation to foreign domiciliaries, the scope of IHT is limited by the excluded property concept, as described in paras **37.9** to **37.15**. A personally held non-UK situs asset is excluded property and thus outside the scope of IHT, provided the beneficial owner is non-UK domiciled (and not deemed to be domiciled in the UK for IHT purposes; see below). To secure this treatment no claim is necessary and it applies whether or not the non-UK domiciliary is a remittance basis user, as described below, and whether or not he is paying the £30,000, £60,000 or £90,000 charge to access the remittance basis. These charges, too, are discussed below.

For IHT purposes, the rules as to the situs of assets are the common law rules outlined in CHAPTER **38**. The overall result is that, at least in principle, investments of a non-UK domiciliary may be kept entirely outside the scope of IHT.

It might be thought that those rules totally preclude UK investments. However, in reality this is not so, for the rules focus on the asset immediately held by the non-UK domiciliary. Interposing a foreign investment vehicle can therefore secure excluded property status for UK assets, albeit that there are risks and technical points that have to be watched (see CHAPTER **15**).

There is also one category of UK assets that is excluded property of a non-UK domiciliary even if held directly, namely shares or units in authorised funds (see para **37.11**). Again, this is subject to the individual not being deemed domiciled in the UK (as discussed below).

It should be noted that the UK Government has announced that with effect from 6 April 2017 a new transparency rule for IHT will apply to foreign companies (and any similar opaque entities) holding UK residential property. This is discussed in CHAPTER **27**.

Deemed domicile

12.5 The beneficial IHT regime for non-UK domiciliaries is subject to one very important qualification, namely that for IHT purposes an individual is deemed to be UK domiciled once he has been resident in the UK for an extended period. Under current law, such deemed domicile arises once it becomes the case that the individual has been UK resident in 17 out of the 20 tax years culminating in the current tax year (IHTA 1984, s 267); so typically at the beginning of the 17th tax year of residence.

However, as already noted, there are proposals to amend the law, with effect from 6 April 2017. The proposed amendments will mean that a deemed UK domicile will typically be acquired once a foreign domiciliary has clocked up 15 prior tax years of residence in the UK; so typically at the beginning of the 16th tax year of residence. The phraseology of the new rule will in fact mean that once an individual has been resident in the UK for 15 consecutive tax years, deemed domicile will be acquired at the beginning of the following tax year, regardless of whether the individual is in fact resident in that year. However, the most important point about the proposed new rules is the fact that from 6 April 2017 the deemed domicile concept will apply to income tax and CGT, as well as IHT. As discussed below, a UK resident individual who is deemed domiciled for all tax purposes under the proposed new regime will not be able to use the remittance basis of taxation.

The current rules, and proposed new rules, are discussed in CHAPTER 45. An important point to remember, which will apply to the proposed new rule for long-term residents with just as much force as it applies to the current IHT rule, is that a year counts as a year of residence even if, by virtue of split year treatment, the individual was only taxable in part of it. For this reason deemed domicile can creep up earlier than expected, and a thorough count should always be made.

One effect of a non-domiciliary being deemed UK domiciled is that the excluded property status of foreign situs assets is lost. However, for the well-advised the adverse implications of deemed domicile can be countered, by virtue of the rules pertaining to settlements. These rules are discussed in CHAPTER 16. Their effect is that foreign situs property of a settlement is outside the scope of IHT, provided that the settlor had neither an actual nor a deemed UK domicile at the time he made the settlement. The foreign situs property remains outside the reach of IHT even if the settlor subsequently acquires a UK domicile, and this is so even if he is a beneficiary of the settlement and/or has reserved a power to revoke the settlement.

The practical result is that a non-UK domiciliary should, where this is practical, consider settling his assets before a deemed UK domicile is acquired. The considerations to be kept in mind in making such a settlement are reviewed in CHAPTER 19. A point to emphasise is that the individual's advisers must satisfy themselves that he has neither an actual nor a deemed UK domicile, for if there is a mistake as to either of these matters, the settlement will result in a 25% entry charge (see para **60.2**). For the same reason it must be verified that the assets settled really are foreign situs.

Spouses

12.6 A married woman does not under current law take her husband's domicile (see para **44.10**) and for this reason mixed domicile marriages are common. Such marriages can create IHT issues.

The IHT spouse exemption applies in the normal way, if a non-UK domiciled individual gives assets to a spouse with an actual or deemed UK domicile (IHTA 1984, s 18). But should the gift be the other way round, ie be a gift by a UK domiciled or deemed domiciled individual to a spouse who is neither actually domiciled nor deemed domiciled, the spouse exemption is (in principle) capped at an amount equal to the nil-rate band, currently £325,000 (s 18(2)). This means the gift in excess of that cap is a potentially exempt transfer, with the result that IHT is chargeable should the donor spouse fail to survive seven years (IHTA 1984, s 34). So too, bequests in excess of the cap are fully charged at the death rate once the nil-rate band ceases to be available.

However, where a non-UK domiciled individual has received a lifetime gift or a bequest from a UK domiciled or deemed domiciled spouse, the IHT legislation allows the making of an election by the recipient. The effect of this is that the recipient is deemed to be domiciled in the UK for IHT purposes but the gift or bequest qualifies in full for the spouse exemption (IHTA 1984, s 267ZA).

INCOME AND GAINS SUBJECT TO THE REMITTANCE BASIS

12.7 In principle, the foreign income and gains of non-UK domiciliaries can also be kept free of UK tax. There is only tax exposure if the income or gains are remitted to the UK.

Under current law the concept of deemed domicile does not apply for the purposes of income tax and CGT. The result is that under current law, the remittance basis regime is available no matter how long the individual has been resident in the UK, provided he has in fact retained his foreign domicile. However, as already noted, the proposed new deemed domicile rules discussed in CHAPTER 45 will apply for all tax purposes, and will therefore remove access to the remittance basis for individuals who have become deemed domiciled.

For non-UK domiciliaries who can, in principle, access the remittance basis, the regime is highly beneficial but also complex, with many traps for the unwary or ill-advised. As discussed below:

(1)   The regime is available only if the non-UK domiciliary qualifies as a remittance basis user. This typically requires a tax return to be submitted and a claim to be made within it.
(2)   It does not apply on a blanket basis to all income and gains generated by foreign situs assets, but instead only applies to items which fall within the defined term 'foreign income and gains'.
(3)   The concept of remittance to the UK extends beyond situations where the non-UK domiciliary himself brings the money to the UK.

Remittance basis user

12.8 To be a remittance basis user, the non-UK domiciliary typically has to make a claim under ITA 2007, s 809B. The claim is an annual event, in that it is required for each year for which the individual wishes to access the remittance basis. The rules regarding claims are explained in Chapter 46, and the point to stress is that each year is viewed separately. In other words, the making of a claim, or omission to make a claim, for one year is unaffected by the decision taken for the previous year.

There are certain *de minimis* instances where a claim is not needed, described in paras **46.10** to **46.13**. However, in general these exceptions are not in point for non-UK domiciliaries with significant income or assets. The term 'remittance basis user' may be used to describe both those who make a claim and those to whom the remittance basis is available without a claim.

The cost of the claim

12.9 Claiming the remittance basis carries a cost. That cost depends on how long the non-domiciliary has been UK resident. For all non-UK domiciliaries use of the remittance basis has the following downsides:

- No personal allowance (£11,000 in 2016–2017);
- No annual exemption for CGT (£11,100 in 2016–17);
- Any foreign dividends remitted are taxed at the rates applicable to interest; they do not qualify for the dividend tax rates (ITA 2007, s 13).

For adult non-UK domiciliaries who have been UK resident in at least seven out of the preceding nine tax years, there is an additional cost, in the form of the remittance basis charge. This is initially £30,000, but rises to £60,000 if the non-UK domiciliary has been UK resident for at least 12 out of the previous 14 tax years and under current law, there is a charge of £90,000 if the non-UK domiciliary has been a UK resident for at least 17 out of the previous 20 tax years. The details of the remittance basis charge are given in Chapter 47.

A section 809B claim potentially carries one further cost, related to losses on foreign situs assets. The basic rule is that foreign losses are not allowable, but this can be overridden if, in his first s 809B claim, the non-UK domiciliary makes an election to use foreign losses under TCGA 1992, s 16ZA. Section 16ZA is explained in para **49.13**. The key point here is that there is a single opportunity to make such an election, and unless the election is made with the first s 809B claim, the ability to set foreign losses against gains is lost forever.

The decision to claim

12.10 For non-UK domiciliaries with modest foreign assets or income, a claim to use the remittance basis may not be worthwhile, particularly where the result is payment of the remittance basis charge. This is particularly so where the foreign income or gains are taxed in the country of source, so that the UK tax if a claim is not made is reduced by foreign tax credits. For such individuals a detailed calculation may be required for each year. The answer in one year may be different to that in the next.

For example, it may be the case that in an ordinary year claiming the remittance basis is not worthwhile, but a claim may make sense in a year in which the non-UK domiciliary realises a large foreign capital gain or receives a substantial trust distribution. Indeed, in planning terms it makes sense to concentrate large receipts in a single tax year, where this is possible, for then the maximum value for the cost of the claim is secured.

The Government has previously considered making it a requirement for a non-UK domiciliary to claim the remittance basis for three tax years at a time, in order to prevent such individuals planning their affairs so that the remittance basis is only used intermittently, thereby avoiding remittance basis charges. However, in the Budget 2015 the Government announced that a decision had been made to leave the position unchanged, presumably reflecting acceptance that this is legitimate planning for a remittance basis user to adopt.

Claim procedure

12.11 Should the remittance basis charge be payable, the non-UK domiciliary has to nominate foreign income and gains which are deemed to have been remitted. This curious procedure is explained in CHAPTER 47. In practical terms what is important is that the non-UK domiciliary nominates less than £10 of foreign income or gains each given year. The reason for this is that a remittance of less than £10 of nominated income and gains for a given year cannot trigger the special ordering rules described in paras **47.7** to **47.9**. Those ordering rules can nullify remittance planning of the kind described in the next chapter and are therefore best avoided.

FOREIGN INCOME AND GAINS

12.12 The term 'foreign income and gains' is a defined term, whose meaning is given in ITA 2007, s 809Z7. As respects investments, it encompasses relevant foreign income and foreign chargeable gains.

Relevant foreign income

12.13 The term 'relevant foreign income' is defined in ITTOIA 2005, s 830 and is explained in paras **48.2** to **48.6**. In broad terms it is investment income which has a non-UK source, and includes all dividends, interest, and rent which have a foreign source.

Because the principal determinant of the tax treatment is the source of the income, rather than the situs of the asset generating the income, not all foreign situs assets generate relevant foreign income. The tax rules on life insurance policies represent a particular trap for foreign domiciliaries, as such policies may generate deemed income which is not eligible for the remittance basis, even where the policy is issued by a foreign insurance company and is itself non-UK situs (see **96.15**). Other potential sources of UK income are dividends paid by foreign registered companies that are managed and controlled in the

UK, and therefore UK resident; and interest payments where the payer is UK resident. The law on source of income is explained in CHAPTER 40 and wherever there is doubt the rules should be checked.

Foreign chargeable gains

12.14 Foreign chargeable gains are gains realised on the disposal of foreign situs assets (see TCGA 1992, s 12 and CHAPTER 49). But as with income there is an important trap, for CGT has special situs rules which often displace the common law. These rules are explained in CHAPTER 39. Perhaps the most important point is that, for CGT purposes, the situs of a debt is typically the residence of the creditor, not that of the debtor. This rule is subject to important exceptions, most notably for registered securities, but it is a trap with bearer bonds and may also be in point in relation to 'immobilised' bonds held through clearing systems (see para 39.15).

REMITTANCE

12.15 The concept of 'remittance', and certain exemptions from tax on remittances, are explained in CHAPTERS 51 to 59. There are several scenarios in which a remittance does not result in tax and these, together with the planning opportunities they afford, form the subject of the next chapter. For present purposes what matters is that the concept of remittance goes far beyond the simple bringing of the income or gains to the UK by the non-UK domiciliary. In certain instances deeming rules mean even a payment abroad is a taxable remittance, and such may be the case even where the payment is made by a person other than the non-UK domiciled taxpayer.

Services

12.16 A remittance basis user who brings foreign income or gains to the UK to pay for services, whether enjoyed in the UK or elsewhere, effects a taxable remittance under general principles. A taxable remittance also occurs if he uses foreign income or gains abroad to pay for services provided in the UK (see para 55.1). An exception to the latter charge is made if the service relates wholly or mainly to property outside the UK (ITA 2007, s 809W; see para 55.13).

HMRC appear to take the view that a service is provided in the UK if it is provided there to any extent. Thus a flight originating from or ending in the UK is, in HMRC's view, a service provided in the UK.

Loans

12.17 A remittance basis user who borrows money in the UK effects a remittance under general principles if he brings foreign income or gains to the UK to pay principal or interest on the borrowing. The same applies if he makes payments of principal or interest outside the UK, should the money borrowed have been brought to the UK or if it is brought to the UK in the future (see para 56.1). It is likely that the same also applies if he uses the foreign income and gains as collateral for a loan used in the UK.

HMRC have recently changed their position on this. It was formerly indicated in HMRC guidance that there was no remittance in this situation, provided that the loan was commercial in nature and any interest or principal due was paid on a timely basis. Now, however, the HMRC view is that there is a remittance (see para **56.13**).

Care is needed over the debt rules in commercial situations. Clearing cheques through the UK does not amount to remittance, provided that the remittance basis user has no control over the banking process (para **51.23**). But the use of foreign income or gains to settle credit or debit cards is a remittance if the card issuer is UK based, for then settlement involves bringing the money to the UK. Foreign income or gains are also remitted if used to settle a foreign credit card debt insofar as the credit card expenditure was incurred in the UK.

GIFTS

12.18 Prima facie, a remittance basis user who gives his foreign income and gains away abroad removes the possibility of the money being taxed if it is subsequently brought to the UK by the donee, for in the donee's hands the money becomes clean capital. However, in certain circumstances a taxable remittance can occur. Such taxation may arise if the remittance basis user subsequently enjoys the income or gains in the UK, but it can also occur as a result of acts by the donee over which the remittance basis user has no control. These difficulties arise because a remittance by what the remittance basis legislation calls a 'relevant person' counts as a remittance by the remittance basis user and because of the anti-avoidance rules comprising Conditions C and D in ITA 2007, s 809L.

CHAPTERS 54 and 57 contain technical analysis of these points. The main risk areas are as follows:

(i)   A remittance by an individual donee is taxable on the (remittance basis using) donor, if the donee is the spouse or cohabitee of the donor, or his minor child or grandchild, as such persons are all 'relevant persons' (see paras **54.2** to **54.5**).

(ii)   The same applies if the donee is a trust under which the donor is a beneficiary or a close company in which he or such a trust is participator. And even if he is not a beneficiary or participator, a trust or company is caught if his spouse or cohabitee, or any minor child or grandchild is. All such trusts or companies are 'relevant persons' (see paras **54.6** to **54.15**).

(iii)   Assuming the donee is not within one of these categories, anti-avoidance Condition C in s 809L renders the remittance basis user taxable if the donee brings the gifted property to the UK and it is enjoyed by the remittance basis user or another relevant person. The same applies if what is brought to the UK and enjoyed is derived from the gift or if it is made available to the remittance basis user as part of some quid pro quo arrangement. This is explained in paras **57.5** to **57.7**.

(iv)   More generally, enjoyment by the remittance basis user of anybody else's property in the UK can result in a tax charge if the remittance basis user's income or gains have found their way to the owner of the property. The precise circumstances in which a remittance occurs turns on the construction of Condition D, which is obscurely worded (see paras **57.11** to **57.16**). But as a general rule caution is required whenever the remittance basis user or another individual who is a relevant person is enjoying somebody else's property in the UK. The same issues arise if what is enjoyed is not property but services provided in the UK.

It should also be noted that even if the donee is an individual who keeps what is gifted abroad, his future actions could still result in tax on the donor. This is the position if the donee makes a further gift of the gifted property and the second donee is the spouse or cohabitee of the original donor or his minor child or grandchild (ie a relevant person in relation to the original donor) and that second donee brings the property to the UK. The point also arises if the second donee is a trust of which the original donor or any other relevant person is a beneficiary.

A crucial point here is that the remittance basis user's income and gains can be taxed even though he has given them away and the act of bringing of them to the UK is beyond his control. No provision gives the remittance basis user a right to recover any tax he has to pay from the donee. This should be explained to any remittance basis user who is minded to make gifts.

There is one final point to make. This applies where what the donee gives away is income or gains of 2007–08 or earlier tax years. In such a case none of the above consequences ensue, except in the event that the income or gains are given back to the non-UK domiciliary or he, personally, enjoys property representing them in the UK. In other words, receipt or enjoyment of property by the donor's spouse, other relatives, trusts and companies can be ignored. This result follows because only the taxpayer is a relevant person in relation to income and gains of 2007–08 and earlier tax years (see para **54.1**).

EARNINGS

12.19 In principle, a remittance basis user can keep his foreign earnings free of UK tax in the same way as applies to investment income and gains, ie by ensuring that they are not remitted. However, in practice this is often difficult to achieve. Onerous conditions are imposed for foreign earnings to be eligible for the remittance basis, at least after the first three tax years of UK residence.

Employments

12.20 The term 'foreign income and gains' includes what are called chargeable overseas earnings, which are thus eligible for the remittance basis. The meaning of this term is explained in CHAPTER 50, and is very restrictive, for it requires the employer to be non-UK resident and all the duties of the employment to be performed abroad. Incidental duties in the UK are allowed, but 'incidental' is narrowly construed and, in HMRC's view, does not include responding to emails or telephone calls from clients.

It is particularly difficult to secure that earnings qualify as chargeable overseas earnings in the perhaps normal case where some at least of the non-UK domiciliary's work is in the UK. The traditional technique for overcoming this difficulty is split or dual contracts. One contract is with a UK company and covers the UK duties. The other is with an associated foreign company and covers the work abroad. The idea is that all the earnings under the latter contract are chargeable overseas earnings, whereas earnings form the former contract are taxable on the arising basis.

HMRC accept that split contracts are effective in appropriate cases, but they expect there to be two distinguishable jobs which are substantially different and not merely different in that one is to be performed in the UK and the other outside the UK. The split of the earnings between the contracts must be reasonable, failing which there can be a re-apportionment of earnings from the foreign contract to the UK contract. In addition, as explained in Chapter 50, foreign earnings may be subject to UK tax on the arising basis if the local tax actually paid on such earnings is less than 65% of the UK tax that would be due if the earnings were from a UK employment and were taxed at the maximum UK income tax rate (so at least 29% of the gross amount). The combined effect of all these rules is that securing the remittance basis on foreign earnings can be very difficult in practice.

However, the position is more straightforward for non-UK domiciliaries in the first three years of UK residence who are performing work outside the UK. Earnings in respect of such work are capable of qualifying for the remittance basis, even if the employer is UK resident. This treatment is provided by a special relief, known as overseas workday relief. This too is explained in Chapter 50.

Self-employment

12.21 The chargeable overseas earnings concept does not apply to earnings from self-employment. But in theory the profits of a trade or profession carried on wholly abroad are relevant foreign income and thus benefit from the remittance basis if the trader is a remittance basis user.

Unfortunately, as is explained in para 40.12, it is generally believed that it is difficult, and probably impossible, for a UK-resident sole trader to carry on a trade or profession wholly abroad. If it is not carried on wholly abroad, the profits do not have a foreign source and so are not relevant foreign income.

The conventional solution to this problem is a partnership whose business is managed and controlled outside the UK. As explained in para 40.12, the non-UK domiciliary's share of the partnership's foreign profits is then relevant foreign income.

An alternative approach is for the non-UK domiciliary to conduct the business through an overseas company, for then his remuneration is chargeable overseas earnings if all the duties are performed abroad (subject to the many caveats discussed above and in CHAPTER 50). The company's profits are in principle outside the scope of UK corporation tax, and dividends from the company are relevant foreign income eligible for the remittance basis. But for these advantages to obtain the company must not be resident in the UK. The applicable test is the central management and control test, which requires care to satisfy (see CHAPTER 43). Care must also be taken to avoid any UK trading profits attributable to a permanent establishment of the company in the UK, as such profits would be subject to UK corporation tax. A further point is that the transfer of assets code can, and typically will, operate to treat the company's profits as the non-UK domiciliary's income (see CHAPTER 69). The remittance basis applies to such deemed income, but the company is likely to be a relevant person for the purposes of the remittance rules, and if so a remittance by the company will result in tax on the company's business profits (see further CHAPTER 72).

Chapter 13
PRE-ARRIVAL PLANNING

13.1 The highly favourable tax treatment available to UK resident, non-UK domiciliaries can be somewhat overshadowed by the complexities of the tax regime and the level of planning required to obtain full advantage from it. However, without doubt, the position is made considerably simpler if the individual has taken steps to optimise his financial affairs, prior to becoming UK resident. The purpose of this chapter is to provide an overview of the kind of pre-arrival planning which should be considered.

TIMING ISSUES

13.2 It is critical to be clear about when the individual will first become a UK tax resident. This is to be determined by reference to the statutory residence test (SRT) discussed in detail in CHAPTER 41.

In the ideal scenario, the individual will plan to move to the UK shortly after 6 April in the chosen year of immigration and will be able to spend sufficient time in the UK either to be an automatically UK resident (see para **41.9**) or resident under the sufficient ties test (see para **41.13**).

If the individual wishes to move to the UK part way through the UK tax year, and he is likely to become UK resident in the tax year, consideration will need to be given to whether he will be eligible for split year treatment (see para **41.34**). Even if he will, it is likely to be desirable to implement any pre-arrival planning in the prior UK tax year if possible. The reason is that split year treatment only disapplies certain UK tax charges in the non-resident part of the relevant tax year, and in particular does not prevent a charge to income tax under Income Tax Act 2007 (ITA 2007), s 720 (see para **69.45**).

It is an unwelcome feature of the SRT that the internationally mobile, with homes in numerous jurisdictions, can find it difficult to spend sufficient time in the UK to become a UK resident, even when they wish to do so (for example in order to obtain the benefit of treaty reliefs vis-à-vis other countries). In some cases, the individual may need to settle for being non-UK resident in the first tax year in which significant time is spent in the UK. Provided that the individual's midnights in the UK in that first tax year exceed 90, achieving a UK tax residence in the following tax year is likely to be easier, by virtue of the '91 day tie' (see para **41.13**).

However, in other cases, taxability in the UK as a resident can commence sooner than anticipated. This applies in particular to individuals with existing UK homes, who start to spend a greater part of the year in the UK. If such an individual ceases to have any overseas homes, or the amount of time spent at overseas homes falls below 30 days over a rolling 91-day period, the individual may become UK resident under the 'only home' test (see para **41.9**). This test is difficult to apply and can be draconian in its effect. Moreover, where an existing UK home becomes an individual's only home, within the meaning of the 'only home' test, split year treatment is typically unavailable; so taxability in the UK is effectively backdated to the beginning of the tax year. For these reasons, it is often important for individuals who intend to become resident in the UK to retain their overseas homes and to continue spending significant amounts of time at them to avoid premature UK residence under the 'only home' test.

REVIEW OF ASSETS

13.3 Once it has been determined when the individual is likely to become taxable in the UK as a resident, the next step is to carry out a review of the assets that are held, whether personally or via corporate structures, partnerships, trusts, foundations, life insurance products etc. The following analysis should then be undertaken.

Characterise any holding structures

13.4 The UK tax treatment of any existing asset-holding entity or arrangement should be considered. Particular attention must be given to any foreign entity or arrangement which is not found under English law, such as a foundation or usufruct, or which may have a different tax treatment in the UK than in the country from which the individual is emigrating, such as a life insurance wrapper or a company which under its domestic law is tax transparent.

There are various considerations here, including:

• whether the entity or arrangement is likely to be treated as fiscally transparent or opaque for the purposes of income tax and CGT, bearing in mind that the position for these two taxes may not be the same;
• whether the nature of the entity or arrangement is such that credit can be claimed against UK taxes in respect of any foreign taxation of its income and gains;
• whether, in the case of an entity or arrangement that is not one that can be created under English law, there is sufficient clarity about its UK tax treatment for it to be a sensible vehicle for use in a UK tax context, or whether ambiguity regarding its treatment is such that it should ideally be replaced by another entity or arrangement which avoids such uncertainty; and
• the extent to which the foregoing issues matter, if the individual plans to use the remittance basis while he is a UK resident.

The general principles regarding characterisation of foreign entities and arrangements are considered in CHAPTER 32. The complexities and uncertainties created by foundations and usufructs are addressed in CHAPTER 33 and CHAPTER 34 respectively.

Consider possible application of the motive defences

13.5 Consideration should next be given to whether the 'motive defences' discussed in detail in CHAPTERS 73 and 88 may be applicable to any of the individual's existing corporate or trust structures, with the advantage that exemptions may be available from certain of the UK's anti-avoidance legislation which would otherwise attribute income or gains of such structures to the individual. It is important to consider the possible application of the motive defences at an early stage, in view of the precarious nature of such defences, as their availability could be inadvertently jeopardised by pre-arrival tax planning. If the motive defences are or may be in point, consideration should be given to leaving the structure untouched, or limiting any pre-arrival planning in relation to the structure to steps which clearly do not constitute UK tax avoidance.

Review company directorships and trusteeships

13.6 A particular trap for the unwary is that the acquisition of UK residence by an individual can trigger an immigration of other entities.

If the individual is a director of a non-UK company, the company may find itself managed and controlled from the UK, if the individual in practice controls the company and does so from the UK. Ideally the individual would therefore resign any such directorships before moving to the UK, in favour of an exclusively non-UK resident board of directors who in practice control the company. If this is not feasible for commercial reasons, the directors should take extreme care to exercise all duties at board meetings held outside the UK, and as best practice there should be a majority of non-UK resident directors on the board (see further at CHAPTER 43).

If the individual is the sole trustee of a trust, or trustee with their spouse (who is also moving to the UK), that trust will become UK resident when the individual(s) become UK resident. Therefore, similarly, the individual(s) should retire before the acquisition of UK residence in favour of a non-UK resident trustee(s), or (if it is certain that no further additions will be made to the trust) a non-UK resident co-trustee could be appointed (see further CHAPTER 42). The former option is preferable, as if the trust has mixed-residence trustees and any additions are made by the individual once he has become UK resident, the trustee residence rules will then deem the body of trustees to be UK resident (ITA 2007, s 476 and TCGA 1992, s 69(2B)). Moreover, a trust with mixed-residence individual trustees can be something of a hostage to fortune, as there is always the risk of the non-UK resident trustee(s) dying unexpectedly, causing the trust to become UK resident.

Trustee residence issues can be a particular trap for individuals moving to the UK from the USA, where individuals are often trustees of so-called 'living' trusts. However, with such trusts there is always the separate question as to whether we would in fact characterise the arrangement as a settlement (see para **32.4**).

If steps are to be taken to avoid the immigration of existing non-UK resident trusts, it should be remembered that while the individual may be planning to move to the UK in, say, July of a particular year, he or she may be treated as UK tax resident from 6 April of that year and so any such steps will need to be completed before 6 April.

Review terms of existing life insurance products

13.7 Finally, it is important to review the terms of any pre-existing single premium life insurance policies which the individual may hold, unless specifically designed for the UK market (which in the circumstances is unlikely). Such products are likely to be classified as personal portfolio bonds for UK tax purposes. If this is the case an extremely penal tax regime will apply once the individual is UK resident (see para **96.36**). As a result, it should be recommended that the individual either encashes the policy, or (if possible) enters into a variation of the policy to take it outside the personal portfolio bond regime, before the end of the insurance year which falls after the individual becomes UK resident (see para **96.35**).

Even where the policy is not a personal portfolio bond, or can be varied so that it will fall outside that regime, deemed income arising on chargeable events will not qualify for the remittance basis. This alone may render a single premium life insurance policy unsuitable for certain foreign domiciliaries who are moving to the UK.

IDENTIFYING AND MAXIMISING PRE-RESIDENCY CAPITAL

13.8 Having confirmed how the individual's assets are held and reviewed them accordingly, the next steps are: (1) identification of pre-residency capital, also known as 'clean capital', and (where this is practicable); (2) maximisation of pre-residency capital by pre-arrival rebasing. Such planning is simplest to implement where assets are directly held, as explained below.

Personally held cash and investments

13.9 Any cash in a personally held bank account when the individual becomes UK resident will clearly represent pre-residency capital. Such funds should be transferred to a new bank account with the individual's offshore bank and be designated as a 'clean capital' account. Instructions should be given to the individual's bank to ensure that any interest earned on such funds after the commencement of UK tax residence is mandated to a separate 'income account', as explained further at para **14.6**. No further additions should be made to the clean capital account after the commencement of residence in the UK, unless the funds added are also demonstrably clean capital.

The clean capital account can then be used for tax-free funding of the individual's UK expenditure. Ideally, this account should therefore contain a sufficiently generous amount to fund the individual's anticipated UK expenditure for the duration of his residence in the UK (since as a non-UK domiciliary he must of course intend to leave at some point), possibly supplemented by UK source income or other immediately taxable receipts.

Additionally, in order to maximise the amount in the clean capital account, consideration should be given to disposing of some or all of any of the individual's personally held investments which are standing at gain (subject to investment considerations and local tax implications) prior to the individual becoming UK resident. This exercise is commonly referred to as pre-arrival rebasing.

It is important to consider the merits of undertaking such planning, as there is no automatic rebasing of assets when an individual becomes UK resident. It follows that if such assets are sold after the individual has become resident, the entire historic gain will be subject to CGT if remitted to the UK, not just the post-residency growth in value. Therefore, even if the individual has sufficient clean capital for anticipated needs in the UK, it may be worth undertaking this rebasing (assuming the local tax implications are palatable) and after an appropriate interval (so as not to fall foul of 'bed and breakfasting' rules) to reinvest the proceeds of sale.

It may also be desirable for the individual to realise any losses on personally held investments prior to becoming UK resident, as once he is UK resident such losses will not be allowable to set against capital gains (assuming the individual will be a remittance basis user and will not make a foreign loss election – see paras **49.14** and **49.15**), and as doing so may mitigate the tax implications in the home jurisdiction of the rebasing exercise.

Cash and other assets held in corporate structures

13.10 While cash held within an individual's investment or trading company when the individual becomes UK resident may represent income/profits earned pre-residency, such funds may only be accessible by the individual if the company declares a dividend or implements a share buy-back. Such a transaction effected after the individual becomes UK resident will convert the cash into post-residency income or capital gains in the individual's hands (depending on which extraction method is used).

Even if the transfer of assets motive defence applies to the company, a dividend receipt will be taxable on the individual in the normal way if remitted to the UK (as the motive defence would only apply to prevent attribution of the company's post-residency income to the individual; it would not protect the income from charge once actually distributed as income to the individual).

The only way to extract pre-residency funds from the company as clean capital would be by way of repayment of any outstanding shareholder loan. If there is no such loan, consideration should be given to declaring a pre-residency dividend (again, subject to local tax implications) which can be added to the individual's personally held clean capital, or all or part of which could be subsequently lent back into the company (unless the motive defence applies, in which case such step may be undesirable, as the defence could be prejudiced). A loan to the company would create a route for re-extraction of such funds as clean capital (if kept segregated from post-residency income/profits of the company) after the individual is UK resident.

Cash and other assets held in trust structures

13.11 As regards existing trust structures, the position is even more complicated. Where such structures include underlying companies, the above considerations are equally applicable and similarly, pre-residency cash held within such structures will be converted to post-residency income or gains if extracted to trust level after the individual has become resident. However, there is a further layer of complexity as a result of the anti-avoidance legislation applicable to trusts.

One major issue here is that the rules that impose taxation on capital payments from non-resident trusts (see CHAPTER 77) do so by reference to capital gains that have been realised by the trust, even if such gains arose long before any beneficiary of the trust was resident in the UK or had any connection to the UK. The result is that there can be tax on pre-residency gains.

Perhaps the biggest trap for the unwary in this context is the fact that a capital payment made to an individual from a non-resident trust before he or she becomes UK resident will not necessarily represent clean capital in the individual's hands, or at least not indefinitely. Indeed, such a payment could cause disastrous tainting of clean capital if the payment from the trust is paid into a clean capital account containing pre-residency capital. This is because, unless the capital payment is fully matched with capital gains realised within the trust before the individual becomes UK resident, any unmatched balance of the capital payment will be available for matching with capital gains that are realised within the trust in subsequent tax years; and as and when such matching occurs, the proceeds of the capital payment will become tainted with such gains. Similarly, if a non-transferor receives such a capital benefit prior to becoming UK resident, any unmatched element can be taxed under ITA 2007, ss 731–735 by reference to any relevant income which may subsequently arise within the structure once the individual has become UK resident.

Consideration should therefore be given to winding up any pre-existing trust completely before the individual becomes UK resident, subject to local tax considerations. The individual can retain sufficient funds in his personal ownership to fund his clean capital account, and then resettle any surplus into a new trust structure.

Banking and investment arrangements

13.12 Finally, having established a clean capital account with sufficient funds for the individual's UK expenditure during his anticipated stay in the UK, it is critical to ensure that this does not become tainted with any post-residency income or gains. Suitable segregated banking arrangements should therefore be put in place in the manner described in Chapter 13. Any existing investment portfolios should also be reviewed, and any new portfolios being established should be designed, so that, ideally, they do not contain any UK investments or investments where it is difficult to segregate income as it arises (see Chapter 14).

OTHER POINTS TO NOTE

13.13 The main pre-arrival planning concerns are those outlined above. However, some additional points to note include the following:

- While the best practice will be for the individual only ever to remit funds to the UK from a clean capital account, it will be critical for the individual to have a good understanding of what constitutes a taxable remittance for UK tax purposes, so that he does not inadvertently trigger a remittance of foreign income or gains, eg by inappropriate use of credit cards (see Chapter 51 for the scope of what constitutes a remittance).
- Similarly, the common law and CGT situs rules (discussed in Chapters 39 and 40) can be a trap for the unwary, as the immigration of the individual may unwittingly result in a shift in the situs of any debts owed to him and by him (for CGT and IHT purposes respectively). Such arrangements should therefore be reviewed.
- If the individual is planning to work in the UK, but with some overseas aspects to his duties, he may be eligible for overseas workday relief during the first three tax years of UK tax residency (see paras 50.2 to 50.4).
- The individual's assumption of UK residence, and possibly also habitual residence in the UK, may affect the succession law position in other countries. Existing testamentary arrangements should be reviewed in the light of this change.
- Finally, one of the first things that an individual moving to the UK will typically wish to do is buy a UK home. In light of recent and prospective changes to the rules regarding the deductibility of debts for IHT purposes and the tax treatment of traditional property holding structures, consideration should be given well before contracts are exchanged to the individual's attitude to IHT and the steps that might be taken to mitigate IHT exposure in respect of the property. The possibility of using bank borrowing or another third-party loan to fund the purchase should be considered, since leveraging the property post-acquisition will generally no longer achieve any IHT saving (see further discussion at Chapter 84). If the borrowing used is commercial bank borrowing, the terms of the facility should also be reviewed carefully if secondary collateral in the form of bankable assets is required (see paras 84.6 and 56.13).

Chapter 14

BRINGING MONEY TO THE UK

INTRODUCTION

14.1 Some remittance basis users do not need or want to remit foreign income and gains to the UK. However, many do. There are two main situations in which this requirement may arise. The first is where the remittance basis user wishes to invest in the UK, whether via a collective investment scheme or by direct investment. The second, which is more common in practice, is where he requires overseas funds for personal spending, whether on houses or chattels or on general living expenses.

This chapter looks at techniques and reliefs that are relevant to both kinds of UK spending. It is an area where significant changes resulted from FA 2012. In relation to investments this chapter focuses solely on remittance issues, as planning for tax liabilities occasioned by the investments themselves is the subject of CHAPTER 15.

DIRECT INVESTMENTS

14.2 The basic rule is that investment in UK assets or a UK business is just as much a remittance as bringing in money for personal spending. This has been widely criticised as irrational, as it means that remittance basis users are discouraged from investing in the UK. The former Conservative/Liberal Democrat coalition government was sensitive to this criticism and in 2012 introduced a relief for investments which would otherwise trigger a remittance, in ITA 2007, ss 809VA–809VO.

This relief, known as business investment relief, is described in detail in CHAPTER 58. It is available where the money brought to the UK is used to subscribe for shares in an unlisted company or to make a loan to such a company. The company may be a trading company or the parent company of a trading group and, in an important extension to the relief, farming companies and property investment companies are also included. There is no minimum or maximum amount of investment and it does not matter whether the remittance basis user works for the company.

The practical result of the relief is that a remittance basis user desiring to invest in a UK business or in UK real estate can do so without effecting a taxable remittance, provided the investment is through the medium of an unlisted company. There has been pressure to extend the relief to listed companies and

LLPs but to date this pressure has been resisted. HMRC operate an informal clearance procedure, of which use should be made in appropriate cases (see para **58.13**).

The principal difficulty with the relief is that it can be clawed back. This may happen if the remittance basis user disposes of the shares or loan, but it can also happen if value is extracted from the company. However, in general the risk of claw-back should not be exaggerated, for the claw-back does not occur if within prescribed grace periods, described in para **58.13**, the proceeds of the investment are taken back abroad or reinvested in another qualifying company.

Caution is required in relation to the anti-avoidance provisions that qualify business investment relief, in particular the provisions regarding 'extractions of value'. The concept of an extraction of value encompasses not only the situation where value is extracted from the investee company but also where there is an extraction of value from any company with which the investee company is connected. For this reason, business investment relief can be more challenging where it results in the investor controlling the investee company, for then he has to ensure that he does not extract value from any other company he controls. That said, the concept of an extraction of value definitely does not include commercial remuneration, interest and dividends, and so in the main it comes into issue in more unusual transactions. The matter is explained more fully in para **58.16**.

The current Government appears to be committed to making the business investment relief in ss 809VA–809VO work and wishes to increase the use that is made of it. For this reason it is to be hoped that the shortcomings of this legislation will eventually be remedied. In the meantime, use of the relief should be considered in appropriate cases.

INDIRECT INVESTMENT

14.3 As indicated above, investments in listed companies do not attract business investment relief. It follows that remittance basis users who buy quoted UK bonds and equities in their portfolios risk making a remittance. Indeed, the traditional view is that if such assets are acquired using foreign income or gains, a remittance of the income or gains is inevitable, and that this is so even if an overseas broker is used, with settlement abroad (see para **51.19**).

However, in reality the position is not always so black and white. Difficult questions as to the situs of investments arise where they are interests in immobilised securities or take the form of depositary receipts (see paras **38.14** to **38.15**). In such cases there may be a technical argument that a debt or equity interest in a UK company is, in fact, a non-UK situs asset at common law.

In any event, indirect investment in UK bonds and equities can be achieved without any risk of a remittance. Most, if not all, asset managers now operate their own in-house mutual funds, and some at least of these are overseas entities such as a Channel Island open-ended investment company or a Luxembourg SICAV. The remittance basis user who buys shares in such a vehicle does not effect a remittance so long as settlement is effected outside the UK. Some such vehicles invest largely or wholly in UK stocks, and often the portfolio reflects much the same spread as would a direct investment portfolio of the same asset manager. So long as the vehicle is not close, it is not a relevant person in relation to the investor (see paras 54.12 to 54.15) and so no remittance occurs when it brings funds to the UK for investment. Exposure to UK bonds and equities can thus be achieved without effecting a taxable remittance.

In all probability the same result is achieved if the overseas entity is not a company but a unit trust. Unit trusts are not relevant persons, and the better view is that remittance by a widely-held unit trust cannot be treated as remittance by the unit holders (see para 54.19).

PARTNERSHIPS

14.4 Given that partnerships are transparent for income tax and CGT purposes, it might be expected that a remittance of funds by a partnership would be treated as a remittance by the individual partners in it. In fact, this is not how HMRC view the matter (see RDRM 33530). This creates theoretical scope for a non-UK domiciliary to use a foreign partnership as a vehicle for investment into the UK, without a taxable remittance of any foreign income or gains contributed to the partnership.

PERSONAL SPENDING

14.5 The reliefs and practices described above are not generally relevant where the UK spending is on consumption or on houses or chattels for personal use. Here reliance has to be placed on a different technique; namely, ensuring that any such expenditure is funded from an account that does not contain unremitted income or capital gains.

Capital and income segregation: cash

14.6 It has long been established that if what is brought to the UK is neither income nor capital gain, there is no taxable remittance. This is so even if the remittance basis user holds foreign income and gains elsewhere abroad. In other words, determining whether a remittance has occurred is a matter of tracing, not accounting. Avoidance of any taxable remittance is achieved even if the capital remitted is from one account and the income or gains are in another account at the same bank.

For the purposes of these principles, funds count as capital if inherited by gift or bequest or, more importantly, if pre-dating arrival in the UK. The latter follows because the charges on remittances do not operate on income or gains which arose or accrued prior to immigration.

The result is that if pre-arrival capital and inheritances are kept in one account, tax-free remittance from that account is possible provided the interest earned on that account is credited directly to another account as it arises. The two accounts thereby operated are known as capital and income accounts. An important point to note is that pre-arrival funds do not have to be remitted prior to immigration. Such money retains its tax-free status provided it is segregated from any future income or gains.

Until 5 April 2012, a procedure such as this was only entirely satisfactory if the capital account was denominated in sterling. The reason was that any foreign currency account was a chargeable asset in its own right, resulting in chargeable gains on withdrawals from the account if the currency concerned had appreciated against sterling (see para **49.18**). Often the amounts of tax thereby generated were modest, but the cost and complexity in computation were formidable. Capital and income accounts were only entirely free of tax complications if the capital account was in sterling. But avoiding foreign currency accounts for this reason came close to avoiding tax by not making a profit.

Now however this problem has gone, for foreign currency bank accounts are not chargeable assets if held, inter alia, by individuals (TCGA 1992, s 252 as substituted by FA 2012, s 35). The practical result is that capital and income account procedures can now be operated on a multi-currency basis. For many remittance basis users that is an entirely satisfactory basis on which to hold the proportion of their assets needed to fund foreseeable UK spending.

One caveat is that the currency exposure must be through bank accounts. Currency instruments such as money-market funds do not enjoy exemption from CGT and so should be avoided where the capital account is held for remittance.

Capital and income segregation: investments

14.7 It may be that a more adventurous strategy is desired involving equities, bonds and mutual funds. Here the capital and income account procedure can still be used, but two capital accounts are normally recommended. The first is for the proceeds of disposals that have generated a chargeable gain and the second is for the proceeds of other disposals. The latter, and not the former, is used for remittance.

The gains account has to include the full proceeds of disposals at a gain rather than just the gain element, as base cost on the one hand and gain on the other are indivisible and so cannot be segregated. The mixed fund rules described in CHAPTER 53 operate, on the basis that the proceeds of any disposal are a mixed fund, and any remittance from that mixed fund will be deemed to be of gain first (see para **53.8**). It follows that if the capital account includes the proceeds of investments which have generated chargeable gains, a remittance from that account is likely to result in tax.

It may be felt that if the gains account is not going to be remitted, the gains account and the income account could be amalgamated. On the assumption that a remittance from such a combined account will never occur, this is right. But unforeseen circumstances can necessitate remittances, and if so it is preferable to have gains separate, for generally gains attract a lesser rate of tax than income, and the base-cost elements may well represent clean capital.

There is one situation where the capital account for remittances can include the proceeds of a disposal realising the gain. This is in point should the remittance basis user have made a s 16ZA election (see paras **12.9, 49.12** and **49.17**). In such a case the allowance of the loss against an unremitted gain is effected as a reduction or elimination of the gain. Where the gain is thereby eliminated, the proceeds of the disposal are effectively clean capital, assuming that the investment was itself bought out of clean capital. In practice it may be difficult, when a disposal is made, to know whether, under the complex loss rules applicable to non-domiciliaries, the gain will be offset. In such a case the proceeds could, pending clarification as to the position, be credited to a special holding account.

If a multiple account approach is adopted, it should generally be followed through to investments made out of the various accounts. Generally the proceeds of an investment should be credited to the account from which the purchase of that investment was funded. The exception, as indicated above, is where an investment has been purchased using capital but has been realised at a gain, in which case its proceeds need to be credited to the gains account rather than the capital account. As noted above, the entire proceeds of a disposal at a gain must be credited to the gains account, not just the gain element. If the portfolio is being managed with the object of generating capital growth (rather than income) the inevitable consequence of the need to segregate gains from clean capital is that, over time, value passes from the capital account to the gains account and the stock of clean capital becomes depleted.

Deemed income

14.8 Should the remittance basis user have three accounts, for clean capital, gains and income, the gains account is likely to include some gains taxed as income. The most notable example is offshore income gains, ie gains realised on the disposal of non-reporting funds (see CHAPTER 95) but another instance is profits arising on the redemption or maturity of 'structured products' where, as is commonly the case, such products qualify as deeply discounted securities for tax purposes. This could be unhelpful should remittance from the gains account ever prove necessary, for the income element will attract tax at income tax rates rather than the 20% CGT rate. In view of this, a separate fourth account for disposals generating income gains can be considered, but, on the assumption that the gains account ought never in fact be remitted, this may be a complication too far.

Offshore funds present one other issue in operating multiple accounts, this time concerning reporting funds. The proceeds of disposal of a reporting fund are a mixed fund if the fund has reported income which has not been distributed (see para **95.24**). The solution to this problem is to ensure that any reporting fund held has a policy of distributing all reported income or, if that is not possible, to ensure that the proceeds of any realisation of such a fund do not go into the clean capital account.

The deemed income issue also arises when bonds are disposed of, insofar as the proceeds include an element taxable as accrued interest. Here however, HMRC allow segregation provided that the selling broker credits an amount equal to the interest directly to an income account of the client (see para **53.41**).

Nominated income

14.9 There is one situation where a remittance from a clean capital account can result in tax, and that is where a remittance has been made of income or gains nominated under the rules relating to the remittance basis charge (see paras **47.7** to **47.9**). Should this happen, ordering rules as described in para **47.9** prevail over any actual identification of what is remitted. For this reason care must be taken to avoid a remittance of nominated income or gains.

Since 2012–13, the ordering rules have not been triggered if what is remitted is less than £10 of a given year's nominated income or gains. As is explained in para **47.8**, this means that the whole problem is now avoided by ensuring that for each year less than £10 is nominated. The difficulties with nominated income are thus only likely to arise in practice in the event that more than £10 has been nominated for some prior year.

Settlements

14.10 Prior to 2008, the conventional way of dealing with the CGT problems posed by capital and income accounts was for investments to be held by a settlor-interested settlement. Non-UK domiciliaries were then outside both the settlor charge in TCGA 1992, s 86 and the beneficiary charge in s 87 and this meant that gains could be realised within settlements without any CGT liabilities being generated. However, since 2008-09 non-domiciliaries have been within s 87 (see CHAPTER 79) and so a remitted capital payment generally results in tax. The role of settlements is discussed further in CHAPTER 16.

Use of borrowed funds to acquire investments

14.11 As noted above, where an investment portfolio is being managed with a capital growth objective (rather than aiming at income generation), it is inevitable that if capital and capital gains are being segregated, value will over time leach from the capital account to the capital gains account, and the capital account will be depleted. This is due to the requirement to transfer the entire proceeds of an investment that has been disposed of at a gain – not merely the gain element – to the capital gains account. It can be argued that segregation procedures are somewhat self-defeating in relation to a typical investment portfolio, as the remittance basis user is unlikely to be able to preserve a significant amount of clean capital, to be used for tax-free remittances to the UK, over anything other than a short timeframe.

There are two possible responses to this. One is to set aside the proportion of capital that may be needed for remittance to the UK and keep it in cash (or other income-producing assets that will not generate capital gains), operate segregation in relation to the cash, but not to attempt segregation in relation to investments that are liable to generate gains (accepting that if there is any unforeseen requirement to remit from the proceeds of such investments, the tax cost will be high).

A second possible response is to utilise bank borrowing, to preserve the maximum amount of clean capital without compromising investment growth. A remittance basis user who holds clean capital can borrow commercially, using that clean capital as collateral. The clean capital is left in the form of cash, with any interest paid by the bank being segregated. The borrowed capital is transferred to a separate account and is used to make non-UK investments (which may be of a kind which would be problematic for a segregated portfolio, eg non-reporting offshore funds). The investment account is managed to generate capital growth, without any attempt being made to segregate income or gains from the original borrowed capital. Capital growth within the investment account is used to pay interest on the bank loan and also, progressively, to repay the principal. Interest from the cash can also be used for these purposes. As the debt is gradually repaid, the portion of the clean capital cash which is required by the bank as collateral is gradually reduced. Cash within the account is 'freed up', and can be withdrawn from the account and used for UK expenditure. In theory, the remittance basis user may end up with 100% of the original clean capital being available for expenditure in the UK, plus a substantial investment portfolio. The above planning relies on the fact that, provided that all of the investments acquired using the bank facility are non-UK situs, the bank debt is not a 'relevant debt'. This concept is discussed in Chapter 56.

MIXED FUNDS

14.12 For some remittance basis users, the above suggestions as to multiple accounts – and other techniques for the preservation of clean capital – represent an unattainable state of perfection. They may have been resident in the UK for a long period, and/or may not have been well-advised regarding account structuring when UK residence commenced. Such individuals may not have any assets that are indentifiable as clean capital. All their assets are mixed funds.

The rules as to mixed funds are explained in Chapter 53. Often a substantial part of a fund may in fact represent capital, but the computation required to demonstrate this may be time consuming and expensive, if indeed records exist at all. Moreover, the ordering rules described in Chapter 53 are likely to mean a partial remittance is not identified with clean capital. The problems are compounded by the fact that until 5 April 2012, gains on foreign currency bank accounts were chargeable to CGT with the result, strictly, that they have to be included in the computational exercise.

Given these difficulties, a remittance from a historic mixed fund is often to be avoided if at all possible. There is however one kind of mixed fund which may represent an exception, namely one where a large proportion of the potentially chargeable items include pre-5 April 2008 investment income. Here such income is not charged if remitted provided that at some point before 12 March 2008 it was invested in assets which were not cash, bonds, or other fixed-interest securities (see paras **59.2** to **59.4**). If such income comprises a large part of the mixed fund the tax charge on the rest, and the computational cost, may be an expense worth paying for remittance. A point to stress is that this relief does not apply to earnings or capital gains.

If that pre-2008 relief is not in point, the best strategy to consider is to confine remittances from the mixed fund to circumstances which do not attract tax even if all of what is remitted is income or gains, ie the circumstances described in the first part of this chapter. Ideally the remittance basis user will meet expenses which cannot be so covered out of UK source income such as UK earnings or it may be he will have at least a modest fund of clean capital.

If that is not possible, the remittance basis user may have to accept some tax. Superficially it may be felt inevitable to remit from the mixed fund and accept not merely the tax but also the computational expense that is entailed. But there is one scenario whereby the computational expense can be avoided and even the tax reduced.

This relates to current income. If the current income is paid directly to the UK, or credited to a separate account from which remittances are made to the UK, there is no doubt that it and it alone is remitted. The problem which used to arise with currency gains if the banking is in a foreign currency has been removed by the 2012 change described above. In this scenario computational complexity is removed.

In addition tax is reduced if the foreign income is subject to withholding tax, for such tax is creditable against the UK tax. Furthermore, dividend tax rates are available for dividend income, if the individual is prepared to forego the remittance basis (see para **12.9**). In cases of withholding tax and dividend tax rates, the combined effect may be to substantially reduce the UK tax, albeit not eliminate it.

It should be noted that the Government's proposals regarding changes to the taxation of long-term resident foreign domiciliaries include a relief to allow mixed funds to be unmixed. At the time writing, the exact scope of this is unclear, but the relief may be available to foreign domiciliaries generally, with the exception of those who have a UK origin, and not merely those individuals who have become deemed domiciled due to long-term residence. The proposed unmixing relief is discussed at para **19.6**.

Borrowing on the security of mixed funds

14.13 Until 4 August 2014, there was one other option for non-UK domicili-aries who needed to bring funds into the UK, for personal expenditure, but did not have any clean capital. This was the option of borrowing on the security of an offshore mixed fund, and bringing the borrowed money into the UK.

As discussed in CHAPTER 56, the remittance code provides for a taxable remittance if foreign income or gains are used in respect of a 'relevant debt', meaning a debt which relates to property that has been brought to or enjoyed in the UK by a relevant person. On the face of it, if a remittance basis user pledges foreign cash or investments as collateral for a loan which is used for

UK expenditure, that is probably a 'use' of the income or gains comprised in the collateral, in respect of a relevant debt. The result is tax on a remittance of the income or gains in question.

Strangely, however, this was not the view that HMRC used to take. For six years or so, HMRC's published position was that there was no remittance of the income or gains in this situation, provided that the loan was 'commercial' in nature and that it was 'serviced' by regular interest payments. This position was couched as an interpretation of the legislation, although many advisers doubted that it was justified by the legislation, and instead treated it as a concession. Whatever its legal basis, a certain number of non-UK domiciliaries took advantage of the ability to raise clean capital by borrowing on the security of offshore mixed funds and using the borrowed money for UK spending, apparently with HMRC's blessing.

However, on 4 August 2014 there was an abrupt change of position by HMRC in relation to this practice. HMRC's current published view is discussed in greater detail at para **56.12**. The upshot is that it is no longer possible for offshore mixed funds to be used as collateral for loans used in the UK, unless a taxpayer is audacious enough to challenge HMRC's current view that the offering of an account as collateral involves a 'use' of the income or gains comprised within it.

Chapter 15

IDENTIFYING SUITABLE INVESTMENTS

INTRODUCTION

15.1 It is standard advice to a non-UK domiciled UK resident who is claiming the remittance basis of taxation (an RBU) to avoid holding UK investments within any offshore investment portfolio. The principal reason for this is that income or gains arising on such assets will not benefit from the remittance basis and, while the individual is non-UK domiciled for IHT purposes, UK assets may create unnecessary IHT exposure.

An RBU may also be advised that it is desirable to avoid holding certain investments which, although they may be 'non-UK', can generate deemed income when they are sold. The potential problem with such investments, if they are acquired using clean capital, is that generally there is no ability to separate out the clean capital and deemed income elements of the sale proceeds. The result is that, typically, they result in clean capital being turned into a mixed fund.

This is unproblematic for as long as the RBU has no wish or need to take money out of the offshore portfolio for remittance to the UK. However, it is rather common for non-UK domiciliaries to end up being resident in the UK for longer than originally intended, or to have heavier spending requirements in the UK than originally envisaged. This can necessitate remittances from sources which it was expected could be left untouched throughout the period of residence. In view of this risk, it often does make sense to avoid investments which can generate deemed income when sold, or at least to be aware of which investments have this characteristic, so that the proceeds of sale can be segregated from other cash that is not tainted by deemed income.

However, identifying investments that are suitable to be held by an RBU is not always straightforward. For example, the question of whether something is a UK investment or not is easily answered with some asset classes but less so with others. There is scope for confusion because the rules for determining whether an investment is 'UK' or not differ, depending on the tax in question.

The purpose of this chapter is to set out some of the basic principles which can be applied when approaching the topic from a remittance basis planning and IHT mitigation perspective; namely, which investments are readily classifiable as 'non-UK' and suitable for acquisition by an RBU, those which require more detailed consideration, and those which are often best avoided.

The difficulties with classifying certain investments from a tax perspective, or with preserving clean capital, should of course be balanced with the investment opportunities potentially afforded by them.

RELEVANT TAXES

15.2 When classifying an investment as 'UK' or 'non-UK', it is necessary to consider its situs for IHT and CGT purposes and the source of its income for income tax purposes.

For IHT purposes, the situs analysis follows common law principles. For CGT, there is a statutory basis for determining situs in most (but not all) circumstances. For income tax, source is determined by the common law. The latter provides reasonably clear answers as to the source of dividends, but rather less clarity about the source of interest payments. A statutory test for determining source would in many ways be preferable. These issues of situs and source are discussed in detail in CHAPTERS **38, 39** and **40**.

If the outcome of applying the analysis for these three taxes to a particular investment is that it has a UK situs for IHT and CGT purposes and would give rise to UK source income then it is a 'UK' investment and should generally be avoided in an RBU's offshore investment portfolio. However, if the particular investment has a non-UK situs for IHT and CGT purposes and would give rise to non-UK source income, it will generally be suitable from a UK tax perspective for inclusion as a 'non-UK' investment in the RBU's offshore portfolio, at least where the RBU does not expect to withdraw funds from the portfolio for remittance to the UK.

INVESTMENTS WHICH ARE READILY CLASSIFIABLE

15.3 The following asset classes are readily classifiable:

Bank accounts

15.4 As noted at para **38.4**, the situs of a bank account for IHT purposes will be where the bank account is maintained. CGT is not relevant for classifying such assets, as foreign currency gains made on bank accounts are now exempt from CGT. Any interest earned on the funds held in the bank account will have its source where it is earned, so again where the account is maintained. Thus an account at a foreign bank, or a foreign branch of a UK bank, is 'non-UK'.

Registered shares

15.5 As noted at paras **38.7** and **38.8**, the situs of registered shares for IHT purposes and for CGT purposes will be where they are registered, and in the unlikely event that there is more than one register, where the primary share register is kept. A dividend paid in respect of the shares will have its source where the company is resident. Accordingly, shares in a listed company incorporated outside the UK can in practice be assumed to be 'non-UK'. It should be noted that where such shares are listed/traded is irrelevant.

Government securities

15.6 Government bonds are normally registered, and therefore do not give rise to the uncertainties as to situs which are created by immobilised securities (see para 15.12). The situs of a government bond for IHT and CGT purposes will be the country of issue and that will also be the source of any interest paid on the securities. Thus a bond issued by a foreign government is 'non-UK'. However, it should be noted that all traded fixed interest securities providing for periodic interest payments, including government bonds, can give rise to segregation issues due to the operation of the accrued income scheme. See para 15.12 below, re corporate bonds.

Physical precious metals

15.7 The IHT situs and CGT situs will be where the precious metals are physically held. As such investments are not income producing, source is not relevant.

INVESTMENTS REQUIRING MORE DETAILED CONSIDERATION

15.8 The following asset classes require more detailed consideration to ascertain whether they would be regarded as UK investments or not.

Offshore funds

15.9 The definition of the term 'offshore fund' is discussed at para 95.2ff. If the fund in question is structured as a corporate then the position is straightforward; it is the same analysis as for registered shares set out above.

If the fund is structured as a unit trust, this is deemed to be a corporate for CGT purposes (TCGA 1992, s 99). However, the treatment of the fund for IHT and income tax purposes is more difficult and may not always be immediately clear. Depending on the precise terms of the unit trust in question, the IHT situs and source for income tax purposes will either be where the trustees are resident or where the underlying assets are held (see para 38.13). For this reason, the prudent approach is to avoid unit trusts which have underlying investments in the UK, so that regardless of the interpretation, the investment is 'non-UK'.

It should be remembered that there are also other tax issues to be concerned with in relation to offshore funds, namely, whether the fund is a reporting or non-reporting fund, which in turn affects whether any gain realised on a disposal of units in the fund will have a CGT or income tax treatment. The tax treatment of offshore funds is a separate topic covered in detail at CHAPTERS 3 and 95.

15.9 *Identifying suitable investments*

As a general rule, it is preferable for an RBU to invest in offshore reporting funds which are structured as corporates, and which distribute all reported income, so that any gain on redemption benefits from CGT treatment.

UK authorised funds

15.10 UK authorised funds have a UK situs as a matter of common law, but in the hands of individuals who are domiciled outside the UK for IHT purposes are given 'excluded property' status, effectively deeming them to be non-UK situs for the purposes of IHT (see para 37.11). The rationale for this special treatment is to encourage non-UK domiciliaries to invest in such funds, rather than be put off by concern about IHT exposure.

However, this special status is limited to IHT. Such investments still have a UK situs for CGT purposes and give rise to UK source income. Therefore, for a UK resident non-UK domiciled investor, they generally only make sense if the individual is not yet deemed domiciled for IHT, and/or has a low mortality risk, and is not claiming the remittance basis of taxation. A further qualification is that, if the individual has previously taken advantage of the remittance basis, he or she must not use historic unremitted foreign income or gains to make the investment, as in that case the investment will typically trigger a remittance of such funds.

Exchange traded funds

15.11 These differ from traditional offshore funds in that they are traded on a secondary market, and investors typically realise the cash value of their investments through a sale on this market, rather than by means of a redemption. However, they are considered to fall within the tax definition of an offshore fund. The tax treatment is therefore as discussed at 15.9 above.

Corporate bonds

15.12 As discussed in detail at paras 38.14 and 39.15, the application of the situs rules to bonds is difficult where the bond is 'immobilised', ie traded electronically through a clearance system. However, for the reasons discussed in those paragraphs, in practice a bond issued by a non-UK resident company is highly likely to be non-UK situs at common law and also for CGT purposes. Similarly, the source of interest payments should be non-UK if the issuer is non-UK resident.

Perhaps surprisingly, in view of their prevalence as an asset class, bonds and other fixed interest securities can be considered something of a problem investment where there is a desire to segregate income; although as discussed below, HMRC practice does permit *ex post facto* segregation. Actual interest payments from a bond are easily segregated from capital, by ensuring that such payments are credited to an income account. But difficulties with the segregation of income can in principle arise if a bond (or other fixed interest security) is sold in circumstances where the sale proceeds reflect the amount of accrued income that will be received by the purchaser on the next interest payment date. Any such sale engages the provisions of the accrued income scheme (ITA 2007, Pt 12), which causes the attribution to the vendor of deemed income equal to the accrued income acquired by the purchaser.

If such proceeds are received in a single sum, those proceeds will include, as a mixed fund, the deemed income element. However, HMRC's published position is that 'for consistency of treatment between the AIS and the remittance basis regime, HMRC will . . . accept that an "income amount" can be transferred to a separate "income account" immediately upon transfer . . . without creating a mixed fund' (RDRM 33550). This is arguably concessionary.

Depositary receipts

15.13 Depositary receipts in respect of shares are generally treated in the same way as the 'underlying' shares for UK tax purposes, discussed above. However, the analysis is not entirely straightforward (see paras **38.15** and **39.9**).

INVESTMENTS WHICH CAN BE DIFFICULT TO CLASSIFY

15.14 There are a number of more sophisticated types of investments which from a tax perspective can be problematic and which, where tax-efficiency is a high priority, may be best avoided in an RBU's investment portfolio. It is of course acknowledged that there may well be very good investment reasons for the RBU to wish to invest in such products and these must be balanced with any tax concerns.

Structured products

15.15 A major issue with structured products is that as an adviser it can be difficult to get enough information about the product, in advance of an investment being made into it, to be confident in determining its situs and otherwise characterising it for tax purposes.

Structured products are a form of derivative. They are contractual arrangements made between an issuer (usually a bank) and subscribers. The document setting out the terms of the contract is usually referred to as a 'note'. Usually, no interest is payable under the note, but it provides for a payout to the subscribers on the maturity of the note or, in some cases, at an earlier date if certain conditions are met. That payout will typically be determined by a mathematical formula. The note may provide subscribers with financial exposure to an index, or a particular security, or a 'basket' of securities. That financial exposure may be positive or negative; in other words, the note may reward subscribers if the underlying investment gains value in the period to the maturity date, or conversely may reward subscribers if the price of the underlying investment falls in that period. A further variable with these products is that while some provide a payout on redemption which is directly correlated to the price of the underlying investment, and offer no element of capital protection, others guarantee that a certain proportion of the amount invested in the product will be returned on the redemption date.

For income tax/CGT purposes, a structured product will typically be treated either as a deeply discounted security (DDS) or as an excluded indexed security (EIS). The rules on DDSs and EISs are at ITTOIA 2005, Pt 4. Very broadly, the distinction is between those products that provide significant capital protection (typically qualifying as DDSs) and those that do not (typically qualifying as EISs). A gain on the redemption of a DDS is within the income tax regime, whereas such a gain in respect of an EIS is a chargeable gain.

The subscribers to a structured product hold a chose in action, exercisable against the issuer. Accordingly, the traditional view is that the situs of such products for IHT purposes is determined by where the issuer of the note is resident for the purpose of suit (see para **38.3**). As such products are quite often issued by UK banks, that may point to a UK situs.

However, in practice it is very common for structured products to be immobilised, and for interests in such products to be cleared and traded through clearance systems, usually Euroclear and/or Clearstream. As discussed at para **38.14**, the most widely held view is that under general law, an interest in an immobilised security is situated where the relevant clearing system is based. That is Belgium in the case of Euroclear, and Luxembourg in the case of Clearstream. Assuming that view is right, most structured products have a non-UK situs for IHT purposes. However, it can be difficult to obtain the documentation regarding these products which is necessary to establish how they are cleared and traded.

A different answer may be reached for CGT. As intangible property, the chose in action held by the subscribers to a structured product will be situated in the UK, for CGT purposes, if the note is governed by the law of any part of the UK (see para **39.18**). If the governing law is foreign, the position will be governed by the common law, and the situs for CGT purposes will follow the situs for IHT. The difficulty here is that it may not be readily apparent which country's law governs the product, and there is always a risk of English law being chosen even where the issuer has no connection with England.

It might be thought that source would be irrelevant to determining the tax treatment of structured products, as they are generally not income producing. However, as noted above, a gain on a product which falls within the definition of a DDS is treated as income. In the hands of an RBU, such deemed income qualifies for the remittance basis if its source is outside the UK (ITTOIA 2005, ss 830(1), 830(2)(h)). There is no case law on the source of deemed income arising under a DDS but presumably it would be treated in the same way as bank interest, so a non-UK resident issuer should ensure that the deemed income is non-UK source.

Structured products are arguably unsuitable where there is a desire to preserve clean capital for possible future remittance to the UK, at least where they fall into the DDS category. The deemed income that results from a redemption at a gain cannot be segregated from the capital that was originally invested in the product.

Options and futures

15.16 These rather simpler derivatives are again choses in action. Their situs for IHT is determined by where the counterparty is resident for the purposes of suit.

For CGT purposes, contractual rights such as options and futures are UK situs if the contract is governed by the law of any part of the UK. An option or future is also treated as a UK situs asset if the underlying subject matter is itself UK situs (see paras **39.18** to **39.19**). However, in the context of the CGT situs rules, the words 'option' and 'future' have the meanings given to them by CTA 2009, ss 580–581 (TCGA 1992, s 275B(3)). These provisions define 'option' and 'future' narrowly, as excluding any contract under which settlement is to be made in cash, rather than through delivery of the underlying subject matter (except where the underlying subject matter is currency, in which case provision for cash settlement does not prevent the contract from being an option or future).

In practice, most 'options' or 'futures' held by individual investors provide for cash settlement. Where this is the case, if the contract is governed by foreign law, the CGT situs rules fail to determine its situs and the common law rules must be resorted to. As noted above, these yield the result that the chose in action is situated outside the UK if the issuer is non-UK resident for the purposes of suit.

It is suggested that, as a general rule, an RBU would be well advised to avoid structured products, options or futures, or other derivatives with UK governing law or with a UK situated underlying subject matter. If such investments are to be made, case by case analysis will be required to avoid unnecessary UK tax exposure.

Chapter 16
MITIGATING TAX ON UK INVESTMENTS

INTRODUCTION

16.1 Non-domiciliaries frequently wish to invest in the UK. Indeed the investment relief discussed in CHAPTER 14 and CHAPTER 58 encourages them to do so. But if a non-domiciliary does invest in the UK, the basic rule is that the income and gains generated by the investments are taxed on the arising basis, for the remittance basis applies only to foreign income and gains (see CHAPTERS 48 and 49). So too the investments are prima facie exposed to inheritance tax, for the general rule is that excluded property status is confined to foreign situs assets (see para 37.10).

This chapter explores how these potential UK taxes may be mitigated. It should be read in conjunction with CHAPTER 26, which reviews investment in real estate. It does not deal with the purchase of residential property for personal use, as the planning issues relevant to such property are different from those applicable to investments (see CHAPTER 28).

THE PREFERRED STRUCTURE

16.2 The tax exposure generated by UK investments is minimised where the investments are owned in an offshore trust and company structure, ie an offshore company owned by an offshore trust. The trust should normally be a conventional excluded property settlement, ie a settlement which satisfies the following three conditions:

(a)   the non-domiciliary made and funded it when he had neither an actual nor a deemed UK domicile;

(b)   it is a discretionary settlement of which he is one of the beneficiaries; and

(c)   the assets held at trust level are all foreign situs.

The reason why this structure is attractive are twofold:

(1)   as the asset held at trust level is shares in or loans to the offshore company, inheritance tax is avoided; and

(2)   as the company is owned by a trust, chargeable gains cannot be attributed to the settlor on an arising basis (see para **76.2**). Instead CGT is only potentially applicable if capital payments are made and even then may in appropriate cases be relieved by the remittance basis (see further CHAPTER **23** for planning techniques).

Points to watch

16.3 As always with structures involving an offshore company, care must be taken to ensure the company does not become UK resident, applying the central management and control test. The practical steps to take are detailed in para **43.11**, the key point being to ensure the board meets at regular intervals where the company is based and genuinely considers and takes all necessary decisions. The risk of usurpation, and thus a finding of UK residence, is perhaps greater than normal where both the investments and the settlor and principal beneficiary are in the UK. For this reason adherence to the recommendations in CHAPTER **43** are of particular importance.

Investment in the UK does, of its nature, entail the bringing of funds to the UK. This means the issues discussed in CHAPTER **14** require consideration. As a general rule, the remittance will result in tax unless what is remitted is clean capital or either business investment relief or 2008 transitional reliefs are in point.

Business investment relief

16.4 The rules governing the availability of investment relief are discussed in some detail in CHAPTER **58**. In principle the relief may be relied on here, since:

(1)   investment relief is available not merely where the remittance-basis user himself makes the qualifying investment, but also where the investor is an entity which is a relevant person in relation to him (see para **58.9**); and

(2)   a close company owned by a trust under which the settlor is a beneficiary is a relevant person in relation to the settlor (see para **54.12**).

It follows that if the investor is a non-UK company owned by the trust, investment relief is available, provided the various conditions described in CHAPTER **58** are met. It should however be noted that any claim for the relief must be made by the non-domiciliary (see para **58.12**). Further it is the non-domiciliary who is taxed in the event that a potentially chargeable event occurs without the appropriate mitigation steps being taken (see para **58.13**). He must, therefore, be satisfied that both the trustees and the directors of the company will have regard to his tax position when making and managing the investment.

It is not necessary that the offshore company owned by the trust is the investor company, because the relief is not confined to UK registered companies (see para **58.3**). Provided that the offshore company meets the various requirements to be an eligible company it can be the investee company, a point particularly worth bearing in mind where the investee is not itself going to be an eligible trading company, but will be an eligible stakeholder company or an eligible holding company (see paras **58.5** and **58.6**). In such cases the money must be sent to the UK and then subscribed for shares or loan in the offshore company (see para **57.11**).

Income tax

16.5 As a general rule the trust and company structure described above does not avoid liability to income tax on an arising basis on the income which the UK investments generate. This is because the structure will normally fall within the transferor charge in the transfer of assets code (see CHAPTER **69**). As the non-domiciliary will be a beneficiary of the trust, he will inevitably have power to enjoy the income of the holding company, and so be taxed on that income on an arising basis to the extent it is UK source.

This point even arises if, as per the previous discussion, the investee company in an investment relief claim is non-UK resident, for then the transferor charge bites on the UK income received by the investee company. The charge is not avoided if the investee company is foreign registered but UK resident, for dividends from such a company have a UK source (see para **40.2**).

Direct investment by the trust

16.6 The use of a trust funded by a non-UK domiciliary for the acquisition of UK investments provides significant CGT advantages. CGT is deferred until distributions or other benefits are received, and distributions outside the UK may be tax-free by virtue of the remittance basis. However, the acquisition by the trust of UK investments directly cannot in general be recommended, for the assets, being UK situs, are exposed to IHT. In fact, the IHT position is worse than with personal ownership, for the structure entails both the 10-yearly charges under the relevant property regime (see CHAPTER **61**) and the risk of tax under the gift with reservation of benefit (GWR) rules, should the non-domiciliary die while the trust still owns the assets (see CHAPTER **86**).

There is one potential qualification to the above, which is often in point where the UK asset is shares in an unlisted trading company. Here IHT business property relief should be available and if so, both the 10-yearly and the GWR charges are avoided (IHTA 1984, ss 103–114). But the conditions for business property relief are not always straightforward and, in particular, the relief does not apply on a GWR charge unless it applied on the gift into trust (FA 1986, Sch 20 para 8). For this reason a structure which removes IHT issues altogether is preferable.

Company without a trust

16.7 A non-UK company in the personal ownership of the non-domiciliary also secures IHT advantages, in that the directly held asset is non-UK situs and therefore outside the scope of IHT, for as long as the individual remains non-UK domiciled under general law and for IHT purposes. However, there are a number of potential issues with this structure, which generally makes an offshore trust and company structure preferable.

The first is company residence. It is generally thought to be more difficult to show that the company is centrally managed and controlled abroad if it is owned directly by a UK resident than if it is owned by an offshore trust (see para **43.14**).

The second is that gains realised by the company may be apportionable to the participators under TCGA 1992, s 13. Section 13 is explained in CHAPTER 88, and is likely to be in point if the acquisition, holding, or disposal of any asset by the company is tainted by a purpose of avoiding CGT or corporation tax. Where the section is in point, UK gains are apportioned to the non-domiciliary under TCGA 1992, s 13 and are taxed on an arising basis, for the remittance basis under s 13 applies only to foreign chargeable gains (see paras **88.26** and **88.27**). Section 13 also applies where the company is in trust, but there the sole result is to turn the gains into trust gains, taxable only insofar as matched with capital payments remitted to the UK.

A third reason for preferring an offshore trust and company structure over a personally held offshore company is that (as discussed in CHAPTER 19) it should continue to provide IHT protection in the event that the non-domiciliary becomes deemed domiciled.

INDIRECT INVESTMENT

16.8 The above discussion has, implicitly at least, largely been couched in terms of direct investment. An alternative approach is to invest in the UK through offshore mutual funds in corporate form, ie through an offshore open-ended investment company or a SICAV. This was recommended in CHAPTER 14 as avoiding a taxable remittance of foreign income or gains (see para **14.3**) and it also brings the following further advantages:

(1)   As the relevant asset is shares in the company, it is excluded properly for IHT purposes provided the owner is neither domiciled nor deemed domiciled in the UK. A fund in corporate form is to be preferred from an IHT perspective as, with certain unit trusts there can be an argument that the fund is transparent for IHT purposes (see para **38.13**).

(2)   As the shares are foreign, any gain on the shares is a foreign chargeable gain and so eligible for the remittance basis, provided that the owner is a remittance basis user. Provided that the mutual fund is widely held, as it will be if it is quoted, the fund's gains will not be apportioned to its participators under TCGA 1992, s 13, as that section is confined to close companies (see para **88.11**).

Income tax

16.9 As the mutual fund is non-UK resident, its dividends are relevant foreign income and so eligible for the remittance basis if the non-domiciliary is a remittance basis user (see para **48.2**).

A more interesting issue is whether the transfer of assets code could ever operate to attribute a proportion of the income arising within the mutual fund to the non-domiciliary who is the investor. This issue is discussed in para 3.11. As explained there, it is reasonably plain the answer is no. An exception might be made where a mutual fund is closely held as part of an artificial avoidance strategy, but this is not the position with the kind of mutual fund envisaged here.

Offshore fund legislation

16.10 A mutual fund of the kind discussed above is almost invariably an offshore fund (see paras 95.2 and 95.3). The above discussion has, implicitly at least, assumed that it is a reporting fund distributing all its income (see paras 95.10 to 95.12). In fact it is much more likely to be a non-reporting fund and if so any gain on realisation will be deemed income under the rules described in CHAPTER 95. However, the remittance basis is still available as such gain is deemed relevant foreign income (see para 95.26).

Should the non-reporting fund be an accumulating fund, the generation of relevant foreign income is thus delayed until realisation. For short stay non-domiciliaries this may be an attractive regime, for realisation can simply be delayed until after departure. At that point the gain is tax-free provided that the non-domiciliary is non-resident for more than five years and the realisation takes place in a complete tax year of non-residence (see para 95.16). In the meantime he has avoided generating remittable income and all the complications entailed in ensuring it does not taint clean capital.

UK authorised funds

16.11 An alternative to investing in offshore mutual funds is the purchase of shares or units in UK authorised funds. These are free from IHT if held by a non-domiciliary (see para 37.11) and so to that extent secure the same advantage as an offshore fund. But the income and gains generated by UK funds do not, of course, qualify as relevant foreign income or foreign chargeable gains. As such the arising basis of taxation applies.

In general this makes UK authorised funds unattractive to resident non-domiciliaries and, certainly, it is fair to say the main attraction of the IHT exemption of authorised funds is for non-resident non-domiciliaries. However, there is one context where authorised funds may be attractive to a resident non-domiciliary, namely where the fund generates little or no income and the investor anticipates being non-UK resident when he realises his investment. In such a case the gain is tax-free provided he is non-UK resident for more than five tax years and the sale is in a tax year of non-residence.

Even where the income tax and CGT implications are acceptable, the purchase of UK authorised funds does, in contrast to offshore funds, entail a taxable remittance, if funded using foreign income or gains. The better view is that the mere UK situs of the shares or units make this so, even if settlement of the purchase is wholly abroad (see para 51.19). It follows that tax is only avoided as a result of the purchase if the funds used are clean capital or protected by the 2008 transitional provisions (see further paras **14.6** and **14.12**).

Trust ownership

16.12 In the foregoing discussion, indirect investment in the UK through a non-UK mutual fund has been presented as an alternative to a trust and company structure. For short-stay non-domiciliaries this is so. But for longer-stay non-domiciliaries an excluded property settlement is likely to be more attractive, due to its long-term IHT advantages.

There is however one point to note, which is relevant if a trust which is not protected by the transfer of assets motive defence makes an investment in an offshore fund. In that scenario, there is strictly no scope to claim the motive defence with respect to income of the fund. The reason for this is that the investment in the fund can be regarded as an associated operation in relation to the original transfer of assets to the trust (see para **68.8**) and the defence is unavailable if the original transfer to the trust was tainted by tax avoidance (see CHAPTER **73**). It follows that prevention of the income of the fund from being attributed to the non-domiciliary has to rely on other arguments (see para **3.11**).

REMOVAL ABROAD

16.13 Certain other strategies may also be considered. They revolve round either the assets, or the individual himself, being removed abroad.

Individual emigration

16.14 It should never be forgotten that non-domiciliary status is predicated upon eventual departure from the UK. If the non-domiciliary starts planning on the basis he is remaining in the UK indefinitely he risks losing his non-domiciled status and will definitely do so if, realistically, he intends to remain for the rest of his life (see CHAPTER **44**).

The CGT and IHT exposure entailed by the holding of UK assets will not turn into actual liability if the following conditions are met:

(a)   The non-domiciliary retains the assets until he leaves the UK.
(b)   He disposes of the assets in a year of non-residence and is non-resident for more than five years.
(c)   He keeps the proceeds or their reinvestment outside the UK.
(d)   If he was in the UK long enough to become deemed domiciled, he survives long enough to lose that status.

The principal risk in such a relaxed strategy is untimely death while still owning the UK assets. But this risk may be covered by life assurance, the cost of which may be cheaper than the offshore structures discussed earlier in this chapter. Also it needs to be remembered that IHT may be avoided if the non-domiciliary is survived by a spouse. The spouse exemption is unlimited unless the non-domiciliary is deemed UK domiciled and his spouse has neither an actual nor a deemed UK domicile (IHTA 1984, s 18). In the latter situation, the restriction on the spouse exemption can be removed by means of an election by the spouse to be treated as UK domiciled, under the rules described in paras **45.6** to **45.9**.

A strategy of this sort does not impact on whether or not funds used to acquire the assets in question are remitted and nor does it prevent income generated by the assets from being taxed. But UK tax on investment income may be avoided if the investment if the investment is in a wrapper which rolls up the income, such as a non-reporting offshore fund. Another example is a life policy, as discussed in CHAPTER 4 (see especially para **4.9**). Life policies are not normally recommended to non-domiciliaries as gains under the chargeable event legislation do not qualify for the remittance basis. But this is of no consequence if the chargeable event is going to be deferred until after the individual has ceased to be UK resident (see para **96.14**).

Change of situs

16.15 There are certain classes of asset which can be exported from the UK in specie, or whose situs can otherwise be changed, so that they are taken outside the ambit of IHT. The most obvious example is chattels such as pictures, cars or fine furniture. A chattel owned by a non-domiciliary who is not deemed domiciled in the UK is within the ambit of IHT if it is within the UK, but not if it is elsewhere.

The ability to protect an asset from IHT by giving it a non-UK situs previously also extended to shares in UK companies, which could be issued in bearer form and taken outside the UK. It is widely thought that bearer instruments are situate where found, allowing their situs to be changed. However, following changes introduced by Small Business, Enterprise and Employment Act 2015, s 84 and Sch 4, it is no longer permitted for a UK company to issue bearer shares, and any pre-existing bearer shares are required to have been cancelled or converted into registered shares. Therefore, such planning is no longer possible.

It is also widely thought that a deed under seal converts a simple debt into a specialty, with the result that, like a bearer instrument, it is situate where the deed is physically located. However, the current HMRC guidance questions the effectiveness of specialties to change the situs of debt obligations, at least in certain circumstances (see para **38.6**). And for CGT purposes the debt may remain UK situs under the rules discussed in CHAPTER 39. In particular, this will be the case if the creditor is UK resident (see para **39.10**).

Removal of chattels abroad does not occasion a deemed disposal for CGT purposes, and a sale abroad after the asset has been taken out of the UK results in a foreign chargeable gain eligible for the remittance basis. However, this technique is of course not available with an asset whose situs for CGT purposes is deemed to be in the UK.

Chapter 17

CREATING OFFSHORE SETTLEMENTS

INTRODUCTION

17.1 Offshore settlements have long played a central role both in the UK tax planning of non-domiciliaries and in their wider asset protection and succession strategies. CHAPTER 16 referred to one particular aspect of their role in tax planning. This chapter reviews the general advantages offshore settlements confer and also the potential drawbacks and complications which may be entailed.

For the most part settlements made by non-domiciliaries are discretionary, with the settlor as a beneficiary, and such is assumed in this chapter. It is also assumed the settlor does not have a deemed UK domicile when he creates and funds the settlement, whether under the current IHT rules until 5 April 2017 or the new general rules applicable thereafter (as to both of which see CHAPTER 45). Settlements of the kind discussed here are often referred to as excluded property settlements as the property in them is, or is meant to be, excluded property for IHT purposes (see CHAPTER 62).

This chapter focuses on the implications for the non-domiciliary of creating the settlement and how such may assist his personal planning. Planning for existing settlements forms the subject of Section IV below. Particular considerations bearing on this issue in the run-up to the changes taking effect on 6 April 2017 are considered at the end of this chapter.

TAX ADVANTAGES

17.2 The principal tax advantage an excluded property settlement brings is long-term protection from IHT. An excluded property settlement also confers CGT advantages, although these are less clear-cut than before 2008.

Inheritance tax

17.3 The IHT advantage an excluded property settlement brings is protection from the tax should the non-domiciliary acquire an actual or a deemed UK domicile after the making of the settlement. As deemed domicile is governed by years of residence (see CHAPTER 45), acquisition is inevitable for the long-stay non-domiciliary. Long-term protection from IHT is therefore of practical importance. Current indications are that this aspect of the regime will be preserved under the changes taking effect on 6 April 2017.

The reason why an excluded property settlement confers long-term IHT protection is that the excluded property status of foreign situs settled property is determined by the domicile and deemed domicile of the settlor when he made the settlement or, in HMRC's view, when he added assets to it (see para **62.2**). If therefore he was neither domiciled nor deemed domiciled on all such occasions, the foreign situs property remains excluded even after his domicile or deemed domicile changes.

An important issue is whether, in addition to protection from charges under the relevant property regime, excluded property status also confers protection from charges under the gift with reservation legislation. The better view in law has always been that it does, and this is accepted by HMRC (see para **83.20**). As a result, an excluded property settlement confers protection from IHT on the settlor's death even if he remains a beneficiary until his death.

There is one exception to the testing of excluded property status by reference to the domicile or deemed domicile of the settlor when he made the settlement. This applies to settlements made before 22 March 2006, and is in point if the settlor and/or his spouse took initial life interests. The exception is explained in para **62.24**.

Although excluded property status generally depends on the asset in question having a foreign situs, it can in practice apply to UK situs assets. As explained in para **62.8**, UK authorised funds are excluded property in their own right if held in a settlement whose settlor was neither actually UK domiciled nor deemed domiciled when the settlement was made. More generally, and as is explained in the previous chapter, excluded property status for UK assets can be achieved by holding them through a non-UK company. This will change in one respect only on 6 April 2017 in that the shares in such companies will not be excluded property insofar as their value is attributable to UK residential property.

An excluded property settlement confers a further IHT advantage, namely protection from IHT after the non-domiciled settlor's death. Excluded property status continues to be available so long as the settlement lasts. Even if the non-domiciliary's family become settled in the UK, excluded property status can continue down the generations.

Strictly speaking, the excluded property settlement confers no IHT advantage while the non-domiciliary is alive and neither domiciled nor deemed domiciled in the UK. This result follows because all assets which would be excluded property in the trust would also be excluded property in his hands. But such considerations should not normally delay creation of an excluded property settlement, for death may not be foreseen and nor, sometimes, can a change of domicile.

Furthermore, if the non-domiciliary has a UK domiciled spouse or a spouse who will become deemed domiciled before them, they may wish to make an election to be treated as deemed domiciled in the event of their spouse's death, in order to benefit from the full spouse exemption from IHT. If such an election is made, they would then be precluded from making an excluded property settlement, whereas if they had made the excluded property settlement during their spouse's lifetime, the trust funds would retain their excluded property status notwithstanding the election made. This is therefore a further reason in such circumstances not to delay the creation of such a settlement.

Capital gains tax

17.4 There is one clear-cut CGT advantage to an excluded property settlement whose settlor remains non-UK domiciled, namely that the rules in TCGA 1992, s 86 attributing trust gains to the settlor on an arising basis are not in point (see para **76.2**). This protection does not survive after the settlor acquires an actual UK domicile. But until then it is available regardless of whether or not the settlor is a remittance basis user. Under current law, the concept of deemed domicile does not apply to CGT. As described in CHAPTER **45**, it will do so from 6 April 2017, but current indications are that if certain stringent conditions are met, s 86 will not apply to settlements created and funded before the settlor acquires a deemed UK domicile.

The protection from s 86 applies to both UK and foreign assets, and so has two attractions compared with keeping the assets in personal ownership. One is that the arising basis charge on UK gains is avoided. The second is that remittance issues do not arise as respects foreign situs gains should the trustees bring money representing such gains to the UK.

The CGT advantages of an excluded property settlement are not, however, completely unqualified, for gains matched under TCGA 1992, s 87 are potentially taxable even if the recipient is non-UK domiciled. However, as explained in CHAPTER **79**, this is subject to transitional reliefs for pre-2008 gains and payments (see paras **79.9** to **79.22**) and in addition the remittance basis is available to recipient beneficiaries who are remittance-basis users. Importantly the test for remittance focuses solely on whether the recipient remits the capital payment or benefit; whether the gain arose on UK or non-UK situs assets is immaterial (see paras **79.2** to **79.7**).

On the face of it these qualifications to the capital payment rules put non-domiciliaries in a favourable position. But in one sense the position with an offshore trust is less attractive than with absolute ownership, for the s 87 rules operate by matching, not tracing. Furthermore, supplemental charges apply to the rate of CGT applicable to gains which have been accumulated unmatched within a settlement for more than two tax years. At current rates, these supplemental charges can increase the CGT liability in the hands of a UK resident beneficiary who remits the capital payment so matched from 20% on a graduated basis up to 32% (depending on the interval between the accrual of gains and the matching of such gains to capital payments).

In the case of personally owned assets a non-domiciliary can avoid a taxable remittance of foreign situs gains by ensuring he never remits the proceeds of disposals generating gains (see paras **12.7** and **14.7**). In a trust, by contrast, the issue of whether a foreign situs gain is remitted by the trust is immaterial to the taxation of the beneficiary. What matters to him is whether he remits the capital payment matched within the gain under the s 87 rules.

This qualification should not, however, be overstated. One reason is that quite complicated procedures are needed to ensure that personal gains cannot be traced into remittances. A second reason is that careful operation of the capital payment rules can reduce or eliminate taxation of remitted capital payments. This subject is discussed in Chapter 23.

A third point is that the issues with capital payments can potentially be avoided if the non-domiciliary keeps back some of the capital he is minded to settle and lends it to the settlement on an interest free, on demand basis. Such a loan still means investment growth is in the trust, but capital to fund the settlor's UK spending can be provided by loan repayment. Capital so repaid and used is without tax consequences provided that the original capital lent was clean and the trustees keep all income generated by the capital lent segregated from it.

Should such a strategy be adopted, care needs to be taken with the trustee borrowing rules described in Chapter 80, but the adverse consequences these generate are avoided provided the trustees avoid making loans or capital distributions while the loan from the settlor is outstanding (see para 80.3). Any underlying company of the trust should thus be capitalised by share subscription or loan stock rather than simple shareholder loan (see para 80.11).

One disadvantage of using loans in this way is that substantial value may, initially at least, remain in the settlor's name. It might be thought the settlor could settle the loan in a second, separate settlement, which would make the requisite capital payments to the settlor using loan repayments from the first settlement. Such an arrangement should however be viewed with caution, as for s 87 purposes the term settlement includes any arrangement, with the result that the two settlements could be viewed as one (see paras 77.52 and 77.53). Alternatively it is conceivable that the settlor might be regarded as having received capital payments from the first settlement indirectly, through the second settlement.

ADVANTAGES OTHER THAN TAX

17.5 Although the above discussion focuses on tax, excluded property settlements also confer non tax advantages. For many non-domiciliaries these are at least as important as tax. The advantages concerned include succession planning and the avoidance of probate in countries where the assets are situated. Settlements can also confer general asset protection from risks such as divorce or bankruptcy, although specialist advice is essential if a trust is to be relied on in these areas.

TAX DRAWBACKS

17.6 Although the tax advantages of an excluded property settlement are clear, the potential drawbacks and tax complications also need to be kept in mind. In general these are not arguments against making a settlement, but issues to be managed by the trustees over time.

Income tax

17.7 In broad terms, an offshore settlement brings no income tax advantage, for the income of a settlor-interested trust and any underlying company is treated for tax purposes as that of the settlor (ITTOIA 2005, s 624; ITA 2007, s 720; see CHAPTERS 75 and 69). In certain cases company income may be protected by the transfer of assets motive defence (see CHAPTER 73) but this is unlikely to be in point where the non-domiciliary is already in the UK or is anticipating a move to the UK, and is making the settlement for UK tax planning reasons.

These conditions are not in themselves a drawback, as the income is taxed in the same way as if the non-domiciliary owned the assets personally. But as both the trust and any underlying company are separate fiscal entities, income arises not merely on underlying investments but also when any company pays a dividend to the trust and when the trust makes income distributions to the settlor. It is possible to avoid any additional tax by ensuring that what the company pays to the trust, and what the trust pays to the settlor, is capital in form. But such exercises are not always straightforward and the possible impact of the transactions in securities rules discussed in CHAPTER 89 has to be considered. These complications do not arise with investments kept in personal ownership. The issue is discussed further in paras 21.9, 69.40, 75.38, and **75.45**.

Under the proposals taking effect on 6 April 2017, UK source income arising after the settlor becomes deemed UK domiciled will continue to be taxed on the settlor. This will be the same as where he owns the assets personally. But as with gains, taxation of the settlor on the foreign income in the trust structure will be avoided if certain conditions are met. Should this proposal figure in the legislation when it is eventually enacted, it will outweigh what are otherwise income tax drawbacks to trust structures.

Offshore income gains

17.8 The tax treatment of offshore income gains realised in a trust or underlying company is complex and counter-intuitive. The rules are explained in CHAPTER 82, and some of the planning issues are identified in paras 21.12 to 21.14. The potential tax problems generated by the holding of non-reporting funds within offshore trust structures can usually be overcome, with skilled advice and careful management. However, if a non-domiciled settlor wants a long-term, 'low-maintenance' structure, an offshore trust holding non-reporting funds may not be appropriate, unless there is no intention that funds from the trust should be brought into the UK.

17.9 *Creating offshore settlements*

Remittance issues

17.9 An offshore settlement of the kind postulated here is a relevant person in relation to the non-domiciliary, as he and his family will be beneficiaries (see para 54.6). An underlying company owned by the trust is also a relevant person (para 54.10). This means that a tax charge may arise should the trustees or company effect a remittance of foreign income to the UK, for example by using funds representing such income to acquire UK situs investments (see para 75.28). So too a taxable remittance may occur if the income is used to pay for services provided in the UK or in respect of debts relating to UK property in the UK (see para 75.33).

None of these heads of charge differs from the position where the income is the settlor's personal income and, as is described in CHAPTER 14, techniques exist for investing in the UK without making taxable remittances. But the remittance position is in one sense unattractive and thus a disadvantage compared with absolute ownership, for the settlor has no control, in law at least, over what the trustees do with the income.

Provision for the family

17.10 A settlement can be unattractive if in due course the non-domiciliary wishes to make provision for members of his family who are UK resident. The desired provision may be for personal spending in the UK, for a UK house purchase, or for funding business ventures.

The reason why the settlement may be unattractive in these contexts stems from the non-transferor charge in the transfer of assets code (ITA 2007, ss 731–735A) and the s 87 capital payment rules described above (see CHAPTERS 70 and 77). General planning techniques to deal with these rules are explained in CHAPTERS 22 and 23 and the point that arises here is that a distribution from a trust can be subject to income tax or CGT by reference to income and gains retained in the trust. A personal gift or bequest by the non-domiciliary both avoids this result and avoids remittance issues, provided that:

(a)   the recipient is adult;
(b)   the gift is completed abroad; and
(c)   the donee does not use the gifted property to benefit the donor (see further para 12.18).

These points mean that outright gifts have advantages. But in reality, they are not an argument against making a settlement. Rather they are an argument for making a division between value which may be required by UK family members for personal spending and assets which can represent a long-term family fund. The latter are what should be settled and, ideally, what the family should enjoy from that (and pay tax on) is current income as and when needed rather than capital.

NON-TAX DRAWBACKS

Cost

17.11 The costs of maintaining and managing offshore trusts and companies are often significant. With large funds these are often no greater than would be incurred if the funds stayed in personal ownership. But this is not so with smaller trusts and certainly there is a level below which an offshore trust is not cost effective.

Loss of control

17.12 Creating a trust has the important non-fiscal implication of putting the trustee in control of the assets. If the non-domiciliary is unlikely to be able to accept this, there is a risk of the trust being a sham and the arrangement is best not entered into at all (see CHAPTER 35). However, in practice many of the concerns non-domiciliaries have may be allayed by reputable trustees and by including in the trust provision for a protector with power to remove and appoint trustees and perhaps also a power of veto over capital distributions or other significant trustee acts such as the exercise of a power of amendment.

Personal law

17.13 At least in the eyes of English law, non-domiciled status means the non-domiciliary's personal law is not English. His personal law may impose forced heirship rules extending to lifetime gifts and it may also be characterised by community of property. Such rules may affect the capacity of the non-domiciliary to make the settlement.

Most offshore jurisdictions have express legislation validating settlements despite any feature of the law applying in the settlor's country of residence or domicile which may fetter his ability to give assets to a trust. However, such legislation is really only effective as respects assets in the offshore jurisdiction whose law governs the trust. Making a settlement in contravention of the law of the settlor's domicile, defeating forced heirship provisions or claims by actual or potential creditors, can open the door to wide-ranging and expensive international litigation. Where there is any risk of such litigation, advice should be taken at the outset, from advisers in the relevant jurisdictions, on the level of risk and whether there are any measures that could be taken to reduce or defuse such risks.

Compliance

17.14 The planning described in this book is predicated on the assumption that what is done is effective in tax terms and all tax liabilities are fully disclosed. But as this book shows, the legislation applicable to offshore structures is complex and often uncertain in meaning, and as a result mistakes may be made. It should be kept in mind mistakes may result not just in tax but also in penalties as described in CHAPTER 97. It is important that mistakes are corrected and reported once identified, and it should also be kept in mind that if penalties are levied their severity may vary according as to which jurisdiction the trust is based in.

For all these reasons ongoing review and advice is required should an offshore trust be created. Such of itself may be a significant additional cost.

CREATING THE SETTLEMENT

Timing

17.15 Self-evidently, an excluded property settlement should be made before there is any risk of the non-domiciliary having acquired an actual or a deemed UK domicile. Deemed domicile should be watched in particular as it can arise sooner than expected (see CHAPTER 45). If HMRC are able to argue the settlor has acquired either an actual or a deemed UK domicile, an IHT entry charge at 20% is normally the result.

In view of the CGT advantages, the settlement should be made as soon as possible. Indeed some domiciliaries are advised to create a settlement before taking up UK residence. In theory this is good advice; however, in practice, establishing a trust prior to UK residence may not be feasible because, prior to the individual's arrival in the UK, he may be subject to the tax rules of another country, under which a gift into a trust may give rise to gift tax and/or tax on capital gains.

Until 22 March 2006, the CGT advantages of an offshore settlement could be achieved without an IHT entry charge even if the non-domiciliary had acquired a deemed UK domicile. This was possible if the non-domiciliary or his spouse took an initial interest in possession (see para **62.22**). Now such a settlement propels the property straight into the relevant property regime and an IHT entry charge results (see para **60.15**).

This entry charge can be avoided should IHT reliefs such as business property relief or normal expenditure out of income be in point, and so in such cases a deemed domiciliary who has previously failed to act can still consider an offshore settlement. Even though it will not have excluded property status, protection from CGT may be secured.

Assets settled

17.16 The assets transferred to the excluded property settlement should be foreign situs, as otherwise an IHT entry charge may result and any latent gain become chargeable. The common law and CGT situs rules apply (see CHAPTERS 38 and 39) and, given the areas of uncertainty, the status of each asset to be settled should be reviewed with care.

One kind of UK asset might be thought to represent an exception to the rule that UK situs assets should not be settled, namely holdings in authorised funds. As explained in para **37.11**, these are excluded property if in the ownership of an individual with neither an actual nor a deemed UK domicile, with the result that their transfer into settlement does not result in an entry charge. However, such holdings have a UK situs for CGT purposes, with the result that any gain triggered by the gift to the settlement will be within the scope of CGT; the remittance basis will not apply. Thus a gift of such assets to a settlement will only be free of CGT in the event that they are not standing at an overall gain.

Assuming the assets settled are foreign situs, the remittance implications need to be watched where the settlor is or has been a remittance basis user. Should the settlor settle property which is or is derived from his personal income or gains, the trustees may trigger a tax charge for the settlor if they or an underlying company bring the funds to the UK. This is as discussed in para 12.18 above and follows because the trust and company are relevant persons in relation to the settlor (see paras 54.6 to 54.10). As explained in para 20.12 below, this difficulty is avoided if the trustees ensure that all the assets concerned are kept abroad, but that strategy may not be a complete solution. Two points need to be kept in mind in particular:

- An absolute bar on investment in the UK may be unattractive commercially.
- As with income arising after the trust is created, the settlor may find it unattractive to be at risk of tax by reason of actions by the trustees, over which he may have little control.

In view of these points, the assets settled are best limited to those which represent clean capital, ie inheritances or gifts to the settlor or funds predating his arrival in the UK (see CHAPTER 13). But in addition they may include income and gains of 2007–08 and prior as such are not taxable unless remitted by the settlor personally, and so these cannot be taxed unless distributed back to him.

As always with remittance planning, the mixed fund rules described in CHAPTER 53 have to be watched to ensure what is settled is not in fact income or gains of 2008–09 or post. Gains on foreign currency bank accounts are a particular concern as sterling depreciated against many currencies after 6 April 2008 and foreign currency bank accounts were not exempted until 6 April 2012 (see para 49.18).

A final issue in selecting assets to settle is that assets settled in specie may aggravate the remittance issues just described. This is because any latent gain on the assets settled may be taxable on the settlor if the assets or its proceeds are remitted by the trustees or another relevant person in relation to him (ITA 2007, s 809T; see para 49.22).

Form of trust

17.17 The trust should be discretionary so as to confer flexibility. As the objective will be to allow the settlor and his family to benefit, they should, as indicated at the beginning of this chapter, be in the discretionary class. Trustee powers to add and exclude persons as beneficiaries, perhaps subject to protector consent, are generally advisable, again so as to confer maximum flexibility to deal with changing circumstances.

FOUNDATIONS

17.18 Many non-domiciliaries come from countries whose law does not include trusts and as a result are uncomfortable about handing assets over to trustees. Such individuals may be more familiar with foundations, and as a result, a foundation may be suggested as an alternative to a trust. The question of whether a foundation is a viable alternative to a trust, in a UK planning context, is discussed in the following chapter. CHAPTER 33 considers in greater detail the characterisation issues raised by foundations.

ACTION BEFORE 5 APRIL 2017

17.19 As will be apparent from this chapter, a settlement may be attractive if made before 6 April 2017 should that date be the one on which the non-domiciliary acquires a deemed UK domicile under the rules then taking effect. But such settlements should not be rushed into. Experience over many years shows that tax planning put in place to counter anticipated tax legislation often has unforeseen consequences. Further the exercise may be so rushed that insufficient attention is given to detail. In addition three specific considerations should be kept in mind.

First, it is essential to be certain the putative settlor really is neither UK domiciled under general law nor deemed UK domiciled for IHT purposes under current law. If he is not, creating the settlement creates a 20% entry charge. HMRC are more robust than they once were in challenging assertions of non-UK domicile, and it should be kept in mind that if a case were litigated to the Supreme Court the present law as to the requisite intention, discussed in para **44.5**, could alter.

Second, under current proposals there may be advantages in retaining assets in the non-domiciliary's personal name. This is because those becoming deemed UK domiciled on 6 April 2017 will enjoy automatic tax-free rebasing of any personal foreign situs asset held both on that date and on 8 July 2015. The attraction of this proposal is that remittance will not result in the latent gain as at 5 April 2017 being taxed, a relief that will not apply if before then the asset is settled in trust.

Third, at the time of writing the proposals taking effect on 6 April 2017 are still very much in evolution. No action should be taken until their form is much clearer, which will certainly not be until the draft 2017 Finance Bill clauses are published in December 2016, and may even be later. Inevitably this carries the risk of rushed action, but as the changes made in 2008 showed, fundamental changes can come at a very late stage.

Chapter 18
FOUNDATIONS

INTRODUCTION

18.1 Many non-domiciliaries are unfamiliar with trusts and uncomfortable at the idea of handing valuable assets to offshore trustees of whom they know little. Such individuals may have greater familiarity with foundations, and as a result may prefer to form a foundation, or retain an existing foundation, where a trust might otherwise be suggested. The question is whether such a strategy can be recommended, in the context of UK tax planning.

CHARACTERISATION

18.2 Historically the private foundation concept was limited to, and indeed synonymous with, Liechtenstein. Private foundations have been allowed under Liechtenstein law since 1926 (*Personen- und Gesellschaftsrecht* ('PGR'), arts 552–570). However, in the last few decades foundation laws have been enacted in many other jurisdictions, among them all three Crown Dependencies.

In general English advisers have not favoured foundations, partly because they have not understood them but mostly, and more legitimately, because there has been uncertainty as to how they should be characterised for the purposes of UK taxation. Given such uncertainty there is always a fear that the tax authority will argue for the characterisation that results in the most tax.

Historically the characterisation debate has tended to be couched in terms of whether a foundation should be equated with an English company or an English trust, and the debate has tended to be inconclusive. Arguably there has until recently been too much emphasis on the corporate nature of foundations, and insufficient attention to the rights or interests that they create for their beneficiaries. It is suggested that fundamentally there are two, or possibly three, kinds of foundation, each of which needs to be considered separately from a UK tax perspective; namely:

- foundations which confer rights of control and enjoyment on their beneficiaries which are tantamount to full beneficial ownership;

- foundations which confer interests on their beneficiaries which are broadly similar to the interests that are capable of being created by settlements, and which the beneficiaries have effective means to enforce; and

- foundations which exist to hold assets for the benefit of a class of beneficiaries, but where those beneficiaries do *not* have any effective means of enforcing their interests. Such foundations are conceptually possible, and appear to be legally possible in certain offshore jurisdictions, but it is uncertain whether any foundations of this nature actually exist.

Foundations of the first two kinds are, it is suggested, likely to be characterised for most UK tax purposes as nominees and settlements, respectively. A foundation of the third kind may, at least for certain UK tax purposes, be characterised as a company. The likely tax implications of the three possible characterisations are discussed in detail in CHAPTER 33.

Liechtenstein foundations

18.3 As a result of developments in 2009 and 2010 the position with respect to Liechtenstein foundations at least is now somewhat clearer. There are two reasons.

One is that Liechtenstein has inserted new provisions into its foundations law, effective from 1 April 2009 (PGR Article 552). The new law uses language much closer to that of trusts than the old, including defining different categories of beneficiaries and giving them rights to information and disclosure. This supports the possibility of a Liechtenstein foundation, particularly one created on or after 1 April 2009, being characterised as a trust for UK tax purposes.

The second reason is that in September 2010 the Liechtenstein government and HMRC issued the Second Joint Declaration, in connection with the Liechtenstein Disclosure Facility, which includes guidance on the UK tax treatment of Liechtenstein entities. The guidance states that any Liechtenstein foundation may be treated as a trust.

The guidance is not, of course definitive, and stresses that the UK tax position on any given foundation will depend on the facts of the case. Nevertheless, the conclusion is inescapable that even if not all Liechtenstein foundations equate in UK tax terms to a trust, at least some do; and thus that by appropriate drafting such a result can be secured with confidence. It follows that the traditional English law objection to using Liechtenstein foundations is weaker than it was.

ADVANTAGES

18.4 In these circumstances, a foundation may, for some non-UK domiciliaries, merit serious consideration. In some cases a foundation may have specific advantages, actual or perceived, over a trust.

Investments in civil law countries

18.5 One advantage concerns the investment of the trust fund. Many countries do not recognise or understand trusts, and so trustees may feel uncomfortable making investments in such countries at trust level. Foundations, by contrast, are much more familiar to civil law jurisdictions. As a result, it could be said that a foundation which in the UK clearly equates to a trust has the best of both worlds, in that its recognition may be clear in both common law and civil law states. A counter-argument here is that a better result may be obtained by using a trust coupled with a company, but this can raise other tax issues, as discussed in para **20.20** and CHAPTER **6**.

Beneficiaries in civil law countries

18.6 A very similar point arises where the entity's beneficiaries will include residents of civil law jurisdictions. It is conceivable that when dealing with reporting of the entity or distributions from it to the relevant tax authorities, fewer issues will arise if the entity is a foundation rather than a common law trust. However, this will not always be the case and clearly this is a point which requires expert advice in the relevant jurisdiction(s).

Other points

18.7 There may also be perceived operational advantages in a foundation. In principle, the founder or members of his family can be on the board or council of the foundation and thus have a degree of involvement or control that is difficult to achieve with a trust. And commercial transactions may be easier to contemplate with a foundation than with a trust, for with a trust there is often concern over the risk of technical and obscure breaches of trust.

A further possible reason why a foundation may be favoured over a trust is that among some non-UK families, trusts have gained the reputation of being the source of prolonged and expensive litigation. This reputation may well not be justified but, such as it is, is not perceived to exist to the same extent with foundations.

POTENTIAL ISSUES

18.8 There are nonetheless a number of drawbacks and caveats which need to be kept in mind.

Recognition in the UK

18.9 The first and most important point is that there must be confidence that UK tax law will recognise the foundation as trust, assuming that such recognition is desired; for otherwise all the inherent uncertainty in the tax treatment of 'non-fiduciary' foundations will arise, as analysed in detail in CHAPTER **33**. Particular caution must be exercised with foundations in jurisdictions which permit beneficiaries to be deprived of information and otherwise disenfranchised.

Non-UK residence

18.10 Secondly, great care must be taken if the founder or other UK residents want to be members of the foundation council or board. As the foundation is a corporate entity, the test of its residence is likely to be the central management and control test described in CHAPTER 43. As a result it is essential to follow the practical disciplines recommended in CHAPTER 43. It may be prudent to ensure that family representation on the council or board is in fact confined to non-UK residents. Whether or not that is done, it is essential to ensure that regular board meetings held in the foundation's home jurisdiction are the key decision-making forum.

Clearly, where the family members who would wish to be involved in decision-making are UK resident, this point eliminates one of the perceived advantages of a foundation over a trust.

Trust law issues

18.11 It should be kept in mind that the law applicable to foundations is unlikely, by nature, to replicate all the subtleties of trust law. This is particularly germane where it is desired, for tax reasons, to have a particular form of trust. At one time the form of a trust was of great importance for IHT, as interest in possession trusts fell outside the relevant property regime. But although in general this is no longer so, it can still be important to distinguish between interest in possession and discretionary trusts for income tax reasons, for, as is explained in CHAPTER 8, the tax treatment of what the beneficiaries receive may be different.

The significance of this to foundations is twofold. The first is that, if subtle distinctions of this sort are important, it may be better not to use a foundation at all. The second is that, if a foundation is used, drafting to address these points may be challenging. In particular it may not be possible to replicate the English position where a life tenant is specifically entitled to trust income. In other words, to use the jargon, it may not be possible to replicate a *Baker* trust in a foundation with any degree of certainty. The income tax distinction between *Baker* and *Archer* trusts is discussed at paras **8.3** to **8.4**.

Nomineeship

18.12 A related point is that care must be taken to ensure that the foundation will not be characterised in the UK as a nominee, unless of course that is for some reason the desired analysis. This characterisation can come about in two scenarios.

The first is where the terms of the foundation give the founder or some other person such extensive powers of control and enjoyment that his rights are tantamount to absolute beneficial ownership of the foundation's assets. This was a particular problem with older Liechtenstein foundations, where the drafting of the by-laws was often rudimentary, and could have the flavour of absolute entitlement. In any modern foundation such problems can be avoided by careful drafting.

The second scenario is where, in English law terms, the foundation is a sham. As is explained in CHAPTER 35, a sham arises where the settlor and trustees intend a different relationship to that in the documentation, and the same point can arise with foundations. Indeed, in the case of older Liechtenstein foundations there can be documentation which makes this explicit, such as mandates signed between the founder and the foundation council. In any modern foundation, care should be taken to ensure that the underlying reality and the documentation are in accord.

Sui generis entities

18.13 A final risk is somewhat different. As discussed above and in CHAPTER 33, it is possible that, in some jurisdictions, foundations either are not equivalent to trusts or are capable of being drafted so that they are not equivalent. As a result there may be a temptation to try and create an entity which in English terms equates neither to a trust nor to any other entity or arrangement recognised by the law of the UK, with the object of taking the entity entirely outside UK anti-avoidance legislation.

Such temptation should be resisted. In the main, this is because, as discussed in CHAPTER 33, key pieces of anti-avoidance legislation apply regardless of the form of the offshore entity. The prime example is the transfer of assets code, but another example is Taxation of Chargeable Gains Act 1992 (TCGA 1992), s 87, which applies to any arrangement which is a settlement for the purpose of the income tax settlement code. A second reason is the reason which has long deterred UK advisers from recommending foundations at all, namely the risk of fiscal uncertainty if there is doubt over characterisation. Such doubt would be almost inevitable if an attempt were made to create an entity with no specific common law equivalent.

EXISTING FOUNDATIONS

18.14 Some non-domiciliaries who become UK resident have already created a foundation or are beneficiaries under one. In these circumstances the UK advice has tended to be to substitute a trust, either by direct transfer or by distribution and resettlement.

It may be suggested that this is often good advice, if there is any doubt about how the foundation will be characterised for the purposes of UK tax, and it may not be possible to resolve such doubt by means of an amendment to the foundation's governing documents. However, such advice is much more questionable where the foundation has been properly set up and managed, and it clearly equates to a trust. Here the advantages of retention may well outweigh those replacing the foundation with an actual trust. One or two points in particular may be made.

First, the whole process of substitution may itself have tax implications. Thus income or gains may accrue and in some cases distributions to beneficiaries may be made.

Second, a long-standing structure may have better prospects of qualifying for the transfer of assets motive defence and (where applicable) the motive defence to TCGA 1992, s 13 (see CHAPTER 73 and para 88.4). Transactions effected at the behest of UK tax advisers are bound to raise concerns under those defences even if no tax avoidance is intended.

Chapter 19

ANTICIPATING DEEMED DOMICILE

INTRODUCTION

19.1 As explained in CHAPTER 45, under current law a non-UK domiciliary may after a significant period of UK residence become deemed domiciled. Such deemed domicile applies for the purposes of IHT only. However, the Government's intention is to bring in new legislation which will mean that, on 6 April 2017 or at the beginning of a subsequent tax year, certain non-UK domiciliaries will become deemed domiciled for all UK tax purposes.

This chapter considers the impact of becoming deemed domiciled, and the steps that foreign domiciliaries should take, or consider taking, before any such change of tax status. At the time of writing (early October 2016) there is relative certainty about the new deemed domicile tests, but less certainty about how deemed domiciliaries will be treated under the new regime, particularly with respect to non-resident trusts that they have settled. It follows that some of the suggestions made below as to possible anticipatory planning steps are tentative.

It is likely that, to some extent at least, the details of the new regime will be evolving throughout the remainder of the 2016–17 tax year. The expectation is that draft legislation for the regime will be issued in December 2016, but the likelihood is that this draft legislation will be incomplete and far from definitive. The months leading up to 6 April 2017 will therefore be a difficult period for affected taxpayers and their advisers, with risks if action is taken on the basis of incomplete draft legislation, but also risks if anticipatory planning steps are left until the last minute, in which case it may be difficult to implement them in time or errors may be made in execution of them. Experience shows that, generally, the greater risk is in proceeding with planning at a time when the future regime is not certain.

LIKELY FEATURES OF THE REGIME

19.2 As a general principle, foreign domiciliaries who become deemed domiciled for all tax purposes on 6 April 2017, or at the beginning of a later tax year, will (if UK resident) be subject to arising basis taxation on personal income and gains, whether such income and gains arise from UK or foreign assets, and will be within the scope of IHT on a worldwide basis. To this extent, deemed domiciliaries will be in the same position as individuals who have an actual domicile within the UK.

However, in certain respects, individuals who have become deemed domiciled for all tax purposes under the new '15 out of 20 years' rule (see para 45.11) will enjoy significantly more favourable treatment than UK domiciliaries. Certain non-resident trusts created by such individuals will have protected status, meaning that where assets have been transferred to such a trust, the position for the settlor, if UK resident and deemed domiciled under the '15 out of 20 years' rule, will be very different from the position he would be in if he was actually domiciled within the UK.

In addition, there will be reliefs designed to ease the transition of individuals who are caught by the '15 out of 20 years' rule from the remittance basis to the arising basis of taxation, and to encourage them to bring their wealth into the UK. One of these reliefs will provide for a selective rebasing of foreign assets. The other will permit foreign mixed funds to be separated into their constituent parts, so that clean capital within the mixed fund can be brought into the UK without foreign income and gains being deemed to be remitted in priority. The latter is of course the normal result under the rules that determine what is remitted if there is a remittance from a mixed fund (see CHAPTER 53).

The Government is evidently committed to introducing these reliefs, although it seems possible that their precise form and the conditions applicable to them will be subject to some modification in the course of the legislative process.

TRUSTS CREATED BEFORE ONSET OF DEEMED DOMICILE: TREATMENT OF INCOME AND GAINS

19.3 At the time of writing, the details of the regime that will apply to non-resident trusts with settlors who have become deemed domiciled remain rather sketchy. However, it is relatively clear that, subject to certain conditions, a foreign domiciliary with deemed domiciled status under the '15 out of 20 years' rule will generally be exempted from arising basis taxation on income and gains of any non-resident settlement created and funded by him before the onset of deemed domicile. In other words, income of the settlement will not be treated as the deemed domiciled settlor's under the settlements code (discussed in CHAPTER 75), and gains of the settlement will not be attributed to the deemed domiciled settlor under Taxation of Chargeable Gains Act 1992, s 86 (TCGA 1992) (discussed in CHAPTER 76).

One probable exception to this relates to UK source income, which is likely to be taxable on the settlor on an arising basis. This is likely to be so unless the settlor and any spouse have been excluded, there are no payments of income to minor children of the settlor, and the capital sum provisions in the settlements code are not engaged (see paras 75.2 to 75.14).

The general protection from tax on the settlor under the settlements code and TCGA 1992, s 86 will be subject to a condition that no additions have been made to the settlement by the settlor after his acquisition of deemed domiciled status. A Treasury consultation document issued in August 2016 indicated that the protection of the settlor from tax under TCGA 1992, s 86 would be subject to a further condition, namely that no 'family benefits' have been received from the settlement after the settlor's change of tax status. The document and accompanying draft legislation indicated that a distribution or benefit would fall within the 'family benefit' concept if received by the settlor himself, the settlor's spouse, or a minor child of the settlor; and that the provision of such a 'family benefit' after the settlor's acquisition of deemed domiciled status would cause the settlement to fall within the s 86 regime in the tax year of the benefit and all subsequent tax years in which the settlor was UK resident and deemed domiciled. However, there is some doubt about whether this kind of 'tainting' provision will feature in the finalised legislation.

What is clear is that any such protection from arising basis taxation on income/gains of the settlement will only, potentially, apply if the settlor has become deemed domiciled under the '15 out of 20 years' test, ie on the basis of long-term residence in the UK. No such protection will be available in the case of a non-resident settlement created by an individual who has become deemed domiciled by reason of a domicile of origin and place of birth within the UK (see para 45.12). Any such individual will be taxable on income of the trust under the settlements legislation, unless both he and any spouse are excluded from benefit. Similarly, he will be taxable on gains of the settlement under TCGA 1992, s 86, as if he were actually UK domiciled, unless the persons who may benefit from the settlement have been restricted to such an extent that the settlement is not settlor-interested for the purposes of s 86. But given the very wide class of related persons who must be excluded to achieve this (see para 76.4), this is unlikely to be practical.

Trusts created before onset of deemed domicile: IHT treatment

19.4 It is also clear that where a settlement has been created and funded prior to the settlor's acquisition of deemed domiciled status, and the deemed domicile has arisen due to long-term residence in the UK, the settlement's non-UK situated assets will qualify as excluded property (see CHAPTER 62). In other words, foreign assets of the trust will enjoy excluded property status even once the settlor has become deemed domiciled, provided that (a) the deemed domicile arose after the creation and funding of the settlement, and (b) deemed domicile has not arisen due to the settlor having a domicile of origin and place of birth within the UK.

Where assets of a settlement qualify as excluded property, they are protected from IHT decennial charges (see para 60.3) and exit charges (see para 60.6). Even more importantly, such assets are protected from a 40% IHT charge on the settlor's death under the reservation of benefit rules, if the trust is settlor-interested (see para 83.20). Under current law, such advantages are subject to certain exceptions, in particular one that applies to assets transferred between settlements at a time when the settlor is deemed domiciled or actually domiciled within the UK (discussed in CHAPTER 62). It seems very likely that such exceptions will continue to apply, and will need to be watched to ensure that these protections from IHT are not forfeited.

The IHT treatment of a settlement will be quite different where the settlor has become deemed domiciled by reason of a domicile of origin and place of birth within the UK. Such a settlement will be within the relevant property regime, with respect to its UK and non-UK situated assets alike, for as long as the settlor has deemed domiciled status – unless the assets are subject to a pre-22 March 2006 interest in possession (see para **61.3**). Accordingly there will be scope for decennial charges and exit charges. There will also be scope for a 40% IHT charge on the settlor's death under the reservation of benefit rules, unless he has been excluded from the settlement. The only potential exception to this is where the settlor is resident or domiciled at the time of his death in a country with which the UK has entered into an IHT double taxation treaty, and is domiciled for the purposes of the treaty in that other country; as in that situation, the treaty may take away the UK's taxing rights (see para **105.4**).

Rebasing relief

19.5 As noted above, the Government has announced a relief to allow non-UK situated assets of certain foreign domiciliaries to be rebased for CGT purposes on 6 April 2017, so that when calculating the gain realised by a subsequent disposal, the rebased asset can be treated as having a base cost equal to its value on that date. For those who are eligible for the relief, it will effectively convert latent foreign gains into clean capital.

However, as explained below, the relief will be conditional on various conditions being met. Most strikingly, the August 2016 consultation document indicated that the relief will only be available to individuals who become deemed domiciled for all UK tax purposes under the '15 out of 20 years' test on 6 April 2017; it is not currently intended that the relief should apply to individuals who acquire a deemed domicile at the beginning of any subsequent tax years. If this odd restriction is carried into the final legislation, it will be very discriminatory, creating a pronounced difference in the treatment of foreign domiciliaries who are in objectively comparable situations. It is hoped that the relief will in fact be available on a rolling basis to any foreign domiciliary who becomes deemed domiciled under the '15 out of 20 years' test in 2017–18 or any later tax year, ie on the basis that the relief will be available at the beginning of the tax year in which a deemed domicile is acquired.

The other key features of the relief, as currently understood, are as follows:

- It will apply, or not, on an asset-by-asset basis, which seems to indicate that some form of election will be required.
- It will be limited in scope to assets that were personally held, and that were non-UK situated, on 8 July 2015 (which was the date on which the April 2017 tax reforms were first announced) and that remain personally held, and non-UK situated, on the date of acquisition of deemed domicile status under the '15 out of 20 years' rule (and, as discussed above, quite possibly only if that date is 6 April 2017).
- The relief will be conditional on the individual having paid a remittance basis charge in one of the preceding tax years.
- It will be a complete rebasing. In the case of an asset rebased on 6 April 2017, no tax will be charged on the pre-6 April 2017 increase in value of the asset, if it is sold outside the UK after the rebasing and the proceeds are remitted.

However, a disposal of a rebased asset will, naturally, give rise to some tax if the asset increases in value in sterling terms between the date of the elective rebasing and the date of disposal. Currency fluctuations will need to be watched.

Moreover, a remittance of sale proceeds may trigger tax if foreign income/gains were originally used to acquire the asset. If the asset was acquired before 12 March 2008 using relevant foreign income, consideration should be given to the availability of the transitional relief discussed at para 59.2, which may mean that the relevant foreign income contained within the proceeds is not taxable if remitted, and is in substance clean capital.

UNMIXING RELIEF

19.6 Like the rebasing relief, the proposed unmixing relief will be withheld from individuals born in the UK with a UK domicile of origin. However, apart from that restriction, it appears that the relief will potentially useable in the tax year 2017–18 by a wide class of foreign domiciliaries, not limited to those becoming deemed domiciled on 6 April 2017 under the '15 out of 20 years' rule, and not even limited to UK residents. It would seem more logical for the relief to apply on a rolling basis, ie for it to be available in any tax year to foreign domiciliaries becoming deemed domiciled under the '15 out of 20 years' rule at the beginning of such year.

There is little available detail on the relief, but the basic concept is that foreign domiciliaries with mixed funds in bank accounts will be able to draw any clean capital element in such funds into a separate non-UK account, which can then be used for tax-free remittances to the UK; or transfer the clean capital element to a UK account, without that resulting in a remittance of the foreign income/gains comprised within the source account. It appears that there will be a period of one year from 6 April 2017 in which such transfers can be made, without engagement of the normal mixed fund rules regarding offshore transfers and s 809Q transfers (see para 53.10 ff).

POSSIBLE ANTICIPATORY STEPS: LONG-TERM RESIDENTS

19.7 For individuals who will become deemed domiciled for all tax purposes on 6 April 2017 under the '15 out of 20 years' test, the possible planning steps can be divided into those that relate to asset-holding structures, either new or existing, and those that relate to personally held assets.

Creation of new trusts

19.8 For individuals in this position who are not already deemed domiciled for IHT purposes under the current '17 out of 20 years' rule, the tax year 2016–17 represents a final opportunity to create and fund a non-resident excluded property settlement. Doing so will only make sense if the individual has non-UK situs assets of a nature suitable for transfer to a trust and which the individual and his family will not need to draw on while the individual remains UK resident. It should be borne in mind that distributions or other benefits to the settlor or close relatives are likely to be taxed on the settlor, and as discussed above, such distributions/benefits may have the draconian consequence that the trust loses its protection from the s 86 regime.

It is worth noting that the IHT benefit of an excluded property settlement can be achieved without the trust being non-resident. This point creates theoretical scope for the trust to be administered at a lower cost than is typically possible with professional offshore trustees. But of course such a trust will be fully within the scope of UK tax on its income and gains, with the settlor being taxed on trust income under the settlements code, assuming that the trust is settlor-interested, and the trustees being taxed on trust gains. This treatment may be felt to be acceptable, particularly if the accrual of taxable income and gains can be deferred through the use of offshore funds or a non-UK life insurance bond. However, it must be remembered that a UK resident settlement is effectively locked into the UK tax system and generally cannot be extracted from it without all latent gains being subjected to tax (see para 30.8 ff). It should not be assumed that if the deemed domiciled settlor and his family become non-resident in future, it will be possible for the trust to follow them out of the UK tax net without a tax cost.

In some cases, it will be too late for the individual to create an excluded property settlement, as he may already be deemed domiciled for IHT purposes under the '17 out of 20 years' rule. However, it appears that a non-resident settlement created by a foreign domiciliary will be capable of qualifying as a protected settlement for income tax and CGT purposes provided that when it was made, the settlor was not yet deemed domiciled for all tax purposes under the '15 out of 20 years' test; and 6 April 2017 is of course the earliest date on which such deemed domicile can be acquired. It seems to follow that deemed domicile under the '17 out of 20 years' rule is not an impediment to the creation of a tax-favoured non-resident settlement, provided that it is understood that the settlement will be within the relevant property regime and, if the individual makes any gift to the settlement and is a beneficiary of it, also the gift with reservation of benefit regime.

The funding of the settlement will of course give rise to an IHT entry charge if effected by way of gift, unless the amount given away falls within the individual's available nil-rate band or the assets qualify for IHT relief as business property. In most cases this will not apply. However, consideration may be given to the settlement being funded by way of a sale of assets to the trustees, in consideration of a debt left outstanding, to be repaid on demand. That arrangement may kill a number of birds with one stone – avoiding an IHT entry charge, potentially mitigating IHT under the relevant property regime (see para 85.5 ff), and potentially allowing the individual to withdraw value from the settlement by way of loan repayments, in tax years in which he is UK resident, without such withdrawals being taxable benefits (see paras 70.18 and 78.2) or causing the settlement's protected status to be forfeited. However, this conclusion is necessarily tentative.

Additions to existing trusts

19.9 There may be some cases where an individual who has already created an excluded property settlement wishes to add assets to it before becoming deemed domiciled under the '15 out of 20 years' rule, to prevent such assets becoming subject to arising basis taxation in his hands. Such intention is obviously unproblematic where the individual is not yet deemed domiciled for IHT purposes.

If the individual is already deemed domiciled for IHT, a gift to the settlement is likely to generate an entry charge, and the assets of the settlement will not qualify as excluded property to the extent that they derive from a gift made after deemed domicile was acquired (see para **62.6**). Consideration should be given to the approach discussed above, involving a sale of assets to the trust in exchange for debt. Such strategy should generally only be used with a new settlement, so that there is clarity about which assets are excluded property and which are not. If for some reason there is a desire not to create a further settlement, the existing settlement could in principle be used, provided that the assets given to the trust after the acquisition of deemed domicile are carefully segregated from the assets that are excluded property, for example by means of separate investment accounts.

Withdrawals from existing trusts

19.10 As well as individuals who wish to put value into settlements, there will undoubtedly also be individuals who will want to take value out. For a foreign domiciliary who is a remittance basis user, and who will become deemed domiciled under the '15 out of 20 years' rule on 6 April 2017, the current tax year almost certainly represents a last opportunity (until he becomes non-resident) to receive a trust distribution or other benefit outside the UK which is not taxable at the point of receipt.

For a number of foreign domiciliaries, therefore, there will be merit in offshore distributions being received, to be kept outside the UK and used to meet foreign spending requirements over the anticipated remaining period of UK residence. Typically such distributions will be treated as comprising foreign income and/or gains, and will give rise to tax if remitted; and this will of course continue to be the case once the recipients have become arising basis taxpayers (see para **46.14**).

The decision whether such a distribution should be made may not be straightforward. From an IHT standpoint a large distribution may be undesirable, as its value will of course add to the individual's taxable estate. In addition, income and gains resulting from any investment of the distribution will, prima facie, be taxable in the individual's hands for as long as he remains resident. There may however be scope to defer, and potentially avoid, such tax charges through investment in non-reporting offshore funds (see CHAPTER 3) or offshore life insurance bonds (see CHAPTER 4). Authorised funds and UK life insurance bonds cannot be used without triggering a remittance of the foreign income/gains represented by the distributed cash.

In principle, there is a potential trap if a large trust distribution is received by an individual who in future will be an arising basis taxpayer. Depending on the facts (including whether the individual is the trust's settlor, the trust's s 2(2) amount and the amount of relevant income in the tax year of the distribution), the distribution may represent an unmatched capital payment for the purposes of TCGA 1992, s 87 or, in the case of an individual who is not a settlor, an unmatched benefit for the purposes of Income Tax Act 2007, s 731. If so, there may be scope for income/gains of the trust realised in later tax years to be taxed on the individual, by reference to the earlier distribution, even if such distribution is never remitted. If on this basis income/gains are treated as accruing to the individual in later tax years, they will not as a matter of general principle benefit from the remittance basis, as the individual will be an arising basis taxpayer when matching occurs (see paras **72.4** and **79.3**). However, it is hoped that the legislation for the 6 April 2017 reforms will include a transitional relief to address this issue. It seems reasonable to hope for this, in view of the exemptions that were granted when capital payments to UK resident foreign domiciliaries were first brought within the scope of s 87 (see in particular para **79.18**).

Other entities

19.11 The approach to be taken with other entities, including non-resident close companies, will need to be assessed on a case-by-case basis. The starting point is to consider how income and gains of the entity will be treated once the individual has become deemed domiciled for all tax purposes, factoring in the availability or otherwise of treaty relief (see CHAPTER **104**), and of motive defences and other provisions that may disapply anti-avoidance legislation (see CHAPTERS **73** and **74**, and para **88.4**). EU law-based defences may, of course, not provide long-term protection against UK tax charges, in light of the UK's referendum vote to secede from the EU.

In some cases it may make sense to liquidate the entity and if possible to utilise the unmixing relief to extract any identifiable clean capital element from the proceeds; and/or to replace it with an entity or arrangement which is capable of achieving a degree of tax deferral going forward. That might be a life insurance bond, or a non-reporting offshore fund, although neither of these options is likely to be feasible where there is a requirement to retain specific underlying investments, eg private equity investments. In that situation, it may be that a company resident in a country with a beneficial DTT (see para **88.24**) would work as well, particularly if the underlying investments are likely to be non-income producing.

Personally held assets

19.12 In general, dealing with personally held assets should be more straight-forward. However, there may still be some difficult calls to make.

Clearly, the rebasing relief should, where possible, be used for non-UK assets that are standing at a gain in sterling terms. Generally, where an asset will qualify for this relief if it is held on 6 April 2017, a disposal of it before that date should be avoided.

It should be remembered that this relief will only be available to foreign domiciliaries who have paid remittance basis charges for prior tax years including 2016–17. There may be cases where the individual has not used the remittance basis at all since remittance basis charges were introduced in April 2008, but where there is an argument in favour of paying a £90,000 remittance basis charge for 2016–17, to qualify for the relief.

For assets standing at a gain that will not qualify for the rebasing relief, consideration may be given to the possibility of 'manually' rebasing the asset, at a time when the individual is still a remittance basis user and when the asset is non-UK situated, so that the gain taxable on a later disposal is limited to the increase in the asset's value since the rebasing transaction. For example, this kind of exercise may make sense in the case of a valuable UK situated chattel, which can be removed from the UK prior to the rebasing transaction. In principle, transfers to companies and trusts can be used to 'manually' rebase assets, but there are various complexities and such exercises should only be undertaken with care.

At the time of writing, it appears that there will be scope in appropriate cases to utilise the rebasing relief with respect to a particular asset, and then use the unmixing relief with respect to the proceeds of its sale. Use of the latter may be beneficial where the asset was originally acquired using foreign income or gains rather than clean capital.

Where personally held cash is to be invested, or reinvested, it may again be attractive to take advantage of entities or arrangements that secure tax deferral, such as non-reporting offshore funds and life insurance bonds. In cases where the individual has managed to identify and segregate clean capital, eg by utilising the unmixing relief, it will be critically important to ensure that such clean capital is kept separate from assets that represent foreign income or gains from the period in which he was a remittance basis user.

This point may necessitate the use of separate investment accounts or vehicles for the clean capital and the foreign income/gains. If life insurance is to be used, there may be a need for two separate life insurance bonds, one subscribed for using clean capital and the other subscribed for using the foreign income/gains (although in reality it is likely that each such life insurance bond will in fact be structured as a number of segments or sub-policies; see para **96.12**). With this approach, withdrawals can be made from the first life insurance bond to cover UK expenses, whereas withdrawals from the second should be kept outside the UK, for non-UK expenditure.

Outright gifts

19.13 Lastly, some individuals who are facing deemed domicile may wish to make gifts to children or other family members, particularly if the donees are resident in zero tax or lower tax jurisdictions. If the donor is not yet deemed domiciled under the '17 out of 20 years' rule, and the subject matter of the gift is cash in a non-UK account or some other non-UK situated asset, there will be no scope for IHT on the gift even if made within seven years of death, as the subject matter will of course be excluded property.

Caution must be exercised with gifts to, or which may be used for the benefit of, the donor's spouse or his minor children or minor grandchildren, if the subject matter represents foreign income or gains of the donor and there is any possibility of something derived from the gift being brought into the UK. This point is discussed at para **12.18**.

POSSIBLE ANTICIPATORY STEPS: INDIVIDUALS WITH A UK ORIGIN

19.14 Some of the possible steps mentioned above will also be relevant to individuals facing the prospect of becoming deemed domiciled due to a combination of UK residence and a domicile of origin and birthplace within the UK. However, it must be remembered that individuals in this situation will not be entitled in any circumstances to the rebasing relief or the unmixing relief.

Where such an individual has created a non-resident settlement, a decision will need to be made whether the settlement should be retained, perhaps on amended terms, or wound up. If the trust is retained, there may be scope to avoid tax for the settlor on income and gains of the trust, in the settlor's period of UK residence and deemed domicile, by switching to indirect investments that are capable of achieving tax-deferral. The most likely candidates are, again, non-reporting offshore funds and life insurance bonds.

However, the IHT issues will remain; in particular, the exposure to IHT at 40% on the trust assets, under the reservation of benefit rules, if the settlor is a beneficiary and his death occurs during the period of deemed domicile. In some scenarios, a complete and irrevocable exclusion of the settlor, perhaps after he has received a distribution of some of the assets, may be acceptable as a means of eliminating this issue. There is an open question whether temporary removal of a settlor from the class of beneficiaries is enough to prevent a reservation, in the period up to any reinstatement of him as a beneficiary. As discussed at para **83.5**, there is a good argument that it is, but HMRC's position is that there is a reservation unless the settlor has been irrevocably excluded from all future benefit. Where the settlor knows that he will be UK resident and deemed domiciled for a finite period, for example for the period of a fixed-term secondment to the UK, a possible response to the GWR issue is to request the trustees to exclude him revocably and, in case that is not sufficient to prevent a reservation of benefit, for the trustees to take out the term life insurance to cover the potential IHT liability should he die in the period of deemed domicile.

Section IV

International Settlements

Chapter 20

GENERAL

INTRODUCTION

20.1 The trust is the global ownership vehicle of choice. A substantial portion of the world's private wealth is owned in trusts based in offshore jurisdictions. Most such trusts are discretionary in form, with the settlor among the beneficiaries until his death. The advantages that a trust of this kind brings are asset protection (including protection against political risk), flexibility in succession, and avoidance of probate on death.

The great majority of international settlements are created by settlors who have no connection with the UK, and most remain unconnected to the UK throughout their existence. But sometimes one or more beneficiaries becomes resident in the UK, either for a finite period or indefinitely, and in some instances beneficiaries become UK domiciled.

A rather greater connection is achieved if it is the settlor who becomes resident in the UK. In some instances the settlor is already resident in the UK and makes the settlement for the reasons discussed in CHAPTER 17. Such settlements are conventionally known as excluded property settlements as, provided the settlor has neither an actual nor a deemed UK domicile when he makes the settlement, the foreign situs property of the trust is excluded property for IHT purposes and so outside the ambit of that tax (see CHAPTER 62).

This section deals with the UK tax issues which may face the trustees of international settlements, both in managing and in investing the trust fund and in making distributions to UK resident beneficiaries. This chapter deals with some general planning points that the trustees need to have in mind. Subsequent chapters address the planning of distributions. It is assumed for the purposes of this chapter that the settlor was neither domiciled nor deemed domiciled in the UK when he made the settlement, and has remained non-UK domiciled or is dead.

It is likely that the fundamental freedoms under EU law require some of the anti-avoidance rules described in this section to be disapplied or modified. The freedoms are discussed in CHAPTERS 106 and 107. Although they are important, they should not be relied on in planning, both because there are many uncertainties as to their application and because they may not survive the UK's departure from the European Union. The impact of the freedoms is therefore only referred to in this section to a limited extent.

In large measure this section is written on the basis of the law as it currently stands. The changes which will take effect on 6 April 2017 are referred to where appropriate. But they are not discussed in detail, for, at the time of writing, the detail of the changes is still far from clear.

INHERITANCE TAX

20.2 The first and most fundamental UK tax requirement for any international settlement is to avoid exposure to inheritance tax. If this requirement is breached the immediate and obvious cost is the 10-yearly charge at 6%, together with exit charges at a lesser rate when capital distributions are made (see CHAPTERS 56 and 63). Much more drastic is the death charge under the gift with reservation rules. This charge is potentially applicable should the settlor be a beneficiary when he dies and here the rate of tax is not 6% but the 40% death rate. This charge is made regardless of whether the settlor is resident in the UK and, indeed, may be in point if he has no UK connection at all, except the fact that the settlement created by him holds assets situated in the UK.

The prime requirement in preventing exposure to IHT is to ensure that the trust never owns UK situs assets. There are two methods by which to achieve this, namely avoiding UK assets entirely and holding any UK assets through one or more non-UK holding companies.

Non-UK holding companies

20.3 If the trust holds all its assets through one or more holding companies incorporated outside the UK, IHT should be avoided because the relevant assets for IHT purposes are the shares in and any debts due from the company. As explained in CHAPTER 38, these assets will be non-UK situs provided the company's share register is maintained outside the UK and any shares or debt in bearer form are kept outside the UK. It is immaterial to the IHT treatment of the trust if some or all of the company's assets are in the UK.

Under the proposals taking effect on 6 April 2017, this freedom from IHT will be eroded to a limited extent. However such erosion will apply only to the extent the underlying asset is UK residential property.

Avoidance of UK assets

20.4 Absent a holding company, ensuring that none of the trust assets is UK situs involves considerable attention to detail. The relevant situs rules are those developed by the common law, explained in CHAPTER 38 and discussed in CHAPTER 15. As these rules are in some respects illogical and uncertain, mistakes are easily made. A particularly common mistake is to overlook the fact that where a loan has been made to a UK resident beneficiary, the resultant debt will be a UK situs asset of the trust. The UK situs of the debt may be displaced if the debt is in the form a of a specialty kept outside the UK, but currently it is unclear how far HMRC accept the specialty rule (see para 38.6).

It is sometimes said that mistakes do not matter, as no IHT is due provided that any UK assets are within the nil-rate band (currently £325,000). But under the relevant property regime there are circumstances, perhaps rare, where this is not true. More importantly a charge under the gift with reservation rules when the settlor dies is only avoided if the UK assets of both the trust and the settlor personally are within the settlor's nil-rate band. Further all the settlor's personal assets are taken into account if he is deemed UK domiciled at the time of his death. For all these reasons even minimal UK assets are best avoided.

An international trust can achieve exposure to the UK economy without IHT cost by investing in UK authorised funds – ie authorised unit trusts and open-ended investment companies. This is because authorised funds are, for IHT purposes, excluded property if held in a trust created by a settlor who was neither domiciled nor deemed domiciled in the UK (see para **62.8**). There used to be a trap with authorised funds in that if UK situs money or other UK assets were used to acquire the investment, an IHT exit charge resulted. This absurd and counter-intuitive charge was abolished with retrospective effect in 2013 (IHTA 1984, s 65(7A); FA 2013, s 175).

There are also a great many offshore funds in corporate form which also provide economic exposure to UK shares or bonds. For technical reasons that are touched on at **20.24** below, non-corporate offshore funds that invest in the UK should be avoided.

Deemed domicile

20.5 As indicated above the settlor of some international settlements may be or become UK resident and in some instances he subsequently remains in the UK long enough to acquire a deemed UK domicile for IHT purposes. As explained in CHAPTER **45**, the changes taking effect on 6 April 2017 mean deemed UK domicile will be acquired after 15 years of residence. However under current law foreign situs property in the trust remains excluded provided the settlor was not deemed UK domiciled when he made the settlement and current indications are the same will remain the position after 6 April 2017. But there are three points to note.

The first is that if the settlor makes additions to the trust when UK deemed domiciled it is likely he will have created a separate, non-excluded property settlement or tainted the excluded property status of the settlement as a whole. HMRC have indicated that they would take a point on these lines and, while there are arguments that their view is wrong, it has been upheld in the Upper Tribunal. The point is explained in para **62.6**.

The second is that on one view a potentially exempt transfer or PET arises if during the settlor's lifetime he is excluded as a beneficiary or capital is appointed to another beneficiary. This is a somewhat anomalous point. If it were correct, IHT may be due if the settlor fails to survive seven years. It is, however, now generally accepted that the point is bad and this acceptance is shared by HMRC (IHTM14396).

The third point comes into issue only if the settlement was made before 22 March 2006 and was subject to an initial life interest conferred on the settlor or his spouse. If when the pre-2006 initial life interest comes to an end the holder has an actual or deemed UK domicile, excluded property status is thereafter lost. The point is explained in para 62.22 and, if material, means that all the assets in the trust come into charge to IHT.

Sale of beneficial interest

20.6 There is an obscure and badly drafted anti-avoidance provision of which trustees of international settlements need to be aware. Excluded property status is lost if a UK domiciliary becomes entitled to an interest in possession as a result of a disposition made for money or money's worth. This rule applies if the disposition occurred after 5 December 2005 and needs to be kept in mind in trust reorganisations. It is explained in para 62.19.

A further anti-avoidance provision, enacted in 2012, applies where a UK domiciled individual acquires an interest in excluded property in an offshore trust, which is not an 'interest in possession'. It applies where the UK domiciled individual acquires an interest in excluded property in such a way that the value of his estate is reduced. Then the reduction in the value of the individual's estate is charged to IHT as if the individual had transferred assets of that value directly to a relevant property trust. The assets settled in the offshore trust cease to be excluded property and instead become subject to the relevant property regime. This is explained in paras 62.20 to 62.21.

THE MOTIVE DEFENCE

20.7 Although the UK tax focus of an international trust is often IHT, income tax also raises difficult issues. The most important point is that the settlement may well be protected from the UK's principal anti-avoidance code directed at income, namely the transfer of assets code (ITA 2007, ss 713–751; see CHAPTERS 68 to 73). It is so protected if it falls within the terms of the motive or purpose defence in ITA 2007, ss 736–742. This defence is explained in CHAPTER 71.

Advantages

20.8 The motive or purpose defence confers two advantages. The first is that, with one exception, distributions of capital to UK resident beneficiaries cannot be taxed as income, such as otherwise happens under ITA 2007, s 731 (see CHAPTER 70). The one exception is if the trust structure realises offshore income gains and these are matched under the rules in TCGA 1992, s 87A with distributions or benefits to a UK resident beneficiary (see CHAPTER 82 and para 20.24 below). The second advantage arises if the settlor is UK resident and he or his spouse are beneficiaries. In such a case the general rule is that income in any underlying company is taxed as his under the transfer of assets code (see CHAPTER 69). But this result is avoided if the motive defence is in point. Unfortunately the motive defence is not complete, as it does not protect income at trust level. Such income is taxed as the settlor's not under the transfer of assets code, but under ITA 2007, s 624, which is not subject to the motive defence (see further para 69.30 and CHAPTER 75).

Application

20.9 Despite the qualifications, the motive defence is worth having and, once secured, preserving. In broad terms, the defence applies if UK tax was not the reason, or at least a reason, for creating the settlement. So stated, it is plain that the defence applies to most international settlements. Indeed, in logic it should apply in all cases where the settlor was not UK resident when he created the settlement and had no immediate plans to become so. But a possible exception would be where some of the other beneficiaries were UK resident or contemplating becoming so and the settlement was created in connection with their tax planning. However in these cases it does have to be kept in mind that the defence is not jeopardised if the UK tax planning can properly be described as mitigation as distinct from avoidance. What is meant by this elusive distinction is explained in para **73.21**.

Loss of the defence

20.10 A particular reason why the motive defence is an important issue for the trustees is that even if it protects the settlement at the outset, protection may be lost if the trustees or any underlying company enter into tax avoidance transactions. Avoidance of any UK tax, including such indirect taxes as stamp duty or VAT, counts for these purposes. Such a transaction may jeopardise the defence, even if relating to only a small part of the trust fund or occurring long after the settlement was created.

The precise extent to which subsequent transactions jeopardise the motive defence is controversial. One reason is the lack of clarity about where the dividing line is to be drawn between avoidance and mitigation. Another is whether all kinds of transaction have to be considered or whether there are implied limitations and, if there are such limitations, whether they differ as between pre and post 2005 settlements. These difficult issues are discussed in paras **73.17** to **73.21**.

In practical terms it is prudent for trustees to avoid entering into transactions which could be characterised as the avoidance of UK tax. There are two particular traps to watch. One is discrete, self-contained investment transactions which may inadvertently contain a tax avoidance element, for example SDLT avoidance on the acquisition of UK real estate or stamp duty avoidance on the acquisition of shares. The other is restructurings or investment decisions initiated for reasons unconnected with UK tax but where the UK tax implications are reviewed. Here it is important to ensure that the UK tax advice is secondary and reactive and does not cross the line and initiate particular transactions or parts of transactions.

UK INVESTMENTS AND INCOME TAX

20.11 As indicated above, the holding of UK investments raises IHT issues, but these can be overcome by use of non-UK underlying companies. UK investments also raise income tax issues which, in contrast to IHT, are less easy to resolve. As a result, for some structures the best advice may be to avoid UK investments entirely and, even where this course is not taken, careful planning is required.

Remittance issues

20.12 The first income tax issue arises from the fact that the UK investments have to be paid for. In general they should not be paid for out of funds traceable back to foreign income.

One reason for this arises out of the rules for taxing capital distributions and benefits under the transfer of assets code. Should the recipient of such a benefit or payment be resident in the UK and a remittance basis user, tax results inter alia if the income related to the benefit or payment has been or is brought to the UK. The rules governing the relating of income and benefits are discussed in CHAPTER 72 and for the reasons indicated above (para 20.8) they are not in point if the motive defence applies. Otherwise the rules are complex and obscure, so the best course is to avoid them by ensuring no income is brought to the UK.

A secondary reason is in point should the settlor be UK resident and a remittance basis user. In this event the bringing of funds to the UK may result in a remittance taxable on the settlor on any of the following scenarios:

(1)   The funds are traceable back to the income of the settlement (see paras 75.28 to 75.36).
(2)   The funds are traceable back to the income of an underlying company and the motive defence referred to above does not apply (see CHAPTER 72).
(3)   The funds are traceable back to personal income of the settlor which was included in the funds he settled.

The reason why remittance taxable on the settlor may occur in these circumstances is that the trust and any underlying company are relevant persons in relation to the settlor (see CHAPTER 54). But this is not so in relation to income which arose before 6 April 2008 as trusts and underlying companies are not relevant persons in relation to such income (see para 54.1). Remittance does not result in tax if the settlor was non-resident when the income arose and the charge on income in the trust or any underlying company is normally also avoided if the settlor and his spouse are entirely excluded as beneficiaries (see CHAPTERS 69 and 75).

These exceptions mean that in many cases the bringing of income to the UK will not result in a tax charge on the settlor even if he is UK resident. But as with the tax charge on beneficiaries the rules are complex, and the complexity is avoided by not bringing income to the UK at all.

UK source income

20.13 A second income tax point is that any income generated by the UK investments can be exposed to UK income tax as it arises. Two situations have to be distinguished, the first where the settlor or his spouse is a beneficiary and resident in the UK and the second where these conditions are not met.

In the first scenario, UK income arising at trust level is taxable as the settlor's as it arises under ITTOIA 2005, s 624 (see CHAPTER 75). UK income in underlying companies is also so taxed, but there the charge is under the transfer of assets code (see CHAPTER 69) and so is displaced if the motive defence applies and on certain scenarios could also be displayed by EU law (see CHAPTER 74 and para 107.8 to 107.12).

In the second scenario, the trustees are taxed on UK income arising at trust level. The rate applicable to trusts applies. The liability of non-resident trusts to tax on UK income is explained in paras 64.7 to 64.11, and the important point to note is that the exemption for dividends and interest in ITA 2007, s 811 does not normally apply. This is because that exemption is not available to trusts if any of the beneficiaries are UK resident (see para 64.8).

Tax in this second scenario is much reduced and may be eliminated where the trust holds the UK investments through an offshore company. Here the non-resident exemption for dividends and interest does apply, and the rate of tax on other categories of income is the 20% basic rate rather than the trust rate (see para 64.5).

Should the settlor be a beneficiary, but non-UK resident, any UK income at trust level falls to be treated as his, with the result that the non-resident exemption for dividends and interest should be available. This difficult point is explained in para 75.26 and does not apply to interest paid gross.

Whether at trust level or in a company, UK source income has a further implication, which is relevant should the motive defence not apply and the trustees make capital distributions or confer other benefits on UK resident beneficiaries. As noted above, such a distribution or benefit may result in tax on the beneficiary under the transfer of assets code (ITA 2007, s 731). On the assumption he is a remittance basis user, the remittance basis does not apply insofar as the relevant income related to the benefit is UK source (see para 72.4). It follows that UK source income potentially jeopardises this remittance basis. As explained in para 22.15, it may be that the problem can be avoided should the UK investments be held through a company, for the UK income can be converted to foreign income by paying it up to the trust in the form of a dividend. This is discussed further in para 71.30.

Authorised funds

20.14 The purchase of and income from UK authorised funds suffers the various tax liabilities described above in the same way as other UK assets. There is no income tax exemption corresponding to the IHT excluded property status. But provided the settlor is not resident or not a beneficiary, use of a holding company avoids liability to income tax on the fund income, as the non-resident exemption for dividends and interest applies.

Investment relief

20.15 In theory, shares or loans which constitute qualifying investments under the business investment relief introduced in 2012 (see CHAPTER 58) avoid the remittance issues discussed in para 20.12 above, for the relief is available if the investment is made by anybody who is a relevant person in relation to the remittance basis user (ITA 2007, s 809VA(3)(c); see also para 16.4). But in practice the relief may be difficult to secure, for it applies only if claimed and the claim has to be made by the remittance user rather than the investor. Further the claim must be made before the next but one 31 January after the tax year in which the income or gains would otherwise be remitted.

These restrictions may be manageable where the remittance would be taxed on the settlor, for normally he will know what the trust is doing and can plan his claim accordingly. Matters are more difficult if the remittance renders or may render benefits or payments to beneficiaries taxable. In part these difficulties arise from the uncertainties of matching income with benefits (see para 72.5) and in part from the fact that the recipient beneficiary may simply not know the remittance which is matched with his benefit is in fact accounted for by a qualifying investment.

CAPITAL GAINS TAX

20.16 Capital gains tax is less of an issue for international trusts than income tax. This is because the trustees, being non-resident, are not subject to the tax, and because TCGA 1992, s 86, the legislation attributing gains to the settlor on an arising basis, does not apply to non-domiciled or non-resident settlors (see para 76.2). As a result, the settlor is not exposed to CGT should the trustees or any underlying company bring funds to the UK for investment, and nor are any of the beneficiaries, as the capital payment rules in TCGA 1992, s 87 look solely at whether the payment is remitted (see paras 79.2 to 79.7).

One exception to the above concerns the settlor and arises if he settled funds after 5 April 2008 and those funds included gains of 2008–09 or post, including any gains crystallised on the settling of assets in specie (see para 21.16). But even this is not in point unless the settlor is UK resident (or non-resident for less than five complete tax years) both when the gains accrued and at the time of remittance.

But despite these points, the trustees of international trusts cannot wholly ignore CGT issues, as the tax has to be considered should distributions or other benefits be provided to UK resident beneficiaries, as is discussed in CHAPTER 23 below. There are certain points to keep in mind as the trustees administer the trust and any underlying company.

2008 rebasing elections

20.17 2008 rebasing is explained in paras 79.9 to 79.15. It is something of a misnomer as it is not a rebasing as such but instead a relief from the CGT charge made under TCGA 1992, s 87 when a resident but non-domiciled beneficiary receives a capital payment. In certain circumstances it also relieves the income tax charge made when offshore income gains are matched with the capital payment (see further para **82.18**).

Its relevance to the trustees is that rebasing is not available unless the trustees have made a rebasing election. The general rule is that a rebasing election is not effective unless it was made before 31 January 2010. But a later election is allowed if since 6 April 2008 the trustees have neither distributed capital nor conferred a benefit on a UK resident beneficiary and have not transferred all or part of the trust fund to another settlement. In any such case, an election is effective if made by 31 January following the tax year in which one of those events first occurs.

It is generally accepted that there is no tax downside to an election, and those trustees who have not so far elected should give the matter consideration if beneficiaries are or may become UK resident. The only reason not to make an election is that it brings the trust to the attention of HMRC, which may be unwelcome if the trust has not hitherto had reporting obligations or if there is concern about information being exchanged under double tax treaties. If in any particular case these issues are significant, an election may be inappropriate and non-domiciled beneficiaries in receipt of capital payments may have to forgo rebasing relief. In such a case, mitigation of tax on any s 87 payment has to rest on the beneficiary being a remittance basis user and not remitting the payment (see paras **79.2** to **79.7**).

The election is made on Form RBE 1. It is likely that receipt of the election will prompt HMRC to seek information about the settlement. But provision of such information is not a prerequisite to the validity of the election. So far, the general experience of practitioners has been that HMRC accept that the making of an election does not, in itself, give HMRC any entitlement to further information.

Trustee borrowing

20.18 The UK has a bizarre anti-avoidance code directed at trustee borrowing. It is explained in CHAPTERS 80 and 81 and becomes an issue should the trustees incur borrowing. A deemed disposal of all or a proportion of the trust assets occurs if, when the borrowing is still outstanding, the trustees make a loan or capital distribution. Borrowing is not outstanding once it is repaid or so long as the borrowed money is invested in ordinary trust assets such as shares, securities, or land.

International settlements are not affected by the principal disadvantage of the trustee borrowing rules, namely attribution of any gain resulting from the deemed disposal to the settlor. As described above, attribution of gains to the settlor applies only if he is both resident and domiciled in the UK.

But even without this consequence there are two reasons why falling foul of the trustee borrowing rules is not in general to be recommended. The first is that any ordinary capital gains or offshore income gains resulting from the deemed disposal go into and thus inflate the s 2(2) or OIG amount of the year in question (see CHAPTERS 77 and 82). The second is that the s 2(2) and OIG amounts of that and all prior years become what is called a Sch 4C pool. The principal downside of this is that they cannot be matched with distributions to non-residents, with the result that capital gains cannot be washed out tax-free by such distributions. A less important consequence is that gains in the pool are matched not merely with capital payments by the subject settlement but also with payments by any other settlement to which it has directly or indirectly transferred funds (see para **81.13**).

In general these considerations mean borrowing by the trustees is best avoided or, if incurred, that care is taken to avoid triggering the deemed Sch 4B disposal. In this context it is to be noted that while the rules may be engaged if the trust borrows from or lends to an underlying company, they are not in point if the borrowing or any lending is by the company itself.

In one situation, infringement of the rules may be attractive. Under the ordering rules, s 2(2) or OIG amounts in a Sch 4C pool are matched before those of subsequent years. This is a reversal of the normal LIFO rule and, going forward, may mean resident but non-domiciled beneficiaries access the transitional rules described in CHAPTER 79 when they would not otherwise do so. But it does need to be kept in mind that all OIG amounts are matched before any s 2(2) amounts. Both for this reason, and on account of the general points noted above, the general conclusion is likely to be that any advantages of engaging Sch 4B do not outweigh the drawbacks, and thus that trustee borrowing should be avoided.

A final point to stress about the trustee borrowing rules is that they are in point even if, when engaged, no beneficiary was UK resident. However, they do not apply if the loan or capital distribution made when the borrowing outstanding predates 21 March 2000 (see para **81.32**).

Appointment and resettlements

20.19 It is not uncommon for the trustees of international settlements to appoint new trusts over all or part of the trust fund, or to transfer some or all of the trust assets to another settlement altogether. The CGT implications of such transactions have to be kept in mind, as they can impact on the CGT treatment of capital distributions or benefits to UK beneficiaries.

For CGT purposes, it is important to distinguish between dispositions which leave the assets concerned in the original settlement and dispositions which remove them into another settlement. The distinction rests on case law rather than statute, notably *Roome v Edwards (Inspector of Taxes)* [1982] AC 279, [1981] STC 96 and *Bond (Inspector of Taxes) v Pickford* [1983] STC 517. In the first instance, a distinction has to be drawn between a power to appoint new trusts, and a power to resettle the trust fund or transfer it to another trust. Exercise of a power of the former kind rarely if ever results in the assets concerned leaving the original settlement whereas exercise of the latter kind of power may do so. A distinction, secondly, then has to be drawn between an exercise which is exhaustive and an exercise which is not, for in general only an exhaustive exercise causes the assets to leave the original settlement. An exercise is not exhaustive if there may be circumstances in which the funds subject to the exercise will fall back into the original settlement. That situation could arise where a power is exercised revocably, or on complete failure of the class of beneficiaries under the new trusts.

Should the assets not leave the original settlement the whole remains a single settlement for CGT purposes. This means that when determining the residence of the settlement one has to take account of the residence of the trustees of all of its funds. It also means that a capital payment or benefit to one beneficiary out of one fund is matched with s 2(2) and OIG amounts across the settlement as a whole and so, depending on where net gains lie, may be wholly matched with gains in other funds. This can permit constructive planning, as where the recipient beneficiary is non-resident, and the fund with gains is principally intended for UK beneficiaries. Equally there are traps, as where the reverse situation obtains, ie the gains are in a fund destined for non-residents and the recipient of the capital payment out of the other fund is UK resident.

Should the exercise of the power remove the assets into a new settlement, the s 2(2) and OIG amounts of the original settlement are split pro rata (see para 77.29). This removes the misallocation problem just described and can create a planning opportunity, explained in para 23.6.

The upshot is that the exercise of fiduciary powers requires careful consideration of the CGT implications if the beneficiaries are or are likely to become UK resident. It should also be kept in mind that the advantages of separate settlement treatment may to some extent be lost if the original trust has previously fallen foul of the trustee borrowing rules or has outstanding borrowing. As described above (para 20.18) in either such event gains in the original settlement can be matched with payments out of either settlement (see para 20.18 above). A further issue to consider is whether, if there is indeed a separate settlement, this could jeopardise the excluded property status of the assets transferred. The relevant considerations are discussed in para 62.11.

NON-UK HOLDING COMPANIES

20.20 As indicated above, non-UK holding companies are to be recommended should the international settlement invest in the UK. They may also be rendered desirable for the investment portfolio as a whole should it be considered that direct investment by the trust in other countries will lead to possible tax risk there.

UK investments apart, the issue of whether holding companies are attractive from the standpoint of UK tax is one of difficulty. Chapter 6 lists a number of factors in relation to non-excluded property settlements and most are also relevant to international settlements. In relation to international settlements the overall balance, absent UK investments, is against holding companies. This is for the following reasons:

- Holding companies potentially double up income and gains. The result is that both s 731 available relevant income and s 2(2) amounts may be unnecessarily inflated.
- Holding companies mean income cannot attract the tax credits which may otherwise apply to dividends if the trust is subject to an interest in possession (ITA 2007, s 397A; see para 8.6).

- Holding companies require the issue of company residence to be addressed (see CHAPTER 43).
- Holding companies require the transactions in securities legislation to be considered should the company be liquidated or sold or should its shares be bought back. Transactions involving loans can also come within the legislation. As explained in para **89.30**, the risks may be remote, but on any view they should be understood.

In certain situations the doubling up of gains is avoided, namely where the holding company enjoys the defences to TCGA 1992, s 13 introduced in 2013 (see paras **88.3** and **88.4**). The motive defence applies if it can be shown that the company and the investment are untainted by avoidance of CGT or corporation tax, conditions which of their nature are met by many companies formed by international settlements. In relation to international settlements the effect of the defence applying is that gains realised by the company are not included in the matching to capital payments under the rules discussed in CHAPTER 23.

With existing companies, this defence gives rise to an important planning point similar to that applicable to the transfer of assets motive defence. The history of all such companies should be checked to see if the defence is in point and, if it is, care taken not to risk losing it by engaging in transactions which could amount to avoidance of CGT or corporation tax.

INVESTMENT

20.21 In general UK tax considerations should not influence the choice of investments, as undue focus on tax can diminish investment return. However certain points need to be kept in mind.

UK investments

20.22 As explained above, the tax issues raised by UK investments may lead to the conclusion that such investments should be avoided.

Capital or income

20.23 As with investment generally, the normal issues as between capital return and income return arise. In general, from a UK tax standpoint, return treated as capital gain is to be preferred. This is for three reasons:

(1)   CGT rates are lower than income tax rates.
(2)   In relation to non-domiciliaries, the treatment of capital distributions matched with gains is much more generous than that of distributions which are income or treated as income under the transfer of assets code. This is explained in detail in the next two chapters.
(3)   Should the trust have a UK resident but non-UK domiciled settlor, UK income is taxed on him on an arising basis whereas gains on UK assets are subject only to the capital payments regime.

Offshore funds

20.24 As explained in CHAPTER 95, offshore funds are categorised as reporting or non-reporting. Reporting funds are the same as any normal investment in that dividends or equivalent distributions are taxed as income, and the return on sale as capital gain. They do not, therefore pose particular issues for international trusts.

The position is otherwise with non-reporting funds, for here the return on realisation is an offshore income gain, or OIG, taxed as income. The rules dealing with OIGs and non-resident settlements are extraordinarily complex, the technical detail being described in CHAPTER 82, and the implications for settlors and other beneficiaries in CHAPTERS 21 and 22 respectively. There is also a fundamental disadvantage with non-reporting funds, namely that the income tax treatment on realisation extends not merely to such gain as represents retained income, but also to the part of the gain representing capital or currency gain. Gains potentially taxable at CGT rates are thus turned into income.

For some international settlements the solution to these problems may be to avoid non-reporting funds entirely. But it may be difficult to construct a balanced and well-performing portfolio without such funds and in that event the complex planning discussed in CHAPTERS 21 and 22, and perhaps some tax, may have to be accepted as the price.

Offshore funds can be either open-ended companies, unit trusts, or analogous civil law arrangements. Unless the fund is a company issues may arise as to whether it could be characterised as transparent, particularly for IHT purposes (see para 38.13). Although in practice this risk is small, certainty can be achieved if the fund is a company.

Banking arrangements

20.25 As a general rule, an international settlement should segregate income and capital through the use of separate bank accounts, if the settlor or any of the beneficiaries is or may become UK resident. This is in part to ensure investment in the UK does not risk remittance (see para 20.12 above), but more importantly to facilitate the income tax planning of the settlor and the beneficiaries, as described in the next two chapters.

General comments on separate bank accounts may be found in CHAPTER 14 and para 53.39. In contrast to individual banking, separate accounts for capital gains are not required, as trust gains are taxed only by reference to capital payments. Disposals generating offshore income gains may represent an exception, insofar as there is any risk of the OIGs becoming income for the purposes of the transfer of assets code (see further CHAPTER 80).

Chapter 21

PROVISION FOR THE SETTLOR

INTRODUCTION

21.1 This chapter focuses on one particular kind of international settlement, namely settlements where the settlor is alive, a beneficiary, and resident but not domiciled in the UK. Such settlements are often known as excluded property settlements and, as explained in CHAPTER 17, form a key planning tool for non-UK domiciliaries who are, or are considering becoming, UK resident. This chapter addresses what is often the key tax issue for the trustees, namely how UK income tax may be minimised when funds are distributed to the settlor.

It is assumed that the trust is discretionary as this is the form most international settlements take. It is also assumed that the settlor is a remittance basis user, either on the basis that he has been UK resident in fewer than seven of the last nine years or because he is paying the remittance basis charge. If the latter is uneconomical for him it is unlikely that the costs and complexity of a trust structure could be justified.

The planning described in this chapter will be affected by the changes taking effect on 6 April 2017, in that settlors who have been UK resident in 15 or more of the past 20 tax years will become deemed UK domiciled for all tax purposes, not just for IHT purposes. However there will be transitional reliefs and, in particular, disapplication of anti-avoidance legislation to certain settlements made by the settlor before he became deemed UK domiciled. At the time of writing the detail of these proposals is unclear and so discussion here would be premature.

UK SOURCE INCOME

21.2 The UK source income of the trust is taxable as the settlor's as it arises. Income arising directly to the trustees is so taxed under ITTOIA 2005, s 624 (see CHAPTER 75). If, as is suggested in the previous chapter, the UK investments are held through an underlying non-UK company, the charge is under the transfer of assets code (ITA 2007, s 720; see CHAPTER 69). But in either event, the remittance basis is not available as the income is UK source. The motive defence is unlikely to protect the company income unless the settlement was made before the settlor was considering UK residence (see para 20.9 and CHAPTER 73). However in appropriate circumstances the possible disapplication of the code under EU law may need to be considered (see CHAPTER 74 and paras **107.8** to **107.12**).

On the basis that the income is in any event taxed as the settlor's, it makes sense to pay it out to him and for him to remit the money to the UK. However, care is needed to avoid creating a further tax liability in doing so.

Capital distribution

21.3 Somewhat counter-intuitively, a further tax liability is most likely to arise if the income is paid out as capital. Such could happen at trust level if the income has first been accumulated. In the case of a company, the income is capital in the hands of the trust if it reaches the trust in repayment of a shareholder loan, on the sale or liquidation of the company, or on a share buy back. But however the UK income is converted into capital, a distribution of it is a capital payment for the purposes of TCGA 1992, s 87 and the rules taxing offshore income gains. This means that it is taxable if the trust has OIG or s 2(2) amounts, the tax being income tax in the case of the former and otherwise CGT (see CHAPTERS 77 and 82). As is explained in paras **79.2** and **82.17**, the remittance basis is available in respect of these charges but it does not avail should the payment be brought to the UK.

Income distribution

21.4 In view of the above, UK income is better distributed to the settlor as income. In the case of income at trust level, a distribution of the income as income does not result in further tax, as such is specifically precluded by ITTOIA 2005, s 685A(5) (see para **75.45**).

Matters are more complicated with UK income at company level. Here ITA 2007, s 743(2B) provides that income charged under ITA 2007, s 720 is not treated as income again if subsequently received by the settlor (see para **69.40**). In practice, it should be possible to rely on s 743(2B) where the income is paid by the company to the trust as dividend, and the trust then makes an income distribution of the dividend to the settlor. But strictly the analysis is not clear cut, as the payment of the dividend to the trust means that there is a supervening further tax charge before the income reaches the settlor, namely a charge under ITTOIA 2005, s 624. This section is in point because the dividend is the income of the trust and, while it is relevant foreign income eligible for the remittance basis, remittance occurs should the settlor bring the money to the UK.

As indicated in para **69.41**, published statements by HMRC suggest that they are unlikely to tax the income both when it arises to the company and in the settlement. But if it is desired to avoid risk there is a method of doing so, namely to give the settlor a life interest in the trust's shares in the company. The effect of this is that under the rule in *Williams v Singer* (see para **8.3**) the dividend is treated as his income ab initio and so clearly comes within the language of s 743(2B).

Banking

21.5 A final point over which care is needed is to ensure that at all stages the UK income is kept separate in banking terms. If it is not, the mixed fund rules described in Chapter 53 may be engaged, with the risk that what is brought to the UK may be treated as a remittance of something other than the UK source income.

DISTRIBUTIONS KEPT ABROAD

21.6 A distribution to the settlor, whether of income or capital, does not result in income tax provided it is made and kept abroad. This is for the following reasons:

(1)   Even if as a matter of tracing, the funds distributed are derived from income, no remittance occurs.

(2)   ITA 2007, s 731, which taxes distributions by reference to retained income, does not apply to transferors and thus do not apply to the settlor.

(3)   The OIG rules, which tax distributions by matching to OIGs, do not apply unless the capital payment is remitted (see Chapter 82).

The result is that a settlor whose foreign spending is funded by trust distributions is no worse off then if he owned the trust assets personally. As with personal assets, he needs to ensure that inadvertent remittance does not occur, the applicable rules being those described in Chapters 51 to 57. Key risk areas are summarised in Chapter 12.

On one view, distributing the income as income is preferable to accumulating it and distributing it as capital. The basis for this view is that unremitted income retained in the trust structure can be available relevant income in relation to other beneficiaries and so create or increase potential tax charges under ITA 2007, s 731 should any of those beneficiaries be UK resident. There are good arguments that this view is wrong in relation to settlor-interested trusts unless the s 731 benefit is in the same tax year as the income arises (see para 71.26). But distribution as income avoids the issue.

FUNDING UK SPENDING

21.7 Save where UK source income is in issue, the settlor's spending in the UK needs to be funded by distributions which are capital in his hands. This is because a distribution which is his income is on any view taxed when remitted.

The fact that a distribution is capital in the settlor's hands does not of itself mean it is free of income tax when he brings it to the UK. The bringing of it to the UK can result in income tax on any of the following scenarios:

(1)   The funds distributed are derived from past foreign income of the settlor which was included in the funds he settled into trust.

(2)   The funds distributed are derived from foreign income in the trust or any underlying company, potentially taxable as his under ITTOIA 2005, s 624 or ITA 2007, s 720.

(3)   The distribution causes OIGs to be treated as accruing to the settlor under the OIG matching rules discussed in CHAPTER **82**.

The settlor's income

21.8 Capital in the trust is derived from the settlor's income if the funds settled by the settlor, or subsequently added by him, were or were derived from his income within the meaning of ITA 2007, s 809L (see further para **12.8**). The fact that in relation to pre-6 April 2008 income the trust is not a relevant person (see para **54.1**) is immaterial as the remittance of the capital distribution is not by the trust but by the settlor. On the face of it this means that it may be difficult to ensure a trust has clean capital, particularly where much of the settlor's personal wealth has resulted from saved income. But in reality two of the reliefs described in CHAPTER **48** mean that this problem is not severe in relation to old trusts. The reliefs are the relief for income which arose in a tax year when the settlor was not UK resident and the relief for relevant foreign income which arose and was invested before 12 March 2008 (see paras **48.10** and **48.11**). Such investment can be by either the settlor or the trust.

For most pre-2008 trusts these reliefs will obviate the need for undue investigation of whether the funds settled derived from the settlor's income. But in relation to the pre-12 March 2008 relief there are two points to watch. One is to ensure that the income was at some point invested in the kind of assets which attract the relief – ie in broad terms any investment other than cash or fixed-interest securities. The other is that it applies only to relevant foreign income and so does not protect pre-2008 chargeable overseas earnings. If these were settled and funds derived from them are included in the distribution, tax results on remittance by the settlor.

As discussed in CHAPTER **52**, there are arguments that the derivation of income does not carry on through multiple ownerships. It can be said that the trust distribution of capital to the settlor is the source of what he remits to the UK, and that accordingly in determining what the remittance is derived from, the chain of derivation stops with the distribution. The argument would in practice be strengthened if at the time of the distribution it was difficult or impossible to identify what part of the trust capital was traceable back to the settlor's income. But although these arguments are compelling, they appear not to be accepted by HMRC and this makes it difficult to rely on them in planning.

Trust and company income

21.9 As a general rule, a capital distribution traceable back to the foreign income of the trust or an underlying company results in that income becoming taxable when the settlor remits the funds distributed. If the income is at trust level, the charge is under ITTOIA 2005, s 624 (see paras **75.28** to **75.36**), and if it was at company level the charge is under the transfer of assets code (see para **72.2**). As with the settlor's actual income, there are arguments the derivation concept would not carry through to the capital distribution. But assuming such arguments are discounted, the basic technique for precluding a tax charge is the same as for individual income, namely segregating the income in separate bank accounts and funding distributions only out of untainted capital accounts.

To this end, the trust must maintain separate capital and income accounts at the bank. All income must be credited directly to the income account and all capital receipts to the capital account. The capital distribution to the settlor should be made in exercise of power over capital and must be effected by debiting the capital account of the trust and crediting a clean capital account of the settlor.

Where an underlying company is involved, the company must also maintain separate capital and income accounts. Any transfer from the company to the trust must be from the company's capital account to the trust's capital account and must be under a transaction which is capital in form. In other words it must not be a dividend but must be a repayment of shareholder loan or liquidation. Alternatively a buy-back or upstream loan may be considered.

As is explained in para 32.12, there can be reasonable confidence that a buy-back results in a capital receipt. An upstream loan is indubitably capital, but when followed by a distribution of capital or a loan by the trust, it results in a deemed disposal under the trustee borrowing rules in TCGA 1992, Sch 4B. As explained in para 20.18, such is in general to be avoided, albeit that the settlor's non-domiciled status means that there is no immediate tax charge.

A liquidation or buy-back may be vulnerable to counteraction under the transactions in securities code. This issue is discussed in para 89.30, and an important point to stress is that counteraction only applies if initiated by HMRC. There are also arguments a counteraction notice served on the trustees could not on any view affect the settlor's tax. But the issues are difficult and even if the risk of counteraction is remote it should be taken into account, particularly where the transaction is a buy-back rather than a sale or liquidation. As explained in paras 89.28 to 89.29, it is unlikely that the code is engaged by simple upstream loans or by repayment of a simple shareholder loan.

The non-applicability of TCGA 1992, s 86 means the capital accounts of the trust and any underlying companies can contain capital gains as well as original capital. In this respect, therefore, segregation is easier than with the personal income and assets. To avoid complications with the IHT exit charge (paras 63.6 to 63.9) it is better if the settlor's account which receives the distribution is outside the UK. This avoids argument about whether, at the moment of distribution, the funds distributed are UK situs.

Income as clean capital

21.10 With long-standing trusts it may be difficult to ensure income has always been segregated from capital and thus that the so-called capital accounts really are untainted by income. This is particularly so where the trust was created before the settlor became UK resident. However in practice these difficulties are less than might be supposed, as there are three categories of trust or company income which are not taxable even if remitted by the settlor. Income of these types effectively counts as capital for the purposes of the remittance rules.

The first category is income which arose to the trust or underlying company in a tax year when the settlor was not UK resident. As indicated in para **21.8** above, a remittance charge cannot be made unless the settlor was UK resident when the income arose.

The second category is income which arose before 12 March 2008 and is protected by the relief for investment in assets. This relief is likely to protect most pre-12 March 2008 income of trusts and underlying companies.

The third category is in point only where the income arose to an underlying company and is operative where the structure is protected from the transfer of assets code by the motive defence in ITA 2007, ss 736–742. As explained in paras **20.7** to **20.10**, this is likely to be in point if the trust was set up before the settlor was considering UK residence. Where the defence is in point it prevents income of the company being taxed as that of the settlor. The same would apply should the application of the transfer of assets code be precluded by EU law (see Chapter **74** and paras **107.12** to **107.15**). But neither point applies to income at trust level because, as explained above, that is taxed under ITTOIA 2005, s 624 instead of the transfer of assets code.

Capital as income

21.11 The segregation exercise is complicated by the fact that UK tax law deems certain categories of capital receipt to include income. The three categories which cause most difficulty in practice are accrued income profits under the accrued interest scheme, offshore income gains (or OIGs) and profits from deeply discounted securities.

Accrued income profits are the interest element when the price at which fixed interest securities are sold includes accrued interest. This element, although capital as a matter of general law, is taxed as income (ITA 2007, ss 615–681). The best way of dealing with the problem is for the selling broker to credit the interest element directly to the income account of the selling company or trust. As explained in para **53.41**, HMRC accept this is an effective segregation of the income.

As explained in the next paragraph, OIGs realised in the trust or an underlying company are income for the purposes of the transfer of assets code unless matched, under the matching rules in TCGA 1992, s 87A, with a capital payment to a UK resident. In the case of trusts of the kind postulated here, which are settlor interested, what this means in practice is that the OIGs are transfer of assets income unless matched in the tax year of realisation with a capital payment to the settlor or some other UK resident.

Both accrued interest and OIGs treated as transfer of assets income are subject to the three reliefs described in the previous paragraph (**21.10**). In two respects these reliefs are enhanced. First, accrued interest cannot result in a tax charge on the settlor at all insofar as the settlement day was before 6 April 2008 (FA

2008, Sch 7 para 160). Second, as OIGs are transfer of assets income at trust as well as company level, trust OIGs are, in contrast to actual trust income, protected by any applicable motive defence.

Assuming such reliefs are not in point, tainting of the capital account by OIGs may be avoided if the entire proceeds of the OIG disposal are kept out of the capital account and credited either to an income account or a special account for OIGs. But such a drastic step is unlikely to be worthwhile with accrued interest, given its modest size relative to overall proceeds. Here tainting and thus modest tax on remittance may have to be accepted unless the selling broker has credited the accrued interest directly to an income account.

Profits from deeply discounted securities, which are deemed to be income under ITTOIA 2005, ss 427–442, are perhaps even more problematic than accrued income profits and OIGs. The term 'deeply discounted security' is defined in s 430. It encompasses most 'structured products' – a class of investment which is increasingly common in practice (see para **15.14**). Deemed income arising on the disposal of a deeply discounted security is transfer of assets income (s 459). The only way to avoid contamination of the capital account by such income is to ensure that, if such a security is disposed of at a gain (in sterling terms), the entire proceeds of redemption are credited to an income or 'tainted capital' account.

OFFSHORE INCOME GAINS

21.12 A remitted capital distribution to the settlor results in income tax if it is matched with OIGs in the trust or an underlying company under the matching rules in TCGA 1992, s 87A. These rules are explained in Chapter 77, and their application to OIGs in Chapter 82. As indicated in the previous paragraph (**21.11**), the matching rules do not as a general rule apply to a settlor-interested trust unless the OIGs are realised in the trust or any underlying company in the same tax year as the distribution. This is a somewhat bizarre result of the rule that OIGs which are not matched on a current-year basis to a distribution to a UK resident become the transfer of assets code income of the settlor. As such they then become incapable of being matched under s 87A (see para **82.13**).

It follows that an income tax charge on the distribution by reason of OIGs can normally be avoided by ensuring that (a) no OIGs are realised in the tax year of the distribution, and (b) the distribution is made from assets of the trust which have not been tainted by OIGs on a tracing basis (see para **21.11** above). However, avoidance of tax on OIGs may not be achieved if in that year the structure does not realise ordinary gains, for then the capital payment is carried forward. It results in OIGs accruing in a future tax year if OIGs are realised in the trust or an underlying company in that future year and the capital payment has not in tax years before then been matched with ordinary gains.

Even if OIGs are treated as accruing to the settlor as a result of the matching rules, tax does not necessarily result. Assuming that the trust has made a rebasing election the OIGs treated as accruing are not taxed save insofar as the trust or company OIGs matched with the capital payment represent increase in value since 6 April 2008 (see paras 20.17 and 82.18) or accrued on investments acquired since then. In applying the rebasing rules, the April 2008 value has to be converted to sterling at exchange rates then prevailing.

As explained in para 82.17, tax is also avoided if the capital payment matched with the trust or company OIGs is not remitted. Strictly such mitigation is not of interest if the object of the exercise is to provide funds for the settlor to spend in the UK. But advantage could be taken of the point if in one year there is an unremitted capital payment by ensuring sufficient OIGs are realised in that tax year to match with it. In the next tax year a remitted capital payment may be made and if so may be matched in its entirety with OIGs or s 2(2) amounts fully covered by rebasing or with s 2(2) amounts brought forward from 2007–08 or prior (see para 82.18).

Past OIGs

21.13 In general a capital distribution to the settlor cannot result in OIGs accruing to him by reason of past year OIGs in the trust or any underlying company, as those OIGs will have been removed from OIG amounts by having become his transfer of assets income. But this is not the position where the settlor was non-resident when the OIGs accrued to the trust or company, for then he would not have been within the transfer of assets code (see para 69.44). However such past year OIGs will not result in tax if of 2007–08 or prior, for OIGs resulting from the matching of a capital payment with an OIG amount of 2007–08 or prior are tax-free provided that the recipient of the capital payment is a non-domiciliary (see para 82.18).

Disinvestment

21.14 The result of these various points is that with careful planning, it may be possible to avoid a tax charge in respect of OIGs realised in the trust structure. But the rules are undoubtedly complex, and as time goes on the likelihood of a charge is increasing as new investments are acquired and values increase above those as at 6 April 2008. For this reason tax considerations may increasingly be an argument against investment in non-reporting funds and for the progressive realisation of existing investments in such funds.

CAPITAL GAINS TAX

21.15 Even if the distribution to and remittance by the settlor is effected without exposure to income tax, CGT may be chargeable. Two possible liabilities have to be considered, namely personal gains of the settlor included in the funds settled and the s 87 capital payment rules. What is to be stressed is that TCGA 1992, s 86 cannot operate to treat gains as the settlor's as they arise, as that section does not apply to non-domiciliaries (see para 76.2). As a result it is not necessary to engage in the kind of tracing exercise which is required for income, as trust gains are taxed only if matched to a remitted capital payment, and not if funds derived from the gains are remitted.

Personal gains

21.16 The reason why a remitted capital distribution can result in a CGT charge in respect of the settlor's personal gains is the same as with his personal income: if the capital distributed is traceable back to funds derived from the settlor's personal gains, remittance of the distribution by the settlor is a remittance of those gains. The gains so brought into account include any realised on the settlement of assets in specie (ITA 2007, s 809T; see para **49.22**).

A tax charge under this head is more likely than in respect of personal income, for one of the circumstances which obviates an income tax charge does not apply to gains, namely the relief for income arising and invested before 12 March 2008. The only relief which does avail is that gains realised when the settlor was non-resident are not charged, although even this is truncated as compared with income tax for, in contrast to income, gains realised in a period of absence of less than five tax years or less are taxed if remitted (see para **49.9**).

As with income, the charge on remitted personal gains applies to personal gains of 2007–08 and prior as well as to subsequent gains. In respect of such gains there may be formidable compliance difficulties with old settlements made by long stay non-domiciliaries as there may be little record of what the settlor settled or where it came from. But two small points may reduce the difficulties and thus the liability. One is that no account is taken of gains realised in 2007–08 and prior on the transfer of assets in specie to the settlement, as ITA 2007, s 809T applies only to disposals in 2008–09 and post (see para **49.23**). The second is that the statutory mixed fund rules do not apply as these are restricted to income and gains of 2008–09 and post (see para **53.2**). Instead the old informal practice is in point of treating a remittance from a mixed fund as gain only in the proportion that aggregate gains in the fund bear to the total fund.

Section 87

21.17 The capital distribution to the settlor results in capital gains if under the rules in TCGA 1992, s 87A it is matched with gains in the trust or any underlying company. Because s 87 operates by matching rather than tracing it is difficult to avoid, as segregated bank accounts and similar procedures do not avail. But a substantial measure of relief can be achieved by the transitional rules and timing. These techniques are the same whether the recipient beneficiary is the settlor or some other beneficiary and are therefore discussed in CHAPTER 23.

Potential double charge

21.18 There is a double tax trap on capital distributions to the settlor. This arises if:

(a)   the distribution results in OIGs or capital gains accruing to the settlor by virtue of the matching rules in TCGA 1992, s 87A; and

(b)   Under the general remittance rules described in CHAPTERS 51 and 52 the funds distributed are derived from either:

(i)   income of the trust or an underlying company treated as the settlor's under ITTOIA 2005, s 624 or the transfer of assets code, or

(ii)   personal income or gains of the settlor comprised in the funds settled.

The double tax trap is simply that when the settlor remits the capital distributed he suffers a taxable remittance of both the s 87 capital gains or OIGs and the trust or personal income or gains from which as a matter of tracing the capital payment is derived. If that is right, the effective rate of tax on the distribution could, in a worst case scenario, be 90% (if he is a 45% rate taxpayer and OIGs are matched).

No statutory relieving provision appears in point as what are taxed on remittance are two entirely separate items of income/gains. The point is avoided by ensuring that the remittance is not taxable under at least one of the above heads or, ideally, both.

There is the same potential for double taxation if the recipient of the distribution is a beneficiary other than the settlor. Here the liability resulting from matching under s 87A is that of the beneficiary rather than the settlor, but the liability resulting from the remittance of the settlor's income or personal gains remains with the settlor. Fortunately cases of this sort are rare, as the point only arises where the other beneficiary is a relevant person in relation to the settlor, ie a spouse or co-habitee, or a minor child or grandchild (see further CHAPTER 54).

There is a good argument this double taxation does not exist, based on the point made in para 21.8, namely that the source of the capital remitted is the trust distribution. If that distribution itself generates a tax liability the argument that the derivation chain cannot go any further back is inevitably stronger. If this is right there is no derivation from either the settlor's personal income or gains or the income of the trust or any underlying company, with the result that the tax at (b) above falls away. But it is far from clear HMRC would accept this analysis. The relevant issues are discussed further in para 52.28.

Business investment relief

21.19 A remittance by the settlor is not taxable if the settlor uses the money to subscribe for shares or loans which qualify for business investment relief. The position is the same as if the income or gains had arisen to the settlor personally and not from funds settled by him, and thus is as described in para 58.9.

Chapter 22

PROVISION FOR OTHER BENEFICIARIES

INTRODUCTION

22.1 This chapter addresses the income tax issues which arise when the trustees of an international settlement make distributions to beneficiaries other than the settlor. It focuses on avoidance of income tax, CGT mitigation being addressed in the next chapter. In some instances the settlor may be alive and resident in the UK, but most of the settlements on which this chapter focuses are ones where the settlor is either dead or non-resident.

One key point is that the beneficiaries may have a variety of different tax statuses. A few may be both resident and domiciled in the UK. Some, perhaps even a majority, may be UK resident but non-domiciled, some of these being remittance basis users and some not. For the great majority of international settlements, the bulk of the beneficial class will normally have no UK connection, the only reason for UK involvement being one or two beneficiaries who are temporarily living or working in the UK or have made UK marriages.

The issue this chapter addresses is how UK income tax is minimised on distributions to, or benefits conferred on, UK resident beneficiaries. In the main, this requires focus on such distributions and benefits themselves. But regard also has to be had to distributions to non-UK beneficiaries as the pattern and structuring of such distributions may impact on the UK tax treatment of the distributions to the beneficiaries resident in the UK.

To a limited extent this chapter will be affected by the changes taking effect on 6 April 2017. Those changes will impact on beneficiaries who become deemed UK domiciled under the proposed rules discussed in CHAPTER 45. They will be in the same tax position as beneficiaries who have an actual UK domicile. At the time of writing there is no suggestion there will be any special transitional rules for non-settlor beneficiaries.

INCOME TAX ISSUES TO CONSIDER

22.2 In planning to minimise UK income tax on distributions, three separate heads of charge have to be considered:

- Distributions which are income in the hands of the recipient are taxed as ordinary income. Assuming that the trust is discretionary, the trust is the source (see para **8.8**).
- Distributions of capital are potentially taxable under ITA 2007, s 731 to the extent of available relevant income in the trust or any underlying company. This legislation is explained in CHAPTERS **82** and **71**.
- Offshore income gains (OIGs) realised by the trust, or any underlying company, may be matched to a capital distribution, and taxed as income in the hands of the recipient beneficiary under the matching rules in TCGA 1992, s 87A. The legislation which secures this is explained in CHAPTER **95**.

All three types of charge are subject to the remittance basis if the beneficiary is a remittance basis user. But the applicable rules differ as between the three heads, income distributions being covered by the normal rules explained in CHAPTERS **51** to **57**, and s 731 and OIGs being covered by rules explained in CHAPTER **72** and CHAPTER **82** respectively.

MOTIVE DEFENCE CASES

22.3 A UK resident beneficiary does not suffer income tax on a distribution or benefit if the following conditions are all met:

(1)   The distribution or benefit is capital;
(2)   The motive defence in ITA 2007, ss 736–742 applies; and
(3)   The distribution or benefit is not taxed as an OIG as a result of the matching rules in TCGA 1992, s 87A.

Provided that these conditions are met, income tax is avoided whether or not the distribution or benefit is remitted. The reason why income tax is so avoided is that tax is not charged on income treated as accruing under ITA 2007, s 731 if the motive defence explained in CHAPTER **68** is satisfied. As suggested in paras **20.7** to **20.10**, it should be satisfied with many international settlements, as UK tax is unlikely to have been an issue unless the settlor or the principal intended beneficiaries were then residing or intending to reside in the UK.

The reason why the distribution must be capital is that the motive defence has no application to distributions which are income in the hands of the recipient. As explained in para **8.8** these are subject to income tax as normal income where the recipient is UK resident, subject to the remittance basis where applicable.

Offshore Income Gains

22.4 The third of the requirements set out above arises from the fact that a distribution or benefit can be treated as an offshore income gain as a result of matching under TCGA 1992, s 87A (see CHAPTER **82**). This charge is not displaced by the motive defence, as that defence is only in issue if the trust or company OIG is treated as income for the purposes of ITA 2007, s 731 such as happens only in the limited circumstances explained in CHAPTER **82**.

Treatment of the distribution or benefit as an OIG is principally avoided by one of two methods:

(1)   Neither the trust nor any underlying company invests in non-reporting offshore funds, or

(2)   The settlor is both resident in the UK and a beneficiary and no capital distribution is made to a UK resident beneficiary in the same tax year as OIGs are realised in the trust or any underlying company. On this scenario, the trust OIGs become transfer of assets income (see para **82.15**) but the tax otherwise payable by the settlor in consequence is precluded by the motive defence.

If neither of these conditions is nor can be satisfied, the distribution or benefit is likely to result in OIGs accruing to the beneficiary. But tax can still be avoided if one of the following conditions is met:

(a)   The beneficiary is a remittance basis user who does not remit the distribution or benefit (see para **82.17**), or

(b)   The recipient is a non-domiciliary and each OIG in the trust or underlying company is nil after 2008 rebasing. 2008 rebasing applies to OIGs, as explained in para **82.18**, or

(c)   The recipient is a non-domiciliary and the distribution or benefit is matched with OIG amounts of 2007–08 and prior (see para **82.18**).

If none of the above conditions can be met, the best way to avoid a tax charge by reason of the trust OIGs is to arrange matters so that OIGs are matched to distributions to non-resident beneficiaries or to a UK resident beneficiary within (a)–(c) above. This can be done as follows:

(i)   In any tax year in which the trust has a current year or brought forward OIG amount (Year 1) a distribution at least equal to the OIG amount is made to a non-resident beneficiary or a beneficiary who satisfies any of conditions (a)–(c) above.

(ii)   Neither the trust nor any underlying company realises OIGs in the next tax year (Year 2).

(iii)   The capital distribution to the resident beneficiary who is not within (a)–(c) above is made in that tax year (ie Year 2).

(iv)   That distribution is matched with s 2(2) amounts as described in CHAPTER 23 in Year 2 or in a future tax year before the tax year in which OIGs are first again realised. This may result in a CGT charge, but avoids income tax (see para **82.4**).

In the light of the above complexity, the conclusion which may be reached is that non-reporting funds should be avoided. Whether this course is right will depend on the balance as between investment and the tax requirements of UK resident beneficiaries.

Motive defence: practical difficulties

22.5 Although as indicated above, the motive defence ought to be available to the great majority of international settlements, there are two reasons why securing it may be difficult.

One is practical and is simply that HMRC resist conceding the defence and do not give advance rulings. The only method of securing agreed treatment is to make a test capital distribution to a UK beneficiary, the beneficiary then ticking the appropriate boxes on his tax return. The hope is that this will trigger an enquiry, thereby enabling the matter to be negotiated.

The second problem is substantive and is that even if a trust structure starts off protected by the defence, it may lose that protection if subsequent tax driven operations are undertaken. This problem is as discussed in para **20.10** above and is considered in more detail in paras **73.17** to **73.20**.

A key issue is how far accumulating income so that it in due course is available for distribution as capital is itself avoidance such as potentially jeopardises ss 736–742. In reality it is most unlikely such an accumulation is avoidance as the mere fact of letting the normal process of income converting to capital takes its course can hardly be said to be frustrating any presumed intention of Parliament.

A similar conclusion may be reached with respect to organising distributions so as to minimise tax under the OIG regime. The point here is that such organisation is taking advantage of express statutory rules and reliefs, not frustrating them.

'DRY' TRUST

22.6 If the above defences are not or may not be available, the next best strategy is for the trust to be 'dry'. The term 'dry' trust is a colloquial expression to describe a trust structure which either never has had income or where all the income has been distributed as income.

A distribution or benefit by a dry trust to a UK resident beneficiary is free of income tax if four conditions are all met:

(1) The distribution or benefit is capital in the hands of the beneficiary (as to which see para **8.9**);
(2) Neither the trust nor any underlying company invests in non-reporting offshore funds;
(3) Neither the trust nor any underlying company receives deemed income; and
(4) Any future income of the trust or any underlying company is distributed as income.

The reason why the distribution is free of tax is that ITA 2007, s 731, which would otherwise subject the distribution to income tax, operates only to the extent of available relevant income (see CHAPTER 71).

A point to keep in mind is that in identifying available relevant income, it is necessary to look not just at the trust but at the income of any underlying company. Further it may be necessary to look at the income of any trust from which any funds in the subject settlement have been received, and at any trust to which the subject settlement has added funds. The extent of these difficult points is explained in paras **71.32** to **71.34**.

Offshore funds

22.7 The reason why investment in non-reporting funds needs to be avoided is that OIGs in the trust or an underlying company can result in tax both under the matching rules in TCGA 1992, s 87A and under ITA 2007, s 731 (see CHAPTER 82). The complex detail of this is explained in CHAPTER 82. As with motive defence cases, the complexity and uncertainty is so great as to be best avoided altogether if a 'dry' trust strategy is adopted. The only way of doing this is not to hold non-reporting funds.

Unmatched past OIGs need not be fatal to a 'dry' trust strategy now. In such case there are methods of washing past OIGs out without causing them to become available relevant income. These are as follows:

(1) In the case of OIG amounts of 2007–08 and prior, matching to a distribution to a non-domiciliary (see para **82.18**).

(2) In the case of OIG amounts of 2008–09 and post, distribution to a remittance basis user who does not remit (see para **82.16**). Alternatively if the OIG amounts are fully covered by rebasing the distribution can be to any non-domiciliary.

As is explained in para **82.15** what must be avoided until a tax year after that in which the OIGs are washed out is a distribution to a non-resident beneficiary. If such a distribution has already occurred the OIGs may already be available relevant income (see paras **82.13** to **82.15**) and thereby make it difficult to make the trust 'dry'. This is because the past OIGs became transfer of assets income save insofar as matched on a current-year basis to a distribution to a UK resident (see para **82.14**).

Should the trust have unrealised OIGs matters are somewhat simpler. These can be washed out without becoming available relevant income, whether or not the settlor is a beneficiary, by matching in the year in which the OIGs are realised to distributions to remittance basis users who do not remit. The distribution can be to any non-domiciliary if the OIG amount(s) are fully covered by rebasing. The detail of this is explained in CHAPTER 82.

Deemed income

22.8 Deemed income can jeopardise the 'dry' status of a trust as it is capital in accounting terms and so cannot be kept separate and distributed as income.

Apart from OIGs which have become available relevant income, the principal category of deemed income is accrued interest under the accrued income scheme. But here the difficulty may be more apparent than real. In part this is because the amounts involved are by definition modest, being only interest accrued at the time securities are sold. More fundamentally, as is explained in para **53.41**, HMRC accept accrued interest can be stripped out if the selling broker pays the interest element direct to the income account of the seller, where it can be distributed as income, thereby keeping the trust dry.

Future income

22.9 The reason why future income must be avoided or distributed is that a distribution or benefit is taxable under s 731 not merely by reference to past available relevant income but, if there is none, by reference to future retained income as well. Future income can thus render the recipient of the benefit taxable at the time such future income arises. This is as explained in para **71.17**. Future income does not result in tax if distributed as income, for then it does not become available relevant income (see para **71.17**). Deemed income in the future should also be avoided or dealt with in the manner indicated above.

There is one scenario in which future income and deemed income can be disregarded. This is where, under the rules in TCGA 1992, s 87A, the capital distribution or benefit is matched with a s 2(2) amount, either in the tax year in which the distribution is made or in a tax year prior to that in which the future income or deemed income arises. In such a case the capital distribution is taxed as a capital payment for the purposes of s 87, and falls out of account for the purposes of s 731. This is as explained in para **78.5**.

On the face of it, taxation under s 87 as distinct from under s 731, is out of the frying pan and into the fire, as CGT is due. But such pessimism ignores a fundamental point. If the recipient is a non-domiciliary, the s 87 gain may be wholly or partly exempt, either because of rebasing or matching with s 2(2) amounts of 2007-08 or prior, or because the recipient is a remittance basis user who does not remit the funds distributed. The planning potential of these reliefs is described in CHAPTER 23 and the important point is that even where they render the capital distribution free of s 87 tax, the s 87 matching prevents it being carried forward under s 731 to future available relevant income.

But in the majority of cases this route involving s 87 will be impractical or there will be CGT cost which, despite the points made above, may be felt to be too great. In these circumstances, therefore, any future income will need to be distributed. It may be objected that doing this defeats the whole object of keeping the trust dry, as if it is implemented the income is taxed on distribution rather than under s 731. But in reality this ignores two important points. The first is that tax is avoided entirely if the recipient of the income distribution is non-resident or a remittance basis user who does not remit. This is so even if he is the settlor. The second is that even if the recipient beneficiary is UK resident and not a remittance basis user, lower rates of tax can be secured by appointing the recipient(s) interests in possession. As explained below (para **22.16**) this secures the dividend rates where the income is dividend income.

'DRYING OUT' A TRUST

22.10 In practice most long-standing international settlements are not 'dry'. Usually this is because s 731 has not in the past been an issue, but sometimes it is because accumulation of income has been the course appropriate for the trust, regardless of tax. In such circumstances the issue arises of what can be done to render the trust dry for the future.

Income distribution

22.11 As explained above there is no doubt that a distribution of income prevents the income from becoming available relevant income (see para 71.14). But this is rarely in point with long-standing trusts, as once income is accumulated it is capital. The issue of when and in what circumstances income is accumulated is explained in para 8.10.

There are two situations in which historic income may be distributable as income. One is if the income is at trust level and has not been accumulated. This rarely occurs, as normally income is presumed accumulated after a reasonable period (see para 8.10). But the presumption may be rebutted if the trustees have had good and genuine reason to defer the decision as to whether to accumulate. Accumulation may also be delayed if the primary trust is to distribute and the ability to accumulate is a mere power. If in such a case the trustees are inactive and the trust accounts do not show accumulation, the power to accumulate may be found to have lapsed and the trust to distribute remains in force as a discretion requiring exercise.

The second situation is if the income is in an underlying company. Here there is an argument, explained in para 71.30, that retained income in the company ceases to be available relevant income in the company if it is paid up to the trust in dividend. Instead it becomes current income at trust level, where it can be distributed to beneficiaries as income on a current basis. Tax is avoided provided such beneficiaries are non-resident or remittance basis users who do not remit.

Most advisers are of the view that the above two techniques are effective to remove relevant income. However in August 2013, HMRC published draft guidance to the transfer of assets code (see para 68.3) and this indicated that HMRC may not take the same view.

Capital distribution

22.12 It may be thought a capital distribution is a self-defeating method of removing available relevant income, as the distribution is itself a benefit and so results in tax under s 731. But this ignores the circumstances which obtain where the recipient is a remittance basis user or non-resident and so, if these circumstances can be secured, capital distributions may 'dry' the trust.

Should the recipient be a remittance basis user, a charge is not made under s 731 provided that the related available relevant income is all foreign source, and neither it nor the related benefit is remitted. This is explained in CHAPTER 72. On the face of it, this does offer a means of stripping out the related available relevant income without tax charge. But there are two points to note:

(1)   The distribution cannot be to the settlor as, being a transferor, he is not within ss 731–735 at all (see para 70.15).
(2)   In practice it may be difficult to ensure that neither the related available relevant income nor the related benefit is remitted.

Should the recipient of the capital distribution be non-resident, it is ignored for the purposes of s 731 and no available relevant income is allocated to it. On the face of it, therefore, such a distribution does not diminish the available relevant income. But this ignores the point, explained in paras **71.15** and **71.28**, that if the distribution removes the relevant income from the trust structure as a matter of tracing, it ceases to be available and ceases to be able to be taken into account under s 731. As is explained in para **71.15**, the better view is that the past income is removed for the purposes of s 731 if it has at all times been kept segregated in banking terms, or is part of a larger fund which is so segregated and is distributed in its entirety. But the draft guidance referred to above indicates that HMRC may not share this view.

Offshore income gains

22.13 Drying out the trust is more complicated if the trust or any underlying company holds non-reporting offshore funds or has realised OIGs in the past.

The best techniques where the trust currently holds unrealised non-reporting funds are those described above (para **22.7**), namely ensuring that when OIGs are realised they are matched under s 87 rules with distributions to remittance basis users who do not remit or to non-domiciliaries able to access the transitional reliefs. But this technique does not work unless the trust has been 'dried out' as respects actual relevant income in prior tax years, for if there is such income it is allocated to the distribution in priority to the OIGs and tax under ITA 2007, s 731 may result.

Should the trust have realised OIGs in the past, it may be possible too to use the matching rules to match the OIGs to distributions to remittance basis users who do not remit or to non-domiciliaries able to access the transitional reliefs. But should there have been a distribution to a non-resident beneficiary the OIGs will have been turned into available relevant income (see para **82.13**). In such a case, a subsequent distribution to a remittance basis user who does not remit may be considered, provided that there is confidence the OIGs which have become relevant income by reason of the distribution have not and will not be remitted and will indeed be the income related under the rules in ITA 2007, s 735A to the subsequent distribution (see CHAPTER 72). A distribution to a non-resident will only wash out OIGs which have become relevant income if the entire proceeds of disposal have been segregated and are distributed and it is right in law that the distribution of segregated funds removes relevant income.

OTHER TRUSTS

22.14 The reality is that many international settlements with UK beneficiaries are not 'dry', cannot be made 'dry' and do not or may not enjoy the benefit of the motive defence. With these trusts it is difficult to avoid exposure to UK income tax when distributions are made to UK resident beneficiaries. However some mitigation may be possible.

Remittance basis users

22.15 As indicated at the beginning of this chapter, a distribution to a remittance basis user which is income in his hands is not taxed unless remitted. This is an application of the normal remittance basis and means unlimited income distributions may be made to remittance basis users without tax cost provided unremitted. The issue of when a distribution is income is discussed in para **8.9**.

The remittance basis under s 731 when capital is distributed is more challenging because, as discussed above, it requires focus on both what is distributed and on the related relevant income. It is not available at all to a beneficiary who remits the distribution to the UK. Tax may be easier to avoid should the beneficiary be a remittance basis user who does not remit what is distributed. Here all that is needed is to ensure that the related income is neither UK source nor remitted and in certain scenarios even these requirements are or may be relaxed, specifically as follows:

- There is the argument that if the related income arose and was invested before 12 March 2008, the transitional relief for income so invested is in point, with the result that a remittance basis user cannot be charged even if the matched income is remitted. But this argument involves the difficult issues discussed in para **72.9**.
- A mitigation technique may be available if the related income is UK source and is in an underlying company. There is an argument, alluded to above (para **22.11**) and explained in para **71.30**, that payment of the income by the company in the form of a dividend converts it into, or back into, unremitted foreign income. If such is done before the benefit is received the related income is foreign.

Interest in possession

22.16 Self-evidently the remittance basis avails only non-domiciliaries who are remittance basis users. For other UK resident beneficiaries, tax is inevitable whether or not they bring the funds distributed to the UK. However if regular distributions are in prospect, the level of tax may be reduced by appointment of an interest in possession. This secures potentially two advantages:

(1) Any foreign withholding tax to which the trust income is subject is available as a credit to the beneficiary.
(2) The dividend rates of income tax apply.

These results follow because, as explained in para **8.3**, income of a life interest trust is treated as that of the life tenant, provided that the proper law of the trust in this regard follows English law. The first advantage is also available to remittance basis users who remit. The second, however, is not (see para **48.13**).

Chapter 23
CGT PLANNING

INTRODUCTION

23.1 This chapter assumes that a capital distribution or benefit to a UK resident beneficiary does not result in an income tax charge under ITA 2007, s 731 either because the beneficiary in question is the settlor or because the charge under ITA 2007, ss 731–735 has been avoided in the manner discussed in the previous chapter. It also assumes that the distribution or benefit does not result in offshore income gains accruing. The point this chapter addresses is that a capital distribution or benefit which does not attract income tax has CGT implications if the recipient is UK resident. But here there is much scope for planning, resulting from the fact that most of the beneficiaries are likely to be non-resident or, if UK resident, non-UK domiciled.

As in previous chapters of this section it is assumed that the settlor is non-resident or dead or, if UK resident, non-UK domiciled. This means that the rules described in CHAPTER 76 attributing trust gains to him as they arise are not in point (see TCGA 1992, s 86 (i)(c)). As a result the CGT rules to consider are those in TCGA 1992, s 87 and Sch 4C, treating gains as accruing insofar as capital payments or benefits are matched with s 2(2) amounts.

The technical detail of these rules is explained in CHAPTERS 77 to 79. The planning techniques appropriate where the settlor and most of the beneficiaries are both resident and domiciled in the UK are explained in CHAPTERS 9 and 10. To some extent what is said here overlaps with those chapters, but as the subject has a very different perspective where the trust is international, it is considered afresh here.

As most UK resident beneficiaries are likely to be non-UK domiciled in this scenario, a key planning issue is ensuring full advantage is taken of both the transitional reliefs afforded to foreign domiciliaries by FA 2008 and the remittance basis allowed to remittance basis users. These various reliefs are explained in CHAPTER 79. In this chapter, the position where no transitional reliefs are available will be considered first. Attention will then focus on the transitional reliefs.

A final preliminary point to stress is that the planning in this chapter is relevant to the settlor where he is UK resident as much as to other beneficiaries. Indeed, in a sense, it is more relevant for, being the transferor, no distribution or benefit to him can be taxed under ITA 2007, s 731.

The planning discussed in this chapter will be affected by the changes coming into force on 6 April 2017 insofar as a beneficiary in receipt of a distribution or benefit becomes deemed UK domiciled under the new rules (see **CHAPTER 45**). In such a case, tax will be charged whether or not the distribution is remitted. But at the time of writing it appears likely the 2008 transitional reliefs will continue to apply to non-domiciled beneficiaries who become deemed domiciled under the new rules.

NO 2008 TRANSITIONAL RELIEFS

23.2 The following categories of trust do not enjoy the 2008 transitional reliefs for foreign domiciliaries explained in **CHAPTER 79**:

- Trusts created after 6 April 2008.
- Trusts with none of the following as at 5 April 2008, namely unrealised gains, surplus capital payments or surplus s 2(2) amounts.
- Trusts where all transitional reliefs have been exhausted.

Taxable beneficiaries

23.3 A capital payment or benefit conferred by one of these kinds of trust on any of the following can result in CGT:

- A beneficiary resident and domiciled in the UK.
- A non-UK domiciled beneficiary who is not a remittance basis user.
- A remittance basis user who remits the capital payment or, where it is a benefit, enjoys it in the UK.

The remittance basis applicable to s 87 and Sch 4C is contained in TCGA 1992, s 87B. As is explained in paras **79.2** to **79.7**, the issue of whether a remittance has occurred focuses solely on the capital payment or benefit. There are technical arguments that the charge under s 87B does not apply in certain cases where the payment or benefit is in fact remitted, but in this chapter it is assumed these technical arguments will not prevail.

Section 2(2) amounts

23.4 A payment or benefit to a beneficiary in one of the categories listed above results in CGT if matched to one or more s 2(2) amounts of the trust – ie if the trust has realised gains not previously matched. The key planning technique is to ensure any given s 2(2) amount is not so matched. Instead s 2(2) amounts should be matched with a payment or benefit to either:

- A non-UK resident beneficiary, or
- A remittance basis user who does not remit.

As is explained in para **10.4** if the current year and all brought forward s 2(2) amounts are fully so matched in one tax year, Year 1, capital payments or benefits in the next tax year, Year 2, are potentially free of tax even if made to a UK resident beneficiary. But the freedom from tax is only potential, because the payments or benefits in Year 2 may be or become subject to CGT if and to the extent that either:

(a)   The trust has a s 2(2) amount in Year 2, ie the trust realises net gains in Year 2, or

(b)   The trust has a s 2(2) amount in a subsequent tax year which is not, under the LIFO rules described in paras **77.21** to **77.23**, matched with more recent capital payments or benefits.

Taxation under this second head, ie in a subsequent tax year, is avoided if by then the recipient beneficiary is non-resident for more than five years. It is also avoided if in a tax year between Year 2 and the year of the accrual of the later s 2(2) amount the entire trust fund has been transferred to another trust. As explained in para **77.29**, such a transfer carries across surplus s 2(2) amounts but not surplus capital payments.

Sch 4C pool

23.5 The techniques described above have to be qualified if and to the extent that the trust's s 2(2) amounts are in a Sch 4C pool. As is explained in CHAPTER 81, a Sch 4C pool is triggered where the trust makes a Sch 4B transfer, ie a transfer of value linked with trustee borrowing (see CHAPTER 80). In such a case the Sch 4C pool comprises all s 2(2) amounts of years up to and including that of the Sch 4B transfer, including any gains realised on the transfer itself.

The main result of s 2(2) amounts being in a Sch 4C pool is that they cannot be matched with a capital payment or benefit to a non-resident beneficiary, and so to that extent washing out gains by distributions or benefits to non taxable recipients is more difficult. But where the Sch 4C pool came into existence in 2008–09 or post, matching is still possible on distribution or benefits to UK residents who are remittance basis users, and so in this respect the planning described above remains possible.

Sch 4C pools are much more of an issue with international settlements than with those discussed in CHAPTERS 9 and 10. This is because the trustees of most international settlements have little awareness of the bizarre UK rules in Sch 4B and so may well at some stage fall foul of them.

Split the trust fund

23.6 In appropriate cases, the washing out techniques described above may be enhanced if part of the trust fund is transferred to another trust. This has the effect of moving a proportion of each year's s 2(2) amounts across to the transferee trust (see para **77.29**). In principle, a capital payment or benefit in a subsequent tax year is matched only with the part of the s 2(2) amounts in the trust from which it is made. This means a smaller capital payment to a non-resident or a remittance basis user is needed to remove s 2(2) amounts from the trust in question.

But although this technique is useful in appropriate cases, there are catches and caveats:

- It does not avail if the transferor trust has a Sch 4C pool, as then s 2(2) amounts can be matched with capital payments from either settlement (see para **81.13**).
- The same result follows if the transferor settlement has outstanding borrowing, for then the transfer to the second trust is itself a Sch 4B transfer (see para **80.17**) which moves all the s 2(2) amounts to a Sch 4C pool.
- If the capital distribution is from the transferee trust, account must be taken of any s 2(2) amounts in that trust.
- If the transfer between trusts is of non-cash assets, any latent gain on such assets will be realised by the transfer. Any such gain will be added to the s 2(2) amount of the transferor trust for the year of the transfer, and split between the two trusts accordingly.
- The distribution made by the transferee trust may be taxed as made by the transferor trust if on the facts the transferee trust is merely an intermediary of the transferor trust. This could be the position if there is agreement between the two sets of trustees as to the distributions the transferee trust will make, or if the transferor trustees are otherwise involved in the decision-making by the transferee trustees. Absent such factors it is unlikely the transferee trust will be an intermediary (see para **78.6**).

Surplus capital payments

23.7 In some cases, the distributions and benefits conferred by a trust exceed its aggregate s 2(2) amounts (if any). This scenario is more common than might be supposed. But it is less usual if a significant number of the beneficiaries are UK resident, for then capital payments and benefits are reduced by available relevant income as well as s 2(2) amounts (see para **78.5**). Nonetheless even then there is one common category of trust where surplus capital payments are the rule, namely the trust where the sole asset or assets are used by one or more beneficiaries in specie, for example a house.

Self-evidently surplus capital payments are not taxed when made. But they are potentially taxable if matched with future s 2(2) amounts. There are three planning points which may be deployed to avoid or reduce this potential tax:

- Taxability is determined by the status of the recipient of the payment in the year of matching, not the year of receipt. Tax is therefore avoided if in that tax year he is non-resident and the period of non-UK residence lasts for more than five tax years.
- Matching of the brought forward surplus payments does not occur if and insofar as capital payments or benefits are conferred in the year when the s 2(2) amount arises or in prior intervening years. This result follows because of the LIFO rule applicable to matching (see para **77.21**). Tax is avoided if such later payments or benefits are to non-residents or remittance basis users who do not remit, albeit leaving the older capital payments carried forward.

- A transfer of some or all of the trust fund to another trust prevents future s 2(2) amounts in the transferee trust from being matched against the brought forward capital payments (see para **77.29**). But matching and thus potentially a tax charge occurs insofar as a net gain is realised on the transfer, as that gain then constitutes a s 2(2) amount of the year of the transfer.

The second of the points made above is of particular value where the brought forward capital payments are enjoyment in the UK of the sole trust asset in specie, for then tax is avoided if, in the year when that asset is sold, capital payments at least equal to any gain are made to non-resident beneficiaries or to remittance basis users who do not remit. This is so even if the recipient of such payments is the former user of the asset in specie.

The obtaining of this advantage can be rendered complicated where the trustees make a Sch 4B transfer in the year of the disposal and a matched capital payment is made to a non-resident in that tax year. In that situation the matched capital payment is disregarded in computing the gains going into the Sch 4C pool (see para **81.4**). But in practice, this point is of little significance as gains in a Sch 4C pool cannot be matched with capital payments made in a tax year earlier than that of the Sch 4B transfer (see para **81.21**).

Underlying companies

23.8 Many international trusts hold investments through one or more underlying companies and in these cases the planning described above needs to take account of gains realised in the company or companies. This is because such gains are prima facie apportionable to the trust under TCGA 1992, s 13. The detailed rules relating to s 13 are explained in Chapter **88**, but what is important here is that there may be a fundamental difference between s 2(2) amounts of 2011–12 and prior and those of 2012–13 and post.

Under UK domestic law, the s 2(2) amounts of 2011–12 and prior tax years always include underlying company gains. However, this is subject to various reliefs described in Chapter **88**, most notably indexation and the exclusion of bank account and other loan relationship gains.

It is also subject to the point that under EU law, s 13 may have fallen to be disapplied. As explained in para **107.13** it has been held s 13 infringed the fundamental freedoms in relation to companies formed in EU Member States and it may be this infringement extended to companies formed elsewhere as well. How far HMRC would accept this, however, may be doubted.

The position is much simpler as respects s 13 gains of 2012–13 and post. Here the s 2(2) amounts include underlying company gains only if the acquisition, holding, or disposal of assets in question is tainted by an intention to avoid CGT or corporation tax. Precisely what this exemption means is a matter for debate, but, as explained in para **88.37**, international settlements set up and operated without regard to UK tax, or with regard only to IHT, are plainly within it. In such cases, s 2(2) amounts from 2012–13 onwards may be smaller than might be supposed, as underlying company gains are excluded.

The trustees of all international settlements with underlying companies need to consider whether the s 13 motive defence is in point, for if it is, it may have a very significant impact on the planning strategies described here. In particular the quantum of capital payments to non-taxable beneficiaries required to remove existing s 2(2) amounts may be less than might be supposed. So too, cases of surplus capital payments may become more common than previously.

REBASING AVAILABLE

23.9 2008 rebasing is explained in paras **79.10** to **79.14**. It applies only to beneficiaries who are non-UK domiciled, but in relation to such a beneficiary operates whether or not he is a remittance basis user. At the time of writing the indications are it will continue to apply after 6 April 2017 and will apply even if the beneficiary concerned is deemed UK domiciled under the new rules.

Rebasing is the only transitional relief available if either:

- As at 5 April 2008 the trust had neither carried forward s 2(2) amounts nor carried forward capital payments, or
- All such amounts or payments have already been matched.

Should an election be made?

23.10 As explained in para **20.17**, there is no downside in making a rebasing election and the trustees of any international trust should give the matter consideration. The normal deadline was 31 January 2010 but this is extended if the trust has not, since 6 April 2008, made a s 90 transfer to another settlement or a capital payment to a UK resident beneficiary (see further para **79.11**).

How to maximise the relief

23.11 The mechanics of the relief are explained in para **79.10**. The key point is to ensure that it is not wasted, a point which requires s 2(2) amounts which benefit substantially from rebasing to accrue in the same tax year as capital payments are made only to non-UK domiciliaries. This ensures, under LIFO, that the s 2(2) amounts are matched with the payments and so result in s 87 gains attracting significant relief. Rebasing is wasted if and to the extent that s 2(2) amounts which attract rebasing are matched with capital payments to non-residents, to individuals both resident and domiciled in the UK, or to remittance basis users who are never going to remit.

In reality most trusts are likely to have a mix of assets, some of which benefit from rebasing and some do not. The latter comprise assets acquired after 6 April 2008, and assets acquired before then whose base cost is more than the April 2008 value. In an ideal world disposals of assets in these latter categories should be concentrated in one tax year, with payments equal to the ensuing s 2(2) amount being made in that tax year to non-resident beneficiaries or to remittance basis users who will never remit. In another tax year the assets which benefit from rebasing should be disposed of and here a capital payment or payments equal to the s 2(2) amount must be made to non-UK domiciliaries who are either not remittance basis users or, if remittance basis users, remit.

In operating the above strategies the following practical points should be kept in mind:

- Account should only be taken of disposals in underlying companies if the motive defence described above (para **23.8**) is not in point.
- As explained above (para **23.5**), distributions to non-residents do not have s 2(2) amounts matched if, by reason of a Sch 4B transfer in the tax year concerned, the s 2(2) amount moves into a Sch 4C pool (see further CHAPTER **81**).
- If it is intended to maximise rebasing in a given tax year's s 2(2) amount, disposals of assets whose April 2008 value was lower than base cost should be avoided. Such assets increase the numerator of the rebasing fraction and so increase the proportion of the non-UK domiciliary's s 87 gain which is chargeable.

SECTION 2(2) AMOUNTS OF 2007–08 AND PRIOR YEARS

23.12 Many international settlements created before 6 April 2008 have unmatched s 2(2) amounts of 2007–08 and prior tax years. Significant further planning opportunities may be available if this element is present. These apply to all foreign domiciliaries and not just to remittance basis users (see para **79.16**). As with 2008 rebasing, the indications at the time of writing are that these opportunities will continue to be available after 6 April 2017 and will be available even if the beneficiary concerned is deemed UK domiciled under the new rules.

Surplus s 2(2) amounts

23.13 As explained in paras **77.26** to **77.28**, all the old s 2(2) amounts have to be computed, an exercise required and valid even if the trust has had no UK connection whatsoever for much of the time in question. With international settlements the start date is normally 17 March 1998 (see para **77.28**).

The old s 2(2) amounts are reduced on a first in first out basis to the extent that gains were treated as accruing to beneficiaries in 2007–08 and prior, ie to the extent of capital payments and other benefits made before 6 April 2008. In general the start date for such capital payments is also 17 March 1998 and the payments or benefits taken into account include those to non-residents. This latter point enhances the payments taken into account, for benefits to non-residents cannot be taken out of s 87 by being taxed under ITA 2007, s 731 (see para **78.5**). The result, in turn, is that the s 2(2) amounts brought forward from 2007–08 may be less than might be supposed.

Use of surplus s 2(2) amounts

23.14 As with rebasing, the key planning issue for s 2(2) amounts brought forward from 2007–08 is to ensure they are not wasted. This is achieved if, under the LIFO rules applicable to s 87, those s 2(2) amounts are matched to capital payments to non-UK domiciliaries. They should not be matched to capital payments to non-residents, to individuals both resident and domiciled in the UK, or to remittance basis users who are never going to remit.

Securing the requisite matching is achieved as follows:

(A)   If at the start of a tax year the trust has no unmatched s 2(2) amount of 2008–09 or later tax years, care should be taken in that year to avoid generating one. Assuming this is achieved, capital payments in that tax year are matched with the s 2(2) amounts of 2007–08 and earlier tax years and so should be made exclusively to non-UK domiciliaries who are not remittance basis users or are remittance basis users who will or may remit. On that basis, the ensuing s 87 gains are tax-free.

(B)   If at the start of a tax year (Year 1) the trust does have unmatched s 2(2) amounts of 2008–09 or later tax years, capital payments should be made in that tax year to non-resident beneficiaries or to remittance basis users who will never remit. These capital payments should equal, but not exceed, any current-year s 2(2) amount plus the brought forward s 2(2) amounts of 2008–09 and subsequent tax years. In the next tax year, Year 2, no further s 2(2) amount should be realised and capital payments should be made exclusively to resident non-UK domiciliaries who are not remittance basis users or are remittance basis users who will or may remit. These will be matched with the s 2(2) amounts of 2007–08 and earlier tax years and so be exempt.

Rebasing may require these procedures to be modified as follows:

• At (A) above, a current-year s 2(2) amount may be realised insofar as wholly covered by rebasing. It will be matched with the capital payments to the non-domiciled beneficiaries and, like the matching with s 2(2) amounts of 2007–08 and earlier tax years, result in a tax-free s 87 gain.

• At (B) above, unmatched amounts of 2008–09 or later tax years may be ignored if wholly covered by rebasing, the trust in effect being treated as the same as those within (A).

There are three important qualifications to the procedures at (A) and (B) above:

• If the trust has available relevant income, such is matched to distributions and benefits to UK residents before any matching under s 87 (see para **78.5**). This does not apply if the recipient is the settlor (see para **70.15**) but otherwise should be taken account of in formulating amounts to be distributed and to whom.

• Any OIG amounts in the trust are matched before s 2(2) amounts (see CHAPTER **82**). Should the matching be to a distribution or benefit to a non-resident, the amount matched becomes available relevant income and so should be taken account of accordingly (see para **82.13**).

• The capital payments to the non-domiciliaries should not exceed the s 2(2) amounts of 2007–08 and prior, as if they do the surplus is carried forward, and is potentially taxable by reference to future OIG or s 2(2) amounts.

In computing s 2(2) amounts account should be taken of underlying company gains within TCGA 1992, s 13. As described in para **23.8** above, unless an EU argument is to be relied on, such gains always need to be included in determining the s 2(2) amounts of 2007–08 and prior. They may need to be excluded in determining whether there are s 2(2) amounts of 2008–09 and post, in that the motive defence referred to in para **23.8** may mean such amounts do not include underlying company gains for 2012–13 and subsequent years.

Trustee borrowing

23.15 The above procedures have to be modified if the trust has fallen foul of the trustee borrowing rules in TCGA 1992, Sch 4B and 4C. As is explained above, these rules have been in force since 21 March 2000 (see para **81.2**). In practice many international settlements have fallen foul of them, as unless the trust has UK beneficiaries, the rules are of no consequence.

If the infringement was in 2007–08 or before, s 2(2) amounts in the ensuing Sch 4C pool, ie those of years up to including that of the infringement, are not matched with capital payments to non-domiciliaries (see para **81.29**). This means that the planning recommended above does not work and so leaves the payment unmatched and available for carry forward, save insofar as s 2(2) amount accrued after the tax year of the s 2(2) infringement and before 6 April 2008.

Should the trust have infringed Sch 4B in 2008–09 or a later tax year, the s 2(2) amounts of 2007–08 and earlier tax years in the Sch 4C pool can be matched to capital payments to non-domiciliaries (see para **81.27**). This means that the planning described above can be undertaken. But two points need to be kept in mind:

- Any s 2(2) amounts of 2008–09 and later years cannot, if in the Sch 4C pool, be matched to distributions to non-residents. Accordingly any removal of such amounts as per B in para **23.14** above has to be by distribution to a remittance basis user who does not remit.
- Section 2(2) amounts in the Sch 4C pool are matched before s 2(2) amounts outside it, ie before s 2(2) amounts of tax years following that of the Sch 4B infringement. This is an exception to the normal LIFO rule, and means that at B in para **23.14** above, the distribution in Year 1 should not only be just to a remittance basis user who does not remit but also should equal only the s 2(2) amounts of 2008–09 and post which are in the Sch 4C pool. So too, the distribution in Year 2 to the non-domiciliary should not exceed the s 2(2) amounts of 2007–08 and earlier years in the pool. If it does so exceed them the excess will be matched with those s 2(2) amounts of 2008–09 and later years which are outside the pool.

SURPLUS CAPITAL PAYMENTS AS AT 5 APRIL 2008

23.16 A trust with surplus capital payments as at 5 April 2008 is one where capital payments or benefits in 2007–08 and earlier tax years exceeded the s 2(2) amounts of those years. As indicated above (para **23.13**), the start date is normally 17 March 1998 and older capital payments of 2007–08 are set against the aggregate s 2(2) amounts of those years in priority to younger ones.

Should such a surplus capital payment be matched with a s 2(2) amount now, the ensuing s 87 gain is tax-free if the recipient is non-UK domiciled in the year of matching. As with s 2(2) amounts of 2007–08 and prior, the indications at the time of writing are that this relief too will continue after 6 April 2017 and will apply even if the non-domiciled beneficiary is deemed UK domiciled under the new rules.

There are certain scenarios in which surplus payments of 2007–08 and earlier years can be wasted:

- If the trust ends without them ever being used.
- If payments in or after 2008–09 are matched with OIG amounts and the payments of 2007–08 and prior are matched with s 2(2) amounts.
- If the beneficiary in receipt of the surplus payments becomes UK domiciled before they are matched.
- If and to the extent that the s 2(2) amount with which the brought forward capital payment is matched is covered by rebasing.

The second of these points requires some elaboration. It would arise if the trust has OIG amounts in or after 2008–09 and these are matched to capital payments in 2008–09 or later tax years to beneficiaries who are resident in the UK and either UK domiciled or non-UK domiciliaries who are not remittance basis users or who remit. In such case the resulting tax is income tax, not CGT. If in a subsequent tax year there is a s 2(2) amount, and the payments of 2008–09 and later years have all been exhausted, the matching is with the brought forward payments of 2007–08 and earlier years. The ensuing s 87 gain is tax-free, but the tax saved is CGT rather than income tax. To have avoided the income tax, the capital payments of 2008–09 and post would have needed delaying until a tax year after that in which the OIG amounts were realised.

So far it has been assumed that the surplus payments of 2007–08 and earlier years were all to non-UK domiciliaries. In reality some may also have been to resident UK domiciliaries and/or to non-residents. In such circumstances the matching is pro rata using LIFO (see para **77.21**). Self-evidently tax will result insofar as the brought forward payments were made to beneficiaries who are, in the tax year of matching, both resident and domiciled in the UK.

As is explained in para **79.19**, one category of brought forward capital payment is excluded from matching in or after 2008–09. This is payments made between 12 March and 5 April 2008 to an individual who was then UK resident but non-UK domiciled, and has remained so. But these capital payments come back into account if the recipient becomes non-resident or becomes domiciled in the UK whilst remaining UK resident. In the latter event the payments represent something of a trap, for if matching then occurs with s 2(2) amounts, tax results without any of the foreign domiciliary reliefs.

Planning

23.17 Should a trust have surplus capital payments the first point to ascertain is whether some date back to before 12 March 2008, and assuming some do, whether some or all of the recipients were and have remained non-UK domiciled. Assuming this latter condition is met, the further point to ascertain is whether there are any surplus payments from 2008–09 or later. Assuming the answer to that question is negative, the trust is then in the happy position of being able to realise gains without risk of matched capital payments rendering the gains taxable. Other things being equal there is much to be said in such circumstances for realising gains now equal to the pre-2008 payments in case the law changes or the foreign domiciled beneficiaries become UK domiciled.

If such gains are to be realised, there is little point in them exceeding the capital payments as such excess gains may be taxed by reference to future capital payments to UK residents. But in computing what s 2(2) amount is fully needed to absorb pre-2008 capital payments, the circumstances in which underlying company gains are excluded should be kept in mind.

It goes without saying that planning of this sort presupposes capital payments are not made in the tax year in which the s 2(2) amount is being realised. Under LIFO such a capital payment would be matched first, and so would defeat the intended matching with capital payments of 2007–08 and prior.

Matters are more complicated if some of the surplus capital payments of 2007–08 were to resident UK domiciliaries or, if in addition to pre-2008 surplus capital payments, there are unmatched capital payments to UK residents of 2008–09 and later tax years. In such cases generating a s 2(2) amount now will generate a CGT charge by reference to such capital payments unless, in the case of payments made in or after 2008–09, the payment is to a remittance-basis user who has not and will not remit. In all these cases, a judgement is needed as to whether the disadvantages represented by such charges outweighs the advantages of accessing the tax-free pre-2008 payments to non-UK domiciliaries.

Section V

Offshore Tax Planning in relation to Business Activities

Chapter 24

SHELTERING BUSINESS PROFITS

The authors would like to thank Robert Birchall of Charles Russell Speechlys LLP for his help with this chapter.

INTRODUCTION

24.1 This chapter considers the extent to which a non-UK resident company can shelter business profits. Typically the issue arises in one of two contexts. The first is where a UK resident individual or company is genuinely carrying on business abroad, or planning to do so, where the question is how the ownership of the overseas business may best be structured. The second is where, commercially, an existing or proposed business could be carried on in a low tax jurisdiction and here the question is whether it is worthwhile doing so, and, if it is, how the operation should best be structured.

This chapter focuses on privately owned businesses rather than quoted companies or groups. The latter have many opportunities for structuring their global operations so as to minimise tax, albeit exposing themselves to the risk of adverse publicity should they do so. But international corporate tax planning of this sort is beyond the scope of this book.

HISTORY

24.2 In the past, so called business operations constituted a large part of what was done in low or nil tax jurisdictions. Often it was felt possible to set up offshore companies to capture all or part of the profit of a business venture and keep it sheltered in a nil tax environment. Perhaps the most common operation of this kind was reinvoicing or double invoicing. In other words, the offshore company either invoiced for so called services or was interposed, with a mark-up, between the buyer and seller of goods or services.

If operations of this kind ever worked, they do not do so now, primarily on account of the rules as to transfer pricing. Transfer pricing is an international issue and most countries now have rules to counter the artificial diversion of profits into low tax jurisdictions. In general, these rules are based on OECD guidelines and the UK rules, which are described in CHAPTER 91, are no exception.

The effect of these rules is that it is unrealistic to expect to take anything other than commercial profit in a low tax jurisdiction. In other words, what is earned in the low tax jurisdiction must represent reasonable recompense for value added there. It follows that the principal area where scope for sheltering business profits arises is where the operations do not require great physical presence. Obvious examples are finance sector business such as insurance but, as is well publicised, e-commerce has potential in this area as well.

Insofar as any company in a low tax jurisdiction is trading with associated UK entities, compliance requirements must be kept in mind as well. The UK entities when filing must consider transfer pricing issues and, if arm's length prices have not been charged, make appropriate adjustments in computing the taxable profit (see para **91.20**).

At one time, offshore companies were widely used to capture profit generated by operations in countries which lacked robust transfer pricing legislation, usually third world countries. To a limited extent such business may still be carried on in some jurisdictions. But as a general rule practices of this sort have had their day, both because there is a global push to stop third world countries from being exploited, and because, for many providers, significant reputational issues arise as well. That is not to say companies based in low tax jurisdictions cannot do business in the Third World but merely that the terms on which they do so must be commercial.

At the time of writing it is unclear how far the tax planning described in this chapter will be affected by the international attack on multinationals which divert profits to low tax jurisdictions. In FA 2015 the UK commenced its implementation of the international attack by enacting Diverted Profits Tax. That tax is described in CHAPTER **92** and referred to in this chapter where it may be relevant.

IS IT WORTHWHILE?

24.3 Before any offshore sheltering of business profits is undertaken, careful consideration is required as to whether it is worthwhile. This entails consideration of three separate issues, namely the effective rate of tax the profits will suffer overall, the disciplines required to ensure any overseas company really is resident where it says it is, and diverted profits tax.

Effective tax

24.4 The issue of overall tax principally arises because the UK's corporate tax rates are now very competitive. Currently the rate of corporation tax is 20% and is due to fall further to 19% from 1 April 2017 and 17% from 1 April 2020.

These rates of corporate tax mean that the issue to be addressed in reviewing offshore sheltering is whether effective overall tax resulting from using a non-UK resident company is going to be significantly less than that using a UK company. It is easy enough for an individual contemplating an overseas venture to see that appropriate structuring may prevent the profits being taxed as his personal income at rates of 40% or 45%. But in reality he can secure the low UK corporate tax rates merely by trading through a UK company. The real question is whether using a non-UK company will deliver a significantly better outcome than a UK company.

A point also to keep in mind is that UK resident companies with a foreign permanent establishment may find themselves in a position to claim that some or all of the permanent establishment profits are exempt from Corporation Tax. This is the effect the foreign permanent establishments exemption, enacted by CTA 2009, ss 18A–18S, which entitles a UK company to irrevocably elect that its foreign permanent establishment profits be exempt from Corporation Tax.

The potential availability of this exemption should always be considered when making the comparison between a UK and a non-UK company. However the exemption is subject to anti-diversion rules in the same terms as those applicable under the Controlled Foreign Company legislation (see para 24.18). More importantly, its availability is restricted if the UK company is small. Small for these purposes means a micro or small enterprise within the meaning of the European Commission Recommendation 2003/3611 EC (CTA 2009, s 18S; see further paras **91.15** and **92.9** to **92.13**). The exemption is not available to a small company unless the permanent establishment is in a country with which the UK has a double tax treaty containing an anti-discrimination clause (ss 18P(1) and 18S).

A further point concerns the tax payable should the owner of any non-resident company wish to access the profits the company has sheltered. Here a dividend attracts tax at the dividend rates. Of course, instead of being distributed, profits can be left in whatever company earned them and eventually taken in capital form when the company is sold or liquidated. However, a sale or liquidation results in CGT whether the company is onshore or offshore. While the rate of CGT is normally 20%, shares in a UK company may attract the lower 10% rate under entrepreneurs' relief (TCGA 1992, ss 169H–169R). That relief applies to gains up to £10m but it requires the disponor to have been an officer or employee of the company. The company residence constraints discussed below make that a difficult condition to meet with an offshore company.

A further consideration should the owner sell or liquidate the company is the anti-avoidance legislation countering transactions in securities. This is described in CHAPTER 89 and is not in point on sales of the company to unconnected parties (see para **89.5**). But in other situations the legislation can be a risk if the sale or liquidation is in part at least tax driven. Should the legislation be in point the proceeds of the sale or liquidation are effectively treated as dividend.

It may be objected that if retention of profits in the company is the strategy, tax on ultimate disposal may in practice be an academic issue as it is avoided if the owner becomes non-UK resident. But this is the same where the company is UK resident. It also has to be remembered that more than five years' non-residence is required to avoid CGT (see para **41.40**) and that the strategy is only effective if emigration is to a country that does not itself tax capital gains. Further, when it comes to the point, emigration may quite simply not be what the owner wants to do.

Company residence

24.5 Should an overseas company be used, it will only be effective to avoid UK corporation tax if it is non-UK resident under the central management and control test. That test is explained in CHAPTER 43 and what it requires is a properly constituted board, meeting where the company is based and genuinely understanding and managing the company's business. Ideally one or more board members should be experienced in the kind of business the company is conducting.

What is generally not to be recommended is that the board include UK resident members, and in particular the board should not include any UK shareholder in either the offshore company or any UK company which owns it. The dangers such board membership entails are either that the UK board members will be found to have usurped the board as a whole or that they will render the company dual resident. In theory a properly run board can avoid these risks, but in practice it may be difficult to persuade either HMRC or the First-tier Tribunal that this has been achieved.

The practical result is that the UK owner may be unable to have a hands-on role in relation to the overseas company. To some extent this difficulty can be overcome by making shareholder 'requests' to the board, in that company residence is not jeopardised just because the board accedes to such requests, provided it has given informed consideration to them. But here the danger is that if the owner acts too much like a shadow director, he will be found to have usurped the board and if so render the company UK resident.

In some instances these risks may be manageable, particularly if the company is carrying on genuine international business and has other investors. Here it may well be possible to create a credible local board and, particularly if the UK shareholder does not have shareholder control, the risks of him being on the board are much less. But as a general rule the fact remains that hands-on control of the business is difficult for any UK owner to achieve and this is a further, commercial, reason favouring a UK company.

Diverted profits tax

24.6 Diverted profits tax is explained in CHAPTER 92. It was introduced in 2015 and in general ought not to be an issue in the present context as it does not apply if the companies concerned are all small or medium-sized enterprises within the EU definition (as to which see paras 92.9 to 92.13). However where it does apply the consequences are penal, for the rate of tax is 25% rather than the normal corporation tax rate.

Diverted profits tax could potentially come into issue if the profits being sheltered in the offshore company are the result of transactions or arrangements with a UK company. Should the UK company and the offshore company not both fall within the definition of small or medium enterprise, it is likely DPT will be engaged and at the very least careful consideration will need to be given to the legislation described in CHAPTER 92. A point to stress is that DPT is engaged even if the arrangements between the UK company and the offshore company are commercial and, if engaged, has the effect of taxing the UK company on the offshore company's profits at the rate of 25%. A further issue is that DPT appears not to give credit for income tax the profits might suffer under other anti-avoidance legislation (see para **92.15**).

If there is any risk of the companies concerned not being small or medium-sized, it is thus important to ensure that the profits accruing to the offshore company will not be attributable to transactions or arrangements with a UK company. Business emanating from the UK clearly poses a risk as potentially could the transfer or relocation of elements of an existing business carried on by a UK company. But a new overseas business with no UK connection is not at risk.

POSSIBLE STRUCTURES

24.7 Despite the points made above there are undoubtedly situations where use of a company in a low tax jurisdiction will prove attractive. In such a case, consideration then has to be given as to how it is best structured. There are three possibilities:

(1)   Direct ownership by one or more UK resident individuals.
(2)   Ownership in an offshore trust.
(3)   Ownership by an existing UK company.

Each of these forms of ownership raises a number of further tax issues, for the most part revolving around anti-avoidance legislation designed to nullify the sheltering potential of offshore companies.

INDIVIDUAL OWNERSHIP

24.8 The key issue with individual ownership is the transfer of assets code discussed in Chapters **68** to **74**. The effect of this code is that the profits of the non-UK company are treated as income of the UK resident shareholder under the transferor charge in ITA 2007, s 720 (see Chapter **69**). This result follows because, by forming or investing in the company, the individual is transferor and by holding shares, he has power to enjoy the company's income.

The effect of the company's profits being treated as the transferor's income is that tax is levied at personal rates, ie 40% higher rate and 45% top rate. This is a dramatically worse outcome than if a UK company had been used, for then the applicable tax is corporation tax at the rates as described above. Since the abolition of close company apportionment in 1989 (see para **87.1**) there has been no provision in the UK tax code attributing the income of UK resident companies to shareholders.

On the face of it, the transfer of assets code means individuals should never use non-UK companies to shelter profits. To some extent this is true and the transfer of assets code certainly reinforces the message that this kind of sheltering is often not worthwhile. But there are exceptions to the transfer of assets code and in appropriate cases these may displace this prima facie conclusion. A point, however, to stress at the outset is that there needs to be some confidence the code is displaced, given the potentially serious consequences of the company's profits being subjected to tax at personal income tax rates.

Motive defence

24.9 On the face of it the motive defence, which is described in CHAPTER 73, ought not be in point. In commercial contexts, it applies only if all relevant transactions are genuine commercial transactions and none is more than incidentally designed to avoid UK tax (see para **73.16**). As such it is clearly not in point where a business is carried on by a company in a low tax jurisdiction specifically because of the more favourable tax regime there.

It may be thought this renders the defence irrelevant in the contexts being discussed here. To a large extent this is true. But one of the scenarios postulated at the beginning of this chapter is where a business is in any event being carried on abroad and here there may be good and genuine commercial reasons to use a company in a tax neutral jurisdiction. Such reasons might include the requirements of non-UK joint venture partners or the need for proximity to target markets. A case where arguments of this sort succeeded is *Carvill v IRC* [2000] STC (SCD) 143, which concerned insurance companies set up in Bermuda.

In appropriate cases arguments of this sort may secure the defence and preclude the transfer of assets code. But anybody planning such an approach should keep three points in mind. First the defence has to be claimed, and HMRC are notorious for their reluctance to concede it. Second, a subsequent tax motivated operation may cause the defence to be lost, for all associated operations must be free of a tax avoidance intent if the defence is to be secured (see para **73.17** to **73.18**). Third, an intention to avoid any UK tax causes the defence to be lost: the enquiry is not restricted to income tax or corporation tax (see para **73.6**).

EU defence

24.10 As is explained in paras **107.7** to **107.12**, the transferor charge infringes EU law. It is reasonably plain that it is precluded where the company concerned is genuinely established and carrying on business in a member state of the EU. This preclusion is carried into UK domestic law by ITA 2007, s 742A which applies to transactions effected after 6 April 2012. Section 742A is explained in CHAPTER 74 and, as discussed in that chapter, its drafting is defective and obscure. However a reasonable inference is that it should be construed so as to bring the transfer of assets code into line with EU law, and even if that were wrong, EU law would have the same result by direct effect. By one means or another, therefore the transfer of assets code is precluded in relation to companies genuinely established and carrying on business in EU Member States.

On the face of it, this is of little relevance here, for EU states are generally jurisdictions with higher corporate tax rates than the UK. As such, the fundamental point discussed in para **24.4** above arises, namely using a foreign company results in a higher effective tax rate than using a UK company. But this is not always so, in that some EU jurisdictions such as Ireland have exceptionally low corporate tax rates and others offer tax incentives in specific contexts. This is not the place for a comparative review of EU taxes, but if on investigation a favourable regime is found, such may offer a context for tax sheltering through a company based in the Member State concerned.

The issue of whether EU law in general, and s 742A specifically, precludes the transfer of assets code where the company is resident outside the EU is discussed in paras **107.10** to **107.12**. In general the freedoms, and thus s 742A, are in point only where the company is established in the EU. But one freedom, capital, extends to movements to and from third countries and the issue which may be debated is whether that freedom gives third country companies protection from the transfer of assets charge.

In the present state of CJEU jurisprudence, this area of the law is very uncertain. However at present disapplication of the transfer of assets code looks unlikely. One reason is that the kind of company being contemplated here is establishment (see para **106.4**) and as such may be within the standstill for third country capital movements described in para **106.23**. If it were, any charge under the transfer of assets code might well be preserved as the code pre-dates 1993, albeit that even this is not clear cut in view of the changes to the code since then (see para **107.10**). The second reason is that the CJEU has proved much readier to uphold justifications in relation to third country capital movements than within the EU (see para **106.25**). As discussed in para **107.10**, it may well be that if the point were litigated the code would be upheld as proportionate in relation to third country capital movements.

On the basis of this analysis, the protections of EU law, and s 742A, can only be relied on within the EU. To this there may be one qualification, namely EFTA countries (Iceland, Norway and Liechtenstein). As is explained in paras **106.27** and **107.11**, all the freedoms are in point in relation to these countries, albeit that the justifications are more stringently applied.

The above points will obviously be subject to future legislative change following the outcome of the referendum to leave the EU in June 2016.

Purchased company

24.11 A completely different qualification to the transfer of assets code is in point should the UK resident purchase shares in an existing company rather than subscribe for the shares. Such a purchase is not a relevant transfer, such as is a prerequisite for the application of the code, as it does not result in income becoming payable to a person abroad (see para **68.5**). The prior formation of the company is, of course, a relevant transfer, but in relation to this transfer the UK resident purchaser would not have been transferor.

The exclusion of purchased companies has not been the subject of a decided case directly in point, but it is consistent with one point in *Vestey v IRC* [1980] STC 10. The transferee in that case had purchased a pre-existing company and it was accepted in the House of Lords that the income of that company was outside the code.

This principle should not be taken too far. If the UK individual had anything to do with the prior formation of the company he would very likely be a quasi transferor (see para **69.50**). As such the transferor charge would apply.

TRUST OWNERSHIP

24.12 Ownership of the company by an offshore trust brings one advantage regardless of the form of the trust, namely an additional defence against it being argued the company is UK resident under the central management and control test. As is explained in para **43.14** ownership by a properly managed and independent trustee makes any contention the company is UK resident hard to sustain as in such a case only the trustees are constitutionally authorised to give instructions to the directors. A finding that the company is UK resident thus carries the implication that both they and the directors have failed to properly discharge their duties.

Settlor-interested trust

24.13 Apart from the above point, ownership by a settlor-interested trust brings no advantage as compared with personal ownership. This is because, as a beneficiary, the settlor retains power to enjoy, with the result that the transferor charge applies, unless precluded by one of the points discussed above. Indeed in one respect a trust can make matters worse. This arises if the company is protected by the motive defence but holding the shares in trust is tainted by a tax avoidance purpose, for then the defence would be lost in relation to the company.

Other trusts

24.14 Where trust ownership has much more potential for tax mitigation is if the settlor and his spouse are completely excluded as beneficiaries, for an offshore discretionary trust from which the settlor and his spouse are wholly excluded should, with appropriate care, mean the settlor does not have power to enjoy and so prevent liability arising under the transferor charge. It follows from this that exclusion from that charge may be achieved in relation to an offshore company if such a trust owns all the shares.

It follows that in income tax terms, an appropriate structure for sheltering foreign business profits is a non-resident company owned by a non-resident trust from which the settlor and his spouse are wholly excluded. Such sheltering of business profits may be part of a wider structure, in which the trust is also used to shelter investments, as is described in CHAPTER 1. Indeed, the business activities of the company may generate the funds from which the portfolio investments are purchased.

Exclusion of the settlor

24.15 There is a price which has to be paid for a trust structure of this kind and this is that the individuals behind the underlying business venture may, as settlors, have to be excluded. In some cases this is not a problem, as where those individuals are already wealthy. Alternatively, the problem may be avoided if the initial capital settled in the trust comes not from those individuals but from parents or from more remote relatives. Such arrangements are discussed in para **1.9** and should be effective to prevent the shareholders from being treated as settlors providing any dealings between them and the offshore company are on commercial terms (see para **75.22**).

The transferor charge should be reviewed with particular care in a structure of this sort, for liability extends to procurers of the offshore arrangements (see para **69.50**). To minimise risk, the UK shareholders should as far as possible be distanced from the setting up of the offshore arrangements, and certainly they should not indirectly provide funds for the trust. The extended meaning of 'power to enjoy' should also be kept in mind as should the importance of ensuring that the UK individuals neither lend to nor borrow from the company or trust (cf paras **69.5** and **69.22**).

Employment income through third parties

24.16 In any case where the company is owned by a trust the legislation directed at employment income through third parties should be kept in mind. This legislation is explained in CHAPTER **94**. It ought not to be in point in relation to trusts of the kind discussed here, for it is confined to arrangements which are, in essence, a means of remunerating employees (ITEPA 2003, s 554(1)(c); see para **94.6**). But it could come into issue if a beneficiary works for the company, and is rewarded not by remuneration but by trust distributions. Such scenarios should be avoided, specifically by ensuring that the remuneration of those who work for the company is such as would be agreed at arm's length.

OWNERSHIP BY A UK COMPANY

24.17 The discussion above has assumed that the offshore company is owned by UK resident individuals or by trusts. Another possibility is that the offshore company is the subsidiary of a UK company or group. Should this be the position, diverted profits tax requires particular consideration, as it is inherently likely there will be transactions between the UK company and the offshore subsidiary. That apart the fundamentals described at the beginning of this chapter remain the same, but the position regarding anti-avoidance legislation and distributions differs.

Anti-avoidance legislation

24.18 It might be thought the transfer of assets code is not in point in this scenario, as the code applies only where the transferor is an individual. But an individual can count as transferor if he procured or was associated with the transfer, such individuals being known as quasi transferors. The quasi transferor concept is explained in para **69.50** and one or more individuals who control a corporate transferor are likely to be treated as quasi transferors (*Fisher v Revenue and Customs Comrs* [2014] UKFTT 804 (TC), [2014] SFTD 1341, 17 ITLR 141; see para **69.51**). In FAQs in relation to employee benefit trusts HMRC indicated that they would so argue (see para **3.6** in HMRC Notice 5 September 2012 reproduced [2012] SWTI, p 2658). It follows that the mere fact that the offshore company is a subsidiary of a UK group does not of itself preclude the risk of the transferor charge.

Ownership by a UK company or group also requires consideration of the controlled foreign company or CFC rules. These were first enacted in 1984 and were consolidated as TA 1988, ss 747–756. Following the ECJ decision in *Cadbury Schweppes plc v Revenue and Customs Comrs* [2006] STC 1908 (see para **107.3**) it became clear that they were not EU compliant and, for accounting periods starting on or after 1 January 2013, a radically different code has been enacted (FA 2012, Sch 20).

The old rules, ie TA 1988, ss 747–756, are described in earlier editions of this work. The more limited nature of the new rules means detailed treatment here is no longer appropriate. However, three key points about the new rules should be noted. The first is that although any foreign company controlled by UK residents is a CFC (TIOPA 2010, s 371AA(3)) attribution under the rules is only made insofar as those with a direct or indirect interest in it are companies resident in the UK (TIOPA 2010, s 371BC).

The second point is that attribution, and thus the CFC rules as a whole, come into issue only if the profits of the CFC pass through one of the five quite tightly defined gateways (TIOPA 2010, s 371BB). Three of the gateways relate to captive insurance companies and trading finance profits (TIOPA 2010, ss 371CE–371CG) and are not normally relevant in the present context.

As a result, the gateways of concern are the first, general gateway (TIOPA 2010, s 371CA) and the second, which deals with non-trading finance profits. But the first gateway is a narrow one, for it is precluded if the CFC satisfies a motive defence and, more importantly, it is also precluded unless risks or assets of the CFC are managed or controlled on a non-arm's length basis from the UK. At the risk of oversimplification, it follows from this that an offshore company of the kind postulated here will rarely pass through this gateway, for such companies are genuinely managed and controlled by their own board, and respect transfer pricing principles. Further, assuming that the general gateway is not passed through, the non-trading finance profits gateway is also closed if those profits are within a 5% de minimis or generated by working capital (TIOPA 2010, ss 371CB and 371CC).

The consequence of all this is that, while the CFC gateways should always be checked, they will rarely be passed through. But should they be passed through the third point to be noted arises, namely that if a CFC charge is made on the UK parent the amount charged cannot be transfer of assets income (ITA 2007, s 725). Bizarrely, in a case where the quasi transferor point means that the transfer of assets code is in point, a CFC charge is thus effectively a relieving provision, for the CFC charge results in tax at corporate rates, whereas a charge under the transfer of assets code is at income tax rates.

Reporting obligation

24.19 There is one other anti-avoidance rule which has to be referred to with offshore subsidiaries, namely that there can be reporting requirements if a non-resident subsidiary creates or issues any shares or debentures or if the UK parent transfers any shares or debentures in the subsidiary (FA 2009, Sch 17). But in the present context these requirements are unlikely to be in point as a report is only required if the value of the transaction is above £100m (Sch 17 para 8(1)).

Repatriation of profits

24.20 As with companies in personal ownership, thought has to be given as to how any profits in an offshore subsidiary will be repatriated. Here the position is more favourable than with companies in personal ownership, at least so far as the repatriated profits are retained in the UK parent.

Should the offshore subsidiary pay a dividend, exemption applies unless the UK parent is a small company (CTA 2009, s 931E). The applicable definition of a small company is the EU definition referred to in para **24.4** above and explained in relation to transfer pricing in para **91.15**. Although many UK recipients of the kind described in this chapter will be small, fewer are than might be supposed as the EU definition requires account to be taken of partner and linked enterprises (as to which see paras **92.11** to **92.12**).

Even if the UK parent *is* small, dividends can still be exempt, but only if the offshore company paying them is resident in a territory with which the UK has concluded a double tax treaty containing a standard non-discrimination article (CTA 2009, s 931B). Further, in such a case the dividend must not be part of a tax advantage scheme. Of their nature few offshore companies of the kind described in this chapter will meet the former of these conditions.

An alternative to dividends is sale or liquidation, where the applicable tax is corporation tax on chargeable gains. Corporate gains are computed with the benefit of indexation (TCGA 1992, ss 52A and 53) and in addition the relief for disposals of substantial shareholdings may be in point (TCGA 1992, Sch 7AC). This relief applies as much where the company invested in is non-resident as where it is resident (Sch 7AC para 26) and the term 'substantial' connotes simply that the investing company must have owned 10% or more of the company invested in for at least 12 months in the two years prior to the disposal (Sch 7AC paras 7 and 8). If the relief applies, any gain on the disposal is tax free (and any loss is an unallowable loss). There is an anti-avoidance provision, but this only applies if arrangements have been put in place from which the sole or main benefit is exemption of the gain (Sch 7AC para 5). The arrangements can either be the acquisition of the company invested in or, more likely, the commencement or alteration of its trade.

The most important limitation on the main relief is that both the investing company and the company invested in must be trading companies or members of a trading group broadly during the two years before and also immediately after the disposal (Sch 7AC paras 18 and 19). A trading company is one whose activities do not to a substantial extent include non-trading activities and a trading group is one where the activities of the group as a whole do not to a substantial extent include non-trading activities (Sch 7AC paras 20 and 21). 'Substantial' is not defined in the legislation but the HMRC view is that it means more than 20% (*Tax Bulletin* 62 (December 2002, p 985); Capital Gains Manual CG53116).

In light of the various exemptions and reliefs, it may be said that the dividends will normally be more attractive where the UK parent is not small. But where it *is* small, capital gains tax treatment on a sale or liquidation will in many cases be more advantageous. It goes without saying that profits reaching the UK parent will not be at the disposal of its shareholders without more tax being payable. Further tax normally has to be found, whether income tax at the dividend rates on dividends or CGT on a sale or liquidation.

CONCLUSION

24.21 In the light of the above analysis, the conclusion must inevitably be that use of an offshore company to shelter business profits is rarely attractive and in some cases significantly increases overall tax as compared with using a UK company. This is particularly so where the offshore company and any related UK company are large enough to come within diverted profits tax. Even where that is not so, there are really only two exceptions to the general unattractiveness of offshore companies, namely companies genuinely formed and carrying on business in an EU Member State and companies owned by trust from which the settlor and his spouse are completely excluded.

CAPITAL GAINS

24.22 So far this chapter has not dealt with capital gains of an offshore company. Here the starting point is that any non-resident company of the kind envisaged here is close and so potentially subject to apportionment of gains under TCGA 1992, s 13. Section 13 is analysed in CHAPTER 88 and at one time it was a significant deterrent to the use of an offshore company, as most gains realised by the company were attributed to UK resident participators. Now, however, its bite is more modest, for a combination of three reasons.

First, s 13 is subject to a motive defence, which has been in force since 6 April 2012. Under that defence, the section does not apply on any given disposal unless the disposal, acquisition, or holding of the asset concerned formed part of arrangements, and one of the main purposes of those arrangement was the avoidance of CGT or corporation tax. It will be noted that this is a much more generous defence than that applicable to the transfer of assets code, inter alia because the only taxes which have to be looked at are corporation tax and CGT.

Second, s 13 does not apply if the asset disposed of was used by the company in a trade or in economically significant activities carried on outside the UK. The concept of economically significant activities was introduced to s 13 by FA 2013 and is discussed in para 88.5. In broad terms it connotes the provision of goods and services to others on a genuine and commercial basis. As will be apparent many if not most of the companies of the kind postulated in this chapter will fall within the concept, particularly if their activities are structured so as to comply with transfer pricing principles.

Third, substantial shareholder relief, as briefly referred to in para **24.20** above, is capable of applying to disposals by companies that are within the scope of s 13 (see para **88.10**). This means that if the non-UK company is part of a group structure, disposals of group members may well be protected from s 13.

The combined effect of these three points is that s 13 is rarely in point in relation to companies of the kind discussed in this chapter. Certainly, it alone is not an argument against using such companies.

REMITTANCE BASIS USERS

24.23 Hitherto in this chapter it has been assumed, implicitly at least, that the UK resident individual behind the company is also UK domiciled or, if non-UK domiciled, is not a remittance basis user. But in reality many of the individuals who consider using a non-UK company for business ventures are remittance basis users. In general the tax issues discussed above apply with equal force in relation to companies held by remittance basis users, as the transfer of assets code still has to be considered and it is also necessary to ensure the company is non-UK resident and ask whether it really will achieve lower overall tax.

Advantages

24.24 There is however one fundamental difference as respects remittance basis users. If a remittance basis user carries on overseas business as a sole trader he is likely to be taxable on the profits on an arising basis; in such a case it is difficult to show that the business is conducted wholly abroad such as is necessary to attract the remittance basis (see para **40.12**). So too if the business is carried on by a UK company its profits are inevitably within the purview of corporation tax and any dividends have a UK source and so are unable to attract the remittance basis (see para **40.2**).

However, the position is different if an overseas company is used. Here, provided that the company is indeed non-UK resident, the company is not subject to corporation tax and any dividends it pays are foreign source and so taxed only if remitted. Moreover, although the transfer of assets code applies unless one of the defences discussed above is in point, it too is subject to the remittance basis. In short, use of an overseas company operates as a genuine tax shelter for a remittance basis user, provided neither he nor the company intends to remit profits to the UK. In such a case, therefore, use of an overseas company should seriously be considered.

Remittance

24.25 Where a non-UK company is less advantageous for a remittance basis user is if in due course the profits are going to be remitted. Remittance of profits by the company results in tax on the remittance basis user himself, unless one of the defences to the transfer of assets code is in point, for the company is inevitably a relevant person (see para **54.12**). So too, remittance of any dividend is either remittance of the underlying transfer of assets income or of the dividend itself. In either event the result is income tax.

It may be thought that remittance issues can be overcome if the profits are retained in the company and the company is in due course sold or liquidated. But here CGT is the applicable tax and so, should there be a gain, remittance of the proceeds results in the gain being charged to CGT at 20%. As indicated in para **24.4** above it is also necessary to consider the possible impact of the legislation directed at transactions in securities (see CHAPTER 89). A further point is that on a liquidation, the proceeds could be identified with the prior corporate profits with the result that the latter count as remitted, with an ensuing income tax charge, should the shareholder bring the funds to the UK (see further para **72.16**).

Chapter 25

EMPLOYEE BENEFIT TRUSTS

The authors would like to thank Robert Birchall of Charles Russell Speechlys LLP for his help with this chapter.

INTRODUCTION

25.1 The term 'Employee Benefit Trust', or 'EBT', encompasses a wide variety of trusts. The common factor is an intention to benefit employees, either by cash distributions or by buying, holding and in due course distributing shares in the employer company. A definition may be found in the former ESC A68, the concession now enacted as ITA 2007, ss 496A and 496B. In the words of that concession 'Employee trusts are discretionary trusts created by funds provided by employers for the benefit of their employees, past, present or future or for the benefit of any dependents or relations of such employees'.

In first decade of the present century, offshore EBTs became common. They raise difficult tax issues and were the principal target of the legislation directed at the provision of employment income through third parties, enacted in 2011 as ITEPA 2003, Part 7A. This legislation is analysed in CHAPTER 94. HMRC have published their view on some of the other tax issues which arise with EBTs. One such publication is HMRC Brief 18/11 'Employment Benefit Trusts: Inheritance Tax and Income Tax issues', reproduced [2011] SWTI 1303 and another is HMRC's 'Employee Benefit Trusts: Settlement Opportunity Guidance August 2012'.

Previously, the Settlement Opportunity for EBTs was available, which essentially involved tax being paid on the basis that contributions to or 'earmarking' within pre-2011 EBTs involved the provision of taxable emoluments. However, this Settlement Opportunity was withdrawn from 31 March 2015. Despite this withdrawal, HMRC remain open to the settlement of historic tax liabilities in respect of EBTs, albeit on less favourable terms to the taxpayer (HMRC guidance entitled 'Employee Benefit Trust settlements after 31 July 2015', published online in August 2016).

INCOME TAX AND CGT

25.2 The test of trust residence is the same for an EBT as for any trust. Assuming one or all of the contributing employer or employers is resident or domiciled in the UK the EBT is only non-resident if all the trustees are non-resident (see CHAPTER 42). Care must be taken to avoid conduct which could be construed as creating a permanent establishment of the trustee in the UK (see para 42.13). Were a resident EBT to emigrate it would be deemed to dispose of its assets at market value for CGT purposes, just like any other trust (TCGA 1992, s 80; see para 30.8).

Assuming an EBT is non-resident, then, as with any non-resident trust, trust gains are generally free of CGT in the hands of the trustees and the liability of the trustees to income tax is restricted to UK source income. UK source income accruing to the trustees is fully subject to tax, for inherently the trust will have UK beneficiaries. As such, the conditions for relief under ITA 2007, s 811 are not met (see para 64.8). The rates are the trust rates.

Sections 720–730

25.3 A key issue with offshore EBTs is the extent to which anti-avoidance legislation applies. Logically the first code to consider is ITA 2007, ss 720–730 (for which see CHAPTER 69). This code, however, only applies if there is an individual transferor, and cannot therefore attribute EBT income to a corporate settlor. Normally this will be the end of the matter save in the unlikely event that the employer (and settlor of the EBT) is an individual or a partnership. But as described in para 69.50, a person can count as a transferor for the purposes of ss 720–730 if he has procured or been associated with the transfer and there is authority that a controlling shareholder or shareholders may be caught in this way (*Congreve v IRC* [1946] 2 All ER 170; *Fisher v Revenue and Customs Comrs* [2014] UK FTT 804 (TC), 17 ITLR 141). Accordingly, ss 720–730 issues could arise in relation to an offshore EBT settled by a company, if that company is controlled by one or perhaps a small group of shareholders.

But in such a case, reliance may be placed on two other features of the transfer of assets code. The first is that liability does not arise unless the transferor receives a capital sum or has power to enjoy. If therefore the controlling shareholders are totally excluded and do not benefit, any possible attack under the section is excluded. Second, ss 720–730 are subject to the motive test described in CHAPTER 73. If the EBT is set up for the commercial reason of motivating employees it ought, in logic, to be within the motive defence. However, the defence may in practice prove difficult to sustain as the EBT is offshore rather than onshore and, in many cases, is quite overtly designed to reward employees in a tax-efficient manner. A specific risk arises if a pre-existing EBT emigrates for tax reasons, for emigration is an associated operation (para 68.17).

HMRC concur both in the conclusion that the transferor charge is unlikely to be applicable where the EBT is a normal commercial arrangement to reward employees and in the view that those who control close companies could be transferors by virtue of having procured a transfer to the EBT by the company (Brief 18/11, para 5.1.1; August 2012 guidance, 3.6). They also point out that an employee who transfers the right to a bonus to the EBT would be the transferor in relation to that bonus.

Settlement code

25.4 The settlement code in ITTOIA 2005, Part 5, Chapter 5 inter alia deems the income of a settlement to be that of the settlor if he is an actual or a potential beneficiary (s 624) (see Chapter 75). The settlor includes any person by whom the settlement is made, whether directly or indirectly (s 620) but, in contrast to the CGT rules described in the next paragraph, there is no provision deeming participators in a corporate settlor to be settlors.

The settlement code does not apply to settlement income which originates from a company (ITTOIA 2005, s 627(4)). Income counts as originating from a company if it is generated by property which the company has directly or indirectly provided (ITTOIA 2005, s 645). The effect of this rule is that the settlement code could only be in point in relation to an EBT if the employer settlor is non-corporate.

But even here the settlement code is unlikely to be material, for the code is subject to a bounty test: for an arrangement to be a settlement and for a person to be settlor there must be some element of bounty. This qualification is not statutory but derives from case law and its precise ambit is unclear (see para **75.17**). HMRC said in *Tax Bulletin* 16 (April 1995 p 204) that a genuine commercial arrangement by a company to attract, retain and motivate good quality staff is protected by the bounty test. A similar position is taken in HMRC's August 2012 guidance (para **3.8**).

It is unclear how far this practice can be relied on where an EBT is used in aggressive tax planning. However if the employer's contributions are allowed as deductions in computing the taxable profit, they are unlikely to be bounteous, for deductibility inter alia requires the expenditure to have been incurred wholly and exclusively for the purposes of the trade. This, presumably, is the basis of HMRC practice as stated in *Tax Bulletin 16*. But if the wholly and exclusively test is not satisfied, the settlement code could be in point and in such cases there must be risk of HMRC invoking it where the employer is not corporate.

If the bounty defence is not or may not be in point, liability under the settlement code can be excluded in the same way as liability under ss 720–730, namely by excluding the employer and any other person who could possibly be described as a settlor. It is also necessary to ensure that such persons do not receive or make loans to the EBT so as to avoid liability under ITTOIA 2005, s 633 (see para **75.9**).

CGT – section 86

25.5 One anti-avoidance section requires consideration in relation to CGT, namely s 86. This attributes the gains of an offshore settlement to the settlor if he is UK resident and domiciled and he, his children, his grandchildren, or their respective spouses or any company controlled by any of them does or could possibly benefit. It is analysed in Chapter 76.

The term 'settlor' is defined in the same terms as in ITTOIA 2005, s 620 (see TCGA 1992, Sch 5, para 8) and for this reason the HMRC statement in *Tax*

Bulletin 16 is equally applicable. Insofar as the bounty defence is not in point, liability under s 86 may be avoided by completely excluding the settlor and all of the other persons listed above.

In that context, an interesting point is who the settlor is. Section 86 defines the settlor as any 'person' and thus on the face of it comprehends an employer company in an EBT context. It is expressly provided that CGT rules apply in determining what gains accrue to companies for the purposes of corporation tax (TCGA 1992, s 8(3)). However, TCGA 1992, Sch 5 contains rules deeming participators in corporate settlors to be settlors where the company is close (paras 7 and 8). Clearly gains cannot be assessed on both the company and the participators, so the inference is that in the case of a close company, the company is not the settlor.

INHERITANCE TAX

25.6 Assuming the EBT is (as is normally the case) a discretionary trust, it is prima facie within the relevant property regime and so subject to the regime of 10-yearly and exit charges (see CHAPTER 60). This result is avoided if the conditions of IHTA 1984, s 86 are met.

The conditions imposed by s 86 are discussed in a recently rewritten section of HMRC's Inheritance Tax Manual which is devoted to EBTs (IHTM42900 to IHTM42991).

Section 86

25.7 Section 86 is difficult to construe with certainty. But its main requirements are twofold:

(1)   The trusts on which the property is held must not allow the settled property to be applied for the benefit of persons who are neither employees nor their spouses, relations or dependants.
(2)   Assuming the beneficial class is defined by reference to employment with a particular body, it must comprise all or most of the employees of that body.

The first requirement does not mean that relief under s 86 is unavailable if there might be circumstances in which persons falling outside the category of employees, spouses, relations and dependants could benefit from the trust fund. The true requirement is that, under the current trusts, the only objects are persons falling within that category. The requirements of the section are not therefore breached if the trustees have power to alter the trusts and in such alteration make persons who are not employees or their dependents beneficiaries or potential beneficiaries (see *Postlethwaite's Executors v Revenue and Customs Comrs* [2007] STC (SCD) 83 at para 68). HMRC accept that a power of amendment or power of appointment which could be used to this effect does not prejudice s 86 relief (IHTM42922).

At one time there were indications that HMRC took the view that the requirement is breached if the trustees have power to pay tax or NICs which fall to be born by the employer. The prime example of such liabilities is the employer's NIC liability occasioned by the conferring of benefits out of the trust (see para **25.13**). This view of HMRC was controversial, and was not found in HMRC's August 2012 guidance (see especially para **4.12**). The IHT Manual comments that an ability for EBT trustees to settle tax or NIC liabilities out of the trust fund 'may' affect whether s 86 relief is applicable, but does not attempt to specify the circumstances in which this point would be taken (IHTM 42935).

At least until the enactment of ITEPA 2003, Part 7A in 2011, it was common for EBTs to appoint separate sub-trusts for each employee and his family. HMRC's view is that this takes the EBT, or rather each sub-trust, outside s 86, for the beneficiaries of any given sub-trust by definition do not comprise all or most of the employees of the employer concerned. This is so even if the sub-trusts are revocable, for, as indicated above, s 86 focuses on the current trusts, not on the trusts that might be appointed in the future (Brief 18/11, Part 3; August 2012 guidance, 4.7). As a matter of law, such a conclusion is supported by the decision of the Special Commissioner in *Postlethwaite's Executors v Revenue and Customs Comrs* [2007] STC (SCD) 83 at para 73.

As an alternative to appointing sub-trusts, the trustees of many EBTs simply 'earmarked' particular funds or assets for particular employees in the internal accounts of the trust. Such allocation does not cause s 86 protection to be lost, for, in law, the trusts of the EBT as a whole remain applicable to the funds so allocated.

Exit charge

25.8 A special form of exit charge arises if a settlement which has hitherto qualified under s 86 ceases to do so (IHTA 1984, s 72). Such would most obviously happen if new trusts outside s 86 were appointed or if events caused the 'all or most' test to be failed. Where such a charge falls to be made the amount charged is the value ceasing to be within s 86 (IHTA 1984, s 70(5) as incorporated by IHTA 1984, s 72(5)).

An exit charge is also levied if any of the following occurs:

(a)   the trustees make a distribution to a person who has provided any of the settled property;

(b)   the trustees make a distribution to any participator holding 5% or more of the shares or any class of shares in the employer company. This applies only where the provider of the settled property is a close company;

(c)   the trustees make a disposition (other than a distribution) as a result of which the value of the settled property is diminished.

The special charge is 0.25% per quarter for the first ten years during which the EBT satisfied the s 86 conditions, 0.20% per quarter for the next ten years, 0.15% per quarter for the next ten years and so on (IHTA 1984, ss 72(5) and 70(6)).

The special charge does not apply to a distribution if it is the income of the person for the purposes of UK income tax or would be such income if the recipient were UK resident (IHTA 1984, s 70(3)(b) as incorporated by s 72(5)). It cannot therefore apply to distributions taxed as employment income or under ITA 2007, ss 731–735. HMRC consider IHT is only precluded by ss 731–735 if a charge is made in the tax year when the benefit is conferred (August 2012 guidance, 4.18).

Should the property comprised in the EBT be excluded property, it is not per se relieved from the exit charge. Instead, in computing the charge any quarter throughout which the property was excluded is ignored (see para **62.26**). This means that if an EBT settled by a non-domiciliary holds UK situs property it cannot avoid the exit charge on such property by replacing it with foreign situs property shortly before the event triggering the exit charge. To be wholly protected from the exit charge it must have held foreign situs property at all times when it was within s 86.

Entry charge

25.9 Just as it is possible for a trust formerly within s 86 to fall out of the section, so too relevant property trusts can be brought within s 86. Should this happen an exit charge under the relevant property regime is made (IHTA 1984, s 65(1)(a); see para **60.8**). There is a relief from this charge, but this only applies where the trust holds more than half the shares in the employer company (IHTA 1984, s 75).

Trusts outside s 86

25.10 As indicated above, if an EBT does not satisfy the somewhat onerous conditions of s 86, it is subject to the relevant property regime. Tax charges under that regime are, in accordance with normal rules, displaced if business property relief applies or the settled property is excluded property. The latter requires the settlor to have neither an actual nor a deemed UK domicile (see CHAPTER 62). The IHT definition of 'settlor' is not restricted to individuals and nor is it purely confined to bounteous provision (IHTA 1984, s 44). A company is domiciled where it is registered (*Gasque v IRC* [1940] 23 TC 210), so where a foreign incorporated company is the settlor of the trust foreign situs trust property has excluded property status (August 2012 guidance, 4.17).

Interest in possession trusts

25.11 As section 86 operates as an exemption from the relevant property regime, it is irrelevant where the EBT is subject to a qualifying interest in possession. The position is the same if the EBT is subject to an interest in possession which is not qualifying – ie an interest created after 22 March 2006 which is not a transitional serial interest. This latter result follows because property subject to such an interest which would otherwise be within s 86, is nonetheless treated as relevant property (IHTA 1984, s 58(1A)). Both this rule, and that relating to qualifying interests in possession, are disregarded if the interest is less than 5% of the settled property.

CONFERRING BENEFIT

25.12 Until the enactment of ITEPA 2003, Part 7A, the key issue in taxing distributions or benefits was whether they were taxable as earnings in the general sense of the term (ITEPA 2003, s 62) or as benefits under the benefits in kind code (see CHAPTER 93). There were certainly some scenarios which escaped both kinds of charge, most notably distributions to family members after the employment had ceased or the employee had died. In such cases other legislation fell to be considered, for example the non-transferor charge under the transfer of assets code, but that charge was avoided if there was no relevant income or the recipient was non-resident (see further CHAPTER 70).

The enactment of Part 7A has changed all this. It remains the case that distributions which are earnings in the general sense of the term are taxable as such. But Part 7A now brings within the compass of employment income virtually all other kinds of distribution or benefit. In addition it taxes as employment income certain other kinds of transaction which are neither distributions nor benefits.

There has also been a further development of, potentially, great importance, in the form of the Court of Session judgment in the Glasgow Rangers case, *Advocate General for Scotland v Murray Group Holdings Ltd* [2015] CSIH 77, [2016] STC 468, 2015 Scot (D) 2/11. The Court of Session has held that, on the facts of the case, an employment income charge was triggered for beneficiaries of the EBT not when payments were made to them by the trustees, but at an earlier stage, when the employer made contributions to the trust. This view was reached on the basis that such contributions amounted to a receipt and then an immediate redirection of the employees' earnings. The apparently broad application of this decision raises a number of concerns that go beyond the historic use of EBTs. The liquidators of the Murray Group have been granted leave to appeal the decision to the Supreme Court and so it is hoped that further clarity will be brought to these issues when the Supreme Court makes its final ruling on the matter.

Except where otherwise indicated, the following discussion is premised on contributions to the EBT not having given rise to employment income tax charges. This may be the case where, on the facts of the case, the view cannot reasonably be reached that the contributions were earnings received by the employees and redirected into the EBT by the employees, or transferred to the EBT by the employer with the employees' consent.

Distributions taxed as earnings

25.13 The general rule is that a distribution from an EBT to an employee is taxed as earnings (*Brumby v Milner* [1976] STC 534). At one time a distribution after the employment had ceased escaped tax as earnings in the general sense of the term under the cessation of source rule (*Bray v Best* [1989] STC 159). But now this is no longer so, for post-cessation earnings are deemed to be earnings of the last year of the employment (ITEPA 2003, s 30(3)).

For PAYE purposes, the trustees are what are called intermediaries of the employer (ITEPA 2003, s 687(4)). This means any distribution which is taxable as earnings is within PAYE and that the employer is responsible for the

PAYE insofar as the trustees do not pay the tax (s 687(2)). The amount which is subject to PAYE is the amount of the distribution (s 687(3)). Any tax paid by the employer is itself treated as earnings unless reimbursed by the employee within 90 days (ITEPA 2003, s 222).

A double tax issue arises insofar as the trust income suffers UK or foreign tax. The law addressing this issue (ITA 2007, ss 496A and 496B) is not in point as that law is confined to resident trusts (s 496A(1)(b)). But during 2010, HMRC informed professional bodies that they apply ESC B18 (CIOT Technical Note 16 July 2009; for ESC B18, see para **8.11**). This means that in computing the tax on the employee, appropriate credit is allowed for tax at trust level.

Part 7A

25.14 If a distribution from an EBT is not taxed as earnings in the general sense of the term, it counts as employment income under Part 7A. This is so regardless of who the recipient is, whether or not the employment still subsists, and whether or not the employee is still alive. In general, the distribution is taxed as the employment income of the employee, but, if he is dead, it counts as that of the recipient provided the recipient is UK resident (see para **94.20**). As with distributions which are earnings in the general sense of the term, the employer is liable under the PAYE system for the tax unless the EBT pays. The amount subject to PAYE is the amount of the distribution and the tax paid by the employer is itself treated as earnings unless the employee reimburses it within 90 days.

Part 7A also catches the transfer or use of assets in specie. Where the EBT transfers an asset to an employee or another beneficiary in specie, the value of the asset or, if greater, its cost counts as employment income (see para **94.10**). The same result can follow if the employee or another person simply benefits from the asset (see para **94.15**). Should such benefit subsist or be created more than two years after the employment has ended, the mere fact of benefit causes the asset to be taxed as if transferred to the person enjoying it. But this result does not follow during the employment and within the two years following it unless the use the trustees allow gives the same benefit as absolute ownership.

As will be apparent from the above, the effect of Part 7A is that the EBT cannot confer benefit, whether on the employee personally or on his family, without generating an employment income charge. As indicated above, this is so even if the recipient is non-resident. The one qualification to this extra territoriality is if the employee was non-resident during part of the employment. In such case, the proportion of the benefit or payment attributable to the non-resident period drops out of charge, save insofar as during that period the employee was performing duties in the UK (see para **94.25**).

Loans and earmarking

25.15 The real sting of Part 7A is that it can generate an employment income charge even if no distribution is made and no benefit conferred. The two principal scenarios where this occurs are loans and what is termed 'earmarking'.

Prior to the enactment of Part 7A, a genuine loan from an EBT to an employee was taxed only to the extent that no interest was charged or the interest was less than the official rate (ITEPA 2003, Pt 3 Ch 7; see para **93.16**). The position was of course otherwise if the 'loan' was, in reality, a distribution and the loan documentation was mere window-dressing (in other words, if the supposed 'loan' was a sham, and the arrangement was not intended by the parties to create a debtor-creditor relationship). This somewhat obvious point was confirmed by the First-tier Tribunal decision in the Glasgow Rangers case, *Murray Group Holdings Ltd v HMRC* ([2012] UKFTT 692 (TC), affirmed on appeal to the Upper Tribunal, [2014] UKUT 0292 (TCC)).

However, the question of whether a loan from an EBT is genuine is now academic, as loans from EBTs are caught by Part 7A. As explained in para **94.12**, a loan (however genuine) is taxed as an outright transfer of the money or other asset lent. This is so whether or not the loan carries interest and regardless of its term. Further, the charge is not reversed if the loan is repaid; the only relief available is that the distribution charge is not made if and when the loan is written off.

There can be a very similar result under Part 7A if there is 'earmarking'. The 'earmarking' charge is described in para **94.16**. In broad terms, it applies both where sub-funds are formally appointed and where assets are allocated to a particular employee without formal appointment. As is explained in para **94.17**, the scope of the 'earmarking' concept is not wholly clear. But if the charge is in point the result is draconian, for the full amount appointed or allocated counts as employment income of the employee, regardless of the fact that at that stage neither he nor anyone else may have received a distribution.

Other tax charges

25.16 As indicated above, prior to the enactment of Part 7A some distributions or benefits potentially fell outside employment income tax and thus fell to be taxed either as income distributions or as benefits under ITA 2007, ss 731–735 (see CHAPTER 70). It is now difficult to envisage scenarios where distributions or benefits fall outside Part 7A and, if so, these other heads of tax are no longer relevant. In particular ss 731–735 only apply if the benefit is not otherwise subject to income tax, and Part 7A itself gives relief where a subsequent event would otherwise give rise to a liability for income tax (ITEPA 2003, s 554Z13; see para **94.23**).

Another head of charge to consider on such distributions is liability to CGT under TCGA 1992, s 87 or Sch 4C (see CHAPTERS 70 and 77). However, that legislation only applies if the EBT is a settlement in the sense that that term is used in ITTOIA 2005, s 620 and so the section is not in point if the bounty defence referred to in para **25.4** above is available. If defence is not available, supplemental tax could mean a tax rate as high as 44.8% (see para **77.48**). ITEPA Part 7A makes no reference to future CGT charges being obviated where Part 7A has previously applied, confirmation perhaps that s 87 is not generally seen as being in point in relation to EBTs.

PAYMENTS INTO THE EBT

25.17 The rules and issues which apply in creating and funding an offshore EBT are the same as where it is onshore.

Liability of employees

25.18 The traditional view is that employees do not receive taxable earnings when payments are made into the EBT for, so long as the trust is truly discretionary, no employee has any vested right to them (*Edwards v Roberts* (1935) 19 TC 618). This point was implicit in *Macdonald v Dextra Accessories Ltd* and was affirmed by Special Commissioners in *Sempra Metals Ltd v HMRC* [2008] STC (SCD) 1062.

In *Edwards v Roberts* HMRC adduced a purposive construction to argue that a contribution became an employee's earnings when and insofar as allocated to him. In practice the money was then available to him in that he could then request a loan or distribution, or request that the money be applied in the purchase of an investment of his choice. The Special Commissioners rejected this argument on the grounds that earnings only arise when money or its equivalent is unreservedly at the disposal of the employee. With a discretionary trust this condition is not met, as in law the final decision on any use of the money rests with the trustee.

However, the Court of Session in *Advocate General for Scotland v Murray Group Holdings Ltd* has taken a radically different view. The Court has ruled that the fact that a trust operates in truly discretionary manner is immaterial in determining whether taxable earnings arise in relation to payments made to an EBT. The critical points are determining whether the payments into trust are derived from the employment (and therefore amount to emoluments or earnings from the employment) and whether such payments constitute a redirection of such earnings.

In the case in question, the Court of Session found that payments by the employer to the EBT were derived from employment of the footballers and other members of staff and were therefore emoluments or earnings, and it appears (it is never made explicit in the Court's decision) that because the payments were made into an EBT at the request of, or at least with the acquiescence of, the employees, this was sufficient to amount to a redirection of earnings. The employment tax charge therefore arose at the point of the payment by the employer into the EBT. Anything that took place afterwards was viewed by the Court as irrelevant. As noted above, the apparent breadth of application of the Court's argument raises issues that go beyond the historic use of EBTs into more topical matters such as the taxation of bonus sacrifice and salary sacrifice arrangements. The liquidators of the Murray Group have been granted leave to appeal this decision to the Supreme Court so it is hoped that a future decision will bring more clarity in this area.

Part 7A of ITEPA 2003 does, not as such, affect the taxability of contributions to EBTs. However the 'earmarking' charge is in point if the contribution is to a specific sub-fund or if, following contribution, the trustees appropriate funds to a sub-fund or otherwise allocate funds to an employee. In this indirect manner, Part 7A can thus cause contributions to suffer an employment income tax charge when made.

Deductibility

25.19 To be deductible, a contribution to an EBT has to satisfy both the general rules as to deductibility and also the specific rules originally enacted in FA 2003, Sch 24 and now consolidated as CTA 2009, ss 1290–1297. The employer must not be under an obligation to make payments to the EBT, for then the payments would be taxable as income in the hands of the EBT.

A series of cases has established that under general rules a contribution to an EBT is deductible in the trading computation of the employer provided that the contribution is revenue in nature and made wholly and exclusively for the purposes of the employer's trade (see for example *Heather v P-E Consulting Group Ltd* [1973] 1 All ER 8; *Jeffs v Ringtons Ltd* [1985] STC 809; *Mawsley Machinery Ltd v Robinson* [1998] STC (SCD) 236; *JT Dove Ltd v Revenue and Customs Comrs* [2010] UKFTT 16 (TC), [2011] SFTD 348, [2011] SWTI 1448).

The 'wholly and exclusively' test requires an investigation of why the contributions to the EBT are made. One context in which the test is likely to be satisfied is if the payments are intended to preserve and maintain the competitiveness of the employer in a market where discretionary bonuses are normal and the payment to the EBT is, on the facts, in lieu of such bonuses (*Sempra Metals Ltd v HMRC* [2008] STC (SCD) 1062).

CTA 2009, s 1290 operates where a deduction would otherwise be allowed under the general rules just described. It prevents the employer from taking the deduction unless within nine months of the end of the accounting period the money is used by the trustees to meet qualifying expenses or provide qualifying benefits. Insofar as a deduction cannot be taken for the accounting period in which the money is paid to the EBT, it may be taken in a subsequent period insofar as qualifying benefits are then provided out of it. To the extent that such benefits are never provided a deduction is never available. Section 1290 is thus both a timing provision and a provision which in some cases wholly denies relief.

Qualifying expenses are trustee expenses which would be deductible if incurred by the employee (CTA 2009, s 1296(1)). There are two kinds of qualifying benefit. The first is an actual payment or transfer which gives rise to both employment income tax and a NIC charge (CTA 2009, s 1292(1)). The second is the taking of a relevant step within ITEPA 2003, Part 7A which results in a tax charge under the rules described above (CTA 2009, s 1292(6A)). As explained above and in CHAPTER 94, the term relevant step inter alia includes the making of a loan or engagement of the earmarking charge.

Section 1290 was enacted in response to schemes such as that in *MacDonald v Dextra Accessories Ltd*. The decision of the House of Lords that the former legislation (FA 1989, s 43) had broadly similar effect is not therefore of ongoing relevance. Section 1290 applies both where the employees are beneficiaries of the EBT and where the beneficial class comprises only their dependants (*Sempra Metals Ltd v HMRC* [2008] STC (SCD) 1062).

Section 1290 applies to corporate employers, the equivalent income tax provisions being ITTOIA 2005, ss 38–44.

IHT

25.20 IHT is relevant in relation to a contribution to an EBT by an employer, if that employer is non-corporate or is a close company (whether or not UK resident). In the latter case, the employer is not in itself subject to IHT, but any value transferred is, in principle, attributed to the participators (IHTA 1984, s 94). The company has secondary liability if the participators fail to pay any IHT due (IHTA 1984, s 202).

In accordance with normal excluded property rules, IHT is not charged if the contributing employer is non-corporate, the employer has neither an actual nor a deemed UK domicile, and the cash or other assets contributed to the EBT are situated outside the UK. And in the case of a closely held corporate employer held by an individual, any value transferred is left out of account if the assets settled are foreign situs and the participator has neither an actual nor a deemed UK domicile (IHTA 1984, s 94(2)(b)). In the event that the contributing employer is a close company held by the trustees of a discretionary trust, protection of the contribution from IHT by virtue of the excluded property concept depends on the trust having been established by a non-UK domiciliary and on the shares in the employing company being foreign situs (IHTA 1984, ss 99(2)(b) and 65(2)(a)).

Where excluded property protection is not available, it may be argued that, provided that the 'wholly and exclusively' test for deductibility is met, payments to the EBT do not amount to a transfer of value at all. The net estate of the employer is not diminished because it is merely providing what it needs to provide to motivate staff. This is particularly so where, on the facts, the payments to the EBT are in lieu of bonus and no greater than the bonus would have been. Indeed on one view tax-efficient remuneration arrangements enhance an employer's net worth, as they increase the value of the employer's business.

In this context, reference may be made to IHTA 1984, s 10, which broadly prevents a disposition from being a transfer of value if it is made without any gratuitous intent. For s 10 to apply, it has to be shown that the parties to the transaction were unconnected or, if not, that the transaction is such as would be made between unconnected parties. In *Postlethwaite's Executors v Revenue and Customs Comrs* [2007] STC (SCD) 83, the Special Commissioners held that this relief was applicable to a substantial payment to an offshore unapproved retirements benefit scheme. HMRC had conceded that the trustee of the scheme was not connected with the employer. The Special Commissioners considered that on the facts the sum could have been paid to the employee as bonus and that such would certainly not have been gratuitous as the employee had given past consideration by his work. The fact that the payment was to the FURBS did not affect the position.

HMRC, however, consider that s 10 rarely protects a transfer of funds to an EBT (Brief 18/11 para 1.3.1.2; IHTM42957). The basis of their view is that a transaction is not protected by s 10 if there is any intention to confer gratuitous benefit. The possibility of even the slightest gratuitous benefit thus infringes s 10. As an EBT is by definition discretionary, with unfettered discretion reserved to the trustees, there is at least some possibility of benefit to those who are not employees, for example their spouses or children.

It may well be that this analysis is right as regards the majority of EBTs, *Postlethwaite* being confined to its own rather peculiar facts. But the real issue, it may be suggested, is not the applicability or otherwise of s 10 but whether payments to the EBT are transfers of value at all. For the reasons given above, there are strong arguments that they are not.

Assuming a payment to an EBT is a transfer of value, business property relief may be in point. *Re Nelson Dance Family Settlement* [2009] STC 802 established that a transfer of value attributable to the gift of a business asset is eligible for business property relief. The judge also indicated that a close company transfer apportioned under IHTA 1984, s 94 would attract relief if the taxpayer's shares were otherwise eligible for relief (ibid at para 28). HMRC accept that s 94 transfers can attract relief, albeit focusing on the company's gift (Brief 18/2011, para 1.4). It follows that the IHT entry charge may be avoided provided the conditions for business property relief are otherwise met.

Until recently the relief normally relied on to preclude IHT was IHTA 1984, s 12. This prevents a disposition from being a transfer of value if it is allowable in computing the disponor's trading profits. However HMRC's view is that s 12 does not apply unless CTA 2009, s 1290 allows the deduction to be taken in the tax year in which the contribution to the EBT is made (Brief 18/11 para 1.3.2.1).

The problem posed by ss 12 and 1290 is that the former was not amended when the latter was first enacted as FA 2003, Sch 24. As a result it is quite unclear, as a matter of strict construction, whether the delay required by s 1290 means that the contribution is allowable or non-allowable for the purpose of s 12. But since s 1290 contemplates that at some stage the contribution will be allowed, the better view is that s 12 should apply, particularly as it makes no provision for cases where the conditions of s 1290 are later satisfied. For this reason HMRC's view may, if the matter is litigated, be open to challenge.

The final relief to refer to is IHTA 1984, s 13. This is a specific relief for disposals by close companies to EBTs and requires the EBT to satisfy the conditions of s 86. In addition the beneficiaries must not include 5% participators in the employer company or persons connected with them. However this restriction is not in point if any benefit which could be conferred on such a person would be taxable as his income (or would be so taxable if he were UK resident). This greatly diminishes the force of this restriction and certainly allows some trusts to qualify which would not otherwise do so (see for example *Postlethwaite's Executors v Revenue and Customs Comrs* [2007] STC (SCD) 83 at para 67).

CONCLUSION

25.21 Until the announcement of what became ITEPA 2003, Part 7A in late 2010, offshore EBTs were widely used in aggressive tax planning. In such scenarios, contributions tended to be earmarked for specific employees and their dependants at the outset, and invested in accordance with their wishes. Often the trustees gave the employee use of the money by making loans to him. The benefit in kind charge on interest-free loans (see paras **93.16** to **93.20**) tended to mean such loans were at interest, but there was a widespread perception that such interest, or the benefit-in-kind charge, was much more tax-efficient than actual remuneration taxed in full up-front.

How tax-efficient such EBTs were in the long term may be debated, particularly given that contributions were non-deductible. Over time the cumulative annual cost of interest, or tax on an interest-free loan, can come to equal the tax payable had the sums lent been taken as remuneration in the first place and the problem of securing tax-free distribution of the capital still remains. But whatever view is taken of these issues, Part 7A has effectively ended such strategies, for, as described above, it imposes an up-front tax charge on the amount lent or earmarked. And, if it is upheld by the Supreme Court, the Court of Session's judgment in *Advocate General for Scotland v Murray Group Holdings Ltd* will, at least in some cases, accelerate employment income tax charges yet further, causing such charges to be treated as occurring when employer contributions are made to the EBT.

In these circumstances, it may legitimately be asked whether offshore EBTs created now have any remaining value for tax planning. In answering this, three points may be made.

The first is that an offshore EBT is in general more attractive than its onshore equivalent. This is because, as described above, the offshore EBT is generally outside the charge to CGT and is not taxed on foreign income. A further point which may be made about foreign income is that it is outside the earmarking charge, even if the funds generating the income are earmarked (see para **94.19**).

The second point is that the symmetry between the earmarking charge under Part 7A and the corporation tax deduction means that an EBT is a tax-efficient means of settling money into trust. It is true that an employment income charge is suffered up-front, but what can often be avoided is the IHT entry charge which would arise if the employee took the money as remuneration and in due course created the settlement himself. Further, and in contrast to settlements he creates, the employee and his spouse can normally be beneficiaries without causing the income and gains to be taxed as his (see paras **25.3** to **25.5** above). In appropriate cases these can be valuable advantages to high-earning employees who would otherwise have surplus income. It is true that, as a result of Part 7A, all distributions and benefits in excess of the value earmarked are likely to suffer a charge to income tax and NIC and that to some extent what is so taxed as income may reflect capital appreciation. But in the case of funds intended for long-term accumulation these drawbacks may be acceptable, albeit, in contrast to a private family trust, not ones avoidable by emigration (see para **94.25**).

A third point is that many EBTs are not set up for aggressive tax planning but as genuine discretionary vehicles to reward deserving employees (or their families) or to hold shares in the employer company. In such cases, tax on distributions has always been accepted, and trusts of this kind are little affected by Part 7A. It remains to be seen whether the view advanced by the Court of Session in *Advocate General for Scotland v Murray Group Holdings Ltd*, discussed above, will affect such trusts. This may be fact-sensitive and vary from case to case.

A final, countervailing, point which must be stressed is that the tax implications of offshore EBTs can be hugely complex. It is not just a matter of employment income taxes, but also IHT and the other taxes material to trusts highlighted in this chapter. Too often in the past insufficient attention was paid to these.

Section VI

UK Real Estate

Chapter 26

INVESTMENT IN REAL ESTATE BY OFFSHORE COMPANIES

INTRODUCTION

26.1 This chapter considers the tax issues which arise when an offshore company acquires UK real estate for investment or development. A significant amount of real estate in the UK is owned by companies registered and managed in low tax jurisdictions and the tax issues which arise are of some complexity. Many such companies are owned by individuals or trusts who otherwise have no UK connection, but in other cases the ultimate owner of the company is a UK resident individual or a trust whose settlor and/or beneficiaries include UK residents.

The real estate may be commercial or residential and can be a pure investment or may be held for development or otherwise as trading stock. The assumption made here is that if residential property is being acquired, this will be for the purpose of letting it on commercial terms to third parties, redeveloping and then selling it, or for some other form of commercial exploitation. The chapter does not, therefore, address the treatment of residential property acquired for use by the owner of the company, or, in the case of trust ownership, by beneficiaries. The tax issues raised by such properties are considered in CHAPTERS 28 and 27.

This chapter focuses on direct taxes and does not cover VAT or SDLT planning. The VAT and SDLT issues which arise are largely the same as where there is no element of offshore ownership. SDLT is now extremely difficult to avoid and thus must normally be factored into any purchase. The various applicable rates are set out in CHAPTER 67.

INHERITANCE TAX

26.2 At the time of writing IHT is not an issue where UK real estate is held by an offshore company as, for IHT purposes, the relevant asset is not the property but the shares in the company which owns it. Those shares have a non-UK situs provided that they are registered and the share register is, as is invariably the case, kept outside the UK (see para 38.7). As such they are excluded property (IHTA 1984, ss 6(1) and 48(3)).

Proposed changes

26.3 As from 6 April 2017 this freedom from IHT is going to change insofar as the UK real estate is residential. On 8 July 2015 the government announced its intention to withdraw excluded property status from shares in close companies insofar as the value of those shares is derived from UK residential property (HMRC Technical Note, 8 July 2015, reproduced [2015] SWTI 2344). This intention was confirmed in a consultative document issued on 19 August 2016, which also indicated that the definition of residential property is likely to be the same as that applicable to non-resident CGT (as to which see CHAPTER 65). The August 2016 document made it clear that the removal of excluded property status will apply on all occasions on which IHT could be charged, including, for example, 10-yearly charges on trusts (see CHAPTERS 60 and 63) and charges under the gift with reservation rules (see CHAPTER 83).

The practical result is that the residential portfolio of an offshore company will no longer be protected from IHT. A point to stress is that this will be so even if the owner of the company is non-UK resident and otherwise has no connection with the UK. The proposed changes in 2017 were announced as part of a package affecting resident non-domiciliaries, but they apply equally to non-residents.

The 2017 changes will not apply to all kinds of property. They do not affect real estate that falls outside the NR CGT definition of residential property, so offshore companies owning portfolios of commercial property are unaffected. So too the August 2016 document confirmed it will only be shares in close companies which will lose their excluded property status.

At the time of writing, an unresolved issue is whether the loss of excluded property status will apply only to investment companies or whether it will extend to companies that deal in or develop residential property. What is clear is that it will be possible for shares to move in and out of excluded property status, for the August 2016 document confirmed that excluded property status will be restored once two years have elapsed from when the company disposed of its residential property.

Other IHT issues

26.4 There are two other IHT points to keep in mind as respects offshore companies. Both arise under the current law, but neither is of anything other than limited application.

The first point arises where a non-resident close company makes a gratuitous disposition of the UK real estate. In such case any resultant transfer of value is apportioned among the participators, or among the indirect participators where the company is owned by intermediate holding companies (IHTA 1984, ss 94–102). Under current law, this is normally of no consequence where the ultimate owner is a trust, for with trusts tax is charged as if the trust had made a disposition of the shares which, by definition, are excluded property unless the settlor was domiciled or deemed domiciled in the UK (see para 62.2). But

should the participator be an individual, tax can result, for apportionment is precluded only where the underlying asset, ie the asset subject to the gratuitous disposition, is non-UK situs (IHTA 1984, s 94(2)(b)). In that case the transfer of value which is apportioned to the individual participator is immediately chargeable. The apportioned transfer of value is not potentially exempt, even if the company's transfer was to one or more individuals (IHTA 1984, s 3A(6)).

The second point arises where individual or trustee shareholders capitalise the company by debt. Here the debt must either be held in another offshore company or care needs to be taken to ensure the debt does not have UK situs. In the case of a debt not governed by a specialty, the borrowing company must be resident outside the UK for the purposes of suit. If the debt is governed by a specialty, the specialty instrument must be kept outside the UK. In both cases it is unwise to secure the debt on the UK real estate, for such security is likely make the debt UK situs. These various issues are discussed further in para **38.4**.

It is not entirely clear how debt will be dealt with under the proposed 2017 changes. A particular issue is whether those changes will catch debt owed by close companies owning UK residential properties or shares in close companies owning such debt. The August 2016 consultative document indicates that debt owed by the property owning company to a connected party will be disallowed.

COMPANY RESIDENCE

26.5 A fundamental point which must not be overlooked is the residence of the company owning the real estate. Care should be taken to ensure that the company does not become UK resident under the central management and control test, for if it does, it will be exposed to UK corporation tax. The concept of central management and control is explained in CHAPTER **43**, and risk should be avoided provided that the company's board genuinely manages the company and conducts regular and properly minuted meetings in the offshore jurisdiction where the company is based.

Central management and control needs to be watched with particular care with UK real estate, for of its nature UK real estate entails activity in the UK. The biggest risk area is where the owner of the company, or beneficiaries of a trust which owns the company, are based in the UK and involve themselves in the management of the real estate. In such cases it is important to be able to demonstrate that the board of the company exercises independent judgement when considering suggestions made by the individual owner or by beneficiaries, and that all decisions are made outside the UK. One way of doing this is to put in place a property management agreement between the owning company and the UK-resident individual(s) or a UK company they own.

TRADING

26.6 A key issue in any tax analysis of UK real estate is whether any profit on a sale of the property is subject to corporation tax as the profit of a trade carried on in the UK. Here the company is within the charge to corporation tax if it carries on a trade of dealing in or developing UK land (CTA 2009, s 5(2)(a)). The term 'dealing in or developing UK Land' is defined as dealing in UK land or developing UK land for the purpose of disposing of it (CTA 2009, s 5B(2)). The term 'UK land' comprehends both bare land and buildings and structures. It also includes estates, rights or interests over the land (CTA 2009, s 5B(3)).

These express definitions were enacted by FA 2016, s 76 and supersede, in relation to non-residents, the old common law tests as to whether activities involving UK land are trading. More importantly, the trade of dealing in UK land is treated as carried on in the UK even if under the common law tests described in para **40.7** it would not be treated. Profits of the trade are subject to corporation tax regardless of whether or not the company has a UK permanent establishment.

Position in practice

26.7 In determining whether a non-resident company's activities amount to trading in UK land, its intention at the time of acquisition is plainly fundamental, as was the position prior to 2016. This conclusion follows because the term 'dealing' must connote an intention to deal and, in the case of development, the legislation expressly specifies that disposing of the land must be the purpose of the development.

It follows that the board of a non-resident company acquiring real estate should be clear as to whether it intends short-term profit or long-term investment. Development and obtaining an advantageous planning consent do not per se point to short-term profit: they do not do so if the intention is to retain and let the property once developed. In practical terms what is important is to ensure that what the board intends is properly documented and that the facts and circumstances are consistent with it. Thus if investment is the intention, the company's objects should be those of an investment company and board consideration should be on the basis of investment. Perhaps most importantly, the financing structure should be consistent with long-term retention rather than being of only short duration such as would require rapid sale to effect repayment.

Double Tax Treaties

26.8 In certain instances, a double tax treaty may operate to eliminate the corporation tax charge. A treaty requires consideration should the offshore company be tax resident in a country or territory with which the UK has concluded a double tax treaty.

Most treaties to which the UK is a party follow the OECD model and give the UK taxing rights over income from UK land and gains generated by alienating the land. But should the offshore company be an enterprise of the treaty partner, the business profits article comes into play. This gives the treaty partner sole taxing rights over the profits of the enterprise save insofar as the business in the UK is carried on through a permanent establishment. If it is so carried on, the UK has taxing rights. The applicable definition of permanent establishment varies from treaty to treaty, but the core definition comprises fixed places of business and dependent agents. Construction sites of a certain duration, normally 6 or 12 months, are also included.

It follows that use of an offshore company in a treaty jurisdiction can be advantageous. But a number of hurdles have to be overcome if this advantage is to be secured and in the majority of cases these hurdles make the advantages theoretical rather than real.

First, it must be clear that the offshore company is an enterprise of the contracting state within the meaning of the applicable treaty, and that the gain on the alienation of the UK land is captured by the business profits article rather than the articles dealing with income and gains from land. These are matters of interpretation of the relevant treaty.

Second, and most important a UK permanent establishment must be avoided. This may be difficult to achieve given that the land is in the UK and decision-making by duly authorised persons may be required on the spot. Such decision-making may result in a dependent agent permanent establishment. In the case of development projects the difficulties are compounded by the inclusion of building sites and construction projects in the definition of permanent establishment. If therefore an offshore company carrying out a development project can be said to be carrying on its business through the building site or construction project, it inevitably has a fixed place of business and thus a permanent establishment in the UK if the project is of the requisite length.

As a matter of plain language a development company carries on its business through its building sites or construction projects and so has a permanent establishment. Against this it may be objected that the reference to building sites and construction projects is directed at contractors rather than site owners. The basis of such arguments are that in the commentary on Article 5 of the OECD model treaty the whole emphasis is on contractors rather than site owners. However it is nowhere explicitly stated in the commentary that site owners are not included and, in Article 5, the reference to building sites and construction projects is not part of the definition of fixed place of business but instead an exclusion where the site or project is of insufficient duration. In all the circumstances, it is difficult to regard the model treaty as displacing the prima facie conclusion that owners of building sites or construction projects do have a permanent establishment.

A third difficulty in relying on treaties is that the treaty partner is likely itself to tax the trading profit, often at rates more severe than UK corporation tax. In the past the Crown Dependency treaties were often used to shelter dealing profits as the Crown Dependencies did not themselves tax the profit. But if strategies of this sort ever worked they no longer do so now, for the treaties with the Crown Dependencies have been amended to preserve the UK's taxing rights (see para 90.6). However some treaty jurisdictions are still considered to offer planning opportunities, for example Cyprus.

The final difficulty is that the changes made in 2016 include a targeted anti-avoidance rule or TAAR (CTA 2009, s 5A). This nullifies arrangements designed to secure a tax advantage and requires the removal of treaty benefits if the advantage is contrary to the object and purposes of the relevant treaty provisions. As discussed in para **90.4**, it is unclear whether and if so to what extent this provision goes beyond purposive interpretation of the treaty. But at the very least it requires serious consideration if the offshore company has little real connection with the chosen treaty jurisdiction.

Should the treaty be relied on an issue which may also arise is whether diverted profits tax could ever come into issue (see CHAPTER **92**). It may be suggested it cannot, for the avoided PE charge only comes into issue if the structure is designed to ensure the overseas company does not carry on its trade in the UK. As a result of the 2016 changes, the company will ipso facto be trading in the UK, albeit the profits are sheltered by the treaty if the treaty planning is effective.

ANTI-AVOIDANCE LEGISLATION AND TRADING PROFITS

26.9 There are certain circumstances in which UK anti-avoidance legislation can treat any trading profit realised by the non-resident company as the income of an individual or a trust. There are two relevant anti-avoidance codes, namely the transfer of assets code and the code dealing with transactions in land.

The transfer of assets code

26.10 The transfer of assets code needs to be addressed if the owner of the offshore company is a UK resident individual or individuals, or if the company is owned by a settlor-interested offshore trust whose settlor is such an individual. In either case, the transfer of assets code operates to treat any trading profit as income of the individual(s) concerned.

Until 2008 there was a very good argument that if the company was resident in a treaty jurisdiction, the treaty precluded a transfer of assets charge on a UK resident transferor (*Bricom Holdings Ltd v IRC* [1997] STC 1179, 70 TC 272; see further para **104.9**). But since then two developments, discussed in para **104.9**, have undermined this argument.

The first is TIOPA 2010, s 130, which precludes the business profits article in a double tax treaty from preventing the income of a UK resident from being charged to income tax. The second is the linguistic changes made to the transfer of assets code in 2013, which were intended by HMRC to tax the transferor on a notional sum rather than on the actual income of the person abroad. Although both developments raise difficult technical issues the conclusion reached in para **104.9** is that they stop treaties from preventing the application of the transfer of assets code.

Where there may be more scope for arguing the code is disapplied is under European law (see paras **107.7** to **107.12**), and the incorporation of that law into the transfer of assets code in ITA 2007, s 742A (see CHAPTER **74**). If the owning company is genuinely established and carrying on business in an EU jurisdiction, the fundamental freedoms may well preclude the transferor charge and the same would follow as a matter of domestic law under s 742A providing the property owning company was set up after 6 April 2012. It is also possible to run similar arguments in relation to companies set up outside the EU, but here there are many more defences against the application of EU law and, at least where the company is in a nil tax jurisdiction, it is difficult to see one or other of them as not prevailing.

Should the transferor be a remittance basis user, the issue arises of whether any profit attributed to him under the transfer of assets code has a UK or a foreign source. It may be suggested the rules introduced in 2016 subjecting the company's profit to corporation tax regardless of where the trade is carried on do not alter the location of the source of the trading profits for other purposes. On this basis, the common law applies in locating the source of the profit attributed to the transferor. But that common law is unlikely to result in a non-UK source for there is persuasive authority to the effect that any dealing or development trade is carried on where the real estate is located. Thus in *IRC v HK-TVB International Ltd* [1992] STC 723, Lord Jauncey said (at p 729):

> 'profits arising to a resident taxpayer from the sale of foreign immovable property are likely to arise in the country where that property is situated, although both the contracts of purchase and sale thereof are made in the country of residence of the taxpayer.'

Transactions in land

26.11 The code directed at transactions in land is explained in Chapter 90. It was recast in 2016 and imposes a corporation tax charge on companies which acquire or develop UK land with a view to realising a profit on its disposal. It applies the same computational rules as apply to actual trading and so on the face of it adds little or nothing to the tax exposure of offshore property traders described above.

In reality however there are two points to watch. The first is the provider charge which operates where a third party provides the value or opportunity to the company that enables it to realise the profit or gain. In such a case the profit or gain is charged on the provider rather than the company. As explained in para **90.11**, this provision was in the pre-2016 legislation and it has never been clear how far it goes and in particular whether it could catch an introducer as distinct from someone who himself sells the land to the company. Nor, under the present legislation, is it clear how the charge operates where the provider is non-corporate and the gain is realised by a company. But at the very least this is a risk area and attention is needed to minimise the risk of an individual falling into the provider charge for were this to happen the result would be tax at the much higher income tax rates.

The second point is that the code can apply if the shares in the company are disposed of rather than the land itself. This risk is explained in para 90.10, and here too the result is the substitution of much higher income tax rates if the selling owner is an individual or a trust. This risk has to be considered should the share disposal occur when over half the company's value is represented by UK real estate. However the charge is only made if a scheme or arrangement is in place and one of the main purposes of that scheme is to realise a profit on the disposal of the shares. This provision principally counters developers who develop multiple residential units and sell the units in corporate envelopes and so should not be a concern to a conventional offshore property trading company. But as ever it should be watched should the owning company be sold.

Should either the provider charge or the share sale charge be in point the ensuing profit is treated as trading in the UK land and so taxable regardless of where the provider resides or the share sale takes place.

An interesting issue is how far any applicable tax treaty can prevent the various charges under the code. In principle a treaty should operate to preclude the charge on the offshore company itself, assuming the applicable conditions for treaty relief are otherwise met. But this is subject to the targeted anti-avoidance rule, discussed above, disapplying treaty relief where relief would be contrary to the object and purposes of the treaty.

The interaction of the provider charge with treaties is more complex. The targeted anti-avoidance rule is certainly in point and so also is TIOPA 2010, s 130 discussed above in relation to the transfer of assets code. It may be suggested s 130 precludes treaty relief if the provider is UK resident and the treaty provision being relied on is the business profits article.

Should the charge under the 2016 legislation be on a share disposal, the business profits article is unlikely to be in point, as the enterprise of the treaty state is carried on by the company, not the owner of its shares. The applicable treaty article is likely to be that dealing with capital gains. In many instances this will give sole taxing rights to the country of the alienator of the shares and if so treaty protection will apply. But here too this is subject to the TAAR.

USE OF A UK COMPANY

26.12 Given all the difficulties, and the certainty of the trading profit being exposed to UK tax in any event, the question may be asked of whether the offshore company should refrain from acquiring the UK property itself, but instead incorporate a UK subsidiary to do so and conduct the trading venture. In many cases, a UK subsidiary represents a better solution, particularly where the underlying owner is UK resident or where beneficiaries of the underlying trust are UK resident. In such a case they may want a hands-on role in relation to the property venture, and such is more readily accommodated with a UK company where they may be board members. Further if a UK company is used, its profits are not caught by the transfer of assets code. It is true that a profit realised by a UK company could attract a provider charge and that a disposal of its shares could be taxed under the share disposal rules described in the previous paragraph. But these risks are inherently less if a UK company is used, if only because subjectively it is less indicative of tax avoidance.

Should a UK company be used, thought does have to be given to the eventual extraction of any profit. A dividend would be caught by the transfer of assets code where the conditions for the code are otherwise met. But even this result is avoided if the profits are retained in the company and in due course the company is sold. On such a scenario a charge under the share disposal rules is avoided provided all the land has been sold or, at the very least, more than half the land has been sold. Thought does have to be given to the transactions in securities code but this is avoided if the buyer is unconnected (see para **89.27**).

An alternative scenario is liquidation of the UK company. Here the transactions in securities legislation is not precluded and consideration needs to be given as to whether HMRC would be entitled to serve a counteraction notice. It is also necessary to consider whether the rules directed at phoenix transactions could be in point (see para **89.19**) albeit these apply only where the shareholder is an individual. It may be suggested the risk is low provided the liquidation is occasioned by the genuine end of the property dealing or development activity.

It should not be thought that the risks on a sale or liquidation arise only if the company is a UK company and are avoided if the dealing or development company is offshore. As explained in CHAPTER **89** those risks apply equally where the company is non-UK resident. Indeed they are greater, for there may be more of a flavour of tax avoidance.

A point also to keep in mind under both the phoenix code and the transactions in securities legislation is that they only result in tax if a dividend paid by the UK company would itself be taxable. This is not the position if the shareholder in the company is a non-resident individual (see para **64.6**). Nor is it the position if the shareholder is an offshore company so long as the owner of that company is not a UK resident individual or a structure under which a UK individual is transferor and has power to enjoy. Indeed in such cases where a dividend would not be taxable extraction of profit by dividend may be preferable.

A practical consequence of using a UK company is that it will be required to keep a register of persons with significant control and make the register available for inspection (Companies Act 2006, ss 790A–790ZG). For some investors this may be unattractive.

Foreign registered company

26.13 In some cases thought may be given to using a UK resident company that is foreign registered. The principal attraction of this is that the shares are then foreign situs and so excluded property in the hands of an individual who is neither domiciled nor deemed domiciled in the UK or a trust created by such an individual (see paras **37.9** and **62.2**). In reality, however, it is unlikely such a company adds much. One reason is the proposed removal of excluded property status insofar as the company's assets are UK residential property. The other is that any available excluded property status can be achieved by an offshore registered parent to the UK trading company.

INVESTING

26.14 Provided it is established that the offshore company is investing rather than trading, the applicable tax on any sale is capital gains tax. This is payable by the non-resident company if and insofar as the property invested in falls within the definition of residential property. The rate of tax is 20% and indexation relief is allowed. The tax is known as non-residents CGT, or NR

CGT, and is explained in CHAPTER **65**. A point to stress is that NR CGT does not extend to commercial property, and is also precluded for institutional property (see para **65.21**). The position as respects all such property remains that non-residents are not subject to CGT save insofar as the property is used or held for the purposes of a trade carried on in the UK through a branch, agency or permanent establishment (see para **65.2**).

Where the owning company is not itself subject to CGT, TCGA 1992, s 13 has to be considered insofar as the owner of the company is UK resident or is a non-UK resident trust. This section is described in CHAPTER **88**, and as there described it attributes gains to participators owning more than 25% of the company. However it is subject to the motive or purpose defence described in para **88.4** and that defence potentially precludes its application in many cases (see para **88.37**). Even where it is in point, it will only result in a tax charge on the gain as it arises if the participator is UK resident or if a non-resident trust participator has a settlor who is resident and domiciled in the UK and so within TCGA 1992, s 86 (see CHAPTER **76**). Absent that s 13 gains apportioned to a trust are only taxable if and insofar as a UK resident beneficiary receives a capital payment (TCGA 1992, s 87; see CHAPTER **77**).

Transactions in land

26.15 An issue which may be raised is whether, if it is an investor, the offshore company or a provider of an opportunity to realise a gain, can be caught by the transactions in land legislation described above (para **26.11**). Under the pre-2016 law it was reasonably clear they could not be, for the leading case, *Yuill v Wilson* [1980] STC 460 made it clear, ss 752–772 applied only if some element of income tax avoidance was involved: such was explicitly stated in the first instance and Court of Appeal judgments approved in the House of Lords. At one time it was felt that the Court of Appeal decision in *Page v Lowther* [1983] STC 799 pointed to a different conclusion, but that case involved what was in substance a development profit.

It is unclear whether this reasoning has survived into the legislation enacted in 2016. The reason for this concern is that ss 752–772 contained a preamble expressly defining their purposes as being preventing the avoidance of income tax by persons concerned with land or the development of land (s 752(1)). There is no such preamble to the 2016 legislation.

In reality it may be regarded as unlikely the 2016 provisions can operate to turn a gain which is not a trading gain into income. The reason is that the preconditions for the 2016 code are still expressed in terms of acquisition or development where the purposes, or one of the purposes, is to realise a profit on the disposal of the land. As described in paras **26.6** and **26.7**, such a purpose stamps the exercise as trading.

But inevitably the position is not as clear cut as would be desirable. In practice what is important is that the decision-making and financing all point to retention as an investment rather than the possibility of selling at a profit. It is also prudent to ensure that the property is retained and generates an income return. There is no hard and fast rule as to how long property should be retained for an intention to realise a profit on disposal is not less an intention just because disposal may be delayed.

If the 2016 legislation were in point in relation to residential property, it would preclude a charge to NR CGT. This is because consideration brought into account for CGT purposes excludes amounts charged to income tax (TCGA 1992, s 37(1)).

Diverted profits tax

26.16 Diverted profits tax could come into issue if the offshore company acquires the property from a connected UK company, for then there would be a material provision (see para **92.3**). In theory at least it could apply to the rental income of the offshore company even if the latter is arm's length and despite the fact such rental income is subject to income tax (see para **92.15**). In practice however DPT will rarely be of concern as it does not apply if all the companies are small or medium-sized entities within the EU definition (see para **92.9**). But as explained in para **92.13** there could be issues where there is underlying trust ownership.

Rental income

26.17 The principal tax issue where the owning company is an investor is the taxation of the rental income. UK rental income is fully taxable regardless of the residence of the owner and has never enjoyed the restriction of UK tax to tax withheld discussed in CHAPTER 64. As is explained in para 64.20, the prima facie rule is that tax is secured by requiring the tenant or managing agent to withhold tax at source. However, the withholding requirement is displaced if the owner is accepted into the non-resident landlord scheme.

The computational rules applicable to rental income are the same as for business profits (ITTOIA 2005, s 272). Expenditure is accordingly deductible, if of a revenue nature and incurred wholly and exclusively for the purposes of the letting business (ITTOIA 2005, s 33 and 34). Repairs, maintenance, and management are thus allowable. For offshore investors much the most important deduction is that for interest. Interest is plainly allowable on commercial loans incurred in connection with the property. In general the same is true of shareholder loans, but the relevant considerations can be more complicated and are discussed further below.

In general, the applicable tax on net rental income is the basic rate tax payable by the owning offshore company. However should the owner of the company be a UK resident individual, that individual is taxable on the rental income under the transfer of assets code (see CHAPTER 69). The same is true should the owner be an offshore settlor-interested trust whose settlor is UK resident. In neither case does the remittance basis apply, as the rental income is by definition UK source.

Should an individual be taxable on the rental income under the transfer of assets code, the deduction for interest against higher rate tax is being progressively restricted (ITTOIA 2005, ss 272A and 274A). This restriction does not apply where the transfer of assets code is not in point and the rent is taxable on the company (s 272A(5)).

ATED

26.18 ATED is explained in CHAPTERS 66. As a general proposition it does not impact on the subject matter of this chapter as it relates only to residential property occupied by the owner of the company or other connected or associated persons. However, companies which own residential property have ATED compliance obligations in that they are required to file an annual relief declaration return (FA 2013, s 159A; see para **66.18**). This return must be filed by 30 April for each year and covers all let residential property owned by the company. It is not needed if all the company's let property is below the ATED threshold of £500,000 (see s 159A(4)(a) and para **66.10**).

A company may have substantive liability to ATED if what is called a non-qualifying person is in occupation of a given property, whether as a tenant or otherwise. In such a case ATED is due unless the property in question is below the ATED threshold. In broad terms non-qualifying persons encompass any individual owners of the company plus the settlor and beneficiaries of any trust owner. But as is explained in para **66.20** a number of persons with connections of varying closeness to such individuals are also comprehended. Should ATED have become payable for all or part of the company's ownership, all or a proportion of the tax payable on any eventual disposal is ATED related CGT rather than NR CGT. This is more onerous than NR CGT as the rate is 28% and there is no indexation (see paras **66.26** to **66.27**).

UK company

26.19 As with dealing and developing, recent tax changes raise the question of whether UK property investment should be conducted through a UK resident company rather than an offshore company. Here three points may be made.

The first point is the same as applies to trading companies, namely that a UK resident company avoids having to comply with the disciplines of ensuring the company is non-resident under the central management and control test. This is particularly apposite where the underlying owner or owners are UK resident.

A second reason operates if there is such a UK connection and the transferor charge under the transfer of assets code is potentially in point. This does not apply if a UK company owns the property generating the rental income. As such tax on the rental income is capped at corporation tax rates.

The third point is more general and operates where the portfolio is residential. Here NR CGT, and the proposed extension of IHT, mean the playing field is virtually level as between the offshore and the onshore company.

The conclusion that may be drawn is that for residential portfolios a UK company merits serious consideration. With commercial portfolios, offshore ownership has advantages, notably freedom from CGT. But even here the practical issues that arise where the underlying owners are UK resident should be kept in mind as should the risk there will be greater temptation for HMRC to invoke the transactions in land code should the property ever be sold.

SHAREHOLDER LOANS

26.20 Whether the company is trading or investing, the individual or trust which owns it may introduce finance by shareholder loan. Indeed, debt financing normally represents good planning as an interest deduction can be secured, thereby reducing the trading profit or rental income taxable in the UK. Shareholder loans do however require account to be taken of several tax issues.

Situs

26.21 As indicated at the beginning of this chapter, care may be needed to ensure the loan does not have a UK situs. This is relevant if the lender is the owning individual or trust, for in such a case a UK situs loan results in exposure to IHT. As indicated above, where the borrower is non-UK resident, a debt secured by a charge over the UK land held by the company is likely to have a UK situs. Concern about the situs of the asset is obviated if the lender is another company, for then the relevant asset for IHT purposes is the shares in that company.

Should the UK land be residential, the impact on debt financing of the IHT changes described in para 26.2 above will need to be considered. At the time of writing the indications are connected party loans will be disallowed in computing the value exposed to the new charge.

Taxability of the interest

26.22 Should the interest have a UK source the borrower, ie the investing or trading company, is typically required to withhold tax at the basic rate when making interest payments (see para 64.15). The interest suffers further tax by direct assessment on the lender if the lender is a trust with UK beneficiaries (see para 64.8). The interest also suffers further tax if it can be attributed to a UK resident under anti-avoidance legislation such as the transfer of assets code. In other cases the general rule will apply to the lender, namely that UK source interest received by non-residents is taxable only to the extent of tax withheld (see further CHAPTER 64).

The issue of whether interest has a UK source can be one of difficulty, and is explained further in para 40.3. However in the context of a loan to an offshore company a finding that the interest has a UK source should be avoided if the loan agreement is governed by non-UK law, a foreign court is given exclusive jurisdiction to settle disputes, payments of both interest and principal are required to be made abroad and the loan is not secured on the UK real estate. It is said by some that security over the real estate does not result in risk, but as explained in para 40.3, this is unlikely to be so.

Deductibility

26.23 As indicated above the key issue, and often the planning rationale, in shareholder loans is the interest deduction. This requires consideration of two points, namely whether the interest is deductible under general principles and whether, if it is, that conclusion is displaced by the UK's transfer pricing legislation discussed in CHAPTER 91.

General principles

26.24 As described above, should the company be trading the applicable tax is corporation tax. In such case deductibility is governed by the loan relationship rules (CTA 2009, Part 5). Reference should be made to specialist works on corporate tax.

In all other cases, the applicable rules are the income tax rules for business profits which require the interest, and thus the loan, to have been incurred wholly and exclusively for the purposes of the trading or letting business (ITTOIA 2005, ss 29, 35, and 272). On one view this condition is not met with shareholder loans as, looking at the matter in the round, the purpose of the shareholder loans may not be to buy the real estate but merely secure the interest deduction. This however is not the right analysis. Lender and borrower have to be viewed separately and the fact of the matter is that the owning company has to have funding if it is to buy the real estate and so have a property business. If its shareholder insists on introducing interest-bearing debt, paying interest is for the purposes of its business, at least so long as the rate of interest is no higher than other lenders would charge.

The result is that the interest is deductible under the wholly and exclusively rule provided that the rate is no higher than commercial lenders are currently charging. In assessing commercial comparables the comparison should be with loans with the same terms and maturity as the actual shareholder loan.

A point sometimes raised is whether the interest is only deductible if it has a UK source and the owning company is withholding 20% tax. There used to be a rule in computing business profits that annual interest paid to a non-resident was normally only allowed if the payer deducted tax at source (TA 1988, s 82). But this rule was specifically disapplied in computing rental income (TA 1988, s 21A(4)). For some reason the rewrite in ITTOIA 2005 appears to have omitted both the general rule and its disapplication to rental income. The upshot is therefore that deduction of source is not material to deductibility. HMRC in the Property Income Manual appear to accept the point in relation to rental income, in that PIM 2110 says simply that the payer of interest to a non-resident should 'normally' deduct tax at source. There is no suggestion that HMRC consider such deduction a precondition.

There is one overarching anti-avoidance provision applicable to the deduction of interest, namely ITA 2007, s 809ZG. This section denies relief if there is a scheme or arrangement and the sole or main benefit to the borrower from the loan is the interest deduction. This provision has been invoked only sparingly by HMRC, and is accepted to be an anti-avoidance provision targeted at artificial schemes (*MacNiven v Westmoreland Investments Ltd* [1998] STC 1131, 1146, as approved at [2001] STC 237, 260). It may be argued that it cannot apply to straightforward shareholder loans as the position of the owning company, as borrower, has to be looked at in isolation. On that basis it will have to enter into the loan for the purposes of its business with the result that the main benefit to it of the loan will be commercial, not the interest deduction. Any attempt by HMRC to invoke s 809ZG in a situation of this sort would be met by the point that such is the job of transfer pricing rules.

Transfer pricing

26.25 The UK's transfer pricing code is discussed in CHAPTER **91**, and its application to property investors in paras **91.24** to **91.26**. But for one point, shareholder loans of the kind discussed here are plainly within the code, for lender and borrower are connected. The one point is that discussed in paras **91.15** to **91.17**, namely that the borrower, ie the advantaged party, is normally a small enterprise and so outside the scope of transfer pricing unless the other party, ie the lender, is liable to tax in a jurisdiction with which the UK does not have a double tax treaty with a standard non-discrimination article. By liable to tax is meant liability by reference to residence or place of management.

It may well be that in some instances the small companies exemption will be in point in that the lender, although based in a territory which lacks a treaty in the requisite form, is not liable to tax there at all. But this line of argument is untested and it also needs to be kept in mind that even if the transfer pricing legislation is not in point, HMRC could argue that the wholly and exclusively rule has much the same effect. For all these reasons, the prudent course is undoubtedly to comply with transfer pricing rules.

On this basis, the following points may be made:

(1) The interest is allowable provided it does not exceed the interest which would be allowable if the offshore company and the shareholder lender were at arm's length.

(2) In HMRC's view all the terms of the loan have to be looked at in determining what is a commercial rate of interest, not merely the rate itself. In particular, in HMRC's view, interest is not allowable if and to the extent the amount of a loan is greater than an independent arm's length lender would lend, having regard to the security offered (ie the LTV ratio) and the strength of the borrower's covenant.

The result is that interest on shareholders' loans is on any view allowable provided the amount of the loan and the rate of interest are commercial.

A controversial issue is whether the loan should be secured. There is a view that if the loan is not secured, the transfer pricing question is whether and to what extent an independent lender would have made an unsecured loan and, to the extent he would not have done, the interest is disallowed. The contrary view is that Sch 28AA looks at the transaction as a whole and compares the actual interest paid with what would have been payable had the transaction been wholly at arm's length. On this basis security is assumed even if not given. As explained in para **91.26**, the wording of the UK legislation indicates that this latter interpretation is correct and this view is supported by the Special Commissioners in the only case decided on Sch 28AA, namely *DSG Retail Ltd v Revenue and Customs Comrs* [2009] UKFTT 31 (TC), [2009] STC (SCD) 397, [2009] 11 ITLR 869.

Chapter 27

UK HOUSES FOR NON-RESIDENTS

INTRODUCTION

27.1 Many houses and flats in the UK are now bought for the personal use of non-residents when visiting the UK. The extent of this phenomenon is politically sensitive and as a result the tax regime is of some complexity. This chapter explains the various forms of ownership and outlines possible planning strategies. It is assumed that the non-resident(s) concerned are also non-UK domiciled.

INDIVIDUAL OWNERSHIP

27.2 The simplest means for a non-resident to effect a house purchase is to buy in his personal name. Among other advantages this avoids the setting up and running costs entailed if corporate or trust structures are used.

Tax on acquisition

27.3 SDLT is charged on the purchase price. SDLT on residential property is now a banded tax, the bands being set out in FA 2003, s 55 as amended by Stamp Duty Land Tax 2015, s 1. In the great majority of cases the house or flat purchased is an additional dwelling of the purchaser with the result that the purchase is a higher rates transaction (see para **67.4**). This means the rates are as follows:

0–£125,000	3%
£125,001–£250,000	5%
£250,001–£925,000	8%
£925,001–£1.5m	13%
Over £1.5m	15%

SDLT is difficult to avoid as the legislation includes robust anti-avoidance provisions and is thus a cost that must be factored into any purchase. Some of the details are given in Chapter **67**.

Tax during ownership

27.4 The only tax the UK currently imposes on owner occupied residential property is Council Tax. The rate of Council Tax is set out locally, but the bands are national, being determined by actual or hypothetical values as at 1 April 1991. The top band is G, starting at a 1991 value of £320,001.

There are, periodically, calls for higher Council Tax bands to be introduced and/or for an additional, national tax to be charged on high value properties, mansion tax as it is sometimes called. To date such calls have been resisted. There is also the possibility that the bands could be revalued to current values, as was envisaged when Council Tax was first introduced. But this too has not happened, although this is more likely than the introduction of a mansion tax.

Tax on sale

27.5 Should the non-resident owner sell his house or flat, non-resident capital gains tax (NR CGT) is payable. Gains subject to NR CGT are upper rate gains and so the rate is 28%, save insofar as the individual has available his annual CGT exemption and his income tax basic rate-band (TCGA 1992, s 2A(b) as inserted by FB 2016, cl 72). The tax is charged on the difference between the sale proceeds and acquisition and enhancement costs, with no allowance for inflation. But in the case of properties acquired before 6 April 2015, the element of gain accruing before then is outside charge, the default position being rebasing as at 5 April 2015.

NR CGT is explained in CHAPTER 65. A principal private residence election is not normally open to non-residents, as a non-resident cannot make the election unless he or his spouse spend 90 or more midnights in their UK residential property(ies) (TCGA 1992, ss 222B and 222C; see para **65.14**).

Tax on succession

27.6 Should the individual die, the house or flat is a chargeable asset for IHT purposes as it is UK situs. It is thus subject to IHT at 40% insofar as its value, and that of the deceased's other UK assets, exceeds the nil-rate band, currently £325,000.

With effect from 1 April 2017 the possible availability of the additional residential property nil-rate band requires consideration (IHTA 1984, s 8D). The rules pertaining this are complicated, but at best the additional exempt amount in 2017–18 is £100,000. To secure the exemption the house must pass to descendants and the deceased's UK estate (including the house) must be worth less than £2m (subject to tapering for estates a little over that value). Only one house can have the exemption, the nomination as to which being made by the personal representatives.

Should the individual give the house away inter vivos, IHT is not payable if the recipient is another individual and the donor survives seven years. This result follows because the gift is a potentially exempt transfer or PET (IHTA 1984, s 3A). But if the donor goes on using the house or otherwise falls foul of the gift with reservation rules described in CHAPTER 83, the property is treated as remaining in his estate for IHT purposes and so remains exposed to IHT in the event of his death (FA 1986, s 102A).

Succession also has CGT implications. On death, there is a good CGT result, for the house is rebased for CGT purposes without tax charge (TCGA 1992, s 62(1)). Inter vivos gifts, by contrast, produce a bad CGT result, in that the gift counts as a CGT disposal at market value (TCGA 1992, s 17(1)(a)). There is thus a charge to NR CGT if the house has appreciated in value since acquisition or, as the case may be, since 5 April 2015. In some cases a gift can produce the worst of all worlds, in that the CGT remains chargeable even if the donor fails to survive seven years and so causes the gift to be chargeable to IHT.

There are various strategies for mitigating the possible IHT charge on death. These are discussed below. But perhaps the simplest point to keep in mind is that, assuming that the owner is not only non-UK resident but also non-UK domiciled, IHT is only in issue if the owner gives the house away or dies while still owning it. IHT falls out of the equation should the owner sell the house and remove the proceeds abroad. A long-term plan of that sort, plus life assurance to cover untimely death, is often the simplest and cheapest means of covering the IHT risk.

Practical implications

27.7 Prima facie, personal ownership by the individual means he appears as owner at the Land Registry. For some this may be undesirable. But in practice the difficulty may be overcome, at least for now, by use of a nominee company. Providing the nominee really is a nominee it is looked through for all tax purposes, so the tax position is no different from the position if the individual was the registered proprietor as well as the beneficial owner.

This approach may not preserve privacy indefinitely. There are proposals for the introduction of a public register of beneficial ownership of companies acquiring or owning UK real estate. The timeframe for this is uncertain. It is also unclear whether the requirement to disclose personal information for the purposes of such a register will apply where the corporate owner of the property is a nominee, as distinct from being the beneficial owner of the property.

A potentially more serious issue arises should the individual die while still owning the house. As the house is UK real estate, UK law as the lex situs governs its devolution and so an English will to cover the house and any other UK assets is prudent. But with or without a will, the executors or administrators will require a grant of probate, and that in turn requires the filing of an IHT return (Form IHT 400) and the payment of any IHT due. Foreign domicile has to be claimed on Form IHT 401, which requires information which may in some instances be regarded as intrusive.

CORPORATE OWNERSHIP

27.8 For many years non-resident buyers have favoured buying UK houses or flats in wholly-owned offshore companies. This has mainly been driven by concern over the IHT risk entailed in personal ownership. But corporate ownership also gives privacy, in that under current law the individual's name does not appear at the land registry and UK probate is not required in the event of death. Company ownership does however raise other tax issues and, as noted above, there are suggestions that the law may at some stage be changed to require disclosure of the beneficial ownership of companies owning UK property.

Tax on acquisition

27.9 As with individuals, SDLT is payable on acquisition. But instead of the banded rates there is a single flat rate of 15%, assuming the purchase price exceeds £500,000 (FA 2003, Sch 4A, para 3). With high value properties this rate is not significantly more burdensome than the higher rates applicable to all purchases of additional dwellings as the latter are also charged at 15% insofar as the consideration exceeds £1.5m.

Tax during ownership

27.10 Corporate owners, or the individual occupier, pay the same Council Tax as an individual owner occupier does. In addition, and much more significantly, corporate owners are likely to be liable to the annual tax on enveloped dwellings, or ATED as it is known. This tax applies only to properties whose value is above £500,000. Currently the valuation date is 1 April 2012 or, if later, the date when the property was acquired. But for the chargeable period which will commence on 1 April 2018, the valuation date will be 1 April 2017.

The amounts of ATED payable are as follows (Finance Act 2013 (FA 2013), s 99):

Value of property	Amount payable
£500,001–£1m	£3,500
£1,000,001–£2m	£7,000
£2,000,001–£5m	£23,350
£5,000,001–£10m	£54,450
£10,000,001–£20m	£109,950
More than £20m	£218,200

These amounts are payable annually. The amounts, but not the bands, are subject to indexation (FA 2013, s 101).

ATED is discussed in more detail in CHAPTER 66. The key point is that it applies only to corporate owners and partnerships with a corporate member.

Tax on sale

27.11 Should the company sell the house, any gain is subject to ATED-related CGT. The same computational rules apply as with individuals, and indexation is not allowed. There is no annual exemption and no possibility of private residence relief. The rate of tax is 28% (TCGA 1992, s 4(3A); see para **66.27**). Assuming the property was acquired before the introduction of ATED rebasing is allowed in computing the ATED related gain. The general rebasing date is 5 April 2013. But if the property was worth less than £2m on that date, the rebasing date is 5 April 2015, or 5 April 2016 if it was worth between £0.5m and £1m.

It is open to the buyer and the seller to agree to transact shares in the company rather than the property itself. Should this be done the seller benefits, for ATED-related CGT does not attach to company shares even if UK residential property is the company's sole asset. The buyer also benefits, for SDLT is similarly not charged on a disposal of shares.

Historically property transactions effected as share sales have been less common than might be supposed on account of buyer nervousness about possible corporate liabilities. But this may change now that residential property taxes are so onerous. Certainly, those owning property through a company have every incentive to keep the company properly run and in order so as to be in the best position to achieve a share sale, should that course prove appropriate.

A share sale is unlikely to work if the company owns other assets, and it should be kept in mind that the government may find a means of looking through companies for the purposes of ATED-related CGT and SDLT. The main reason why the government has not attempted this so far is thought to be a concern about compliance with EU law and in particular the need to avoid the politically unacceptable complication of looking through purely domestic transactions.

Tax on succession

27.12 As noted above, corporate ownership of residential property has historically avoided the IHT issues raised by personal ownership. As of today, that remains the law, and indeed it will remain so until 5 April 2017. But as from 6 April 2017 shares in close companies will not be excluded property insofar as their value is attributable to UK residential property. This proposal was first announced on 8 July 2015 (see HMRC technical note reproduced [2015] SWTI 2344). A consultation document was published by HM Treasury on 19 August 2016.

The practical consequence is that corporate ownership now looks unlikely to be a long-term IHT shelter for UK residential property. This change, assuming that it is enacted, will remove the principal advantage of corporate owner-ship. Corporate ownership will only be advantageous if and to the extent that the possibility of avoiding SDLT and CGT on a sale by selling shares outweighs the certainty of the annual ATED charge and the higher SDLT charge on initial acquisition.

Practical implications

27.13 If the property is to be held in an offshore company, the company has to be formed and run in an offshore jurisdiction. Directors and very likely annual accounts will be required. All this carries a cost. Should a share sale ever be a possibility it will be important to ensure corners are not cut, even assuming regulation in the chosen offshore jurisdiction might otherwise allow this.

It is important to ensure there is no risk of the company becoming UK resident under the central management and control test described in CHAPTER 43. Where the shareholder is non-UK resident, the risks may not be great. However, by definition the principal asset will be in the UK and to that extent the risks may be greater than might be supposed. If risk is to be avoided on this front, there must be evidence that any decisions relating to the property have been taken in properly minuted board meetings and that instructions to third parties have been given by the board, not the shareholder. A meeting twice a year as a minimum is prudent, and certainly once a year.

Another risk to keep in mind is the shadow director benefit in kind risk described in CHAPTER 93 (ITEPA 2003, s 102). This risk makes it unwise for the shareholder/occupier to be a director of the company himself. Assuming he is not a director, the benefit in kind risk arises only if on the facts he is a shadow director and he can be said to perform duties in the UK. It is difficult to see how a shadow, who has no actual duties, can be said to perform any such duties in the UK. Certainly the experience of practitioners is that shadow director issues have not historically been raised with non-residents.

If there is felt to be a risk, possible ways of reducing it are for the company shares to be held in trust, and to have the property managed commercially by agents acting on the instructions of the board. Use of an agent means that if anybody is performing UK duties in relation to the property, it is the agent rather than the occupier.

The practical consequences of the company residence and shadow director issues are often to require more formalities such as board meetings in the offshore jurisdictions. The extra costs are additional points to take into account in considering whether offshore corporate ownership is appropriate.

IHT PLANNING

27.14 It may well be concluded, in the light of the various points made above, that individual ownership is to be preferred to corporate ownership. If that decision is made, it may be that, as indicated above, the view will be taken that the house will be sold and the proceeds removed abroad before any IHT charge will arise. But in many instances there is a desire to put IHT mitigation in place and a review of at least the more straightforward options is worthwhile.

Spouse exemption

27.15 The spouse exemption (IHTA 1984, s 18) applies as much to non-resident non-domiciliaries as to anybody else. The restriction where the transferor is UK domiciled and the transferee is not should not be in point as, in the circumstances postulated here, both are non-UK domiciled.

At its simplest, the spouse exemption operates to defer the IHT charge until the second death. Save in unfortunate circumstances there will be ample time after the first death to sell the house and remove the proceeds abroad. Should the first death be that of the owning spouse, a further advantage is that the death rebases the property for the purposes of NR CGT (TCGA 1992, s 62(1)). But probate and an IHT return are still required. The latter is necessary even though the spouse exemption obviates IHT as the estate does not count as an excepted estate (see IHT (Delivery of Accounts) (Excepted Estates) Regulations 2004, SI 2004/2543).

It may be the decision of the spouses to buy the property jointly. Should they do so as joint tenants in equity, the interest of the first to die passes by survivorship, and no grant of probate is required. But an IHT return is still required (IHTA 1984, s 216(2)).

Commercial borrowing

27.16 The general IHT rule is that a debt which is secured on property is a deduction in the IHT value of the property (IHTA 1984, s 162(4)). If therefore the non-resident mortgages his UK house or flat, his IHT exposure is reduced by the amount of the mortgage.

In practice this treatment is normally only available as respects debts incurred to buy the property or effect works to it. This is on account of the rules, introduced in 2013, disallowing debts incurred to finance the acquisition of excluded property (IHTA 1984, s 162A). These complicated rules are explained in para 84.15 and they make the charging of debt against the property to finance other expenditure challenging. In an era of rising property values, therefore, use of debt normally cannot prevent increases in the property's value from being exposed to IHT.

Should death occur while the property is still owned, the debt is not allowable unless it is discharged out of the deceased's estate. This is the effect of IHTA 1984, s 175A. Provided that this is remembered, the rule should not be an issue in the present context, for non-UK as well as UK assets can be used to discharge the debt (s 175A(1)(a)), which is explained in para 84.20. Further HMRC accept that the personal representatives can themselves borrow to discharge the debt (IHTM 28028).

An issue which sometimes arises is that a lender may require additional security, particularly where the loan is high relative to the value of the property. The point raised here is that the IHT deduction is only available to the extent the debt is an encumbrance on the UK property (IHTA 1984, s 162(4)). If therefore it is also secured on other property, is it still an encumbrance on the UK property? The safest solution is to avoid other security entirely. If this is not done, it should be clear the lender can only have recourse to the other assets should the UK property prove insufficient.

As the borrowing is commercial, interest will be payable. The issue that arises here is that if the lender is non-UK resident, deduction of basic rate tax is required if the interest has a UK source (ITA 2007, 874(1)(d)). The Upper Tribunal decision in *Ardmore v HMRC* [2016] STC 1044 indicates a multifactorial test is applied in determining whether interest has a UK source, the key factors being the residence of the debtor, the location of the security, and the ultimate or substantive source of the discharge of the debtor's obligations. Here one of the factors is in the UK, namely the security, and a second may also be if in reality the debt is going to be paid off out of the proceeds of the house.

If this point is felt to be of concern, the simplest solution is a UK resident lender. That avoids the problem, because withholding is only required where the lender is non-UK resident. Another solution to consider is borrowing from a lender in a treaty jurisdiction and applying to have the interest paid gross, assuming the treaty gives sole taxing rights to the treaty partner (see para **64.15**).

Private borrowing

27.17 Particularly when faced with the prospect of paying interest to a commercial lender, some non-residents may try and secure the tax advantage of borrowing secured on the property by private borrowing. In reality two situations have to be distinguished. One is where the borrowing is genuine third-party borrowing, and the other is where the non-resident borrows from a structure, for example a trust, he has himself set up.

Borrowing of this latter kind is aggressive and may well not work. There are a number of points that need to be watched. The first and most important is that the exercise may fall foul of the GAAR (see CHAPTER 83). One of the examples in the GAAR guidance (D31) involves house structures. It is true this example mainly concerns trust purchase, but the overall message is that an individual who generates a deduction by effectively borrowing his own money is likely to be at risk. There are also more technical concerns, inter alia as to whether FA 1986, s 103 would preclude the deduction. This obscure section is discussed in paras **84.12** to **84.13** and while there are very good arguments it is precluded if the previous gift to the lender was of excluded property, such has never formally been accepted by HMRC.

Certain further points have to be watched whether the borrowing is from a structure created by the individual or from a genuine third party. Perhaps the most important is that, for the reasons explained above, the borrowing has to be secured on the property to be a deduction (IHTA 1984, s 162(4)). As such the issue is raised of whether the lender's asset, ie the debt, has a UK situs, with the result the lender is exposed to IHT if he or it is a trust.

The relevant law on the situs of debts is discussed in paras **38.3** to **38.6**. Much the better view, shared by HMRC, is that a debt secured on UK property is UK situs. This is so whether or not the debt is a specialty.

The conventional, and simple solution to the problems posed by the situs of debts is to interpose a non-UK resident company as lender. This however raises another set of problems. First there are the technical points of benefit in kind and company residence, albeit these ought not to be too troublesome on account of the points made above. More serious is a regulatory concern arising out of the Financial Services and Markets Act 2000. This makes it an offence to carry out a regulated activity without authorisation (s 18). Various activities specified by statutory instrument are regulated if carried on in the course of a business (s 22). One activity so specified is making a loan secured by first legal mortgage on a dwelling used by the borrower or by a beneficiary of a trust who is a borrower (Financial Services and Markets Act 2000 (Regulated Activities) Order 2001, art 61). The FCA perimeter guidance (s 4.3) indicates that loans between family members are not caught, on the basis that such loans will not be made in the course of a business; but it is not immediately clear that this extends to companies owned by family members, still less to loans from companies owned by other parties.

The overall conclusion must be that private loans raise too many difficult issues to be worth considering in the generality of cases, although there may be specific cases which represent exceptions. A final point to keep in mind is that if the loan is interest-bearing, deduction at source may be required unless the lender is UK resident (see above and para **64.15**).

Multiple ownership

27.18 Another approach to the potential IHT exposure is to share ownership round the family. Thus the property could be owned in equal shares by, say, father, mother and three adult children. This delivers a number of IHT advantages most notably:

(a)   Multiple nil-rate bands. When coupled with commercial borrowing these can reduce potential IHT exposure to modest or even non-existent levels.

(b)   Delay in the IHT charge in the case of the children (assuming normal life expectancy).

The major tax issue raised by such co-ownership is the IHT gift with reservation rules. These are analysed in CHAPTER 83 and they potentially come into play if the parents directly or indirectly fund the children's shares.

In reality however, there are two contexts in which the rules are normally precluded. The first is in point if the parent(s) gives undivided shares in the property itself to the children. Here IHTA 1984, s 102B precludes GWR exposure provided both donor and donees occupy the land and there is no collateral benefit to the donor. This route thus potentially works if and so long as all the family genuinely use the property. But difficulties can arise if, as often happens, the children acquire UK properties of their own and no longer use the original property. The requirement to avoid collateral benefit to the donor means that the donor must bear at least his share of the property's running expenses. Often he might bear all the expenses so as to avoid argument about what his share of the expenses should be.

Section 102B is often thought of as being confined to cases where the undivided shares are equal and HMRC in the IHT manual provide an illustration on this basis (IHTM 14360). But on the wording of the legislation the shares need not be equal, albeit that in such cases greater HMRC scrutiny may be anticipated.

The second context is where the initial purchase is by the co-owners, each providing his or her share of the purchase price. Here the children may well have been given the necessary cash by the parents, the gift being made abroad and so not subject to IHT. But as described in para **83.10**, a gift of cash to individuals normally breaks the GWR rules, with the result the GWR rules are not engaged if the donor uses or enjoys whatever the donee buys with the cash. There is a concern that a reference to associated operations in the GWR legislation (FA 1986, Sch 20, para 6(1)(c)) calls this into question but the better view, set out in para **83.10**, is that it does not. This view appears to be shared by HMRC, who indicate that associated operations are only likely to be in issue if in reality the gift is of the purchased property (IHTM 14372). It may be suggested a cash gift is not in reality a gift of the purchased property if it is unconditional and made before negotiations to buy the property commence.

If the gift is of cash, the rationale applies equally well regardless of what shares in the property the co-owners take. Indeed, the original donor need not be a co-owner at all, albeit that this leaves one less applicable annual exemption.

Any co-ownership solution involves practical issues. Each co-owner will by definition own a UK situs asset and probate and an IHT return are required in the event of his death. An English will is prudent. Also the senior members of the family need to keep in mind that any share in the property belonging to a child may be exposed to those with claims against that child, including business creditors and divorcing spouses. In many cases such non-tax considerations make co-ownership solutions unattractive.

A final point to keep in mind is NR CGT. CGT is an argument in favour of the original purchase being in shares rather than the original owner making subsequent gifts of undivided shares. This is because gifts of the latter kind are CGT disposals. If therefore a gain has accrued tax will result.

Timely gift

27.19 In the context of planning within the family it is also worth keeping in mind that even if the parent buys the house wholly himself he can give all of it away inter vivos to his family. As explained above, should he then survive seven years no IHT is chargeable.

Also as indicated above, the GWR rules normally make this unattractive, for, in the absence of co-ownership as described above, the donor has to cease using the house if it is to be out of his estate for IHT purposes. With some elderly donors this may be practical, but usually it is not.

A possible solution is for the donee to grant a lease back at a commercial rent to the donor. As explained in para **83.14**, such a lease avoids GWR issues provided that the rent is kept at commercial levels. A drawback with a lease is that it generates rent, taxable on the donee. But with high value property such rent is normally modest relative to capital value and often it can largely be offset by allowable expenditure on the property.

Any gift of the property is a disposal for the purposes of NR CGT. If therefore there is a gain such will be chargeable on the donor and potentially makes a gift unattractive.

Artificial solutions

27.20 There are a number of more artificial solutions to the IHT problem posed by personal ownership of UK property. These include reversionary leases, based on the decision in *Buzzoni v Revenue and Customs Comrs* [2011] UKFTT 267 (TC), [2011] SFTD 771. It is however essential that specialist advice is taken before such solutions are adopted. Three points in particular need to be kept in mind. First, the efficacy of the scheme may not be tested until many years hence and when it is tested, the outcome may turn on fine distinctions (see *Viscount Hood (Executor of the Estate of Lady Diana Hood) v Revenue and Customs Comrs* [2016] UKFTT 59 (TC), [2016] SFTD 351, [2016] SWTI 1159). Second, tax planning involving houses has historically proved provocative, thereby inviting greater scrutiny. Third, strategies to save IHT may have other tax implications, particularly as respects CGT. With the introduction of NR CGT and ATED-related CGT the latter is a live issue for non-residents.

OTHER OWNERSHIP STRUCTURES

27.21 Other forms of property ownership may be considered for houses and flats, most notably trusts and partnerships.

Settlor–interested trust

27.22 The kind of trust normally thought of for house ownership is a settlor-interested trust. The settlor is the principal beneficiary and occupier of the house and often the trust is created for the purposes of the purchase.

In reality, such a trust makes the IHT position worse, not better. This is because it is subject both to the IHT relevant property regime of 10-yearly charges and to the death charge in the event of the settlor/occupier's death (see CHAPTERS 60 and 63). The latter follows because inescapably the settlor's position as beneficiary means the trust assets are GWR property (para **83.5**). In reality the GWR death charge is potentially worse than with outright ownership, for it is difficult to secure the spouse exemption in relation to GWR property (para **83.23**). Also HMRC are thought to argue, at last in some contexts, that debt is not deductible in determining the GWR charge. The GWR problems are not avoided by the settlor funding the settlement by cash gift, for the restriction on tracing through cash does not apply to settled property (para **83.12**).

The IHT issues posed by trust ownership are, under current law, obviated if the trust owns the house through a company. However a company entails the various SDLT, ATED, and practical drawbacks discussed above. More importantly the IHT proposal to look through companies with effect from April 2017 applies equally to companies held in trust. As a result, the IHT position will then be as described above, involving both death and relevant property charges.

Other trusts

27.23 Many trusts are not settlor-interested, either because the settlor is excluded from benefit or because he is dead. The IHT analysis should such a trust acquire a UK property for a beneficiary to live in is much more attractive than where the trust is settlor-interested. This is because, by not being settlor-interested, the trust is not GWR property. As a result, the only IHT exposure is to 10-yearly charges.

The rate of 10-yearly charge is 6% and it may be felt this is a substantial burden to bear. But should the trust take borrowing to buy or improve the property, the value exposed to IHT is *pro tanto* reduced.

In general the borrowing should be secured on the property, but if the house is the only trust asset it need not be, as then it operates as a deduction in computing the net value of the trust on 10-yearly charges in any event. However whether secured or unsecured, the deduction is not normally secured unless the borrowing is spent on the house. This is on account of the rules in IHTA 1984, s 162A, discussed above, and generally means top-up borrowings to reduce the net IHT value of the house are not possible.

A trust purchase may also have non-fiscal attractions as compared with personal ownership by the beneficiary, for it protects the house from claimants against the beneficiary. A further point is that as the trust is the owner probate is not required should the occupying beneficiary die. But the 10-yearly charge does require the filing of IHT returns, and for some the disclosure and expense entailed in that exercise may be unattractive.

Trust ownership entails the same exposure to NR CGT and SDLT as individual ownership. But there is no ATED as the ownership is not corporate.

A point to remember with trust ownership is that sometimes some users of the property can temporarily be UK resident. This might, for example, happen with younger members of the family attending university in the UK. Contrary to a widespread assumption, study at a UK university typically entails residence in the UK. Occupation by UK residents is a benefit for the purposes of the income tax non-transferor charge and the CGT capital payments code (ITA 2007, ss 731–735 and TCGA 1992, s 87). The issue of whether liability arises under one or other of those codes would therefore need to be considered.

Partnerships

27.24 The rationale advanced for having a partnership acquire the house or flat is that the partnership is not a company, and so avoids the adverse ATED and SDLT consequences discussed above, and yet is opaque for IHT purposes.

This latter point follows because, for IHT purposes, a partner's asset is his partnership interest rather than an aliquot share in each partnership asset. The situs of this asset is the place where the partnership business is carried on and so, if that place is abroad, a non-UK situs asset is secured.

In reality it is very difficult to recommend a partnership as the vehicle to acquire a UK house or flat. One reason is that the proposals taking effect on 6 April 2017 envisage that partnerships will be looked through as respects UK residential property in the same way as companies. An equally compelling point is that partnership connotes the carrying of business with a view to profit and it is difficult if not impossible to see this condition as being met if the only partnership asset is an owner-occupied house. Further, even if the condition were met, the issue would then arise of whether the partnership business was in reality carried on in the UK, given that its sole asset would be in the UK. The likely outcome, therefore, even under the current law, is that the value of the home is within the IHT net. This is either on the basis that the partnership business is carried on in the UK, so that the partnership interests are UK situated; or (more likely) that there is no partnership at all, and the supposed partnership is in reality a co-ownership arrangement, such that the supposed partners actually hold shares in the UK home directly.

LLP

27.25 A variant on the partnership theme is to use an offshore LLP. As with UK LLPs, such LLPs are normally companies as a matter of general law. But the UK LLP rules apply only to LLPs incorporated under the UK Limited Liability Partnerships Act 2000 (see s 1(2)). So the way is left open for the offshore LLP to be a company for IHT purposes and so on this basis a foreign situs asset is secured for IHT with some certainty.

But precisely because the LLP is a company as a matter of general law, the general rule is it suffers the ATED, SDLT and practical drawbacks of a company described above. To this general rule there is an exception, namely that a non-UK LLP is treated in the same way as a UK LLP for the purposes of ATED and SDLT if it is 'of similar character' to a UK LLP (FA 2003, Sch 15, para 1; FA 2013, s 167(1)(d); see further para 66.2).

Such an LLP has on occasion been perceived as a kind of Holy Grail in property structuring, ie an entity which is company for IHT purposes and is not a company for ATED and SDLT. But like the Holy Grail of Arthurian legend it will prove illusory if the proposals announced on 8 July 2015 are enacted. And even under current law it is likely to be illusory. In part this is because it is unclear what is required to satisfy the 'of similar character test'. More importantly, as with a general partnership, a UK LLP requires two or more persons carrying on a business with a view to profit (Limited Liability Partnerships Act 2000, s 2(1)(a)). It is difficult to see an entity whose sole asset is an owner-occupied house so carrying on business.

EXISTING PROPERTIES

27.26 Many non-residents already own UK homes through corporate structures. As explained above, these structures will become exposed to IHT by reference to the underlying residential property with effect from 6 April 2017. They are already exposed to ATED and ATED-related CGT. In the circumstances the issue arises of whether these structures should be collapsed and the property vested in individuals.

A liquidation of the company triggers ATED-related CGT insofar as, after allowing for ATED rebasing, there is an ATED-related gain on the property. Should there be external debt finance, liquidation results in an SDLT charge on value equal to the loan. This charge is certainly made if the liquidator transfers the property subject to the loan and may be made if the loan is cleared first (see para **67.11**).

Should the company be owned in trust, consideration is needed as to whether any of the beneficiaries are or have been UK resident and if so whether liquidation will result in gains accruing to them under TCGA 1992, s 87 (as to which see CHAPTER **77**). This problem arises because liquidation will crystallise the trust's gain on its shares in the company and so cause that gain to go into the trust's s 2(2) amount. The pre-ATED gain on the house may also go into the s 2(2) amount if the conditions for the motive defence to TCGA 1992, s 13 are not met (as to which see para **88.37**). This s 2(2) amount will trigger a CGT liability if a UK resident beneficiary (or one non-UK resident for five years or less) has an unmatched benefit or capital distribution. Such unmatched benefit could include rent-free occupation of the house itself and, while techniques described in CHAPTER **23** can enable this issue to be overcome, at the very least the problem requires consideration.

These tax complications arising on liquidation of the company may mean the better course is to retain the company and continue paying ATED. Such a course may prove attractive if in due course the decision is to sell the property. In such event, it may then be possible to sell the company. As described in para **27.11**, under current law that avoids both ATED related CGT for the seller and SDLT for the buyer.

When the IHT proposals taking effect on 6 April 2017 were first announced there was a suggestion that the tax issues raised by the liquidation of the owning company might be ameliorated by some form of de-enveloping relief. The consultative document issued on 19 August 2016 indicates that this suggestion will not be taken forward.

Chapter 28

UK HOUSES FOR RESIDENT NON-DOMICILIARIES

INTRODUCTION

28.1 A key tax planning issue for many non-UK domiciliaries is the ownership and funding of their UK home. The issues that arise are similar to those raised by houses owned by non-residents (see CHAPTER 27). But where the non-domiciliary is UK resident matters are in many respects more complicated than those discussed in CHAPTER 27.

An initial point is that remittance issues have to be considered when funding the purchase, as funds brought to the UK to buy the house are taxable if derived from foreign income and gains. The techniques for avoiding taxable remittance are the same as for bringing any other funds to the UK save that, self-evidently, business investment relief can never be in point (see further para **14.5**). Much the best solution is to bring the money in pre-arrival or ensure that the non-domiciliary maintains a pool of pre-arrival cash untainted by income or capital gains. The need to avoid capital gains means it has to be cash, but now that currency gains on bank accounts are not chargeable (TCGA 1992, s 252), the funds can be multi-currency provided held in bank accounts as distinct from money market funds or structured products.

PERSONAL OWNERSHIP

28.2 As a UK situs asset, a UK home owned by the non-domiciliary in his personal name is prima facie within charge to IHT. So too CGT on its disposal is chargeable without the benefit of the remittance basis. However these potential charges have to be kept in perspective.

IHT

28.3 IHT only comes into issue should the non-domiciliary die while still owning the home or having given it away inter vivos. Given the whole premise of non-domiciled status is that he will leave the UK, departure from the UK may well occasion sale of the UK home and removal of the proceeds from the UK. Such removal eliminates the IHT charge, at once if the non-domiciliary is not deemed UK domiciled, and otherwise once he has lost deemed UK domicile (see further CHAPTER 45).

CGT

28.4 CGT too may be manageable. A PPR election is open to the non-domiciliary as, by being UK resident, it is not precluded by the new rules introduced in 2015 (see para **65.14**). There are time limits for the election, in that it has to be made within two years of the acquisition (TCGA 1992, s 222(5)(a)) and there are also practical limits in that the non-domiciliary may have another UK residence that he wishes to elect. But the first of these points may not represent an insurmountable difficulty, for the house may on the facts be the only or main residence and in any event the time for an election starts to run again on any occasion on which the combination of residences changes, albeit that backdating by more than two years is not possible.

Until 2015, all CGT difficulties could be overcome by delaying any sale of the house until after departure from the UK. Now however NR CGT precludes this, at least insofar as any gain represents growth in value since 5 April 2015 (see further CHAPTER **65**).

OFFSHORE COMPANIES AND TRUSTS

28.5 At one time the conventional solution to the tax problems posed by home ownership was to have the house owned in an offshore company owned by an offshore trust. The attraction of this was protection from both IHT and CGT. Trust ownership of the company was normally recommended because a company owned by the individual personally would be vulnerable to the argument it was UK resident under the central management and control test (see CHAPTER **43**) and/or that the individual was a shadow director of the company (see para **93.2**). The former would expose any gain on the property when sold to corporation tax and the latter would result in a benefit in kind charge (see paras **93.6** to **93.23**).

In practice in more recent years, ownership through trust and company structures ceased to be recommended. This was for three main reasons. First, it was difficult to be certain the company residence and shadow director risks were removed. Second, occupation of the house was a benefit under the CGT capital payment rules which meant possible liability under TCGA 1992, s 87 had to be considered once non-domiciliaries were brought within that section in 2008. This was a real risk where the trust held other assets (see further CHAPTER **26**, **81** and **82**). In many cases there were ways of managing the s 87 exposure, but such exercises were potentially complicated and thus expensive in fees. Third, from April 2013, the house in such structures came within ATED and ATED-related CGT.

As a result, modern advice was normally against ownership through a trust and company structure. The final nail in the coffin of trust and company structures has now been administered by the IHT proposals coming into effect on 6 April 2017. Under these proposals shares in non-UK close companies will not enjoy excluded property status insofar as their value is attributable to UK residential property. This means the typical trust and company structure will be exposed to 6% ten-yearly charges under the IHT relevant property regime (see CHAPTERS **60** and **63**). More importantly there will be a 40% charge under GWR rules should the settlor still be a beneficiary when he dies and the house still retained (see para **83.5**).

The end result is that the traditional trust and company structure cannot be recommended for house purchases. This is essentially the same conclusion as is reached in CHAPTER **27** as respects non-residents buying UK property for their own use. But the conclusion is much stronger for resident non-domiciliaries in view of the drawbacks of corporate ownership that already existed prior to the publication of the new proposals on 8 July 2015.

Direct trust ownership

28.6 For completeness it may also be added that ownership by a trust without a company cannot be recommended either. This is because such a trust is exposed to both 10-yearly charges and the GWR death risk in the manner described above. Non-trust individual ownership is, as noted above, exposed to IHT in the event of untimely death. But it does not also suffer 10-yearly charges. Trust ownership thus makes the position worse, not better.

IHT MITIGATION

28.7 Assuming the decision is for individual ownership, IHT mitigation is the key issue. As emphasised above, the problem is not an inevitable tax charge but a tax charge that arises only on untimely death, ie death before the non-domiciliary has left the UK, lost any deemed UK domicile, and removed the proceeds of the house abroad. In paras **27.14** to **27.20** a number of strategies are identified whereby non-residents can minimise the IHT risks. In general these can also avail resident non-domiciliaries, but there are a number of important qualifications.

First, the spouse exemption may be restricted if the non-domiciliary has a deemed UK domicile and his spouse does not (Inheritance Tax Act 1984 (IHTA 1984), 18(2)). However in practice this problem may be avoided if the surviving spouse is able to and does elect to be treated as UK domiciled (IHTA 1984, s 267ZA; see para **45.6**).

Second, commercial borrowing carries the cost that servicing the loan is a remittance. This result follows under general principles if servicing is in the UK and otherwise under the debt rules discussed in CHAPTER **56** if the servicing is outside the UK. In view of this, commercial mortgages may make sense only if the loan can be serviced out of clean capital or taxed UK income. A further point is that the interest will almost inevitably have a UK source as the borrower will be UK resident (see para **38.4**). This means deduction at source will apply if the lender is non-resident unless the interest is able to be and is paid gross under a treaty (see para **64.15**).

Third, co-ownership solutions are unlikely to be attractive. In the case of gifts of undivided shares this is because indefinite occupation by donees and donor is much less likely to be realistic in the long term if the house is the donor's main home, as distinct from a London base used on occasion by all members of a wide family. In the case of cash gifts, it is because, in relation to UK residents, POAT has to be considered and could well catch such gifts (see Chapter 86).

TRUST PURCHASE

28.8 As noted above, purchase by a settlor-interested trust is not to be recommended. But as described in para **27.23** in relation to non-residents the position may be different if the transaction is one of the trustees buying a residence for the use of a beneficiary and the trust is not settlor-interested. A number of issues arise should the occupying beneficiary be UK resident.

Funding

28.9 First, funds sent to the UK by the trustees to pay for the house will count as remitted. This will be without CGT consequences, as taxation under TCGA 1992, s 87 is not impacted by whether or not the trustees remit the s 2(2) amount (see para **79.4**). But the position is otherwise as respects the non-transferor charge under ss 731–735. Here remittance could cause an unremitted benefit to a non-UK domiciled beneficiary to become taxable (ITA 2007, s 735; see para **72.15**). This result follows if what the trustees remit is or is derived from the income matched with the benefit under the matching rules in s 735A (see para **72.5**). These rules can be very difficult to operate in practice. An important point to note is that the remittance-basis user whose benefit is at risk of becoming taxable need not be the same beneficiary as the one for whom the UK house is being bought.

IHT

28.10 Once the house is bought, the trustees have ongoing IHT exposure. But where the trust is not settlor-interested, the exposure is restricted to 10-yearly charges.

At 6% every ten years these are not insignificant and mitigation strategies may be considered. The most obvious is if the trustees borrow. The borrowing could be a simple commercial mortgage but it could also be from another trust. Example D31 in the GAAR guidance indicates such borrowing may not be seen as abusive (see para **98.16**). However if the trust also holds other assets, the borrowing might have to be secured on the property so as to secure a deduction for the borrowing trust under IHTA 1984, s 162(4) and if so HMRC might argue the lending trust is likely to have a UK situs asset. This point is discussed in para **27.17**, and the point there made is that it may not be possible to overcome the problem by interposing an offshore company as lender, on account of regulatory concerns.

Secured borrowing may thus raise difficulties. If the trust has no other assets a practical solution may be an unsecured loan from another trust. Normally this would not be set against the UK property (IHTA 1984, s 162(5)) but where there are no other trust assets it has to be, as the ten-yearly charge cannot be on more than the net value of the trust fund. It is in any event very undesirable for other reasons for a UK home to be held by a trust that also holds other assets, which may give rise to income or gains, if the user of the home is or may become UK resident. This issue is discussed below.

It goes without saying that the lending trust must not be one funded by the occupier of the house as otherwise issues would have to be considered under the GAAR, the GWR rules and POAT. Whether the borrowing is commercial or from another trust, it should be spent on buying or improving the property, so as to avoid issues under IHTA 1984, s 162A (see para **85.3**).

Benefits and capital payments

28.11 Occupation of the house is a benefit under the non-transferor charge and a capital payment under the capital payment rules (see paras **70.19** and **78.12**). If therefore there are gains or undistributed income in the owning trust liability under one or other of those sections may arise. These liabilities are those of the occupying beneficiary rather than the trustees.

Risks of this kind are minimised if the UK home is the sole asset of the trust for then there is no income and even if eventually there is a gain on the house, it could be covered by principal private residence relief (TCGA 1992, s 225). But in reality the kind of trust postulated here may have held other assets in the past and, even if the house is its first and only asset, it is always possible the house will be sold and the proceeds invested. In such a case income and gains generated by the investments can bring the benefit represented by the earlier occupation into charge (see Chapter **71** and para **77.21**). This is certainly so if the occupying beneficiary has remained UK resident and may be so as respects income even if he has not (see para **70.14**).

Should the owning trust borrow from another trust in the manner described above, income in the lending trust can be taken into account in taxing the benefit from the borrowing trust. The analysis is that the relevant transfer is the original transfer of assets to the lending trust, with the loan being an associated operation enabling the benefit represented by the house to be provided (ITA 2007, s 732(1)(c); see Chapter **71**).

It is unlikely the same analysis applies to CGT and capital payments as s 2(2) amounts do not move between trusts if the transfer is for full consideration (TCGA 1992, s 90; see para **77.29**). But the loan raises a different CGT issue, namely it is borrowing by the borrowing trust for the purposes of the trustee borrowing rules (TCGA 1992, Sch 4B; see Chapter **80**). This ought not to pose a problem if the entire loan proceeds are invested in the property as such as expenditure on ordinary trust assets (see para **80.11**). But the detail needs watching to ensure there is not inadvertent falling foul of Sch 4B.

EXISTING CORPORATE STRUCTURES

28.12 As may be apparent from the historical discussion in para **28.5** above, some existing non-domiciliary homes are owned in trust and company structures of the kind discussed in para **28.5** above. Such structures may so far have been retained, on the basis the IHT protection they confer outweighs the cost of ATED and the other drawbacks outlined in this chapter.

With IHT protection ceasing on 6 April 2017 the case for retaining these structures will require revisiting. The points bearing on this issue are, in general, the same as those discussed in para 27.26 in relation to non-residents. But the tax complications entailed in winding up the structure are likely to be greater for resident non-domiciliaries, principally for one reason. This is that, by definition, there is a UK resident beneficiary who will potentially be taxable insofar as he has received, or receives, capital distributions or benefits matched with the gains generated by the winding-up exercise. Such potentially matchable benefits include rent-free occupation of the house and would also include the capital distribution occasioned by any distribution of the house from the trust. Benefits of this nature are received in the UK and so do not attract the remittance basis.

The result of these considerations is that in some cases it may be best to retain the structure. Given he is non-UK domiciled, the occupying beneficiary will in due course leave the UK and at that point the house or the company can be sold, and the proceeds kept abroad. However, in all such cases a careful calculation needs to be carried out of the tax costs of winding up the structure compared with retaining it over the likely period of residence of the occupying beneficiary.

Section VII

Emigration from the UK

Chapter 29
EMIGRATION

INTRODUCTION

29.1 This chapter outlines the tax planning opportunities afforded by emigration from the UK. At the outset it must be emphasised this chapter is concerned only with UK tax. Most emigrants move to countries which also impose direct taxes, and in all such cases it is essential local tax advice is taken prior to emigration.

LEAVING THE UK

29.2 The issue of whether or not an individual is tax resident in the UK is determined by the statutory residence test, in force since 6 April 2013 (FA 2013, Sch 45). This test is complicated, but in contrast to previous law, it does make it possible to identify fact patterns which, if achieved, ensure an individual leaving the UK can be confident he is indeed non-UK resident.

Key scenarios

29.3 The statutory test is explained in CHAPTER 41, with the steps required to ensure a leaver is non-UK resident being detailed in paras **41.19** to **41.24**. There are perhaps three scenarios which are most likely to be encountered in practice.

The first scenario is full time work abroad (see paras **41.6** and **41.20**). The rules pertaining to this are complicated and, if it is to be relied on, must be studied with care. But the essence is that the individual must move abroad and work full time. Assuming he satisfies the various conditions set out in the legislation he can visit the UK for up to 90 midnights each tax year and his non-resident status is not jeopardised if he retains a home in the UK and his wife and children continue to be based there.

The second scenario is where the individual and his spouse and any minor children settle permanently in a new country (see para **41.22**). Here too it is possible to spend up to 90 midnights in the UK and it is also possible to retain a flat or house there. But it is necessary to restrict work in the UK to 40 days or less and it is also essential that the individual's spouse does not in her own right remain UK resident.

The third scenario is where the individual spends 15 or fewer midnights in the UK and ensures that his single day visits to the UK and days of departure from the UK are below 31 (see para **41.21**). Here the existence of family or other ties with the UK is irrelevant, as is the question of whether or not the individual settles permanently in one particular country.

An issue with the second and third of these scenarios, but not the first, is that the individual can be clawed back into residence in a given tax year should he die during the year. Self-evidently the consequences of this will have to be faced not by the individual himself but by his executors. In the case of the second scenario, the problem only arises if the UK visits are concentrated in the early part of the year, or if he dies in the first tax year following departure. These bizarre points are explained more fully in paras **41.21** to **41.22**.

Cessation of taxability in the UK

29.4 The statutory test looks at tax years as a whole (see para **41.2**). As a result an individual who satisfies the conditions for UK residence for part of a tax year is UK resident for the whole of it. This means that in most cases, 6 April is the day on which the individual ceases to be taxable in the UK as a resident of it.

The statutory test does provide for eight split year cases, three of which relate to leavers (see para **41.36**). Should any of these three cases be in point, the year of departure is split into a UK part and an overseas part. For most tax purposes, the individual is then treated as if he were non-UK resident in the overseas part but only for the purposes of certain charging provisions. Split year treatment does not mean he is in fact non-UK resident in the overseas part, and so in the case of any given charging provision it has to be checked if it is in fact one to which split year treatment applies.

Two of the three split year cases relating to leavers relate to full time work abroad, Case 1 applying to the full time worker and Case 2 to accompanying spouses (Sch 45 paras 44 and 45). The third case, Case 3 is of general application and applies if the following conditions are met (Sch 45 para 46).

(1) The individual has no home in the UK in the overseas part of the year.
(2) The individual spends fewer than 16 midnights in the UK in the overseas part of the year.
(3) Within six months of leaving, the individual becomes tax resident in another country or establishes his only home there.

As will be apparent this case is not in point where an emigrant retains a house or flat in the UK. Should an individual be within both Cases 1 or 2 and Case 3, Cases 1 and 2 determine when the overseas part of the tax year starts (Sch 45 para 54).

AVOIDING CGT

29.5 In many respects the principal tax opportunity afforded by emigration is the sheltering of gains. This opportunity is available because of two fundamental features of the CGT code. The first, described in para **37.5**, is that non-residents are not in general subject to CGT. The second is that the UK does not require latent gains to be brought into charge when an individual becomes non-UK resident.

As a result of these two features, an individual owning assets pregnant with gain can avoid the CGT otherwise payable by deferring any disposal of the assets until he is non-UK resident. There are however certain points that need to be kept in mind in planning of this sort.

Short-term migration

29.6 The CGT advantages of emigration are not usually achieved unless the migrant is non-UK resident for more than five years. This is the effect of the special anti-avoidance rule directed at those who are temporarily non-UK resident. This rule, contained in TCGA 1992, s 10A, is explained in paras **41.39** to **41.40**, and, unless split year treatment is in point, requires non-residence for six complete tax years.

Effect of the 5-year rule

29.7 As the statutory test applies to tax years as a whole, disposals are normally only free of CGT if made in or after the first complete tax year of non-residence. But where a split year case is in point, disposals in the overseas part of the year of departure are also free of CGT as split year treatment applies generally to CGT (TCGA 1992, s 2(1B)). It goes without saying that if reliance is being placed on a split year case, care should be taken to ensure the facts fall fairly and squarely within it.

The anti-avoidance rule for temporary non-residents does not apply unless the period of non-residence is five years or less. In other words, it is not a general rule catching disposals made by all emigrants in the first five years following departure. It follows that disposals made in the first tax year of non-residence or the overseas part of the split year are free of CGT in the same way as disposals made subsequently, provided that the individual ensures that he remains non-resident for more than five years.

UK branch or agency

29.8 An exception to the rule that non-residents are not liable to CGT arises where the non-resident is carrying on business in the UK through a branch or agency (TCGA 1992, s 10). In these circumstances gains are chargeable to the extent that they accrue on UK situs assets used for the purposes of either the branch or the business. At one time the charge was restricted to trades carried on through a branch or agency, but since 1989 it has extended to professions (s 10(5)).

A migrant may find he is trading in the UK through a branch or agency if he retains a UK business and runs it through a manager. Perhaps the most common example is farming but the problem can arise with any kind of business. A branch or agency trade also exists if the migrant is a partner in a UK partnership, for in law any one partner is the agent of all the others (Partnership Act 1890, s 5). Accordingly, the migrant is chargeable on his proportion of any gains realised by such a mixed residence UK partnership.

At one time, the charge on branch or agency gains could be avoided by removing the assets from the UK or by not disposing of them until after the branch or agency trade had ceased. These avoidance possibilities were blocked in 1989, and now a deemed disposal occurs if assets are removed from the UK or the branch or agency trade ceases (TCGA 1992, s 25(1)). Roll-over relief is not available on the disposal of branch or agency assets unless the new assets are also branch or agency assets (TCGA 1992, s 159).

For compliance purposes the branch or agent is the non-resident's UK representative (TCGA 1992, s 271B).

Charges on migration

29.9 Although the general rule is that migration goes not result in a CGT charge there are certain exceptions where gains have previously been deferred. The principal such exception arises if (1) the migrant has been the recipient of a gift and (2) a gain accruing on the making of the gift was held over under either of the two regimes for hold-over relief, namely that for business assets in TCGA 1992, s 165, and that involving trusts in TCGA 1992, s 260. If these conditions are satisfied, migration causes the held-over gain to be assessed on the migrant and charged at his marginal rate of tax (TCGA 1992, s 168).

Fortunately there are two important reliefs from this charge:

(1) The charge does not arise if migration occurs more than six years after the end of the tax year in which the hold-over disposal occurred (s 168(4)).
(2) The charge is also avoided if the taxpayer goes abroad for full time employment and returns within three years without having disposed of the assets (s 168(5)).

An exit charge can also arise where the migrant has deferred a gain under the Enterprise Investment Scheme. In such a case emigration triggers a charge on the postponed gain, but only if it occurs within three years (TCGA 1992, Sch 5B para 3(1)(C)). The charge is not made if the emigration is for less than three years and for full time employment.

It is unclear whether an argument could be run that these charges breach European law. The cases discussed in para 107.26 indicate that European law could be breached if the emigrant moves to the European Union or the European Economic Area. On these scenarios, the implication of those cases may be that the held over gains should not be charged until the asset is disposed of.

The death risk

29.10 As explained above (para **29.3**) death can in certain circumstances cause an individual who would otherwise have been non-resident in the year of death to be treated as UK resident. This point inter alia arises where, under the sufficient ties test, the individual is restricting his midnights in the UK to 45 or 90 and concentrates those midnights in the early part of the year and then dies.

The relevance of this point to CGT planning is that disposals in March in the tax year avoid this risk and disposals in the month or two previously minimise it. This is because in such cases death between the date of the disposal and the end of the tax year results in no or little reduction in the permitted day count.

This point means that, other things being equal, delaying disposals until the last month or two of the tax year can make sense. Equally if visits to the UK are spread evenly over the tax year the point does not arise at all and in such cases there is no reason to delay disposal until the end of the year.

CGT PLANNING

Postponing disposals

29.11 As indicated above, CGT is avoided if a permanent emigrant delays any disposal until the tax year following that of his departure. The date of disposal for CGT purposes is normally the date of contract (TCGA 1992, s 28). Accordingly, if a disposal needs to be postponed until a subsequent tax year, no contract should be entered into until after the following 6 April.

It should be remembered that a contract can be oral, save where the asset disposed of is land in England and Wales. Save as respects such land, HMRC may contend in provocative cases that there is an oral contract prior to emigration. Care should be taken to avoid giving a factual basis to support such a contention.

Delaying a binding contract can be unacceptable commercially, but in such situations advantage may sometimes be taken of two exceptions to the rule that the date of the contract is the date of disposal. These exceptions are, first, that a disposal under a conditional contract only occurs when the condition is satisfied, and second, that where an option is granted, the disposal only takes place when the option is exercised (TCGA 1992, s 28(2)).

In theory conditional contracts are the better means of postponing a disposal, for both sides are bound. Unfortunately it is often unclear whether a contract is in fact conditional. A contract is only conditional if (a) the condition is precedent to performance and (b) it is contingent in the sense that neither party covenants to bring it about (*Eastham v Leigh* [1971] Ch 871). The best example of a conditional contract is one whose performance is subject to an unconnected third party consent, for example, the grant of planning permission.

The difficulties with conditional contracts mean that options are frequently used to postpone the date of disposal. Options can either be call options, whereby the purchaser is entitled to call on the vendor to sell the asset, or put options, under which the vendor can require the purchaser to buy the asset. The disadvantage in both cases is that only one side is bound. Sometimes this disadvantage is overcome by using cross options, ie having both a call and put option. If these options are exercisable at the same price and at the same time, it may be that HMRC could argue they constituted a concluded contract, entered into when the options are granted. But such an argument is inconsistent with *J Sainsbury plc v O'Connor* [1991] STC 318, CA. It is on any view much less convincing if the periods of exercise for the options are successive and the price varies slightly.

In appropriate cases, cross options merit serious consideration. However, HMRC scrutiny should be expected, particularly as to whether, notwithstanding the documentation, there was a binding oral agreement prior to emigration. The possible impact of the GAAR should also be considered (see CHAPTER 98)

Company sales

29.12 Where the taxpayer sells a company he owns, CGT may be deferred under TCGA 1992, s 135 if the consideration is shares or loan stock rather than cash. In such case, the date of disposal for CGT purposes is deferred until the replacement shares or loan stock are disposed of. Over the years many individuals have emigrated before disposing of the replacement shares or loan stock and thereby sheltered gains.

It does however have to be remembered that the relief in s 135 is subject to a motive defence. Under TCGA 1992, s 137, the relief is precluded unless the exchange is effected for bona fide commercial reasons and does not form part of arrangements one of whose main purposes is the avoidance of CGT or corporation tax. This test thus has two requirements, one that the exchange be effected for commercial reasons and the other that it not form part of a tax avoidance scheme or arrangements. It has been considered in two emigration cases.

In the first, *Snell v HMRC* [2007] STC 1279, the taxpayer sold his company on 21 December 1996 in return for loan notes. The evidence was that at that time he intended to become non-resident and redeem the loan notes when non-resident and so avoid CGT. On 21 December he had not decided where to go, but in due course, on 2 April 1997, he emigrated to the Isle of Man and thereafter redeemed the loan notes.

The Special Commissioners and, on appeal, the High Court, decided the exchange was commercial, as the transaction to be looked at was the sale, regardless of the form it took. But they then decided there was a scheme or arrangement involving redemption of the loan notes when non-resident and as such that the motive defence was failed.

The case is curious in that the High Court refused to consider the distinction between avoidance and mitigation (as to which see paras 73.7 and 73.21 to 73.24). The taxpayer argued that emigration was mitigation, to which the

High Court responded that the distinction was not relevant to s 137. It is difficult to follow the logic of this.

In the second case, *Coll v HMRC* [2010] STC 1849, the evidence was again that the loan notes were taken as consideration with a view to avoiding CGT when non-resident, albeit that here too the taxpayer had not decided where to go. The Special Commissioner found that the test in s 137 was not satisfied, and the Upper Tribunal held this was a conclusion he was entitled to reach. It did however stress that the question was one of fact, with the implication that a contrary finding would also have been open to the Special Commissioner.

The moral of both *Snell* and *Coll* is that an individual selling a company who thinks emigration might be attractive should not develop or investigate such plans until the sale is concluded. However, if on the facts the purchaser has only ever been prepared to pay in shares or loan stock, an intention to emigrate should not be material.

Section 137 is subject to a clearance procedure in TCGA 1992, s 138. It should be remembered that a clearance does not hold good unless all relevant facts and considerations are disclosed. If therefore an applicant for clearance has considered becoming non-resident such should be referred to in the application.

Business assets

29.13 It is difficult for an individual to use migration to shelter gains accruing on the disposal of an unincorporated UK business. This is because once he migrates, the business will be a branch or agency trade, and gains on the business assets will accordingly remain in charge.

There are two ways round this difficulty. One is to sell the business before migration and invest the proceeds in the assets of a new business situated abroad. In these circumstances roll over relief is available (TCGA 1992, s 152). That relief is not clawed back when the individual migrates, and indeed it is even possible for the new assets to be purchased after migration. Since the new assets are foreign situs, no branch or agency charge can arise on their disposal, and accordingly, so long as the migrant remains non-resident, the gain is completely sheltered.

The second avoidance technique is to transfer the business to a company as a going concern prior to migration. If the transfer includes all the assets of the business and shares in the company are the sole consideration received by the individual, the gains on the business assets are rolled into the company shares (TCGA 1992, s 162). Since the shares are not a business, they can be sold after migration without fear of a branch or agency charge. To avoid attack under the *Ramsay* principle, the transfer to the company should take place before the sale of the company is negotiated. It should also take place before migration, since otherwise the cessation occasioned by the transfer could result in a branch or agency charge (TCGA 1992, s 25(3)), although HMRC said in 1990 they would not take this point (*Taxation Practitioner* (May 1990) p 232).

INCOME TAX

29.14 In general the main income tax advantage of emigration is that foreign income and some UK income drops out of charge. In many cases this advantage is more apparent than real, for the absence of UK tax is counter-balanced by tax in the jurisdiction to which the emigrant moves. But this is not always so as some jurisdictions do not levy direct tax and others offer incentives to immigrants.

Investment income

29.15 Once the emigrant is non UK resident his foreign investment income is free of UK tax (see para **37.2**). The tax exposure of his UK income is as described in para **64.6**. In general, UK income remains in charge but an exception is made for dividends and for interest paid gross. Emigration thus shelters not merely foreign investment income but also UK dividends and interest.

Should the emigrant attract split year treatment in the year of departure, foreign investment income in the overseas part of the year is not taxed (ITTOIA 2005, ss 368(2A)). The same applies to foreign rental income, the apportionment between the UK and the overseas part of the year being on a just and reasonable basis (ITTOIA 2005, s 270(3)). But split year treatment does not apply to UK dividends and interest, as such treatment is not available to the relief under ITA 2007, s 811 (for this relief see further para **64.6**).

In general it is immaterial to the above treatment if the emigrant is only temporarily non-resident. However an exception is made for close company dividends. These are taxed in the year of return if the emigrant returns having been non-resident for five or fewer years, whether the paying company is UK or non-UK (see para **41.41**).

Offshore income gains

29.16 Emigration takes unrealised offshore income gains out of charge for, as with capital gains, there is no deemed disposal of material interests in offshore funds when an individual emigrates. Should the emigrant enjoy split year treatment in the year of departure, OIGs realised in the overseas part of the year are free of tax, for OIGs are charged under ITTOIA 2005, Pt 5 chapter 8, which is subject to split year treatment (SI 2009/3001 reg 18(2), ITTOIA 205 s 577(2A)). OIGs are however one of the categories of income taxed in the year of return where the individual is only temporarily non-resident (see para **41.42**). This means permanent or long term emigration is required to shelter OIGs.

Business income

29.17 A migrant who has been engaged in a trade or profession in the UK is treated as permanently discontinuing the trade when he migrates (ITTOIA 2005, s 17). If in fact the business continues it is treated as newly started up.

The notional discontinuance takes place at the start of the overseas part of the year of departure should split year treatment be in point (s 17(1B)(b)). Otherwise it occurs at the beginning of the first tax year of non-residence.

The individual remains in charge to UK tax if and insofar as the business operations continue in the UK, for then he is trading in rather than with the UK (cf para **40.7** and *IRC v Brackett* [1986] STC 521). If as is normal the UK business operations amount to a branch or agency, the branch or agent is assessable as UK representative (ITA 2007, ss 835E and 835U). Losses of the period of UK residence are able to be brought forward (ITTOIA 2005, s 17(3)).

Should the migrant be in partnership there is no discontinuance of the migrant's trade under the partnership if the partnership business is carried on wholly in the UK. But if this is not the case, the migrant suffers a discontinuance and recommencement of his notional trade (ITTOIA 2005, s 852).

Employment income

29.18 A non-resident is only liable to UK tax on employment income insofar as duties are performed in the UK (ITEPA 2003, s 27). These rules apply whether the employer is foreign or UK based and are subject to any applicable double tax treaty. Tax is recovered by the PAYE system and it is possible to obtain a direction as to the proportion of the earnings which are to be treated as taxable for the purposes of operating PAYE (ITEPA 2003, s 690).

In the year of departure, split year treatment may be claimed for earnings from an employment carried on wholly abroad, with the result that post departure earnings from such employment are not taxable (ITEPA 2003, s 15(1A). This inter alia protects individuals who emigrate and immediately take up a new foreign employment.

The employment related securities legislation remains in point so long as the securities (or option) were acquired while the taxpayer was UK resident. Assuming the tax charges arise after emigration a form of remittance basis may apply as respects the post-emigration period (see paras **50.13** to **50.16**).

Planning opportunities

29.19 The principal income planning opportunity is deferring receipts until after departure. As a general rule such deferral is not practical, as the timing of most categories of receipt is outside the control of the individual. However there are exceptions to this, most notably offshore income gains and close company dividends. In the case of OIGs, the timing of the receipt is when the investor sells his interest in the fund and is thus within his control. So too if the individual controls a close company, he can decide when dividends are paid.

The only limitation on these types of planning is the temporary residence rule discussed above. But as indicated above, this is only in point should the individual in fact be non-resident for five or fewer tax years. Provided he remains non-resident for longer it does not preclude realisation earlier provided he is definitely non-resident at the time of realisation.

NON-RESIDENT TRUSTS

29.20 Emigration can impact on the emigrant's position under non-UK resident trusts.

Settlor

29.21 Should the emigrant have settled a non-resident trust which is within TCGA 1992, s 86, cessation of UK residence precludes further liability, for UK residence is a prerequisite of liability under that section (see para **76.2**). But freedom from s 86 comes only from 6 April following departure, split year treatment not being available (TCGA 1992, s 86(4)(a)). Section 86 is subject to the rule for temporary non-residents described above, as that applies generally to CGT.

Should the settlor or his spouse be beneficiaries under the trust, emigration takes foreign income out of charge but UK source income remains taxed as the settlor's under the income tax settlement code (see para **75.26**). Should the year of departure be a split year, foreign source settlement income in the overseas part of the year is outside the settlor charge (ITTOIA 2005, s 577(2A)).

As indicated in para **69.20**, the transfer of assets code is in point in relation to company income should a settlor-interested settlement own its investments through a company. Here emigration removes both UK and foreign income from the transferor charges (see para **69.44**). But split year treatment is not in point (see para **69.45**).

Beneficiaries

29.22 Once a beneficiary has emigrated, income distributions from a foreign discretionary trust are free of UK tax, as the distribution is foreign source (see para **40.13**). Should the year of departure qualify for split year treatment income distributions in the overseas part of the year are free of tax (ITTOIA 2005, s 577(2A)).

Capital distributions are not taxed as income under the non-transferor charge provided the recipient is non-UK resident in the year of receipt (see para **70.14**). Split year treatment is not available in the year of departure but the rule for temporary non-residents does not apply as the non-transferor charge is not one of the provisions within that rule.

The CGT charge under TCGA 1992, s 87 is not in point either should the recipient be non-UK resident (see para **77.46**). But here, in contrast to income tax, tax is clawed back in the year of return if the individual is non-UK resident for five or fewer years as that is the general rule for CGT. Also in contrast to income tax, a form of split year treatment applies if the year of departure qualifies for split year treatment. Here the s 87 gains are not split according as to the timing of capital payments. Instead a proportion of the year's s 87 gains are exempt, the proportion being the proportion the overseas part of the year bears to the whole year (TCGA 1992, s 87(7)).

The rules relating to trust distributions offer scope for planning. In particular, if income is the sole tax in issue, short term non-residence can allow tax fee distributions. But it should be remembered that if the distribution is capital, removal of the transfer of assets charge by non-residence leaves the way open for the distribution to be matched with trust gains under s 87 and be taxed on return should the beneficiary be temporarily non-resident. This result is only avoided if the trust has no s 2(2) or OIG amounts or some other relief from s 87 is in point.

INHERITANCE TAX

29.23 An individual with an actual UK domicile who leaves the UK remains liable to inheritance tax until three complete years have elapsed after he has acquired a domicile of choice in a new country. As is described in CHAPTER **44**, he only acquires such a domicile of choice if he fixes his chief residence in the new country with the intention of remaining there permanently or indefinitely. In the case of a federal country, his intention must be to remain permanently or indefinitely in the particular state, province etc in which he has his new residence.

A migrant remains liable to IHT until three tax years have elapsed because for IHT purposes he has a deemed UK domicile during that period (see CHAPTER **45**). Once the three-year period is up, all foreign situs assets of the migrant are taken out of the ambit of IHT. UK situs assets are still within the scope of IHT, but this difficulty can be overcome by owning those assets through a foreign registered holding company.

As discussed in CHAPTER **45**, it is likely that the IHT deemed domicile rules will be amended with effect from 6 April 2017. One result of this change will be that an individual who has been resident in the UK for 15 or more tax years will typically be deemed domiciled under a different rule from that referred to above; and if the individual ceases to be UK resident, such deemed domicile will typically persist for a minimum of four tax years after the last tax year of residence (and then only if he remains non-UK resident for a further two tax years). This other rule may lengthen the IHT 'tail' that applies when an individual emigrates from the UK, depending on how quickly the individual acquires a new domicile of choice in the new country.

As is described in para **37.13**, there are certain assets where liability to IHT is not determined by domicile. The most notable is British government securities, most of which are outside the ambit of IHT provided the owner is not resident. It follows that an emigrant can secure IHT protection by switching his assets to appropriate government securities once he has lost residence, regardless of domicile. Such switching should not, of course, be effected until the tax year after that of departure if it would result in capital gains being realised and nor should it effected if there is any likelihood of falling foul of TCGA 1992, s 10A (para **29.6** above).

Chapter 30
MIGRATION OF TRUSTS

INTRODUCTION

30.1 The migration of a trust does not usually entail the UK trustees moving abroad, although if this happened, the trust would become non-resident. Instead, the UK trustees retire, and non-residents are appointed in their place. As is described in CHAPTER 42, all the new trustees should be non-resident unless all persons who have contributed funds to the settlement were neither resident nor domiciled in the UK when they did so.

CAN THE TRUST MIGRATE?

30.2 The essence of trusteeship is a personal obligation binding the conscience of the trustee. The courts of equity enforce the trust at the instance of the beneficiaries, but in order to do so, the trustees need to be in the jurisdiction. These fundamental principles mean difficult issues may, at least in theory, be raised by the appointment of foreign trustees of a trust governed by English law.

Express power

30.3 There is little doubt that the courts will in appropriate cases sanction the appointment of non-resident trustees. There are several cases where this has happened, and in view of those cases it necessarily follows that the appointment of non-resident trustees can be expressly authorised by a settlement. Most modern settlements do contain such authorisation, coupled with a provision preventing the removal of a trustee on the grounds of absence for more than twelve months. It is generally accepted that such provisions make the appointment of a foreign trustee subject to the same considerations as apply where a resident trustee is appointed.

No express power

30.4 At one time the law where there is no express power is thought to have been summarised by Sir John Pennycuick V-C in *Re Whitehead* [1971] 2 All ER 1334 at 1337:

'the law I think has been quite well established for upwards of a century, that there is no absolute bar to the appointment of persons resident abroad as trustees of an English trust. I say "no absolute bar", in the sense that such an appointment would be prohibited by law and would consequently be invalid. On the other hand, apart from exceptional circumstances, it is not proper to make such an appointment. That is to say, the court would not, apart from exceptional circumstances, make such an appointment, nor would it be right for the donee of the power, apart from exceptional circumstances, to make such an appointment out of court. If they did, presumably the court would be likely to interfere at the instance of the beneficiaries. There do, however, exist exceptional circumstances in which such an appointment can properly be made.'

Two points follow from this dictum. First, it is plain that an appointment of foreign trustees can never be invalid in the sense that it is void. Accordingly, it is effective unless and until upset by the beneficiaries and thus, if they accept the appointment, binds HMRC. However, according to Pennycuick V-C, the appointment is 'improper' unless special circumstances exist.

The following cases are material in deciding what special circumstances suffice:

(1) In *Meinertzhagen v Davis* (1844) 1 Coll 335 the court approved the appointment of US trustees where the beneficiaries were US domiciliaries moving to the US.

(2) In *Re Long's Settlement* (1868) 19 LT 672 the court refused the appointment of New Zealand trustees where the beneficiaries were about to go, but had not yet gone, to New Zealand.

(3) In *Re Smith's Trusts* (1872) 26 LT 820 the court appointed Canadian trustees where the beneficiaries had lived in Canada since 1858.

(4) In *Re Liddiard* (1880) 14 Ch D 310 the court appointed Australian trustees where all the beneficiaries lived in Australia.

(5) In *Re Seale's Marriage Settlement* [1961] 3 All ER 136 Buckley J sanctioned an arrangement under the Variation of Trusts Act 1958 involving the appointment of Canadian trustees and an advance into an identical Canadian settlement where the beneficiaries had lived in Canada for many years.

(6) In *Re Weston's Settlements* [1969] 1 Ch 223 the Court of Appeal refused to sanction a similar arrangement in relation to Jersey. The beneficiaries were young, had only lived in Jersey for three months and could easily move.

(7) In *Re Windeatt's Will Trusts* [1969] 2 All ER 324, Pennycuick V-C distinguished *Re Weston* on the grounds that the beneficiaries had lived in Jersey for nearly 20 years.

(8) In *Re Whitehead's Will Trusts* [1971] 2 All ER 1334 itself Pennycuick V-C approved the appointment of Jersey trustees where the beneficiaries had lived in Jersey since 1959.

More recent decisions

30.5 The effect of these cases is that in the absence of an express power the only circumstances in which it is established as 'proper' to appoint non-resident trustees is if the beneficiaries live in the jurisdiction in which the proposed trustees reside. Certain unreported decisions, however, suggest that this approach is too restrictive (see *Capital Taxes* [1992] 81). The decisions are as follows:

(1)   In *Re Chamberlain*, an arrangement was approved under the Variation of Trusts Act 1958 for the export of a trust to Guernsey. The beneficiaries were domiciled in Guernsey and Indonesia.

(2)   In *Richard v Hon A B Mackay* Millet J sanctioned an advance to a new Bermuda trust. The beneficiaries were all UK domiciled although some had Far Eastern connections.

(3)   In *Re Beatty*, Vinelott J sanctioned the appointment of Jersey trustees of a Will trust, where one of the three principal beneficiaries lived in Australia and another was about to move to Spain.

In the latter two cases, both Millet J and Vinelott J drew a distinction between cases where the court is appointing new trustees and cases where the appointment is being made out of court. They suggested that in the latter situation Pennycuick V-C's language is too restrictive. All that is required is that the appointor can properly form the view that the appointment of non-resident trustees is for the benefit of the beneficiaries. That suggestion is highly persuasive, as it brings the considerations in relation to the proposed appointment of non-resident trustees into line with the considerations in relation to any other proposed exercise of a fiduciary power.

Millet J referred with approval to a decision of Mann J in Australia (*Re Kay, MacKinnon v Stringer* [1927] VLR 66). Mann J identified the two relevant considerations as being:

'First, that the proposed transaction should not put the trust fund at risk or deprive the beneficiaries of appropriate protection from a court armed with the necessary powers; and, secondly, that the transfer of funds or the appointment of foreign trustees is appropriate.'

Millet J then concluded:

'Certainly in the conditions of today, when one can have an international family with international interests, and where they are as likely to make their home in one country as in another, and as likely to choose one jurisdiction as another for the investment of their capital, I doubt that the language of Sir John Pennycuick is really in tune with the times. In my judgment, where the trustees retain their discretion, as they do in the present case, the court should need to be satisfied only that the proposed transaction is not so inappropriate that no reasonable trustee could entertain it.'

Where are we now?

30.6   It is tempting to conclude in the light of these three cases that Sir John Pennycuick's dictum in *Re Whitehead* can be disregarded. However, it is to be observed that none of the three cases concerned the typical and straightforward case where it is proposed to appoint non-resident trustees of an English trust, with exclusively UK beneficiaries. The three cases make it likely that such an appointment would, if challenged, be upheld as proper. But in none of the three cases was the point so decided on the facts, and the strong language of the Court of Appeal in *Re Weston's Settlements* must not be forgotten. For the present, caution, where there is no express power, should still be the watchword, coupled with a hope that the issue will at some stage be concluded by a properly reported decision directly in point.

FORM OF MIGRATION

30.7 Section 37(1)(c) of the Trustee Act 1925 must be watched when a trust governed by English law migrates. It provides as follows:

> 'it shall not be obligatory, save as hereinafter provided, to appoint more than one new trustee where only one trustee was originally appointed, or to fill up the original number of trustees where more than two trustees were originally appointed, but, except where only one trustee was originally appointed, and a sole trustee when appointed will be able to give a valid receipt for all capital money, a trustee shall not be discharged from his trust unless there will be either a trust corporation or at least two persons to act as trustees to perform the trust;'

A trust corporation is a corporation entitled to act as a custodian trustee by rules made under the Public Trustee Act 1906 (Trustee Act 1925, s 68). Under these rules it must be incorporated under the law of the UK or some EU country and have a place of business in the UK. Such a corporation, therefore, will not be found in offshore jurisdictions.

As a result, the practical effect of s 37(1)(c) on trust migration is that the resident trustees do not get a good discharge unless there are at least two non-resident trustees. Until 1 January 1997, the non-resident trustees had to include at least two individuals, but the law was changed by the Trusts of Land and Appointment of Trustees Act 1996, Sch 3 para 3(12). If there is no good discharge, the resident trustees remain trustees and the trust is likely to remain resident (cf *Adam & Co International Trustees Ltd v Theodore Goddard* [2000] 2 ITELR 634 and *Jasmine Trustees Ltd v Wells and Hind* [2007] STC 660).

Section 37(1)(c) can be excluded by express provision in the settlement (Trustee Act 1925 s 69(2); see also *London Regional Transport Pension Fund Trust Co v Hatt* [1993] PLR 227 and *Lewin on Trusts* (17th ed, 2000), pp 14–25).

HMRC used to take a point on s 37(1)(c) prior to 1 January 1997 where two individuals were not appointed. It may be assumed they would now take the point if two persons are not appointed.

TAX ON MIGRATION

30.8 When a trust migrates the trustees are deemed to have disposed of and immediately reacquired all the settled property at its market value immediately before the relevant time (TCGA 1992, s 80). The relevant time is the time at which the trustees become not resident in the UK. Since the deemed disposal takes place immediately before the relevant time, any gains on the deemed disposal accrue to the UK trustees rather than to their non-resident successors.

The deemed disposal does not extend to UK situate assets which immediately after the relevant time are branch or agency assets of a trade carried on in the UK by the trustees: such assets remain in the charge by virtue of TCGA 1992, s 10. Nor does the deemed disposal extend to assets if, before the relevant time, gains accruing on them would have been protected by a double tax treaty (s 80(5)).

A further restriction prevents the trustees from claiming roll-over relief under TCGA 1992, s 152 if the new assets are acquired after the relevant time (s 80(6)). An exception is made where the trustees are trading in the UK and the new assets are branch or agency assets.

Reliefs

30.9 Relief from the s 80 charge is available where the trustees of a resident settlement become non-resident as a result of the death of a trustee. Where this relief applies the deemed disposal under s 80 is restricted to certain assets provided the trustees again become UK resident within six months. The assets to which the charge is restricted are assets disposed of between the death and the resumption of UK residence and such assets (if any) as on the resumption of residence are protected from UK CGT by a double tax treaty.

Relief from the s 80 charge is also conferred where (1) the death of a trustee causes non-resident trustees to become UK resident and (2) the trustees again become non-resident within six months. In these circumstances the deemed disposal under s 80 is restricted to assets which the trustees acquired while resident and in respect of which a hold-over relief claim has been made.

Recovery of tax from past trustees

30.10 TCGA 1992, s 82 empowers HMRC to recover CGT assessed under s 80 from certain past trustees. They are able to invoke this section if the CGT is not paid by the migrating trustees within six months from the time when it becomes payable. That time is 31 January in the following year of assessment.

The tax may be recovered from a past trustee if two conditions are satisfied. First, he must have retired within 12 months of the migration. Second, at the time of his retirement there must have been a proposal that the trustees might become non-resident. A retired trustee who has to pay the tax has a right of recovery against the migrating trustees.

Section 82 must be remembered whenever the trustee of a resident trust retires. If the export of the trust is even remotely in contemplation, he will need to see that he is satisfactorily indemnified against liability under this section. The section is open to criticism, for tax is recoverable from a past trustee whether or not he personally retired with a view to facilitating migration. Its effect is particularly harsh where a trustee is involuntarily removed, as can happen under many modern settlements.

European law

30.11 As a result of decisions of the European Court of Justice there is a live issue as to whether the s 80 charge is compatible with European law. This issue is discussed in para **107.26**.

The bed and breakfast rule

30.12 Should the UK trustees sell shares prior to resigning in favour of non-resident trustees, the shares sold are not identified with shares of the same class acquired within the next 30 days if such acquisition takes place after the non-resident trustees are appointed (TCGA 1992, s 106A(5A)). This rule disapplies the normal anti bed and breakfasting rule in TCGA 1992, s 106A(5) and counteracts the scheme for avoiding the exit charge upheld in *Davies v Hicks* [2005] EWHC 847 (Ch), [2005] STC 850.

OTHER CGT CONSEQUENCES OF MIGRATION

Disposals in year of migration

30.13 Gains accruing on disposals after migration but in the same tax year are fully chargeable. This is because gains are chargeable if the taxpayer is resident in the UK during any part of the year (TCGA 1992, s 2(1A)(c)). Split year rules have never applied to trusts.

The chargeability of gains realised in the year of departure applies even if the new trustees are resident in a treaty territory whose treaty with the UK gives the territory sole taxing rights over capital gains. This has been the law since 16 March 2005 (TCGA 1992, s 83A as inserted by F(No 2)A 2005, s 33). Once a new tax year starts the overseas trustees are fully within the regimes for offshore trusts in TCGA 1992, ss 86 and 87 (see CHAPTERS 76 and 77).

Capital payments

30.14 As is described in CHAPTERS 77 and 82, the OIG and s 2(2) amounts of a non-resident trust are attributed to beneficiaries who receive capital payments in the same year as the gains accrue, or who have received hitherto unallocated payments in earlier years. When a trust migrates it should be remembered that a capital payment is brought into account for these purposes if it was received when the trust was resident and was made in anticipation of a disposal by the trustees when non-resident (see para **77.34**). So too a capital payment received from a resident trust can be taxed by reference to a Sch 4C pool if made after or in anticipation of the Sch 4B transfer (TCGA 1992, Sch 4C para 9; see para **81.6**).

As explained in CHAPTER 78, capital payments include advances in specie and the free use of property. Furthermore, unless a sub-fund election has been made, a beneficiary is taxed even if the settlement is a single settlement divided into funds, and the gain accrues in a fund from which he is excluded. Thus a beneficiary who is paid out in full in anticipation of a disposal after migration can be taxed in full on subsequent trust gains even though he cannot benefit from them.

Beneficial interests

30.15 As is explained in para **7.11**, the exemption for disposals of beneficial interests under settlements does not apply if the trustees of the settlement are non-resident when the disposal takes place. TCGA 1992, s 85 gives a measure of relief where the settlement was formerly UK resident and has migrated. This relief applies to any beneficiary whose interest was created or acquired before the relevant time, that is, the date of migration. Where it applies, any gain accruing on a subsequent disposal of the beneficial interest is computed on the basis that the beneficiary acquired the interest at its market value at the relevant time. This does not apply if prior to being resident in the UK the trust was previously non-resident and at the relevant time it has unallocated s 2(2) amounts or a Sch 4C pool (TCGA 1992, s 85(10)).

Trustee borrowing

30.16 So long as the settlement is UK resident and has not previously been non-resident, outstanding trustee borrowing within the meaning of TCGA 1992, Sch 4B is immaterial (see para **80.29**). But this ceases to be so once the settlement becomes non-resident. Ideally any borrowing should be repaid before emigration or, if not, great care is needed to ensure the non-resident trustees do not make a transfer of value. This subject is discussed in CHAPTER 80.

INCOME TAX IMPLICATIONS

30.17 The emigration of a trust does not generally trigger recognition of income. However, one important exception is offshore income gains, as a disposal for the purposes of the offshore fund legislation takes place whenever it occurs for CGT purposes (see para **95.13**).

Emigration does not affect the income tax exposure of actual income (as distinct from deemed income) if the trust is a fixed-interest trust, as such income is taxed by reference to the life tenant (see para **8.2**). But if the trust is discretionary, emigration renders the foreign income of the trust free of tax (see para **37.2**). Post-emigration foreign income in the year of emigration is free of UK tax as the rules pertaining to the residence of trusts do not render the trust tax resident for the tax year as a whole but merely for that part of it during which the conditions for UK residence are met (ITA 2007, s 475). UK income of the trust remains in charge unless none of the beneficiaries is UK resident (see para **64.8**).

WHEN SHOULD A TRUST MIGRATE?

30.18 In the 1980s many trusts migrated in order to shelter prospective gains from CGT. Migration has only occasioned a deemed disposal of trust assets since 1991: before then the only CGT consequence of migration was that any gain held over on the transfer of an asset into the trust became chargeable. Once the trust was non-resident, gains were free of tax on an arising basis, for it was also only in 1991 that the rules attributing gains to the settlor were introduced.

Since 1991 the migration of trusts has been much less common. The deemed disposal on migration means migration should generally only be considered where the trust is free of latent gains or where the tax charge on those gains is acceptable. Such may be the position if the assets concerned are going to be sold in any event, particularly if further growth before sale is anticipated and after emigration the gains will not be attributed to the settlor under TCGA 1992, s 86. However, there is of course scope for a 'dry' tax charge in this scenario, and the anticipated further growth may not materialise, in which case more tax will be paid than necessary.

Where s 86 is in point after emigration, emigration may on any view be seen as pointless as exposure to CGT remains. It should however be remembered that s 86 only catches gains. If, therefore, the trust's return when non-resident will be mainly actual or deemed income, emigration may be attractive, provided the settlor and his spouse are wholly excluded.

Where s 86 is not in point, for example because the settlor is dead, non-resident, or non-domiciled, emigration of the trust may still be regarded as unattractive on account of the taxes on distributions, summarised in CHAPTER 9. But these drawbacks may be more apparent than real, as distributions are free of all tax if the recipient is non-resident for more than five years (see para 10.2). Self-evidently, tax on distributions is also avoided if none are made.

Looking at the position overall, the arguments in CHAPTER 1 deployed in favour of newly created trusts being offshore apply equally to existing trusts. If, therefore, emigration is possible without significant tax charge, it should be given serious consideration.

Chapter 31
COMPANY MIGRATION

INTRODUCTION

31.1 A UK resident company migrates when one of two conditions is fulfilled:

(1)   it becomes non-resident under the central management and control test; or

(2)   it becomes dual resident.

Central management and control

31.2 A company can now only become non-resident under the central management and control test if it is foreign registered (CTA 2009, s 14; see para **43.15**). For such a company migration can be effected easily and without uncertainty, for all that is required is for the directors to cease meeting in the UK and commence meeting in a foreign territory (assuming, of course, that the strategic decisions in relation to the company's business and assets are indeed being made by the board, rather than a shadow director). Provided the board meets in the new territory and properly discharges its functions the company will be resident there (see para **43.11**).

Dual residence

31.3 A company becomes dual resident if it is resident in the UK and some other country under their respective domestic laws, and under a double tax treaty between the UK and the other country it becomes treated as resident in the other country for the purposes of the treaty (CTA 2009, s 18). A company becomes so treated if the place of effective management moves to the other country. Under this test both foreign and UK registered companies can become non-resident (para **43.16**).

Criminal offences

31.4 Until 1988 company migration without Treasury consent was an offence. Now consent is no longer required, but migration does occasion certain tax and compliance consequences.

TAX CONSEQUENCES OF MIGRATION

The deemed disposal

31.5 A company is deemed to dispose of its assets for CGT purposes immediately before it ceases to be resident (TCGA 1992, s 185). The fact that the disposal is before rather than on migration is significant, for it means any resultant gains belong to the accounting period which ends with the migration. The cessation of residence in the UK is one of those events which causes an accounting period to end (CTA 2009, s 10(1)(g)).

The deemed disposal and ensuing reacquisition take place at market value, and they extend to all the company's assets. There is, however, one exception and this is where the company continues to carry on a trade in the UK through a permanent establishment (s 185). In these circumstances assets situate in the UK and used in the trade or for the purposes of the permanent establishment are excepted from the deemed disposal. But this exception is not as generous as it appears, for the assets concerned remain within the charge to CGT even after the migration (TCGA 1992, s 10B).

Postponement of the charge

31.6 In certain circumstances gains accruing on the deemed disposal can be postponed. This is possible if, and only if, the migrating company is the 75% subsidiary of a UK parent (TCGA 1992, s 187). For the postponement to apply both the parent and the migrating subsidiary must give notice of election to HMRC within two years of the migration.

If an election is made, all the gains and losses arising in respect of the assets deemed to be disposed of are aggregated. The resultant figure is then treated as a single gain and this is treated as (a) not accruing to the migrating company but (b) accruing to the parent if and at such time as one of three events take place:

(1)   the parent itself migrates, or
(2)   the migrating company ceases to be a 75% subsidiary of the parent by reason of the parent disposing of some or all of its shares in the subsidiary, or
(3)   the parent disposes of shares in the subsidiary after the latter has ceased to be a 75% subsidiary otherwise than on a disposal of its shares.

The postponed gain can also accrue to the parent if the subsidiary disposes of any of the assets which were subject to the deemed disposal (s 187). But such disposals only trigger a charge if they occur within six years of the migration, and, where some only of the assets are disposed of, only a proportion of the postponed gain is charged.

In certain circumstances the postponed gain can be reduced (s 187(5)). This happens where the subsidiary has allowable losses which have not otherwise been relieved and requires an election by both the parent and the subsidiary. This relief is of restricted effect because (1) allowable losses cannot accrue to non-residents save in respect of UK permanent establishment assets (TCGA

1992, s 16(3)) and (2) any losses accruing prior to migration will have already been relieved by a reduction in the postponed gain. As a result the relief appears to operate only if the non-resident trades in the UK through a permanent establishment and the losses accrue there.

Loss of roll-over relief

31.7 One of the quirks of roll-over relief is that new assets count as new assets even if the trader becomes non-resident before they are acquired (TCGA 1992, s 152 passim).

Unfortunately companies cannot take advantage of this, for when a company migrates no asset acquired subsequently can count as a new asset (TCGA 1992, s 185(2)). The only exception is the same as that made for the deemed disposal on migration: an asset can count as a new asset if (a) the company trades in the UK through a permanent establishment, (b) the asset is UK situate and (c) it is used in the permanent establishment.

European law

31.8 The issue of whether the deemed disposal on migration could be in breach of European law is discussed in para **107.26**, as is the relief applying where the migrating company becomes resident and carries on business in the EU or EEA.

COMPLIANCE OBLIGATIONS

31.9 Although the criminal sanction preventing company migration has gone, some obligations still have to be complied with (TMA 1970, ss 109B–109F). These obligations are normal compliance obligations and failure to honour them results not in prosecution but in penalties.

Notifying HMRC

31.10 The following conditions must be satisfied by the company before it migrates:

(1) It must notify HMRC of (a) the time at which it intends to migrate and (b) the tax outstanding or payable in respect of accounting periods beginning before that time.
(2) It must make arrangements for securing the payment of all the tax and those arrangements must be approved by HMRC. If a dispute arises as to the amount of the tax it is settled by the First-tier Tribunal. The tax outstanding or payable includes interest on tax and any corporation tax occasioned by the deemed disposal on migration. It also includes PAYE, and other tax deductible at source (s 109F).

The penalty for failing to comply with these obligations is a sum equal to the tax outstanding at the time of migration (TMA 1970, s 109C). This penalty may be recovered from:

(1)   The migrating company itself.
(2)   Any director of the migrating company or of any company which controls it.
(3)   Any person who has instructed or directed the directors to cause the relevant obligations to be breached.

For a director or other person to be caught, he has to be a party to an act which to his knowledge will result in breach of the compliance obligations. But directors are rebuttably presumed to be parties to any act of the migrating company and they are also rebuttably presumed to know the effect of any act which in fact breaches the company's obligations. The term 'director' bears the same meaning as in the income tax benefits code and therefore includes shadow directors (s 109F(3); see further CHAPTER 93).

HMRC guidance notes

31.11 In 1990 HMRC published guidance notes for migrating companies, which explain how the compliance rules operate in practice (SP 2/90). The advance notification of migration should be sent to HMRC, CT and VAT International (Company Migrations), Floor 3c, 100 Parliament Street, London SW1A 2BQ. Two or more months should be allowed. A resident solicitor or accountant should be appointed to act for the company after the migration and the unpaid tax should be secured by a guarantee from a bank or a suitable resident company. If the guarantee is to be unlimited, the tax liabilities do not need to be computed in detail, and as a result the approval will be speeded up.

Securing unpaid tax

31.12 The main method by which the outstanding tax is secured is by the compliance obligations just described (TMA 1970, s 109E). However, in case those provisions do not prove watertight, HMRC have further powers to recover tax due from the migrating company. The following persons may be required to pay any unpaid tax:

(1)   Any company in the same group as the migrating company.
(2)   Any individual who is or was a controlling director of either the migrating company or a company which controls it. A controlling director is a director who controls the company concerned. For these purposes, a shadow director counts as a director and control bears its close company definition discussed in CHAPTER 87 (TMA 1970, s 109F(4)); CTA 2010, ss 450 and 451.

HMRC may require these persons to pay the tax if the tax is outstanding more than six months after it is payable. Written notice must be served, specifying the amount of the tax and requiring payment within 30 days. No notice can be served more than three years after the amount of the tax has been finally determined.

Part B

THE DOMESTIC
LEGAL FRAMEWORK

Section I

Characterisation

Section 1

Characterisation

Chapter 32
CHARACTERISATION

INTRODUCTION

32.1 As will be apparent from the discussion of situs and source in CHAPTERS 38 and 40, a key issue in offshore tax planning can be deciding how, for UK tax purposes, a foreign entity or receipt should be characterised. This chapter outlines the salient principles established by the decided cases.

GENERAL

32.2 The leading modern cases on characterisation are *Memec plc v HMRC* [1998] STC 754 and *Revenue and Customs Comrs v Anson* [2015] UKSC 44, [2015] STC 1777, 17 ITLR 1007. In *Memec* the Court of Appeal referred with approval to a dictum of Rowlatt J in *Garland v Archer-Shee* (1929) 15 TC 693, 711. Rowlatt J said:

'The question of American law is, what exactly are the rights and duties of the parties under an American trust, and when you find what those rights and duties are, you see what category they come in, and the place they fill in the scheme of the English Income Tax Acts which the Courts here must construe.'

At first instance in *Memec*, Robert Walker J made the same point ([1996] STC 1336, 1348):

'When an English tribunal has to apply the provisions of a United Kingdom taxing statute to some transaction, arrangement or entity which is governed by a foreign system of law, the tribunal must take account of the rules of that foreign system (properly proved if not admitted) in order to determine the nature and character-istics of the transaction, arrangement or entity. But having informed itself in this way, the tribunal must then apply the taxing statute as part of English law.'

This part of Robert Walker J's judgment was referred to with approval by the Supreme Court in *Anson*. In delivering the sole judgment, Lord Reed emphasised that exercise has two stages, the first of which, being a matter of foreign law, is a question of fact in the English Court. At para 51 of his speech Lord Reed said:

'First, the questions whether the members had a right to the profits, and as to the nature of that right, were questions of non-tax law, governed by the law of Delaware. The FTT's conclusion, whether correctly construed as a finding that Delaware law had the effect of conferring on the members of the LLC an automatic statutory (or contractual) entitlement to the profits of the LLC, or as a finding that

Delaware law vested the members with a proprietary right to the profits as they arose, was on either view a finding of fact. Secondly domestic tax law – in this case, the relevant double taxation agreement as given effect in UK law – then fell to be applied to the facts as so found.'

The most dramatic illustration of the two stage exercise required is represented by the *Archer-Shee* cases, where essentially the same legal dispute came before the House of Lords within the space of five years. It concerned the rule in the income tax legislation as it stood at that time, to the effect that income of a UK domiciliary from foreign stocks, shares or rents was taxed under the arising basis but income arising from other 'foreign possessions' was taxed on the remittance basis.

The facts were that the taxpayer was life tenant of a trust formed under the law of New York. The trust fund was entirely comprised of foreign securities, stocks, and shares, but the taxpayer argued that her entitlement was not to specific dividends but merely to due administration of the trust. As such it was a foreign possession to which the remittance basis applied.

In the first case, *Baker v Archer-Shee* [1927] AC 844 there was no evidence as to New York law, and the House of Lords held that, under English law, the life tenant is specifically entitled to the income of the trust investments as it arises. As described in CHAPTER 8, it is for this reason that life tenants now enjoy the favourable tax rate applicable to dividends. But in *Baker v Archer-Shee*, the analysis worked against the taxpayer, for it meant that she did not secure the remittance basis on the income of the trust.

In the second case, *Archer-Shee v Garland* [1931] AC 212, she relitigated the point for subsequent tax years, and this time did provide evidence as to what the applicable law of New York was. The evidence was that, under the law of New York, she did not have a specific interest in the dividends, but merely the right to have the balance of the income after expenses paid to her or applied for her benefit. This, it was held, was a foreign possession and so entitled the taxpayer to the remittance basis.

COMPANY OR PARTNERSHIP

32.3 Several of the decided cases turn on whether an arrangement governed by foreign law should be treated as a company or a partnership. In fact the issue has normally proved to be whether the arrangement is a partnership, for partnerships are deemed to be transparent for income tax and CGT purposes (ITTOIA 2005, s 848; TCGA 1992, s 59). Accordingly a finding that a foreign entity is a partnership is tantamount to a finding that its income or gains are for UK tax purposes those of its members.

An early case was *Dreyfus V IRC* (1929) 14TC 560, which concerned a French *société en nom collectif*. This owed its existence not to agreement between the parties but to a written document deposited with the Registrar of the French Commercial Court. It had separate legal personality and was owner of its assets, but its members could be made liable for its debts. The Court of Appeal held that as it was a separate legal person owing its existence to the deposited document, it could not be construed as a partnership.

Lord Hanworth MR stated a general principle as follows:

> 'If there has been a body established by foreign law, the courts will recognise the juristic status of that body and thus the Court says that the principle of the liability of members of a foreign corporation to third parties is to be referred to the law under which that corporation was established, and if the law does show it was established as a separate entity effect should be given to it.'

In modern times, the flexibility of business entities makes it difficult to determine whether a particular entity should or should not be treated as a partnership. Thus in *R v IRC ex p Bishopp* [1999] STC 531 a dispute arose as to the status of a Jersey LLP. HMRC had indicated in a pre-transaction informal ruling that this, despite its name, should be regarded as a company. The Court refused to review this ruling, Dyson J stating the applicable principles as follows (at p 545):

> 'It is common ground that, in determining whether a Jersey LLP is a partnership for purposes of United Kingdom taxation, the nature of the rights, obligations and other features of the organisation must be determined according to Jersey law; but the characterisation of its status, i.e. whether a body of that kind should be treated as a partnership or not for UK tax purposes, will be determined according to the law of the relevant part of the United Kingdom (see *Rae (Inspector of Taxes) v Lazard Investment Co Ltd* [1963] 1 WLR 555, 41 TC 1).'

The difficulty in determining whether a foreign arrangement is a partnership is compounded by the fact that both English and Scottish partnerships count as partnerships for UK tax purposes and yet the legal nature of the two is not the same. In *Anson (under the name Swift v Revenue and Customs Comrs* [2010] UKFTT 88 (TC), [2010] SFTD 553), the First-tier Tribunal saw a spectrum between partnership and company, not a clear dividing line. It described the spectrum as running from:

(1)   'the English partnership: not a legal person, with the partners owning the assets jointly and incurring the liabilities, carrying on the business, and being entitled to the profits; through

(2)   the Scots partnership: legal person (in consequence of an agreement) owning the assets and incurring the liabilities with a secondary liability on the partners, with the partners nevertheless carrying on the business (since that is the definition of partnership) and being entitled to the profits; to

(3)   the UK company: legal person (in consequence of registration) owning the assets and incurring the liabilities with no liability on the members (or a liability only on winding-up for an unlimited company) and carrying on its business with the members holding shares and being entitled to profits only after either payment by the directors or recommendation by the directors and a resolution to declare dividends by the members.'

In *Anson* the entity was a Delaware LLC. The First-tier Tribunal considered it stood:

> 'somewhere between a Scots partnership and a UK company, having the partnership characteristics of the members being entitled to profits as they arise and owning an interest comparable to that of a partnership interest, and the corporate characteristics of carrying on its own business without liability on the members and there

being some separation between managing members and other members falling short of the distinction between members and directors.'

The Tribunal concluded:

'Since we have to put it on one side of that dividing line we consider that it is on the partnership side particularly in relation to its income.'

The Supreme Court referred to the spectrum identified by the First-tier Tribunal without criticism (at para 32). Lord Reed then commented (at para 40) that the rights of a partner under a Scottish partnership are:

'broadly analogues to those of a member of the LLC under the LLC Act, as found by the FTT: an interest, which is personal property, entitling the member to share in the profits of the LLC in accordance with the LLC agreement, and to share in the net proceeds of sale of the LLC's assets in the event of a dissolution of the LLC. There are, of course, also some differences: in particular, the partners in a Scottish partnership, other than a limited partnership, have an unlimited liability for its debts, whereas the members of the LLC had no liability for its debts beyond their initial capital contributions, prior to their repayment. Nevertheless, given the points of similarity, the comparison made by the [First-tier Tribunal] between the LLC and a Scottish partnership was understandable . . . '

It is difficult to avoid the conclusion that had this kind of analysis been applied in *Dreyfus* the result would have been a finding the French entity equated to a partnership. This is particularly so as, in contrast to the members of the LLC in *Anson*, the members in *Dreyfus* did not have limited liability. It is also interesting to speculate where in the spectrum a UK LLP formed under the Limited Liability Partnership Act 2000, would fall. Strictly the question is academic as such entities are deemed for most tax purposes to equate to partnerships (ITTOIA 2005, s 863; TCGA 1992, s 59A). But the question is far from academic in relation to offshore entities which, whether by design or otherwise, mimic UK LLPs.

TRUSTS

32.4 Common law jurisdictions recognise trusts and their trust law is based on English law. Typically, therefore, what is characterised as a trust in a common law offshore jurisdiction falls to be so characterised in England. However, many offshore jurisdictions have by legislation allowed forms of trust to be created which are not recognised as valid at common law. The most notable example is the non-charitable purpose trust. No decided case exists on how such a trust would be characterised in England but, there can be little doubt such purpose trusts count as trusts for UK tax purposes. This is because their essentials correspond to charitable purpose trusts, which are permitted by English law, and to the rare categories of non-charitable purpose trust that English law does recognise.

Many offshore jurisdictions expressly allow the settlor to reserve extensive powers, for example to direct investment, to direct distributions, and to hire and fire trustees. The issue powers of this sort raise is whether, in a common law jurisdiction such as England without the relevant legislation, the relationship would be characterised not as a true trust but as one of nomineeship. It is, however, unlikely that the relationship would be characterised as nomineeship provided the trustees are left with genuine responsibilities over the trust assets. Authority for this is cases such as *Perry v Astor* [1935] 19 TC 255 where, even though a trust was revocable, it was still treated as a trust for tax purposes. In such cases it is of course essential that the trustees do genuinely and independently discharge the functions reposed in them. If they do not, such inertia may, when coupled with the extensive powers reserved to the settlor, render a sham finding likely (see CHAPTER 35).

Foundations

32.5 Foundations are characteristic of civil law jurisdictions and have been introduced to various common law jurisdictions by statute. They are considered further in CHAPTER 33.

OPAQUE OR TRANSPARENT

32.6 An issue which is closely related to entity characterisation is whether an entity or arrangement is opaque or transparent. This issue normally arises in connection with income tax. In that context the issue is whether the source of the investor's income is his share of the underlying income of the entity, or whether the source is his rights against, or interest in, the entity.

Memec plc v IRC [1996] STC 1336, 71 TC 77 and *Revenue and Customs Comrs v Anson* [2015] UKSC 44, [2015] STC 1777, 17 ITLR 1007 both turned on whether a foreign entity was transparent for UK tax purposes. The issue was whether a UK taxpayer could claim credit under a double tax treaty for foreign tax.

Memec

32.7 In *Memec*, the foreign tax was German tax borne by German subsidiaries of the active partner in a *stille Gesellschaft* (or silent partnership) established under German law. Under the Double Tax Treaty between the UK and Germany that foreign tax could be claimed as a credit by the UK silent partner if, as a matter of law, the silent partnership was transparent so that the silent partner could be treated as entitled to a proportion of the dividends as they arose.

The first issue was whether the silent partnership equated to a UK partnership, and the Court of Appeal decided it did not, on the basis there was no carrying on of the business with a view to profit. But that still left open the issue of whether the silent partnership was transparent as a matter of general principle, and here the Court of Appeal decided it was not, on the grounds that the source of the silent partner's income was the silent partnership agreement rather than the underlying assets. The distinction drawn was between arrangements which have independent vitality and those which are mere machinery. This distinction was originally made by Robert Walker J at first instance [1996] STC 1336, and among the illustrations he gave were *Garland* trusts or discretionary trusts which do have independent vitality as respects trust income, and *Baker* trusts which do not.

Anson

32.8 *Anson* is discussed in detail in para 103.5. The issue for decision was whether the UK tax payable by Mr Anson was computed by reference to the same profits or income as the US tax he had suffered on his share of the LLC's profits. Mr Anson was UK resident but non UK domiciled so the issue arose as respects such part of his share of the LLC profits as he had remitted.

The First-tier Tribunal (hearing the case under the name *Swift v Revenue and Customs Comrs* [2010] UKFTT 88 (TC), [2010] SFTD 553) noted that the Delaware LLC legislation required the profits and losses of the LLC to 'be allocated among the members in the manner provided' in the LLC agreement. Article IV of the LLC agreement provided that:

> 'all gross income and gains . . . realised during the period in question . . . shall . . . be credited, and all losses, deductions and expenses . . . during the period in question . . . shall . . . be debited, to the respective capital accounts of the members pro rata, in accordance with ratios prescribed in the agreement, and subject to specified adjustments.'

On the basis of these provisions, the First-tier tribunal concluded the profits belonged to the members as they arose with the result that the income on which the member's tax was computed was the same as that on which the US tax was computed. They encapsulated their reasoning as follows:

> 'In summary, our conclusion in relation to the LLC operating agreement is that the combined effect of section 18-503 of the Act and the terms of article IV means that the profits must be allocated as they arise among the members. It follows that the profits belong as they arise to the members.'

The Supreme Court decided that these findings were decisive of the case and open to the Tribunal.

The Supreme Court made it clear (at para 121) that the member's share of the profits was his income for UK tax purposes and not what was in fact distributed to him. The LLC agreement gave the LLC managers some discretion over whether and when to distribute profits from members' capital accounts. But this discretion, regardless of its extent, was not held to vitiate the conclusion that as a matter of construction the members were entitled to their shares of profit as the profit arose rather than when it was distributed.

A question left open in *Anson* was the question at issue in *Memec*, namely whether the transparency of the LLC would have extended to treat each item of the underlying income of the LLC as the income of the members. The Supreme Court regarded this question as different from entitlement to profits, expressing itself as follows (at para 109):

> 'The issue in this case is not whether the receipts of the LLC from third parties are to be regarded as having been paid to the members of the LLC, but whether the income on which Mr Anson paid tax in the US is the same as the income on which he is liable to tax in the UK. As I shall explain, answering that question involves considering whether income arises to Mr Anson, for the purposes of UK income tax, when his share of profits is allocated to his account, or when he receives distributions of profits. That issue is different from the issue considered in *Memec*. The answer to the question whether the receipts and expenditure of an entity are paid to and by its members does not necessarily determine whether, when a profit

arises in a given accounting period, that profit constitutes the income of the members. The answer to the latter question depends on the respective rights of the entity and it members in relation to the profit, and therefore on the legal regime governing those rights.'

In practice the answer to this question may not be as difficult as the Supreme Court implied, for if the LLC indeed equated to a partnership (para 32.3 above) it would be transparent for income tax purposes.

HMRC practice

32.9 HMRC published the practice they adopt in deciding, for income tax purposes, whether an entity is opaque or transparent. This practice is now set out in paras INTM 180010 and 180020 of the International Manual, having previously been in *Tax Bulletin 83*.

HMRC stress that the issue of whether an entity is opaque or transparent is not necessarily the same as determining whether it is a company or a partnership. In the light of the discussion above, this must surely be right. In considering transparency, HMRC express themselves as having regard to *Memec plc v IRC* and itemise several factors they consider relevant. The most important are whether any business is carried on by the entity or by the persons having an interest in the entity and whether those persons are entitled to share profits as they arise or whether the distribution of profits requires a decision by the entity or its members.

In the International Manual, para INTM 180030, HMRC list entities on which they have given a view, with respect to tax transparency or opacity. As a result of *Anson* this list must be viewed with reservation as Delaware LLCs are classed as opaque. Indeed *Anson* may well go much wider than Delaware LLCs if, as appears the true ratio is that any entity is opaque if as a matter of construction, members or participators are entitled to profits as they arise. HMRC, however, consider the decision in *Anson* is specific to its own facts. Any claims made in reliance on *Anson* will be considered on a case-by-case basis (HMRC Brief 15/2015, 25 September 2015, reproduced [2015] SWTI 2856).

CAPITAL OR INCOME

32.10 The issue of whether a receipt is capital or income is determined by the same process as is used to characterise entities. In other words the nature of the recipient's rights are determined by the relevant foreign law and then English law is applied to the rights as so found (*Rae v Lazard Investment Co Ltd* (1963) 41 TC1, 27, per Lord Reid).

Company distributions

32.11 Dividends paid by non-UK companies are only charged to income tax if not capital (ITTOIA 2005, s 402(4)). The term 'dividend' connotes the payment out of a part of the profits of a company in respect of a share in a company. It may be a fixed amount on a preference share or a fluctuating amount on an equity share (*Esso Petroleum Co Ltd v Ministry of Defence* [1990] Ch 163, [1990] 1 All ER 163, as cited in *Memec plc v IRC* [1996] STC 1336, 1357).

In determining whether a dividend is capital or income the key issue is whether the taxpayer's shareholding remains intact. Lord Reid put the matter as follows in *Rae v Lazard Investment Co Ltd* (supra, at p 41):

> 'The question is whether "the corpus of the asset" or "shares of the company" or "the capital of the possession" did or did not remain intact after the Bestwall shares were distributed: or whether the Bestwall shares were merely fruit or had they in their fall taken part of the tree with them.'

The point was illustrated by the earlier House of Lords decision in *IRC v Reid's Trustees* (1949) 30 TC 431. Here a South African company had realised a capital profit on the sale of fixed assets and declared a dividend from those profits. The House of Lords held this was income in the hands of a UK resident shareholder, on the grounds that the shareholder's shares remained intact. A similar approach was taken by the First-tier Tribunal in a recent case concerning a UK company, *Trustees of the Bessie Taube Discretionary Settlement Trust v Revenue and Customs Comrs* [2010] UKFTT 473 (TC), [2011] SFTD 153, [2011] SWTI 268. Here the company paid a dividend on a class of ordinary shares which extinguished the value of those shares, but the shares remained in existence and so the dividend was income.

In applying the tree and fruit test, account is often taken of how a distribution is treated under the proper law of the company. Thus in *Rae v Lazard Investment Co Ltd*, a company incorporated in Maryland effected a distribution in specie in a partial liquidation. Such a transaction was not at the time possible under English law, and the evidence was that under Maryland law, the original shares did not remain intact, with the result that the transaction was capital. The House of Lords held the same result followed under English law, despite the fact that the taxpayer continued to hold the original shares, albeit much diminished in value.

In a couple of cases, the company's proper law has proved decisive in determining whether dividends of share premium are income or capital. *Courtauld Investments Ltd v Fleming* (1969) 46 TC 111 concerned an Italian company and the evidence was that Italian law treated share premium as paid up capital. On this basis, Buckley J regarded share premium as an accretion to the 'tree' and so capital, with the result that a dividend paid out of the share premium was capital. In *First Nationwide v Revenue and Customs Comrs* [2012] EWCA Civ 278, [2012] STC 1261, [2012] 13 LS Gaz R 24, by contrast, the evidence was that the share premium of a Cayman company was, under Cayman law, profit available for distribution and not capital. On that basis the Court of Appeal confirmed the Upper Tribunal's view that dividends paid out of share premium were income, despite the fact that the dividends amounted to 98% of the value of the shares in respect of which they were paid.

Share buy-backs

32.12 Application of the above principles demonstrates that when a company buys back its own shares, the ensuing receipt by the shareholder is capital. To use Lord Reid's language in *Rae v Lazard Investment Co Ltd*, the buy-back takes part of the tree with it.

That this is so, is confirmed by pre corporation tax cases on UK companies. These cases are not directly in point as, in those days, UK companies could not in general buy in their own shares. But capital treatment was secured when reserves were capitalised as bonus shares or redeemable debentures (*IRC v Blott* [1921] 2 AC 171, 8 TC 101; *IRC v Fisher's Executors* (1926) 10 TC 302). One of the early cases on transactions in securities code affirmed that the redemption of such debentures was, absent anti-avoidance legislation, capital (*IRC v Parker* (1966) 43 TC 396; see further para **89.7**).

Trust distributions

32.13 The issue of whether a trust distribution is income or capital is discussed in CHAPTER 8.

Chapter 33

FOUNDATIONS AND TRUST REGS

INTRODUCTION

33.1 This chapter addresses the question of how foundations and Liechtenstein trust regs are liable to be characterised for UK tax purposes. The focus is on foundations. Liechtenstein trust regs, which raise rather similar issues, are considered at the end of this chapter.

Foundations may loosely be described as dedicated funds with separate legal personality. Liechtenstein was the first jurisdiction to enable the creation of non-charitable foundations (*Stiftungen*), by virtue of Articles 552–570 of the Liechtenstein company law of 26 January 1926 (the *Personen- und Gesellschaftsrecht*, or PGR). Recent years have seen a rapid spread of the private foundation concept. Offshore jurisdictions which have enacted their own foundations' laws include all three Crown Dependencies, the Bahamas and Mauritius.

Foundations have never formed part of English law, and are not specifically addressed in the UK's tax legislation, a fact which gives rise to the characterisation issues that are discussed in this chapter. For this reason, as well as the fact that advisers in the common law world have historically been much less familiar with foundations than they are with trusts, foundations have rarely, if ever, been recommended by UK advisers. And generally it continues to be the case that a trust is to be preferred over a foundation where the creator of the entity and/or its beneficiaries are or may in future become UK resident, because of the potential for ambiguity about the UK tax treatment of a foundation.

However, UK advisers do need an understanding of foundations and the characterisation issues that they raise. This is firstly because foundations are reasonably common vehicles for the holding of wealth for families from certain civil law countries, who may be more familiar or comfortable with the concept of a foundation than a trust; and secondly because foundations have in recent years been promoted with some enthusiasm in a number of offshore jurisdictions, to clients from the Middle East or Far East who might otherwise have created a trust. In these cases family members may become UK resident or some other nexus with the UK may be created, giving rise to a need to establish how the foundation should be characterised for the purposes of English law or UK taxation.

LAW ON CHARACTERISATION

33.2 In principle, the process to be followed when determining how a foundation should be characterised is the same as for any other foreign entity which lacks a precise equivalent under the law of any part of the UK. This is discussed in general terms in Chapter 32.

It is thought that, in principle, there are two stages to the exercise. First, the nature of the foreign law entity and the rights and obligations that it creates must be established, having regard to the characteristics which it derives from its proper law and, where relevant, those which it derives from its constitutional documents. Second, there must be an analysis of the laws that apply within the UK, to identify the domestic entity which, in substance, shares that nature and creates substantially the same rights and obligations. The primary modern authorities for this are *Memec plc v IRC* [1998] STC 754 and 71 TC 77; *Revenue and Customs Comrs v Anson* [2015] UKSC 44, [2015] STC 1777, 17 ITLR 1007 (see **32.7** and **32.8**).

It is worth noting that these cases concerned a slightly narrower point than is typically required to be addressed regarding foundations. For example, in *Memec* the court was not, strictly, determining whether the 'silent partnership' should be characterised as a partnership, for the purposes of a provision of UK tax law applying specifically to partnerships. It was only answering the more limited question of whether the 'silent partnership' was transparent or opaque for the purposes of tax on its income. And in *Anson* the court was determining whether the LLC was transparent for certain tax purposes, not strictly whether it should be characterised as a company or a partnership. There was no doubt that it was a body corporate and it may be that for certain UK tax purposes, it would have been characterised as a company. The possibility of different characterisations for the purpose of different taxing provisions is discussed below.

The two-stage exercise above sounds quite simple, but in practice the difficulties of this process can be formidable. The following three points must be kept in mind.

Approximation

33.3 Almost by definition, a foreign law entity which cannot be created under the law of any part of the UK will not have the same set of properties as any single domestic entity. A foreign law entity frequently has some characteristics which it shares with one domestic entity, and some which it shares with another. Moreover, where in broad terms there is a sharing of characteristics with an entity that can be created under the law of a part of the UK, it will often be found that the equivalence is imprecise. There may be differences in detail between the rights and obligations created by the foreign entity and the superficially similar rights and obligations created by the domestic analogue. It appears that what is required is to find the domestic entity whose properties are the closest to those of the foreign law entity, ie the closest analogue.

That this is the correct approach that is suggested by the Court of Appeal's judgment in *Memec plc v IRC* [1998] STC 754, 71 TC 77. Peter Gibson LJ stated:

'What in my judgement we have to do in the present case is to consider the characteristics of an English or Scottish partnership which make it transparent and then see *to what extent* those characteristics are shared or not by the silent partnership in order to determine whether the silent partnership should be treated for corporation tax purposes in the same way.' (Italics ours.)

Nomenclature

33.4 The second point is that the mere fact that the foreign law entity which is being analysed is called a particular thing is not decisive as to how it should be characterised for English law or UK tax purposes. This much is evident from *Memec*, where an entity referred to as a 'silent partnership' was found *not* to be a partnership, as that term is understood in English law.

Of course, there is no risk of a foreign law private foundation being inappropriately equated with an English law private foundation, as there is no such thing. However, the nomenclature point does have relevance in relation to foundations: the fact that a foundation established under one country's laws has a particular characterisation for UK tax purposes does not mean that the same characterisation will necessarily apply to a foundation formed under the law of another country. Indeed, the point goes further, as the laws of a given country may be sufficiently flexible to allow the creation of foundations with divergent characteristics. It follows that foundations must be analysed on a case-by-case basis to arrive at the correct characterisation.

Tax context

33.5 The third point is equally crucial. It is that, when seeking to characterise a foreign law entity for the purposes of UK tax, it is necessary to focus on the particular tax or taxing provision in question. It cannot be assumed that the same characterisation or treatment will apply for all UK tax purposes. This is recognised in HMRC's International Manual, which notes that:

'The expressions "transparent" and "opaque" are not interchangeable with "partnership" and "company" or "body corporate". A fiscally transparent entity is not necessarily a partnership. A fiscally opaque entity is not necessarily a "body corporate" or a "company" for UK tax purposes.' (INTM 180020).

The point is particularly pertinent in relation to non-UK resident entities for the holding of family wealth, such as foundations. As discussed below, such entities may, depending on their characteristics, engage the UK anti-avoidance provisions regarding settlements, persons abroad and/or close companies. Many such provisions rely on deliberately broad definitions of the entities which they are seeking to catch, and this point may render rather academic the discussion about whether a foundation is capable of being characterised for English law purposes as a trust. Where a foundation is concerned it makes sense to consider each of the UK taxing provisions which is potentially applicable, having first sought to establish the nature of the foundation under its proper law and its constitutional documents, and the rights and duties that it creates.

NATURE OF THE FOUNDATION

33.6 All foundations are corporate. They thus have separate legal personality; they are managed by boards or councils, which are similar to the board of directors of a company; and liability to creditors is limited to the foundation assets. Historically, this fact has sometimes drawn UK advisers towards the conclusion that a foundation should be characterised for the purposes of English law and UK taxation as a company. However, it is suggested that, in reality, other characterisations are generally more appropriate, and that only limited weight should be given to the corporate nature of a foundation when seeking to characterise it.

It is suggested that there are at least two, and possibly three, types of private foundation.

Nominee-like foundations

33.7 Certain foundations give extensive rights to the founder or, occasionally, some other person. In Liechtenstein and Panama, the person with such rights is often termed the 'first beneficiary'. He may have the right under the foundation documents to direct how the foundation's assets are managed, to call for its capital to be transferred to him at any time, and pending any such transfer to receive the income from the investments or otherwise to enjoy the capital, without restriction. In such cases, the relationship between the foundation and the beneficiary is very close to the relationship between a nominee and the person for whom the nominee holds its assets.

The similarity may only be approximate, because the foundation's proper law may not recognise the concepts of bare trusteeship, nomineeship or beneficial ownership (this is understood to be the case in Liechtenstein and Panama). The obligations of the foundation vis-à-vis the beneficiary may not, therefore, be fiduciary, but owed under contract or statute. However, it is doubtful whether the legal mechanics which underlie such rights are relevant. If, under contract or statute or on some other basis, the 'first beneficiary' has enforceable rights against the foundation which are in effect the same as the rights of a beneficiary under a nominee arrangement, it is suggested that it would be appropriate to characterise the foundation as a nominee.

As foundations of this type provide for other beneficiaries to acquire entitlements on the death of the 'first beneficiary', they can be regarded as functional equivalents of wills.

Trust-like foundations

33.8 Certain other foundations appear to confer rights on beneficiaries, and obligations on the foundation itself, which are broadly similar to the rights and obligations created by a trust. A beneficiary under such a foundation may have a right to income, and therefore be in broadly the position of a life tenant of a common law trust, or may be a member of a class of beneficiaries who are eligible to receive payments from the foundation but have no entitlement to them, in which case clearly the beneficiary's status is very similar to the status of an object of a common law discretionary trust.

Again, a UK adviser should not fall into the trap of assuming precise equivalence; the foundation's proper law may not recognise trusts and fiduciary duties in any situation, or the provisions of the law allowing the creation of foundations may expressly exclude the possibility of fiduciary duties being owed by a foundation (which is the case with certain of the Crown Dependencies' foundation laws). However, it is suggested that what is key is whether the beneficiaries, either individually or collectively, have some means of holding the foundation or its board to account, to ensure that it is managed for their collective benefit. Arguably, it does not matter, for the characterisation question, whether the mechanism which can be used to achieve this relies on fiduciary duties.

'Non-fiduciary' foundations

33.9 It is possible, at least in theory, that there is a further type of foundation. Certain countries' laws may permit the creation of private foundations under which the assets are ostensibly held for the benefit of a class of persons but those persons do not, individually or collectively, have any legal ability to compel the making of payments to them or otherwise to hold the foundation or its board to account.

Such a foundation is arguably not a contradiction in terms, but it is uncertain whether, in reality, one can be created. As discussed below, the Jersey foundations law expressly excludes fiduciary duties and information rights for beneficiaries, but seems nevertheless to provide legal mechanisms which a disgruntled beneficiary can use to seek redress in a case of malpractice by the foundation's board. It may be that an English court would consider these mechanisms to be sufficiently similar in effect to the rights afforded by a common law trust to allow characterisation of a Jersey foundation as a trust. However, another theoretical possibility is characterisation as a non-UK resident company without shareholders, which holds its assets beneficially.

Foundations that are not characterised as nominees or trusts are sometimes referred to as 'non-fiduciary' foundations. This terminology is potentially confusing, as it might suggest that the distinction between 'fiduciary' and 'non-fiduciary' foundations turns on whether they give rise to fiduciary interests and obligations, whereas (as discussed above) no foundation gives rise to such interests and obligations in the strict common law sense.

Surrounding circumstances

33.10 As noted above, the starting points when seeking to characterise a foundation are the foundations law of the relevant country and the constitutional documents of the particular foundation. However, these will not necessarily tell the whole story.

There are some cases, encountered not infrequently in relation to Liechtenstein and Panamanian foundations, where the regulations or by-laws are misleading as to the true relationship with the beneficiaries, and a different conclusion is reached if the surrounding circumstances are taken into account. This may be the case where the regulations or by-laws are trust-like, but the reality is that the foundation has been operated on the basis that a particular individual has complete control over the assets, including the ability to call for them if required. Alternatively, the regulations or by-laws may purport to give one individual rights of a 'first beneficiary', whereas in reality those rights are held by someone else. In any such case the real relationship may approximate to nomineeship, and the assets of the foundation should generally be treated for UK tax purposes as the assets of the person who, in reality, has the ability to control and benefit from them.

The scope for Liechtenstein foundations to obscure and mislead was touched on in *Hamilton v Hamilton* [2016] EWHC 1132 (Ch), one of the very few reported English legal decisions concerning foundations. The judgment of Henderson J makes reference to a report prepared by Professor Martin Schauer, a professor at the University of Vienna and an expert on private foundations. The report discusses various features which have helped to ensure the success of Liechtenstein foundations, including their lack of transparency:

'A further point mentioned by Professor Schauer is that an investor hardly ever establishes a foundation by himself, but rather uses the services of a Liechtenstein-based professional who will act as a fiduciary. The fiduciary will establish the foundation in his own name, as legal founder, although acting on behalf of his client, the so-called economic founder. There will then be a contract of mandate between the fiduciary and the client, under which the fiduciary will manage the foundation by nominating the members of the board and instructing them how to make use of their powers. All of this forms part of the machinery designed to make the real operation of the foundation as opaque as possible to outsiders.'

JERSEY FOUNDATIONS

33.11 This chapter is not the place for an extended discussion of the features of foundations that can be created under any particular law. However, some consideration of Jersey foundations is arguably merited here, as the Jersey foundations law brings into sharp relief the distinctions between foundations and trusts, and the scope for these distinctions to create uncertainty as to the UK tax treatment of foundations.

Jersey foundations are governed by the Foundations (Jersey) Law 2009. As one would expect, a Jersey foundation is a corporate body, under the control of a board (referred to in the Law as the 'council'). The foundation must specify its objects in its charter. Those objects can be either to benefit a person or class of persons, or to carry out a specified purpose.

The Law specifically provides that the beneficiary of a foundation has no interest in the foundation assets, and that neither the foundation itself nor any person appointed under the foundation's governing documents owes any beneficiary a fiduciary or analogous duty (Article 25(1)). The Law also provides that beneficiaries are not entitled to information, save insofar as the foundation's governing documents provide otherwise (Article 26(1)).

In light of these provisions, there are good reasons to question whether it is appropriate for a Jersey foundation to be characterised as a trust. There is no doubt that beneficiaries can lawfully be deprived of the information which they might require to bring any claim, and it might be assumed that there is no legal mechanism for enforcement or protection of their interests.

However, the reality of the situation is more complex. Article 25(2) of the Law provides that a beneficiary entitled to a benefit under the terms of the foundation may apply to court for an order, ordering the foundation to provide the benefit. This provision may well be in point where a beneficiary has an absolute entitlement under the terms of a foundation's governing documents, but probably does not assist a beneficiary who has only a right to be considered. But in that scenario, the beneficiary may be able to obtain redress by petitioning the foundation's guardian. The appointment of a guardian is mandatory, and any guardian has an obligation to 'take such steps as are reasonable in all the circumstances to ensure that the council of the foundation carries out its functions' (Article 14(4)), and is empowered to hold the council to account (Article 14(5)).

Should a petition to the guardian fail, the beneficiary may be able to apply to court under Part 5 of the Law. This allows 'persons with standing' (including beneficiaries) to apply to court for various specific remedies. The remedies which are potentially available under Part 5 include:

- an order against any person who has failed to comply with an obligation imposed by the Law or the foundation's governing documents, requiring such person to comply with the obligation (Article 44(1));
- an order against the foundation itself, if it has failed to carry out its objects, requiring that the objects be carried out (Article 44(2)); and
- a direction as to the meaning of a provision of the foundation's governing documents, or the manner in which the council is required to administer its assets or carry out its objects, or the question of whether a person is a beneficiary, or as to the rights of beneficiaries between themselves or against the foundation (Article 46(2)).

These various rights do not, of course, completely mirror the rights of beneficiaries of a common law trust. However, in very broad terms they provide means for beneficiaries to enforce their interests, and they undoubtedly reduce the practical impact of the elimination of fiduciary duties to beneficiaries.

Notwithstanding all this, it is difficult to be confident that a Jersey foundation is sufficiently trust-like to be characterised as a trust. It may be that, in any given case, the question turns on the precise terms of the foundation's constitutional documents.

At the time of writing, there have been only a couple of reported cases in the Royal Court concerning the Jersey foundations law. The first was *In the Matter of the Representation of A Limited* [2013] JRC 075. The case was chiefly concerned with a procedural issue, namely the stance that a Jersey foundation should take in relation to commercial litigation. Where the issue of English law characterisation is concerned, the most interesting aspects of the judgment are the following:

(1)   It was confirmed that the members of the council of a Jersey foundation have the ability to apply to court for directions with respect to the management of the foundation, and the court is required to give a direction if it is satisfied that it will assist the foundation in the administration of its assets or the carrying out of its objectives, or the giving of a direction is 'otherwise desirable'. The court does therefore have a supervisory jurisdiction over Jersey foundations, which is loosely analogous to the court's jurisdiction to approve, or to disapprove, proposed acts by the trustees of Jersey law trusts which might be considered momentous. There is no equivalent jurisdiction in relation to companies.

(2)   Although council members do not owe fiduciary duties to beneficiaries, they do owe fiduciary duties, and duties of care and skill, to the foundation. They may be sued by the foundation in the event of a breach of such duties. In this respect it would appear that the position of council members is similar to the position of the directors of a company, who do not owe fiduciary duties to the company's members, but do owe such duties to the company itself.

The second reported case regarding the Jersey Foundations law was *Representation of the C Trust Co Ltd* [2016] JRC 144. It concerned an application by a member of the council of a foundation, for directions regarding a proposed change to the class of beneficiaries of the foundation. The Royal Court affirmed its jurisdiction under the foundations law to approve proposed steps in relation to Jersey foundations and generally to supervise their management, which is similar to the supervisory jurisdiction that it exercises over Jersey law trusts.

Arguably, both these reported cases provide some support for the view that the differences between Jersey foundations and trusts are less dramatic than might, initially, be thought.

One last point must be made here, which may have a significant impact on the characterisation issue. This is that the founder of a Jersey foundation is permitted to retain founder's rights (Article 18). These rights can be made assignable by the foundation's governing documents and, if not assigned, pass to the guardian on the founder's death. The Law is silent as to the nature of such rights, and imposes no fetters on the rights that may be reserved. The result may be that the founder or another person may, in principle, hold powers over the foundation that equate to those exercisable by a controlling shareholder. If so, this may be an indication that some Jersey foundations, at least, should be equated to a company owning its assets beneficially.

UK TAX ANALYSIS: TRUST-LIKE AND NON-FIDUCIARY FOUNDATIONS

33.12 In practice, the key issue for UK tax purposes is not how a foundation may be characterised in the abstract, but whether, and if so how, specific fiscal legislation applies. In many cases the central question is whether, for the purposes of the relevant tax, the foundation is a settlement.

The following paragraphs address the likely UK tax analysis with respect to trust-like foundations and also 'non-fiduciary' foundations, making the assumption that such foundations can indeed be created.

Inheritance tax: is the foundation a settlement?

33.13 For IHT, 'settlement' is defined as any disposition of property whereby the property is:

(a)   held in trust for persons in succession,

(b)   held on trust to accumulate the income of the property or with power to make discretionary payments out of that income, or

(c)   charged or burdened with the payment of any annuity or periodical payment payable for life or some other limited period

or whereby the property (i) would be so held, charged or burdened if the disposition was regulated by the law of any part of the UK, or (ii) is governed by provisions equivalent in effect to those which would apply if the property were so held, charged or burdened (IHTA 1984, s 43(2)).

If a foundation is characterised as a trust for English law purposes, other than a bare trust, it must fall within the definition above. Such a foundation must fall within (a), (b) or (c) above, or perhaps several of these heads at once, and will therefore be a settlement for IHT purposes even without the extension of the definition regarding dispositions 'governed by provisions equivalent in effect'.

It is, in fact, a moot point whether this extension, which has been a feature of the IHT legislation since its first enactment in 1975, ever draws a foundation within the meaning of a settlement, where it would not be within that meaning in any event. It is sometimes suggested that, in this context, the extending wording has no real effect, being an unnecessary statutory articulation of the general law as to characterisation, as summarised above.

However, it is arguable that the extending wording does have a function, in rendering a foundation of the hypothetical third type a settlement for IHT. It may be that a discretionary foundation which does not give its beneficiaries any means of holding the foundation or its board to account, ie a so-called 'non-fiduciary' foundation, would not be characterised as a trust for the purposes of English law generally, but would nevertheless be a settlement for IHT purposes. This might on the basis that its provisions could be said to be 'equivalent' to those of a trust even if the beneficiaries have no ability to enforce their rights or interests. Perhaps the better argument, though, is that such a foundation falls within the 'settlement' definition for IHT on the basis that if the arrangement were regulated by the law of any part of the UK, it would be a trust.

Inheritance tax analysis

33.14 A gift of assets to a foundation which is not characterised as a nominee for the founder may be a chargeable transfer for IHT purposes (IHTA 1984, s 3A(1)). However, this is not the case if the donor is non-UK domiciled and not deemed domiciled, and the assets fall within one of the categories of excluded property (see paras **37.9** to **37.13**).

A foundation that is a settlement for IHT purposes may be subject to the relevant property regime described in CHAPTER 60. If the founder is living and is not entirely excluded from benefiting, the foundation's property will also be within the charge to IHT on the founder's death, under the reservation of benefit rules (see CHAPTER 83). However, in either case, liability to IHT will be avoided insofar as the foundation's assets are excluded property (see CHAPTER 62).

The rules for pre-22 March 2006 interests in possession are in point if the foundation was created before that date and the foundation's constitution conferred a right to income on a beneficiary, which is still subsisting, or that right to income was replaced before 6 October 2008 by another such right which is still subsisting (see CHAPTER 61). In such cases the rules that apply on the termination of qualifying interests in possession should be kept in mind, as should the special rules applicable where the settlor or his spouse has an initial qualifying interest in possession but the trust then moves into the relevant property regime (see CHAPTER 62).

CGT position on funding of foundation

33.15 A gift of assets to a foundation which is not characterised as a nominee for the founder is a disposal for CGT purposes, so any latent gains on the assets given to the entity will be crystallised. In practice the foundation will almost certainly be non-UK resident, as discussed below, which precludes a claim to holdover relief (TCGA 1992, ss 166 and 261). It follows that if non-cash assets are given to a foundation by a UK resident, and those assets are standing at a gain, CGT is likely to be triggered, subject to two qualifications.

One is that the donor may conceivably have losses that can be set against the gains. The other qualification is that if the assets are non-UK situated and the donor is non-UK domiciled, the remittance basis may protect the donor from an immediate CGT charge. In the latter case, the rule regarding disposals otherwise than for full consideration (ITA 2007, s 809T) will need to be watched (see para **49.22**), bearing in mind the fact that, if the foundation is characterised as a trust, it may be a relevant person in relation to the donor (see paras **54.6** to **54.11**).

Taxation of the foundation itself on its income and gains

33.16 If the foundation is trust-like, there may in principle be UK tax for the foundation itself on its income and gains, under the income tax and CGT provisions dealing with the taxation of trustees.

These provisions apply by reference to settled property, which means property held in trust, other than property held by a nominee or property to which another person is absolutely entitled (ITA 2007, s 466; TCGA 1992, s 68). Property of a foundation is thus settled property for these purposes, if the foundation is characterised for English law purposes as a trust.

Generally, these provisions only impose a charge to tax on a trust whose trustees who are UK resident. This raises the question of how, in the case of a foundation which is characterised as a trust, the residence of the deemed body of trustees is to be determined. The trustee residence rules (see CHAPTER 42) do not specifically address this point. However, it is likely that the foundation itself must be treated as a single corporate trustee and that the residence of the deemed trustees follows the residence of the foundation. It is sometimes suggested that the individual members of the foundation's board should be treated as its trustees, but this is unlikely to be correct, since those persons do not themselves hold the assets of the deemed trust.

Assuming that the foundation is managed and controlled in the country where it has been created, and is not under the de facto control of a UK resident shadow director (see CHAPTER 43), the deemed trustees will be non-UK resident. If so, the foundation itself will generally be outside the scope of UK tax on income and gains.

Possible exceptions to this are if the foundation receives UK-source income, particularly if it has UK resident beneficiaries (see CHAPTER 64), or the foundation makes a disposal of UK residential property (see CHAPTER 65).

Income tax for the founder or beneficiaries

33.17 There is also scope for UK tax on foundation income for the founder, if he is UK resident, or for UK resident beneficiaries.

Where income of the foundation is concerned, any tax for the founder is likely to be under the settlements code, discussed in CHAPTER 75. As explained in that chapter, the concept of a settlement for the purposes of that code is wide, encompassing any disposition, arrangement or transfer of assets (see 75.14). The definition is therefore wide enough to embrace not only a foundation which is characterised as a trust, but also a discretionary foundation which does not give its beneficiaries any means of holding the foundation or its board to account, and which may not be treated as a trust for English law purposes more generally. However, the settlements code is only applicable if the founder or any spouse can benefit from the foundation, or the foundation's income is paid to minor children of the founder.

If the foundation has UK resident beneficiaries, there will also be scope for them to be taxed by reference to payments or benefits received by them. Discretionary distributions of income to UK resident beneficiaries will be within the charge to income tax on annual payments or income not otherwise charged, under ITTOIA 2005, s 683 or 687 (see 8.8). These provisions are not specific to trust distributions, so are capable of applying in relation to a discretionary foundation that is not characterised as a trust, as well as a trust-like foundation.

Distributions of capital, too, may give rise to income tax for UK resident beneficiaries, under the transfer of assets non-transferor provisions (ITA 2007, s 731; see CHAPTER 70). The transfer of assets code is agnostic about whether the entity to which assets have been transferred is a settlement, so in this context the code potentially applies to both trust-like foundations and discretionary foundations that are not characterised as trusts. However, income tax charges under this code are precluded if the conditions of the motive defence are met (see CHAPTER 73).

It might be thought the latter defence is rarely in point as, in popular imagination at least, foundations are associated with aggressive tax planning and indeed tax evasion. But this reaction is ill-founded. Globally most foundations are created by people unconnected with the UK, UK tax only becoming an issue when they or relatives subsequently move to the UK.

CGT for the founder or beneficiaries

33.18 Where gains of a foundation are concerned, any tax for a UK resident founder is likely to be under the settlor charging provision in TCGA 1992, s 86 (discussed in CHAPTER 76) or the beneficiary charging provision in TCGA 1992, s 87 (discussed in CHAPTER 77). The latter also creates scope for CGT charges for other UK resident beneficiaries of the foundation. Of course, s 87 can only give rise to tax for a founder or other beneficiary if capital payments are received.

Both these sections operate by reference to settlements, but employ different definitions of this term. Section 86 is limited in scope to trusts, whereas for s 87 purposes, 'settlement' has the same artificially extended meaning that it has for the purposes of the income tax settlements code.

The narrow meaning of 'settlement' that applies for s 86 does not mean, of course, that this section has no relevance for gains of a foundation, because a trust-like foundation will be characterised as a trust and s 86 may apply accordingly. However, under current law s 86 requires a settlor, or in this case a founder, who is not only UK resident but also UK domiciled, and it is relatively unusual for a UK domiciliary to create a foundation that is trust-like. Section 86 may begin to apply more commonly to foundations from 6 April 2017, when certain foreign domiciliaries will become deemed domiciled for all UK tax purposes (see CHAPTER 45).

If it is possible to create a discretionary foundation which does not give its beneficiaries any means of holding the foundation or its board to account, and such a foundation is characterised as something other than a trust, s 86 will not apply to its gains, even if the founder is both UK resident and UK domiciled. In such a case there will, however, be scope for CGT charges for the founder under s 87, if he receives capital payments from it.

Relevance of close company provisions?

33.19 It is sometimes suggested that, if it is possible to create a discretionary foundation which is not characterised as a trust, there might be scope for certain anti-avoidance provisions to apply which operate by reference to closely held companies. The thinking is that if a foundation is characterised as neither a nomineeship nor a trust, it might be characterised as a guarantee company, leading to these provisions being invoked.

The provisions in question are TCGA 1992, s 13, which can cause gains of a closely held non-UK resident company to be attributed for CGT purposes to UK resident participators in it; and IHTA 1984, s 94, which can cause a transfer of value by a closely held company to be attributed for IHT purposes to the participators in the company.

For the purposes of both these provisions, 'participators' has the meaning given to it under CTA 2010, s 454(1) (see 87.3). The definition includes not only holders of share capital, but also persons who possess or are entitled to acquire the right to participate in distributions, and persons who are entitled to secure that income or assets of the company are applied for their benefit. In principle, then, the anti-avoidance provisions referred to above can apply even where the company, or deemed company, has no shareholders or other persons with voting rights.

However, there is no indication that HMRC take this line of argument and generally, it seems unlikely that it would succeed in court. The difficulty with the argument is that if the foundation's nature is such that its beneficiaries have no ability to enforce their interests, such that the foundation cannot be equated with a trust, it is hard to see how the beneficiaries could actually be considered to be participators in it, within the definition referred to above. They would have no right to distributions, because at the most they would have a mere hope of benefit, with no means of compelling the foundation to make any payments to them. And similarly they would have no means of securing that income or assets of the foundation are applied for their benefit.

Generally, therefore, the better view is that these close company anti-avoidance provisions do not, in practice, apply to discretionary foundations which cannot be characterised as trusts. However, one possible exception to this is where founder's rights have been reserved and the holder of these rights has the power to cause the foundation to be wound up in his favour, or to require distributions to be made to him. As noted above, this scenario seems possible where Jersey foundations are concerned. The holder of such rights would fall within the 'participator' definition.

UK TAX ANALYSIS: NOMINEE-LIKE FOUNDATIONS

33.20 As already noted, a significant number of foundations are functional nominees for their founders or, more occasionally, other persons. Effectively, the founder or other 'first beneficiary' is the full beneficial owner of the foundation's assets, although as the governing law of the foundation may not recognise the concept of beneficial ownership, the legal basis for this may be different from that which applies to a nominee arrangement under English law.

Where a foundation is characterised as a nominee, the income tax and CGT analysis is straightforward. No disposal occurs when assets are transferred to the foundation, unless the foundation is a functional nominee for a person other than its founder. If he is UK resident, the founder or other 'first beneficiary' is taxable on the foundation's income and gains, subject of course to the remittance basis if the foundations assets are non-UK and he is non-UK domiciled and is using that special basis of taxation.

However, the position is perhaps less clear where IHT is concerned.

Inheritance tax: is the foundation a settlement?

33.21 The suggestion is sometimes made that a foundation of this type is a settlement for IHT purposes, despite its nominee-like characteristics. The reasoning seems to be that:

- a foundation of this type creates succession rights for other persons, which become enforceable under the governing law of the foundation on the 'first beneficiary's' death; and
- as already noted, the definition of 'settlement' in IHTA 1984, s 43(2) includes a disposition whereby property is held in trust for persons in succession, or would be so held if the disposition was regulated by the law of any part of the UK, or the administration of the property is governed by provisions that are equivalent in effect to those that would apply if the property were so held. Clearly, a foundation does not hold its assets on trust, but it might conceivably be said that, if the disposition was regulated by English law, it would take the form of a gift to a trust conferring a life interest on the founder, with remainder interests for the individuals who are entitled on the founder's death; or that the provisions of a nominee-like foundation are equivalent in effect to such a trust.

This appears to have been the view of Henderson J in *Hamilton v Hamilton*, who asserted that it 'would have been very hard to resist' an HMRC argument that the nominee-like foundation in that case was a settlement, 'within the very wide meaning of that section 43(2) of IHTA 1984' (see para 20). However, this assertion is clearly *obiter*.

If this view were correct, the transfer of assets to a foundation of this kind made after 22 March 2006 would, of course, create scope for an immediately chargeable transfer, unless the assets transferred qualified as excluded property (see paras 37.9 to 37.13). Where the founder is the 'first beneficiary' one would perhaps expect no value to be transferred at all, on the basis that functionally, the founder has not given anything away, so it might be assumed that there would be no loss to the estate. However, this ignores a requirement to exclude from the value of the founder's estate his interest in possession (see para 34.12) and also any other rights exercisable over the foundation, which would qualify as settlement powers (see IHTA 1984, ss 5(1), 47A and 272). The result seems to be that if it were correct to regard a nominee-like foundation as settlement for IHT, the creation of such a foundation would involve a chargeable transfer of an amount equal to the value of the assets transferred to it, except insofar as excluded property.

It is very doubtful whether this view is, in fact, right. By far the better view is that where a foundation is a functional nominee for its founder, it falls outside the 'settlement' definition discussed above (unless and until it becomes trust-like on the founder's death). If the disposition was regulated by English law, it would not take the form of a gift to a trust conferring a life interest on the founder, with remainder interests for the individuals who are entitled on his death; it would instead most probably take the form of a transfer to a nominee for the founder, coupled with a will dealing with the assets held by the nominee. And the provisions of a nominee-like foundation are clearly *not* equivalent in effect to a life interest trust for the founder; they are equivalent in effect to a nomineeship.

CASE LAW

33.22 To date there have been few, if any, English cases regarding the characterisation of foundations. *Hamilton v Hamilton*, mentioned above, is at bottom about a succession dispute, rather than the issue of how a foundation should be viewed as a matter of English law or UK tax.

The question of how a foundation should be characterised in a common law country which lacks a foundations law has, however, been considered in Canada, in *Sommerer v R* [2011] 13 ITELR 952. This concerned the tax treatment in Canada of a family foundation, the SPF, formed under the Austrian Private Foundations Act of 1993. At para 59 of his judgment Miller J said:

> 'What needs to be analysed, however, is not what the SPF is, but what relationship exists amongst the SPF (a separate legal person), Mr Herbert Sommerer, and Mr Peter Sommerer and the Sommerer family. Is there a trust relationship? Can Mr Herbert Sommerer be seen as a settlor? Can the SPF be seen as a trustee, perhaps a corporate trustee? Can Mr [Peter] Sommerer be seen as a beneficiary? Do the three certainties, certainty of intention, certainty of subject matter and certainty of objects exist? Are there any other characteristics of the Canadian trust that are missing in the Sommerer arrangement?'

This arguably suggests rather too narrow an approach to the question, as clearly no foundation creates an actual trust relationship, and it is doubtful whether a foundation needs to meet the three certainties test for a trust characterisation to be appropriate. However, later in his judgment, Miller J emphasised that a key question was whether the beneficiaries under the SPF had the right to call the foundation to account. This approximates to the concept, familiar to English trust lawyers, of the irreducible core of the trust.

HMRC PRACTICE

33.23 Generally, there is little in the way of published HMRC guidance or practice in relation to the characterisation of foundations. There is nothing of value on the subject in the International Manual.

There was a statement that Liechtenstein foundations are to be treated as trusts for UK tax purposes in an appendix to the Second Joint Declaration by the UK and Liechtenstein, which was issued in 2010 in connection with the Liechtenstein Disclosure Facility (LDF). However, this statement was very heavily qualified:

'For the avoidance of doubt, nothing contained in this appendix is to affect the ability of affected persons to rely on UK law or practice permitting alternative characterisation, recognition and treatment. The parties further recognise that the ultimate UK taxation consequences for UK tax payers will depend on the particular facts relating to specific entities or fiduciary relationships. Nothing in this appendix affects how those entities or relationships are treated for any purposes outside the MOU.'

Ultimately, therefore, the statement in the Second Joint Declaration has limited value, as a confirmation that HMRC accept that in certain situations a foundation should be characterised as a trust. The experience of practitioners dealing with LDF disclosures was that Liechtenstein foundations were, in fact, most commonly characterised by HMRC as nominees rather than as trusts. This is likely to reflect the nature of the situations requiring such disclosures, which involved many foundations established for the purpose of asset concealment, and a certain number of sham foundations which purported to give interests to persons who were not, in reality, their beneficiaries.

There was formerly some published HMRC guidance on the Tax Deduction Scheme for Interest, in which it was stated that 'the current HMRC view is that Stiftungs [ie Liechtenstein foundations] are Trusts for UK tax purposes'. This was clearly incorrect, insofar as certain foundations are certainly best characterised as nominees rather than trusts. In any event the guidance has been withdrawn.

TRUST REGS

33.24 There is a further Liechtenstein law entity which has some similarities to a foundation, namely the *Treuunternehmen* (trust enterprise), more commonly known as the trust reg. If anything, trust regs raise even greater difficulties in terms of the correct English characterisation and UK tax treatment than foundations.

The trust reg entity is provided for under Article 932a of the PGR. A trust reg can be thought of as an incorporated trust. Unlike a common law trust it has legal personality and the assets are held by the trust itself, rather than being vested in the trustees subject to fiduciary obligations owed to the beneficiaries. (Although Article 932a of the PGR permits trust regs to be created with or without legal personality, trust regs without legal personality are rare.)

As with older Liechtenstein foundations, the governing documents of trust regs tend to be very laconic. The wording can be suggestive of a discretionary entity, under which beneficiaries have no entitlement to income or capital distributions, or it may indicate that a given beneficiary has rights which would enable him or her to direct the making of investments and to call for capital. In the latter case the trust reg is liable to be characterised as a nomineeship. In the former case, it may be thought that the closest English law analogue is a discretionary settlement.

However, with trust regs there is an additional complication for the characterisation exercise, in the form of founder's rights (*Treugeberrechte*; sometimes also called 'trustor's rights'). Such rights may be very extensive, including rights to appoint trustees, to direct the making of distributions to beneficiaries and to direct that the trust reg be wound up by a transfer of all assets to the founder (whether or not he or she is a beneficiary). Such rights are assignable by the founder inter vivos, and moreover do not necessarily fall away on his or her death, but are transmissible by will or under intestacy rules.

It might be argued that such rights are not necessarily inconsistent with a characterisation of the entity as a trust. An English law trust can be created with a reservation of a settlor power to appoint and remove trustees, an overriding power of appointment for the settlor and a settlor power of revocation. However, clearly there is a limit to the powers that can be reserved by a settlor without creating a risk of a finding that what appears to be a trust is in fact, as a matter of law, a nomineeship. As with a foundation the manner in which a trust reg is operated in practice, including the degree of personal involvement of the founder or other holder of founder's rights, may need to be taken into account in determining whether the entity is closer to a settlement or a nomineeship.

Chapter 34

USUFRUCTS

INTRODUCTION

34.1 This chapter addresses the controversial issue of how usufructs should be characterised for UK tax purposes. The approach to be taken to the problem is of course exactly the same as for foundations, whose characterisation is discussed in CHAPTER 33.

As with foundations, usufructs are alien to England law and are not specifically addressed in the UK tax legislation. It is necessary to try to establish the closest analogue to a usufruct that can be created under the law of the UK, and then to apply the relevant UK tax provisions accordingly. This is, however, easier said than done.

The usufruct concept is common in civil law systems and is derived from Roman law. They may be created under the laws of many countries on the European mainland, many Latin American countries, South Africa, Thailand and also, in the United States, Louisiana. There may be subtle differences between the nature of a usufruct in one civil law country compared to another. However, there appears to be a broad similarity in usufruct laws across the civil law world.

Usufructs are often compared with life interest trusts. As discussed below, there are certainly some points of similarity, but also significant differences which are material to the UK tax analysis. Usufructs are also sometimes compared with proper liferents, which are arrangements that can be created under Scots law and are thought to have the same historical origins.

CHARACTERISTICS

34.2 A usufruct might be described as an arrangement under which one person has ownership of an asset, but that ownership is encumbered by rights of use or enjoyment held by another person, called the usufructuary. The first person, who owns the asset subject to obligations due to the usufructuary, is commonly called its bare owner.

In the case of income-producing property, the usufructuary will be entitled to receive the income from the asset. He may also have control powers, for example power to exercise voting rights over shares that are subject to the usufruct, although such powers are not instrinsic to the usufruct concept. If, on

347

the other hand, a usufruct is created over unlet real property or chattels, the usufructuary will be entitled to occupy or otherwise enjoy the asset.

The usufructuary's interest is usually an interest for life, but it can be for a fixed period instead. The usufruct arrangement can normally be terminated by agreement of the bare owner and usufructuary, through a partitioning of the capital, with the usufructuary receiving a proportion of the capital broadly reflecting the net present value of his income right. In some countries, eg France, the split between bare owner and usufructuary is determined by civil code provisions, whereas in others it is left to the parties to agree the division, perhaps following expert advice as to the net present value of the parties' respective interests.

Unlike a foundation, the arrangement does not give rise to a legal person which is separate from the bare owner and the usufructuary. The legal position seems to vary across the civil law world as to how, in the case of an asset that is transferred by registration, the respective interests of the parties are shown on the title register. It seems to be most usual for the bare owner to be the registered proprietor, but the usufructuary's interest may also be registered as an encumbrance.

A usufruct over an asset is commonly created by a lifetime gift of the asset to another person, most often a child of the donor, subject to a reservation of rights – so a usufructuary is often the donor of the asset in question, and the bare owner the donee. This contrasts with life interest trusts, where it is usual for both the life tenant and the remainderman to be persons other than the settlor.

However, it is also possible for a usufruct to be created on death. This may be by express provision in the deceased's will. In certain systems that create community of property between spouses, a bequest of community property to descendants where there is a surviving spouse automatically takes effect as a bequest to them as bare owners, subject to a usufruct for the spouse. Here the practical effect of the usufruct is of course similar to the statutory trust which can arise under English law where an individual dies intestate, leaving a spouse and descendants.

POSSIBLE ANALOGUES

34.3 As discussed in relation to foundations (see **33.5**), it is possible for a foreign law entity to have one characterisation for the purposes of one taxing provision, and a different characterisation for the purposes of another. Care therefore needs to be taken with any generalised equation of a usufruct with a particular entity or arrangement that can be created under the laws of the UK. But having noted that caveat, there are a number of candidates for the closest domestic analogue of a usufruct.

Interest in possession trust

34.4 A usufruct is superficially similar to an interest in possession trust, in that it is a succession arrangement, without legal personality, which confers an income right or right to enjoy on one person, and a remainder interest on another. However, a key difference is that once it has been created, a usufruct arrangement has two parties (usufructuary and bare owner) whereas a trust has three (life tenant, remainder beneficiary and trustees). With a trust, legal ownership and control rests with the trustees, who are legally distinct from the income beneficiary and the capital beneficiary. There is no real equivalent of the trustee role in a usufruct and no fiduciary duties are involved.

Proper liferent

34.5 As noted above, this is a Scots law institution which has the same Roman law 'roots' as the usufruct and is considered to be very similar in nature. It creates separate property interests for the 'liferenter' (ie usufructuary) and 'fiar' (ie bare owner), which do not involve the property in question being held subject to any trust.

Lease

34.6 There are obvious similarities between a usufruct over real estate and a lease, for example a lease for life. The arrangement creates legal rights and obligations between the parties which do not involve any trust. However, it is thought that a lease, in the strict sense, is only capable of being created over real property. One cannot grant a lease, as such, over shares or other financial assets. Usufructs on the other hand can be created over a wide range of assets.

Other contractual arrangement

34.7 Where financial assets are concerned, a further possible analogue is a contractual arrangement between transferor and transferee, whereby the assets are transferred subject to a contractual right for the transferor to receive all income from them for the duration of his life or a shorter period. Such arrangements are rarely, if ever, used in the UK but there is no obvious reason why such an arrangement would not be possible as a matter of law.

Range of views possible

34.8 It is suggested that the absence of trustees in a usufruct makes it unlikely that an interest in possession trust should *generally* be considered to be the closest domestic analogue. The other legal arrangements discussed above, which are bipartite instead of tripartite, are arguably closer in nature to the usufruct. However, at least where IHT is concerned, it may not matter.

UK TAX ANALYSIS

Inheritance tax: is a usufruct a settlement?

34.9 The main IHT definition of 'settlement' in IHTA 1984, s 43(2) has already been summarised in the context of foundations (see para **33.13**). HMRC's current view (IHTM 27054, updated 15 August 2016) is that:

> 'a usufruct should be treated as a settlement for IHT purposes given the closing words of IHTA84/S43(2), " . . . .or would be so held charged or burdened if the disposition were regulated by the law of any part of the UK . . . .". This creates a fiction solely for the purposes of charging IHT and requires us to look at the outcome of the disposition and then consider how that outcome could be achieved under the law of any part of the UK. Bearing in mind the nature of the split in ownership that a usufruct achieves, the closest equivalent under UK law is a life interest settlement, with the bare owners holding the property for the benefit of the usufructuary (life tenant) with remainder to themselves.'

This is tenable. It is not certain that the rationale is right, because as noted above there are a number of other legal mechanisms which are, in principle, available under the law of the UK to create a relationship between two parties which is broadly equivalent to the relationship between a bare owner and usufructuary. However, even if HMRC are incorrect in saying that a usufruct is a settlement for IHT on this basis, there are other bases from which the same result can be reached.

If a usufruct is characterised as a proper liferent, it may be that it is caught by a separate limb of the 'settlement' definition, which 'in relation to Scotland' applies to any disposition 'creating or reserving a proper liferent of any property whether heritable or moveable', and deems any property affected by such disposition to be the property subject to the settlement (IHTA 1984, s 43(4)(c)). However, it is perhaps not a very natural reading of the IHT legislation to say that a foreign law usufruct affecting property outside Scotland falls within this subsection. The words 'in relation to Scotland' arguably confine the subsection to actual Scots law proper liferents.

If, on the other hand, a usufruct over real property is characterised as a lease, it is likely to be caught by a further separate limb of the 'settlement' definition in IHTA 1984, s 43(3). This catches leases for life and other leases terminable on the tenant's death, unless granted for full consideration.

Lastly, if a usufruct over a financial asset is characterised as a contractual arrangement of the kind postulated at para **34.7**, it may be a disposition whereby the property is burdened, otherwise than for full consideration, with the payment of an annuity 'or other periodical payment payable for a life or any other limited or terminable period' (IHTA 1984, s 43(2)(c)). If so, it falls within the main IHT definition of 'settlement'. One potential argument against this is that the income payable to the usufructuary is obviously not an annuity, and the words 'or other periodical payment' should arguably be construed according to the *ejusdem generis* rule, as referring to periodical payments having some similarity to an annuity. This would exclude payments of an irregular nature and/or fluctuating amount, such as dividends, which are of course dependent on the profitability of the company.

The IHT treatment is therefore very uncertain, although on balance it seems more likely than not that HMRC are correct in saying that a usufruct is a settlement for IHT purposes. HMRC themselves recognise that their stance is contentious, and the internal guidance suggests that some pragmatism may be shown:

> 'The correct treatment of a usufruct for IHT purposes is not universally accepted. One leading commentator refers to it as a "toss of a coin matter" . . . Each case will need to be considered on its own merits.' (IHTM 27054).

Generally, if a usufruct is a settlement for the purposes of IHT, it is irrelevant which limb of the IHT definition of 'settlement' it falls within. However, there is one qualification to that. A reversionary interest under a settlement is typically excluded property, but not where it is the interest expectant on the determination of a lease for life (IHTA 1984, s 48(1)(c)). It follows that the interest of a bare owner under a usufruct arrangement would be within the scope of IHT if the usufruct was properly characterised as a lease for life. However, as discussed above, that is not HMRC's rationale for treating a usufruct as an IHT settlement, and HMRC accept that, generally, the interest of a bare owner is excluded property (see IHTM 27054).

If one proceeds on the basis that a usufruct is indeed a settlement for IHT purposes, it makes sense to consider separately (1) usufructs created on death, (2) usufructs created *inter vivos* before 22 March 2006, and (3) *inter vivos* usufructs created on or after that date. The analysis needs to be considered afresh if one takes the view that a usufruct is not a settlement for IHT.

Inheritance tax analysis if a settlement: usufructs created on death

34.10 Usufructs created on death are not usually problematic where IHT is concerned. If such a usufruct is treated as a settlement for IHT purposes, it may be an excluded property settlement. This will be so if at the time of death the deceased was neither actually domiciled in the UK nor deemed domiciled, and the assets are non-UK situated.

Even if the assets are not excluded property, the relevant property regime will not apply, as the usufructuary's interest is an immediate post-death interest, and therefore a qualifying interest in possession (see CHAPTER 61). The corollary of this is that the assets subject to the usufruct are treated as being in the usufructuary's estate for IHT.

It follows that if the usufructuary is the widow or widower of the deceased, the spouse exemption can be claimed with respect to the assets in the deceased's estate that have become subject to the usufruct (subject to the usual condition as to the recipient spouse's domicile for IHT purposes – see para 45.5). And in principle there may also be an exemption from IHT on the death of the usufructuary, if the bare owner is the usufructuary's spouse, or a charity. However, those scenarios are uncommon.

As noted above, while the usufruct is subsisting, the interest of the bare owner will be treated as a reversionary interest under a settlement and therefore as excluded property. The bare owner can therefore give away his interest, including to a trust, without IHT being charged.

Inheritance tax analysis if a settlement: pre-22 March 2006 *inter vivos* **usufructs**

34.11 It will be recalled that if a usufruct is created *inter vivos*, this is typically done by means of a gift of the asset to another person such as a child of the donor, subject to a retention by the donor of a right to income from or other enjoyment of the asset. Prior to the FA 2006 IHT reforms, this did not usually give rise to the acute problems which may be generated by the current legislation.

Under the pre-FA 2006 legislation, treating the usufruct as a settlement resulted in the gift being, at worst, a non-event for IHT, where the donor was the usufructuary. This was on the basis that the donor's retained right to income or other enjoyment was an interest in possession. Under the law at that time, this resulted in the usufruct assets being treated as part of the donor's estate for IHT (IHTA 1984, s 49(1)). One implication of this was that if the donor was UK domiciled, or deemed domiciled, at the time of the gift, then the gift did not secure any IHT advantage, compared to simply retaining full ownership of the asset and bequeathing it by will. However, there was no upfront IHT charge or scope for periodic charges.

The position was even more benign if the donor was neither actually domiciled in the UK nor deemed domiciled at the time of the creation of the usufruct. In that case there would be no scope for IHT on the creation of the usufruct, if the donor was himself the usufructuary, and there would also be no IHT on the usufruct assets on his death, provided that the assets were non-UK situated at that time (IHTA 1984, s 48(3); see para 61.13).

In either case, in the event of the bare owner's death during the subsistence of the usufruct, no IHT would be due on his interest under the arrangement, as it would qualify as a reversionary interest and therefore as excluded property (IHTA 1984, s 48(1)).

Inheritance tax analysis if a settlement: *inter vivos* **usufructs created on or after 22 March 2006**

34.12 The FA 2006 reforms were implemented without thought about the impact they might have on usufructs. If a usufruct is a settlement for IHT purposes, there is now a stark contrast between (on the one hand) usufructs created by individuals who are neither domiciled nor deemed domiciled in the UK, whose assets should qualify as excluded property, and (on the other hand) usufructs created by UK domiciliaries and deemed domiciliaries.

A usufruct over excluded property remains unproblematic, avoiding any IHT charge on its creation, on the death of the donor/usufructuary or indeed if the donee/bare owner dies whilst the usufruct is subsisting. However, for assets which are not excluded property, the IHT analysis re post-21 March 2006 usufructs is difficult, if one accepts the HMRC view that they are settlements.

It is no longer generally the case that the holder of an interest in possession created under an *inter vivos* settlement is treated as the beneficial owner of the assets in which that interest subsists (IHTA 1984, s 49(1A)). The result is that if a usufruct is created by lifetime gift, and the usufruct is deemed to be a settlement for IHT purposes, and the assets are not excluded property, a transfer of value occurs.

Quantifying that transfer is not straightforward. A transfer of value is of course calculated by reference to the loss to the transferor's estate (IHTA 1984, s 3(1)). It might be expected that an individual creating a usufruct would be permitted to take account of the net present value of his retained rights when determining the value transferred, which would of course reduce that value.

However it is very unclear whether such discounting is actually allowed. Under IHTA 1984, s 5(1), a person's estate is the aggregate of all the property to which he is beneficially entitled, but subject to certain exceptions. It is specifically provided that a person's estate does not include an interest in possession in settled property to which he became entitled on or after 22 March 2006 (s 5(1)(a)(ii), s 5(1A)). The result appears to be that, strictly, the value of the retained rights has to be disregarded when calculating the value transferred, although it is conceivable that these provisions are intended to disapply the former rule in IHTA 1984, s 49(1), discussed above, but do not prevent the value of the retained rights from being factored in.

It is clear in any event that not all of the value transferred is immediately chargeable. Part of the value transferred is potentially exempt, as the net present value of the bare property interest must be part of the donee's estate (IHTA 1984, s 3A(2)). This is the case notwithstanding that the bare property interest is excluded property in the donee's hands, as the value of excluded property is only left out of an estate on his death (IHTA 1984, s 5(1)(b)). The proportion of the value that this applies to will of course turn on the donor's life expectancy; the creation of a usufruct by an elderly donor or one who is in poor health should to a large extent be a PET.

The HMRC guidance ignores both of these subtleties, stating that 'On creation of a usufruct, the donor will be making an immediately chargeable transfer of the full value of the property . . . ' (IHTM 27054). This is clearly wrong, at least where s 3A(2) is concerned.

The assets of a post-21 March 2006 *inter vivos* usufruct are within the relevant property regime unless, as noted above, they qualify as excluded property. There is therefore scope for IHT charges at 10-yearly intervals and on termination of the usufruct. Such charges are on the value of the property comprised in the deemed settlement (IHTA 1984, s 64(1) and 64(2)) and are therefore on the entire value of the assets that are subject to the usufruct, at a rate of up to 6%.

It is a matter for debate whether, in this scenario, the person primarily liable for relevant property regime charges is the usufructuary or bare owner. The latter seems more likely, as arguably the assets are 'vested' in the bare owner (see IHTA 1984, s 45). But this is likely to be academic, as the usufructuary will have secondary liability (IHTA 1984, s 201(1)(b)).

A further point of controversy is whether, where the assets of a post-21 March 2006 *inter vivos* usufruct are relevant property, the gift with reservation of benefit rules are engaged where the income right has been retained by the donor, such that the entire value of the assets that are subject to the usufruct is treated as being within the donor/usufructuary's estate on his death. HMRC say that 'If the donor has retained a usufruct over the property, they may well have reserved a benefit in the property . . . ' (IHTM 27054). Generally, the analysis turns on whether the creation of the usufruct is viewed as a gift of the asset subject to a reservation of rights, or as a gift of an asset from which rights to income or enjoyment have been shorn. This perspectival issue is discussed at para **83.17**. On balance, it more seems likely that the GWR rules are engaged. They certainly apply where the subject of the usufruct is land, as then the test for whether a benefit has been retained is different (see para **83.6**).

It follows from the above that the death of the donor/usufructuary may, in principle, give rise to three simultaneous IHT charges: there may be IHT on a failed PET and/or additional IHT on a chargeable transfer made within seven years of death; IHT on termination of the deemed settlement, under the relevant property regime; and IHT under the GWR rules. The Inheritance Tax (Double Charges Relief) Regulations 1987 (SI 1987/1130) are likely to permit the IHT on the failed PET and/or additional IHT on the chargeable transfer to be credited against the IHT triggered by FA 1986, s 102 (reg 5). However, there is no statutory ability to credit the IHT triggered by the termination of the settlement.

The baroque complexity of this analysis, and its penal implications, may be factors that a court would take into account if required to decide whether a particular usufruct is a settlement for IHT purposes.

Inheritance tax analysis if not a settlement

34.13 If a court found a way to say that a usufruct is not a settlement for IHT, the analysis would be somewhat simpler. The *inter vivos* creation of a usufruct by an actual or deemed UK domiciliary would be a PET to the extent of the net present value of the bare property interest conferred on the donee. There would be no further transfer of value, as there would be no statutory obstacle to including the net present value of the donor/usufructuary's retained rights in his estate. There would of course be no scope for relevant property regime charges. However, there would probably be a GWR, resulting in an IHT charge on the donor/usufructuary's death on the entire value of the assets subject to the usufruct.

CGT: is a usufruct a settlement?

34.14 Generally, in the CGT legislation 'settlement' is used in the narrower sense of a trust – excluding arrangements with equivalent effect to a trust. As discussed above, although a usufruct has some similarities to a life interest trust, there is also a major difference in that a usufruct has no trustee, nor any other person with an equivalent office or role. For this reason it is generally thought that for CGT purposes, a usufruct is not a settlement.

HMRC agree. They say that 'A usufruct governed by French law would be regarded as a non-trust arrangement as it is broadly similar to a Scottish proper liferent.' (CG 31305).

CGT position on creation of usufruct

34.15 The creation of a usufruct obviously involves a disposal of the assets for CGT purposes. The position with regard to holdover relief is rather complex, but in practice such relief is only likely to apply in relation to a gift of business assets (under TCGA 1992, s 165) and only if the bare owner is UK resident (TCGA 1992, s 166).

If gains are realised on the gift, CGT is likely to be triggered for the donor if he is UK resident, subject to two qualifications. One is that he may conceivably have losses that can be set against the gains. The other qualification is that if the assets are non-UK situated and the donor is non-UK domiciled, the remittance basis may protect the donor from an immediate CGT charge. In the latter case, the rule regarding disposals otherwise than for full consideration (ITA 2007, s 809T) will need to be watched (see para **49.22**), bearing in mind the fact that the bare owner may be a relevant person in relation to the donor (see paras **54.2** to **54.5**).

Taxation of income from usufruct assets

34.16 If the usufruct assets generate income, such income can only be taxed on one of two parties, namely the usufructuary or the bare owner. Logic would demand that the usufructuary should be taxed as he is the beneficial owner of the income.

It is suggested that this is indeed the result, if the usufructuary is UK resident and has created the usufruct. Technically, this result is usually secured by the income tax settlements code. A usufruct falls within the artificially wide definition of 'settlement' that applies for the purposes of that code (see CHAPTER 75), which includes dispositions, arrangements and transfers of assets. The creator of a settlement in this wide sense is deemed to be its settlor (ITTOIA 2005, s 620(1)). Thus a UK resident individual who has created a usufruct, with himself as usufructuary, is taxable on its income as a settlor of a settlor-interested settlement.

It is possible, although in practice rarely done, for an individual to create a usufruct inter vivos by giving assets to one person subject to an income right for another (i.e. not reserving income rights for himself). In that scenario there is still a settlement for the purposes of the income tax settlements code, but it is not settlor-interested unless the donor's spouse or civil partner is the usufructuary or bare owner, or income is paid to minor children of the donor. Assuming that is not the case, so that the usufruct is not a deemed settlor-interested settlement, the usufructuary (if UK resident) is the person who is taxable on income generated by the usufruct assets, on the simple basis that he is entitled to such income.

Taxation of gains on disposals of usufruct assets

34.17 In the event that there are disposals of usufruct assets during the subsistence of the usufruct, liability for CGT on any resultant gains must fall on the bare owner. This is of course subject to the remittance basis if they are foreign gains and he is a remittance basis user. There is no scope for the creator of the usufruct to be taxed on such gains under TCGA 1992, s 86 (see CHAPTER 76) as that section requires a settlement in the traditional, narrow sense, ie a trust (see para **76.3**).

Quantifying such gains can be challenging. It might be expected that the bare owner's base cost in the usufruct assets would be the market value of those assets when the usufruct was created, under the ordinary rule for transactions otherwise than at arm's length (TCGA 1992, s 17). However, the creator of the usufruct and the bare owner will usually be connected persons, and if so a special rule requires the bare owner's base cost to be reduced by reference to the depreciatory effect of the usufructuary's retained rights (TCGA 1992, s 18(6)).

CGT position on termination of usufruct

34.18 A usufruct may be terminated by the death of the usufructuary, the death of the bare owner, or a partitioning of the usufruct so that the usufructuary's interest is commuted.

No chargeable gain arises on the death of one of the parties to a usufruct. There is no deemed disposal and reacquisition if the bare owner becomes absolutely entitled to the usufruct assets on the death of the usufructuary, as TCGA 1992, s 71 is limited to settled property, and for these purposes 'settled property' means property held in trust (TCGA 1992, s 68).

The corollary of this is that there is no tax-free rebasing of the assets on the usufructuary's death, even in the case of a usufruct that was created on death or before 22 March 2006 (TCGA 1992, s 73(2A)). A subsequent disposal of usufruct assets by the absolute owner is likely to raise difficult issues about his base cost in the assets, for the reason mentioned above.

Similar CGT issues arise if the usufruct is partitioned. A partition is likely to involve disposals by the bare owner, to allow the usufructuary to receive a capital sum in commutation of his income rights. It seems likely that there is a disposal by the usufructuary too, of his chose in action against the bare owner. If that is the right analysis, determining the usufructuary's base cost in the chose in action is difficult. At first sight, there is no base cost at all. However, if the usufructuary was the creator of the usufruct, it seems to be arguable that some proportion of the market value of the assets that were given away by him can be treated as base cost in his retained rights, under the provisions of the CGT legislation regarding part-disposals (TCGA 1992, s 42).

COMMENT

34.19 It will be evident from the above that the UK tax treatment of usufructs is highly uncertain, exquisitely complicated and potentially penal. Where any of the parties is or may become UK resident, a usufruct should only be created with great circumspection. And, bearing in mind the significant risk that a usufruct is an IHT settlement, a usufruct should never be created by a UK domiciliary or deemed domiciliary.

Chapter 35
SHAM TRUSTS

35.1 If a trust is characterised as a sham, the legal analysis is that the trustee holds the assets not on the trusts laid down in the trust instrument, but as nominee of the settlor or on some other basis. A finding that a trust is a sham is often the result of family litigation and in that context can be serious for the trustee, for he may end up being found to have misapplied money that was not his, particularly where the settlor is dead. In a fiscal context the sham concept can also have criminal implications (*R v Allen* [2001] STC 1537).

WHAT IS A SHAM?

35.2 In English law the generally accepted definition of what constitutes a sham was given by Diplock LJ in *Snook v London and West Riding Investments Ltd* [1967] 2 QB 786, 802. His words are as follows:

> 'As regards the contention of the plaintiff that the transactions between himself, Auto Finance and the defendants were a "sham", it is, I think, necessary to consider what, if any, legal concept is involved in the use of this popular and pejorative word. I apprehend that, if it has any meaning in law, it means acts done or documents executed by the parties to the "sham" which are intended by them to give to third parties or to the court the appearance of creating between the parties legal rights and obligations different from the actual legal rights and obligations (if any) which the parties intend to create. One thing I think, however, is clear in legal principle, morality and the authorities (see *Yorkshire Railway Wagon Co v Maclure* (1882) 21 Ch D 309 and *Stoneleigh Finance Ltd v Phillips* [1965] 2 QB 537), that for acts or documents to be a "sham", with whatever legal consequences follow from this, all the parties thereto must have a common intention that the acts or documents are not to create the legal rights and obligations which they give the appearance of creating'.

Further elucidation of what is meant by sham was given by the Court of Appeal in *Hitch v Stone* [2001] STC 214, 230. Here Arden LJ stressed that an inquiry as to whether a document is a sham requires a careful analysis of the facts and then said that the authorities establish the following points (at paras 65–69):

> 'First, in the case of a document, the court is not restricted to examining the four corners of the document. It may examine external evidence. This will include the parties' explanations and circumstantial evidence, such as evidence of the subsequent conduct of the parties.
>
> Second, as the passage from *Snook* makes clear, the test of intention is subjective. The parties must have intended to create different rights and obligations from those

appearing from (say) the relevant document, and in addition they must have intended to give a false impression of those rights and obligations to third parties.

Third, the fact that the act or document is uncommercial, or even artificial, does not mean that it is a sham. A distinction is to be drawn between the situation where parties make an agreement which is unfavourable to one of them, or artificial, and a situation where they intend some other arrangement to bind them. In the former situation, they intend the agreement to take effect according to its tenor. In the latter situation, the agreement is not to bind their relationship.

Fourth, the fact that parties subsequently depart from an agreement does not necessarily mean that they never intended the agreements to be effective and binding. The proper conclusion to draw may be that they agreed to vary their agreement and that they have become bound by the agreement as varied (see for example *Garnac Grain Co Inc v HMF Faure and Fairclough Ltd* [1966] 1 QB 650 at 683–684 per Diplock LJ . . .

Fifth, the intention must be a common intention (see *Snook*).'

The Jersey Court of Appeal has defined how the principles formulated in *Snook* and *Hitch v Stone* apply to trusts. In *MacKinnon v The Regent Trust Company* [2005] JCA 066 Southwell P said (at para 20):

"In order to succeed in showing that the three settlements are shams [the Plaintiff] must establish that:
(i)   both [the settlor] and [the trustee] intended that the true position would not be as set out in the settlement deeds, but that either the settlements were invalid and of no effect or that the assets of the settlements were held for [the settlor] absolutely so that the assets were simply held to her order, and
(ii)   both [the settlor] and [the trustee] intended to give a false impression to a third party or parties (including other beneficiaries and the Courts) that the assets had been donated into the settlements and were held on the terms of the deeds".

The plaintiff in *MacKinnon* sought leave to appeal to the Privy Council, but leave was refused. It is thus clear that a trust is only a sham if both the settlor and the trustee share the shamming intention at the outset and both intend to deceive third parties.

In an English divorce case, *A v A* [2007] EWHC 99 (Fam), [2007] 2 FLR 467, [2007] Fam Law 791, Munby J analysed whether what is a genuine trust at the outset can later become a sham or vice versa. He stated that 'as a matter of principle a trust which is not initially a sham cannot subsequently become a sham'. He then went on to say that 'the only way, as it seems to me, in which a properly constituted trust which is not, ab initio, a sham could conceivably become a sham subsequently would be if all the beneficiaries were, with the requisite intention, to join together for that purpose with the trustees'.

He then considered whether a trust which is initially a sham can subsequently lose that character. He said that he could see no reason in principle why that should not be possible in circumstances where a trustee who is a party to a sham retired and a new trustee, who believed the trust to genuine, took over in their place. He concluded 'I cannot see any reason why, in that situation, what was previously a sham could not become, even if for the future, a genuine trust.'

SOME OFFSHORE CASES

35.3 A number of cases illustrate how in practice the sham concept has been applied to offshore settlements. A point these cases emphasise is that in determining whether a trust is a sham, it is not simply a question of looking at what happened when the trust was created. It is also necessary to look at the subsequent conduct of the parties to see whether their conduct signifies a true trust or whether in reality they are behaving as nominee and absolute owner.

Rahman

35.4 The first case, *Abdel Rahman v Chase Bank (CI) Trust Co Ltd* [1991] JLR 103 (*Spitz and Clarke: Offshore Service Vol 1*, p 433) concerned a Middle Eastern settlor who wished to protect his assets from forced heirship claims. On English legal advice, a trust was formed, which inter alia gave the settlor a right to revoke the trust as respects one-third of the assets in any one year. The income was payable to the settlor, he had power of appointment over what was to happen after his death, and the trustee had power to appoint all the capital back to him, exercisable solely in his interest.

The dispossessed heirs duly attacked the trust after the settlor's death, and their principal line of argument was that the trust fell foul of an old Jersey maxim '*donner et reteinr ne vaut*'. This maxim applies where a donor retains power to dispose of what he has given or where what is given remains in his possession. The Royal Court in Jersey held that the maxim applied to trusts, and that the Rahman trust did indeed fall foul of it. Trusts established since the amendments to the Trust (Jersey) Law in 1989 no longer have the concept of '*donner retenir ne vaut*'.

What is of significance in the present context is that the Royal Court went on to consider how the settlor and the trustee in fact conducted themselves. After a lengthy review of the facts the Court concluded the trust was a sham in the following terms:

> 'Therefore, having taken into consideration the whole of the evidence and documentation, we were able to reach but a single and unanimous conclusion. KAR retained dominion and control over the trust fund throughout his lifetime. The settlement was a sham in the sense that it was made to appear to be what it was not. The *don* was a *don* to an agent or nominee. The trustee was never made the master of the assets. KAR intended to and in fact retained control of the capital and income of the trust fund throughout his lifetime and used the trust and the deed of appointment made under the trust to make testamentary dispositions. In our opinion, KAR's advisers and the trustee lent their services to the attainment of his wishes.'

The factual findings which led the Royal Court to this conclusion included the following:

(1) Chase Bank in Switzerland opened the trust account on terms requiring it to make or change investments on the direction of the settlor.

(2) The settlor negotiated and gave instructions for the replacement of Chase by Advicorp as investment manager in May 1978.

(3) $1m was diverted from money due to the trust in February 1978 on the orders of the settlor. Similar diversions were made subsequently.

(4)   Chase Bank took investment instructions from the settlor.

(5)   The settlor orally stated that the trust fund was his own money to use as he wanted.

(6)   Reversionary beneficiaries were not told about the trust.

(7)   All distributions were made on the settlor's orders, without the trustee considering which power was being exercised or executing proper documentation.

(8)   The settlor regularly took money from the trust bank without consulting the trustee.

(9)   On the evidence there was no circumstance in which the trustee would have refused a request from the settlor.

(10)   The trustees made loans to settlor's wife on the instructions of the settlor on terms that only the settlor could call in the loans.

(11)   The trustees acted in relation to a Liechtenstein Establishment to the order of the settlor.

(12)   Advicorp managed the investments on the instructions of the settlor and in practice regarded themselves as answerable to him.

Allen

35.5 The second case is *R v Allen* [2001] STC 1537. Here, as part of a tax investigation, the accused had been asked to list his assets and he had omitted any reference to assets held in two offshore trusts. Subsequently those trusts came to the attention of HMRC, and they prosecuted the taxpayer, inter alia claiming that the trust assets should have been included in the list of his assets. The basis of this claim was that the trusts were shams, so that the accused was beneficial owner of the assets held by the trustees.

The accused was convicted in a jury trial in London, and appealed to the Court of Appeal on the grounds that the jury had been misdirected by the trial judge. This appeal was rejected on the grounds that there was overwhelming evidence that the assets were the accused's 'to dispose of as he would' (see *R v Dimsey* [1999] STC 846). The accused treated the assets as his and there was 'no question of the trustees possessing any real power or discretion in the matter'. The evidence is not set out in the report of the case, but once again, the key point is what in practice happened after the alleged trusts were created.

Abacus

35.6 *Re Abacus (CI) Ltd* [2004] 6 ITELR 368 was one of many cases arising out of the litigation between Grupo Torras SA and Sheikh Fahad Mohammad Al Sabah. According to the case report, Grupo Torras was, between May 1988 and June 1990, defrauded of $430m of which $120m was Sheikh Fahad's share.

Sheikh Fahad had previously created a Jersey discretionary trust, known as the Esteem Trust, for the benefit of himself, his second wife and their son. US$1m was comprised in the initial settlement in August 1981, and in April 1982, Sheikh Fahad added further cash which was used to acquire the family's main home. Sheikh Fahad added much more substantial value to the trust between 1988–92, starting with a gift of £5m in 1989–90. By the time *Re Abacus* was heard, Grupo Torras and Sheikh Fahad's trustee in bankruptcy had recovered all assets added to the settlement after 1988, by virtue either of proprietary claims or under a Pauline action in Jersey. There remained the assets settled in 1981 and 1982 and this Grupo Torras sought to secure in *Re Abacus*.

Their primary attack was that the trust was a sham. However, it was clear on the facts that the trust was a bespoke trust drawn up by London solicitors with the advice of Counsel to achieve specific tax planning and asset protection objectives. There was evidence that the settlor had understood he was putting the trust assets beyond his legal control, for he rejected advice that other assets of which he did wish to retain control should be settled. The terms of the trust were expressly modified to ensure it did not fall foul of the 'donner et retenir ne vaut' maxim. The trustee was a reputable trustee company whose files and evidence disclosed no evidence that it took on the trusteeship on any basis other than that set out in the trust deed.

Given this evidence it is scarcely surprising that the Royal Court concluded, as it did, that the trust was not a sham. The only serious point Grupo Torras was able to advance was that one attendance note of the solicitors referred to the settlor having 'control' of the trustees. However, the Royal Court construed this note as referring to the ability of the settlor to remove the trustees rather than any ability of his to control their actions.

In reaching its conclusion, the Royal Court affirmed that it is legitimate to take account of subsequent conduct in ascertaining what was intended when the trust was set up ([2004] 6 ITELR 368, 462). In this context the Court was pressed with the fact that the trustee had always implemented requests made by Sheikh Fahad and also with evidence that on occasion proposed transactions had been put to the trustee virtually as a fait accompli on a take it or leave it basis.

The Court accepted that this was correct on the facts but also found that the trustee had always given genuine consideration to the requests or transactions put to it. This, the Court held, confirmed the trustee had, at the time the settlement was executed, intended to act as a proper independent trustee.

In the course of reaching its decision, the Royal Court issued trenchant general observations on the relationship between trustee, settlor and beneficiaries. It initially cited *Letterstedt v Broers* (1884) 9 App Cas 371 as authority for the basic proposition that all trustee powers must be exercised only in the interests of the beneficiaries. It then explained the duty of the trustees in dealing with requests by the settlor or beneficiaries in the following terms:

> 'In our judgment there is nothing untoward in beneficiaries making requests of a trustee as to the investment of the trust fund, the acquisition of properties for them to live in or for the refurbishment of properties in which they already live. In our judgment many decisions of this nature are likely to arise because of a request by a beneficiary rather than because of an independent originating action on the part of a trustee. The approach that a trustee should adopt to a request will depend upon the nature of the request, the interests of other beneficiaries and all the surrounding circumstances. Certainly, if he is to be exercising his fiduciary powers in good faith, the trustee must be willing to reject a request if he thinks that this is the right course.

But when a trustee concludes that the request is reasonable having regard to all the circumstances of the case and is in the interests of the beneficiary concerned, he should certainly not refuse the request simply in order to assert or prove his independence. His duty remains at all times to act in good faith in the interests of his beneficiaries, not to act against those interests for improper reasons.

In our judgment, where the requests made of trustees are reasonable in the context of all the circumstances, it would be the exception rather than the rule for trustees to refuse such requests. Indeed, as Mr Journeaux accepted, one would expect to find that in the majority of trusts, there had not been a refusal by the trustees of a request by a settlor. This would no doubt be because, in the majority of cases, a settlor would be acting reasonably in the interests of himself and his family. This would particularly be so where there was a small close-knit family and where the settlor could be expected to be fully aware of what was in the interests of his family.'

The approach implicit in this passage was endorsed by the English Court of Appeal in *Charman v Charman* [2005] EWCA Civ 1606, [2006] 1 WLR 1053 (see especially para 70) and in *Charman v Charman (No 2)* [2007] 9 ITELR 913 (at para 50). In has also been endorsed by the Court of Final Appeal in Hong Kong (*Kan Lai Kwan v Poon Lok to Otto* [2015] 17 ITELR 843, para 35). The conclusion which may be drawn is that a trust cannot be attacked as a sham just because on the facts the trustee has always accommodated the wishes of the settlor or beneficiaries. For conduct to be evidence of sham, an additional element has to be present, namely failure when any given request is made to give it genuine consideration.

Minwalla

35.7 *Minwalla v Minwalla* [2004] EWHC 2823 (Fam), [2005] 7 ITELR 457 was a bitterly contested divorce case in England, in which the former wife of an Asian businessman was claiming capital in ancillary relief proceedings. The husband had for many years owned a Panamanian company administered in Jersey which received his earnings, discharged payments on his behalf, and held assets. In 1998 the husband had settled a Jersey discretionary trust to which the company was transferred and the trustees also acquired a second company which owned the London flat in which the couple lived. The trust was discretionary and the only named beneficiary was a charity. The trustee held two contradictory letters of wishes from the husband which appeared to bear the same date.

In the ancillary relief proceedings the husband argued that the trust and the companies had nothing to do with him and should be left out of account. In the English High Court, Singer J rejected this, holding the trust to be a sham.

The following two passages in his judgment indicate the facts which led him to that conclusion.

'What are the factors here that support the proposition that the trust is a front, and that H, at least, had no intention of treating it as such? First, the assets of the trust comprise only the shares in DM and the shares in MM. As to the former, it is clear that H has treated the bank accounts of DM as if they were his own. He has caused to be paid into them the funds to which he was entitled under his various consultancy agreements with Cathay Pacific. He has withdrawn money from those accounts as if it were his own. No formal trading accounts for DM have been drawn up, at least since the execution of the trust deed in 1998. Transfers have been made from DM to MM, without any accounting ever being undertaken between the two companies. Transfers have been made from DM to Jealott Investments Limited, as if the money were H's own funds to move around as he chose, which is precisely as he has always regarded them, a practice from which the trustees/directors have been unwilling or unable to restrain him.'

'In his testimony in Jersey Mr Morgan conceded in answer to questions from Mr Kingscote that DM was in truth H's alter ego; that H had total investment control over that company and, in Mr Morgan's own words, H treated DM as his own "personal fiefdom". Not only had Mr Morgan never seen any consultancy agreement between H and DM, he had not until this summer seen any of DM's bank accounts, and could not be sure at which banks accounts were operative. He was until shortly before he gave evidence in July wholly ignorant about a series of three agreements between Cathay and DM concluded as long ago as May 2001 under which DM would receive up to a total of \$4,750,000 in one-off fees contingent upon securing certain deals, plus an annual fee income until April 2006 of \$850,000.'

The judge was faced with the requirement that for a trust to be a sham both the settlor and the trustees must have so intended. However, he founded himself on an earlier English case, *Midland Bank v Wyatt* [1995] 3 FCR 11, in which the judge had held the test was satisfied if one of the parties to the sham 'merely went along with the shammer, not either knowing or caring about what he or she was signing'. Singer J held that the trustees satisfied the test, observing that they did not attempt at any stage to rein him in.

Singer J also gave a trenchant statement of what is and is not effective in an offshore context (at para 51):

'The nature and structure of sophisticated offshore arrangements such as have been deployed by [the husband] is well understood in this Division. No doubt the professional advisers and trustees of wealthy individuals wish honestly to strive to construct a network of interwoven trusts and companies able successfully to withstand the scrutiny of the internal revenue services of the parts of the world relevant to the interested parties. That shelter is dependent upon there being properly constituted corporate and trust structures in place; and there being a level of competence and of formality in the production of minutes of board meetings, powers of attorney and so on. There must also be supporting evidence (if and when questions arise which must be answered) for the proposition that proper consideration has been given by the trustees to the exercise of their discretionary powers. Two divergent letters of wishes do not fit anywhere into such a structure. I do not see how any professional trustee can properly have in his possession two such contemporaneous documents without there being the clearest instructions in writing as to which prevails.'

Minwalla is not a wholly satisfactory case, as the husband did not attend the ancillary relief hearing and the trustees were not represented. However a clearer contrast with *Re Abacus (CI) Ltd* could not be imagined, as almost all the features that in the latter case led the Royal Court to uphold the trust were absent. It is also to be observed that in *Re Abacus (CI) Ltd*, the Royal Court endorsed the proposition that a trustee has the necessary intention if he goes along with the sham neither knowing or caring what he is signing (see [2004] 6 ITELR 368, 400, at para 58).

As the trust in *Minwalla* was a Jersey trust, Singer J's order fell to be enforced in the Royal Court in Jersey. As an interesting postscript to the English case, the Royal Court asserted trenchantly that it is a matter for Jersey law as to whether a Jersey trust is a sham and reiterated the applicable principles as set out earlier in this chapter. Nonetheless, it ended up by enforcing the English judgement, on the grounds that the trustee had voluntarily submitted to the jurisdiction of the English Court (*CI Law Trustees Limited v Minwalla* [2005] JRC 099).

CONSEQUENCES

35.8 Even though it may be difficult to prove a trust is a sham, the consequences if the allegation is upheld are severe. Thus in *Rahman, Abacus* and *Minwalla*, the result was or would have been that the assets were at the disposal of the creditors, or as the case may be, the heirs or the former wife. A question of particular difficulty for any trustee would be if after the death or bankruptcy of the settlor he had incurred fees or even made distributions in accordance with the fictitious trust. In all probability the trustee would have to make these good, for he would have been dealing with the property without the authority of the beneficial owner.

Allen was a tax case and it illustrates the obvious point that if a trust is a sham any hoped-for fiscal advantages are not achieved. Perhaps more seriously, it demonstrates that criminal liability can arise as well.

Allegations made by HMRC that a trust is a sham may impact not only on the tax payable as a result of the effectiveness or non-effectiveness of the impugned transaction but also on the rights of other parties and on the ability of HMRC to enforce other tax liabilities. In such cases the appropriate forum for resolving the issue may be the High Court rather than the tax tribunal (*Stow v Stow* [2008] EWHC 495 (Ch), [2008] STC 2298).

MINIMISING RISK

35.9 Examination of the facts of the cases described above shows the risk areas to avoid. The classic danger is where the settlor is a non-domiciliary from a civil law country who thus has little familiarity with trusts. The trustee is a bank who manages his assets, and submits a standard form trust document. The bank says that although this document confers wide discretion on the trustee, in practice nothing will change and the settlor's wishes will continue to be followed. The only difference will be that on the settlor's death the assets will devolve in accordance with the trust and not in accordance with the heirship rules of the settlor's home country or his will. Once the trust is set up, the reality is that in fact nothing changes, and the trustee in practice regards itself as bound by settlor's instructions. Indeed, as in *Minwalla*, he may often be referred to as 'the client' and his wishes as 'instructions'.

There is no doubt that such a trust is vulnerable to a sham attack. The best way of avoiding such risk is to ensure:

(a)   The settlor fully understands what a trust is and, in particular, that it is the trustee who is in the driving seat.

(b)   A trust is in fact the kind of legal relationship the settlor wishes to enter into.

(c)   Once set up, the trustee behaves as a trustee. That is not to say he cannot follow the settlor's wishes, but it must be clear that the settlor can do no more than make requests, to which, on each occasion, the trustee must give genuine consideration.

Postscript: Petrodel

35.10 The widely publicised case of *Prest v Petrodel Resources Ltd* [2013] UKSC 34, [2013] All ER (D) 90 (Jun) was not decided on grounds of sham but is a further warning of what can go wrong when trusts and companies are not properly managed and the steps recommended above to avoid risk are not taken.

The case was an English divorce case and concerned an Isle of Man company which was owned by the husband personally or by an offshore structure he had created. He was director and chief executive and it was found neither of the other two directors were independent. During the 1990s, five properties were transferred to the company for the nominal consideration of £1, in each case by or at the behest of the husband. Both the company and the husband declined to give evidence and the Supreme Court concluded that in the absence of any evidence to rebut it, the normal inference should apply, namely that the husband remained beneficial owner of the properties. A similar conclusion was drawn in relation to two other properties which were paid for, but where the inference was that the husband had provided the funds.

The appeal to the Supreme Court arose out of an order by Moylan J that the properties be transferred to the wife as part of the financial provision in the divorce. As the properties were on the facts owned beneficially by the husband, this order was upheld. The position would have been otherwise if the properties had been validly vested in the company, for then, contrary to the decision of Moylan J, the corporate veil could not have been pierced.

It appears that in such cases, a company is nominee for the provider of funds if it holds the funds or purchased property on resulting trust for him. The presumption is that the company is resulting trustee, but this presumption is easily rebutted by the evidence. The issue, therefore, is one of fact (see the discussion in *M v M and others* [2014] 16 ITELR 391).

Chapter 36

TAX MISTAKES

The authors would like to give special thanks to Catrin Harrison of Charles Russell Speechlys LLP for her assistance with this chapter.

INTRODUCTION

36.1 In offshore tax planning, mistakes can be made as to the tax consequences of a course of action. Such mistakes may arise because no tax advice is taken or because the tax advice turns out to be wrong. The unforeseen tax consequences may be in the UK or abroad, although the case law in this area relates very largely to mistakes as to tax consequences in the UK. The issue is whether, if a disposition generates unforeseen tax liabilities, it can be set aside.

Under English law, this question must be answered by reference to equitable doctrines. There is a large body of case law. The key modern judgment in the English courts, which includes a detailed discussion of previous cases, is the Supreme Court decision in the joined cases of *Futter v HMRC* and *Pitt v HMRC* [2013] UKSC 26, delivered by Lord Walker (referred to below, for brevity, as *Futter/Pitt*).

As set out in Lord Walker's judgment, there are three main bases on which voluntary dispositions can be set aside:

(1)   Excessive execution: A voluntary disposition made, or purportedly made, by a fiduciary can be set aside if it is established in court that, under the terms of the relevant document or general law, the fiduciary lacked the power to make it. In such cases the purported disposition is deemed to be void *ab initio*.

(2)   Inadequate deliberation, also known as the rule in *Hastings-Bass*: A voluntary disposition made by a fiduciary can be set aside if, when reaching his decision to make it, the fiduciary failed to take into account all relevant considerations, or alternatively he took into account irrelevant decisions; and this flaw in the decision-making process was causative, ie it resulted in a disposition being made which would not have been made had the fiduciary taken all relevant considerations, and no irrelevant ones, into account. As discussed below, it has now been established that under English law there is a further requirement,

369

namely that the fiduciary is guilty of a breach of duty. A disposition which is within this category is not void *ab initio*, but becomes void if and when relief is granted by the court.

(3) Mistake: A voluntary disposition by any person, including but not limited to a fiduciary, can be set aside if it was made on the basis of a mistake, made without recklessness, of such gravity that it would be unconscionable for the person in question to be held to his mistaken act. Again, the disposition becomes void if and when relief is granted.

There is a possible fourth category of dispositions that can be set aside, namely voluntary dispositions by fiduciaries that fall within the doctrine of fraud on a power, ie where the relevant power has been exercised for an improper purpose. There is Court of Appeal authority that such a disposition is void rather than voidable (*Cloutte v Storey* [1911] 1 Ch 18). But reservations have been expressed about the correctness of this decision, and in the Supreme Court judgment in *Futter/Pitt* Lord Walker suggested that *Cloutte v Storey* might need to be 'revisited' (para 62). Unless and until this happens, it is arguable that fraud on a power can be regarded as a particular form of excessive execution, or at least that there is no practical difference between them. In any event, the fraud on a power doctrine is relatively unlikely to be relevant in the context of a tax mistake.

Where a remedy is potentially available on the basis of inadequate deliberation or mistake, the equitable relief is considered to be discretionary. In *Futter/Pitt*, Lord Walker commented that 'we are in an area in which the court has an equitable jurisdiction of a discretionary nature, although the discretion is not large, but must be exercised in accordance with well-established principles' (para 93). It is well-established that a claimant may forfeit equitable relief by laches, ie excessive delay in bringing proceedings. And a beneficiary may forfeit relief by complicity in the trustee decision which he would wish to set aside (para 43). An issue of obvious interest in the present context is whether, and to what extent, questions of public policy or morality regarding tax avoidance may affect the availability of the equitable relief.

The English cases of *Futter v Futter* and *Pitt v Holt*, culminating in the Supreme Court judgment, are considered a landmark. They have corrected what is now considered to be a previous wrong turn in the law in relation to inadequate deliberation cases, ie the so-called rule in *Hastings-Bass*. They have also erased from the law of mistake a supposed distinction between the effect of a disposition and its consequences, which was widely considered to be philosophically incoherent and practically unworkable. Both these points are discussed further below.

Futter/Pitt has triggered a wave of new case law, with most applications after *Futter/Pitt* being pleaded in reliance on the law of mistake rather than the reformulated rule in *Hastings-Bass*. Where fiduciary mistakes are concerned, the broad effect of *Futter/Pitt* has been to restrict the availability of relief for inadequate deliberation, because there is now considered to be a requirement to show a breach of fiduciary duty for the disposition to be set aside on this basis. This not only reduces the ambit of the rule, but also makes it unattractive for a trustee to bring a *Hastings-Bass* claim (although it is a striking feature of some of the previous *Hastings-Bass* cases that they were brought by trustees who seemed to have little embarrassment in relying on their own defaults to found their claims to relief). At the same time, *Futter/Pitt* has helped to clarify that it is open to fiduciaries, as much as non-fiduciaries, to rely on the doctrine of mistake.

These cases have also prompted legislative change and judicial comment outside of England. The reaction to *Futter/Pitt* in the offshore territories is important, not only because the validity of many dispositions relating to offshore tax planning is governed by the laws of such territories, but also because offshore courts are very willing to accept jurisdiction in such cases, whether on the basis that they will apply their own laws or on the basis that English law will be applied.

In certain offshore jurisdictions the trust law has been amended to 'undo' the reformulation of the so-called rule in *Hastings-Bass*, preserving the ability of trustees and beneficiaries to rely on the rule as it was understood prior to *Futter/Pitt*. In other jurisdictions, there are indications that the courts will not regard themselves as being bound to follow *Futter/Pitt* when applying the local law, and may continue to apply the rule as it was previously understood, even in the absence of any specific statutory authority for such divergence from English law.

In summary, where tax mistakes are concerned, the offshore jurisdictions are generally ploughing their own furrows. It is clear that public policy in these jurisdictions differs from that in the UK. The offshore jurisdictions have a natural interest in protecting their fiduciary industries, which results in a willingness for trustee mistakes to be set aside, where the result of not allowing such relief might be a substantial negligence claim against the trustee in question. Equally naturally, these jurisdictions tend to have a different perspective from the English courts on the morality of UK tax avoidance or mitigation. As Commissioner Bailhache memorably stated in *Re S Trust* 2011 JLR 375 (at para 39):

> 'We entirely accept that it is open to the courts of any country to lay down their own judicial policy in relation to the exercise of an equitable jurisdiction. The preference accorded to the interests of the tax authority in the United Kingdom is not one, however, with which we are sympathetic. In our view, Leviathan can look after itself.'

TRUSTEE MISTAKES

36.2 As noted above, mistakes by trustees and other fiduciaries can be set aside under the general doctrine of mistake, which is discussed in some detail below. However, other remedies may also be available, depending on the circumstances.

Excessive execution

36.3 The concept of excessive execution is potentially relevant where trustees exercise a power conferred on them by a settlement, such as a power of appointment or advancement. The exercise is excessive if it goes beyond what is authorised by the power.

Excessive execution renders the purported disposition void. In other words, the legal position is not a matter for the court's discretion; the purported disposition is deemed to have been a non-event, from the outset. It seems to follow that where it is clear that a power has been exceeded, no application to court is strictly required for the purported disposition to be treated as void. However, in doubtful cases, an application to court may be required for a declaration that the relevant power has indeed been exceeded.

In a passage approved by the Supreme Court ([2013] STC 1148, para 60), Lloyd LJ in *Pitt v Holt* [2011] EWCA Civ 197 (at para 96) described the concept of excessive execution and set out a number of scenarios in which it might arise:

> 'The purported exercise of a discretionary power on the part of trustees will be void if what is done is not within the scope of the power. There may be procedural defect, such as the use of the wrong kind of document, or the failure to obtain a necessary prior consent. There may be a substantive defect, such as an unauthorised delegation or an appointment to someone who is not within the class of objects. Cases of a fraud on the power are similar to the latter, since the true intended beneficiary, who is not an object of the power, is someone other than the nominal appointee. There may also be a defect under the general law, such as the rule against perpetuities, whose impact and significance will depend on the extent of the invalidity. *Re Abrahams' Will Trusts* and *Re Hastings-Bass* together show that the effect on an advancement of invalidity by reason of something such as the rule against perpetuities may be such that what remains of the advancement is not reasonably capable of being regarded as for the benefit of the advancee. In that case the advancement will be void, since the power can only be used for the benefit of the relevant person and the purported exercise was not for his or her benefit. That is an example of an exercise outside the scope of the power. Otherwise, as in *Hastings-Bass* itself, it will be valid.'

Lloyd J acknowledges here that in some cases the purported exercise of a power is valid to some extent but not wholly so. In such a case, the valid part may be severed and upheld. Indeed, as Lloyd LJ indicated, this was what happened in *Re Hastings-Bass* [1974] 2 All ER 193 itself.

The passage quoted above also makes clear that, in certain scenarios, the concept of excessive execution is potentially more useful for undoing tax mistakes than is immediately obvious. Where trustees hold a power to appoint or transfer trust property for the benefit of one or more beneficiaries, and they purport to exercise such power but overlook the tax implications of doing so, it appears that the appointment or transfer will fail on the basis of excessive execution if the unforeseen tax implications are such as to eliminate any benefit to the beneficiary, or beneficiaries, in question. Absent any benefit to the object or objects of the power, the exercise of it is excessive. As stated by Buckley LJ in *Re Hastings-Bass*, a case concerning a purported appointment in exercise of the power in the Trustee Act 1925, s 32:

> 'If the resultant effect of the intended advancement were such that it could not reasonably be regarded as being beneficial to the person intended to be advanced, the advancement could not stand, for it would not be within the powers of the trustees under section 32.'

Inadequate deliberation

36.4 The concept of inadequate deliberation derives from the general principles of the duties of care owed by fiduciaries, including their duty to 'inform themselves, before making a decision, of matters which are relevant to the decision' (*Scott v National Trust for Places of Historic Interest or Natural Beauty* [1998] 2 All ER 705 at 717).

The so-called rule in *Hastings-Bass* was developed from this concept. It can be argued that the rule should really be called the rule in *Mettoy*, as it was in *Mettoy Pension Trustees Ltd v Evans* [1990] 1 WLR 1587 that the rule was expounded. As discussed above, *Re Hastings-Bass* is best regarded as a case about excessive execution rather than the trustee decision-making process. However, the usage has stuck.

Prior to *Pitt v Holt*, it was considered that where a trustee or other fiduciary failed to take into account relevant considerations when making a decision, or took into account irrelevant considerations, and the flaw in the decision-making process was causative, that decision could be set aside (see the formulation in *Sieff v Fox* [2005] EWHC 1312 (Ch) at para 119). There were no further requirements for the relief. There was a lack of clarity as to whether the relief was on the basis that the act was void *ab initio* or merely voidable.

Until 2011, trustees relied on this principle to have their actions set aside in circumstances where they had sought tax advice, but unforeseen adverse tax consequences had nevertheless arisen from the exercise of a trustee power or discretion. However, in *Pitt v Holt*, the Court of Appeal significantly narrowed the scope of the rule. Lloyd LJ stated ([2011] EWCA Civ 197, para 127) that:

> 'the principled and correct approach to these cases is, first, that the trustees' act is not void, but that it may be voidable. It will be voidable if, and only if, it can be shown to have been done in breach of fiduciary duty on the part of the trustees. If it is voidable, then it may be capable of being set aside at the suit of a beneficiary, but this would be subject to equitable defences and to the court's discretion. The trustees' duty to take relevant matters into account is a fiduciary duty, so an act done as a result of a breach of that duty is voidable. Fiscal considerations will often be among the relevant matters which ought to be taken into account.'

The Supreme Court in *Futter/Pitt* approved this statement of the principle (para 91) and reiterated that breach of duty was an essential requirement (para 85) for the rule to apply.

It is clear that trustees will not be in breach of duty if they have taken professional advice from an apparently reputable and suitable source, and implemented it correctly, and that advice turns out to be wrong. In both *Pitt v Holt* and *Futter v Futter* the fiduciaries had taken and followed supposedly proficient, but in fact flawed, advice. In neither case was the fiduciary found to have committed any breach of duty, although there was apparent negligence on the part of the fiduciaries' advisers. It followed that there was no relief under the so-called rule in *Hastings-Bass* in either case. However, as discussed below, in *Pitt v Holt* there was relief under the parallel doctrine of mistake.

One slightly bizarre implication of the reformulation of the rule, therefore, is that beneficiaries are more likely to be able to avoid unwanted tax consequences of trustee actions if the trustees in question have not troubled themselves to take tax advice, or have been inattentive as to whether they implement it correctly. This might suggest to some that there are advantages in appointing slapdash trustees. But it should be remembered that relief under the so-called rule in *Hastings-Bass* is discretionary. It is likely that a court would disallow such relief if there was evidence that the beneficiaries were complicit in a strategy of proceeding without tax advice on the understanding that doing so might allow any adverse tax consequences to be undone.

Prior to *Futter/Pitt*, it was common for claims relying on the so-called rule in *Hastings-Bass* to be brought by the trustees themselves. It was suggested in *Futter/Pitt* that, in general, any setting-aside of trustee actions under this rule should be at the instance of a beneficiary who has been prejudiced, rather than trustees (see [2013] STC 1148 at para 69). However, following *Roadchef (Employee Benefits Trustees) Ltd v Hill* [2014] EWHC 109 (Ch), it is clear that there will remain circumstances where the English courts are prepared to accept the standing of a trustee to bring a claim for relief under the reformulated principle in *Hastings-Bass*.

Offshore perspectives

36.5 Offshore jurisdictions had enthusiastically embraced the so-called rule in *Hastings-Bass* as it was previously understood, ie with no requirement for a breach of duty on the part of the fiduciary. The Supreme Court decision in *Futter/Pitt* has not been well received.

Jersey and Bermuda have taken the most robust approach in response (despite indications from the Jersey Royal Court in *Re the Onorati Settlement; A v Confiance Ltd* [2013] JRC 182 that the Supreme Court's judgment should be followed). The Trusts (Amendment No 6) (Jersey) Law, which inserts new ss 47A–47J into the Trusts (Jersey) Law 1984, and the Bermudian Trustee Amendment Act 2014, which has similarly inserted a new subsection 47A(1) into the Bermudian Trustee Act 1975, both serve to put the previous view of the *Hastings-Bass* rule on a statutory footing. Both give the court the discretion to set aside dispositions of fiduciaries without the need for a breach of duty and without any seriousness requirement. Each expressly permits trustees to apply for the setting-aside of their actions, and each applies retrospectively to dispositions made before their respective enactments. The Jersey provisions also cover mistakes by non-fiduciaries, but there a seriousness test is applied.

The Bermudian law has already been tested in the courts in *Re F Trust; Re A Settlement* [2015] SC (Bda) 77 Civ, where it was held that 'the application of the discretion provided for in s 47A should not be trammelled by the imposition of any particular "test" but rather should be applied on the facts of each particular case' (para 26).

It had been suggested that the Isle of Man too might legislate on this point, but as yet the Tynwald has declined to do so. However, in the recent case of *AB v DC* [CHP] 16/007, Deemster Doyle firmly reserved the position of the Isle of

Man courts to reject a requirement for breach of duty, even suggesting that the Privy Council, sitting as a Manx court, may not follow *Pitt v Holt*. He observed that:

> 'The Isle of Man is not, and has never been, a part of the United Kingdom. Its public policy is in certain areas different to the public policy of the United Kingdom, especially in the area of tax. It would be a mistake to assume that Manx law would automatically follow English law especially in respect of a decision which appears largely driven by UK policy and UK tax revenue considerations.'

MISTAKE

The doctrine in general

36.6 The requirements for a voluntary disposition to be set aside under the general doctrine of mistake were set out in *Ogilvie v Littleboy* (1897) 13 TLR 399 at 400:

> 'Gifts cannot be revoked, nor can deeds of gift be set aside, simply because the donors wish they had not made them and would like to have back the property given. Where there is no fraud, no undue influence, no fiduciary relation between donor and donee, no mistake induced by those who derive any benefit by it, a gift, whether by mere delivery or by deed, is binding on the donor . . . In the absence of all such circumstances of suspicion a donor can only obtain back property which he has given away by showing that he was under some mistake of so serious a character as to render it unjust on the part of the donee to retain the property given to him.'

In the influential, albeit first-instance, case of *Gibbon v Mitchell* [1990] 3 All ER 338 a distinction was introduced into the doctrine between mistakes as to the legal effect of a disposition, which could create grounds for it to be set aside, and mistakes as to the consequences of a disposition, which could not. Following this, it was generally understood that a disposition involving a mistake as to its tax consequences could not be set aside. The Court of Appeal in *Pitt v Holt* extended this distinction, which was incomprehensible to many, and reformulated it as a requirement under the doctrine for there to be 'a mistake on the part of the donor either as to the legal effect of the disposition or as to an existing fact which is basic to the transaction' (para 210).

To widespread relief, the Supreme Court disapproved these unworkable distinctions in *Pitt v Holt* [2013] STC 1148 and reaffirmed the test of 'a causative mistake of sufficient gravity', as set out in *Ogilvie v Littleboy* above. The principles of the general doctrine of mistake can now be summarised as follows (see *Van der Merwe v Goldman* [2016] EWHC 790 (Ch) at para 26 and *Kennedy v Kennedy* [2014] EWHC 4129 (Ch) at para 36):

(1) There must be a distinct mistake, rather than mere ignorance or inadvertence, but the court may infer a conscious belief or tacit assumption where the evidence so permits.

(2) A mistake may still be a relevant mistake even if it was due to carelessness on the part of the person making the disposition, unless the circumstances are such as to show that he or she deliberately ran the risk, or must be taken to have run the risk, of being wrong.

(3)   The causative mistake must be sufficiently grave as to make it unconscionable on the part of the donee to retain the property.

(4)   The evaluation of whether retention of the property by the donee would be unconscionable must be objective, with an intense focus on the facts of the particular case.

As noted above, relief on grounds of mistake is potentially available not only to persons making voluntary dispositions of property to which they are beneficially entitled, but also to persons acting in a fiduciary capacity. *Pitt v Holt* itself is an example of this. Mrs Pitt was the receiver of her husband following his injury in a serious road accident. When settling the damages she received on his behalf, she was not adequately advised and the trust was not drafted so that it would qualify for the special relieving provisions for trusts for disabled persons (IHTA 1984, s 89). As a result, the creation of the settlement gave rise to an IHT entry charge which was not foreseen. While the court would not grant her relief under the rule in *Hastings-Bass*, as she had not breached her duties as receiver (having taken professional advice), it was prepared to set aside the creation of the settlement on the basis that it would be unconscionable for the trustees to retain the property on those terms, in view of the very adverse tax consequences of the settlement.

Tax mistakes

36.7   The extent to which relief on grounds of mistake should be available in cases of errors as to tax consequences was questioned by Lord Walker in *Futter/Pitt* [2013] STC 1148. Lord Walker rejected an argument raised on behalf of HMRC that 'a mistake which relates exclusively to tax cannot in any circumstances be relieved' (para 129); and indeed, as noted above, the Supreme Court's decision was that the gravity of the consequences of Mrs Pitt's mistake, in terms of the tax treatment of the settlement, entitled her to set the settlement aside. However, Lord Walker commented that it is 'necessary to consider whether there are some types of mistake about tax which should not attract relief' (para 132). He added (at para 135) that:

> 'in some cases of artificial tax avoidance the court might think it right to refuse relief, either on the ground that such claimants, acting on supposedly expert advice, must be taken to have accepted the risk that the scheme would prove ineffective, or on the ground that discretionary relief should be refused on the grounds of public policy. Since the seminal decision of the House of Lords in *WT Ramsay v IRC* there has been an increasingly strong and general recognition that artificial tax avoidance is a social evil which puts an unfair burden on the shoulders of those who do not adopt such measures.'

Lord Walker suggested that even if mistake (rather than the principle in *Hastings-Bass*) had been pleaded in *Futter v Futter*, the Court might not have granted the relief (para 135). *Futter v Futter* primarily concerned a distribution of approximately £142,000 from a non-resident trust to its settlor, Mr Futter. The trust had stockpiled gains. It was believed or assumed that if Mr Futter realised latent losses on certain personally held investments, he would be able to set such losses against the gains that would be attributed to him under s 87.

However, this was incorrect (see para **77.42**). The result was that although it was anticipated that the distribution would be free of tax, in fact it attracted a CGT charge at approximately 64%.

Lord Walker remarked that 'the scheme adopted by Mr Futter was by no means at the extreme of artificiality . . . but it was hardly an exercise in good citizenship' (para 135). However, utilising genuine economic losses to mitigate tax on gains is, in principle, rather commonplace and uncontroversial planning. Indeed, it is so straightforward that it seems strange to refer to it as a 'scheme'.

Arguably, it was entirely reasonable for Mr Futter to have expected that he would be able to set his personal losses against the s 87 gains that would be triggered by the distribution, as it is irrational for the statute to prohibit this. Indeed, until 1998 the legislation *did* allow personal losses to be used in this way, and it remains the case that gains matched to a capital payment can be set against personal losses where such gains are within Sch 4C, rather than s 87 (see para **81.26**). It is to be questioned whether, objectively, it was appropriate for the trustees in *Futter v Futter* to be denied relief against an unforeseen 64% CGT charge when Mrs Pitt was allowed relief against her unforeseen IHT liability, which would have been at an effective rate of, at most, 25%.

Several cases decided in the English courts following *Futter/Pitt* have indicated a more liberal, and more rational, attitude to tax mistakes. The general doctrine of mistake was successfully invoked in *Lobler v HMRC* [2015] UKUT 0152 (TCC) to set aside a step which had produced an 'outrageously unfair result' for the claimant, Mr Lobler. An unusual aspect of the case was that the step in question was not a gift or an exercise of a fiduciary power, but a notice to an insurance company, to effect a partial surrender of an offshore life policy (see para **96.28**).

Proudman J found that 'the withdrawal was so affected by the tax consequences that the effect of the withdrawal was entirely different from that which Mr Lobler believed it to be' (para 70). She commented (at para 68) that:

'It is clear from *Pitt v. Holt* at [129]–[132] that a mistake as to the tax consequences of a transaction may, in an appropriate case, be sufficiently serious to warrant rescission and thus rectification. There is no justification for a different approach to mistakes about tax and other types of mistake.'

Proudman J repeated this point in the High Court in *Freedman v Freedman* [2015] EWHC 1457 (Ch). However, it is worth observing that in *Freedman*, Proudman J suggested that she might have had more sympathy with HMRC's submissions if the only consequence of not setting aside the mistake had been the payment of IHT. She commented (at para 41) that 'the fact that the tax charge means that the loan [to the settlor from her father] cannot be repaid makes all the difference'.

Even more recently, in *Van der Merwe v Goldman* [2016] EWHC 790 (Ch), the proceedings concerned an interest in possession trust which the claimant had settled on 27 March 2006, unaware of the overhaul of the taxation of trusts which took effect on 22 March 2006. As a result of that reform, an IHT entry charge of £1.3m arose. Despite noting that the claimant saw IHT mitigation as the 'principal advantage' of creating the settlement, Morgan J set aside its creation.

Offshore cases

36.8 Mistake cases in the offshore territories divide into two categories, namely those where the court is applying the local law, and those where the court is applying English law, in reliance on expert evidence as to the same.

The Guernsey case of *Nourse v Heritage Corporate Trustees Ltd* 18 ITELR 502 is an example of the latter. It concerned a gift by a UK resident individual to a Guernsey resident trust, governed by English law, of shares in a UK resident company. Although the application for relief was brought under the Trusts (Guernsey) Law 2007, s 69, which empowers the Royal Court to make an order as to the validity or enforceability of a trust or in respect of any trust property, it was agreed amongst all advocates involved in the case that whether the gift should be set side on grounds of mistake had to be determined applying English legal principles (para 11).

Generally, the offshore courts have welcomed the abolition of the supposed effect/consequences distinction in the law of mistake, but have distanced themselves from Lord Walker's comments about the social evil of 'artificial tax avoidance'. Chief Justice Smellie of the Cayman Islands had much to say in response to Lord Walker's comments in a 2014 article (Trusts and Trustees, Vol 20, No 10, pp 1101–1110). He commented that '"artificiality" in this sense—like beauty its antithesis—must be in the eyes of the beholder' and that 'In the socio-political context of the Cayman Islands, there can be no presumption that an arrangement, which is otherwise within the law not only of the Cayman Islands, but also of the relevant domiciliary jurisdiction, is to be deemed "artificial" simply because its primary aim is to mitigate the incidence of tax.'

The Manx courts had sensibly rejected the supposed distinction between effect and consequences and so had accepted, even before *Futter/Pitt* that voluntary dispositions could be set aside on the grounds that they gave rise to adverse tax consequences that had not been foreseen. The Manx cases *Re Betsam Trust* [2009] WTLR 1489 and *Clarkson v Barclays Private Bank and Trust (Isle of Man) Ltd* [2007] WTLR 1703 both involved individuals who had established settlements believing themselves to be outside the scope of UK IHT, when they were in fact still deemed UK domiciled under the 17 out of 20 years rule, so that an IHT entry charge was triggered. In each case, the Manx High Court set aside the creation of the settlement.

The Jersey Royal Court in *Boyd v Rozel Trustees (Channel Islands) Ltd; Re the Strathmullan Trust* [2014] JRC 56 commented that the decision of the Supreme Court in *Futter/Pitt* 'seems to us broadly to align the approach to be taken by the English courts in the future with that adopted by the Royal Court' and confirmed that the applicable test under Jersey law was that in *Ogilvie v Littleboy*, as more recently affirmed in *Re the Lochmore Trust* [2010] JRC 068. It is clear from the *Strathmullan Trust* case that mistakes as to the tax consequences of a disposition may suffice for the disposition to be set aside.

The Royal Court noted that 'artificial tax avoidance' is liable to be perceived differently where it is another country's tax which has been avoided (para 25).

The Guernsey courts also appear to have accepted the principles set out by Lord Walker in *Futter/Pitt* as the correct test for the doctrine of mistake, whilst making clear that a disposition motivated by tax mitigation may still be set aside under this doctrine.

However, a 2016 case, *Gresh v RBC Trust Company (Guernsey) Ltd* 18 ITELR 753, resulted in a surprisingly severe decision by the Guernsey Royal Court. The case concerned a request by the beneficiary of a pension trust for a lump sum payment from the trust, which was based on a mistaken belief that such payment would be free of tax. In fact, a pension from the trust would have been free of tax, but a lump sum was not. The beneficiary's mistake resulted from incorrect professional advice.

All other elements required for the general doctrine of mistake as set out in *Futter/Pitt* were present, but the Bailiff did not find it unconscionable to allow the disposition to stand, and so refused to grant the relief sought by the claimant, warning that 'it is not every serious error that will be corrected by the courts' (para 54). The Bailiff distinguished the facts of *Gresh* from those in *Pitt v Holt, Freedman* and other cases, where parties other than the individual who made the disposition would have been affected if the mistake were not corrected, notwithstanding the fact that the affected third parties were often affected only as a result of the unexpected tax due. Even *Strathmullen Trust* was distinguished, on the basis that Mr Gresh had a contractual relationship with his tax advisers and so could bring a claim for professional negligence, whereas the claimant in *Strathmullen Trust* had no such recourse. It will be interesting to see whether the case is appealed.

TAX EFFECT OF MISTAKES

36.9 Implicit in all of the above is the fact that if a disposition is declared void, it is treated as not having occurred and the UK tax position follows this. This is so even in cases where the equitable remedy is discretionary, as where a disposition is avoided on grounds of mistake, and in principle it is regardless of the length of the interval between the disposition and its setting-aside.

This principle has a statutory footing in the case of inheritance tax. IHTA 1984, s 150 provides that where a chargeable transfer is set aside as being voidable, any IHT paid or payable by the taxpayer that would not have been payable if the transfer had been void *ab initio* shall be repaid to him, or shall not be payable, as the case may be; and the IHT position in relation to any later chargeable transfers shall be determined as if the transfer which has been set aside had been void *ab initio*. However, a claim for such relief from IHT must be made within four years of the date on which the claimant became aware, or ought to have become aware, that the disposition had been set aside (s 150(3)).

There is no equivalent provision within the income tax or CGT legislation. However, Mostyn J in *AC v DC* [2012] EWHC 2032 (Fam) stated (at para 31) that:

'The law of tax is not an island entire of itself. Unless a taxing statute says to the contrary the right of the state to charge tax in relation to a given transaction is subject to the effect of that transaction as defined by the general law. In the specific context with which I am concerned there is long-standing authority from the Court of Session (First Division) in Scotland, *IRC v Spence* (1941) 24 TC 312, never doubted in subsequent tax cases in the English courts, which says that the tax effects of a transaction will be annulled retrospectively if it is subsequently found to be voidable, and is declared void.'

MISTAKES BY AGENTS

36.10 The discussion on above has focused on tax mistakes by trustees and individuals. However, mistakes resulting in unforeseen tax liabilities or undesirable tax outcomes can be made by banks and other agents. This typically arises in the case of bank accounts of remittance basis users, where payments or transfers may result in unwanted remittances or 'training' of clean capital. Where this occurs but the payment or transfer was effected in contravention of express instructions by the account-holder, HMRC accept that the payment or transfer can be reversed and that the account-holder can treat it as not having happened (HMRC Residence, Domicile and Remittance Basis Manual, RDRM33560). Such acceptance appears to be based on the principles in *Roxburghe's Executors v IRC* (1936) 20 TC 711. However, in the absence of clear instructions to the bank or other agent, this principle cannot be relied upon.

Section II

The Territorial Limits of UK Taxation

Chapter 37

TERRITORIAL LIMITS

INTRODUCTION

37.1 There is a presumption that all UK legislation is subject to territorial limits. Lord Scarman put the matter thus in *Clark v Oceanic Contractors Inc* [1983] STC, 35, 41:

'... Unless the contrary is expressly enacted or so plainly implied that the courts must give effect to it, United Kingdom legislation is applicable only to British subjects or to foreigners who by coming to the United Kingdom, whether for a short or long time, have made themselves subject to British jurisdiction.'

Lord Scarman also cited *Re Sawers, ex p Blain* (1879) 12 Ch D 522. Here at p 526 James LJ referred to the:

'... broad, general, universal principle that English legislation, unless the contrary is expressly enacted or so plainly implied as to make it the duty of an English Court to give effect to an English statute, is applicable only to English subjects or to foreigners who by coming into this country, whether for a long or short time, have made themselves during that time subject to English jurisdiction . . .'

In recent years it has been emphasised that the territorial principle is ultimately a rule of construction. Thus in *Agassi v Robinson* [2006] 1056, 1063 Lord Scott cited words of Lord Wilberforce in *Clark v Oceanic Contractors*, to the effect that British tax liability has never been exclusively limited to British subjects and foreigners resident in the jurisdiction. In all cases the question to be asked is 'who is within the legislative grasp, or intendment, of the statute under consideration'.

INCOME TAX

37.2 It has long been accepted that income tax legislation recognises the territoriality principle. The position was encapsulated in one sentence by Lord Herschell in *Colquhoun v Brooks* (1889) 14 App Cas 493 at 503, a sentence subsequently approved by the House of Lords inter alia in *National Bank of Greece SA v Westminster Bank Executor and Trustee Co (Channel Islands) Ltd* [1971] AC 945 at 954. Lord Herschell's words were as follows:

'The Income Tax Acts, however, themselves impose a territorial limit, either that from which the taxable income is derived must be situate in the United Kingdom or the person whose income is to be taxed must be resident there.'

Source and residency

37.3 As will be apparent from Lord Herschell's dictum, the key issues are the residence of the taxpayer and where the income is derived from, or source as it is usually known. These concepts are considered in CHAPTERS 40 to 43.

Exceptions and qualifications

37.4 There are some important exceptions and qualifications to the general rule:

(1)   The relevant foreign income and certain earnings of remittance-basis users are not taxed save insofar as remitted. The remittance basis is explained in Section IV.

(2)   UK source investment income arising to non-residents is for the most part exempt from UK tax save insofar as tax is withheld.

(3)   In many instances, double tax treaties curtail the UK's taxing rights where the taxpayer is non-resident or the income is foreign source.

(4)   In many cases, anti-avoidance legislation deems the income of a non-resident to be that of a resident, or attributes income to a resident by reference to income of a non-resident. Prime examples are the settlement code discussed in CHAPTER 75 and the legislation concerning transfers of assets abroad. The latter is discussed in Section I of Part C.

It is also to be stressed that, as the general rule is one of construction, specific legislative provisions can be construed as prevailing over it. *Agassi v Robinson* itself was an example of such construction process.

A further qualification concerns trusts. As is explained in CHAPTER 42, statute attributes a residence status to trusts for income tax purposes. But where a beneficiary is entitled as of right to the trust income, the residence of the trustees is immaterial and instead income tax liability turns on the residence and domicile of the beneficiary. This principle is explained in paras **8.2** and **40.13**. It does not apply to capital receipts which are deemed to be income, which are taxed as the trust's income whatever form the trust takes.

CAPITAL GAINS TAX

37.5 In contrast to income tax, the territorial limits of capital gains tax are, with limited exceptions, defined solely by residence. The basic rule is that a person is chargeable to capital gains tax in any tax year if he is resident in the UK during all or any part of the year (TCGA 1992, s 2(1)). In the case of companies, the charge is to corporation tax, for gains are included in total profits. All forms of trust (other than nomineeship) are treated as a separate taxable entity and so, in contrast to income tax, it is not necessary with fixed-interest trusts to look through to the beneficiaries.

Non-residents

37.6 With three exceptions and one important qualification, there is no liability to CGT in respect of gains realised by non-residents, including gains on UK situs assets.

The first exception is that an individual who emigrates but returns to the UK after a period of five or fewer years remains subject to capital gains for his period of non-residence (TCGA 1992, s 10A). This rule is discussed in para **29.6**.

The second exception is that a non-resident trading in the UK through a branch or agency or a permanent establishment is chargeable to CGT to a limited extent (TCGA 1992, s 10). The charge is on assets which are situate in the UK and used in the trade or held for the purposes of the branch or agency. This charge is discussed further in para **65.2**.

The third exception concerns UK residential properties. Gains realised by non-UK resident individuals and trusts on such properties are chargeable, as are gains realised by any non-UK resident company that is not diversely held. The charge is to Non-resident CGT and is explained in CHAPTER **65**.

The qualification alluded to above is that, as with income tax, there are a number of anti-avoidance provisions which deem the gains of a non-resident to be gains of a resident, or which attribute gains to a resident by reference to gains realised by a non-resident. Prime examples are TCGA 1992, ss 13, 86 and 87 (see CHAPTERS **88, 76** and **77**).

UK residents

37.7 There are two situations in which the liability of UK residents to CGT is qualified. The first is where a double tax treaty is in point and either exempts the gain from CGT or requires the UK to give credit for foreign tax.

The second concerns non-UK domiciled individuals who are using the remittance basis. A remittance-basis user disposing of an asset situated abroad is liable to CGT only if and insofar as the gain is remitted (TCGA 1992, s 12). This, the CGT remittance basis, is explained in CHAPTER **49**.

Situs

37.8 The CGT legislation includes special rules as to the situs of assets. These are explained in CHAPTER **39**.

INHERITANCE TAX

37.9 The territorial limits of inheritance tax are expressed in terms of excluded property. There are several classes of asset which, if specified conditions are satisfied, are excluded property.

37.9 *Territorial limits*

The IHT legislation gives effect to the excluded property concept by two principal rules:

(1)   The estate of a person immediately before his death does not include excluded property (IHTA 1984, s 5(1)).

(2)   No account is taken of excluded property which leaves a person's estate in determining whether an inter vivos disposition is a transfer of value (IHTA 1984, s 3(2)).

Foreign situs assets

37.10 Property which is situated outside the UK is excluded property if the beneficial owner is not domiciled in the UK. The common law rules described in CHAPTER 38 apply in determining the situs of property.

As from 6 April 2017, current government proposals are that certain forms of foreign situs asset will cease to be excluded property. The assets concerned are shares in close companies and interests in foreign partnerships. But such an asset will only cease to be excluded property to the extent its value is attributable to UK residential property. It is likely that UK residential property will be defined in the same way as for NR CGT. This proposal was first announced on 8 July 2015 and more details were given in a Consultation Document issued by HM Treasury on 19 August 2016 (Reform to the Taxation of non-domiciliaries: further consultation).

Authorised funds

37.11 FA 2003 created an important class of UK situs excluded property. A holding in an authorised unit trust or a share in an open-ended investment company is excluded if the owner is not domiciled in the UK (IHTA 1984, s 6(1A). This rule has applied since 16 October 2002 (FA 2003, s 186(8)). It will be noted that, as with foreign situs assets, eligibility for it is determined solely by domicile.

For these purposes the term open-ended investment company has the meaning given in s 236 of the Financial Services and Markets Act 2000. To qualify as one, a company must be incorporated in the UK. An authorised unit trust is a unit trust scheme approved under s 243 of the Financial Services and Markets Act 2000 (IHTA 1984, s 272). Open-ended investment companies and authorised unit trusts may be given the generic name authorised funds.

UK bank accounts

37.12 A UK bank account is excluded property if it is denominated in foreign currency and the account holder is an individual who is neither resident nor domiciled in the UK (IHTA 1984, s 157).

This exemption is restrictive in that it applies only on death. It does not extend to sterling accounts and nor does it protect any account of a non-domiciliary who is resident in the UK.

UK government securities

37.13 Each issue of UK government securities is or is deemed to be subject to a condition that the stock is exempt from taxation if in the beneficial ownership of a person of a description specified in the condition (F(No 2)A 1915, s 47; F(No 2)A 1931, s 22; FA 1996, s 154; FA 1998, s 161). For IHT purposes, a government security is excluded property if it is in the beneficial ownership of an individual of a description specified in the condition applicable to its issue (IHTA 1984, s 6(2)).

What the applicable conditions are is difficult to discern from the legislation, the principal points of difficulty being whether being not ordinarily resident in the UK is the sole criterion or whether, in the case of some issues, there is also the requirement of not being UK domiciled. HMRC give some guidance in the IHT Manual (IHTM0291) but this is not totally clear,

The Manual indicates that any security issued after 29 April 1996 is excluded property provided the beneficial owner is not ordinarily resident in the UK. Some securities issued before then carry the additional requirement of the beneficial owner not being UK domiciled as well, but it is unclear from the Manual whether this is confined to 3½% War Loan 1952 or applies more generally. If domicile is relevant, it is only actual domicile that need be looked at, as the deeming in IHTA 1984 does not apply to the legislation authorising exemption for government securities.

The Manual has not been updated to reflect the abolition of ordinary residence. For government securities acquired after 6 April 2013, residence is the test for exemption, but for earlier acquisitions ordinary residence applies (FA 2013, Sch 46, para 114).

In cases where excluded property status is important the status of the particular gilts held or being acquired should be checked.

Deemed domicile

37.14 For IHT purposes, an individual is domiciled in the UK in all cases where under the general law described in CHAPTER 44 he is in fact domiciled there. In addition a non-domiciliary is deemed to be domiciled in the UK if:

(1)   he was in fact domiciled in the UK at any time in the preceding three years; or

(2)   he has been resident in the UK in 17 out of the 20 years of assessment ending with and including the current year (IHTA 1984, s 267); or

(3)   he has made an election to be treated as domiciled in the UK for IHT purposes so that a gift or bequest to him qualifies in its entirety for the spouse exemption (IHTA 1984, s 267ZA).

The details of these rules and their consequences are described in CHAPTER 45.

On 8 July 2015 prospective changes to the deemed domicile rules were announced. These changes will take effect on 6 April 2017 and are explained in an HMRC Technical Note.

Settlements

37.15 Special rules apply in determining whether, if the classes of asset listed in paras 37.10 to 37.13 above are settled property, they are excluded property and so outside the scope of IHT. These rules are described in CHAPTER 62.

Chapter 38

SITUS OF ASSETS: GENERAL RULES

INTRODUCTION

38.1 This chapter addresses the common law rules concerning the situs of assets. Some of the legal principles, for example regarding the situs of obligations governed by specialties, have their origins in case law of great antiquity. The classic textbook treatment of the subject is in *Dicey, Morris and Collins on the Conflict of Laws*.

The situs of property under the common law rules is important for inheritance tax, in that foreign situs property is not subject to that tax if it is owned by a person who is neither domiciled nor deemed domiciled in the UK, or by a settlement created by such a person (see paras **37.10** and **62.2**). Such property is termed 'excluded property'. The IHT legislation does not include any statutory code to determine situs, so the issue of whether a particular asset constitutes excluded property must generally be resolved by reference to the common law rules.

IHTA 1984, s 5(1) provides that an individual's estate on his death comprises all property to which he is beneficially entitled, with the exception of excluded property. It is clear from the reference to beneficial entitlement that where an asset is held by a nominee, the IHT treatment is determined by the situs of the asset rather than the situs of the individual's rights as against the nominee; the nomineeship is looked through.

Situs is also relevant to capital gains tax, chiefly in that gains accruing on the disposal of foreign situs assets of remittance basis users are subject to the remittance basis (see CHAPTER 49), whereas gains accruing on the disposal of UK situs assets are taxed on the arising basis. However, the CGT legislation includes a statutory code at TCGA 1992, ss 275–275C to determine the situs of assets. This is described in CHAPTER 39. As explained in that chapter, the statutory code that applies for CGT purposes is not comprehensive.

TANGIBLE PROPERTY

38.2 Tangible property does not, in general, occasion difficulty under the situs rules. Not surprisingly it is situate where found. This applies both to real estate and to chattels (see for example (*IRC v Stype Investments* [1982] STC 625, 633 and *Young v Phillips* [1984] STC 520, 534, passim).

INTANGIBLE PROPERTY

38.3 The general rule, as stated as Rule 120 in *Dicey*, is as follows:

'Choses in action generally are situate in the country where they are properly recoverable or can be enforced.'

This rule was cited with approval by the Privy Council in *Kwok Chi Leung Karl v Comr of Estate Duty* [1988] STC 728, 732. It is however only a general rule and it is modified and in some cases disapplied with respect to many types of intangible. Moreover, as discussed in the following paragraph, the general rule is potentially somewhat misleading.

DEBTS

38.4 A debt is perhaps the most obvious chose in action. The relevant rule was stated in the following terms by the Privy Council in *Kwok*:

'It is clearly established that a simple contract debt is locally situate where the debtor resides the reason being that that is, prima facie, the place where he can be sued'

Early case law indicates this rule applies whether the debt is secured or unsecured (*Payne v B* [2002] AC 442). But HMRC's comments on specialties (para **38.6** below) indicate that debts is secured on UK real estate may represent exception in that such debts may have a UK situs even if the debtor is non-UK resident.

As will be apparent from the reference to being sued, what is being referred to is residence for the purposes of suit rather than tax residence. The position is complicated in relation to corporate debtors, as for the purposes of suit a company resides wherever it carries on business in its own name. In that event the situs of the debt is the country in which the debtor's obligations fall to be performed (*New York Life Insurance Co v Public Trustee* [1924] 2 Ch 101, CA, *Re Russo-Asiatic Bank* [1934] Ch 720, [1934] 103 LJ Ch 336). There is a body of case law elaborating on this principle. For example the debt has been held to be situated:

(a)   In the case of a debt due under an insurance policy: where monies were payable under the policy, rather than where the insurance company had its head office (*New York Life Insurance Co*, supra);

(b)   In the case of a bank account: where the account was maintained, at a particular branch, rather than where the bank had its head office (*R v Lovitt* [1912] AC 212); and

(c)   In the case of a promissory note that was payable in one country on presentation and in another after 60 days: where the note was payable on presentation (*Kwok*, supra).

There is no modern authority on the position where, applying general principles, the debtor resides for the purposes of suit in country X but the loan agreement confers exclusive jurisdiction on the courts of country Y, and that contractual choice of jurisdiction is effective, whether under the domestic law or under an international convention. The case of *Raiffeisen Zentralbank Osterreich AG v Five Star General Trading LLC* [2001] 3 All ER 257 refers to the issue. The position is not free from doubt, but it seems most likely that the old authorities continue to apply, without reference to any exclusive juris-diction clause and without regard to international conventions – ie that what is material is where the debtor is subject to the jurisdiction of the courts, applying general principles rather than looking at specific jurisdictional issues raised by (hypothetical) proceedings to enforce the debtor's obligations.

Negotiable instruments

38.5 A negotiable instrument is an instrument transferable by delivery or by delivery coupled with endorsement to the back of the instrument. A debt enshrined in a negotiable instrument is thus assignable by delivery of the instrument and upon such delivery the assignee obtains title good against the world. He does not have to give notice to or otherwise involve the debtor. Negotiable instruments are regarded as a form of chattel – ie the debt is the piece of paper. Accordingly their situs is governed by the rules pertaining to chattels and thus they are situate where found.

This principle was established as long ago as 1838 in the leading case of *A-G v Bouwens* (1838) 4 M & W 171. It has been affirmed in recent years in cases such as *Kwok* (at p 732) and *Young v Phillips* [1984] STC 520 p 534). However, those recent cases do indicate that for the principle to apply there must, where the document is situate, be a market in which its value can be realised.

An instrument is rendered negotiable and thus within this rule either by statute or by commercial custom. An example instanced in *A-G v Bouwens* is foreign bills of exchange traded on the Royal Exchange. But far and away the most significant category of negotiable instrument is the bearer bond – ie debt issued by a public authority or by a company in the form of bonds payable to bearer and expressed as transferable by delivery. This was exemplified in *Winans v R* [1908] 1 KB 1022 (affirmed) [1910] AC 287, where foreign bonds payable to bearer and traded on the London Stock Exchange had been deposited in the Bank of England. These, the Court of Appeal held, were UK situs.

Specialties

38.6 A second exception to the basic rule regarding debts concerns specialty debts. The classic definition of a specialty debt is 'an obligation under seal securing a debt, or a debt due from the Crown or under statute' (*R v Williams* [1942] AC 541, 555). The basic meaning of 'an obligation under seal' is one governed by deed as, historically, a deed could only be created by seal.

Under the Law of Property (Miscellaneous Provisions) Act 1989, a document entered into by an individual is a deed if it is 'clear on its face that it is intended to be a deed' and is signed, witnessed and delivered. English company law allows a document to be executed by two authorised signatories of the company, or by a director in the presence of a witness; if so, and the document is 'delivered as a deed', it has the status of a deed (Companies Act 2006, ss 44 and 46). Thus, under English law, a deed generally no longer requires a seal, and it is very unlikely that there is any surviving requirement, generally, for a seal to make a deed a specialty. However, the same is not the case in other common law countries which recognise the concept of a specialty (see below), and if a document subject to foreign law is to be a specialty, a seal may be needed.

It is considered by many practitioners, although the source of the doctrine is unclear, that a document that is subject to the law of a country other than England can only qualify as a specialty if that country's law recognises the concept of a specialty, or at least the concept of a deed. Thus a loan agreement which is subject to the law of Guernsey, for example, may not qualify as a specialty even if it describes itself as such. If correct, this principle restricts the permissible governing laws for specialty loan agreements to those of common law countries.

It is sometimes said that the situs of a specialty debt only follows that of the document if the document is kept in a country whose law recognises the concept of a specialty or deed. However, there is no authority for this proposition. It may be suggested that the only relevant questions are: (1) does the governing law recognise the concept of a specialty/deed?; and (2) has the document been executed as a specialty/deed?

It is clear that a debt does not have to be secured to be a specialty: this is apparent from *Gurney v Rawlins* (1836) 2 M & W 87, where an unsecured obligation under seal to pay insurance monies was held to be a specialty and so situate where the policy was found. Equally it is also clear that a mortgage debt can be a specialty if the mortgage is by deed: see *Stamps Comr v Hope* [1891] AC 476. This latter case also shows that the execution of a deed containing an express covenant to repay the debt converts a simple debt into a specialty.

Until 2013, it was generally accepted that a specialty debt is located where the deed enshrining the debt is found. The law was widely believed to have been settled in Australian Privy Council decisions such as *Stamp Comr v Hope* (supra). The position was enshrined in a succinct and unqualified dictum in the *Privy Council in Kwok Chi Leung Karl v Comr of Estate Duty* [1988] 1 WLR 1035, [1988] STC 728:

> 'a specialty debt is situate where the deed is physically situate'.

More recently HMRC have expressed reservations as to whether it is correct all specialities are situate where found. At IHTM 27079 it is said:

> 'We now believe this may not be the correct approach in all cases involving specialty debts; specifically that many such debts are likely to be located where the debtor resides or where property taken as security for the debts is situated.'

It is widely accepted that HMRC's reservations have force where the debt is secured and that the situs of the debt in such cases is the location of the security. *Stamps Coms v Hope* is often cited as authority for the proposition that a mortgagor's debt is situate where the mortgage deed is situate rather than where the land is situate. But many advisers consider what *Hope* decided was solely whether the document was a specialty and not the wider issue of whether it or the land determined the situs of the debt. And on any view, where there are duplicate deeds securing the debt, the situs of the land, together with factors such as the residence of the debtor, may be taken into account in choosing which of the deeds determines situs: *Toronto General Trusts Corpn v R* [1919] AC 679.

In the light of this, it is prudent to proceed on the basis a debt is UK situs where it is secured on UK land. With unsecured debts, by contrast, it is difficult to see the law as stated in *Kwok* being successfully challenged below the Supreme Court.

It is occasionally queried whether planning involving the use of a specialty is liable to counteraction under the GAAR, on the basis HMRC have expressed their opposition to the use of specialties to change the situs of obligations. It may however be doubted whether this is a correct analysis. A specialty is nothing more than a deed, which the common law imbues with the power to affect the situs of obligations. Even if this interpretation of the case law is subsequently proved to be wrong, or is overridden by a new authority, it cannot possibly be unreasonable, in itself, to use specialties to document obligations, and to seek to rely on what is understood to be their effect.

SHARES

38.7 A share is part of the capital of a company, to be distinguished from a security or loan stock, which is an obligation of the company (*Singer v Williams* [1921] 1 AC 41). The basic rule is that a share is situated where it can be effectively dealt with as between the owner and the company (*Brassard v Smith* [1925] AC 371). For these purposes a share only counts as effectively dealt with if and at such time as the transferee becomes legally entitled to all rights of a member (*R v Williams* [1942] AC 541). The question of where a share can be effectively dealt with has to be determined by the constitution of the company. However, where only registration on the register of members constitutes a person a member as against the company, the situs of the register is the situs of the shares (*Brassard v Smith* [1925] AC 371).

Multiple registers

38.8 It may be that the company's constitution allows the maintenance of more than one registered office or the keeping of branch registers in two or more separate countries. In this event the choice between those countries is made on rational grounds, which in practice means selecting the country where the owner is more likely to deal in the shares (*Ontario Treasurer v Blonde* [1947] AC 24; *Standard Chartered Bank Ltd v IRC* [1978] STC 272). It is, however, important to distinguish multiple registry offices or branch registers from mere copy registers. This distinction was drawn in *Standard Chartered Bank Ltd v IRC*, where the company register was at its head office in South Africa, with a duplicate register listing UK members in the UK. The evidence was that a transferee only became a member as against the company when entered in the head office register and this meant the shares were situate in South Africa.

Bearer shares

38.9 There is no English authority directly in point on bearer shares. These are shares where simple delivery of the share certificate or other documents of title gives the transferee all rights of membership as against the company. Title to the shares is not subject to registration. Application of the rules relating to negotiable instruments described above (para **38.5**) indicates that such shares are situated where the certificates or other documents are found, for the shares can only be dealt in there. Such has been held to be the law in Canada (*Secretary of State of Canada v Alien Property Custodian for United States* [1931] 1 DLR 890). This conclusion does not however extend to renounceable letters of allotment (*Young v Phillips* [1984] STC 520).

A UK company may issue share warrants to bearer. The effect of such warrants is that the bearer of the warrants is entitled to the shares, the shares being transferable by delivery of the warrant rather than by registration (Companies Act 2006, ss 779–780). On the basis of the above analysis it is arguable that the shares which are subject to the warrants are situate where the warrants are found. However, in *Chandrasekaran v Deloitte & Touche Wealth Management Ltd* [2004] EWHC 1378 (Ch), [2004] All ER (D) 128 (Jun), Patten J suggested this may not be so where no obvious market exists for the shares in the foreign jurisdiction concerned (at para 16). However, he expressly forbore from deciding the point and it appears from the later case of *Hossein Mehjoo v Harben Barker (a firm)* [2013] EWHC 1500 (QB), [2013] All ER (D) 132 (Jun) that the use of bearer warrants to affect situs is effective, albeit nullified in relation to CGT by the statutory rules described in the next chapter.

Transfers endorsed in blank

38.10 Bearer shares must be distinguished from registered shares whose certificates are endorsed with transfers executed by the shareholder in blank. In *R v Williams* [1942] AC 541, the testator had so endorsed his share certificates, and it was accepted that a delivery of the endorsed certificates was a good assignment of the shares, since it passed legal title to the assignee. The endorsed certificates were fully marketable in New York where they were kept by the testator. However, it is clear from the judgment of the Privy Council both in that case and in *Ontario Treasurer v Blonde* [1947] AC 24 that the situation of the certificates could not prevail over the location of the register, for delivery of the certificates merely conferred the right to registration. However, since in *R v Williams* there were two registers the situs of the endorsed certificates was material in deciding between registers on rational grounds, and resulted in the situs of the shares being in New York.

It is noteworthy that in *R v Williams* the registered owner of the shares was the person who held the certificates and signed the blank transfer. In *Stern v R* [1896] 1 QB 211, shares in US companies were freely marketable in England on delivery of a certificate with the transfer endorsed on the back completed. In contrast to *R v Williams*, the owner of the shares was not the person in whose name the shares were registered in the US. The Court held that, as the endorsed certificates were freely marketable in the UK, they fell to be treated in the same way as other negotiable instruments in accordance with *A-G v Bouwens* (1838) 4 M & W 171. The shares were thus rendered UK situate.

Unless the distinction noted above is a valid one, *Stern v R* is not consistent with *R v Williams*. The distinction, however, is not drawn in *R v Williams* or any of the other decided cases, and in the Canadian case of *Royal Trust Co v R* [1949] 2 DLR 153, *Stern* was not followed. *Stern* may be inconsistent with *IRC v Stype Investments (Jersey) Ltd* [1982] STC 625 in that the latter case indicates that the beneficial owner's right to nominee property has the same situs as the property itself (see para **38.1**). But *Stern* was referred to without disapproval in *Winans v A-G* [1910] AC 27 and in *Young v Phillips* [1984] STC 520, 534.

HMRC consider that *Stern* is good law where the beneficial owner is not the registered holder of the shares (IHTM 27150). This does not apply if the registered holder is a good Marking Name or a Street Name – ie a financial institution such as a broker, bank or discount house.

BENEFICIAL INTERESTS

38.11 A distinction has to be drawn between beneficial interests in the underlying property and personal rights against the trustee or legal holder of the property. In the case of the former, the relevant asset is the underlying property and its situs is the situs of the beneficial interest (*Re Clore* [1982] STC 625). But where the asset is a personal right, it is simply a chose in action and its situs is determined by the rules pertaining to choses in action.

The distinction is illustrated by cases relating to unadministered residue. It has been held that the residuary legatee is not entitled to any particular asset in the estate so long as administration is continuing, but instead merely has the right to compel due administration (*Sudeley (Lord) v AG* [1897] AC 11; *Stamp Duties Comr (Queensland) v Livingston* [1964] 3 All ER 692; *Marshall (Inspector of Taxes) v Kerr* [1995] 1 AC 148, [1994] STC 638). Accordingly the situs of the residuary legatee's asset is not that of the assets in the estate, but the jurisdiction where the deceased was domiciled and the executors reside.

The principle was applied in a trust context in *Re Smyth, Leach v Leach* [1898] 1 Ch 89. Here the deceased owned a reversionary interest under an English trust holding Jamaican real estate. Romer J held that, as reversioner, the deceased owned merely the right to have the trust duly performed when the reversion fell in. As such, he held a chose in action situate in England rather than an asset in Jamaica.

It can be difficult to determine whether what a person owns is an interest in the underlying assets or a chose in action. However, an analogy may be drawn with the CGT concept of absolute entitlement. Should a person be absolutely entitled as against the trustee or nominee, or should two or more persons be jointly so entitled, the property is treated as theirs for CGT purposes (TCGA 1992, s 60). Case law has established that the interests have to be concurrent rather than successive, ie ownership as joint tenants or tenants in common, rather than life-tenant and remaindermen (see for example *Kidson v Macdonald* [1974] STC 54). But absolute entitlement is preserved even if several beneficial owners accept contractual fetters such as voting restrictions or pre-emption rights, provided it is clear that each co-owner remains entitled to recover at the end of the arrangement the same property as he put in (*Booth v Ellard* [1980] STC 555).

Assuming the CGT principles are a good analogy, the result is that a beneficiary becoming absolutely entitled to settled property ceases to own a chose in action but instead acquires an aliquot share in each trust asset, situate where those trust assets are situate (*Stephenson v Barclays Bank Trust Co Ltd* [1975] STC 151). But by analogy with the CGT cases, this would be displaced if the trust asset is land or private company shares until all the trust interests have vested absolutely (*Crowe v Appleby* [1975] STC 502; *Pexton v Bell* [1976] STC 301).

PARTNERSHIP INTERESTS

38.12 It is well settled that a partner in a partnership does not hold an aliquot share of the assets of the partnership, but holds a chose in action which is situated where the partnership business is carried on. Case law makes it clear that the place where the business is carried on is not necessarily the same as the place where all or a majority of the partners reside (*Laidlay v The Lord Advocate* (1890) 15 App Cas 468; *Beaver v Master in Equity* [1895] AC 251; *Stamp Duties Comr v Salting* [1907] AC 449, 76 LJPC 87, PC).

The above cases do not identify a single factor which will determine where a partnership business will be regarded as being carried on. It appears that the situs of the assets used in the partnership business, the place where day-to-day decision-making takes place and the place where the partnership's business accounts are maintained are all relevant factors. However, the place at which 'strategic' decisions take place does not seem to be relevant. Thus it seems clear that the test to determine the situation of a partnership business is different from the central management and control test which is used to identify the tax residence of a non-UK incorporated company. It seems clear also that the law governing the partnership is irrelevant, as each of the above cases appears to have concerned a partnership established under English law.

UNIT TRUSTS

38.13 Unit trusts are a form of nomineeship. The trustee holds a portfolio of investments and cash. The units issued to the investors are equitable interests under the trust and each unit confers an undivided share in whatever the fund of the unit trust consists of from time to time (see *M&G Securities v IRC* [1999] STC 315, 319, per Park J).

For many tax purposes unit trusts are deemed to be separate fiscal entities. Thus for CGT purposes all unit trusts, wherever situate, are deemed to be companies, and the units shares (TCGA 1992, s 99). So too, special income tax rules apply to UK-resident unit trusts, both authorised and unauthorised (CTA 2010, ss 617 and 621).

For inheritance tax purposes, however, there is no provision deeming unit trusts to be separate entities. However, there is one very important indication, namely the rule that units in authorised unit trusts are excluded property if owned by a non-domiciliary or owned by a trust settled by a non-domiciliary (IHTA 1984, ss 6(1A) and 48(3A)). This is an indication that unit-holders are seen for IHT purposes as owning a chose in action constituted by their units rather than aliquot shares in each underlying investment.

Without this indication there would be difficulty in being certain that the unit-holder's asset is not an aliquot share of each underlying asset. The dictum from *M&G Securities* referred to above may be adduced in this context. But at least in the normal case, the unit-holder is not entitled to call on the trustee to transfer investments of the unit trust to him in specie. He is merely entitled to call on the manager to redeem his units for cash. This, it may be suggested, places him on the chose in action side of the line on the basis of the cases cited in para **38.11** above.

The position may be otherwise if the unit-holder is entitled on redemption to call for an aliquot share of the unit trust's investments in specie (as was the position in the *M&G Securities* case itself). Here it may be suggested the situs of what he owns is much more likely to be that of the underlying investments. Despite IHTA 1984, ss 6(1A) and 48(3A), there must be some risk that situs would be that of the underlying investments.

IMMOBILISED SECURITIES

38.14 The term 'immobilised securities' is a technical name for securities held in international settlement systems, principally Euroclear and Clearstream. Euroclear is based in Brussels and Clearstream in Luxembourg. Originally Euroclear and Clearstream settled Eurobonds, but now they are used for a wide range of securities.

Major financial institutions hold cash and securities accounts at Clearstream and Euroclear. Securities in an institution's account are held either for its clients or itself, or for other institutions which themselves hold their securities for themselves or their clients.

Securities held on Euroclear and Clearstream are issued by crediting each participating institution's securities account with the amount of the stock it or its principals have subscribed for. Transfers are effected by debiting the securities account of the transferor and crediting that of the transferee. Corresponding debits and credits are made in the respective cash accounts of the institutions concerned. Interest and the proceeds of redemption are also paid through the cash accounts.

So far there is no paper in the system. However the company or governmental body issuing the security does issue a single instrument to a depositary, who then holds the instrument to the order of the clearing systems, ie Euroclear and Clearstream. This instrument is known as a global bond, and while in form it is a bearer bond, in substance it is never envisaged that it will leave the custody of the depositary. Further it is a single bond representing the whole issue: the depositary does not hold separate bearer bonds representing the separate holdings of each holder of the issue. In certain circumstances those holders are entitled to be issued with what are called definitive bonds, ie a physical bearer bond corresponding to their respective holdings. But normally such right arises only on default of the issuer or the clearing system.

The situs of immobilised securities is a much debated topic, of relevance to far wider issues than just tax. In a tax context, the debate has historically been expressed by reference to Eurobonds. The question is rendered complex by two factors in particular, namely the fact that Euroclear and Clearstream are governed by Belgian and Luxembourg law respectively and by the fact that there is no standard documentation package for immobilised securities.

No case law bears on the question. However the preponderance of textbook opinion is that the situs of immobilised securities is that of the clearing system in which they are held – ie Belgium or Luxembourg. This is the view taken in *Dicey* (at p 1125). It was also the conclusion reached, after extensive discussion with fellow lawyers, by Joanna Benjamin in her book *Interests in Securities* (Oxford, 2000) pp 158–159. In support of this view is the fact that Euroclear and Clearstream are registration systems on which the securities are effectively dealt. As such they are analogous to share registers, albeit that what is being dealt in is mainly debt rather than shares.

A contrary view fastens on the nature of the immobilised security and, where the securities are in fact debt, focuses on the position of the debtor. The debtor company or institution is under an enforceable obligation to pay interest and principal, and is also subject to default obligations such as that to issue definitive bonds. The whole bundle of obligations could be seen as a chose in action, situate where the issuing company resides.

A third view is that the relevant asset is the global bond, in which all holders of the security have an interest by virtue of the depositary holding it to the order of the clearing systems. As the global bond is in the form of a bearer bond, its situs on this analysis determines the situs of the security. This analysis, however, is rejected by both *Dicey* and *Benjamin*. In a technical sense, the fallacy in it is that the owners of the security are never entitled, even collectively, to have the global bond transferred to them. Instead, the most that they can require is the separate issue of definitive bonds (and the cancellation of all or a corresponding part of the global bond).

A further argument against the global bond determining the situs is that even though in form bearer, in practice it is never dealt in. As noted above (para **38.5**), marketability is required for a negotiable instrument to determine situs. A final, practical, point, is that no investor is likely to know where the global bond is, many of them in fact being in London. It is difficult to see HMRC, or the Courts, being attracted by a solution which could damage the UK as a financial centre.

In the result, the choice as to situs is between the place of residence of the issuing institution and that of the relevant clearing system. Given that the clearing systems are outside the UK, the only practical area of difficulty is securities issued by UK companies or institutions. If it is desired to avoid UK situs assets, immobilised securities so issued should be avoided.

HMRC have given little guidance on this issue. In 1994 they implied that investors holding Eurobonds would be treated as holding rights to and interests in a bearer security (see *Private Client Business* [1994], 139–140). This might be thought to imply that the situs of immobilised securities is that of the global bond. If so, it is at variance with the conclusions reached above, and, for the reasons there given, wrong. But HMRC's comments were prefaced by the caveat that the position depends on the terms of the issue. In any event their more recent comments indicate their position has altered, for in para IHTM 27077 of the Inheritance Tax Manual they say situs is determined by the terms of issue of the particular security in question.

ADRS AND GDRS

38.15 Depositary receipts are issued by financial institutions. The institution concerned is holder of shares in a company, the shares being registered in either its name or that of a nominee. The institution issues depositary receipts to investors, each receipt representing a given number of the underlying shares. The depositary receipt concept was evolved in the United States, where the purpose of ADRs ('American Depositary Receipts') is to enable US investors to hold foreign securities in a form which can be traded on a US stock market. Normally the depositary maintains a register on which the receipts are transferable but in the case of GDRs ('Global Depositary Receipts'), a single receipt may be deposited with a depositary to the order of Euroclear and Clearstream. This then enables dealings in the GDRs to be cleared on those systems.

Given the trust relationship the logical conclusion, in the light of the previous discussion, would be that the investor's asset is the underlying shares rather than the depositary receipts. However, Joanna Benjamin, in her book *Interests in Securities* suggests that where depositary receipts are transferable on the register maintained by the financial institution, that register determines situs (see paras 11–14). In the case of GDRs traded on Euroclear or Clearstream, the same issues would arise as with other immobilised securities (see para **38.14**).

Joanna Benjamin's analysis finds support in the tribunal decision in *HSBC Holdings plc v HMRC* [2012] SFTD 913. This was a SDLT case where the tribunal subjected ADRs issued under the law of New York to exhaustive analysis. It concluded (at para 148):

> 'Overall our conclusion is that we are not satisfied as a matter of fact that under the law of the State of New York the holder of an HSBC ADR has a beneficial interest in the underlying fund of HSBC shares held by BNY Nominees as custodian for BNY.'

Whatever the legal position HMRC has revised its guidance in the Capital Gains Manual at CG50240, after the HSBC decision, to say what line it takes in practice. In summary:

- Where the depositary receipt is issued in the UK, HMRC will treat the holder as the beneficial owner of the underlying shares.

- Where the depositary receipt is issued outside the UK and the relevant overseas law determines that the holder of the receipt is not the holder of a beneficial interest in the underlying shares, HMRC will treat the receipt and underlying shares as separate assets.
- Where the depositary receipt is issued outside the UK and the beneficial ownership of the underlying shares cannot be conclusively determined by reference to the law governing the issue of the receipt, HMRC will treat the holder as the beneficial holder of the underlying shares.

The ADRs in the HSBC case were issued under the terms of a Deposit Agreement that was governed by the law of the State of New York. The HMRC guidance confirms they accept the ADRs in that case fall within the third bullet above. So those ADR holders were accepted as the beneficial holders of the underlying shares.

The HMRC guidance on DRs does not specifically talk about situs of assets. Where a DR falls within the first or third bullet above it is reasonable to assume the situs will be that of the underlying shares. Where the depositary receipt is within the second bullet it appears the situs of the receipt will be determined independently from the situs of the underlying shares.

Although HMRC's revised guidance appears in the CGT Manual it is stated to apply generally to all direct taxes (HMRC Brief 14/2012 15 May 2012, reproduced [2012] SWTI 1651).

OTHER FINANCIAL PRODUCTS

38.16 Many financial products exist apart from those discussed above. Some raise equally difficult issues as to situs. But, in most cases, the difficulty is not identifying the relevant legal principles, but determining what legal relationships are entailed in the product. Careful analysis is needed, often on a case by case basis.

Chapter 39

CGT SITUS RULES

INTRODUCTION

39.1 The situs of assets is relevant to CGT in two respects:

(1)   Gains accruing to non-UK domiciled remittance basis users on the disposal of foreign situs assets are taxable only insofar as remitted to the UK (TCGA 1992, s 12; see CHAPTER 49).

(2)   Non-residents carrying on a trade or profession in the UK are taxed on gains accruing on certain assets situated in the UK (TCGA 1992, ss 10 and 10B; see paras 37.6 and 65.2).

In contrast to inheritance tax, TCGA 1992 contains express statutory rules determining the situs of assets for the purposes of CGT. These rules, contained in TCGA 1992, ss 275–275C, are the focus of this chapter. The rules are by no means a codification of the common law situs rules. In some cases the result they point to is unexpected, and for this reason they need to be watched with care.

It should be noted that the statutory rules are not entirely comprehensive. They fail to determine the situs of certain assets, and in such cases (by implication) situs must be determined by applying the common law situs rules discussed in CHAPTER 38.

In relation to remittance basis users, the statutory situs rules determine whether a gain qualifies as a foreign chargeable gain, but have no part to play in establishing whether the gain has been remitted to the UK. As discussed at the end of this chapter, there is a special statutory rule which can, in effect, alter the situs for CGT purposes of carried interest investments. In relation to a fund manager who is a remittance basis user, this rule can turn what would otherwise be a foreign chargeable gain into a UK gain that is taxable on the arising basis.

LAND

39.2 The situs of land is governed by the common law and thus is where the land is (cf para 38.2). Section 275(1)(a) provides that the situation of rights or interests in or over immovable property is the same as that of the property itself. However, an exception is made for rights by way of security, which are therefore covered by the rules as to debts discussed below.

TANGIBLE MOVEABLE PROPERTY

39.3 As with land, the situation of tangible moveable property is left to the common law: it is where the property is (see para **38.2**). This is a point which has to be watched by remittance basis users, for it means that the bringing of a chattel to the UK for sale generally results in any gain in the value of the chattel being taxed on an arising basis. However, there is an exception to this, discussed at para **59.7**.

As with land, s 275(1)(b) provides that rights or interests over tangible moveable property have the same situation as the property itself.

SHARES

39.4 For the purposes of the CGT situs rules, the term 'share' includes the interests in a company owned by the members if the company is of a kind which has no share capital (s 275(2)(a)), such as an LLC or a company limited by guarantee. The term 'company' is defined for CGT purposes as including any body corporate or unincorporated association, but not a partnership (TCGA 1992, s 228(1)). As unit trusts are deemed for CGT purposes to be companies, save insofar as excluded by regulations, units in unit trusts also count as shares for these purposes (TCGA 1992, s 99).

Municipal or governmental authority

39.5 A share which is issued by a municipal or governmental authority is situated in the country of the issuer (s 275(1)(d)). The same applies if the share is issued by a company created by such an authority. It is of course unusual for municipal or governmental authorities to issue shares.

UK incorporated company

39.6 Shares of a company incorporated in the UK are, in all circumstances, treated as situate in the UK (s 275(1)(da)). This follows the common law, save perhaps as to warrants to bearer. As is explained in para **38.9**, it is widely believed the latter convert UK shares to foreign situs under the common law (where the warrant is held outside the UK). Such is not the position for CGT purposes.

Registered shares

39.7 Subject to the two foregoing rules, registered shares are situate for CGT purposes where the register is situate or, if there is more than one register, where the principal register is situate (s 275(1)(e)). This follows the common law (see para **38.7**).

The term 'registered shares' is not defined. But it must mean shares where registration of subscription or transfer is required to constitute the holder a member as against the company. Such shares contrast with bearer shares (see below) where legal title to the shares passes by delivery of the share certificate and is not subject to registration.

Bearer shares

39.8 The CGT code makes no express provision as respects bearer shares, other than insofar as issued by a UK company or by a governmental or municipal authority (see paras 39.5 and 39.6). It follows that the common law applies (as to which see para 38.9).

ADRs and GDRs

39.9 The CGT code does not make express provision as to ADRs and GDRs (as to which see generally para 38.15). However, it may be suggested that if the underlying shares are registered in the name of the depositary or its nominee, they count as registered for the purposes of the above situs rules. This conclusion follows because it is difficult to see the owner of the ADRs or GDRs as otherwise than absolutely entitled to the underlying shares. Under TCGA 1992, s 60, property to which a person is absolutely entitled is treated as belonging to the beneficial owner.

It appears HMRC do not see ADRs and GDRs as nominee property if under the proper law of the instrument, the owner is not the beneficial owner of the underlying shares (CG 50240). In such a case, the implication of HMRC's view is that the situs for CGT purpose of the ADRs or GDRs would be determined under the rules for intangibles discussed below.

DEBTS

39.10 The CGT situs rules differ most markedly from the common law in their application to debts. This is because, for CGT purposes, the basic rule is that a debt is situate in the UK if and only if the *creditor* is resident in the UK (TCGA 1992, s 275(1)(c)). This is so whether the debt is secured or unsecured, and is in contrast to the common law, where the basic determinant is the residence of the *debtor* (see para 38.4). But although the basic CGT rule looks to the residence of the creditor, there are important exceptions.

Judgment debts

39.11 A judgment debt is treated as situate where the judgment is recorded (s 275(1)(k)).

Foreign currency bank accounts of non-UK domiciliaries

39.12 A bank account owned by a UK resident non-UK domiciliary which is not denominated in sterling is situated in the UK if, and only if, the branch at which it is maintained is in the UK (s 275(1)(l)). If follows that all non-UK foreign currency accounts of non-UK domiciliaries are situate outside the UK and are therefore eligible for the remittance basis, where this basis of taxation is being claimed or is otherwise available (see CHAPTER 46).

Clearly, this provision does not, in itself, determine the situs of an account of such an individual that is denominated in sterling. It is difficult to avoid the conclusion that, under the general CGT rule for debts (see para **39.10**), such an account has a UK situs for CGT purposes, even if held at a non-UK bank/branch. Generally, this is something of a non-point, because a disposal of a sterling-denominated debt cannot give rise to a chargeable gain.

Debentures

39.13 The term debenture is not defined for CGT purposes. It therefore bears its common law meaning. That meaning is itself not wholly clear but the definition in *Halsbury* is that a debenture is a document which either creates or acknowledges a debt (*Halsbury's Laws*, vol 7(2) para 1533). This formulation derives from the judgment of Chitty J in *Levy v Abercorris Slate and Slab Co* (1887) 37 Ch D 260. The recent Court of Appeal judgment in *Fons HF v Corporal Limited* [2014] EWCA Civ 304 contains a useful synopsis of previous cases which have considered the meaning of this term.

A debenture can be registered or bearer and in the latter event is negotiable (ibid para 1537). Section 275(2)(b) extends the definition in one respect, in that in relation to a person other than a company, the term debenture includes securities.

The situs rules as to debentures are similar to those pertaining to shares. They are as follows:

(1)   debentures issued by a municipal or governmental authority (or by a body created by such authority) are situated in the country of that authority (s 275(i)(d));
(2)   debentures of a UK incorporated company are situate in the UK (s 275(i)(da));
(3)   registered debentures of any other kind are situated where the register is situated or, if there is more than one, where the principal register is situated (s 275(i)(e)).

Bearer bonds

39.14 As with bearer shares, the CGT rules make no express provision for bearer bonds (cf para **38.5**). The rules listed above are, however, in point in two respects. First, government bonds are plainly securities if not debentures and so fall in the category of governmental debentures situate in the country of such government. Second, bonds issued by UK companies are situated in the UK assuming, as will almost invariably be the case, that they can correctly be characterised as debentures.

But there remains an important category of bearer bond not covered by the above rules. This is bonds issued by non-UK companies and these, therefore, are covered by the basic creditor rule and so are situate in the UK if the creditor, ie the owner of the bond, is UK resident.

Immobilised securities

39.15 The difficulties which arise in establishing the common law situs of immobilised securities are explained in para **38.14**. The application of the CGT situs rules is equally difficult.

It is perhaps worth restating here the essential characteristics of an immobilised security. This is that a debt is due from the issuer of the security to (collectively) the various holders of beneficial interests in that debt. Such interests are traded on an electronic system (Euroclear or Clearstream). The debt as a whole is evidenced by a bearer instrument, typically governed by English law, which is deposited in a vault and held to the order of the institution which operates the trading system. The situation of the vault will be unknown to investors acquiring interests in the debt (and may be in the UK). The institutions which operate the trading systems are non-UK companies (Euroclear SA/NV is a Belgian company; Clearstream Banking SA is a Luxembourg company). Essentially, these companies maintain registers of beneficial ownership of interests in immoblised securities that are traded through these systems. However, such registers are purely electronic; there is no physical register.

Immobilised securities may be issued by a company, a government, or a municipal authority.

The CGT situs provisions which are potentially relevant here are:

- s 275(1)(b), which provides that (subject to the following provisions of s 275(1)) a right or interest in or over tangible movable property is situated where that property is situated;
- s 275(1)(c), which is the general rule (subject to the following provisions of s 275(1)) that a debt is situated in the UK if and only if the creditor is resident in the UK;
- s 275(1)(d), which is the rule that shares or debentures issued by a governmental or municipal authority are situated in the country of that authority;
- s 275(1)(da), which says that shares or debentures issued by a company incorporated in the UK are UK situated; and
- s 275(1)(e), which provides that (subject to s 275(1)(d) and (da)) registered shares or debentures are situated where they are registered.

It is clear that government or municipal bonds, even where immobilised, fall within s 275(1)(d) and therefore have the situs of the country of issuer. It is clear also that a bond issued by a UK incorporated company falls within s 275(1)(da), even where such bond is immobilised. It is hard to see why the bearer instrument that is held to the order of the institution which operates the trading system would not qualify as a debenture (see para **39.13** above).

The difficulty arises in identifying the situs of immobilised bonds issued by non-UK companies. At first sight, such bonds fall within s 275(1)(c) – under which a debt is situated where the creditor is resident. But that would be an extremely surprising result. It would mean that any interest in an immobilised bond issued by a non-UK company and held by a UK resident non-UK domiciliary would have a UK situs, and a gain realised on the disposal of such a bond would be taxable on the arising basis. If that conclusion is correct, it is widely ignored in practice; there is a widespread assumption that such bonds have a foreign situs for CGT as well as IHT purposes.

One other possible analysis which might be suggested, but must be discounted, is that immobilised bonds issued by non-UK companies fall within s 275(1)(b). A bearer instrument can be thought of as a form of chattel. But 'tangible property' has been defined as property that has a 'tangible and corporeal existence and intrinsic value because of it' (Merriam-Webster's *Dictionary of Law*); whereas 'intangible property' has no intrinsic value but is representative or evidence of value. On this basis, a bearer instrument is intangible property.

On balance, perhaps the most plausible analysis is that an immobilised bond issued by a non-UK company falls within s 275(1)(e), as a registered debenture. At first sight, this seems wrong: the bearer instrument is a debenture, but that instrument is not itself registered; conversely, the debt interests held by investors under the trading system are undocumented, and are not, therefore, debentures in the traditional sense (see para **39.13**). In addition, the term 'registered' has historically been used to refer to paper-based systems used to record transfers of securities, whereas under the Euroclear and Clearstream systems transfers of securities are paperless. But arguably the term needs to be construed in light of modern technologies, rather than being confined by Victorian usage. The debt interests traded through Euroclear and Clearstream can, reasonably, be considered to be registered, as those institutions maintain electronic registers of the holders of such interests. If that is right, it is arguably not too great a stretch to treat the registered interests in the debenture, which are held by investors, as registered debentures. It has, after all, been recognised in a number of cases that although the term 'debenture' is most commonly used to denote a document which creates or acknowledges debt, the word has no well-defined meaning. It derives from the Latin *debentur mihi*, 'There are owed to me . . . ', so the word's root meaning is simply 'indebtedness' (see eg *Lemon v Austin Friars Investment Trust Ltd* [1926] Ch 1, 95 LJ Ch 97, CA). On that basis, it might be suggested that the debt interests that are traded through the Euroclear and Clearstream systems are registered debentures, and are situated where they are registered (Belgium or Luxembourg) except where this rule is overridden by the specific rules for debentures issued by UK incorporated companies and for debentures issued by governmental or municipal authorities.

It may be worth noting, parenthetically, that the reference in s 275(1)(e) to registered debentures was inserted in 2005, replacing a reference to 'registered securities'. It is unclear why the amendment was made – it may well have been an attempt to harmonise the language used in s 275, and was probably not intended to affect the situs of immobilised securities. It is possible that before this change was made, it was more obvious that the situs of such securities was governed by s 275(1)(e). It is perhaps clearer that an investment can be a 'security' without the investment being documented (the primary meaning of 'security' being a debt or claim, the payment of which is in some way secured; see *Singer v Williams* (1921) 7 TC 419, 431 per Viscount Cave.)

INTELLECTUAL PROPERTY

39.16 Patents, trademarks, and registered designs are situated where they are registered or, in the case of multiple registration, where any register is situate (s 275(1)(h)). Licences or other rights are situate in the UK if exercisable there (ibid). Copyright, design right, and franchises therefrom are situate in the UK if exercisable in the UK or if any right derived therefrom is exercisable in the UK (s 275(1)(j)).

GOODWILL

39.17 The goodwill of a business is situate where the business is carried on (s 275(1)(g)).

OTHER INTANGIBLES

39.18 The CGT situs of many forms of intangible property is given by the rules described above. But where this is not so, s 275A provides that the intangible is situate in the UK for CGT purposes if at the time it is created it is subject to UK law (s 275A(3)). An intangible is treated as being subject to UK law if it or any right or interest forming part of it is governed by or enforceable under the law of any part of the UK (s 275B(2)). Thus, for example, an interest in a partnership governed by the law of any part of the UK is a UK situs asset under s 275A(3).

Options and futures

39.19 An option or future which is not subject to UK law is deemed to be so subject, and thus situate in the UK, if the underlying subject matter is treated as UK situate under any of the CGT situs rules other than s 275A itself (s 275A(8)). Although the wording of s 275A is obscure, it appears that the same result follows with options and futures where the underlying subject matter is an intangible whose situs is deemed to be in the UK under s 275A itself.

For the purpose of these rules, the terms 'future' and 'option' bear the meanings given to them in the corporation tax rules pertaining to derivative contracts (s 275B(3); Part 7). Thus a future is a contract for the sale of property at an agreed date and price (CTA 2009, s 581). The term 'option' includes warrants, warrants being defined as instruments entitling the holder to subscribe for shares or corporate debt (CTA 2009, ss 580 and 710). A contract is neither a future nor an option if it provides for cash payment rather than the delivery of any property (s 580(2)).

Intangibles not subject to UK law

39.20 Should an intangible be neither in fact subject to UK law, nor deemed to be so under s 275A, its situs is not affected by s 275A. Unless therefore the intangible falls within one of the categories described earlier in this chapter, its situs for CGT purposes is governed by the common law. As explained in para **38.3**, this is normally the place of residence of the person against whom the right is enforceable.

Relevance to non-UK domiciliaries

39.21 Many investment products are intangibles which are neither shares nor debt. As such their CGT situs is likely to be governed by the rules just described. In some cases, the result will be that investment products which might be expected to be non-UK situate are, for CGT purposes, in fact situate in the UK. Careful analysis of the product in question is required.

CO-OWNERS

39.22 TCGA 1992, s 275C expressly provides that a co-ownership interest has the same situs as that of the underlying asset.

Trust interests

39.23 It is sometimes suggested that s 275C governs the situs of beneficial interests under trusts. But in reality it is most unlikely that it does, as the language of s 275C(4) connotes co-ownership and nomineeship rather than settled property in the CGT sense. The intangible rule discussed at para **39.18** above is in point in relation to trusts governed by English law and produces the result that beneficial interests in such trusts have a UK situs even if all the trustees are non-resident and all the assets foreign situs. This is material where a remittance basis user disposes of a beneficial interest in the trust in circumstances where the normal exemption for such disposals is not in point (as to which see para **7.11**).

Carried interests

39.24 Finance Act (No 2) 2015 introduced a special CGT rule which applies to certain carried interests (as defined at ITA 2007, ss 809EZC and 809EZD). This rule (at TCGA 1992, s 103KA) applies to chargeable gains realised by remittance basis users on or after 8 July 2015 on the disposal of carried interests in collective investment schemes, where the arrangements involve at least one partnership. 'Arrangements' for these purposes is given a broad meaning and so would include not just the fund vehicle but also any investment or management vehicle for the fund.

A chargeable gain accruing in respect of such a carried interest is treated as a foreign chargeable gain for the purposes of TCGA 1992, s 12, only to the extent that the manager has performed the investment management services to which the carried interest relates outside the UK. Implicitly, there is an additional requirement that the carried interest investment which has been disposed of is non-UK situated under the situs rules discussed above. Where the investment management services have been performed both inside and outside the UK, a 'just and reasonable' apportionment of the gain is permitted, although there is currently little guidance from HMRC on how this apportionment should be made. Pending clarification of this point, it is safest to assume that where the carried interest investment is non-UK situated, and services are being performed both within and outside the UK, a strict time apportionment exercise will be required, along the lines of the exercise that is required where a foreign domiciliary wishes to take advantage of overseas workday relief (see para **50.2**).

Chapter 40

SOURCE

INTRODUCTION

40.1 As explained in para **37.2**, territorial limits have been implied to income tax since its earliest days. The definitive statement was and remains that of Lord Herschell in *Colquhoun v Brooks* (1889) 2 TC 490, 503:

> 'The Income Tax Acts, however, themselves impose a territorial limit, either that from which the taxable income is derived must be situate in the United Kingdom or the person whose income is to be taxed must be resident there.'

For non-residents, therefore, the prerequisite is that whatever the income is derived from must be situate in the UK. So too, at the time of *Colquhoun v Brooks*, income from foreign securities or possessions, the former Cases IV and V of Schedule D, was taxed only insofar as remitted.

The word 'source' does not appear in Lord Herschell's formulation. However it was used in the same case by Lord Macnaghten who said, with reference to the former Case V:

> 'I am therefore forced to conclusion that in the expression "foreign possessions" as used in the Act of 1799 the word "possessions" is to be taken in the widest sense possible, as denoting everything a person has as a source of income.'

The term 'possession' was thus equated with source and this led to the point of decision in *Colquhoun v Brooks*, namely that a trade carried on wholly abroad was a foreign possession. As Lord Herschell put it (at p 502):

> 'I cannot see why [possessions] may not fitly be interpreted as relating to all that is possessed in Her Majesty's dominions out of the United Kingdom or in foreign countries.'

Over time the issue as to whether income was within Cases IV and V came to be not whether it was income from foreign securities or possessions but whether it had a non-UK source. If it had a non-UK source it was ipso facto slotted into Case IV or V as appropriate. This was made explicit in *Westminster Bank v National Bank of Greece SA* (1970) 46 TC 472. Here the issue was whether the payer of interest was required to deduct tax at source, such as would not have been necessary if the interest fell within Case IV or Case V rather than Case III. The House of Lords endorsed the following submission on behalf of HMRC:

'the only question of substance in the case was whether or not the source of the payments by the Appellants . . . was or was not situated within the United Kingdom . . . If this source were within the United Kingdom the income would be taxable under Case III . . . but . . . if it were not . . . it would then be either a foreign security within Case IV or a foreign possession within Case V and not taxable in the hands of a recipient not resident in the United Kingdom.'

When the income tax legislation was rewritten, the abandonment of the scheduler system meant that the terms foreign possessions and foreign securities were dropped. Instead, the territorial limits of income tax are now directly expressed by reference to source. Thus ITTOIA 2005, s 368(2) provides that investment income arising to a non-resident is chargeable only if it is from a source within the UK and similarly ITTOIA 2005, s 830 provides that the various categories of income there listed are only relevant foreign income if arising from a source outside the UK. Limitations in similar terms apply to trades (s 6(2)) and rental income (s 269(2)). However, in *Ardmore v HMRC* [2016] STC 1044, the Upper Tribunal affirmed s 368 does no more than give effect to Lord Herschell's formulation set out above.

What is also clear is that any decision under the old scheduler system that income was from a foreign possession also signifies it had a foreign source. This is apparent from Lord Macnaghten's words set out above and also from cases such as *Bradbury v English Sewing Cotton Co Ltd* (1923) 8 TC 481. Here Lord Wrenbury said (at p 517):

'To ascertain whether a possession is a foreign possession or not I must look to see what is the "source of income" from which the profits of the possession arise . . . A profit arising from a foreign possession . . . must be a profit coming from a source out of Great Britain.'

As a result there is much case law on what constitutes the source of income and whether that source is outside the UK and thus, under the former scheduler system a foreign possession. Two general points are apparent from this case law.

The first is that the source of income is not simply the situs of the asset or obligation which generates the income. This inter alia is apparent from the rules applicable to shares and debts, discussed below.

The second point is that the case law is not expressed in terms of a single governing principle governing all kinds of income. Instead particular cases were decided with reference to particular categories of income and formulate rules for the category concerned.

DIVIDENDS

40.2 ITTOIA 2005, s 383 charges the dividends and other distributions of UK resident companies, and s 402 of the same Act charges dividends of non-UK resident companies. Neither section contains an express territorial limit. Instead this is found in the general words of ss 368 and 830 referred to above, and the issue therefore is whether and in what circumstances dividends have a non-UK source.

The law is laid down in *Bradbury v English Sewing Cotton Co Ltd* (1923) 8 TC 481. Here the English taxpayer company owned a US incorporated subsidiary. The US subsidiary was UK resident under the central management and control test for three years ending in 1916–17 and then removed its residence back to the United States. HMRC sought to assess dividends paid by the US company to the English company in 1917–18 by reference to the average dividends of the previous three tax years, in accordance with the computational rules then in force. This was resisted by the English company on the grounds that its shares in the US company were not foreign possessions in the three years in which the US company was UK resident.

It was accepted on all sides that the shares in the US company were foreign possessions when the company was non-UK resident. But the decision of the House of Lords was that the shares were not foreign possessions during the period in which the company was UK resident. Lord Wrenbury put the matter thus (at p 518):

'If a company is foreign by incorporation and foreign by residence, no doubt shares in the company are foreign possessions . . . But for the purpose of the Income Tax Acts the company ceases to be a foreign company as soon as by residence it becomes amenable to all the provisions of the Acts.'

More specifically Lord Cave said (at p 508):

'A share or a parcel of stock is an incorporeal thing, carrying the right to a share in the profits of a company, and where the company is, there the share is also, and there is the source of any dividend paid upon it.'

The result is that dividends paid by a company that is both incorporated and resident outside the UK have a non-UK source, while dividends paid by a company that is resident in the UK have a UK source, regardless of where the company is incorporated. The position where the company is incorporated in the UK but resident abroad (see paras 43.15–43.16) is less clear, but the logic of *Bradbury v English Sewing Cotton Co Ltd* is that such dividends have a non-UK source, and the contrary has never seriously been suggested.

It is clear that dividends paid by a non-UK resident company have a foreign source even if paid in the UK or from funds generated in the UK. This is apparent from *Gilbertson v Fergusson (Surveyor of Taxes)* (1881) 7 QBD 562 and *Canadian Eagle Oil Co Ltd v The King* (1945) 27 TC 205. In the first case, the Imperial Ottoman Bank traded partly in England and party in Turkey, and was taxed on its English trading profits. The Court of Appeal held that dividends it paid to UK resident shareholders were not taxable insofar as attributable to its taxed English profits. *Gilbertson v Fergusson (Surveyor of Taxes)* (1881) 7 QBD 562 was overruled in the second of the two cases, where a core part of the ratio was that dividends paid by a foreign company were a source separate from the underlying profits of the company and as such income from foreign possessions within the former Case V.

INTEREST

40.3 Modern authority on where interest is sourced is represented by *Ardmore Construction Ltd v HMRC* [2016] STC 1044. *Ardmore* is a decision of the Upper Tribunal and is based on and follows the House of Lords decision in *Westminster Bank v National Bank of Greece SA* [1971] AC 945 ('the Greek case').

According to *Ardmore*, a multifactorial test must be applied and requires examination of three factors, namely:

- The residence of the debtor.
- The location of the security.
- The ultimate or substantive source of discharge of the debtor's obligation – ie where the funds used to pay interest and principal have or will come from.

The Upper Tribunal also referred to other factors and said these either carry little or no weight or do not outweigh the three factors listed above. These factors are as follows:

- The residence and/or place of activity of the creditor.
- The place where the credit was advanced.
- The place of payment of the interest.
- The jurisdiction in which enforcement proceedings might be brought.
- The proper law of the loan contract.

The Upper Tribunal made it clear that the situs of the debt is not per se relevant. This inevitably follows from the Greek case for that case concerned bearer bonds and yet that fact had no bearing on the eventual decision of the House of Lords.

In *Ardmore* (and *Perrin*, the case heard with it) the debts were unsecured. However in both cases the debtor was UK resident and in both cases the substantive source of funds used to pay interest and principal was found to be in the UK. Not surprisingly, therefore, in both cases the interest was held to have a UK source.

In one sense, the reliance placed in *Ardmore* on the Greek case may be misconceived. This is because the relevant passages in the Greek case, from which the three factors are taken, are descriptive rather than analytical. In a narrow sense, the interest in the Greek case was plainly Greek source under the original facts, and strictly the only issue was whether, in the events which had happened, the fact that the debtor's obligations could only be enforced against the guarantor altered the location of the source. The House of Lords decision was that the location of the source was not so altered. But unless and until *Ardmore* is reversed or overruled the multifactorial test emphasised in *Ardmore* case represents the law.

The multifactorial test gains support from two earlier authorities. In the first, *IRC v Viscount Broome's Executors* (1935) 19 TC 667 an individual resident in both Kenya and England had incurred a debt to a Kenyan resident. The security was in both Kenya and England and under the terms of the contract the interest was payable in Kenya. But when the debtor died his executors were English and they paid interest in England out of English assets. Finlay J stated that interest has a UK source if paid by a UK resident out of a source in the UK and decided that on the facts those conditions were both met.

The second case is *Hafton Properties Ltd v McHugh* [1987] STC 16. Here a UK company purchased a US property subject to two mortgages. One of the mortgages was assumed by the company and serviced in the US out of the US rental income. The other it paid off, funding the payment with a short-term unsecured facility from a Swiss bank, which it serviced from the UK out of its UK resources. The Special Commissioner decided that the interest on the first loan did not have a UK source, whereas the interest on the Swiss facility did. His decision on these points was not appealed.

As *Ardmore* itself affirms, it is plain under the multifactorial test that if the residence of the debtor and the source of the funds used to pay interest and principle is in the same country, that country is the location of the source. But what is the position if the debtor's residence is in one country and the source of the funds is in another?

Here *Hafton Properties* indicates the country where the funds are is the source if the debt is secured and the security is also in that country. But where the debt is not secured, just two of the three factors highlighted in *Ardmore* are present, with one being in one country and one in another. There is thus a tie, with which a multifactorial approach is not well equipped to deal.

Two solutions may be suggested. One is that in the event of a tie the residence of the debtor prevails. In *Ardmore*, the Upper Tribunal specifically said residence was not more important than the other factors. But it would be logical to give it a casting vote in the event of a tie.

The other solution is to look at the factors referred to in *Ardmore* as carrying little or no weight. On the basis they have at least some significance they could be looked at to see if they are more focussed on one country than another. This, it may be suggested is consistent with the multifactorial nature of the *Ardmore* approach.

HMRC practice

40.4 In *Tax Bulletin 9* (1993) 100 HMRC stated that their view on the location of source was based on the Greek case. They extrapolated from the case four factors which they regard as important, namely the residence of the debtor, the source from which the interest is paid, where it is paid, and the nature and location of any security. HMRC stated that if all four factors point to the UK, the interest has UK source. What was not indicated in *Tax Bulletin* is the position if some only of the factors are in the UK, but a reasonable inference was that HMRC would not necessarily assert a UK source.

HMRC's Savings and Investment Manual (para SAIM 9090) states that the most important factors are the residence of the debtor and the location of his assets. Residence, however, means not tax residence but residence for the purposes of jurisdiction. Other factors are the place of performance of the loan contract, the method of payment, the competent jurisdiction for legal action, the place of performance of the contact, the residence of any guarantor, and the location of the security for the debt. HMRC consider this list of factors to be derived from the Greek case.

HMRC consider that interest paid by a company is sourced where the company carries on business as this is where it is resident for the purposes of jurisdiction. If the company carries on business in several jurisdictions the source of the interest is the place where, under the loan agreement, interest and principal are payable. Thus interest paid by the UK branch of a foreign company has a UK source if the loan agreement is entered into in the UK for the purposes of the UK business and the UK branch pays the interest (see para SAIM 9095). These views of HMRC reflect the law as to the situs of simple debts (see para **38.4**).

The difference in emphasis between *Tax Bulletin* and the Manual indicates HMRC practice has never been wholly clear. In any event it is now subject to *Ardmore*, which has not at the time of writing been reflected in the Manual. Inter alia *Ardmore* indicates that SAIM 9090 is wrong in giving priority to the residence of the debtor.

Possibility of reform

40.5 It may be suggested that this is an area of law which would, in principle, benefit from statutory intervention. In December 2003, the government initiated a consultation on replacing the present rules as to the source of interest with a statutory rule. However, this did not result in legislation.

Much more recently, the government consulted on proposed changes to the income tax legislation in relation to interest and 'disguised interest' payments, and amendments to the ITA 2007 were duly made by Schedules 11 and 12 to the FA 2013. The changes included ITA 2007, s 874(6A), which is concerned with the requirement to deduct income from certain payments of yearly interest arising in the UK, most importantly payments of yearly interest to persons whose 'usual place of abode' is outside the UK. Section 847(6A) provides that in determining for these purposes whether a payment of interest does arise in the UK, no account is to be taken of the location of any deed recording the obligation to pay the interest. This new provision is curious, since (as explained above) it has never been seriously arguable that the location of a specialty affects the source of interest payable under the specialty. No attempt was made to make more substantial changes to the law governing the source of interest for income tax purposes.

TRADING INCOME

Non-residents

40.6 The profits of a trade carried on by a non-resident have a UK source and so are taxable if he is trading in the UK (ITTOIA 2005, s 6(2)). If, however, he is merely trading with the UK, there is no UK source and the trade is not taxable in the UK.

The basic test

40.7 The test of whether or not a person is trading in the UK is a common law one. At one time the place where the contracts of sale were made was thought to be decisive (*Grainger & Son v Gough* [1896] AC 325, 3 TC 462). If the contracts of sale were made in the UK the trade was carried on in the UK and if they were not it was not. Now, however, it is clear that this is only the position where the trade is pure merchanting. The general test is where the operations take place from which the profits in substance arise (*Firestone Tyre and Rubber Co Ltd v Llewellin* [1957] 37 TC 111). Thus a manufacturing trade is carried on in the UK if the manufacturing takes place there and a trade involving the provision of services is carried on in the UK if the services are performed there (cf *IRC v Brackett* [1986] STC 521).

In *IRC v Hang Seng Bank Ltd* [1990] STC 733 at 739 the Privy Council gave useful guidance. Lord Bridge expressed himself as follows:

'The broad guiding principle . . . is that one looks to see what the taxpayer has done to earn the profit in question. If he has rendered a service or engaged in an activity such as the manufacture of goods, the profit will have arisen or derived from the place where the service was rendered or the profit making activity carried on. But if the profit was earned by the exploitation of property assets as by letting property, lending money or dealing in commodities or securities by buying and reselling at a profit, the profit will have arisen in or derived from the place where the property was let, the money was lent or the contracts of purchase and sale were effected.'

The case concerned the question of whether, for Hong Kong tax purposes, profits generated by dealing in certificates of deposit were arising in or derived from Hong Kong. But Lord Bridge's observations apply equally to the distinction between trading in and with the UK (cf *Yates v GCA International Ltd* [1991] STC 157 at 172 and *IRC v HK-TVB International Ltd* [1992] STC 723 at 729). In the latter case Lord Jauncey affirmed that the proper approach is to ascertain what were the operations which produced the relevant profits and where those operations took place.

Non-trading activities

40.8 Case law has established that two forms of activity do not amount to trading in the UK:

(1)   Purchasing goods or services in the UK for use in the business abroad (*Sulley v A-G* (1860) 2 TC 149).
(2)   Representative offices, sales promotions, or after-sale services, provided the contracts of sale and other trading activities are made or carried on abroad (*Greenwood v FL Smidth & Co* (1922) 8 TC 193 HL).

Extent of charge

40.9 If a non-resident is trading in the UK, the profits are fully in charge to UK tax if the trade is carried on wholly in the UK. But if the trade is partly carried on abroad, only the profits arising from the part carried on in the UK are taxable (ITTOIA 2005, s 6). This gives statutory effect to previous practice as published in *Tax Bulletin 18* (August 1995 p 238).

In such cases, there is obviously scope for disagreement in determining what proportion of the overall profit is attributable to the UK. In practice HMRC apply the same criteria as are laid down in the Permanent Establishment Article of Double Tax Treaties. Accordingly, it is necessary to ascertain what the profits of the UK operation would be if it was a separate enterprise dealing on arm's length terms with the rest of the business (*Tax Bulletin 18* (August 1995) p 238). Accordingly, the transfer-pricing criteria discussed in CHAPTER 91 apply.

Branch, agent, or permanent establishment

40.10 Assuming the trading in the UK is being carried on by an individual through a branch or agency, the branch or agent is assessable on behalf of the non-resident as his UK representative (ITA 2007, ss 835E and 835U). In the case of companies the charge is to corporation tax and arises if the trade is being carried on through a permanent establishment (CTA 2009, s 5; see para **64.3**). Certain types of investment trade carried on by a non-resident through a broker or investment manager are excepted from these charges. This is discussed further in CHAPTER **64**.

Dealing in or developing land

40.11 A trade of dealing in or developing UK land is treated as carried on in the UK even if under the common law test described above (para **40.7**) it is carried on outside the UK. Should the trader be a company, the profits are charged to corporation tax regardless of whether the company has a UK permanent establishment. These rules, which were introduced in 2016, are explained in para **26.6**.

Resident trading abroad

40.12 The converse question as to whether a non-resident is carrying on a trade in the UK is whether a UK resident trading abroad can ever be said not to be carrying on the trade, at least in part, in the UK. An old Scottish case is generally taken as authority that he cannot and that the profits of the trade are fully in charge to UK tax (*Ogilvie v Kitton* (1908) 5 TC 338). The true principle appears to be that the person carrying on the trade governs and directs the whole commercial adventure with the result that the trade is carried on where he is based, even if all the operations are in fact performed somewhere else (*San Paulo (Brazilian) Rly Co Ltd v Carter (Surveyor of Taxes)* [1896] AC 31, 3 TC 407).

The position is qualified where a remittance basis user is trading in partnership. Where a partnership is trading wholly or partly abroad and is controlled and managed abroad, a partner who is resident in the UK and a remittance basis user can treat his share of the trading profits arising outside the UK as relevant foreign income (ITTOIA 2005, s 857). As such they attract the remittance basis.

INCOME FROM TRUSTS

40.13 The discussion of trust distributions at para 8.2 indicates that a life tenant is treated as directly entitled to the trust income if the trust is governed by English law or a law which in this matter follows English law.

In such a case, the source of the life tenant's income is that of the underlying trust investments, determined as per the rules outlined earlier in this chapter. Thus in *Archer-Shee v Baker* (1927) II TC 749, which was determined on the basis of English law, the life tenant's income was held to arise from the underlying trust investments.

With a discretionary trust, it is clear that the trust is the source of income distributions to a beneficiary. Thus in *Memec v IRC* [1996] STC 1336, 1351 Robert Walker J said:

'A discretionary trust, on the other hand, is not transparent. No beneficiary is entitled unless and until the trustees exercise their discretion in his or her favour, and the trustees' exercise of discretion is regarded as having . . . . independent vitality and creating a new source of income.'

The location of that source is established by the cases of *Archer-Shee v Baker* (1927) II TC 749 and *Garland v Archer-Shee* (1930) 15 TC 693. The facts of these cases are explained in para 32.2 and here the important point is that the law of New York was that the beneficiary had no right to the income of the underlying investments as such. Instead the trustee had discretion as to the manner and timing of payments or applications for her benefit. In the light of New York law as so found, the House of Lords decided the income paid to the beneficiary was income from a foreign possession and thus had a non-UK source.

The matter was put succinctly by Lord Tomlin as follows (at p 736):

'the assessable income . . . is income arising from a possession out of the United Kingdom . . . , viz a chose in action available against the American trustee . . . .'

So too, in *Archer-Shee v Baker*, Viscount Sumner, in the dissenting judgment endorsed in *Garland* said (at p 771):

'the learned Lord Justice says that Lady Archer-Shee has not any specific right to any particular item of income but . . . only an equitable right to have handed over to her the net income of the estate subject to all proper deductions, which right of hers is property situate in New York in whose Courts it would have to be asserted. I think the reasoning of this judgment is correct'.

The trust in *Archer-Shee* was different from the conventional discretionary trust, for in *Archer-Shee*, the beneficiary was entitled to have all the net income paid to her or applied for her benefit. Nonetheless discretionary beneficiaries too have rights against the trustees, for example the right to due consideration and such rights are enforceable in the court having jurisdiction over the trust.

On this basis it is clear discretionary trust distributions have a non-UK source if the rights of the beneficiaries against the trustee are enforceable abroad.

Such is certainly the position if the trustees are resident in the jurisdiction of the governing law of the trust. It may be suggested that if the residence of the trustee and the proper law diverge, it is the residence of the trustees that is decisive, for that is where they would be sued. Thus it has never been suggested that non-resident trusts governed by English law give rise to UK source income.

DISTRIBUTIONS FROM MUTUAL FUNDS

40.14 As described in CHAPTER 3, non-UK mutual funds represent an increasingly large part of most investment portfolios. For the most part mutual funds are in form either open-ended investment companies or unit trusts.

OEICs

40.15 As an open-ended investment company is a company, any income paid out to the investor is dividend. The location of its source is therefore determined by the rules given in para **40.2** above.

Unit trusts

40.16 In contrast to CGT, the income tax code does not deem non-resident unit trusts to be companies. As a matter of general law, the legal form is that each unit-holder owns an undivided share in the investments and cash which from time to time comprise the funds in the unit trust (*M & G Securities v IRC* [1999] STC 315, 322, per Park J). Accordingly the issue is whether the source of the unit-holder's income is the underlying investments or his right against the trustee or manager of the unit trust.

A unit trust differs from a private, family trust in that the relationship is a mix of trust and contract. But as the case of *Memec plc v IRC* [1998] STC 754 shows, the family trust cases may be applicable in commercial contexts. The identity of the unit-holder's income should therefore be determined in accordance with the principles applicable to life-interest trusts, described in para **40.13** above. In other words if, as a matter of construction, the unit-holders are entitled to have the income after expenses paid out to them, the source is the underlying investments. But if the terms of the unit trust require the income to be retained and invested, any distributions are a new source, located where the trustee resides and the payment is made.

The conclusion that certain types of unit trust are opaque is, of course, without prejudice as to how capital receipts on the sale or redemption of units are taxed. As described elsewhere (CHAPTERS 3 and 95), unless the fund is a reporting fund these are subjected to income tax under the offshore fund legislation. That legislation represents further confirmation that unit trusts which retain income are opaque, for if all offshore unit trusts were transparent the inclusion of unit trusts in the definition of offshore fund (para **95.2**) would be otiose. Equally that legislation also recognises that some unit trusts are transparent.

IMMOBILISED SECURITIES

40.17 Immobilised securities are discussed in relation to situs in para **38.14**. No special rules apply to determine where the source of the interest they generate is located. The matter should thus be determined by the principles outlined in para **40.3**. The choice is between the residence of the issuing company and the situs of the relevant clearing system (cf para **38.14**). As the latter is abroad, this means issues as to source really only arise with securities issued by UK companies.

In practice, as is noted in para **40.3**, it is generally accepted that if the borrowing company is a UK company, the interest has a UK source. It never seems to have been suggested that the holding of securities through an overseas clearing system moves the source of the interest abroad. As explained in para **64.15**, ITA 2007, s 882 removes the requirement to deduct tax at source on quoted Eurobonds, but it does not mean the interest ceases to have a UK source.

ADRS AND GDRS

40.18 It is generally accepted that the source of dividends received by the holders of American Depositary Receipts and Global Depositary Receipts is the underlying shares. As a matter of law, this may be regarded as correct, for the owner of the ADR or GDR has a specific entitlement to dividends in the same sense that a life tenant does under an English law trust.

Section III

Residence and Domicile

Chapter 41

THE RESIDENCE OF INDIVIDUALS

INTRODUCTION

41.1 The test of whether an individual is resident in the UK for tax purposes is determined by statute (FA 2013, Sch 45). The statutory residence test, or 'SRT' as it is called, has been in force since 6 April 2013 (Sch 45 para 153).

Tax residence is relevant in determining liability to income tax and capital gains tax. As is explained in CHAPTER 37, those resident in the UK are taxable on their world-wide income and gains. Non-residents, by contrast, are taxable only on certain sources of UK income, and their capital gains are in general free from tax.

Tax residence is not in general material to inheritance tax. As is explained in para 37.9, liability to that tax is principally governed by domicile.

The statutory test has no effect on provisions in double tax treaties which determine where an individual is resident for the purposes of the treaty. Such provisions operate where the individual is resident in both the UK and the treaty partner under their respective domestic laws. They mean that an individual who is UK resident under the statutory test may nonetheless fall to be treated as non-UK resident for the purposes of an applicable treaty.

The statutory test has been criticised for its complexity. In some respects the draftsman gives the impression of barking at shadows, and to that extent the complexity is unnecessary. But in general, the complexity does no more than reflect the complexity of real life. In planning terms it is essential to see the wood for the trees, and, rather than becoming bogged down in the minutiae of definitions, identify the fact patterns which, if achieved, produce an unequivocal outcome. The ability to do this was the objective and is in large measure the achievement of the statutory test.

HMRC publish guidance entitled 'Guidance Note: Statutory Residence Test (SRT)'. This was updated in August 2016.

UNDERLYING CONCEPTS

Tax years

41.2 Individual residence is determined by tax years, in that an individual is either resident or non-resident for a given tax year as a whole (Sch 45 paras 3 and 4). In certain circumstances years of arrival and departure can be split, but these circumstances are restricted and relief is effected not by reference to residence status but by disapplying specified charging provisions in the non-UK part of the year. The split year rules are explained in paras **41.34** to **41.37** below.

Arrivers and leavers

41.3 The statutory test draws a distinction between individuals who have been UK resident in one or more of the three prior tax years and individuals who have not. It is convenient to refer to the first category as 'leavers' and the second as 'arrivers' or 'visitors'. Separating the two categories is the best way of understanding the statutory test, as the rules which enable a visitor or arriver to remain non-UK resident are simpler and less onerous than those which enable a leaver to become non-resident.

It is important to remember that a visitor loses the benefit of the simpler and less onerous rules once he has been UK resident for a single tax year, even if such UK residence is through inadvertence. He does not regain the advantages of being a visitor unless three tax years have elapsed since his year of residence or, as the case may be, his last year of residence. These consequences follow because the more favourable rules for arrivers require non-residence in all three of the prior three tax years.

Days counted

41.4 In large measure residence under the statutory test turns on the number of days in the tax year an individual is present in the UK. The general rule is that the individual does not count as present on a day unless he is present at the end of the day (Sch 45 para 22). It is thus convenient to express day counts in terms of midnights.

FRAMEWORK

41.5 The way the statutory test works is in three stages. The first is the automatic overseas tests (Sch 45, paras 11–16). If any one or more of those tests is met, the individual is non-UK resident for the tax year concerned come what may (Sch 45, paras 5(b) and 17(i)(a)). The second stage is the automatic UK tests (Sch 45, paras 6–10). These only require consideration if one or more automatic overseas tests is not in point. Subject to that caveat, if any one or more of the automatic UK tests is met, the individual is ipso facto UK resident for the tax year concerned (Sch 45, para 5).

The third and final stage is the sufficient ties test which only has to be addressed if the individual is neither non-resident nor resident under the automatic tests (Sch 45, para 17). The sufficient ties test is a day-count test, but the number of days that results in UK residence varies according as to whether the individual is an arriver or leaver and according to the number of ties he has with the UK (Sch 43, paras 17–20).

AUTOMATIC OVERSEAS TESTS

41.6 Although the legislation refers to five automatic overseas tests, in practical terms there are just two, a day-count test and a full-time work abroad test.

Day-count test

41.7 The day-count test differs as between visitors and leavers. A visitor is automatically non-resident, without any exception, if his midnights in the UK in the tax year are fewer than 46 (Sch 45, para 13). For leavers the position is more complicated, in that the general rule is that fewer than 16 midnights in the UK results in non-residence (Sch 45, para 12). But this does not apply if the individual dies in the year, and, in certain circumstances, explained in para **41.21**, single day visits and days of departure can count towards the 15 midnights.

Full-time work abroad

41.8 Full-time work abroad is a convenient shorthand to refer to a test of some complexity (Sch 45, para 14). It requires the individual's midnights in the UK in the tax year to be fewer than 91 and the days on which he does more than three hours work in the UK to be fewer than 31. If these threshold conditions are met, it is then necessary to compute the net overseas hours and the reference period.

The net overseas hours are the total hours the individual works overseas in the tax year, less any hours so worked on a day when he also works more than three hours in the UK. The reference period is the 365 days in the tax year, less days on which the individual works more than three hours in the UK and days when he is on holiday or ill.

With these details ascertained the reference period is divided by seven to give a number of weeks. The net overseas hours are then divided by that number of weeks and if the result is 35 or more the test is met. The availability of the test is however subject to there not being a significant break in the overseas work, a term defined as a period of at least 31 days on none of which the individual works more than three hours overseas (or would have done but for being ill or on holiday) (Sch 45, para 29(2)).

What is meant by work, and where it is carried on, is tightly defined (see para **41.32**). As a general rule, full-time work abroad is relevant to employees of governments and multi-nationals, with personnel departments to undertake the extensive record-keeping required. It is much harder for the self-employed to rely on and it has no relevance at all to those not in full-time work.

AUTOMATIC UK TESTS

41.9 The principal automatic UK tests are a day-count test, a home test and a full-time work test.

Day count test

41.10 Under the day-count test, an individual who spends 183 or more midnights in the tax year in the UK is UK resident for the whole year, come what may (Sch 45, para 7).

The home test

41.11 The home test is in essence an only home test, although the detail is confusing (Sch 45, para 8). However what is relatively simple is that the test is not engaged unless two fundamental conditions are met. The first is that the individual has a home in the UK at some point during the tax year concerned (para 8(1)(a)). The second is that he must be present in that home on at least 30 days in the tax year (para 8(1)(b)).

This 30-day requirement means that an individual who first acquires a UK home in March when the tax year has fewer than 30 days to run can never be UK resident in that tax year. In computing the 30 days, any time in the house during the day counts: in contrast to SRT generally the focus is not on midnights. Should the individual have more than one UK home, they are not aggregated so the 30-day requirement is not met unless he spends time on at least 30 days in at least one of them (para 8(6)(a)). Further, a day only counts towards the 30 if it is a day on which the property is a home (para 8(6)(b)). Thus days viewing the house prior to buying it are disregarded and so, it would appear, would days spent refurbishing it prior to moving in.

Satisfying the 30-day requirement only opens the door to automatic UK residence: for the home in fact to have that result a further requirement must be met. The simplest way of expressing what is a very confusing rule is to express it as a negative, namely that automatic residence cannot occur if the individual also has an overseas home in which he spends at least 30 whole or part days during the tax year (para 8(5)). Provided these 30 days are within the tax year some or all of them can precede the acquisition of the UK home, but in such a case the individual must retain the overseas property as a home until the end of the tax year or, at least until fewer than 30 days of the tax year are left unexpired (para 8(1)(c)).

As with the UK property, days visiting the overseas property when it is not the individual's home are ignored, and the test in counting days is whole or part days as distinct from midnights. Should the overseas home cease to be a home more than 30 days before the end of the tax year, automatic UK residence is avoided if another overseas home is acquired within 90 days and that home meets the 30-day presence test in either or both of the current or the next tax year (para 8(1)(c)).

Work test

41.12 The work test in large measure mirrors the full-time work abroad test (Sch 45, para 9). However it uses as its base period not the tax year but any period of 365 days, provided that period includes one day that is both in the tax year and a day on which the individual does more than three hours' work in the UK. The reference period is 365 days, less days when the taxpayer does more than three hours' work abroad and holiday and sick days. The net UK hours is the total hours worked in the UK in the 365 day period, but excluding any hours worked in the UK on days when the taxpayer has also worked more than three hours overseas. The reference period is divided by seven to give a number of weeks. The net UK hours is then divided by that number of weeks and if the answer is 35 or more the test is met.

To qualify under the work test, there cannot be a significant break in the work, by which is meant a period of at least 31 days during none of which the individual does more than three hours' work in the UK (Sch 45, para 29(1)). The work test does not apply at all unless during the 365-day period at least 75% of the individual's working days are days on which he does more than three hours' work in the UK.

SUFFICIENT TIES

41.13 As indicated above, the sufficient ties test is a mixture of day counting and ties to the UK. The UK ties are as follows (Sch 45, para 31):

- Family: a member of the individual's family is UK resident, family being spouse or minor children (see further para **41.30**);
- Accommodation: the individual has accommodation in the UK available for his use (see further para **41.31**);
- Work: the individual performs more than three hours' work in the UK on 40 or more days in the tax year (see further para **41.32**);
- Past years: the individual spent 91 or more midnights in the UK in one or both of the two prior tax years.

In addition, for leavers there is a fifth potential tie, namely that the individual spends more midnights in the UK in the tax year concerned than in any one other country.

For arrivers or visitors the day counts which result in residence are as follows (Sch 45, para 19):

- 4 ties: 46–90;
- 3 ties: 91–120; and
- 2 ties: 121–182.

For leavers the day counts which result in residence are more stringent (Sch 45, para 18):

- 4 ties: 16–45;

- 3 ties: 46–90;
- 2 ties: 91–120; and
- 1 ties: 121–182.

A point to reiterate is that these day counts result in residence only if the individual is not non-resident under an automatic overseas test. So too an individual who is below these day counts can still be UK resident if he meets an automatic UK test.

A point also to keep in mind is that the day counts are reduced in the year of death. The reduction is by a fraction, of which the denominator is 12 and the numerator is the number of whole calendar months left in the tax year after the end of the month in which the death occurs (Sch 45, para 20).

ARRIVERS OR VISITORS

41.14 With the framework explained it is now possible to move to what matters in planning terms, namely ensuring residence status as a matter of certainty. Here it is convenient to start with visitors or arrivers.

Minimum day count

41.15 As explained above, a visitor or arriver cannot be UK resident unless he spends 46 or more midnights in the UK in the tax year concerned (Sch 43 para 13). This is the second automatic overseas test and there are no exceptions. Visitors who wish to have absolute certainty thus have one totally safe harbour.

90-day maximum

41.16 In practice a visitor who ensures his day count never exceeds 90 midnights in any tax year is not UK resident either. The reason for this is that under the sufficient ties test, a day count in the range 46–90 only results in UK residence if the individual has four UK ties. For arrivers, there are only four possible ties, one of which is the past years tie, ie the individual has spent more than 90 midnights in the UK in one of the two prior tax years (Sch 43 para 31(3) and 37). This tie is by definition not present if the individual never exceeds 90 midnights in any given tax year.

There are two qualifications to this 90 midnight principle. The first is in point if the individual spends 46 or more midnights in the UK in the year and comes within either the only home test or the test based on working full time in the UK. As explained in para **41.9**, on either of these scenarios he satisfies an automatic UK test.

In general it is unlikely that an individual could have his only home in the UK or work full-time in the UK without spending over 90 midnights there. But there is one scenario in which such eventualities do come about, namely if the only home or the work commence sufficiently late in the tax year for there to be insufficient time left in the year to spend 90 midnights in the UK, albeit that the midnight total still exceeds 45. In such a case, the ensuing satisfaction of the automatic UK tests causes the individual to be UK resident for the tax year as a whole.

The second qualification is bizarre and is in point only should the individual die during the tax year. As explained above on this scenario the minimum numbers of days that result in UK residence under the sufficient ties test are pro rata reduced to reflect the number of whole months in the year during which the individual was not alive. This does not impact if the individual's midnights in the UK before he died are below 46, for then he is within the automatic overseas test which is not subject to abatement in the event of death. Nor does it impact if the individual has only one UK tie in the year of death, for then he is not UK resident unless he satisfies one of the automatic UK tests. But in other cases the pro rata reduction of the 91 midnight threshold can result in UK residence in the year of death should the time in the UK be concentrated in the early part of the tax year, ie in the spring and summer.

Higher day counts

41.17 A visitor or arriver can spend up to 120 midnights in the UK year in year out provided he has only one of the family, accommodation or work ties. He is only able to have one of these ties as, once he has exceeded 90 midnights in one year, he has the prior year tie for the next two years and, once he has three ties a day-count in excess of 90 results in residence.

In practice much the most likely tie is accommodation. It therefore follows that a visitor or arriver with a flat or house in the UK can spend up to 120 midnights in the UK each year without risk of UK residence provided he is certain he has neither a work nor a family tie. He must also ensure he is not inadvertently trapped by the only home and full-time work automatic UK tests, and he also has to accept the risk of a lower permitted day-count in the event of his death during the year.

On a one-off basis a visitor or arriver can spend up to 182 midnights in the UK in a single year provided he has no more than one tie, in practice usually accommodation. This can be of advantage to those undergoing extended medical treatment. But 121–182 midnights is difficult if not impossible to sustain for more than a single year, for on that day count two ties result in residence. The past year tie is by definition present after the first year, and the wide meaning of the term accommodation (para **41.31** below) means the accommodation tie may be very difficult to avoid in practice.

Becoming UK resident

41.18 Should a visitor or arriver cross the threshold into UK residence, the rule is, as indicated above, that he is UK resident for the whole tax year in which the threshold is crossed. The split year treatment referred to above exempts most categories of pre-arrival income and gains from tax, but only if the facts fall within one of the Cases for split year treatment. These rules are explained in para **41.35** below.

LEAVERS

41.19 As indicated above (para **41.3**), the term 'leaver' may be used to describe an individual who has been UK resident in one or more of the prior three tax years.

Full-time work abroad

41.20 There is only one category of leaver for whom the rules are exceptionally generous, namely those who satisfy the full-time work automatic overseas test (see para **41.6** above). These individuals fall to be treated as non-UK resident come what may, and, in addition, split year treatment is potentially available in both the year of departure and the year of return (Cases 1 and 6: Sch 45 paras 44 and 49; see para **41.36**).

For those leavers lucky enough to have both the work and the record-keeping capacity, full-time work abroad is the simplest and safest means of ensuring non-residence. Three features of the regime are particularly generous:

(1) Up to 30 days may be worked in the UK in a given tax year (Sch 45 para 14(1)(c)).

(2) Up to 90 midnights may be spent in the UK in a given tax year and, in contrast to other rules for leavers, there are no circumstances in which single day visits and days of departure are counted (Sch 45 para 14(2)(b)).

(3) As non-resident status is under an automatic overseas test, it is achieved even if the individual retains a home in the UK and his spouse and children go on living there.

Minimum day count

41.21 For the many leavers who cannot rely on full-time work abroad, there is a minimum day count which results in non-residence. As explained above, a leaver who spends 15 or fewer midnights in the UK satisfies the first automatic overseas test and so is non-UK resident. However as noted in para **41.6**, the rule is subject to two qualifications.

The first is that the 15 midnight automatic overseas test does not apply at all in the year of death (para 12(c)). Second and more substantive, there are circumstances in which single day visits and days of departure count towards the day count. This rule applies only to leavers, ie only to those who were UK resident in one or more of three prior tax years. It is in point should the individual have three or more UK ties, and have more than 30 single day visits and days of departure across the year as a whole. In such a case, the single day visits and days of departure in excess of 30 count as midnights (Sch 43 para 23).

This qualification impacts on those leavers who make frequent short visits. In the first and second years following departure, the past years tie, namely 91 or more midnights in the UK in one of the two prior tax years, is likely to be present, so for those years the rule is engaged unless the other ties are restricted to just one.

90-day maximum

41.22 A leaver who spends 46–90 midnights in the UK is UK resident if he has just three ties. This again is more severe than for visitors or arrivers, where the threshold is four. So too the rule counting single day visits and days of departure in excess of 30 as midnights is in point as the three tie prerequisite for that rule is by definition present.

As just indicated, a leaver is likely in the first two years to have the past years tie. So only one other tie is possible with a midnight count of 46–90 and, assuming there is indeed only one other tie, the three tie threshold for counting single day visits and days of departure is not engaged either. In practice the most likely tie is accommodation, and so the position is reached that restricting midnights in the UK to 90 enables non-UK residence to be achieved provided family and work in the UK are avoided. This is a workable scenario for what is perhaps the principal category of individuals affected, namely retirees moving abroad.

As with visitors or arrivers, a leaver spending up to 90 midnights in the UK does not secure non-residence in the unlikely event his only home is in the UK or if he is present in his foreign home for fewer than 30 whole or part days: in either such event he is UK resident under the second automatic UK test (see para **41.9**). Perhaps more significant is the extra potential UK tie, namely the country tie. Under this tie, a leaver has a UK tie if in the tax year he spends more midnights in the UK than in any one other country or territory (Sch 43 para 38 and 143). This tie does not catch those genuinely moving to and then living in a particular place abroad but could catch those who leave the UK to enjoy a nomadic lifestyle, for example on a boat cruising around the world.

Leavers relying on a day-count of below 91 midnights are exposed to the risk of inadvertent residence should they die during the year and their time in the UK be concentrated in the early part of the tax year (ie spring and summer). In addition an equally bizarre rule can apply should the individual die in the first complete tax year following his departure. In such a case, he is UK resident under an automatic UK test should he have retained a UK home and should he not have spent at least 30 days in his foreign home (or been there for at least part of every day between the start of the tax year and the date of his death) (Sch 45 para 10).

45-day maximum

41.23 A leaver may consider he is at risk of having three UK ties. Such may be particularly so in the first two tax years following departure where the past years tie is present. Assuming accommodation is in any event a tie it may for some be difficult in practice to be sure the work tie is not infringed, or, in the case of the very mobile, that the country tie is not infringed. In such a case, the leaver may restrict his midnights to 45, and in that event, three ties (including the past year tie) are permissible. However such an individual does need to keep in mind that with three ties, his single day visits and days of departure count towards the 45 maximum if and insofar as they exceed 30. He is also at risk of a posthumous claw-back into residence in the manner described above, should he die during the year.

Year of departure

41.24 As indicated above, an individual remains UK resident for the whole of the tax year in which he departs. But full-time work abroad enables the year of departure to be split and one other split-year case is also material. These rules are discussed in para **41.36** below.

DAY COUNTING

41.25 As will be apparent from the above discussion, day counting is of great importance in determining residence.

Records

41.26 As in most tax matters, the onus of proof in the event of dispute with HMRC is on the taxpayer. For this reason, an accurate record of movements and more particularly midnights in the UK is essential. For leavers, the risk of having single-day visits and days of departure in excess of 30 counted means all visits to the UK should be recorded rather then merely midnights. Indeed it may be prudent to record all travel movements and not just those involving the UK. For leavers, this is a safeguard against the issue being raised of whether the individual has spent more midnights in the UK than in any one other country. For both leavers and visitors a complete record of movements may be necessary to demonstrate that any accommodation the individual has in the UK is not his only home.

In many cases, the record keeping needs to go beyond mere dates of visits. What is done on those visits can be important. The prime instance of this is where the individual needs to establish whether and if so on which days he did or did not do three or more hours work in the UK. But another example is the need to record time spent in the UK with minor children at school there (para **41.30**).

Margin for error

41.27 The second general point is that in planning terms it is prudent always to allow a margin for error. There are two reasons for this.

One is that many of the concepts used in the statutory test can be uncertain and may therefore give rise to argument with HMRC. Much the best position to be in, is to be able to say that even if HMRC win a disputed point, the individual is still non-UK resident. In relation to the sufficient ties test, the course of prudence is undoubtedly to base day-count on the basis of one more tie than is in fact planned for.

The second reason is that travel arrangements can be disrupted. It is unfortunate, to say the least, if travel disruption pushes an arriver or leaver into unplanned residence.

At this point it is apposite to note that a midnight in the UK can be disregarded if the individual would not have been present in the UK but for exceptional circumstances beyond his control (Sch 45 para 22(4)). The examples given of exceptional circumstances are national or local emergencies and sudden or life threatening illness or injury. The key point about this disregard is that the circumstances must be both exceptional and beyond control. Weather disruption to travel is not exceptional and visits to the UK for medical treatment are within the individual's control. Neither therefore provide a basis for ignoring midnights.

The overall conclusion is that the relief for exceptional circumstances is not one that should be counted on in planning. This reinforces the necessity of allowing a reasonable margin for the unexpected and the unforeseen.

Travelling through the UK

41.28 The third general point is that a midnight in the UK can be disregarded if the individual is in transit (Sch 45 para 22(3)). However this relaxation too is restricted in that it is not available if when in the UK the individual engages in activities unrelated to his passage through the UK. Examples given in the guidance (RDR 3 para 39) indicate regular travellers may find their view of what constitutes unrelated activities differs from that of HMRC. And for leavers a point to keep in mind is that this transit relief does not apply in determining whether and to what extent single day visits and days of departure exceed 30.

DEFINITIONS

41.29 As will be apparent, although day counting is at the core of the statutory test, many other concepts are material as well. Definitions are thus of crucial importance.

Family

41.30 What constitutes an individual's family is material to the sufficient ties test, as family in the UK is one of the ties. As already noted, family is a restricted concept, the term being confined to the individual's spouse and such of his children as are under 18 (Sch 45 para 32(2)). Those living together as spouses are also comprehended although precisely how this can be policed is unclear. Separated spouses are excluded.

The family tie is engaged if a member of the individual's family as so defined is tax resident for the tax year concerned. However in determining for these purposes whether a given member of an individual's family is UK resident the fact that that member is related to the individual is ignored (Sch 45 para 33(2)). Thus in the case of Mr and Mrs X, neither has a family tie by virtue of their marriage unless the other is otherwise UK resident.

There are two circumstances in which children under 18 may be ignored. The first is where the number of whole or part days the individual spends in the UK with the child is less than 61 (Sch 45 para 32(3)). The second is where the child is in full-time education in the UK and would not be UK resident if the time spent in education were disregarded (Sch 45 para 33(3)). In this case the child does not give rise to a family tie unless present in the UK for 21 or more midnights outside term-time. Term is defined as including half-term breaks, and HMRC regard the days on which term begins and ends as part of the term (see example 13 on page 31 of the guidance).

In practice the 61 day rule ensures that non-residents who send children to UK boarding schools do not have a family tie. It should however be stressed that all whole or part days count towards the 61 including days in transit.

Accommodation and home

41.31 The statutory test uses both the term accommodation and the term home. Accommodation is the concept used in the sufficient ties test, in that accommodation in the UK is a tie. Home by contrast is the term applicable in the automatic UK test, in that a home in the UK makes the individual UK resident if, in broad terms, it is his only home.

In view of its importance, the term 'home' ought to be defined comprehensively but it is not. Instead, the legislation offers merely elliptical comments, to the effect that any structure of vessel can be a home, and that whether there is sufficient permanence or stability about its use for it to be a home depends on all the circumstances (Sch 45 para 25). To add to the confusion it is then said that somewhere used periodically as a holiday home or temporary retreat does not count as a home.

The definition of accommodation is somewhat more robust, in that an individual has an accommodation tie if he has a place to live in the UK and that place is available to him for a continuous period of at least 91 days (Sch 45 para 34). Whether and if so in what circumstances such accommodation falls outside the term 'home' is unclear, although it is said that the term 'place to live' includes holiday homes and any accommodation otherwise available to the individual.

An important point about accommodation is that accommodation (whatever it is) does not give rise to the accommodation tie unless the individual spends at least one night there in the tax year (Sch 45 para 34(1)(c)). This means the difficulties which would otherwise arise with empty property and investment property are avoided. A comparable provision is made in the definition of home in that a property does not count as a home if the individual has moved out (Sch 45 para 25(5)).

An issue of difficulty is how far rooms available in the house of a friend or relative can count as an accommodation or even a home. In relation to accommodation, a safe harbour is provided where accommodation is owned by the parents or adult children of the individual. Such accommodation is disregarded unless the individual spends at least 16 nights there in the tax year (Sch 45 para 34(5)).

Hotels can also raise difficulties in relation to the accommodation tie. Concern is raised in particular by a rule that provides that accommodation is deemed to be available in any period when it is not in fact available if the period is less than 16 days and the accommodation is in fact available both before and after (Sch 46 para 34(2)). The concern is this catches regular visitors who always use the same hotel when in the UK. In fact it may be doubled whether this provision has this result, for accommodation only counts if it is a place to live. Hotels are not this unless, at the very least, a room is always reserved for the individual regardless of whether or not the hotel is otherwise full. HMRC consider that a hotel stay does amount to an accommodation tie if the individual books a room for at least 91 days, either continuously or with gaps of fewer than 16 days (Guidance Annex A, para A42 and example A17).

Work and location of work

41.32 Work embraces both the employed and those carrying on a trade profession or vocation (Sch 45 para 26). Whether what an employee does is in fact working turns on whether any payment received would be taxable as employment income. For the self-employed, the test is whether any expenses incurred would be deductible.

Travel time counts as work if the costs of the travel are deductible or insofar as the individual is in fact working as he travels. Time spent in training counts as work if the training is paid for by the employer or, in the case of the self-employed, the cost is deductible.

It is clear that time an individual spends in managing his investments is not work for the purposes of the statutory test, for such activity is neither employment nor trading. But the position is otherwise should the investments be held in a company of which the individual is a paid director for then the remuneration is employment income.

A specific rule prevents voluntary posts for which there is no contract of service from counting as work (Sch para 26(8)). This plainly protects charity trustees and the like. It is unclear whether this rule embraces unpaid company directors. Arguably it does not, for any director owes duties to the company and thus, implicitly at least, owes contractual obligations.

The location of work is where it is in fact done as distinct from where any contract might require it to be done (Sch 45 para 27). Insofar as travel to or from the UK constitutes work, it is treated as performed abroad up to the moment of disembarkation on arrival in the UK or, as the case may be, embarkation on departure from the UK. In these cases time spent at airport terminals thus counts as work (see RDR3 para 3.24). Special rules, however apply to those working on ships or aeroplanes (Sch 45 para 30).

The rules addressing travel can increase otherwise modest amounts of work in the UK. Thus an employee based in say Switzerland who makes a single day tax deductible visit to the UK for a 2-hour meeting will find his work in the UK will exceed three hours, for his travel time to and from the UK airport is included as work. Indeed even his time at the airport may count as work, for the embarkation rule means travel counts as UK travel from the moment he leaves the aeroplane on arrival to the moment he boards it on departure.

An issue of some difficulty is how far reading or responding to emails or taking telephone calls counts as work. In both cases the answer is such activities are work. This follows because any payment to an employee for these activities is or would be employment income and any costs are deductible by the self employed. It follows that such activities carried on in the UK are work in the UK.

In this area there are self-evidently policing and record-keeping difficulties. However many of the difficulties are in practice avoided by the fact that a day does not count as worked in the UK unless more than three hours' work is done. This means occasional responding to emails or business calls do not of themselves impact on residence status.

Country

41.33 The term 'country' is material to leavers under the sufficient ties test, for the fifth tie is engaged if the individual spends more midnights in the UK in the tax year than in any one other country. So too the tie is engaged if the number of midnights in the UK and the other country is the same (Sch 45, para 38).

For these purposes the term 'country' includes a state or territory (Sch 45, para 45). The terms state or territory are not further defined, but HMRC say in the guidance (at paragraph 2.18) that presence in any state, territory or canton into which a country is divided is regarded as presence in the country.

SPLIT YEARS

41.34 As explained above, residence is determined for tax years as a whole, and so, once an individual meets the conditions for residence at some point in a tax year he is resident for the year as a whole. But there are eight scenarios on which the tax year may be split, three for leavers and five for arrivers. Where the conditions for one or more of these scenarios are met, the tax year is split into a UK part and an overseas part and most charging provisions then operate as if the overseas part were a period of non-residence.

Arrivers

41.35 Five cases concern arrivers, namely Cases 4, 5, 6, 7 and 8.

All five require the arriver to have been non-UK resident in the tax year prior to that of arrival. Case 6 concerns those returning from having satisfied the automatic overseas work test and, rather bizarrely, is only in point if the arriver was UK resident in one of the prior four tax years (Sch 45, para 49). Case 7 is related to Case 6, in that it covers spouses accompanying the returning worker. Cases 6 and 7 both require the returnee to remain UK resident for at least the tax year following the return.

Case 5 is in point where the individual comes to the UK to work and satisfies the automatic UK work test (Sch 45, para 48). He must not be resident under the sufficient ties test in the part of the year prior to his arrival, the various day counts being reduced proportionately, and, there is no requirement he be resident in the following tax year.

Cases 4 and 8 focus on UK homes. In broad terms Case 4 is in point where the individual first has his only home in the UK, and Case 8 where he first has his home in the UK. But a point to stress with these cases, as with all others, is that they split the year only where residence results under the automatic UK test or the sufficient ties test. If the individual is not so resident under one or other of these tests, the split year rules cannot make him UK resident in what would otherwise be the UK part of the arrival year.

In detail, Case 4 is satisfied if at some point in the tax year, the individual's only home is in the UK, and that state of affairs continues until the end of the tax year (Sch 45, para 47). In contrast to the automatic home test for residence, there is no minimum time the individual must be present in the home and, more importantly, the existence of an overseas home precludes the UK home from counting as the only home regardless of how many days the individual spends there. Indeed, it would seem the mere existence of the overseas home prevents the UK home from being the only home. This point can have unfortunate results for arrivers who are resident in tax year of arrival under the automatic home test, for it means that some such arrivers do not attract split year treatment under Case 4. This is the position if there is an overseas home, but the individual has spent fewer than 30 whole or part days in it in the year of arrival.

Case 4 also requires one further condition to be met relating to the part of the tax year prior to the date on which the individual first has his only home in the UK. For that part of the year the individual must not be resident under the sufficient ties test (for which see para 41.13). But in applying that test the various day count thresholds are proportionally reduced to reflect the number of complete months that elapsed between the date when the UK home starts being the only home and the end of the tax year.

It will be noted that Case 4 does not preclude the individual from previously having had a UK home. All that matters is that that home was not previously his only home. It should also be noted that there is no requirement that the taxpayer be UK resident in the following tax year.

Case 8 is like Case 4 in focusing on the existence or otherwise of a UK home. However it is fundamentally different in two respects. The first is that the UK home does not have to be the only home: thus the existence or retention of an overseas home does not preclude Case 8. Second and more important, is that Case 8 does not apply unless at the start of the tax year the individual had no UK home at all. What Case 8 requires is for the individual to first have a UK home at some point in the tax year, and then to continue to have a UK home for the rest of that tax year and all of the following year. However there is no minimum requirement of days present in the home: all that matters is that on the facts the property is a home of the individual.

Case 8 also requires the individual to be resident throughout the following tax year and not qualify for split year leaver treatment. It is thus potentially available to all arrivers who have not previously had a UK home. Like Case 4 it is subject to the additional requirement that the arriver does not have sufficient UK ties for the part of the tax year prior to first having his UK home.

Where Case 4 is in point, the overseas part of the year ends when the taxpayer first has only a UK home and where Case 8 is in point it ends when he first has a UK home (Sch 45, para 53). Should Case 5 be in point, the overseas part ends when the 365 day begins – ie the first day of the continuous period or more than three hours being worked overseas. Where more than one of these cases applies, the overseas part ends on the earliest of the applicable dates (Sch 45, para 55(5)).

Leavers

41.36 Cases 1, 2 and 3 deal with leavers.

Case 1 is engaged if the individual satisfies the automatic overseas work test. The rules are expressed in terms of a period, which starts on a day on which the individual works more than three hours overseas and ends at the end of the tax year. During that period the individual must work overseas for an average of 35 or more hours per week. As with the overseas work test, in computing this average days worked in the UK are disregarded as are holiday and sick days. And also, as with the overseas work test, there must be no significant break from the work – ie more than 30 days.

The benefit of Case 1 is not lost if the individual makes return visits to the UK in the tax year of departure, provided two limits are not exceeded. The first is that the total post departure midnights in the UK must not exceed a limit of 90, reduced pro rata by the number of complete months in the tax year prior to departure. So too days worked in the UK must not exceed 30, this number also reduced pro rata by the number of complete months prior to departure.

As with the overseas work test generally, Case 1 is mostly of relevance to those working for governments or multi-nationals, with appropriate record keeping capacity. The benefit of the case is lost unless the individual continues to satisfy the overseas work test throughout the tax year following departure (Sch 45 para 44(4)).

Case 2 applies to accompanying spouses and operates where an individual satisfies Case 1 and his spouse moves abroad to join him. This move must take place either in the tax year when the Case 1 individual departs or in the following tax year (Sch 45 para 45) and the spouse must remain non-UK resident for all the tax year following the year of her departure. To come within Case 2, the spouse must either have no home in the UK or both a UK and an overseas home. In the latter event she must spend the greater part of her time living in the overseas home. She is allowed to make return visits to the UK in the year of her departure, the 90-day limit being reduced in proportion to the number of complete months prior to departure. In contrast to the position of the working spouse, departure days and single days in excess of 30 count as midnights in the UK.

The third and final case, Case 3, is not tied to any of the automatic overseas tests. It requires the leaver to cease having a home in the UK on a given date in the year of departure, and not to resume having such a home at any time in the rest of that tax year (Sch 45 para 46).

There are also three further requirements under Case 3, of which the first is that the individual must not spend more than 15 days in the UK between the UK home ceasing to be a home and the end of the tax year. Single day visits and departure days in excess of 30 are counted here so, while 15 midnights on their own do not infringe this requirement, it is infringed if in addition there are 31 or more single days and days of departure.

The second requirement is that the individual must remain non-UK resident throughout the next tax year. The third and most important requirement is that the individual must come to have a sufficient link with a specific country overseas. This link does not need to exist ab initio but must be in place within six months of departure. There are three methods by which a sufficient link can be proved:

(1)　Tax residence in the new country under its domestic laws.
(2)　Physical presence in the new country on each midnight in the six months following departure.;
(3)　No home in any country other than that specific country.

With Case 1, the overseas part of the year starts on the first day on which the individual works more than three hours overseas, provided he thereafter satisfies the overseas work criteria for the rest of the tax year (Sch 45 para 53(1)). For accompanying spouses, the overseas part of the year begins when the working spouse's overseas part starts or, if later, the date when they start living together overseas. Under Case 3 the overseas part starts when the leaver first ceases to have a UK home – ie when he moves out (Sch 45 para 53(4)). However if Cases 1 or 2 is also in point, the start of the overseas part is as determined for those cases (Sch 45 para 55).

Consequences of split year treatment

41.37 As indicated above, most charging provisions treat the overseas part of a split year as a period of non-residence. But there are some exceptions, most notably the transfer of assets code (see paras **69.45** and **70.14**). As a result the charging provisions at issue should always be checked if split year treatment is being relied on.

ANTI-AVOIDANCE

41.38 The statutory test includes one general anti-avoidance rule. This counteracts tax advantages which might otherwise be achieved should an individual be UK resident for a short period only. As the statutory test operates separately in relation to each tax year it is possible for an individual to be non-UK resident for one or a limited number of tax years even if he is UK resident both before and after.

Temporarily non-resident

41.39 The anti-avoidance rule is contained in FA 2013 Sch 45 paras 109–144. It is expressed as operating where an individual is temporarily non-resident. The definition of 'temporarily non-resident' is confusing because the anti-avoidance rule and thus the definition, are attempting to do two things (Sch 45 para 110). The first is to capture individuals who become non-UK resident under the statutory test, and the second is to embrace individuals who, while remaining UK resident under the statutory test, are treated as non-resident for the purposes of a double tax treaty under the tie breaker clause in the treaty.

So far as the statutory test is concerned, the definition is expressed in terms of residence periods. The general rule is that a residence period is a tax year but should one of the split year cases be in point, the UK and overseas parts of the year are each separate residence periods (Sch 45 para 111). An individual is temporarily non-resident if, following a residence period, he is non-UK resident for a period of five years or less. In addition he must have been UK resident in at least four of the seven tax years prior to the year in which non-residence commences.

As explained above, the statutory test operates by whole tax years, so normally an individual is temporarily non-resident if he is non-UK resident for five years or less. As a matter of language, the formulation 'five years or less' includes a period of exactly five years and so individuals who do not enjoy split year treatment must remain non-UK resident for six complete tax years to avoid the anti-avoidance rule. But as the rule imports the split year cases, the requisite period where the departure cases 1–3 are in point runs for five calendar years from the date of departure.

CGT consequences

41.40 The most important component of the anti-avoidance rule is directed at gains. Should an individual be temporarily non-resident, chargeable gains and allowable losses realised in the period of absence are treated under TCGA 1992, s 10A as accruing in the tax year in which he returns (TCGA 1992 s 10A(2)). As they are treated as then accruing, the rate at which tax is charged is the rate applicable in the year of return. So too losses realised in the period of absence may be offset even if in fact realised in a tax year prior to the gains. But as what are treated as accruing are chargeable gains and allowable losses, the computational rules are those applicable in the tax year during the period of absence when the gains or losses were in fact realised.

It should be noted that the gains charged on return are the total gains realised and not simply the part of each gain that was unrealised as at the commencement of the period of non-residence. However gains realised on assets acquired during the period of non-residence are in general excluded (TCGA 1992, s 10AA). But this exclusion is itself subject to exceptions, most notably for assets acquired under a roll-over disposal or on a no gain/no loss disposal such as that between spouses.

Close companies

41.41 A second component of the anti-avoidance rule is directed at dividends paid by UK and non-UK close companies. Should the anti-avoidance rule be in point, any such dividend received during the period of absence is treated as received in the period of return (ITTOIA 2005, ss 408A and 689A; ITA 2007, s 812A). This rule is expressed as applying only to material participators in the company, but as the term material connotes ownership of 5% or more of the company (ITA 2007, s 457) few close company participators fall outside it.

A limited exception is made for trading companies in that the rule does not apply to dividends paid in respect of post departure trading profits. This fully protects trading companies formed after departure. In the case of companies already in existence and trading, a just and reasonable basis is used to allocate dividends between pre and post departure profits.

This exception applies only to trade profits and thus does not relieve any form of investment income. The just and reasonable basis is used to allocate a dividend as between trading income and investment income where the company has both. Perhaps more significantly, the exception for trading profits does not appear to embrace group structures. It follows that dividends paid by a non-trading parent with trading subsidiaries do not attract the exception as the income in the hands of the parent is dividends from the subsidiaries.

An issue which arises is whether the rule applies only if the individual is himself a participator in the distributing company or whether it catches dividends paid to a non-resident trust which then distributes the money as income to the individual. It is clear that if the trust is a fixed interest trust the rules do apply for, provided the trust is a *Baker* trust, the dividend is treated as the income of the life tenant (see para 8.6). With discretionary trusts the position is more complex, but since any income distribution is from a source different from the dividend (see para 8.8) the rule ought not to apply. That this is right is confirmed by the requirement in the rule that the recipient receive the dividend or distribution by virtue of being a participator in the company or an associate of a participator (see ss 408A(3)(c) and 689A(3)(c)). Much the better view is that a discretionary beneficiary is not a participator (see para 87.5) and, while the trustees are often associates of his (see para 87.8), there is no countervailing provision deeming him to be an associate of theirs.

Other income tax provisions

41.42 In contrast to CGT, the anti-avoidance rule is not of general income tax application. It applies to certain pension-related receipts and otherwise in three contexts.

The first is where a UK close company writes off a loan it has made to a participator. Such write-offs are taxed under ITTOIA 2005, s 415. Should the write off be during the borrower's temporary period of non-residence, the write-off is treated as occurring in the tax year of return (ITTOIA 2005, s 420A).

The second concerns chargeable event gains under the legislation directed at life policies.

The third concerns offshore income gains. Here Regulation 23 of the Offshore Funds Regulations (SI 2009/3001) replicates TCGA 1992, s 10A, and provides that OIGs realised in the period of non-residence are treated as accruing in the period of return. As with s 10A, there is an exception for interests in offshore funds both acquired and disposed of in the period of non-residence (Regulation 23A). Regulation 23 in its present form has been in force since 6 April 2013 (SI 2013/1810 Reg 2(b)); before then it operated by incorporating the former TCGA 1992, s 10A directly.

Remittances

41.43 A further application of the anti-avoidance rule concerns remittance basis users. As explained in paras **48.10** and **49.8**, remittances of relevant income and foreign chargeable gains do not in general result in tax unless the remittance basis user is UK resident in the year of remittance.

ITTOIA 2005, s 832A applies the temporary non-resident rule to remittances of relevant foreign income and requires such income remitted during the period of absence to be treated as remitted in the year of return. However, with one exception, it does not apply if what is remitted is income arising in the period of absence. The one exception is dividends of non-UK close companies caught by the rule described in para **41.41** above: these are treated as remitted in the year of return if they both arise and are remitted in the period of absence (ITTOIA 2005, ss 408A(5) and 689A(5)).

As respects gains, the general charging provisions (TCGA 1992, s 12) treats foreign chargeable gains as accruing when remitted, with the result that TCGA 1992, s 10A, as described in para **41.40** above, catches remittances of pre-departure gains during the period of absence. Gains both realised and remitted in the period of absence are also treated as remitted in the tax year of return (s 10A(9)).

Treaty non-residence

41.44 As indicated above, the anti-avoidance rule caters also for treaty non-residence. The main consequence of this is that the rule overrides treaties in certain cases where a treaty might otherwise disapply UK legislation to an individual who remains UK resident under UK domestic law. However there is a further consequence, namely that periods of treaty non-residence are included in computing the period in which the individual is temporarily non-resident (Sch 45 paras 112 and 113). It follows that the rule can be disapplied in certain cases where an individual is non-resident under the statutory test for five or fewer tax years. Such cases are those where, before or after the period of non-residence, the individual is treaty non-resident and inclusion of the treaty non-residence period causes the five years limit to be excluded.

TRANSITIONAL

41.45 As indicated at the start of this chapter, the statutory test came into force on 6 April 2013. It is not given retrospective effect and as a result, the residence of individuals for earlier years remains determined by the old combination of case law, limited statutory rules, and HMRC practice. That combination was described in the 18th and earlier editions of this book, but of its nature that description takes no account of subsequent case law, most notably the Supreme Court decision in *R (on the application of Davies) v Revenue and Customs Comrs* [2011] UKSC 47, [2012] 1 All ER 1048.

As will be apparent from earlier paragraphs of this chapter, residence status in a prior year can impact on residence status in the current year, the prime example of this being the distinction between arrivers and leavers, where anybody who was UK resident in one of the prior three tax years is a leaver. The default position is that for these purposes residence in a prior year which pre-dates the statutory test is determined by the old law and practice. However it is possible to elect out of this in determining residence for any of the five tax years 2013–14 to 2017–18. Such election is on a year by year basis and must be made during the tax year following that to which it relates (Sch 45 para 154).

Careful analysis will be needed before making such an election. Most elections will no doubt be made where, under the statutory test, the individual would definitely have been non-UK resident in the prior year. The danger is that the making of the election may signify a concern in the individual's mind that he might have been UK resident in the prior year in question under the old law, albeit that he did not file on that basis for the year concerned.

The anti-avoidance rule described in paras **41.39** to **41.43** above do not apply unless the first year of non-residence is 2013–14 or a later year (Sch 45 para 153(3)). However, prior to the enactment of the statutory test a similar five-year rule applied inter alia to capital gains, offshore income gains, and remittances (see TCGA 1992, s 10A (as originally enacted) and ITTOIA 2005, s 832A (as originally enacted)). This law continues to apply where the year of departure was 2012–13 or prior (Sch 45 para 158). One important point of difference is that the old law is engaged in any case where the period of absence is fewer than five complete tax years: there is no provision for calendar years to operate where the former split-year concessions applied.

ORDINARY RESIDENCE

41.46 Before 6 April 2013, taxpayers and their advisers had to contend with the concept of ordinary residence as well as residence simpliciter. The law was that an individual became ordinarily resident in the UK if he adopted UK residence voluntarily and for settled purposes as part of the regular order of his life (*Shah v Barnet London Borough Council* [1983] 2 AC 309, [1983] 1 All ER 226, HL). In law most arrivals became ipso facto ordinarily resident as the necessary intention normally existed at the outset. However as a matter of practice some arrivals were treated as not ordinary resident for the two or three years following arrival.

41.46 *The Residence of Individuals*

Ordinary residence as a connecting factor has been removed from the tax code with effect from 6 April 2013 (FA 2013, Sch 46). However transitional relief is afforded for certain limited purposes, most notably the transfer of assets code (as to which see CHAPTERS 69 to 74). Here the code can be disapplied for the first three years of residence provided that the individual is not ordinarily resident in those years under old law (Sch 46 para 73). However this relief only applies up to 2015–16 and is restricted to 2013–14 where the individual first became UK resident in 2010–11, and to 2013–14 and 2014–15 where he first became UK resident in 2011–12.

Chapter 42

RESIDENCE OF TRUSTS

INTRODUCTION

42.1 The residence of trusts is material to income tax and CGT but not, in general, to IHT. As is described in CHAPTER 62, the liability of trustees to IHT turns on the nature of the assets and the domicile of the settlor rather than the residence of the trustees.

For both income tax and CGT purposes, the trustees of a settlement are deemed to be a single person distinct from whoever might from time to time in fact be the trustee or trustees (Income Tax Act 2007, s 474 (ITA 2007); Taxation of Chargeable Gains Act 1992, s 69(1) (TCGA 1992)). In contrast to IHT, the term 'settlement' is not defined for the purposes of CGT. It thus bears its common law meaning (for which see *Roome v Edwards* [1981] STC 96 and *Bond v Pickford* [1983] STC 517).

Since 6 April 2007, the substantive rules for determining the residence of the notional single person have been the same for the two taxes, albeit that the rewrite in ITA 2007 has created linguistic differences (see ITA 2007, s 475, rewriting TA 1988, s 685E, and TCGA 1992, s 69(2)–(2E)). In July 2009, HMRC published 'Trustee Residence Guidance' giving their interpretation of the rules. In 2010 further guidance, in the form of worked examples, was agreed under the title Tax Guide 3110 between HMRC and three professional bodies, ICAEW, CIOT, and STEP (reproduced [2010] SWTI p 2459). The 2009 Guidance constitutes Appendix 1 to the Trusts Settlements and Estates Manual.

THE RULES

42.2 The residence rules require the residence status of each of the actual trustees to be looked at. The enquiry is restricted to those who are validly appointed trustees under the terms of the settlement or under any applicable legislation. Persons invalidly appointed are simply nominees for the true trustees and so do not count (*Jasmine Trustees Ltd v Wells and Hind* [2007] STC 660). However, by the same token, a trustee *will* count if he sought to retire or an attempt was made to remove him, but such purported retirement or removal was ineffective as a matter of trust law.

Individual trustees

42.3 The statutory residence test described in CHAPTER **41** applies in determining the residence status of a trustee who is an individual (FA 2013, Sch 45 para 2(2). Should an individual trustee become or cease to be UK resident, his change of personal tax status can thus affect the residence status of the trust.

If an individual trustee becomes resident in the UK but benefits from one of the split-year rules described in para **41.18** in the first tax year of residence, his move does not impact on the trust's residence provided that he resigns or is removed in the overseas part of the year. So too, if split-year treatment applies to an individual in a tax year prior to a period of non-residence, an assumption of trusteeship by the individual in the overseas part of the tax year does not affect the residence of the trust (TCGA 1992, s 69(2DA); ITA 2007, s 475(8)).

In some instances property comprised in a single settlement may be comprised in separate funds vested in different sets of trustees. In such cases the residence of all the trustees of all the funds has to be taken into account unless a sub-fund election under TCGA 1992, Sch 4ZA has been made (*Roome v Edwards* [1981] STC 96).

All trustees UK resident

42.4 If all the trustees are UK resident the notional separate person is also UK resident (ITA 2007, s 475(2); TCGA 1992, s 69(2A)). There is now no exception to this. Prior to 6 April 2007 an exception applied to CGT in that professional trustees could be treated as non-resident if the settlor was neither resident nor domiciled in the UK when he made the settlement.

All trustees non-resident

42.5 If all the trustees are non-resident, the notional separate body is non-resident (ITA 2007, s 475(3); TCGA 1992, s 69(2E)). In contrast to the pre-2007 position for CGT there is now no requirement that the place of general administration be abroad.

Mixed residence trusts

42.6 A mixed residence trust is a trust where one or more trustees is UK resident and one or more is not. The general rule is that the notional separate body is UK resident. But the body is non-resident if no settlor of the settlement was resident or domiciled in the UK at the time he made the settlement (ITA 2007, s 476; TCGA 1992, s 69(2B)).

MIXED RESIDENCE TRUSTS: THE SETTLOR TEST

42.7 The residence or domicile of the settlor is relevant if and only if the trust is a mixed residence trust. A mixed residence trust is UK resident if any settlor was resident or domiciled in the UK, and as a result the rules determining who should be considered a settlor are important.

A point to make at the outset is that the residence and domicile of any given settlor are tested only at the time he makes the settlement. Subsequent changes of status are immaterial, provided that there are no further acts by the settlor that could qualify as further acts of settlement by him (discussed below).

A further point to make is that, for these purposes, the settlor's status is determined by reference to his residence in the relevant tax year and his actual domicile at the time of the act of settlement. In the event that an act of settlement occurs at a time when an individual is UK resident but in the overseas part of a split year, no account is taken of the split year; regard is only had to the fact that the individual has made the settlement at a time when he was UK resident.

Moreover, under current law, no account is taken of deemed domicile, which is not a concept that applies to income tax and CGT. However, this is due to change (see CHAPTER 45) and the provisions discussed below will no doubt be amended by the Finance Act 2017, so that if a settlement is made on or after 6 April 2017, and it has mixed residence trustees, the body of trustees will be UK resident if the settlor was UK resident, actually domiciled or deemed domiciled when the settlement was made.

Who is a settlor?

42.8 The basic rule is that a person is a settlor if either:

(a)   He has in fact made the settlement; or
(b)   Property is comprised in the settlement by reason of an event which causes him to be treated as settlor (ITA 2007, s 467(2); TCGA 1992, s 68A(2)).

A person is treated as a settlor if:

(a)   He has entered into the settlement directly or indirectly.
(b)   He has provided property for the purposes of the settlement, whether directly or indirectly.
(c)   He has entered into reciprocal arrangements whereby another party makes the settlement.

The terms 'entered into' and 'provided' are not defined. However, in the context of the income tax anti-avoidance code 'provided' has been construed as connoting bounty (see para 75.20) and there seems no reason why that principle should not apply here. But even if that is so, non-bounteous persons are not excluded from the definition provided that they can be said to have 'made' the settlement. This is because a person counts as settlor if he has made the settlement, regardless of whether he falls within the categories of those treated as making it.

The most difficult issue is how inadvertent bounty towards the settlement can render a person settlor. Typically this arises where somebody who is not the settlor as a matter of trust law transacts with the settlement, and there is uncertainty over what, commercially, are the correct price and other terms of the transaction. But here it may be suggested that the person will not become a settlor provided the intention is to transact at arm's length and reasonable attempts are made to secure that result. This conclusion follows because provision of property only results in a person being settlor if it is for the purposes of the settlement. 'For the purposes of' connotes some intention to benefit the settlement. Support for this point comes from a dictum of Lord Keith in *Fitzwilliam v IRC* [1993] 3 All ER 184, [1993] STC 502, set out at para **75.23**.

Testamentary settlements

42.9 Settlements arising on death, whether by will or intestacy, are treated as made by the deceased and his domicile and residence are tested as at the moment before death (ITA 2007, ss 467(4) and 476(2); TCGA 1992, ss 68(2)(b) and 69(2C)(a)).

ITA 2007, ss 472–473 and TCGA 1992, s 68C deal with variations of a will or intestacy which are treated for CGT purposes as having been effected by the deceased under TCGA 1992, s 62(6). If the result of the variation is that the property becomes or remains settled, the rules identifying the settlor are as follows:

(1)   If the property is not settled under the will or intestacy, the person or persons making the variation are treated as settlor or settlors of the trust thereby constituted.

(2)   If the property is settled under the will or intestacy the deceased is treated as settlor of any settlement resulting from the variation.

Multiple settlors and multiple additions

42.10 Should there be more than one person who is a settlor under the above rules then, as indicated above, the status of each such person at the relevant time must be determined. If any person who made the settlement (or who is treated as having done so, for example due to a provision of property to the trust) was resident or domiciled in the UK at the relevant time, the body of trustees is deemed UK resident.

The effect of this is to create a form of 'tainting' for mixed residence trusts, and may be regarded as a reason for considering mixed residence trusteeships undesirable where any person transacting with the trust is resident or domiciled in the UK. However, a subsequent addition would not taint the trust if on the facts it constitutes a separate settlement. Whether this point can be relied on turns on the application of the common law concept of 'settlement' as propounded by Lord Wilberforce in *Roome v Edwards (Inspector of Taxes)* [1982] AC 279, [1981] STC 96.

The legislation is not wholly clear about the position if a settlement has a single settlor who is non-UK resident and non-domiciled when the trust is first created, but who makes a subsequent addition at a time when he has become

UK resident and/or UK domiciled. But since a person is treated as settlor if he has provided property for the purposes of the settlement, the better view must be that he is treated as making the settlement at each time he provides property. On this basis his residence and domicile on each such occasion is material, and the facts outlined above lead to the settlement being deemed UK resident if it has mixed residence trustees.

Transfers between settlements

42.11 It is expressly provided that when property is advanced or appointed from one settlement to another, the settlor or each settlor of the transferor settlement is treated as having made the transferee settlement or a proportionate part of it (ITA 2007, ss 470–471; TCGA 1992, s 68B). In such a case the settlor's residence and domicile is tested at the time when he provided property to or otherwise constituted himself settlor in relation to the transferor settlement (s 476(4); s 68(2C)). This, it may be suggested, is a logical provision, in that it focuses on the moment when the settlor conferred bounty, regardless of the vehicle through which he initially did so.

An issue which has been debated is whether this rule also requires the residence and domicile of the settlor of the transferor settlement to be tested at the time of the transfer. The reason why the issue arises is that it is only at that moment that property he provides becomes comprised in the transferee settlement. It is however reasonably clear that testing at that time is not required. This is because ITA 2007, s 474(4) and TCGA 1992, s 69(2C) focus on the time or times when the settlor made the transferor settlement.

Ceasing to be settlor

42.12 Both the income tax and the CGT legislation contemplate that a person can cease to be settlor (ITA 2007, s 469; TCGA 1992, s 68A(6)). Such happens if a time comes when no property which he has provided is comprised in the settlement, such as would happen if, for example, all property he had provided is appointed to beneficiaries absolutely. The income tax legislation expressly provides that a settlor who has ceased to be settlor is ignored in determining the residence of the trust (ITA 2007, s 476(2), (3)). The same result follows under the CGT legislation by implication (TCGA 1992, ss 68A(6) and 69(2B)(c)).

BRANCH AGENCY AND PERMANENT ESTABLISHMENT

42.13 A non-resident trustee of a settlement is deemed to be UK resident if:

(a)   it or he is carrying on business in the UK through a branch, agency, or permanent establishment; and

(b)   it or he is acting as trustee of the settlement concerned in the course of that business (ITA 2007, s 475(6); TCGA 1992, s 69(2D)).

This rule did not apply to either income tax or CGT prior to 6 April 2007.

When enacted it generated concern among offshore trustees and their UK professional advisers. In the main the concern stemmed from two factors:

(1)   Although widely used and commented on, permanent establishment is an ill-defined term in its application to businesses such as the provision of trustee services.

(2)   The consequences of a trustee becoming UK resident through inadvertence can be draconian, for the assumption of the UK residence locks all latent gains into CGT. The trust can emigrate without difficulty but, as explained in para **30.8**, migration occasions the deemed disposal of all the trust assets at market value.

In part the concern has been addressed by the HMRC guidance referred to at the beginning of this chapter. Such guidance cannot alter the law, but what it has done is confirm that HMRC will not take points which most advisers consider bad but where in the nature of things the law is uncertain.

The key issues

42.14 As is recognised in HMRC's 2009 guidance, the rule requires three questions to be asked:

(1)   Is the trustee carrying on business in the UK?

(2)   If so, is it or he doing so through a branch agency or permanent establishment?

(3)   If so, is it or he acting as trustee of the trust whose residence is at issue in the course of that business?

Putting the issue in this way highlights a key point about the rule. It is directed at non-resident trustees who conduct a business in the UK of providing trustee services. It is hardly objectionable that a trustee acting in the course of such a business should be classed as UK resident, given that the profits of the branch, agency, or permanent establishment would themselves be taxed in the UK (see CHAPTER **64**).

Carrying on business in the UK

42.15 Read literally, the reference to business could be to business of any kind. HMRC, however, indicate that they read 'business' in this context as the business of providing professional trustee services for a fee.

An interesting issue is whether the same distinction can be drawn with reference to business as with trade, namely the distinction between trading in the UK, and trading with the UK (see para **40.6**). It is thought not, as 'business' is a wider term than 'trade', embracing both professional activities and investment (*American Leaf Blending Co Sdn Bhd v Director General of Inland Revenue* [1979] AC 676, [1978] STC 561). Case law also indicates that a trader may be carrying on business in the UK even if his acts do not amount to trading there (*Greenwood (Surveyor of Taxes) v F L Smidth & Co* [1922] 1 AC 417, 8 TC 193, per Atkin LJ). An example would be a representative office which solicits orders but does not conclude contracts (ibid).

An important distinction is between the trustee's own business, and the business of any particular trust it is carrying on as trustee of that trust. It is clear that the legislation is looking only at the trustee's own business and this is accepted by HMRC in the 2009 guidance. The fact, therefore, that a particular trust is carrying on UK business is immaterial.

Branch, agency or permanent establishment

42.16 On a literal reading of the legislation any trustee carrying on business in the UK is caught if a branch agency or a permanent establishment can be identified. However as is explained in CHAPTER 64, a non-resident company is subject to corporation tax only if trading in the UK through a permanent establishment, and other non-residents are only assessable in the name of a UK representative if that representative is a branch or agency. It is therefore a reasonable inference that a corporate trustee can only be treated as UK resident if it has a permanent establishment in the UK, and a non-corporate trustee only if he has a branch or agency. HMRC's guidance confirms that they share this view (para 5).

Meaning of permanent establishment

42.17 Both ITA 2007 and TCGA 1992 incorporate the definition of 'permanent establishment' contained in CTA 2010, ss 1141–1153 (ITA 2007, s 989; TCGA 1992, s 288). That definition requires there to be either:

(a) a fixed place of business in the UK through which all or part of the business of the company is carried on, or
(b) an agent acting on behalf of the company who has and habitually exercises in the UK authority to do business on behalf of the company.

The legislation does not in terms state this definition must be construed in accordance with OECD commentary, but such an approach must be regarded as likely in practice. Somewhat curiously, HMRC do not in their guidance refer to this statutory definition. However they do confirm that the OECD commentary is in point, and set out salient points in Annex A to the guidance.

The first limb of the statutory definition, focusing on a fixed place of business, principally connotes an owned or rented premises, and the examples in HMRC's guidance all assume such ownership or renting. But according to the OECD guidelines, a place of business does not have to be owned or leased to be fixed. Accordingly de facto availability of premises in the UK for meetings or other purposes could amount to a permanent establishment. This would be particularly so if the accommodation is owned by an affiliate of the non-resident trustee.

The second limb of the statutory definition, that concerning agents, is subject to two important limitations, both of which are recognised by HMRC in the guidance. They are as follows:

(a) Agents of independent status acting in the ordinary course of business are excluded (CTA 2010, s 1142(3)).

(b)   Under the investment manager exemption described in para **64.21**, investment managers are deemed to be of independent status in relation to particular kinds of investment transactions. The investment transactions in question are listed in para **64.22**, and comprehend all transactions normally undertaken by portfolio managers acting for trusts.

The first of these limitations means that UK professionals providing services to a non-resident trustee do not expose it to the risk of having a permanent establishment in the UK, so long as the terms of the engagement are commercial. This is recognised by HMRC in example 3 to the 2009 guidance, and it appears from that example that HMRC accept that the analysis is the same even if the trustee and the service provider are members of the same group.

With investment managers the position is as follows:

(1)   The investment manager cannot be a permanent establishment of the trustee provided that he acts on commercial terms and all the transactions are investment transactions of the kinds listed in para **64.22**.

(2)   In the unlikely event of the manager acting on behalf of the trustee in other transactions, he will not be a permanent establishment either, provided he stays within the general meaning of the term 'agent of independent status acting in the ordinary course of his business'.

Where the second limb of the definition can impose difficulty is where a non-resident corporate trustee has one or more UK resident directors or employees or where it is represented by a UK relationship manager in dealings with the settlor or beneficiaries. Both scenarios are best avoided. Directors and employees are of their nature dependent agents and thus a permanent establishment if they have authority to bind the trustee and do in fact act on its behalf whilst in the UK. In principle at least, a relationship manager is capable of counting as an agent of independent status provided that he is in fact remunerated on commercial terms. But in reality independent status may be difficult to demonstrate in practice.

Branch or agency

42.18 The terms 'branch' and 'agency' are not defined in the income tax legislation. For CGT purposes they mean any factorship, agency, receivership, branch, or management (TCGA 1992, s10(6)). The CGT definition is expressed as excluding persons within TMA 1970, s 82. That section inter alia excluded agents not carrying out the regular agency of the non-resident and brokers acting in the ordinary course of business. It was repealed in 1995 and it is unclear whether the continuing reference to it in TCGA 1992 is of any effect (see *Tax Guide 3/10* example 28).

General guidance as to what a branch or agency is may be derived from *IRC v Brackett* [1986] STC 521, 540 where Hoffmann J found it difficult to envisage that a non-resident carrying on a trade in the UK with any degree of continuity would not be doing so otherwise than through a branch or agency. A point he also made is that it is not necessary for there to be an agent in the UK empowered to enter into contracts on behalf of the non-resident. It may be extrapolated from this that if on the facts an individual non-resident trustee is carrying on business in the UK at all, he is likely to be doing so through a branch or agent.

As a matter of practice, HMRC apply the permanent establishment rules to individual trustees who are resident in a country with which the UK has concluded a double tax treaty. This practice is set out in paras 13–15 of the Trustee Residence Guidance. The applicable definition of the term 'permanent establishment' in such cases is the definition in the relevant treaty.

Which trusts become UK resident?

42.19 A point which is not clear on the wording of the legislation is whether, if a trustee is carrying on business in the UK through a branch, agency or permanent establishment, it or he is deemed to be UK resident in respect of all trusts of which it or he is trustee or just those of which it or he acts through the branch, agency or permanent establishment. As a matter of strict construction there is much to be said for the former view, on the basis that the business of trustee is a single business and that once there is a UK branch, agency or permanent establishment the business as a whole is in part at least being carried on through it. HMRC, however, take the latter view in the Guidance.

In determining whether a corporate trustee's UK permanent establishment renders a particular trust UK resident, HMRC look to whether the trustee carries out what it terms 'core activities' in relation to the trust in the UK. They regard the core activities of a trustee as including the general administration of the trust, investment strategy and performance, and decisions as to distributions.

Interestingly, HMRC take the view that a non-resident corporate trustee with a UK resident director can use the core activity concept to avoid a trust being UK resident. It does so by ensuring that the UK director does not carry out any core activities in relation to the trust in question (see example 4.2 in the 2009 Guidance).

Practical steps

42.20 It is difficult to formulate rules which will be appropriate for all types of professional trustee. However the following may be suggested:

- There is no risk in using UK professional services provided that the engagement is on commercial terms.
- There is no risk in using UK investment managers provided that the manager comes fully within the terms of the investment manager exemption.
- UK directors, employees, and relationship managers are best avoided.
- UK premises should be avoided, whether owned, leased or de facto available from affiliated companies or otherwise.

Provided that the above points are respected, non-resident trustees can safely meet investment advisors and beneficiaries in the UK. However decisions should not be taken at such meetings, a report back being made with a view to decision making where the trustee is based.

PROTECTORS

42.21 Protectors are persons who are not trustees but have certain powers in relation to the trust. They generally have the power to appoint new trustees and often they are given the power to dismiss trustees. Their consent may be required to the exercise of major dispositive powers over capital and they may also have power to add or exclude beneficiaries.

A question which may be raised is whether, if the protector of an offshore trust is UK resident, his residence can make the trust as a whole UK resident. At present this question is academic, in that it has not been raised in any reported case, but the fear of it leads most advisers to discourage the appointment of persons as protector if they are, or may in future become, UK resident.

In fact these fears are generally ill-founded. It is highly unlikely that a protector can be classed as a trustee, for he is not appointed as such and the trust property is not vested in him. Further, he does not normally have power to initiate action, but merely power to veto actions proposed by the trustees proper. If there is any risk at all of a protector being characterised as a trustee, it must be reduced if the matters which require the protector's consent are restricted to major fiduciary appointments or advances of capital, the trustees being unfettered in their discretions over income and investment.

Chapter 43

RESIDENCE OF COMPANIES

INTRODUCTION

43.1 The companies which feature in offshore tax planning are almost always incorporated under the law of an offshore jurisdiction. But even if incorporated in an offshore jurisdiction, a company may be resident, for UK tax purposes, in the UK, and accordingly subject to UK tax on its profits.

CENTRAL MANAGEMENT AND CONTROL

43.2 The test for determining where a foreign-registered company resides was formulated in *De Beers Consolidated Mines Ltd v Howe* [1906] AC 455. Lord Loreburn said that a company resides where its real business is carried on. He then said:

> 'the real business is carried on where the central management and control actually abide.'

In the later case of *Unit Construction Co Ltd v Bullock* [1960] AC 351, [1959] 3 All ER 831, HL, this test was described as being 'as precise and unequivocal as a positive statutory injunction'. All cases since 1906 have so treated it, including *Wood v Holden* [2006] STC 443.

But although the test may be a positive injunction, its meaning is not immediately clear. In fact what was meant at the time was the place where the board of directors met and directed the operations of the company. This is apparent from the approval in *De Beers* of the decisions in *Calcutta Jute Mills Co Ltd v Nicholson* (1876) 1 TC 83 and *Cesena Sulphur Co Ltd v Nicholson* [1874–80] All ER Rep 1102 to the effect that a company resides where its board meets rather than where its operations are carried on.

In *De Beers* itself, the company was registered in South Africa, the preponderance of its operations were carried on there, and some members of the board resided and met there. But other members of the board resided and met in the UK and it was found as a fact that:

> 'the head and seat and directing power of the affairs of the . . . Company were at the office in London, from whence the chief operations of the Company, both in the United Kingdom and elsewhere, were in fact controlled, managed, and directed.'

On this basis, central management and control was found to abide in the UK.

The primacy of the place where the board meet was affirmed in *Wood v Holden*. In his first instance judgment, upheld by the Court of Appeal, Park J said ([2005] STC 789, 824 para 21):

> 'In all normal cases the central control and management is identified with the control which a company's board of directors has over its business and affairs, so that the principle almost always followed is that a company is resident in the jurisdiction where its board of directors meets.'

AUTHORISED AND UNAUTHORISED CONTROL

43.3 Despite the fact that in all normal cases, a company resides where the board meets, it is to be observed that in *De Beers*, Lord Loreburn stated that the issue of where central management and control abide:

> 'is a pure question of fact, to be determined not according to the construction of this or that regulation or byelaw, but upon the scrutiny of the course of business and trading.'

This emphasis on what happened in fact was the ratio of the House of Lords decision in *Unit Construction Co Ltd v Bullock* [1960] AC 351, [1959] 3 All ER 831, HL. Here the memorandum and articles of Kenyan subsidiaries of a UK group vested control of their businesses in the directors and specified that board meetings could not take place in the UK. In fact the subsidiaries got into severe difficulties and the parent board in London took over the running of them. It is unclear whether the Kenyan boards met, but if they did, their minute book was no more than a formal record of the implementation of decisions made in London. On these facts, the House of Lords held that central management and control abided in London.

Usurpation and dictation

43.4 In the half century following the *Unit Construction* decision, there was much uncertainty as to its implications, and HMRC used it to argue that offshore companies with shadowy boards were UK resident. In *Wood v Holden*, however, the extent of the decision was clarified. Chadwick LJ put the matter thus in the Court of Appeal (at para 27):

> 'It is essential to recognise the distinction between cases where management and control of the company is exercised through its own constitutional organs (the board of directors or the general meeting) and cases where the functions of those constitutional organs are usurped – in the sense that management and control is exercised independently of, or without regard to, those constitutional organs. And, in cases which fall within the former class, it is essential to recognise the distinction (in concept at least) between the role of an outsider in proposing, advising, and influencing the decisions which the constitutional organs take in fulfilling their functions and the role of an outsider who dictates the decisions which are to be taken.'

It is apparent from this that there are only two scenarios where the meeting place of the board is displaced as the residence of the company. The first is when the board is usurped, and the second is when it is dictated to.

Usurpation

43.5 *Unit Construction* is the paradigm case of a usurped board. Another instance is a criminal case, *R v Dimsey* [2000] QB 744, [1999] STC, 846. This was a decision of the Court of Appeal, where on this point leave to appeal to the House of Lords was refused: [2001] STC 1520, para 26. By implication, the jury found Jersey companies had become UK resident and so should have been filing tax returns. They did so on the basis of the following direction by the trial judge, which the Court of Appeal found to be proper:

> 'You may think that possibly the simplest way of formulating a test in the circumstances of this case is are you sure that [the UK resident individual] was in reality managing and controlling these companies or may it have been [the Jersey director] or some other person or persons.'

Dictation

43.6 It is difficult to identify what constitutes dictation to the board. However the distinction drawn in *Wood v Holden* is, in the words of Park J (at para 66), as follows:

> 'If directors of an overseas company sign documents mindlessly, without even thinking what the documents are, I accept that it would be difficult to say that the national jurisdiction in which they do so is the jurisdiction of residence of the company. But if they apply their minds to whether or not to sign the documents, the authorities ... indicate that is a very different matter.'

The authorities to which Park J refers include *Untelrab Ltd v McGregor* [1996] STC (SCD) 1. Here an offshore group finance company at all times acceded to requests from its UK parent as to what to do with its funds. However the evidence was that all requests were considered by the board and that the board would have refused to carry out any proposal which was unreasonable or improper. On this basis the board was found to have genuinely exercised its discretion with the result that the company was resident in Bermuda, where its board met, and not in the UK.

The decision in *Little Olympian Each Ways Ltd, Re* [1994] 4 All ER 561, [1995] 1 WLR 560 was to the same effect. This was not a tax case but turned on whether the company was resident outside the UK for the purposes of security for costs. Half the shares were owned by a Greek intestate estate and half by a Foundation, but in practice a UK resident purported to give instructions to the board and was one of the signatories to the company's bank account. But the board did meet and was the source of instructions regarding the litigation. The directors were four Jersey lawyers, one of whose evidence was that he would act in accordance with the UK resident's instructions provided they were consistent with Jersey company law and the interest of the actual shareholders. On these facts Lindsay J found the company was not UK resident.

Information

43.7 An issue of difficulty is whether a board is acting mindlessly if it lacks a minimum level of information in reaching its decisions. In *Wood v Holden*, there was no evidence that the board understood how the price had been arrived at in transactions the company were entering into and this led the Special Commissioners to find their meeting place did not determine the residence of the company. But this conclusion was quashed by Park J and the Court of Appeal on the grounds that, regardless of information, the board had in fact made a decision and so not acted mindlessly. Somewhat curiously the requirement of a certain basic level of information resurfaced in a later tribunal case, *Laerstate BV v Revenue and Customs Comrs* [2009] UKFTT 209 (TC), [2009] SFTD 551, [2009] SWTI 2669. In reality, however, the dispute may be semantic, for, if a board is to satisfy itself a request is reasonable and proper, it needs at least some information.

What is clear beyond peradventure is that in determining company residence, the level of application of the board does not have to be such as to free it from the risk of an allegation of breach of duty. As Chadwick LJ put it in *Wood v Holden* (at para 43):

> 'a management decision does not cease to be a management decision because it might have been taken on fuller information; or even . . . because it was taken in circumstances which might put the director at risk of an allegation of breach of duty. Ill-informed or ill-advised decisions taken in the management of a company remain management decisions.'

In practice of course, company directors meeting as a board should have sufficient information and give full consideration to matters before them so as to properly discharge their duties under the applicable company law. Should they do this, it is plain from the above analysis they are neither being dictated to nor usurped and thus the place where they meet is the place where the company resides.

DUAL RESIDENCE UNDER THE CENTRAL MANAGEMENT AND CONTROL TEST

43.8 In one respect, the central management and control test in *De Beers* has been qualified. The circumstances in which this arises were specified by Lord Radcliffe in *Unit Construction* as follows:

> 'the facts of individual cases have not always so arranged themselves as to make it possible to identify any one country as the seat of central management and control at all. Though such instances must be rare, the management and control may be divided or even at any rate in theory, peripatetic.'

These days, it may be suggested, dual residence under the central management and control test is potentially more common than when *Unit Construction* was decided, for many boards, particularly of offshore companies, are peripatetic.

Assuming one country is not the sole seat of central management and control, the issue then arises of how it is determined which countries are. Here the best guidance is two cases cited in *Unit Construction*.

In the first, *Swedish Central Railway Co Ltd v Thompson (Inspector of Taxes)* [1925] AC 495, [1925] 9 TC 342, HL, a UK company existed merely to receive rent from a Swedish railway. Its business was controlled from its head office in Sweden, but three members of the board constituted a committee in the UK to seal share certificates and sign cheques. The company banked in the UK and prepared accounts there. On these facts the company was held to be resident in the UK as well as Sweden. In *Unit Construction*, this decision was rationalised as follows:

> 'the Swedish Central Railway Company's business and administration were of such a nature that what managing and controlling had to be done was in fact done as much on English as on Swedish soil.'

The second decision comprised three cases heard together as *Union Corpn Ltd v IRC* [1953] AC 482, [1952] 34 TC 207, HL. In two of these three cases, the facts were similar to *De Beers* in that the companies were South African, with some directors running the company's operations in South Africa but the main board in London. On these facts, the Court of Appeal held the companies were resident in South Africa as well as in the UK.

The third of the three cases in *Union Corporation, Trinidad Leaseholds Ltd v IRC* [1953] 1 All ER Rep 729, concerned a UK company exploiting oil in Trinidad. The directors all resided in England and all board meetings took place there. But the chairman and managing director regularly visited Trinidad for the purpose of supervising the company's affairs and took decisions at minuted informal meetings. This, the Court of Appeal held, meant the company was also resident in Trinidad. It is unclear whether this aspect of the case was approved in *Unit Construction*, but the prudent view is to assume it was. *Trinidad Leaseholds* emphasises that what is important in dual residence cases is the activities of board members in the second country. Thus the manager in Trinidad had a power of attorney to run the company's business in the widest possible terms but this, it was held, would not have made the company resident in Trinidad. The company would on that scenario simply have been an absentee owner.

The only modern case on dual residence, *Laerstate BV v Revenue and Customs Comrs* [2009] UKFTT 209 (TC), [2009] SFTD 551, [2009] SWTI 2669, is in line with the above. Here, one member of a two-man board was UK resident and one not, and board meetings, of a rudimentary nature, took place outside the UK. However the UK resident director was the owner of the company and the Tribunal found his activities in the UK were 'concerned with policy, strategic, and management matters and . . . included decision-making'. On this basis it found the company was UK resident.

An important point is whether the mere presence of a director in a country carries the risk of dual residence. In *Laerstate* the Tribunal said it does not and this is consistent with the earlier cases. Thus, in *Unit Construction*, Lord Radcliffe summarised the decision in *Union Corporation* as being to the effect that:

> 'residence arose in any country in which 'to a substantial degree' acts of controlling power and authority were exercised.'

So too, in *News Datacom Ltd v Atkinson* [2006] STC (SD) 732, two members of an eight-man board were UK resident, including the chief executive, and an executive committee met in the UK. HMRC argued that the chief executive and other colleagues were effectively exercising central management and control in the UK and had usurped the board. But the Special Commissioners rejected this, finding that the board continued to direct the business of the company, and did so from outside the UK.

A related point is whether, if the main board is in one country, the company can only be resident in another country if some part of its business is carried on there. In the *Union Corporation* case, Evershed MR suggested this is a requirement for he said:

> 'there must, in order to constitute residence, be not only some substantial business operations in any given country, but also present some part of the superior and directing authority.'

A point which may also be raised is whether a company is only dual resident if some part of its board control is split. The answer, it may be suggested, is that a finding of dual residence may be possible if a board is being usurped or dictated to. But if there is no usurpation or dictation, it is, on the authority of *Wood v Holden*, the board alone which determines residence.

HMRC PRACTICE

43.9 HMRC published a statement of practice on company residence in 1983 (SP 6/83). It was reissued in 1990 (SP 1/90). Three points require comment.

First, it is stressed that company residence is ultimately a question of fact, turning on where central management and control is in fact exercised. It means HMRC will, in a disputed case, investigate the facts of how the company has operated, studying Board minutes and other documents and, if available, interviewing witnesses.

Second, HMRC indicate the approach they adopt in investigating the factual position. First, they try to ascertain whether the directors of the company in fact exercise central management and control. Next, if the directors do exercise central management and control, HMRC seek to determine where they in fact do this. Lastly, in cases where the directors apparently do not exercise central management and control, HMRC look to establish where and by whom it is exercised.

The final point to emphasise about HMRC practice is that they sound a warning about company residence in a tax-avoidance context. HMRC examine the facts particularly closely where 'it appears that a major objective underlying the existence of certain factors is the obtaining of tax benefits from residence or non-residence'.

SP 1/90 was not updated to reflect *Wood v Holden*. Given that HMRC fought *Wood v Holden*, it is a reasonable inference that, on the criteria set out in SP 1/90, HMRC thought the company at issue in that case was UK resident. To that extent, therefore, what is said in SP 1/90 needs to be qualified. However, in its emphasis on the factual position, and in particular where offshore avoidance is involved, it is still a salutary warning.

The only recent guidance HMRC has given relates to subsidiaries of UK groups based in treaty jurisdictions (INTM 120150). This guidance includes comments on the implications of some directors being UK resident and of participation in board meetings by telephone from the UK. It appears HMRC accept that neither, of itself, renders the company UK resident.

PRACTICAL CONCLUSIONS

The position now

43.10 It is clear from *Wood v Holden* that an offshore company is resident where its board meet, if the board do indeed meet and give genuine consideration to the transactions put before them. It is not necessary for them to meet more often than there are transactions for them to consider and from a company residence standpoint, it is not necessary for them to consider and understand the transactions in detail. All that is required is that they are satisfied the transactions proposed are in the interests of the company, in accordance with its governing law, and proper. Provided the directors give genuine consideration to these issues, it is immaterial that the transactions are proposed by the shareholder or some third party and that the board never in fact refuses 'requests' made by such persons.

Practical steps

43.11 In practice prudent advisers ensure the boards of offshore companies go further than this. Two steps in particular are prudent:

(1)   The board should meet, at a minimum, yearly or half-yearly and conduct a review of the company's business and investments.

(2)   In reaching any decision the board should have sufficient material before it to properly discharge its duties as a matter of the applicable company law and should have genuine understanding of that material. Even if not necessary to establish company residence, failure to conform with such practice is likely to expose the directors to personal risk under the applicable company law.

In addition, the following common-sense steps are prudent:

(a)   Most if not all board meetings should take place in the same jurisdiction, so that the company can positively be said to be resident there.

(b)   Board meetings should be properly minuted, the minutes reflecting reasoning as well as simply decisions.

(c)   All directors minuted as present must in fact have been present.

(d)   Any requests from the shareholder or third parties should be expressed as requests for consideration rather than instructions.

(e)   In the case of complex transactions, the main terms and draft documents should be considered and approved by the board well in advance of actual signing.

(f)   Any instructions as to implementation should be given by or on behalf of the board.

Telephonic meetings and written resolutions

43.12 In terms of how meetings are conducted, there is plainly no difficulty under UK company residence rules if the meetings are telephonic, provided none of the participating directors is in the UK. Written resolutions signed by all the directors are in practice frequently used, partly because the participation of all the directors is then proved. It is reasonably clear from *Wood v Holden* that the mere signing by the directors of written agreements was sufficient and if so, the signing of an antecedent written resolution plainly is as well. But in cases of controversy, most practitioners regard it as helpful to have evidence of properly minuted meetings and certainly, if written resolutions are to be used, it must be clear on the facts that each director understands what he is agreeing to and why it is in the interests of the company. A further point is that no director should sign or consider a written resolution whilst in the UK.

UK resident directors

43.13 In the light of the decision in *Wood v Holden*, the issue may be raised of whether the board of an offshore company can include UK resident individuals. As indicated above (para **43.8**), strictly there should be no objection to this, provided the board does meet outside the UK, and is the genuine decision-making forum. But extra care is needed, particularly where the UK resident owns or is interested in shares in the company. In such cases, HMRC scrutiny and challenge must be anticipated and to counter this it must be clear on the facts that the board as a whole is the decision-making body which genuinely meets regularly abroad. It must never meet in the UK.

Trustee shareholders

43.14 Where the shares in offshore companies are held in an offshore trust *Re Little Olympian Each Ways Ltd* (para **43.6** above) suggests there is an added line of defence against the company being found to be UK resident. This is that if anybody is constitutionally authorised to give 'instructions' to the directors it is the trustee shareholders. Nonetheless, as central management and control is ultimately a question of fact, the residence of a company could be found to be in the UK if both directors and trustees stand aside in favour of a UK resident settlor or UK resident beneficiaries. For this reason, and because it accords with trust and company law, any requests or suggestions from the settlor or the beneficiaries should be directed to the trustees. The trustees can then, if thought fit, communicate with the directors (even if in reality the same individuals are involved).

UK REGISTERED COMPANIES

43.15 As a result of legislation enacted in 1988, incorporation is the test of residence for UK registered companies (CTA 2009, s 14). The case law on central management and control is therefore of relevance only to foreign registered companies.

An exception to the incorporation rule operates if the UK registered company was carrying on business before 15 March 1988 and had become non-resident before then pursuant to a general or a specific Treasury consent obtained under now repealed provisions of TA 1988, s 765 (CTA 2009, Sch 2 paras 13–15). If the consent was a specific consent, the company can remain non-resident regardless of where it is based, and it only becomes UK resident if it in fact becomes resident under the central management and control test.

If the consent was a general consent, a further condition had to be satisfied. This condition is that the company was taxable in a foreign territory. By 'taxable' is meant being liable to tax on income by reason of domicile, residence, or place of management, but not simply being liable to a flat-rate sum or fee (see CTA 2009, Sch 2 para 15(1) and SP 1/90, para 6). Provided a company which migrated before 15 March 1988 pursuant to a general consent was taxable in a foreign state it may remain non-resident, but only so long as it is so taxable. There was in fact only ever one general consent, which applied where the company was formed after 1951 to carry on new business and over half its share capital was owned by non-residents.

The exception for companies which became non-resident pursuant to a specific consent applies also to companies which migrated after 15 March 1988 pursuant to a specific consent applied for before then. Such a company does however have to have commenced business before then.

DUAL RESIDENCE FOR TREATY PURPOSES

43.16 As indicated above, a company can be dual resident as a matter of UK domestic law under the central management and control test. Somewhat confusingly the term 'dual residence' is also used in another sense when considering the position under double tax treaties.

Meaning of dual residence

43.17 A company is dual resident in the treaty sense if the following conditions are satisfied:

(1) It is resident in the UK under UK domestic law whether as a UK registered company or under the central management and control test.
(2) It is liable to tax in some other state by reason of residence, domicile, or place of management.
(3) There is a double tax treaty between the UK and the other state.
(4) Under the tie-breaker clause in the treaty it is treated as resident in the other state for the purposes of the treaty. In other words the company is 'treaty resident' in the other state.

Effect of dual residence

43.18 A company which is dual resident in the sense described here is deemed for all UK tax purposes to be non-UK resident (CTA 2009, s 18). This is so regardless of whether the company has claimed treaty relief. The normal case of a dual resident company is a UK registered company whose effective management is in the treaty state. Dual residence is thus a further exception to the incorporation rule being decisive of residence for a UK registered company. But a foreign registered company can, in theory at least, also be dual resident, as was argued in *Wood v Holden*. According to HMRC, an example of a dual resident foreign registered company would be where the company's business is run by executives abroad with the final directing power resting with a non-executive board in the UK.

Most treaties follow the OECD model and have the tie-breaker provision expressed in terms of effective management and located in a separate paragraph in the residence article. Certain old colonial treaties are different and there is simply a provision to the effect that the company is regarded as resident in the UK if its business is managed and controlled in the UK, and in the treaty partner if its business is managed and controlled there. Such a provision was not thought to operate as a tie breaker, but on 30 November 2015 HMRC said they now consider 'the better interpretation' is that it does (Policy Paper 'change of view on the interpretation of residence articles in sixteen Double Taxation Agreements').

The treaties in question include those with all three Crown Dependencies. The result is that a UK registered company is resident in the treaty partner concerned for UK tax purposes generally if its business is managed and controlled there. But this does not apply if on the facts management and control is split, and in such a case there is no operative tie breaker, with the result that UK residence by incorporation stands.

Meaning of effective management

43.19 In the OECD Model Treaty, the test under the tie-breaker article is where the company's place of effective management is situated. Effective management is where the key management and commercial decisions are actually made (*Trevor Smallwood Trust, Re, Smallwood v Revenue and Customs Comrs* [2010] EWCA Civ 778, [2010] STC 2045, para 48, [2010] 80 TC 536). In *Wensleydale's Settlement Trustees v IRC* [1996] STC (SCD) 241, a Special Commissioner considered that effective management is 'where the shots are called', implying realistic positive management. HMRC consider that the place of effective management may, in some cases, differ from the place of control (SP 1/90, para 22).

In *Wood v Holden* [2005] EWHC 547 (Ch), [2005] STC 789, the taxpayer argued that even if the company in question had been resident in the UK under the central management and control test, its place of effective management was in the Netherlands. The Special Commissioners rejected this argument, holding that on the facts of the case there was no difference between effective management and central management and control. The Court of Appeal found it very difficult to see how, in the circumstances of the case, the effective management test and the central management and control test could lead to different results (see [2006] STC 443 para 44).

In *Indofood International Finance Ltd v JP Morgan Chase Bank NA* [2006] EWCA Civ 158, [2006] STC 1195, [2006] 8 ITLR 653, Sir Andrew Morritt C laid stress on the OECD commentary, to the effect that effective management refers to the place where key decisions are taken. He then concluded, on the facts of the case, that the Indonesian parent of a Netherlands company was taking key decisions and thus that Indonesia was the latter's place of effective management. Chadwick LJ, however, tentatively disagreed with this conclusion.

The place of effective management test is considered further at para **100.6**.

Chapter 44

DOMICILE: GENERAL PRINCIPLES

WHAT IS DOMICILE?

44.1 Domicile is a legal status which plays an important role in English law, and UK tax law, as a connecting factor. It determines whether English or some foreign law regulates personal relationships, eg marriage, legitimacy and succession. Domicile has also been adopted by the UK tax system as a determinant of the scope of various personal taxes, but it should be remembered that it is a general legal concept, and not one created merely for tax purposes.

In relation to income tax and CGT, the sole determinant at present is domicile under the common law principles which are discussed in this chapter. Where IHT is concerned, the basic concept is again domicile under common law, but there are statutory modifications which may mean that, for IHT purposes, an individual who is not domiciled in any part of the UK under the common law principles is deemed to be domiciled within the UK. These statutory modifications in relation to IHT are discussed in CHAPTER 45.

There are Government proposals to introduce unified deemed domicile rules that will apply for the purposes of all UK taxes to which domicile is relevant, ie to income tax and CGT as well as IHT. Assuming such rules are indeed introduced, they will apply from 6 April 2017 (see para 45.10 ff). Until then, the availability of the remittance basis (see CHAPTER 51) will continue to be determined solely by the common law domicile rules.

Under common law, an individual can have only one domicile at any time: a domicile of origin; a domicile of choice; or a domicile of dependency. The place in which an individual is domiciled is not necessarily a nation in a political sense, but any geographical area governed by a single system of law (*Re Fuld's Estate (No 3)* [1968] P 675 at 682–684). Thus an individual is domiciled in 'England' or 'Scotland', rather than in 'the United Kingdom' and in one of the several states which make up such federal countries as Australia or the United States.

The concept of domicile evolved in relation to individuals and for tax purposes is generally material only in relation to individuals. It has been held that a company has a domicile where it is registered, but no aspect of corporate tax liability turns on domicile (cf *Gasque v IRC* (1940) 23 TC 210).

DOMICILE OF ORIGIN

44.2 An individual acquires a domicile of origin when he is born (*Henderson v Henderson* [1967] P 77, [1965] 1 All ER 179). Normally, this is his father's domicile at the date of his birth, but if his parents are unmarried, it is the mother's domicile. A domicile of origin continues unless and until the individual acquires either a domicile of dependency or a domicile of choice: upon his acquiring one or other, that will remain his domicile until abandoned. If it is abandoned without another domicile of choice or dependency being acquired, the domicile of origin revives (*Udny v Udny* (1869) LR 1 Sc & Div 441). An individual's domicile of origin is thus his default domicile (*Henwood v Barlow Clowes International Ltd* [2008] EWCA Civ 577, [2008] All ER (D) 330 (May), para 21).

A person's domicile of origin is often described as having an adhesive quality. There are two reasons for this. First, the burden is on whoever alleges a person has acquired a domicile of choice to prove it. Second it is variously said either that the burden is heavy (*Winans v A-G* [1904] AC 287, 291) or that the acquisition of a domicile of choice is regarded as a serious matter, not to be lightly inferred from slight indications or casual words (*Re Fuld's Estate (No 3)* [1968] P 675 at 684; *Buswell v IRC* [1974] 2 All ER 520, [1974] STC 266). But the standard of proof is still the civil standard, ie balance of probabilities (*Henwood v Barlow Clowes International Ltd* [2008] EWCA Civ 577, [2008] All ER (D) 330 (May), 88; *Holliday v Musa* [2010] EWCA Civ 335, para 67).

DOMICILE OF CHOICE

44.3 The modern law on domicile of choice is founded on Scarman J's judgment in *Re Fuld's Estate (No 3) Hartley v Fuld* [1968] P 675. In a much-quoted passage, he expressed himself as follows:

> 'a domicile of choice is acquired when a man fixes voluntarily his sole or chief residence in a particular place with an intention of continuing to reside there for an unlimited time.'

This formulation was followed by the Law Commission in their 1987 report on the law of domicile (Cmnd 200). That report states the individual must both reside in the new country and have an intention 'to make his home in [the new] country permanently or indefinitely'. This passage of the Law Commission's report was cited with approval in Lady Hale's speech in *Mark v Mark* [2005] UKHL 42, [2005] 3 All ER 912 (at para 39), and as a result now has the authority of the House of Lords.

An individual can only acquire a domicile of choice once he has attained the age of 16.

Residence

44.4 As the Law Commission report makes clear, in the context of the law domicile the concept of residence has nothing to do with tax residence. For the purposes of the law of domicile, an individual resides in a country if it is in that country that he has his sole or main home. The acquisition of a domicile of choice involves the fact of residence as well as intention, and a residence only counts as such if it is the person's sole or chief residence. Thus in *Plummer v IRC* [1988] 1 All ER 97, [1987] STC 698, a young lady who intended to reside permanently in Guernsey did not acquire a domicile of choice there because her chief residence was in England, her home in Guernsey being on the facts merely secondary. So too in *IRC v Duchess of Portland* [1982] STC 149, a lady failed to abandon an English domicile of choice because, although she did not intend to remain permanently in England, her chief residence was there.

Most cases on the law of domicile were decided when travel was much slower and as a result it was usually clear where an individual's main home was. The speed of modern travel means that this is no longer so and as a result it may be difficult to determine which of two or more homes is the individual's main home.

In making the determination the quality of the individual's residence has to be looked at, the issue being which country he intends to reside in permanently (*Henwood v Barlow Clowes International Ltd* [2008] EWCA Civ 577, (2008) Times, 18 June, para 104). There is thus an overlap between the fact of residence and the intention to reside permanently. Both the individual's actions at the time of the alleged change and his subsequent conduct are material in determining which residence is his chief residence (*Gaines-Cooper v HMRC* [2007] EWHC 2617 (Ch), [2008] STC 1665, at para 44).

Retention of accommodation in the country of origin does not preclude the acquisition of a domicile of choice elsewhere if, on the facts, the new country is the main home (*Shaffer v Cilento* [2004] EWHC 188 (Ch), [2004] All ER (D) 122 (Feb)). But it may be difficult to show that the new country is the individual's chief residence if his accommodation in the old country is his former home, particularly if his social and business activities there continue and statements made on his behalf indicate that he is looking forward to resuming permanent residence there (*Gaines-Cooper v HMRC* [2007] EWHC 2617 (Ch), [2008] STC 1665, at paras 64–65).

Even if accommodation is not retained in the country of origin, the availability of homes in more than one other country may mean that none can be said to be the individual's chief residence. All could, on the facts, be temporary or holiday homes (*Henwood v Barlow Clowes International Ltd* [2008] EWCA Civ 577, (2008) Times, 18 June, para 140). It is most unlikely that a particular home will be the chief residence if that home is rented rather than owned, if the individual has no right of residence in the country of question, and if he spends more of his time in one of his other homes (*Henwood v Barlow Clowes International Ltd*, passim).

Intention

44.5 The use of the word 'indefinitely' in the formulation of the intention requirement might be thought to imply the test is satisfied in any case where the individual does not know when he will leave the new country. But in reality indefinitely carries much the same implications as permanently. It is not enough that at any given time the length of the individual's stay in the new country has not been determined. Rather the new country must be the place where he intends to end his days (*Henwood v Barlow Clowes International Ltd* [2008] EWCA Civ 577, (2008) Times, 18 June, paras 10 and 14).

Two Court of Appeal decisions illustrate that the threshold connoted by permanent or indefinite intention is high. The more recent, *Cyganik v Agulian* [2006] 8 ITELR 762 concerned a Greek Cypriot who died in 2003 having lived in the UK for 43 years. The Court of Appeal cited passages in Scarman J's judgment in *Re Fuld*, to the effect that the necessary intention is lacking if the individual intends to return to the land of his birth 'upon a clearly foreseen and reasonably anticipated contingency', such as the end of his job. But the position is otherwise if what he has in mind is only a vague possibility, such as making a fortune or some sentiment about dying in the land of his fathers. Applying this test, the Court of Appeal decided that the individual in *Cyganik v Agulian* was still domiciled in Cyprus.

The other, much earlier, decision of the Court Appeal is *IRC v Bullock* [1976] STC 409. Here the taxpayer, who was Canadian, had come to England in 1932 to serve in the RAF, and he had married an English lady in 1947. He had lived in England since 1932, and HMRC asserted for 1971–72 and 1972–73 that he had acquired an English domicile of choice. His wife, who was four years younger, would not contemplate moving to Canada, but the evidence was the taxpayer would go back there if she predeceased him. The Court of Appeal decided in these circumstances that he still had a Canadian domicile.

In the course of reaching this decision the Court of Appeal reviewed nineteenth century cases as well as *Re Fuld*. The Court concluded that a domicile of choice is only acquired if the individual 'intends to make his home in the new country until the end of his days unless and until something happens to make him change his mind' (at p 415). The existence of a contingency on which he would return to his country of origin negatives the necessary intention provided the contingency is not doubtful or indefinite and there is a sufficiently substantial possibility of it happening.

Return to the country of origin

44.6 Despite what is said in some of the passages cited above, the intention which has to be proved is the intention to remain permanently or indefinitely in the new country. It does not have to be proved that the contingency on which the individual would leave entails his return to his country of origin (*Cyganik v Agulian* [2006] 8 ITELR 762 para 49)). It is important that the individual has the necessary intention to remain in one particular country as his main home: it is not sufficient to acquire a domicile of choice if the individual is unclear which of several countries he will finally settle in even though he has no intention of ever returning to his country of origin (cf *Surveyor v IRC* [2002] STC (SCD) 501; *Henwood v Barlow Clowes International Ltd* [2008] EWCA Civ 577, (2008) Times, 18 June).

Length of stay

44.7 Both *Cyganik v Agulian* and *IRC v Bullock* show that an individual can live in a country for many years without acquiring a domicile of choice there, as each concerned residence in the UK for 40 or more years. However, in *Holliday v Musa* [2010] EWCA Civ 335 the Court of Appeal said that it would be a strong starting point in demonstrating the acquisition of a domicile of choice if the individual had clearly set up his home for a very long time in the new country, had his family there, and did not have his home elsewhere (at para 67).

Evidence of intention

44.8 A person only acquires a domicile of choice in the new country if his intention to remain there is firm and settled (*Re Clore, Official Solicitor v Clore (No 2)* [1984] STC 609). Another way of putting the same point is that the intention must be clear and unequivocal (*Cyganik v Agulian* at para 51). What an individual intended has to be ascertained as a fact by a process of inference from all the available evidence (*Cyganik v Agulian* at para 13). All that the individual has said and done must be looked at. Account can be taken of what the individual said and did after the alleged change of domicile as well as what he said and did before (*Bheekhun v Williams* [1999] 2 FLR 229).

The task which has to be undertaken was described in graphic terms by Megarry J in *Re Flynn; Flynn v Flynn* [1968] 1 All ER 49, 51:

> 'In one sense there is no end to the evidence that may be adduced; for the whole of a man's life and all that he has said and done, however trivial, may be prayed in aid in determining what his intention was at any given moment in time. The state of a man's mind is as much a fact as the state of his digestion, but, as Harman LJ is reputed to have observed, "the doctors know precious little about the one and the judges know nothing about the other". The difficulty is as old as the Year Books and the celebrated dictum of Brian CJ in 1477, uttered in theological terms which have waned in fashion: *"Le Diable n'ad conusance de l'entent de home"*. All that the courts can do is to draw inferences from what has been said and done; and in doing this, too much detail may stultify.'

Statements the person has made are not necessarily conclusive in determining whether he has acquired a domicile of choice. Thus in *Wahl v A-G* [1932] 147 LT 382, HL, a German applied for British naturalisation and stated to the Home Secretary that he intended to reside permanently in the UK and had no intention of leaving it. This, however, was held to be insufficient to displace other evidence that a domicile of choice had not been acquired. Statements to HMRC that the individual intends to remain indefinitely in the UK are not conclusive as to domicile either. Nor even are statements in an HMRC affidavit that the deceased was UK domiciled if there is no evidence that the issue had been properly considered by the person swearing the affidavit (*Buswell v IRC* [1974] STC 266; *Re Furse; Furse v IRC* [1980] STC 596).

The acquisition of nationality and a passport in the new country can point to the acquisition of a domicile of choice there but it is not conclusive evidence. Thus in *Bheekhun v Williams* [1999] 2 FLR 229 the deceased was a Mauritian who had come to the UK in 1960, and chose to retain a British passport when Mauritius became independent in 1968. The trial judge and the Court of Appeal accepted evidence that the deceased was then considering remaining in the UK and concluded he had acquired a UK domicile of choice. But in *F v IRC* [2000] STC (SCD) 1, an Iranian exile with long-standing UK connections, including a UK home, obtained indefinite leave to remain in the UK in 1980 and British citizenship and a passport in 1982. On the evidence he intended always to return to Iran when it was safe to do so, and had acquired a British passport merely for travel convenience. On these facts, a Special Commissioner found he retained his Iranian domicile.

The fact that the individual is in the new country illegally does not, per se, prevent him from acquiring a domicile of choice there although it is clearly relevant in determining his intention (*Mark v Mark* [2005] 3 All ER 912).

Abandonment

44.9 A domicile of choice may be abandoned. For this to happen, the country of choice must cease to be the individual's main residence and he must cease to intend to resume main residence there (*Re Flynn; Flynn v Flynn* [1968] 1 All ER 49; *IRC v Duchess of Portland* [1982] STC 149). The change of intention need not be a positive decision not to return but may simply be a withering of intention so that at some point it can be said the intention has gone (*Shaffer v Cilento* [2004] EWHC 188 (Ch), [2004] All ER (D) 122 (Feb)). Nonetheless, the absence of intention must be unequivocal and, as with the acquisition of a domicile of choice, is not to be lightly inferred.

A practical question of some importance is whether an individual with a domicile of origin in the UK who has acquired a foreign domicile of choice loses that domicile if he has to return to the UK for medical reasons and eventually dies there. The Special Commissioner's decision in *Allen v Revenue and Customs Comrs* [2005] STC (SCD) 614 indicates that the domicile of choice is not lost if the foreign home is kept and maintained ready for occupation and it is clear on the facts the individual would return there, if, for example, the family members caring for him would accompany him. But the domicile of choice can be lost if the foreign home is let on a long-term basis, even if the letting is to members of the individual's family (*Henwood v Barlow Clowes International Ltd* [2008] EWCA Civ 577, (2008) Times, 18 June, 118).

The UK Government in Budget 2015 announced proposals affecting individuals with a UK domicile of origin and a place of birth in the UK who have acquired a foreign domicile of choice and resume tax residence in the UK (which under the statutory residence test would be possible without the individual having necessarily abandoned their foreign domicile of choice). If these proposals are introduced, with effect from 6 April 2017, for UK tax purposes the individual's UK domicile of origin will be treated as immediately reviving upon the resumption of their UK residence, regardless of their intentions. The likely tax implications of this are discussed in CHAPTER 45.

DOMICILE OF DEPENDENCY

44.10 A domicile of dependency can be attributed only to a child under 16. A child's domicile of origin is displaced by a domicile of dependency if the domicile of the parent upon whom the child's domicile depends changes. If this happens the domicile of choice, which the parent thereby acquires, becomes the child's domicile of dependency. On attaining 16 a domicile of dependency is retained by the child as a domicile of choice. But if the child does not live in the territory and never intends to live there, this acquired domicile of choice is forthwith abandoned. Normally in these circumstances the child's domicile of origin revives but if he is living in a third territory with the intention of remaining there, that territory becomes his domicile of choice (*Re Scullard, Smith v Brock* [1957] Ch 107).

The domicile on which a child under 16 normally depends is that of his father, but his mother's domicile is the relevant domicile if the child is illegitimate, the father is dead, or the parents are separated and the child has no home with the father (see Law Commission report on the Law of Domicile, Cmnd 200 (1987) pp 4–5).

Until 1974, a married woman did not enjoy an independent domicile but took her husband's domicile as a domicile of dependency. This rule was abolished in 1973 (Domicile and Matrimonial Proceedings Act 1973, s 1). A married woman's domicile is now determined independently in the same way as that of her husband. But a woman who on 1 January 1974 had her husband's domicile, as a domicile of dependency, retained that domicile as a domicile of choice and must abandon it before she can acquire, or reacquire, her own domicile (*IRC v Duchess of Portland* [1982] Ch 314, [1982] STC 149). It appears from the *Duchess of Portland* case that, where the woman is residing in the UK, such abandonment is only possible by leaving the UK to make her home (or chief residence) abroad.

ESTABLISHING AN INDIVIDUAL'S DOMICILE

Practice

44.11 HMRC has published guidance giving their view of the law of domicile and indicating questions they may ask and information they may seek if looking into an individual's domicile (Business Brief 17/2009, reproduced [2009] SWTI 806).

Those leaving the UK

44.12 Where a UK domiciliary migrates he may wish to establish that he has acquired a foreign domicile of choice before entering into a particular transaction. In this situation HMRC will not give a hypothetical ruling, and so the best solution is for the taxpayer to wait until three complete tax years have elapsed and then make a gift of foreign situs assets in excess of the IHT nil-rate band to a trust.

In general HMRC expect a taxpayer to be able to decide for himself whether he is UK domiciled and, assuming he has neither an actual nor a deemed UK domicile, not trouble HMRC should he make gift of foreign situs assets into a settlement. In the past, if an IHT account was submitted, HMRC would give a decision on domicile if at least £10,000 of tax was at stake (Business Brief 17/2009). Now however HMRC will only consider making a determination where there is a significant risk of UK tax being lost. The amount of tax required to cross this threshold is not stated, and a balance is struck between the tax 'at risk' and the potential cost of the enquiry. If an enquiry is opened, personal information about the taxpayer and his family may be required (HMRC Brief 34/2010, reproduced [2010] SWTI p 2452).

It is necessary to wait for three complete tax years before making a gift into settlement because, for IHT purposes, a UK domicile is deemed to persist for three years after it is in fact lost (see CHAPTER 45 regarding the IHT deemed domicile rules). Provided the gift consists of foreign situs assets, IHT will be chargeable unless the taxpayer has lost both his actual and his deemed UK domicile. Accordingly, if in fact HMRC do not seek to charge IHT, it will be clear that they accept he has acquired a foreign domicile.

In practical terms, HMRC are prepared to accept that migrants from the UK have acquired a foreign domicile if the facts warrant this. One point, however, is important. Once the three-year period has elapsed, the foreign domicile of the taxpayer should if practical be established immediately. This safeguards the position if, later, the taxpayer has to return to the UK for medical or other reasons, for, once he has returned, it may be difficult to prove an intention to remain abroad indefinitely (and note also the proposed change to the tax treatment of returning UK domiciliaries discussed at **44.9** above).

UK residents

44.13 In past years, HMRC would accept foreign domicile claims on Forms DOM 1 or P86. Now however, Form DOM 1 has been withdrawn and HMRC deal with claims to foreign domicile by enquiring into the individual's self-assessment return. The risk-based approach described above applies (Brief 34/2010).

PROPOSALS FOR CHANGE

44.14 The 1987 Law Commission paper referred to above recommended changes to the law of domicile (Cmnd 200). The recommendations were enshrined in a draft Bill, the main points of which were as follows:

(1)   The domicile of origin should be abolished.
(2)   A child's domicile should be that of the country with which he is most closely connected. In the absence of evidence to the contrary, this country would be presumed to be the country where his parents are domiciled.
(3)   On attaining adulthood, a person should retain his childhood domicile unless and until he acquires another domicile.

(4)   An adult should acquire a new domicile if he is present in a new country and intends to remain there for an indefinite period. He should keep that domicile unless and until he acquires another one.

At the time of writing there is no proposal to give effect to these recommendations or otherwise reform the law of domicile. The changes made in 2008 were to the tax consequences of foreign domicile, not to the law of domicile itself. Similarly, the April 2017 changes mentioned above will not impact upon the law of domicile itself.

Chapter 45

DEEMED DOMICILE

The authors would like to give special thanks to Sangna Chauhan of Charles Russell Speechlys LLP for her help with this chapter

INTRODUCTION

45.1 Under current law, the concept of deemed domicile only has relevance for inheritance tax (IHT). The question of whether an individual is domiciled in the UK for income tax and CGT, and accordingly whether he is entitled to use the remittance basis of taxation as a foreign domiciliary, is currently determined solely by the common law principles discussed in the last chapter.

However, this is due to change. The Government intends to introduce new deemed domicile rules which will govern the question of whether an individual is treated as domiciled in the UK for the purposes of all three taxes, from 6 April 2017. These proposed new rules are considered at the end of this chapter, but the focus of the chapter is on the current deemed domicile rules which, as noted above, only affect an individual's tax status for the purposes of IHT.

Under the existing IHT legislation, there are three separate deeming rules. An individual who is not actually domiciled in any part of the UK under the common law principles will be deemed to be UK domiciled on a particular date if:

(a)   17 or more of the 20 tax years culminating in the tax year in which the relevant date falls are years of UK residence (IHTA 1984, s 267(1)(b)) (this is sometimes referred to as 'the 17 years rule');

(b)   at the relevant date, fewer than three calendar years have elapsed since the individual ceased to be actually domiciled in any part of the UK under the common law principles (IHTA 1984, s 267(1)(a)) (this is sometimes referred to as 'the 3 years rule'); or

(c)   the individual has made a valid election to be treated as domiciled in the UK, which is still in effect (IHTA 1984, s 267ZA).

This chapter considers the application of the rules in s 267(1). It also considers the 'domicile mismatch' issue which domicile elections are intended to address, and the details of how domicile elections are made and their effects. The effect of treaties on the deemed domicile rules for IHT is examined in CHAPTER 105.

THE '17 YEARS RULE'

45.2 Under the common law principles discussed in the last chapter, it is possible for an individual with a foreign domicile of origin to reside in the UK and remain non-UK domiciled for a number of decades, provided that he does not form the intention to reside in any part of the UK permanently or indefinitely. However, such individuals are not permitted to enjoy the IHT benefits of non-UK domiciled status without time limit. Indefinite enjoyment of such benefits is prevented by the '17 years rule' in s 267(1)(b).

The maximum period in which non-UK domiciled status for IHT can be preserved, as a UK resident, is 16 years from the date of 'arrival' in the UK. However, in practice the period is usually shorter than this. Deemed domiciled status under s 267(1)(b) may be acquired in as little as 15 years and two days after 'arrival'. This is because residence for the purposes of s 267(1)(b) is determined in accordance with income tax principles (s 267(4)) but without regard for the split year concession which sometimes applied under the pre-April 2013 law of residence, and likewise without regard for any division under the current statutory residence test of a tax year into a resident and non-resident part. Residence for income tax purposes in any part of a tax year is treated for the purposes of the '17 years rule' as residence throughout that tax year. Thus if an individual becomes resident in the UK on 5 April in one year, he will clock up two tax years of UK residence for the purposes of the '17 years rule' in the space of two days, and the beginning of the 17th tax year of residence will arrive a year sooner than he may expect.

Similarly, if a non-UK domiciled individual is in his 16th consecutive tax year of UK residence, and he wishes to avoid the acquisition of a deemed UK domicile under s 267(1)(b), it is essential that he ceases to be UK resident before the end of the 16th tax year of residence. Tax residence in the following tax year will cause the test in s 267(1)(b) to be satisfied, and bring the deeming rule into play. This is so even if split-year relief applies in that tax year, and even if the effect of such relief is that the period of taxability as a resident is minimal.

The availability of relief from UK taxation under an income/gains/profits DTT, on the basis that the individual may have been treaty resident in another country in some or even all of the tax years in which he was resident in the UK (see CHAPTER 100) is also irrelevant for the '17 years rule'. The rule looks at the number of tax years of residence in the UK as a matter of domestic law.

Once it becomes the case that, of the 20 tax years culminating in the present tax year, 17 or more are years of UK residence, a significant period of non-UK residence is needed to 'break' the deemed domicile under s 276(1)(b). Four complete tax years of non-UK residence are required. If this can be achieved, the deemed domicile falls away at the end of the third such year.

THE '3 YEARS RULE'

45.3 The common law allows an individual to abandon a domicile in the UK (whether a domicile of origin or a domicile of choice) for a domicile in another jurisdiction (see CHAPTER 44).

However, s 267(1)(a) imposes a delay of three years between the date on which an individual loses a domicile in the UK for general purposes and the date on which (subject to the possible application of s 267(1)(b), as discussed below) he ceases to be UK domiciled for IHT purposes. Any non-exempt gifts made within this three-year period will continue to be within the scope of IHT, and in the event of death within this period IHT will be charged on the entire estate, subject to the exemptions for transfers to spouses and charities.

Unlike the '17 years rule', s 267(1)(a) does not specifically refer to 'years of assessment' and so it is generally accepted that the rule refers to calendar years.

This rule is not without its traps. Consider the example of an individual with a UK domicile of origin who has moved to (for example) Monaco and established a domicile of choice there. Suppose that he has been a Monegasque domiciliary for long enough to have escaped the effect of s 267(1)(a) following the cessation of his UK residence; but that he then decides that Monaco is not for him and that he would much prefer to live in (for example) Canada and make that his permanent home. As discussed in the previous chapter, by leaving Monaco and ceasing to intend to reside in Monaco permanently, the individual will abandon his domicile of choice there. Until he arrives in a province or territory of Canada and makes it his permanent home, the individual's domicile of origin in the UK will revive. The three-year clock for the purposes of s 267(1)(a) will restart, with the effect that the individual must acquire a domicile of choice in a particular province or territory of Canada, and retain that domicile for a further three years, before he is able to claim he is no longer within the UK IHT net.

However, as explained below, in some cases there may be scope to claim treaty protection against the effects of the deemed domicile rules.

OVERLAP BETWEEN THE RULES

45.4 As noted above, where an individual has become deemed domiciled under the '17 years rule', the deemed domicile persists until the end of the third complete tax year of non-UK residence, provided that the individual does not become a UK resident again in the following tax year.

The '17 years rule' is often thought of as being limited in scope to individuals who are not, and never have been, domiciled in the UK as a matter of common law. However, it is not in its terms so limited, and is therefore capable of applying also where a former UK domiciliary has taken on a new domicile as a matter of common law, on or after ceasing to reside in the UK. In other words, there can be overlap between the '17 years rule' and the '3 years rule'.

This overlap can necessitate extra care when calculating the date on which the deemed domicile will cease to apply. Take the example of an individual with a common law domicile in the UK, who has been UK resident for the last 20 tax years. If this individual moves to a new jurisdiction with the intention of residing there permanently or indefinitely, then under common law principles he or she will acquire a new domicile of choice. The individual will cease to be deemed domiciled in the UK under the '3 years rule' three calendar years after the change of common law domicile. However, under the '17 years rule', the individual will continue to be deemed domiciled until there have been three complete tax years of non-UK residence. At best, deemed domicile will fall away simultaneously under the two rules. At worst, the effect of the '17 years rule' will be a postponement of the loss of deemed domicile until nearly four years have elapsed since the change of common law domicile.

DOMICILE MISMATCHES

45.5 Transfers of value between spouses and civil partners are generally exempt from IHT, without limit (IHTA 1984, s 18). However, where a UK domiciliary, or a non-UK domiciliary who is deemed to be domiciled in the UK for IHT purposes, makes a transfer of value to a non-UK domiciled spouse or civil partner (who is not deemed domiciled in the UK), the exemption is limited by the operation of s 18(2). Transfers of value between spouses and between civil partners are treated identically. In the interests of brevity, the following discussion is couched in terms of spouses, but all references to spouses should be taken as including civil partners. Similarly, the chapter refers to UK domiciled individuals as shorthand for individuals who are actually UK domiciled or are deemed domiciled for IHT purposes, whereas references to non-UK domiciled individuals should be taken to mean individuals who are neither actually UK domiciled nor deemed domiciled.

Until 6 April 2013, the exemption for a transfer of value from a UK domiciled individual to his or her non-UK domiciled spouse was capped at a mere £55,000 (which represented the nil-rate band as at March 1983, when the provision was introduced). For transfers of value since 6 April 2013, however, the limited spouse exemption has been increased to the prevailing nil-rate band amount (IHTA 1984, s 18(2A)), ie £325,000 at present.

DOMICILE ELECTIONS

45.6 To cater for couples with domicile mismatches, in cases where the limited spouse exemption is insufficient to prevent IHT arising on lifetime gifts or transfers on death from UK domiciled individuals to their non-UK domiciled spouses, Finance Act 2013 introduced two forms of domicile election, intended for use where a non-UK domiciled individual has received, or expects to receive, a gift or legacy from a UK domiciled spouse. Once such an election has been made, the elector will be treated as domiciled in the UK and transfers of value made by the UK domiciled spouse in the period of validity of the election will benefit from the unlimited spouse exemption contained in IHTA 1984, s 18(1).

As with the deeming rules in IHTA 1984, s 267, such elections have effect for IHT purposes only; an election will not alter the elector's domicile under common law principles, so it will not prejudice the availability of the remittance basis.

There are two types of election: one which can be made during the lifetime of a UK domiciled spouse (known as the 'lifetime election') and one which can only be made following the death of a UK domiciled spouse (known as the 'death election'). The relevant provisions are in IHTA 1984, s 267ZA and s 267ZB.

Death elections

45.7 A death election may be made by a non-UK domiciliary within two years of the death of a UK domiciled spouse (although this two-year period can be extended with the consent of HMRC).

When making a death election, the elector can specify the date on which the election should take effect: either from the date of the spouse's death or from a date up to seven years preceding the date of death. If no date is specified, it will be valid from the date of the spouse's death. It is not possible to make an election for an effective date earlier than 6 April 2013.

The ability to backdate the election by up to seven years before the death of the UK domiciled spouse means that it can be used not only to prevent an IHT charge on assets passing to the non-UK domiciliary on the death of the UK domiciled spouse, but can also be used to convert, retrospectively, lifetime gifts made by the UK domiciliary to the non-UK domiciled spouse from 'failed' potentially exempt transfers into exempt transfers.

Initially, the 6 April 2013 longstop date referred to above will limit the usefulness of elections to deal with 'failed' PETs, but the ability to backdate will of course become more useful as time goes on.

Lifetime elections

45.8 A lifetime election can be made at any time by the non-UK domiciled spouse of a UK domiciliary. The effective date can be up to seven years preceding the date on which the election is made, but (again) not earlier than 6 April 2013. If no date is specified, the election will be valid from the date that it is made.

As with the death election, backdating the lifetime election by up to seven years will allow PETs made after 6 April 2013 by a UK domiciliary to his or her non-UK domiciled spouse to be treated as exempt. Given the ability to backdate death elections, the advantages of making a lifetime election may not be immediately obvious. There are, however, a few circumstances in which a lifetime election will be preferable to a death election:

- One such is where the UK domiciliary has made a lifetime gift to the non-UK domiciled spouse but has continued to benefit from the subject matter of the gift, so that the gift with reservation rules are in point. Where a gift qualifies for the spouse exemption, the GWR rules are generally excluded (FA 1986, s 102(5)(a)). However, the GWR rules are not excluded to the extent that a transfer of value between spouses is non-exempt, due to the limited spouse exemption discussed above. Making a domicile election can eliminate a domicile mismatch at the time of such a gift, thereby taking the subject-matter of the gift outside the GWR rules. A death election may not be sufficient for these purposes: if the domiciled spouse made the gift more than seven years before their death, it will be too late to wait until his or her death to make the election.

- As explained below, an elected UK domicile will persist until the elector has been non-UK resident for four complete tax years from the date on which the election is made (not, it should be noted, from when it takes effect). In the event that the non-UK domiciled spouse is non-resident, a lifetime election will start this four-year run-off earlier than waiting until death to make the election. This may be especially useful in situations where assets are unlikely to pass from the UK domiciled spouse to the non-UK domiciliary on death, thereby eliminating the need for a death election.

Practical implications

45.9 For an election to be made under s 267ZA, the elector must have had a UK domiciled spouse at the date on which the election takes effect. There is no requirement that the couple remain married for the duration of the deemed domicile and so a backdated election may be made even if the marriage has, by the date of the election, been dissolved. There is also no requirement that the UK domiciled spouse remains UK domiciled after the election has been made. The elector may have become UK domiciled for IHT purposes (eg under the '17 years rule') by the time that he or she makes the election, provided that a domicile mismatch subsisted on the effective date of the election.

Elections have been available since 6 April 2013. As noted above, it is not possible to make an election for a death prior to 6 April 2013, or to make an election which is capable of changing the status of any 'failed' PETs made by the UK domiciled spouse to the non-UK domiciled spouse before that date. In the event that a lifetime gift by the UK domiciled spouse has been made which was a PET, and which cannot be converted into a spouse-exempt transfer through the making of an election, term insurance may be considered to cover the IHT risk in the seven years from the gift. However, this will not, in itself, address any GWR issues.

Once made, the election is irrevocable. A non-UK domiciliary who has made an election will only cease to be deemed domiciled under the election regime once he or she has been non-UK tax resident for four complete tax years from the date on which the election was made. Note that the date on which the election was *made* may be different than the date on which the election is treated as having *taken effect*.

The decision to make an election should not be made without careful consideration and due diligence. The entire estate of the elector will of course be brought within the scope of IHT whilst the election remains valid. The start of the election period can be up to nine years before the date the election is actually made, and any gifts of non-UK assets made by the elector during the period of validity of the election (other than gifts to the UK domiciled spouse or to charity) will be brought within the scope of IHT, either as PETs (which will of course only be chargeable in the event of the elector's death within seven years) or as immediately chargeable transfers (in the case of gifts to settlements).

If the non-UK domiciled spouse has established and funded an excluded property settlement in the period, the effect of making the election will be particularly far-reaching, as not only will any gift to the trust be rendered chargeable to IHT, retrospectively, but there will also be a loss of excluded property status of non-UK assets of the trust, for as long as the trust subsists. The settlement will be pushed into the relevant property regime. However, on one view, this impact on the ongoing tax treatment of the trust is avoided in the event that the trust was settled by the non-UK domiciliary before the start of the period of validity of the election, albeit funded substantively within that period. There is a strong technical argument that in this latter scenario, the excluded property status of all non-UK assets of the trust is unaffected by the settlor's UK domicile when gifts were made to the trust, provided that he or she was non-UK domiciled on the date of commencement of the settlement. However, HMRC are known to take a different view (see para **53.6**).

If the effect of an election is to render earlier gifts by the elector subject to IHT, s 267ZB(8) makes provision for the filing of an IHT account, payment of the IHT and calculation of interest.

Both types of election are to be ignored in relation to any of the existing IHT treaties (s 267ZA(6)). Therefore an election to be treated as UK domiciled under s 267ZA will not affect the elector's domicile for the purposes of any the treaties that are discussed below.

PROPOSED REFORM

45.10 The discussion above is based on the legislation as it now stands. However, in the 2015 Summer Budget, the Government announced its intention to make significant changes to the tax rules regarding foreign domiciliaries. This announcement has now been followed up with an initial consultation published in September 2015 and a further consultation on various aspects of the draft legislation that was issued on 18 August 2016. Following the Autumn Statement on 23 November 2016, further draft clauses for consultation prior to inclusion in the Finance Bill 2017 will be published on Monday 5 December 2016. This consultation will be open until Monday 30 January 2017.

New '15 years' rule

45.11 The Government has proposed that from 6 April 2017, individuals will be treated as deemed domiciled for *all* tax purposes, including IHT, once they have been resident in the UK for 15 or more out of the preceding 20 tax years. In a typical case, this will mean that deemed domicile for all tax purposes will apply from the start of the 16th tax year of residence in the UK.

Because the new rule will look at the number of tax years of residence in the *preceding* 20, it will have the effect that an individual who is currently in his 15th consecutive tax year of residence will not be able to avoid the acquisition of deemed domiciled status merely by not being resident in the following tax year. A deemed domicile within the UK will be acquired at the start of the following tax year even if that is a year of non-residence, and this will of course affect the individual's IHT position, even if the deemed domicile is, at least for the time being, irrelevant to his status for income tax and CGT. Foreign domiciliaries wishing to ensure that they do not become deemed domiciled under this rule will therefore have to 'leave' the UK before the end of their 14th year of tax residence.

On the face of it, the phrasing of this '15 years rule' also increases the number of years of non-UK residence that are required before such deemed domicile can be 'broken' to six. Whilst this will remain the case for income tax and CGT, following consultation, the Government has stated that deemed domicile for IHT purposes will fall away after a continuous period of four tax years of non-residence, provided that residence in the UK is not resumed in the six-year period. To reflect the general IHT position, the Government has also confirmed that domicile elections will remain unaffected and that, as under the current law, their effect will persist for four complete tax years.

Whether or not a particular tax year counts as a year of residence for the purposes of the '15 years rule' will need to be determined by reference to the residence rules and HMRC practice that applied in the tax year in question. As is currently the case, tax years of residence will be counted without regard to any treaty relief, and a tax year of residence will count towards the total even if in a large part of it the individual was non-taxable by virtue of split-year treatment.

New UK origin rule

45.12 In addition to the above, the new legislation will also treat as UK domiciled any individual who is domiciled outside the UK as a matter of common law, but who had a domicile of origin within the UK, who was born within the UK and is, in the relevant tax year, UK resident. It is possible for an individual who had a domicile of origin within the UK to have acquired a foreign domicile of choice, and for the individual to have retained that foreign domicile under the common law rules even though he may be spending time in, and even be tax resident in, the UK (see para **44.9**). However, the availability of the tax benefits of non-UK domiciled status for such individuals is regarded as unacceptable by the Government.

From 6 April 2017, such individuals will be deemed domiciled in the UK, for income tax and CGT purposes, in any tax year in which they are UK resident. For IHT the position will be broadly the same, but there will be an exemption from the deemed domicile if the individual was not UK resident in either of the preceding two tax years. The effect of this, in relation to an individual who has become UK resident following a non-resident period, is to provide a one year 'grace period' before the onset of deemed domicile for IHT purposes.

Where IHT is concerned, the consequences of any such deemed domicile will be severe. It appears that if the individual has established a settlement after the loss of IHT domicile in the UK, so that the non-UK assets of the settlement enjoy excluded property status (see CHAPTER **62**), such status will be withdrawn from the beginning of the first tax year in which the individual is treated as UK domiciled for IHT purposes.

This will bring the settlement into the relevant property regime (see CHAPTER **60**) and also, much more seriously, will remove the protection from the gift with reservation of benefit rules which is available for any settlement whose assets are excluded property (see para **83.20**).

Section IV

The Remittance Basis

Chapter 46

ELIGIBILITY FOR THE REMITTANCE BASIS

INTRODUCTION

46.1 This part of the book explains technical details of the remittance basis. As is explained in CHAPTER 12, the foreign income and gains of non-domiciliaries are not taxed unless remitted. But this treatment is only available if certain conditions are met, and the law as to what constitutes a remittance is technical and wider than might be supposed.

This and the next chapter deal with eligibility for the remittance basis, including details of the remittance basis charge. CHAPTERS 48 to 50 examine the categories of income and gains that are eligible for the remittance basis, and then CHAPTERS 51 to 57 explain what is meant by remittance. Finally, CHAPTERS 58 and 59 consider a number of reliefs which render certain kinds of remittance tax free.

ELIGIBILITY

46.2 The starting point in considering the remittance basis is to identify who is eligible, and what income and gains qualify.

Foreign domicile

46.3 Under current law, any UK resident non-UK domiciliary can use the remittance basis. However in the great majority of cases the remittance basis does not apply unless a claim is made, as described below.

For these purposes domicile is governed by English general law, as explained in CHAPTER 44; in relation to income tax and CGT, there is yet no concept of deemed domicile such as applies to inheritance tax. However, as CHAPTER 45 explains, significant reforms to the taxation of non-UK domiciliaries have been proposed, and are expected to take effect on 6 April 2017. They include a new rule under which a non-UK domiciliary will be deemed domiciled for all tax purposes, and thus ineligible for the remittance basis, once it becomes the case that 15 or more out of the preceding 20 tax years were years of UK residence.

Change of domicile

46.4 The question is sometimes raised whether an individual can use the remittance basis in a tax year in which he is initially non-UK domiciled, but in the course of which he acquires a domicile within the UK. The sections of the legislation which allow the remittance basis to apply (ITA 2007, ss 809B, 809D and 809E) apply in a given tax year if the individual 'is not domiciled in the United Kingdom in that year'. It seems a reasonable inference that the individual must be non-UK domiciled throughout the tax year. There is no provision in the legislation for tax years to be split into non-UK domiciled and UK domiciled parts; the remittance basis either applies for the entirety of a tax year or not at all.

Other ineligible persons

46.5 Historically, certain categories of foreign income accruing to those who were resident but not ordinarily resident in the UK attracted the remittance basis regardless of domicile. However, this is no longer the law, and now domicile is the sole determinant of eligibility for the remittance basis. UK domiciliaries are no longer able to use the remittance basis in any circumstances.

The remittance basis applies only to the income and gains of individuals. It is not available to UK resident trustees even if all the trustees are non-UK domiciled. However, should the trust be subject to an interest in possession, the remittance basis is available as respects trust income, assuming the life tenant is non-UK domiciled and makes the necessary claim. This is because the income is taxed as his (see para **8.2**).

Qualifying income and gains

46.6 Assuming a non-domiciliary claims or is otherwise entitled to the remittance basis, it applies to his foreign income and gains. That term is defined as follows (ITA 2007, s 809Z7):

- Relevant foreign income. In broad terms this means investment income which has a foreign source, but the term extends to certain gains in respect of foreign assets, which are treated as income for the purposes of the UK tax code, and also to foreign trading income and foreign rental income. The term is explained further in paras **48.2** to **48.6**.
- Chargeable overseas earnings. This term is explained in para **50.5** and in summary means earnings from employments with foreign employers where all the duties are performed abroad.
- Foreign specific employment income. This term refers to certain kinds of income treated as arising under the employment-related securities legislation (see para **50.14**).
- Foreign chargeable gains. These are gains accruing on assets whose situs is foreign under the CGT situs rules (see further para **49.1** and Chapter 39).

THE CLAIM

46.7 As a general rule, the remittance basis is not available unless the taxpayer makes a claim under ITA 2007, s 809B. The general rules as to claims apply (s 809B(3); TMA 1970, ss 42 and 43) and so a claim to the remittance basis must be made within four years of the end of the relevant year of assessment. It should, where possible, be made in the non-domiciliary's return (TMA 1970, s 42(2)).

All claims under s 809B must include a statement that the taxpayer is non-UK domiciled. A further requirement is imposed if the taxpayer was UK resident in at least seven of the preceding nine tax years (s 809C). This is that the claim must nominate income or gains for the purposes of the remittance basis charge discussed in CHAPTER 47.

Withdrawal of claim

46.8 Where a claim to the remittance basis has been made, it can be withdrawn subsequently within the usual statutory time limits, ie:

- Within 12 months after the filing date for a claim made in the self-assessment return (TMA 1970, s 9ZA(2)) and
- Within 12 months of the date on which a claim was made outside a self-assessment return (TMA 1970, Sch 1A para 3(1)(a)).

It is not possible to extend these time limits for withdrawal by making an overpayment relief claim (TMA 1970, Sch 1AB para 2(2)(b)). For example, suppose that a claim to the remittance basis for 2011–12 was made in a self-assessment return which was submitted to HMRC at the normal time. In that scenario, the time limit for a subsequent withdrawal of the claim is 31 January 2014. A changed view, say in December 2014, that there had been a mistake on the return in making a remittance basis claim would not result in any overpayment relief. That is because the overpayment relief legislation does not cover mistakes in making a claim.

Extended time limits for claim or withdrawal

46.9 The general time limits for making or withdrawing a claim are extended when:

- An assessment is made by HMRC (TMA 1970, s 36(3) and s 43A(2)), or
- A self-assessment is amended by HMRC (TMA 1970, s 43C(1) and (2)), or
- An enquiry is concluded by contract settlement (HMRC practice, set out in the Self-Assessment Claims Manual at SACM9005).

A claim to the remittance basis (or withdrawal of such a claim) can be made within 12 months of the end of the year of assessment in which HMRC make the assessment or amend a return in an self-assessment enquiry closure notice (TMA 1970, ss 43(2), 43A(2) and 43C(2)). But the extension of the general time limit for withdrawing claims only applies where the loss of tax to the

Crown is not brought about carelessly or deliberately by the taxpayer or someone acting on his behalf (TMA 1970, ss 43A(1)(b) and 43C(1)(b)).

Where a claim to the remittance basis is made or withdrawn under these extended time limits the relief that can be given is limited broadly to the additional liability to tax resulting from the HMRC assessment or amendment (TMA 1970, ss 36(3), 43B(3) and 43C(1)).

WHEN A CLAIM IS NOT REQUIRED

46.10 In two circumstances the remittance basis is available without a claim. The term 'remittance basis user' is widely used to denote both those who have made a claim and those who are entitled to the remittance basis without need for a claim.

De minimis relief

46.11 No claim is required if the aggregate amount of the individual's unremitted foreign income and gains for the year is less than £2,000 (ITA 2007, s 809D(2)). It is important to stress that the total foreign income and gains can be more than £2,000: what matters is how much remains unremitted. HMRC's practice is to apply the £2,000 limit by converting unremitted foreign currency at exchange rates prevailing on the last day of the tax year (RDRM para 31190). Prior remittances may be debited in the foreign currency.

Nothing taxable

46.12 Certain categories of individual do not need to make a claim if they have no UK source income or gains and none of their foreign income and gains is remitted to the UK (ITA 2007, s 809E). Minors qualify for this treatment provided that they are under 18 throughout the tax year in question. An adult attracts this treatment only if he has been UK resident in less than seven of the preceding nine tax years.

One trap here is that the ability to use the remittance basis without claim is lost not merely if current year income and gains are remitted but also if, in the tax year in question, past year income and gains are remitted (s 809E(3)). But no account is taken of income and gains arising in tax years prior to the assumption of UK residence as they do not fall within the definitions of the constituent elements of foreign income and gains (s 809E(3)(b)).

In one limited respect the requirement that the individual have no UK source income is qualified. He is allowed to have up to £100 of UK source interest income, provided income tax has been deducted at source from it (ITA 2007, s 809E(1)(c), (2A)).

Opting out

46.13 An individual who would otherwise be entitled to the remittance basis as of right under one or other of the above heads may disclaim it when filing (ss 809D(1B) and 809E(1)).

CONSEQUENCES OF A CLAIM

46.14 The primary consequence of a claim is that the taxpayer's foreign income and gains are not taxed unless and insofar as remitted to the UK (ITA 2007, s 809H). As noted at the beginning of this chapter, the meaning of 'remittance' is highly technical and is explained in CHAPTERS 51 to 57.

A key point for any UK resident non-UK domiciliary to understand is that once the remittance basis has been used in any given tax year, his foreign income and gains from that tax year will remain taxable if remitted, for as long as he remains UK resident. The exposure to UK taxation on a remittance of the income/gains will persist even if the individual ceases, in a later tax year, to be a remittance basis user – whether this is because he has chosen not to make any further claims to use the remittance basis, or has become deemed domiciled and therefore ineligible for the remittance basis, or even because he has become actually domiciled in the UK. Any such change of status will of course affect the treatment of future income/gains, but will not affect the treatment of the foreign income/gains that date from the period in which the remittance basis was used. The individual will need to continue to take care not to remit these, if tax on the historic income/gains is to be avoided. See also para **48.8**.

Making a s 809B claim to the remittance basis is not necessarily to a taxpayer's advantage, in that it usually carries certain penalties. With one exception, these do not apply in the circumstances described in paras **46.11** and **46.12** where the remittance basis is available without claim.

Allowances

46.15 A taxpayer who has claimed the remittance basis forfeits the income tax personal allowance and the CGT annual exemption in the tax year in question (ITA 2007, s 809G). Currently (2016–17) the former is £11,000 and the latter £11,100.

Dividend rates

46.16 The dividend rates do not apply to foreign dividends insofar as the dividends arise in a tax year in which the taxpayer has made a s 809B claim (ITA 2007, s 13(2)(c)). This means that the 'headline' rate of tax on the remittance of such dividends is 20% within the basic rate band, 40% within the higher rate band and 45% at the top rate, rather than the dividend rates applicable to dividends taxed on the arising basis.

The non-application of the dividend rates is the one cost of the remittance basis which applies to those who do not need to claim as well as to those who make a claim.

Long stay non-domiciliaries

46.17 The principal cost of claiming the remittance basis is that the remittance basis charge described in the next chapter must be paid. But this cost does not apply to all those who claim: it catches only those who have been UK resident in at least seven of the preceding nine tax years. Where it is payable it is additional to, and not a substitute for, tax on UK income and gains and tax on remitted foreign income and gains.

For some long-stay non-domiciliaries the charge renders the remittance basis unattractive, particularly when coupled with the loss of the personal allowance and the CGT annual exemption. But a point to emphasise is that the claim, and thus the charge, is made on a year by year basis. Thus if no claim is made for a particular tax year, no remittance basis charge is payable, even if a claim is made and the charge paid for the year before and/or the year after. The Government did look at making it a requirement for a remittance basis user to claim the remittance basis for three consecutive years at a time, but in the Budget 2015 announced that it had decided to leave the position unchanged.

Capital losses

46.18 The presumption is that losses accruing on the disposal of foreign situs assets are not allowable for CGT purposes (TCGA 1992, s 16ZA(3)). This disallowance of losses applies from the first tax year in which the taxpayer makes a claim to the remittance basis under s 809B. However, the presumption is displaced if, for the first year for which the taxpayer makes a s 809B claim, he makes an election under TCGA 1992, s 16ZA. This important relief is explained in paras **49.12** to **49.17**. The critical point here is that the opportunity to make an election under s 16ZA is a once-only opportunity, only available for the first tax year for which a claim under s 809B is made; and is lost if not taken at that time.

Chapter 47

LONG-TERM RESIDENTS: THE ANNUAL CHARGE FOR THE REMITTANCE BASIS

INTRODUCTION

47.1 The remittance basis charge is payable for a tax year if the following conditions are met (ITA 2007, s 809H):

(1)   The non-UK domiciliary claims the remittance basis for that tax year.
(2)   He has been UK resident in at least seven of the preceding nine tax years.

The amount of the charge starts off at £30,000. But if the non-UK domiciliary has been UK resident for at least 12 of the preceding 14 tax years it rises to £60,000, and under current law, once he or she has been UK resident for at least 17 out of the preceding 20 tax years it rises to £90,000.

As noted in the previous chapter, and addressed more fully in CHAPTER 45, significant reforms to the taxation of non-UK domiciliaries are expected to take effect from 6 April 2017. They include a new rule under which a non-UK domiciliary will be deemed domiciled for all tax purposes, and thus ineligible for the remittance basis, once it becomes the case that 15 or more out of the preceding 20 tax years were years of UK residence. As a result, the £90,000 charge will cease to apply.

The remittance basis charge is not payable unless the non-domiciliary is aged 18 or over in the tax year (s 809H(1)(b)).

NOMINATED INCOME AND GAINS

47.2 The remittance basis charge is in form a tax on what is called the nominated income and gains for the year. The taxpayer can decide which income and gains are nominated; he is entitled and bound to make such nomination when he files his s 809B claim (s 809C(2)). Tax is charged on the nominated income and gains as if the non-domiciliary had not made a s 809B claim for the year in question and the remittance basis did not apply (ITA 2007, s 809H(2)). This formulation makes it clear that the nominated income and/or gains are taxed notwithstanding that they have not been remitted.

Provided that some income or a gain is nominated, it does not matter if what is actually nominated fails to yield tax, or yields tax of less than the required £30,000, £60,000 or £90,000. If the tax payable as a result of the nomination falls short of the required sum, tax is deemed to be payable on additional income, which is deemed to have been nominated for the purpose, of an amount sufficient to make up the shortfall (s 809H(4)). It is unnecessary, therefore, for a taxpayer to ensure that he nominates income or gains which will actually give rise to the required sum if taxed in the ordinary way.

THE NOMINATION

Minimum

47.3 There is no minimum amount which must be nominated, so a nomination of £1 of some item of foreign income or gains is effective. However, some income or a gain (or part of one) must be nominated, for the rule that the s 809B claim contain a nomination is mandatory (ITA 2007, s 809C(2)). It may be inferred that HMRC are entitled to ignore a s 809B claim, and thus disapply the remittance basis, if the claim does not include a nomination.

Provided that a nomination is made, it does not matter whether this actually generates a tax charge. As explained above, in such cases the tax charge is generated by the deemed top-up nomination.

The ordering rules described below mean that generally any nomination should be of income or gains of an amount not exceeding £10. The one circumstance where this might not be so is where it is desired to secure a credit for the UK tax on the nominated income and gains against some foreign tax on the same items. As explained in para **47.16** below, this is unlikely to occur in practice.

Maximum

47.4 Although there is no minimum amount, the amount nominated is subject to a maximum. This is expressed in terms of the 'relevant tax increase'. This is defined so that, in effect, the relevant tax increase is the tax payable on the nominated amount, assuming it to be taxable on the arising basis and also assuming it to form the 'top slice' of the non-domiciliary's income or gains. The rule is that the relevant tax increase caused by the nomination must not exceed £30,000, £60,000 or £90,000 (as applicable) where the higher remittance basis charge applies (ITA 2007, s 809C(4)).

HMRC consider that in computing the relevant tax increase, the personal allowance and dividend rates are not applicable (RDRM32350).

Consequences of exceeding the maximum

47.5 It is unclear whether a nomination giving rise to tax in excess of the relevant tax increase is invalid and thus renders the claim invalid. Although it is at least arguable that this is the case, the government said at the report stage of the 2008 Finance Bill that this point would not be taken. HMRC practice in cases of excessive nomination is to contact the taxpayer and invite amendment to the return (RDRM para 32330).

In practice it is likely that most advisers will recommend minimal nominations. In general such a course is to be recommended. But it does carry one risk, if in due course the taxpayer remits all his foreign income and gains. Actual nomination franks remittances, whereas a deemed top-up nomination does not. However, as explained below, nominated income and gains are deemed to be remitted last, so the point is unlikely to arise often.

What can be nominated?

47.6 A nomination of a particular item of income or a particular gain is valid. There is no requirement that the nomination extend to all income of a given type or all gains. Accordingly, the nomination can be of dividends from particular shares or interest from a particular bank account, as distinct from all dividends or all interest.

An argument in favour of nominating gains rather than income is that nominated income is taken into account in determining payments of tax on account under the self-assessment regime (TMA 1970, s 59A). Gains, by contrast, are not so taken into account. If gains are nominated, the nominated gains should if possible generate the full remittance basis charge as, if the nomination is topped up, what is deemed nominated is income (s 809H(4)(a)).

There is no reason why part only of an item of income or a gain should not be nominated. This is because of the general rule that the nomination can be of part only of the taxpayer's income or gains (s 809C(3)).

REMITTANCES OF NOMINATED INCOME AND GAINS

47.7 Special ordering rules may apply in any tax year in which the non-domiciliary remits income or gains which he has nominated. The purpose of these rules is to prevent non-domiciliaries from nominating foreign income or gains and then bringing that money into the UK, thereby avoiding the need to make taxable remittances.

The effect of the ordering rules is that the income or gains identified by the rules are treated as remitted and income or gains in fact remitted are treated as not remitted or, if caught by the ordering rules, as remitted in accordance with those rules. However, the actual income and gains do have some relevance, in that the total amount treated as remitted under the ordering rules is equal to the actual aggregate remittances of remittance basis and nominated income and gains (ITA 2007, s 809J(1), step 1). This aggregate is termed the relevant amount.

In determining whether and if so which actual income and gains have been remitted, the mixed fund rules described in CHAPTER 53 apply. This means that the ordering rules being described here cannot come into play unless, under the rules described in CHAPTER 53, what is actually remitted is or includes nominated income or gains. Further as the ordering rules apply only to the extent of actual remittances of income and gains of 2008–09 and later tax years, they cannot have the effect of turning what, under the rules in CHAPTER 53, is a remittance of clean capital or pre-6 April 2008 income or gains into something else.

Preconditions

47.8 The special ordering rules operate in a tax year if the following conditions are met:

(1)   Any of the individual's nominated income and gains is remitted to the UK in the tax year.

(2)   As at the end of the tax year some at least of individual's remittance basis income and gains have not been remitted.

(3)   What might be called the £10 test is met for the year.

For the purpose of these conditions, the individual's remittance basis income and gains are his foreign income and gains for all tax years in which he is or has been a remittance basis user, up to and including the tax year of the remittance of nominated income/gains, except that the term excludes any income or gains which have been nominated (ITA 2007, s 809I(4)). As the term is defined with reference to the applicability of ITA 2007, ss 809B, 809D, and 809E, it excludes income and gains of 2007–08 and earlier years.

The £10 test requires each tax year for which the individual has made a nomination to be looked at separately. In relation to each such year it operates as a *de minimis*. The test is not met unless total remittances of that year's nominated income and gains exceed £10. In determining whether this threshold is met all prior and current year remittances of the year's nominated income and gains are aggregated. So too the test is met, and the ordering rules are triggered, if the £10 threshold is exceeded as respects the nominated income and gains of either the current tax year or those of any prior tax year.

Ordering rules

47.9 In the event that the above preconditions are met, two ordering rules are in point.

The primary rule is that the relevant amount is treated as a remittance of the remittance basis income and gains of the current year, ie all foreign income and gains of the year other than the nominated income or gains. If it is less than those income and gains it is treated as a remittance first of income and gains not subject to a foreign tax and then of income and gains which are subject to foreign tax. Within these two categories, income is taken before gains, and employment income before relevant foreign income (s 809J(2)). Income and gains are included even if at the time of the remittance they have not arisen but do so before the end of the tax year. They are also included even if in fact previously spent abroad.

The secondary rule applies if the relevant amount exceeds current year unnominated income and gains. In this event it is carried back and matched with unnominated income and gains of prior years back to 2008–09, the prior years being taken in reverse date order. The different categories of income and gains are ordered within each prior year on the same basis as for the current year.

PRACTICAL IMPLICATIONS

47.10 The key point about the ordering rules is that, if triggered, they cause a re-characterisation of all remittances of post-6 April 2008 income or gains in that tax year. In theory, there may be opportunities for manipulation, for example if actual remittances are of past year income and the rules would cause those remittances to be recharacterised as remittances of capital gains. However, it is unusual for a remittance of nominated income or gains to be advantageous, and the more common result of the rules is that ill-advised taxpayers end up paying more tax than they should.

There are two particular traps. One concerns individuals who remit what they believe to be chargeable gains, kept untainted by income by being in a separate bank account. The trap is that if nominated income or gains are remitted, a remittance of gains may be taxed as a remittance of the otherwise segregated income.

The second trap is that the ordering rules look at all the income or gains of a given category for the year, regardless of what the taxpayer has done with the money, and regardless indeed of whether he has spent it all abroad on consumables. The result is that the taxpayer may be taxed on income which, in the event, could never in fact be remitted.

Avoiding the ordering rules

47.11 The £10 test provides a means of ensuring the ordering rules are avoided. All that is required is to ensure that the actual nomination for each tax year is of £10 or less of income and gains, in practice £1. In that event, the £10 test will never be met for that year, for it will by definition be impossible for more than £10 of nominated income and gains for that year to be remitted.

The £10 test means that in practice nominations should always be less than £10. On the face of it this offers a means of avoiding the whole ordering problem. In general it does, but there is one caveat. This is that the £10 test took effect only from 2012–13 onwards. It follows that nominations in earlier years will not have been made with knowledge of the test. If those nominations exceeded £10 care must still be taken to ensure what was nominated is never remitted or, if it is, such a remittances do not exceed £10.

OTHER ISSUES

47.12 Although the £10 test should mean remittances of nominated income and gains are rarely encountered, a number of further issues require consideration should such a remittance occur.

Impact on future years

47.13 HMRC consider that once a remittance of nominated income or gains has engaged the ordering rules, those ordering rules govern how remittances are taxed thereafter. HMRC appear to consider that the imposition of the ordering rules continues until there has been complete remittance of all the income and gains of the year in which the nominated income or gains are remitted and of the income and gains of all prior years back to 2008–09 (RDRM para 35110). It is unclear how in future years this interacts with actual remittances of current year income and gains or how account is taken of the fact that some income and gains will be incapable of remittance as having been spent abroad.

Many practitioners are of the view that HMRC are incorrect. The view those practitioners take is that the ordering rules apply only to determine what is to be treated as remitted in the subject tax year, ie the year in which the remittance of nominated income or gains occurs. The basis for this view is that s 809I(2) charges tax as if the income and gains treated under s 809J as remitted in that tax year had in fact been remitted. The reference to 'that' tax year is clearly a reference to the tax year referred to in s 809I(1), ie the tax year in which the nominated income or gains are remitted. It is true that s 809I(2) refers to tax being charged for that and subsequent years, but the reference to subsequent years does no more than ensure that the alterations to what has actually been remitted in the current tax year are taken into account in subsequent years.

If this view is right, there is a trap, applicable where income or gains which have in fact been remitted in the subject year are treated as not remitted in that year. Assuming that such income or gains or assets derived from them are still in the UK in a subsequent tax year they can be treated as remitted then, insofar as they or derived assets can be said to be used in the UK by or for the benefit of the taxpayer or another relevant person. This result follows from the general definition of remittance in s 809L (see para 51.7).

It is clear, at the very least, that there are acute practical difficulties and legal uncertainties when nominated income and gains are remitted and the ordering rules are triggered. For that reason most advisers are of the view such remittances should at all costs be avoided. Up to 2011–12, this was best done by ensuring that the nominated income or gains were credited to, or arose within, a bank account from which no withdrawals were made, and which could not be said to be collateral for current or future borrowing. Since 2012–13, the 'de minimis' exemption discussed above has rendered this procedure unnecessary.

Remittance in error

47.14 HMRC allow accidental remittances of nominated income and gains to be reversed provided the following conditions are met (RDRM para 35140):

- The remittance is reversed before the end of the tax year in which it is made.

- It is reversed without unreasonable delay.
- There have been no relevant transactions or benefits conferred on the taxpayer or any other relevant person in the interim.

Payment of charge using nominated income or gains

47.15 A direct payment to HMRC in respect of a tax year in which the remittance basis charge is payable is not taxed as a remittance if the amount does not exceed the amount of charge (ITA 2007, s 809V(1)). The money must go directly from the taxpayer's foreign bank account to an account of HMRC, whether by cheque or bank transfer. The payments relieved can be a single payment or several and thus can either be included in payments on account or in a final balancing payment. HMRC advise taxpayers to retain information documenting the payments and where they were made from (RDRM34020). The exemption does not apply in the event that a payment which would otherwise fall within it is repaid by HMRC (s 809V(2)) and in that event the ordering rules would be engaged if nominated income or gains had been used.

A payment on account made in reliance on this exemption loses the exemption should it be decided when filing for the year in question not to claim the remittance basis. This follows because the failure to claim means the remittance basis charge is not payable and thus that the basic precondition for the exemption is not met.

This point can cause problems for taxpayers who do not claim the remittance basis every year. Possible solutions are (a) to use capital for all payments on account (although there may then be wastage of the exemption in s 809V), or (b) to use current year income or gains for such payments (which will be taxable in any event if the arising basis is used, and exempt if the remittance basis is claimed).

CREDITABILITY OF CHARGE

47.16 The question of the creditability or otherwise of the remittance basis charge against foreign tax arises most frequently in relation to US citizens living in the UK, with resident but non-domiciled status. This is because the USA taxes by reference to citizenship as well as residence, so the potential for double taxation is not limited to dual residence.

Most practitioners were, originally, sceptical about the creditability of the remittance basis charge against US income tax, but the IRS announced in August 2011 that it considers the total charge to tax under the remittance basis, including the remittance basis charge itself, to be a 'single levy' which is creditable against US tax liabilities. Accordingly, US citizens who are remittance basis users are able to secure credit for the £30,000, £60,000 or £90,000 (as applicable) even if only a nominal amount of income is nominated and the deemed top-up nomination is relied on to generate £30,000 or £50,000 of tax (see para 47.2).

However, the creditability of the remittance basis charge against tax in other countries, in dual residence situations, remains doubtful. The general experience of practitioners is that claims to treaty relief for the charge are unsuccessful, even where the taxpayer has nominated income and/or gains of sufficient quantum to generate £30,000, £60,000 or £90,000 (as applicable) in tax. It is worth noting the HMRC guidance in the International Manual (at INTM153270) regarding the assistance that HMRC can provide in liaising with foreign tax authorities.

Chapter 48

RELEVANT FOREIGN INCOME

INTRODUCTION

48.1 This chapter explains the application of the remittance basis to relevant foreign income. It uses the term 'remittance basis user' to describe a person who has validly claimed the remittance basis for the tax year in which the income arises or is otherwise eligible for the remittance basis in that year (see para **46.10**).

DEFINITION

48.2 Relevant foreign income is defined in ITTOIA 2005, s 830 as income arising from a source outside the UK which is chargeable under one of a number of specified provisions.

Actual income

48.3 The principal categories of actual income which, if the source is foreign, are relevant foreign income are as follows (ITTOIA 2005, s 830):

(1)   Trade profits;
(2)   Rental income;
(3)   Interest;
(4)   Dividends;
(5)   Royalties; and.
(6)   Annual payments and other income not otherwise charged.

In determining whether income arises from a source outside the UK, and thus is relevant foreign income, the normal rules as to source apply. These rules are explained in CHAPTER 40.

Deemed income

48.4 In addition, certain forms of deemed income are treated as relevant foreign income (ITTOIA 2005, s 830). The most important instances are:

(1)   Offshore income gains (see para **95.26**); and
(2)   Profits realised on the disposal of deeply discounted securities.

It should also be noted that foreign investment income (or deemed income) of a non-UK person may be deemed to be that of a UK resident individual under the transfer of assets legislation (see Part C Section II) or the income tax legislation regarding settlements (see CHAPTER 75).

Irish income

48.5 The remittance basis used not to apply to relevant foreign income arising in the Republic of Ireland (ITTOIA 2005, s 831(5)). The European Commission raised the issue of whether this infringed EU law (EC Press Release 30 March 2007, reproduced [2007] SWTI 1251). As a result, the legislation was amended so that since 2008–09 Irish income has been eligible for the remittance basis (cf Finance Act 2008, Sch 7 para 83(3) (FA 2008)).

Deductions

48.6 In relation to relevant foreign income arising in 2008–09 and subsequent years it is expressly provided that in applying the remittance basis, no deductions are allowed in computing the relevant foreign income (ITTOIA 2005, s 832B(1); FA 2008, Sch 7 para 81). An exception is made for trades, professions and vocations, where the same deductions are allowed as if the business were carried on in the UK (s 832B(2)).

Arguably this rule disallows what would otherwise be allowable expenses such as repairs and interest where the relevant foreign income is foreign rental income. This follows because although the profits of letting businesses are calculated in the same way as trading profits, they are not in fact trading profits (ITTOIA 2005, s 272). HMRC, however, have made it clear that in their view the allowable expenses of the letting business may be deducted (RDRM para 31150).

THE CHARGE TO TAX

48.7 If in the year in which the income arises the taxpayer is a remittance basis user, he is charged only on such of the income as is remitted or treated as remitted (ITTOIA 2005, s 832(2)).

Remittance in subsequent tax year

48.8 A remittance is taxable not only if it is made in the year in which the income arises, but also if it is made in a subsequent tax year in which the individual is UK resident. Should a remittance be made in a subsequent year of UK residence, it is charged as income for that year and so is subject to the rates and allowances applicable to that year. This is the case even if, in the tax year of the remittance, the taxpayer is taxable (with respect to that tax year's income and gains) on the arising basis rather than the remittance basis. Before 2008–09 this situation was relatively uncommon. It now arises much more frequently, because the remittance basis charge makes it desirable for some non-UK domiciliaries to opt in and out of the remittance basis.

Meaning of remittance

48.9 The term 'remittance' has the extended meaning explained in CHAPTERS 51 to 57.

Territorial limits

48.10 A remittance is not charged if in the tax year in which it is made the individual is not UK resident (s 832(2)(a)). Nor is a remittance charged if it is in the overseas part of a split year (s 832(2)(b)).

A remittance when the individual is UK resident is not charged if what is remitted is actual income which arose when the individual was non-resident. This result follows because foreign income is only relevant foreign income if it is chargeable under specified chapters of ITTOIA 2005, Parts 2–5. All those parts charge only UK residents on non-UK income (ITTOIA 2005, ss 6, 269(2), 270(3), 368 and 577).

Should the year of arrival be a split year, actual income arising in the overseas part is not taxed if remitted after arrival. The reason for this is that the charging provisions in ITTOIA 2005, Parts 2–5 all treat a split year as a period of non-residence.

The treatment of remittances of pre-arrival deemed foreign income turn on the rules specific to that category of deemed income.

Source-ceasing

48.11 It was generally accepted prior to 6 April 2008 that a remittance was not chargeable if effected in a tax year after that in which the source of the income ceased. Thus there was no charge to tax if a remittance basis user remitted cash representing non-UK bank interest received in a previous tax year, if the bank account giving rise to that interest had been closed before the beginning of the tax year in which the remittance occurred. This is no longer the law, as ITTOIA 2005, s 832(3) expressly provides that the charge is made regardless of whether the source exists when the income is remitted.

Double tax relief

48.12 Remittance basis users enjoy any double tax relief applicable to the remitted income. But where credit relief is claimed the amount remitted is treated as increased by the creditable foreign tax (TIOPA 2010, s 32). The same applies if the income is interest subject to withholding tax under the EU Savings Directive; if the interest is remitted, tax is calculated by reference to the gross (pre-withholding) amount of the interest, albeit with credit for the tax withheld (TIOPA 2010, s 143).

Treatment of dividends

48.13 In general, remittances of relevant foreign income are charged at the same rate of tax as other income. Remittances of foreign dividends paid to remittance basis users do not attract the normal dividend rates, the applicable rates being the normal income tax rates of 20%, 40% and 45% (ITA 2007, ss 13(1)(c) and 13(2)(c)).

Between 6 April 2008 and 5 April 2016, dividends typically attracted a notional tax credit equal to one-ninth of the actual amount of the dividend, under ITA 2007, s 397A. This tax credit could be applied to reduce the tax on a remittance of a foreign dividend which was received in a year in which the taxpayer was a remittance basis user. However, the notional tax credit has been abolished, replaced by a dividend nil rate of £5,000 (ITA 2007, s 13A). This nil rate is not applicable on a remittance of foreign dividends, as the nil rate can only be used for the first £5,000 of dividends which, absent the nil rate, would be subject to tax at the dividend ordinary rate, dividend upper rate or dividend additional rate (ITA 2007, s 13A(1)). On a remittance of foreign dividends, none of these rates is applicable.

TEMPORARY NON-RESIDENTS

48.14 Income remitted during a period of temporary non-residence is taxed in the year of return insofar as the income arose while the individual was UK resident (ITTOIA 2005, s 832A). Temporary non-residence bears the meaning it has under the statutory residence test (see para **41.39**). However income which arises in the period of temporary non-residence is not taxed if remitted unless it falls within one of the categories caught by the temporary non-residence rule, most notably dividends paid by close companies (see ITTOIA 2005, s 408A(5) and paras **41.41** and **41.43**).

INCOME ARISING BEFORE 6 APRIL 2008

48.15 The issue of whether a taxpayer's relevant foreign income of 2007–08 or prior years is chargeable as remitted is determined under the law as enacted by FA 2008 rather than by the law in force when the income arose. This fundamental principle is laid down by FA 2007, Sch 7 para 83.

A remittance of relevant foreign income arising in 2005–06, 2006–07 and 2007–08 is taxable only if a claim to the remittance basis was made under the (now repealed) ITTOIA 2005, s 831, as without such a claim the income was taxed on the arising basis. Under the law prior to 6 April 2005 a claim as such was not needed, although the taxpayer did have to have made a claim that he was not UK domiciled (TA 1988 s 65(4)). Income of 2007–08 or earlier tax years which arose in the Republic of Ireland is not taxable if remitted, as such income was taxed on the arising basis (FA 2008, Sch 7 para 83(3)).

Dividends

48.16 Should the income of 2007–08 or prior years be dividends, a remittance of the income in 2008–09 or subsequently does not attract the dividend rates

(ITA 2007, s 13; FA 2008, s 68(2)). The tax credit under ITA 2007, s 397A referred to above does not apply here, as it can only be claimed on dividends received between 6 April 2008 and 5 April 2016 (FA 2008, s 34(2)).

Mixed fund rules

48.17 The current, statutory, mixed-fund rules do not apply to relevant foreign income arising before 6 April 2008 (FA 2008, Sch 7 para 89). This means that the common law, with all its uncertainties, has to be resorted to in determining whether income has in fact been remitted (see paras **53.2** to **53.4**).

Old reliefs

48.18 One consequence of the remittance rules enacted in 2008 applying to income of 2007–08 and earlier is that reliefs which may have rendered the income free of tax if remitted before 6 April 2008 are no longer applicable. The prime example of this is source-ceasing (para **48.11** above). Another example is the rule that a remittance of income received by a non-domiciliary was only chargeable if in the tax year when it was made the individual was still non-UK domiciled.

TRANSITIONAL EXEMPTIONS

48.19 There is a couple of transitional exemptions which apply to relevant foreign income of 2007–08 and earlier years. These continue to have some practical importance for taxpayers who were remittance basis users before the 6 April 2008 reforms.

Property acquired before 12 March 2008

48.20 There is a broad exemption for relevant foreign income of 2007–08 or earlier tax years which was converted into 'property' before 12 March 2008. The exemption has the effect that in many cases pre-2008–09 income can be treated as clean capital for the purposes of remittance planning.

Paragraph 86(3) of FA 2008, Sch 7 provides that relevant foreign income is not treated as remitted if before 12 March 2008 'property' consisting or deriving from the relevant foreign income was acquired by a relevant person. To attract this relief, the 'property' does not have to have been retained until 12 March 2008, and nor does it have to have been brought to the UK before then. It is sufficient that before 12 March 2008 the income was spent and that what it was spent on was 'property'. It is also clear that the exemption is engaged if funds derived from the income, rather than the income itself, were used to acquire the 'property'.

The term 'property' excludes 'money'. This is less straightforward than it sounds, as 'money' is given an artificial definition which encompasses various instruments that are readily convertible into cash (ITA 2007, s 809Y). The term includes:

(a)   traveller's cheques;

(b)   promissory notes;
(c)   bills of exchange;
(d)   any other instrument that is evidence of a debt; and
(e)   vouchers, stamps, and similar tokens or documents which are capable of being exchanged for money goods or services.

This definition of 'money' plainly includes bank accounts. Whether it includes loan notes and corporate or government bonds is not completely clear, but the cautious view is that it does, on the basis that all of these can reasonably be regarded as instruments evidencing a debt. However, assuming that in general this is right, there is likely to be an exception for immobilised bonds, as there no instrument is issued to the investor (see para **38.14**).

Much relevant foreign income which arose before 12 March 2008 should fall within the scope of the above exemption. All that the non-domiciliary needs to show is that at some point before 12 March 2008 it was invested in or represented by an asset which does not fall within the definition of 'money' set out above.

As indicated above, the relief does not apply unless the property consisting or deriving from the relevant foreign income was acquired by a relevant person. It might be assumed that such acquisition must have been by the taxpayer himself, as s 809L applies to pre-6 April 2008 income on the basis that the only relevant person is the taxpayer (see para **54.1**). But in reality this is not the case, because the rule relating to 'property' acquired before 12 March 2008 is not in s 809L.

It is sometimes suggested that words should be implied into para 86(3), to the effect that the exemption applies only if the 'property' acquired before 12 March 2008 has been retained by the remittance basis user and it is this 'property' which has been remitted to the UK. However, that it is not what para 86(3) says. There is no need to construe the provision purposively to achieve this more restrictive result. It is reasonably clear that the broad purpose of para 86(3) is to ensure that income which arose before the remittance rules were changed in 2008 counts as capital if genuinely invested. Without such a provision the computations required for long-stay non-domiciliaries would be impossible and, in view of the ending of source-ceasing, issues as to retrospection would arise. Example 1A in RDRM, para 31470 shows that the construction of para 86(3) adopted here is shared by HMRC.

It should be noted that the exemption is limited to relevant foreign income and does not provide protection for chargeable overseas earnings or foreign chargeable gains.

Property remitted before 6 April 2008

48.21 A second transitional relief applies if relevant foreign income or property deriving from it was brought to or used in the UK before 6 April 2008 (FA 2008, Sch 7, para 86(2)). The bringing in or use must have been by or for the benefit of a relevant person and here too the restriction of the relevant person concept to post-6 April 2008 income does not apply. Where this condition is met, the income cannot be treated as remitted after 6 April 2008 if it otherwise would be.

In view of the relief for property acquired before 12 March 2008, the compass of this relief is small. It does however protect income arising and brought to the UK between 12 March and 5 April 2008. It means that income cannot be charged in 2008–09 or later years provided that it was remitted in 2007–08 or earlier years, even if such remittance was tax-free under the law as it then stood.

For the purposes of this relief, it is specifically provided that items falling within the definition of money count as property and so attract the relief. Provided that the property was in the UK at any time on or before 5 April 2008, it does not matter if the asset is subsequently exported and reimported.

Foreign chargeable gains and chargeable overseas earnings are not protected from tax by this measure.

Payment of interest to offshore lender

48.22 In 2007–08 and earlier years, special rules countered the use of loans to avoid what would otherwise be a taxable remittance. These were much less comprehensive than the present rules described in CHAPTER 56 and there was one noteworthy gap. The use of foreign income to pay interest on a loan made abroad did not count as a remittance even if the proceeds of the loan were brought to the UK.

Accordingly, a technique became widely used, whereby UK resident non-UK domiciliaries borrowed money abroad, spent it in the UK (frequently, but not exclusively, on the acquisition of UK residential property), paid interest using foreign income, and eventually repaid the loan either out of capital, or when they ceased to be UK resident. Under current, law this 'loophole' is closed – where foreign income is used to pay interest on a debt relating to property in the UK, the income is treated as remitted (see CHAPTER 56). However, in 2008 the Government made a concession to non-UK domiciliaries who had borrowed offshore to finance expenditure on UK residential property. Under FA 2008, Sch 7, para 90, relevant foreign income used to service interest payments may be 'grandfathered' so that it is not treated as remitted.

The conditions which must be met for this relief to apply are as follows:

(1) The loan was made to the taxpayer before 12 March 2008.
(2) It was made outside the UK.
(3) The purpose of the loan was to fund the taxpayer's acquisition of residential property in the UK.
(4) The money was received in the UK before 6 April 2008.
(5) The taxpayer used the money before 6 April 2008 to acquire the residential property.
(6) The debt was secured on the property before 6 April 2008.

Where all such conditions are satisfied, relevant foreign income used outside the UK to pay interest on the loan is not taxed as a remittance. This remains the position until 5 April 2028. The relief also applies to replacement loans taken out before 12 March 2008 provided that the money was used to clear the earlier loan before 6 April 2008 (FA 2008, Sch 7, para 90(4)).

The relief is lost if after 12 March 2008 any terms of the loan have been or are varied or waived. It is also lost once the taxpayer no longer owns the property, or if either the loan ceases to be secured on the property or the property is used as security for other loans. A point to stress is that this relief is confined to Interest payments and so does not cover repayments of principal.

A point of some curiosity is that the relief is limited to payments made using relevant foreign income: the law pre-6 April 2008 allowed foreign earnings and chargeable gains to be used to pay the interest as well.

A key issue for those who qualify for this relief is ensuring that the terms of the loan are not waived or varied. It may be suggested that variation connotes a consensual arrangement between lender and borrower and a waiver occurs only if made by deed or accompanied by detriment so as to be enforceable. HMRC consider a variation to have occurred if the lender and borrower agree that, on the maturity of a fixed-term loan, the debt shall be left outstanding, so a loan extension of this nature will cause the relief to be forfeited from the expiry of the original term. Conversely, HMRC accept that the automatic continuance of a loan under its original terms does not prejudice the relief (RDRM31510). There is clearly no 'variation' of a loan if there is a change to the interest rate (whether triggered by a change to the base rate or by the expiry of a discounted rate period) where the change was provided for in the terms and conditions applicable to the loan as at 12 March 2008.

Chapter 49

FOREIGN CHARGEABLE GAINS

GENERAL

49.1 This chapter explains the application of the remittance basis to foreign chargeable gains. The law is principally contained in TCGA 1992, s 12. Section 12 was recast in 2008 (FA 2008, Sch 7 para 60).

WHAT ARE FOREIGN CHARGEABLE GAINS?

49.2 Foreign chargeable gains are gains which accrue on the disposal of assets situated outside the UK (TCGA 1992, s 12). Situs is determined by the CGT rules in TCGA 1992, ss 275–275C; these are explained in CHAPTER 39.

As mentioned in that chapter (see para **39.24**), there is one situation in which a gain realised by a remittance basis user on the disposal of an asset which is non-UK situated under the CGT situs rules may not be a foreign chargeable gain. This is under a special rule regarding certain carried interests where the individual has performed investment management services in the UK.

However, in general whether a gain is a foreign chargeable gain is determined by the CGT situs rules. These rules are not the same as the common law rules that apply for the purposes of IHT. In particular, there is a counter-intuitive general rule regarding the situs of a debt, namely that the debt is situated in the UK if the creditor is UK resident. This may render a debt due to a UK resident, non-UK domiciled taxpayer a UK asset, with the result that a gain on the disposal of the debt is ineligible for the remittance basis even though the debtor is non-UK resident.

Deemed foreign gains

49.3 As explained at para **59.7**, if an item of 'exempt property' is sold in the UK, then (unless the taxpayer elects otherwise) any resultant gain is treated as a foreign chargeable gain rather than a UK gain. This treatment is subject to various conditions. In particular, tax on the deemed foreign gain will only be avoided if the proceeds of disposal are removed from the UK or used to make a qualifying investment (see CHAPTER 58) within 45 days of receipt of those proceeds.

Computation of the gain

49.4 As with all foreign assets, gains accruing to remittance basis users are computed by comparing the proceeds of disposal converted into sterling at exchange rates prevailing at the date of disposal with the acquisition costs, these each being converted to sterling at the rate prevailing when incurred (*Bentley v Pike* [1981] STC 360; *Capcount Trading v Evans* [1993] STC 11). It is not possible to express the gain in foreign currency and convert that amount to sterling.

THE CHARGE TO TAX

49.5 The foreign chargeable gains of a remittance basis user are treated as accruing when remitted (TCGA 1992, s 12(2)). The legislation does not in terms say they are not charged when the disposal giving rise to them occurs, but that follows by necessary implication.

The meaning of remittance is governed by the general rules in ITA 2007, ss 809L–809Z. It is thus as explained in Chapters 51 to 57.

Rate of tax

49.6 Since foreign chargeable gains do not accrue until remitted, the rate of CGT is determined by rates then prevailing. Gains remitted are therefore in general subject to the 20% rate even if the disposal generating the gain took place when CGT rates were different.

A remittance basis user who is not a higher rate taxpayer qualifies for the 10% rate insofar as his basic rate band is available. But that rate never applies to a remittance basis user who nominates or is treated as nominating income for the purpose of the remittance basis charge (see Chapter 47). This follows because the nomination ipso facto uses up the basic rate band.

Annual exemption

49.7 A non-domiciliary is not, generally, given the annual exemption in any tax year in which he is a remittance basis user (TCGA 1992, s 3 (1A)). But this preclusion does not apply to those who qualify as remittance basis users without need for a claim (see paras 46.10 to 46.13). The annual exemption is available in any tax year in which the non-domiciliary is not a remittance basis user and so, somewhat surprisingly, it can be set against remittances of prior year gains.

TERRITORIAL LIMITS

Immigrants

49.8 The charge on remittances is restricted to gains realised when the non-domiciliary was UK resident. This follows because s 12 is expressed only as applying to gains accruing in years when ITA 2007, ss 809B, 809D, or 809E is in point. Those sections are all restricted to years when the taxpayer is UK resident (see para **46.3**).

Emigrants

49.9 A remittance of gains is not charged if the non-domiciliary is non-resident throughout the tax year of remittance. This follows because the gains are treated as accruing in the year of remittance and the charge to CGT is restricted to tax years in which the taxpayer is UK resident (TCGA 1992, s 2(1)).

This is, however, subject to the rule applicable to temporary non-residents in TCGA 1992, s 10A (as to which see para **29.6**). This treats the gains or losses accruing during the period of absence as accruing in the year of return. In relation to non-domiciliaries it catches both gains resulting from disposals during the period of absence and gains resulting from remittances during that period. The former follows because, during the years of absence, the non-domiciliary cannot be a remittance basis user, so the general rule in s 10A applies to postpone the accrual of the gain to the year of return (s 10A(2)(a)). The latter follows because gains realised when the non-domiciliary was UK resident and a remittance basis user are treated as accruing when remitted, regardless of chargeability (TCGA 1992, s 12(2)). Gains both realised and remitted in a year of absence are treated as remitted in the year of return (s 10(9ZA)).

The remittance basis applies to gains realised during the period of absence provided those gains are foreign and the non-domiciliary is a remittance basis user in the year of return. This result follows because under s 10A those gains are treated as accruing in the year of return and, under s 12, the remittance basis applies to gains accruing in a tax year when the non-domiciliary is a remittance basis user.

None of this applies if the absence is long enough to fall outside the temporary non-residence rule, and, provided it is of at least that length, remittance is tax-free provided that it is effected in the period of non-UK residence.

Temporary non-residence bears the same meaning as it has under the statutory residence test (s 10A(10); see para **41.39**). However, in relation to individuals who became non-resident in or at the end of 2012–13, the term bears the meaning it had prior to the statutory test and means at least five tax years.

Split years

49.10 Save in cases of temporary non-residence, gains remitted in the overseas part of the split year are not taxed (s 12(2A)). Should the year of arrival be a split year, gains accruing in the overseas part of the split year are not taxed if remitted after arrival unless the prior period of non-residence is temporary. This is expressly enacted by s 12(1A), which did not apply until 2013–14 (FA 2014, s 59).

Change of domicile

49.11 As with relevant foreign income, a remittance is chargeable even if, by the time it is made, the taxpayer is UK domiciled or has otherwise become an arising basis taxpayer (TCGA 1992, s 12 passim).

LOSSES

49.12 Until 6 April 2008, a loss accruing to a non-domiciliary on the disposal of a foreign situs asset was not allowable in any circumstances. This was widely criticised and as a result, the present law affords somewhat more generous treatment.

Losses fully relievable

49.13 As under previous law, losses accruing on UK situs assets are relievable in full. Losses accruing on foreign situs assets are now also fully relievable provided the non-domiciliary does not claim the remittance basis under s 809B for the year in which the loss accrues and has not done so in any prior year. As the regime of s 809B claims only started on 6 April 2008, it is not necessary to look further back than that date.

Election by remittance basis users

49.14 In the first tax year for which the non-domiciliary does make a s 809B claim he has a once only right of election under TCGA 1992, s 16ZA. If he decides not to avail himself of that right, his losses on foreign situs assets for that and all future years are not allowable (TCGA 1992, 16ZA(3)). This is so even as respects losses accruing in future years in which he does not make a s 809B claim. The allowability of foreign losses is only restored if and at such time as he becomes UK domiciled.

As just indicated, the election is only effective if made for the first year for which the non-domiciliary claims the remittance basis under s 809B. The rules as to claims in TMA 1970, ss 43 and 43A govern the procedure for making the election (s 16ZA(4); see further para **46.7**). The election is irrevocable (TCGA 1992, 16ZA(4)).

Treatment of losses if election made

49.15 Assuming the non-domiciliary makes a s 16ZA election, both UK and foreign losses are deductible. But in tax years in which he is a remittance basis user, special rules apply (TCGA 1992, s 16ZC). These rules apply both to current year losses and unused brought forward losses. They apply to UK as well as foreign losses.

The effect of these rules is that the losses are set first against foreign chargeable gains which both accrue and are remitted in the tax year. They are next set against the foreign chargeable gains of the year which are not remitted in the year. Obviously losses which are so offset are not relieved on a current year basis. Instead, they are relieved if and when the foreign chargeable gain is remitted, the mechanism being that the loss is treated as a deduction from the gain (s 16ZB(3)). Should the losses be less than the unremitted gains of the year, they are allocated to the unremitted gains of the year in reverse date order (s 16ZC(2)).

UK gains of the year are relieved only if the brought forward and current-year losses exceed all the remitted and unremitted foreign chargeable gains of the year. Should the losses exceed all the gains of the year they are carried forward (s 16ZD(2)).

Brought forward losses do not for these purposes include any foreign losses of 2007–08 and prior years. This is because the repeal of TCGA 1992, s 16(4), the section disallowing such losses, took effect only in 2008–09 (FA 2008, Sch 7 paras 61 and 81).

The ordering rules described above mean that it is not always obvious whether a non-UK domiciled taxpayer should take the opportunity to make a s 16ZA election, where he is still in time to do so. An election will be advantageous if the taxpayer can be expected to remit foreign gains and not to have any UK gains; conversely, a taxpayer who expects to realise UK gains and to avoid the remittance of foreign gains would be well advised not to make the election. Many non-UK domiciled taxpayers will, in the absence of a compelling argument either way, take the default option (ie will not make the election). It may be argued that this makes sense, given that a remittance of foreign gains is (in theory at least) itself elective.

Allowability of losses in years when the non-domiciliary is not a remittance basis user

49.16 The legislation does not make provision for those years following an election in which the non-domiciliary is not a remittance basis user. It is therefore to be inferred that for such years UK and foreign losses are allowed in the normal way.

Subsequent year remittance of gains

49.17 A section 16ZA election has one further consequence. This applies to any foreign chargeable gains which accrue when the non-domiciliary is a remittance basis user and are remitted in a subsequent tax year. In such a case, the gain so remitted cannot be relieved by losses otherwise allowable in the year of remittance (s 16ZB). This does not mean such a gain is devoid of loss relief for, as indicated above, it may be reduced by losses in the year of accrual.

FOREIGN BANK ACCOUNTS

49.18 Until 5 April 2012, the disposals that were capable of generating foreign chargeable gains included withdrawals from foreign currency accounts at non-UK banks, insofar as the currency concerned had appreciated against sterling. This was because foreign currency is a chargeable asset (TCGA 1992, s 21(1)(b)). The only exception was where the account represented currency acquired for personal expenditure abroad, including expenditure on a residence abroad (TCGA 1992, s 252(2)).

This rule was capable of generating immense computational complexity and substantial compliance costs, and the tax at stake was usually modest. As a result, the law was amended in relation to disposals occurring on or after 6 April 2012 (FA 2012, s 35).

The rule which has applied since 6 April 2012 is that a withdrawal from a foreign currency bank account does not generate a foreign chargeable gain provided that the beneficial owner of the account is the original creditor of the bank, or is a personal representative or legatee of the original creditor (ie is not an inter vivos donee or purchaser of the balance of the account). This is the effect of TCGA 1992, s 251(1), combined with s 252(1) as amended.

A corollary of the rule is that, since 6 April 2012, a withdrawal from a foreign currency bank has not been capable of giving rise to an allowable loss (TCGA 1992, s 16(2)).

The change was not retrospective and does not exempt bank account gains comprised in remittances of 2012–13 and post save insofar as the gains themselves were realised after 6 April 2012. This means it will, strictly, still be necessary to carry out computations to establish the chargeable gains realised on bank account disposals before 6 April 2012, where the funds are now remitted to the UK. However, it may be possible to take advantage of certain concessionary practices published by HMRC in relation to foreign currency bank accounts. These were discussed in the eighteenth edition of this book.

GAINS REALISED BEFORE 6 APRIL 2008

49.19 As with relevant foreign income, gains realised before 6 April 2008 are subject to the law as to remittances enacted in 2008 insofar as unremitted as at 6 April 2008 (FA 2008, Sch 7 para 84). However, and again as with relevant foreign income, remittance by any relevant person who is not the taxpayer may be disregarded.

Indexation

49.20 On disposals prior to 5 April 2008 indexation was allowed insofar as the asset was acquired before 6 April 1998, the indexation allowance being frozen as at April 1998 in the case of disposals after that date (TCGA 1992, s 53 prior to amendment by FA 2008, Sch 2 para 79). Any applicable indexation allowance is not withdrawn should gains of 2007–08 or an earlier tax year be remitted now. This result follows because the ending of indexation is as respects disposals on or after 6 April 2008 (FA 2008, Sch 2 para 83).

Taper

49.21 Taper relief applied on disposals up to 5 April 2008. Should such a gain be remitted in 2008–09 or subsequently, taper relief is not allowed. This result follows because the gain is treated as accruing when remitted and taper relief does not apply to gains accruing in 2008–09 and post (see FA 2008, Sch 2 para 56(3) and TCGA 1992, s 12(2)).

DISPOSALS FOR LESS THAN FULL CONSIDERATION

49.22 Prior to 6 April 2008, tax was avoided if a non-domiciliary gave away a foreign situs asset abroad. Any gain thereby accruing was taxable only if remitted to the UK. However the non-domiciled donor was left with nothing to remit as he received no actual consideration. The donee owned an asset with an updated cost which, if sold, would generate a remittable gain equal only to any increase in value since the gift.

Since 6 April 2008, the loophole has been closed by ITA 2007, s 809T. The approach that s 809T takes is to treat the asset in the hands of the donee as derived from the chargeable gain realised by the donee. This means that the gain is remitted if the donee brings the asset to the UK. However, this does not result in tax for the donor unless the donee is a relevant person, for the remittance by another party of the donor's income and gains is not taxable unless the other party is a relevant person (see CHAPTER 54).

The main category of donee where remittance of the gifted asset results in tax is trusts, which are inter alia relevant persons if the donor or his minor children or grandchildren are beneficiaries (see para 54.6). A remittance by a corporate donee is also caught if the donor or a relevant person trust is a participator, as in such case the company is a relevant person (see para 54.12). But this would not apply if the transfer to the company was in exchange for shares or loan stock of a value equal to the asset transferred to the company; clearly, in such a case there is no gift.

The rule can also trigger a taxable remittance by the donor if the donee gives the asset back to him. This is particularly in point where the donee is a trust which subsequently appoints the asset back to the donor.

As with other cases of deemed derivation (see para 52.15), the issue arises of whether derivation from the gain extends to the proceeds of the gifted asset or to investments purchased with those proceeds. There is an argument that the deemed derivation does not go this far, as s 809T states simply that the asset is derived from the chargeable gains (see para 52.16).

Section 809T applies not merely on gifts but also on any transaction where the consideration received for the disposal of the asset is less than market value. In theory this is something of a trap for it can be difficult to know what market value is, and there is no disapplication for transactions by way of bargain at arm's length. The trap is compounded in that the asset disposed of is treated as derived from the full amount of the gain, and not just that part representing the undervalue.

Transitional issues

49.23 An issue of some difficulty is whether, in relation to the remittances in 2008–09 and later tax years, s 809T applies where the gift was in 2007–08 or earlier tax years. If it did so apply its compass would be limited, as a remittance of the gifted asset by the donee would not be caught, since the only relevant person in relation to pre-6 April 2008 income and gains is the taxpayer himself (see para **54.1**). But the rule could still be in point if the gifted asset was passed back to the donor, as on an appointment back to the settlor out of a settlor-interested trust followed by remittance by the settlor.

The better view, adopted by HMRC, is that s 809T does not apply in such circumstances (see RDRM para 31180). It is one of the sections inserted into ITA 2007 by FA 2008, Sch 7 para 1, and that paragraph has a general commencement date of 2008–09 (para 81). The rule that the present version of TCGA 1992, s 12 applies if a gain realised in 2007–08 and prior is remitted in 2008–09 or post could be read as importing s 809T. But if so it is difficult to reconcile this with the use of the present tense in s 809T and the lack of an express transitional provision incorporating it.

Chapter 50

EARNINGS

INTRODUCTION

50.1 This chapter explains the application of the remittance basis to earnings of non-UK domiciliaries. Except where otherwise stated, it assumes that the non-UK domiciliary has validly claimed the remittance basis for the tax year in which the earnings arise or is otherwise eligible for the remittance basis (see para **46.10**).

Where this is the case, the remittance basis applies to earnings attributable to duties performed outside the UK which qualify for 'overseas workday relief', or which qualify as 'overseas chargeable earnings'. As explained below, securing the remittance basis on earnings by virtue of overseas workday relief is fairly straightforward, but this relief is only available for the first few years of UK residence. By contrast, it is possible, in theory, to secure the remittance basis indefinitely under the regime for overseas chargeable earnings. However, this regime is subject to a number of restrictions and for some years has been very difficult to access in practice. FA 2014 has increased these difficulties further.

OVERSEAS WORKDAY RELIEF

50.2 Prior to FA 2013, there was a special regime for foreign earnings of individuals who claimed the remittance basis by virtue of non-ordinarily resident status. The regime applied whether or not such individuals were also non-UK domiciled. The regime was known as overseas workday relief, although this term was not used in the legislation.

FA 2013 abolished the concept of ordinary residence for tax purposes. FA 2013 included saving provisions which effectively 'grandfathered' the old regime for individuals who were (a) UK resident in the tax year 2012–13, but (b) not ordinarily resident on 5 April 2013 (FA 2013, Sch 46, para 26(1)). This 'grandfathering' has in all cases ceased to apply.

However, the broad effect of the old regime for non-ordinarily resident taxpayers has been preserved by the current regime for non-UK domiciliaries contained in ITEPA 2003, s 26. Again, this is widely known as overseas workday relief, although the legislation does not call it such.

Unlike the old regime, the current form of overseas workday relief is restricted to non-UK domiciled taxpayers. It is available if the taxpayer is a remittance basis user and (broadly) has been UK resident for no more than three tax years (including the current year) and the tax year(s) of UK residence follow at least three tax years of non-UK residence (ITEPA 2003, s 26A).

Where the relief is available, the remittance basis applies to earnings in respect of duties performed outside the UK, regardless of the residence status of the employer. Remuneration can be paid under a single contract of employment. If duties have been performed both within the UK and abroad, the remuneration will be apportioned between general earnings taxable on the arising basis (being those earnings that are 'in respect of' the UK duties) and general earnings that are taxable only if remitted (being those earnings that are 'in respect of' the non-UK duties).

The statute does not specify how such apportionment is to be carried out. There is some case law in relation to the old regime, which required the same apportionment exercise. Generally, the apportionment is to be performed on a time spent basis, employing units of days rather than hours (*Platten v Brown* [1986] STC 514). However, HMRC practice is to allow the time apportionment exercise to be carried out on the basis of half-day units (see EIM77020).

Whether particular earnings are 'in respect of' duties performed in the UK is a matter of fact, and in certain circumstances time-apportionment may not be the correct approach. For example in *Taylor v Provan* (49 TC 579) it was held that a reimbursement of travel expenses of a director who had travelled to the UK to perform duties there was an emolument 'in respect of' UK duties and therefore taxable on the arising basis. Similarly, in *Perro v Mansworth* (SpC 286) a payment by the employer of the employee's tax liabilities in respect of earnings for UK duties was itself an emolument 'in respect of' UK duties.

Where overseas workday relief is applicable, remuneration will need to be paid to a non-UK account of the employee to avoid an immediate remittance of the earnings relating to non-UK duties.

Special mixed fund rules

50.3 Many individuals in receipt of earnings which qualify in part for overseas workday relief will, in practice, want or need to use such earnings for UK expenditure. In such cases, the issue arises of how to determine the tax status of the monies that have been brought into the UK – ie whether such monies are treated as comprising, in priority, earnings 'in respect of' UK duties (taxable on the arising basis and therefore, in a sense, clean capital which can be brought to the UK without any additional tax charge) or earnings 'in respect of' non-UK duties (in which case there will be tax on the remittance).

Absent any special provision in the legislation, this issue would be determined by the normal mixed fund rules, contained in ITA 2007, ss 809Q–809R and discussed in CHAPTER 53. However, the remittance basis legislation now includes special mixed fund rules, which are limited in scope to determining the above issue, and apply provided that certain conditions are met (ITA 2007, ss 809RA–809RD). Such rules are intended to be simpler to operate than the normal mixed fund rules, although the drafting is elaborate and the rules are not entirely straightforward. HMRC published FAQs in 2013 (HMRC Notice 3 October 2013, reproduced SWTI [2013] 3211).

The conditions are that the account is a non-UK account, in the name of the individual, and that the account has a balance of £10 or less on the date on which earnings from the relevant employment are first credited to it. Details of the account must be notified to HMRC in the individual's tax return for the relevant tax year. The individual must not deposit other sums into the account and so transfers into the account must be limited to payments of remuneration by the employer and, if applicable, interest paid by the individual's bank on the account balance.

Assuming that at all times the account contents are limited to (a) earnings taxable on the arising basis, and (b) earnings qualifying for the remittance basis (in some combination), and that transfers out of the account have occurred in the course of the tax year which include (i) transfers to a UK account (or other transfers involving a remittance to the UK), and (ii) transfers for non-UK expenditure (or other transfers not involving a remittance to the UK), then the simplified mixed fund rules have the effect that the individual can proceed as follows:

- The individual needs to establish the value of arising basis earnings and remittance basis earnings, respectively, received by the end of the tax year.
- The individual then needs to establish the total value of transfers to a UK account and other remittances from the account in the course of the tax year. All such remittances are treated as having occurred on the last day of the tax year. Such remittances will be treated as remittances of arising basis earnings (ie remuneration that has already been taxed) in priority to remittance basis earnings.
- The individual also needs to establish the total value of transfers to a non-UK account and other transfers not involving a remittance ('off-shore transfers'), in the course of the tax year. All such transfers are treated as having occurred on the last day of the tax year (but immediately after the remittances referred to above). If the account contents at such point comprise a mixture of arising basis earnings and remittance basis earnings, the offshore transfers will be deemed to have carried out of the account arising basis earnings and remittance basis earnings on a pro rata basis.

It will be apparent that for maximum tax-efficiency, the individual should limit remittances to the UK from the notified account to the expected value of arising basis earnings in the course of the tax year.

Interaction with PAYE

50.4 A further complication with the overseas workday relief regime is its interaction with the Income Tax (Pay As You Earn) Regulations 2003 (SI 2003/2682), under which employers have obligations to deduct income tax at source. Such obligations typically go hand-in-hand with obligations to deduct national insurance contributions, although the rules are not entirely harmonised.

An employer is subject to PAYE withholding obligations in relation to an employment if it has a place of business in the UK (regardless of whether it qualifies as UK resident) and earnings from the employment will be taxable for the employee. The rules are awkward to apply in relation to individuals whose earnings may, to some extent, qualify for overseas workday relief, as the proportion of earnings that are taxable will not be determined until after the end of the relevant tax year. In these circumstances a PAYE settlement agreement may be made between the employer and HMRC (under reg 105) to the effect that the income tax deductions at source will be limited to the tax due on the proportion of the earnings that the employer reasonably anticipates will be attributable to duties of the employee in the UK.

CHARGEABLE OVERSEAS EARNINGS

50.5 Where overseas workday relief does not apply, it may still be possible for an individual to secure the remittance basis on earnings which fall within the definition of chargeable overseas earnings. This definition requires the following conditions to be met (ss 22(1), 23(2)):

(1)   the individual is not domiciled in the UK;
(2)   he is a remittance basis user for the year in question;
(3)   the employer is non-UK resident;
(4)   the duties of the employment are performed wholly outside the UK (although see para 50.7 below, re incidental duties); and
(5)   the employee does not meet the requirements for overseas workday relief to be available.

Key differences between overseas workday relief and the chargeable overseas earnings regime is that the latter can only apply where the employer is non-UK resident, and is precluded if non-incidental work under the employment is performed in the UK.

Assuming the earnings are chargeable overseas earnings, they become taxable if and when remitted to the UK. The general rules as to the meaning of remittance in ITA 2007, ss 809L–809S apply (ITEPA 2003, s 22(6); see further CHAPTERS 51 to 57). For these purposes, the treatment of a remittance from a mixed fund is determined under the normal mixed fund rules (discussed in CHAPTER 53), not the special mixed fund rules outlined above.

Remittances after termination of employment

50.6 A remittance of chargeable overseas earnings is taxable whether or not the employment is still held (s 22(3)). In principle, this is so even if the employee is dead when the earnings are remitted, his personal representatives being the party liable for the tax due (ITEPA 2003, s 13(4)). However, HMRC comment (in the Residence, Domicile and Remittance Basis Manual, at para 33600) that 'Foreign Income and Foreign Chargeable Gains of a remittance basis user that arose or accrued before his or her death but which are brought to the UK after the date of his or her death will generally not be regarded as a taxable remittance.' HMRC appear to include chargeable overseas earnings within the term 'Foreign Earnings' and therefore not to differentiate between the tax treatment of remittances of chargeable overseas earnings and relevant foreign income after the death of the remittance basis user.

In contrast to relevant foreign income, a remittance is taxable even if the employee has become non-UK resident when remittance occurs.

Incidental duties

50.7 Statute provides that in determining whether any duties are performed in the UK, incidental duties may be disregarded (ITEPA 2003, s 39). However, the concept of incidental duties has been strictly defined by case law: for example it has been held that an airline pilot working for a foreign airline whose schedule includes occasional UK stopovers performs more than incidental duties in the UK (*Robson v Dixon* (1972) 48 TC 527). As discussed below, HMRC rely on *Robson v Dixon* in taking an extremely hard line where the employee has carried out activities in the UK in connection with the foreign employment, even if such activities might in isolation be considered trivial.

Split contract arrangements

50.8 Many non-UK domiciliaries have – at least historically – been employed under what are called dual or split contracts. One of these contracts would be with a UK employer and would cover UK duties. The other would be with an associated foreign company and would cover duties outside the UK. Historically, it has been the case that the earnings under the contract with the foreign company would qualify as chargeable overseas earnings provided that all the duties under it were in fact performed abroad and the split of aggregate earnings was reasonable (see para **50.9** below).

HMRC have published their practice on split or dual contracts (*Tax Bulletin* 76 (April 2005) p 1201; Employment Income Manual, appendix 3). Their position may be summarised as follows:

(1) They accept that split contracts can be used in appropriate cases and, where they are appropriate, the tax issues raised are whether non-incidental duties under the foreign employment have been performed in the UK, and whether the spilt of earnings is commercial.

(2) HMRC do not consider that split contracts are appropriate unless there are two distinguishable jobs. Unless there are two distinguishable jobs, HMRC are likely to argue there is in reality a single employment partially carried on in the UK and so wholly taxable on an arising basis. In particular HMRC take this line where the sole division of functions between the two employments is according as to where the functions are performed.

(3) Particular scrutiny is to be expected where originally there was a single employment or self-employment or where the job was originally advertised as one.

(4)   If the two contracts are in reality one, the UK employer is responsible for PAYE and NIC on the whole.

HMRC practice repays detailed study by those minded to take up split contracts. Both for tax and for commercial reasons it is important to remember that the arrangements adopted will have employment law as well as tax implications. Specialist employment law advice is essential, both in the UK and in the jurisdiction of the foreign contract. Furthermore, even where a robust split contract arrangement is feasible, it may still be defeated by the special provision for associated employments discussed at para 50.10 below.

The distinction between the incidental and non-incidental duties of the foreign employment can prove troublesome. HMRC tend to take a very tough line on activities in the UK which might be regarded as incidental, and in particular consider that responding to a telephone call or email from a client whilst in the UK is not incidental to the foreign employment if the employee's duties under the foreign contract included servicing the client in question (*Tax Bulletin 76*, pp 1202–1203).

Associated employments

50.9 Special provisions apply where the employee has one or more associated employments and the duties under those employments include UK duties. In such a case, it is necessary to look at the aggregate earnings under all the employments. The chargeable overseas earnings are such proportion of that aggregate as is reasonable (ITEPA 2003, s 24), having regard to all relevant circumstances and in particular to the nature of and time devoted to duties in the UK and duties outside the UK.

Employments count as associated if the employer is the same, or if the employers are associated (ITEPA 2003, s 24(4)). Corporate employers under common control are treated as associated. For this purpose, 'control' bears its close company definition, discussed in CHAPTER 87 (ITEPA 2003, s 24(5); CTA 2010, s 450).

The effect of these provisions is that it is not possible for the overall remuneration to be weighted towards the foreign employment, unless that is justified by the circumstances, including in particular the split of workdays between the UK and overseas. If the earnings payable by the foreign employer are disproportionate, bearing in mind how much time is spent in the UK and abroad and all other relevant factors, a portion of such earnings are in effect re-allocated, for tax purposes, to the UK employment.

Further restrictions

50.10 Further, significant restrictions on the scope of the chargeable overseas earnings regime were introduced by FA 2014, Sch 3 as ITEPA 2003, ss 24A–24B. They are potentially applicable, with effect from 6 April 2014, in any case where there are two associated employments and one of them involves the performance of UK duties ('associated' having the same meaning as for the purposes of ITEPA 2003, s 24, discussed above). However, there is an additional requirement for these provisions to be in point, namely that the associated employments be 'related' to each other (s 24A(8)). The legislation sets out various circumstances in which the employments are considered to be 'related' to each other (s 24A(9)), including:

(a)   where it is reasonable to suppose that the employee would not hold one employment without holding the other employment, or that the employments will cease at the same time or one employment will cease in consequence of the other employment ceasing;

(b)   where the terms of one employment operate to any extent by reference to the other employment;

(c)   where the performance of duties of one employment is wholly or partly dependent upon, or otherwise linked to, the performance of duties of the other employment;

(d)   where the duties of the employments are wholly or mainly of the same type (ignoring the fact that they may be performed in different locations);

(e)   where the duties of the employments involve to any extent the provision of goods or services to the same customers or clients;

(f)   where the employee is (i) a director of either employer, and has a 'material interest' in either employer; or (ii) a 'senior employee' of either employer; or (iii) one of the employees of either employer who receives the higher or highest levels of remuneration.

'Material interest' has the meaning given to it in ITEPA 2003, s 68; essentially this means ownership or control over 5% or more of the relevant company's ordinary shares, whether such ownership or control is direct or via intermediate companies. The legislation makes no attempt to define 'senior employee'.

It will be noted that many of the above conditions are subjective in nature, or are potentially open to various interpretations, so that it may be difficult to say categorically whether they are met.

Where the view is reached that any of these conditions apply, so that the employments are not only associated but also 'related', s 24A may cause earnings received under the foreign employment to be reclassified as general earnings which are not eligible for the remittance basis. Whether such reclassification occurs depends on the amount of foreign taxation, if any, which is payable in respect of the foreign earnings. Specifically, the test is whether the amount of foreign taxation which would be allowed as a credit against UK income tax on the earnings is 65% or more of the UK income tax that would be payable on the earnings, assuming them to be subject to the additional rate (ie 45%). If not, the remittance basis will be withdrawn from such earnings.

The broad thrust of s 24A, therefore, is that unless the chargeable overseas earnings attract local tax, which is actually payable, of at least 29% of the gross amount received from the foreign employer, they will be subject to UK tax on the arising basis.

BENEFITS IN KIND

50.11 Amounts treated as earnings under the benefits in kind code in ITEPA 2003, Pt 3 are included within the term general earnings (ITEPA 2003, s 7(3)(b)). This means, in the case of remittance basis users, that they enjoy the reliefs described above. The main points in the benefits in kind code which are applicable to offshore tax planning are discussed in CHAPTER 93.

EMPLOYMENT-RELATED SECURITIES

50.12 Part 7 of ITEPA 2003 contains an extensive code taxing securities and securities options acquired by reason of employment. Any securities or options made available by the employer or a person connected with him are deemed to be acquired by reason of employment (ITEPA 2003, ss 421B(3) and 471(3)). Securities and options caught by this legislation are given the generic name employment-related securities.

Territorial limits

50.13 Amounts which are taxable under this legislation are not general earnings but are referred to as specific employment income and as such count as employment income (ITEPA 2003, s 7(4) and (6)). As specific employment income is not general earnings neither the general territorial limits in ITEPA 2003 nor the remittance basis described above apply. Instead specific territorial limits operate.

The general rule is that employment-related securities are not taxable unless the employee is UK resident when the securities or option are acquired (ITEPA 2003, ss 421E and 474). Prior to 2008–09 most of the code was also precluded if at the time of acquisition a resident employee was not ordinarily resident, but ordinary residence as a limiting factor was repealed in 2008 as respects acquisitions in 2008–09 and subsequent years (FA 2008, Sch 7 para 80).

Certain provisions, namely those in chapters 3A to 3D of ITEPA 2003, Pt 7 are not limited by residence at the time of acquisition. These provisions are those relating to securities whose market value is artificially depressed or enhanced, and securities acquired at an under or over value. The territorial limit applicable in each such case was and is that at the time of acquisition the employee is subject to UK tax on earnings from the employment. Thus non-residents working in the UK and, before 6 April 2008, those not ordinarily resident are caught.

Both under the general rule and chapters 3A–3D the focus is thus on status at the time of acquisition. Status at the time of charge is immaterial which means those then non-resident may be caught.

Remittance basis

50.14 Historically, specific employment income arising under the employment-related securities legislation did not qualify for the remittance basis. This anomaly was recognised and redressed as part of the 2008 reforms to the remittance basis, but the relief is available only as respects securities and options acquired in 2008–09 and subsequently (FA 2008, Sch 7 paras 22 and 80). It follows that specific employment income arising from securities and options acquired before then is subject to previous law and practice.

The new remittance basis applies to all charges on employment-related securities other than those in respect of securities with enhanced market value and securities with artificially depressed market value (ie those caught by chapters 3A and 3B of Pt 7: see ITEPA 2003, s 41A(2)). It is also precluded if under the anti-avoidance rule in ITEPA 2003, s 446UA a charge is made on acquisition, where securities are acquired at an undervalue.

The new remittance basis applies to such part (if any) of specific securities income as falls within the term foreign securities income. To arrive at the foreign securities income a time apportionment exercise is required over what is called the relevant period. In general this is the period over which the securities or option have been held (ITEPA 2003, s 41B). But in the case of the charges under chapters 3D and 4 of Pt 7 on securities disposed of for more than market value and on post-acquisition benefits, the relevant period is the tax year in which the chargeable event occurs (s 41B(4)).

The specific securities income is treated as foreign if and to the extent that the employee has qualified for the remittance basis during the relevant period. The part of the specific securities income which is foreign is the part attributable on a pro rata basis to years in which he was a remittance basis user and all the duties were performed outside the UK (s 41C(3)). Adjustment may be required if there are associated employments, on the lines explained in para 50.9 above (s 41D). In addition an apportioned part of the securities income attributable to years when the duties were performed partly in and partly outside the UK is foreign if in those years the employee qualified for overseas work day relief (s 41C(5); see para 50.5 above).

The part of the specific securities income which is treated as foreign also includes any attributable to tax years when the employee was not UK resident all. This is achieved by deeming him to have been a remittance basis user in such years (s 41C(7)).

It will be noted that the availability of the remittance basis turns on status during the whole relevant period and not on status when the securities or options are acquired or when the chargeable event occurs. It is thus possible for specific securities income to be in part foreign securities income even if the employee is not a remittance basis user in the year of charge. This would be the position if the employee was either non-resident for part of the relevant period or resident but a remittance basis user.

Meaning of remittance

50.15 Assuming some part of the securities income is under these rules foreign, the general remittance rules described in Chapters 51 to 57 apply in determining whether it is remitted to the UK (ITEPA 2003, s 41A(8)). As with earnings generally, a remittance is taxable whether or not the employment is still held and whether or not the employee is UK resident (s 41A(7)).

The securities or option giving rise to the charge are in general deemed to be derived from the foreign securities income (s 41A(8)). But this rule is displaced if the chargeable event is a disposal or assignment of the securities or option for a consideration equal to or exceeding their market value. In that event the consideration, and not the securities or option, is treated as derived from the foreign securities income (s 41A(9)).

Nothing in the rules disapplies the new relief where the securities or option is issued by a UK company. But as is indicated in para **51.19**, the better view is that remittance occurs if and insofar as the asset held by the employee is UK situs, and this is the view taken by HMRC (Employment-related Securities Manual para ERSM 16110). The applicable rules as to situs are the general rules described in Chapter **38**, and so, if the remittance basis is to be secured, what is treated as derived from the foreign securities income must be non-UK situs under those rules. This will be easy to achieve where it is the consideration which is the derived property but less easy, in UK cases, where the derived property is the securities or option itself.

HMRC practice

50.16 HMRC have published their analysis of the remittance basis applicable to employment-related securities in the Employment-Related Securities Manual (at para 160600 et seq).

EXEMPTION FOR MINIMAL FOREIGN EARNINGS

50.17 In certain limited circumstances foreign earnings (and other foreign income) of a UK resident non-UK domiciliary may be completely exempt from tax, under ITA 2007, ss 828A–828D. The requirements for the exemption are fairly involved. It only applies if the individual has not made a claim to the remittance basis under s 809B, so essentially only if the individual has opted to be taxed on the arising basis.

The exemption requires there to be earnings from a UK employment. If there are also earnings from a foreign employment, which would qualify for the remittance basis if a claim were made under s 809B, such earnings must not exceed £10,000 and they must be subject to foreign tax. HMRC practice is to treat earnings as being subject to foreign tax if they are, in principle, taxable, even if no actual tax is payable due to a tax allowance in the relevant country (see the HMRC publication 'Paying tax on the remittance basis – an introduction'). The exemption is precluded if there is foreign investment income in excess of £100, if such income is not subject to foreign tax, or if there are any other forms of foreign income or gains. Various other conditions apply. Where all conditions are met, the earnings from the foreign employment (and other foreign income) are effectively left out of account in determining the individual's UK tax liability.

Section V

The Meaning of Remittance

Chapter 51

CORE MEANING OF 'REMITTANCE'

INTRODUCTION

51.1 This chapter explains the core meaning of 'remittance'. Until April 2008, the concept of 'remittance' was largely contained in case law. It now has a statutory basis, being governed by the complex rules in ITA 2007, ss 809L–809S.

HMRC has published guidance on this in the Residence, Domicile and Remittance Basis Manual ('RDRM'). The HMRC guidance contains many worked examples. What follows here is an analysis of the law, so the guidance is referred to only sparingly. Nonetheless it should always be kept in mind that the guidance may in a given case impact on compliance or planning and that it may and has changed.

Section 809L

51.2 Section 809L contains the basic law as to what constitutes remittance. It conflates a number of different kinds of remittance and so needs to be unpicked before it can be understood. Although s 809L is expressed in terms of four conditions, A, B, C, and D, it in fact prescribes three kinds of remittance, namely the core definition in Conditions A and B and two anti-avoidance provisions, respectively Conditions C and D. A further source of difficulty is that the conditions combine remittance in the general sense of the term with two kinds of deemed remittance, namely payment abroad for UK services and payments abroad in connection with certain debts.

Consequently, s 809L needs to be unpicked as follows:

(1)   The core definition of remittance in Conditions A and B.
(2)   Services, which are discussed in CHAPTER 55.
(3)   Debts, which are discussed in CHAPTER 56.
(4)   Conditions C and D, which are considered in CHAPTER 57.

Relevant persons

51.3 Conditions A–D are expressed in terms of relevant persons rather than the individual taxpayer to whom the foreign income or gains accrued. The term 'relevant person' comprehends the taxpayer himself, together with his spouse, his minor children and grandchildren, trusts of which individual relevant persons are beneficiaries and companies in which such individuals or trusts are participators. The definition of relevant person is set out in ITA 2007, s 809M and is explained in Chapter 54.

Inclusive or comprehensive definition

51.4 An issue which may be raised is whether there are any circumstances in which a taxable remittance can occur even if, on a strict construction, there is no remittance under the terms of s 809L. In other words, has any of the pre-2008 case law as to the meaning of remittance survived, and are there circumstances in which such case law would produce a remittance where the provisions of s 809L do not?

The answer to this point comes from the charging provisions discussed in Chapters 48 to 50, for these state simply 'See Chapter A1 of Part 14 of ITA 2007 for the meaning of "remitted to the United Kingdom" (ITEPA 2003, s 26(5); ITTOIA 2005, s 832(4); TCGA 1992, s 12(5))'. This directive language does, it may be suggested, require s 809L and the following sections to be construed as comprehensive.

Pre-2008 income and gains

51.5 As explained in Chapters 48 to 50, remittances of income or gains which arose or accrued before 6 April 2008 are, subject to exceptions, taxed under the present rules in s 809L and the following sections. The most important exception to this general rule is that, in relation to such income and gains, the term relevant person comprehends only the taxpayer himself (FA 2008, Sch 7, para 86(4)). Other exceptions, applicable to pre-2008 relevant foreign income, are considered in paras **48.19** to **48.22**.

THE CORE DEFINITION

51.6 There are two elements to the core definition of remittance in s 809L, one in Condition A and one in Condition B. Both conditions must be met for a taxable remittance to arise under the core definition.

Condition A

51.7 Condition A imposes two alternate requirements as follows:

(1)   The taxpayer or another relevant person has brought money or other property to the UK or has received or used it in the UK, or

(2)   Money or other property is used in the UK for the benefit of the taxpayer or another relevant person or it is brought to or received in the UK for such a person's benefit.

Condition B

51.8 Condition B also postulates two alternate requirements. These are as follows:

(1)   The property is the taxpayer's foreign income or gains, or
(2)   The property is derived from the taxpayer's foreign income or gains and belongs to a relevant person.

It is to be observed that Condition B refers just to the property, using the definite article. It thus refers to the property brought to or used in the UK as specified in Condition A. But in contrast to Condition A, Condition B does not additionally refer to money. This does not, however, mean that money is not covered, for Condition A refers to money or other property and thus makes it clear that property comprehends money.

Under the pre-2008 law, there was no remittance of relevant foreign income if such income was used abroad to purchase an asset and that asset was brought into the UK. But a remittance did occur, and a tax charge arose, if the asset was sold while still in the UK (*Scottish Provident Institution v Farmer* (1912) 6 TC 34). The reason why a taxable remittance did not occur until the asset was sold in the UK was that the old law referred to 'sums' received in the UK (ITTOIA 2005, s 832(1) as originally enacted). As Condition A refers to property rather than sums, the position now is that remittance occurs when the property is brought to the UK. (See para **51.19** below.)

Basic structure

51.9 An important general point about Conditions A and B is that the starting point is Condition A and requires that the question asked is whether money or other property has been brought to or received in the UK. Only having identified such money or other property does one then ask whether it is foreign income or gains or derived from such income or gains. In contrast to pre-2008 law, one does not start with the income and gains and ask what sums or amounts have been received in the UK in respect of them. Because Conditions A and B are structured in this way the concept of derivation is of critical importance. It is discussed in the next chapter.

FOREIGN INCOME OR GAINS

51.10 As noted above, the legislation distinguishes between property which 'is' the foreign income or gains (s 809L(3)(a)) and property which 'derives' from the foreign income or gains (s 809L(3)(b)).

Property which is the foreign income and gains

51.11 HMRC refer to remittances which are the foreign income and gains as 'direct' remittances (RDRM 33140). They consider direct remittance occurs only where the income or gains themselves are transferred to the UK whether as cash, by cheque or by bank transfer (ibid). Should the income or gains be invested, any remittance of the investment is derived from the income or gains, as is any remittance of the proceeds of the investment (RDRM 35030, example 6).

In earlier editions of this book it was suggested income and gains retain their character as income and gains even if invested and that accordingly a bringing of the investment or the proceeds of its sale to the UK was not a direct remittance. The authority given was *Patuck v Lloyd* (1944) 26 TC 284 and *Walsh v Randall* (1940) 23 TC 55. These cases determined that under pre-2008 law mere investment of the income did not prevent remittance of the proceeds of the investment from being taxed as a remittance of the income. In a graphic phrase in *Walsh v Randall*, Wrottesley J said (at p 61):

'The fact is that if a man resides here he cannot, by investing for the time being his income abroad, change its character vis a vis the Income Tax collector.'

It is however clear that these cases are authority only for the remittance being taxable and not for whether what was remitted was the income or was derived from the income. In *Thomson v Moyse* (1960) 39 TC 291, Lord Radcliffe made it clear (at p 335) that a remittance was taxable if the sums received were 'sums of money derived from the application of the income to achieving the necessary transfer'. It thus appears that even under pre-2008 law, taxable remittance could occur if what was remitted was derived from the income rather than being the income itself.

HMRC's construction is more in accordance with the language of Condition B, in that it is difficult to see property as being the income or gains once invested. In these circumstances, it may be regarded as correct.

Property derived from the foreign income and gains

51.12 The term 'derives' is not defined in the legislation. As indicated above, the better view is that it covers cases where the income or gains are invested by the taxpayer, and what he remits is the proceeds of the investments. That apart, the derivation concept means taxable remittance can occur where the taxpayer has passed the foreign income and gains to another relevant person and that person remits. Under pre-2008 law, a gift abroad converted income or gains in the hands of the donor into clean capital in the hands of the donee, with the result that remittance by the donee did not attract tax (*Carter v Sharon (Inspector of Taxes)* [1936] 1 All ER 720, 20 TC 229; *Grimm v Newman* [2002] EWCA Civ 1621, [2003] 1 All ER 67, [2002] STC 1288). The combined effect of the relevant person and the derivation concepts reverses this where the donee is a relevant person.

The concept of derivation is not however an easy one, and it is unclear how far tracing should go where gift and remittance are not part of pre-planned arrangements or otherwise closely identified with each other. These and other issues attaching to the meaning of derivation are discussed in CHAPTER 52.

There is one qualification to the non-definition of derive. This is that in certain instances where there is plainly no derivation in the normal sense of the term, derivation is deemed to occur. The legislation enacts several types of deemed derivation and this subject too is discussed in CHAPTER 52 (see para **52.15**).

The belonging requirement

51.13 As indicated above, property derived from the income or gains only results in taxable remittance under Conditions A and B if it belongs to a relevant person when brought to or received or used in the UK. This is point of some significance given that, under Condition A, such receipt or use can be for the benefit of a relevant person rather than by him personally. The point means that in the case of derived property Condition B is not satisfied just because there is some benefit in the UK to a relevant person: in addition the property must also belong to a relevant person.

But this point does not preclude remittance in all cases. It does not avail if what is brought to the UK is the income and gains, as then there is no belonging requirement. And even if the point does avail, enjoyment by a relevant person may result in remittance under Condition C (see CHAPTER 57).

Mixed funds

51.14 In reality foreign income and gains often pass through many bank accounts and investments prior to remittance and normally end up mixed up both with each other and with other funds.

There are rules, the mixed funds rules, for tracing items of income or gains through such mixed funds. These rules, which do not apply to pre-2008 income and gains, are enacted by ITA 2007, s 809Q and described in CHAPTER 53 .

AMOUNT REMITTED

51.15 Where the property remitted is the foreign income or gains, the amount remitted is equal to the income or gains (ITA 2007, s 809P(2)). The same rule applies where the property remitted is derived from the foreign income or gains (s 809P(3)). In other words the amount taxed is not the value of what is remitted but the amount of the income or gains from which what is remitted is derived. The only limitation placed on this is that the amount taxed cannot exceed the income or gains, this cap being applied to aggregate remittances where there are more than one (s 809P(12)).

This rule works harshly where foreign income and gains are invested and the value of the investment falls. Should the investment be brought to the UK, the ensuing tax charge is not on its value but the amount of foreign income or gains used to buy it. So too if, having fallen in value, the asset is sold and the proceeds are brought to the UK, the tax charge is not on what is brought to the UK but on the original cost of the bad investment.

This rule is not confined to investments. It applies also where foreign income or gains are spent on assets for enjoyment, for example cars or other chattels.

If these, or their proceeds, are brought to the UK, the tax charge is effectively on cost rather than value.

If only a proportion of the income or gain is brought to the UK, only that proportion is taxed as remitted. Less clear is the position where what is brought to the UK is not part of the income or gain but property derived from that part. On a literal reading the property is derived from the whole gain or item of income, in which case remittance of the property results in remittance of that whole. But the reality is that the property remitted is derived from part only of the gain or income and the rules should clearly be read as requiring only that part to be taxed as remitted. It is difficult to see a purposive construction as requiring any other conclusion. It is implicit from examples in RDRM that such is accepted by HMRC.

An interesting and unresolved issue is how far these rules as to quantum are implicitly displaced by the mixed fund rules discussed in CHAPTER 53. The issue arises because those rules require the amount of the various categories of income and capital in the mixed fund prior to the transfer to be ascertained and are expressed as operating inter alia for the purposes of determining amounts remitted (see ss 809QA(1)(b) and 809Q(3), step 1). One reading of those rules is that the amounts are fixed by values immediately prior to the transfer out of the mixed fund. But it is difficult to see this surviving a purposive construction.

CURRENCY FLUCTUATION

51.16 Most foreign income and gains are received in foreign currency and only converted to sterling on remittance. A difficult and controversial issue is whether remittances have to be converted to sterling at exchange rates prevailing when the income or gains arose or at rates prevailing when the remittance occurs. Most professional bodies take the former view. HMRC takes the former view in relation to gains, but the latter view in relation to income. Their view is stated in RDRM31190, and in a notice issued on 24 December 2009 (reproduced in [2010] SWTI p 37).

The basis of the view taken by professional advisers is two rules applicable to CGT:

(1)   Bank accounts are assets for CGT purposes (TCGA 1992, s 21). In most cases gains or losses on foreign currency bank accounts are neither chargeable nor allowable (TCGA 1992, s 252; see para 52.18). But this exemption does not detract from the general rule that such accounts are assets.

(2)   Where investments are bought and sold in foreign currency the gain or loss takes account of currency fluctuation as well as the investment gain or loss. Accordingly for CGT purposes the gain or loss is computed by comparing the sterling equivalent of the cost of acquisition at exchange rates prevailing on acquisition with the sterling equivalent of the proceeds of disposal at exchange rates prevailing at the time of disposal (*Capcount Trading v Evans* [1993] STC 11).

On the basis of these two rules, it may be suggested the correct analysis is as follows:

(a)   Assuming income or gains accrue in a foreign currency their sterling amount is fixed at exchange rates prevailing at the time of accrual.

(b)   If the income or gains are invested before being remitted, and the disposal of the investment results in a gain, the proceeds of disposal fall to be analysed in sterling terms and as so analysed comprise the sterling gain computed as per the rules described above plus the original income or gains converted at the date when they accrued. These are taxed in their original sterling amounts if remittance then occurs.

(c)   If instead of being invested the original income or gains are until remittance simply held in a bank account denominated in a currency which appreciates against sterling, the same rule applies, but the gain element on the disposal represented by withdrawal from the bank account is tax-free on remittance.

(d)   If the investment or bank account generates a sterling loss, a subsequent remittance of the proceeds is a remittance equal to the original income or gains. The rule in s 809P, described above, means the amount taxed as remitted is the full amount of such income or gains.

In support of this analysis is the fact that the rules defining what constitutes remittance and the amount of such remittance applies to both income and gains. It would therefore be illogical if the rules ignored the CGT treatment of currency gains and bank accounts.

HMRC's position that conversion should occur only at the date of remittance appears to be based on little analysis other than that such was the practice prior to the 2008 changes. Their position produces odd results. If income is received in the form of a foreign currency bank balance, which appreciates prior to remittance, in HMRC's view the income tax charge is on the sterling value at remittance, which is greater than the income which, in sterling terms, the taxpayer in fact received. This is difficult to reconcile with the rule that the amount remitted is the amount of the original income.

It is clear from all this that the currency issue is a mess. In practical terms the key requirement is to ensure that whatever approach is adopted is used consistently and fully disclosed.

CONDITION A

51.17 It is perhaps inevitable that in discussing remittance the focus is on Condition B and, in particular, derivation. But the requirements of Condition A should not be overlooked.

Acts of the relevant person

51.18 As indicated at the beginning of this chapter Condition A is engaged if the money or other property is brought to or received or used in the UK either by a relevant person or for the benefit of a relevant person. What therefore has to be identified is either a bringing to the UK, or receipt or use in the UK.

The incorporation of this language in Condition A means the mere existence of a UK situs asset does not of itself engage Condition A. It might be thought unlikely that a relevant person could have a UK situs asset without coming within the terms of Condition A. But one example would be a chattel stolen abroad. If the thief subsequently brings the chattel to the UK, Condition A is not engaged, as no relevant person has brought the chattel to the UK and what the thief does is certainly not for the benefit of a relevant person. Should the stolen property be recovered in the UK it would be remitted if then used in the UK by the rightful owner. But it may be suggested there would be no remittance if the police return the chattel by sending it directly to the rightful owner abroad.

In its reference to use, Condition A creates the concept of continuing remittance, with the condition potentially being met in a number of tax years with respect to the same asset. This would be so, for example, if the person concerned brings foreign income and gains to the UK to buy a house, and then lives in the house. In such cases, multiple taxation is avoided because of the rule that what is taxed cannot exceed the original income and gains (ITA 2007, s 809P(12); see para **51.15**).

Remittance in specie

51.19 As indicated above (para **51.10**) in relation to Condition B, it is clear that the bringing of a chattel or other physical asset to the UK counts as a remittance of any income or gains from which the chattel is derived. Condition A is engaged by the bringing in of the chattel, albeit, for the reasons given above, this would not apply if the bringing in was unauthorised and not by a relevant person. A similar analysis would apply if the income or gains had been invested in a bearer bond or specialty whose situs determines the situs of the creditor's asset (see paras **38.4** to **38.6**). Here remittance of the income or gains would occur if the bond or specialty were brought to the UK by or for the benefit of a relevant person.

Receipt in the UK

51.20 An example of receipt in the UK occurs if the payer of foreign source income credits it to the taxpayer in the UK. Such could occur if a non-UK resident company credited a dividend directly to the UK account of the remittance basis user. Here there would be no bringing to the UK but there would be receipt in the UK.

A similar issue arises where an employee is taxed on shares issued to him as part of his remuneration package. HMRC consider receipt of such shares to be a remittance of the foreign securities income. The basis of this view is said to be that the shares are used in the UK for the benefit of the employee (see ERSM 162930). This analysis, it may be suggested, is incorrect, as it is not a natural use of language to describe intangibles as used. The correct analysis is, it may suggested that the shares are property received in the UK.

UK assets paid for abroad

51.21 HMRC consider that Condition A is engaged if foreign income or gains are used abroad to purchase a UK asset such as a UK house or shares or bonds in a UK public company (RDRM33050). On this scenario, payment of the price is to a non-UK account of the seller, with the result the taxpayer's funds do not come to the UK. In these circumstances it is not immediately clear that Condition A is engaged, the case being one where the taxpayer has a UK situs asset without remittance having occurred.

In the case of land or chattels the point is normally academic, for if the asset is in the UK, it will very likely be used there by or for the benefit of the taxpayer. In the case of UK land or shares in a UK company, where legal title is obtained only by registration in the UK, it might be argued that such registration constitutes receipt of the property in the UK but this would depend on an extended and very artificial interpretation of 'receipt'. In any event in the case of shares it is unclear whether this argument could prevail where ownership is completed abroad, as may be the case with ADRs or immobilised securities (as to which see paras **38.14** and **38.15**).

Loans to UK residents

51.22 It is sometimes suggested that a remittance-basis user who makes a loan abroad to a UK resident is within Condition A even if the borrower never brings the money to the UK. The basis of the argument is that the loan results in the creation of a UK situs asset, namely a debt owed by the UK resident (see para **38.4**). It is, however, most unlikely Condition A is engaged, for there is no bringing to or receipt in the UK by the lender of anything and any use of the money by the lender takes place outside the UK. The transaction consists of the creation of a new asset, the UK situs debt, but that does not involve the use of any existing asset in the UK.

Essentially the same analysis applies where the remittance-basis user sells a foreign asset to a UK resident or provides a service abroad to a UK resident. The buyer may owe the purchase price and, by virtue of the buyer's residence, that debt may have a UK situs. But as with loans, nothing has been brought to or received or used in the UK.

A loan abroad does of course engage Condition A if the borrower is a relevant person and brings the money lent to the UK. Such might for example happen if the borrower is the remittance-basis user's spouse and she brings the borrowed money to the UK. But it would be very odd if, in such a case, remittance occurred if the loan was made abroad and the spouse spent all the money abroad and did not bring any of it to the UK. Such a result is avoided by the construction indicated above.

The only published comment HMRC have made on the point is to confirm that a loan abroad of income made by the remittance user to a relevant person results in a remittance if the borrower brings the money to the UK. In the example given (RDRM33050) the borrower is a company controlled by the remittance-basis user. It is not stated whether the company is UK resident or non-UK resident.

Concerns that a loan abroad to a UK resident could engage Condition A have led to suggestions that such loans should be documented as specialties, so as to ensure the debt does not have a UK situs provided the deed is kept abroad. On the basis of the analysis above, this step is not necessary. In any event it may not work if HMRC's doubts about the specialty rule are well-founded or the various technicalities surrounding that rule are not complied with (as to which see further para **38.6**).

Banking arrangements

51.23 International banking arrangements mean that a movement of funds from one foreign bank account to another may be reflected in debits and credits in London. If, for example, the remittance basis user wants to use his offshore sterling account with bank A to make a payment to a non-UK resident person, bank A may well effect the payment by instructing a bank in London, bank B, to debit bank A's account with bank B, and credit the London bank used by the non-resident's bank.

Under pre-6 April 2008 law, such arrangements did not result in remittance provided that the funds were never at the disposal of the non-domiciliary in the UK. The basis for this analysis was the formulation of the remittance basis in *Thomson v Moyse* (1960) 39 TC 291, where Lord Radcliffe characterised remittance as the turning of the non-domiciliary's resources abroad into expendable resources in the UK (at p 334). Reference could also be made to *Parkside Leasing Ltd v Smith* [1985] STC 63, which established that an individual 'gets' money not when he is handed a cheque but when the proceeds of the cheque are credited to his bank account.

On one view Condition A may imply that the above analysis does not now hold good as Condition A postulates simply that money which is or is derived from the income or gains is brought to the UK (s 809L(2)(a)). The use of the passive tense indicates that the bringing in can be by anybody, provided that the bringing is for the benefit of the taxpayer. But in reality remittance does not occur. The correct analysis, it may be suggested, is that the remittance basis user's offshore account with bank A is or represents his income and gains. The account bank A has with bank B may be derived from such income and gains, but even if it is, it does not satisfy Condition B in s 809L for it is not the property of the remittance basis user or any other relevant person. His property is his rights against bank A a point which would become painfully apparent should bank A default, for then his status would merely be that of unsecured creditor. He would have no right in rem, as against bank A's other creditors, to any part of bank A's account with bank B.

The position would of course be otherwise if bank A had deposited the remittance basis user's funds with bank B as his nominee. In that situation his funds are off bank A's balance sheet, and belong beneficially to the remittance basis user. Here remittance occurs not because London is being used for clearing but because the remittance basis user, through bank A, owns a bank account with a UK bank, bank B.

The key distinction in all this is thus whether the remittance basis user's rights against bank A are contractual or whether bank A is, to use lawyer's language, a bare trustee or nominee. Although in most simple banking cases the relationship is plainly contractual in more complex cases it may not be so and careful analysis is required.

HMRC have indicated agreement to the conclusion that passage of funds through the UK does not result in taxable remittance (RDRM 33560). They stress that the remittance basis user has no right to payment at any intermediate point and no control over the funds in transit.

Clearing systems

51.24 Many transactions in non-UK situs securities are cleared through systems which involve payments being made to or by UK resident entities, to or from UK accounts. For example, many Irish corporate mutual funds are traded through the Euroclear UK & Ireland Ltd securities settlement system, which is popularly known as CREST. This system, and other systems like it, involve a company acting as central counterparty, ie acting as a seller for every purchase made and as a buyer for every sale made through the system. In the case of CREST, the central counterparty is a UK company. In the course of transactions effected through CREST credit entries arise in UK bank and custody accounts. However, it is suggested that this does not, in itself, result in a taxable remittance, if foreign income or gains are used to make a purchase, or conversely if a sale is made of securities that represent foreign income or gains. The remittance basis user has no right to payment at any intermediate point and no control over the funds or contractual rights that arise under the clearance system. This is equivalent to the passage of funds through the UK pursuant to international banking arrangements.

Settlement of UK debts

51.25 A remittance-basis user or other relevant person may bring funds to the UK and then use the money to settle a debt. Here the bringing of funds to the UK engages Condition A and remittance occurs if the funds are or are derived from the remittance-basis user's income or gains. Equally the remittance-basis user or other relevant person may use income or gains to settle a debt abroad. Here remittance occurs under the rules discussed in CHAPTER 56 if the debt is a relevant debt.

But what if the remittance-basis user or other relevant person instructs his foreign bank, bank A, to send funds directly to a UK creditor's UK bank account? Here there may not be a remittance under the general rules, for the analysis will be the same as that described above in relation to banking instructions. The remittance-basis user simply has a contractual right against bank A, and that bank will effect the payment by directing a bank in London, bank B, to debit its account with that bank and credit the account of the remittance-basis user's creditor or that of the bank where the creditor banks.

However, the conventional view is undoubtedly that the instruction to the foreign bank to send funds to the creditor's UK account causes Condition A in ITA 2007, s 809L to be met. It is suggested that a court would be rather likely to uphold that conventional view, perhaps on the basis that, whatever the technical underpinnings of the transaction, the commercial substance is that the remittance-basis user's money has been transferred to a UK account through the actions of one or more banks, acting as his agent.

Even if, contrary to the conventional view, there is no remittance in this situation under the general language of Conditions A and B, there is remittance under the debt rules described in CHAPTER 56, provided that the debt being settled is a relevant debt. This result follows because of the very point implicit in the banking analysis given above, namely that use of the income and gains occurs when bank A debits the remittance-basis user's offshore account, and that use is outside the UK.

The possibility that in such cases there is no remittance under the general language of Conditions A and B may be thought to be at variance with some of the pre-2008 case law, notably *Timpson's Executors v Yerbury* (1936) 20 TC 155, which was referred to with approval in *Thomson (Inspector of Taxes) v Moyse* [1961] AC 967, [1960] 3 All ER 684, HL. In the former case the funds represented by a bank draft were held to be the property of the payer when the drafts reached the UK, rather than the payee. But as was recognised by Lord Radcliffe in *Thomson v Moyse*, this case is not really material to banking matters as it turned on the rules of English law as to the effecting of voluntary dispositions (see 39 TC, at p 336).

If it is correct to say that in the case of a payment from a non-UK account to a UK account of a creditor, Conditions A and B are not met unless the debt which is being settled is a relevant debt, then a payment of a debt which relates to neither property nor services is not caught. An obvious example of such a debt is a tax debt to HMRC. But here the legislation appears to assume that a direct transfer from the remittance-basis user's foreign bank account to HMRC is a remittance, for ITA 2007, s 809V expressly provides that payment of the remittance-basis charge is not a remittance if made directly from abroad (see further para 59.5). Arguably this provides support for the conventional view discussed above.

EXEMPT REMITTANCES

51.26 Certain remittances of foreign income and gains are exempt from tax if conditions laid down in the legislation are met. The most important of these exemptions is business investment relief, discussed in CHAPTER 58. Chattel reliefs are explained in CHAPTER 59.

Chapter 52

DERIVATION

INTRODUCTION

52.1 The words 'derives' and 'deriving' are central to the remittance law enacted in 2008. Further that law includes the concept of deemed derivation as well as actual derivation. But apart from such deeming, 'derives' and 'deriving' are not defined and so their meaning has to be inferred from the context and from cases decided on other legislation. This chapter analyses the relevant law, and takes as its starting point cases on pre-2008 remittance law.

PRE-2008 REMITTANCE LAW

52.2 The words 'derives' and 'deriving' were not used in the remittance legislation prior to 2008. But they did figure in two important cases.

Thomson v Moyse

52.3 *Thomson (Inspector of Taxes) v Moyse* [1961] AC 967, [1960] 3 All ER 684, HL is the leading pre-2008 case on remittance. It concerned an American who had received US income in his New York bank account. He drew dollar cheques on this bank and then sold those cheques to an English bank, the consideration being the immediate crediting to his English account of the sterling equivalent of the dollars. The bank then collected the dollars in New York and at that point the taxpayer's income account there was debited, ie after his English account had been credited. The taxpayer argued that he had not received his dollar income in the UK and, surprisingly in today's terms, was successful in the Court of Appeal. The House of Lords however reversed this decision.

In the present context the significance of the case lies in a dictum of Lord Radcliffe which uses the word 'derived'. Lord Radcliffe said, in discussing the remittance basis under Case IV of the old Schedule D:

> 'The computation in respect of income from foreign securities depends simply on the question, what is the amount of sums which have been or will be received in the United Kingdom in the year of assessment. No doubt proper construction of those words requires that the sums computable must be sums "of" the income, by which I would understand sums of money derived from the application of the income to achieving the necessary transfer. But that is all. If sterling sums are received and are so attributable, that is enough for liability.'

Harmel v Wright

52.4 In *Harmel v Wright (Inspector of Taxes)* [1974] STC 88 the taxpayer was a non-domiciled South African in receipt of what would now be called chargeable overseas earnings. He used the earnings to subscribe for shares in one South African company, Artemis, in which he owned all the shares. This company lent the money interest free to a second South African company, Lodestar, which was not owned by the taxpayer. Lodestar then lent the money to the taxpayer in London. The taxpayer argued his earnings had become and remained the shares in Artemis, his receipt in the UK being something entirely different, namely the loan from Lodestar.

Templeman J rejected this analysis and held the sums lent were the earnings. He characterised the true nature of the arrangements as follows:

> 'Of course there is no obligation on the taxpayer to invest money in Artemis, and if he invests money in the shares in Artemis there is no legal obligation on Artemis to lend it to Lodestar, and when Lodestar borrows the money from Artemis there is no legal obligation on Lodestar to lend it, in turn, to the taxpayer. But this is what always happens; that it shall happen lies entirely within the control of the taxpayer.'

He then focused on the passage in Lord Radcliffe's speech in *Thomson v Moyse* cited above:

> 'Applying the test adumbrated by Lord Radcliffe, have the sums of money received derived from the application of the taxpayer's income in South Africa to achieving the necessary transfers which led to his receiving money from Lodestar? The question turns on the meaning of the word "derivation". Can you, as I think, start with the £25,000 trace it through to the taxpayer and say the one is derived from the other, or must you, as counsel for the taxpayer says, trace the money as far as the shares in Artemis and, having got there, say it stays there. I see no reason why derivation should stop at the shares . . . '

Templeman J did however emphasise his decision turned on the facts of the case stating:

> 'In my judgement, on the peculiar circumstances of this case – and I say nothing about other cases where it may be possible that the money does, en route disappear and it is not possible to follow with the same certainty as in the present case – the sums which the taxpayer eventually receives represent and are the [earnings].'

Wider context

52.5 In evaluating both *Thomson v Moyse* and *Harmel v Wright* the wider context of pre-2008 law should be kept in mind:, specifically two points. The first is that, as explained in para **51.10**, a remittance was taxable even if the income was invested first. Thus in *Harmel v Wright*, there is no doubt that the proceeds of the sale or liquidation of Artemis would have remained the income for remittance purposes. Second, as described in para **53.39**, segregation of income and capital meant that remittances of capital were not taxable. This presumably was the point relied on by the taxpayer in *Thomson v Moyse* in that at the moment when he received sterling in the UK his dollar income in New York was intact.

THE CGT CASES

52.6 Under TCGA 1992, s 22, a disposal is deemed to occur where a capital sum is derived from an asset. This provision generated a surprising amount of litigation between 1974 and 1988 and a number of the cases are relevant here.

IRC v Montgomery

52.7 In *IRC v Montgomery* [1975] Ch 266, [1975] 1 All ER 664 an insurance claim in respect of fire damage to real property had been agreed in the sum of £75,192. However instead of taking payment from the insurer themselves the taxpayer trustees sold their rights under the policy to a third party assignee and he collected. The taxpayer trustees argued that the proceeds of sale were consideration for the assignment of the policy and thus free of CGT as the law then stood. HMRC, by contrast, argued that the proceeds were a capital sum derived from the real property.

Walton J decided in favour of the taxpayer. He first of all commented:

'The relevant dictionary meaning of "derivation" is to trace or show the origin, and that is what I think it means here.'

He then said:

'There is no doubt at all but that the only reason [the purchase monies] were paid to the trustees was in exchange for the disposal of their rights under the policies, which rights are quite obviously, from the point of view of [s 22] "derived" from the underlying real property of the trustees. Is it right to trace derivation back in this way? In my view it is not. It appears to me quite clear that the capital sum paid by [the third party assignee] was derived from the sale of the rights under the policies and that it is not right to go back any further. If it were legitimate to embark on an exercise of tracing the derivation of assets back in the manner of an abstract title, I do not know where the line could ever properly be drawn.'

Walton J had *Harmel v Wright* and *Thomson v Moyse* cited to him, but pointed out that they were of no assistance as they did not concern the interpretation of the word 'derive' as found in a statute. But this disregard of those cases does not mean the s 22 cases are immaterial to the present remittance code on account of the very point implicit in what Walton J said, namely that both s 22 and the present remittance code do use 'derive' and 'derived' in statute.

O'Brien v Benson's Hosiery Ltd

52.8 In *O'Brien (Inspector of Taxes) v Benson's Hosiery (Holdings) Ltd* [1980] AC 562, [1979] 3 All ER 652, HL the taxpayer was the holding company of two trading companies. The marketing director was a key employee and he paid £50,000 to be released from his employment contract. The House of Lords decided that the holding company's rights under that contract were an asset, from which the sum of £50,000 derived. Of significance in the present context is the Commissioners' inference that the main reason why the taxpayer could extract the sum of £50,000 was the possible diminution of the value of the holding company's shares in its subsidiaries which would result from the employee's departure. On this basis, the taxpayer argued the sum of £50,000 was derived from those shares.

Fox J and the Court of Appeal rejected this argument, the Court of Appeal stating [1978] STC 549, 557:

> 'The commissioners felt themselves to be prohibited by the decision of Walton J in *IRC v Montgomery* [1975] Ch 266, [1975] 1 All ER 664 from accepting this . . . . argument and Fox J said that there was no more justification for going behind the service agreement than there was for going behind the policies of insurance in *Montgomery*. We agree with this view . . . .'

This reasoning was endorsed by the House of Lords, who also rejected the argument.

Davenport v Chilver

52.9 In *Davenport (Inspector of Taxes) v Chilver* [1983] Ch 293, [1983] 3 WLR 481, the taxpayer had owned land in Latvia which had been expropriated by the Soviet Union in 1940. In 1969 a compensation fund was established under a Foreign Compensation Order, which conferred on the taxpayer the right to payment provided she established her claim. Nourse J held that the taxpayer's rights under the Order were an asset, from which the sums paid to her were derived. More importantly he also considered whether the sums were derived from the expropriated land. He followed Walton J in *IRC v Montgomery* in concluding not, stating:

> 'To express it in my own words, I do not think one thing can be said to derive from another unless it is in some sense the fruit of the tree. In Latvia the tree is dead. The tree has dropped from one rooted in loftier soil to which the blight cannot attain.'

Drummond v Austin Brown

52.10 In *Drummond (Inspector of Taxes) v Austin Brown* [1985] Ch 52, [1984] 2 All ER 699, CA , solicitors had a business tenancy with security of tenure under the Landlord and Tenant Act 1954. The landlord was entitled to possession under one of the permitted grounds, and under the terms of the 1954 Act, became liable to pay the solicitors compensation determined under a statutory formula. HMRC argued that the compensation was a capital sum derived from the tenancy, but this argument was rejected in the Court of Appeal. The Court stated:

> 'The word "derive" suggests a source. The right to the payment was, in our view, from one source only, namely the statute of 1954. The lease itself gives no right to such payment.'

Zim Properties Ltd v Proctor

52.11 In *Zim Properties Ltd v Proctor (Inspector of Taxes)* [1985] STC 90, 58 TC 371, the taxpayer company had contracted to sell property, but was unable to force the buyer to complete as a key conveyance required to show good title could not be found. The taxpayer sued the solicitors acting in respect of the loss they had suffered by losing the sale and in due course the solicitors paid £69,000 to compromise the action.

Here the taxpayer argued that the £69,000 was a capital sum derived from the property, which would have meant not all of it was taxable on account of the property's base cost. HMRC by contrast argued that the sum was derived from the right of action against the solicitors. Warner J agreed with HMRC stating:

> 'It seems to me that if one is to search for "the reality of the matter", the reality is that the taxpayer derived the £69,000 from the right to sue the firm.'

Pennine Raceway Ltd v Kirklees MBC

52.12 *Pennine Raceway* is the final case in the CGT series (*Pennine Raceway Ltd v Kirklees Metropolitan Council (No 2)* (1989) 58 P & CR 482, [1989] STC 122). Here the taxpayer owned a licence over a disused airfield for drag motor racing. The local council revoked the planning permission authorising this use, and the taxpayer became entitled to compensation. In determining the amount of compensation one of the issues was whether it would be subject to CGT as a capital sum derived from the licence.

The Court of Appeal held it would be so subject. All three members of the Court followed Warner J in *Zim Properties* and held that the Court must:

> 'Look for the real source from which the capital sum is derived rather than the immediate source.'

On the facts the licence was the real source of the compensation because it was the licence:

> 'through which the [taxpayer] was injured by the withdrawal of the planning permission and were entitled to be paid compensation in respect of that injury.'

CGT cases: conclusion

52.13 Four clear points can be extracted from the CGT cases, namely:

(1)   'Derive' connotes a source.
(2)   In looking for source, one looks for the real source.
(3)   Seeking the real source requires identification of the asset or right which gave rise to the payment.
(4)   Once that asset is identified further tracing back is precluded.

Such conclusions are consistent with Templeman J's approach in *Harmel v Wright*, specifically his emphasis that it was possible to follow the money with some certainty through the various elements in the structure the taxpayer had set up.

THE 2008 LEGISLATION

52.14 As indicated at the beginning of this chapter, the 2008 legislation does not define 'derive'. There are however occasional pointers which may be taken as indicative of what, in the 2008 legislation, the term is intended to mean. A key issue is whether these indications displace the meaning which may be inferred from the cases discussed above.

Directly or indirectly

52.15 In most places where the word 'derives' is used, it is prefaced by the adverbs 'directly or indirectly'. It may however be doubted whether 'indirectly' adds much to the concept that 'derives' requires identification of the real source.

Deemed derivation

52.16 As already noted, the remittance code makes wide use of the concept of deemed derivation (see further para **52.29**). It could be said that this deeming means there is no obligation in construing 'derive' to give much if any scope to actual derivation. Given that the case law discussed above points to such scope being narrow, this point is not without significance. But it is at best only an indication and cannot of itself be decisive as to meaning.

Mixed fund rules

52.17 The mixed fund rules are discussed in CHAPTER 53. It might be thought they require a mathematical tracing exercise, for they provide rules by which the mixed fund is dissected between the various elements in it. As such it could be said they override any requirement implicit in the cases discussed above, namely that what has to be looked for is the real source.

In truth however, it may be doubted whether the mixed fund rules bear such an implication. Two facts point to the conclusion they do not. First, as explained in para **53.2**, the mixed fund rules are not of universal application in that they do not apply to Conditions C and D (see CHAPTER 57) and nor do they apply to income and gains of 2007–08 and prior. The term 'derive' is used in both those contexts and it would be odd if it had one meaning where the mixed fund rules are applicable and one where they are not.

Second, as explained in para **53.8**, the concept of derivation is fundamental to the preconditions for the mixed fund rules. This may be gathered from the following points:

- The definition of mixed fund is expressed in terms of money or other property which 'contains or derives from' more than one of the specified categories of income and capital (ITA 2007, s 809Q(6)).
- Property is treated as containing a given item of income or capital if it 'derives' from that income or capital (s 809R(2)).
- The precondition for the operation of the mixed fund rules is that the property brought to the UK that satisfies Condition A in s 809L is or derives from a transfer from the mixed fund (s 809Q(1)).

In a sense, therefore, the mixed fund rules beg the very question now being discussed, namely when does derivation occur, and operate only when such derivation is established. In this sense, therefore, there may be an inherent conflict in the rules between their apparent purpose of dissection and tracing, and the derivation precondition fundamental to their operation. The next few sections of this chapter consider a number of specific scenarios in which this conflict arises.

HMRC view

52.18 HMRC say at several points in the Residence, Domicile and Remittance Basis Manual that the concept of derivation is wide, most notably in RDRM35030. Here it is said that income and gains can be traced through any series of subsequent investments or transactions, including through relevant persons. It may be suggested, however, that this reference to tracing is misconceived. The structure of Conditions A and B is that one starts with the money or other property received or used in the UK and then asks whether it is or is derived from the foreign income and gains. The exercise does not start with the income and gains and then trace them.

ACTS OF THE TAXPAYER HIMSELF

52.19 As noted in paras **51.11** and **52.5** an investment is derived from any foreign income or gains used to pay for it, as are the proceeds of selling the investment. If therefore the foreign income and gains pass through a number of investments before being brought to the UK they still count as remitted. However as explained in para **51.15** the amount taxed is not the amount remitted but the amount of the original income and gains. The mixed fund rules then operate well enough, for each item in the various mixed funds represented by the successive investments is an item of the taxpayer's income or capital and, if the often formidable mathematical complexity can be faced, what is comprised in the remittance to the UK can be determined.

What is also equally clear is that taxpayers who engage in the kind of operations highlighted in *Thomson v Moyse* or *Harmel v Wright* will find what is brought to the UK is a remittance of the income and gains. Such income and gains, on the facts of those cases, were the real source if only because each step in the operation was planned at the outset. On such facts derivation is plainly established.

But what if the facts are less clear cut? Suppose a taxpayer, A, gives the income or gains to a third party, X, who mixes the funds with his own money and at all times keeps all the money outside the UK. Somewhat later X passes funds back to A, as a completely independent transaction, and A remits that money to the UK, perhaps even unaware that some of the money may have had as its ultimate origin his prior gift.

In these circumstances the RDRM indicates that HMRC may well say that what comes back to A is his income and gains. But in reality it is difficult to see how the real source of the funds gifted back to A is anything other than X's own money. On one view the mixed fund rules could go against this, as they can as a matter of construction be operated on the basis that what X gives to A is, in part at least, traceable to the income and gains in A's prior gift. But the fact that they can be so operated does not mean they should be if the necessary element of derivation is not present. Further, as is explained in para 53.21, the mixed fund rules contain no express provision at all covering mixed funds containing income or capital from more than one taxpayer.

COMMERCIAL TRANSACTIONS

52.20 As indicated above, investments bought with income and gains are derived from the income and gains, as are the proceeds of their sale. But this addresses only the position in the hands of the taxpayer. What about the other party to the various transactions?

Independent third parties

52.21 Where the other party to the transaction is an independent third party, it is difficult to see the cash he receives on a purchase by the taxpayer, or the asset on a sale, as derived from whatever the taxpayer provides. The real source of what the other party gets, in his hands, is what he has to pay or transfer in return.

In most cases, of course, this issue of remittance is academic, as it is rare for the other party to the transaction to be a relevant person or pass what he gets back to the taxpayer or another relevant person. Absent that, remittance issues cannot arise as even if the other party remits, Condition B cannot be engaged in relation to the taxpayer as what is brought to the UK will not be the property of a relevant person. So too Conditions C and D could not be engaged unless what is brought to the UK is enjoyed by the taxpayer or another relevant person.

Relevant person parties

52.22 Matters may have a different complexion if the other party to the transaction is a relevant person, albeit that the transaction is still on arm's length terms. Typically this arises where a trust or company which is a relevant person in relation to a remittance basis user sells an asset to the remittance basis user. The purchase price the remittance basis user pays is, or is derived from, his foreign income or gains; but the asset is not. It is clear that following the transaction the asset in the hands of the remittance basis user is derived from his income or gains. But are the proceeds in the hands of the trust or company also so derived?

It may strongly be argued that they are not, for in the hands of the seller the real source of the proceeds of sale can hardly be anything other than the asset itself sold. It may be suggested that this is so even if the object of the exercise is to generate clean capital cash, provided the exercise in on arm's length terms. Particular reliance may be placed on Walton J's analysis in *IRC v Montgomery* (see para 52.7 above).

Share and loan subscriptions

52.23 A variant on the arm's length transaction theme occurs when the taxpayer or another relevant person uses foreign income and gains to subscribe for shares in a company or make a loan to the company. Here, plainly, the shares or debt in the hands of the lender or subscriber remains the income or gains. But what of the money now held by the company? In most cases this is a far from academic issue as the subscriber or lender is likely to be a participator thereby rendering the company a relevant person and so the cause of tax if it remits (see para **54.12**).

Here, although the transaction is arm's length, it is difficult not to regard the subscription or loans, and thus the income and gains, as being the real source of the company's funds. Put colloquially the real source of money subscribed into or lent to a company is the funds provided by the shareholder or lender. In contrast to arm's length sales there is no pre-existing asset of the company that can instead be regarded as the real source.

This conclusion is shared by HMRC (RDRM33050). It may be objected that there is scope for remittances to far exceed the original income and gains. In one sense this is true, for the company could remit the money subscribed or lent and the shareholder or lender could subsequently remit the proceeds of the shares or loan. But in reality there is nothing in this point for, as explained in para **51.15**, the total amount taxed as remitted cannot exceed the original income and gains. Thus if the company remits that full amount, remittance thereafter by the shareholder or lender is not taxable.

Distributions and buy-backs

52.24 Similar issues arise should a company in which the remittance basis user is a participator effect a share buy-back, or make a distribution, whether by way of dividend or in liquidation. The income or gains of such a company are treated as the participator's should the transferor charge under the transfer of assets code apply or, as the case may be, should TCGA 1992, s 13 be in point (see CHAPTERS 69 and 88). In such a case the distribution or buy-back could well be funded out of such income or gains and, should the remittance basis user then remit, the issue would arise of whether the remittance was derived from the company's income or gains.

Here common sense would indicate not, for on almost any view the real source of the remittance would be the shareholders' shares as it is they which give him legal entitlement to the distribution or buy-back. Moreover, were the remittance to be treated as derived from the company's income or gains, there would be the risk if not the certainty of it being taxed twice, once by reference to the dividend income or the gain on the buy-back and a second time by reference to the company's income or gains.

RELEVANT PERSON GIFTS

52.25 As described in CHAPTER 54, individual relevant persons are confined to spouses (and their various equivalents) and minor children or grandchildren.

Non-individual relevant persons include trusts of which an individual relevant person is a beneficiary and close companies in which such an individual or trust is a participator.

Individual donees

52.26 As explained in para 54.1 prior to 2008, a gift completed abroad converted income or gains of the taxpayer into clean capital of the donee. Under the present law it is clear from the relevant person concept that this is no longer so where the donee is a relevant person. It is also to be inferred that in such a case the property in the hands of the donee is at least capable of being derived from the income and gains comprised in the gift and so taxable on the donor if remitted.

The issue, however, is whether this derivation is confined to cases of actual pre-planning or whether a tracing exercise is required and any remittance by the donee results in tax if, by such tracing, it is traceable back to the gift. This issue is essentially the same as that discussed in para 52.19 above, and turns on whether the real source concept breaks the link with the income and gains and whether, even if it would otherwise do so, such a result is prevented by the mixed fund rules.

The issues principally arise in relation to spouses, as spouses and co-habitees are the only category of individual adult relevant person. The issues are discussed in para 54.4 and the conclusion there reached is similar to that suggested in para 52.19 above in relation to gifts back. In other words the mixed fund rules can be made to work if tracing is required, but the legislation does not expressly contemplate mixed funds derived from more than one taxpayer and anomalies are thrown up.

In the light of this it could be argued the meaning of 'derive' suggested by case law should prevail to the effect that the link is broken unless there is pre-planning or it is otherwise clear that the real source of what the donee remits is the donor's gift rather than the donee's undifferentiated fund of his or her own money.

It is unlikely that HMRC would accept this, and examples in RDRM indicate that they do not. However it is perhaps worth noting that the examples they give are ones where it may not be not difficult to say the real source is the donor's income and gains.

Gifts to trusts

52.27 In practical terms, the analysis may be regarded as clearer where the gift is to a trust. It would be difficult to argue that the real source of settled property is anyone other than the economic settlor and, on this basis, capital in the trust does count as derived from any income and gains which, under the mixed fund rules, are comprised in the funds settled. This means any remittance by the trust from such capital is taxable on the settlor if it is a relevant person in relation to him. So too if the trust distributes funds back to the settlor it is difficult not to regard the trust, and thence the settlor himself, as the real source.

But even with trusts the interaction of the derivation scope and the mixed fund rules is not without difficulties. As is explained in para **54.11**, retained trust income can be deemed derived from notional income of non-transferors under the transfer of assets code (see CHAPTER **72**). Such income can easily find itself in a mixed fund with trust capital derived from the settlor's income or gains. On this scenario, remittance by the trust from that mixed fund could result in tax on both the settlor and the beneficiaries. This issue is discussed further in para **54.11** and demonstrates that even a narrow view of what is meant by the term 'derive' would not remove all difficulties posed by the mixed fund rules.

DOUBLE DUTY REMITTANCES

52.28 An interesting issue is whether a single bringing or use of funds in the UK can do double duty. In other words can the remittance be derived simultaneously, from two sums, each representing the taxpayer's foreign income or gains? Were this possible a single bringing of funds to the UK could effectively result in double tax.

It may be suggested such doubling up is not contemplated by the general language Conditions A and B, on the basis there can be only one real source. If there are two or more sources the real one has to be found, in the manner indicated in the CGT cases discussed above.

A context in which this point arises is where the taxpayer or another relevant person keeps foreign income or gains abroad and invests them to generate income. He then remits that income. The issue which arises is whether such income is derived from the capital which generated it and thus from any income or gains which that capital represents. It may strongly be argued not, as the real source of what is remitted is plainly the income rather than the capital which generated the income.

Another context in which the point arises is that described above, namely where a close company pays a dividend or effects a buy-back. As indicated above here the real source is the dividend or shares, not whatever the company used to fund payment.

The point also arises in a comparable situation involving trusts, namely where a settlor-interested trust makes a capital distribution to the settlor which, if it were a capital payment, would be taxable under TCGA 1992, s 87, and which is funded directly or indirectly out of trust foreign income. Should the settlor remit the payment, the remittance is potentially taxable both as a remittance of the notional s 87 gain and of the income taxable under ITTOIA 2005, s 624. Here it may be argued that in reality there is no scope for double taxation of remittance, as a distribution to the settlor of trust income is (potentially) chargeable to income tax on him, and accordingly falls outside of the 'capital payment' concept. On that basis, it is only the trust income which is taxable if the distribution is remitted.

It might be thought a discussion of whether a remittance can result in double tax is an absurdity as such would never have been the intention of Parliament.

However in another context, namely collateral (see para **56.13**) HMRC are contending that a remittance can do double duty, so the point does have to be addressed. However that context is not one involving the general rule in Conditions A and B and so, even if HMRC are right in relation to collateral, the points cited above in relation to Conditions A and B still hold good.

DEEMED DERIVATION

52.29 As indicated at the beginning of this chapter, in many instances derivation is deemed to occur. Deemed derivation takes at least three different forms.

The first is where anti-avoidance legislation treats the actual income or gains of another person as the income or gains of the taxpayer, or an amount equal to the actual income or gains is so deemed. Examples include the attribution of income to the transferor under the transfer of assets code (see CHAPTER 72) and the attribution of gains to participators under TCGA 1992, s 13 (see para **88.27**). Here deemed derivation operates by deeming the actual income or gains of the other person to be derived from the deemed income or gains of the taxpayer. The result of such deeming is that a remittance of the actual income or gains is taxed as a remittance of the deemed income or gains provided that the owner of the actual income or gains is a relevant person.

A second form of deemed derivation is that an item of property owned by the taxpayer or another person may be deemed to be derived from actual income or gains. Examples include gifted assets, in that on any disposal of a foreign asset at less than market value, the asset in the hands of the donee is deemed to be derived from the gain realised by the donor on the gift (see para **49.22**). Another example is employment related securities, where the securities are deemed to be derived from the foreign securities income (see para **50.15**). In all these cases remittance of the property is treated as a remittance of the income or gains from which it is deemed to be derived.

The third use of deemed derivation is where an actual benefit to the taxpayer is deemed to be derived from income or gains treated as accruing to him by reason of the benefit. The prime examples of this are under ITA 2007, s 735 and TCGA 1992, s 87B (see paras **72.17** to **72.22** and **79.4** to **79.7**). Here considerable difficulties exist in applying the remittance basis, for Condition A in s 809L requires what is brought to or enjoyed in the UK to be money or other property, not a benefit. The point is discussed further in paras **72.22** and **79.6**.

Extent of deemed derivation

52.30 An important general point needs to be made about deemed derivation. This is that the deeming is not in terms extended to anything derived from the actual income or gains or, as the case may be, the item of property or benefit. Thus in the case of a gifted asset, what the legislation says is derived from the donor's gain is the asset, not the proceeds of its sale or the investment of such proceeds.

This is a surprising gap, but the result may be less significant than might be supposed. This is because a purposive construction would very likely conclude that in the first category of deemed derivation the deeming would extend to any investment of the actual income and gains by the person to whom they in fact accrued, or the proceeds of such investment. But it is less easy to see such a purposive construction as applying after that person has transferred the assets concerned to another party. Here there may be a gap.

Chapter 53

MIXED FUNDS

INTRODUCTION

53.1 The impression given by Conditions A and B is that taxpayers keep each item of foreign income or gains separate. Each such item, or property into which it is invested, is then remitted to the UK, or not as the case may be.

In reality this is not the way the world works, as capital, income and gains are frequently mixed with each other. As discussed in CHAPTER 14, it is relatively easy to ensure that actual income is kept separate from other monies, by means of banking procedures which are, at least in theory, straightforward. However, contamination of capital by gains or deemed income is, to some extent, inevitable with almost any investment strategy. And the mixing problem can be compounded by errors in operating the required banking procedures, whether such errors are the taxpayer's own or those of his bank.

The result of all this is that mixed funds are common, and not infrequently there are remittances from them, in some cases deliberate and others accidental. The treatment of mixed funds is therefore a subject of practical importance.

THE POSITION AT COMMON LAW

53.2 Until 5 April 2008, the treatment of mixed funds rested on a mixture of case law and HMRC practice. This law and practice remains important for two reasons:

(1)   The statutory rules described below do not apply to the income and gains of 2007–08 and earlier tax years (FA 2008, Sch 7 para 89).
(2)   The statutory rules described below do not apply to remittances treated as occurring by virtue of Conditions C and D in s 809L. This conclusion follows because the statutory mixed-fund rules are expressed only as applying in relation to Conditions A and B (s 809Q(1) and (2)).

Income

53.3 A remittance from a mixed fund was presumed to be income to the extent that income had been paid into the fund. This was established in *Scottish Provident Institution v Allan* (1903) 4 TC 591, where the taxpayer had made a loan in Australia. Substantial amounts of interest had accrued and both this and the repayments of principal had been intermixed. In remitting money back to England the company's Australian agents designated the remittances as repayment of principal but this was held to be ineffective in the House of Lords. In a memorable phrase, Lord Halsbury LC observed that 'mere nicknaming' could not alter the taxability of what was in substance profit earned abroad.

An unresolved issue was the position if the non-domiciliary drew on the mixed fund for foreign spending before effecting any remittance to the UK. Logical application of *Scottish Provident Institution v Allan* suggested that if foreign spending preceded UK spending, it should be regarded as having drawn off income rather than capital in the account. But there was neither authority nor published HMRC practice on the point.

A related point arose where the account consisted of some income taxed on the arising basis and some on the remittance basis. The now withdrawn Inspector's Manual indicated that HMRC treated the income taxed on the arising basis as remitted first (see para 1568). Dicta in *Roxburghe's Executors v IRC* (1936) 20 TC 711 suggested that this accorded with the legal position.

It was sometimes suggested that a large one-off remittance made from a mixed fund to meet capital expenditure was a remittance of the capital in the fund and so tax-free. Such a proposition lacked authority and was questionable, as income was taxable even if capitalised prior to remittance (see para 51.10).

Capital gains

53.4 Where a payment was made out of an account containing a mixture of capital and capital gains, HMRC practice was to treat the payment as carrying capital and gains out of the account on a pro rata basis (the payment would be treated as comprising capital and gains in the same proportions as in the source account, and if remitted would be taxed accordingly). This was a pragmatic approach, but was untested by case law.

THE PRESENT LAW

53.5 The present law applies if the following conditions specified in s 809Q(1) are met:

- Condition A in s 809L is met – ie money or other property is brought to or received or used in the UK by or for the benefit of a relevant person;
- The money or other property is a transfer from a mixed fund or is derived from such a transfer.

The purpose of the present law is stated to be to determine whether Condition B in s 809L is met, ie whether the property or money is or is derived from the taxpayer's income or chargeable gains. Assuming Condition B is met, the mixed fund rules also determine the amount remitted. They thus determine whether a tax charge is made and if so on what amount.

The present law also extends to cases within Condition A because services enjoyed in the UK by a relevant person have been paid for abroad (see CHAPTER 55). The application of the mixed fund rules to debts related to UK property is considered in para 56.7.

MEANING OF MIXED FUND

53.6 The starting point with the present law is to identify what a mixed fund is. The term is defined twice, in ss 809Q(6) and 809R(7), but both definitions are in essentially the same terms. The definitions apply by reference to categories of income and capital listed in s 809Q(4) and these therefore have to be considered first.

Categories of income and capital

53.7 The specified categories of income and capital are set out in the following order in s 809Q(4):

(a)   UK employment income.
(b)   Relevant foreign earnings (see CHAPTER 50).
(c)   Foreign specific employment income, ie foreign income treated as arising under the employment related securities legislation (see paras 50.12 to 50.16).
(d)   Relevant foreign income (see CHAPTER 48).
(e)   Foreign chargeable gains (see CHAPTER 49).
(f)   Employment income also taxable in some other country.
(g)   Relevant foreign income also taxable in some other country.
(h)   Foreign chargeable gains also taxable in some other country.
(i)   Income or capital not within any of the above paragraphs.

The last of these categories is considered further below, para 53.38.

Definition of mixed fund

53.8 A mixed fund can be either money or other property (s 809Q(6)). Such money or other property is a mixed fund if it contains:

(1)   Income for more than one tax year; or
(2)   Capital for more than one tax year; or
(3)   Both income and capital; or
(4)   Income or gains of more than one of the categories listed in para 53.7 above.

The concept of income or gains for a tax year is reasonably clear: it is income or gains arising in the tax year. What is less clear is what capital for a tax year is. This difficult issue is discussed below (para 53.37).

That fact that a mixed fund can be either money or other property means that the concept is not confined to bank accounts. An asset is thus a mixed fund if the money used to pay for it answers any of the descriptions at (1)–(4) above, it being expressly provided that property which derives from income or capital is to be treated as containing or consisting of that income or capital (s 809R(2)).

A related point is that a single transaction can generate a mixed fund. The sale proceeds of a foreign situs asset are inevitably a mixed fund if a gain is realised on the sale, as the proceeds contain at least two of the categories listed in para 53.7 above, ie whatever the original purchase price was or was derived from, and a foreign chargeable gain or (if the asset was one of those which are capable of giving rise to deemed income if disposed of at a gain) relevant foreign income.

Debts

53.9 The mixed fund concept is extended where a debt relates to property (s 809R(3)). The meaning of the term 'relates' to property is considered in paras 56.8 to 56.11, an obvious example being a debt incurred to buy the property. The extension of the mixed fund rules comes into operation when the debt is satisfied and requires the property to be treated as containing the income or capital used to satisfy the debt. However this treatment is required only to the extent that it is just and reasonable.

Where this treatment is in point, the result is that property which is not a mixed fund can be converted into such a fund or, where it is already a mixed fund, the kinds of income or capital in it are increased. This rule applies to debts relating to foreign rather than UK property, as a mixed fund within s 809Q is by definition abroad.

TYPES OF TRANSFER

53.10 Once a mixed fund is identified, attention has to focus on transfers from it. There are in fact two kinds of transfer, transfers within s 809Q and offshore transfers.

In distinguishing between s 809Q transfers and offshore transfers, the key definition is that of s 809Q transfers as a transfer from a mixed fund is an offshore transfer if and to the extent s 809Q does not apply to it (s 809R(5)). As noted above (para 53.5) s 809Q applies if Condition A in s 809L is met. It follows that any transfer from a mixed fund is a s 809Q transfer if either:

(a)   The funds transferred or property derived from them are brought to or used or enjoyed in the UK by or for the benefit of a relevant person (see para 51.7); or

(b)   The funds are used abroad to pay for a service provided in the UK to or for the benefit of a relevant person.

Of itself this definition is unsatisfactory, for at the time of a transfer from a mixed fund, it may not be known what is going to happen to the transferred funds. This gap is met by s 809R(6), which applies a test at the end of the tax year in which the transfer occurs. The transfer is presumed to be a s 809Q transfer if either:

(a)   Condition A has already applied to it, ie remittance has already occurred, or

(b)   On the best estimate that can then be reasonably made Condition A will apply at some point in the future.

Any transfer which does not satisfy one or other of these two conditions is an offshore transfer. A point to stress is that the distinction between the two types of transfer is not simply whether the money or other property transferred is or will be brought to the UK. The requirement is that Condition A be met. This means that if the bringing to or use or enjoyment in the UK is not by a relevant person, the transfer remains an offshore transfer.

A point also to stress is that 'offshore' in the term 'offshore transfer' is a misnomer. Offshore transfers are not just transfers within or to or from offshore jurisdictions. The term embraces any transfer which is not a s 809Q transfer even if no part of the transaction goes anywhere near an offshore jurisdiction.

The term 'transfer' is also something of a misnomer. It is not defined, but its genesis is plainly bank accounts where transactions involving the movement of money to the UK, or from one overseas account to another, can aptly be described as transfers. But as s 809Q is expressed in terms of other property as well as money, it plainly comprehends the transfer of property in specie. And in reality, the term has to go still further, for when property is sold the term must comprehend the receiving of the proceeds of sale in exchange. Were this not so, the rules as to offshore transfers would be largely confined to transfers from bank accounts, which would be quite contrary to the overall intent of the legislation.

A final point to emphasise is that a transfer is not prevented from being a s 809Q transfer just because remittance has not occurred by the end of the tax year in which it is made. As indicated above, future remittance means the transfer is a s 809Q transfer provided that at the end of the tax year of the mixed fund transfer the future s 809Q transfer will, on the best estimate that can then reasonably be made, happen.

Hybrid transfers

53.11 In practice many transfers from mixed funds may partly satisfy the s 809Q conditions and partly not. In such a case s 809Q is applied to the part which does meet those conditions and the balance is an offshore transfer (s 809R(8)).

Amount transferred

53.12 As is explained in para **51.15** the amount taxed where a remittance is derived from foreign income and gains is not the amount remitted but the amount of income and gains the remittance is derived from. In relation to mixed funds, the issue which arises is whether this rule carries over into determining the composition of the fund. It is a particularly important issue if the fund is not denominated in sterling, for then the proportion of the fund representing a given item of income or capital is unlikely, in sterling terms, ever to correspond to the original sterling value of the income or capital.

The only guidance the legislation gives on this point is s 809R(2) which simply requires that property which derives from an individual's income or capital is to be treated as containing that income or capital. Although this subsection is not particularly clear, it is certainly not in terms requiring the amount of the income or capital in the mixed fund to equal the original sterling value of the income or capital. The natural reading is that what is being looked for is whatever in the mixed fund is derived from the original income or capital, such item by implication being taken at its then value in the mixed fund.

COMPUTATIONAL RULES

53.13 Once it is clear whether the transfer is a s 809Q transfer or an offshore transfer, the relevant computational rules have to be applied.

Section 809Q transfers

53.14 The computational rules under s 809Q essentially involve identifying the transfer to the UK with income and capital in the mixed fund from which the transfer is made on a 'last in, first out' basis. However the 'last in, first out' rule is not absolute, for tax years are looked at as a whole and within each tax year income and capital is taken in the order listed in para **53.7**.

In detail, the rules look at the mixed fund immediately before the transfer and identify the amount of each category of income and capital for the tax year of the transfer which is then in the fund. The transfer from the fund is matched with the categories in the order set out in para **53.7** above. If it exceeds all the income and capital then in the fund for the tax year of the transfer, the process is repeated as respects the income and capital in the fund for prior years, taking each year separately in reverse chronological order.

Once the ordering rules have applied in relation to one transfer, the amount treated as transferred to the UK is left out of account in applying the ordering rules on subsequent transfers (s 809R(9)).

As will be apparent from the order listed in para **53.7**, in general the ordering takes items which result in a higher effective rate of tax when remitted before those which attract a lower rate. However this is qualified in two important respects. First and principally, all items for one tax year must be exhausted before those in the prior tax year can be looked at: thus clean capital of the current year is identified before foreign income of the preceding tax year. Second, the first category of income identified for any given tax year does not result in remittance tax at all as that category is UK source employment income. This anomaly is the result of the informal predecessor to overseas work day relief being grandfathered into the present statutory remittance code (see paras **53.28** and **50.2**).

Offshore transfers

53.15 The rule in relation to offshore transfers is much simpler in that the transfer is treated as containing a pro rata proportion of each kind of capital or income as was in the account immediately before the transfer (s 809R (4)). What is meant by 'each kind of income or capital' is not defined but it may reasonably be inferred it connotes the categories listed in para **53.7**, separated out by each year represented in the account.

SPECIFIC TRANSACTIONS

53.16 The operation of the mixed fund rules in relation to particular kinds of transactions is not always clear.

Purchases and sales

53.17 As explained in para **51.11**, the general rule on the purchase of an asset is that the income or gains in the purchase price carry forward into the asset bought. So too, on a sale, income and gains contained in the asset carry forward into the sale proceeds.

The logical implication of this is that a purchase carries forward into the purchased assets a pro rata proportion of each category of income and capital in the fund from which the purchase price is derived. But would this be so if at the time of the purchase there is the intention to bring the asset bought to the UK, in circumstances such that Condition A is met? It may be suggested not, and in such circumstances the purchase is a s 809Q transfer. The same applies mutatis mutandis on sales.

In certain artificial situations discussed in para **52.22**, the purchase price may in the hands of the seller be regarded as derived from the income and gains. In the unlikely event that this is the case the transaction will in that aspect be a s 809Q transfer if the proceeds are brought to the UK in circumstances where Condition A is met. Because of the requirement in Condition A that the bringing, use, or enjoyment be by a relevant person this issue is normally only live where, as discussed in para **52.22**, the purchaser is a relevant person. Here too the same applies mutatis mutandis on sales as respects the asset sold.

Spending the money

53.18 Funds abroad may well be spent on services abroad or consumables such that no asset is received in return. In such a case the spending is plainly an offshore transfer, as by definition the funds transferred out of the mixed fund are never going to find their way to the UK. Services may be thought to be an exception to this in view of the special rules for services, but this exception is only in point as respects services provided in the UK to a relevant person (see CHAPTER 55).

Gifts

53.19 In general gifts are in the same category as services – ie they are offshore transfers. The one exception to this arises if two conditions are met:

(a)   The donee is a relevant person; and
(b)   He remits to the UK by the end of the tax year of the transfer or then intends to do so.

If these conditions are met, the conditions for the gift to be a s 809Q transfer are satisfied, and s 809Q takes effect accordingly.

MULTI-PERSON MIXED FUNDS

53.20 The term multi-person mixed fund may be used to describe a fund which contains income and capital belonging to or derived from more than one taxpayer. Such funds undoubtedly exist for, as explained in CHAPTER 52, funds or property held by one person can count as derived from another person, albeit that there is scope to debate how extensive such derivation is. Funds or property held by one person can also be deemed to derive from income and gains of another (see para 52.29) or indeed from those of several others.

In discussing multi-person mixed funds it is convenient to refer to the present owner of the fund as the fund holder and anyone else whose income or capital is in it as a contributor.

Application of the mixed fund rules

53.21 There is no express provision in the mixed fund rules dealing with multi-person mixed funds. As explained in para 52.19 this is one reason for inferring that derivation from one person to another is not as wide as might be supposed. But in some cases such derivation undoubtedly exists, and also there is the whole issue of deemed derivation. On any view, therefore, the omission is surprising.

Given the omission, the application of the mixed fund rules to multi-person mixed funds is a matter of inference. Here two points are significant. The first is that the definitions of mixed fund (ss 809Q(6) and 809R(7)) do not in terms say that the various categories of income and capital must have arisen to the taxpayer. The second is that in applying s 809Q rules to a s 809Q transfer there is an express direction, for each of the various categories, to focus on 'the amount of the relevant income or capital of the individual . . . ' (s 809Q(3), step 1).

As a result of these two points, it can be inferred that any transfer from a multi-person mixed fund that is an offshore transfer carries out a pro rata proportion of all categories of income and capital, regardless of whose income or capital they originally were. Equally if in relation to one of the persons whose income or capital is in the fund the transfer is a s 809Q transfer, s 809Q rules require his income or capital to be identified with the transfer first. Self-evidently, a given transfer can be an offshore transfer in relation to the fundholder or one of the contributors to the account and a s 809Q transfer in relation to the other or others. In such a case, s 809Q rules have to be operated in relation to one, and the offshore transfer rules in relation to the rest.

A point that should also be noted is that, even if the transfer is an offshore transfer in relation to both fund holder and contributor(s), the categories of income and capital in it will be different in relation to each. Thus what are the different categories of income and capital in relation to the contributors will all be the residual category of capital in relation to the fund holder save in those relatively rare circumstances where his own income and capital can be traced into what he receives from the contributor(s) (see para **52.19**).

Operation of the rules

53.22 In the great majority of cases where trusts or companies are not involved, the fund holder is not a relevant person in relation to the contributor(s). In such cases, almost all transfers out of the fund are offshore transfers in relation to all parties. The only situation where that is not so is where a transfer is back to a contributor or to a relevant person in relation to him and that person remits or intends to remit. In such circumstances the transfer satisfies s 809Q in relation to that contributor and s 809Q rules apply to him accordingly, but not of course to the fund holder or any other contributor.

Typically this last scenario arises where an ex-spouse or an adult child of the contributor is the fund holder and the transfer is to a settlement of which minor children or grandchildren of the contributor are beneficiaries. In such a case, the transfer to the settlement may be a s 809Q transfer, but even then only if the transferee settlement remits or intends to remit.

The way in which the mixed fund rules work in these cases can on occasion accelerate remittance. This might occur if the fund holder brings funds to the UK by way of partial remittance. So far as he is concerned this transfer is a s 809Q transfer and is identified first with his income and gains in the mixed fund. But assuming he is not a relevant person in relation to the contributor, the remittance to the UK is an offshore transfer so far as the contributor is concerned, and thus carries out only a pro rata proportion of the contributor's income and gains. Should the fund holder later give the balance of the fund back to the contributor or someone else who is a relevant person in relation to the contributor, that gift will operate in relation to the contributor as a s 809Q transfer if remittance to the UK is intended and be identified first with such of the contributor's income and gains as are left after applying the offshore transfer rules to the fund holder's prior remittance.

The mixed fund rules pose rather broader problems where the fund holder is a relevant person in relation to the contributor(s). These issues are discussed in CHAPTER 54 under the respective categories of relevant person.

COMMENT

53.23 The complexity implicit in the mixed fund rules is mind-bending. The following points may be made in relation to just bank accounts:

(1)   The rules have to be operated on each occasion when money is withdrawn from a non-UK bank account.

(2)   Such occasions include not merely the remittance of money to the UK but also spending abroad and the purchase of foreign investments as all such transactions are offshore transfers.

(3)   On each occasion on which the rules are operated, account has to be taken of any intervening credits to the account as, depending on the derivation of the funds credited, such will alter the quantum of some of the categories of income and capital in the account and perhaps add new ones.

(4)   On each occasion on which the rules are operated, a decision has to be taken as to what will be done with the money, to identify whether the applicable rules are s 809Q or those pertaining to offshore transfers.

It may be doubted whether the compliance costs entailed in operating these rules could ever be justified, either for taxpayers in preparing computations or HMRC in checking them. In many instances, no doubt, pragmatic approaches may be taken, although if this is done, full disclosure should be made of the basis used.

PRACTICAL POINTS

Possible shortcuts

53.24 An important point to keep in mind is that the complexity results not from the fact that money or property is a mixed fund but from what categories of income or capital it in fact consists of. Something that is strictly a mixed fund may contain sums which, if remitted, would all be treated in the same way. In practice it is generally possible to treat such a fund as unmixed.

By way of example, an income account may contain income of many different kinds and years, but if it has only ever contained income, income tax will result on any remittance to the UK, regardless of what particular item of income is deemed to be remitted under the mixed fund rules. So too a capital account may contain capital from many different sources, but if all income has been effectively segregated and no gains have been credited to the account, no tax will result if there is a remittance from the account.

One possible fly in this ointment is CGT on currency gains. Under the law which applied up to 5 April 2012, a foreign chargeable gain could be realised not merely on the disposal of an investment but also on the operation of a foreign currency bank account. The practical result is that a 'clean' capital account may turn out to have some, usually modest, historic currency gains, with the result, strictly, that the horrendous rules described above must be operated.

A second potential fly in the ointment is tax credits. Tax credits need to be considered where there is a transfer from an account containing foreign dividends received before 6 April 2016, as prior to that date, foreign dividends of remittance basis users usually attracted a 10% domestic tax credit. Even with respect to a dividend received on or after 6 April 2016, there may be a credit in respect of foreign tax withheld at source (whether such credit is available under a treaty or the UK's unilateral relief provisions). Tax credit issues also arise where interest or income from mutual funds has suffered withholding tax under foreign domestic law or under the EU Savings Directive.

In all such cases it is, strictly, necessary for the history of the account to be investigated and for the mixed fund rules to be applied, to establish whether and to what extent transfers from the account comprise income that carries a tax credit and will therefore be taxed less harshly on a remittance than income that carries no such credit. However, taxpayers cannot reasonably be criticised for ignoring tax credits, and reporting on the basis that none are available, if they or their advisers consider that the compliance costs involved in carrying out this exercise are likely to exceed the financial benefit of claiming the credits.

Former remittance basis users

53.25 A subject of considerable importance already, and which is likely to become more important as time goes on, is the application of the mixed fund rules to taxpayers who have in the past used the remittance basis, but who are now arising basis taxpayers. This category includes some foreign domiciliaries who are eligible for the remittance basis, but for whom making a claim under Income Tax Act 2007, s 809B (ITA 2007) is not cost-effective (see para **12.10**). It also includes a small number of taxpayers who were formerly domiciled outside the UK but who have abandoned their intention to leave (see para **12.3**). And from 6 April 2017 these individuals will be supplemented by a number of deemed UK domiciliaries who, although foreign domiciled as a matter of law, will be treated for all tax purposes as if domiciled in the UK, and who will be precluded from using the remittance basis (see CHAPTERS **19** and **45**).

Taxpayers in these categories may have investment accounts outside the UK, containing non-UK situs investments which to a large extent represent foreign income or gains that would be taxed if they were remitted, but which now give rise to income or gains that are taxed on an arising basis. There will usually be a desire to draw out of such accounts sums equal to the income and gains that have been taxed on the arising basis, firstly to pay the tax and secondly for personal expenditure, without remitting the income and gains that date from the period in which the individual was a remittance basis user.

In principle, this is perfectly feasible, as a s 809Q transfer from the account will be treated as carrying out of the account the current-year income and gains in priority to sums 'for' previous tax years. However, in practice, achieving this may be challenging if income receipts or sale proceeds are reinvested within the account. The reason is that it is strictly incorrect to treat the investment account as a single mixed fund. Arguably, it is necessary to treat each investment held within the account, as well as any cash that is held pending reinvestment or pending transfer to the taxpayer, as a discrete mixed fund.

One possible response to the problem is to ensure that any income receipt is immediately transferred to the taxpayer's UK account, and that if an investment is sold at a gain, the gain element of the proceeds (only) is likewise immediately transferred to the taxpayer's UK account. If desired, there can be reinvestment of these sums within a UK investment account.

As discussed at para 19.6, it is expected that there will be an opportunity in 2017–18 for certain foreign domiciliaries, not necessarily limited to those who have become deemed domiciled for all tax purposes, to unmix their mixed funds to facilitate tax-free remittances from them. This may reduce, to some extent, the problems created by the mixed fund rules for deemed domiciled taxpayers. However, it is unlikely that the issue outlined above will be eliminated entirely.

EXCEPTIONS TO THE RULES

53.26 There are three circumstances in which the mixed fund rules described above are modified. The first two are more fully described elsewhere.

Remittance of nominated income or gains

53.27 As explained in para 47.7, the question of whether nominated income and gains have been remitted is determined using the rules in this chapter, as is the total of the taxpayer's remittances of post-2008 income and gains in the year in question. But once that total has been arrived at, the income and gains treated as remitted are not those arrived at using the rules described in this chapter but those artificially determined by the ordering rules in ITA 2007, s 809J.

This is all as explained in para 47.7, as is the uncertainly over how long the taxpayer remains in s 809J. The problem is avoided by ensuring no nominated income and gains are ever remitted, specifically by nominating less than £10 of actual income each year.

Overseas workday relief

53.28 This relief is described in para 50.2 and is available to employed remittance basis users in the first three years of UK residence. As described in para 50.3, a special mixed fund rule applies where a single employment has both UK and overseas duties. The rule operates where earnings are credited to a nominated overseas bank account which does not receive any other credits (apart from interest on the account). The effect of the rule is that all s 809Q transfers made from the account during the tax year are deemed to be a single s 809Q transfer made at the end of the tax year and all offshore transfers a single offshore transfer made immediately afterwards.

The rationale of this seemingly bizarre rule may be seen from the ordering rules described in paras 53.7 and 53.14, which identify s 809Q transfers first with UK employment income of the current tax year. The consequence is that the single s 809Q transfer at the end of the tax year is of that year's taxed employment income save insofar as it exceeds that income. Save as to that excess the remittances are thus free of tax regardless of the state of the account before any given remittance during the year.

Section 809S

53.29 ITA 2007, s 809S is an anti-avoidance rule of somewhat uncertain scope. It applies if an arrangement is entered into and one of the main purposes is to secure a tax advantage. If as a result a mixed fund contains income or capital within the final residual category or income or capital taxed abroad, it is treated as only containing such amount of that income or capital as is just and reasonable.

The term 'tax advantage' comprehends relief from tax, repayment of tax, avoidance of or reduction of tax and avoidance of possible liability to tax (s 809S(4), (5)). Tax for these purposes is confined to income tax and CGT.

The purpose of this rule is to prevent manipulation of the offshore transfer rules. Thus a mixed fund of half income and half capital would be fully taxable if remitted as to half. But an offshore transfer of half the fund would, if effective, mean that a subsequent remittance of either all the transferor fund or all the transferee fund would result in just half the income being taxed.

COMPARISON WITH OLD LAW

53.30 The 2008 rules differ in several important respects from the old law.

Ordering

53.31 Under the old law, income was presumed remitted before capital, regardless of the tax year in which the income arose. Section 809Q operates that system only within tax years: in other words capital and capital gains of later years are treated as remitted before income of earlier years. The curious result is that it is not uncommon for the 2008 rules to be more beneficial than the old ones.

UK income

53.32 Although in a given tax year UK employment income has priority over foreign income, other categories of UK income go to the back of the queue, behind not merely foreign income of the tax year but also foreign gains. As a result particular care will be needed to keep UK-source income segregated.

Capital gains

53.33 The old pro rata rule has gone in that a remittance which is equal to or less than the gain is now all gain. But this only applies within years and so, as with income, capital or UK income or gains of later years are treated as remitted before foreign gains of earlier years.

Offshore transfers

53.34 The rules dealing with offshore transfers are explicit rules covering an area where the old law was uncertain.

Priority as between old law and 2008 rules

53.35 The legislation is silent as to the position where the mixed fund contains income and capital of both 2007–08 and prior and of 2008–09 and post. However s 809Q requires all income and capital for 2008–09 and post to be identified, and this carries the implication that the new rules are applied until the income and gains of 2008–09 and post are all treated as remitted. Such is the view taken by HMRC. But there is a potential difficulty with offshore transfers, for these carry out only the pro rata portion of each category of income and capital (s 809R(4)). As the term mixed fund is defined by reference to the whole fund, the result is that an offshore transfer carries out only a proportion of the 2008–09 income and gains even if in amount it exceeds such income and gains.

THE RESIDUAL CATEGORY

53.36 As indicated in para **53.7** above, the residual category is income or capital not within any of the other categories listed in s 809Q(4). Its significance is that if the income or capital is 'for' a given tax year it is treated as remitted in priority to foreign income or gains of earlier tax years. In appropriate circumstances the result is tax-free remittance even though the fund contains substantial amounts of income or gains from earlier years.

Capital 'for' a tax year

53.37 It is clear that income or gains are 'for' a tax year if they arise or are realised in the year. But when is capital 'for' a tax year?

The obvious example of capital for the purpose of the remittance basis rules is capital received by gift or bequest. But is it 'for' the tax year when the taxpayer receives the gift or bequest or 'for' the year in which it is credited to the mixed fund? The former is surely correct given that income and gains are clearly 'for' the year in which they arise or are realised.

What is the position when an asset is sold? Are the proceeds capital 'for' the year of the sale, save insofar as a foreign gain is realised? If there is a gain it is indubitably 'for' that year, which might lead one to the conclusion that the element of the proceeds that does not represent the gain must be capital 'for' that tax year. However, that conclusion must be incorrect; if it were correct, it would mean that income or gains would lose their character as such if reinvested. As discussed in para **51.10**, that is not the case. The position must be that, while any gain realised on the disposal is a gain 'for' the year of the disposal the balance of the proceeds will represent the capital, income or gains that were used to acquire the asset. The composition of the funds used to acquire the asset will need to be established using the mixed fund rules.

What is comprised in the residual category?

53.38 HMRC consider that the residual category includes items which are 'lost' in computation, eg indexation in the case of corporate gains or allowable expenditure not traceable into the asset (for example incidental expenses on disposal).

The principal type of income in the residual category is UK income which is not employment income. But the category also includes life policy gains taxed as income as these are not relevant foreign income even if the policy is foreign (see para **96.14**). In HMRC's view 'tax-free' 5% withdrawals are taxable remittances if and to the extent that the monies used to pay the premium represented foreign income and gains (see RDRM33540).

SEGREGATION OF INCOME

Old law

53.39 Under old law, remittance of income could be avoided if the income was credited directly to a separate income account and remittance was effected only from the account containing original capital or the proceeds of asset disposals. So too remittance of capital gains or deemed income was avoided if the proceeds of disposals generating such gains or deemed income were kept separate from the account containing clean capital, and remittance was effected only from the latter.

HMRC challenged the capital and income account procedure in *Kneen v Martin* (1934) 19 TC 33. Here the taxpayer was a UK citizen who commenced residence in the UK in 1925. She had several bank accounts in New York. One was credited with the income from her US investments, and the others, from which remittances to the UK were made, with the proceeds of capital realisations. The Special Commissioners found she had not remitted income and this finding was affirmed in the Court of Appeal. The key findings of the Special Commissioners were as follows:

> 'the proper inferences for us to draw were that the actual sums remitted to the [UK] were all derived from the proceeds of realisation of investments owned by [the taxpayer] before 1925 and not from income, or the proceeds of realisation of investments acquired out of income, arising since that date, and that she was not resident in the United Kingdom before 1925. We also thought it a reasonable inference that the investments sold had been largely replaced by other investments acquired out of income arising in America.'

House of Lords approval of capital and income account procedures could be inferred from the leading case of *Thomson v Moyse* (1960) 39 TC 291, 335. Here Lord Radcliffe said the sum remitted must be attributable to the income.

The findings in *Kneen v Martin* showed that the capital and income accounts could be at the same branch of the foreign bank, and that it mattered not that the accumulated foreign income was reinvested abroad. It was, however, important to remember that the capital account could not contain the proceeds of all investments sold; it could only be credited with proceeds of investments not directly or indirectly acquired out of foreign income. This was an application of the principle in cases such as *Patuck v Lloyd*, noted above (para **51.10**).

The present position

53.40 It is clear from the mixed fund rules, and Conditions A and B themselves, that the old law as described above remains good. Condition B requires what is remitted to be the income or gains, or derived from them. So too, the definition of the term mixed fund requires the money or other property to be derived from more than one of the enumerated categories or more than one tax year. It follows that the mixed fund rules are avoided, and tax-free remittance achieved, if clean capital is kept separately in one account from which remittances are made. But as indicated above, for this to be effective, income and the proceeds of disposals generating gains or deemed income must be credited directly to income or gains accounts. Planning steps are discussed further in CHAPTER 14.

A point which was raised under the old law, and may be raised in relation to the 2008 rules, is whether effective segregation is achieved if the relevant accounts are at the same bank. The argument under the 2008 rules is that bank accounts are debts owed by the bank to the customer, with the result that all a customer's accounts constitute a debt owed to him by the bank and thus, on one view, a single item of property. If there is a single item of property it is a mixed fund insofar as it contains capital and income.

It was established in *Hart v Sangster* (1957) 37 TC 321 that the source of interest is the deposit of money upon the terms of the contract, ie on the terms agreed between the bank and the customer. It was held in that case that an addition to an existing account is an addition to a pre-existing source and not the creation of a new source. Implicit in this decision is that a deposit in a separate account would be a separate source. The effect of *Hart v Sangster* was thus that capital and income accounts at the same bank did achieve effective segregation under old law, and such was recognised in *Kneen v Martin* itself, where at least some of the accounts in question were at the same bank.

It may be suggested that the position is the same under the 2008 rules and HMRC accept this is indeed so (RDRM33560). The definition of mixed fund refers to money or other property and thus signifies that money is viewed differently to other property. The issue, therefore, is not what property the customer owns but what his money is. Both natural use of language, and the cases cited above, indicate that each account is separate money.

Other practical points

53.41 HMRC also accept that income remains separate in two circumstances where there used to be doubt:

- Interest credited on the maturity of a deposit to the same account as the principal is treated as segregated provided that it is immediately and identifiably transferred to an income account (RDRM33560).
- Accrued interest under the accrued income scheme is treated as segregated if it is segregated by the selling broker and credited directly to the remittance basis user's income account (RDRM33550; see also para **15.12**).

Chapter 54

RELEVANT PERSONS

INTRODUCTION

54.1 The relevant person concept has two main functions in the remittance code. The first is to counter a feature of the pre-2008 law, commonly referred to as the alienation abroad rule. This applied where the taxpayer gave his income and gains away abroad and was to the effect that a remittance by the donee was not taxable, save insofar as the donor received financial equivalence (*Carter (Inspector of Taxes) v Sharon* [1936] 1 All ER 720, 20 TC 229; *Grimm v Newman* [2002] EWCA Civ 1621, [2003] 1 All ER 67, [2002] STC 1388). The rule was widely exploited before 2008 reforms, for example through gifts by non-domiciliaries to their spouses and children. The relevant person concept counters the technique of alienating income or gains abroad so that they may be bought into the UK by third parties, on the basis that where the donee is a relevant person in relation to the taxpayer, a remittance by the donee is treated as a remittance by the taxpayer. However the counteraction is only partial, for it is not in point unless the donee is in fact a relevant person. Where he is not, remittance only occurs if the rules contained in Conditions C and D are engaged (see CHAPTER 57).

The second function of the relevant person concept is where income and gains of another person are deemed to be derived from those of the taxpayer. This kind of deemed derivation is described in para **52.29** and it requires the relevant person concept for, unless the other person is a relevant person, his remittance of the actual income and gains does not result in the taxpayer being taxed.

The principal topic of this chapter is the definition of relevant person. However it also considers some of the implications of property held by particular categories of relevant person being, or being derived from, the income or gains of the taxpayer.

As indicated in para **51.5**, the relevant person concept is subject to one important transitional rule. FA 2008, Sch 7 para 86(4) provides that s 809L has effect in relation to income and gains of 2007–08 and prior as if the only person who is a relevant person is the taxpayer.

INDIVIDUAL RELEVANT PERSONS

54.2 The taxpayer is a relevant person and so too are his spouse, his minor children and his minor grandchildren (ITA 2007, s 809M(2)(a)–(d)). A point to stress is that adult children and grandchildren, and all remoter relatives, are not relevant persons.

Spouses

54.3 The term relevant person includes civil partners as well as spouses (s 809M(2)(c)). Moreover, two persons living together as husband and wife or as civil partners are treated as married even if in fact they are not (s 809M(3)(a) and (b)). This remarkable extension of the concept of marriage raises issues of uncertainty as to what is meant by living together as husband and wife. It also raises issues of enforcement in that it is difficult to see how HMRC can police it without being intrusive.

Spouses cease to be relevant persons in relation to each other when the marriage ends, ie on decree absolute. In contrast to the CGT spouse exemption (TCGA 1992, s 58) there is no requirement in the relevant person definition that the spouses be living together, so spouses remain relevant persons after separation unless and until decree absolute is pronounced. However the definition of relevant person in s 809M(2) is expressed in the present tense and this means the definition is applied at the moment of remittance. It follows that a divorcee can, once decree absolute is pronounced, remit property given to her by her husband prior to divorce without risk of him being taxed.

There are however two caveats to this. The first is that if the divorcee gives property back to her former husband, or someone else who is a relevant person in relation to him, remittance by that person results in tax if, contrary to the suggestion in Chapter 52, the derivation concept is wide enough to embrace tracing through multiple gifts. The main practical instance where this might be a risk is where the divorcee creates a settlement, for then the settlement is a relevant person in relation to her former husband should their minor children or grandchildren be beneficiaries and under 18.

The second caveat is that Condition C can catch use by the divorcee of the funds given to her by her former husband if those funds are derived from his income and gains. Such use can be remittance if it amounts to enjoyment in the UK by someone who is a relevant person in relation to her former husband, ie principally their minor children and grandchildren. But this is in point only if the gift to the divorcee is post decree absolute, as Condition C is not engaged if the recipient is a relevant person at the time of the gift (see para 57.9).

Some implications

54.4 As is explained above, the main function of the relevant person concept is to render taxable remittances by the relevant person of property derived from the taxpayer's income or gains. In Chapter 52, it is explained there is much uncertainty as to how far the derivation concept goes, but HMRC's view is that tracing is required, using the mixed fund rules described in Chapter 53.

The implications of this where the relevant person recipient is an individual raise interesting issues. As in practice these issues are unlikely to arise where the recipient is a child, the discussion here is expressed in terms of spouses.

The first point to make is that, as respects the donee spouse, the gift from the donor is in the residual category under the mixed fund rules, ie capital not within another paragraph. This means that, so far as the donee is concerned, the mixed fund rules identify remittance with that gift after the donee's income and gains of the year of the gift have been exhausted and, in the case of subsequent year remittance, those of subsequent years as well. It follows that, as respects the donee spouse, the spousal gift delays the time at which income and gains of prior years are remitted.

The second point is that as respects the donor spouse, the key requirement is that in s 809M(3), step 1, namely that what has to be looked for is the amount of the different categories of *his* income and gains in the mixed fund. As explained in para 53.21 there is no requirement that the mixed fund be owned by him, and so the effect is that remittances from the mixed fund are, so far as he is concerned, identified first with such of his income and gains as by derivation are traceable into the mixed fund. What appears not to be required, in relation to each year, is to look at income and gains of both donor and donee.

The above two points pre-suppose the transfer from the mixed fund is a s 809Q transfer, ie is a transfer to the UK or expected to be so. What happens if the transfer is an offshore transfer – ie not expected to be remitted to the UK (see para 53.10)? Here much the better view is that the offshore transfer carries out a proportion of the capital and income across the account as a whole. In a wider context, this solution is likely to be right for, if in relation the donor the offshore transfer were exclusively identified with his income and gains, an offshore transfer equal to them would remove them from the mixed fund and render the balance of the latter able to be remitted without tax cost to the donor.

Assuming all these points are right there is a sting in the tail. This is in point if the donee spouse retains the gift, generates income and gains by investing it, and then remits part of the enhanced fund in a future tax year. In that event the logical implication is that the partial remittance is taxed twice, first as a remittance by the donee of her income and gains of the year of the gift and subsequent tax years and second as a remittance by the donor of his income and gains comprised in the gift.

There is no absolute reason on the terms of the legislation why a single remittance to the UK should not do double duty but one might expect a judge to try and avoid this result. Limiting the extent of the derivation concept in the manner described in CHAPTER 52 would be one way of achieving this.

Children and grandchildren

54.5 As indicated above, children and grandchildren are not relevant persons unless under 18. It is pretty clear that, once a minor child or grandchild reaches 18, he immediately ceases to be a relevant person in relation to the taxpayer.

The restriction of the relevant person category to minor children and grandchildren means that gifts of income and gains to the taxpayer's adult children do not result in tax if the recipient remits. But as with ex-spouses, onwards gifts to someone who is a relevant person, for example minor grandchildren or a trust of which they are beneficiaries, can result in tax if that onward recipient remits and a wide view is taken of the derivation concept (see CHAPTER 52). Indeed, HMRC specifically state that remittance by a minor grandchild in these circumstances does result in tax (see RDRM33050). A further point is that use in the UK by the recipient adult child for the benefit of his minor children could result in tax under Condition C, for they are the taxpayer's grandchildren. This difficult point is discussed further in CHAPTER 57.

In contrast to other legislation, step-children and step-grandchildren are not deemed to be children or grandchildren.

TRUSTS

54.6 The trustees of a settlement are relevant persons if an individual relevant person is a beneficiary (s 809M(2)(g)).

Settlement

54.7 The term 'settlement' bears the same meaning as it is given in ITA 2007 Pt 9 chapter 2 (s 809M(3)(d)). That part is the legislation providing the general rules as to the taxation of trusts. It does not define 'settlement' as such, but instead describes settled property as any property held in trust other than property held by a person as nominee for another (ITA 2007, s 466). In relation to the equivalent CGT provision (TCGA 1992, s 68) it has been held that the term 'settlement' bears its general common law meaning (*Roome v Edwards* [1981] STC 96). By this somewhat roundabout route, it may be inferred that the term bears this meaning for the purposes of the relevant person rule also. The important point is that the term does not have the anti-avoidance meaning given in the income tax settlement code (see paras 75.14 to 75.17).

Rather curiously s 809M(3)(d) provides a definition of the term 'settlor'. This is puzzling because the word 'settlor' is not otherwise used in s 809M.

Trustee

54.8 The term 'trustee' bears its normal meaning save where the settlement has no trustees. In such a case the term comprehends any person in whom the settled property is vested or any person having the management of it (ITA 2007, s 809M(3)(f) applying ITA 2007, s 994(3)). As with income tax and CGT generally, the trustees are treated as a single person distinct from the particular persons who happen to be trustees (ITA 2007, s 474).

This reference to s 994(3) is curious, given that the normal meaning of 'settlement' applies for the purposes of the definition of 'relevant persons'. Section 994(3) is intended to apply to 'settlements' in the broad sense used in

ITTOIA 2005, Pt 5 chapter 5, which include trusts but also other entities and arrangements, of which there may well not be any trustees in the ordinary sense. It seems likely that by extending the meaning of 'trustee' in s 809M, the draftsman was intending to catch persons having responsibility for the management of trust-like entities, such as foundations, which have boards rather than trustees. The question of whether, for the purposes of English law and UK tax laws, a foundation should be regarded as a trust is considered in CHAPTER 33.

Beneficiary

54.9 The term 'beneficiary' is defined as any person who, under or by virtue of the settlement:

(a)   receives any benefit; or
(b)   may receive any benefit (s 809M(3)(e)).

The natural meaning of this definition is that the first limb connotes beneficiaries under a fixed interest trust and the second limb reversioners and discretionary beneficiaries. However there are points of difficulty.

The first concerns the many trusts where the trustees or some other person have power to add persons to the class of beneficiaries. Sometimes such power of addition is restricted to a narrow class, but normally it extends to the whole world, subject to limited exceptions, for example the trustees themselves. The issue raised is whether, assuming the named class of beneficiaries excludes relevant persons, the settlement is nonetheless a relevant person in relation to a given individual if any possible object of the power of addition is a relevant person or, in other words, unless all such relevant persons are excluded from the scope of the power of addition.

The prudent view is undoubtedly to assume that in such cases the settlement is a relevant person and this should certainly be the line taken in planning. But there are arguments that this view is too conservative, the most cogent of which are the natural reading of the two limbs, as indicated above and the fact that until a person is added as a beneficiary he cannot, under the terms of the settlement, benefit. Further it is to be noted that the definition in s 809M is not in the same terms as those in ITTOIA 2005, s 624 and TCGA 1992, Sch 5, para 2 (see paras **75.2** and **76.4**) which expressly refer to persons who could benefit in any circumstances whatsoever. It can reasonably be argued that had Parliament intended such an all-embracing meaning it would have said so. For all these reasons it can be argued with some force that, in determining whether a settlement is a relevant person, one ignores those who could be added in exercise of the power of addition.

The second point is whether the first limb of the definition includes the receipt of a benefit or benefits in breach of trust. In other words, if the settlement excludes all relevant persons, is it nonetheless a relevant person should the trustees confer benefit on a non-beneficiary who is a relevant person. Here it seems reasonably clear such benefit does not make the settlement a relevant person, both because the definition is expressed by reference to the terms of the settlement and because any such purported benefit would be in breach of trust and so liable to be returned and not a benefit at all.

But to this there is one qualification, applicable where the settlement does not comprehensively exclude relevant persons from any possibility of benefit but has a narrow class of non-relevant person beneficiaries with no power of addition. Here it is possible as a matter of trust law for the trustees to benefit a non-beneficiary if such is for the benefit of a beneficiary, and, were that non-beneficiary a relevant person, the first limb would be engaged.

In such a case an interesting issue would arise of the period for which the settlement is a relevant person. The legislation is silent on this point. The answer it may, be suggested, is the tax year of the benefit as it is by tax year that remittances are charged.

The third point is related and concerns the position where the settlement excludes relevant persons, but a beneficiary who is not a relevant person receives a distribution and passes it on to an individual who is a relevant person. This is a variant of the onward gift problem, discussed in other contexts in paras **70.28** to **70.30**. Here it may be concluded the onward gift does not make the settlement a relevant person as it is not under or by virtue of the settlement.

A fourth and final issue is whether some of the impact of the relevant person concept can be circumvented where the taxpayer and his spouse (and all those treated as spouses) are excluded but his children and grandchildren are beneficiaries but cannot receive benefit until 18. This circumvention however is most unlikely to work, for a child under 18 still may benefit in the future even if he cannot do so until 18.

But what does seem clear is that such a settlement is not a relevant person unless a child or grandchild is in existence and under the age of 18. The mere prospect of future children or grandchildren cannot of itself make the settlement a relevant person for, until such a child or grandchild is born, he is not a person at all.

Bodies connected with the settlement

54.10 Any body connected with a settlement is a relevant person if the settlement itself is a relevant person (s 809M(2)(h) applying ITA 2007, s 993(3)). The term connected bears its normal definition as given in ITA 2007, s 993 (ITA 2007, s 809M(3)(g)). The following thus count as bodies connected with the settlement and so relevant persons:

(1) Any resident or non-resident company in which the trustees are a participator; and
(2) Any body corporate controlled by such a company.

In applying this definition of connection, control does not bear its anti-avoidance meaning as given in the close company code but instead means simply voting control (ITA 2007, ss 993(3)(e) and 995). The term participator bears its normal close company definition (see CHAPTER 87).

There is one other type of body connected with the trustees which is regarded as a relevant person. This is any sub-fund settlement of which the settlement is principal settlement. As is explained in para **10.20** sub-fund settlements require stringent conditions to be met and an election on the part of the trustees concerned (TCGA 1992, Sch 4ZA). They are therefore rarely encountered in practice.

Some implications

54.11 The primary significance of a settlement being a relevant person arises if the settlor is a beneficiary and so taxable on the income under the income tax settlement code (see CHAPTER 75). As indicated above, it is not the fact of him being settlor that makes it a relevant person. Instead the settlement is not a relevant person unless he, or some other individual who is a relevant person in relation to him falls within the definition of the term 'beneficiary'.

It might be thought that the kind of mixed fund issues that arise in relation to individual relevant persons do not arise in relation to settlements, on the grounds that the only person from whom funds in the settlement, and thus income and gains, are derived is the settlor (see para **52.27**). So too if any income of the settlement is attributed to an individual it is attributed to the settlor. As a result the mixed fund rules can be operated across the settlement on the basis of 100% derivation from a single remittance basis user.

But in reality the position may not be as simple as this. One reason is that on occasion settlements can have multiple settlors. Here, if all the funds end up in mixed funds, remittances to the UK would, if derivation connotes a tracing exercise, be identified with the income or gains of each settlor and suffer multiple tax accordingly.

More cogent is the non-transferor charge under the transfer of assets code. As is explained in CHAPTER 72, this identifies benefits with trust income on a first in first out basis and, in all cases, the trust is a relevant person in relation to each non-transferor as they are by definition beneficiaries. For remittance purposes the s 732 income is deemed derived from the income so identified on the first in first out basis. Self-evidently one could have a mixed fund comprised of income so identified in relation to benefits to multiple beneficiaries and, if so, remittance by the trust from that mixed fund would, on the analysis put forward here, be remittance of the s 732 income of each of the multiple beneficiaries.

The same point arises as between settlor and beneficiaries on the assumption unremitted income attributable to the transferor can unless remitted also be relevant income in relation to the non-transferor charge (as to which see para **71.26**).

COMPANIES

54.12 A company is a relevant person if:

(a)   it is close or would be close if UK resident; and

(b)   the participators include any individual or settlement which is a relevant person (ITA 2007, s 809M(2)(e) and (f)).

Close company

54.13 The term close company bears its normal tax definition (ITA 2007, s 809M(3)(c)). This definition is explained in CHAPTER 87.

Participator

54.14 The term participator bears the same meaning as in the close company rules (s 809M(3)(ca)). It thus includes anybody who possesses or is entitled to acquire share capital or voting rights in the company (CTA 2010, s 454; see para **87.3**). Non-bank loan creditors are also included (CTA 2010, s 454).

There is no de minimis threshold of participant which has to be crossed before a person counts as a participator for these purposes, which means that even a shareholder with less than 5% of the company will find it is a relevant person in relation to him. In such a case, the more important issue is likely to be whether the company is close.

Subsidiaries

54.15 Two overlapping provisions make subsidiaries relevant persons. The first forms part of the definition of participator (s 809M(3)(ca)) and is to the effect that the term bears the meaning it has for the purposes of CTA 2010, s 455. That section charges loans to participators and requires a participator in one company to be treated as participator in any company which that company controls (s 455(5)). Control bears its normal close company definition (see para **87.9**) and the result is that where the taxpayer or another relevant person is a participator in the top company of a group, both that top company and all close companies controlled by it are relevant persons.

The second provision is in the list of categories of relevant person and is to the effect that any 51% subsidiary of a company which is a relevant person is also a relevant person (ITA 2007, s 809M(2)(f)). The term 51% subsidiary bears its corporation tax meaning (s 809M(3)(cb)) and is thus any company in which the top company owns more than 50% of the ordinary share capital, either directly or indirectly (CTA 2010, ss 1154–1157).

It might be wondered whether there are any companies covered by this second provision which are not also within the first. The answer is that there are, for the subsidiaries referred to in the second provision need not be close. It is possible for a close company to own more than 50% of the shares of a non-close company, as where more than 35% of the shares of the latter are listed and dealt in on a recognised stock exchange (CTA 2010, s 446).

In its form originally enacted s 809M did not in general include subsidiaries as relevant persons. The defect was rectified in relation to subsidiaries of resident close companies with effect from 22 April 2009 (FA 2009, Sch 27 paras 7(2) and 15(2)). It was rectified in relation to subsidiaries of non-resident close companies with effect from 6 April 2010 (FA 2010, s 33). A subsidiary has always been a relevant person where a trust which is a relevant person is participator in the top company, for companies connected with such trusts are relevant persons in their own right (para 54.10 above).

Implications

54.16 The practical result of the above definitions is that a surprising number of companies will turn out to be relevant persons in relation to a surprising number of remittance basis users. It is true that, as noted above, a company can only be a relevant person if close. But as explained in CHAPTER 87, even quite widely held private companies can turn out to be close on account of the aggregation of participations held by associates. A particular sting in commercial contexts is the fact that all partners are associates of each other. Further the associate concept is so wide that in some cases it may be impossible to know for certain that a company is not close, for there may be relationships between participators that are not apparent from the share register.

But wide though this definition is, the implications in practice are not always great. This is because relevant person status is material only if there are income or gains which are taxable if remitted. In the case of the company's income and gains this condition is met only if they are attributable to the taxpayer under ITA 2007, ss 720 or 727 or under TCGA 1992, s 13 (see CHAPTERS 69 and 88). Both these sections are subject to motive defences (see CHAPTER 73 and paras 88.4 and 88.37). In addition, ss 720 and 727 are in any event unlikely to be in point if the remittance basis user acquires the shares by purchase or gift rather than by subscription and s 13 is subject to a de minimis, now 25%. These points mean that relevant person status is not as significant as might be supposed. But one point to note with s 13 is that, until 5 April 2012, the de minimis was just 10% and the motive defence did not apply. Gains realised in the company prior to that date are thus more likely to be within s 13 and, despite the subsequent change of the law, would still attract tax now if the company remits at a time when it is a relevant person in relation to any participator to whom such gains were apportioned.

The relevant person status of close companies is also potentially significant if the remittance basis user subscribes for his shares or loan stock. Should the funds subscribed be or be derived from his income and gains remittance by the company results in tax if the company is a relevant person in relation to him (see para 52.23).

With multiple participators the same issue arises with the mixed fund rules as has been discussed above in relation to spouses and trusts. As described in para 53.20 to 53.22 those rules operate on each remittance basis user separately and require, in relation to him, that any remittance by the company is identified first with what is derived from him. Assuming this is right, a close company with eight remittance basis subscribers that remits one eighth of the funds subscribed would cause each of the eight subscribers to be taxed as having remitted the full amount subscribed.

The same point also arises if the company itself generates income or gains attributable to participators under s 720 and/or s 13. Here partial remittance from the mixed fund would be taxed on each participator concurrently and, in contrast to the subscription position, this would be the result of express deemed derivation. There would thus be no room for reducing the potential multiple taxation by a restrictive construction of 'derive'.

ENTITIES WHICH ARE NOT RELEVANT PERSONS

54.17 Certain kinds of entity are omitted from the list of relevant persons, most notably partnerships and unit trusts.

Partnerships

54.18 The general rule is that a partnership is transparent for tax purposes (ITTOIA 2005, s 848; TCGA 1992, s 59). In the light of this, the logical conclusion is that partnerships do not need to be addressed by the relevant person rules, on the grounds that remittance by the partnership is treated as remittance by the partners in proportion to their respective shares in the partnership.

HMRC, however, do not view the matter in this way. Their position is that a remittance by a non-UK partnership is not a remittance by the partners. An individual partner who is a remittance basis user does not, therefore, make a taxable remittance, unless what is remitted is used to benefit him (RDRM para 33530).

Unit trusts

54.19 Non-UK resident unit trusts are generally regarded as opaque for income tax purposes (see para 40.16) and are treated as companies for CGT purposes (see para 3.4). It is a reasonable inference from this that remittance by the unit trust does not fall to be treated as pro rata remittance by each of the unit holders. But the position may be otherwise in the event that the unit trust is transparent for income tax purposes (see para 40.16).

The fact that unit trusts are companies for CGT purposes does not make them relevant persons, for the CGT treatment of unit trusts as companies is not extended to the remittance rules. Even if it were it would only be in point insofar as the unit trust could be regarded as close.

Chapter 55

SERVICES PROVIDED IN THE UK

INTRODUCTION

55.1 Under the core definition in Conditions A and B in s 809L a service results in a taxable remittance if the following conditions are met:

(1)   The service is provided to or for the benefit of the taxpayer or another relevant person.
(2)   It is so provided in the UK; and
(3)   The consideration for the service is foreign income and gains of the taxpayer or is derived from such income or gains.

To the uninitiated, this special rule for services may appear pointless, for if the taxpayer brings foreign income or gains to the UK to pay for services, he effects a remittance under the general rules described in CHAPTER 51. But this overlooks the fact that the taxpayer may make payment to a non-UK account of the service provider, and it is this situation which the rule described here is designed to catch. It was generally accepted prior to 6 April 2008 that a remittance did not occur in such circumstances. This view was founded on the House of Lords decision in *IRC v Gordon* [1952] AC 552, [1952] 1 All ER 866, and the fact that statute reversed that decision only as respects debts for money lent (see ITTOIA 2005, s 833 as originally enacted).

The mixed fund rules described in CHAPTER 53 apply in determining what is remitted. The term 'relevant person' bears the meaning discussed in CHAPTER 54 and thus, in relation to income and gains of 2007–08 and prior, means only the taxpayer.

Amount of the remittance

55.2 As with Conditions A and B generally (para 51.15), if the consideration for the service is the foreign income or gains the amount remitted is the amount of the income or gains. If the consideration is derived from the income or gains it is the amount of the income or gains from which it is derived. Not surprisingly, therefore, the amount remitted is not the value of the services but the amount of foreign income or gains used to pay for them.

The distinction between consideration which is the income and gains and consideration which is derived from them is explained in para 51.7. The discussion in CHAPTER 52 of the extent of derivation is in point here also.

Consideration derived from the income or gains

55.3 Should the consideration used to pay for the service be derived from the income or gains it must belong to the taxpayer or some other relevant person (s 809L(3)(b)(ii)). As explained in CHAPTER 52, one instance of derivation is where the taxpayer gives the income or gains away, and the effect of the relevant person limitation is that Conditions A and B do not apply unless the donee who pays for the service is a relevant person. But that is not to say that the taxpayer escapes tax, for Condition C is in point provided it can be said that the taxpayer is enjoying the service (see para 57.17).

MEANING OF SERVICE

55.4 The term 'service' is not defined, with the result that it is a question of fact as to whether what is provided in the UK is a service.

An area of some difficulty is whether the making available of an asset for use by a relevant person is properly characterised as a service provided to that person. It seems very unnatural to describe a lessor of land as a provider of a service, but it is more arguable that a service is provided if land or a chattel is licensed, and the conservative view must be that there is, or may be, a service in these situations.

It follows that a licence fee paid abroad is a remittance if the land or chattel for which the licence fee is paid is in the UK. This is so even if the land or chattel had itself occasioned a taxable remittance. The latter could be the position if the property in question belongs to someone who is a relevant person in relation to the payer of the licence fee, for example a trust of which he is a beneficiary or a company owned by such a trust. In a case of this sort the full value of the land or chattel may itself have been taxed as a remittance, as where the trust paid for the property out of income deemed to be that of the licence-fee payer. The fact that a taxable remittance occurred at this point does not prevent payment of the licence fee itself also being a remittance.

In ordinary parlance, loans fall within the term 'financial services', so the provision of a loan might also be considered a service. This point arises most commonly in relation to loans from non-resident trusts (see para 55.6 below, and para 79.6).

To or for the benefit of the taxpayer

55.5 It should be noted that the service need not be provided to the taxpayer or another relevant person, it being sufficient if it is provided for the benefit of such person. This means, inter alia, that a UK service to a non-UK entity may be caught if the provision of that service benefits the taxpayer.

UK services provided to non-UK entities and paid for abroad most frequently result in remittance where the service is paid for out of income which is attributed to the taxpayer under ITTOIA 2005, s 624 or ITA 2007, ss 720–730 (see CHAPTERS 69 and 75). In such cases, remittance occurs not because the service benefits the taxpayer but because the recipient is almost invariably a company or trust that is a relevant person in relation to him (see CHAPTER 53).

Such services so paid for can also result in remittance of s 732 income under the non-transferor charge if the income used to pay for them is matched to the s 732 income under the s 735A matching rules (see CHAPTER 72). Here too remittance occurs not because the UK service benefits the taxpayer but because the person to whom it is provided is almost invariably a relevant person in relation to him (see CHAPTER 53). But were that person for some reason not a relevant person in relation to the taxpayer, then the services would only be a remittance if it could be said they benefited him.

Service 'is' the income or gains

55.6 Condition B includes a puzzling provision to the effect that remittance occurs not only if the consideration for the UK service is the income or the chargeable gains but if the UK service itself 'is' the foreign income or gains or derives from them. At first sight this offends against logic, as it is hard to see how foreign income or gains could constitute a service, as distinct from being what is used to pay for the service.

However, in at least two instances a benefit from a trust or other overseas structure is deemed to be derived from income or gains treated as accruing to a beneficiary. These instances are ITA 2007, s 735(4) and TCGA 1992, s 87B(4), which deal respectively with benefits and capital payments (see paras 72.22 and 79.6). If therefore a benefit from a trust can be said to be a service to the recipient, the present provision would be in point if the benefit is conferred or enjoyed in the UK.

Most benefits provided by trustees are not apt to be described as services. A distribution is certainly not a service. But some benefits clearly are; for example the provision by the trustee of a guarantee to a bank in support of a loan to a beneficiary of the trust, can reasonably be characterised as a service to the beneficiary. As discussed at para 77.6, it may be that a direct loan from the trust to the beneficiary is also a service.

PROVIDED IN THE UK

55.7 It is a question of fact as to whether the service is provided in the UK. The legislation does not include 'place of supply' provisions comparable to those in the VAT legislation. A practical solution is to ensure that services provided in the UK are recorded and invoiced separately from those provided elsewhere.

Travel

55.8 The concept of a service being provided in a particular place is cogent in relation to manual labour. However, other forms of service may be difficult to categorise as UK or non-UK services. For example, if a car is hired in Calais, taken on a ferry to Dover, and then returned to Calais, is the service provided in the UK because the car has been brought to the UK? It seems somewhat unnatural to say that it is. It is suggested that the service in this case consists in the making available of the car for use, and that act takes place in Calais, so this is a non-UK service. HMRC's published view, which arguably does not answer the question posed here, is that a travel service is provided in the UK if the travel is to or from the UK (RDRM33130, Example 3).

Service provider based outside the UK

55.9 If a foreign business provides all its services outside the UK, no remittance issues arise provided it is paid abroad. More difficult is the position, where, as part of its overall service, employees make occasional visits to the UK for meetings or similar functions. Can it then be said those meetings are a service provided in the UK? The better view is not, so long as those meetings are ancillary to the main tasks performed where the service-provider is based. It appears this view is shared by HMRC who say at RDRM 34040:

'A service is regarded as having been provided in the UK if the providers of the service are based in and give that service in the UK.'

It may be suggested the position might be different if the whole service was provided in the UK, for example a UK construction project carried out by a foreign contractor.

Sub-contractors

55.10 A non-UK service-provider may engage a service-provider in the UK as part of his service to the client. Here the UK service-provider will very likely be seen as indirectly providing services to the client, or at least as providing services for the benefit of the client. On this basis payment of the foreign service-provider is a remittance insofar as the payment reimburses the fees of the UK provider.

Intangibles

55.11 The difficulty of answering the question of where a service is provided may be acute where there is an international element to the service, and the 'work product' is intangible (save that it may be presented or communicated by tangible means, eg in the form of a letter or report). This problem commonly arises in relation to legal, accountancy, financial and marketing services.

One possibility is that the question must be determined by looking at the residence of the service-provider, ie the person who is bound, as a matter of contract law, to provide the service. That would provide legal certainty. But it would open the door to the avoidance of remittances through back-to-back arrangements, whereby a non-UK entity would agree to provide the service to the taxpayer, but would sub-contract to a UK entity, which would, in the UK, employ the individuals ultimately responsible for the provision of the service. As just indicated, it seems unlikely that a court would favour this interpretation.

Another possibility is that the situs of the service depends on where the 'work product' is delivered to or received by the client. But this interpretation is unattractive. It would make the situs of the service unpredictable in relation to internationally mobile clients and could render the situs of a service in the UK even though it might have no connection to the UK other than the client's physical presence in the UK when, for example, an email was opened.

A more plausible interpretation would focus on the physical presence of the individuals responsible for the provision of the service – ie one which says that the service is provided in the UK if that is where the relevant workers perform their work. This would seem the most natural interpretation, but it may leave open the question of where a service is provided in the (now very common) scenario of a 'work product' developed by individuals or teams in different countries, within a multinational concern. It might be reasonable to conclude that, in that scenario, the service should be regarded as having been provided in the UK if the relevant workers were in the UK when they did their work, to a more than minimal extent.

Apportionment

55.12 It may be suggested that apportionment is possible if an identifiable part of a service is provided in the UK and the rest is not. This is because Conditions A and B focus on the service provided in the UK and the consideration given for that service. But where identifiable elements cannot be split out, the service has to be looked at a whole and if overall can be said to be provided in the UK, all is so treated even if some work was performed outside the UK.

EXEMPTION FOR SERVICES RELATING TO NON-UK PROPERTY

55.13 ITA 2007, s 809W prevents consideration given for a service from being a remittance if the following conditions are met:

(1)   The service relates wholly or mainly to property situate outside the UK.
(2)   The service provider holds a bank account outside the UK.
(3)   All the consideration due for the service is discharged by payment to that bank account.

In what follows, the shorthand 'the property condition' has been used for the requirement at (1) above, and 'the banking condition' for the requirements at (2) and (3).

As discussed below (para **55.17**), there is an exception, which may in theory disapply the exemption in s 809W. It is, however, rarely relevant.

The property condition

55.14 The first of the above conditions requires two questions to be asked: does the service relate to property and, if it does, is the property situate outside the UK? The adjectives 'wholly or mainly' qualify both of these requirements. It follows that the test stipulated by the legislation is: (1) does the service relate wholly or mainly to property, and (2), if so, is that property wholly or mainly outside the UK?

HMRC take a 'broad brush' view of how the property condition works. They state (at RDRM34040) that 'for the purposes of applying the exemption "wholly or mainly" means more than half. Wholly or mainly relates to the service provided, not the property, and is, in general, judged by reference to work done, normally time spent'.

It is clear that a limited relationship between the service and property will not satisfy the property condition, even if all of the property in question is non-UK. For example, where a remittance basis user engages an accountant to prepare his tax return, the property condition will not be satisfied if the tax-payer's main source of income in the tax year was employment income, and most of the work involved in preparing the return relates to this (even if the employment was outside the UK). However, if the main source of income was investments, and most of the work involved relates to the investment income, the first part of the two step test is passed and one turns to the question of whether the investments were wholly or mainly outside the UK. (See RDRM34060, Example 6.)

The same analysis is required if a UK service is provided to a non-UK entity, and the entity makes payment for the service using funds that are deemed to be the taxpayer's income under ITTOIA 2005, s 624 or ITA 2007, s 720 (see CHAPTERS **69** and **75**). For example, a non-UK company may obtain advice from a UK bank regarding a proposed disposal of its shares in a subsidiary. Such advice clearly relates to property, so whether the property condition is satisfied turns on the situs of the shares (see para **55.15**).

Deciding whether a service relates to property can be difficult. For example, if a non-UK trust company engages UK solicitors to prepare and negotiate a deed effecting its appointment as trustee of a trust, does the service relate wholly or mainly to property? It might be assumed that it does, because on one level it is concerned with the arrangements under which the assets of the trust will be transferred to the trust company. But a narrower view is possible, viz that the service is chiefly concerned with legal relations between the outgoing and incoming trustees (specifically the scope of the indemnities that are typically required by outgoing trustees) and not, strictly, with the property of the trust. It is suggested that this narrower view is the correct one. If so, legal work for an incoming trustee, relating to the wording of a deed of appointment, does not relate wholly or mainly to property as it is mainly related to the negotiation of the trustee's obligations under the deed. However, there must be a good argument that such work for an *outgoing* trustee *does*, predominantly, relate to property, namely the rights of indemnity against the incoming trustee that are reserved under the deed.

If work performed by the UK solicitors for an incoming trustee encompasses not only preparation and negotiation of the deed of appointment and retirement but also advice as to the transfer of the trust assets to it, that work can reasonably be construed as two discrete services and the second element will satisfy the property condition, provided of course that the trust assets are wholly or mainly non-UK situated.

It is similarly difficult to apply the property condition in relation to professional services in connection with divorce, other legal proceedings, and tax. The most one can say here is that it is always a question of fact whether the service in question relates to property. Taxpayers and their advisers should be alive to the possibility of the work done being characterised as a 'bundle' of discrete services so that some, at least, of the payment for that work qualifies for the exemption. In borderline cases it may be helpful, evidentially, for the division of the work into discrete services to be reflected in separate engagement letters or contracts and separate invoices.

Situs rules

55.15 The rules for determining the situs of the property to which the service relates are the CGT rules described in Chapter 39 (s 809W(6)). These rules are not entirely the same as the common law rules, the most important point of difference being that simple debts have a UK situs for CGT purposes if the creditor is UK resident. This means that overseas bank accounts of non-domiciliaries which are denominated in sterling have a UK situs, with the result that services relating to them are not within the exemption. But this does not apply to overseas bank accounts denominated in foreign currency as the situs of these is an exception from the normal creditor rule (see para **39.12**).

The banking condition

55.16 The exemption in s 809W also requires the banking condition to be met, ie all the consideration for the service must be paid to the service provider's non-UK account.

This requirement serves no purpose other than to support, to some minor extent, the offshore banking industry. It is a relic of the pre-2008 law (see para **55.1** above), which has been incorporated into the statutory rules. However, for as long as this rule stands, a service-provider which wishes to attract or retain the custom of non-domiciliaries will need to offer the facility of payment to a non-UK bank account, where the exemption in s 809W may otherwise be in point.

The existence of the banking condition is a further reason for contracting and invoicing separately, as otherwise it may be difficult to see which payment relates to which part of a given invoice.

THE EXCEPTION

55.17 The relief under s 809W is disapplied if the UK service relates to the provision in the UK of a benefit that is treated as deriving from the income under ITA 2007, s 735. The same result follows if the service relates to a UK benefit that is treated as deriving from the gains under TCGA 1992, s 87B. It appears that the relationship of the service to the benefit can be modest, for the disapplication operates if the service relates to any extent to the benefit. The disapplication is effected by s 809W(5).

UK benefit derived from gains

55.18 Section 87B is the section which applies the remittance basis to capital payments from trusts as described in Chapter 77. It provides that the capital payment or benefit is derived from the s 87 gain and thus treats the s 87 gain as remitted if the capital payment is remitted or, where the capital payment is a benefit in kind, if the benefit is enjoyed in the UK.

In relation to s 87 gains, the s 809W relief is engaged if the recipient of the capital payment uses it outside the UK to pay for services provided in the UK that satisfy the s 809W conditions, ie relate wholly or mainly to property situate outside the UK. The effect of s 809W(5) is to disapply the relief if, to any extent, the UK services also relate to the provision in the UK of a benefit. However it is not all benefits provided in the UK which jeopardise the s 809W relief but merely those which:

(a)   amount to a capital payment within s 87; and
(b)   are derived from the same s 87 gains as accrue by reason of the capital payment used to pay for the services.

This last point is a surprising limitation on s 809W(5) but is clearly required by the subsection, for the subsection uses the definite article in relation to the chargeable gains from which the benefit is derived. At first impression it is difficult, in relation to a given s 87 gain, to see how the capital payment generating the gain can be both a sum of money used to pay for services within s 809W and a benefit provided in the UK. The obvious example of a benefit provided in the UK is the rent free use of a house or chattel, but it is difficult to see how that gives rise to the same s 87 gain as some separate distribution of cash which is then used to pay for the services.

The answer, however, appears to be that matching under s 87A is on an annual basis, ie total capital payments to the beneficiary are matched to trust s 2(2) amounts and the result is a single gain accruing to the recipient beneficiary in the tax year concerned. If so, s 809W(5) operates to deny s 809W(5) relief where:

(a)   In the same year the trust both distributes capital cash to the beneficiary and provides benefits to him in the UK.
(b)   The distribution and benefit result in a s 87 gain.
(c)   The beneficiary uses the cash to pay for the s 809W services, ie services relating wholly or mainly to property abroad.
(d)   The services, at least to some extent, relate also to the benefit provided in the UK.

In other words, if the services are legal or accountancy, they must relate mainly to property abroad for s 809W to be in issue at all. But if, at least to some extent, they extend also to advice on the benefits provided by the trust in the same year in the UK, s 809W(5) disapplies the s 809W relief.

UK benefit derived from income

55.19 Section 735 is part of the code which treats benefits to non-transferors as income to the extent of available relevant income in the overseas structure (see CHAPTER 70). Under ITA 2007, s 733 the total benefits received by a given individual in a tax year are treated as his income of that tax year to the extent that there is available relevant income in the structure (see further in CHAPTER 71). Section 735 treats both the benefit and the matched relevant income as derived from the beneficiary's notional income and thus the latter is remitted if either the benefit or the matched income is remitted (see further paras **72.14** to **72.24**).

In these regards it differs from s 87B, where remittance of the notional gain occurs only if the capital payment is remitted. Section 735 also differs from s 87 in that there are specific rules for matching the beneficiary's notional income of a given year with specific items of relevant income and specific benefits. As explained in para **72.5**, first in first out is applied, both between tax years and within tax years. Accordingly it is possible to know which item of relevant income is matched with which benefit.

With this established, it is apparent that a payment abroad for services provided in the UK is, absent s 809W, a remittance of the beneficiary's notional income if either:

(a)   the payment is by the person abroad and is made out of the matched relevant income or funds derived from it; or

(b)   the payment is by the beneficiary and is made using the benefit or funds derived from it.

Section 809W prevents a payment in one or other of these categories from causing the notional income to be remitted if the payment is made abroad and the services relate wholly or mainly to non-UK property. Section 809W(5) in turn disapplies the relief if a benefit provided in the UK can be identified which is also derived from the beneficiary's notional income. Such a benefit could be identified as arising in the following circumstances:

(1)   The matched benefit is a benefit provided in the UK.

(2)   The relevant income matched to that benefit under s 735A is used to pay for s 809W services rendered to the person abroad.

If these conditions are met s 809W(5) disapplies the s 809W relief if the services rendered to the person abroad to any extent relate to the matched benefit. This they might easily do if for example the services are legal or accountancy which, while mainly concerned with the foreign situs property of the person abroad, also encompass the provision of the benefit in the UK. However on this scenario disapplication of the relief is of no consequence for the benefit being provided in the UK means the beneficiary's notional income is in any event remitted.

But as with s 87 benefits, it is also possible for the beneficiary to use a matched s 735 benefit to pay for UK services. Ipso facto this normally only happens where the benefit was an outright distribution of cash. Here s 809W(5) is engaged if there is the provision of a benefit in the UK derived from the same notional income as the outright cash distribution. In logic it is possible for there to be such a benefit, namely one provided by the person abroad using the matched relevant income. Were the services rendered to the beneficiary to any extent related to that benefit, s 809W(5) would deny s 809W relief.

An interesting point is whether this denial operates only if the benefit provided in the UK is one provided to the beneficiary whose notional income is being taxed. It may be suggested the answer to this question is yes, as s 809W(5) requires the benefit to be derived from the notional income by virtue of s 735. Sections 735 and 735A are then expressed in terms of the basic rules for calculating notional income in s 733, which focus on the recipient beneficiary alone.

The conclusion therefore is that in s 735 cases, s 809W(5) operates in relation to the recipient beneficiary and denies relief where the services he uses the benefit to pay for to any extent related to another benefit provided to him in the UK out of the matched relevant income.

Section 735 is part of the code which treats benefits to non-transferors as income to the extent of available relevant income in the overseas structure (see CHAPTER 70). Under ITA 2007, s 733 the total benefits received by a given individual in a tax year are treated as his income of that tax year to the extent that there is available relevant income in the structure (see further in CHAPTER 71). Section 735 treats both the benefit and the matched relevant income as derived from the beneficiary's notional income and thus the latter is remitted if either the benefit or the matched income is remitted (see further paras **72.14** to **72.24**).

In these regards it differs from s 87B, where remittance of the notional gain occurs only if the capital payment is remitted. Section 735 also differs from s 87 in that there are specific rules for matching the beneficiary's notional income of a given year with specific items of relevant income and specific benefits. As explained in para **72.5**, first in first out is applied, both between tax years and within tax years. Accordingly it is possible to know which item of relevant income is matched with which benefit.

With this established, it is apparent that a payment abroad for services provided in the UK is, absent s 809W, a remittance of the beneficiary's notional income if either:

(a)   the payment is by the person abroad and is made out of the matched relevant income or funds derived from it; or

(b)   the payment is by the beneficiary and is made using the benefit or funds derived from it.

Section 809W prevents a payment in one or other of these categories from causing the notional income to be remitted if the payment is made abroad and the services relate wholly or mainly to non-UK property. Section 809W(5) in turn disapplies the relief if a benefit provided in the UK can be identified which is also derived from the beneficiary's notional income. Such a benefit could be identified as arising in the following circumstances:

(1)   The matched benefit is a benefit provided in the UK.

(2)   The relevant income matched to that benefit under s 735A is used to pay for s 809W services rendered to the person abroad.

If these conditions are met s 809W(5) disapplies the s 809W relief if the services rendered to the person abroad to any extent relate to the matched benefit. This they might easily do if for example the services are legal or accountancy which while mainly concerned with the foreign situs property of the person abroad, also encompass the provision of the benefit in the UK. However on this scenario disapplication of the relief is of no consequence for the benefit being provided in the UK means the beneficiary's notional income is in any event remitted.

But as with s 87 benefits, it is also possible for the beneficiary to use a matched s 735 benefit to pay for UK services. Ipso facto this normally only happens where the benefit was an outright distribution of cash. Here s 809W(5) is engaged if there is the provision of a benefit in the UK derived from the same notional income as the outright cash distribution. In logic it is possible for there to be such a benefit, namely one provided by the person abroad using the matched relevant income. Were the services rendered to the beneficiary to any extent related to that benefit, s 809W(5) would deny s 809W relief.

An interesting point is whether this denial operates only if the benefit provided in the UK is one provided to the beneficiary whose notional income is being taxed. It may be suggested the answer to this question is yes, as s 809W(5) requires the benefit to be derived from the notional income by virtue of s 735. Sections 735 and 735A are then expressed in terms of the basic rules for calculating notional income in s 733, which focus on the recipient beneficiary alone.

The conclusion therefore is that in s 735 cases, s 809W(5) operates in relation to the recipient beneficiary and denies relief where the services he uses the benefit to pay for to any extent related to another benefit provided to him in the UK out of the matched relevant income.

Chapter 56

DEBTS RELATING TO PROPERTY ENJOYED IN THE UK

INTRODUCTION

56.1 This chapter is concerned with the provisions in s 809L that apply to debts. The core rule is that the taxpayer's foreign income and gains are treated as remitted if the following conditions are met:

(1)   Either the income or gains, or something derived from them, is used in respect of the debt. This is Condition B in s 809L as it applies to debts.

(2)   Such use is outside the UK.

(3)   The debt relates either to property brought to or received or used in the UK by the taxpayer or another relevant person or to services provided to or for the benefit of such a person. This is Condition A in s 809L as it applies to debts.

The key words in these conditions are 'in respect of' in the first and 'relates to' in the third. A debt which satisfies the third condition is termed a 'relevant debt' (Income Tax Act 2007, s 809L(7) (ITA 2007)).

As with s 809L generally, the term relevant person bears the meaning considered in CHAPTER 54 and thus, in relation to income and gains of 2007–08 and prior, means only the taxpayer.

Services

56.2 As indicated in para 56.1, a remittance can also occur if, instead of the relevant debt relating to property brought to or used in the UK, it relates to services provided in the UK. As with Conditions A and B generally, the service must be one provided in the UK to or for the benefit of the taxpayer or another relevant person.

Quantum

56.3 Where there is a remittance under these rules, the quantum of the remittance is the amount of income or gains used in respect of the relevant debt or, where derived property is used, the amount of the income or gains from which the property so used is derived (s 809P(4)(5)). However, if the relevant debt is only partly in respect of the property brought to or used in the UK, the amount remitted is restricted to what it would be if the debt were wholly in respect of such property (s 809P(10)).

Timing

56.4 For there to be a remittance under Conditions A and B, both of those conditions must be met. It follows that a use of income or gains in respect of a debt results in remittance if the property to which the debt relates is already in the UK. But if the property to which the debt relates is outside the UK a remittance does not occur unless and until it is brought into or used in the UK.

Use outside the UK

56.5 The rules regarding relevant debts address the use of foreign income and gains outside the UK in respect of a relevant debt – they are not engaged in the event that foreign income or gains are used in the UK in respect of such a debt. However, that does not mean there would be no taxable remittance in the latter scenario. The use of foreign income or gains in the UK in respect of a debt incurred by the taxpayer or another relevant person entails the bringing of such income or gains into the UK, by or for the benefit of that person, and that involves a remittance in the general sense of the term.

DERIVED PROPERTY

56.6 As indicated above, the requirements of Conditions A and B are satisfied not only if the income or gains are used in respect of the debt but also if anything deriving from the income or gains is so used. The derivation can be direct or indirect and in whole or in part. It is clear from this that the use in respect of the debt need not be by the taxpayer personally: as explained in CHAPTER 52, property given away can count as derived property in the hands of the donee and there are also many instances of deemed derivation.

Generally, for there to be a remittance of income and gains under Conditions A and B by reference to money or other property that derives from the taxpayer's income and gains, the derived property must belong to a relevant person (see para **51.8**). However, there is no such requirement in relation to relevant debts; there can be a remittance under Conditions A and B in relation to a relevant debt where derived property belonging to any person whatsoever is used outside the UK in respect of that debt.

In theory there is a trap here, which needs to be borne in mind when advising on planning which involves gifts or other transfers to non-relevant persons, such as adult children. If a remittance basis user gives a UK house to an adult child, subject to a debt secured on it which is due to a non-UK bank, and also makes an offshore gift to the child of money which represents his foreign income or gains, it might be assumed that the child could safely use that money to repay the debt. However, on the assumption that, at some point prior to the gift, the house was used by the remittance basis user, the debt is likely to be a relevant debt (even though it is no longer a debt owed by the remittance basis user) and a repayment of the debt outside the UK using money deriving from the foreign income or gains will, on the face of it, trigger a remittance under s 809L(3)(d) (or alternatively under Condition C, as discussed in CHAPTER 57). Bizarrely, though, a remittance would be avoided if the child made the repayment to a UK account of the bank, because the rules in relation to relevant debts only catch 'use' of income, gains or derived property outside the UK in respect of such debts.

The derivation concept is not used in relation to the property to which the debt relates. In other words, the property brought to or received or enjoyed in the UK must be the same property as the debt relates to. On the face of it, this leaves a gap where the property to which a debt relates is kept outside the UK and sold. If the proceeds of sale are not used to repay the debt but are used to buy other property which is brought to the UK, does the debt relate to that second property? It may be suggested it does, as a debt is relevant inter alia if it relates indirectly to the property brought to the UK.

MIXED FUND RULES

56.7 The mixed fund rules described in CHAPTER 53 apply if the money or property used in respect of the debt is transferred from a mixed fund or is derived from a transfer from a mixed fund (s 809Q(1)(b)). They so apply in determining whether income or gains have been used in respect of the debt and if so in what amount.

The mixed fund rules do not, it may be noted, apply at the different and subsequent stage of tying the income or gains used in respect of the debt with the property brought or used in the UK. If part only of the property to which the debt relates is brought to the UK, the rule in point is that in s 809P(10), as described above, namely that the amount remitted cannot be greater than what it would be if the debt related wholly to the property brought to the UK. This somewhat obscure provision appears to mean that the amount remitted is the full amount of the income and gains used in respect of the debt, save insofar as that amount exceeds the amount of the debt relating to the property brought to the UK.

RELATIONSHIP TO PROPERTY

56.8 As explained above, a debt is a relevant debt if it relates to property that is brought to, received or used in the UK by or for the benefit of a relevant person. The issue of whether a debt 'relates to' property is therefore central. The legislation does not attempt to define this expression, which must be construed according to ordinary linguistic usage and the legislative context.

Use to purchase property

56.9 The paradigm case of a debt relating to property is where it is incurred to buy the property and is secured on the property. However, the common sense view must be that a debt incurred to fund the purchase of property, or indeed the enhancement of property, relates to the property even if not secured on it.

Collateral

56.10 The position is clearly different where a debt is secured by a charge, pledge or other 'security interest' over property, but there is no other connection between the debt and that property and the debt has not been used to purchase or enhance the property. It is suggested that such a debt does not relate to the property on which it is secured: if it relates to anything, it relates to whatever is bought using the money borrowed. There is nothing in a purposive construction which offends against this conclusion, as securing a debt on property in or brought to the UK does not involve bringing anything to the UK: what is remitted to the UK when the property is brought to or used in the UK is what was used to buy it, not what is secured on it.

A variant of this point arises where the taxpayer uses foreign assets ('portfolio A') as collateral for borrowing to acquire further foreign investments ('portfolio B'). In due course income and gains on portfolio B are used to repay the debt and then portfolio A is brought to the UK. Can it in those circumstances be said that the debt related to property brought to the UK, ie portfolio A? It is suggested not, both because the debt did not relate to portfolio A and because it had in any event been repaid before the assets in portfolio A were brought to the UK.

Debt due to UK creditor

56.11 Repayment in the UK of a debt owed to a UK resident creditor is a remittance in the general sense of the term. A point sometimes raised is whether such a debt of itself relates to UK property and so is a relevant debt. If this argument were right, repayment of a UK resident creditor would be a remittance even if effected abroad, ie to a non-UK account of the creditor. Such repayment may, of course, be a remittance if the debt relates to a service provided in the UK, or to property brought to the UK. But the issue is whether the mere fact that the creditor is UK resident means that repayment out of foreign income or gains ipso facto results in a taxable remittance.

The basis of the argument that it does is that the debt is property (in the hands of the creditor). If it is owed by the taxpayer and is a simple debt it is likely to have a UK situs as the situs of simple debts is normally that of the debtor's residence (see para 38.4).

This argument cannot be right. One reason is that it is difficult to regard the debt as having been brought to or used in the UK for the benefit of the taxpayer. Another reason is that a debt is only a relevant debt if it *relates* to property used or brought to the UK. The definition does not say it is relevant debt if it *is* such property. There is nothing in a purposive construction against such a result, for, as indicated above, remittance does result if the debt is in respect of UK services or property brought to the UK.

This point normally arises in relation to foreign property bought from a UK resident, for example foreign securities bought from a UK broker, with settlement to a non-UK account of the broker. Here there is nothing brought to the UK which can offend against the principle of the remittance rules.

USE IN RESPECT OF A RELEVANT DEBT

56.12 As with 'relates to', the expression 'used ... in respect of' is not defined and so the issue of whether the taxpayer's income or gains are used in respect of the relevant debt is one of fact. It is however expressly provided that the payment of interest is use in respect of a debt (s 809L(9)).

Apart from interest, money or other property is plainly used in respect of a debt if it is used to repay it. Describing repayment as 'use in respect of' a debt is a somewhat odd use of language, but it is inconceivable that a court would construe 'use in respect of' a debt as excluding repayment of the debt. To do so would defeat the obvious intent of the legislation.

Collateral

56.13 An issue of difficulty is whether the charging or pledging of money or other property as collateral security for a debt is 'use' of the money or property 'in respect of' the debt; and if it is, whether there is also 'use' of money or other property 'in respect of' a debt if the property or money is made available as collateral security in a less formal manner, for example by means of a right of set-off. If there is 'use' of the property 'in respect of' the debt in these cases, there is a remittance if the debt is (or subsequently becomes) a relevant debt and the property in question is or derives from foreign income or gains.

It is easy to accept that income or gains specifically charged or pledged as collateral for a particular debt are used in respect of the debt. But what is the position where a bank can have recourse to all monies and assets of the taxpayer in support of any borrowing? Does this mean that any income and gains in any of the taxpayer's accounts with the bank are necessarily 'used in respect of' any debt due from the taxpayer to the bank?

It might be suggested that in law two situations should be distinguished, namely where monies are available to the bank by way of set-off and where assets or monies are charged or pledged to the bank. In the former case it can be argued that the monies are not 'used' in respect of the debt unless and until the right of set-off is exercised; until that time they are simply available for use, and their availability for use does not in itself have the potential to cause a remittance. However, this is not clear beyond doubt, and the counsel of ultimate caution would be to ensure that a non-UK bank releases its set-off rights if there will be both a loan or overdraft account used to fund money brought to the UK and an account holding monies representing foreign income or gains.

Nor is there certainty about the position in the latter scenario, ie where assets have been charged or pledged. It might be argued that, commercially, there is no real difference between a bank having the ability to deduct funds from accounts by exercise of set-off rights and a bank having the ability to secure repayment through the realisation of charged or pledged assets. In either case property is available to the bank as security but, it might be argued, there is no 'use' of it in respect of any debt unless and until such security rights are exercised.

One possible conclusion here is that, as a matter of law, there is no use of property in respect of a debt where a right of set-off can be exercised (but has not), but there is (in all cases) use of property in respect of a debt where the property has been charged or pledged and that security may be exercised to ensure repayment of that debt. However, unless and until there is a judgment on the point or an amendment to the legislation to clarify its scope the law remains uncertain.

In the former para RDRM33170, HMRC made the point that if collateral security for a relevant debt is a taxable remittance of what is pledged, the same debt may result in two remittance charges, once by reference to the collateral and once if and when other funds are used to pay principal and interest. The double charge will arise if both the collateral and the funds used in repayment are income and gains. HMRC took the position that the payment of interest and principal 'masks' the collateral, with the result that only principal and interest payments were taxed as a remittance. In their view this 'masking' of the collateral applied even if the principal and interest payments are funded out of capital. Situations where they considered the collateral was remitted were those where the loan is non-commercial and payments of interest or principal were not being made, with the result that the collateral was effectively a substitute for such payments.

It is open to question whether this 'masking' doctrine was supported by the legislation. Arguably, the grant of a security interest to a lender in connection with a loan is either 'use' of the charged/pledged assets, in respect of the debt, or it isn't. The pattern of subsequent payments of interest and principal cannot, logically, affect whether the collateral has been used in respect of the debt or not (unless, possibly, the taxpayer has defaulted and the lender has resorted to the security).

HMRC have now revoked the former para RDRM33170 and take the position that despite the 'masking' point, the use of overseas collateral to secure a relevant debt can result in double remittance, once insofar as the collateral is foreign income and gains and again if monies used to service the loan are also foreign income and gains (see HMRC Notice 4 August 2014, reproduced [2014] SWTI 2624). Whether the revised practice is any more firmly rooted in law than its predecessor will no doubt be a matter for legal argument. So too it is unclear whether the new practice applies only where the collateral is charged to the lender as distinct from simply being available for set off. The HMRC statement uses the word 'secured' in relation to the collateral which perhaps indicates that only formal charging is comprehended.

The HMRC Notice issued on 4 August 2014 advised that taxpayers who had relied on HMRC's previous practice and used foreign income and gains as collateral had until 5 April 2016 to unwind the arrangement. Furthermore, such taxpayers had until 31 December 2015 to give a written undertaking either that the loan would be repaid or that the foreign income and gains used as collateral would be replaced by clean capital collateral, the requisite steps being required by 5 April 2016 in both cases. Rather belatedly in view of these deadlines, on 15 October 2015, HMRC issued a further announcement that they would not in fact seek to apply the change announced on 4 August 2014 to arrangements where the loan was brought into or used in the UK before that date. Loans brought into or used in the UK on or after 4 August 2014 will, however, be affected.

This grandfathering of pre-4 August 2014 arrangements, whilst no doubt good news for those taxpayers who were still considering their options in relation to their borrowing, raises further questions about HMRC's interpretation of the word 'use' in these arrangements and in what circumstances a pre-4 August 2014 loan arrangement will be regarded as having lost the benefit of this grandfathering. In particular, HMRC has yet to clarify whether, in addition to straightforward pledges of foreign income and gains, rights of set off against or secondary collateral over such funds will be regarded as 'use' for these purposes. Arguably, such arrangements should be regarded as 'use' if the lender would not be making the loan on its terms but for the right of recourse which they have to such funds.

Interest

56.14 As indicated above, payment of interest on a debt is use in respect of the debt. An interesting point arises regarding interest paid when the debt is not yet a relevant debt – ie before the property to which it relates has been brought to or used in the UK. At that stage income or gains used to pay the interest are not remitted. But on the face of it a remittance of the funds used to make the interest payments does occur when the property is brought to the UK, for at that point all the requirements of Conditions A and B are met. The position is thus the same as if income or gains had been used to pay off part of the principal prior to the remittance of the property.

DIVORCE ORDERS

56.15 The question of whether foreign income or gains of a remittance basis user have been used outside the UK in respect of a relevant debt sometimes arises in the context of divorces. A party to the divorce, who is a current or former remittance basis user, may be ordered by the matrimonial court to make a payment or transfer to the other party. He may wish, or need, to make such payment or transfer using cash/assets that represent his foreign income or gains. It may be possible to ensure that once the payment or transfer has been made, there is no remittance of the cash/asset by the other party until a decree absolute has been issued, ie until she has ceased to be a relevant person in relation to the remittance basis user (see para 54.3). But the issue is whether there could be a remittance by him when the payment or transfer is made, on the possible basis that the obligation under the court order is a relevant debt.

Arguably, this cannot possibly be the case if the payment or transfer is made before the deadline stipulated by the court order, as until that time there is no debt at all. Until the deadline has expired, the remittance basis user has no more than a prospective liability.

If this argument is wrong, or is unavailable because the payment or transfer occurs after the deadline, the issue is essentially whether the debt relates to property brought to or received or used in the UK, by or for the remittance basis user or any other relevant person (ITA 2007, s 809L(2)(a)). It is difficult to see how the debt could relate to any property at all, unless the other party's rights under matrimonial law can be regarded as a form of property. In *Haines v Hill* [2007] EWCA Civ 1284, [2008] 2 All ER 901, [2007] 3 FCR 785, Sir Andrew Morritt indicated that an entitlement under matrimonial law was not a proprietary right (para 29). But even if the other party's rights under matrimonial law can be regarded as a form of property, it is hard to see how such rights could have been brought to or received or used in the UK.

There was some correspondence on this topic in 2012 between HMRC and the Chartered Institute of Taxation. It is understood that HMRC accepted in that correspondence that a payment or transfer pursuant to a court order, made after the issuance of decree absolute, does not give rise to a taxable remittance of any income/gains represented by the cash or assets transferred to the former spouse. However, the technical rationale for this view was unclear.

Chapter 57

ANTI-AVOIDANCE PROVISIONS: CONDITIONS C AND D

INTRODUCTION

57.1 As explained in para **54.1**, under old law tax was avoided when the non-domiciliary gave income and gains away abroad and the donee then brought the money to the UK. Tax was avoided even if the non-domiciliary benefited from what he had given away save, perhaps, where such benefit could be said to have been financially equivalent to the asset given away. This technique was generally referred to as 'alienation abroad'.

The present law counters alienation abroad by the relevant person concept, combined with the derivation concept. This is as explained in CHAPTER 54. But these concepts do not fully address the potential for tax avoidance through alienation abroad, for derived property only results in tax if it belongs to a relevant person at the time of the receipt or use in the UK. What is not covered is benefit from UK property which is not owned by a relevant person. It is this which is the subject of two further conditions in s 809L, Conditions C and D.

In contrast to Conditions A and B, Conditions C and D are alternate rather than cumulative. They have certain common requirements, which relate to the benefit in the UK, and then diverge in the manner in which that benefit is linked to the taxpayer's income and gains. Like Conditions A and B, they apply also to services and debts.

It follows that in common with s 809L generally, Conditions C and D conflate several different matters. In this chapter they will be unpicked by concentrating mainly on the basic rule, with the common requirement considered first, and then the requirements under which the two Conditions diverge. After this has been done, services and debts will be considered.

THE COMMON REQUIREMENT

57.2 The common requirement is as follows (ITA 2007, s 809L(4)(a) and (5)(a)):

(1)   Property is brought to or received or used in the UK.
(2)   It belongs to a person who is neither the taxpayer nor anybody else who is a relevant person.

(3)   It is enjoyed by the taxpayer or some other relevant person.

There are three circumstances in which enjoyment is disregarded (ITA 2007, ss 809N(9) and 809O(6)):

(a)   The property is enjoyed virtually to the entire exclusion of all relevant persons – ie de minimis enjoyment is disregarded.

(b)   The taxpayer or other relevant person gives full consideration for his enjoyment.

(c)   The taxpayer or other relevant person enjoys the property in the same way and on the same terms as the public at large or a section of the public.

Enjoyment

57.3 Conditions C and D contrast with Conditions A and B in requiring the property in the UK to be enjoyed by the relevant person as distinct from being used by him or for his benefit. Enjoyment is not defined but it might be presumed that the draftsman intended to convey different meaning by using the word enjoy rather than the words use and benefit.

One clue as to what he had in mind is that the language of Conditions C and D is redolent of the IHT gift with reservation rules. Thus enjoyment is the core test of liability under those rules, and those rules are also subject to exemptions for full consideration and de minimis use.

It might be suggested that enjoyment is a narrower concept than benefit. Arguably, enjoyment connotes control over and possession of what is enjoyed, whereas benefit can be entirely in the discretion of another party. In the gift with reservation rules, it is noticeable that enjoyment by the taxpayer is not the prerequisite of liability; rather the rules come into play if the donee does not enjoy the property or, if he does, if the donor can benefit by contract or otherwise.

The contrary view is that the distinction between enjoyment and benefit is one without a difference. In support of this view is the dictionary meaning of enjoy, which, in the Shorter Oxford English Dictionary includes 'have the use or benefit of'. Further support may be gained from the exclusions, particularly the first, which only operates if all relevant persons are excluded or virtually excluded. This does not make a great deal of sense if there can be situations in which a relevant person can benefit from the property without enjoying it.

The distinction between the two views becomes material when the owner of the UK property allows the relevant person to use it as his guest or licensee when he himself is in possession and enjoyment. Typically this arises in two contexts:

(1)   An adult relevant person, ie the remittance basis user or his spouse, stays in the property as the guest of the owner, deriving benefit from both the property and its contents and being there long enough to fall outside the de minimis exemption.

(2)   A minor relevant person, ie a grandchild of the taxpayer, lives in a house owned by his parent, who is not a relevant person, being an adult child of the taxpayer.

If indeed enjoyment is a narrower concept than benefit, the adult or, as the case may be, the grandchild, would not in these circumstances be enjoying the property. But if enjoyment and benefit are the same, they probably would be.

HMRC consider that Conditions C and D are not normally engaged where minor grandchildren live with their parents in a house whose purchase was funded from a gift out of the grandparent's income or gains (RDRM para 33270). But the basis of their view is that the grandchildren come within the de minimis exemptions, not that they are not enjoying the property.

Time of remittance

57.4 Where Condition C or D do result in income or gains being treated as remitted, the rule governing the time of remittance is the same under both (s 809L(6)). It is when the property is first enjoyed by the taxpayer or other relevant person.

CONDITION C

57.5 The requirements specific to Condition C are as follows (ITA 2007, s 809N):

(1)   The taxpayer must have made a gift to the owner of the enjoyed property.
(2)   The property so given away must have been derived from the taxpayer's income or gains or must have comprised the income or gains themselves.
(3)   The enjoyed property must be either the property the taxpayer gave away or property derived from that property.

Put in summary form, the requirement of Condition C is that the enjoyed property must be or be derived from the taxpayer's gift of his income or gains. There is however one situation in which such tracing is not required (s 809N(7)(c)). This is where the enjoyment of the property by the relevant person is by virtue of an operation effected with reference to the taxpayer's gift or with a view to enabling or facilitating it. Situations thus caught are those where it is intended that the taxpayer will benefit from his gift, but where as a matter of tracing other property of the donee is substituted in conferring the benefit. The concept is thus quid pro quo and, to judge by examples in RDRM35060, will where appropriate be invoked by HMRC.

Ownership of the donee

57.6 The legislation refers to the donee as a 'gift recipient' and to the enjoyed property which satisfies the requirements of Condition C as 'qualifying property'. These terms probably confuse rather than clarify. But they are significant in one important respect, namely that the key words of Condition C require that 'qualifying property of a gift recipient . . . is enjoyed by a relevant person'. The use of the present tense carries the clear implication that at the time of enjoyment, the enjoyed property must be owned by the donee.

It may be thought that this conclusion is displaced by the fact that the property enjoyed can be derived from the gift and need not be comprised in the gift itself. But here 'derived' plainly refers to the case where the particular item of property which the taxpayer gives the donee is sold or converted to other assets. Given the clear requirements of the opening words of Condition C, it cannot refer to property which at the time of enjoyment belongs to somebody other than the donee.

Identity of the donor

57.7 Condition C requires the gift to the donee to have been made by the taxpayer himself. This is made clear by the definition of 'gift recipient' in s 809N(2): it is the person to whom the taxpayer makes the gift of income or gains or derived property.

The significance of this is that Condition C is not engaged in the following scenarios:

(1)   The person who makes the gift to the owner of the enjoyed property is a relevant person other than the taxpayer.
(2)   The person who makes that gift is not a relevant person at all.

These scenarios in turn mean that Condition C does not catch either of the following:

(1)   A person such as a trust which holds assets abroad treated as derived from the taxpayer's deemed income (see para **52.29**) transfers those assets to another person, say a beneficiary, who then brings them to the UK and allows the taxpayer to use them.
(2)   A person to whom the taxpayer has given income or gains makes an onward gift and the taxpayer enjoys the property in the UK when in the hands of the second donee.

In both these instances HMRC would probably argue that remittance would be treated as occurring under Conditions A and B if the recipient under the transfer or second gift is a relevant person in relation to the taxpayer (see para **52.19**). But otherwise remittance occurs only if Condition D is in point, as discussed below.

Meaning of gift

57.8 The taxpayer is treated as making a gift if he disposes of the income or gains or derived property for no consideration or for consideration which is less than market value (s 809N(5)). But in the latter event only the undervalue is treated as gift. A gift is still a gift if the taxpayer retains an interest in what is given away or reserves the right to benefit from it (s 809N(6)).

The use of consideration as the test for whether there is a gift generates uncertainty if property is passed between spouses as part of the financial arrangements following a divorce. There is some authority that in such contexts consideration is not given despite the fact the property transfers are in satisfaction of obligations under matrimonial law (see *G v G (financial provision: equal division)* [2002] EWHC 1339 (Fam), [2002] 2 FLR 1143 and *Haines v Hill* [2007] EWCA Civ 1284, [2008] 2 All ER 901, [2007] 3 FCR 785). If it is indeed the case that consideration is not given, the former spouse in such circumstances is a gift recipient for the purposes of Condition C and benefits she subsequently gives to minor children of the marriage in the UK have to be watched.

Identity of the donee

57.9 Condition C is not engaged if the donee is a relevant person in relation to the taxpayer. This is logical, as if the donee is a relevant person, Conditions A and B apply to any remittances he makes.

The time at which it is tested whether the donee is a relevant person is when the gift is made (s 809N(3)). This means Condition C cannot operate even if subsequently the donee ceases to be a relevant person, for example a spouse on decree absolute (see para **54.3**). The converse however is not true: if the donee is not at the time of the gift a relevant person, he ceases to be a gift recipient should he become a relevant person, for example on marriage to the donor.

The fact that a spouse remains a relevant person until decree absolute (see para **54.3**) means the consideration problem noted above (para **57.8**) can be avoided by ensuring any property adjustment required on divorce is made prior to decree absolute. In such a case, it can never be within Condition C.

Amount treated as remitted

57.10 If Condition C is engaged the amount treated as remitted is not determined by the value of the enjoyment. Instead the focus is on the income or gains which are traceable into the enjoyed property, and the amount remitted is the amount of such income or gains (s 809P(11)). This is draconian, for it means that enjoyment may result in substantial tax if the property enjoyed is valuable, even if the enjoyment is limited in extent or by time. For this reason Condition C should be watched and avoided.

A particular trap is the fact that enjoyment is caught if by a relevant person rather than the taxpayer personally. The limited range of individual relevant persons (para **54.2**) means that this trap is not as great as it might be, but it still needs to be watched.

CONDITION D

57.11 As will be apparent from the above analysis of Condition C, it does most of the work needed to counter the former alienation abroad technique. In these circumstances, it may be wondered why a further condition is needed at all, and such mystification is compounded by the fact that the language of Condition D is obscure. It is plainly anti-avoidance, but the avoidance at which it is directed is difficult to discern.

Requirements

57.12 Condition D applies only if the common requirement is satisfied (see para 57.2) and the enjoyed property is not caught by Condition C. It requires three further conditions to be met:

(1) A relevant person must have made a disposition to or for the benefit of the owner of the property.

(2) The property comprised in that disposition must have been derived from the taxpayer's income or gains.

(3) An operation must have been effected with reference to the disposition or so as to enable or facilitate it.

The legislation refers to the disposition at (1) as the qualifying disposition and to the operation at (3) as the connected operation (s 809O(3), (4)). The amount remitted is the income or gains comprised in the qualifying disposition (s 809P(8)).

The disposition

57.13 It is not immediately clear whether the term disposition refers only to bounteous transactions. But it is likely that it does not, for a disposition for full consideration is specifically excluded if it is consideration for the relevant person's enjoyment of the property (s 809O(5)).

It is clear that the relevant person who makes the disposition need not be the same relevant person as enjoys the property. This is evident from the use of the indefinite article in both references to relevant persons.

Connected operation

57.14 The formulation of Condition D in s 809L(5) refers to enjoyment of the property by the relevant person in circumstances where there is a connected operation. This raises the question of whether, in addition to being linked with the qualifying disposition, the operation has also to be connected to the relevant person's enjoyment of the property. In other words, does the requirement that the enjoyment be in circumstances where there is a connected operation carry the implication that the operation be in some way connected to the enjoyment? Or is the term 'connected operation' exhaustively defined by reference to its linkage with the relevant person's qualifying disposition?

In a strict sense the latter construction is plainly right, for the definition in s 809O(3) states when an operation is to be regarded as connected and so states only by reference to the qualifying disposition. But three points of construction indicate there must be some association between the operation and the enjoyment of the property:

(a)   The reference in s 809L(5) itself is to the enjoyment being in 'circumstances' where there is a connected operation.
(b)   The definition in s 809O(3) is expressed as being 'in relation to' the property enjoyed.
(c)   The definition of connected operation echoes the IHT definition of associated operation (IHTA 1984, s 268). That definition too is on one view very wide but has been construed as confined to operations which form part of and contribute to the scheme which confers benefit (*MacPherson v IRC* [1988] 2 All ER 753, [1988] STC, 362, 369 per Lord Jauncey).

For these reasons there can be some confidence that the connected operation must have some association with the enjoyment. HMRC's comments in the remittance basis manual on Condition D are unhelpful (RDRM para 33410), but comments in the CGT manual indicate that they concur in the view that there must be linkage between the connected operation and the enjoyed property (CG25343).

Enjoyment as a connected operation

57.15 Assuming that conclusion is right, a further and rather different point has to be addressed, namely whether the owner's acquisition of the property can itself be the connected operation or whether the relevant person's enjoyment can be. As to the former, there appears no reason why not: indeed in many cases, if the construction above of connected operation is right it will be the acquiring of the property which has the necessary association with the enjoyment.

Equally it is difficult to regard the enjoyment as of itself being a connected operation, for two reasons:

(1)   Enjoyment is not an operation.
(2)   If enjoyment alone were sufficient to bring Condition D into play, s 809L(5) would simply have provided for there to be linkage between the enjoyment and the qualifying disposition. There would be no need to have a connected operation in the middle.

Application of Condition D

57.16 It is difficult to specify in advance circumstances in which Condition D might apply. The approach inevitably has to be to start with given facts or proposals, and then see whether the requirements of Condition D fit. The implications of the analysis above is that in carrying out this exercise a three stage exercise is required:

(1)   Ascertain whether the taxpayer or some other relevant person is enjoying property in the UK which does not belong to him or to any other relevant person.

(2)   Ascertain whether the taxpayer or some other relevant person has transferred income or gains to the owner (otherwise than in payment for use of the property).

(3)   Identify an operation which is in some way associated with the enjoyment and facilitates the transfer or is made with reference to it.

In the light of this formulation it is clear that some at least of the scenarios identified above (para 57.7) as outside Condition C are caught. One such would be where the gift to the owner of the enjoyed property is made not by the taxpayer personally but by another relevant person. Condition D would apply here if the taxpayer's antecedent gift to the relevant person was with a view to the subsequent gift, as then it would be the connected operation.

Another scenario caught would be where the owner of the enjoyed property funds its acquisition out of a distribution from a settlor-interested trust of which the person enjoying the property is settlor. Here the trust is a relevant person in relation to the settlor and the distribution by the trust is thus the qualifying disposition insofar as what is distributed includes income treated as the settlor's. The owner's acquisition of the enjoyed property would then be the connected operation.

A situation where Condition D would *not* apply is if the taxpayer gives his income and gains to someone who is not a relevant person. That person then gives the money to another individual who is the owner of or acquires the enjoyed property. Here the taxpayer's gift is not a qualifying disposition, as the owner of the property is not the recipient. Condition D would only be engaged if the taxpayer's gift was mere machinery, so as to be said to be for the benefit not of the immediate donee but of the owner of the property.

The fact that the qualifying disposition can be commercial could be a trap. Suppose the taxpayer uses his income or gains to buy investments from an individual who owns property in the UK. This is a qualifying disposition. There is risk under Condition D if the taxpayer or some other relevant person subsequently enjoys the property. The risk will materialise if a connected operation is identified, ie if an operation can be identified which was effected with reference to or with a view to the purchase of investments and is in some way associated with the enjoyment of the property.

The practical consequence of Condition D is that care should be taken if the taxpayer, or any other individual relevant person, enjoys or is likely to enjoy property in the UK belonging to someone else. Transactions with the owner should be avoided insofar as funded out of the taxpayer's actual or deemed income or gains.

SERVICES

57.17 As indicated at the beginning of this chapter, Conditions C and D apply to services. Condition C so applies if the service is enjoyed in the UK by the taxpayer or another relevant person and is paid for by somebody who is not a relevant person using funds given to him by the taxpayer or as a quid pro quo for such a gift. But the condition is not in point insofar as the taxpayer's gift is neither income nor gains or property derived from them.

Condition D also requires the service to be enjoyed in the UK by the taxpayer or another relevant person. The party paying for the service must be in receipt of the qualifying disposition, ie a disposition of the taxpayer's income and gains made by a relevant person. And as with Condition D generally a connected operation must be identified, ie an operation effected with a view to the disposition.

As generally with remittances under Conditions C and D, there is a contrast with Conditions A and B in that the latter focus on the service provided to or for the benefit of the relevant person rather than his enjoyment. The comments made above (para 57.3) on the distinction between benefit and enjoyment are thus in point, although how they operate in relation to the services is less clear.

As indicated above, the enjoyment of the service must be in the UK. The consideration for the service can be given either in the UK or abroad. Thus the paradigm case of Condition C applying to services is a gift recipient who is not a relevant person paying for services contracted for by somebody who is.

An issue raised is whether Conditions C and D catch school fees. A typical situation is where the taxpayer's adult child pays his children's school fees using income or gains given to him by the taxpayer. The children are grandchildren of the taxpayer and so relevant persons. Here a service is indubitably rendered in the UK – ie education of the minor grandchildren and so a remittance is in point if Condition C is otherwise satisfied. But can the education be said to be a service enjoyed by the grandchildren? Apart from the obvious, and perhaps rather flippant, point that children rarely enjoy schooling, a more fundamental issue is that the person who enjoys the service is the party who contracts for it, ie the parent. An equally fundamental point is that if the education can be said to be enjoyed by the child, such enjoyment is available on the same terms to the public generally, ie on payment of fees.

On this basis, school fees are not caught, but in view of the doubts, prudence would dictate assuming otherwise in planning.

DEBTS

57.18 As indicated at the beginning of this chapter, Conditions C and D apply to debts. However there are particular difficulties of construction.

Condition C

57.19 It is clear under Condition C that the donee must use the income or gains given to him by the taxpayer, or the quid pro quo property, in respect of a relevant debt – in other words he must use the taxpayer's income and gains abroad to pay interest or principal. What is not so clear is the circumstances in which a debt becomes a relevant debt so as to trigger this treatment.

The legislation defines the term as any debt which relates either to property or services enjoyed in the UK by a relevant person as per Conditions C and D or to property or services brought to or used in the UK by or for the benefit of a relevant person as per Condition A (s 809L(7)). One is tempted to infer that the only part of the definition relevant to Condition C is property or services enjoyed in the UK but this is not what the legislation says and, if so, the distinction between benefit and enjoyment discussed in para 57.3 above is not material to debt remittances.

Where the debt relates to property, it is unclear whether the property has to be owned by the gift recipient. The answer appears to be yes if only debts related to Condition C property are within Condition C, but no if debts related to Condition A property are included. This result follows because para (c) of s 809L(7) refers to qualifying property, whereas para (a) does not.

A related issue is whether the property to which the debt relates can be owned by the taxpayer or any other relevant person. Here the answer is yes if, as suggested above, that property can be Condition A property.

Despite the uncertainties, a typical case where Condition C would be in point is as follows:

(1)   A person who is not a relevant person owns UK property ('the owner').
(2)   The owner has incurred debt abroad to buy the property.
(3)   The owner allows the taxpayer or some other relevant person to enjoy (or perhaps use) the property.
(4)   The taxpayer gives income or gains to the owner.
(5)   The owner uses funds traceable back to the gift to service the debt.

If the conclusions above are right, Condition C would also be in point if the taxpayer or another relevant person owns the property and incurs the debt. The condition would be engaged if:

(1)   A donee who is not a relevant person pays interest or principal; and
(2)   What the taxpayer gave the donee, and what the donee then used, was income or gains.

Condition D

57.20 Like Condition C, Condition D requires use of property abroad in respect of a relevant debt. But the property so used cannot be or be derived from a gift by the taxpayer of his income and gains or be quid pro quo property. This result follows because Condition D is not engaged if the qualifying property of a gift recipient is used in respect of the debt.

The term 'relevant debt' bears the same meaning as under Condition C and so the same issue arises of whether the property or service to which the debt relates must be enjoyed by the relevant person or whether use or provision for the benefit of the relevant person counts as well. In relation to enjoyment of property a further point arises which is that the property enjoyed must be qualifying property (s 809L(7)(c), (e)). 'Qualifying property' is defined in relation to gift recipients as the property given to the donee by the taxpayer, or derived or quid pro quo property (s 809N(7)). The incorporation of the concept into Condition D is odd, and means that if enjoyment is the sole test, the only debts which, for Condition D, are relevant debts are those incurred in connection with property given away by the taxpayer or derived or quid pro quo property. But the point is of little significance if, as suggested above, a debt is also relevant if the property is merely used for the benefit of the taxpayer.

Once the relevant debt is identified the normal requirements of Condition D come into play, namely:

(a)   A relevant person must make the qualifying disposition, ie the disposition of property which is or is derived from the taxpayer's income and gains.
(b)   The recipient of that disposition must use other property of his in respect of the debt, ie pay interest or principal.
(c)   A connected operation must be identified.

As with Condition D generally, the connected operation must be made by reference to or to facilitate the qualifying disposition. Under the debt rules in Condition D it is the use in respect of the debt which must be in circumstances where there is a connected operation. It follows that if linkage for the connected operation is required beyond the qualifying disposition (see para 57.14) it is with payment of interest or principal on the debt rather than with the relevant person's use or enjoyment of the property.

Use and enjoyment

57.21 If it is correct that a debt is a relevant debt if it relates to property within Condition A there may be an important distinction between Conditions C and D as they apply to debts and those conditions as they apply to general remittances and services. Thus in the child/grandchildren example given above, use for the benefit may well catch school fees paid by the parent. If so, settlement by the parent of a debt for the school fees would result in taxable remittance if effected out of income or gains given to him by the taxpayer (ie the grandparent). But payment at or before the contractual due date would not, on the basis that until the contractual date for payment has passed, there is no debt.

MIXED FUND RULES

57.22 Both Conditions C and D require income or gains of the taxpayer to be identified as it is these income or gains that are then treated as remitted. Under Condition C, the income and gains so treated are those given by the taxpayer to the gift recipient, and under Condition D it is those comprised in the relevant person's qualifying disposition.

The chances are that the income and gains the taxpayer uses will emanate from a mixed fund but, despite this, the mixed fund rules described in Chapter 53 do not apply (see para 53.2). It is to be inferred from this that identification of what is comprised in the gift or qualifying disposition is as per the old law as described in paras 53.2 to 53.4.

The difficulty this poses is how this interacts with remittances made by the taxpayer within Conditions A and B. If such a remittance is in the same tax year as the Condition C or D remittance, or a prior tax year, it is easy to see that the rules described in Chapter 53 should be operated first to determine what is comprised in it. The old common law then works on what is left in relation to Conditions C and D.

But matters are more difficult if the Condition C or D remittance comes first. Here there is nothing which requires what is allocated to such remittance under common law to be taken into account when it comes to applying the rules described in CHAPTER 53 to subsequent Condition A and B remittances. In theory at least the same income or gains could end up being taxed as remitted twice.

COMMENCEMENT

57.23 It is clear that Conditions C and D are not engaged unless the enjoyment by the taxpayer in the UK, or the use in respect of the relevant debt, is on or after 6 April 2008. What is unclear is the position if the bringing to the UK was before that date, or indeed if the enjoyment in the UK began before that date. Equally unclear is whether the gift under Condition C, or the qualifying disposition under Condition D, must have been after 6 April 2008 or whether prior transactions count. The basic commencement rule (FA 2008, Sch 7 para 81) and the use of the present tense in ss 809N and 809O provide an argument in support of the former position.

Conditions C and D are subject to the transitional rule to the effect that s 809L has effect in relation to income and gains of 2007–08 and prior as if only the individual taxpayer is a relevant person (FA 2008, Sch 7 para 86(4)). This means that where the gift or, under Condition D, the qualifying disposition is of income and gains of 2007–08 and prior, the only enjoyment of the property in the UK which counts is that of the taxpayer himself.

The corollary of the term relevant persons being restricted to the taxpayer means that Condition C can apply if the enjoyed property is owned by someone else who would otherwise be a relevant person. Condition D can similarly so apply if the property is owned by someone who otherwise falls within the definition of relevant person.

An interesting issue in relation to Condition D is whether, if the income and gains are of 2007–08 and prior, a disposition will only be treated as a qualifying disposition if made by the taxpayer personally. The definition of 'qualifying disposition' is in ITA 2007, s 809O, whereas the transitional rule (para 86(4)) is expressed in terms of s 809L. This might suggest that the transitional rule has no effect on the meaning of 'qualifying disposition'. However, the better view is probably that the transitional rule does affect the interpretation of 'qualifying disposition', so that dispositions by relevant persons other than the taxpayer do not count. This view is based on the fact that s 809O is self-evidently supplemental to s 809L.

Section VI

Remittance Basis Reliefs

Chapter 58

BUSINESS INVESTMENT RELIEF

INTRODUCTION

58.1 The 2012 Finance Act introduced a potentially important qualification to the taxation of remittances. Its effect is that a remittance is not taxable if used to make an investment of a type and in the form prescribed by the legislation. It applies to remittances occurring on or after 6 April 2012 (FA 2012, Sch 12 para 17).

The legislation comprises ITA 2007, ss 809VA–809VO. It was inserted into ITA 2007 by FA 2012, Sch 12 para 7. Some advisers feel that in present form ss 809VA–809VO are too complex and hedged in by anti-avoidance rules for use of the relief to be recommended, but the government is committed to this relief and hopefully necessary amendments will be made. A consultation document issued by HM Treasury in August 2016, regarding proposed changes to the taxation of foreign domiciliaries, invited comments on how the relief might be developed.

HMRC published guidance on 28 May 2012 ('Guidance Note: Changes to the Remittance Basis', pp 9–36). The relief is generally referred to as Business Investment Relief or BIR.

FORM OF INVESTMENT

58.2 An investment is only capable of attracting the relief if it is a qualifying investment. To make a qualifying investment, the investor must either make a loan to a company or he must be issued with shares by the company (s 809VC(1)). The company is referred to in legislation as the target company (s 809VC(2)) and the investor's loan or shares as the holding (s 809VC(3)).

The target

58.3 The target company must be what is called a private limited company (s 809VD). That term requires that none of the company's shares be listed on a recognised stock exchange (s 809VD(11)(c)). As the reference is to listing, AIM shares are allowed, as AIM shares are quoted, not listed.

The term private limited company otherwise requires that the target be a body corporate with limited liability (s 809VD(11)(a)). In its reference to body

621

corporate the legislation makes it clear that both UK and foreign companies are comprehended. Limited liability partnerships are specifically excluded (s 809 VD(11)(b)).

The simplest form of target company is a single ungrouped company. Such a company qualifies for the relief if it is what is called an eligible trading company (s 809VD(1)(a)). A more complex form of target company is the eligible stakeholder company. This is a company whose sole purpose is the making of investments in eligible trading companies (s 809VD(3)). The final and most complex type of target is the eligible holding company (s 809VD(1)(a)). This, in broad terms, is the holding company of what is called an eligible trading group (s 809VD(5)).

Eligible trading company

58.4 To be an eligible trading company, the target must carry on one or more commercial trades and the carrying on of those trades must be all or substantially all of what it does (s 809VD(3)). 'Substantially all' is not defined, but in HMRC's view means 80% or more (Guidance Notes para 2.17).

A trade counts as commercial if it is carried on on a commercial basis with a view to profit. The term 'trade' otherwise bears its normal meaning, but includes both anything deemed to be a trade for corporation tax purposes and rental businesses (s 809VE). The business of generating income from land is treated as a trade for most computational purposes (CTA 2009, s 210) and this deeming thus carries over into the present relief. There is no restriction on the type of property investment which may be carried on, and thus residential portfolios attract the relief as much as commercial portfolios.

Allowance is made for start-up companies in that a target company can be eligible if it is preparing to carry on a commercial trade and does so within two years (s 809VD(2)(b)).

Eligible trading group

58.5 The term 'group' means a parent and its 51% subsidiaries (s 809VD(6)). To be eligible, all or substantially all of the group activities must be the carrying on of commercial trades (s 809VD(9)). The parent company and each of its 51% subsidiaries must be private limited companies.

It is not necessary that the investor's investment be in the top company. It can be in an intermediate holding company in the group or even in a trading subsidiary. In the latter event, the subsidiary is an eligible trading company in its own right. Intermediate holding companies qualify because the term 'eligible holding company' requires merely that the target be a member of an eligible trading group, not that it be the top company.

Eligible stakeholder company

58.6 As with single companies and groups, the eligible stakeholder company must be a private limited company. The investments it makes in eligible trading companies can be of any size and can be shares or loan. However the concept of investment is the same as for the relief generally and so the form of investment must either be the making of the loan or subscribing for the shares (s 809VD(4)). As the company's purpose has to be wholly making investments it cannot also be a trading company.

INVOLVEMENT WITH TARGET

58.7 There is neither a minimum nor a maximum percentage of the target which the investor can subscribe for. Thus the relief is available as much where he owns 100% of the target as where he is a small minority shareholder. Indeed, there is no requirement that he hold shares at all, for, as described above, the qualifying investment can be a loan.

There is no objection if the investor makes the qualifying investment into a company which he already owns or in which he is already an investor. There is no obligation on him to work for or be a director of the company, and equally the relief is not precluded if he does work as director or employee.

The one qualification to this is that an investment cannot be qualifying if the investor obtains or is expecting to obtain what is called a related benefit (ss 809VC(4) and 809VD). A benefit counts as related if it is attributable to the making of the investment or would not have been available without the investment (s 809VF(3)).The term benefit is defined in rather an odd way in that the definition is not comprehensive but expressed in terms of inclusion of certain things and exclusion of others (s 809VF(2)). What is expressly included is anything that would not be provided in the ordinary course of business or would be provided on less favourable terms. Excluded is anything provided to the investor in the ordinary course of business on arm's length terms.

In the light of this it is clear that the rent-free use of property or other assets is caught, and thus precludes the relief if at the time of the investment there is expectation of such benefit. Equally it is plain there is no benefit if arm's length rent or other consideration is paid. So too arm's length remuneration to an employee who works for the target company does not preclude the relief (and nor do dividends or interest paid at commercial rates). Excessive remuneration or excessive dividends or interest, by contrast, do.

These provisions as to related benefits apply also if the recipient of the benefit is anybody who in relation to the remittance-basis user is a relevant person. Relevant person has the meaning it normally has for remittance purposes (see CHAPTER 54), and thus includes spouses, minor children, trusts under which any individual relevant person is a beneficiary and close companies in which any other category of relevant person is a participator.

AVAILABILITY OF RELIEF

58.8 The availability of the relief depends on the occurrence of what is called a relevant event (s 809VA(1)(a)). A taxable remittance of foreign income or gains is only prevented if, but for the relief, the income or gains would be regarded as remitted by virtue of the event (s 809VA(1)(b)).

Relevant events

58.9 There are two types of relevant event, namely where:

(a)   A relevant person uses money or other property to make the qualifying investment, ie to subscribe for shares in the target or make a loan to it (s 809VA(3)(a)); and where

(b)   The money or other property is brought to the UK in order that a relevant person may make a qualifying investment (s 809VA(3)(b)).

As in the provisions described above, the term relevant person has its normal meaning under the remittance basis code. It follows that the relief is available not merely where the taxpayer makes the qualifying investment, but also where the investor is a trust of which he is a beneficiary or a close company in which he or the trust is a participator.

It will be noted from the formulation of the relief above, that it is not income or gains but simply money or other property that must be brought to the UK or used to make the qualifying investment. The linkage with foreign income or gains comes with the operative provision conferring the relief. This provides that any income or gains which would otherwise be treated as remitted to the UK by virtue of the relevant event are not to be so treated (s 809VA(2)).

It might be thought that the definition of relevant event, and the requirement that there be a remittance of foreign income or gains by virtue of the relevant event, require the target to be a UK company. In fact this is not so. There is nothing to stop a non-UK company from having a UK bank account to which a share subscription or loan is sent. So too if money is brought to the UK with the intention of making a qualifying investment, that investment could be effected by sending the money to a foreign bank account of the target abroad.

HMRC in practice allow relief where the investor takes out a loan to fund the qualifying investment and then uses the foreign income and gains to repay the investment. This is so even if the repayment occurs in a tax year subsequent to that in which the investment is made (CIOT press release 15 August 2012, reproduced [2012] SWTI 2563).

It is sometimes suggested that the investment must be in the name of the investor. This is because s 809VA(3)(a) refers to use by a relevant person and so, read literally precludes use by a nominee for that person. In 2013, however, HMRC confirmed to CIOT that they look through nominees.

Where income or gains are brought to the UK prior to the qualifying investment, relief is dependent on two further conditions. One is subjective, namely that the income or gains are brought to the UK in order to make the qualifying investment. The second is objective and requires the investment in fact to be made within 45 days (s 809VA(5)). But a failure to meet this latter condition is not inevitably fatal, as the income and gains do not count as remitted if they are removed from the UK within the 45-day period (s 809VB).

In applying the 45-day condition, the income or gains may be split up. In other words, if part breaches the 45-day condition and part not, only the latter counts as remitted (s 809VA(6)). Where the qualifying investment is pursuant to a loan agreement, separate drawdowns over a period counts as separate investments made when each drawdown occurs (s 809VC(7)).

Transactions attracting the relief

58.10 In the light of the points made above it is possible to identify which kinds of transaction attract the relief. Here the position is not entirely straightforward, because of the rule that the relief only operates if, but for the relief, there would be a taxable remittance by virtue of the relevant event (s 809VA(1)(b)). For brevity, we refer to this rule in the following as 'the remittance condition'.

The simplest form of transaction is one where the income or gains are first brought to the UK, causing the remittance condition to be met, and are then used to make the investment. Here the facts plainly fall within the second type of relevant event, ie that described in s 809VA(3)(b), provided of course that the 45-day time limit is met, and the purpose of the remittance is to make the investment.

A second form of transaction is where the investment is effected by a money transfer from the foreign account of the investor directly to the account of the investee company. Here the relief will plainly apply if the company's account is in the UK, for then the remittance condition is met at the time of the investment.

Difficulties arise if on a subscription or loan, the monies are sent to a non-UK account of the investee company, and the company then brings the money to the UK. In this scenario, remittance of the monies occurs then, but the relevant event is the subscription or loan. At first sight, therefore, the remittance condition is not met, unless in the case of a UK investee company it can be argued that the shares or loan have a UK situs and as a result their acquisition of itself engages Condition A in ITA 2007, s 809L. As explained in para **51.22** such an argument is unlikely to prevail and should not be relied on in planning.

It seems unlikely that Parliament intended the relief not to be available in this situation; and there is an argument that, in fact, the relief is available if the investee company proceeds to transfer the invested sum to the UK. The argument rests on the language used in s 809VA(1)(b), which imposes a requirement for there to be a remittance 'by virtue of' the relevant event. There is no necessary implication that the remittance be triggered by the relevant event immediately; arguably, a remittance may arise 'by virtue of' a relevant event not only where the remittance is an immediate and unavoidable consequence of that event, but also where the event leads in due course to the remittance. Such is the case where a taxpayer's foreign income/gains are invested in a company, which becomes a relevant person in relation to the taxpayer, and the income/gains are in due course used to make an investment into the UK. In this situation, the eventual remittance is 'by virtue of' the taxpayer's investment in the company, in the sense that had he not made that investment, no remittance would have occurred. Arguably, s 809VA(1)(b) imposes a 'but for' test of causation, but does not require an immediate remittance.

Despite this, there can be little doubt that much the safest way of securing relief is to transfer the money to the UK first and then (within the 45-day period allowed by s 809VA(5)) use it to make the investment. No other course should be taken unless cleared in advance under the informal clearance procedure referred to in para **58.13**.

Purpose test

58.11 The relief is subject to a perplexing purpose test, in that it is precluded if either the relevant event or the investment are part of a scheme or arrangement, and one of the purposes of that scheme or arrangement is the avoidance of tax (s 809VA(7)). The term 'avoidance of tax' is not specifically defined and so must bear its normal meaning, under which it connotes conduct designed to frustrate or defeat the intention of Parliament (see further paras **73.21** to **73.30**). The contrast drawn is with tax mitigation, which is where the taxpayer avails himself of a relief which the legislation confers and suffers the economic consequences entailed in that relief (see *IRC v Willoughby* [1997] 4 All ER 65, [1997] STC 995, HL).

This purpose test was widely criticised when the legislation was first published in draft, as the uncertainty it generates deters potential investors. However, mere use of the relief does not carry risk under the test, as such use is taking advantage of an expressly conferred relief. Moreover, some at least of the uncertainty may in practice be removed by the informal clearance procedure described below.

The claim

58.12 The relief is not available unless claimed (s 809VA(1)(c)). The time limits for the claim are tight, in that the claim must be made either in the tax year in which the income or gains would otherwise be treated as remitted, or in the next tax year, or before 31 January in the tax year after that (s 809YA(8)). There is no discretion to extend the time limit.

The claim must be made by the remittance basis user claiming the relief (s 809VA(1)(c)). This works well enough where that individual is the person making the qualifying investment. But it is unsatisfactory where the investor is not the remittance basis user but someone who in relation to him is a relevant person. Here he may not know until it is too late either that the relevant person has effected a remittance or that relief could have been claimed to avoid the tax otherwise due.

In certain cases a remittance can occur prior to the income arising, most notably where gains are treated as accruing to a beneficiary under TCGA 1992, s 87 and/or where income is treated as arising to an individual under the transfer of assets non-transferor charge. Here a remittance is deemed to occur when the gains or income are treated as arising (ITA 2007, s 809U; see paras **79.4** and **72.24**) and so it is from this moment that the beneficiary or non-transferor's time to claim runs. This works well enough in s 87 cases where for remittance purposes the focus is solely on the capital payment (TCGA 1992, s 87 A) and in non-transferor cases where remittance is by virtue of remittance of the matched benefit (ITA 2007, s 735). But there may be difficulty in non-transferor cases where remittance is of the matched relevant income, particularly in view of the difficulties of operating the matching rules in s 735A (see para **72.5**).

Clearance

58.13 There is no formal advance clearance procedure whereby it can be determined conclusively than an investment is qualifying. However, HMRC will, if requested, give a view under the CAP I procedure and, provided the proposed transactions are correctly described, this view can generally be relied on (*CAP I – obtaining HMRC's advice on non-business activities*, 20 July 2012, reproduced [2012] SWTI 2271). Where the investor is not the remittance basis user, but another relevant person, the CAP I application should be made by the remittance basis user (Guidance Notes, para 2.29).

CHARGEABLE EVENTS

58.14 The relief is prima facie lost, and a taxable remittance is treated as occurring, should what is called a potentially chargeable event occur (s 809VM). In such a case the taxable remittance is deemed to take place at the time of the event. But a taxable remittance may be avoided if appropriate mitigation steps are taken within what is called the relevant grace period.

There are four kinds of potentially chargeable events, namely:

(1)   Disposal of some or all of the shares or loan,
(2)   Extraction of value,
(3)   Change in the target's status, and
(4)   Breach of the two year start-up rule.

There are two kinds of appropriate mitigation steps, namely:

(1)   Reinvestment, and
(2)   Taking money back abroad (s 809VI).

There are two kinds of grace period, namely 45 days in relation to disposals and 90 and 45 days in relation to other events. In relation to other events, the 90 and 45 days are consecutive, in that the holding must be disposed of within the 90-day period and the proceeds then removed abroad or reinvested within the 45-day period.

Disposal

58.15 A disposal causes the income or gains comprised in the original investment to be treated as remitted unless within the 45-day period the proceeds of the disposal are taken abroad or reinvested in another investment which qualifies for relief (ss 809VH(1)(b) and 809VI(1)). Should the disposal be of part only of the original shares or loan, part only of the income and gains are treated as remitted if the proceeds are not removed abroad or reinvested.

The term 'disposal' is not defined. The term does not obviously cover the repayment of a loan where the investment is loan rather than shares. But the context indicates repayment is covered and such is assumed by HMRC (Guidance Notes para 2.34).

The term 'disposal proceeds' is defined and means the consideration for the disposal less the costs of the disposal (s 809Z8)(1)). It is clear that non-arm's length disposals count for these purposes as disposals, for such disposals are expressly deemed to be made at market value (s 809Z8(4)). In such a case what has to be reinvested or taken abroad may be money or other property of equivalent value (s 809Z9(6)). The same applies where there is full consideration for the disposal but it is not money (s 809Z8(3)).

To satisfy the appropriate mitigation steps, the prima facie rule is that what has to be taken abroad or reinvested must be, or, as the case may be, be equal to the proceeds or deemed proceeds. But if the proceeds or deemed proceeds exceed the amount invested the excess can stay in the UK (s 809VI(3)).

On a part disposal, all the proceeds must be taken abroad or reinvested save insofar as the proceeds of just the part disposal exceed the original investment. But credit is given for the part disposal on subsequent disposals. (s 809VI(4)).

Extraction of value

58.16 The extraction of value rule is the core concept in ensuring the relief is not vulnerable to abuse. However in many important respects it goes too far, and makes the relief very difficult to use if the investor or persons connected with him control the target.

The basic rule is that value is extracted if the investor receives money or money's worth from the target company (s 809VH(2)(a)). But what is meant by extraction of value is not defined. However, it is provided that the rule is not breached if the value is received under a disposal that is a potentially chargeable event in its own right (s 809VH(2)(c)). There is also an exclusion for transactions in the ordinary course of business and on arm's length terms. But this exclusion is restricted to value that is income for income tax purposes or would be income if the recipient were amenable to such tax (s 809VH(3)).

It seems reasonably plain from these exclusions that the draftsman envisaged value can count as extracted even if full consideration is given by the extractor. It is however unclear why the exclusion for commercial transactions requires the value extracted to be income, albeit that that exclusion confirms that arm's length remuneration and commercial dividends and interest are permitted.

What is perhaps most odd is the contrast between the extraction of value concept used here and the benefit concept used in determining whether the relief is available in the first place (para 58.7). One wonders whether the draftsman's left hand knew what his right hand was doing. On the assumption it did, the different phraseology must carry the implication that the term extraction of value does not comprehend all forms of benefit. In particular, it may be argued that the rent-free use of property, which is plainly a benefit, is not an extraction of value as nothing is extracted from the company.

The mitigation steps that prevent extraction of value from being remittance of the original income and gains are two fold (s 809VI(2)). First the investor must dispose of the shares or loan within 90 days of the value being extracted. Second he must within 45 days take the entire proceeds abroad or reinvest them.

An important point about extraction of value is that once value is extracted, all the original income or gains are treated as remitted. There is no de minimis allowance and no provision for the withdrawal of relief to be proportionate to the value extracted. So too if taxable remittance is to be avoided it is the entire loan or shareholding which must be disposed of and the entire proceeds which must be taken abroad or reinvested.

The principal difficulty with the extraction of value rule is that it is not confined to value extracted from the target company by the investor. Instead, the value can be extracted by any person who is a relevant person in relation to the remittance basis user being taxed. So too the company from which the value is extracted can be any company which falls within the term 'involved company'. The latter is a term specific to this legislation and includes any company which is connected with the target. Should the target be an eligible stakeholder company, any investee company of the target is also an involved company.

The key concept in all this is 'connected' and this bears its normal tax meaning (ITA 2007, s 993). It thus includes not merely subsidiaries of the target, but companies under the same control as the target. Accordingly, where the investor controls the target, any other company he controls is an involved company. So too is any company controlled by persons connected with him, such as close relatives or trusts of which he is settlor (s 993(5)). The breadth of the connected concept means the relief carries risk if the investor controls the target and is the reason why the extraction of value rule is a deterrent to the relief in such cases.

It might be thought that this problem with connected companies is avoided if neither the individual nor trusts or other persons connected with him control the target. In general this is true. However it should be noted that under ITA 2007, s 993(7) persons acting together to secure or exercise control of a company are treated as connected with each other. The extent of this difficult provision is not clear (see for example *Foulser v MacDougall* [2006] STC 311). But it plainly catches consortia of individuals acting together in relation to an investee company and means the problem with the extraction of value rule described above can apply even where the investor is a minority shareholder.

A particular issue is whether value is extracted if an investor receives a capital distribution from an involved company, as in a liquidation or on the repayment or redemption of a loan or shares. On the face of it value is extracted. This result is precluded if the shares or loan are deemed part of the holding under the rules described below, for then there will be a disposal which is a potentially chargeable event. But this is not so if the paying company is not in the same group as target (and is not an investee of an eligible stakeholder company).

Change of status of target

58.17 A chargeable event occurs if and at such time as the target company first becomes neither an eligible trading company, an eligible stakeholder company, nor an eligible holding company (s 809VH(1)(a)). In the main this happens if the company becomes listed on a recognised stock exchange. But it would also happen if the activities of the company or group ceased to meet the trading requirement.

In such a case remittance of the original income or gains occurs unless the investor disposes of the investment within 90 days and reinvests the proceeds or removes them abroad within 45 days. Should the investor not be aware of the change in status, the 90-day period does not start to run until he becomes aware of the change or ought reasonably to have become so (s 809VJ(1)(b)).

Breach of the two-year start-up rule

58.18 The two-year start-up rule is material only where, at the time of investment, the target has not met the appropriate condition as to the activities of it or its group. If the target is still non-operational on the second anniversary of the making of the investment, a potentially chargeable event occurs (s 809VH(5)). Remittance of the original income and gains is triggered unless the investor disposes of the shares or loan within 90 days and reinvests the proceeds or removes them abroad within 45 days. As with change of status, the 90-day period is extended if the investor does not know of the breach until he becomes aware of it or could reasonably have become so.

Insolvency

58.19 A chargeable event is not triggered merely because the target company enters into administration or is wound up or dissolved (s 809VH(9)). However, a liquidation distribution counts as an extraction of value (s 809VH(9)). This potentially has severe consequences, for it prima facie means all the original income and gains are treated as remitted. Such a result is only avoided if, as per the general rules applicable to extraction of value, the investor disposes of all the shares or loan in the insolvent company within 90 days, and removes the proceeds abroad or reinvests them within 90 days.

A potentially more helpful relief is that no chargeable event occurs just because a subsidiary of target goes into liquidation, and nor does one occur just because an investee company of an eligible stakeholder company goes into liquidation. This means that such a liquidation does not of itself trigger a chargeable event under the change in status rule.

MULTIPLE INVESTMENTS

58.20 Section 809VN contains surprisingly wide aggregation rules. These rules aggregate loans and shares that fall within them and treat them as a single investment. The rules are expressed in terms of income and gains of an individual not being remitted to the UK. As a result they aggregate not merely loans and shares held by the individual personally but any held by relevant persons where the relief has prevented the individual from being taxed on a remittance by the relevant person.

Aggregation

58.21 The aggregation rules are as follows (s 809VN(1)):

- All loans to and shares in the same company are treated as a single investment.
- All loans to and shares in member companies of an eligible trading group are treated as a single investment.
- Loans to and shares in an eligible stakeholder company are treated as the same investment as loans to or shares in any eligible trading company in which the stakeholder company has invested.

These aggregation rules aggregate both loans and shares which have attracted the relief and those which have not (s 809VN(4)(a)).

Identification rules

58.22 These artificial aggregation rules are accompanied by equally artificial identification rules. There are two:

- Any disposal of any loans or shares in the aggregate holding is identified with loans or shares which attracted the relief before other shares or loans (s 809VN(4)(b)).
- Loans or shares which attracted the relief are identified on a first in first out basis (s 809VN(2)(b)).

These rules have the bizarre result that a disposal of shares or loans which did not attract the relief may be taxed as if it was a disposal of shares or loans which did attract the relief. Unless the proceeds are removed abroad within 45 days, remittance of all or a proportion of the original income or gains occur. It is true that this treatment is simply an acceleration of remittance rather than creating remittance. But it is still a trap.

Other chargeable events

58.23 The aggregation rules are even more capricious in relation to other kinds of chargeable events, ie extraction of value, change of the target company's status, or breach of the two-year rule.

The effect of the rules is that engagement of one of these kinds of chargeable event in relation to any one company in the aggregate holding prima facie cause all income and gains in the aggregate holding to be treated as remitted.

This result follows because the remittance required by reason of the chargeable event is of the affected income and gains (s 809VG(2)). The affected income and gains are in turn defined as the portion of income and gains which reflects the portion of the investment affected by the chargeable event (s 809VG(5)). The portion of the investment so affected is then defined as the whole (s 809VG(6)(b)). As the aggregation rules require all shares and loans to be treated as a single qualifying investment, the result is reached in aggregation cases that all are affected by a chargeable event in relation to any.

The practical result of this in multiple investment cases is that extraction of value from one company in the aggregate investment is fatal to all. The same applies if just one company breaches the two-year rule or changes its status.

The aggregation rules do not treat as part of the aggregate holding shares in or loans to involved companies which are not within the categories listed in para 58.21, ie companies which are not in the same group as the target or investees of the same eligible stakeholder company. But, as explained in para 58.16, extraction of value from any such involved company still causes all the relief to be lost unless appropriate mitigation steps are taken and, as those steps require disposal of the whole holding, all shares and loans in the aggregate holding must be disposed of.

TIME LIMITS

58.24 The 45-day period, which applies to disposals, does not start to run on the date of the disposal. It starts when the proceeds first become available for use by the investor (s 809VJ(2)).

HMRC have discretion to extend both the 45-day and the 90-day period. There are two overlapping provisions (s 809VJ(3) and (4)).

The first applies in exceptional circumstances and gives HMRC discretion to extend the time limit in a particular case. The second allows HMRC to make regulations specifying non-exceptional circumstances in which the grace period may be extended. To date this regulation-making power has been exercised to cover cases where the target is listed or becomes a subsidiary of a listed company and a lock-up agreement restricts the disposal of the shares (Business Investment Relief Regulations (SI 2012/1898)).

ONGOING TAX EXPOSURE

58.25 Once the investment is made in the eligible company normal tax rules apply. Thus the company is subject to corporation tax on its worldwide profits unless it is non-UK resident. Even if non-resident it is subject to corporation tax on permanent establishment profits if trading in the UK.

So long as the company is UK resident any dividends or interest it pays to the investor are subject to income tax, and being UK source, are not eligible for the remittance basis. Any disposal by the investor of shares in the company attracts CGT, and that tax is due regardless of whether the disposal is a chargeable event by reference to the income or gain originally invested. A disposal does not attract the remittance basis unless the company is foreign registered.

The shares in the company will potentially be exposed to inheritance tax if the investor is an individual, unless the company is foreign registered and the individual does not have a deemed UK domicile. In practice IHT may be avoided on equity investments by business property relief, but this will not apply in all cases, most notably where the target company or group is engaged in property investment. Where the investment is a loan, IHT exposure will be present if the investor is an individual and the company is UK resident.

A special relief applies should the investor's disposal cause a gain to be realised. This operates on part disposals and applies where the proceeds of the part disposal are less than the CGT due on the part disposal and the amount invested. It allows the shortfall to be used to buy a certificate of tax deposit. The certificate must be bought within the 45-day grace period. Detailed rules as to this are set out in ss 809VK and 809VM.

MISCELLANEOUS RULES

Mixed funds

58.26 Income and gains attracting the relief which have been transferred from a mixed fund are treated as having been so tansferred under the offshore transfer rules (s 809VO). This means a pro rata proportion of all income and gains in the mixed fund passes into the qualifying investment rather than such income and gains as would be identified if a taxable remittance had occurred (see further CHAPTER 53).

Should the qualifying investment be disposed of, the income and gains identified with it remains the same, even if the proceeds are taken abroad (s 809VO(7)).

Taking proceeds abroad

58.27 The proceeds of any disposal of a qualifying investment count as taken abroad once circumstances exist under which they would not be treated as remitted (s 809Z9(2)). The proceeds of the disposal can first be paid into a UK bank account, but if so, the money removed abroad must be taken from the same account (s 809Z9(3)). As indicated above, an exception to this is made where the proceeds is not money, for here what is removed abroad need only be money of equivalent value.

Chapter 59

CHATTEL RELIEFS

INTRODUCTION

59.1 Section 809X of ITA 2007 provides that certain kinds of property are not treated as remitted to the UK even if Condition A of s 809L is satisfied. Such property is referred to as exempt property and comprises the following:

- Property which satisfies the public access rule.
- Clothing, footwear, jewellery and watches which satisfy the personal use rule.
- Property which meets the repair rule.
- Property which meets the temporary importation rule.

In practical terms all the above items are chattels. This is reinforced by the definition of the term 'property' as that term excludes money (ITA 2007, s 809Z6(2)). Money is in turn defined as including travellers cheques, promissory notes, bills of exchange, vouchers capable of being exchanged for money or goods and services, and any other kind of instrument that evidences debt (s 809Z6(3)).

There is one other category of exempt property, namely any property where the notional remitted amount is less than £1,000 (s 809X(5)(c)). The notional remitted amount is the amount that would otherwise be taken to be remitted to the UK if the exemption was not in point (s 809Z5).

Form of relief

59.2 The language of s 809X is in one sense curious for the exemption operates by treating the exempt property as not remitted. In so providing there is inconsistency with s 809L, for when Condition A is satisfied it is not the property that is remitted, but the foreign income and gains from which the property is derived (s 809L(1)). Clearly s 809X must be read as exempting such income and gains, but, as is explained below, this drafting imprecision makes certain aspects of the exempt property regime difficult to construe.

PUBLIC ACCESS RULE

59.3 The public access rule requires the property to be available for public access at an approved establishment (ITA 2007, s 809Z(3)). In addition, the property is allowed to be in transit to or from the public access premises or in storage at those premises. But if reliance is being placed on transit or storage such transit or storage must precede or succeed actual availability for public access.

Public access

59.4 Public access has a somewhat wider meaning than the term normally connotes. It is satisfied not merely if the property is on public display at the approved establishment but also if it is available for viewing or educational use on request (s 809Z(4)(b)). Property is also available for public access if it is held by the establishment in connection with its sale (s 809Z(4)(c)). This last means property can count as exempt property even if the sole reason for bringing it to the UK is to sell it.

As indicated above, the public access has to be at an approved establishment. That term is principally defined by reference to VAT legislation and means a museum, gallery or other institution that has been approved for the purposes of Group 9 of Schedule 2 to the VAT (Imported Goods) Relief Order 1984. Group 9 exempts approved museums and other institutions from import VAT when they import items themselves. In addition the term approved establishment includes any other person, premises, or institution approved by HMRC (s 809Z(5)(b)). There is no published list of approved establishments and any questions as to how an establishment gains approval or whether it is approved are directed to HMRC's Remittance Basis Technical Team (RDRM 34130). The major auction houses are known to be approved and for that reason the bringing of art objects to the UK for sale at auction can avoid remittance.

Storage

59.5 If the chattel is in storage it must either be in store at the approved establishment or at other premises which falls within the term 'public access premises'. Other premises so comprehended are any commercial premises used for storage before or after public access.

Time limits

59.6 The general rule is that the public access rule ceases to be satisfied once the conditions have been satisfied for more than two years (s 8097(7)). But HMRC have discretion to allow a longer time and here too the contact is HMRC's Remittance Basis Team (RDRM 34150). Also the public access rule is not precluded if the property is exempt under other heads before or after the public access period.

PERSONAL USE RULE

59.7 To understand the personal use rule it is necessary to focus on the individual whose income and gains would otherwise be treated as remitted. To attract the exemption, the clothing footwear, jewellery or watch must be his property or the property of someone who is a relevant person in relation to him (see CHAPTER 54). In addition the item must be for the personal use of a relevant person who is an individual, ie the remittance basis user himself or his spouse or minor children or grandchildren (ITA 2007, s 809Z2).

REPAIR RULE

59.8 To be within the repair rule, the property must meet the repair conditions throughout its time in the UK (s 809Z3). These conditions require that the property is undergoing repair or restoration. It is permissible for the property to be in storage before or after repair provided the storage premises are commercial premises used by the repairer for storage. It is also permissible for the object to be in transit, but only to the repair or storage premises from outside the UK before repair or from such premises to somewhere outside the UK following completion of the repair.

There is no time limit under the repair rule as to how long the property can be in the UK. The repair rule combines with the public access rule, in that the repair rule is treated as satisfied for the whole period in the UK if part of the period is repair and the rest satisfies the conditions for the public access rule (s 809Z3). However the repair rule cannot be combined with the temporary importation rule, as the repair rule requires the repair conditions or the public access conditions to be satisfied throughout the time in the UK.

TEMPORARY IMPORTATION RULE

59.9 The temporary importation rule is much the simplest rule as it focuses only on the number of countable days. The rule is satisfied provided the total number of countable days is 275 or fewer (ITA 2007, s 809Z4(1)). The simplicity of this rule means it is normally the rule relied on when chattels are brought to the UK for sale, but in such cases it is necessary to check previous countable days with some care.

Countable days

59.10 The term 'countable day' means any day on which the following conditions are met (s 809Z4(2)):

(a)   The property is in the UK.
(b)   It is in the UK by virtue of being brought to, or received or used in, the UK.
(c)   The circumstances in which it is so brought to or received or used in the UK are those in which Condition A, ie ITA 2007, 809L(2)(a) applies.

The reference to Condition A applying is significant in two respects. First, Condition A operates only if the bringing, receipt or use is by or for the benefit of a relevant person. It follows that time in the UK when no relevant person either owned, benefited from or used the property can be ignored. Second, s 809L, and thus Condition A, had effect only from 2008–09 (FA 2008, Sch 7, para 81). It follows that time in the UK before 5 April 2008 can be ignored.

But subject to those two qualifications, countable days include not merely the number of days on which the chattel is in the UK in the current period, but also any prior time in the UK when the chattel was in the ownership of a relevant person. Such prior time could have been when the non-domiciliary concerned was not a remittance basis user or even when he was non-UK resident. It could also have been when another relevant person owned the property. For these reasons a check as to the movements of the property since 6 April 2008 is essential if the temporary ownership and importation rule is to be relied on.

Disregarded days

59.11 Certain days are not countable days, most notably any day on which the public access or repair rule is met or when the personal use rule is met (s 809Z4(3)). However there is a wrinkle with the disregard of public access rule days, which is that the public access rule was widened with effect from 6 April 2013 (FA 2013, Sch 7, paras 5 and 6). It is unclear whether, in computing countable days after 5 April 2013, satisfaction of the public access rule before then is determined by the present public access rules or the more restrictive pre 2013 rules.

A special issue arises with property in the UK on 6 April 2013, to the effect that the present law disregarding public access days takes effect from when the property was first removed from the UK thereafter (FA 2013, Sch 7, para 10). Until then the disregard of public access days is governed by the more restrictive pre-2013 law, this law being more restrictive both as to the public access rule itself and the circumstances in which days that satisfied the rule were not countable.

Loss and theft

59.12 A day is not a countable day if the property has been lost, stolen or destroyed (s 809Z4(3A)). But if lost or stolen property is recovered, days again become countable, and, if the 275 days has nearly expired, up to 45 days are allowed for removal from the UK.

PROPERTY CEASING TO BE EXEMPT PROPERTY

59.13 Remittance occurs should exempt property cease to be exempt property while still in the UK. Under s 809Y(1), it, ie the exempt property, is then treated as having been remitted to the UK. This provision contains the same linguistic quirk as the exemption itself, for strictly it is the income or gains from which the property is derived that are remitted. The amount of such income and gains of its nature will not be exactly equal to the value of the property and, as noted in para 51.15, it is the amount of the income and gains that is the amount remitted.

There are two main circumstances in which property ceases to be exempt. The first and most obvious is where the property is sold while still in the UK (s 809Y(3)). This applies not merely if all the property is sold but if part of it is, and the term sale includes conversion into anything that counts as money within the definition explained in para **59.1** above.

The second circumstance is where the property ceases to meet the rule on which its exemption is based and does not at the same time meet one of the other rules. Thus exemption for property in the UK under the temporary importation rule is lost if the 275 countable day limit is breached. But in determining whether the limit is breached days in the UK which satisfy the conditions for the public access rule are ignored, even if days before or afterwards do not and so go towards the 275 days. But the same is not true of the repair rule for here the repair conditions have to be satisfied throughout the time the property is in the UK. Thus repair days are only excluded from countable days if they comprise a period in the UK separate from that giving rise to the countable days.

Loss or destruction

59.14 Exempt property does not cease to be exempt if it is lost, stolen or destroyed (s 809Y(4A)), and days during which it is lost, stolen or destroyed are not countable days for the purposes of the temporary importation rule (see para **59.9**). But receipt of insurance monies or other compensation causes remittance to occur unless all the monies are taken abroad within 45 days of receipt (ss 809Y(4B) and 809YF).

RELIEF ON SALE

59.15 The remittance which would otherwise occur on sale is disapplied under s 809YA if the disposal proceeds are taken offshore within 45 days of being released to the seller. Should the proceeds be released in instalments, the 45-day limit applies separately to each instalment. There is also a final deadline which is expressed in terms of the tax year in which the sale occurs. The deadline is 5 January 21 months after the end of that tax year (s 809YA(5),(6)), and all the proceeds must have been taken offshore by then regardless of when released. HMRC do not have power to extend this deadline, albeit they do have power, in exceptional circumstances, to extend any 45-day deadline (s 809YB).

For the purpose of these rules proceeds count as released when made available for use by or for the benefit of anybody who is a relevant person in relation to the remittance basis user concerned (s 809YA(10)). The entirety of the disposal proceeds must be taken offshore. The term 'disposal proceeds' means the consideration for the sale less agency fees deducted before the consideration is made available (s 809Z8). The term 'agency fees' is itself defined as fees and other incidental costs charged by the person through whom the sale is effected (s 809Z8(6)).

The requirement that the proceeds be taken offshore means simply that they must be taken outside the UK. In addition they must not be available for use or enjoyment in the UK (s 809Z9). Should the proceeds first be received in a UK bank account, that account must be debited with the removal abroad (s 809Z9(3)).

The legislation contemplates that the proceeds of the sale can be property other than money. In such a case either what is received or equivalent money must be taken offshore (s 809Z9(4)).

The relief on a sale is subject to a TAAR, in that does not apply if the sale is part of tax avoidance arrangements (s 809YA(11)). A further restriction is that the sale must be at arm's length and the buyer must not be a relevant person. The sale must also be outright, in that after the sale relevant persons must not have any interest in the property or any right to benefit from it or acquire an interest in it (s 809YA(2)–(4)).

The relief where the proceeds of the sale are taken offshore can also apply should the proceeds be used to make an investment qualifying for business investment relief (s 809YA(7); see CHAPTER 58). In contrast to the general relief a claim is required (s 809YA(9)).

CGT RELIEF

59.16 Section 809YA does not, in itself, remove all tax disincentives to the sale of 'exempt property' in the UK since, where the property is standing at a gain, a sale will crystallise that gain and it will not be a foreign chargeable gain as the property will be in the UK at the time of disposal. In other words there could be a charge to CGT even if the proceeds of sale are removed from the UK within the 45-day period.

This issue is addressed by s 809YD. It applies where a chargeable gain accrues to the taxpayer on the sale of an item of exempt property, where the property would have been treated as remitted to the UK under s 809Y but for the application of s 809YA. Section 809YD is in point both where the sale was made by the taxpayer himself or where it was made by a foreign closely held company and the gain was apportioned to him under TCGA 1992, s 13 (see CHAPTER 88). In either of these situations the gain is deemed to be a foreign chargeable gain. The result is that, if the taxpayer is a remittance basis user in the relevant year, an immediate charge to CGT is avoided.

However, the taxpayer has the ability to disapply this deeming, by notice to HMRC, so that the gain is treated as a UK gain (s 809YD(9)). Such an election might be made by a non-domiciliary who, but for the deemed foreign gain, would be entitled to the remittance basis without payment of the £30,000 or £50,000 charge, on the basis that, disregarding the gain realised on the sale of the 'exempt property', his unremitted foreign income and/or gains are within the £2,000 limit in s 809D (see para **46.11**).

The deeming in s 809YD is of somewhat broader application than might first appear. It applies in respect of any gain accruing on a sale in the UK of property which falls within the definition of 'exempt property' (in s 809X). That definition is not expressly limited to property representing or derived from foreign income or gains. Thus s 809YD can operate to convert a UK gain into a foreign chargeable gain where the asset sold was acquired using clean capital of the taxpayer. For the section to have this effect, and for a taxable remittance of the foreign chargeable gain to be avoided, the conditions of s 809YA must all be met, including taking the proceeds offshore.

Although as stated above, the deeming under s 809YD is, as a matter of construction, of broader application, HMRC are thought to consider it only applies if the property sold is derived from foreign income and gains which, in the absence of the remittance relief under s 809YA, would have been chargeable when the property was sold. The difficulty with this construction is that s 809YD is expressed in terms of s 809Y(1) otherwise applying. As noted above (para **59.13**) that section postulates simply that the property is treated as remitted to the UK, not that any particular income or gains from which it is derived are.

Section VII

Inheritance Tax and Settlements

Chapter 60

THE RELEVANT PROPERTY REGIME

INTRODUCTION

60.1 The general rule is that IHT is charged on settlements in accordance with the rules detailed in IHTA 1984, ss 64–69. As the property to which those rules apply is termed relevant property, the rules themselves are normally referred to as the relevant property regime.

Certain categories of settled property are not relevant property (IHTA 1984, s 58). The principal categories are as follows:

(1)   Excluded property. This is property which is taken out of the scope of IHT under the excluded property rules applicable to settlements. These rules are explained in CHAPTER 62.

(2)   Property subject to a qualifying interest in possession. Such property is treated as being in the beneficial ownership of the holder of the interest in possession. This is dealt with in the next chapter.

(3)   Limited categories of property held on trust for children. This also is explained in the next chapter.

(4)   Employee benefit trusts which qualify under the somewhat restrictive provisions of IHTA 1984, s 86. These are discussed in CHAPTER 25.

THE ENTRY CHARGE

60.2 Save where one of the exceptions referred to above applies, property becomes relevant property when it is settled. An immediately chargeable transfer occurs save insofar as specific reliefs such as business property relief or normal expenditure out of income are in point (IHTA 1984, ss 21 and 104). In general the rate of tax is 20% (IHTA 1984, s 7(2)). But in certain circumstances the rate may be either less or greater.

The rate is less insofar as the settlor's nil-rate band is available. Currently that band is £325,000. It is available provided the settlor has not made any other chargeable transfers in the seven years prior to the transfer of assets to the settlement (IHTA 1984, s 7(1)).

The rate is greater should the settlor die within five years of transferring the assets to the settlement (IHTA 1984, s 7(4)). It is the full death rate of 40% should he die in the first three years. Otherwise it is 32% in year 4, and 24% in year 5.

Settlements frequently arise on death by virtue of provisions in the deceased's will. Save insofar as exemptions apply, property passing into settlement on death is charged at the death rates of IHT – ie 40% once the nil-rate band is exhausted.

THE 10-YEARLY CHARGE

60.3 The 10-yearly charge is a key feature of the relevant property regime. It is made on the tenth anniversary of the date on which the settlement commenced and on each 10-yearly anniversary thereafter (IHTA 1984, ss 61 and 64). This date is used even if on the date the settlement commenced the settled property was not relevant property but only became so subsequently. The date on which a settlement commences is the date on which property first became comprised in it (IHTA 1984, s 60).

The 10-yearly charge is made on the value of the relevant property as at the ten-yearly anniversary concerned. In other words all the property in the settlement is charged, save insofar as it is not relevant property or a specific relief, such as business property relief, is in point (IHTA 1984, s 64). The rate is three-tenths of the lifetime rate of IHT (IHTA 1984, s 66). As the latter is currently 20%, the 10-yearly rate is 6%.

In many cases the effective rate is less. This is because the mechanics of determining the rate involve postulating a hypothetical transfer, and then determining what three-tenths of the effective lifetime rate on that transfer would be. As the hypothetical transfer presupposes a nil-rate band, the result is that normally three-tenths of the effective rate is somewhat less than 6%. Indeed, if the value of the settlement as a whole is below the nil-rate band, the effective rate, and thus the tax, on the 10-yearly anniversary may be nil.

However, the benefit of the nil-rate band is not always available, or wholly available. This is for the following reasons:

(1) The hypothetical transfer presupposes previous transfers equal to chargeable transfers made by the settlor in the seven years prior to the creation of the settlement (IHTA 1984, s 66(5)(a)).
(2) It also presupposes previous transfers equal to any amounts on which an exit charge was made in the previous ten years under the rules described below (IHTA 1984, s 66(5)(b)).
(3) The amount comprised in the hypothetical transfer includes not merely the relevant property in the settlement on the 10-yearly anniversary, but also relevant property comprised in any other settlement made by the same settlor on the same day (IHTA 1984, s 66(4)(c)). This property is included at its value when the related settlement was made rather than at its value on the 10-yearly anniversary date.

A further addition to the property included in the hypothetical transfer is in point if the settlor has made an addition both to the subject settlement and to another settlement on the same day (IHTA 1984, s 62A). Such additions are referred to as same-day additions and are in point unless both additions represent the commencement of the two settlements, in which event the settlements are relevant settlements and so in any event taken into account in relation to each other under point (3) above.

An important limitation to the same-day addition concept is that it does not extend to what are called protected settlements (IHTA 1984, s 62B(1)(c)). These are settlements made before 10 December 2014 which have not been added to since then (IHTA 1984, s 62C). The same-day addition rule is also precluded if the addition to either of the two settlements concerned is less than £5,000 (s 62B(2)).

Where the same-day additions rule is in point, two additional elements are included in the hypothetical transfer. The first is the value of the same-day addition to the other settlement as at the date the addition was made (s 66(4)(d)). The second is the value of whatever relevant property was comprised in that settlement on the date it commenced (s 66(4)(e)).

In almost all cases with which this book is concerned, the same-day additions rule is of limited impact, for the only impact it can have is to increase the size of the hypothetical transfer and so diminish the impact of the nil-rate band on the effective rate. Most offshore settlements are valued at figures so far in excess of the nil-rate band that its impact is immaterial. The same-day additions rule has applied to 10-yearly anniversaries since 18 November 2015 (F(No 2)A 2015, Sch 1, para 7). There is a transitional relief for testamentary additions on deaths before 6 April 2017 if the will was made before 10 December 2014 (s 62C(3)).

Many settlements, both onshore and offshore, still exist which were created before 27 March 1974, this being the date of the introduction of IHT (or Capital Transfer Tax as it was then known). In determining the hypothetical transfer in such a case, no account is taken of the transfers made by the settlor in the seven years prior to the creation of the settlement, and nor is account taken of other settlements created by the same settlor on the same day, or of same-day additions (IHTA 1984, s 66(6)).

Additions

60.4 Should the settlor have added property to the settlement, such addition may affect the rate of tax on subsequent 10-yearly anniversaries. This is the position if the settlor's total chargeable transfers in the seven years prior to the creation of the settlement are less than his total in the seven years prior to the addition. In such case the greater cumulative total is used in computing the effective rate at subsequent 10-yearly anniversaries (IHTA 1984, s 67). However, in computing the settlor's cumulative total as at the date of the addition, his previous transfer or transfers to the settlement are ignored (IHTA 1984, s 67(5)).

On the 10-yearly anniversary next following an addition, the rate of tax on added property is reduced. This is so whether the property was added by the settlor or someone else. The rate is reduced by as many fortieths as there are complete quarters in the 10-year period during which the property was not comprised in the settlement or not relevant property (IHTA 1984, s 66(2)).

The addition may impact on the rate on future anniversaries in another respect if on the same day the settlor makes an addition to another settlement. In this event the same-day additions rule described above will come into play, unless one of the exceptions to that rule is in point.

Accumulations

60.5 Many settlements subject to the relevant property regime generate income and often such income is accumulated. This is particularly so with offshore trusts, for almost all offshore trust laws are free of fetters on accumulation.

HMRC practice is to treat accumulated income as becoming a taxable asset of the trust on the date on which accumulation is made (SP 8/86; IHTM42088). It is so treated for the purposes of the fortieths rule described above. It cannot however be characterised as added by the settlor, as additions by the settlor are only taken into account if by way of chargeable transfer.

The effect of the above is that on a 10-yearly anniversary IHT can be reduced by determining what part of the value is attributable to accumulations over the past ten years and when such accumulations were made. The tax can also be reduced by delaying decisions as to what to do with income in the period leading up to the 10-yearly anniversary, for unless and until the income is accumulated it is not subject to the 10-yearly charge (*Gilchrist (as trustee of the J P Gilchrist 1993 Settlement) v Revenue and Customs Comrs* [2014] STC 1713, 164 NLJ 7605). However there are two reasons why delaying accumulation cannot be taken too far. The first is that de facto accumulation or distribution may occur, as described in para **8.10**. The second is that if unaccumulated income as at a 10-year anniversary is more than five years old it is deemed to be relevant property which has been comprised in the settlement for the whole of the past ten years (IHTA 1984, s 64(1A)).

This second reason did not apply to 10-yearly anniversaries occurring before 6 April 2014 (FA 2014, Sch 25 para 4(4)). It means that it is preferable to ensure that income which will be more than five years old on the date of the anniversary is accumulated before the anniversary, as then the fortieths reduction in rate is potentially available. The legislation is silent as to how distributions are allocated between income of different years. HMRC's practice is to take the amount standing on income account as at the anniversary and deduct what has arisen in the previous five years. The balance (if any) is then relevant property (IHTM42166).

The treatment of unaccumulated income described above applies only to receipts of the trust which are income as a matter of general trust law. It does not apply to capital receipts which are deemed to be income for income tax purposes (*Gilchrist v HMRC*).

THE EXIT CHARGE

60.6 As well as the 10-yearly charge, the relevant property regime imposes exit charges (IHTA 1984, s 65). An exit charge is made when property in the settlement is distributed to beneficiaries. An exit charge is also in point should the trustees effect a depreciatory disposition or omit to exercise a right (IHTA 1984, ss 65(1)(b) and 65(9)). But no charge is made on dispositions on arm's length terms that are not intended to confer gratuitous benefit (s 65(6); *Macpherson v IRC* [1988] STC 362).

Where an exit charge is in point, the amount charged is the amount by which the value of the property in the settlement is reduced. The rate of tax is based on the effective rate charged at the last anniversary – ie the rate of 6% or less (IHTA 1984, s 69). But the actual rate used is a fraction of that effective rate, the fraction being as many fortieths as there are complete quarters since the last 10-yearly anniversary (s 69(4)). It follows that in the first quarter following an anniversary there is a nil charge, and indeed an event during that quarter is not returnable as an occasion of charge at all (s 65(4)).

Should relevant property have become comprised in the settlement since the last 10-yearly anniversary, the rate of tax on the anniversary is adjusted for these purposes to what it would have been had the settlement then included the added property (IHTA 1984, s 69(2)). The same applies where property comprised in the settlement on the last anniversary was not relevant property but has become so since (IHTA 1984, s 69(2)). In both cases the value brought into account is the value of the property when added or, as the case may be, when it became relevant property (s 69(3)). Should an addition have engaged the same-day addition rule (see para **60.3** above) the value brought into account also includes the value of the addition to the other settlement and the value of the relevant property in the other settlement when the latter commenced (s 692A(b)).

As noted above, accumulations count as new property becoming comprised in the settlement on the date on which the accumulation is made. For the purposes of the exit charge, there is no deeming of unaccumulated income as having been accumulated if it arose more than five years before the exit event.

In the event that added property is included in the distribution occasioning the exit charge, the rate of tax on the property is reduced to reflect the number of complete quarters since the anniversary and before the property was added to the settlement (IHTA 1984, ss 69(4) and 68(3)). These rules would seem to apply both where the added property is a genuine addition and where it is the result of accumulation.

Before the first 10-yearly anniversary

60.7 Should the exit charge occur before the first 10-yearly anniversary, the hypothetical transfer used is the value of the initial property settled and the value of any subsequent additions (IHTA 1984, s 65). In both cases the value used is the value as at the date the property became comprised in the settlement and no account is taken of property which was not relevant property. However property which has become relevant property by the time of the exit charge is included. Should the same-day addition rule (para **60.3** above) have been engaged the hypothetical transfer includes the value of the addition to the other settlement and the value of the property initially comprised in that settlement (s 65(5)(e)(f)).

In computing the rate on the exit charge, previous transfers are assumed, equal to chargeable transfers made by the settlor in the previous seven years. The resultant rate, of 6% or less, is then reduced to a fraction, this being as many fortieths as there are complete quarters since the property became comprised in the settlement or became relevant property.

Property ceasing to be relevant property

60.8 The rules as to the exit charge state that the charge is made whenever property ceases to be relevant property. Prior to FA 2006, property ceased to be relevant property not merely when it was distributed to beneficiaries absolutely, but also when it was appointed on fixed interest or accumulation and maintenance trusts as such trusts were then outside the relevant property regime. Now however they are in the relevant property regime, insofar as appointed after 22 March 2006. As a result, exit charges where the property remains settled are rare. The principal examples are property appointed on charitable trusts and property becoming held on employee trusts within IHTA 1984, s 86 (see para 25.9).

Business property

60.9 An exit charge does not arise insofar as the distributed property is eligible for business property relief (IHTA 1984, s 103(1)). Even where the distributed property is not so eligible, the relief may impact on the exit charge. This is the position if business property relief applied on the previous 10-yearly anniversary, for the rate of tax charged on the distribution is governed by the tax charged on the anniversary (IHTA 1984, s 69(1)). The position is otherwise on distributions before the first 10-yearly anniversary, for here the rate is based on the valued settled (IHTA 1984, s 68(5)(a)).

Income distributions

60.10 An exit charge does not arise should a distribution be a payment which is the income of any person for the purposes of income tax (IHTA 1984, s 65(5)(b)). The same result follows if the payment will be the income of any person or, should the recipient be non-resident, if it would be his income were he UK resident. This relief extends to distributions in specie as the term payment includes any transfer of assets other than money (IHTA 1984, s 63).

This rule self-evidently protects income distributions from the exit charge. A more interesting question is whether it relieves distributions taxed as income under Income Tax 2007 (ITA 2007), s 731 (see CHAPTER 70). The answer would appear to be that it does, as such distributions are treated as the recipient's income (ITA 2007, s 732). However, an exception would be made if, through insufficiency of relevant income, the payment is taxed as a capital gain under TCGA 1992, s 87 or Sch 4C as then the payment is not treated as income (cf para 78.5). But this exception would itself not be in point if the payment were taxed as an offshore income gain, for then again it is treated as income (see CHAPTER 82).

An interesting point would arise if, at the time of distribution, there is neither relevant income nor any gains pool with which to match it. In such case, arguably an exit charge would still not be in point if it could be said that the distributed property 'will' be the income of the recipient – ie that it will be if and when there is relevant income.

In the context of employee benefit trusts, HMRC have confirmed that a capital distribution or benefit which is taxed under s 731 when made avoids the IHT exit charge. But in their view an exit charge is in point if insufficiency of relevant income means the distribution is not, or is not fully, taxed under s 731 in the year in which made (see 'EBT Settlement Opportunity FAQs', August 2012, para 4.18).

IDENTIFYING THE SETTLEMENT

Definition of settlement

60.11 As will be apparent, the relevant property regime requires identification of the settlement, the property comprised in it, and the date on which it commenced.

The term 'settlement' is defined for IHT purposes (IHTA 1984, s 43(2)). It means any disposition or dispositions of property whereby the property is held either:

(a)   for persons in succession, or
(b)   for any person subject to a contingency, or
(c)   on trust to accumulate the income and/or distribute it at the discretion of the trustees.

It is not always clear whether a given arrangement should be treated for IHT purposes as a single settlement or multiple settlements. For example, this question may arise where:

(1)   part of a trust fund is held on discretionary trusts and part on fixed-interest trusts, or
(2)   property is added to a trust on separate occasions, whether by one settlor or by several.

In *Rysaffe Trustee Co (CI) Ltd v IRC* [2002] EWHC 1114 (Ch), [2002] STC 872, Park J held (at para 20) that the issue of whether there is one settlement or several is to be answered in accordance with the general understanding of trust practitioners. The reference in s 43 to dispositions comprehends cases where property is contributed to the settlement on more than one occasion. Park J's analysis was approved by the Court of Appeal (see [2003] EWCA Civ 356, [2003] STC 536, 541, para 25).

That this is right is confirmed by provisions in the relevant property regime. The rules noted above as to additions contemplate a single settlement. So too the rules as to property comprised in the settlement not being relevant property imply that property subject to different trusts can be relevant property of the same settlement.

Commencement of the settlement

60.12 As indicated above, the commencement of the settlement is the date from which 10-yearly anniversaries are computed. The date on which a settlement commences is the date on which property is first comprised within it (IHTA 1984, s 60). This is so even if the settlement is one of those in which an initial life interest of the settlor or his spouse otherwise causes the making of the settlement to be treated as postponed until the life interest ends (IHTA 1984, s 61(2); see further IHTA 1984, s 80 and para 62.23 post).

Property moving between settlements

60.13 Where property is appointed or advanced from one settlement to another, it is treated for the purposes of the relevant property regime as remaining comprised in the transferor settlement. This means that 10-yearly anniversaries in respect of the transferred property are computed by reference to the commencement date of the original settlement (IHTA 1984, s 81).

THE SETTLOR

60.14 The term 'settlor' is defined for IHT purposes in substantially the same terms as ITTOIA 2005, s 620 (IHTA 1984, s 44). Reference should therefore be made to the discussion in para 75.18. Where under the rules described in para 62.23 the commencement of the settlement is treated as deferred until the termination of the settlor's spouse's interest in possession, the spouse is treated as the settlor (IHTA 1984, s 80).

LIFE INTERESTS

60.15 Unless an interest in possession is a qualifying interest in possession (see paras 61.2 to 61.15), settled property subject to a life interest is relevant property and so subject to the rules described above. As a result the creation of a fixed interest inter vivos settlement occasions an entry charge under the current IHT regime, and thereafter it is subject to 10-yearly charges. This is so even if the settlor or his spouse is the life tenant (save in the unlikely event that the trust is a disabled trust (para 61.10)). So too, an exit charge is levied on any capital distribution even if the recipient is the life tenant (save insofar as the distribution is taxable on the recipient under ITA 2007, s 731; see para [60.10] above).

One potential advantage that the present regime has, in contrast to that before FA 2006, is that the creation of a life interest within an existing settlement is a non-event for IHT purposes. This is as explained in para 60.8 and follows because the property is relevant property both before and after. So too the termination of a life interest is a non-event unless the life interest is a qualifying interest in possession, in which case the termination is immediately chargeable or potentially exempt (see para **61.3**).

Chapter 61

EXCEPTIONS TO THE RELEVANT PROPERTY REGIME

INTRODUCTION

61.1 This chapter deals with certain exceptions to the relevant property regime, namely that for qualifying interests in possession and those for certain kinds of settlement in favour of children. The present form of these exceptions largely results from FA 2006. Some significant points of uncertainty were addressed in an exchange of questions and answers between STEP and CIOT on the one hand and HMRC on the other. At the time of writing the most recent published version of this is that issued on 8 August 2008 (reproduced [2008] SWTI 1929).

QUALIFYING INTERESTS IN POSSESSION

61.2 The term 'qualifying interest in possession' is used in IHTA 1984, s 58 to denote interests in possession not subject to the relevant property regime. The following kinds of interest in possession qualify (s 59(1)):

(1)   Interests in possession to which the holder became entitled before 22 March 2006.
(2)   Transitional serial interests ('TSIs').
(3)   Immediate post-death interests ('IPDIs').
(4)   Disabled person's interests.

PRE-22 MARCH 2006 INTERESTS IN POSSESSION

61.3 The inclusion of pre-22 March 2006 interests in possession reflects the pre-2006 law, when all interests in possession were outside the relevant property regime. An interest in possession is only qualifying under this exception if it is the same interest as the life tenant held before 22 March 2006. If the pre-22 March 2006 interest is revoked or terminated, as may happen on an appointment or resettlement, any ensuing interest in possession does not count as having been held on 22 March 2006 even if the holder of the interest is the same.

This point particularly arises where a beneficiary is entitled to capital on attaining a particular age and until then is entitled to the income. If the trust is resettled to delay absolute vesting, HMRC consider any ensuing interest in possession in favour of the beneficiary is a post-22 March 2006 interest. The same applies if the vesting of capital is delayed by appointment rather than resettlement (see STEP/CIOT questions answer 6).

TRANSITIONAL SERIAL INTERESTS

61.4 There are three species of TSI, defined respectively by IHTA 1984, ss 49C, 49D, and 49E.

22 March 2006–5 October 2008

61.5 An interest in possession qualifies as a TSI under s 49C if the following conditions are met:

(1)   The settlement commenced before 22 March 2006 and immediately before that date was subject to an interest in possession.

(2)   That interest, referred to as the prior interest, came to an end before 6 October 2008.

(3)   On its coming to an end, it was replaced by another interest in possession, which is the TSI.

The TSI can be held by the same person as held the prior interest, or by a different beneficiary. A point to stress is that the prior interest and the TSI must be under the same settlement: an interest in possession resulting from a resettlement cannot be a TSI.

An interest in possession is only a TSI if it took effect on the termination of the interest subsisting on 22 March 2006. In other words, an interest is not a TSI if it replaced an earlier TSI, even if such replacement was before 6 October 2008.

It is unclear on the wording of the legislation whether the interest subsisting on 22 March 2006 had to be terminated in its entirety or whether it could be terminated as respects some of the settled property but not the rest. So too it is unclear whether the TSI had to subsist in all the settled property in which the prior interest subsisted. HMRC however accept that in such cases any ensuing interest is a TSI (STEP/CIOT Questions 1–5).

Surviving spouse

61.6 An interest in possession qualifies as a TSI under s 49D if the following conditions are met:

(1)   The settlement commenced before 22 March 2006 and immediately before that date was subject to an interest in possession, 'the prior interest'.

(2)   The prior interest terminates on the death of the holder of that interest.

(3)   On the death, the surviving spouse of the interest-holder takes an interest in possession, the TSI.

To attract this treatment it is immaterial whether the holder of the prior interest and the spouse were married before 22 March 2006; all that matters is that they were married immediately before the death. So too, the TSI need not have been provided for under the terms of the trust before 22 March 2006; what matters is that it arises on the death, whether under the original terms of the trust or a subsequent appointment.

The surviving spouse's interest is not a TSI unless it is under the same settlement as the prior interest. Moreover the prior interest must have existed since before 22 March 2006: it cannot be a TSI arising under s 49C. This may be a trap, in that an appointment of new trusts on or after 22 March 2006 may have caused a prior interest to be replaced by a new interest which would not qualify as a 'prior interest' for the purposes of s 49D. In such case any successive spouse's interest on death cannot be a TSI.

Life policies

61.7 Special provisions apply under s 49E to life policies held on interest in possession trusts on 22 March 2006. In such a case, subsequent interests in possession in the policies are TSIs indefinitely, unless and until non-interest in possession trusts supervene (IHTA 1984, s 49E). Each interest must be held until death for this treatment to apply to the successive interests.

POST-22 MARCH SETTLEMENTS

61.8 IPDIs and disabled persons' interests represent the two kinds of interest in possession which are qualifying under settlements created after 22 March 2006. Neither is likely to be encountered much in offshore tax planning.

IPDIs

61.9 The following conditions must be met for an interest to be an IPDI (IHTA 1984, s 49A):

(1) The settlement must be effected by will or intestacy.
(2) The interest in possession must arise on the death of the testator or intestate.

In contrast to TSIs for surviving spouses, there is no requirement that the interest be held by the deceased's widow. Nor is there any requirement as to whether the property remains settled on termination of the IPDI. However, if on a resettlement or appointment the IPDI is replaced by another interest in possession, such is not a qualifying interest in possession even if the holder of that interest is the surviving spouse of the former life tenant.

Disabled person's interest

61.10 A disabled person's interest is an interest in possession to which a disabled person is entitled, the term disabled person requiring the disability to exist when the property is transferred into settlement (IHTA 1984, ss 89(4) and 89B(c)). For these purposes, an individual counts as disabled if incapable under the Mental Health Act 1983 or if in receipt of an attendance allowance or disability allowance (IHTA 1984, s 89(4)).

The term 'disabled person's interest' also includes the settlor's life interest under a settlement created by him in reasonable anticipation of his incapacity (IHTA 1984, s 89A). The term extends as well to the deemed interest in possession which subsists in discretionary trusts where during the life of a disabled person over half of any applications of the settled property must be for his benefit (IHTA 1984, s 89).

The provisions relating to disabled person's interests are not confined to UK resident trusts. It will be interesting to see whether any offshore trusts take advantage of them.

MEANING OF 'INTEREST IN POSSESSION'

61.11 To fall within one of the categories described above, the beneficiary's interest must in fact be an interest in possession. That term is not defined in the legislation. Case law indicates that the holder of the interest must have a present right of present enjoyment (*Pearson v IRC* [1980] STC 318, HL). In other words any income of the settled property must be his as it arises. Should the trustees have power to accumulate the income, or pay it to other beneficiaries, it is not his as it arises, for the trustees must have reasonable time within which to consider and, if thought fit, exercise those powers (cf para 8.10).

The most common form of interest in possession is a life interest. But an entitlement to income for a term of years or during somebody else's life is also an interest in possession. It is clear too that an interest is not prevented from being an interest in possession just because the trustees have overriding powers over the capital. What matters is that the holder is entitled to all income that arises before the power is exercised.

An area of controversy has been whether an interest in possession is created if trustees simply allow a beneficiary to use property, as where the trustees provide the beneficiary with a home. HMRC's view is that a licence by trustees to a beneficiary to occupy property, whether formal or otherwise, can result in an interest in possession unless the beneficiary pays at least some consideration (SP 10/79). Case law indicates that if the settlement obliges the trustees to allow the beneficiary to occupy the property he does indeed have an interest in possession (*IRC v Lloyds Private Banking Ltd* [1998] STC 559). But he has no such interest if his occupation is in the discretion of the trustees. A Special Commissioner so decided in *Judge v Revenue and Customs Comrs* [2005] STC (SCD) 863, a decision not appealed by HMRC.

TREATMENT OF QUALIFYING INTERESTS IN POSSESSION

61.12 As indicated at the beginning of this chapter, property in which a qualifying interest in possession subsists is not relevant property. Instead, for IHT purposes, the holder of the interest is treated as beneficial owner of the underlying trust assets (IHTA 1984, s 49).

This has two principal IHT consequences:

(1)   On death, the property subject to the life interest is included in the life tenant's estate.

(2)   The termination of the life interest is treated as an inter vivos transfer of the underlying settled property (IHTA 1984, s 52).

Death

61.13 As the settled property is treated as being in the life tenant's estate it is subject to IHT at 40% (once his nil-rate band is exceeded) unless some relief such as business property relief is in point. Liability for the IHT is primarily that of the trustees (IHTA 1984, s 200(1)(b)).

The spouse exemption applies provided that the property passes to the life tenant's spouse absolutely on his death and the spouse is domiciled or deemed domiciled in the UK (IHTA 1984, s 18). The spouse exemption does not apply if she takes a successive life interest unless her interest counts as a TSI. As explained above (para **61.6**), that condition is only met if the deceased's interest in possession arose before 22 March 2006. Save where that condition is met, the death of the interest holder results in IHT at the death rate and entry into the relevant property regime.

Inter vivos termination

61.14 The inter vivos termination of a qualifying interest in possession does not result in IHT if or to the extent that the holder of the interest becomes absolutely entitled to the property (IHTA 1984, s 53(2)). The same applies where the life tenant's spouse becomes absolutely entitled to the property (IHTA 1984, s 53(4)). But this does not apply if the spouse does not have an actual or a deemed UK domicile or if she had acquired the reversionary interest for money or money's worth (IHTA 1984, s 53(5)).

Where somebody else becomes absolutely entitled to the property on the termination, the exercise is a potentially exempt transfer or PET. This result follows because the termination is treated as a gift by the life tenant under the PET rules (IHTA 1984, s 3A(7)) and the property, being the absolute property of the reversioner, becomes comprised in his estate (IHTA 1984, s 3A(2)(a)). As a PET, IHT is only chargeable should the former life tenant fail to survive seven years.

Where the property remains settled, the termination of the qualifying interest in possession causes the property to move into the relevant property regime. An entry charge at 20% results insofar as the former life tenant's nil-rate band or other reliefs such as business property relief are not available. Now that the time limit for creating transitional serial interests has expired, this is so even if there is a successive life interest. There was an argument that this result was avoided where the same life tenant took the successive interest in possession but an amendment introduced in 2008 removed this argument (IHTA 1986, s 53(2A) as amended by FA 2008, s 140).

Excluded property

61.15 All the above IHT charges are avoided if and to the extent that the settled property is excluded property. The life tenant's domicile is immaterial in determining excluded property status. As explained in CHAPTER 62, the issue instead turns on the domicile or deemed domicile of the settlor when the settlement was made.

ACCUMULATION AND MAINTENANCE TRUSTS

61.16 Accumulation and maintenance trusts were a feature of the original CTT legislation. For a trust to qualify one or more beneficiaries had, on or before attaining 25, to become entitled to the settled property or to an interest in possession in it (IHTA 1984, s 71(1)(a)). Until then the income had to be accumulated save insofar as used for the maintenance, education, or benefit of the beneficiaries (IHTA 1984, s 71(1)(b)).

All accumulation and maintenance trusts created on or after 22 March 2006 are now within the relevant property regime and thus do not qualify for any special treatment. This is so whether the accumulation and maintenance trust was created by way of original settlement or by appointment under existing trusts.

Accumulation and maintenance trusts created before 22 March 2006 remained outside the relevant property regime until 5 April 2008. But on 6 April 2008, all such accumulation and maintenance trusts become relevant property and so subject to 10-yearly and exit charges (FA 2006, Sch 20 para 3). But uniquely, and generously, no entry charge was made on this deemed entry into the relevant property regime (FA 2006, Sch 20 para 3(3)).

As such trusts therefore no longer have any special status, they are not discussed any further here. Readers are referred to the nineteenth and earlier editions of this book, which contained a more detailed discussion of them.

TRUSTS FOR CHILDREN CREATED AFTER 22 MARCH 2006

61.17 As indicated above (para **61.16**), a trust for minors created after 22 March 2006 cannot secure relief as an accumulation and maintenance trust. It is within the relevant property regime save where two limited exceptions apply.

Absolute gifts

61.18 An absolute gift to a child is outside the relevant property regime because it does not fall within the IHT definition of settled property. HMRC accept that this is so even if Trustee Act 1925, s 31 is not excluded (CIOT Press Release 26 March 2007, reproduced [2007] STI 1120).

Bereaved minor trusts

61.19 What is called a bereaved minor trust is also outside the relevant property regime (IHTA 1984, s 71A). This is unlikely to be of relevance to offshore tax planning as such a trust can only arise under the will or intestacy of a parent of a bereaved minor or under the Criminal Injuries Compensation Scheme. The property must vest absolutely in the minor on attaining 18 (s 71A(3)(a)). But vesting can be delayed until 25, at the price of an exit charge when vesting does occur (IHTA 1984, s 71D).

Chapter 62

EXCLUDED PROPERTY AND SETTLEMENTS

INTRODUCTION

62.1 This chapter explains when property comprised in a settlement is excluded property and thus free of IHT. In general the rules apply both where the property would, if not excluded, be relevant property (see CHAPTER 60), and where the property is subject to a qualifying interest in possession (see paras **61.2** to **61.15**). It explains the law as it now is, and does not take account of proposed changes taking effect on 6 April 2017.

FOREIGN SITUS PROPERTY

62.2 Foreign situs property is excluded property provided the settlor was not domiciled in the UK when the settlement was made (IHTA 1984, s 48(3)(a)). This rule applies regardless of the form of the settlement and even if the settlor is among the beneficiaries. It also applies regardless of subsequent changes to his domicile.

Situs

62.3 The common law rules as to situs apply in determining where the settled property is situated. A point to emphasise is that the relevant assets are those held directly by the trustees. Thus in the common case of a trust holding its investments through a holding company, it is the shares in the company, as distinct from the investments the company holds, which must be non-UK situs.

Domicile

62.4 The rules as to deemed domicile described in CHAPTER 45 apply in determining what the settlor's domicile was at the time the settlement was made. However this is not so if the settlement was made before 9 December 1974 save insofar as property has been transferred to the settlement after that date (IHTA 1984, s 267(3)).

Who is the settlor?

62.5 The term 'settlor' bears its normal IHT meaning (IHTA 1984, s 44(1)). As explained in para **60.14** this definition is in substantially the same terms as the income tax anti-avoidance definition in ITTOIA 2005, s 620 (as to which see para **75.18**). It is expressly provided that where more than one person is settlor, the settled property is treated as comprised in separate settlements (IHTA 1984, s 44 (2)), although this is only insofar as circumstances so require. Thus a single settlement for the purposes of trust law may constitute two or more settlements for the purposes of IHT.

In *Hatton v IRC* [1992] STC 140, 159, Chadwick J pointed out that circumstances would require property provided by multiple settlors to be treated as separate settlements if it had to be determined whether any of the settled property enjoyed excluded property status. He further commented that where each settlor provided an identifiable or proportionate part of the settled property, each is the settlor of a notional settlement comprising what he has provided. But where what is provided cannot be sensibly apportioned or partitioned, each settlor must be treated as the settlor of the entire trust fund. Thus, on the facts of the case, where a reversionary interest had been settled as part of a pre-planned arrangement, both the original settlor and the settlor of the reversion fell to be treated as a settlor of the entire fund comprised in the settlement.

Additions after change of domicile

62.6 As noted above, under the terms of s 48(3), the settlor's domicile is tested only at the time when the settlement is made, and if he is non-UK domiciled and does not have a deemed UK domicile at that time, the subsequent acquisition of an actual or deemed domicile in the UK does not affect the excluded property status of non-UK situs property within the settlement.

However, HMRC take the position that if the settlor adds to the settlement after he has acquired an actual or a deemed UK domicile, its excluded property status is jeopardised (see *Tax Bulletin 27* (February 1997) p 398). The extent of the jeopardy is gauged by applying the provisions as to separate settlors in s 48(3) and the reasoning of Chadwick J in *Hatton* (para **62.5** above). If therefore the added property can be separated out, HMRC's view is that it represents a separate settlement whose assets do not enjoy excluded property status (even if situated outside the UK). If, on the other hand, the original property and the added property are intermingled and cannot be separated out, the implication is that HMRC would regard the whole settlement as having lost its excluded property status.

The HMRC view is very difficult to support as a matter of construction. This is because HMRC's position is based on the proposition that, for IHT purposes, a settlement is made in relation to any particular asset at the time when that asset is transferred to the trustees. But the case of *Rysaffe v IRC* [2003] EWCA Civ 356, [2003] STC 536 indicates that such reasoning is in error. As noted in para **60.11**, at first instance Park J expressly held that, where property is added to an existing settlement, both the original fund and the added property form a single settlement for IHT purposes (see [2002] EWHC 1114 (Ch), [2002] STC 872, 892). The Court of Appeal upheld Park J's judgment and nothing in their judgment indicates disagreement with this point.

There are also two further arguments against HMRC's view. One is that s 44(2), and *Hatton*, deal on their terms with the position where there are two settlors, not where there is one settlor who just changes his status. Second, the relevant property regime expressly provides that the commencement of a settlement is when property first becomes comprised in it (IHTA 1984, s 60). It thus implies that other property can subsequently become comprised in the same settlement.

Despite the strength of these arguments the Upper Tribunal has upheld HMRC's view. In *Barclays Wealth v Revenue and Customs Comrs* [2015] EWHC 2878 (Ch), the first settlement had been made when the settlor was non-UK domiciled and a second when he was deemed UK domiciled. The property had passed from the first settlement to the second and then back to the first. The Upper Tribunal held that the retransfer back was a disposition and thus itself the making of a settlement for the purposes of s 48(3). As the settlor was then deemed UK domiciled, excluded property status was not available. This case is discussed further in paras **62.11** to **62.16**.

UK ASSETS AS EXCLUDED PROPERTY

62.7 The categories of UK asset listed in paras **37.11** to **37.13** which are capable of being excluded property if owned by an individual can also be excluded property if settled.

Authorised funds

62.8 The rules in relation to authorised funds are the same as those which apply to foreign situs assets. Accordingly, shares in a UK open-ended investment company or units in an authorised unit trust are excluded if the settlor had neither an actual nor a deemed UK domicile when he made the settlement (IHTA 1984, s 48(3A)). The terms open-ended investment company and authorised unit trust have the meanings discussed in para **37.11**.

One of the provisions described above does not operate in relation to authorised funds, namely that described in para **62.11**, which requires the domicile of the settlor of both the transferee and the transferor settlement to be tested when property has been transferred between settlements (IHTA 1984, s 82). However, the settled property is still treated as comprised in the first settlement (IHTA 1984, s 81) and so the relevant domicile in testing excluded property status is that of the settlor of that settlement when it was made.

The rules described in para **62.19** below relating to interests in possession acquired for consideration by UK domiciliaries apply also to holdings in authorised funds (IHTA 1984, s 48(3B)).

FOTRA securities

62.9 Should FOTRA securities be settled the residence of the beneficiaries is the criteria for determining excluded property status (cf para **37.13**). The basic rule is that the securities are excluded property subject to satisfying the condition that all the known persons for whose benefit the capital or income of the settled property has been or might be applied are not UK resident (IHTA 1984, s 48(4)(b)). Prior to FA 2013, this condition was met if such persons were not 'ordinarily resident'. Since the concept of 'ordinary residence' was removed from the tax legislation by FA 2013, this condition (contained at Finance (No. 2) Act 1931, s 22) is now read as omitting the word 'ordinary', subject to one exception. FOTRA securities issued before FA 2013 was passed (on 17 July 2013) are subject to the original wording of the condition and therefore benefit from grandfathering. The wording of the condition is therefore less generous for FOTRA securities issued on or after 17 July 2013 than it is for those issued previously.

The condition requires the whole settlement to be looked at, and not just the trusts on which the FOTRA securities are held. Should the settled property have been transferred from another settlement the other settlement must be taken into account too, unless the transfer was before 19 April 1978 (IHTA 1984, s 48(5)).

These conditions are stringent and inter alia bar FOTRA securities from being excluded property where the only UK resident beneficiaries are long-stop beneficiaries who are realistically most unlikely in fact to benefit (*Montagu Trust Co (Jersey) Ltd v IRC* [1989] STC 477). But it appears that wide powers of adding beneficiaries do not breach the conditions as it is not known who might be added. Such is implicit in the Court of Appeal's decision in *Von Ernst & CIE SA v IRC* [1980] STC 111.

The domicile of the settlor is immaterial to the excluded property status of FOTRA securities. However, it can come into issue in determining whether investment into such securities triggers an exit charge under the relevant property regime (see para **63.9**).

There is one situation in which the residence of all the known beneficiaries does not have to be looked at. This is if the securities are subject to a qualifying interest in possession. In such case, only the life tenant needs to be non-UK resident (or non-ordinarily resident, in the case of FOTRA securities issues before 17 July 2013) (IHTA 1984, s 48 (4)(a)). In practical terms this means that FOTRA securities held by interest in possession trusts on 22 March 2006 qualify for excluded property status so long as the interest in possession existing on 22 March 2006 subsists or it is replaced by a transitional serial interest. But once those conditions cease to obtain the much more rigorous rules hitherto applying only to non-interest in possession settlements are in point. As a result some settlements may lose excluded property status.

Foreign currency bank accounts

62.10 The relief afforded to non-domiciliaries who are also non-resident in respect of foreign currency bank accounts (see para **37.12**) is in limited circumstances extended to settlements (IHTA 1984, s 157). It applies where the settlement is subject to an interest in possession and the holder of that interest is non-UK resident and non-UK domiciled. However, the relief only applies if, in addition, the settlor was non-domiciled when he made the settlement and the trustees are non-resident and non-domiciled.

Where it applies, the relief removes the account from charge on the life tenant's death. It does not relieve liabilities under the relevant property regime and so it is point only as respects qualifying interests in possession.

PROPERTY TRANSFERRED BETWEEN SETTLEMENTS

62.11 Most offshore trusts contain powers to transfer all or part of the trust property to another settlement. Normally such powers are expressly phrased as power to transfer funds to another settlement, but the same result may be achieved in exercise of widely drawn powers of advancement. It has been well settled since 1981 that as a matter of general law, the effect of such powers is to remove the property in question from the transferor settlement and subject it to the transferee settlement (*Roome v Edwards (Inspector of Taxes)* [1982] AC 279, [1981] 1 All ER 736, HL).

The issue that arises in the context of excluded property is how to apply the requirement that the settlor be neither domiciled nor deemed domiciled in the UK at the time the settlement is made. Does this requirement focus on the settlor's domicile at the time the transferor settlement is created, on his domicile at the time of the transfer, or on the domicile of the settlor of the transferee settlement at the time that settlement was created.

In investigating the issue a complication has to be faced, namely that a transfer between settlements can take one of two main forms. The first is where the transferee settlement is a genuine pre-existing settlement, sometimes also created by the settlor of the transferor settlement, but often created by somebody completely different. The second is where the new settlement is an ad hoc settlement created at the time of the transfer. This ad hoc settlement may be created by act of the trustees of the transferor settlement or by the settlement of some notional sum by a third party.

Relevant legislation

62.12 The legislative provisions that are relevant to this issue are as follows:

(1)   As explained in para **60.11**, IHTA 1984, s 43(1) defines the term 'settlement' as meaning 'any disposition or dispositions of property' whereby property is held inter alia in trust for persons in succession or subject to discretionary trusts.

(2)   As discussed in para **62.5**, the term settlor is defined in s 44(1) as including any person by whom the settlement was made, whether directly or indirectly, and anybody who has provided funds for the purposes of the settlement.

(3)   As explained above foreign situs property is excluded property unless the settlor was UK domiciled or deemed UK domiciled 'at the time the settlement was made' (IHTA 1984, s 48(3)).

(4)   The settled property is treated as comprised in separate settlements if more than one person is the settlor and circumstances so require (s 44(2)). As indicated in para **62.5**, circumstances would so require if property provided by one settlor would be excluded property and that provided by the other not.

(5)   As indicated in para **60.12**, the commencement of a settlement for the purposes of the relevant property rules is when property first becomes comprised in it (IHTA 1984, s 60).

(6)   When property passes from one settlement to another, IHTA 1984, s 81 treats it as remaining comprised in the first settlement.

(7)   Where s 81 applies, s 82 stipulates that the property transferred is not thereafter excluded property unless the settlor of the transferee settlement was neither domiciled nor deemed domiciled in the UK 'when that settlement was made'. This stipulation is stated to be in addition to the requirement that the settlor of the transferor settlement was neither domiciled nor deemed domiciled in the UK when the transferor settlement was made.

The first four of these rules apply generally and have formed part of the IHT code since the legislation was first enacted in 1975 (FA 1975, Sch 5 paras 1(2), 1(6), 2, 1(8)). The fifth, sixth and seventh rules apply only for the purposes of the relevant property regime and were first enacted in 1982 (FA 1982, ss 104, 121 and 122).

Who is settlor of the transferred property

62.13 The starting point in any discussion must be to establish whether the original settlor remains the settlor of the transferred property once the transfer has occurred. It is unlikely, at least in the majority of cases, that the settlor of the transferor settlement is a provider of funds in relation to the transferee settlement, as the reference to purposes and connection implies some conscious association between the provision and the settlement (*Fitzwilliam v IRC* [1993] 3 All ER 184, [1993] 1 WLR 1189; see para **75.23**). This may exist in some cases, but definitely does not in others, for example when the settlor of the transferor settlement has died before the transfer is effected.

This then leaves the more general words in the definition referred to above, namely that a person is a settlor if he has made the settlement directly or indirectly. Here, there is good authority that these words do mean the settlor of the transferor settlement remains settlor of the funds transferred even after the transfer. Thus in *Pilkington v IRC* [1964] AC 612, [1962] 3 All ER 622, the House of Lords was quite clear that on an advance into a new settlement the settlor of the original settlement remained the settlor of the funds advanced. Such was taken as given in *Barclays Wealth v Revenue and Customs Comrs* [2015] EWHC 2878 (Ch).

Lord Wilberforce analysed the position graphically in the latter case of *Chinn v Collins (Inspector of Taxes)* [1981] AC 533, [1981] 1 All ER 189, HL. His words were as follows:

> 'If it be said that there must be an act of bounty of the settlor and that the latter had fully divested himself of his settled property when he made the settlement, I would reply that his bounty was at that point incomplete, and became completed only when an appointment was made, thereby, as it were, filling in the names of the intended beneficiaries.'

The general rules

62.14 *Barclays Wealth v Revenue and Customs Comrs* [2015] EWHC 2878 (Ch) (supra) is authority that the excluded property status of the transferred property is tested by the domicile and deemed domicile of the settlor of the transferor settlement when the transfer is made. As explained in para **62.6**, the basis of the decision is that the transfer is itself a disposition and thus itself is the making of a settlement within the meaning of the IHT definition in s 43(1).

There is however a very real difficulty with this conclusion where the settlor has died, for the definition of excluded property provides that foreign situs settled property is excluded property unless the settlor was UK domiciled at the time the settlement was made. Self-evidently a dead settlor cannot be said to have a UK domicile. So if excluded property status is tested by the settlor's domicile at the time of the transfer all cases where the settlor was then dead would result in foreign situs transferred property becoming excluded property regardless of the domicile of the settlor when alive. That would be an absurd result. As explained below (para **62.15**) it may be displaced in relation to relevant property by IHTA 1984, s 82. But s 82 applies only to relevant property and so cannot affect the construction of the general rules. Indeed, as explained in para **62.15**, the terms of s 82 itself only make sense on the basis the construction offered here for the general rules is correct.

This point about dead settlors highlights a more general concern about the approach taken in *Barclays Wealth v Revenue and Customs Comrs* [2015] EWHC 2878 (Ch). On its terms, the legislation focuses on the domicile and deemed domicile of the settlor and this carries at least an implication that the focus is on actions he himself has taken. Why should subsequent events affect the issue, particularly as in some cases, even if alive, he may have neither knowledge nor input into those events?

There is plainly no clear and easy answer to these difficulties. However a possible solution is to fasten on the approach taken in *Barclays Wealth v Revenue and Customs Comrs* [2015] EWHC 2878 (Ch), but note that the IHT definition of settlement also refers to dispositions in the plural. It may be argued that the trusts on which the property is held following a transfer to another trust result not just from the transfer but also from the original settlement, for the latter defines the applicable perpetuity period (*Pilkington v IRC*, supra). There are thus two dispositions as a result of which the transferred property is held on the operative trusts, and it may not unduly strain construction to say the settlement is made at the time of the first disposition rather than the second.

It may be wondered why there is so much difficulty over the general IHT position on transfers between settlements. The answer, it may be suggested, lies in the fact that until *Hoare Trustees v Gardner* [1978] STC 89 it was far from clear, at least in the case of ad hoc settlements, that any exercise of a fiduciary power could result in a separate settlement.

Impact of the relevant property rules

62.15 As noted above, s 81 deems the transferred property to remain in the transferor settlement. This rule is expressed as applying for the purposes of the relevant property rules and principally has the function of determining when ten-yearly anniversaries fall. It has no impact on the definition of excluded property, as the definition of excluded property (s 48(3)) is not in the relevant property code (*Barclays Wealth v Revenue and Customs Comrs* [2015] EWHC 2878 (Ch), supra, para 37).

Section 82, of course, does impact on the definition of excluded property as it expressly so provides. But perhaps the most important point about s 82 is that it presupposes the excluded property status of the transferred property would otherwise be tested by reference to the domicile of the settlor of the transferor settlement at the time that settlement was made. As such it appears to presupposes the doubts raised above in para **62.14** have force. It may be objected that in fact all s 82 is doing is referring to s 81, and that regardless of the general analysis, s 81 alone would require excluded property status to be tested solely by the domicile of the settlor of the transferor settlement when that settlement was made. But this ignores the point noted above, namely that s 81 does not, when read strictly, apply to s 48(3) at all.

Regardless of whether that point is right, there are two views which may be taken of the construction of s 82. The first, which represents a natural reading, is that it focuses on genuine pre-existing transferee settlements and does no more than require the excluded property status of the transferred property to be subject to two testings, namely the domicile of the settlor of the transferor settlement when it was first made and the domicile of the settlor of the transferee settlement when that settlement was first made. To this view it may be objected that separate settlement treatment would apply under s 44(2) where the settlor of the transferee settlement is a person different to the settlor of the transferee settlement. But s 44(2) does only applies where circumstances so require and on no view operates where the same person was the settlor of both settlements.

The alternative view is that in referring to the time at which the settlement is made, s 82 is referring to the time at which the transferred property becomes comprised in the transferee settlement. On the basis of *Barclays Wealth v Revenue and Customs Comrs* [2015] EWHC 2878 (Ch), it is this view which is correct. The dead settlor point referred to in para **62.14** is not of itself an argument against this view, for if the settlor is dead he is by definition not domiciled in the UK at all, with the result that, s 82 has no effect and the sole determinant of excluded property status is the domicile of the now deceased settlor when he made the original settlement. But on this scenario there would then be fundamental differences of treatment according as to whether the settlor was alive or dead when the transfer was made. It is curious, to say the least, that a transfer between settlements causes excluded property status to be lost if made in the lifetime of the settlor, but not if made after he has died. This illogicality falls away if the natural construction suggested above were correct.

In practice

62.16 On any view the law in this area is a mess. It must be kept in mind that views as respects both relevant and non-relevant property are divergent and that as matters now stand *Barclays Wealth v Revenue and Customs Comrs* [2015] EWHC 2878 (Ch) is Upper Tribunal authority that excluded property status is lost if at the time of the transfer the settlor of the original settlement has become domiciled or deemed domiciled in the UK. However, even on this view, the problem falls away if the transfer is after the settlor has died for, as indicated above, then he cannot satisfy the condition of being domiciled in the UK.

Authorised funds

62.17 As noted above, the deeming in s 82 does not apply to exclude property represented by authorised funds. The issues discussed here are therefore governed by the factors identified in para **62.14** above.

PURCHASED INTEREST

62.18 As explained in para **62.2**, excluded property status for non-UK property within a settlement depends only on the settlor being non-UK domiciled at the time the settlement was made – IHTA 1984, s 48(3). So it was possible, subsequently, for a UK domiciled individual to acquire an interest in the settled property without affecting its excluded property status. Legislation enacted in 2006 and 2012 counters the potential advantages arising from this.

The 2006 changes

62.19 The 2006 changes apply when a disposition is made for a consideration in money or money's worth and, as a result, an entitlement to an interest in possession arises, either directly or indirectly. If the holder of that interest in possession is UK domiciled, the trust property is not excluded property (IHTA 1984, s 48(3B)).

This provision does not apply if the disposition took place before 5 December 2005, and it applies only from the time of the disposition. But once it does apply, it operates for all time, even if the UK domiciled holder of the interest in possession ceases to be entitled to that interest or becomes non-UK domiciled. When read strictly, this rule is expressed in terms of the UK domiciliary being entitled to an interest in possession in 'the' property which would otherwise be excluded property. It is therefore arguable that if his interest terminates, and then the property comprised in the settlement is sold, the provision no longer bites.

This provision needs to be watched wherever excluded property settlements with UK beneficiaries are reorganised, as consideration may be given in money's worth, in the form of other interests under the same trust. Further, the consideration does not have to have been given by the UK domiciliary who has acquired the interest in possession.

The term 'interest in possession' bears its normal meaning and is not restricted to qualifying interests in possession.

The 2012 changes

62.20 There are five conditions that all have to be met before the 2012 changes apply (IHTA 1984, s 74A(1)):

(1)   One or more persons enter into arrangements. 'Arrangements' are widely defined to include any scheme, transaction, agreement or understanding (IHTA 1984, s 74C(5)).
(2)   In the course of the arrangements a UK domiciled individual acquires, or becomes able to acquire, an interest in settled property.
(3)   Consideration is given by at least one of the people entering into the arrangements.
(4)   At any time, there is a reduction in the value of the UK domiciled individual's estate over what it would have been in the absence of the arrangements.
(5)   The settlor was non-UK domiciled when making the settlement and the settled property is foreign situs at any time during the course of the arrangements. Alternatively the settlor was neither an individual nor a close company at the time the settlement was made.

Where these five conditions are all met excluded property status is lost for the settled property in which the interest is acquired, the 'relevant settled property' as it is termed in the legislation (IHTA 1984, s 48(3D)). This applies from the time the conditions were first satisfied onwards. Consequential changes (IHTA 1984, s 201(4A)) make it clear that the UK domiciled individual who acquired the interest is thereafter liable for 10-yearly charges (see para 60.3) and exit charges (see para 60.6).

The 2012 changes were enacted to counter some highly artificial schemes and their ambit is far from clear. A particular issue is what is meant by acquire: does it mean the UK domiciliary must proactively acquire the interest in the relevant settled property from somebody else who previously owned it, or does a mere fiduciary act by the trustees suffice? It may be suggested the former is right, for, if the trustees are able to make an appointment in favour of the UK domiciliary he already has an interest under the extended definition discussed above.

Another oddity in the 2012 changes concerns the giving of consideration. The giver does have to be one of the persons who enter into the arrangements, but, as is expressly provided, the giving does not have to be in any way connected with the UK domiciliary's acquisition of the interest. In theory at least, consideration given in an entirely separate transaction could be embraced, albeit that the giver has to be a party to the arrangements in the course of which the interest is acquired.

Despite these uncertainties the practical impact of the 2012 legislation may be narrow. The reason for this is the provision defining when a UK domiciliary has an interest in the relevant settled property (IHTA 1984, s 74C (2)). This is expressed in the same terms as in the income tax settlement code (see para 75.2) and thus includes any case where there are any circumstances in which the property or its income could be paid or applied to or for the benefit of the UK domiciliary. It follows that unless the trust has an overriding exclusion clause which excludes the UK domiciliary in all circumstances he has an interest in the relevant property for the purposes of the 2012 changes (see para 75.2).

The significance of this point is that under the second of the conditions enumerated in para 62.20, the 2012 changes bite only if the UK domiciliary acquires an interest in the relevant settled property. If, under the extended definition he already has such an interest, can any future event ever amount to the acquisition of such interest? It may be suggested not, for the definition of interest does not differentiate between interests: thus no distinction is drawn between an individual who could possibly be added in exercise of a power of addition and someone who really is a beneficiary enjoying income or capital.

Should the 2012 changes be engaged two further consequences follow. First, the UK domiciled individual is treated as having made a transfer of value of the amount of the reduction in the value of his estate over what it would have been in the absence of the arrangements (IHTA 1984, s 74A(4)–(8)). This transfer of value is not a potentially exempt transfer (IHTA 1984, s 74B(1)). There are detailed rules about the calculation of the transfer of value in s 74B. Further transfer of value charges can arise if there are subsequent further reductions in the value of the UK domiciled individual's estate over what it would have been in the absence of the arrangements (IHTA 1984, s 74C(3)).

The second consequence is that where conditions 1, 2, 3 & 5 in para 62.20 are met together with both the conditions below, then, any reversionary interest acquired by the UK domiciled individual is not excluded property (IHTA 1984, s 48(1)(d)). The two additional conditions which must both be met are:

- The interest acquired by the UK domiciled individual is a reversionary interest in the settled property to which the individual is beneficially entitled.
- The individual has, or is able to acquire, another interest in that settled property.

Authorised funds

62.21 The 2006 and 2012 changes both operate in relation to foreign situs settled property which would otherwise be excluded property. UK authorised funds, by contrast, are only caught by the 2006 changes. This is because under the fifth of the conditions listed in para **62.20**, the 2012 changes are engaged only if the relevant settled property is foreign situs. The only exception to this is where the settlor is a company which is not close.

INITIAL LIFE INTEREST OF THE SETTLOR AND/OR HIS SPOUSE

62.22 Trusts where the settlor or his spouse enjoy an initial interest in possession create difficulties in applying the excluded property rules. In the main the difficulties apply only where the trust was created before 22 March 2006.

IHTA 1984 s 80

62.23 Section 80 applies where the settlor or his spouse became beneficially entitled to an interest in possession in property when it was first settled. The rule it imposes is that the property is treated as becoming settled not then, but when the property is first held on trusts under which neither the settlor nor his spouse is entitled to an interest in possession. On that occasion it is treated as being settled by whichever of them last had an interest in possession. Section 80 thus not merely alters the timing of the settlement but also, where the spouse has a life interest, the identity of the settlor.

Section 80 applies only for the purposes of the relevant property regime. It is subject to three exceptions:

(1)   It does not apply if the property was first settled before 27 March 1974.
(2)   It does not apply if the property is first settled after 22 March 2006 unless the settlement is a disabled trust or a testamentary settlement giving the settlor's widow an immediate post-death interest (see para **61.9**).
(3)   It does not apply unless the interest is a qualifying interest in possession.

The last of these conditions was imposed in 2015 (F(No 2)A 2015, s 13(2)). By requiring the interest to be a qualifying interest in possession it restricts s 80 to:

(1)   Interests in possession subsisting since before 22 March 2006.
(2)   Interests in possession arising after that date which qualify as transitional serial interests. As it is explained in paras **61.4** to **61.7**, an interest in possession which came into existence between 6 April 2006 and 5 October 2008 can be transitional serial interest if the conditions in IHTA 1984, s 49C are met. So too can an interest in possession which came into existence after that date, but only if the life tenant's spouse had a prior interest in possession which ended on his death and that interest had subsisted since before 22 March 2006 (IHTA 1984, s 49D, see para **61.6**).

Non-qualifying interests in possession which would otherwise fall outside s 80 by reason of this change are grandfathered if existing on 18 November 2016 (F(No 2)A 2016, s 13(4)). Where settled property is subject to one of these grandfathered interests in possession, it is, as in all s 80 cases, outside the relevant property regime as s 80 deems the property to have not yet been settled. Equally the interest is not qualifying and so does not occasion a charge on the interest holder's death.

Impact on excluded property rules

62.24 As section 80 applies only for the purposes of the relevant property regime, it might be thought it has no bearing on whether or not the settled property is excluded. This point was made, in the context of IHTA 1984, s 81, in *Barclays Wealth v HMRC* [2015] EWHC 2878 (Ch) (see para **62.15**). On this analysis, the sole issue would be the domicile or deemed domicile of the actual settlor when the actual settlement was first made.

But IHTA 1984, s 82 assumes that s 80 does apply in determining excluded property status and thus that the issue of whether the settled property is excluded assumes the settlement is treated as made when the qualifying interest in possession of the settlor or the successive qualifying interest of his spouse ends and was made by the holder of the qualifying interest so ending. It then imposes an additional requirement, namely that the actual settlor was non-UK domiciled when the actual settlement was made. As a matter of inference at least, s 82 thus requires domicile to be tested at two different times and, where the final qualifying interest in possession is of the settlor's spouse, the test is on two different individuals.

It is unclear what domicile is tested if the final interest in possession is a grandfathered non-qualifying interest. Section 82 clearly requires the domicile or deemed domicile of the actual settlor to be tested as at the time the actual settlement was made. But it is unclear whether the second test is made when the grandfathered non-qualifying interest ends or when the prior qualifying interest ended. This problem did not exist prior to 18 November 2015, for then it was clear that the second test was made when the non-qualifying interest ended. But in such cases, it is unclear when the second test should be applied in determining excluded property status in periods after 18 November 2015. At the time of writing there is no published HMRC guidance on these obscure points.

A further difficulty with s 82 is that on its terms it applies only in testing whether foreign situs property is excluded property. UK authorised funds are not covered. As respects such funds, it is unclear whether the deeming in s 80 applies, so that domicile is tested when the qualifying interest in possession ends, or whether domicile is tested when the actual settlement was made.

A point to emphasise is that as s 80 applies only for the purposes of the relevant property regime, it does not alter whose domicile is taken account of, and when, so long as the settled property is not subject to that regime. Thus if the property is subject to a qualifying interest in possession, s 80 is not in point on the termination of that interest. In such cases, the only relevant domicile is that of the actual settlor when the actual settlement was made.

The FA 2006 trap

62.25 Prior to FA 2006, a non-domiciled settlor could ensure excluded property status was preserved in spite of s 80 by ensuring that after his initial life interest and (where appropriate) that of his spouse, the trusts were interest in possession or accumulation and maintenance trusts. They thus kept the settled property from being relevant property. As such s 80 was prevented from applying and accordingly it was immaterial if by the time the initial or successive interest ended the settlor or his spouse had an actual or a deemed UK domicile.

FA 2006 created two difficulties for trusts of this sort. The first concerns those trusts where an interest possession of the settlor or his spouse has been subsisting at all times since 22 March 2006, whether qualifying or non-qualifying. Here the property will move into the relevant property regime when the interest in possession ends or, in appropriate cases, where the successive qualifying interest in possession of the spouse ends. Once the initial or (as the case may be) the successive life interest ends, excluded property status is lost if the settlor (or as the case may be) his spouse then has an actual or a deemed UK domicile.

It is to be emphasised that this potential loss of excluded property status does not apply on the termination of the settlor's or the spouse's interest, for in neither case is the property at that time subject to the relevant property regime.

The second area of difficulty is trusts where the interest or successive interest terminated before 22 March 2006 and the ensuing trusts were interest in possession trusts in favour of some other beneficiary. If on termination the holder of the initial or successive interest had an actual or a deemed UK domicile, the settled property will in due course lose its excluded property status. If the present trusts confer an interest in possession, excluded property status will be lost once the interest in possession subsisting on 22 March 2006 and any transitional serial interest has ended. But the assets will still enjoy excluded property status (assuming the settlor indeed had neither an actual nor a deemed UK domicile when he created the settlement) at the moment of termination of such interests.

SPECIAL CHARGING REGIME

62.26 Several categories of trust which would otherwise be relevant property are not relevant property so long as they satisfy special conditions. Examples include charitable trusts (IHTA 1984, s 70), accumulation and maintenance trusts (IHTA 1984, s 71), 18–25 trusts (IHTA 1984, s 71D), and certain kinds of employee benefit trust (see para 25.8). Should any of these trusts cease to meet the requisite conditions a charge is made on the then value of the property (IHTA 1984, s 70(3)–(9)). The rate is 0.25% per quarter for each quarter of the first ten years during which the special conditions were met, 0.2% for each such quarter in the next ten years, and so on.

In contrast to the relevant property regime this charge is not in terms precluded where the property subject to it is excluded property. Instead the excluded property concept is recognised in computing the rate. A quarter is excluded if throughout that quarter the property was excluded property (IHTA 1984, s 70(7)).

This represents a trap for excluded property trustees who hold UK assets and replace those assets with foreign assets shortly before the moment of charge. A similar rule applies in computing the special exit charge on 18–25 trusts under IHTA 1984, s 71E.

Chapter 63

EXCLUDED PROPERTY AND THE RELEVANT PROPERTY REGIME

INTRODUCTION

63.1 The interaction of the relevant property regime with excluded property is of some complexity. This chapter explains the main points. It should be read with the general explanation of the relevant property regime in CHAPTER 60.

An important point to keep in mind is that the issues discussed in this chapter can arise even if the settlor and beneficiaries have no connection with the UK. What matters is whether or not the assets are excluded property. Inadvertence can mean trusts with no UK connection can own non-excluded assets on an occasion of charge.

As is explained in CHAPTER 62, settled property cannot be excluded property unless the settlor was neither domiciled nor deemed domiciled in the UK when he settled it. So too property owned by an individual cannot be excluded property unless the owner is neither domiciled nor deemed domiciled in the UK (IHTA 1984, s 48(3), see paras 37.8 to 37.14). Provided the domicile condition is satisfied it is conventional to assume foreign situs assets are excluded property and UK assets are not. But in reality the position is and increasingly will be more nuanced. This is for two reasons:

(1) Certain UK situs assets can be excluded property. As is explained in paras 37.11 and 62.8, the principal category of UK assets so treated is authorised funds, but in certain circumstances FOTRA securities can be comprehended as well (see paras 37.13 and 62.9).

(2) It is proposed that as from 6 April 2017, shares in non-UK close companies will not be excluded property to the extent their value is attributable to UK residential property.

Given these complexities, in this chapter the term 'chargeable asset' will be used to describe assets which are subject to tax regardless of the domicile or deemed domicile of the owner or settlor. Assets which are not so chargeable may be referred to as non-chargeable assets or, more simply, as excluded property.

An assumption made in this chapter is that any settlement is discretionary. In other words it is assumed any chargeable assets are within the relevant property regime described in Chapter 60, and that the only one of the exceptions to that regime listed in para 60.1 which in point is that for excluded property.

ENTRY CHARGE

63.2 On the assumption the settlor is neither domiciled nor deemed domiciled in the UK, the settling of assets into the settlement only attracts an entry charge to the extent the assets are chargeable. If therefore chargeable assets are avoided, the entry charge is avoided.

Interestingly, and in contrast to reliefs such as business property relief, there is no 'claw-back' should the individual making the transfer die within seven years having in the meantime acquired an actual or a deemed UK domicile. Nor is there a 'claw-back' if at the moment of such death the property is chargeable. Excluded property status in all these circumstances is tested solely at the time of the transfer into the settlement.

There however is one important respect in which the settlor is concerned with whether or not property in the settlement remains excluded. This is in point should the trust be settlor-interested. In that event the trust property is in his estate under the gift with reservation rules described in Chapter 83. When he dies such assets attract IHT at the death rates. So too any chargeable assets in the trust should he release his interest inter vivos comprise a PET.

10-YEARLY CHARGE

63.3 As is described in Chapter 60, the principal occasion of charge once the property is settled is the ten-yearly charge. But if on a 10-yearly anniversary all the property in a settlement is excluded property there is no charge. The result follows because the charge is made only on relevant property and that term excludes excluded property (IHTA 1984, s 58(1)(f)).

If, on a 10-yearly anniversary, some only of the property is excluded only the chargeable assets are taxed. As with all relevant property the rate of tax cannot exceed 6% as that is the maximum rate under the regime (see para 60.3). But the issue which may arise is whether the availability of the nil-rate band reduces that rate or even results in a nil charge. As is explained in para 60.3, the rate is the effective rate, arrived at by postulating a hypothetical transfer, with the result the benefit of the nil-rate band is available only if the nil-rate band applies on that hypothetical transfer. Here the law changed on 18 November 2015 (F(No 2)A 2015, Sch 1, para 7) and the present position is the nil-rate band is normally fully available.

This result follows because in almost all cases the sole element comprised in the hypothetical transfer is the actual chargeable assets as at the 10-yearly anniversary concerned (IHTA 1984, s 66(4)(a)). The hypothetical transfer is assumed to be of those assets and the rate is three-tenths of the inter vivos rate that would apply on a lifetime transfer of those assets. If therefore those assets are within the nil-rate band, the hypothetical transfer does not result in tax and the effective rate is therefore nil. So too if the chargeable assets exceed the nil-rate band, the latter is fully available in the hypothetical transfer and so reduces the effective rate.

There are however three exceptions, admittedly unusual, where the hypothetical transfer includes other elements. The effect of these other elements may be to eat into or remove the nil-rate band on the hypothetical transfer and so increase the effective rate, in some cases to the full 6%.

The first exception is in point if the settlor made another settlement on the same day as the subject settlement. As is described in para 60.3, the general rule is that the initial value of that settlement is included in the hypothetical transfer. This is of no consequence if only excluded property was in that settlement, for account is taken of only relevant property. But if there were chargeable assets, their value is taken into account, at their values on the date the other settlement was created.

The second exception is if the same-day addition rule has been engaged. This rule is described in para 60.3 and is engaged if on the same day there was both an addition to the subject settlement and an addition to another settlement. However the rule is engaged only if both additions were transfers of value and so is not in point unless both additions were of chargeable assets (IHTA 1984, ss 3(2) and 62A(1)). This excludes the rule in the great majority of excluded property settlements. But in the unlikely event both additions have been of chargeable assets, the addition to the other settlement is included in the hypothetical transfer and so too are any chargeable assets in the other settlement when that settlement first created, these assets being taken at their value as at that date.

The third exception is that two kinds of disposition are treated as previous transfers on the hypothetical transfer and so pre-empt the nil-rate band if and to the extent in point (para 60.3). The first is amounts on which exit charges have been levied in the past ten years, ie the value of any chargeable assets comprised in any exit charges in the past ten years. The second is amounts comprised in chargeable transfers, ie only transfers of chargeable assets, made by the settlor in the seven years prior to the making of the settlement. Should the settlor have subsequently added UK assets to the settlement, chargeable transfers in the seven years prior to such addition can also be taken into account.

As indicated above in the great majority of cases the result is account only taken of the chargeable assets in the settlement on the anniversary concerned. But a check is needed on the exceptions noted above to confirm this is indeed correct treatment.

Accumulations

63.4 Unaccumulated income which would otherwise be relevant property by virtue of having been kept in hand for more than five years (see para 60.5) is excluded property provided it is situate outside the UK (IHTA 1984, s 64(1B)). Its status as excluded property thus turns on its situs as at the 10-yearly anniversary and not on that of the property from which it arose.

Reduction by fortieths

63.5 As described above, once the rate of tax on the 10-yearly anniversary has been arrived at, it is applied to the chargeable assets. But where property which has previously been excluded is involved that may not be the end of the matter. This is because the rate is reduced as respects any particular item of property if that property was not relevant property throughout the previous ten years (IHTA 1984, s 66(2)). The reduction is by one fortieth for each complete quarter between the last 10-yearly anniversary and the date on which the property became, or last became, relevant property. The practical application of this, in relation to excluded property settlements, is that the rate of tax on chargeable assets will not be the full rate unless those assets or the assets they represent have been chargeable throughout the previous ten years. If for part of that time the value they represent was excluded property, fortieth reductions fall to be made.

THE EXIT CHARGE

63.6 As the exit charge is levied on the amount by which the value of the relevant property is reduced, a distribution of excluded property is not subject to the charge (IHTA 1984, s 65(2)). But if what is distributed is chargeable, the same computational complexity arises as with the 10-yearly charge.

Exit charge before the first 10-yearly anniversary

63.7 The hypothetical transfer used in computing the rate of tax for an exit charge before the first ten-yearly anniversary assumes a hypothetical transfer equal to chargeable assets in the settlement when first created and chargeable assets in any other settlement made by the same settlor on the same day (IHTA 1984, s 68(5)(a), (b)). The restriction to chargeable assets follows because the legislation looks only at relevant property comprised in the settlements concerned. The hypothetical transfer also includes the value of any chargeable assets added to the settlement, at their value when added, and more importantly, any chargeable assets which have been acquired in replacement of excluded property, valued as at the date acquired and taken into account regardless of whether subsequently disposed of (IHTA 1984, s 65(5)(a), (b)).

This last point is in contrast to the rules in computing the 10-yearly anniversary, where no account is taken of value which ceased to be excluded property over the prior ten years. As with the 10-year charge, same-day additions can be taken into account but only if and to the extent the addition to both settlements were chargeable transfers, ie comprised chargeable assets.

As explained in para 60.7, the rate of the exit charge before the first 10-yearly anniversary is as many fortieths of what would otherwise be the rate as there are complete quarters which have elapsed since the making of the settlement. A further reduction is made if the property comprised in the exit charge has not been relevant property throughout that period (IHTA 1984, s 68(3)). The number of fortieths is reduced by each complete quarter during which the property was excluded. In other words, if the chargeable assets comprised in the exit charge replace property which was excluded, the rate of exit charge is correspondingly reduced.

Between 10-yearly anniversaries

63.8 As is explained in para 60.6, the rate of tax on an exit charge in the 10 years following any 10-yearly anniversary is as many fortieths of the rate on the anniversary as complete quarters have elapsed since the anniversary. In light of this it might be thought that if on the last 10-yearly anniversary an absence of chargeable assets meant the rate was nil, such nil rate would also apply on the exit charge. But in reality this is not so.

The reason why is, that for the purposes of the exit charge, the rate on the ten-yearly anniversary is recomputed to what it would have been had chargeable assets acquired after the anniversary been held on the anniversary. This is so even if the chargeable assets have been subsequently disposed of and, at the very least, means the rate on the ten-yearly anniversary must take account of the chargeable asset comprised in the exit charge. The value used is the value when the assets in question first became relevant property, ie when the chargeable assets were acquired or first acquired.

In the unlikely event there have been same-day additions since the last ten-yearly anniversary, account is taken both of the addition to the other settlement and of the initial value of that other settlement. But as generally in this chapter, this is only required if both additions were of chargeable assets.

As with exit charges before a 10-yearly anniversary, the rate is reduced if the chargeable assets comprised in the exit charge represent property which was not relevant property throughout the period since the most recent 10-yearly anniversary. In such case, reduction is the same – complete quarters during which the property was excluded property are ignored in computing fortieths (IHTA 1984, s 69(2)).

Conversion of relevant property into excluded property

63.9 Generally, a reduction in the value of the relevant property of a settlement triggers an exit charge (IHTA 1984, s 65(1)). It might therefore be assumed that the conversion of relevant property into excluded property – for example on the transfer by the trustees of a cash balance from a UK bank account to an account with a foreign bank – would potentially give rise to IHT. In reality, this is not the case, as IHTA 1984, s 65(7) precludes an exit charge where relevant property becomes excluded property by reason of its foreign situs.

There is also express relief from the exit charge where the trustees use money in the UK to buy holdings in authorised funds (IHTA 1984, s 65(7A)). This change was made by FA 2013 and corrected an omission in s 65 which had existed since 15 October 2002 when authorised funds were first granted excluded property status. This new provision has retrospective effect (FA 2013, s 175) and HMRC, in their August 2013 newsletter, confirmed that where tax has been paid as a result of this omission, an application may be made for repayment.

A similar express relief applies where excluded property status results from investment in FOTRA securities and, again, this is available provided that the settlor had neither an actual nor a deemed UK domicile when he made the settlement (IHTA 1984, s 65(8)).

Section VIII

UK Income and Assets

Chapter 64

UK INCOME OF NON-RESIDENTS

INTRODUCTION

64.1 This chapter details what tax is suffered by non-residents on UK source investment income and how such tax is collected. The issue of whether income has a UK source is addressed in the previous chapter.

NON-RESIDENT COMPANIES

64.2 Both corporation tax and income tax have to be considered in relation to non-resident companies.

Corporation tax

64.3 A non-resident company is liable to corporation tax only if it is trading in the UK through a permanent establishment (CTA 2009, s 5(2)). If it is, corporation tax attaches to such of its profits as are attributable to the permanent establishment (CTA 2009, s 5(3)). The following profits are treated as so attributable (s 19(3)):

(a)   Trading income of the establishment.
(b)   Income from property or rights of the establishment.
(c)   Chargeable gains accruing on UK assets of the establishment or the trade carried on through it.

In determining its profits, the permanent establishment is deemed to be an enterprise separate from the rest of the non-resident company. Normal transfer-pricing principles then apply (CTA 2009, s 21).

Meaning of permanent establishment

64.4 CTA 2010, s 1141 gives the meaning of the term 'permanent establishment'. The definition reflects that in the OECD model double-tax treaty, although, interestingly, s 1141 is not expressly required to be construed in accordance with that treaty.

A company only has a UK permanent establishment if one of two conditions is met (s 1141(1)):

(a)   It has a fixed place of business in the UK; or
(b)   An agent has and habitually exercises in the UK authority to do business on behalf of the company.

In line with the OECD model, a place of management, a branch, or an office is deemed to be a fixed place of business (s 1141(2)). So too are building sites and construction projects. An agent is not regarded as constituting a permanent establishment if he is an agent of independent status acting in the ordinary course of business (s 1142).

In an important extension of the independent agent concept, not found in the OECD model, brokers and investment managers are deemed to be independent agents if certain conditions are met (CTA 2010, ss 1145 and 1146). This extension forms part of what is generally termed the investment manager exemption, or IME, and the conditions which must be satisfied are explained in para 64.21. The IME applies in relation to what are termed investment transactions, the meaning of which is also discussed in para 64.21. In relation to such transactions the exemption is exhaustive: in other words if the transaction is an investment transaction the broker or investment manager is not treated as an agent of independent status unless the conditions discussed in para 64.21 are met. Should the non-resident company engage in other transactions which do not fall within the exemption, the issue of whether in relation to those transactions he is an agent of independent status is governed by the general meaning of the term.

Income tax

64.5 Prior to the introduction of corporation tax in 1965, companies were, like all other taxpayers, subject to income tax. Liability was at the basic rate only, as no provision imposing higher rates extended to companies.

Corporation tax now displaces the liability to income tax of companies resident in the UK and of the permanent establishments of non-UK companies (CTA 2009, s 3; ITA 2007, s 5). But otherwise income tax remains chargeable on UK source income of non-resident companies. However, in practice, the liability of non-resident companies to UK income tax is limited.

Under current law, the reasons for this are as follows:

(1)   UK dividends are, in theory, taxable in the hands of a non-resident company at the dividend ordinary rate (ITA 2007, s 14). However the company is deemed to have paid this tax by virtue of ITTOIA 2005, s 399(2). The result is that no tax is in fact due from the company.
(2)   Tax on what is called 'disregarded company income' is restricted to tax withheld or deducted at source (ITA 2007, s 815). The principal categories comprised in disregarded company income are disregarded savings and investment income and disregarded annual payments, the meaning of which is given in para 64.13 below.
(3)   Apart from dividends, the most important type of disregarded company income is interest. As is described in para 64.15, most categories of interest paid to non-resident companies are free of withholding tax.

The practical result is that there are only two categories of income on which a non-resident company is likely to be subject to income tax, namely rental income from UK real estate and profits from trading in the UK otherwise than through a permanent establishment. In both cases, there being no contrary provision, the rate is the basic rate (ITA 2007, s 11).

The rental income of non-residents is discussed in para **64.20** below. Trading income subject to income tax is rarely encountered in practice as, if there is trading in the UK at all, it is likely to be through a permanent establishment. One potential exception to this, namely trading carried on through brokers and investment managers attracting the investment manager exemption, is removed from income tax liability as the income from such trading transactions is deemed to be disregarded company income (ITA 2007, s 816(1)(c) and (d)).

NON-RESIDENT INDIVIDUALS

64.6 In principle, a non-resident individual is fully subject to income tax on his UK source income. If the income is in excess of the individual's basic rate band, the excess is subject to higher-rate tax, and, if the amount is sufficient, the top rate may also apply. The general rule is that personal allowances are not available, but this rule is displaced for residents of the Channel Islands and the Isle of Man and EEA nationals (ITA 2007, s 56), and also where the effect of a double taxation treaty is to give UK personal allowances to residents and/or nationals of the relevant country. HMRC publishes details of the arrangements under which non-residents may claim personal allowances in its Residence, Domicile and Remittance Manual, at RDRM10340.

As with companies, the general rule is that non-residents are liable to income tax on UK source income, but the reality is that relatively few forms of such income actually give rise to tax charges. This is because the tax is limited to what it would be if:

(a)   tax on what is called disregarded income were restricted to tax withheld, deducted at source or given as a credit; and

(b)   any personal or similar allowances otherwise available were not made (ITA 2007, s 811).

As with companies, disregarded savings and investment income and disregarded annual payments count as disregarded income (ITA 2007, s 813(1)(a) and (b)). The meaning of these terms is discussed in para **64.13**, the main categories being dividends and interest. Also as with companies, disregarded income includes profits on trading transactions where the trade is carried on through a broker or investment manager qualifying for the investment manager exemption (ITA 2007, ss 813(1)(e) and 814). In addition, the term includes certain categories of pension and social security income (ITA 2007, s 813(1)(c) and (d)).

Where interest is concerned, the effect of the above rule is generally an exemption from tax. This is because, as respects most categories of interest, freedom from withholding tax mostly applies automatically or can be claimed (see para **64.15**).

In practical terms, UK source dividends paid to non-resident individuals are similarly exempt from tax. This is because the UK does not charge withholding tax on dividends. Dividends received by such individuals are in theory taxable at the dividend ordinary rate, but such tax is deemed to have been paid, so there is no actual liability (ITTOIA 2005, s 399 and ITA 2007, s 811(4)(b), as amended by the Finance Act 2016).

The overall effect of the above rules is the same as with non-resident companies, namely that the principal categories of UK source income on which non-resident individuals are chargeable are rent from UK real estate and profits of trades carried on in the UK (other than investment-type trades attracting the investment manager exemption).

The taxation of rental income is discussed in para **64.20**. Should the non-resident be trading in the UK through a branch or agency, the branch or agent is the non-resident's UK representative for tax purposes and as such is required to discharge the non-resident's compliance and payment obligations (ITA 2007, ss 835E and 835U). The term branch or agency is given a rather antiquated definition as being any factorship, agency, receivership, branch, or management (ITA 2007, s 835S(2)). The branch or agent is responsible not only for tax on the trading profits but also for tax on any income from branch or agency assets (ITA 2007, s 835E(2)(b)) and such cannot count as disregarded income (ITA 2007, s 813(2)). This is thus the one instance where dividends and interest accruing to a non-resident are fully exposed to UK tax.

NON-RESIDENT TRUSTS

64.7 The tax treatment of the UK income of non-resident trusts turns on whether any of the beneficiaries is resident in the UK.

Trusts with UK beneficiaries

64.8 Trusts with UK beneficiaries are the one exception to the reliefs for disregarded income (ITA 2007, s 812). All UK source income of such trusts is charged to UK tax at the dividend trust rate or the trust rate in the same way as if the trust were UK-resident.

The precise conditions which must be met for this treatment to apply are set out in ITA 2007, s 812. Section 812 is expressed in terms of liability for a tax year, so it is clear that the test falls to be applied on a year by year basis. Section 812 applies if in the tax year concerned there is a beneficiary of the trust who is either a UK resident individual or a UK resident company. Just one UK resident beneficiary, therefore, brings the trust into s 812.

Perhaps surprisingly s 812 then defines the term 'beneficiary'. It means any actual or potential beneficiary of the trust who satisfies one of two conditions. These conditions are as follows:

(A)   The beneficiary is or may become entitled under the trust to receive some or all of the income of the trust.

(B)   Some or all of the income could be paid or used for the benefit of the beneficiary in exercise of a discretion conferred by the trust.

On the face of it, Condition A addresses fixed-interest trusts, and Condition B discretionary trusts. But there is overlap between the conditions, as Condition A also embraces any discretionary trust under which the trustees have power to appoint interests in possession.

One issue that is not immediately clear is whether 'beneficiary' includes just those persons within the class of beneficiaries in the tax year concerned, or whether it includes anybody who could become a beneficiary at some time in the future pursuant to an exercise of a power of addition. The extension of the term 'beneficiary' to encompass any 'potential beneficiary' might at first sight suggest the latter construction. But in reality this cannot be right, for until a person is added he is not a beneficiary at all. The term 'potential beneficiary' is better construed as meaning a member of the class who could benefit but has not done so yet. HMRC have accepted the correctness of this in relation to the comparable definition in ITA 2007, s 873 (see para **64.15** post). It is noteworthy as well that the term has been used in this sense judicially inter alia by Lord Wilberforce in *Vestey v IRC* [1980] STC 10, 15.

Another issue which is not immediately clear is whether s 812 affects the tax treatment of income enjoyed by a fixed-interest beneficiary, eg a life tenant. It must be regarded as fairly certain that it does, both because of Condition A and because s 812 is not in terms restricted to discretionary trusts. But on its terms s 812 applies only to income tax for which the trustees are liable. With fixed interest trusts the liability of the trustees is only to tax at the basic or dividend ordinary rate (cf ITA 2007, ss 479 and 480). Higher rate tax is the responsibility of the fixed-interest beneficiary, and so it follows that, if he is non-resident, he escapes this tax on such trust income as it is disregarded income. Further, the implication of cases such as *Baker v Archer-Shee* [1927] AC 844 is that any basic rate tax suffered by the trust can be claimed back by him (cf para 8.2).

Computational issues

64.9 In general, if a trust is within s 812 its UK income is taxed in the same way as that of resident trusts. However, two points should be noted as respects discretionary trusts.

The first is that only a proportion of the trustees' allowable expenses is available for set-off against the trust's UK income (ITTOIA 2005, s 487). The proportion is the same proportion of the expenses as the UK income bears to the total income. Allowable expenses in this context are those expenses which are not allowable in computing specific items of income but are set against income as a matter of general trust law (ITTOIA 2005, s 484). The law as to what expenses are allowable in this way is represented by *Trustees of The Peter Clay Discretionary Trust v HMRC* [2009] STC 469. HMRC's view is in the Trusts, Settlements & Estates Manual (TSEM8000 onwards).

The second point is that if the trust is discretionary, bank and building society interest must be paid under deduction of tax (see para **64.15**).

Other trusts

64.10 Non-resident trusts not caught by ITA 2007, s 812 (ie those without any UK resident beneficiaries) are treated in the same way as individuals in relation to UK income which is disregarded income. In other words, UK tax is restricted to tax withheld or deducted at source.

This does not mean such trusts are entirely free of UK tax. As with individuals, other categories of UK income are fully taxable, most notably trading profits (other than where the investment manager exemption applies) and rental income. Trusts with such income can offset it by allowable trustee expenses, but here the proportion of such expenses allowed is reduced. It is reduced by the part of the UK income which is disregarded income not subject to withholding tax or tax deducted at source (ITA 2007, s 487(5)).

Starting rate

64.11 The first £1,000 of the income of a discretionary or accumulation trust is not charged at the rate for trusts. Instead it is charged at the basic or dividend ordinary rate, as the case may be (ITA 2007, s 491).

This relief *does* apply to non-resident trusts. This conclusion follows because the rate is expressed as applying to the first £1,000 of the trust's trust rate income, which, while not defined, may be inferred to refer to income that would otherwise be taxed at the rate applicable to trusts. It follows that, in the case of non-resident trusts, it is fully available against UK source income and is not reduced pro rata by reference to foreign income. Further, where the trust is not within ITA 2007, s 812, it is fully available against the taxable UK income.

Should the settlor have made more than one settlement, the £1,000 limit is divided between them or, if there are more than five, reduced to £200 (ITA 2007, s 492). Non resident trusts are counted for these purposes, even those with no taxable UK-source income.

Settlor-interested trusts

64.12 Should a non-resident trust be settlor-interested, the income is deemed to be that of the settlor if it would have been taxable by deduction or otherwise if it had been his in fact (see para **75.25**). If the settlor is non-resident, the reliefs for disregarded income should be in point even if the trust has UK beneficiaries. An exception is however made for those categories of excluded income which are paid gross, for then, as no tax is paid, the income is not treated as the settlor's. These difficult issues are discussed further in para **75.26**.

DISREGARDED INCOME AND PAYMENTS

64.13 'Disregarded income' can be relevant for a non-resident company (para **64.5**), a non-resident individual (para **64.6**) and a non-resident trust (para

64.10). It consists of 'disregarded savings income' and 'disregarded annual payments'.

The term 'disregarded savings and investment income' is defined in ITA 2007, s 825. It comprises the following categories of UK income:

(1)   Dividends and stock dividends.
(2)   Interest.
(3)   Purchased life annuity payments.
(4)   Profits from deeply discounted securities.
(5)   Distributions from unauthorised unit trusts (distributions from authorised unit trusts are taxable as dividends: CTA 2010, s 617 and para 64.16).
(6)   Transactions in deposits.

There are three categories of 'disregarded annual payment', namely:

(1)   Annual payments not otherwise charged, ie those taxable under ITTOIA 2005, s 683.
(2)   Royalties from intellectual property.
(3)   Certain telecommunication rights, ie income within ITTOIA 2005, s 614.

TAX DEDUCTED OR WITHHELD AT SOURCE

64.14 The UK has several regimes for the collection of income tax on the UK-source income of non-residents. The more important are discussed below.

Interest

64.15 The principal section requiring deduction at source is ITA 2007, s 874. Section 874(1)(d) applies to yearly interest paid to a person whose usual place of abode is outside the UK. It requires the person by or through whom the interest is paid to deduct tax at the basic rate (currently 20%) and account for it to HMRC.

There are a number of exceptions to section 874(1)(d), of which the following are the most important:

(a)   It does not apply to 'short' interest, ie interest on a loan which cannot last more than a year.
(b)   It does not apply to relevant foreign income (ITA 2007, s 884). This means it only applies if the interest has a UK source (ITTOIA 2005, s 830). The exemption seems otiose, as s 874(1) is restricted in terms to interest arising in the UK, which must mean UK source interest. The issue of when interest has a UK source is discussed in para 40.3.
(c)   Interest paid by banks in the ordinary course of their business is expressly excluded (ITA 2007, s 878).
(d)   Interest on all quoted Eurobonds is exempted (ITA 2007, s 882). The term 'quoted Eurobond' means any corporate security which is listed and admitted for trading on a recognised stock exchange and carries interest (ITA 2007, s 987; see also HMRC Brief 21 (7 April 2008, reproduced SWTI [2008] 1175)).

(e) Interest on all gilt-edged securities is payable gross (ITA 2007, ss 877 and 893). Interest on other public revenue dividends is, however, subject to withholding tax unless the Treasury direct to the contrary (ITA 2007, ss 893 and 894).

(f) The element of discount on the redemption of deeply discount securities is not subject to withholding tax (ITTOIA 2005, ss 427–460).

(g) Section 874 does not apply to building society interest (ITA 2007, s 880).

(h) Section 874 does not apply to interest paid by a dealer in financial instruments who is authorised under the Financial Services and Markets Act 2000 (ITA 2007, s 885).

(i) Withholding at source may be precluded, or the rate of the withholding may be restricted, under a double taxation treaty between the UK and the country where the recipient of the interest is resident. In such cases the recipient may apply for the rate of withholding tax to be reduced to the level prescribed by the treaty (see Double Taxation Relief (Taxes on Income) (General) Regulations 1970 (SI 1970/488)).

Prior to 6 April 2016, bank and building society interest was excluded from s 874, but deduction at source was required under a different rule if the recipient was either an individual or a discretionary or accumulation trust (ITA 2007, s 851). However, this rule was abolished by the Finance Act 2016.

The rule in s 874 is displaced for non-resident interest in possession trusts if the life tenant is not resident in the UK and makes the declaration applicable to individuals. This result follows because the relief for non-resident individuals applies wherever the individual is beneficially entitled to the interest (see ITA 2007, s 858(1)(a) and para 8.3).

The rule in s 874 is displaced for discretionary or accumulation trusts if the trustees declare that the trust is not UK resident and that they have no reasonable grounds for believing that any beneficiary is UK resident. The term 'beneficiary' is defined in ITA 2007, s 873, in the same terms as apply in determining whether the trust income is disregarded income (see para **64.8** above). As with that definition, the issues arises of whether the reference extends the definition to persons who could be added as beneficiaries in exercise of a power to that effect. In this context, HMRC have stated publicly that it does not (see the Financial Intermediaries and Claims Office Newsletter No 3, January 1999).

Authorised investment funds

64.16 A distribution from an authorised fund is either shown as interest or as dividend. Should the distribution be shown as interest, the general rule is that tax must be deducted at source (The Authorised Investment Funds (Tax Regulations 2006 (SI 2006/964) (reg 26)). But this is disapplied if a reputable intermediary receives the interest on behalf of a non-resident or if the recipient is an individual and has made a declaration in the prescribed form that he is non-resident (regs 26(4), 27 and 30). Fixed-interest trusts can satisfy this latter condition if the life-tenant is non-resident. Such a declaration may be made by the trustees of a discretionary trust if the trustees are also non-resident and all actual or potential beneficiaries known to the trustees are non-resident (regulations 30(6) and 32).

Other income

64.17 Deduction at source is required from certain other categories of income, including annual payments, patent royalties and copyright royalties (ITA 2007, ss 898–917). The instance most frequently encountered used to be rent. It used to be the case that a tenant of UK property always had to deduct tax at source if he made payment direct to a non-resident landlord. Now, however, rental payments are governed by the rules regarding non-resident landlords described at para **64.20** and (as explained there) the landlord may now be entitled to receive rent free of any withholding.

UK REPRESENTATIVES

64.18 Many non-residents investing or trading in the UK use a UK representative of some kind. Such a representative may be a fund manager managing a portfolio, or a property professional looking after investment property. In either event the issue arises of whether the representative is assessable to tax on behalf of the non-resident.

Two sets of provisions have to be considered as regards this. One, ITA 2007, ss 835C–835Y and CTA 2010, ss 969–972, applies where the non-resident is carrying on any trade, profession or vocation in the UK. The other, ITA 2007, ss 971–972, applies to rental income. It is to be stressed that, apart from these two sets of provisions the investment income of a non-resident cannot be assessed in the name of a UK resident.

Traders in the UK

64.19 ITA 2007, s 835U applies to the branch or agency through which a non-resident individual or trust carries on the trade, profession or vocation in the UK. The branch or agency is what is called the non-resident's 'UK representative' and is assessable on behalf of the non-resident in respect of:

(a)   trading profits arising directly or indirectly through the branch or agency, and
(b)   income and capital gains from property or rights used by, or held by or for the branch or agency.

As UK representative, the branch or agency is under the same compliance obligations as the non-resident principal (s 835X). The UK representative has an express right to a full indemnity from the principal.

CTA 2010, s 969 makes comparable provision in relation to companies trading in the UK through a permanent establishment. The permanent establishment is the UK company's representative for the purposes of corporation tax as respects the establishment's chargeable profits.

These rules do not catch investment income or gains unless the income or gain accrues on assets of the branch or agency or permanent establishment. In theory they can apply where the investment activities themselves amount to trading in the UK. But this is precluded where the investment manager exemption is in point (see para **64.20**).

Rental income

64.20 A special scheme operates to secure the UK tax due from non-residents on UK rental income (ITA 2007, ss 971–972). As all non-residents are fully taxable on UK rental income, all categories of non-resident are subject to this scheme.

The scheme applies wherever the usual place of abode of the person receiving the rent is outside the UK. The legislation is largely enabling, permitting the necessary regulations to be made. The regulations in question are The Taxation of Income from Land (Non-residents) Regulations (SI 1995/2902). Somewhat confusingly, these regulations are expressed in terms of non-residents, but the term 'non-resident' is defined as a person who has his usual place of abode outside the UK.

Regulation 3 defines the UK representative of the property owner as:

(a)   such person as HMRC prescribe by notice, or (if none is prescribed)
(b)   such agent of the non-resident as receives or has control of the rent, or (if there be none)
(c)   the tenant.

The UK representative is required to make quarterly and annual returns. The quarterly return is a calculation of basic rate tax due on rent paid for the quarter and is accompanied by payment of the tax. Where the agent makes the return, deductible expenses are allowed in calculating the tax (reg 9). Where the tenant makes the return, the tax is calculated on the gross amount of the rent (reg 8). The UK representative is entitled to an indemnity from the non-resident in respect of any tax he pays (ITA 2007, s 971(4)). If the tenant is the UK representative, he does not have to deduct tax if the rent is less than £100 per week.

The non-resident can receive rent gross under the non-resident landlord scheme. To do this, he must make an application to HMRC and inter alia satisfy them either that he has complied with all his UK tax obligations to date, or that he has so far had none (reg 17). The non-resident must undertake to operate self-assessment in respect of his rental income and otherwise comply with his tax obligations. Any authorisation HMRC give for payment gross is revoked if these undertakings are breached. The non-resident landlord scheme is administered by HMRC Personal Tax international. They have produced a long 'Guidance note for letting agents and tenants' on the scheme which is available on HMRC's website.

THE INVESTMENT MANAGER EXEMPTION

64.21 The investment manager exemption (IME) was originally enacted in 1995 as FA 1995, s 127. Its prime and original purpose was and is to ensure that investment managers acting for non-resident clients cannot be assessed as the non-resident's branch or agent. It has since been extended to exclude assessment as a permanent establishment (CTA 2010, ss 1145–1150) and, as is explained above (paras **64.5** and **64.6**) where the exemption is in point, the non-resident client cannot be charged to tax either. The result of the exemption performing a multiplicity of functions is that it is now enacted, in more or less identical terms, in three other places, namely ITA 2007, ss 817–824, ITA 2007, ss 835H–835Q and CTA 2010, ss 1145–1150.

The IME is of great practical importance to the City of London and for that reason many of the concepts used in it are explained in a published statement of practice. This was first issued in 2001 and revised in 2007 (SP 1/01 revised).

One important point is that the IME as such is in point only where the non-resident's activities amount to trading (SP 1/01 revised, para 14). If this condition is not met, there can be no permanent establishment exposed to corporation tax (para **64.3**) and any branch or agent falls outside the definition of UK representative. It follows that in the context of offshore tax planning, the relevance of the exemption is limited to situations where a non-UK resident individual, trust or company is, or may be, trading in investments, where the transactions are arranged or executed by a person who might otherwise be regarded as a UK branch or agent. The revised SP 1/01 acknowledges that active management of an investment portfolio does not of itself normally amount to trading (para 19). However, modern investment strategies involving securities being held for short periods, a high turnover of investments and/or heavy use of derivatives arguably mean that there is a greater risk of trading through investments than was formerly the case.

The IME applies to brokers and investment managers. The following conditions must be satisfied:

(1)   The broker must be carrying on the business of broker or, as the case may be, the investment manager must be in the business of providing investment management services.

(2)   He must be acting for the non-resident in the ordinary course of that business.

(3)   His remuneration must be not less than is customary for business of the kind concerned.

In addition the following further conditions have to be satisfied by investment managers:

(a)   The transactions carried on through the investment manager must be investment transactions.

(b)   The relationship between the investment manager and the non-resident must be one between independent businesses dealing with each other at arm's length.

(c)   The requirement of what is called the 20% rule must be met. This is discussed below (para **64.23**).

Neither brokers nor investment managers qualify for the IME if otherwise a permanent establishment of the non-resident. But this requirement is relaxed as respects investment managers, in that the chargeable profits taxable by reason of such a permanent establishment exclude any otherwise within the investment manager exemption (CTA 2010, s 1152).

Investment transactions

64.22 As indicated above, investment managers only secure the relief insofar as the transactions are investment transactions. HMRC has power to designate by statutory instrument which transactions are to count as investment transactions.

This power has been exercised by the Investment Manager (Investment Transaction Regulations 2014 (replacing the Investment Manager (Specified Transactions) Regulations 2009 with effect from 8 April 2014, and operate by reference to the Investment Transactions (Tax) Regulations 2014 (SI 2014/685)).

Transactions in the following are investment transactions:

*   Stocks and shares
*   Securities
*   Units in collective investment schemes
*   Foreign currency
*   Debts arising from the lending of money
*   Relevant contracts as defined by CTA 2009, s 577
*   Life policies
*   Carbon emission trading profits

CTA 2009, s 577 defines relevant contracts as options, futures, and contracts for differences. Contracts relating to land cannot be relevant contracts and nor can other contracts whose underlying subject matter would not be an investment transaction (SI 2014/685 reg 3).

Other requirements only applicable to investment managers

64.23 In applying the independent relationship test, regard must be had to the legal, financial, and commercial characteristics of the relationship. HMRC consider the test is met inter alia if less than 70% of the investment manager's business comprises services to the non-resident (SP 1/01 revised para 40). They also accept that a parent and subsidiary are not per se debarred from satisfying the test.

The last of the requirements applicable to investment managers, the 20% rule, is primarily directed at hedge funds. In essence at least 80% of the non-resident or its income must be beneficially owned by persons who are not connected to the UK investment manager. But even if this condition is failed, the IME still applies to such part of the non-resident's trading profit as is attributable to the other connected parties.

Chapter 65

UK GAINS OF NON-RESIDENTS

INTRODUCTION

65.1 In general non-residents are not subject to CGT (TCGA 1992, s 2(1)). To this there are three principal exceptions:

(1)   non-residents with a UK branch, agency, or permanent establishment;
(2)   temporary non-residents; and
(3)   non-resident owners of UK residential property.

In addition, certain anti-avoidance legislation deems gains realised by a non-resident to accrue to a resident taxpayer. The principal examples are TCGA 1992, s 13, dealing with non-resident close companies, and TCGA 1992, s 86, which concerns non-resident trusts where the settlor is both resident and domiciled in the UK (see respectively Chapters 87 and 76).

BRANCH AGENCY OR PERMANENT ESTABLISHMENT

65.2 A non-resident individual or trust is subject to CGT if he or it is carrying on a trade, profession or vocation in the UK through a branch or agency (TCGA 1992, s 10). The charge does not extend to all the non-resident's assets, but merely to UK assets which are used for the purposes of the trade or are used or held for the purposes of the branch or agency. A deemed disposal of such assets occurs if the UK business ceases or in the event that the non-resident removes the asset from the UK (TCGA 1992, s 25).

The term 'branch or agency' has an old fashioned definition: it is any 'factorship, agency, receivership, branch or management' (TCGA 1992, s 10(6)). However any taxpayer wishing to overanalyse this definition should keep in mind Hoffmann's J observation in *IRC v Brackett* [1986] STC 521, 60 TC 134, to the effect that it is difficult to imagine a non-resident carrying on a trade in the UK with any degree of continuity doing so otherwise than through a branch or agency.

There is a curious carve-out to the definition of branch or agency, to the effect the definition does not include any person within the exemptions for general agents and brokers in Taxes Management Act 1970 (TMA 1970), s 82. This is curious because s 82 was repealed in 1995. It is unclear whether this repeal means the carve-out is of no effect, or whether it is it still effective and incorporates the former s 82 by reference. It may be suggested the latter is correct.

As described in para 45.3, non-resident companies are liable to corporation tax if trading in the UK through a permanent establishment. The charge extends to gains on assets situate in the UK and used in the trade or used or held for the purposes of the permanent establishment (TCGA 1992, s 10B).

TEMPORARY NON-RESIDENTS

65.3 The charge on short-term non-residents applies only to individuals and is described in paras 41.38 to 41.44.

UK RESIDENTIAL PROPERTY

65.4 UK residential property represents much the biggest exception to the general exclusion of non-residents from CGT. A limited move towards this exception was made in 2013, when ATED-related CGT was imposed on high value residential property which had suffered the annual tax on enveloped dwellings, or ATED. This is described in paras 66.23 to 66.28. A more general exception was introduced in 2015, in the form of non-resident CGT, or NR CGT; and it is with this that the remainder of this chapter is concerned.

NR CGT: PROPERTY CHARGED

65.5 The key point about NR CGT is that it is not a tax on all forms of UK real estate. The tax applies only if what is disposed of is a UK residential property interest (TCGA 1992, s 14A(1)(a)).

UK residential property interest

65.6 An interest in land is a UK residential property interest if it consists of or includes a dwelling (TCGA 1992, Sch B1, para 1(2)(b)). It is not however necessary that it be a dwelling at the time of the disposal. All that is required is that it was a dwelling at some point during the relevant ownership period. The general rule is that that period begins with the date on which the disponor acquired his interest in the land and ends the day before the date of disposal (Sch B1, para 1(4)). However, an exception is made where the disponor acquired his interest before 6 April 2015: in such a case the relevant ownership period starts on that date.

The legislation enacting NR CGT forms part of TCGA 1992. As a result the normal CGT rules apply in determining the date on which a disposal or acquisition occurs (TCGA 1992, s 28). The default position in relation to a disposal or acquisition pursuant to a contract is that the date of the contract is the date of the disposal/acquisition. But if the contract is conditional, including if it is conditional on an option being exercised, the date of disposal/acquisition is when the option is exercised or any other condition is satisfied.

The term 'interest in land' also extends to contracts for the purchase of properties 'off plan' (Sch B1, para 1(3)).

Dwelling

65.7 As will be apparent, the word 'dwelling' is the key component in the definition of residential property interest. The definition of this word presupposes a building and then provides that the building is a dwelling at any given point in time if it is used or suitable for use as a dwelling (Sch B1, para 4(1)). A building also counts as a dwelling if it is in the course of construction or adaption. A point to stress is that a building counts as a dwelling and so is within NR CGT whether it is owner-occupied or not.

A dwelling is taken to include any land which is occupied or enjoyed with it as garden or grounds. The language of this extension to the dwelling concept is similar to that in the CGT principal private residence exemption (TCGA 1992, s 222(1)(b)). But in contrast to that exemption there is no limitation by acreage. Thus owners of grand houses with extensive grounds will find that the entirety of the grounds count as part of the dwelling. So too does any building or structure on such land.

It will be apparent that the issue of when a building is a dwelling is left by the legislation as a question of fact. In most if not all cases the answer to the question will be obvious.

Exclusions

65.8 Certain types of residential building are deemed not to be used as dwellings and so are taken outside NR CGT (para 4(3)). The common feature these buildings share is that they are institutional or commercial and the list of exclusions thus specifically itemises schools, old people's homes, hospitals, prisons and hotels. There is also a sweep up provision that deems any residential building that is an institution not to be a dwelling (Sch B1, para 4(4)). It is however unclear what kinds of building qualify as institutional if not one of those specifically itemised.

Special rules apply to student accommodation. A building managed or controlled by the university does not count as a dwelling (Sch B1, para 4(5)). Other student accommodation does count as a dwelling unless it includes at least 15 student bedrooms (Sch B1, para 4(8)). It must be either purpose-built or the result of a conversion.

Temporary non-use

65.9 The general rule is that a dwelling remains a dwelling even if it is out of use or unsuitable for use (Sch B1, para 4(10)). But an exception is made for unsuitability if the unsuitability extends over at least 90 days and is involuntary (Sch B1, para 6).

Further exceptions apply to demolition or conversions. Should the building be entirely demolished it is regarded as ceasing to exist once demolished and so not as dwelling. The same applies where the demolition leaves the façade of the building in place if such retention is a condition of a planning consent (Sch B1, para 7). A building is also regarded as having ceased to be a dwelling if it is undergoing works to convert it to another use or is empty pending such works (Sch B1, para 8). But this treatment is only available if any necessary planning consent has been obtained or is granted retrospectively (Sch B1, paras 8(6) and 9).

Mixed use and change of use

65.10 In the real world many buildings are mixed use, for example shops with flats above, and the use of a building can change. As described below (para 65.11) these issues are dealt with by the computational rules.

NR CGT: COMPUTING THE GAIN

65.11 Fundamentally, NR CGT gains are computed in the same way as any other gain. This is because the general rules in TCGA 1992 are incorporated by reference (see particularly TCGA 1992 Sch 4ZZB, para 9(2), step 1).

There is one general modification, but this applies only in the circumstances referred to above, namely where the property is mixed use or has changed use. In cases of change of use straight-line apportionment applies, the gain subject to NR CGT being arrived at by applying to the gain a fraction of which the denominator is the total days in the ownership period and the numerator the number of days on which it is a dwelling (Sch 4ZZB, para 9). In the cases of mixed use the apportionment is not based strictly on the area which is subject to residential use, but is made on a just and reasonable basis.

A key feature of NR CGT is that it is not retroactive. For that reason, unrealised gains as at 5 April 2015 are not charged. The default method by which this is achieved is to deem the the disponor's interest in the property to have been acquired on 5 April 2015 at its then market value (Sch 4ZZB, para 6). In such a case only the period after 5 April 2015 is looked at to see if and when the building has been a dwelling, and the days taken into account in the time apportionment fraction are only those after 5 April 2015 (Sch 4ZZB, para 6(2)).

A disponor can elect for one of two alternative computational rules for property owned since 5 April 2015. The first is to use the actual acquisition date and the actual cost or, if the property has been owned since 5 April 1982, to treat that date as the date of acquisition, and to treat the acquisition cost as the market value of the property on that date (Sch 4ZZB, para 9). The second is to use the actual acquisition date and cost and then time-apportion the gain (Sch 4ZZB, para 8). The time apportionment is on a straight-line basis, using a fraction of which the denominator is the total number of days in the disponor's ownership and the numerator the days since 5 April 2015. It appears this time-apportionment is done before an apportionment for mixed use or changes of use, albeit that the days taken into account in the latter are just those since 5 April 2015.

One or other of these alternative methods is only in point if the disponor so elects (Sch 4ZZB, para 2). The election is irrevocable and must be made in the NR CGT return or the self-assessment return (para 3). If the property is or has been within ATED (see Chapters 66) time-apportionment is not available and any election to use actual cost and time of acquisition for the purposes of ATED related CGT applies also to NR CGT (para 2(2), (5)).

Losses

65.12 NR CGT losses are computed by the same rules as gains (TCGA 1992, s 14D(5) and Sch 4ZZB, paras 6(1), 8(1) and 9(1)). Losses may be deducted from NR CGT gains of the same tax year and, to the extent that they are unused, carried forward (TCGA 1992, s 14D). In the case of emigrants from the UK it is possible also to offset NR CGT gains with unutilised losses from the emigrant's period of UK residence, but only insofar as such losses arose on disposals of UK residential property interests (s 14D(2)(b)).

NR CGT: NON-CORPORATE DISPONORS

65.13 All non-resident individuals and non-resident trusts are within the charge to NR CGT (TCGA 1992, s 14B(2)). So too an individual is charged if the disposal takes place in the overseas part of a split year (s 14B(3)).

PPR relief

65.14 An individual using the dwelling as a residence can, in principle, avoid a charge to NR CGT on its sale by making a principal private residence election s 222(5). The same applies to trustees if a beneficiary so uses the dwelling (TCGA 1992, s 225). However, in practice, the scope for a PPR election is restricted. This is because the dwelling does not count as a residence in a tax year unless the occupier or his spouse is UK resident or he or his spouse spend at least 90 midnights in the tax year in that residence or in another UK dwelling which is owned by one or the other of them (TCGA 1992, ss 222B and 222C). In practice non-residents rarely meet this condition, as more than 90 midnights in the UK on a sustained basis is quite likely to entail UK residence (see paras **41.17** and **41.22**).

There is a trap for those who do spend more than 90 midnights per tax year in the UK without becoming UK tax resident. This is that the test for PPR purposes is not 90 or more midnights in the UK, but 90 or more midnights in the tax year in a dwelling the individual or his spouse own. This a trap that those with active nocturnal social lives need to be aware of, albeit that a midnight of absence counts as a midnight in the dwelling if the next midnight is spent in the dwelling (s 222C(8)).

However, it should be noted that a dwelling counts as a residence if the disponor's spouse spends more than 90 midnights in it or is UK resident. This is helpful for disponors whose family may be UK resident but themselves have a day count sufficiently low to avoid UK residence, or achieve the same result by the full-time work automatic overseas test (see para **41.6**).

Where the right to make a PPR election is available, it is exercisable in the NR CGT return (TCGA 1992, s 222A(6)). Emigrants from the UK who have made a PPR election when UK resident can vary such election when filing the NR CGT return (s 222A(5)). But such variation cannot apply if another residence affected by the previous election has already been disposed of (s 222A(4)).

Annual exemption

65.15 NR CGT is subject to the basic annual exemption in the same way as ordinary CGT. Thus in 2016–17 a non-resident individual's first £11,100 of NR CGT gains in a tax year are exempt (TCGA 1992, s 3(5)(b)). With trusts the exemption is half the individual exempt amount, or less if the trust is one of more than one made by the same settlor (TCGA 1992, Sch 1). The annual exemption is applied after current-year losses but before brought-forward losses (TCGA 1992, s 3(5BA) and (5D)).

Rate of tax

65.16 For individuals and trustees, NR CGT is charged at the same higher rates as apply to gains realised by UK resident individuals and trustees on disposals of residential property interests (TCGA 1992, s 4(2A)). Trustees therefore pay NR CGT at 28%. For individuals too, the general rule is that the rate is 28%. But the 18% rate applies if and to the extent that the individual's income tax basic rate-band for the tax year is unutilised (TCGA 1992, s 4(4)).

The basic rate-band is currently £32,000. In practice it is likely to be unutilised by many non-residents as it is applied after the personal allowance, and for non-residents only UK source income is taxable and so taken into account. But account should be taken of UK dividends and interest which otherwise count as disregarded income (see para **64.6**), as such income still attracts withheld tax or tax credits.

NR CGT: COMPANIES

65.17 In contrast to individuals and trusts, not all non-resident companies (or entities that are treated as companies for corporation tax purposes) are subject to NR CGT. Two categories may claim exemption from NR CGT, namely diversely held companies and widely marketed unit trusts and OEICs (TCGA 1992, s 14D). These important exemptions are discussed below.

Liability to tax

65.18 Where a non-resident company is subject to NR CGT, the liability is to CGT rather than corporation tax (TCGA 1992, s 14D(1)). In this there is thus a contrast with the charge where the company is trading in the UK through a permanent establishment, for in the latter case gains in charge are subject to corporation tax (see para **65.2** above).

But this contrast is a distinction without a difference. One reason is that in computing gains and losses, corporation tax rules apply. For the most part the corporation tax rules are the same as the normal CGT rules (TCGA 1992, s 8(3)), but there is one important distinction, namely that in computing gains, indexation is allowed (TCGA 1992, s 52A). Indexation thus applies to the NR CGT gains of companies.

Second and equally important, the rate of NR CGT payable by companies is 20%, ie a rate approximating to corporation tax rates rather than the normal CGT rate (TCGA 1992, s 4(3B)).

Groups

65.19 The normal CGT group relief does not apply as that relief applies only for the purposes of corporation tax (TCGA 1992, s 171(1)) and in computing gains subject to TCGA 1992, s 13. Instead there is a special relief allowing non-resident group members who hold UK residential properties to make a pooling election (TCGA 1992, s 188A). Once such election is made, no gain/no loss treatment applies on transfers of UK residential property between group members. More importantly NR CGT gains and losses across the group are consolidated (s 188D) and one group member may be nominated as representative company to handle compliance (s 188J).

ATED-related CGT

65.20 ATED-related CGT is explained in paras **66.23** and following. It applies to dwellings which are or have been within ATED and thus is of potential relevance to many non-resident companies owning UK residential property. In some respects it differs from NR CGT, most notably as follows:

- the start date for properties worth more than £2m was 6 April 2013 rather than 6 April 2015;
- corporation tax computational rules do not apply, so there is no indexation; and
- there is a fixed rate of tax, of 28%.

Perhaps because of these distinctions, ATED-related CGT has been retained alongside NR CGT. In the great majority of cases, a gain accruing to a non-resident company will be either wholly ATED-related or not ATED-related at all. But where this is not so, computational rues split the gain between NR CGT and ATED. Such splitting of gain between the ATED-related and NR CGT regimes is most commonly required where the dwelling has been subject to commercial letting to third parties for some of the relevant period but there have also been periods of occupation by the company's ultimate beneficial owner or connected persons (see para **66.19**).

The basic principle is that s 14D chargeable days are identified. These are days when the property was a dwelling but was not subject to ATED (TCGA 1992,

Sch 4ZZB, para 12(5)). The NR CGT gain is then a fraction of the overall gain on the disposal, the numerator being the s 14D chargeable days in the disponor's ownership period and the denominator the total days in his ownership period (Sch 4ZZB, para 12). But where the dwelling was held on 5 April 2015 and the default rule described in para 65.11 applies, account is taken only of days after 5 April 2015 (Sch 4ZZB, para 13).

If part of the gain is ATED-related, straight-line apportionment cannot be elected for in relation to a property held on 5 April 2015 (Sch 4ZZB, para 2(2)). Special rules apply to ATED-related gains where the dwelling only came within ATED on 5 April 2016 as a result of the reduction of the ATED threshold to £500,000 (Sch 4ZZB, para 15).

Diversely held companies

65.21 As noted above, diversely held companies can elect out of NR CGT. A diversely held company is simply a company that is not closely held (TCGA 1992, s 14F(10)).

For some reason, the familiar corporation tax definition of close company in CTA 2010, ss 439–454, described in para 87.2, is not applicable in construing the term closely held. Instead a separate schedule, TCGA 1992, Sch C1, paras 1–9 is devoted to the matter and in addition there are two anti-avoidance rules.

In broad terms the effect of Sch C1 is the same as ss 439–454, albeit there are distinctions which could prove material in marginal cases. Perhaps the main distinction is that in Sch C1 a company is not deemed to be closely held if it is under the control of participators who are directors. The question is thus whether the company is controlled by five or fewer participators or whether five or fewer participators would be entitled to over half the assets in any winding up. However, in most respects the same extended definition of control and attribution of associate rights apply as under ss 439–454.

The first anti-avoidance rule is that the separate divisions of what are called divided companies can be looked at separately to see if they are closely held (TCGA 1992, s 14G). The essence of a divided company is that the shares are in different classes and particular assets and liabilities of the company are allocated to particular classes of share. This rule is therefore directed at companies which, looking at the company as a whole, are diversely held, but where the various classes of share are closely held when viewed in isolation. It counters the potential for protected cell companies and similar cellular companies to be used to avoid CGT in this context.

The second anti-avoidance rule is a TAAR. It counters arrangements entered into if one of their main purposes is to avoid NR CGT by rendering a company diversely held (TCGA 1992, s 14F).

Widely marketed schemes

65.22 As noted above, widely marketed unit trusts and OEICs are also outside NR CGT. To count as widely marketed the unit trust or OEIC marketing must not be to a limited number of specific persons or groups of connected persons (TCGA 1992, Sch C1, para 11). Perhaps more importantly the unit trust or OEIC must produce documents explaining the intended category of investor and undertaking the shares or units will be widely marketed to such investors. This documentation must be available to HMRC.

The claim

65.23 As noted above, the exclusion of diversely held companies and widely marketed schemes requires a claim. It appears a separate claim is required whenever a disposal that would otherwise be within NR CGT is made (s 14F(1)).

COMPLIANCE

65.24 Whenever a non-resident makes a NR CGT disposal he must file a NR CGT return (TMA 1970, s 12ZB). This return must be filed within 30 days of completion (s 12ZB(8)). In practice such a short timeframe can be challenging, as the return requires a computation of the gain and valuations may be required.

The default position is that the NR CGT return must be accompanied by a self-assessment and payment of tax (TMA 1970, ss 12ZE and 59AA). But this does not apply if the disponor is already filing self-assessment returns (as he will be if the property was let) or has filed an ATED return for the preceding chargeable period (TMA 1970, s 12ZG). In that event the deadline for payment is the normal deadline of 31 January in the following tax year.

Chapter 66

ATED AND ATED-RELATED CGT

INTRODUCTION

66.1 The Annual Tax on Enveloped Dwellings or ATED was enacted by FA 2013, ss 94–174 and took effect as respects dwellings worth more than £2m from 1 April 2013. It was extended to lower value dwellings by FA 2014, ss 109 and 110 with effect from 1 April 2015 (£1m threshold) and 1 April 2016 (£500,000 threshold). Liability to ATED is not confined to non-UK resident entities, but non-resident companies were its primary target.

ATED is accompanied by a further tax, ATED-related CGT, also enacted in 2013 (TCGA 1992, ss 2B–2F). Despite the fact that all foreign owned properties within ATED-related CGT would otherwise be within NR CGT, ATED-related CGT was retained when NR CGT was introduced in 2015. ATED-related CGT applies to properties that have been subject to ATED at some point in the existence of that tax, and is described at the end of this chapter.

Useful practical guidance to ATED is provided by HMRC's returns guidance notice, HMRC's basic guidance, and HMRC's guidance on valuations of property. All this guidance was published on 24 August 2015 (HMRC Guidance Notes 24 August 2015, reproduced [2015] SWTI, pp 2591–2608).

WHO IS LIABLE TO ATED

66.2 Liability to ATED is confined to three categories of person (FA 2013, s 94(2)), namely:

* companies;
* partnerships; and
* collective investment schemes.

Such entities are subject to ATED whether resident or non-resident. However, a partnership is only caught if one or more partners is a company (s 94(5)).

The term collective investment scheme bears the meaning given by s 235 of the Financial Services and Markets Act 2000 (FA 2013, s 174(1)). The term thus includes onshore and offshore unit trusts and OEICs. In contrast to NR CGT, there is no exclusion of widely marketed schemes.

The term company includes any body corporate other than a partnership (FA 2013, s 166). Again in contrast to NR CGT, there is no exclusion of diversely held companies. Corporate trustees acting as such are expressly excluded (s 95(2)).

The term partnership includes partnerships formed under the Partnership Act 1890, limited partnerships formed under the Limited Partnerships Act 1907 and LLPs formed under the Limited Liability Partnership Act 2000 (FA 2013, s 167). The term also extends to a firm or entity formed under non-UK law if the same is of similar character to any of the above types of UK partnership (s 167(1)(d)). This means that non-UK entities which might otherwise be regarded as companies count as partnerships for ATED purposes if they are of similar character to a UK LLP. As for ATED purposes, the term 'company' excludes partnerships. Such entities are therefore entirely outside ATED, unless one of the members is itself a company.

WHAT IS LIABLE TO ATED

66.3 ATED is not chargeable unless a person within one of the above categories holds a chargeable interest which is a single dwelling interest (FA 2013, s 94(2)). In broad terms a chargeable interest is simply an estate or interest in land in the UK (FA 2013, s 107). So the key issue is what is meant by single dwelling interest.

Single dwelling interest

66.4 An estate or interest in land is a single dwelling interest if the land consists of a single dwelling (FA 2013, s 108(2)). If the interest is in two or more dwellings it is treated as a separate single dwelling interest in each of them (s 108(3)). If the interest is in both residential and non-residential land, it is treated as being a separate single dwelling interest in just the residential part (s 108(4)).

Dwelling

66.5 As with NR CGT, the key concept is the term dwelling. And again as with NR CGT, the definition of dwelling is something of a non-definition: a building is a dwelling if it is used or suitable for use as a single dwelling (FA 2013, s 112(1)). As the definition is expressed in terms of part of a building as well as a building as a whole, it catches individual flats as well as houses.

Gardens and grounds are dealt with in the same way as under NR CGT (s 112(2)): land occupied with the dwelling as garden or grounds counts as part of the dwelling. There is no limitation by area.

Certain types of institutional use are excluded from the term dwelling. The list of exclusions is formulated by reference to the SDLT rules in FA 2003, s 116 (see para 67.4). But the overall effect is that the exclusions cover much the same ground as the equivalent exclusions for NR CGT, albeit that the rules for student accommodation differ.

Unavailability for use

66.6 Where a property is temporarily unsuitable for use as a dwelling, because of accidental damage, repairs or other physical change to the building, that temporary unsuitability is ignored (FA 2013, s 112(6)). While a property might, for example, therefore be uninhabitable during major renovation works, it is nonetheless still regarded as a dwelling for ATED purposes.

A demolished dwelling may be treated as still in existence depending on the intentions for the site. If the intention is to replace the dwelling with a new dwelling or dwellings, the original dwelling is deemed to be still in existence until the new dwelling or dwellings are regarded as coming into existence for Council Tax purposes or, if earlier, are first occupied (FA 2013, s 128). If there is no intention to replace the dwelling, the dwelling ceases to be within the scope of ATED from the date that demolition is begun and the building has become unsuitable for use. The owning company must notify HMRC that there is no proposal to construct any dwelling or dwellings on the site in its ATED return or by amendment to the return (FA 2013, s 127).

Associated dwellings

66.7 Where there is more than one dwelling within the grounds of a single property, the main dwelling and any 'associated dwelling' are aggregated and treated as a single dwelling. But this only applies if the associated dwellings do not have their own separate access and if they are in 'common ownership' (FA 2013, s 116). It does not apply if either of the dwellings are within the reliefs for relievable days (para **66.18** below).

Buildings are regarded as in common ownership not only if they are owned by the same company, but also if one is owned by the company and the other by a person connected with the company. The term 'separate access' means a separate access directly from the highway or a formal right of way from the highway to the dwelling (FA 2013, s 116(9)).

It is sometimes beneficial for the two properties held by the same company to be aggregated, for example, where one dwelling is worth £2.5m and the other £2.2m. If aggregated, they will be within the £2m to £5m band, whereas if they were regarded as separate dwellings, but both still owned by the same company, they would each be in the same band and each charged, resulting in double the charge.

Linked dwellings

66.8 What are termed 'linked dwellings', for example, two or more apartments within the same building, may be treated as a single dwelling if they are all owned by the company and persons connected with the company. Such treatment applies if there is private access between the dwellings and the use condition is met (FA 2013, s 117).

The use condition is met if each of the dwellings is occupied by a relevant individual, is intended to be occupied by a relevant individual or is not occupied at all (FA 2013, s 118(4)). A 'relevant individual' for these purposes means an individual connected with the company, someone who occupies on less than commercial terms, or an employee of the person in occupation of the other dwelling (FA 2013, s 118(5)). A typical example of linked dwellings would be adjacent apartments with interconnecting doors, one owned by a company and the other by the company or by the controlling shareholder or his relative.

Time of acquisition or disposal

66.9 In contrast to CGT, the time at which a chargeable interest is treated as disposed of or acquired for ATED purposes is, by default, completion of the sale/purchase rather than the date of contract (FA 2013, s 121). But an exception applies where the contract is substantially performed prior to completion; in such a case, the date of substantial performance is the date of acquisition or disposal (FA 2013, ss 122 and 123). Substantial performance bears the same meaning as for SDLT and thus connotes either the purchaser taking possession of the property or paying a substantial amount of the consideration (FA 2003, s 44).

The date on which an acquisition takes place under these rules is referred to as the effective date (FA 2013, s 121).

THE VALUATION THRESHOLD

66.10 For ATED in fact to be chargeable, a single dwelling interest must meet one further condition, namely that its taxable value must exceed a prescribed valuation threshold (FA 2013, s 94(2)(a)). When ATED was first introduced, this threshold was £2m. With effect from 1 April 2015 the threshold was reduced to £1m, and since 1 April 2016 the threshold has been £500,000.

TAXABLE VALUE

66.11 The taxable value of a single dwelling interest is its market value (FA 2013, s 102(1)). The term market value bears the same meaning as it has for CGT purposes and thus means the price which the chargeable interest might be expected to realise in a sale on the open market (FA 2013, s 98(8); TCGA 1992, s 272(1)).

Valuation dates

66.12 The taxable value is not determined each year. Instead a quinquennial regime applies, ie a valuation date occurs every five years. The first valuation date was 1 April 2012 (not 2013) and the next one is thus 1 April 2017 (FA 2013, s 102(2)). The 2012 valuations apply until 31 March 2018, and then the 2017 valuations kick in (s 102(2A)). The five-year periods for which valuations apply are thus one year in arrear to the valuations themselves.

There are important exceptions to the quinquennial regime, in that certain events between valuation dates can require a different valuation to be substituted for the remainder of the applicable five-year period. Thus if a taxable entity acquires a single-dwelling interest between quinquennial valuation dates, the effective date of that transaction is treated as the valuation date for the purposes of ATED, under the 'substantial acquisition' rule at FA 2013, s 103.

This rule extends to any 'substantial acquisition' of a chargeable interest in a dwelling, ie any acquisition where the consideration given by the person acquiring the interest exceeds a de minimis threshold of £40,000. As such, the acquisition of a parcel of neighbouring land or an adjacent property, to be used and enjoyed with the existing dwelling, or the extension of an existing lease, is a substantial acquisition if the consideration exceeds £40,000. Transactions between persons who are connected to each other or not at arm's length are treated as made at market value. Self-evidently a revaluation pursuant to this rule can result in the property in question moving up to the next ATED band for the reminder of the quinquennial period.

There is a similar rule for 'substantial disposals' of part of a single-dwelling interest between quinquennial valuation dates, again subject to the £40,000 de minimis threshold (FA 2013, s 102(3)). Thus the disposal of the part of a garden or the grant of a lease can be a substantial disposal and so trigger a revaluation. Even though the new valuation is triggered by a part disposal it may result in the property moving up to a higher ATED band if the property has increased in value since the last valuation.

A point to stress is that the valuation resulting from the substantial acquisition or disposal is superseded once the next quinquennial valuation kicks in.

Aggregation

66.13 Different interests acquired by the same company in the same dwelling are aggregated for valuation purposes (FA 2013, s 109). Their value is taken to be the value of the interests as an aggregate rather than the sum of the parts (s 109(3)). Marriage value is thus included in determining whether the combined interest is within ATED, and if it is in what band.

Where one interest in a single dwelling is owned by a chargeable person and another interest in the same dwelling is owned by a connected person, the taxable value of the connected person's interest is aggregated with the taxable value of the interest held by the chargeable person for ATED purposes (FA 2013, s 110). Thus where a company has a lease of a single dwelling and the shareholder of the company personally holds either the freehold or a reversionary lease (or vice versa), the value of the shareholder's interest in the property is aggregated with that of the company. Similarly, where the company owns 50% of a single dwelling and the shareholder the other 50%, the value of the shareholder's interest in the dwelling is aggregated with that of the company. In both cases the whole value of the property is subject to ATED.

Aggregation with other interests owned by individuals cannot apply if the value of the company's interest is worth less than £250,000. Should the dwelling be worth more than £2m, aggregation is precluded unless the company's interest is worth more than £500,000 (FA 2013, s 110(2), (2A); see also Valuation of Property Guidance). This protects inter alia cases where a company owns the freehold and the individual(s) one or more long leases.

Aggregation is not precluded under the de minimis rule where the other interest or interests are owned by trusts. However it appears that in such cases aggregation is not in point at all, regardless of how valuable the company's interest is. This is because the aggregation rule is expressed in terms of the connected person being entitled to the other interest(s) (s 110(1)). Entitlement is specifically defined for ATED purposes as excluding entitlement as a trustee or a beneficiary (FA 2013, s 95(2)).

Where separate interests in the same single dwelling are held by two connected companies, there is no applicable de minimis rule. However, although the companies' respective interests are aggregated, this cannot give rise to a double charge (FA 2013, s 104). HMRC's guidance notes advise that in such circumstances the two companies should decide between themselves which of them will submit the ATED return and pay ATED on the aggregated value of the two interests (para 11.3 of the guidance notes).

Connected persons

66.14 In applying the aggregation rule, the issue of whether an individual or another company is connected with the company is determined by the corporation tax definition of connected persons (FA 2013, s 172(1); see further CTA 2010, s 1122). Under that definition, an individual is connected with a company if he has control of it, either alone or with other connected persons (s 1122(3)). The applicable definition of control is that as discussed in para 87.9. The wide definition of associate generally has the result that a company held by a trust is deemed to be under the control of, and therefore to be connected with, the trust's beneficiaries (see para 87.8).

THE CHARGE TO TAX

66.15 Tax is potentially chargeable should the single dwelling interest, aggregated as necessary, have a taxable value in excess of the ATED threshold. The tax is an annual tax, payable for each chargeable period in which the conditions for its application are met. Chargeable periods start on 1 April and end on the following 31 March (FA 2013, s 94(8)).

Amount of tax

66.16 For 2016–17, the amounts of ATED are as follows (FA 2013, s 99 as amended):

Taxable value	ATED payable each year
£500,000–1,000,000 (from 1 April 2016)	£3,500
£1,000,001–2,000,000	£7,500
£2,000,001–5,000,000	£23,350

Taxable value	ATED payable each year
£5,000,001–10,000,000	£54,450
£10,000,001–£20,000,000	£109,050
More than £20,000,000	£218,200

The amounts, but not the rate bands, are indexed-linked (FA 2013, s 101). However, the amounts payable for 2016–17 are the same as for 2015–16, due to there having been no increase in the consumer prices index in the reference period.

Filing and payment

66.17 ATED is self-assessed. The ATED return must be filed on or before 30 April in the chargeable period to which it relates (FA 2013, s 159(2)) and the amount of tax due for the period must then be paid (FA 2013, s 163). ATED thus contrasts with most other taxes in requiring filing and payment to be at the beginning of the chargeable period, and not after it or towards its end.

Should the chargeable interest be acquired during the chargeable period, the ATED return for that period must be filed within 30 days of the acquisition. The ATED payable from then until the end of the chargeable period is a straight line proportion of the amounts listed above (FA 2013, s 99(3)).

Should the chargeable interest be disposed of, the full amount for the chargeable period in question will have been paid at the beginning of the period under the self-assessment procedure described above. But the proportion of the tax attributable to the post-disposal part of the chargeable period can be recovered by filing an amendment to the ATED return (FA 2013, s 106). Such amendment is only effective if made during the chargeable period concerned or in the following chargeable period (s 106(6)).

A point to stress is that an ATED return is required each year for each single dwelling interest owned by the non-resident entity which is within ATED (s 159(1)). Should the ATED payable in respect of the single dwelling interest for a chargeable period turn out to be more than the amount in the return, a return of the adjusted chargeable amount must be filed (FA 2013, s 160). This must be filed in the 30 days following the end of the chargeable period (s 160(2)).

Taxpayers must specify in the return what the value of the single dwelling interest is. If the valuation is within 10% of the top or bottom of the applicable band, HMRC can be asked for a pre-return banding check (see Valuation of Property Guidance and Returns Guidance Notice para 24).

RELIEVABLE DAYS

66.18 ATED is not chargeable in a period insofar as any days in that period are relievable. A relievable day is any day on which one of a whole series of reliefs specified in FA 2013, ss 133–150 is in point (s 132(2)). The effect of these reliefs is, in broad terms, to confine ATED to residential property that is occupied by persons in some way linked to the owning entity.

Originally, the reliefs required the filing of ATED returns for each single dwelling interest to which they applied, and then the claiming of that relief on the return as interim relief (FA 2013, s 100). But since 1 April 2015, it has been possible for the owner to file a Relief Declaration Return. Such returns are required for each category of relievable property but cover all properties of that category the owner owns, without the need to list them (FA 2013, s 159A).

Property rental business

66.19 The most important relief is that for property rental businesses (FA 2013, s 133). This relief requires the following conditions to be met:

(1)   The property rental business must be run on a commercial basis with a view to profit.
(2)   The subject single dwelling interest must be being exploited by the owning entity as a source of rents or similar receipts.
(3)   The occupier of the dwelling must not be what is termed a non-qualifying individual.

The relief is also available if the property is empty, provided steps are being taken to secure that the single dwelling interest will be exploited as a source of rental income (s 133(1)(b)). In other words void periods are allowed provided a tenant is being actively sought. Periods when the property is being marketed for sale or prepared for demolition or conversion are also relievable if previously the property was let otherwise than to non-qualifying individuals (s 134).

Non-qualifying individual

66.20 The non-qualifying individual concept is important, because occupation by such an individual precludes the days of such occupation from being relievable. So too any subsequent void periods are prevented from being relievable days unless and until a subsequent letting is made to someone who is not non-qualifying (FA 2013, s 135).

The main category of non-qualifying individual is an individual who is connected to the owner of the single dwelling interest (FA 2013, s 136(1)(b)). As explained above (para **66.14**), connected bears its normal tax definition, set out in CTA 2010, s 1122. It thus includes any individual who, with or without associates, controls the owning company. It normally includes beneficiaries of any trust which controls the owning company. In all these cases control can be direct or through intermediate companies.

There are also other categories of non-qualifying individual, some of which duplicate what is already comprehended by the term connected person. In relation to companies these categories are as follows:

(1)   The spouse of any individual who is connected to the owning company.
(2)   Any relative of a person connected with the owning company, and any spouse of such relative.
(3)   Any relative of the spouse of a person who is connected with the company, and any spouse of such relative.
(4)   Any settlor of a settlement that controls the owning company together with:
       (i)   his spouse; and
       (ii)   his relatives and their spouses.

For the purpose of these rules relatives are siblings, ancestors and descendants (s 136(7)). Settlement bears the wide income tax anti-avoidance definition discussed in CHAPTER 76.

Property trading and development

66.21 Days on which single dwelling interests are held by dealers or developers are relievable (FA 2013, ss 138, 139 and 141). However as with rental businesses, occupation by a non-qualifying individual precludes this result.

Other relievable days

66.22 Other types of use or occupation can also result in relievable days (FA 2013, ss 137 and 144–150). For present purposes the only one likely to be significant is where the dwelling is open to the public on a least 28 days in any year (FA 2003, s 137). However, for this relief to apply, the opening to the public must be in the course of a trade that exploits the dwelling as a source of income.

ATED-RELATED CGT

66.23 ATED-related CGT is enacted by TCGA 1992, ss 2B–2F, supplemented by computational rules in Sch 4ZZA. It forms part of the CGT code and thus the concepts used are, in the absence of definitions to the contrary, CGT concepts.

What is taxed

66.24 ATED-related CGT is only capable of applying if there is disposal of a chargeable interest which is a single dwelling interest, these terms bearing their ATED definitions (TCGA 1992, s 2B, Conditions A and B). It is also necessary for the single dwelling interest to have been within charge to ATED on at least one day in the disponor's ownership period (s 2B, Condition C). In determining whether the interest was in charge to ATED, all relievable days are ignored, and as a result the many cases where all days in the ownership period are relievable are outside ATED-related CGT.

A final requirement is that the proceeds of disposal exceed the threshold amount (s 2B, Condition D). The basic rule is that the threshold amount is

£500,000, ie the threshold above which ATED is payable (s 2D(1)). However the threshold amount is reduced on a pro rata basis if either the disposal is a part disposal or if there have been previous part disposals out of the interest in the previous six years and after 6 April 2013. The threshold is also reduced on a pro rata basis if what is disposed of is an undivided share in an interest in the dwelling.

Who is taxed

66.25 ATED-related CGT is not in its terms restricted to the categories of entity that are subject to ATED, ie companies, collective investment schemes and partnerships with a corporate member. However, the exclusion of other entities from the scope of the tax follows by implication, because ATED-related CGT is in point only if the interest disposed of has given rise to an ATED liability. There is one express rule as to who is liable, to the effect that ATED-related CGT does not apply to the non-corporate members of partnerships within ATED (s 2B(2)).

How the gain is computed

66.26 As ATED-related CGT is part of the CGT code, CGT rules apply in computing the gain. The rules are those applicable to CGT rather than corporation tax on chargeable gains, and as a result indexation is not allowed. Nor is CGT group relief, with the result that disposals between member companies of a group cause any ATED-related gain to be recognised (TCGA 1992, s 171(2)(ba)). The basic rule is that the gain subject to ATED-related CGT is the gain as so computed. But there are two important qualifications.

The first arises if not all days in the relevant ownership have been ATED chargeable days. By ATED chargeable day is meant a day on which the single dwelling interest was within the scope of ATED, but excluding therefrom all relievable days. Where some but not all the days in the relevant ownership period are ATED chargeable days, the ATED-related gain is a pro rata fraction of the total gain (Sch 4ZZA, para 6(2)).

Self-evidently, if all the days in the relevant ownership period are ATED chargeable days and not relievable, the whole gain is ATED-related. If, by contrast, all are relievable, for example on the basis that the dwelling has always been let and never occupied by non-qualifying individuals, none of the gain is ATED-related.

The second refinement is if the single dwelling interest has been owned since before the commencement of ATED. Here the default position is that the interest is treated as having been acquired on the commencement day (see below) at its then market value (Sch 4ZZA, para 3). However, the disponor can elect for the actual date and cost of acquisition to be used instead (Sch 4ZZA, paras 5 and 6). In such a case ATED chargeable days and relievable days are computed on the basis that the first chargeable period was the year 31 March 1982 to 31 March 1983. Nevertheless, the first valuation date remains 1 April 2012 and so it is the value of the single dwelling interest on that date that determines whether before 2012 it would have been within ATED, had ATED then been in force.

The rules determining the commencement day vary according to the value of the property. This variation is the result of ATED having initially applied only where the taxable value is £2m, and then been extended down to taxable values of £1m and £500,000. The basic rule is that the commencement day is 5 April 2013 (Sch 4ZZA, para 2(2)). But if the property first came within ATED on 1 April 2015 the commencement day is 5 April 2015, and if it first came within ATED on 1 April 2016 the commencement day is 5 April 2016 (para 2(3)(4)). For these purposes a property counts as having been within ATED even if all days were relievable (para 2(5)).

As respects the first commencement date, ie 5 April 2013, a slightly irritating feature is that this is one year after the first quinquennial valuation date for ATED, ie 1 April 2012 (see para **66.12**). In theory at least, a disponor of a £2m plus property acquired pre-commencement may be faced with having to commission two separate valuations, albeit that the ATED valuation can be confined to ascertaining which band the property falls in.

The charge to tax

66.27 All ATED-related gains are taxed at 28% (TCGA 1992, s 4(3A)). There is no annual exempt amount, as that amount applies only to individuals and trusts.

ATED-related allowable losses are available. Such a loss arises in the event that a company or other owning entity makes a relevant high value disposal and the formula in Sch 4ZZA produces a negative figure. If such a loss accrues, it may be set against an ATED-related gain arising in the same tax year or a later tax year (s 2B). Such a loss may be carried forward, but cannot be carried back to an earlier tax year (s 2B(5)), nor can it be set against an ATED-related gain realised by any other company, even if the companies are in the same corporate group.

In contrast to ATED itself, the tax charge is by tax year and is on the balance of ATED-related gains and allowable ATED-related losses. Normal self-assessment rules apply, to the effect that the deadline for filing of an ATED-related CGT return and payment of the CGT is 31 January following the tax year. However, for most disponers this is rather academic, as disposals giving rise to ATED-related CGT are most commonly realised by non-resident companies. Being non-resident, such companies are within the scope of the much more demanding NR CGT filing regime (see para 65.24). That regime may require submission of a return within 30 days of the disposal, even if there is no NR CGT to pay.

Other CGT regimes

66.28 ATED-related CGT has priority over NR CGT and TCGA 1992, s 13 (see Chapters 65 and 87). The general rule is that the ATED-related gain is deducted in computing the gain subject to NR CGT or s 13. But that deduction is made prior to the giving of the indexation allowance, the available indexation allowance excluding the proportion otherwise attributable to the ATED-related part of the gain (Sch 4ZZA, para 6(3)). Should the chargeable interest be treated as acquired on the relevant commencement date for the purposes of ATED-related CGT, the pre-commencement gain is separately computed and added to such part (if any) of the post-commencement gain as is not subject to ATED-related CGT. That aggregate is then, after deducting the applicable indexation allowance, subject to NR CGT and/or s 13.

Chapter 67

STAMP DUTY LAND TAX

INTRODUCTION

67.1 Stamp duty land tax, or SDLT as it is normally known, is a tax on dealings in UK real estate, which was introduced in 2003. Its predecessor was stamp duty, which still exists, albeit with much more limited scope than before; its most important application now being in relation to instruments transferring UK situs shares and debt securities.

Stamp duty was a document-based tax, and relatively easy to avoid. In the context of real estate transactions, such avoidance was achieved primarily through the device known as 'resting on contract', whereby properties were sold in equity but there was an indefinite postponement of the transfer of legal title. The transfer of the beneficial interest in the property to the purchaser was not, in itself, stampable.

This scheme became popular, partly because of its simplicity and partly driven by significant increases in stamp duty rates. In 2003 the Government blocked this avoidance through the replacement of stamp duty by SDLT. SDLT is fundamentally different from stamp duty, in that it is transaction-based, rather than document-based, and looks at the substance of a transaction rather than its form. In particular, SDLT catches the sale of an interest in land, whether that interest is legal or equitable, precluding any tax advantage from 'resting on contract'.

SDLT is a vast subject, and this book is not the place for a comprehensive discussion of it. This chapter aims to provide an overview of selected aspects of the SDLT regime, which are particularly relevant in the context of dealings in UK residential property by internationally mobile individuals and offshore entities.

BASIC PRINCIPLES

67.2 SDLT is charged on 'chargeable transactions'. A chargeable transaction is any 'land transaction' which is not exempt from charge (FA 2003, s 49(1)).

The term 'land transaction' is defined as any acquisition of a 'chargeable interest' (s 43(1)). This latter expression is defined very broadly, to cover any interest in or right over UK land, freehold or leasehold, legal or equitable, and the benefit of any obligation, restriction or condition affecting the value of UK land (s 48(1)). The only significant carve-outs are that licences to occupy land are not chargeable interests, and nor are interests or rights held as security for the payment of money or the performance of any other obligation (s 48(2), (3)).

In the legislation, a number of terms are given extended or artificial meanings. In particular, the term 'purchaser' is used to denote a person acquiring a chargeable interest, and 'vendor' to denote a person disposing of a chargeable interest (s 43(4)). This applies whether or not the transaction is actually a sale. In this chapter, the terms 'transferee' and 'transferor' are used. It is the transferee who is liable to pay SDLT, where it is chargeable (s 85).

Various exemptions from charge are contained in Sch 3. The most important of these is where there is no 'chargeable consideration' for the transaction (Sch 3, para 1).

The concept of chargeable consideration is developed in Sch 4. This provides that the chargeable consideration for a transaction is, except where otherwise provided, any consideration in money or money's worth given for the subject-matter of the transaction, by the transferee or a connected person (Sch 4, para 1).

There are special rules in Sch 5 to determine the chargeable consideration for the grant of a lease under which rent will be payable. In essence, SDLT is charged on the net present value of the rent payable over the term of the lease, such rent being discounted by 3.5% per year to account for the reduced present value of future receipts.

RATES OF SDLT

67.3 The rates of SDLT differ according as to whether or not the property comprised in the land transaction is residential.

Residential

67.4 SDLT on residential property is now a banded tax. The rates vary according as to whether or not the property purchased is the only residential property owned by the purchaser or replaces his only or main residence (FA 2003, Sch 4ZA as inserted by FA 2016, s 128). Should one or other of these conditions be met, the rates are 3% lower than would otherwise be the case. In applying these rules, account is taken of residential property outside the UK (Sch 4ZA, para 17) and companies and discretionary trusts are ipso facto precluded from the lower rates (Sch 4ZA, paras 7 and 13). For these reasons the lower rates are rarely applicable to purchases in circumstances contemplated by this book.

On this basis the rates of SDLT applicable to residential property are as follows (Sch 4ZA, para 1(2)):

Chargeable consideration	Rate
£0–£125,000	Nil

Chargeable consideration	Rate
£125,001–£250,000	5%
£250,001–£925,000	8%
£925,001–£1,500,000	13%
Over £1,500,000	15%

Residential property is defined as a building used or suitable for use as a dwelling (FA 2003, s 116), a definition that is broadly comparable to the equivalent definitions applicable to ATED and NR CGT. There are the exceptions for certain types of institutional use. These are not all the same as apply to ATED in that schools and student accommodation (other than halls of residence) count as residential for SDLT purposes (s 116(2), (3)).

Exceptions

67.5 There are several exceptions to the rates listed above.

First in certain instances, the rates of SDLT are those applicable to non-residential property as described below. This rule is in point of the transaction comprises both residential and non-residential property or if it comprises six or more separate dwellings (FA 2003, ss 55(2)(b) and 116(7)).

Second a transaction comprising two or more dwellings is charged at the effective rate that would be applicable if each of the dwellings was transacted separately (FA 2003, Sch 6B). The average rate is used if (as will be likely) the dwellings are each of different values.

Third a single, 15% flat rate applies in certain cases where a single dwelling is worth more than £500,000 and the purchaser is a company, a partnership with a corporate member or a collective investment scheme (FA 2003, Sch 4A). This is part of the same anti-avoidance regime as ATED and is discussed below (para **69.5**).

Non-residential

67.6 SDLT on property which is or is treated as non-residential is also a banded tax. The rates are as follows (FA 2003, s 55(1B), Table B):

Chargeable consideration	Rate
£0–£150,000	Nil
£150,001–£250,000	2%
More than £250,000	5%

Leases

67.7 Rent payable under leases is not charged under the above rules. As indicated above, SDLT is charged on the net present value of the rent payable over the term of the lease. In general the rate of tax is 1% (Sch 5, para 2). But a higher rate of 2% applies to non-residential leases insofar as the net present value of the rent exceeds £5m (Sch 5, para 2, Table B, as amended by FA 2016, s 127(9)). The first £150,000 of net present value is not charged, or the first £125,000 in the case of residential leases.

TRANSFERS FOR NO CONSIDERATION

67.8 A gift of UK land from one person to another, where the transferee does not assume any obligations in connection with the transfer, is free of SDLT. Although a chargeable interest has been acquired, and therefore a land transaction has occurred, it is not a chargeable transaction because no chargeable consideration has been given. There are however two important exceptions from the general rule that a gift of UK land is not a chargeable transaction.

Debt

67.9 The first exception is that a transferee is treated as having given chargeable consideration if the transaction involves the release of a debt due to the transferee or due from the transferor, or the assumption of an existing debt by the transferee (FA 2003, Sch 4, para 8(1)). In such a case, the chargeable consideration is the amount of the debt released or assumed. This principle applies regardless of whether the debt is secured on the property, although typically in such a case it is.

Corporate transferee

67.10 The second exception concerns corporate transferees. Such a transferee is generally deemed to have given chargeable consideration, even if in reality no consideration has been provided, if the transferor is connected with it for corporation tax purposes (CTA 2010 s 1122). In such a case, the market value of the land transferred to the company is treated as chargeable consideration (FA 2003, s 53). This provision effectively imposes an 'entry' charge to SDLT where land is transferred gratuitously to a connected company, but it does not work the other way round – ie it does not impose an 'exit' charge where land is transferred gratuitously by a company to a connected transferee which is not itself a company.

The market value acquiring rule is excluded where the company will hold the land as trustee in the course of a business of managing trusts (s 54(2)). In the event that the company will hold the land as trustee but cannot be said to be doing so in the course of such a business, there is a second exclusion (in s 54(3)) which applies if the transferor and the company are connected by virtue of CTA 2010, s 1122(6) but there is no other connection. Section

1122(6) is the provision which deems the trustees of a settlement to be connected to its settlor.

By virtue of these exclusions, the settlor of a trust can generally give land to a trust corporate trustee without SDLT being triggered, provided that there is no assumption of debt, and provided also that the settlor does not hold the shares in the trustee or otherwise control it. However, there is no corresponding relief for a transfer from a trustee to a company held by the trust. Such a transfer will generally be caught by the deemed market value consideration rule.

A further exclusion from the market value rule applies where the transferor is also a company and is 'a distribution of the assets of that company (whether or not in connection with its winding up)', provided that the land in question has not within the last three years been subject to a claim to group relief (s 54(3)). In this scenario, land can be transferred by way of in specie dividend or, if the company has been put into liquidation, by way of liquidation distribution, without the transfer attracting SDLT. This is sometimes known as distribution relief.

Debt and distribution relief

67.11 Should the company distributing the land distribute it subject to a debt, the debt is chargeable consideration and subject to SDLT accordingly. It may be the recipient shareholder injects funds into the company to enable it to discharge the debt first and so distribute the land free of debt. On this scenario the debt is still likely to be chargeable consideration if its discharge is part of the same arrangements as the in specie distribution (FA 2003, s 75A; HMRC Notice 20 December 2013, reproduced [2014] SWTI 228).

A different situation is where the debt is shareholder loan owed to the recipient shareholder. Here HMRC appear to accept that if the loan simply falls away, it is not chargeable consideration (Notice 20 December 2013). This would be in point on a liquidation distribution but is less easy to apply to a dividend as then the loan may need to be released if, as a matter of applicable company law, the company is to be in a position to declare the dividend.

Problems with debt are central to the issue of de-enveloping, ie the issue of whether residential property owned in corporate structures should be taken into shareholder ownership. HMRC's Technical Note published on 8 July 2015 indicated some consideration was being given to de-enveloping relief. ("Non-domiciled persons IHT residential property charges" reproduced [2015] SWTI 2344). However the consultation document published in August 2016 appeared to rule out de-enveloping relief (HM Treasury 'Reform to the taxation of non-domiciliaries: further consultation', 19 August 2016, para 2.4).

THE 15% RATE

67.12 The flat 15% SDLT rate applies if the following conditions are met (FA 2003, Sch 4A):

(1)   The subject matter of the transaction is a single dwelling interest, a term which bears essentially the same meaning as for ATED (Sch 4A para 7; see para **66.4**).

(2)   The consideration exceeds £500,000.

(3)   The transferee is a company, a collective investment scheme or a partnership with one or more corporate members.

However even if these conditions are met, the 15% rate is precluded if the acquisition is exclusively for one of certain specified purposes (Sch 4A, para 5). These comprise:

(1)   Letting as part of a rental business.

(2)   Development and resale as part of a trading business.

(3)   Resale as part of a property trading business.

These exclusions are the same as those applicable to ATED (see para **66.18** to **66.22**) and thus mean that the 15% rate and ATED cover essentially the same territory. As with ATED the exclusions are precluded if the intention is to let the property to a non-qualifying individual (Sch 4A, para 5(2)). That term is defined in the same terms as for ATED (Sch 4A, para 5A).

These exclusions are disapplied if at any time in the three years following the acquisition the conditions for their application cease to be met (Sch 4A, para 5G). It is sometimes thought that this means once the three years have expired, relief from the 15% rate in such cases is secure, regardless of what is then done with the property. Strictly however this is not true if whatever changes are then made were envisaged at the time of acquisition. This is because relief from the 15% rate turns on a purpose test, ie relief applies only if the acquisition is exclusively for one of the prescribed purposes (Sch 4A, para 5(1)).

In practice the increase of general residential SDLT rates to 15% above £1.5m has made the 15% rate a much less draconian outcome than it was when first enacted, when the top rate was 7%. However it may be still burden on properties at the lower end of its range, where the effective rate where it does not apply is under 15%.

The 15% rate cannot be avoided by introducing non-residential property into the transaction. This is because the 15% rate focuses specifically on interests in single dwellings, and requires mixed transactions to be treated as separate transactions (Sch 4A, para 2(3)).

Application of 15% rate to transfers for no consideration

67.13 It might be assumed that the 15% rate need only be considered where a residential property is being purchased, ie where consideration is being provided for the property. However, that would be incorrect. As explained above, a transfer for no consideration made to a company by a connected person attracts SDLT, based on the market value of the property. SDLT may, therefore, be chargeable at 15% if an individual who already owns a residential property contributes the property to a wholly-owned company.

In principle, the 15% rate may also apply to a transfer of a residential property for no consideration where the transferor and transferee are both companies, within the same group. However, in this scenario, an SDLT charge may be avoided by distribution relief (discussed above), where the property is being distributed by one company to its parent, by way of dividend or on a liquidation.

An SDLT charge on a transfer of a property within a corporate group may also be prevented by group relief, which applies generally to SDLT and is dealt with in FA 2003, Sch 7. In essence the relief applies where one of the companies holds at least 75% of the ordinary shares of the other, whether directly or through intermediate companies, or both companies are held as to at least 75% of their ordinary shares by a third company, again whether directly or otherwise (Sch 7, para 1). There are fairly elaborate provisions governing when the relief will apply and providing for clawback of the relief in the event of a degrouping of the companies.

ADMINISTRATION

67.14 The SDLT legislation imposes a short deadline for reporting and payment of tax liabilities. Where a transaction is notifiable, the transferee is required to submit a land transaction return within 30 days of the effective date of transaction. Payment of the SDLT must be made within the same 30-day period.

In theory, SDLT is a self-assessment tax and it is the transferee's responsibility to ensure that a notifiable transaction is reported and that the tax is paid. In reality, however, payment of the tax is to a large extent professionally enforced. Where a purchaser is represented by a solicitor or licensed conveyancer, that professional will ensure that the purchaser provides sufficient cash to pay the SDLT, and that the land transaction return is submitted.

Part C

UK ANTI-AVOIDANCE
LEGISLATION

Section I

The Transfer of Assets code

Chapter 68

RELEVANT TRANSFERS

INTRODUCTION

68.1 Chapter 2 of Part 13 of Income Tax Act 2007 (ITA 2007) is entitled 'Transfers of assets abroad'. It contains three separate charging sections, namely ss 720 and 727 which impose tax on the transferor, and s 731 which imposes tax on other persons who receive benefits. Sections 720–726 are a rewriting of the charge in TA 1988, s 739(2) on transferors with power to enjoy, and s 727–730 are a rewriting of the charge under TA 1988, s 739(3) on transferors in receipt of a capital sum. Sections 731–735 rewriting TA 1988, s 740.

In addition to the charging provisions, Chapter 2 contains preconditions, definitions, and supplemental provisions in ss 714–719 and 743–751. There is also a motive or purpose defence in ss 736–742, which rewrites the provisions of TA 1988, ss 741–741D, and a newer defence in s 742A, which was inserted in 2013 and is intended to ensure that the transfer of assets provisions are compliant with EU law requirements concerning the fundamental freedoms.

History

68.2 The charge on transferors with power to enjoy was first enacted in 1936 and that on transferors in receipt of a capital sum in 1938 (FA 1936, s 18; FA 1938, s 28). The motive or purpose test featured in the legislation at the outset, being recast into the form taken by TA 1988, s 741 in 1938.

The early years of the code were characterised by judicial decisions, in the war years and the immediately post-war years, which disproportionately strained normal principles of construction in favour of HMRC. The process culminated in *Congreve v IRC* (1948) 30 TC 163, where the House of Lords decided, in contradiction to ministerial statements when the legislation was enacted, that ss 720–730 caught not merely transferors, but anybody else who had power to enjoy or received a capital sum.

Congreve, however, represented a judicial high-water mark and just a year later a retreat began in the first of two Vestey cases to come before the House of Lords. This case, *Vestey's Executors v IRC* (1949) 31 TC 1, emphasised that the language of the code is precise and must be examined with rigour to see if the taxpayer comes within it. A more dramatic step back came with the second

Vestey case in 1979, when the House of Lords overruled *Congreve* and decided that ss 720–730 were restricted to transferors (*Vestey v IRC* [1980] STC 10).

That case led to the enactment in 1981 of what became TA 1988, s 740 and is now ITA 2007, ss 731–735 (FA 1981, s 45). 1981 also saw other changes to the code, notably the conferral of the remittance basis on non-domiciliaries. 1981 apart, the only other years which saw significant amendment to the code were 1969, 2006, 2008 and 2013.

The changes in 2006, which took effect from 5 December 2005, principally involved the motive or purpose defence (see CHAPTER 73) and the 2008 changes recast the remittance basis (see CHAPTER 72). The changes in 2013 introduced the new EU defence, ITA 2007, s 742A, this being necessary as the EU Commission had brought infraction proceedings in the European Court. Section 742A is explained in CHAPTER 74 and the relevant EU issues in CHAPTER 107.

HMRC practice

68.3 Historically HMRC has refrained from publishing its internal guidance on the transfer of assets code. But in April 1999 they gave their view on certain aspects of the legislation, in an article published in *Tax Bulletin 40* (RI 201). More recently, in August 2013, an exposure draft of comprehensive guidance was issued for consultation. This exposure draft should be referred to when planning transactions but it should be kept in mind that it is very much a draft and may change as a result of the consultation. As at the time of writing, HMRC have not issued final guidance or a further draft.

ISSUES OF CONSTRUCTION

68.4 The language of the predecessor legislation to chapter 2 (TA 1988, ss 739–746) was unclear in many respects and, given that most of it dated back to 1936–38, was not drafted with modern offshore structures in mind. A particular problem is that whereas the 1936–38 legislation was primarily focused on non-resident companies and fixed-interest trusts, the modern target is as likely as not to be, or at least involve, discretionary trusts. The non-transferor charge was drafted with discretionary trusts in mind, for a discretionary trust was at issue in *Vestey v IRC*. But the legislation did little more than put into statutory form some judicial observations in *Vestey v IRC*, and its consequent brevity made it difficult to construe with certainty.

Perhaps emboldened by the war-time judicial decisions, HMRC have tended to regard the code as a catch-all weapon which can be relied on to counter all forms of offshore avoidance. The experience of many practitioners is that the code is adduced as a blunt instrument without regard to whether as a matter of construction it is in point. Perhaps for this reason, HMRC have recently had poor success rate in the courts: of seven cases on the code to reach the House of Lords in the years following *Congreve*, only three have resulted in victory to HMRC (*Bambridge v IRC* (1955) 36 TC 313; *Chetwode v IRC* [1977] STC 64; and *IRC v McGuckian* [1997] STC 908). Given these circumstances, taxpayers should respond with vigour when HMRC rely on the code, and concede liability only if such is clear as a matter of reasonable construction.

It has to be said that the rewriting of the transfer of assets code in the ITA 2007 has compounded rather than diminished the difficulties of construction and thus the uncertainty. In part this is because the rewriting process, by unpicking and reassembling the legislation, has made explicit ambiguities and inconsistencies which previously were latent. But also, the very process of unpicking and reassembly has resulted in subtle changes which, with legislation as complex as this, can have the result of changing meaning or rendering it uncertain.

It is the rewritten code which is now in force, and so it is that which has to be considered. In addressing all the uncertainties and ambiguities, the approach to be adopted must be that of purposive construction. Thus the issue is 'whether the relevant statutory provisions, construed purposively, were intended to apply to the transactions, viewed realistically' (*Collector of Stamp Revenue v Arrowtown Assets Ltd* [2004] 6 ITLR 454 at para 35, per Ribeiro PJ, as approved by the House of Lords in *Barclays Mercantile Business Finance Ltd v Mawson* [2005] 1, at para 36 and *UBS v HMRC* [2016] STC 934, para 66). Indeed, a case on s 739 was one of the decisive steps in applying purposive construction to taxing statutes (*IRC v McGuckian*, supra).

This chapter deals with the key precondition for the application of the code, namely that there be a relevant transfer, together with the associated general definitions. Subsequent chapters deal with the charge on transferors, the charge on non-transferors, the relief for non-domiciliaries, the motive or purpose defence and the EU defence.

THE KEY PRECONDITION

68.5 As stated above, the precondition for liability under the code is that a relevant transfer occurs (ITA 2007, s 714(2)). The term 'relevant transfer' was not used in TA 1988, ss 739–746. Instead in that legislation each charging section set out the precondition in full: there had to be a transfer of assets, by virtue or consequence of which, either alone or in conjunction with associated operations, income became payable to a person abroad.

The term 'relevant transfer' is defined in ITA 2007, s 716 and essentially reflects this language. It is as follows:

(1)   There must be a transfer of assets.
(2)   Income must become payable to a person abroad.
(3)   It must become so payable as a result of:
    (1)   The transfer alone,
    (2)   One or more associated operations, or
    (3)   The transfer and one or more associated operations.

All the above terms are defined in the ensuing sections of ITA 2007 (ss 717–719). It will be noted that the phrase 'by virtue or in consequence of' has been replaced by 'as a result of'. It will also be noted that s 714(2) uses the present tense and thus postulates that a relevant transfer occurs. Read literally this would confine the code to transfers in the tax year of charge. But the context makes it clear this cannot be right, 'occurs' in fact meaning 'has occurred'.

Section 714(2) introduces what appears to be one further precondition. This is that the code operates by reference to the income of a person abroad that is connected with the transfer or an associated operation. The term 'connected' is not defined and the concept of connectedness was not an express feature of the TA 1988 provisions.

TRANSFER OF ASSETS

68.6 The term 'transfer of assets' was used in TA 1988, ss 739–746 and all the predecessor legislation and so case law on the meaning of the term remains good. Both in TA 1988 and in ITA 2007, the term 'assets' is defined as including property or rights of any kind and the term transfer, in relation to rights, is defined as including the creation of the rights (ITA 2007, ss 716(2) and 717(a); TA 1988, s 742(9)(b)).

It is essential, in any analysis of the transfer of assets code, to be clear which transaction is the transfer. Among examples in recent cases are the following:

(1)   In *Vestey v IRC*, the members of the Vestey family had transferred valuable properties to non-resident trustees. This was the transfer, the rental income being the income becoming payable to the trustees as a result of the transfer (see [1980] STC, 10, 14, per Lord Wilberforce).

(2)   In *IRC v Willoughby* [1997] STC 995, the transfer of assets was the transfer by the taxpayer of cash to a life office in consideration of the issue to him of a personal portfolio bond (see para **4.6** above). The income arose from the investment of the monies by the life office (see [1995] STC 143, 153, 154, and 157).

(3)   In *IRC v McGuckian* [1997] STC 908 the taxpayers had transferred shares in a private company to non-resident trustees. This was the transfer, and the dividends were the income payable as a result.

(4)   In *Carvill v IRC* [2000] STC (SCD) 143, the transfer was the transfer of shares in a UK holding company to an offshore holding company in consideration of a share issue by that company. The dividends payable by the UK company was the income payable as a result.

The view is sometimes expressed that the code does not apply if the assets transferred are already abroad when the transfer is made. The code is headed 'Transfer of Assets Abroad' and s 716(1)(b) requires income to have become payable to a person abroad as a result of the relevant transfer and/or associated operations. Semantically it is difficult for assets to be transferred abroad if they are already abroad, and for income to become payable to a person abroad if it is already so payable. However, common sense indicates that such an interpretation is unlikely to be right, and a Special Commissioner has so held (*IRC v Willoughby* [1995] STC 143, 161).

It is unclear whether if an individual's assets pass by will or intestacy to an offshore entity, he has made a transfer. The case of *Bambridge v IRC* [1955]

3 All ER 812 decided that a will could be an associated operation (see below), but the issue of whether the will and/or the death was a transfer was not decided.

In all the decided cases, the person who effected the transfer of assets was an individual. That this should be so may be regarded as inevitable, for all those cases involved the transferor charge, which is a charge on individuals (see paras **68.2** and **69.1**). Given that the legislation was originally devised to tax transferors, it might be thought that a transaction is only a transfer if effected by an individual, or procured by an individual in such circumstances as makes him a quasi transferor (see para **69.50**). But the definition of 'relevant transfer' does not in terms impose such a requirement.

Employment contracts

68.7 An issue which is debatable is whether an individual effects a transfer of assets if he enters into a contract of employment with a non-UK resident employer. In a sense he does, as entering into the contract creates rights exercisable by the employer company, and s 716(2) provides that the creation of rights is to be treated as a transfer. Such an analysis was adopted in *IRC v Brackett* [1986] STC 521, where the taxpayer had agreed to provide services to a Jersey company, but had no entitlement to remuneration until he attained 70. Hoffmann J held this agreement was a transfer of assets and that the profits generated by the taxpayer's activities were income payable to the company as a result of the transfer.

Brackett was an avoidance case in which a trust the taxpayer had created owned all the shares in the employer company and the avowed object of the arrangements was to generate funds for the trust. By comparison with most employments, the consultancy contract at issue was unusual in that the employee received no immediate remuneration for his activities. It was also a case where the taxpayer was unrepresented. For all these reasons it may strongly be argued that *Brackett* is confined to its facts and does not extend to normal remuneration arrangements. Indeed, were it to do so, all UK resident employees of non-resident employers would have to rely on, and claim, the motive defence (see CHAPTER **73**).

Despite these points, an employment contract has been found to be a transfer of assets in one tribunal case (*Boyle v HMRC* [2013] UKFTT 723 (TC)). However this too was an avoidance case, involving an offshore employment intermediary and artificial arrangements to write off loans.

ASSOCIATED OPERATIONS

68.8 The term 'associated operation' is defined in relation to a transfer of assets in ITA 2007, s 719. It is an operation of any kind effected in relation to:

(a)   Any of the assets transferred, or
(b)   Any assets directly or indirectly representing those assets, or
(c)   The income arising from the assets transferred or the assets representing them, or

(d)   Any assets directly or indirectly representing the accumulations of such income.

Shares or obligations of a company are deemed to represent assets transferred to the company (ITA 2007, s 717(b)). The same applies to the obligations of any non-corporate person to which assets are transferred.

One occurrence which has not been regarded as an associated operation is death (*Bambridge v IRC* [1955] 3 All ER 812). But since it was held that making a will was an associated operation, the exclusion of death is of little practical significance. An interesting issue is whether there would be an associated operation if the deceased died intestate. Dicta of Jenkins LJ in *Bambridge* suggest not.

Timing issues

68.9 Originally the legislation did not specify any time at which an operation must occur if it is to be associated. But since 5 December 2005 it has been expressly provided that the operation can be effected before, after, or at the same time as the transfer (ITA 2007, s 719(2)). In its reference to operations before the transfer, this reflects what had previously been HMRC's view (*Tax Bulletin* 40 (April 1999) p 652).

The legislation does not specify how much earlier than the transfer an associated operation can be, or any period after the transfer beyond which it cannot be associated. On a literal reading this means there are thus no limits as to how far back, or how far forward, the hunt for associated operations must be conducted. The issue of whether some limitation should be implied is discussed in para **68.14** below.

Operations by third parties

68.10 The legislation expressly says that an operation effected by any person can be associated with the transfer. Thus an associated operation may be effected by someone who is not the transferor.

This is illustrated by *Corbett's Executrices v IRC* [1943] 2 All ER 218, where the taxpayer and others had transferred investments to a UK company. Subsequently that company incorporated a Canadian company and trans-ferred some of the investments to it. The latter transfer was an operation associated with the original transfer to the UK company. So too the accumu-lation of income by a transferee company and the management of the transferred assets have been held to be operations associated with original transfer to the company (*IRC v Herdman* [1968] NI 74, 45 TC 394). The activities of a partnership in which the transferee was partner have been held to be associated with the transfer of the partnership share to the transferee (*Latilla v IRC* [1943] AC 377, [1943] 1 All ER 265).

Omissions

68.11 The concept of associated operations also figures in the IHT legislation (IHTA 1984, s 268). The IHT definition expressly provides that 'operations' include omissions. However, there is no equivalent provision in the transfer of assets code and as a result it may be argued that omissions are not included (cf *Nichols v IRC* [1973] STC 497, 5050 per Walton J).

Other assets

68.12 It is important to stress that to be associated, operations must be effected in relation to the assets transferred, the income from those assets, or assets representing the same. If operations are effected in relation to assets falling outside these categories, they are not associated.

The case of *Fynn v IRC* [1958] 1 All ER 270, 37 TC 629 illustrates this point. Here the taxpayer in 1947 sold securities to an overseas investment company in consideration of the issue of shares to him, and the company charged the securities in support of borrowing from the bank. The charging of the securities was admitted to be an operation associated with the original transfer. Some years later, in 1952, the taxpayer made an informal loan to the company to enable it to reduce its debt to the bank. Upjohn J held that the loan could not be described as having been made in respect of the assets transferred and so was not an associated operation.

A similar approach in relation to subsequent transactions by the taxpayer was taken in *Carvill v IRC* [2000] STC (SCD) 143. Here the taxpayer controlled a UK company. He and the minority shareholders transferred their shares to a company incorporated in Bermuda, in consideration of an issue of shares. Subsequently the taxpayer bought the shares of one of the minority shareholders and then the Bermudian company bought back the shares of the remaining minority shareholders. A Special Commissioner decided these subsequent operations were not associated with the taxpayer's transfer of assets, as they did not relate to the shares he had transferred. For the same reason, various employment arrangements entered into by the taxpayer with the Bermudian company were not associated operations either.

An issue of some difficulty is whether a transfer of assets can also be an operation associated with an earlier transfer of other assets to the same transferee. In logic it should not be, as if an operation is a transfer the transfer of assets code operates in relation to it in its own right. If an operation is a transfer, it is illogical to see it as an operation associated with some other transfer.

Representation of assets

68.13 Decided cases give little guidance on when assets 'represent' the assets transferred or the income generated by such assets. But as assets transferred to a company are deemed to be represented by the shares or obligations of the company, under s 717(b), an operation is associated if it is effected in relation to such shares or obligations. This rule catches cases where a transfer is made to offshore trustees, who transfer the assets they have received to an offshore holding company in return for shares or a receivable, and then effect transactions in relation to such shares or receivable. But such representation may not extend to shares in any further company to which such shares or receivable are themselves transferred.

Guidance as to the general meaning of representation is given, albeit in another context, in *West v Trennery* [2005] UKHL 5, [2005] STC 214 (see para **75.4**). Here the trustees of one settlement had raised money by mortgaging the trust assets, and then advanced the cash to another settlement. In the House of Lords, Lord Millett observed that the cash directly represented the proceeds of the trust assets. Had the trustees of the second settlement invested the cash, the ensuing investments would have indirectly represented the proceeds.

It is clear from this that if cash is comprised in the transfer, investments bought with the cash represent the assets transferred. If assets are transferred in specie and then sold, assets bought with the proceeds directly or indirectly represent the original assets.

But in a case of the latter kind, the question which arises is whether only operations effected with reference to the 'representing' assets – ie the assets owned by the transferee – are associated, or whether operations effected on the original assets are associated as well, despite the fact that these have ceased to be owned by the transferee. A further question is whether, if 'representing' assets are themselves sold, it is necessary to continue to look at operations effected in relation to them, or whether the focus is solely on the new 'representing' assets. Common sense would indicate that, where assets have come to be represented by other assets, it is only operations effected in relation to the latter which are relevant. Were this not so, operations effected by complete strangers would count as associated, with irrational implications as respects the motive defence (see CHAPTER 73).

But if this is right, the position where the transferee sells assets to a company in return for shares or loan stock has to be considered. For the reasons already noted, the shares or loan stock represent the original assets. But if so does this then mean operations effected with reference to the assets held by the company cannot be associated? As a matter of common sense it is difficult to see this being the position where those assets are the original assets transferred and, as noted in para **68.12**, it was accepted in *Fynn v IRC* that the charging of the assets transferred by the transferee company was an associated operation.

Implied limitation

68.14 As will be apparent from the above, on a literal reading, the definition in s 719 is wide. As indicated in para **68.9**, there is on the terms of s 719 no limit to how long before the transfer an operation might have taken place or how long after. Indeed on such a literal reading an operation can be associated even if effected by someone other than the transferor in circumstances quite unconnected with the transfer.

In reality, some limit must be implied to the definition in s 719 and the issue is what. The issue is far from easy, but two possible approaches are indicated by decided cases.

The first is that actual association may be required. This is suggested by observations in *Corbett's Executrices v IRC* (1943) 25 TC 305. Here the initial transfer to the UK company took place in 1933 and the ensuing transfer by that company to the Canadian company followed in 1935. The taxpayers argued that the gap in time meant that the latter transaction was not an associated operation. The Court of Appeal rejected this, on the grounds that the Commissioners had found the transactions were associated. The Court went on to make the following observation:

> 'The interval during which the [transferors] were thinking about their "associated operations" could not make any difference to the legal conclusion unless the Special Commissioners had found as a fact that it negatived the "conjunction" or association between the two operations.'

Another route to the same conclusion is indicated by fact that the definition of 'associated operation' is expressed to be 'in relation to a transfer of assets' (ITA 2007, s 719). In *Fisher v HMRC* [2014] SFTD 1309, para 238, the First-tier Tribunal held the words 'in relation to' impose a requirement that has to be satisfied before a transaction can be considered an associated operation. But the Tribunal appear to have thought a transaction satisfies this requirement if it is effected in relation to the assets transferred or assets representing those assets. As such this view of the requirement does not take the argument much further.

The second approach accepts the definition of associated operation is very wide but holds that account need only be taken of relevant associated operations in applying the provisions of the transfer of assets code. *Herdman v IRC* (1967) 45 TC 394 is the origin of this approach. Here the transfer of assets was to a company which then accumulated the income generated by the assets and used the retained profits to repay debt owed to the transferor. The House of Lords decided the accumulation was an associated operation but was not a relevant operation. This conclusion followed because the then equivalent of Condition A in ITA 2007, s 721 (see para **69.5**) required the taxpayer to have power to enjoy the income by virtue of the transfer alone or the transfer in conjunction with associated operations. Where, as in *Herdman*, the transfer alone gave the transferor power to enjoy, the associated operations did not have to be looked at and so were not relevant.

The issue in *Herdman* was whether the purpose defence described in Chapter 71 applied, it being accepted it did if the accumulation of income was a relevant associated operation. In a latter IHT case, *Macpherson v IRC* [1988] STC 362 (at p 368) the House of Lords summarised the effect of *Herdman* as follows (at p 368):

> 'The only associated operations which were relevant to the subsection were those by means of which, in conjunction with the transfer, a taxpayer could enjoy the income and did not include associated operations taking place after the transfer had conferred on the taxpayer the power to enjoy the income.'

The concept of whether an associated operation is relevant was picked up by the Special Commissioner in *Carvill v IRC* [2000] STC 143, 165. As is described in para **68.12**, the Special Commissioner decided that certain transactions were not associated operations at all. But then he added that even if they were, they were not relevant because:

'No income becomes payable to [the person abroad] by virtue or in consequence of any of them . . . . Nor do any of these transactions give the taxpayer power to enjoy the income of [the person abroad].'

There are thus two approaches. The first would narrow the category of transaction that are associated operations at all. The second accepts that the concept of associated operations is very wide, but then says some only are relevant. Most of the case law on the two approaches concerns the purpose test discussed in CHAPTER 73. In relation to that defence the issue of which approach is right is on one view highly significant (see para **73.13**).

Assuming the second approach is correct, a further issue, in relation to the transferor charge, is whether, as *Herdman* indicates, the focus is only on operations which confer power to enjoy or whether, as *Carvill* indicates, operations are also relevant if they give rise to a new source of income. Strictly the House of Lords authority represented by *Herdman* suggests the former is right.

The cases referred to above were all decided on the transferor charge and power to enjoy. It is not immediately clear how the second approach would apply in relation to the non-transferor charge as that charge does not turn on anybody having power to enjoy. But the equivalent requirement to power to enjoy is that the benefit to the non-transferor must be provided out of assets which are available for the purpose by reason of the transfer and/or associated operations. It may therefore be suggested that the relevant associated operations as respects the non-transferor charge are those which render assets available for the purpose and, if *Carvill* is right, also those which give rise to relevant income (see further paras **70.11** and **70.17**).

The cases referred to above were also all decided in relation to the pre-rewrite legislation. But it is inherently unlikely that rewriting the legislation has altered their impact, inter alia because the present legislation itself uses the term relevant transaction, a term which one can infer was inspired by *Herdman* and the other cases referred to above.

INCOME PAYABLE TO A PERSON ABROAD

68.15 The requirement that income becomes payable to a person abroad is fundamental to the definition of relevant transfer. If no income has become so payable, the transfer is not a relevant transfer, with the result that the transfer of assets code is not engaged.

This point is particularly important to ss 731–735 (see para **70.25**) and is much clearer in the rewritten ITA 2007 provisions than it was in TA 1988. It is relevant to the many cases where the asset transferred is non-income producing. Unless and until the asset produces income, or is sold and reinvested in income producing assets, the code does not apply.

Person abroad

68.16 The core meaning of the term 'person abroad' is a person who is resident outside the UK (ITA 2007, s 718). It should be noted that the test is residence outside the UK: thus a person who is resident in the UK can, in principle, still be a person abroad if he is also resident in another territory. If the dual resident is taxable in the UK on the income, ie there is no treaty exemption, double taxation should be avoided under ITA 2007, s 745 (see para **69.36**).

Save in the case of trustees and personal representatives, the transfer of assets code provides no rules for determining whether a person resides outside the UK and so the general rules described in CHAPTERS **41** to **43** apply. Thus a foreign registered company is resident outside the UK if its central management and control is outside the UK and this is so even if central management and control is split between a foreign territory and the UK, so that the company is dual resident (see para **43.8**). UK incorporated companies are by contrast resident only in the UK (CTA 2009, s 14) and so cannot be persons abroad. It would appear that this is so even where a UK company is treaty non-resident, as the rule deeming such companies to be non-UK resident applies only for the purposes of corporation tax (CTA 2009, s 18(2)).

Trustees and personal representatives are treated as non UK resident for the purposes of the transfer of assets code if they are so treated under the general income tax rules relating to the residence of trusts (ITA 2007, ss 718 and 475(3); see also CHAPTER **42**).

An individual, but only an individual, is also a person abroad if he is non-UK domiciled (s 718(1)(b)). Until 5 April 2012 a UK resident company was a person abroad if it was incorporated outside the UK but this rule was repealed from 6 April 2012 (FA 2013, Sch 10 paras 2 and 9(1)).

There is no doubt that the code applies if income is payable to non-resident discretionary trustees (*Vestey v IRC* [1980] STC 10). The position is less clear with fixed interest trusts, on account of the general principle that the trust income is treated as that of the life tenant (see para **8.2**). In *IRC v McGuckian* [1997] STC 908 the taxpayer had created an offshore trust of which his wife was life tenant. The offshore trustee then sold the right to a dividend for a substantial capital sum. The assignment fell to be disregarded under the *Ramsay* principle, and the House of Lords held that this meant that the dividend was income payable to the trustee for the purposes of s 720. The point that it was the life tenant's income if the sale was disregarded was not discussed. It has subsequently been suggested that the point may be good (*R (Huitson) v HMRC* [2010] STC 715, paras 61–63 as approved [2011] EWCA Civ 893 para 93).

Causality

68.17 The income must be payable to the person abroad as a result of either the transfer, or one or more of the associated operations, or the transfer combined with one or more associated operations. It is clear that the person abroad to whom the income is payable need neither be nor include the original transferee (*Corbett's Executives v IRC* (1943) 25 TC 305). So too the transferee need not be a person abroad when the transfer is made: subsequent emigration is sufficient to engage the code (*Congreve v IRC* (1948) 30 TC 163).

As indicated above, the phrase 'as a result of' replaces 'by virtue or in consequence of'. There is little case law on the meaning of the latter term. However what is clear is that if the income is payable to the person abroad as a result of a transaction which is neither the transfer nor an associated operation the code is not engaged.

MEANING OF INCOME

68.18 As the transfer of assets code forms part of UK tax legislation, the term 'income' means income computed as per UK tax rules (*Chetwode v IRC* [1977] STC 64). Thus expenses or costs are not allowable save insofar as specifically allowed under UK tax legislation.

This means that (to take one example) where a non-resident company derives income from the letting of property owned by it, the costs of maintaining the property are deductible, as are any interest payments under loans taken out for the acquisition or improvement of the property. However, the costs of running the company, as distinct from managing the property letting business, are non-deductible.

Trading profits

68.19 It has, in the past, been argued that the transfer of assets code does not extend to trading profits, on the grounds that what a trading transferee receives are gross receipts rather than income payable to him. Such arguments have been rejected by the courts (*Latilla v IRC* [1943] AC 377, 25 TC 107; *Chetwode v IRC* [1977] STC 64; *IRC v Brackett* [1986] STC 521). HMRC allow trading profits to be offset by past trading losses, but only insofar as losses and profits accrue to the same company (*Tax Bulletin* 40 (April 1999) p 652).

Accrued income profits

68.20 The general rule is that the accrued income scheme does not apply to non-residents (ITA 2007, s 643). However income for the purposes of the transfer of assets code includes accrued income profits which would have been within the scheme had the person abroad been UK resident (ITA 2007, s 747).

Offshore income gains

68.21 Offshore income gains count as income for the purpose of the transfer of assets code. However this rule is displaced if under the rules in TCGA 1992, ss 13 or 87, the offshore income gain is treated as accruing to a UK resident.

These difficult rules, and the practical issues they raise, are discussed in CHAPTER 82 and para 95.27.

Life policy gains

68.22 Gains computed under the chargeable event legislation can count as income for the purposes of the transfer of assets code (see para 96.22).

Chapter 69

TRANSFERORS

INTRODUCTION

69.1 There are two separate sets of provisions applicable to transferors. The first, ITA 2007, ss 720–726, applies where the transferor has power to enjoy the income of the person abroad. The second, ITA 2007, ss 727–730, operates where the transferor is entitled to, receives or has previously received a capital sum. Sections 720–730 together constitute a rewriting of legislation that was formerly in TA 1988, s 739, subject to amendments made in 2008 and 2013.

Structure of the legislation

69.2 The structure of the two sets of provisions, namely those applicable where the transferor has power to enjoy and those applicable where he is entitled to, receives or has previously received a capital sum, is the same. The charging sections, ss 720 and 727, charge the income which is treated as arising to the transferor under ss 721 and 728 respectively. Sections 721 and 728 define the circumstances in which the income is treated as arising and the amount of the income. Changes made by FA 2013 make it clear that the income charged on the transferor is the notional sum treated as arising under ss 721 and 728 and not the actual income of the person abroad (see ss 721(3B) and 728(1A) as inserted by FA 2013, Sch 10 paras 10(3) and 14(2)).

The notional income arising under ss 721 and 728 is exempted from charge where the conditions for the motive defence or the EU defence described in CHAPTERS 73 and 74 are met (ss 720(7) and 727(6)). In addition, the charging sections are subject to the remittance basis in the case of remittance basis users, as described in CHAPTER 72 (ss 720(4) and 727(3A)). In the case of power to enjoy, the charging section is subject also to special rules where the transferor has power to enjoy solely as a result of enjoying a benefit provided out of the income of the person abroad (s 720(4); see para **69.39**).

EU issues

69.3 The European Commission has expressed the view that the transferor charging provisions infringe the fundamental freedoms conferred by EU law where the person abroad is a company based in another EU Member State (EC

Press Release 24 October 2012, reproduced [2012] SWTI 3080). As a result it referred the UK to the European Court of Justice.

In reality, the infringement of EU law may be much wider than cases where the person abroad is a company in the EU. This issue is discussed in CHAPTER 107. The new EU defence referred to above is not a complete answer to these concerns, if only because it applies only to income arising under transactions effected after 6 April 2012 (see para 74.2). The result is that the transferor charging provisions are, in addition to being subject to the EU defence described in CHAPTER 74, also subject to the risk of wider disapplication under general principles of EU law. This risk is considered in more detail in CHAPTER 107.

Avoidance of income tax

69.4 Both charging provisions are expressed to apply 'for the purpose of preventing the avoiding of liability to income tax by individuals ...'. In the light of this it might be thought that the sections apply only if income tax has in fact been avoided.

However, as a matter of domestic law this is not so. In *IRC v McGuckian* [1997] NI 157, [1997] 3 All ER 817, HL the House of Lords held that the words cited above state the purpose of the sections and do not impose a requirement that a purpose of the transfer must be the avoidance of income tax. The subjective element of this is now reflected in the legislation (ss 721(5)(c) and 728(3)(c)). In reality, perhaps, two separate issues have to be distinguished: namely whether in making the transfer the transferor intended to avoid income tax and whether, regardless of intention, income tax has in fact been avoided. *McGuckian* conflates these two issues, but a fair reading is that it applies to both, and this conclusion has been adopted by the First-tier tribunal (*Fisher v Revenue and Customs Comrs* [2014] UK FTT 804 (TC), 17 ITLR 141 para 127).

POWER TO ENJOY

69.5 Section 721 specifies the circumstances in which income is treated as arising to the transferor under the power to enjoy provisions. It is expressed in terms of tax years and applies if in a given tax year three conditions, A, B and C are met. But in reality, condition A encapsulates two points, so s 721 is best seen as imposing four requirements:

(1)   In the tax year concerned the transferor has power to enjoy the income of the person abroad.
(2)   The power to enjoy is as a result of the relevant transfer, one or more associated operations, or both the transfer and associated operations.
(3)   The income would be taxable if it were in fact the income of the transferor.
(4)   The transferor is UK resident in the tax year concerned.

The terms 'relevant transfer', 'associated operation', and 'person abroad' are defined terms, explained in CHAPTER 68.

Meaning of 'power to enjoy'

69.6 The transferor has power to enjoy income if any of five enjoyment conditions is met (ITA 2007, s 722). These are described as Conditions A to E and, save in one respect in Condition C, their wording replicates that of the predecessor legislation in TA 1988, s 742(2). Consequently, the extensive body of case law on the meaning of 'power to enjoy' under the former legislation remains good.

In evaluating that case law, it needs to be kept in mind that significant changes to the former legislation were made in 1969 (FA 1969, s 33). Until that year, the legislation applied only if as a result of the transfer and/or associated operations the transferor had acquired rights by virtue of which he had power to enjoy the income. However, in 1969 the reference to the acquisition of rights was deleted.

General rules of construction

69.7 In determining whether the transferor has power to enjoy, regard must be had to the substantial result and effect of the transfer and associated operations (ITA 2007, s 722(3)). All benefits which may at any time accrue to the transferor must be taken into account, irrespective of their nature or form and whether or not he has any legal or equitable right to them (ITA 2007, s 722(4)). In *Vestey v IRC (No 2)* [1979] Ch 198, [1978] STC 567576 Walton J suggested that this provision enlarges, and can never restrict, the circumstances under which an individual has power to enjoy.

In some of the decided cases, reliance has been placed on these provisions to confirm that there is power to enjoy where there might otherwise be doubt (eg *IRC v Brackett* [1986] STC 521). But in the current era it may be doubted they do much more than purposive construction would in any event require.

These provisions may however have another significance. Their application is not in its terms limited to cases where it is in favour of HMRC, and so it is open to taxpayers also to rely on them. This is particularly apposite in those all too common cases where it is clear on the facts that the transferor was never intended to and is never going to benefit but HMRC look for obscure scenarios or hidden back doors by which he might do so. The answer to such attempts may simply be that as a matter of substantial result and effect the taxpayer does not have power to enjoy. Such an answer is not inconsistent with Walton J's comment in *Vestey v IRC* cited above, as that comment was directed at whether an individual who could only in fact benefit from a small part of the income of the person abroad nonetheless had power to enjoy all of it.

The disregard of legal or equitable rights may be thought to allow account to be taken of what might happen in breach of trust or otherwise in breach of legal obligation. However, HMRC have accepted that regard could only be had to proper use of powers, and this acceptance was referred to with approval by Morritt LJ (*IRC v Botnar* [1999] STC 711, at p 721).

Spouses

69.8 ITA 2007, s 714(4) provides that references to individuals include their spouses or civil partners. As explained in para **69.52**, this indicates that the transferor has power to enjoy if his spouse does, even if the transferor himself is excluded.

AMOUNT OF INCOME TREATED AS ARISING

69.9 Since 6 April 2013 it has been expressly provided that the amount of income treated as arising under s 721 is equal to 'the income of the person abroad' (s 721(3B)). At first sight, this might be construed as meaning that all the income of the person aboard is taken into account, regardless of whether the transferor has power to enjoy *all* such income.

However, in reality, the income of the person abroad which is taken into account is clearly confined to the income which the transferor personally has power to enjoy. This is because s 721(3B) uses the definite article in relation to the income. Thus the income mentioned in s 721(3B) is the same income as is mentioned in s 721(2); in other words, the income of the person abroad which the transfer has power to enjoy.

Prior to 6 April 2013, there was no equivalent to s 721(3B), and so its effect had to be inferred. What was clear under the pre-6 April 2013 legislation was that all income that the transferor had power to enjoy fell to be attributed to him, regardless of the extent of any actual benefit. This was established in *Howard De Walden (Lord) v IRC* [1942] 1 KB 389, [1942] 1 All ER 287, CA and, it may be suggested, plainly remains good law under s 721(3B).

Income attributable to transfer

69.10 A separate question is whether the income treated as arising under s 721 is all the income of the person abroad which the transferor has power to enjoy, or only so much of it (if any) as is attributable to the assets transferred by him. Section 721 itself makes it clear the latter is correct, for the second of the requirements listed in para **71.4** above is that the transferor's power to enjoy is as a result of the transfer and/or associated operations.

That this is correct is supported by *Vestey v IRC* [1980] ST 10, where passages from Lord Wilberforce's speech cited in para **69.52** below indicate that there must be a linkage between the assets transferred and power to enjoy. Such was accepted by HMRC in Tax Bulletin 40 (RI 201) and by a Special Commissioner in *Carvill v IRC* [2000] STC (SCD) 143, 169.

Timing issues

69.11 It is expressly provided that the transferor falls within the enjoyment conditions even if enjoyment is postponed (s 721(4)). However, what is also clear is that the transferor must satisfy one or other of the enjoyment conditions in the tax year in issue. He is not caught merely because he had power to enjoy in some previous year. But if a previous power to enjoy was given effect to by the payment to the transferor of a capital sum, the lack of any current power to enjoy will be academic, as there will be liability under s 727 (as discussed below).

THE ENJOYMENT CONDITIONS

Condition A

69.12 Condition A is that the income concerned is in fact so dealt with as to be calculated at some time to enure for the benefit of the transferor. The application of this condition has been held to be a question of fact. In *Vestey's Executors v IRC* (1949) 3 ITC Lord Simonds said the paragraph required precise findings of fact and in *Vestey v IRC (No 2)* [1978] STC 567 at 579 Walton J considered that 'calculated' meant 'reckoned' or 'estimated' rather than 'likely'.

IRC v Botnar [1999] STC 711 is the leading case on Condition A. Here the taxpayer had created a Liechtenstein settlement under which the only named beneficiaries were persons in the legal profession connected with the protector. The taxpayer was named as an excluded person and as such clause 23 of the settlement prevented him from taking 'any benefit in accordance with the terms of this Settlement'. However, clause 3 of the settlement contained wide overriding powers including power, by clause 3(c), to transfer the trust fund to another trust, freed and discharged from the trusts of the original settlement, and notwithstanding that persons who were not beneficiaries of the original settlement might be beneficiaries of the transferee settlement. Clause 3(c) did not contain any express provision preventing the taxpayer from benefiting under any such transferee settlement. A memorandum made when the original settlement was created indicated that it was envisaged that the power in clause 3(c) could at some stage be exercised to transfer the trust fund to another trust under which the taxpayer and his wife would either be, or be added, as beneficiaries. There was also evidence that leading English counsel had advised that this would be a proper course to take. During the years 1974–1990, no income accrued to the trustees but dividends in excess of £100m were received by underlying holding companies from a UK company run by the taxpayer.

The Court of Appeal held that the retention of the income by the holding companies amounted to dealing with the income and that the Commissioners were entitled to find, as they had, that it had been so dealt with as to be calculated to enure at some point in time for the benefit of the taxpayer, as Condition A requires. However, a more fundamental point arose because it was accepted by HMRC that Condition A could only be invoked if the trustees' purpose in so dealing with the income was proper – in other words if their intention to transfer the trust fund to a new trust from which the taxpayer could benefit was proper. Two members of the Court of Appeal held that as a matter of construction it was and the third held that while as a matter of construction it was not, the scheme could still have been effected lawfully, for the settlement gave the trustees power to take and act on the opinion of suitably qualified counsel.

A question raised by Condition A is whether it extends to income accumulated and beneficially owned by a natural person. This question would arise if the taxpayer had given the assets to a natural person on the understanding, albeit not the obligation, that the donee would deal with them as the taxpayer directed. Such arrangements may be vulnerable, if in reality the income will at some stage be paid over to the taxpayer. Similarly, prearranged devices to route payments out of trusts or companies through natural persons to the taxpayer could be caught for, as explained above (para **69.7**) potential benefits can be taken into account, even if the taxpayer has no legal entitlement to them.

Condition B

69.13 Condition B operates where the income increases the value to the taxpayer of assets held by him or for his benefit. It catches the classic operation at which the transfer of assets code was originally aimed: the sale of income-producing assets to a foreign company in consideration of the issue of shares or debentures to the transferor. It extends to situations where the purchase price is simply left outstanding or is secured by promissory notes. Here Condition B applies because the income increases the company's assets, thereby enhancing the security, and hence the value of the loan notes or debt held by the transferor (*Howard de Walden v IRC* (1941) 25 TC 121; *Ramsden v IRC* (1957) 37 TC 619; *IRC v Brackett* [1986] STC 521).

IRC v Brackett [1986] STC 521 is the leading modern case on Condition B. Here the taxpayer had formed a Jersey discretionary trust of which the beneficiaries were his illegitimate children and their mother. That trust owned a Jersey company which entered into an employment contract with the taxpayer. Under this contract, the company provided the taxpayer's services to clients but the taxpayer was to receive no remuneration until he was 70, at which point he would be paid whatever the directors considered the company could afford. It was also envisaged that the company would buy properties from the taxpayer to provide him with liquidity. This the company did, the purchase price being left payable to the taxpayer by instalments.

In due course the taxpayer's activities generated profits for the company. It used this money both to pay the instalments on the property purchases, and also to put the properties into repair and to provide accommodation and other benefits for the taxpayer's children and their mother. Hoffmann J held that Condition B gave the taxpayer power to enjoy the company's profits, on the grounds that the profits enhanced both the value of the taxpayer's right to the instalments of the purchase price and the value of his right to be considered for remuneration when he attained 70.

It is sometimes said that *Brackett* means that s 720 can be invoked in relation to offshore structures from which the settlor is otherwise excluded if companies in the structure enter into any sort of consultancy or employment contract with him. It does however have to be born in mind that *Brackett* had the special features that all remuneration was deferred and that money was owed to the taxpayer for the properties. It is difficult to see how Hoffmann J's reasoning could apply in the absence of those features, provided the remuneration is commercial with no element of deferral.

Condition C

69.14 Condition C applies if the transferor receives or is entitled to receive a benefit. The benefit must be provided out of the income or out of the funds available as a result of associated operations on the income. As explained in para **68.10**, accumulation or retention of income is an associated operation, as is its investment.

The paradigm case where Condition C is in point is where the taxpayer receives a benefit in kind. Thus in *IRC v Botnar* [1999] STC 711, a flat was made available to the taxpayer rent-free. This, it was held, engaged Condition C.

IRC v Brackett concerned this condition as well as Condition B. Hoffmann J held that the taxpayer was receiving or entitled to receive several benefits, notably the provision of liquidity, the putting of the properties in repair, the potential payments of salary, and the discharge of moral obligations by providing for his children and their mother. It is, however difficult to see any of these items as benefits in the strict sense, as the various items were either for full consideration or not to the taxpayer personally. To that extent the case could be seen as a significant widening of Condition C and thus s 720. However, as indicated in para **68.7**, *Brackett* is a case on its own somewhat extreme facts and that it was the combination of factors, rather than any one individually, which proved fatal. Perhaps significantly, it is a case where the taxpayer was not professionally represented.

Under TA 1988, s 739, the term 'benefit' was defined as including a payment of any kind (s 742(9)(c)). This inclusive definition is not reproduced in ITA 2007. The point may be significant, as the word 'payment' was relied on to invoke Condition C in cases such as *Howard de Walden v IRC* (1941) 25 TC 121. Here the Court of Appeal held that sums payable under the loan notes were benefits because they were payments. This proposition, it may be suggested, is now no longer good as the mere repayment of a debt is simply repayment of what is owed rather than a benefit in the general sense of the term. Indeed the proposition may not have been good even before the removal of references to payment, for in *Vestey's Executors v IRC*, Lord Simonds construed the word 'payable' in the settlements legislation as connoting an out and out parting with trust property (see 31 TC, 1, at p 83 and para **75.7**). When a loan is repaid there is no out and out parting with property as the debtor's obligation is pro tanto reduced. For all these reasons, loan or debt cases such as *Howard de Walden* are, it may be suggested, Condition B cases rather than Condition C cases.

Condition C catches distributions from discretionary trusts. Viscount Dilhorne so stated in *Vestey v IRC* [1980] STC 10, 31, his speech being concurred in by Lord Keith and referred to with approval (on this point) by Lord Edmund Davies (at p 34). It follows that if the transferor is a beneficiary of a discretionary trust, Condition C is engaged. However the distribution must be out of income or accumulated income and, unless a distribution is made in the year in question, Condition C is not in point. This last point follows because a discretionary beneficiary has no right, and thus no entitlement to anything (cf

Walton J's comments on whether discretionary beneficiaries have rights in *Vestey v IRC* [1978] 567, 577, as approved in the House of Lords [1980] STC 10, 17 (per Lord Wilberforce)).

Were Condition C to stand alone it would mean that where the transferor is a discretionary beneficiary of a trust, he has power to enjoy only in a tax year in which he receives a benefit. However, as is explained below, the decision in *IRC v Botnar* means that Condition D applies in any event.

Condition D

69.15 Condition D is in point if the transferor may become entitled to the beneficial enjoyment of the income if one or more powers are exercised or successively exercised. It does not matter who may exercise the powers or whether some consent is required.

The term 'power' is used here in the technical sense as denoting the power vested in a person, the donee of the power, to deal with or dispose of property which is not his own (*IRC v Botnar* [1999] STC 711). It is thus directed at powers vested in trustees and other fiduciary powers.

In *IRC v Vestey* [1978] STC 567, 578, Walton J construed this condition as referring to income proper rather than income which had been turned to capital by accumulation. This analysis appears not to have been shared in the House of Lords (see especially Lord Dilhorne's speech [1980] STC 10, 31). *IRC v Botnar* is now clear authority that it is wrong for the Court of Appeal to have held that the income need only have the attribute of income in the year in which it arises. The Court also held that it is immaterial that the income can only be enjoyed by the taxpayer after it has been removed from the entity to which it first arose.

In *IRC v Botnar*, the income arose in various companies underlying the trust from which the settlor was excluded. The taxpayer could only have become beneficially entitled to the income if the trust fund had been transferred to another trust of which he was a beneficiary, the income had been extracted from the underlying companies, and it had been appointed or distributed to him. This was held, on the facts of the case, to be sufficient to engage Condition D.

A similar analysis was adopted in *Chetwode v IRC* [1977] STC 64. This case concerned an investment company owned by a revocable trust. The company had incurred management expenses and the issue was whether the transferor had power to enjoy such part of the company's income as was used to pay the management expenses. The House of Lords held that Condition D was engaged as the power of revocation meant the transferor could at any time have obtained for himself beneficial enjoyment of the full amount of the company's gross income.

A question posed by the decision in *Botnar* is whether the income of any discretionary trust is caught by Condition D, on the grounds that even if the transferor is wholly excluded, it could be distributed to other trusts to which in due course the settlor might be added as a beneficiary. This question was considered by Mance LJ in *IRC v Botnar* and left open. It may be suggested, however, that this analysis would not obtain save in cases, such as *Botnar* itself, where the intention all along was to benefit the transfer. This conclusion follows from the requirement in s 722(3), that regard must be had to substantial result and effect (see para **69.7**). A further point is that any such benefit would be the independent act of a third party, namely the transferee trustees. In *West v Trennery* [2003] STC 580, the High Court held account could not be taken of such acts, albeit in the context of different statutory provisions (see para **75.5**).

Condition E

69.16 Condition E applies if the transferor is able in any manner to control the application of the income. Such control may be direct or indirect, and as a result the condition was in point in *Lee v IRC* (1941) 24 TC 207, where the taxpayer owned all the voting shares in a Canadian company. He was not a director and so could not directly control the income. But his power to determine the composition of the board gave him indirect control.

Two important limitations were placed on Condition E in *Vestey's Executors v IRC* (1949) 31 TC, 1. The first is that powers exercisable by two or more persons jointly do not engage Condition E in relation to either of them. In *Vestey's Executors v IRC*, the reasoning is expressed in terms of the pre-1969 legislation, which referred to the transferor having power to enjoy by virtue of rights. But it is clear that the reasoning applies to Condition E as it now stands, both because, in referring to entitlement, Condition E connotes rights, and because the underlying reasoning in *Vestey's Executors* is that each transferor must be looked at separately.

The second limitation is that the holder of a special power of appointment does not have control if the power is in favour of a class which does not include him or his spouse (see 31 TC, 1, 86, per Lord Simonds). This proposition was relied on by Vinelott J in *IRC v Schroder* [1983] STC 480, where the transferor effectively had power to appoint and remove trustees. This, Vinelott J held, did not satisfy condition E as the trustees' fiduciary obligations would mean that the transferor could not control what any new trustees subsequently did with the trust income.

HMRC frequently seek to invoke Condition E on the basis of de facto control. This approach was rejected in *IRC v Schroder* and also in *IRC v Botnar* [1998] STC 38. Here HMRC argued that the taxpayer had de facto control of the protector of the settlement and the protector had de facto control of underlying companies. The Special Commissioners decided that this did not amount to indirect control, as the transferor did not have the ability to ensure compliance with his wishes (see [1998] STC at p 72). HMRC did not appeal on this point.

In *IRC v Schroder*, Vinelott J left open the question of whether Condition E can apply where the settlor's control is not sufficient to enable the income to be used for his benefit (see [1983] STC 480 at 505). It may however be suggested that Condition E could not possibly apply in these circumstances.

One reason is the emphasis in ITA 2007, s 722(4) on benefits which may accrue to the transferor which, coupled with the very phrase 'power to enjoy' signifies beneficial enjoyment of the income. The other is that in contrast to legislation such as TCGA 1992, s 86 (see CHAPTER 76) there is no statutory power for the settlor to require or be allowed reimbursement of any tax he has to pay.

POWER TO ENJOY IN PRACTICE

69.17 As will be apparent, the language of the enjoyment conditions can be obscure and difficult. It is worth summarising how they apply to typical offshore structures.

Directly owned company

69.18 Directly owned companies are caught by Condition B, as income generated in the company increases the value of shares held by the taxpayer. The same applies if and to the extent that he owns loan stock.

Settlor interested trust

69.19 Condition D applies to settlor interested discretionary trusts because the trust income could in exercise of the trustees' fiduciary powers be paid to the settlor, either as income or as capital having been accumulated. Should the trust confer an interest in possession on some beneficiary other than the settlor, it may be that Condition D would not be in point. But the issue would be academic if the trust fund could in any circumstances be appointed to the settlor, since ITTOIA 2005, s 624 would catch it (see CHAPTER 75).

Company owned by settlor-interested trust

69.20 Condition D applies because the trustees can procure a dividend from or liquidation of the company and then distribute the proceeds to the settlor.

CAPITAL SUMS

69.21 Sections 728 and 729 together specify the circumstances in which income is treated as arising to the transferor. As under s 721, they are expressed in terms of a given tax year.

The conditions which must be met are as follows:

(1)   Income has become the income of the person abroad as a result of the relevant transfer and/or associated operations.
(2)   The transferor receives or is entitled to receive a capital sum in the tax year or has received a capital sum in a prior tax year.
(3)   The payment of the capital sum is in some way connected with the transfer or an associated operation.
(4)   The transferor is UK resident in the tax year.

Meaning of capital sum

69.22 The term 'capital sum' means any of the following (ITA 2007, s 729(3)):

(a)   Any sum paid to the transferor by way of loan.

(b)   Any sum paid to him by way of repayment of loan.

(c)   Any other sum which is neither income nor paid for full consideration in money or money's worth.

A capital sum is treated as received by the transferor if another person receives it at his direction or as a result of an assignment by him (ITA 2007, s 729(4)). If the capital sum is a loan made to the transferor in an earlier tax year, it does not count as a capital sum if he has wholly repaid it before the beginning of the current tax year (s 729(2)).

A loan is to be distinguished from a sale where the purchase price is left outstanding, even if the price is outstanding for many years and is described as a loan account (*Ramsden v IRC* [1957] 37 TC 619). The same applies where an asset has been sold in exchange for a promissory note (*Lee v IRC* [1941] 24 TC 207).

The fact that the sum paid is capital when paid is sufficient for it to count as capital. It is irrelevant whether or not it is funded by accumulations of what had previously been income (*Vestey v IRC* [1977] STC 414).

The natural meaning of the term 'sum paid or payable' is that a sum of money is paid (*Irving v HMRC* [2008] STC, 597, para 38). However, in other legislation, the context in which the phrase is used may lead to the conclusion that it has a wider meaning and thus includes the transfer of assets in specie (*Irving v HMRC* [2008] STC, para 39). It may be suggested that there is no such context in the transfer of assets code, as where that code intends to comprehend assets in general it says so, as in the core term 'transfer of assets'.

In relation to the comparable provision in the settlement code, ITTOIA 2005, s 633 the Court of Session held that the satisfaction of an agreement to lend a cash sum by means of a transfer of assets in specie was the payment of a capital sum (*McCrone v HMRC* (1967) 44 TC, 142, 46 ATC 85, Ct Sess). It may be suggested that this reasoning would apply also to a loan caught by ss 727–730. But the position would be otherwise if the subject of the loan agreement was an asset in specie, and also, it may be suggested, if the transaction was an out and out transfer of an asset in specie.

In contrast to s 633, ss 727–730 do not specify that the capital sum is caught if paid indirectly. The term 'indirectly' may add little to the general meaning of payment (*Pott's Executors v IRC* [1950] 32 TC 211; see para 71.7). But insofar as it does, such extended meaning is not relevant to ss 727–730.

Connection

69.23 The fact that the capital sum must be in some way connected with a relevant transaction is a limitation. In *Fynn v IRC* [1957] 37 TC 629, the transferor had transferred investments to a company and the investments had been pledged to a bank to secure monies advanced to pay for the acquisition of further investments. Some years later, the transferor lent the company £12,000. Upjohn J held that neither this nor the transferor's right to repayment were connected with the original transfer or the pledging of the transferred securities.

The requirement for a connection is also illustrated by *Vestey v IRC* [1977] STC 414. Here a settlement was made by joint settlors in 1942, and the income of the settled property had to be accumulated and formed a capital fund. In the events which happened, the income of the capital fund was divided into two. Each half of the income of the capital fund had itself to be accumulated if the appointor of that half so directed, and the appointor also had power to direct that capital be distributed to beneficiaries. The appointor exercised both powers, so that the income of the income fund was accumulated and thus capitalised and then capital distributions were made to beneficiaries out of the ensuing capital.

Until this case reached the House of Lords, what are now ss 720 and 727 were not thought to be confined to transferors (see para **68.2**) and what are now ss 731–735 had not been enacted. Further until amendments made to the legislation in 1969 the enjoyment conditions were not thought to catch discretionary trusts (see para **69.6**). For these various reasons HMRC relied on what is now s 727 to assess the various non-transferor beneficiaries who had received the capital distributions. The Special Commissioners addressed the issue of whether the distributions were in any way connected with the transfer, ie the creation of the settlement, or any associated operation, and concluded they were. Their reasoning was that the investment of the income, and the accumulation of the income of the income fund, were associated operations. The necessary connection was provided by the appointor's direction to make capital appointments out of the accumulations.

These findings were accepted both in the High Court and the House of Lords. It is difficult to see any other conclusion as possible, for it is difficult to see a distribution of capitalised income as not in some way connected to the prior accumulation.

Entitlement

69.24 As indicated in para **69.21**, income is treated as arising not merely if the transferor receives a capital sum, but also if he is entitled to receive one. However here entitlement in a prior tax year is disregarded: the entitlement to a capital sum must exist in the tax year itself. It follows that a transferor who lends money to the person abroad is caught so long as the loan is outstanding or if he is repaid. But if he releases the loan he ceases to be within s 727 from the beginning of the following tax year.

The mere fact that the settlor and his spouse are discretionary objects of capital under a trust does not bring s 727 into play for, as a matter of trust law, a discretionary beneficiary is not entitled to anything. But once either of them receives a capital distribution s 727 is in point. Section 727 is not in point merely because the settlor or his spouse is a life tenant, for then their entitlement is to income.

Spouses

69.25 For the reasons given in para **69.52**, s 727 is likely to be in point if the capital sum is received by the transferor's spouse rather than the transferor himself.

Quantum of deemed income

69.26 Since 6 April 2013 it has been expressly provided that the income treated as arising under s 728 is equal to the income of the person abroad (s 728(1A). As with the equivalent provision in s 721, the use of the definite article in s 728(1A) indicates that the income of the person abroad taken into account is that within s 728(1), ie the income deriving from the original transfer. Prior to 6 April 2013 there was no express provision equivalent to s 728(1A) and so it had to be inferred that the income treated as arising under s 728 was equal to the income of a person abroad.

A point to stress, both before and after 6 April 2013, is that receipt of a single small capital sum can cause an amount equal to the entirety of the income of the person abroad to be treated as arising to the transferor. This point was fundamental in *Vestey v IRC* (supra) where it was accepted, on the then view of the law, that each beneficiary in receipt of a capital distribution could be assessed on the whole income of the trust. Further it was also made clear that liability as respects the entire income continued as respects all future years. By restricting ss 720 and 727 to transferors, the House Lords removed non-transferors from these consequences. But in relation to transferors they remain.

In two respects the impact in future years is tempered, but absent these two respects, income of future years in caught. One of these two reliefs for future years applies where the capital sum is constituted by the receipt of a loan, and is to the effect s 727 ceases to apply in the tax year after which the loan is repaid (s 729(2)). The other relief is implicit and is where the transferor has not in fact received a capital sum but is merely entitled to do so. Here liability does not carry forward to a tax year after such entitlement ceases (s 729(1)(a)(ii)).

Practical implications

69.27 In the majority of cases where s 727 might otherwise be in point, the transferor in any event satisfies the enjoyment conditions, so the applicability or otherwise of s 727 is of no practical consequence. It normally only comes into issue in relation to structures from which he and his spouse are entirely excluded and typically arises in loan cases, ie either a genuine commercial loan has been made to the transferor or an inadvertent payment to him has been made which he is bound to repay.

Here the loan or inadvertent payment is indubitably an associated operation. But that fact, it may be suggested, is not relevant, for s 727 requires the capital sum to be connected with an associated operation and not that it itself is an associated operation. Instead the correct analysis should be, as per *Vestey v*

IRC, to see if there is some other associated operation with which the loan or inadvertent payment is connected. If there is none, it may reasonably be concluded that s 727 is not in point.

In logic the same analysis ought to apply where the transferor has made a loan to the offshore structure. Here it will be a question of fact as to whether use of the money lent will be an associated operation in relation to the original relevant transfer. In many cases it will not be and liability under s 727 should be avoided. It should also be kept in mind, for the reasons given above, that releasing the loan would on any view avoid liability for the future.

A context where s 727 is a particular issue is where the transferor and/or his spouse can benefit initially, but later are completely excluded. Typically this can happen as part of the planning of those coming to the UK or that of long-stay non-domiciliaries. Here the transferor may well have had capital distributed to him while a beneficiary, particularly as, if UK resident, such distributions may have been good remittance planning (see paras **21.7** to **21.14**). Here, if s 727 applies, the income of the overseas structure continues to be taxed as his even after he is excluded, which may be regarded as counter intuitive and unjust. Indeed the injustice is all the greater for s 727 gives the transferor no right of recovery as against the transferee.

This last point is a pretty clear indication that s 727 was never intended to apply in such cases. It may be suggested a purposive construction would, when applied to the connection requirement, lead to the result that the requisite connection simply was not there. But the point is far from clear and, unless and until the law is clarified there is clearly risk and thus on one view at least a very nasty trap.

To date HMRC have given no clear published view on these issues.

INCOME OF THE PERSON ABROAD

69.28 A number of rules are common to both sets of provisions in determining the income of the person abroad taken into account. Some of these exclude certain categories of income.

Income and deemed income

69.29 As is explained in para **68.18**, the income of the person abroad is computed in accordance with normal income tax rules. The income includes accrued income profits under the accrued interest scheme (see para **68.20**) and, in the circumstances described in CHAPTER 82 and para **95.27**, offshore income gains.

Income otherwise taxed

69.30 Since 6 April 2013, it has been expressly provided that the income treated as arising under ss 721 and 728 excludes any income of the person abroad on which the transferor is otherwise taxable, provided that all the tax due on that income has been paid (ss 721(3C) and 728(2A)). Prior to 6 April

2013, such exclusion had to be inferred from the general principle that HMRC are not allowed to tax the same income twice. The main application of this rule is to income taxed as the settlor's under the income tax settlement code (as to which see CHAPTER 75). That code deems income so taxed to be the settlor's for all tax purposes (s 624(1)) and thus precluded ss 720 and s 727 even before 6 April 2013, as, by being deemed to be that of the settlor, it had ceased to be that of the person abroad.

These various provisions do not of course mean trust income can never be within the transferor charge. Such a charge would be in point under s 727 if the settlor had received a capital sum from the trust but the trust income fell outside the settlement code because he had been excluded as a beneficiary after receiving the capital sum and a charge under ITTOIA 2005, s 633 was not in point (see para 75.9).

Allocation rules

69.31 No income of the person abroad can be taken into account more than once in charging tax under the transfer of assets code (ITA 2007, s 743(1)). If there is a choice, HMRC are empowered to make a just and reasonable apportionment (s 743(2)). Any apportionment they make is subject to appeal to the First-tier tribunal (s 751).

There are two circumstances in which these provisions operate. The more obvious is where the transferor is within ss 720 or 727 and a non-transferor has received a benefit and so is within ITA 2007, s 731 as is described in the next chapter. Here the impact of the allocation rules is discussed in more detail in CHAPTER 71.

The second situation exists where two individuals are transferors in relation to the same income and each is within ss 720 or 727. Here s 743 provides a means of allocating the income between them. It appears to reverse a suggestion made in *IRC v Pratt* [1982] STC 756, 57 TC 1 to the effect that the transferor charge may fail where the relevant transfer is effected by more than one individual and it is not possible to identify the income which is referable to any single individual's relevant transfer. Section 743 was applied to this effect in *Fisher v Revenue and Customs Comrs* [2014] UK FTT 804 (TC), 17 ITLR 141. Here, three individual quasi transferors were found to be transferors in relation to the entire income of the person abroad and s 743 was relied on to allocate the income between them.

Purchased companies

69.32 It may be that the person abroad used some or all of the assets transferred to purchase shares in an existing company. This point arose in *Vestey v IRC* [1980] AC 1148, where the trustees had purchased a pre-existing Jersey insurance company. Walton J held that the income of the insurance company was not assessable under s 720 or s 727 on the grounds that it did not arise by virtue of the transfer or any operation associated with the transfer ([1977] STC 414, 438; [1978] STC 567, 584). This point was conceded by

HMRC in the House of Lords. It is clear that the position would have been different if and insofar as the trustees had subscribed for shares in the insurance company (see especially [1980] STC 10, 30 per Viscount Dilhorne).

THE CHARGE TO TAX

69.33 As indicated at the beginning of this chapter, the transferor is charged to tax on the income treated as arising under ss 721 and 728. As explained in para **69.2**, this is subject to the motive defence and EU exemption and also the remittance basis. In addition there are a number of further reliefs and rules.

Rate of tax

69.34 In general the income treated as arising to the transferor is taxed at normal income tax rates, ie 20%, 40% or 45% as appropriate. But the income is treated as dividend income if and insofar as the income of the person abroad is dividend income (ITA 2007, s 745(4)). This means that, where the income is taxable on the arising basis, the dividend rates are available.

Deductions and reliefs

69.35 In determining what deductions and reliefs are available, the transferor is treated as if the actual income of the person abroad were his. This means, inter alia, that unilateral or credit relief for foreign tax is in principle available. See para **104.10**.

A difficult issue is whether the transferor is allowed deductions for items incurred by the person abroad and deductible against general income, for example trading losses and interest payments. The logic of s 746 suggests that these items are allowable, the transferor's deemed income being the person abroad's total income as computed for UK tax purposes. Dicta in *Carvill v IRC* [2000] STC (SCD) 143, 169 however, indicate that this is not the correct analysis. Instead, each item of the person abroad's income must be separately attributed to the transferor with no credit for general deductions. This approach is also that adopted by HMRC, in that they do not allow the transferor to credit the person abroad's trading losses against the person abroad's other income (*Tax Bulletin 40* (April 1999) p 652).

Income already taxed

69.36 Sections 720 and 727 can apply even if the income of the person abroad is subject to UK tax in the hands of the transferee (*R v Dimsey* [2001] STC 1520, HL). The main situations where the income is so subject is if it is UK source income or if the transferee is resident in the UK without being domiciled there. This latter situation used to come about with foreign registered companies resident in the UK, which until 6 April 2012 were deemed to be persons abroad (s 718(2); see para **68.16**).

ITA 2007, s 745(1) provides that income tax is not charged at the basic, savings, or dividend rates to the extent that it has already borne income tax at such rates by deduction or otherwise. In *R v Dimsey* [2001] STC 1520, 1530 HMRC assured the House of Lords that in taxing the transferor, credit would always be given for any UK tax that had been borne by the person abroad, and vice versa. In the Court of Appeal, Laws LJ suggested that if HMRC proceeded otherwise in any particular case, the High Court might be invited to prohibit it as an abuse of power ([1999] STC 846, 867).

Double taxation treaties

69.37 The person abroad to whom the actual income accrues may be resident in a jurisdiction with which the UK has concluded a double taxation treaty. Normally the treaty gives the other contracting state sole taxing rights over certain categories of income, and the issue which arises is whether such exemption protects those categories of income from ss 720 and 727. This complex issue is discussed at para 104.9. It may be concluded treaty relief is not available as a matter of law, and a claim to relief is unlikely to be accepted.

The position is different where the transferor, although UK resident, is resident for the purposes of a double taxation treaty in another country. In that scenario it is considered that deemed income under s 720 or 727 falls under the 'other income' article of the treaty, and the treaty is likely to exclude the UK's taxing rights with respect to it (see CHAPTER 101).

Overlap with CFC code

69.38 Chargeable profits caught by the controlled foreign company legislation cannot be taxed on the transferor (ITA 2007, ss 725 and 728(2)). The CFC legislation is in point only if the person abroad is a company. The relief applies insofar as the CFC's profits are apportioned to chargeable UK companies (s 725(2)) and would be in point where a UK company is the actual transferor and one or more shareholders in it can be regarded as quasi transferors.

Actual benefit

69.39 ITA 2007, s 724 imposes a special rule where the transferor has power to enjoy under Condition C because he has received an actual benefit provided out of the income or monies representing it. It charges the full amount or value of the benefit to income tax in the year of receipt, save insofar as the transferor has already been taxed on the income from which it is derived. In *IRC v Botnar* [1999] STC 711, the Court of Appeal decided that where Condition C applies solely by reason of actual receipt of benefit, s 724 substitutes a charge on the amount or value of the benefit for one under s 720 on the whole income of the person abroad. This decision, it should be noted, will only be of advantage to the transferor where the benefit is not a capital sum within s 727 for, if it is within s 727, that section will, as noted above, attach to all the transferee's income.

The Court of Appeal in *IRC v Botnar* did not have to consider how the benefit should be valued, but the Special Commissioner did ([1998] STC 38). The benefit in question consisted of the rent-free occupation of a flat under licence and the Special Commissioner held that the value of the benefit for each of the two years in question was the rent the taxpayer would have had to pay under an arm's length letting.

SUBSEQUENT RECEIPTS

69.40 Relief is given where the taxpayer subsequently receives the income of the person abroad. This relief applies if (a) the income is taken into account in computing the notional income under ss 721 or 728, and (b) it is subsequently received by him. If this occurs the income received is deemed not to form part of his income again for income tax purposes (ITA 2007, s 743(2B)).

New source

69.41 The relief for subsequent receipts applies notwithstanding the fact that the receipt is a new source of income, for if the receipt was not a new source, there would be no separate entity to which the income was originally payable, and thus no charge under ss 720 and 727 at all. Accordingly, the relief exempts income distributions from a transferee company or trust.

A difficult issue arises where the income charged under ss 720 or 727 is received by a company and subsequently paid up to a trust which owns the company in the form of a dividend. Assuming that the trust is discretionary, the dividend is not received by the settlor unless and until the trust distributes it, and yet it is charged as his income under the settlement code, as described above (para **69.30**). There is no express provision preventing a double charge in these circumstances. In 1999 HMRC implied that they would not in this situation tax twice where the company income is distributed to the trust immediately (*Tax Bulletin* 40 (April 1999) p 652). But the position is less clear where there is delay and so the prudent course in cases where the point is applicable is to ensure timely payment of dividends.

Charged or chargeable

69.42 The relief for subsequent receipts applies whether or not, at the time of the subsequent receipt, the transferor has paid the tax due under s 720 or s 727. This follows because s 743(2A) refers to income taken into account in charging income tax rather than to income on which tax has been paid. It is thus clear that the provisions refer to chargeability rather than the fact of payment.

In *Aykroyd v HMRC* (1942) 24 TC 515, one transferee company received debentures taxable as income under s 720 in 1936–37, and in 1937–38 itself paid the value represented by the debentures as a dividend to a second transferee company. Macnaghten J held that this prevented the taxpayer from being charged under s 720 on both receipts. But in the 1930s, what is now s 743 was expressed as applying if the transferor 'has been charged with income tax'. Macnaghten J held that this language required tax to have been paid for 1936–37 before an assessment could be precluded in 1937–38. His decision on this point is not applicable to s 743(4) in its present form as, for the reasons given above, the wording is different.

Capital receipt

69.43 No relief from double taxation is given where the settlor receives the income in capital form. Thus in a company case income tax may be charged on the transferor under s 720 when the income arises to the company and CGT may be charged when the company is sold or liquidated. Here too timely dividends may be a remedy.

TERRITORIAL LIMITS

The transferor

69.44 As noted above (paras **69.5** and **69.21**), income is not treated as arising under ss 721 or 728 unless the transferor is resident in the UK in the tax year of charge. His residence status in the year in which he made the relevant transfer is immaterial (s 721(5)(b).

In the predecessor legislation to s 727 (TA 1988, s 739(3)) it was clear that liability only arose if the transferor was ordinarily resident in the tax year of charge and (if earlier) the tax year in which he received the capital sum. In what appears to have been an inadvertent change, the only territorial limit under s 727 is that the transferor must be resident in the tax year of charge. Should the capital sum have been paid in an earlier tax year his residence status in that year is therefore now immaterial (see s 729, passim). This may be of some practical importance to immigrants with offshore structures not protected by the motive defence.

Should an individual who has been caught by s 727 emigrate, he falls outside the charge. This is because s 727(2) is expressed in terms of the individual who is UK resident.

Until 5 April 2013 the residence criteria for liability under ss 720 and 727 was ordinary residence. There is limited transitional relief for those who under old law would have been treated as not ordinarily resident in one or more tax years up to 2015–16. This is described in para **41.46**, and where the conditions for relief are met, the individual is not taxed under ss 720 or 727 for the tax year or years in question.

Split years

69.45 The circumstances in which an individual arriving in or leaving the UK can split the tax year of arrival or departure are described in paras **41.34** to **41.37**. Split-year treatment does not apply to income treated as that of the arriver or leaver under the transfer of assets code. This conclusion follows because split year treatment applies only if a charging provision expressly applies it, and ITA 2007, ss 720–730 make no such provision. That split year treatment was deliberately withheld from the transfer of assets code is indicated by ITA 2007, ss 726(5) and 730(5), which withhold split year treatment from remittances.

Temporary non-residence

69.46 It may be suggested that the temporary non-residence rule described in paras **41.39** to **41.42** applies insofar as the income of the person abroad is dividend income from a close company (see para **41.41**). This is because notional income under ss 720 and 727 is treated as dividend income if the actual income of the person abroad is dividends (ITA 2007, s 745(4)).

Non-UK domiciled transferor

69.47 The rules applicable to non-UK domiciled transferors are explained in Chapter 72.

THE TRANSFEROR

69.48 The limitation of ss 720 and 727 to transferors is implicit in the language of the sections. Under sub-s (1), the sections are expressed as applying:

> 'for the purpose of preventing the avoiding of liability to income tax by individuals who are ordinarily UK resident by means of relevant transfers' (ss 720(1) and 727(1)).'

The ensuing sections are then expressed in terms of 'such an individual' and thus make it clear that they apply to the individual who effected the relevant transfer or the transferor as he is referred to.

Section 720(1) and 727(1) reflect the provisions of sub-s (1) of TA 1988, s 739. In relation to that section the House of Lords said the legislation is:

> 'directed against persons who transfer assets abroad; who by means of such transfers avoid tax, and who manage when resident in the United Kingdom to obtain or to be in a position to obtain benefits from those assets'. (*Vestey v IRC* [1980] STC 10, 20 per Lord Wilberforce, as approved in *IRC v Willoughby* [1997] STC 995, 999 per Lord Nolan).

As the history of ss 720 and 727 makes clear (para **68.2**) the limitation of the sections to transferors was the principal point of decision in *Vestey v IRC*. But that decision did not define the term 'transferor' or even as such use it, and as a result identifying the transferor is not always straightforward.

Multiple transferors

69.49 In *IRC v Pratt* [1982] STC 756 Walton J explored the issue of multiple transferors. Here a private company made the actual transfer but HMRC sought to treat as transferors three directors who together only owned a minority of the shares. Walton J was clearly of the view that if more than one person transferred assets to an offshore entity each would be liable under ss 720 or 727 on an appropriate proportion of the income, and this is accepted by HMRC in practice (*Tax Bulletin* 40 (April 1999) p 651). The same is the position if there is a single transfer and each transferor owns an identifiable part of the asset transferred, as where they are tenants in common.

The position is more complicated if it is impossible to separate out what each transferor has transferred. Such is the position if several transferors are the beneficiaries of a discretionary trust who together direct the trustees to make the transfer. The implication of Walton J's remarks is that assessment under s 720 or s 727 would not then have been possible. But today the better view is that the allocation rules described in para **69.31** permit apportionment. Such is the view of HMRC in the draft guidance published in August 2013, and the same view has been taken by the First-tier tribunal (*Fisher v Revenue and Customs Comrs* [2014] UK FTT 804 (TC), 17 ITLR 141 paras 186–189).

Quasi transferors

69.50 The problem of quasi transferors stems from a subsidiary ratio in the case overruled in *Vestey*, namely *Congreve v IRC* [1946] 2 All ER 170, 30 TC 163. The central dramatis personae of *Congreve* were the taxpayer, her father, and a successful trading company the father had built up and ran. Initially, in 1928, the father transferred 60% of the shares in the trading company to a Canadian holding company and in 1932 he transferred all the shares in that company to the taxpayer. The next stage, also in 1932, was the interposition of a second holding company between the original holding company and the trading company shares. The original holding company was then liquidated, leaving the second holding company directly owned by the taxpayer.

At the same time as these events were taking place, both the taxpayer and the trading company transferred foreign portfolio investments they held to further Canadian holding companies. The final transaction in this series was the sale by the taxpayer's father of another 28% of the trading company to the second holding company, increasing its interest in the trading company.

The result of all these transactions was that foreign income which would otherwise have accrued to the taxpayer and the trading company, and the dividends paid by the trading company, were payable free of income tax to assorted holding companies abroad. The taxpayer had power to enjoy this income because the consideration for the transfers consisted mainly of debentures repayable on demand.

The Commissioners accepted that everything done in relation to the transactions was brought about by the taxpayer's father, the taxpayer merely signing as she had been instructed. The issue was whether the taxpayer could escape liability under s 720 in respect of the trading company dividends or its transferred portfolio investments, on the grounds that the investments were transferred by the trading company, and the shares in the trading company by the original holding company and the taxpayer's father.

Lawrence J considered that s 720 extended to transfers effected by an agent of the taxpayer or by her wholly-owned company, and this brought the transfer by the original holding company into the section. But he held that the father's transfer was not caught with the result that the dividends attributable to the 28% of the shares transferred by him to the second holding company escaped. He appears also to have considered that the trading company's transfer escaped, for at the time of the transfer the taxpayer only controlled 65% of the company.

In the Court of Appeal and the House of Lords all the difficulties were brushed aside for, in the ratio overruled by *Vestey*, it was held that the taxpayer was liable under s 720 regardless of whether she had been the original transferor. But in the Court of Appeal, Cohen LJ formulated a subsidiary ratio, to the effect that even if s 720 were restricted to the original transferor, it applied if he or she had procured the transfer. For these purposes Lawrence J's identification of wholly-owned companies with the taxpayer was rejected, but on the facts the Court of Appeal held that the taxpayer had, through her father as agent, procured all the transfers concerned.

Close reading of the speeches in *Vestey* makes it clear that only the principal ratio of Congreve was in terms overruled. The survival or otherwise of Cohen LJ's subsidiary ratio is a matter of difficulty, for while Lords Dilhorne and Keith affirmed it, the other three law lords did not as such endorse it. Instead Lord Wilberforce merely contemplated, as an aside, that ss 720 and 727 'may be' extended to persons 'associated' with the transfer. The better view must be that Lord Wilberforce's aside, in conjunction with the affirmation by Lords Dilhorne and Keith, does preserve the subsidiary ratio and such was accepted by Walton J in *IRC v Pratt* [1982] STC 756. Accordingly the issue is what exactly Cohen LJ meant in the subsidiary ratio. Undoubtedly the best, perhaps the only, guide to this is to look at the father's role in *Congreve*. Effectively he was the person who devised and set up the schemes, and accordingly it is such persons, the promoters, who are best regarded as quasi transferors.

Such a conclusion is confirmed by *IRC v Pratt* [1982] STC 756, for here Walton J accepted the proposition that the subsidiary ratio could render a person who procured the transfer taxable under s 720. Indeed the term 'quasi transferor' comes from *Pratt*. However, Walton J rejected the proposition that the three directors who were minority shareholders were quasi transferors. He held that the subsidiary ratio applied only to persons who procured the transfer, and that procurement could only take place if the alleged transferor had the power to procure. In a company context this means that he has to have control of the company, as in *Congreve* itself.

Walton J's approach in *Pratt* indicates that a person cannot be a quasi transferor if the party who in fact effected the transfer is an individual and the alleged quasi transferor merely used persuasion. In *Carvill v IRC* [2000] STC (SCD) 143, 163, a Special Commissioner accepted this in principle. However, he contemplated that there might be exceptional cases where the alleged quasi transferor's influence over the actual transferor is so strong as to make him a quasi transferor.

HMRC, in addressing the issue of quasi transferors, follow the decided cases. Their stated position, following Lord Wilberforce's words in *Vestey*, is that ss 720 and 727 can potentially apply to someone who was associated with the transfer, and that such would include a person who procured the transfer (*Tax Bulletin* 40 (April 1999) p 651).

Fisher

69.51 The quasi transferor concept has been significantly extended by the First-tier tribunal in *Fisher v Revenue and Customs Comrs* [2014] UK FTT 804 (TC), 17 ITLR 141. Here the three taxpayers owned respectively 26%, 26% and 24% of a UK trading company and all three were directors of it. The UK company sold its tele-betting business to a Gibraltar company in the same family ownership and the tribunal found that transfer was jointly procured by the three individuals who were accordingly quasi transferors.

It may be doubted whether this extension of the quasi transferor concept is consistent with either *Congreve* or *Pratt*. It should also be kept in mind that the quasi transferor concept is not found in the legislation but is a judicial gloss. It is clear from the facts of *Fisher* that income tax was not avoided and that there was no intention to avoid income tax. In these circumstances the extension of the quasi transferor concept goes against the stated purpose of the transferor charge (see para **69.4**) and on that basis alone is unwarranted. It is to be hoped that the issue will be considered on appeal.

SPOUSES AND CIVIL PARTNERS

69.52 ITA 2007, s 714(4) states that, for the purposes of the transfer of assets code, references to individuals include their spouses or civil partners. The case law indicates two possible meanings for this reference.

The first is indicated by *Vestey's Executors v HMRC* (1949) 31 TC 1. Here the settlors and their wives were excluded from benefit under the trusts concerned, but one of the settlors had a special power of appointment exercisable in favour of his widow. One of the issues in the case was whether that power brought that settlor within the enjoyment conditions for purposes of the transfer of assets code or constituted an interest in the settlement under predecessor legislation to ITTOIA 2005, s 624 (see CHAPTER 75). The House of Lords decided it did not, on the grounds that 'wife' did not comprehend 'widow'.

Lord Morton, who gave the leading judgment, said:

> 'I think that the treatment of husband and wife by the legislature for Income Tax purposes rests on the view that any income enjoyed by one spouse is a benefit to the other. It is not surprising, therefore, that in the sections now under consideration a benefit to the wife of the settlor is treated as being a benefit to the settlor, but it seems to me unlikely that this principle is being extended by these sections to the widow of the settlor.'

It is clear from this that Lord Morton regarded the reference to spouses and civil partners as signifying merely that the enjoyment conditions are satisfied if the spouse, as distinct from the transferor himself, has power to enjoy. The then version of the transferor charge (FA 1936, s 18) is set out in the judgment and in that version it is difficult to read the provision any other way.

The second possible meaning is indicated by Lord Nolan in *IRC v Willoughby* [1997] STC 995. *Willoughby* was not concerned with the spouse issue at all, but in the course of summarising the law Lord Nolan said (at p 999):

> 'It has now been made clear, by the decision of your Lordships House in *Vestey v IRC* [1980] STC . . . . that the charging provisions of the section can be applied only to the individual (or the wife or husband of the individual) who has made the relevant transfer of assets.'

What this means, if right, is that the reference to spouses means not merely that the enjoyment or capital sum conditions can be satisfied by the spouse, but that in such a case the spouse can be assessed on the income of the person abroad rather than the transferor himself. Further the implication would be that assessment on the spouse is possible even if the spouse does not satisfy the enjoyment or capital receipt conditions, but the transferor does. This construction is possible under the present language of s 714(4) in a way that was not so under FA 1936, s 18. However it is unclear how far, on this narrow spouse point, what Lord Nolan said is really supported by *Vestey v IRC* [1980] STC 10. Lord Wilberforce, who gave the leading speech, made no mention of spouses, although the point is referred to by Lord Dilhorne, Edmund-Davies and Keith.

In the draft transfer of assets guidance HMRC appear to take the position that the wider construction indicated by Lord Nolan is correct and that in law the spouse can be assessed (INT M 600640 and 600660). However the draft guidance also says (at 600460):

> 'In general (unless there are wider arrangements) HMRC will not use transfer of assets to charge tax on one spouse or civil partner in respect of income arising to the other spouse or civil partner, where that spouse or civil partner has made a transfer of assets but is, for example, outside the charge because say of the application of non-UK domicile provisions. In effect the general approach will be to apply the word individual (where the individual has a spouse or civil partner) . . . in a way that is consistent with the individual who has the power to enjoy income of a person abroad, entitlement to capital sums . . . '.

This statement reflects an earlier statement published in *Tax Bulletin 40*, dealing with mixed domicile marriages.

It is clear HMRC have difficulty in the point. It may be suggested that if the point were ever litigated, Lord Nolan's dictum in *Willoughby* would, on this point, not be followed and instead the approach in *Vestey's Executors* preferred.

One reason for so suggesting is that the legislation contains no provision determining how any assessment should be allocated between spouses. In one sense this point may not be material, for the allocation rule in s 743(2) (see para **69.31**) gives HMRC authority to make a just and reasonable appointment. But this provision was not introduced until 1981 (FA 1981, s 46) and so can hardly be an indication of what the spouse provision was meant to mean when first enacted in 1936. It would be necessary to say that consolidation in 1988, or perhaps the rewrite in 2007 had switched the meaning of the spouse provision from that implicit in *Vestey* to that stated by Lord Nolan. It would be odd for a consolidation or the rewrite to make such a fundamental change.

A second reason for so suggesting is that if Lord Nolan's dictum is right, there would be curious results where the transferor is non-UK resident but his spouse is UK resident. Here, on Lord Nolan's formulation all the income would be assessable on the spouse, even if the spouse herself did not satisfy the enjoyment or capital sum conditions. The allocation rules in 743(2) would not be in issue for, if the transferor is non-UK resident, no income is taken into account in relation to him under the code for the code operates on him only if he is UK resident (see para **69.44**). The passage from the draft guidance set out above indicates HMRC would not take the point, but the fact they would not do so is not relevant to the legal analysis.

For all these reasons it may cogently be suggested the approach in *Vestey's Executors* is the correct one. Indeed were Lord Nolan's dictum right, the point at issue in *Vestey's Executors* would not have needed to be discussed at all, for the wife would have had power to enjoy in her own right. This would have resulted in attribution of the income to the transferor in any event as the law then stood, prior to the introduction of independent taxation for spouses.

A final point to note is the position of widows or divorcees if, contrary to the above, Lord Nolan's dictum is right. Here it may cogently be said that once the spouse is no longer married assessment on her ceases on any view to be possible. This is on account of the actual point of decision in *Vestey's Executors*, namely that 'wife' does not include 'widow'. It is clear from an earlier sentence in Lord Morton's speech that divorcees also are comprehended:

> 'To my mind, if a payment is to come within the sub-section it must be made to a lady who answers the description of a wife at the time of payment.'

Future spouses and civil partners

69.53 If the conclusion reached above is correct, a difficult question, in relation to power to enjoy, is whether s 720 is in point even if the person to whom the settlor is currently married or in civil partnership is excluded, but benefit could be conferred on some future spouse or civil partner, at a time when such individual is a spouse or civil partner of the settlor. In other words, does the reasoning in *IRC v Tennant* (1942) 24 TC 215 and *Unmarried Settlor v IRC* [2003] STC (SCD) 274 extend to s 720? The impact of those cases is explained in para **76.10** and, while the point is not wholly certain, the better view must be that they could extend to s 720. Their reasoning is, it may be suggested, particularly apposite in relation to enjoyment condition D (see para **69.15**).

On the basis that this is right, a settlement which excludes the transferor and his current spouse or civil partner is still within s 720 unless future spouses or civil partners are also prevented from benefiting at a time when they are married to or in civil partnership with the settlor. In relation to spouses, this is achieved by any well-drawn settlor exclusion clause, and in any new settlement such can and should be extended to civil partners. This is typically achieved by defining 'spouse' so that it includes any spouse or civil partner for the time being. But settlements made before the Civil Partnership Regulations 2005 do not refer to civil partners and so, as a matter of strict construction, it may be that all settlements with living UK resident settlors previously thought to be outside s 720 came within the section on 5 December 2005, the date on which the Regulations took effect.

Fortunately HMRC indicated that they would not take this point, at least in relation to settlements in existence on 23 November 2005. The relevant correspondence is summarised in para **76.11**. But as stated in para **76.11**, and despite the correspondence, all trustees would be well advised to extend any existing spouse exclusion to civil partners in all cases where they have power to do so.

Further theoretical problems have been created by the Marriage (Same Sex Couples) Act 2013 (MSSCA), which since 13 March 2014 has required all references to spouses in previous legislation to be read as including same-sex spouses (Sch 3, para 1). As a matter of strict construction, it may be that settlements made before the MSSCA came into force, which were not previously settlor-interested, became settlor-interested on that date due to the possibility of benefits being provided to a future same-sex spouse of the settlor, at a time when such individual is married to the settlor. This is highly debatable, as it is uncertain whether a reference to a spouse in a pre-MSSCA exclusion clause might, reasonably, be read as including a same-sex spouse. The MSSCA provides that the extension of the meaning of 'marriage' 'does not alter the effect of' any private legal instrument made before the MSSCA was brought into force (Sch 4, para 1), but arguably that does not answer the question. It is to be hoped that HMRC will take the same line here as in relation to the introduction of civil partnerships. But it would certainly be prudent for trustees (who have the power to do so) to amend any pre-MSSCA trust to make it clear that a spouse includes a same-sex spouse. To avoid ambiguity and ensure that s 720 is not applicable (where that is the intention), the definition of 'spouse' in new trusts should expressly include a same-sex spouse.

COMPLIANCE

69.54 HMRC expect taxpayers to draw HMRC's attention to the implications of ss 720 and 727 when submitting details of transactions to which it may potentially apply (*Tax Bulletin* 40 (April 1999) p 652). Disclosure must be made in box 46 of the Foreign Pages if the taxpayer is relying on the motive defence described in CHAPTER 73.

Chapter 70

NON-TRANSFERORS

INTRODUCTION

70.1 ITA 2007, s 731 imposes a charge to tax in certain circumstances where a relevant transfer of the kind described in CHAPTER 68 has occurred. In contrast to the rules described in the previous chapter, it charges non-transferors – ie individuals who neither made the transfer nor can be classed as quasi transferors (see para 69.50).

Section 731 charges the income which is treated as arising under s 732. That section lays down certain preconditions and then provides that, if those preconditions are met, s 733 specifies whether any income is in fact to be treated as arising and, if so, in what amount. It is convenient to refer to the income which is treated as arising as s 732 income.

This chapter deals with the charge to tax under s 731 and the preconditions set out in s 732. The next chapter addresses the rules in s 733 determining how the s 732 income is computed.

A few years ago there was consultation as to whether (and if so how) ITA 2007, ss 731–735 might be amended. Draft legislation was published in December 2012 but this was withdrawn for further consideration. At the time of writing the most recent development is a document issued on 18 July 2013 entitled 'Reform of an anti-avoidance provision: Transfer of Assets Abroad. Summary of responses and further consultation'.

THE CHARGE TO TAX

70.2 The person charged to tax under s 731 is the individual who satisfies the preconditions set out in s 732. But there are four circumstances in which the s 732 income may not be charged, namely where the motive defence applies, where the EU defence applies, where the individual is a remittance basis user, and where the individual is resident in another country for the purposes of a double taxation treaty.

Motive defence

70.3 The motive or purpose defence is explained in CHAPTER 73. It does not stop deemed income from arising under s 732 but instead operates as an exemption from the charge under s 731 (s 731(4)). It operates provided that the conditions for the defence are satisfied in the tax year in which the s 732 income is treated as arising.

EU defence

70.4 Like the motive defence, the EU defence in ITA 2007, s 742A operates not by preventing s 732 income from arising but by exempting it from charge (s 731(4)). This defence is described in CHAPTER 74 and is only in point if charging the s 732 income would breach the fundamental freedoms. Section 742A applies only to income arising from post-2012 transactions but if the fundamental freedoms are breached in pre-2012 cases the charge on s 732 income is in any event precluded by EU law (see further CHAPTER 107, especially para 107.24).

Remittance basis user

70.5 Where the individual to whom the s 732 income arises is a remittance basis user, the income escapes charge if and to the extent that (a) the relevant income to which it relates is relevant foreign income and (b) the benefit to which the s 732 income is matched is not remitted to the UK. Where condition (a) is met, the s 732 income is itself treated as relevant foreign income and so strictly any tax charge for the remittance basis user is charged under ITTOIA 2005, s 832, rather than under s 731 (ITA 2007, s 735). This complex matter is explained in CHAPTER 72.

Treaty relief

70.6 Section 732 income is typically not charged to tax in the event that the individual is dual resident, and resident for the purposes of a double taxation treaty in the other contracting state. The deemed income is considered to fall within the 'other income' article of a typical treaty, and the usual result is that the other contracting state has exclusive taxing rights (see CHAPTER 101).

PRECONDITIONS

70.7 The preconditions for income to arise under s 732 are as follows (s 732(1)):

(1)   A relevant transfer occurs.
(2)   An individual receives a benefit.
(3)   That individual is resident in the UK, is not taxable under ss 720 or 727 by reference to the transfer, and is not otherwise chargeable to income tax on the benefit.
(4)   The benefit is provided out of assets which are available for the purpose as a result of the relevant transfer or one or more associated operations.

THE RELEVANT TRANSFER

70.8 The term 'relevant transfer' is as defined in ITA 2007, s 716 and thus bears the meaning discussed in CHAPTER 68. The key requirement is that income must have become payable to a person abroad as a result of the transfer or one or more associated operations.

Identity of the transferor

70.9 A point to stress is that the transfer can be effected by anybody, for ss 731–735 are not concerned with the taxation of transferors. There is no requirement that the person who made the transfer be resident in the UK or in any way connected with the UK.

Timing issues

70.10 Section 732(1)(a) refers to the relevant transfer in the present sense, by postulating that it 'occurs'. Read literally, and as income tax is an annual tax, this might suggest that the transfer has to occur in the tax year in which the benefit is conferred. As indicated in para **68.5**, the context and, in particular the computational rules in ITA 2007, s 733, make it clear this cannot be right.

One transfer or several

70.11 As explained in para **68.6**, the term 'relevant transfer' requires there to be focus on a specific transfer of assets (or creation of rights). The associated operations concept emphasises this, for as explained in para **68.8** to **68.13**, an operation is only associated if effected in relation to the assets transferred, assets representing those assets, or income any of those assets generate.

The result is that it is possible for the same person abroad to hold assets resulting from more than one transfer. This would not be the position where all the original assets are transferred by the same person at the same time or where multiple transfers are so closely linked as to be a single transaction in the *Ramsay* sense. But if the various transfers of the original assets are separate transactions decided on at separate times, there are genuinely multiple transfers and it is difficult and, in most cases, impossible to regard the later transaction as part of the same transfer as the earlier (see para **68.12**).

The significance of this is that, under s 732(1)(c), the assets out of which the benefit is provided must be available for the purpose by virtue of the transfer or one or more associated operations – ie operations effected in relation to the assets originally comprised in the transfer or assets representing them. Further, income is only relevant income under the computational rules described in the next chapter if as a result of the same transfer it can be used to provide a benefit for the recipient of the benefit. This follows because s 733(1) refers to benefits being provided as mentioned in s 732(1)(c), and by the fact that the definite article prefaces the words 'relevant transfer or associated operations' in steps 2 and 3.

The point may be illustrated by postulating an offshore settlement, to which the settlor transferred an income-producing portfolio of investments. Some years later, he or some other person transferred to the trust a parcel of real estate which has never produced income. For the reasons given above, the transfer of the portfolio is one relevant transfer and the transfer of the real estate another. If, still having produced no income, the real estate is distributed to a beneficiary it may be concluded that no s 732 income arises, for the benefit provided is not provided out of assets resulting from the transfer of the income-producing portfolio or any operation associated with that transfer.

Transfer or associated operation

70.12 A related issue is whether a given transaction is itself the relevant transfer or whether the legislation applies on the basis that it is merely an operation associated with another transaction which is the relevant transfer. To take the typical case of trustees who incorporate a holding company to hold investments, is the income payable to the holding company so payable because of the transfer of assets to the holding company? Or is it so payable because of the transfer of assets to the settlement together with an associated operation represented by the transfer to the holding company?

An argument based on authority may be made in favour of the former view. In *IRC v Herdman* (1967) 45 TC 394, the House of Lords held that associated operations were not relevant to the transferor charge where power to enjoy the income of the person abroad resulted from the transfer alone (see para **73.13**). Parity of reasoning suggests that where there is a transfer which on its own causes income to become payable to a non-resident, that is the transfer of assets which brings s 731 into play. If this view is right it is normally a transfer alone which causes the income to become payable to the relevant foreign entity. However, one instance where this would not be so is where the transfer is to a resident trust and the trust then migrates. Migration is not a transfer but it is an associated operation (*Congreve v IRC* [1948] 1 All ER 948).

The contrary view is that the whole tenor of the transfer of assets code predicates that the transferor be an individual. Without such a limitation, the transferor charge does not work (see para **68.6**). If this view is right, onward transfers by the transferee are operations associated with the original transfer of assets and not new transfers.

The issue as to whether a subsequent transaction is the transfer or an associated operation also arises where the trustees of one settlement make an out and out appointment of trust assets to another settlement. Is the advance the transfer of assets or is it simply an operation associated with the transfer of the assets by the settlor to the original settlement. Here, in addition to the arguments canvassed above, there is the further point that once the assets are in the transferee trust the operative trusts are those of that trust. In these circumstances the argument that the relevant transfer is the transfer to that trust is perhaps stronger.

THE INDIVIDUAL

70.13 The preconditions listed above (para **70.7**) place three requirements on the individual:

(1)   He must be resident in the UK.
(2)   He must not be taxable as transferor.
(3)   He must be not otherwise chargeable to income tax on the benefit.

Residence

70.14 Section 732 requires that the individual be UK resident for the tax year in which the benefit is received. Split year treatment is not applied to the transfer of assets code and so a benefit received in the non-UK part of a tax year may be taxed. However, the rule for temporary non-residents described in paras **41.38** to **41.43** does not apply and so a benefit received in a tax year of non-residence is outside s 732 even if the recipient is non-resident for a period not exceeding five years (see further paras **41.38** and **29.22**).

Until 2012–13 ordinary residence was the connecting factor applicable under s 732. There is limited transitional relief, described in para **41.46**, for those who, under old law, would not have been considered ordinarily resident. In appropriate cases this is available up to 2015–16.

Not taxable as transferor

70.15 The transferor charge is explained in the previous chapter. Where the individual is taxable as transferor, he is not within s 732. It is expressly provided that this result follows even if he is a remittance basis user who escapes charge because of the remittance basis.

Difficulties can arise where the income arising to the person abroad is the result of transfers by more than one individual. This is an aspect of the multiple transferor issue, discussed in para **69.49**. It would seem that where what each transferred can be separated out, benefits to any given individual would be disregarded if attributable to what he transferred but otherwise would be taken into account under s 732. Should it be impossible to separate out what each transferred, benefits would be disregarded if attributable, on a just and reasonable basis, to what the individual had transferred (see para **69.49**).

It is sometimes said that the exclusion of benefits to the transferor extends also to the spouse of the transferor. The basis for this argument is ITA 2007, s 714(4), which states that in the transfer of assets code, reference to individuals include their spouses. But as explained in para **69.52**, the better view is that this subsection does not render the spouse of the transferor liable as transferor and, if so, she is not excluded from the benefits charge under s 731.

Not otherwise chargeable to income tax

70.16 The requirement that the benefit not be chargeable to income tax is couched not in terms of whether the benefit is income but of whether the recipient is liable to income tax. Strictly an income benefit taxed as somebody else's income could still be a s 732 benefit. An example of this is income or accumulated income paid to a minor child of the settlor (see para 75.8). But in this instance HMRC have said they would not tax the benefit both under s 731 and under ITTOIA 2005, s 629 (*Tax Bulletin* 40 (April 1999) p 652).

THE BENEFIT

70.17 Sections 732 and 733 do not define the term 'benefit'. The previous TA 1988 provisions stated that 'benefit' included a payment of any kind, but this inclusive definition does not feature in the present legislation. Perhaps the only guidance is the requirement that the amount or value of the benefit is brought into account in the computation under s 733. This indicates that the benefit must be one which is capable of valuation. That apart, the question of what (if any) benefit there is is one of fact, to be determined on the normal meeting of the term.

As indicated in para 70.7, a benefit is only caught if it is provided out of assets which are available for the purpose. It is this requirement which links the benefit to the relevant transfer. Assets count as available for the purpose if so available as a result of the relevant transfer alone, or as a result of one or more associated operations. For this reason, the definition of associated operations, discussed in paras 68.8 to 68.13, is crucial in linking benefit and transfer.

The most important practical point arising out of the linkage requirement occurs where there have been multiple transfers to the same transferee. As explained above (para 70.11) each should be looked at separately and, if the income arises under one and the benefit under the other, no s 732 income arises.

Must the benefit be bounteous?

70.18 The word 'benefit' connotes bounty and so it is reasonably clear that bounty must be involved. As indicated above, before the re-writing of the legislation in 2007, the term 'benefit' was defined as including a payment of any kind (TA 1988, s 742(9)(c)) and in relation to enjoyment Condition C in the transferor charge, a repayment of loan notes was held to be a benefit (see *Howard de Walden v IRC* (1941) 25 TC 121 and para 55A.8). But, as suggested in para 69.14 above, such repayment would not now be considered a benefit, both because of the omission of the definition of 'benefit' as including payments of any kind from the current iteration of the legislation, and because more recent judgments indicate that for an action to be a benefit, it must involve the conferment of bounty or the transfer of value.

It follows that the repayment of a debt owed by a non-resident is not a benefit. Such a scenario is not common with non-transferors as normally the person repaid is the original creditor and thus the transferor. But the debt may have been sold, given away or bequeathed on death.

A further implication is that receipts resulting from a fair bargain are not caught. The point is analogous to that arising under ITEPA 2003, s 201 where the word 'benefits' is used. Here it was held in relation to the predecessor to s 201 (TA 1988, s 154) that receipts from fair bargains are outside the charge (*Mairs v Haughey* [1992] STC 495; affd [1993] STC 569).

Assuming that is right, an individual does not receive a benefit when he sells an asset, unless the consideration for the sale clearly exceeds the value of what is sold.

Free use of property

70.19 The free use of property is an annual benefit equal to the rent or licence fee that would be chargeable were the arrangement at arm's length. Such has always been HMRC's view (*Tax Bulletin* 40 (April 1999), p 651) and it is supported in *IRC v Botnar* [1998] STC 38. Here the Special Commissioner decided that the value of the benefit for the purposes of ITA 2007, s 724 was the market rent of the flat (see para **69.39**).

In determining market rent, comparable arm's length lettings have to be looked at and valuation advice is required. It may be that the terms under which the occupier occupies require him to insure, redecorate and keep the property in repair. Should his obligations in these respects be greater than the arm's length comparables, the rent under those comparables should be discounted to reflect the greater level of obligation. An extreme example of this occurred in *Carter v Hunt* [2000] STC (SCD) 17, where the property concerned was a Grade I listed building. The occupier was obliged under the terms of the licence to keep it in repair and ended up spending more than the annual rental value. HMRC accepted in these circumstances there was no benefit.

In some cases it can be difficult to tell whether there is a one-off benefit when the licence arrangement starts or an annual benefit as it continues. The latter however, is the correct analysis if the licence is terminable, for then the annual benefit is forbearance from termination. A similar point arises if the occupier also co-owns a share in the property. Here the annual benefit, assuming the occupier has exclusive use, is the forbearance of the offshore entity from asserting its rights to joint occupation (*Carter v Hunt*, supra).

Valuing the benefit is relatively easy with real estate, as in practice there are arms' length rental comparables. With chattels and in particular fine art, the exercise can be challenging, as commercial leases or licences of art objects are rare. On one view, a custody arrangement whereby the custodian takes full responsibility for housing the art and for insurance and repair, is if anything a benefit to the owner as absent such an arrangement he would have to pay to have the objects securely stored. It is noteworthy that in the case of *Macpherson v IRC* [1988] STC 362, a long-term custody arrangement for valuable pictures was accepted as being on arms' length terms even though it required a payment by the custodian to the owner of just £40 per year.

In practice it is normally accepted that use of art or other chattels is a benefit and in practice one per cent of insurance value is often used as a measure. However ultimately the valuation of the benefit is a question of fact, and so the prudent course if it is desired to avoid a benefit is to have professional advice and an adjuster clause.

A point to keep in mind with chattels is that there are no express quantification rules comparable to those applicable to benefits in kind under employment tax legislation (see CHAPTER 93). That legislation, rather than the transfer of assets charge, is in point should the owner of the chattels be a company and the user on the facts a shadow director.

Loans

70.20 As with the free use of property it has always been HMRC's view that interest free loans are an annual benefit equal to the interest forgone (*Tax Bulletin* 40 (April 1999), p 651). This view is supported by *Billingham v Cooper* [2001] STC 1177 where the Court of Appeal decided that an interest-free loan was a benefit within the meaning of the capital payment rules in TCGA 1992, s 87 (see para **78.12**). The benefit was the trustee's successive acts in not calling in the loan, to be valued retrospectively as equal to the interest which would have been charged had the loan been at a commercial rate. The draft transfer of assets guidance indicates that HMRC apply the official rate in determining the quantum of the annual benefit where the loan is interest-free (INTM 601620). It is accepted in the draft guidance that there is no benefit if commercial interest is paid.

Frequently interest on loans is rolled up. Here the reality may be that the interest is unlikely ever to be paid and in these circumstances HMRC might well argue that there is a benefit equal to the interest rolled up (INTM 601620, supra). Such a result should be avoided where the loan is secured and the interest is compounded. But it is important that the loan to value ratio is such that the rolled up interest as well as the principal is adequately secured. HMRC's argument that the rolled up interest is a benefit could have considerable force if the loan is unsecured, particularly if the beneficiary has insufficient personal assets to be in a position to secure such a loan from a commercial lender.

In an extreme case, it would be open to HMRC to argue that the benefit of what appears to be a loan is in fact equal to the amount lent. This might be the position if on the facts there is no realistic possibility of the loan being repaid, as where the recipient uses the loan to fund current spending and has few personal assets. HMRC instance a case on the transactions in securities legislation, *IRC v Williams* [1980] STC 535 as one where the reality was the loan would not be repaid (see further para **89.10**). In that case the lender was a company and as part of the scheme it came to have the taxpayers as directors and indirect controlling shareholders.

What emerges from all this is that it must be clear that the beneficiary will repay the loan if the benefit is going to be computed on the basis only of interest forgone. If the benefit charge on interest is also to be avoided either the interest must be paid at the official rate as it falls due, or the arrangements for rolling it up must be commercial.

Benefits under trusts

70.21 An obvious example of an individual receiving a benefit is where he receives a distribution from a trust in cash or in specie. For the reasons just noted (para **70.16**), the distribution does not count as a benefit if it is otherwise taxed as income, but if not it does.

HMRC do not in practice regard the conferring of a life interest on a beneficiary as a benefit within ss 731–735 and nor do they regard those sections as applying should a life tenant sell his life interest (*Tax Bulletin* 40 (April 1999) p 651).

Companies

70.22 It may be suggested that a distribution by a company is not a benefit under s 732. In the case of dividends, this result follows because in general such dividends are taxable as the recipient's income. The position on liquidation or in the rare cases where a distribution is otherwise capital is more complex. But there are arguments for concluding there is no benefit. This is because a liquidation distribution is simply payment to the shareholders of what already belongs to them (*IRC v Laird Group* [2003] STC, 1349, 1358).

However, this does not mean companies are outside s 732. A benefit in kind which is not a dividend is a s 732 benefit, albeit only in circumstances where the employment income benefit-in-kind charge is not in point (cf CHAPTER 93).

RECEIVES

70.23 Section 732 does not define the term 'receives' and nor is there any category of deemed receipt or extension of receipt to indirect receipt. It follows that, as with the definition of benefit, the issue as to whether the non-transferor has received the benefit is a question of fact, to be determined by reference to the normal meaning of the term.

Time of receipt

70.24 As with the requirement that a relevant transfer 'occurs', the benefit requirement is expressed in the present tense, ie that the individual 'receives' the benefit. On the face of it this indicates that s 732 income can only arise in the tax year in which the benefit is received. But in reality this cannot be right, as the computational rules described in the next chapter make it clear that surplus benefits must be carried forward.

Benefit received prior to income arising

70.25 It may cogently be argued that s 732 is not engaged if the receipt of the benefit occurs before any income has arisen to the person abroad, and that a benefit so received should not be included in the computational rules described in the next chapter as and when income does arise. This conclusion is based on the following analysis:

(a)   Step 1 in s 733 refers to benefits received by the individual 'in any earlier tax year in which s 732 has applied'.

(b)   Under s 732(1), section 732 applies if the preconditions listed in para 70.7 are met.

(c)   One of those preconditions is that a relevant transfer occurs (s 732(1)(c)).

(d)   A transfer is a relevant transfer if as a result of it and associated operations 'income becomes payable to a person abroad'.

This conclusion is of some significance to trusts or other entities which hold solely non income-producing assets, such as houses. If it is right, it means occupation of the house before the tax year in which income first arises does not fall to be included in the total untaxed benefits (para **71.3**) when income does arise. Moreover, for the reasons given in para **70.11**, income would not count if it results from a transfer separate from that of the house, for example an addition to fund expenses. However once the transfer of the non income-producing asset has produced even a minuscule amount of income, from that tax year on, any benefit is included in the total benefits.

Benefit received before 6 April 2007

70.26 Section 732 first took effect only on 6 April 2007 and in certain respects changed the former law in TA 1988, s 740. In these circumstances, the issue arises of whether s 732 income can arise now by virtue of a benefit received in 2006–07 or prior. Doubts over this issue are increased by the fact that step 1 in the computational rules in s 733 (see para **71.3**) refers to benefits received in tax years when s 732 applied. In reality, however, such doubts are almost certainly ill-founded on account of the continuity provisions in ITA 2007 (Sch 2 para 4(1)).

Receipt prior to non-residence

70.27 As explained above, the individual must be resident in the UK at the time he receives the benefit. But there is no express requirement that he be resident at the time the s 732 income arises. It follows that there is theoretical exposure to tax under s 731 for a non-UK resident who previously received a benefit when UK resident, if such benefit has not already been brought into account under the s 733 computational rules. In principle, s 732 income will be treated as arising to him as and when the person abroad receives income in the future.

However, it may be doubted whether, in such a case, the attribution of income under s 732 would actually result in tax for the non-resident individual. A court might well adopt the view that there is an implied limitation of the tax charge under s 731 to UK residents. Even if this is not the case, if the non-UK resident individual is resident in a country with which the UK has entered into a double taxation treaty, that treaty will normally prevent any UK income tax charge. For the purposes of a treaty based on the OECD Model Treaty, s 732 income is dealt with under the 'other income' article, which typically limits taxing rights to the country of treaty residence (see CHAPTER 101).

INDIRECT RECEIPT

70.28 As indicated above, s 732 does not extend the term 'receives' to indirect receipt. But that does not mean indirect receipt is not per se caught. In reality, the issue turns not so much on what is meant by receipt as on the associated operations concept. As indicated in para 70.7 above, the assets out of which the benefit is provided can be available both as a result of the transfer itself and as a result of associated operations. It follows that if the person abroad passes the assets transferred to another party, and that party benefits the individual, the assets used to benefit him may be available by virtue of an associated operation, ie the passing of the assets to the third party. On this basis, s 732 is engaged.

This analysis plainly operates where the assets are passed from one trust to another, as explained in para 70.12. HMRC take the position that the analysis is in point where the recipient trust which confers the benefit is UK resident. This is clearly right, albeit that HMRC's reasoning, namely that there has been indirect receipt, may be wrong.

The analysis becomes more difficult where the assets are distributed to an individual and he makes an onward gift. The donee may be another individual, in which case the issue is whether that individual can be regarded as receiving the benefit. Or the donee may be a legal person, such as a new trust on which the original recipient settles the benefit. In such a case the issue is whether recipients of benefits under the new trust are caught under s 732 not in relation to that trust but in relation to the transfer to the original trust.

Mostly these issues arise where the individual in receipt of the original benefit is not UK resident, so that s 732 is not then in point on the distribution of the assets to him. But the analysis, it may be suggested, should be unaffected by the residence status of the original recipient.

Onward gifts to individuals

70.29 The issue of onwards gifts to other individuals may be expressed by describing the original recipient , the donor, as A, and the donee as B.

Assuming the person providing the benefit to A is a trust, the first question is whether the distribution to A is a valid distribution to him as a matter of trust law. If the distribution is not validly made to A, and B is also a beneficiary under the trust, the correct analysis should be that the distribution had been made to B and so was a benefit received by B. If in such a case B is not a beneficiary of the trust, the distribution is likely to be a fraud on the power and should thus be a nullity. This ought to mean the money could be returned to the trust without fiscal consequences.

The test of whether the distribution to A is a valid distribution to him is likely to be the same in both cases (cf *Re Dick* [1953] 1 All ER 559, CA). It may be suggested it will not be such a valid distribution if:

(a)   the gift to B is a condition of the distribution;
(b)   the purpose of the trustees in making the distribution is to benefit B; or
(c)   on receiving the distribution A was under 'irresistible moral suasion' to make the onward gift.

Assuming it is established that as a matter of trust law the distribution was validly made to A, there are two good reasons to say that B should not be treated as indirectly receiving a benefit from the trust. The first is the requirement that benefit be provided out of assets available for the purpose. It is difficult to see how assets in the ownership of one individual, ie A, can be said to be 'available' for the purpose of providing a benefit to another.

The second reason is the wider context of s 732. If the onward gift to B were treated as a s 732 benefit from the trust, both A and B could on this construction (if UK resident) be assessed under s 731, or HMRC would have to make a choice between them. In *Vestey v IRC* [1980] STC 10, the House of Lords recoiled from such duplication and discretion and it was one of the reasons which led to the restriction of ss 720 and 727 to transferors. A similar approach should be taken to s 732, to the effect that it bites only on A, ie the individual who as a matter of trust law is the object of the exercise of the trustee's discretion. The rule allowing just and reasonable apportionment where income could be taken into account more than once is not in point, as that rule operates in relation to relevant income not benefits (see ITA 2007, ss 743 and 744(4)).

The only means by which this second reason could be countered would be to say that A is a mere intermediary and so has not enjoyed a benefit at all. This would be close to the concept of indirect receipt formulated for the CGT capital payments code in *Bowring v HMRC* [2016] STC 816 (see para **78.6**). But it is difficult to see A being an intermediary if, under the tests described above, the distribution is a valid distribution to him as a matter of trust law.

Onward gifts to trusts

70.30 Should the onward gift by A be to another trust, s 732 issues arise in relation to B if he receives a benefit from this trust. It is convenient to refer to this trust as Trust 2, and to the original trust as Trust 1. On this basis, the issue is whether the benefit to B is for s 732 purposes a benefit from Trust 1.

It is suggested that the analysis is the same as above, ie:

(1)   If the distribution from Trust 1 to A is not a valid distribution to him, it is either a nullity or treated as direct to Trust 2. In either event the benefit is tied to the relevant transfer to Trust 1, the onward transfer being an associated operation.

(2)   In all other cases, the benefit to B is a s 732 benefit from Trust 2, the role of s 732 in relation to Trust 1 having been spent by the benefit to A.

Were this analysis not right there would effectively be two relevant transfers in relation to Trust 2, that of A and that of B. Such would offend against the duplication principle referred to above and so on that ground alone is unlikely to be right.

COMPLIANCE

70.31 As indicated above there is great uncertainty as to the construction of ss 731–735. In completing a self-assessment return a taxpayer is entitled to adopt a favourable construction if reasonably satisfied it is correct. But he should explain to HMRC very clearly the position he has adopted. In *Tax Bulletin* 40 (April 1999) HMRC included the following statement:

> 'It is incumbent on taxpayers or their advisers to draw [HMRC's] attention to the implications of the legislation when submitting details of transactions to which it may potentially apply.'

Chapter 71

THE S 733 COMPUTATION

INTRODUCTION

71.1 As explained in the previous chapter, ITA 2007, s 733 determines what income is treated as arising under s 732 and its amount. This chapter explains the concepts and steps required by s 733. The draft guidance on the transfer of assets code published in August 2013 (see para **68.3**) addresses some of the issues raised in this chapter and in some places reaches different conclusions to those indicated here. However, perhaps reflecting its draft status, it is not always easy to follow. It is to be hoped the final guidance will achieve greater clarity.

THE SIX STEPS

71.2 Section 733 is expressed in terms of six steps. The first two relate to the benefit and require what is called the total untaxed benefits received by the individual to be identified. The next three steps require the ascertainment of the available relevant income. Step 6 then requires a comparison between the total untaxed benefits and the total available relevant income and the lesser of the two is the s 732 income. If one or other is nil, there is no s 732 income for the tax year concerned.

TOTAL UNTAXED BENEFITS

71.3 The benefits are the total amount or value of the benefits received by the non-transferor in question in the current tax year and in any prior year in which s 732 has applied. As prior year benefits are taken into account only if s 732 has applied, benefits received if and when the non-transferor was not resident in the UK are excluded. The issue of whether a benefit has been received, and if so its amount, is determined by the rules discussed in the previous chapter.

From these cumulative benefits two sums must be deducted to give the total untaxed benefits:

- The non-transferor's s 732 income of prior years.
- Certain benefits taxed under the capital payments code.

71.3 *The s 733 computation*

The practical result is that the total untaxed benefits are the non-transferor's total s 732 benefits which have neither been taxed under s 732 in a prior year nor been taken into account as a capital payment.

Capital payments

71.4 The capital payment issue arises only if the person providing the benefit is a trust, as the capital payment codes are applicable only to trusts (see CHAPTERS 77, 81, and 82). The definition of capital payment discussed in CHAPTER 78 in broad terms encompasses anything which is a benefit within s 732 and so, in general, a benefit provided by a trust also falls within the definition of capital payment.

But as explained in para 78.5, it is not in fact treated as a capital payment for tax purposes if it is chargeable to income tax (TCGA 1992, s 97(1)(9)). Although the language of ss 732 and 733 is a little elusive there is little doubt that a benefit must for these purposes be regarded as chargeable to income tax to the extent that s 732 income arises. But a capital payment or benefit is not subject to income tax in the tax year in which it arises to the extent that total untaxed benefits exceed available relevant income and, on this scenario, it remains treated as a capital payment. If where this happens, it is matched with a s 2(2) or OIG amount, it ceases to be a benefit for the purposes of ss 732 and 733 (s 734) and a reduction is therefore made in the total untaxed benefits going forward.

This treatment can also occur where the matching is not in the current year, so that the payment is carried forward. In such a case, in each subsequent year the carried forward benefit or payment is first matched with any relevant income of that year and, to the extent of that income, it remains a 732 benefit and ss 732 and 733 apply. But if there is no or insufficient income it is matched against any available OIG or s 2(2) amount of that year. To the extent that there is no such amount it is carried forward. To the extent that it is so matched, it ceases to be a s 732 benefit.

It is to be noted that the exclusion of benefits in this way results from matching under the capital payment rules. It is not a precondition that the s 87 or offshore income gain generated by the matching is taxed. Such a gain would inter alia be tax-free if the recipient of the benefit or capital payment is a non-domiciliary enjoying the transitional reliefs described in CHAPTER 79.

AVAILABLE RELEVANT INCOME

71.5 The available relevant income is the relevant income of the current and prior tax years less two deductions required by step 5.

Current year relevant income

71.6 Under step 3 of s 733(1), income of the current tax year is relevant income if it satisfies the following conditions:

(1)   It must arise to a person abroad.

(2)   It must be able to be used for providing a benefit to the non-transferor in question.

(3)   Such ability must be as a result of the relevant transfer or associated operations.

As explained in para **70.11**, the associated operations referred to in the third of these conditions are those which have, with the relevant transfer, caused the income to be payable to a person abroad or rendered the assets out of which the benefit is provided available for the purpose.

Past tax years

71.7 Step 4 of s 733(1) states simply that the relevant income of prior tax years must be identified in the same way as the relevant income of the current tax year. Income which arose before 10 March 1981 is excluded, that being the start date of the original legislation (ITA 2007, Sch 2 para 133(1)). Income is not excluded even if it arose when the recipient non-transferor was non-resident or when the structure was protected by the motive defence (see para **73.19**).

The deductions

71.8 The total relevant income for the current and past tax years is reduced by two amounts to give the available relevant income:

- Amounts previously treated as the non-transferor's income under s 732.
- Amounts which cannot be taken account by virtue of allocation rules in ITA 2007, s 743.

The allocation rules are explained in para **71.18**. They are important in practice for they are the mechanism for excluding income taxed as the transferor's and income taken into account in computing the s 732 income of other non-transferors.

MEANING OF INCOME

71.9 As is explained in para **68.10**, income in steps 3 and 4 of s 733 means income as computed for UK tax purposes. It includes accrued income profits under the accrued income scheme and also, in the circumstances explained in CHAPTER 82 and para **96.22**, offshore income gains and life policy gains accruing under the chargeable event legislation.

Dividends

71.10 In cases where the income of the person abroad included dividends from a UK company, the issue arose of whether the income should be grossed up by tax at the dividend ordinary rate (ITTOIA 2005, s 399). It may be suggested that where a non-resident company received the income beneficially, grossing up was not required, for the general rule was that grossing up did not apply to UK dividends paid to non-resident companies. The position is otherwise where the recipient was a trust, for here grossing up by the dividend ordinary rate was required (ITTOIA 2005, s 399(3)).

These issues as to grossing up apply only in computing relevant income of 2015–16 and prior years. From 2016–17 grossing up ceases to apply to dividends paid to non-residents (ITTOIA 2005, s 399 as amended by FA 2016, Sch 1, para 11).

In the case of non-UK dividends, the issue of grossing up for the tax credit under ITTOIA 2005, s 397A did not arise. This is because s 397A applied only to UK resident individuals. The exemptions for dividends in CTA 2009 ss 931A–931W are not in point even if the person abroad is a company, as those exemptions apply only to corporation tax.

Tax paid by the person abroad

71.11 Sections 732 and 733 make no express provision as to whether (and if so how) account is taken of tax paid by the person abroad on the income received by it. In practice HMRC do not allow tax paid by the person abroad as a credit against tax payable by the recipient of the benefit (see para **104.12**). But as described in para **71.14** below, such tax is a deduction in computing relevant income.

Losses

71.12 Issues also arise if after applying UK computational rules the non-resident has losses, for example trading losses or allowable losses on rental income. In a domestic UK context, a variety of reliefs result from such losses, and the issue which arises is how far they are available in computing available relevant income. One point which is reasonably clear is that if a loss is incurred in one company or trust it cannot be set against income in another entity, even though income in both entities could be relevant income in relation to the same benefit. This result follows because step 3 in s 733 refers to the income which arises to 'a person abroad', and thus focuses on each separately.

The more difficult question is whether a loss in one entity may be set against general income in the same entity or carried forward against future profits. Setting against general income is an issue which arises with trading losses, and would appear to be precluded in computing relevant income, as the relevant relieving section, ITA 2007, s 64, is expressed in terms of relieving the person who incurred the loss from income tax. With carry forward the position is different in that HMRC do allow the loss to be carried forward (*Tax Bulletin* 40 (April 1999) p 652). It is suggested that this is correct in law and accords with ITA 2007, s 83. It should be noted that strictly such carry forward is subject to a claim being made by the entity incurring the loss.

INCOME WHICH IS AVAILABLE

71.13 When it comes to determining which income is available, the brevity of the legislation leaves many important practical points unanswered. Some guidance as to how HMRC interpret the legislation was given in the 1999 *Tax Bulletin* article (issue 40 (April 1999)).

Current year income

71.14 Step 3 in s 733 might be read as encompassing all income of the person abroad even if it is used to meet expenses or distributed as income, on the basis that at the moment of receipt, any such income could have been used to provide benefits.

In reality this cannot be right. In the case of expenses this is because what is used in expenses is not available to benefit anybody. In the case of income distributions the implication of the literal reading would be double taxation, for the income would be taxed when distributed as income (assuming the recipient is UK resident) and again when matched with total untaxed benefits. The correct reading, it may be suggested, is that what can be used for providing a benefit is what is not absorbed by expenses or distributed. Where distributed income is concerned, this is accepted by HMRC, who stated in 1999 that relevant income 'is treated as not including such part of the income as has already been genuinely paid away to a beneficiary or to a bona fide charity' (*Tax Bulletin* 40 (April 1999 p 651). The draft transfer of assets guidance confirms that income counts as genuinely paid away if it is used to pay expenses or taxes or if it is distributed as income (para INTM 601680). There is no suggestion that the expenses or taxes allowed are restricted to income expenses or taxes on income.

There is a suggestion in the draft guidance that the income is only excluded from relevant income if paid away in the same accounting period as it arises. This, it may be suggested, is too restrictive, particularly in relation to trusts, where generally a year is allowed before income has to be accumulated (see para **8.10**).

It is unclear whether income counts as paid away if what is paid out is traceable to the income in banking terms, or whether it is sufficient to debit the expense or distribution to the income in the financial statements of the trust or company concerned. It may be suggested that the latter is right, as the legislation contains no requirement to trace.

With trusts, conventional trust accounting differentiates income from capital and so it is easy to see if an expense or distribution is debited to income. With companies, the profit and loss account normally does not distinguish income proper from gains and so the accounts do not as such show expenses or dividends as debited to income. It may be suggested that in computing relevant income taxpayers are entitled to take the favourable position of debiting all the expenses to actual income. Any computation submitted to HMRC should make clear the position adopted.

Income of past tax years

71.15 Step 4 of s 733 requires the relevant income of previous tax years to be 'identified as mentioned in Step 3'. It must thus have arisen in a past tax year to the person abroad and be capable of being used to provide a benefit for the recipient individual. The issue raised by this is whether ability to provide a benefit is tested in the year in which the income arose or in the year in which the benefit is conferred.

The difference between these two interpretations is that under the first, the available relevant income is a floating pool which can be diminished only by allocation to untaxed benefits. Once an amount equal to the income is included in the floating pool the fate of the actual income is irrelevant. On the second interpretation, by contrast, it is necessary to look at what has actually happened to the income and it is only available relevant income if at the time the benefit is conferred it is still available to benefit the recipient of the benefit.

The draft transfer of assets guidance and the July 2013 consultation document indicate HMRC favour the first interpretation (see paras **68.3** and **70.1**). In favour of this interpretation is the fact that, read literally, steps 3 and 4 focus on each tax year separately and ask whether the income of that year can be used to benefit the recipient individual.

But when the matter is looked at in a wider context, the first interpretation could be difficult to sustain. Three points in particular suggest it may be wrong.

The first focuses on the fact that, were the first interpretation right, s 733 would effectively have matching rules similar to those applicable to TCGA 1992, s 87 (see Chapter **77**). Section 87 replicates legislation first enacted by FA 1981, as does the s 733. It would be surprising if two pieces of legislation in the same Finance Act used radically different wording to enact similar computational systems.

The second point is that s 733 uses the epithet 'available' to describe the relevant income. The word 'available' appears at step 5 and, read naturally, indicates that the income must in fact be available for the provision of benefits at the time when the s 733 matching falls to be done.

The third point is related and may be illustrated by taking a trust with resident and non-resident beneficiaries. In year 10 the trust distributes capital to a UK resident beneficiary. If in years 1–9 a non-resident had had an interest in possession there would be no relevant income. But if there was no such interest but the income was accumulated in a separate bank account would it be relevant income in year 10 if the funds in that bank account were in year 9 distributed as capital to the non-resident? On the first interpretation the answer would be yes. But were the answer yes, the result would hardly be reasonable or proportionate.

In *Tax Bulletin* 40 (1999), p 651 there are indications that HMRC at that time supported the second interpretation. The comment that relevant income does not include income which has been genuinely paid away to a beneficiary is not restricted to payment as income. It is further stated that once relevant income has arisen 'and continues to be available to provide a benefit' it must be carried forward until extinguished by a benefit. There are similar indications in the explanatory notes to ITA 2007. Here it was stated under change of s 113 that 'relevant income is defined as income that can directly or indirectly be used to provide a benefit in the tax year'. It then indicates that 'if it continues to be available' surplus relevant income must be carried forward.

It may be concluded that recipients of benefits are, with full disclosure, entitled to take the position that the relevant income calculation looks at the amount of income received in previous tax years which is currently available for the provision of benefits, net of amounts distributed or absorbed by expenses at any time since the income was received.

Historic income

71.16 The income taken into account as relevant income includes income back to the inception of the overseas structure or, if later, 10 March 1981 (ITA 2007, Sch 2, para 133). As indicated in para **71.7**, it includes income which arose when the recipient of the benefit was non-UK resident even though such income would not have been taxed had that income arisen directly to the recipient.

An interesting issue is whether the relevant income includes income which arose before the recipient was born. If availability to provide a benefit falls to be tested solely by when the income arose, it could be argued such income is excluded. But on any view this income is included if the test of availability is when the benefit is conferred.

Many offshore structures are ones where the transferor can benefit and, during his lifetime, is generally the main individual who does benefit. But all income arising while the transferor is non-UK resident is relevant income, for the transferor charge does not operate unless the transferor is UK resident. This too is a harsh result as a UK resident receiving capital from such a structure is in a worse position than if the transferor had kept the assets which generated the income and made a personal gift. The position as respects relevant income where the transferor is UK resident is covered by the allocation rules discussed in para **71.18**.

The harshness of some of these rules as respects historic income may be tempered if the purpose defence can be claimed. But as explained in CHAPTER 73, that defence may be difficult to sustain.

Future income

71.17 As noted in para **71.2**, if at the time a s 732 benefit is conferred there is no or insufficient available relevant income, the benefit is carried forward and included in untaxed benefits when relevant income arises in the future. Here the construction of s 733 is rather simpler, for the time when the income arises is the sole time at which it has to be considered whether income is capable of being used to benefit the recipient of the benefit. As with current year and past income the theoretical issue arises of whether income distributed as income or used in expenses is caught, and for the reasons given above the answer is not. Accordingly the answer is that relevant income of a future year is the capitalised or retained income of that year.

There are however two important qualifications. The first stems from the fact that step 3 requires relevant income to be capable of being used to benefit the recipient of the benefit. It follows that if by the time there is relevant income – ie by the time income arises and is capitalised – the recipient of the benefit is wholly excluded, the income cannot be relevant income in relation to him. The same, it may be suggested, would apply if he was just excluded from income, but was still able to benefit from original capital.

The second qualification is if the recipient of the benefit has died. It is difficult to see future relevant income as resulting in a tax charge on a deceased person.

ALLOCATION OF INCOME

71.18 As will be apparent, ss 732–733 focus on the resident individual in receipt of the benefit, and the exercise required is to identify relevant income in relation to that individual. This approach works well enough where only one individual ever receives s 732 benefits, for step 5 in s 733 requires the available relevant income brought forward to be reduced by the individual's prior s 732 income. But problems arise where more than one individual receives benefits so that the same income is available relevant income in relation to more than one taxpayer.

A similar problem arises where the transferor is taxable on the income under ITA 2007, ss 720 or 727 (see CHAPTER 69). Nothing in the definition of relevant income in step 3 of s 733 requires the exclusion of income so taxed.

These difficulties are addressed by rules as to duplication in ITA 2007, s 743. There are two rules as follows:

(1)   No amount of income may be taken into account more than once in charging tax under the transfer of assets code.

(2)   HMRC must make a just and reasonable apportionment if there is a choice as between persons in relation to whom income can be taken into account.

Meaning of taken into account

71.19 In the case of the transferor charge, the term 'taken into account' means simply the amount otherwise taken into account in computing the transferor's notional income under ss 721 or 728 (see CHAPTER 69). For non-transferors it means the amount of relevant income taken into account under s 733 in calculating 'the amount to be charged in respect of the benefit for the tax year in question'.

Issues of construction

71.20 In this context, the concept of relevant income being taken into account raises difficult issues of construction. A literal construction of ss 743 and 744 focuses on the steps in s 733, and in particular steps 3–5. These steps arrive at the total available relevant income and, as noted in para **71.8**, that total, in relation to any given recipient of a benefit, is net of amounts deducted under s 743. The logical implication of this is that relevant income is allocated as between recipients of benefits at that stage, and once so allocated ceases to be capable of being relevant income when some future s 732 benefit is conferred on another recipient.

The point may be illustrated by postulating a discretionary trust with six UK resident beneficiaries, A, B, C, D, E and F. If after say ten years of accumulation a benefit is in year 11 conferred on A, an exercise is at that stage required to determine, under steps 3–5, how much of the income of years 1–11 should be allocated to A. Once so allocated, that income is available relevant income only in relation to A even if the benefit in year 11 is vastly less. It would follow that when a benefit is conferred subsequently in year 13 on B, the allocation is at large for the income of years 12 and 13, but as respects years 1–11 all that is capable of being available relevant income in relation to B is what was left after the allocation in year 11 to A. This would be so even if the benefit conferred on B is greater than the income left available for allocation.

The alternate view of s 744(4) focuses solely on the amount of available relevant income in fact matched with the benefit. In the example in the previous paragraph, this would mean only an amount equal to the benefit conferred on A would be unavailable for allocation to B. That amount, and that amount alone, would be deducted under step 5 when computing B's s 732 income.

As a matter of common sense, this latter construction is clearly to be preferred. Without it, large amounts of benefit and available relevant income would potentially be unmatched and thus untaxed. This latter construction represented the natural reading of the predecessor legislation, ie TA 1988 s 740, this result following because the latter did not have inflicted on it the steps in s 733.

But as a matter of strict construction of s 744(4), when read with s 733, the first alternative has much to commend it. In support is the proposition that ss 732 and 733 focus on the particular individual in receipt of the benefit, and the income available to him and do not explicitly provide for pooling and matching. It also appears that the ordering rules for non-domiciliaries would work much better with this construction (see para 72.5) and it is, indeed, a possible inference that the draftsman of those rules based himself on that construction being correct.

What is allocated?

71.21 The duplication rules in s 743 are expressed in terms of amounts of income being taken into account. It is unclear whether the word amount refers simply to a given amount of the total available relevant income or whether it is looking at particular items of the relevant income. In s 743(2), there is reference to 'any amount' of income and this perhaps favours the latter construction.

If this is right, the result is somewhat odd, for it may imply after the event allocation. This would be the position if the second of the two constructions of s 744(4) outlined above is right. Such follows because it would not be until a benefit is conferred on a second recipient that the duplication issue would arise at all. With reference to the example given above, allocation would not fall to be made until year 13 when benefit is conferred on B. At that stage it would have to be decided which particular items of available relevant income had been allocated to A, and in what proportion, so that what is left for B is known. This issue, of course, would not arise on the first construction of s 744(4) above, for then allocation would have had to be dealt with in year 11 when the benefit was allocated to A.

The issue of what is allocated is important for at least two reasons:

(1)   Using the example, if B is a remittance basis user, what has previously been allocated to A may determine whether UK income is related to B's s 732 income, and thus the extent to which B suffers an immediate tax charge (see CHAPTER 72).

(2)   Some of what is capable of allocation to A may not be available relevant income in relation to B. This would be the position if the person abroad is a trust in two funds, where B is a beneficiary of one and A of both.

Income which is not allocated

71.22 There is one important category of income not subject to the allocation rules. This is income arising directly to a trust which is taxed on the settlor under the income tax settlement code, described in CHAPTER 75. As explained in para 75.37, that code deems the income to be that of the settlor for all tax purposes with the result it cannot also be treated as the income of the person abroad.

In general income is taxed on the settlor under the settlement code if he or his spouse are beneficiaries and he is UK resident. But if he is a remittance basis user, foreign income is not treated as arising under the code unless and until remitted (see para 75.28) and so until then is potentially within the transfer of assets code and able to be allocated (see para **71.26** below). Equally, if the transferor is non-UK resident, UK source income can be caught by the settlement code (see para 75.26) and, if so, it may be suggested is not available for allocation under the rules being discussed here.

THE HMRC DISCRETION

71.23 As indicated above, the choice between persons, and the amount allocated to each, is at the discretion of HMRC. This does not sit well with self assessment, as under that system it is taxpayers who have to decide what to return.

Offshore trustees who are aware of the need to do so will keep a record of available relevant income and, despite the strict view of the law, treat it as a sort of pool, reducing it whenever a benefit is conferred. But for the reasons indicated above this is not correct and, in at least the instances given above, may not produce a complete answer. More fundamentally, there are cases of structures with multiple beneficiaries. Some of them may not know what benefit has been conferred on others. In such cases self assessment with any degree of confidence is difficult if not impossible. For all these reasons, some discussion of the scope of HMRC's discretion and the parameters within which it may properly be exercised is appropriate.

When is the discretion exercisable?

71.24 It may be suggested that the discretion to allocate arises only in computing the s 732 income of two or more non-transferors for a given tax year, or in computing both such s 732 income and the transferor's income for the year. This result follows because there is no choice to be made in a given tax year if the case is not a transferor case and in that year only one non-transferor receives a benefit, or if the case is a transferor case and no non-transferor receives a benefit. In any such case, all the income must be allocated to the non-transferor recipient, or the transferor. In the next tax year, there may be other non-transferor recipients, but here the income allocated or taxed in the prior tax year must be excluded, not because there is a choice but because it has already been taken into account.

Transferor cases

71.25 As indicated above, the allocation rules apply between transferor and non-transferors as well as solely among non-transferors. In transferor cases they are thus in point in any tax year in which a benefit is provided to a resident non-transferor. Such can easily happen if the person abroad is a company owned by a settlor-interested discretionary trust. Here the company's income is taxable as that of the transferor under s 720, but there is no reason why the trustees should not trigger s 732 income for the same tax year by distributing capital to another UK resident beneficiary.

In such a case there is nothing in the legislation which states that the company income must all be taxed as that of the transferor, leaving none to be included as relevant income in relation to the non-transferor. Here, therefore, a just and reasonable allocation of that year's company income should be made.

Remittance basis users

71.26 As explained in para 70.5 and CHAPTER 72, the s 732 income of a remittance basis user is, if matched with relevant foreign income of the person abroad, taxed not under s 731 but under ITTOIA 2005, s 832. So too the transferor is taxed under s 832 if the income of the person abroad is relevant foreign income (see para 72.1)

The issue which arises is whether the income of the person abroad is allocated when income is treated as arising under the transfer of assets code, or only when such income is remitted. In other words, should relevant foreign income of the person abroad be allocated to the transferor in that year even though it is not remitted and may never be remitted? A similar question is whether relevant foreign income is taken into account under s 733 in determining a non-transferor's s 732 income then or only when the s 732 income is treated as remitted.

In the case of non-transferors the position is plain. Section 744(4) refers to the relevant income taken account under s 733 in calculating the amount to be charged, and thus envisages allocation at that stage. It may also be suggested that what is allocated must be the income matched under the ordering rules in s 735A (see para **72.13**) since anything else would be unjust and unreasonable.

In relation to transferors, HMRC's published view is that unremitted transferor income can be taken into account as relevant income under the allocation rules (*Tax Bulletin* (April 1999) RI 201).

It may be suggested that this view accorded with the legislation, at least in the form it took until the changes made in 2013. Thus ITA 2007, s 743 applied the duplication rules 'in charging income tax' and s 744(2)(b) defined transferor income taken into account as 'the amount of income charged'. This emphasis on charging and charged indicates HMRC's view was right, and similar language is found in the pre-rewrite provisions (TA 1988, s 744(1) and 744(2)(a)). The practical result is that relevant income includes unremitted transferor income arising before 5 April 2013.

Whether this view remains right under the legislation in its present form is debateable, for as a result of the changes made in 2013, s 744(2) now defines income taken into account as the income mentioned in s 721(2), ie the income of the person abroad which the transferor has power to enjoy. If the 2013 change did inadvertently change the law, unremitted transferor income of 2013–14 and post is excluded from relevant income.

A further comment made by HMRC in *Tax Bulletin* is that trust income is not in practice charged both on the settlor under the settlements code and on a non-transferor in receipt of a benefit. This appears to indicate that in practice unremitted transferor income taken into account in taxing a non-transferor would not if subsequently remitted be taxed under the settlement code.

WHEN RELEVANT INCOME CEASES TO BE AVAILABLE

71.27 The discussion above has indicated that what would otherwise be available relevant income in relation to a particular non-transferor ceases to be so in three circumstances:

(1)   It has previously been taken into account under s 733 in computing the income treated as arising to that individual.

(2)   Using the just and reasonable rules just described it has been taxed on the transferor or taken into account under s 733 in computing income treated as arising under s 732 to another individual.

(3)   At the time the individual receives a benefit, the income is no longer able to be used to confer a benefit on him.

As indicated in para **71.15**, the last of these circumstances is a matter of inference and may not be supported by HMRC. But assuming it is correct, it requires further elaboration.

Trusts

71.28 In relation to trusts, the following facts require consideration:

(1)   Distribution of the capitalised income to another beneficiary.
(2)   Exclusion of the beneficiary from the fund of capitalised income.
(3)   Transfer of the capitalised income to another trust.

If the capitalised income is distributed to another resident beneficiary s 743 is likely to render what is distributed removed from the available relevant income. But if the other beneficiary is non-resident, it does not as s 732 does not apply to benefits conferred on non-residents. Nonetheless, the conclusions reached in para **71.15** indicate that in such case the distributed funds would not remain relevant income if the capitalised income had at all times been kept in a segregated account.

Greater difficulty arises if the capitalised income has not been segregated, so that the distribution to the non-resident in accounting terms is out of accumulated income but in banking terms is undifferentiated. In such a situation is it possible to identify such a distribution with the retained income or at least argue the distribution is pro rata retained income and original capital? When read literally the legislation does not support such an approach.

Suppose a trust with assets worth £1m has ten beneficiaries and £100,000 in accumulated income. Suppose one of the beneficiaries is UK resident and the rest are not, and the trust is wound up by equal distribution to the ten beneficiaries. On the literal reading the entire £100,000 accumulated income would be attributed to the UK beneficiary and he would suffer tax on the full amount of his distribution. But if a pro rata approach were adopted, the only available relevant income in relation to him would be one tenth of the accumulated income, £10,000, and that is what he would be taxed on.

The conservative view must be that a distribution to a non-resident does not diminish relevant income unless the income has been clearly segregated. If the pro rata approach is taken in filing, it must be accompanied by full disclosure and explanation.

Broadly similar considerations apply if the capitalised income is retained in trust but the beneficiary concerned has previously been excluded from it. Such a situation postulates that capitalised income and original capital have been segregated in banking terms and that the beneficiary is excluded from the former but not the latter, the latter then being used to fund the benefit. In this scenario the analysis offered in para **71.15** indicates that this would prevent the income being relevant income. But it may be difficult to see this analysis holding up if the capitalised income has not been segregated.

In relation to a transfer of income or capitalised income to another trust, it is clear that the income remains relevant income in relation to a beneficiary if he is an actual or potential beneficiary of the transferee trust, for then, as steps 3 and 4 require, the income is still available to benefit him. But the position would be otherwise if he is wholly excluded from the transferee trust and the income had at all times been segregated in banking terms. The position is then the same as on an appointment within the original trust.

Trust expenses

71.29 As noted above (para **71.14**), income used in expenses is not available to the beneficiaries in any form. The comment in *Tax Bulletin* 40 about income continuing to be available having to be carried forward indicates that HMRC consider both income and capital expenses should be deducted, for what is paid in expenses is patently not available.

Companies

71.30 On the basis of the analysis above, the income of a company becomes relevant income if it is retained by the company and added to reserves rather than being used in expenses or distributed as it arises. However, it is perfectly open to a company subsequently to distribute past income – ie accumulated profits – and the issue then is whether the reserves so distributed cease to be available relevant income. On the basis of the above conclusions the answer is yes. The point may be reinforced by the fact that, absent a liquidation or buy-back, such a distribution is an income receipt of the recipient shareholder. This is in contrast to the position with trusts, where distributions of accumulated income are, as a matter of trust law, capital. It is inherently difficult to see retained income remaining as available relevant income if it has in fact been distributed as income and HMRC's comments in *Tax Bulletin* 40 are certainly not inconsistent with this view.

This leads on to a point that commonly arises in practice where an offshore trust owns an offshore company. Does retained income at the level of the company cease to be available relevant income if it is paid up as dividend to the trust? If it does not, there is double counting, in that the same item of value received by the company enters the available relevant income total for a second time, in the form of the dividend received by the trust. Indeed there could be triple counting if there are several levels of company. The correct analysis, it may be suggested, is that this double or triple counting does not in fact occur. The technical solution is that steps 3 and 4 postulate income arising to a particular person resident or domiciled outside the UK which is capable of being used to benefit the recipient of the benefit. Once the retained income at company level has been distributed up it is no longer so capable, and instead has changed its character into income of the shareholder trust or company where, if retained, it again becomes relevant income.

Tax Bulletin 40 does not in terms deal with the potential double counting issue, although the remark about income being genuinely paid away supports the above conclusion. In practice HMRC are widely believed not to double count where income is paid up as income to another higher level in an offshore structure, and this is reflected in the draft guidance referred to at para **71.1**.

It is unclear whether such informal practice, or the legal analysis offered above, apply only where the company has segregated the retained income from capital in banking terms, or whether it is sufficient if the treatment is as per the company's accounts. In contrast to trusts it may be argued that the latter is correct given the rules applicable to company accounting under most systems of company law.

Sale or liquidation

71.31 Should the company be liquidated, it may be doubted whether any relevant income in the liquidation proceeds loses its character as relevant income when paid to the shareholders. It does not become income from another source in the same way as happens when a dividend is paid.

The position may be otherwise should the company be sold, for here the relevant income remains held by the company. Two situations should perhaps be distinguished. The first is where the sale is to a party which either is the recipient non-transferor or a trust or other entity from which he can benefit. Here, plainly, the income remains relevant income in relation to him, albeit that ability to benefit him is by a different route. The second is where the sale is to an unconnected third party from which the non-transferor cannot benefit. Here, on the basis of the analysis above, the income ceases to be relevant income.

Against this latter conclusion it is sometimes argued that on a sale any income retained by the company should be traced into the proceeds of sale. As a general proposition this is difficult to sustain, for the income remains in existence in the company. Nothing in s 733 suggests that relevant income can double itself up, ie in the situation postulated here, being represented both by the income in the company and by the proceeds of sale. Indeed on the first of the scenarios in the previous paragraph this doubling up would be a real issue, in that both the actual income and the proceeds of sale are capable in that situation of being used to benefit the recipient non-transferor.

On one view rejecting the tracing of relevant income into the proceeds of sale offers scope for avoidance. But in reality such scope is more apparent than real, as if the sale and benefit are planned together it would not be difficult to say the relevant income indirectly enables the benefit to be provided even if the actual provision is after the sale. This would be particularly so if sale and benefit are in the same tax year.

The above discussion has been predicated on the assumption that the second interpretation discussed in para **70.16** is correct – ie ability to use the income to confer benefit is tested when the benefit is conferred. If, contrary to the conclusion in para **70.16**, the correct analysis is there is a floating pool, then even if the company were sold the income would remain in the pool. But in relation to companies this second interpretation raises other difficulties, most notably where profits which constitute relevant income are paid out in the form of dividends to the new owners and taxed as such. Could it then be right that the profits should remain relevant income?

EXERCISE OF FIDUCIARY POWERS

71.32 Most settlements confer on the trustees wide powers to appoint or create new trusts. Sometimes these may be exercised so as to leave the assets in the original settlement and sometimes so as to advance or transfer the assets to a new or different settlement (*Roome v Edwards (Inspector of Taxes)* [1982] AC 279, [1981] 1 All ER 736, HL; *Bond (Inspector of Taxes) v Pickford* [1983] STC 517, 57 TC 301, CA; *Swires (Inspector of Taxes) v*

Renton [1991] STC 490, 64 TC 315; SP 7/84). The appointment or advance may relate to all the assets in the original settlement or just some of them and in some cases one part of the trust fund may be subject to one appointment or advance and other parts to others. In the case of any such appointment or advance, issues of the kind discussed above arise if a benefit is conferred out of one settlement or fund and income has been retained in another.

Relevant income prior to exercise

71.33 The most common situation is where income is accumulated prior to the exercise of the fiduciary power and a capital distribution is made out of the appointed or advanced fund. In this situation, s 732 plainly catches the distribution. The analysis is that the relevant transfer is the transfer to the settlement. The distribution out of the appointed or advanced fund is out of assets available for the purpose for those assets are so available by virtue of the appointment or advance which is an associated operation. The previously accumulated income is available relevant income because it is still able to be used to benefit the beneficiary in receipt of the benefit.

There are, however, two situations where this result may not follow. The first follows on from that described in para **70.11** above and is where there have been separate transfers to the original trust. If the appointment or advance is solely of the non income-producing assets, a subsequent distribution from that fund will not, if what is said in para **70.11** is correct, be taxable by reference to the income in the original settlement. The second is if, after the appointment or advance, but before the distribution, the beneficiary in receipt of the distribution is excluded from any funds still held on the trusts of the original settlement. If on the facts those funds comprise all the retained income it may be argued as per para **71.28** that it is not available relevant income in relation to the recipient beneficiary, for it is no longer able to be used to benefit him. But this argument is self-evidently not available if some or all of the previously retained income is included in the appointed or advanced fund, as would invariably be the case if the appointment or advance was of the whole trust fund.

Benefit prior to exercise

71.34 Another scenario is where a distribution is made from the original settlement at a time when there is no or insufficient available relevant income and the appointment or advance takes place before such income arises in the future. The issue then is whether, if income does thereafter arise in the appointed or advanced fund, it is available relevant income in relation to the earlier benefit.

The answer is yes, assuming that the transfer to the original settlement is the relevant transfer, for then the appointment or advance is an associated operation as a result of which the income arises. In this scenario, the benefit is provided out of assets which are available for the purpose by virtue of the transfer, and the income in the appointed or advanced fund is available to benefit the benefited beneficiary by virtue of the transfer and the associated operation.

However, there are two situations where liability under s 731 will be avoided. The first is the situation postulated in para **70.11** where there were two separate transfers to the original settlement, one of income-producing assets and one of non income-producing assets. If the distribution was from the latter and the advance or appointment is of the former then liability under s 731 is avoided. Second, if the recipient of the distribution is totally excluded from the appointed or advanced fund he should escape liability, for the income arising in that fund will ipso facto not be able to be used to benefit him and so cannot be included in available relevant income (see para **71.17**).

Chapter 72

NON-UK DOMICILIARIES

INTRODUCTION

72.1 The transfer of assets code includes special rules for non-UK domiciliaries who are remittance basis users (ITA 2007, ss 726, 730 and 735). The effect is that certain income treated as arising under the code is removed from the code and instead deemed to be relevant foreign income, and so charged under ITTOIA 2005, s 832 when remitted to the UK (for s 832, see Chapter 48).

The rules differ according to whether the transferor or the non-transferor charges are in issue. Moreover the rules for transferors are separately iterated for transferors chargeable under s 720 by reason of having power to enjoy, and those chargeable under s 727 by reason of receipt or entitlement to a capital sum (see further paras **69.5** and **69.21** respectively). But the relevant sections are in all material respects identical (ITA 2007, ss 726 and 730).

This chapter considers the law now in force. The proposals taking effect on 6 April 2016 will affect the subject matter of this chapter in that certain transferors and non-transferors will become deemed UK domiciled for all tax purposes. As respects transferors it is envisaged there will be some protection from the charge on non-UK income, which, in the absence of special provisions, would become taxable on the arising basis on deemed UK domiciled transferors. At the time of writing the form these protections will take is unclear.

TRANSFERORS

72.2 Income treated as arising to the transferor is turned into relevant foreign income if two conditions are met:

(a)   The transferor is a remittance basis user in the tax year in which the income arises.

(b)   The actual income of the person abroad would be relevant foreign income if it were in fact the transferor's.

The issue of whether the notional relevant foreign income is remitted is determined by what happens to the actual relevant foreign income of the person abroad. This is achieved by deeming that actual income to be derived from the notional relevant foreign income (ITA 2007, ss 726(4) and 730(4)).

The effect is that if the actual income is paid out to the transferor, he is taxed if he remits the income while still UK resident. So too a remittance by the person abroad results in tax for the transferor if the person abroad is a relevant person in relation to the transferor and the transferor is still UK resident at the time of the remittance. The person abroad will normally be a relevant person, as the term embraces settlements under which the remittance basis user is a beneficiary and companies in which he or such a settlement is a participator (see paras **54.6** to **54.15**).

Actual benefits

72.3 As explained in para **69.39**, a special rule applies if the transferor receives an actual benefit provided out of the income of the person abroad as per enjoyment condition C. Under ITA 2007, s 724, the transferor is liable to income tax for the tax year in which the benefit is received on the whole amount or value of the benefit. This is a charge in substitution for that in ITA 2007, s 720, applicable in cases where there is no power to enjoy apart from the receipt of the benefit (*IRC v Botnar* [1999] STC 711 at para 53).

On one view s 724 is not subject to the remittance basis, as s 724(2) provides that the charge is made on the full amount of the benefit for the year in which it is received. No provision expressly makes the s 724 charge subject to the remittance basis even where the benefit is received and kept abroad. To this extent s 724 may constitute a trap for non-UK domiciliaries.

But even assuming it exists, the trap is of limited compass, provided it is right to restrict s 724 to cases where there is otherwise no power to enjoy. As this restriction has the authority of the Court of Appeal (*IRC v Botnar*, supra) there can be confidence in regarding it as right. If so, any absence of a remittance basis under s 724 is immaterial provided that the transferor otherwise has power to enjoy.

Were this conclusion wrong, the result would be surprising for it would mean a distribution from a settlor-interested offshore discretionary trust to the settlor would be taxable on an arising basis if made out of income or accumulated income. It would apply even if the distribution were an income distribution, as 724 is not restricted to capital benefits. Section 724 would thus have the result of imposing tax on the arising basis even though without it the distribution would be taxable on the remittance basis or exempt. Such considerations reinforce the correctness of the conclusion that s 724 has only limited scope.

NON-TRANSFERORS

72.4 As in CHAPTER 70, it is convenient to refer to the income treated as arising to non-transferors as s 732 income. Such income is deemed to be relevant foreign income if two conditions are met (ITA 2007, s 735):

(a)   The non-transferor is a remittance basis user in the tax year in which the s 732 income arises.

(b)   The relevant income, ie the actual income of the person abroad, to which the s 732 income relates is relevant foreign income.

As explained in para **71.2**, the tax year in which the s 732 income arises is normally the tax year in which the non-transferor receives the benefit. But if an insufficiency of relevant income means that the benefit has to be carried forward, the s 732 income arises as and when there is relevant income in a future year. In such cases it is in that later year that the non-UK domiciliary has to be a remittance basis user.

The s 732 income is an arithmetical construct and so cannot as such be remitted. Instead the law as to remittances applies on the basis that both of the following are derived from the s 732 income:

(a)   The relevant foreign income of the person abroad which relates to the s 732 income.
(b)   The benefit which relates to the s 732 income.

The ordering rules

72.5 ITA 2007, s 735A contains rules determining which benefits and which relevant foreign income relate to the non-transferor's s 732 income. These rules apply on a first in first out basis.

What is required is as follows:

(a)   All s 732 benefits which the non-transferor has ever received are taken in chronological order.
(b)   Each tax year's relevant income is taken in chronological order.
(c)   All s 732 income of the non-transferor is placed in chronological order.
(d)   Benefits, relevant income, and s 732 income are then identified with each other on the first in first out basis.

Within each tax year, UK income is taken before relevant foreign income and, within those categories, income is taken in the order in fact received (s 735A(3)). Income which accrues over a period is treated as received at the end of the period (s 735A(5)).

The ordering rules recognise that some income may have been taken into account in taxing other individuals under the transfer of assets code, whether the transferor or other non-transferors. It does so by reference to the allocation rules in ITA 2007, s 743 (see paras **71.18** to **71.26**). It requires income which cannot be taken into account because of the allocation rules to be excluded from the relevant income used in the ordering process.

The key point about the ordering rules is their bias towards the old. A particular point is that the relevant foreign income included in the ordering includes income of the person abroad of tax years when the non-transferor in receipt of the s 732 income was non-resident. But the benefits do not extend to such years, for under s 732, a benefit is only taken into account if the non-transferor is UK resident at the time of receipt (s 732(1)(b); see para **70.14**).

Effect

72.6 As is explained in para **71.2**, s 732 income normally involves either brought forward benefits or brought forward relevant income. Much the more common scenario is brought forward relevant income – ie more income has arisen as a result of the relevant transfer than has been disbursed in benefits to UK residents.

In this situation the effect of the ordering rules is that all the non-transferor's s 732 income of prior years is deducted from past relevant income, starting with the oldest years first. The oldest year left with relevant income after this process is the year whose relevant income, or what is left of it, relates to the current year's s 732 income. If that relevant income is less than the s 732 income, the latter is carried forward against the relevant income of the next oldest year, and so on.

Once the related income is established, it is necessary to see if it is UK source or if it has already been remitted, in which case the s 732 income is charged at once. If it has not already been remitted a tax charge arises if the benefit is remitted or if the related income is remitted in the future. Remittance by the person abroad or other related entities counts if, as is likely, such are relevant persons in relation to the transferor. This they normally will be, in view of the wide definitions discussed in paras **54.6** to **54.15**.

TRANSITIONAL ISSUES

72.7 The substitution of the present rules for remittance basis users has had effect since 6 April 2008 (FA 2008, Sch 7 para 170). The issue as to how far it impacts on earlier income or benefits is of some difficulty.

The transferor charge

72.8 Prior to 6 April 2008, the rule was that a non-UK domiciled transferor was not charged under the transfer of assets code if and to the extent he would have escaped charge had the income of the person abroad in fact been his. Until 5 April 2007, this was delivered by TA 1988, s 743(3) and for 2007–08 by the original versions of ITA 2007, ss 726 and 730. It was generally accepted that the effect of these rules was to remove unremitted relevant foreign income of the person abroad from charge.

There was a strong argument that the relevant foreign income was charged only if remitted in the tax year in which it arose to the person abroad. The basis for this argument was that neither s 743(3), nor ss 726 and 730, contained provision charging subsequent year remittances. The prescriptive language of the original ss 726 and 730 made this argument particularly compelling in 2007–08.

The issue posed by the 2008 changes is whether a remittance of income dating from 2007–08 or earlier tax years can now be taxed under the present law. As explained in para **48.15**, the general rule is that the present law as to remittances applies as if it had been in force when the income arose (FA 2008, Sch 7 para 83). But no such provision was specifically enacted in relation to transfer of assets income, and so the issue of whether remittances of such income now are taxed is governed by the extent to which the general rule applies.

At the outset, it must be stressed that a remittance of income dating from 2007–08 or earlier cannot on any view be taxed unless the remitting party is the transferor. This is because of the restriction of the term 'relevant person' to transferors as respects pre-6 April 2008 income (see para **54.1**).

It follows that the issue of whether remittances of pre-6 April 2008 income are taxable arises only if the remittance is effected by the transferor himself as a result of distribution to or enjoyment by him. Until 2006–07, the income of the person abroad was deemed for all income tax purposes to be that of the transferor, with the result that the transferor's income can without difficulty be seen as relevant foreign income caught by the general transitional rule. For 2007–08, the effect of the rewrite may have been that what the transferor had was a notional sum of deemed income equal to the actual income of the person abroad (see para **69.37**). If so, it would be less clear that the transferor's income was relevant foreign income and the general transitional rule imposing a charge may not be in point.

In any event, in many cases, a tax liability will not arise, on account of FA 2008, Sch 7 para 86(3). This is the rule which exempts pre-12 March 2008 relevant foreign income insofar as invested in non-money assets prior to that date (see paras **59.2** to **59.4**). It is in point here precisely because, at least in relation to 2006–07 and earlier tax years, the transferor's income was the actual relevant foreign income of the person abroad.

A final point to note applies where the person abroad is a trust. In such a case a remittance of pre-6 April 2008 income may cause such income to be taxable under the settlement code, as discussed in para **75.31**.

Non-transferors

72.9 With non-transferors, there are two distinct transitional issues. The first is how far s 732 income dating from 2007–08 or earlier tax years is taxable if remitted, and the second is how the ordering rules impact on relevant income or benefits received in 2007–08 or earlier tax years.

The analysis of the first point is relatively straightforward. It may strongly be argued that s 732 income dating from 2007–08 or earlier is not taxed now if it was not remitted before 6 April 2008. In other words tax does not result if either benefit or relevant income are remitted. The basis of this analysis is as follows:

(1)   As indicated above in relation to the transferor charge, no provision specifically applicable to the transfer of assets code deals with income of 2007–08 or earlier tax years.
(2)   The general transitional rule (FA 2008, Sch 7 para 83) applies on its terms only to relevant foreign income.
(3)   Until 6 April 2008, no s 732 income was deemed to be relevant foreign income or, prior to 2005–06, case IV or V income.

That s 732 income dating from 2007–08 or earlier should not be taxed if remitted now should not occasion great surprise. As with the transferor charge it was strongly arguable that only current year remittances were taxable, particularly in 2007–08 following the rewrite.

The second issue, how far back the ordering goes, is more complex. However there seems little doubt that the ordering exercise requires account to be taken of income and benefits of 2007–08 and earlier tax years. In the case of income, the analysis leading to this conclusion is as follows:

(1)　　The only transitional rule in the 2008 legislation relating specifically to the transfer of assets code is that the substitution of the present s 735 and 735A for the original s 735 has effect from 2008–09 onwards (FA 2008, Sch 7 para 170).

(2)　　Section 735A(1)(c) requires the income mentioned in step 3 for the tax years mentioned in step 4 to be placed in the prescribed order.

(3)　　Steps 3 and 4 are those prescribed in s 733 (s 735A(2)).

(4)　　Step 4 of s 733 refers simply to 'the relevant income of earlier tax years'.

Assuming this analysis is right, it is thus necessary with old structures to go back many years, the only limitation being the inception of the structure or the original start date of the non-transferor legislation, namely 10 March 1981. The income in the structure of each past year has to be computed and then reduced by past benefits to the subject non-transferor when he was UK resident. What in effect is required is a reconstitution of the past income and distribution history of the structure.

A remittance of the actual income by the person abroad will count, as the restriction of relevant persons to the taxpayer (in relation to pre-6 April 2008 income) applies only to the taxpayer's income, ie the non-transferor's income (FA 2008, Sch 7 para 86(4)). Any such remittance will count whether effected before or after 6 April 2008. So too where it is the related benefit which is carried forward, remittance of the benefit will count, whether effected before or after 6 April 2008.

If the related income arose and was invested before 12 March 2008, the relief for investment before that date should be in point (FA 2008, Sch 7 para 86(3); see paras 59.2 to 59.4). The argument that the relief applies is that the literal requirements of the relief are satisfied, namely that the investment was made before 12 March 2008 and was paid for out of income treated as derived from the s 732 income. A purposive approach supports this construction, for all the circumstances rendering the investment relief fair and appropriate apply equally where the relevant income was invested before 12 March 2008, particularly as the relief plainly applies where such income is treated as that of the transferor.

The fact that ordering under s 735A has to go back to 10 March 1981 or the inception of the structure raises practical difficulties. Even assuming records exist, extensive historical investigation may be required to determine the available relevant foreign income of the person abroad for the old years, and what (if any) is not relevant foreign income. This is particularly in point where the person abroad is a trust which has hitherto had little or no UK connection.

The investigation is required even if the relief for pre-12 March 2008 investment is in point, for that relief applies when the related income has been determined and does not obviate the need to determine what the related income is.

ALLOCATION

72.10 As explained in paras **71.18** to **71.26**, the income of the person abroad is not treated as a pool. Instead the transferor and each non-transferor are looked at separately, a just and reasonable basis being used to ensure income is not taken into account more than once. These allocation rules pose particular problems in operating the remittance basis.

The transferor

72.11 An important point is that in transferor cases not all income of the person abroad is necessarily allocated to him. As explained in para **71.25**, a non-transferor may in the same tax year be in receipt of s 732 income resulting from the same relevant transfer. In such a case, the income of the person abroad has to be allocated between transferor and non-transferor on a just and reasonable basis. It could be just and reasonable to allocate some or all of the income to the non-transferor if the transferor is a remittance basis user who does not remit.

Allocation issues of this sort do not, of course, arise if the transferor is non-resident, for then he is not within the transfer of assets code at all (see para **69.44**). So too the non-transferor has to be UK resident when he receives the benefit as otherwise there is no s 732 income.

Non-transferors

72.12 A difficulty with non-transferors is reconciling the allocation rules described in paras **71.18** to **71.26** with the ordering rules discussed above. This difficulty arises because the ordering rules apply only for the purposes of ITA 2007, s 735 (s 735A(1)), ie in determining whether the s 732 income of a remittance basis user is relevant foreign income and, if it is, whether it is remitted.

The difficulties principally arise if in prior tax years, some of the available relevant income has been taken into account in computing the s 732 income of other non-transferors. To operate the ordering rules it is necessary to identify the relevant income so taken into account with particular tax years, and within each tax year to identify as between UK and foreign income and, within foreign income, between remitted and unremitted foreign income. Neither the allocation rules nor the ordering rules specify how this is to be done. However it may strongly be argued that the clear implication of s 735A is that its ordering rules are to be used in determining what is comprised in each prior allocation of relevant income to other non-transferors.

A similar issue arises if in the current or a future year another non-transferor is in receipt of a s 732 income. Unless he is a remittance basis user, the ordering rules in s 735A do not apply to him. Here however, the position is reasonably clear: it would not be just and reasonable to allocate to him anything which has under the ordering rules been allocated to the remittance basis user.

Reallocation

72.13 A rather different issue arises with both transferors and non-transferors. It is whether the income of the person abroad can be reallocated if, by reason of non-remittance, it has not been taxed in the hands of the transferor or, as the case may be, the non-transferor in receipt of the s 732 income. This issue is discussed in para **71.26**.

REMITTANCE OF THE ACTUAL INCOME

72.14 What happens to the actual income of the person abroad is relevant in determining whether the transferor's income or, as the case may be, the s 732 income is remitted. In the case of s 732 income it is only the related income which has to be looked at. With the transferor all the relevant foreign income of the person abroad is material, other than any allocated to a non-transferor's s 732 income.

The taxpayer himself

72.15 In a transferor case, tax results if the taxpayer himself remits the income following a distribution or transfer of such income to him. In non-transferor cases the position is more difficult. Typically, a non-transferor might remit a benefit and in so doing the s 732 income resulting from that benefit is remitted. But as a matter of tracing, the person abroad might have funded the benefit to the non-transferor out of relevant income which was previously matched to other unremitted benefits and so resulted in earlier s 732 income. Does the remittance of the later benefit mean that earlier s 732 income counts as remitted as well? It may strongly be argued not, for two reasons. One is that it would be absurd to have a single remittance of benefit resulting in a double remittance charge. The second is that the immediate source of the later benefit is the act of the person abroad in conferring it, with the result derivation cannot go further back than that act (see further CHAPTER 52). This second reason is supported by the limited scope of the deeming of derivation in s 735, as discussed in the next paragraph.

Derivation issues

72.16 As noted above (paras **72.2** and **72.4**), the actual income of the person abroad is deemed to be derived from the transferor's notional income or, as the case may be, the non-transferor's s 732 income. As with all deemed derivation, issues as to the extent of the deeming arise. It is however noteworthy that the language of the relevant provisions, ss 726(4), 730(4) and 735(4), is prescriptive. It is clear that what is treated as derived from the deemed income is such of the actual income abroad as would be relevant foreign income were it the individual's. There is no inclusion of anything derived from such income and, with such prescriptive legislation, it is difficult to see why such further deeming should be inferred.

Should the income have been generated in a company, liquidation of the company followed by liquidation distributions to the shareholders are unlikely to cause the income to lose its character, for such distributions return to the shareholders what already belongs to them (*IRC v Laird Group plc* [2003] STC 1349, para 37). It follows that if the shareholder is a relevant person in relation to the transferor or non-transferor, for example a trust of which he is a beneficiary, a remittance by that person results in tax. But the position is otherwise if the company is sold for then the original relevant foreign income remains in the company and, in normal cases, cannot be equated with any particular element in the sale proceeds.

Remittances by persons other than the taxpayer do not, of course, on any view result in tax on the transferor insofar as the income is of 2007–08 or prior. The same does not apply to the s 732 income of non-transferors (para **72.9** above) save insofar as the s 732 income itself arose in 2007–08 or prior (in which event it is in any event unlikely to be taxable).

Should the person abroad be a trust, the remittance in transferor cases is likely to be taxable under the settlement code as that code has priority (see para **75.28**).

Extended meaning of remittance

72.17 As explained in CHAPTER 55, remittance has an extended meaning and this applies in determining whether the income of the person abroad or, as the case may be, the related income is remitted. Thus a remittance occurs if the income is used to pay for services enjoyed in the UK or in respect of a debt related to UK property. Such acts are certainly caught if effected by the person abroad or, subject to the derivation point in para **72.16**, by any of the other relevant persons listed above. The exemption for services in ITA 2007, s 809W (paras **55.13** to **55.17**) applies to services provided to the person abroad, provided that the conditions of that relief are otherwise met, and the disapplication relating to benefits in the UK (para **72.23**) is not in point.

Mixed fund rules

72.18 The relevant foreign income of the person abroad may find itself mixed with other monies of that person. In that event the mixed fund rules described in CHAPTER 53 require the relevant foreign income or, as the case may be, the related relevant foreign income to be identified first. The mixed fund rules are in point in relation to s 732 income even if the related foreign income is of 2007–08 or earlier tax years, as the s 732 income itself is post-5 April 2008 income (see FA 2008, Sch 7 para 89).

As explained in para **54.11**, the mixed fund rules can represent a trap. This arises if relevant income related to the s 732 income of more than one non-transferor is in a single mixed fund. Here the rules relating to s 809Q transfers (see para 53.10) mean that a remittance is identified in relation to each non-transferor first with his related relevant income. This works well enough where the whole mixed fund is remitted, for then each non-transferor's s 732 income is taxed as it should be. But each non-transferor's s 732 income is also taxed in the case of partial remittance and the result may be reached that the combined remittance of s 732 income by all the non-transferors exceeds the actual amount remitted from the mixed fund.

Conditions C and D

72.19 As described in CHAPTER 57, conditions C and D come into issue if the transferor or, as the case may be, the non-transferor, enjoys property in the UK, or any individual who is a relevant person in relation to him does so. Condition C, however requires a gift by the taxpayer himself and so, in transfer of assets cases, operates only if the transferor or non-transferor makes a gift.

Condition D, by contrast is wider. Its meaning is very obscure, but in broad terms it could come into issue if the person abroad makes a disposition of the income or, as the case may be, the related income. There would be a risk of such income being treated as remitted if the disposition is linked to the enjoyment of property or services in the UK by the transferor or, as the case may be, the non-transferor (see para 57.16).

REMITTANCE OF BENEFIT

72.20 The issue of whether a s 732 benefit is remitted is of course relevant only to non-transferors. It determines whether the s 732 income related to the benefit is remitted.

Section 735A states simply that the related benefit must be treated as derived from the deemed s 732 income. It gives no further indication as to how the remittance rules in ITA 2007, s 809L are then to be applied.

Outright transfers

72.21 Where the benefit is the payment of money or the transferring of property, it is reasonably plain that a remittance of the s 732 income occurs if that money or property is brought to the UK. However, s 735A only deems the benefit, ie that money or other property, to be derived from the s 732 deemed income. Accordingly if the money or property comprised in the benefit is converted into another asset, a remittance of that asset is only a remittance of the benefit which was originally received if that asset itself comes within the term benefit. On a purposive construction it plainly should.

If the recipient of the benefit gives the money or property comprised in the benefit to a third party and that third party remits, tax will not on any view result for the beneficiary unless that party is a relevant person in relation to the beneficiary, or the facts fall within conditions C and D (see CHAPTER 57). And where a remittance might otherwise occur because the other party is a relevant person, the point remains that no provision deems what is derived from the benefit to be derived from the s 732 income. If this point is good, a remittance by the third party would only result in tax if the money or property in his hands could be said to be the benefit itself.

Benefits in kind

72.22 The remittance analysis is somewhat different if the s 732 benefit is not an outright transfer but a benefit in kind, for example an interest-free loan or the rent-free use of a house. If the benefit in kind is enjoyed in the UK, a remittance of the s 732 income ought to be treated as occurring.

But as explained in para **79.6** in relation to capital payments, this result does not follow under the rules as to the general meaning of remittance. It is true that if the property is in the UK it is enjoyed by the recipient. But for Condition B in s 809L to apply (see para **51.8**) the property has to be derived from the income. In a benefit in kind case, this condition is not met as it is the benefit, not the property over which the benefit is conferred, which is treated by s 735(4) as derived from the s 732 income.

One way round this analysis would be to argue that the benefit enjoyed in specie is a service, for Condition B is engaged if the service is derived from the income. As is explained in para **55.6**, some benefits in kind may aptly be described as services, but not all are. The same point arises with capital payments within TCGA 1992, s 87A and, in that context, HMRC have indicated that they do equate benefits in specie with services (see para **79.6**).

Even if the analysis is right, a benefit such as a loan conferred outside the UK and subsequently brought to the UK may not be caught. This is because Condition A in s 809L requires the provision of the service to be in the UK.

Services

72.23 As explained in para **55.17**, the exemption for UK services (s 809W) does not apply if the service relates to any extent to a benefit which satisfies the following conditions (s 809W(5)):

(a)   The benefit is provided in the UK.
(b)   It is treated as derived from the income by virtue of s 735.

The second of these conditions uses the definite article in relation to the income and thus harks back to the opening words of s 809W, which refer to the income and gains which would otherwise be treated as remitted to the UK. The meaning of this obscure provision is considered further in para **55.17**.

Timing

72.24 The effect of the ordering rules is that s 732 income can arise by reference to a benefit received in an earlier tax year. In such a case a remittance of the benefit prior to the s 732 income arising means that the s 732 income is treated as remitted when it does subsequently arise (ITA 2007, s 809U).

Chapter 73

THE MOTIVE DEFENCE

INTRODUCTION

73.1 Ever since first enacted, the transfer of assets code has been subject to a motive or purpose defence. The onus of proving the defence is on the taxpayer but, if he discharges it, ITA 2007, ss 720–730 cannot render the income of the person abroad taxable as his. The defence applies also to ss 731–735, with the result that where it applies, income treated as arising under s 732 is not taxable either.

The motive or purpose defence has always been a crucial part of the transfer of assets code. Without it, the income of any overseas company would be taxable as that of its controlling individual UK shareholders under s 720 unless those individuals had played no part in funding the company.

The motive defence was originally contained in TA 1988, s 741, and is now ITA 2007, s 739. On 5 December 2005 the defence was amended, but the amendment did not repeal what is now s 739. Instead a new version of the defence was enacted for post 4 December 2005 transactions in what was TA 1988, s 741A and is now ITA 2007, s 737. There are also transitional provisions, now ITA 2007, ss 740–742. The result is that the original defence in ITA 2007, s 739 has to be looked at in relation to pre 5 December 2005 structures, and the new version in s 737 in relation to transactions since then.

Satisfying the motive test does not, it should be stressed, mean tax is necessarily avoided altogether. Income arising directly to the trustees of a settlement is assessed under ITTOIA 2005, s 624 if the settlor is capable of benefiting, regardless of motive (see para 75.2). So too a capital distribution from a trust may be subject to income tax under the OIG rules or to CGT under TCGA 1992, s 87 or Sch 4C even if the motive test displaces ss 731–735 (see CHAPTERS 77, 81 and 82). This result follows because, in relation to UK residents, the definition of 'capital payment' excludes payments chargeable to income tax as distinct from payments treated as income (see TCGA 1992, s 97(1)).

THE STATUTORY CONDITIONS

73.2 Under both ss 737 and 739, one of two conditions, Condition A or Condition B, must be met. The conditions differ slightly as between the two sections.

Section 739

73.3 In s 739, Condition A is that avoiding liability to taxation was neither the purpose, nor one of the purposes, for which the relevant transactions or any of them was effected. Condition B is that the transfer and any associated operations were (i) genuine commercial transactions, and (ii) not designed for the purpose of avoiding liability to taxation.

In condition A, the term relevant transaction bears the same meaning as in the transfer of assets code generally, namely the relevant transfer or an associated operation (ITA 2007, s 715). It is unclear why condition A is expressed in terms of relevant transactions whereas condition B refers in terms to the transfer and any associated operations.

Section 737

73.4 The conditions in s 739 are essentially replicated in s 737. The differences are as follows:

(a) In s 737, both conditions require the taxpayer to show 'that it would not be reasonable to draw the conclusion, from all the circumstances of the case' that Condition A or, as the case may be, Condition B is met.

(b) Condition B in s 737 is expressed in terms of relevant transactions.

(c) Condition B in s 737 includes the words 'more than incidentally' as a prefix to 'designed'. More significantly, certain types of transaction are expressly deemed not to be commercial (see para **73.16** below).

(d) Section 737(2) provides that Condition B has to be considered only if Condition A is not satisfied. The logic of this is that Condition A is failed if just one of the purposes was tax avoidance. As just noted, an incidental tax avoidance purposes is permitted in Condition B.

AVOIDING LIABILITY TO TAXATION

73.5 The key phrase in both s 739 and s 737 is 'avoiding liability to taxation'.

Meaning of taxation

73.6 In s 739, the word 'taxation' is not defined. However, it has been held to include any form of UK tax, including taxes on capital (*Sassoon v IRC* (1943) 25 TC 154). But the term 'taxation' does not extend to foreign taxes, and so foreign tax planning does not jeopardise s 739. This is so even if the foreign tax avoided is as close to home as the Republic of Ireland (*IRC v Herdman* [1969] 1 All ER 495).

Section 737, in contrast to s 739, does define taxation: it includes any revenue for whose collection HMRC is responsible (s 737(7)). Revenue is then defined as including taxes, duties, and national insurance contributions. It thus clear that, as under s 739, all forms of UK tax are caught. But, in addition, imposts such as customs duties and NICs, which might not normally be designated taxes, are counted as taxes for these purposes.

In s 737(7) the definitions of taxation and revenue are inclusive. At first sight this raises the question of whether foreign taxes could count as 'revenue' or 'taxation' within the general meaning of the term. It is, however, unlikely that s 737 would be construed as imposing such a fundamental change so obliquely and HMRC have given no indication that they so construe it.

Meaning of avoidance

73.7 There is House of Lords authority on what is meant by tax avoidance. The case concerned, *IRC v Willoughby* [1997] STC 995, 1003, distinguished between tax avoidance and tax mitigation. In the course of argument in the House of Lords, Counsel for HMRC formulated the distinction as follows:

> 'The hallmark of tax avoidance is that the taxpayer reduces his liability to tax without incurring the economic consequences that Parliament intended to be suffered by any taxpayer qualifying for such reduction in his tax liability. The hallmark of tax mitigation, on the other hand, is that the taxpayer takes advantage of a fiscally attractive option afforded to him by the tax legislation, and genuinely suffers the economic consequences that Parliament intended to be suffered by those taking advantage of the option. Where the taxpayer's chosen course is seen upon examination to involve tax avoidance (as opposed to tax mitigation), it follows that tax avoidance must be at least one of the taxpayer's purposes in adopting that course, whether or not the taxpayer has formed the subjective motive of avoiding tax.'

The significance of this formulation is that, in the only reasoned speech, Lord Nolan described it as generally helpful and said he accepted the essence of HMRC's submissions. Later he encapsulated in his own words what is meant by tax avoidance:

> 'Tax avoidance within the meaning of s [739] is a course of action designed to conflict with or defeat the evident intention of Parliament.'

PURPOSE

73.8 Both ss 739 and 737 focus on the purpose of the transactions or, in the case of Condition B, the purpose for which they were designed.

Section 739

73.9 The case of *Philippi v IRC* [1971] 47 TC 75 is authority that in determining under s 739 what the purpose of the transfer was, it is necessary to ascertain what the transferor in fact intended; and that in carrying out that process all relevant evidence may be considered. In *Philippi*, the transferor had in 1951 formed an Irish trust and holding company and then in 1952 transferred UK securities to the company. By the time of the Special Commissioners hearing in 1966 the transferor was aged 87 and unable to travel from Switzerland where he then lived.

The Special Commissioners found the defence was not proved. In the Court of Appeal the taxpayer argued that in the absence of the transferor it was not possible to establish what he had intended and that a reasonable inference was that he had not on the facts intended to avoid UK tax. The reason given for this inference was that the transferor was at the time of the transfer living in Ireland. He was therefore outside the UK tax net.

The Court of Appeal rejected those arguments, stating that the transferor's intentions may be inferred not just from the evidence he gives. The evidence of others can be drawn on, for example that of his spouse or his solicitors, as can correspondence or what transpired at meetings. In the circumstances the Commissioners were entitled to find that, by not calling any evidence, the taxpayer had failed to discharge the burden on him. Only then did it address the issue of inference, commenting that objectively there plainly had been UK tax advantages in the transfer of shares to the holding company.

Philippi is authority as respects s 739 for a further point. The taxpayer, who was the transferor's son, had also himself transferred UK securities to the holding company in 1961 at a time when he was UK resident. He was then aged 23 and serving in the army. His evidence was that he made the transfer because his father and mother had told him to do so and that he had no thought of avoiding taxation. The Special Commissioners accepted his evidence and applied s 739 to that transfer. HMRC appealed this point but their argument collapsed during the hearing in the High Court. As a result it was sometimes said that the ignorant or naïve taxpayer had better prospects under s 739 than the astute or well-informed.

Section 737

73.10 Section 737 expressly amplifies how purpose is to be ascertained. First, as noted above, Conditions A and B require one to look at all the circumstances of the case and then ask what conclusion as to purpose it would be reasonable to draw. Second, s 737(5) provides that account must be taken of the intentions and purposes of advisers and of those who design or effect any of the transactions.

In one limited sense, s 737(5) indubitably differs from s 739, for, by requiring the purpose of those who design transactions to be taken into account, it would in *Philippi* have caught the son's transaction. But otherwise it is difficult to see s 737(5), and the language in Conditions A and B, as doing anything more than codify what the Court of Appeal said in that case.

HMRC practice

73.11 HMRC stated in 1999 that if a transaction involves tax avoidance, that must be considered as one of its purposes even if the transferor did not have the subjective intention of avoiding tax (*Tax Bulletin* 40(April 1999) p 651). In so asserting HMRC were relying on the last sentence of the first quotation from *IRC v Willoughby*, cited in para 73.7 above, specifically the words 'whether or not the taxpayer has formed the subjective motive of avoiding tax'. But those words come in Counsel for HMRC's formulation of law and, while the formulation was described by Lord Nolan as generally helpful, it was so described not generally but in relation to what is meant by tax avoidance.

Three subsequent decisions bear on this issue. In *Beneficiary v IRC* [1999] STC (SCD) 134, the Special Commissioners distinguished the question of whether a transaction amounts to tax avoidance from its purpose. In their view, Lord Nolan's words were directed at the former question, and the latter requires a subjective test. In *Carvill v IRC* [2000] STC (SCD) 143, 148, another Special Commissioner took the view that the relevant words of Lord Nolan were doing no more than summarise the HMRC argument and that there was clear authority that the test is subjective. Thirdly, in *HMRC v Anson* [2012] STC 1014 para 19, the Upper Tribunal stated in terms that:

'The taxpayer's purpose must be determined by reference to the evidence of what that subjective purpose was.'

It follows that on this point HMRC's published disregard of the transferor's subjective intention has regularly been found to be wrong and it appears that HMRC now accept this (*Fisher v Revenue and Customs Comrs* [2014] UK FTT 804 (TC), 17 ITLR 141 paras 256–257).

Factors to take into account

73.12 In *Fisher v Revenue and Customs Comrs* [2014] UK FTT 804 (TC), 17 ITLR 141 para 287 the tribunal summarised a number of factors which may or may not be relevant to purpose. This is a useful summary taking in many of the points made above. The tribunal said:

'From the above, we summarise the following propositions in relation to the motive defence:

(1) The test is subjective. (*Carvill*)
(2) Evidence of a person's reactions to what is said to them and circumstances as well what they say their purpose is may be relevant. (*Philippi*)
(3) It is not enough to show a tax avoidance effect.
(4) Knowledge that less tax is paid does not equate to a tax avoidance purpose (but knowledge is a pre-requisite to having a purpose).
(5) Awareness of tax aspects does not equate to having a tax avoidance motive. (*Willoughby*)
(6) The mere fact of taking tax advice does not mean there is a tax avoidance motive. (*Beneficiary v IRC*)
(7) Picking a lower tax route over a higher tax route does not equate to tax avoidance (but equally does not preclude tax avoidance). (*Brebner/Willoughby*).'

TRANSFER AND ASSOCIATED OPERATIONS

73.13 As indicated in paras 73.3 and 73.4, the purpose defence requires associated operations as well as the transfer to be looked at, the defence not been made out if any of them is tainted by a tax avoidance purpose. Section 737 and Condition A in s 739 bring in associated operations by being expressed in terms of the relevant transactions. Condition B in s 739 has the same effect, albeit for some reason referring specifically to the transfer and associated operations.

As explained in para **68.14**, the House of Lords decision in *Herdman* was that only relevant associated operations had to be considered in determining whether the purpose defence is made out. Also as explained in para **68.14**, there is some ambiguity as to whether, in determining under the transferor charge which operations are relevant, the enquiry is confined to transactions conferring power to enjoy or whether operations generating a new source of income are looked at as well. But the decision in *Herdman* is clear authority the former was correct. Thus in *Macpherson v IRC* [1988] STC 362 at para 368 Lord Jauncey summarised the position in the following terms:

> ' . . . the only associated operations which were relevant to the subsection were those by means of which, in conjunction with the transfer, the taxpayer could enjoy the income, and did not include associated operations taking place after the transfer had conferred upon the taxpayer the power to enjoy income.'

It appears that this view of the *Herdman* decision was adopted by HMRC, for *Tax Bulletin* 40 (April 1999), p 652 stated their then practice as follows:

> '[It] has been [HMRC's] practice in considering whether a defence under Section [739] is available to consider only the transfer and any associated operations which directly establish a power to enjoy the income of the overseas person under any particular [enjoyment condition].'

Although the rewrite means ITA 2007 uses language different from that in the legislation previously, there is no reason to suppose the *Herdman* principle does not apply to s 739. In relation to the transferor charge this means:

(1)   If the transfer alone gave power to enjoy it alone is looked at in considering whether the purpose defence applies.

(2)   Otherwise the only associated operations looked at are those which give power to enjoy

With s 737 the position is different on account of a most mysterious provision in s 737, first enacted as part of the FA 2006 changes and now appearing as s 737(8). This provides that if an associated operation would not otherwise be taken into account in applying the purpose defence it must be taken into account if so doing means the conditions for the defence are not made out. Section 737 is the section that applies where all relevant transactions are post-4 December 2005 and on any view it must mean that in such cases more transactions must be tested than under s 739.

The issue of difficulty is how extensive the extra associated operations so taken into account are. Here there are three views. One view accepts the definition of associated operations is not subject to any implied limitation and holds that s 737(8) simply removes the requirement that only relevant associated operations are considered when applying the purpose defence. This view requires any transaction to be taken into account if it falls within the literal wording of the definition in ITA 2007, s 720 (as to which see paras **68.8** to **68.14**). It appears from the draft guidance published in 2013 that HMRC believe this to be its effect (INTM 602800), but such a result is very odd for, as explained in para **68.14**, the literal definition in s 720 could extend to transactions quite unconnected with the transfer and effected by completely different parties.

The second view of s 737(8) also accepts the definition of associated operations is very wide, but allows that only relevant operations are taken into account. On this view, s 737(8) simply reverses the narrow view of the relevance concept, as expressed in *Macpherson* and *Tax Bulletin* 40. It thus means associated operations which create new income can be taken into account as well as those which give rise to power to enjoy. The third view is different in that it accepts there is an implied limitation on the term associated operations. But it then has a similar result to the second view for it holds s 737(8) means all associated operations within the implied limitation can be taken into account, and not just those creating power to enjoy.

It may be suggested that as a matter of construction either the second or the third view is more likely to be right and certainly one or other would be the correct analysis if the First-tier Tribunal was right in *Fisher v Revenue and Customs Comrs* [2014] UKFTT 804 (TC), [2014] SFTD 1341. The Tribunal concluded an operation is not an associated operation at all unless it results in new power to enjoy or new income (see further para **68.14**). But pending the likely appeal in *Fisher* the point remains far from clear.

The above discussion has all been focused on the transferor charge and power to enjoy. With the capital sum charge and the non-transferor charge the analysis may be different. However what may suggested is that on any view s 737 requires consideration of all associated operations which either generate income or enable benefits to be provided or, as the case may be, are connected with the capital sum. Whether it goes wider turns on the issues discussed above.

THE COMMERCIAL DEFENCE

73.14 In both s 737 and s 739, condition B focuses on whether the transfer and any associated operations were commercial and what they were designed for.

Section 739

73.15 The term 'commercial' is not defined in s 739. But *Carvill v IRC* [2000] STC (SCD) 143 gives some guidance. In that case, the Special Commissioner considered that a transaction can be described as commercial if it implements or facilitates a business end or if it is in furtherance of commerce (at para 87). He said that the reference to design requires that the main purpose was not the avoidance of taxation (at para 89). In this it is more accommodating to tax avoidance than Condition A, for the latter only operates if none of the purposes is tax avoidance.

Section 737

73.16 Under s 737, certain transactions are deemed not to be commercial (s 738). Thus a transaction is only commercial if it is in the course of a trade or business or with a view to setting up a trade or business. The making and management of investments does not count as trade or business unless the person by whom it is done and the person for whom it is done are independent persons dealing at arm's length (s 738(4)). Further, a transaction is deemed not to be commercial if either its nature is such that it would not have been entered between independent persons dealing at arm's length or if any of its terms are non arm's length (s 738(3)).

As noted above (para **73.4**), section 737 qualifies Condition B by the word 'incidentally'. Assuming the construction of Condition B of s 739 in *Carvill* is correct, this represents a significant difference between ss 737 and 739. Instead of it being necessary to show merely that tax avoidance was not a main purpose, s 737 requires it to be shown that tax avoidance was, at most, incidental.

On the basis that the motive or purpose test is subjective (para **73.10** above), it is difficult to envisage cases where a transaction which fails Condition A as having a tax avoidance purpose will pass Condition B by showing that that purpose was merely an incidental part of the design. It may be that the use of the word 'incidental' has its origins in HMRC's view on the subjective/objective issue, in that if Condition A is failed because objectively some tax is avoided, Condition B is not failed if such avoidance was merely an incidental part of the design.

But assuming HMRC are wrong on the subjective/objective point, Condition B in s 737 will, by virtue of the insertion of 'incidentally', rarely apply where Condition A does not. If so, the restrictions in it on what counts as commercial will prove to be of little practical significance.

WHICH SECTION?

73.17 As indicated at the beginning of this chapter the old law, now represented by s 739, remains in force alongside the new law as represented by s 737. It is plain from the terms of s 737 itself that if the transfer and associated operations were all subsequent to 4 December 2005, all are tested by s 737 (s 737(1)). But where the transfer predated 5 December 2005 the position is more complex.

The reason for the complexity is that s 739 on its own applies only if *all* the relevant transactions predated 5 December 2005 (s 739(1)). Where some of the relevant transactions occurred before that date, and some afterwards, ITA 2007, s 740 requires the transactions before 5 December 2005 to be tested by s 739 and those after 4 December 2005 by s 737 (ITA 2007, s 742). As the motive defence applies only if all relevant transactions satisfy the requirements, the motive defence is only available if each relevant transaction satisfies the section applicable to it.

With structures dating back before 5 December 2005, a difficult issue arises in determining whether s 740 applies. The issue is whether an operation after 4 December 2005 only brings s 740 into play if it is within the *Herdman* limitation that still applies to s 739 (see para **73.13**). Or can an operation be taken into account if it is one that would be taken account were s 737 applicable? In other words does the mysterious provision in s 737(8) apply in determining where s 740 is engaged?

As a matter of strict construction, s 737(8) does not apply, for on its terms it requires the additional operations to be taken into account only for the purposes of s 737 itself. Section 740 contains no incorporation of s 737(8) by reference. Such a result may not be contrary to a purposive construction for it is a reasonable inference the intention of ss 737 and 739 is to allow the *Herdman* limitation to apply to pre-2005 structures. Clear wording, it may be suggested, would be required if a post-2005 transaction that is not within the *Herdman* limitation were to cause a structure to cease to be wholly within s 739.

It is not wholly clear from the draft guidance what view HMRC take of this point, but it appears they do not share the conclusion reached here (see INTM 602840). However the point is not discussed in any detail.

TAINTING

73.18 It is plain that an associated operation can take place that causes a structure hitherto protected by s 737 or 739 to lose that protection. Should the structure be one that predates 2005, the effect of such an operation will be to move it out of s 739 and into s 740, with the result that the post-2005 transaction will be tested against the somewhat tighter rules in s 737 rather than those in s 739. A form of tainting is thus created, in that such a transaction causes the whole structure to lose the defence.

Effect of tainting

73.19 Should a later associated operation cause a structure to lose the protection of ss 737 or 739, income arising in and after that tax year is taxable as the transferor's if the conditions of ss 720–730 are otherwise met. Income of earlier years is unaffected as in relation to those years the displacement of the charging provisions in ss 720 and 727 was still of effect.

Section 740(4), which contains an express exemption for income arising before 5 December 2005, might be thought to imply that where a pre-5 December 2005 structure loses the motive defence some years later, all income since 5 December 2005 becomes taxable on the transferor. But that cannot be right, as it ignores the basic exempting provision in ss 720(7) and 727(5) which must be applied to each year on a year-by-year basis. The correct construction of s 740(4) is that it was a transitional provision governing the position in 2005–06 alone. HMRC indicated to professional bodies at the time that this was their view.

The motive defence does not stop s 733 operating to compute the income treated as arising under 732. Instead, it comes into play at the subsequent stage, namely in determining whether the s 732 income is chargeable (see 731(4)). As a result, relevant income and benefits are still allocated to each other, and insofar as so allocated, fall out of the available relevant income and total untaxed benefits.

Unallocated available relevant income or total untaxed benefits carry forward and can result in a tax charge if allocated under s 733 in or after a tax year in which the structure loses the protection of s 737 or s 739. In the case of pre-5 December 2005 structures this is specifically applied to relevant income arising before the defence is lost (s 740(5)). But the position with regard to benefits in pre-2005 cases is different in that s 740 expressly requires benefits conferred before 5 December 2005 to be disregarded (s 740(6), (7)). In fact this provision may be otiose and imply the disregard is more time limited than it should be. Such a conclusion follows because until 2007–08, the pre-rewrite legislation caused the motive defence to switch the predecessor legislation to ss 731–735 off, rather than simply rendering income computed under that legislation non-taxable (see TA 1988, s 741). The effect of this is that benefits conferred when the motive defence was in point should be left out of account when the motive defence is subsequently lost (TA 1988, s 740(1)(b)).

All or nothing

73.20 As indicated above, the general rule is that an associated operation which causes the protection of s 737 or s 739 to be lost means it is lost as respects all income resulting from the original relevant transfer. This is so even if the operation which falls foul of s 737 only impacts on a small part of the structure.

A limited exception is made for transferors where Condition B is in point. Here the charge under ss 720 and 727 is restricted to such income as, on a just and reasonable basis, is attributable to the offending associated operation (ITA 2007, s 742). It is unclear whether relief applies just to cases protected only by Condition B or those protected by Condition A as well as Condition B.

AVOIDANCE AND MITIGATION

73.21 The meaning of 'tax avoidance' is the critical point in applying the motive defence. In applying the defence to any given transaction the question to be asked is what the purpose of the transaction was and whether that purpose amounted to or included avoidance of UK taxation. The first of these questions is one of fact but the second is one of law, turning on the all-important distinction between avoidance and mitigation. The basic law on the distinction is the passages from *Willoughby* set out in para **73.7** above, but both the facts of *Willoughby* and other cases give further guidance.

Willoughby

73.22 *Willoughby* itself concerned offshore personal portfolio bonds, which are life policies where the return on maturity is linked to a portfolio of investments selected by the policyholder (see para **4.11**). HMRC had always accepted that policies linked to general funds were protected by the motive defence. However, in *IRC v Willoughby* they sought to bring personal portfolio bonds within s 720, on the grounds that in substance the position is no different from where the policyholder owns the investments directly. This contention was rejected by the House of Lords, on the simple ground that a policyholder merely has a right in contract against the life office, and not a right in rem against the assets held by the life office to which his policy is linked.

The underlying reasoning which led the House of Lords to apply the motive defence was that offshore bonds are a means of saving, with a tax regime specifically provided by Parliament, namely the chargeable event legislation described in Chapter 96. On the facts Professor Willoughby had genuinely incurred the expenditure involved in buying the bonds and had in fact bought them to provide for his retirement. As such the bonds fell within the category of tax mitigation rather than tax avoidance.

An issue raised by both this reasoning, and by the passages in Lord Nolan's speech cited above (para 73.7), is that two tests are potentially applicable in distinguishing mitigation from avoidance. The first is whether the taxpayer has, in economic terms, genuinely incurred the consequences of what, in tax terms, he has done and the second is whether what he has done conflicts with or defeats the intention of Parliament. In reality these tests mean the same thing, in that it is a reasonable inference that Parliament intends tax consequences to follow economic reality. But there is clearly a risk that even where the economic reality test is met, HMRC, and perhaps judges, will speculate on whether Parliament had some other intention.

Challenge and Ensign Tankers

73.23 The origin of the distinction between avoidance and mitigation lies in two judgments of Lord Templeman, in *IRC v Challenge Corpn Ltd* [1986] STC 548 and *Ensign Tankers (Leasing) Ltd v Stokes* [1992] STC 226. These were not cases on the transfer of assets code, but they were cited in *Willoughby*. In *Challenge* Lord Templeman defined avoidance as follows:

'Income tax is avoided and a tax advantage is derived from an arrangement when the taxpayer reduces his liability to tax without involving him in the loss or expenditure which entitled him to that reduction. The taxpayer engaged in tax avoidance does not reduce his income or suffer a loss or incur expenditure but nevertheless obtains a reduction in his liability to tax as if he had.'

Lord Templeman then gave examples of mitigation in the following terms:

'When a taxpayer executes a covenant and makes a payment under the covenant he reduces his income. If the covenant exceeds six years and satisfies certain other conditions the reduction in income reduces the assessable income of the taxpayer. The tax advantage results from the payment under the covenant.

When a taxpayer makes a settlement, he deprives himself of the capital which is a source of income and thereby reduces his income. If the settlement is irrevocable and satisfies certain other conditions the reduction in income reduces the assessable income of the taxpayer. The tax advantage results from the reduction of income.

Where the taxpayer pays a premium on a qualifying insurance policy, he incurs expenditure. The tax statute entitles the taxpayer to reduction of tax liability. The tax advantage results from the expenditure on the premium.'

In *Ensign Tankers* Lord Templeman elaborated on what he regarded as tax mitigation, as follows (at p 240):

'A taxpayer who carries out a "bed and breakfast" transaction by selling and repurchasing shares establishes a loss for capital gains tax purposes because he has actually suffered the loss at the date of the transaction. In "back to back" transactions the taxpayer is entitled to any reduction in tax which Parliament has attached to each transaction.'

Section 685 cases

73.24 Another angle on what is meant by tax avoidance may be gleaned from cases decided on the pre-2010 tax code concerning transactions in securities. These cases are discussed in paras **89.13** to **89.18** and inter alia show that a commercial transaction is not per se tax avoidance just because account is taken of tax. The dictum of Lord Upjohn from *IRC v Brebner* [1967] 2 AC 18 set out at para **89.14** was cited in the Court of Appeal in *IRC v Willoughby* [1995] STC 143, 183. The principle enshrined in that dictum is clearly relevant, particularly when ss 737 and 739 are being relied on to protect commercial structures.

DECISIONS SINCE WILLOUGHBY

73.25 Since *Willoughby*, the distinction between avoidance and mitigation has been considered in several Commissioners or tribunal cases.

Carvill

73.26 In *Carvill v IRC* [2000] STC (SCD) 143 the Special Commissioner adopted the Parliamentary intention approach (at para 91), referring to tax avoidance as a course of action designed to conflict with or defeat the intention of Parliament. The case largely turned on what the taxpayer had intended rather than whether it was avoidance or mitigation. But one issue was split contracts (see para **50.8**) which had been put in place to enable the taxpayer to secure the remittance basis on earnings attributable to his overseas duties. The Special Commissioner found the purpose of the split contracts was tax mitigation not tax avoidance. He concluded:

'The [remittance basis] reliefs are available to persons in the taxpayer's circumstances and he was not misusing the reliefs.'

Beneficiary

73.27 In *Beneficiary v IRC* [1999] STC (SCD) 134, the Special Commissioners cited at length from *Challenge*, including the passages set out in para **73.23** above. The case concerned a non-resident Japanese settlor with a granddaughter resident in the UK, and two transactions arose for consideration.

The first was that, following English advice, the individual had transferred sterling from a UK account to Jersey. The express purpose of moving the money was to protect it from IHT. The Commissioners considered such a transfer was no different from switching the UK account to a foreign currency account at the same bank, which would have been protected from IHT by IHTA 1984, s 157 (see para **37.12**). As such, the switch would plainly be tax mitigation, for it simply takes advantage of an express relief. The Commissioners considered the movement of funds to Jersey was no different and similarly protected by s 739.

The second transaction was the creation of a Jersey discretionary settlement in favour of the granddaughter. The settlor had taken some UK tax advice, but the Commissioners found his purpose was to secure the financial independence of his granddaughter and ensure she did not have to rely on her mother. This part of the case turned on what the settlor in fact intended, rather than on the distinction between avoidance and mitigation, the key finding being that UK tax was a matter of indifference to the settlor.

Burns

73.28 In *Burns v Revenue and Customs Comrs* [2009] STC (SCD) 165 two young women became absolutely entitled to UK real estate on attaining their 18th birthdays. Their parents were settled in Jersey but the women in question were or could well become UK resident. On her 18th birthday each woman transferred her interest in the real estate to a Jersey company in which she owned the shares. The Special Commissioner found the purposes of these transfers included avoidance of higher rate income tax on the rental income and sheltering of the capital value from IHT in the event that the women were or became non-UK domiciled. He then held that both these purposes were avoidance rather than mitigation. In relation to the second he gave the following helpful guidance as to when conversion to excluded property status is or is not avoidance, guidance which is consistent with *Beneficiary* (at para 59):

'I would certainly accept that if a non-domiciled person arranged to hold foreign situs, rather than UK situs, assets, and then died, no tax advantage would have been sought. Thus if a UK house was sold, and a French house purchased, that would simply be a case of genuinely changing the assets held, and were some s 739 point to hinge on whether the change was effected for the purpose of avoiding UK tax, the answer would be that it was not. And if UK bank deposits were withdrawn and deposits placed elsewhere, then again, that would be a pure investment switch, and not step the purpose of which would involve the purpose of achieving a UK tax advantage. Indirectly retaining a UK real property, and simply achieving the technical change in status by putting the property into a non-UK resident company in a case where one of the purposes is to achieve the potential inheritance tax ("IHT") advantage, implicit by effecting those steps, does seem to me to cross the border between mitigation and tax avoidance. This is because it has involved no real change of investment, as in the two previous examples, but the retention of the UK property, accompanied by a step to change the normal tax consequences of that'.

Fisher

73.29 In *Fisher v Revenue and Customs Comrs* [2014] UK FTT 804 (TC), 17 ITLR 141 a UK tele-betting company had been rendered uncompetitive because its competitors were avoiding betting duly by conducting their operations from Gibraltar. The owners of the UK company therefore formed a Gibraltar company and caused the UK company to sell the tele-betting business to it. The tribunal found that preventing bets from suffering betting duty was one of the purposes of the transfer. The taxpayers argued that this was not avoidance but mitigation as they had accepted the economic consequences of operating outside the UK. The tribunal however decided that in enacting betting duty Parliament had intended that the economic consequences of not paying betting duty should be forgoing UK customers. On the facts the taxpayers had not foregone UK customers and had not intended to do so. On that basis, they had crossed the line into avoidance.

Anson

73.30 The facts in *HMRC v Anson* [2013] STC 557 are summarised in paras **32.8** and **103.5**. The transfer of assets point arose on the basis that, as the Court of Appeal decided, the LLC was opaque and thus a person abroad. On that basis, the taxpayer would have suffered 45% US tax at LLC level and then, when the LLC distributed the net profits, UK tax at 40% on the net distribution. The taxpayer, however, argued that a share of the LLC's trading income was attributable to him under the transfer of assets code, with the result he was entitled to the same reliefs as if the income had in fact been his and so he was entitled to credit for the US tax (see para **69.35**). He further argued that what is now ITA 2007, s 743 prevented the income from being taxed again when it was distributed to him by the LLC (see para **69.40**).

HMRC took the position that the taxpayer's purposes in participating in the LLC had not included the avoidance of UK tax. Despite the taxpayer not having invoked the motive defence, HMRC determined that it applied and the Upper Tribunal decided it was open to HMRC to do this (*HMRC v Anson* [2012] STC 1014).

As described in paras **32.8** and **103.5**, the litigation was resolved in the taxpayer's favour, as the Supreme Court determined that he did (as originally found by the First-tier Tribunal) have an entitlement to a share of the LLC's profits with the result the LLC was transparent rather than opaque. Accordingly the aspects of the case concerning the transfer of assets code fell away. But there was no disapproval of the lower courts' acceptance of the HMRC's contention that the motive defence could be raised by HMRC against a taxpayer.

PROCEDURE

73.31 Neither s 739 nor s 737 apply automatically. Instead they are expressed as applying if HMRC are satisfied that Condition A or Condition B is satisfied. But HMRC do not have an unfettered discretion in the matter, for on any appeal, the First-tier Tribunal has jurisdiction to affirm or replace HMRC's decision (ITA 2007, s 751). It is clear from the decided cases that this gives the tribunal an original jurisdiction to make its own decision, as distinct from exercising a judicial review type function.

It might be thought that the decision as to whether or not to invoke ss 739 or 737 is one for the taxpayer alone. But *HMRC v Anson* shows HMRC can determine the defence applies on their own initiative.

The Foreign pages of the self-assessment tax return indicate, at box 46, that if the motive defence is in point, the taxpayer should enter the amount of income protected by the defence and supply full details of why it applies. Such full disclosure is undoubtedly the course of prudence as it gives protection should HMRC not initiate an enquiry. But in complex cases, quantifying the income may be difficult and expensive, particularly where the non-transferor charge is in issue. In such a case an estimate may have to be given, albeit accompanied by full details of why the defence is in point.

Chapter 74

EUROPEAN DEFENCE

INTRODUCTION

74.1 As is explained in paras **107.7** to **107.12**, the transferor charges under ITA 2007, ss 720 and 727 engage two of the fundamental freedoms in EU law, namely the freedom of establishment and the freedom of movement of capital. Given the term 'transfer of assets', it may reasonably be argued that capital is the principal freedom engaged. The significance of this point is that the capital movement freedom can be engaged not merely if the movement is within the EU but also if it involves third countries. This last point makes the freedoms of great materiality to the transfer of assets code.

As is explained in CHAPTER 106, once the freedoms are engaged, anti-avoidance legislation is disapplied save to the extent it can be justified by overriding reasons in the public interest. However, to be so justified, it must be proportionate to the reason by which it is justified. In the context of tax anti-avoidance legislation, the formulation adopted is that legislation cannot be justified unless it is restricted to wholly artificial arrangements with no purpose other than the avoidance of tax (see paras **106.19** to **106.20**).

The concept of 'wholly artificial arrangements' is, as explained in para **106.20**, one whose meaning is open to debate. Nonetheless two points are clear. First, it is most unlikely that the motive defence described in the previous chapter restricts ss 720 and 727 to 'wholly artificial arrangements', for the whole language of ss 736–42 indicates a much more curtailed defence. Second, it is highly likely that a more expansive view of 'wholly artificial arrangements' will be taken where third countries and in particular low tax jurisdictions are involved (see para **106.25**).

The European Commission initiated infraction proceedings against the UK in respect the transfer of assets code. Prompted by this threat the UK government introduced a new defence to the transfer of assets code, ITA 2007, s 742A, which was intended to bring the code into compliance with EU law (or at least, to reduce the risk of it being challenged on EU law grounds). This section forms the subject matter of this chapter. The wider issue of compliance with EU law is discussed in CHAPTER 107.

This chapter is written on the basis of the law as it currently stands and takes no account of the fact that the UK has voted to leave the European Union. However it should be noted that if on leaving the EU, the UK remains in the single market the analysis in this chapter will continue to be relevant. This is because, at least in the absence of special agreement, remaining in the single market entails membership of the European Economic Area.

THE RELIEF

74.2 Section 742A operates by requiring income to be left out of account if it is attributable to a relevant transaction effected on or after 6 April 2012. A relevant transaction can be either the original transfer or an associated operation (ITA 2007, s 715; see CHAPTER 68). Income is left out of account if the transaction satisfies two conditions, conditions A and B (s 742A(2)). The relief is not entirely objective, in that the taxpayer has to satisfy HMRC that the income is attributable to the transaction. But the taxpayer does have the right to appeal to the First Tier Tribunal should HMRC decline to be satisfied (ITA 2007, s 751(da)).

Condition B

74.3 Condition B, which it is logical to consider first, requires the transaction giving rise to the income to be a 'genuine transaction' (s 742A(5)). Genuineness must be determined objectively, and regard must be had to any relevant circumstances and any arrangements under which the transaction is effected. The onus is on the taxpayer to persuade HMRC of the genuineness of the transaction, albeit with a right of appeal.

Condition A

74.4 Condition A operates on the assumption that, viewed objectively, the transaction is 'genuine'. On that assumption, the condition is met if liability to tax by reference to the transaction would constitute an unjustified and disproportionate restriction of a freedom protected under either Titles II and IV of Part 3 of the Treaty on the Functioning of the European Union or under Part II or III of the European Economic Area agreement (as to which see further para 106.27). The freedom of establishment and the freedom of movement of capital are included in these provisions as they form part of Title IV.

INCOME LEFT OUT OF ACCOUNT

74.5 An initial reading of s 742A gives the impression that the reference to income being left out of account is a reference to the actual income of the person abroad. So read, the concept of income being attributable to a transaction is easier to operate.

But in reality, the income left out of account is the deemed income of the transferor. That this is so is indicated by the inclusion of s 742A in the exemptions to the two charging sections, ss 720 and 727 (see ss 720(7) and 727(5)). This makes the exercise of determining whether income is attributable to a particular relevant transaction more challenging, as it becomes necessary to first identify the income of the person abroad to which the deemed income is equal and then ascertain whether that actual income is attributable to a relevant transaction which satisfies Conditions A and B.

DEEMING PROVISIONS

74.6 The relative clarity of s 742A is jeopardised by a series of bizarre provisions which first of all deem a whole range of transactions to be non-genuine, and then exempt a subset of transactions within that range from the deeming.

Transactions deemed non-genuine

74.7 Under s 742A(6), a transaction is deemed not to be genuine unless it is of a form and on terms such as would be entered into by persons at arms length. In determining whether this condition is met regard must be had to the arrangements under which the transaction is effected and other relevant circumstances.

Even if a transaction is on arm's length terms, it may be prevented from being a genuine transaction by s 742A(7). This provision requires, as a first step, the relevant transfer to be identified, ie the original transfer of assets as described in para 68.6. That transfer may be the relevant transaction itself, but equally, where that transaction is merely an associated operation, it is necessary to identify the original transfer with which the relevant transaction is associated (s 742A(13)).

With the relevant transfer identified it is then necessary to identify two elements (s 742A(12)). The first is the assets comprised in the original transfer and any assets directly or indirectly representing those assets. The second is income arising from such assets together with any assets representing accumulation of the income.

With those two elements identified, ie assets and income derived from the original transfer, the substance of s 742A(7) can be approached. The subsection applies if any such asset or income is used or received in the course of activities carried on by a person in a territory outside the UK through a business establishment there. The issue of whether activities amount to a business establishment is determined by the rules applicable in determining the existence or otherwise of a permanent establishment (s 742A(10)). The term thus includes fixed places of business and dependent agents (see para 64.4).

In the event that this business establishment test is met, the relevant transaction cannot be genuine unless the activities carried on through the business establishment involve the provision by the person concerned of goods or services to others on a commercial basis. Further the activities must involve commensurate staff, premises, equipment, and addition of economic value (s 742A(8)).

In essence, what s 742A(7) requires is ascertainment of whether any assets or income derived from the original relevant transfer are used or received in a business establishment. If any are so used or received, the additional tests required by s 741A(8) must be satisfied before the relevant transaction can be considered genuine. Among the many curiosities of s 742A(7) is the absence of a link between the relevant transaction and the business activities: in theory at least, the relevant transaction could be one operation associated with the relevant transfer and the business establishment could be the result of another.

Exemption from deeming

74.8 An exemption from the deeming rule is set out in s 742A(11).

For s 742A(11) to apply, the transferor must have made the relevant transfer wholly for personal, not commercial reasons, and wholly for the personal benefit of other individuals. In addition, the transferor must not have received any consideration for the transfer.

It is fairly plain that s 742A(11) is directed at relevant transfers which are gifts for the benefit of other individuals. Absent s 742A(11), s 742A(6) would deem such transfers to be non-genuine transactions, as they are by definition not commercial. It must be remembered here that the transferor charge is normally only engaged if the transferor can benefit, for absent an ability to benefit he is unlikely to have power to enjoy (see paras **69.12** to **69.16**). In view of this, the scope of s 742A (11) seems fairly small, as there is little overlap between arrangements under which the transferor has power to enjoy and arrangements made wholly for the benefit of other individuals. A revocable settlement of which the transferor is not a beneficiary is, perhaps, one example of an arrangement falling with this overlap, provided of course that such settlement can be considered a 'genuine transaction'.

COMMENT

74.9 Section 742A is an extraordinary piece of legislation. The general issue of whether it renders the transferor charge EU compliant is discussed in para **107.9**. Some specific issues are noted below.

Application of EU law

74.10 It is appropriate to start with a positive. Condition A, in making an express reference to EU law, is to be welcomed, for it avoids the unedifying spectacle of the draftsman attempting to encapsulate a freedom in domestic legislation and getting it wrong. As will be apparent from CHAPTERS 106 and 107 that has happened on many occasions in relation to other legislation. Condition A may be criticised as introducing EU uncertainty into UK tax law, but in view of the primacy of EU law, such is inevitable.

A further consequence of Condition A is that the greater application of the justifications in relation to third country capital movements is fully incorporated into s 742A. In other words, Condition A may disapply the transfer of assets code where the person abroad is a resident of the EU in circumstances where it would not disapply the code had the person been resident outside the EU.

Start date

74.11 Given the EU context, it is bizarre, however, that s 742A applies only if the relevant transaction, ie the transaction giving rise to the income, post-dated 5 April 2012. EU law has been part of UK law since the 1970s, and the freedoms have been in broadly their present form for at least 20 years. In determining the issue of whether the transfer of assets code infringes EU law the issue of whether or not a transaction took place after 5 April 2012 is irrelevant.

Condition B

74.12 Perhaps the biggest problem with s 742A is Condition B. It is clear that transactions only engage EU law if they are 'genuine', within the meaning given to that term by EU jurisprudence.

The difficulty comes with the provisions deeming certain transactions not to be genuine. It may be suggested that these are, in their entirety, pointless verbiage, for, if under EU law income is taken out of the transfer of assets code because such code is overridden by a treaty freedom, the freedom prevails and it does not matter whether under domestic law the relevant transaction is deemed to be non-genuine.

It may be suggested that the correct approach to s 742A is that proposed in para **107.9**, namely to accept that, insofar as it purports to curtail treaty freedoms, it falls to be construed in a manner that is EU compliant. This, the principle of conforming construction, is explained in para **106.21**. In the case of s 742A, its effect is to confirm that all the language of sub-ss (6)–(10) purporting to cut down the 'genuine transaction' concept can be disregarded insofar as such language would take a transaction outside s 742A where the transaction otherwise satisfies Condition A.

One particularly bizarre aspect of Condition B is that activities of a person abroad involving the provision of goods and services are less likely to come within the literal wording of s 742A than investment activities. This is because the former will normally involve a business establishment and so have to satisfy s 742A(7). Investment activities by contrast do not, and, assuming they do not, merely have to be on arm's length terms as required by s 742A(6).

An equally bizarre aspect is that on the face of it, a non-commercial original transfer, for example a gift into settlement, could be cured by a subsequent commercial associated operation, for example the capitalisation of an investment company with a commercial mix of equity and loan capital. The transferor's deemed income would then be equal to the actual income of the company and it could cogently be argued that such income is attributable to the capitalisation of the company rather than the original settlement.

NON-TRANSFEROR CHARGE

74.13 So far the discussion in this chapter has been expressed in terms of the transferor charge. However s 742A is expressly applied to the non-transferor charge also; any s 732 income attributable to a relevant transaction satisfying Conditions A and B cannot be charged (s 731(4)).

It is less easy than with the transferor charge to see how deemed s 732 income can be attributed to a given transaction effected by a person abroad, given that (remittance basis users apart) ss 731–735 do not include matching rules. A particular issue not covered by s 742A would be if some relevant income in a structure does arise from a relevant transaction satisfying Conditions A and B and some does not. In such a case there is no guidance as to which of the two kinds of relevant income should first be matched.

In practice these points are not of great significance insofar as ss 731–735 are EU compliant. But in view of the fact that ss 731–735 find no equivalent in relation to distributions from UK trusts, their compliance with EU law may be questioned (see para **107.24**).

The exemption in s 742A(11) is pertinent to non-transferor cases and it clearly brings trusts from which the settlor is excluded at the outset within s 742A. What on a literal reading s 742A(11) may not do is cover trusts which are initially settlor-interested but later cease to be so, either because the settlor dies or because he is excluded. On this scenario, a conforming construction would, it may be suggested, remedy the defect.

Section II

The income tax and CGT legislation concerning settlements

Chapter 75

ATTRIBUTION OF INCOME TO THE SETTLOR

INTRODUCTION

75.1 Chapter 5 of ITTOIA 2005, Part 5 contains legislation counteracting the income tax advantages of settlements. Where it applies, it deems the income arising under the settlement to be that of the settlor, and it applies whether the settlement is resident or non-resident. It applies in the following circumstances:

- where the settled property is, or will, or may become payable to, or applicable for the benefit of the settlor or spouse in any circumstances whatsoever. This is covered in paras **75.2** to **75.7**;
- where the settlement income is paid to, or for the benefit of a minor child of the settlor. This is covered in para **75.8**; and
- where the settlor receives a capital sum from the settlement. This is covered in paras **75.9** to **75.13**.

In the 1970s the income of resident discretionary or accumulation and maintenance trusts was taxed at 45% and that of individuals at 83%, so the tax sheltering potential of UK resident trusts was significant. Now the rate applicable to trusts and the top rate of income tax applicable to individuals are aligned at 45%. The primary impact of the legislation is therefore on non-resident settlements with UK resident settlors.

Until 1995, the predecessor legislation to what is now Chapter 5 (TA 1988 Part XV) consisted of a whole series of overlapping provisions which had been enacted piecemeal over the previous 60 or 70 years. The 1995 Finance Act recast Part XV, and this reformulated version of Part XV which forms the basis of Chapter 5. There are three principal charging sections, dealing respectively with retained interests, children, and capital sums.

The following discussion is based on the legislation as it stands at the time of writing. It is possible that changes will be made to the settlements code, with effect from 6 April 2017, at least insofar as it applies to settlors who are UK resident and deemed domiciled for all tax purposes (see CHAPTERS 19 and 45).

RETAINED INTEREST

75.2 The primary charging section is ITTOIA 2005, s 624. This deems the income arising under the settlement to be that of the settlor if it arises from property in which he has an interest.

The settlor is regarded as having an interest in the settled property if it is or will or may become payable to or applicable for the benefit of him or his spouse in any circumstances whatsoever. This definition, in ITTOIA 2005, s 625, is in substantially the same terms as that in the former TA 1988, s 673. In relation to that definition it was held that the settlor had an interest if under the terms of the trust there was some contingency, however remote, that he could benefit. Thus in *Muir v IRC* (1966) 43 TC 367 the trustees of a settlement of which the settlor was not a beneficiary could apply income in paying premiums on any policy in which any beneficiary might have a beneficial interest. It was held that such a policy might be held in another settlement under which the settlor was a beneficiary and accordingly that he had an interest in the settlement so long as that power remained exercisable.

Another example of where the settlor has an interest in the settlement is where the trusts are non-exhaustive. In such a case there is a resulting trust to the settlor and, however remote the possibility of the prior trusts failing, he has an interest.

Income is not treated as that of the settlor under s 624 unless he is an individual (s 627(4)).

Exceptions

75.3 There are some exceptions to s 625. The first is that the settlor does not have an interest in the settlement if he or his spouse can only benefit in the event of one or more of the following:

(1)   the bankruptcy of a beneficiary;

(2)   an assignment or charge by a beneficiary of his interest;

(3)   in the case of a marriage settlement, the death of both parties to and any children of the marriage; or

(4)   the death under 25 of a child of the settlor who is beneficially entitled to the settled property or the income from it (s 625(2)).

The second exception covers some cases where the settlor would otherwise be treated as having an interest in the settlement because property may become payable or applicable to him or his spouse at some time in the future. The exception is that the settlor is not regarded as having an interest in the settlement if he or his spouse cannot benefit during the life of another person whilst that other person is aged under 25. The possibility that that person might go bankrupt or assign his interest is disregarded (s 625(3)).

A third group of exceptions concern spouses (s 625(4)). The term 'spouse' does not include a person whom the settlor might marry in the future but to whom he is not currently married (s 625(4)(d)). This disapplies the decision in *IRC v Tennant* (1942) 24 TC 215, the effect of which is explained in para **76.10**. The term 'spouse' also excludes a spouse from whom the settlor is separated and any former spouse. It is thus possible for a settlement to allow the settlor's spouse to benefit in the event of his death, without that causing the settlor to be treated as having an interest in his lifetime.

As from 5 December 2005, references to spouses were extended to civil partners (Tax and Civil Partnership Regulations 2005 (SI 2005/3229)). This means that if the settlor is in fact in civil partnership, he is treated as having an interest in the settlement unless the terms of the settlement expressly exclude civil partners in the same way as spouses. However, in contrast to ITA 2007, ss 720–730 and CGT, it is not necessary for the terms of the settlement to exclude civil partners if the settlor is not currently in civil partnership (ITTOIA 2005, s 625(4)(d)).

Since 13 March 2014, references to spouses in the settlements legislation have also included same-sex spouses, pursuant to the Marriage (Same Sex Couples) Act 2013 (MSSCA). It is debatable whether a reference to the settlor's spouse in a pre-MSSCA trust instrument can ever be construed as encompassing a same-sex spouse (see para 76.12 for a discussion of this point). The prudent course therefore, where the intention is for the trust to remain non-settlor-interested, is for steps to be taken before any same-sex marriage, to ensure that the exclusion from benefit is expressly extended to the same-sex spouse when he or she becomes a spouse. However, s 625(4)(d) (discussed above) makes it unnecessary to exclude from benefit an individual of the same sex whom the settlor might marry in the future but to whom he or she is not currently married.

Income is also prevented from being treated as that of the settlor if it arises from property which he has given to his spouse or civil partner outright (ITTOIA 2005, s 626). For this exception to apply the gift must be truly outright and must not be subject to conditions. Nor must it be wholly or substantially a right to income. As will be apparent, these limitations mean this exemption is not material to settlements in the true sense of the term.

Related property

75.4 The settlor has an interest in the settlement not only if the settled property is applicable for his benefit but also if what is called related property is so applicable. Related property is defined, inter alia, as income from the settled property and property directly or indirectly representing the proceeds of the settled property (ITTOIA 2005, s 625(5)). The term used for related property in TA 1988 Part XV was derived property (TA 1988, s 660A(10)).

In *West v Trennery*, [2005] UKHL 5, [2005] STC 214, the House of Lords held in relation to the comparable CGT definition in TCGA 1992, s 77(8) that property can be related or derived property even if it is no longer in the subject settlement. The facts of *West v Trennery* were that two UK resident settlements in apparently identical terms had been used to effect an old-style flip-flop scheme (cf para 80.2) so as to reduce the rate of CGT on a subsequent disposal from 40% to 25%. The settlements were created on 1 April and 4 April 1995 respectively and both gave the settlor an initial interest in possession. On 4 April 1995 the settlor transferred shares to the first settlement and elected, as he was entitled to do, that the gain be held over. On the same day the trustees borrowed 75% of the value of the shares and transferred this sum to the second settlement. The loan was secured by a mortgage of the shares. On 5 April 1995, a deed was executed by the trustees of the first settlement excluding the settlor as beneficiary. On 13 April 1995, in the new tax year, the trustees of the first settlement sold the shares.

The effect of TCGA 1992, s 77, which has since been repealed, was that the gain on that sale would have been taxable at 40% as the settlor's if it could have been said that in the tax year 1995–96 the settled property of the first settlement or any derived property was payable or applicable for the benefit of the settlor in any circumstances whatsoever. The primary argument of HMRC, and the only one maintained in the House of Lords, was that on the facts of the case the cash transferred on 4 April 1995 to the second settlement remained derived property in relation to the first settlement.

The decision of the House of Lords was that it did. Lord Millett's analysis was that the mortgage of the shares meant the money borrowed was proceeds of the shares. The money transferred to the second settlement directly represented those proceeds and any investment of the money in the second settlement would have indirectly represented the proceeds. As such the money or investments were derived property. But on Lord Millett's analysis they ceased to be derived property once the first settlement sold the shares, for then the property which they represented had gone.

Independent act of third party

75.5 The settlor does not have an interest in the settlement just because he could benefit by an independent act of a third party. The High Court so decided in *West v Trennery* [2003] STC 580, 601 and its decision on this point was not appealed.

The point arose in the context of the power in the first settlement to transfer funds to another settlement, the power that was in fact used on 4 April 1995 as part of the scheme. It was admitted that once the settlor was excluded the power could not be exercised with a view to conferring benefit on him. But it was at least theoretically possible that it could be used to transfer the trust fund to a transferee settlement which could later add him as a beneficiary, or that he could benefit incidentally as a dependant of those who were in fact beneficiaries. In the High Court, HMRC argued that these possibilities meant the settlor still had an interest in the original settlement even after 5 April 1995. In so arguing they relied on *IRC v Botnar* [1999] STC 711 where the Court of Appeal had held that similar possibilities meant the settlor was taxable under TA 1988, ss 720–726 (see para 69.15). Peter Smith J, however, rejected the argument, stating that if the settlor could only benefit by the independent act of a third party, s 77 should not apply.

The point of distinction between *Botnar* and *West v Trennery* is that in *Botnar* the evidence was that the trustees and the settlor did intend that the power to transfer funds to another settlement would be used to enable the money subsequently to be passed to the settlor, and the drafting of the settlement itself contained subtle pointers to this conclusion. In *West v Trennery* and indeed in all normal cases these factors are not present. Unless therefore they are present or a power to transfer is in fact exercised with a view to benefiting the settlor, standard clauses excluding the settlor and his spouse from any benefit under the settlement may be regarded as effective. It is, however, prudent to provide in the settlement that the trustees' power to transfer assets to another settlement may only be exercised if the settlor and his spouse are excluded from any possibility of benefit under that settlement also.

Collateral arrangements

75.6 The rules defining whether the settlor has an interest in settled property do not say that such interest has to arise under the terms of the settlement. It can be under any circumstances whatsoever. In *Muir v IRC* (1966) 43 TC 367 Pennycuick J qualified the apparent breadth of this phrase by saying that it is confined to cases where the income or property will or may become so payable either 'under the trusts of the settlement itself or under some collateral arrangement having legal force'. He held that the former TA 1988, s 673 could not apply simply because there was doubt as to the true construction of the settlement and on one construction the settlement would be void and the income would belong to the settlor by way of resulting trust.

However, the inclusion of collateral arrangements having legal force can trigger liability under ITTOIA 2005, s 624 even where the terms of the settlement exclude the settlor. Thus in *Jenkins v IRC* (1944) 26 TC 265, the trustees were expressly empowered to apply income in repaying any loan they had incurred and they borrowed money interest-free from the settlor. The Court of Appeal held that in these circumstances the settlement income was applicable for the benefit of the settlor. *Jenkins v IRC* was followed in *IRC v Wachtel* (1970) 46 TC 543, where the settlor made an interest-free deposit with the bank to support a borrowing by the trustees at a nominal rate of interest. Trust income was applied in reducing the borrowing and corresponding reductions were made in the settlor's deposit.

The principle which emerges from these cases is that if the settlor or his spouse enters into some arrangement in favour of the trust, the settlor has an interest if there are circumstances in which they could be reimbursed out of trust income or capital. Such arises in the case of interest-free loans to the trustees, or if the settlor or his spouse guarantees some obligation of the trust and has a right to be indemnified out of the trust assets.

Payments and commercial transactions

75.7 It might be thought that the settlor could have an interest if the trustees enter into a commercial transaction with him. For example, a purchase by the trustees from the settlor would render the purchase price payable to him. It is, however, clear that the words 'payable to' connote out and out parting with the trust property (*Lord Vestey's Executors v IRC* (1949) 31 TC 1 at 83, HL). Accordingly, transactions with a settlor only give him an interest in the settlement if they involve some benefit to him. The case of *Lord Vestey's Ex-*

ecutors v IRC is authority for the proposition that a loan on commercial terms to the settlor is not an application for his benefit. By contrast comments by Lord Morton in that case support the view that a loan to the settlor on less than commercial terms is an application for his benefit.

This principle was applied by a Special Commissioner in *Trustees of the Eyretel Unapproved Pension Scheme v HMRC* [2009] STC (SCD) 17. Here trustees of an unapproved pension scheme had created a children's sub-fund from which the settlors were excluded. This sub-fund was used in a capital loss scheme to obviate a CGT charge otherwise falling to be made on the settlors. Such use did not give the settlors an interest in the sub-fund, that question being determined solely by the terms of the sub-fund.

MINOR CHILDREN

75.8 Trust income paid to or for the benefit of a child of the settlor who is under 18 is treated as the income of the settlor (ITTOIA 2005, s 629). Where the settlement was made after 8 March 1999 or funds were added to it after that date, the same applies to income appropriated to the child without being paid to him (ITTOIA 2005, s 629(1)(b) and Sch 2 para 133). The term 'child' includes a stepchild (s 629(7)).

These rules cannot be circumvented by accumulating income and distributing it as capital. A capital distribution to a child of the settlor is taxed as the settlor's income, save to the extent that it exceeds retained income in the trust which has not been applied towards income expenses or otherwise treated as the income of the settlor (ITTOIA 2005, s 631). This rule only applies, however, if at the time of distribution the child is under 18; once he is over 18 a distribution to him cannot be treated as his parent's income.

In the case of a UK resident trust, ITA 2007, s 494 allows the settlor credit for tax borne by the trust. Section 494 does not apply to non-resident trusts but ESC A93 by concession allows such treatment, insofar as the trust has UK source income. To claim this treatment the trust must be fully compliant. ESC A93 is in broadly the same terms as ESC B18 (as to which see para **8.11**).

CAPITAL SUMS

75.9 A capital sum paid by the trustees of a settlement to the settlor may fall to be treated as his income under ITTOIA 2005, s 633. However, it only falls to be so treated to the extent of the income available up to the end of the tax year in which the sum is paid. It is carried forward to the extent it exceeds such income.

Capital sum

75.10 The term capital sum means any capital sum paid otherwise than for full consideration and any loan or repayment of a loan (ITTOIA 2005, s 634). A loan to the settlor cannot be carried forward against future available income once the settlor has repaid it (ITTOIA 2005, s 638). A capital sum paid to the settlor by a company connected with the settlement counts as paid to the settlor by the trustees, but only insofar as the trustees have made a loan to or repaid a loan from the company or otherwise made a payment to it on non-commercial terms (ITTOIA 2005, s 641).

Income available

75.11 The income available as at the end of a tax year is defined as the undistributed income arising under the settlement (ITTOIA 2005, s 635). In the year in which the capital sum is paid, the income available also includes undistributed income of previous years.

The available income is not the full amount of the undistributed income. From it is deducted income previously taken into account under s 633 and income which has otherwise been taxed as that of the settlor (s 635(3)). There is also deducted an amount equal to tax at the rate for trusts on the income otherwise available (s 635(3)(d)). This deduction is made even if the income has not borne the tax, as where the income is the foreign-source income of non-resident trustees. The rate for trusts used is the rate as at the time the exercise is being done.

The charge to tax

75.12 The charge to tax is on the grossed-up capital sum. But as noted above, if the capital sum exceeds the income available, the excess is carried forward and taxed against the available income (if any) of future years.

The grossing up is at the rate applicable to trusts (ITTOIA 2005, s 640(1)). As with the deduction in computing income available, grossing up occurs regardless of whether the available income has borne tax and is at the current rate applicable to trusts.

In computing the settlor's tax liability, a deduction is taken for tax at the rate applicable to trusts (s 640(2)). The deduction is capped at the tax actually paid by the trustees on the income available (s 640(3)(c)). Income of past years is allocated on a first-in first-out basis (s 640(4)).

The practical result of this in relation to the foreign income of non-resident trustees is that the settlor is taxed on the grossed-up amount of the capital sum. This is not a greater charge than would be applicable to the income available under s 624, as tax at the trust rate is treated as deducted in computing the available income. It is considered that credit can be claimed for foreign withholding tax suffered by the income (see para **104.8**).

Application

75.13 As s 624 catches income wherever the settlor is able to benefit, s 633 is principally in point where the trust makes a loan to the settlor or the trust repays the settlor. Such loans are caught even if fully commercial. There is a wide overlap between s 633 and ITA 2007, ss 727–730 (see para **69.21**), but the latter would not apply where, for example, the motive defence in ITA 2007, ss 736–742 is in point.

MEANING OF 'SETTLEMENT'

75.14 The term 'settlement' is given an extended definition which goes far beyond trusts (ITTOIA 2005, s 620(1)). It is defined as including any disposition, trust, covenant, agreement, arrangement, or transfer of assets.

This definition is of great importance, for it is copied or incorporated referentially into other legislation, for example the CGT capital payments code (see para 77.2). The definition follows that in the pre-1995 legislation and has been the subject of much litigation, most of it concerning the issue of whether transactions which are not settlements in the normal sense of the term fall to be treated as such.

Outright gifts

75.15 The inclusion of dispositions and transfers of assets in the definition means outright gifts are caught (*Thomas v Marshall* (1953) 34 TC 178, HL). So too is the release by a life tenant or other beneficiary of an interest under a settlement (*IRC v Buchanan* (1957) 37 TC 365).

As noted above (para **75.3**), an outright and unconditional gift by one spouse to another does not result in the income being taxed as that of the donor under s 624.

Arrangements

75.16 The ambit of the word 'arrangement' is wide. In *IRC v Mills* [1974] STC 130 the taxpayer was an infant film star. Her father created a company to supply her services and she engaged herself to it for a modest salary. He then settled the shares in the company on trusts benefiting the taxpayer and in due course, lucrative contracts were made by the company for the provision of the taxpayer's services. The House of Lords held that all these transactions were an arrangement.

In *Butler v Wildin* [1989] STC 22 two brothers used monies in their children's deposit accounts to acquire £1 shares in an off-the-shelf company at par value. They were appointed directors of the company and caused the company to enter into a development project, inter alia carrying out all negotiations themselves, lending money to the company and guaranteeing bank borrowings. Vinelott J held this whole exercise was an arrangement.

A third illustration is provided by cases such as *Copeman v Coleman* (1939) 22 TC 594 and *Young v Pearce* [1996] STC 743. Such cases involve the controlling shareholder of a private company causing the company to create preference shares and issuing them to children or other relatives. The controlling shareholder then causes the company to pay exceptional dividends on those shares, either by paying the dividend solely to those shareholders or because the shares carry exceptional dividend rights. In such cases, the creation and issue of the preference shares is an arrangement.

The most recent case is *Jones v Garnett* [2007] UKHL 35, [2007] STC 1536. Here a husband with considerable earning potential caused a company to be formed in which he held half the shares and his wife the other half. He engaged himself to work for the company at a salary which was modest in comparison with the income he generated for the company. The ensuing profits were then paid out as dividend, half of them being his wife's income by virtue of her shareholding. The House of Lords held that as all this was envisaged at the outset, the whole was an arrangement.

The bounty test

75.17 An important limitation to the definition, which has been held to be implicit within it, is that some element of bounty must be present (*IRC v Plummer* [1979] STC 793). What that element is must be determined on the facts of each case. However, one test which has been proposed is whether or not the recipient under the transaction benefits without the assumption by him of any correlative obligation (*Chinn v Collins* [1981] STC 1, 12 per Lord Roskill; *IRC v Levy* [1982] STC 442).

A more recent formulation of the test is that of Lord Hoffmann in *Jones v Garnett (Inspector of Taxes)* [2007] UKHL 35, [2007] 4 All ER 857, [2007] STC 1536 at para 7, namely whether the taxpayer would have entered into the transaction in question with someone with whom he was dealing at arm's length. This formulation was followed by the Special Commissioner in *Bird v Revenue and Customs Comrs* [2009] STC (SCD) 81 at para 24.

Normally the bounty test comes into issue when HMRC seek to bring a transaction which is not a settlement in the normal sense of the term into the statutory definition. Thus in *Bulmer v IRC* (1966) 44 TC 1 a group of shareholders sold shares at an undervalue to a company controlled by a friendly party. The terms were that in due course the shares would be retransferred at the same price and in the meantime the dividends would be used to repay loans incurred to purchase further shares. HMRC claimed the arrangement was a settlement but this argument was rejected on the grounds that it was a bona fide commercial transaction.

Jones v Garnett is a further illustration of the bounty principle. Although in that case the wife paid for her shares, the reality was that their value to her was much greater than what she paid. This was on account of the reasonable expectation of what her husband would generate for the company and be prepared to accept in remuneration (see para 88 per Lord Neuberger).

MEANING OF 'SETTLOR'

75.18 The term 'settlor' is defined as meaning any person by whom the settlement is made (ITTOIA 2005, s 620(2)). A person is deemed to have made a settlement if any of the following conditions is satisfied:

(a)   he has made or entered into the settlement, directly or indirectly;

(b)   he has provided or undertaken to provide funds directly or indirectly for the purposes of the settlement; or

(c)   he has made with any other person a reciprocal arrangement for that other person to make or enter into the settlement.

Multiple settlors

75.19 The original legislation initially made no provision where more than one person fell within the definition of settlor in relation to the settlement. In *Lord Herbert v IRC* (1943) 25 TC 93 Macnaghten J held that as a result none could be assessed, for there was no machinery for apportionment between them.

As a result, rules were enacted providing that in relation to any given settlor the property and income comprised in the settlement is restricted to that originating from him (ITTOIA 2005, ss 644 and 645). The term 'originating' is defined so that the property 'originating' from the settlor is the property which the settlor concerned himself provided, whether directly or indirectly, together with property representing that property and income derived there-from.

These rules are not comprehensive, in that they do not cover the position where one person provides property directly and another indirectly. That lacuna was noted but not resolved in *IRC v Mills* [1974] STC 130, 137.

Bounty test

75.20 The bounty test qualifies also the definition of settlor and in particular its extension to providers of funds. The authority for this is *IRC v Leiner* (1964) 41 TC, 589, where Plowman J said that 'provided' implies some element of bounty. His judgment was later referred to with approval in the House of Lords (*IRC v Plummer* [1979] STC 793, 80, 814).

Identifying the provider

75.21 In both *IRC v Buchanan* (1957) 37 TC 365 and *d'Abreu v IRC* [1978] STC 538, an individual who released an interest under the settlement was held to be its settlor despite the fact that the actual settlor of the original settlement was somebody completely different. It has never been decided whether the holder of a prior interest whose consent is required before a fiduciary power is exercised constitutes himself a settlor if he gives such consent.

Providers of services

75.22 In *IRC v Mills* the House of Lords held that the child film star provided the funds, on the grounds that the source of the dividends paid to the trust was money paid for her work and that, but for the arrangements, this money would have been received by her. In *Butler v Wildin* the brothers were held to be settlors in relation to the arrangement, on the basis that by their skill, services, and temporary loans, they had provided the child shareholders with income-producing shares free of either risk or cost. Likewise in *Copeman v Coleman* and *Young v Pearce*, the controlling shareholder was held to be settlor of the arrangement on the grounds that he had provided the necessary funds indirectly.

In *IRC v Mills* the point was raised as to whether a person who provides services as an employee or a professional adviser can be treated as a settlor. The position of such persons was distinguished by the House of Lords, on the grounds that it is the provision of funds, not the provision of services, that renders a person settlor. For that reason it may be said that a person is not a settlor if he provides services to a trust or to a company underlying a trust. However the services must be on arm's length terms, for if they are not, the non-arm's length provision may, with the settlement proper, be seen as part of a non-bounteous arrangement. This is certainly so if the non-arm's length provision is envisaged at the outset and it is at least possible that the same result follows, on a year by year basis, if the provision is the result of a subsequent decision (*Jones v Garnett* [2007] UKHL 35, [2007] STC 1536 paras 88 and 89 per Lord Neuberger).

For the purposes of the settlement

75.23 A person can only be regarded as providing funds for the purposes of a settlement if he is consciously associated with the settlement in question. In *Fitzwilliam v IRC* [1993] STC 502, as part of a complex and pre-arranged IHT avoidance scheme, will trustees on 14 January 1980 appointed funds on trust to pay the income to the testator's widow until 15 February 1980 and subject thereto upon trust for his daughter absolutely. On 7 February 1980, the daughter settled this reversion upon trust to pay the income to the widow until 15 March 1980 and subject thereto on trust for the daughter absolutely. HMRC contended that the testator was settlor of this latter settlement on the grounds that by virtue of the appointment on 14 January 1980 he provided funds for the purposes or in connection with it.

The House of Lords rejected this argument in the following terms ([1993] STC 502 at 516 per Lord Keith):

> 'The words "for the purpose of or in connection with" connote that there must at least be a conscious association of the provider of the funds with the settlement in question. It is clearly not sufficient that the settled funds should historically have been derived from the provider of them. If it were otherwise anyone who gave funds unconditionally to another which that other later settled would fall to be treated as the settlor or as a settlor of the funds.'

UNDERLYING COMPANIES

75.24 Where liability arises under s 624 because the settlor has an interest in the settlement an issue arises of whether the income of a company owned by the settlement can be attributed to the settlor. Until 1989 it was expressly provided that it could be (TA 1988, s 681(3), (4)) but this provision was repealed on abolition of the rules providing for apportionment of the income of close companies.

Following such repeal it has generally been accepted that the income of an underlying company is not income arising under the settlement. The authority cited is *Chamberlain v IRC* (1943) 25 TC 317. Here the taxpayer had transferred assets to a holding company in return for shares and loan stock. The company then created a special class of preference share which were subscribed for at a cost of £10 per settlement by four children's settlements created by the taxpayer. Subsequently the taxpayer caused the company to pay each settlement over £2,000 in dividends.

HMRC argued that the incorporation and structuring of the holding company, together with the actual settlements, were an arrangement and that the property and income comprised in such notional settlement were the property and income of the company. Lord Thankerton, with whom Viscount Simon and Lord Atkin concurred, conceded that the incorporation and operation of the holding company could be part of the arrangement. But then he said that the crucial point was 'what the property comprised in the settlement consists of'. His view that such property was not the assets of the company, but merely the assets of each of the four trusts. The formation of the company provided an investment for the trusts but 'such investment was not essential to the continuance of the trusts under the deed of settlement'.

There is clearly one situation in which income in a company owned by a settlement could be caught. This is if the settlor makes a gift direct to the company. As it is established that an outright gift falls within the statutory definition of 'settlement', it is difficult to see how the donor would not have an interest in the gifted property within s 624 if he was a beneficiary under the settlement.

The more normal situation is where the trustees transfer assets to an underlying company in return for shares or a shareholder loan. If such a transfer was envisaged by the settlor when he created the settlement, it may well be part of a single arrangement, particularly as an arrangement can in part be made up of commercial or non-bounteous transactions (*Chinn v Collins* [1981] STC 1, 7 per Lord Wilberforce). But, following *Chamberlain* the true analysis is that investment into the holding company is merely an investment of the assets settled by the settlor and is not essential to the continuation of the settlement. As such the assets in the settlement are the shares in and loans to the company, not the company's assets.

To date HMRC have never given any indication of invoking s 624 in relation to company income in the case of a straightforward trust and company structure. It is noteworthy that in *IRC v Mills*, the company income was not assessed on the taxpayer. Likewise in *Jones v Garnett* [2007] UKHL 35, [2007] STC 1536 it was the dividends payable to the wife which were potentially taxable as the husband's income, not the profits of the company.

FOREIGN ELEMENT

75.25 The term 'income arising under a settlement' is defined as including (ITTOIA 2005, s 648(1)):

(a) Income chargeable to income tax, whether by deduction or otherwise.
(b) Income which would have been so chargeable if the recipient of it had been resident and domiciled in the UK.

On the face of it this brings within the settlement code all trust income, wherever arising, regardless of the residence of the settlor or the trustees. In reality, however, territorial limitations are imposed. These operate not by exempting certain categories of income treated as arising to the settlement but by treating certain categories of income as not having arisen under the settlement at all.

The rules were not altered when the taxation of non-UK domiciliaries was reformed in 2008. Instead they were put into their present form with effect from 22 April 2009 (FA 2009, Sch 27 para 13). The description below is of the rules in the form they now take.

NON-UK RESIDENT SETTLORS

75.26 If the settlor is non-resident, income is excluded from the term 'income arising under a settlement' if it satisfies the following conditions (ITTOIA 2005, s 648(2)):

(a) Had the income in fact arisen to the settlor, he would not have been chargeable to income tax by deduction or otherwise; and
(b) The reason why he would not have been so chargeable is that he is not resident in the UK.

The effect of s 648(2) is that if the settlor is not resident in the UK, the foreign income of the settlement is not deemed to be his. Conversely, UK income of the settlement is treated as his. These rules apply whether the settlement is resident or non-resident (*IRC v Kenmare* (1957) 37 TC 383, HL).

There is however one category of UK income which is not treated as the settlor's. This category comprises income which satisfies two conditions namely:

(a) It is disregarded income within the meaning of ITA 2007, ss 811 and 813 (see para **64.13**).
(b) It is subject neither to withholding tax nor a tax credit.

The reason why such income falls outside the term 'income arising under a settlement' is that, had such income in fact been the settlor's, he would, as a non-resident individual, have suffered no tax on it (ITA 2007, s 811; see para **64.6**).

One result of these rules is that if the settlor is non-resident, a non-resident settlement with UK source income may be in a better position if settlor-interested than if not. This is so if the settlement has UK beneficiaries, for here the trustees do not enjoy the relief for disregarded income (ITA 2007, s 812; see para **64.8**). The settlor by contrast does. An exception arises for UK interest payable gross to non-residents, for here such income would not have been charged to tax by deduction had it arisen directly to the non-resident settlor. This exception is not in point in relation to dividends, as the mechanism for taxing UK dividends paid to non-residents means tax at the dividend ordinary rate is treated as having been paid at source (ITTOIA 2005, s 399; see also para **64.15**).

Settlor resident in split year

75.27 The split-year rules which form part of the statutory residence test (see CHAPTER **41**) make no provision for income arising under settlements. At first sight, therefore, it might appear that settlement income is taxable on a UK resident settlor even in the overseas part of a split year, as it is the case with income arising to a transferor under the transfer of assets code (see para **69.45**).

However, in reality this is not so. Unlike the transfer of assets code, the settlements code does not include any charging provisions; it simply deems the income of the settlement to have arisen to the settlor, and relies on other provisions of the tax legislation to impose a charge to tax on the imputed income. The split-year rules do make provision for savings and investment income, overseas property income and income from a trade carried on outside the UK, exempting such forms of income from tax in the overseas part of a split year (Finance Act 2013, Sch 45, paras 74–88). This exemption from tax applies not only to personally-received income but also income that is attributed under the settlements code.

NON-UK DOMICILED SETTLORS

75.28 If the settlor is UK resident but not domiciled in the UK, he is fully taxable on the settlement income unless he is a remittance basis user in the tax year in which the income is received by the trust. If he is a remittance basis user a form of remittance basis applies to such of the trust's income as is relevant foreign income (see para **48.2**). The UK income of the trust, and any foreign income which is not relevant foreign income, is taxable in full.

The remittance basis is provided with respect to relevant foreign income of the settlement on the basis that the term 'income arising under the settlement' includes only such of the relevant foreign income as meets the following conditions (s 648(3)):

(a)   it is remitted to the UK; and
(b)   the circumstances in which it is so remitted are such that, if the settlor remitted it, he would be chargeable.

It is expressly provided that the relevant foreign income is so treated whether remitted in the tax year in which it arises or a subsequent tax year. Should it be remitted in a subsequent tax year, it is treated as arising under the settlement then (s 648(5)).

Remittance of foreign income

75.29 Section 648 expressly states that the issue of whether the trust's relevant foreign income is remitted to the UK is determined by the general rules in ITA 2007, Pt 14, chapter A1, described in Chapters 51 to 57 (s 648(4)). At a literal level there is a non sequitur, in that the definition of what constitutes a remittance in ITA 2007, s 809L is expressed in terms of an individual's income and gains (s 809L(1)). But until the trust income is remitted it is not income arising under the settlement and so not that of an individual at all. It may, however, be suggested that the express incorporation of chapter A1 makes the intent of the legislation clear and that chapter A1 has to be operated as if the individual referred to in the definition of the term 'relevant person' is the settlor. Without such inference chapter A1 cannot be operated.

It follows that a remittance causes income to be treated as arising under the settlement provided that the remitting party is a relevant person in relation to the settlor. As explained in paras 54.2 to 54.15, such persons include the following (see Chapter 54):

* The settlor.
* His spouse or cohabitee.
* Minor children or minor grandchildren.
* The trustees or any underlying company.
* Any other trust to which the income is transferred (unless all individual relevant persons are excluded as beneficiaries).

The second requirement

75.30 It is not immediately clear why the second requirement requires the remittance to be in such circumstances as to be chargeable if the settlor had effected it. The answer, however is quite simple. The term 'income arising under a settlement' is without territorial limit. Without more the settlor would be chargeable if non-resident in the tax year of remittance. The requirement that the remittance only be taxable if it would have been taxable had the settlor effected it reinstates the basic territorial limit applicable to the remittance basis (see ITTOIA 2005, s 832 and paras 48.10 and 48.14).

Transitional issues

75.31 Section 648(3)–(5) in their present form came into force on 22 April 2009 (FA 2009, Sch 27 para 15). It is unclear to what extent they apply to income arising before then, as s 648 does not include transitional provisions comparable to the 2008 general transitional dealing with relevant foreign income (FA 2008, Sch 7 para 83; see para 48.15). But what is clear is that the subsections cannot apply to income which arose in 2007–08 and before, as s 648(3) is expressed as applying only to income arising in a tax year in which ITA 2007, ss 809B, 809D or 809E apply to the settlor. Those sections first applied in 2008–09.

It follows that income of 2007–08 and earlier tax years is only chargeable under the settlement code if the old version of s 648(3)–(5) has remained in force in relation to income of the trust received before 22 April 2009. The old version broadly resembled the present law, and to that extent would treat relevant foreign income received by the trust in 2007–08 and earlier tax years as income arising under the settlement when remitted. The same point arises as respects trust income of the period between 6 April 2008 and 22 April 2009 if the present version cannot be taken as applying to such income either. A purposive construction would no doubt strain to fill these gaps, but it is odd that the points are not expressly dealt with.

In most cases the point is academic for, if the income is not treated as arising under the settlement and so as the settlor's under the settlement code, it is caught by ITA 2007, s 720 (see para **75.38** below). Here the better view is that remittances of income of 2007–08 and earlier tax years do result in tax, albeit only if effected by the settlor personally, on account of the transitional relevant person rule (see para **72.8**). Section 720 would not, of course, be in point if the settlement is within the transfer of assets motive defence.

Relevant persons

75.32 The effect of s 648(3)–(5), under both former and present law, is to defer the time the income arises to the moment of remittance. In relation to income of 2007–08 and earlier tax years this would, without more, mean that if such income is now caught by one or other version of s 648 at all, the restriction of the term 'relevant person' to the settlor himself may not apply (see further FA 2008, Sch 7 para 86(4)). In reality, however, this point is addressed, for the rule treating the income as arising when remitted is disapplied in determining whether the term relevant person is restricted to the settlor (para 86(4A)).

This means, as should be expected, that relevant foreign income which arose to the trust before 6 April 2008 is, if taxable at all, taxed only if distributed to and remitted by the settlor. It is not taxed if it is brought to the UK by the trustees or by any other relevant person.

Although only enacted in 2009, para 86(4A) is deemed to have had effect from 6 April 2008 (FA 2009, Sch 27 paras 14 and 15(1)). It is, perhaps, an indication that, one way or another, either the old or the new version of s 648(3)–(5) should be seen as catching remittances of income arising to the trust before 22 April 2009.

Meaning of 'remittance'

75.33 As indicated above the general rules in ITA 2007, Pt 14, chapter A1 are in point in determining whether the trust income is remitted to the UK and thus treated as arising under the settlement. These rules are discussed in CHAPTERS 51 to 57. Remittance by the settlor himself following distribution should be easy to spot, but the same will not necessarily be so as respects the trust.

Acts of the trustees which will cause income to be treated as remitted and so as arising under the settlement include any of the following:

• Bringing the income or funds derived from it to the UK for investment. From 6 April 2012 there is an exception for making a commercial investment in a qualifying company – see CHAPTER 58.

• Bringing to the UK of assets in specie insofar as purchased out of income.

• Use of the income abroad to pay for services provided to the trust in the UK.

• Use of the income abroad in respect of a debt relating to property in the UK.

Income transferred to an underlying company or to another trust will be treated as arising under the transferor settlement if the company or transferee trust uses the income in any of the above ways. The derivation issues arising from how far deemed derivation extends (see para 52.16) do not arise, as the issue under s 648 is whether the trust income itself is remitted. It is not a case of it being deemed derived from some other income and the issue being whether that other income is remitted. In this there is a clear contrast with the transfer of assets code (see paras 72.14 to 72.18).

In view of the transitional provisions none of the acts described above result in trust income of 2007–08 or earlier tax years being treated as arising under the settlement (even assuming such is still taxable at all). It follows that such income is effectively a class of clean capital while in the trust, taxable only if distributed to and remitted by the settlor and then only on the assumption that either old or new s 648 catches remittances of pre-6 April 2008 income at all.

Services

75.34 A payment for services provided to the trust in the UK does not result in remittance if the conditions of s 809W are met (see paras 55.13 to 55.17). In relation to s 648, these may in practice be wider than in relation to services rendered to individuals. This is because a core function of a trust is the holding of the trust property. Accordingly most, if not all, services provided to trustees can be said to relate to property. On that basis the important issue is whether the trust property is wholly or mainly in the UK or, even if it is not, whether the services in reality relate to the UK property of underlying companies. With all services there is the issue of whether to any extent they relate to benefits which are within TCGA 1992, s 87 or ITA 2007, s 732 and enjoyed in the UK (s 809W(5)). This issue is discussed in paras 55.17 and 72.23, the better view being it is narrow in compass.

Mixed funds

75.35 The mixed fund rules in ITA 2007, s 809Q (see CHAPTER 53) operate at the first stage of the exercise required under s 648(3), ie in determining whether the trust income has been remitted to the UK. They are expressly included in the provisions applied to s 648 in determining whether a remittance has occurred (s 648(4)). Once they have identified the trust income which has been remitted, they have no further function to discharge, as once the income is treated as arising under the settlement it is no longer on the remittance basis. For this reason, income treated as the settlor's under s 648 is not treated as arising in the year of remittance when applying the s 809Q ordering results.

There is a literal oddity, in that the steps in s 809Q require the amount of the individual's income to be found and, until income is treated as arising under the settlement, it is not the individual's at all. However, as with s 648(3)–(5) generally, it is clear s 809Q is meant to apply, and must so apply on the basis that the trust income is treated as if it were the individual's.

On the basis that is right, the mixed fund rules apply to identify whether income within the trust is remitted as well as whether income distributed to the settlor is remitted. In applying the rules it should be kept in mind that account must be taken of actual income and gains of the settlor which he has transferred to the trust and other categories of his deemed income. The latter would include income caught by the transfer of assets code (see CHAPTER 70), for example income of an underlying company which has been moved up to the trust as capital. A given trust account might contain income of all these categories, all of which must be taken into account in deciding whether any of the income at trust level is to be treated as arising under the settlement. Thus if the youngest income in the account is company income paid up to the trust in capital form, such is deemed remitted before the older income at trust level.

Conditions C and D

75.36 As described in CHAPTER 57, the prerequisite of a remittance under Conditions C and D is enjoyment by a relevant person of property in the UK belonging to a third party. Condition C cannot be engaged by acts of the trustee, as it requires a gift by the individual himself, ie by the settlor (see para 57.7). Condition D is not subject to this limitation and so could come into issue if the trust distributes assets derived from income to a beneficiary who is not a relevant person and what is distributed is enjoyed in the UK by the settlor or some other relevant person. This is discussed further in para 57.16. In relation to income of 2007–08 and prior, if such is taxable at all if remitted, the point would arise only if the enjoyment is by the settlor, but subject to that could arise if the recipient of the distribution is anybody other than the settlor.

THE SETTLOR'S LIABILITY

75.37 Income treated as the settlor's under ITTOIA 2005, ss 624 and 629 is treated for all income tax purposes as that of the settlor and the settlor alone (ITTOIA 2005, ss 624(1) and 629(1)). The settlor is chargeable under whichever provision of the UK tax code would have applied had it in fact been his income (ITTOIA 2005, s 619(2)). The income is treated as the highest part of his income. Save where the settlor is a remittance basis user, the dividend rates apply.

Transfer of assets code

75.38 Income taxed as the settlor's under the settlement code is not also taxable as his under the transfer of assets code (ITA 2007, ss 721(3C) and 728(2A)). This was expressly stated in 2013 and, it may be suggested, accords with previous law. This follows because under s 624 the income is treated as that of the settlor alone for income tax purposes. This means that it is not the income of the trustees and so fails to satisfy a basic precondition of the transfer of assets code.

The position is more complicated if the settlor is a remittance basis user, for then, as indicated above, the income is not treated as his under the settlement code until it is remitted. This means that until the income is remitted, it is taken into account in computing income under the transfer of assets code, albeit that it is not taxed due to the non-remittance of it.

There is no express provision dealing with the interaction of the two codes when a remittance does occur. The logic of the analysis above is that the income moves when remitted from being transfer of assets income to being settlement code income. In terms of tax payable by the settlor, this is all academic. But issues can arise if and insofar as the just and reasonable appointment rules in ITA 2007, s 743 might have treated the income as relevant income under ITA 2007, s 733 rather than income of the transferor under s 721 (see para **71.25**). In such a case the remitted income could end up being both relevant income and income taxed on the settlor. This is discussed further in para **71.26**.

A possible duplication with the transfer of assets code arises where trust income is a dividend paid out of income that has already been taxed as the settlor's under the transfer of assets code. The changes made in 2013 do not prevent the dividend being taxed under the settlement code. There is a rule in the transfer of assets code preventing income being taxed again if it is actually received by the settlor (ITA 2007, s 743(3)). But in law this is not in point unless the trust distributes the income to the settlor, for until it does so the precondition of the relief, namely actual receipt by the settlor, is not met. The point is discussed further in para **69.40**.

Who pays the tax?

75.39 As the income is treated as that of the settlor and the settlor alone, logic would suggest that the settlor alone should return the income and pay the tax on it. This is supported by ITTOIA 2005, s 646, which empowers the settlor to recover from the trustees any tax he pays under ss 624 and 629.

In fact the system does not work in this way. This is because s 646(8) expressly states that ss 624 and 629 do not exclude a charge on the trustees as the persons by whom the income is received. This rather odd provision echoes Viscount Cave's language in *Williams v Singer* (1920) 7 TC 387, 411, where he said that in a trust context, the person charged with income tax is the person in actual receipt and control of the income. But he went on to say that where the trustees are so charged they are charged on behalf of the beneficiary.

Accordingly, in the context of the rule deeming the trust income to be that of the settlor, the effect of s 646(8) is that the trustees are charged on behalf of the settlor. As per *Williams v Singer*, the settlor is then entitled to claim any relief or exemptions appropriate to his circumstances.

The general rule is that the trustees are not liable to tax at the higher rate as higher rate tax applies only to individuals (ITA 2007, ss 10 and 11). In the case of fixed interest trusts, this general rule is unqualified. Higher rate tax in such cases is a matter for the life tenant, but where the settlement code applies, the effect of the income being deemed to be that of the settlor is to take the life tenant out of the picture and leave the settlor chargeable.

But with discretionary and accumulation trusts, liability to higher rate tax is imposed on the trustees by ITA 2007, s 479. On the face of it this liability does not apply to income caught by the settlement code, for income is excluded from such liability if before being distributed it is the income of any person other than the trustees (s 480(3)(a)). Where the settlement code applies it is such income by virtue of the deeming in ss 624 and 629.

HMRC do not however read the legislation in this way and therefore consider that s 646(8) renders the trustees of settlor-interested discretionary or accumulation trusts liable to higher as well as basic rate tax (*Tax Bulletin* 84 (August 2006) p 1306). The basis for this view is that the predecessor legislation (TA 1988, s 686(2)(b)) expressly excluded income deemed to be that of the settlor and that this express exclusion was removed in 2006 (FA 2006, Sch 13 para 2). So far professional bodies have not been disposed to challenge HMRC's view.

The practical result of this is that non-resident trustees in receipt of UK source income are accountable to tax at higher rates even if the trust is settlor-interested. The settlor is then left to claim any overpaid tax back or have it set against his personal income tax liability. When first introduced, the legislation did not impose any obligation on him to hand tax so recovered, or set off, back to the trustees, which is, perhaps, an argument that HMRC were misunderstanding how the system should work. But since 2010–11 there has been an obligation on the settlor to make this repayment (revised s 646(4)–(5)). The settlor can obtain a certificate from HMRC specifying the amount of repayment to be made, which is conclusive evidence of the amount to be repaid (s 646(6A)–(6B)).

The changes to s 646 were introduced by F(No 3)A 2010, s 7. HMRC guidance is in their Trusts Manual at TSEM04550+. This guidance confirms that there is no transfer of value for IHT purposes when the settlor makes a reimbursement payment to the trustees (TSEM04554).

Trustee expenses

75.40 Trust management expenses do not go to reduce the income taxable as the settlor's where the settlement is settlor-interested (ITTOIA 2005, s 624(1A)). This means that the amount charged on the trustees to higher rate tax may be less than the amount charged on the settlor.

Accrued interest

75.41 Accrued interest taxable under the accrued interest scheme is treated as income arising under the settlement (ITA 2007, s 667). If, therefore, Chapter 5 applies, the accrued interest is included in the income deemed to be the settlor's. But this does not result in a tax charge if the settlor is non-resident, as non-residents are not within the scheme (ITA 2007, s 643). It applies to accrued interest on foreign securities if the settlor is non-domiciled, as non-domiciliaries are within the scheme.

Payments made by settlor to settlement

75.42 Where income arising to the settlement includes payments made by the settlor, those amounts of settlement income are still taxable on the settlor. This was the decision in *Rogge v Revenue and Customs Comrs* [2012] UKFTT49 (TC), [2012] SWTI 1206. In that case the two types of trust income involved were:

- Rent paid by the settlor to trustees for use of a property owned by the trust.
- Interest paid by the settlor to the trustees on a loan from the trust.

DISTRIBUTIONS

75.43 In the absence of the settlement code, the life tenant under a fixed-interest trust is taxable on the trust income, the extent of his liability depending on his residence and domicile status (see para **8.3**). Where the trust is discretionary, UK resident beneficiaries are taxed if and to the extent they are in receipt of income distributions, the remittance basis applying to remittance basis users if the trust is non-resident (see para **8.8**). The interaction of these charges with the settlor's liability where the settlement code is in point can be complex both where he has an interest in the settlement and where he is taxed because his minor children benefit.

Fixed-interest trusts

75.44 If the settlor is both resident and domiciled in the UK, the effect of the settlements code is that he is taxable on the trust income in place of the life tenant. This follows because the income is treated as the settlor's alone (ITTOIA 2005, ss 624 and 629(1)). In practice the non-deductibility of expenses means that the settlor is likely to have a higher tax burden than would have attached to the life tenant (para **75.40** above). Where the settlor is himself the life tenant, the effect of the settlement code is thus to render the settlor taxable on the trustee expenses in addition to what he would be taxable on as the life tenant.

If the settlor is a remittance basis user, the above treatment applies to any UK source income of the trust. But the position is otherwise with relevant foreign income. As this does not count as arising under the settlement unless remitted, it is not the settlor's until remitted. Until then, therefore, it can thus be taxed as the life tenant's if the life tenant is someone other than the settlor, and is a UK resident. The remittance basis does not then apply, unless the life tenant is himself a remittance basis user.

Should the remittance basis-using settlor himself be the life tenant, the relevant foreign income is taxed as his when he remits it. But a remittance by a life tenant who is not the settlor is not taxed as the settlor's income except where the life tenant is a relevant person in relation to the settlor, ie a spouse, cohabitee, or minor child or grandchild (see paras 54.2 to 54.5). In such event, the remittance is taxed as the settlor's income, and this would be so even if the income had previously been taxed as the life tenant's on an arising basis. There appears to be no provision relieving this potential double charge, which is most likely to arise where the life tenant is a minor child.

Discretionary trusts

75.45 Express relief applies to the charge on income distributions insofar as the settlor is taxed under the settlement code on the trust income out of which the distribution is made (ITTOIA 2005, s 685A). The distribution is not treated as income at all where the recipient of the distribution is the settlor himself. Otherwise, the recipient beneficiary enjoys a non-refundable tax credit at the higher rate.

Should the settlor be non-resident this credit is only available to the extent of the UK source income which is treated as his (s 685A(2); para 75.26). Where the settlor is a remittance basis user, the credit applies only to the extent that what is distributed is UK source income or remitted foreign income, as unremitted foreign income is not treated as the settlor's at all.

Remittance of a distribution by a beneficiary who is not the settlor is not treated as a remittance by the settlor of the trust income comprised in the distribution unless the beneficiary is a relevant person in relation to the settlor, ie unless he is a spouse or cohabitee or a minor child or grandchild. Where the beneficiary is a relevant person possible issues of double taxation can arise, particularly where the beneficiary is not a remittance basis user, and does not remit until a tax year subsequent to that of the distribution. In such a case, the beneficiary could be taxed on an arising basis in the year of distribution and the settlor in the year of remittance.

It is possible double tax could also arise on income distributions to UK residents who are not relevant persons. This would be the position if as a matter of tracing the income remains in the hands of the trustees, but as a matter of accounting the distribution is debited to the income. Assuming such is possible the income would be treated as arising under the settlement and so taxed on the settlor if remitted by the trustees or any underlying company. But it is unclear if the beneficiary would be able to recover any tax paid on the distribution.

DOUBLE TAXATION TREATIES

Trustees treaty resident elsewhere

75.46 The income of a settlement may be exempt from UK tax under the terms of a double taxation treaty, if the trustees of the settlement (or any other person receiving income under an arrangement that falls within the definition of a settlement in s 620) are resident for the purposes of that treaty in the other contracting state. If so, it is considered that the exclusion of the UK's taxing rights enures for the benefit of the settlor, who should claim treaty relief accordingly. This issue is discussed at para **104.7**.

Settlor treaty resident elsewhere

75.47 The income of a settlement may also be exempt from UK tax, or there may be a cap on the amount of UK tax that can be levied, under the terms of a double taxation treaty if the settlor (although UK resident) is resident for the purposes of the treaty in the other contracting state. Here the position depends on the nature of the income in question and its source. See CHAPTER **101**.

Chapter 76

ATTRIBUTION OF GAINS TO THE SETTLOR

INTRODUCTION

76.1 From 1981 until 1991 gains arising to a non-resident settlement were not in any circumstances charged to UK CGT as they arose. The sole respect in which they were exposed to UK taxation was under the capital payments code, described in CHAPTERS 77 and 78.

In 1990 and early 1991 there was widespread press comment on the tax avoidance possibilities of offshore settlements. This comment led to legislation in the 1991 Finance Act attributing the gains of certain offshore settlements to the settlor. In 1998 embarrassment on the part of a government minister led to an enlargement of the categories of settlement caught by the 1991 legislation.

The legislation is severe. Until 1991, no anti-avoidance legislation had attributed either income or gains of any settlement to the settlor unless he or his spouse were actual or potential beneficiaries or enjoyed a benefit. The 1991 legislation breached this sensible principle, for since 1991 attribution has been possible even if the settlor and his spouse are wholly excluded. In this respect the gains of offshore settlements are more severely taxed than their income.

The present legislation is in Taxation of Chargeable Gains Act 1992 (TCGA 1992), s 86 and Sch 5. It applies if at any time during the tax year in which the gains arise two principal conditions are satisfied:

(1) The settlor has what is called an interest in the settlement.
(2) The settlement is a qualifying settlement.

It can be argued that, for as long as the UK remains a member of the European Union, s 86 is disapplied by European law. This issue is discussed in paras **107.18** and **107.19**.

THE SETTLOR

76.2 Gains can only be attributed to the settlor of a qualifying settlement if in the year in which gains accrue to the trustees the settlor is both resident and domiciled in the UK (TCGA 1992, s 86(1)(c)). Under current law, an actual domicile in part of the UK is required. However, the Government intends to introduce new rules under which a foreign domiciled individual may be deemed domiciled in the UK for all tax purposes, with effect from 6 April 2017 (see CHAPTER 45). It is anticipated that s 86 will at the same time be extended to apply to certain settlements with settlors who are UK resident, non-UK domiciled but deemed domiciled under these proposed new rules (see CHAPTER 19).

Self-evidently, gains of a qualifying settlement can only be attributed to its UK resident and domiciled settlor if he is alive during the year, and, in a curious relieving provision, they cannot be attributed in the tax year of his death (TCGA 1992, Sch 5 para 3). Under current law, attribution of gains is precluded in all cases where the settlor is non-UK domiciled: there is no requirement that he be a remittance basis user or that the assets on which the gains accrue be foreign situs.

A person is a settlor in relation to a settlement if the settled property consists of or includes property originating from him (ibid, Sch 5 para 6). The term 'originating' is further defined, so that the property originating from the settlor includes property provided by him and property representing property so provided. The term 'provided by' figures in the income tax settlement code in ITTOIA 2005, Part 5, Chapter 5 and connotes bounteous provision (see para 75.20). As in the income tax code, the provision can be direct or indirect, and reciprocal arrangements are countered.

THE SETTLEMENT

76.3 The term 'settlement' is not given the artificial, extended income tax definition which applies under ITTOIA 2005, Part 5, Chapter 5 (cf para 75.14). Accordingly, s 86 applies only to settlements in the true sense of the term – ie trusts, and foreign entities which are properly characterised as trusts for the purposes of English law. However, for a settlement to be within s 86, bounty must have been involved in the making of the settlement for, as noted above, a person is only settlor if he has made bounteous provision in some form. It follows that a settlement made to attract and motivate staff is outside s 86 (*Tax Bulletin* 16 (April 1995) p 204; see further para 25.5).

Section 86 is precluded in a tax year if the settlement is UK resident for all or part of the tax year (s 86(2)(a); *Smallwood v Revenue and Customs Comrs*, [2010] STC 2045, para 6). In such circumstances any gain realised by the trust is charged as that of the resident trustees, as residence in the UK during part of the year renders the trustees taxable on gains realised at any time during the whole year (TCGA 1992, s 2(1)). To this there is one exception, namely where the resident trust is dual resident, for here special rules do apply s 86.

INTEREST IN THE SETTLEMENT

76.4 Gains can only be attributed to the settlor if he has what is called an interest in the settlement at some time in the year in which the gains accrue. The settlor is treated as having an interest in the settlement if one of two conditions is satisfied (TCGA 1992, Sch 5 para 2(1)):

(1)   property or income in the settlement is or will or may become applicable for the benefit of a defined person or payable to a defined person in any circumstances whatsoever; or

(2)   a defined person enjoys a direct or indirect benefit from any property or income in the settlement.

The following individuals are defined persons (TCGA 1992, Sch 5 para 2(3)):

(a)   the settlor;
(b)   the settlor's spouse;
(c)   any child of the settlor or of his spouse;
(d)   the spouse of any child;
(e)   any grandchild of the settlor or of his spouse; and
(f)   any spouse of such grandchild.

For these purposes step relationships are treated as natural (TCGA 1992, Sch 5 para 2(7)).

Subject to the exceptions described below, the principal effect of the rules is that the settlor has an interest in the settlement if he, his children, his grandchildren or any of their spouses is an actual or potential beneficiary. But it should be remembered that the settlor can have an interest in a settlement even where the class of beneficiaries wholly excludes such persons. Under head (2) above, the settlor has an interest in the settlement in any year in which a defined person receives a benefit – for example a benefit that is provided in breach of the terms of the trust.

Exceptions

76.5 There are three important exceptions to these rules. The first is that the settlor does not have an interest in the settlement if a defined person can only benefit in the event of:

(a)   the bankruptcy of a beneficiary;
(b)   an assignment or charge by a beneficiary of his interest;
(c)   in the case of a marriage settlement, the death of both parties to and any children of the marriage; or
(d)   the death of a beneficiary under 25 (TCGA 1992, Sch 5 para 2(4)).

76.6 The second exception is that gains are not attributed to the settlor if a defined person has an interest in the settlement in a year of assessment but that person dies during the year (TCGA 1992, Sch 5 paras 4 and 5). Gains are not attributed either if the only defined person with an interest in the settlement is the spouse of the settlor, or the spouse of one of his children or grandchildren, and the marriage ends during the year concerned (TCGA 1992, Sch 5 para 4).

76.7 The third and very important exception concerns the inclusion of grandchildren and their spouses in the class of defined person. This exception applies if two conditions are satisfied:

(a)   the settlement was created before 17 March 1998; and
(b)   all individual defined persons apart from grandchildren and their spouses are completely excluded from actual or potential benefit.

Where these conditions are satisfied, the settlor is not treated as having an interest in the settlement unless and until it becomes 'tainted' ie one of four conditions specified in Sch 5 para 2A are met on or after 17 March 1998. Those four conditions are:

(1)   Property or income was provided directly or indirectly for the purposes of the settlement otherwise than under a transaction entered into at arm's length (Sch 5 para 2A(2)).

(2)   The settlement, having previously been resident, became neither resident nor ordinarily resident in the UK or Treaty non-resident (Sch 5 para 2A(4)).

(3)   The terms of the settlement are varied so that a person within para 2A(7) became for the first time a person who would or might benefit from the settlement (Sch 5 para 2A(5)).

(4)   A person within para 2A(7) who was not capable of benefiting from the settlement before 17 March 1998 enjoyed a benefit for the first time (Sch 5 para 2A(6)).

The class of persons within para 2A(7), mentioned in the third and fourth conditions above, is restricted to:

•   grandchildren and their spouses, and
•   companies (and associated companies) controlled by grandchildren and their spouses alone, and
•   companies (and associated companies) controlled by grandchildren and their spouses together with anyone within the definition of 'defined person' in Sch 5 para 2(3) – see para **76.13**.

There was a more detailed discussion of the meaning of the 'tainting' conditions in the 18th edition of this book (and earlier editions), which included a separate chapter on 'Tainting'.

Effectively, this exception prevents gains from being attributed to the settlor if the settlement was made before 17 March 1998 and it is a grandchildren's settlement from which the settlor, his children and their respective spouses are totally excluded. It should be noted that it is not necessary for them to have been excluded on or before 17 March 1998; provided the tainting conditions have not been breached since then, all that is necessary is that the settlor, his children, and their respective spouses are excluded throughout the tax year in which the gains are realised.

Independent act of third party

76.8 The definition of interest in the settlement does not, in contrast to that in ITTOIA 2005, s 625, make reference to derived property. This means the House of Lords decision in *West v Trennery* [2005] STC 214 is not relevant (as to which see para **75.4**).

At first instance in *West v Trennery*, Peter Smith J indicated that in deciding whether the settlor had an interest in the settlement for the purposes of the now repealed TCGA 1992, s 77, no account should be taken of what an independent third-party transferee of the settled property might do. In the context of s 86, the point may be material where all defined persons are excluded from benefit, but the trustees have power to transfer all or part of the trust fund to another settlement. Although it would be prudent to ensure that such a transfer is only permitted if all defined persons are expressly excluded from the transferee settlement, *West v Trennery* indicates this is not essential so long as there is no scheme or intention on the part of the transferor trustees to use the transfer as a means of benefiting any of the defined persons. The point is discussed further at para 75.5.

Collateral arrangements

76.9 Head (1) in the definition at the beginning of para **76.4** above does not in terms require the settled property to be applicable for the benefit of, or payable to, the defined person under the terms of the settlement. The wording is similar to that in its income tax equivalent (ITTOIA 2005, s 625(1)). It has been held in relation to the predecessor to that wording (TA 1988, s 673(2)) that the property or income can be payable or applicable under some collateral arrangement having legal force (*Muir v IRC* (1966) 43 TC 367 at 381 per Pennycuick J). This is discussed further in para **75.6**.

Future spouses

76.10 Even if the settlor, his children and grandchildren, and their respective spouses are excluded, the settlor still has an interest in the settlement if the settlement allows benefit to be conferred on a future spouse at a time when such person is a spouse. This is the effect of the decisions in *IRC v Tennant* (1942) 24 TC 215 and *Unmarried Settlor v IRC* [2003] STC (SCD) 274.

In the first of these cases the settlor held an overriding power of appointment and in the second the trustees had an unrestricted power to add beneficiaries. In both cases the settlor was unmarried, but had he or she married in the future the power could, as a matter of construction, have been exercised in favour of the future spouse. This, it was held, was sufficient to render the settlement settlor-interested within the meaning of the then provisions attributing the income and gains of the resident settlements to the settlor, namely FA 1938, s 38 and TCGA 1992, s 77.

Before it was repealed, TCGA 1992, s 77 was amended so as to exclude from the term 'spouse' any person to whom the settlor is not currently married but may later marry. Unfortunately, equivalent exclusions are not found in TCGA 1992, Sch 5. The result is that if attribution of gains under Sch 5 is to be avoided the terms of the settlement must preclude benefit to a future spouse at any time when she is a spouse. Any well-drawn exclusion clause should achieve this.

Civil partners

76.11 Regulation 126 of the Tax and Civil Partnership Regulations 2005 (SI 2005/3229) extended all references in Sch 5 to spouses to include civil partners. This regulation came into force on 5 December 2005 (reg 1(1)).

Its obvious effect is that if, under any settlement, the settlor, his children and grandchildren, and their respective spouses are all excluded, the entry of one of them into civil partnership will give the settlor an interest in the settlement unless, before the entry into civil partnership, the trustees amend the terms of the settlement to exclude civil partners. But as a matter of strict construction the effect of the regulations is wider, for the decisions in *IRC v Tennant* and *Unmarried Settlor v IRC* are in point. The effect of those decisions is that unless the terms of the settlement preclude any benefit to a future civil partner at a time when he is civil partner, the settlement is within Sch 5.

It is improbable that any English law settlement drafted before the Civil Partnership regulations were mooted would have excluded civil partners from benefit, as the concept of civil partnership was then alien to English law. The logical result is that on 5 December 2005 all (or at least the great majority of) non-resident settlements with a living settlor in which the settlor did not have an interest for the purposes of TCGA 1992, Sch 5 became ones in which he did.

Rather surprisingly this point is not covered in the *Tax Bulletin* article on the Tax and Civil Partnership Regulations (*Tax Bulletin 80* (December 2005 p 1252). But in correspondence with STEP dated 23 November 2005, HMRC recognised the correctness of the analysis outlined above. HMRC indicated that in relation to settlements drafted thereafter, civil partners should be expressly excluded in the same way as spouses.

As respects existing settlements HMRC gave an assurance in the letter that 'the introduction of the Civil Partnership Act 2004 will not alone result in a change of status for non-resident settlements that are not regarded as settlor-interested under existing law'. It may be felt that this provides the requisite level of comfort, but as HMRC also say, trustees may, where the terms of the settlement so permit, wish to amend its terms by appointment or exclusion to reflect the change in the law.

Whether a private letter to STEP is a satisfactory means of granting what is, in effect, an extra-statutory concession, is open to question.

Same-sex spouses

76.12 Essentially the same issue has been created by the Marriage (Same Sex Couples) Act 2013 (MSSCA), which since 13 March 2014 has required all references to spouses in previous legislation to be read as including same-sex spouses (Sch 3, para 1). It follows logically that on 13 March 2014 any non-resident settlement with a living settlor in which the settlor did not have an interest for the purposes of TCGA 1992, Sch 5 became one in which the settlor did have an interest, except in any case where it is correct to construe references to spouses in the exclusion clause as including same-sex spouses.

It is questionable whether references to spouses in pre-MSSCA English law trust instruments can properly be construed as including same-sex spouses, given that the concept of same-sex marriage was foreign to English law until the enactment of the MSSCA. However, it is suggested that the meaning of 'spouse' in an exclusion clause in a pre-MSSCA trust instrument is a question of fact – specifically, the intention of the settlor, or of the trustee or any other party effecting the exclusion.

The MSSCA itself does not provide any assistance in interpreting trust instruments made before its enactment, as it merely provides that the extension of the meaning of 'marriage' 'does not alter the effect of' any private legal instrument made before the MSSCA was brought into force (Sch 4, para 1). There is, perhaps, an argument that absent intrinsic or extrinsic evidence as to the intended meaning of 'spouse' in a pre-MSSCA trust instrument, such references should be given the wider of the two possible interpretations, consistently with the overriding aim of the exclusion clause, viz to avoid the settlor being deemed to have an interest for the purposes of TCGA 1992, Sch 5.

Logically, the HMRC concession regarding the introduction of civil partnership, expressed in the letter to STEP referred to above, should also apply in relation to the introduction of same sex marriage. Of course, any new non-resident settlement should define 'spouse' as including a same-sex spouse, if the object is to avoid settlor-interested status under Sch 5.

QUALIFYING SETTLEMENT

The original condition

76.13 When TCGA 1992, s 86 and Sch 5 were first enacted a settlement was only a qualifying settlement if either:

(a)   it was made on or after 19 March 1991; or

(b)   it was made before that date but one of the four 'tainting' conditions in Sch 5 para 9 had been satisfied since then.

The four 'tainting' conditions were:

(A)   Property or income was provided directly or indirectly for the purposes of the settlement otherwise than under a transaction entered into at arm's length.

(B)   The settlement, having previously been resident, became neither resident nor ordinarily resident in the UK or Treaty non-resident.

(C)   The terms of the settlement were varied so that a person within para 9(7) became for the first time a person who would or might benefit from the settlement.

(D)   A person within para 9(7) who was not capable of benefiting from the settlement before 19 March 1991 enjoyed a benefit for the first time.

In conditions (C) and (D), the persons within para 9(7) were as follows:

(i)   any settlor;

(ii)   any spouse of any settlor;

(iii)   any child or stepchild of any settlor;
(iv)   any spouse of such child;
(v)   any company controlled by all or any of the above, and any company associated with such a company.

An exception to condition (A) was made in the following circumstances:

(1)   the settlement's expenses relating to administration and taxation for a year of assessment exceeded its income for that year; and
(2)   the added property did not exceed the shortfall.

There is a more detailed discussion of the meaning of the 'tainting' conditions in the 18th edition of the book (and earlier editions) which had a separate chapter on 'Tainting'.

Protected settlements

76.14 As a result of the amendments introduced by FA 1998, s 132, all settlements have since 17 March 1998 been qualifying settlements, regardless of when made. There is, however, one transitional exception, for what are termed protected settlements.

Under Sch 5 para 9(10A), a settlement can only be a protected settlement if the beneficiaries are confined to children of the settlor who are under 18, unborn children of the settlor, and persons who are not defined persons at all. A child counts as under 18 if he is under 18 at the beginning of the tax year concerned. Future spouses of the settlor or his children are also allowed to be included as beneficiaries.

A protected settlement is not a qualifying settlement provided that:

(a)   it was created before 19 March 1991,
(b)   it was a protected settlement on 6 April 1999, and
(c)   none of the five conditions set out in Sch 5 para 9 has been breached since 19 March 1991 (Sch 5 para 9(1B)).

The five conditions are the four described in para **76.13** which applied to all pre-1991 settlements until 17 March 1998 plus one additional one. This is that the settlement has not ceased to be a protected settlement at any time after 5 April 1999 (Sch 5 para 9(6A)). The main circumstance in which a protected settlement would cease to be a protected settlement is if a child of the settlor attained the age of 18 and was not excluded before the end of the tax year in which he did so.

On a strict construction of para 9(10A), a settlement is not protected if the settlor's grandchildren are beneficiaries. In practice, however, HMRC allow the beneficiaries to include grandchildren (*Tax Bulletin* 38 (December 1998) p 620).

COMPUTATION OF THE GAINS ATTRIBUTED

76.15 Where the conditions for the operation of s 86 are satisfied, a computation is made of the amount on which the trustees would have been chargeable to CGT for the tax year concerned if they were UK resident (TCGA 1992, s 86(1)(e)). Certain rules apply in determining this amount (TCGA 1992, Sch 5 para 1):

(1)   It is assumed no annual exemption is available.

(2)   Current year losses are allowed. Losses carried forward from previous years are also allowed, but only if in the year concerned any gains would have been attributable to the settlor under s 86.

(3)   No account may be taken of either losses or gains which accrued before 19 March 1991.

Underlying companies

76.16 Where the trustees are participators in a non-resident close company, gains realised by the company may be taken into account as if they had accrued in the settlement, if two conditions are satisfied. First, the gains must be such as would be apportioned under TCGA 1992, s 13 if the trustees were resident in the UK, and second, the trustees must be participators in the company in respect of property which originated from the settlor (Sch 5 para 1(3)). This latter phrase is not at first sight wholly clear, but the likely meaning is that the share or loan capital which renders the trustees participators must be, represent or derive from assets which the settlor has transferred to the trust. Accordingly, gains in the company can be taken into account under s 86 insofar as the trustees' participation was settled by the settlor or was acquired using funds or other assets derived from him.

If that is right, there may be a gap in the legislation, highlighted in *Coombes v Revenue and Customs Comrs* [2007] EWHC 3160 (Ch), [2008] STC 2984. Here a foreigner had settled £1,000 in an Isle of Man settlement which in due course acquired an offshore company. The taxpayer then gave £700,000 to the company, which used the money to buy UK land. On the subsequent sale of the land, HMRC sought to charge the taxpayer on the gain thereby realised. The High Court held that s 86 was not in point, specifically rejecting the argument that the increase in the value of the shares which resulted from the gift of £700,000 meant that the money was an indirect addition to the settlement.

Coombes is an unsatisfactory decision, as it contains an assertion that the legislation contains no provision deeming company gains to be realised on disposals by the trustees, whereas such provision is in fact contained in Sch 5 para 1(3). Nonetheless the decision can be supported on the ground that the trustees' participation in the company was not property which originated from the taxpayer, for on the facts the participation originated from the £1,000 settled by the foreign settlor. The only way for HMRC to get round this point would be to rely on the point the judge rejected, namely that the increase in the value of the shares resulting from the gift meant that they were property which originated from the taxpayer, ie to use the words of Sch 5 para 8(1), they were property which he had provided, or represented such property.

If the judge's decision is right, a means of sheltering future gains from s 86 is opened up. But it may be doubted whether the decision would survive a purposive construction in a higher court.

discussed in CHAPTER **88**. As generally under s 13, losses in the
: only taken into account insofar as they offset gains in the
: another s 13 company in the same tax year (para **88.19**). Tax
the settlor by virtue of s 13 may be credited against any tax due
from .... in respect of distributions from the company made within the
specified period of the s 13 gain accruing (see para **88.32**).

CHAPTER 88 also discusses an exemption from s 13 which was introduced by FA
2013, to disapply s 13 where (in broad terms) the use of a non-UK company
to hold assets was not motivated by avoidance of CGT or corporation tax. The
new exemption is intended to ensure that s 13 does not infringe European law.
It could, conceivably, be relevant to a trust structure established by a non-UK
resident foreign domiciliary who has since become UK resident and domiciled.

THE CHARGE ON THE SETTLOR

76.17 The result of the computation described above is that there is either a
net gain or a net loss for the year concerned. If there is a net loss it is *not*
attributed to the settlor and is only able to be relieved by being carried forward
and set against future trust gains as described above. If there is a net gain, it is
included in the net gains on which the settlor is chargeable to tax (TCGA 1992,
s 2(2)).

In computing the settlor's CGT liability, the net gains attributed under s 86 are
treated as the top slice of his overall gains for the year concerned (TCGA 1992,
s 86(4)). His basic annual exemption is available if not otherwise utilised. In
general the rate of tax is the standard 20% rate, but the 10% rate is available
to the extent the settlor's income and personal gains have not absorbed his
basic rate band.

Personal losses of the settlor are set in the first instance against personal rather
than trust gains, as the latter form the top slice of gains. But assuming the
losses exceed the personal gains they can be offset by s 86 gains (TCGA 1992,
s 2(4)). The losses are allocated pro rata if in any given tax year gains are
attributed to the settlor from more than one settlement and are insufficient to
absorb all the losses (s 2(7)).

Reimbursement by the trustees

76.18 The settlor has a statutory right to recover any tax he pays under s 86
from the trustees (TCGA 1992, Sch 5 para 6). HMRC do not regard this right,
or any provision in the trust deed recognising it, as causing the trust income to
be assessable on him under ITA 2007, ss 720–726, ITTOIA 2005, s 624 or as
a reserved benefit for IHT purposes (SP 5/92 paras 8–10).

In practice few offshore trusts expressly recognise the right of recovery. In
many cases the settlor is a beneficiary, and so the trustees can reimburse him
in exercise of their fiduciary powers. But where he is not a beneficiary, and
there is no express right of reimbursement or trustee power to reimburse the
settlor for taxes suffered by him in respect of gains of the trust, it is widely
believed that the settlor is in difficulty in enforcing the statutory right of
recovery. This is because the right to recovery is conferred by a UK statute, and

so, unless the proper law of the settlement is that of part of the UK, it is not part of the trust's governing law. As such it is generally believed that a court outside the UK would have some difficulty in recognising it (see for example *Re T Settlement* [2002] 4 ITELR 820, 822).

A possible solution for an English resident settlor may be to bring proceedings in the English courts and then serve the trustees out of the jurisdiction. Assuming this is possible and that he then obtains judgment, one of two courses is likely to be open to him:

(1)   If the trust or the trustees have English assets he could enforce against those.
(2)   If the trust is based in a jurisdiction with which the UK has a convention for the mutual recognition of judgments, he could enforce the judgment against the trustees in their home jurisdiction.

The difficulty with this solution is that it may not be possible to serve the trustees out of the jurisdiction. In *Prestwich v Royal Bank of Canada Trust Co (Jersey) Ltd* [1998] 1 ITELR 565 Judge Howarth held that such service was possible as of right under the former RSC Ord 11 r 1(2)(b) or, failing that, that the settlor was entitled to leave under Ord 11 r 1(1)(n). But under the present Civil Procedure Rules, the conditions for service out of the jurisdiction as of right are not satisfied, and in Practice Direction 6B, which sets out the circumstances in which leave may be granted for service out of the jurisdiction, the wording of the equivalent to rule 1(1)(n) is restricted to claims by HMRC (paragraph 17), so it is difficult to see how an English court would grant leave to serve out.

A second solution is suggested by a Jersey case, *Re T Settlement* [2002] 4 ITELR 820. Here a standard exclusion clause excluded the settlor from all possibility of benefit under the settlement. The Royal Court approved a variation of this clause to permit reimbursement of tax liabilities incurred by the settlor as a result of the operation of the settlement. This variation was approved by all the adult beneficiaries and was sanctioned by the Court under Article 43 of the Trusts (Jersey) Law 1984 on behalf of minor and unborn beneficiaries. Article 43 only applies if the court is satisfied the proposed variation is for the benefit of the beneficiaries concerned. The benefit relied on was the discharge of the beneficiaries' moral obligation to the settlor and increased investment flexibility. Those seeking to follow this case should however note that the facts were exceptionally strong in that the settlor was a lady aged 98 who had transferred all her assets to the settlement for the benefit of her family prior to moving back to the UK.

Should the trustees end up reimbursing the settlor by one means or another, HMRC do not regard such reimbursement as a capital payment within TCGA 1992, s 87 (SP 5/92 paras 8–10).

Sch 5 makes no provision requiring trustees to give the settlor information about gains. Where he is not a beneficiary, issues may arise of whether he is entitled to such information, particularly if the result of such information would be a tax charge on the settlor and a claim against the trust.

The difficulties the settlor may experience in enforcing his indemnity is a reason for supposing that at some stage the application of s 86 to settlements from which the settlor is excluded may be held to breach European law. This point is discussed in paras **107.18** and **107.19**.

Temporary non-residence of the settlor

76.19 If the settlor is non-resident for a period not exceeding five years, all gains which would have been attributed to him under s 86 had he not emigrated are treated as accruing to him in the year of his return. This is the same as with gains accruing to him directly (see para **29.6**) and is expressly provided for by TCGA 1992, s 10A, which incorporates by reference the definition of 'temporarily non-resident' in FA 2013, Sch 45 para 110.

TCGA 1992, s 86A addresses a problem this poses. This problem is that until the settlor returns, gains in the trust realised in the intervening years go into the trust's s 2(2) amount under TCGA 1992, s 87 (discussed in CHAPTER 77) because, as the settlor is then non-resident, s 86 does not apply. Should capital payments be made to resident beneficiaries, they are taxed by reference to the trust gains and yet, when the settlor returns, he is then assessable on those gains under a combination of ss 10A and 86.

Section 86A addresses this problem by defining two sums (sub-s (1)(b)). These are:

(a)   The pool of trust gains carried forward for the purposes of s 87 as at the end of the year of the settlor's departure.
(b)   Distributions during the intervening years actually charged to CGT as gains accruing to resident beneficiaries under the capital payment rules.

If the distributions at (b) exceed the pool carried forward at (a) there is an 'excess'. Where there is such an excess, gains realised by the trust in the intervening years cannot be assessed on the settlor save insofar as they exceed the excess. Should they exceed the excess, the amount by which they exceed it is assessable on the settlor. It then drops out of the pool of trust gains carried forward to the year of return for the purposes of s 87.

The amount so assessed drops out of the trust gains carried forward to the year of return for the purposes of s 87. This is provided for by s 87(7), but neither that nor the following subsection appear to have been amended to reflect the 2008 changes to s 87 (as to which see CHAPTER 77). As a result it is unclear whether the s 2(2) amounts of earlier or later intervening years are reduced first.

MULTIPLE SETTLORS

76.20 Since the definition of 'settlor' includes any person who has provided property, it is perfectly possible for a settlement to have more than one settlor. In this event any given settlor only has an interest in the settlement if property originating from him could be used to benefit a person who is a defined person in relation to him, or if such a person receives a benefit from such property (TCGA 1992, Sch 5 para 2(2)). A particular settlor is only chargeable on gains accruing on disposals of property originating from him (s 86(1)(e)). So too he is only credited with losses on property originating from him. Gains in an underlying company are attributed to him if the shares in the company originated from him (Sch 5 para 1(2)).

CORPORATE SETTLORS AND BENEFICIARIES

76.21 Unlike other anti-avoidance legislation, TCGA 1992, s 86 and Sch 5 make express provision for the position where a company is the settlor or where one or more companies are beneficiaries.

Corporate settlor

76.22 An individual is treated as having provided property, and thus as a settlor, in certain cases where a company provides the property (TCGA 1992, Sch 5 para 8(4)). An individual is treated as providing all the property provided by the company if he is the only person who controls it. If two or more persons each control the company separately, each is taken to provide the property in equal shares. If two or more persons only control the company by taking them together, they are each treated as providing an apportioned part of the property, subject to a de minimis limit of 5%. For these purposes provision by a company is taken into account whether the company is resident or non-resident, but the company must be close.

The applicable definition of control is that in CTA 2010, ss 450 and 451, the close company definition (para 8(8)). This is discussed in para **87.9**. The core rule under this definition is that an individual has control of a company if he has control at the level of general meetings (*Steele v EVC International NV* [1996] STC 785, 794–795, CA). Control can be direct or indirect, which means an individual who controls the parent also controls its subsidiaries (*Kellogg Brown and Root Holdings (UK) Ltd v Revenue and Customs Comrs* [2009] EWHC 584 (Ch), [2009] STC 1359, para 42). In determining whether an individual has control, the rights and powers of his associates are attributed to him (s 451(4)); see paras **87.2**, **87.9** and **87.10**.

If the income tax definition of control stood alone in determining who is settlor, an individual could be the settlor in relation to a settlement even if he personally owned no shares in the providing company. The legislation attempts to remove this possibility by providing that a person is not for these purposes treated as controlling a company unless he is himself a participator (TCGA 1992, Sch 5 para 8(8)). Unfortunately this provision does not fully hit its target, for the term 'participator' includes actual shareholders and loan creditors, and anybody having a share or interest in the capital or income of the company (CTA 2010, s 454); see para **87.3**. The word 'interest' in this definition certainly brings in fixed-interest beneficiaries in relation to trust shareholdings (*R v IRC, ex p New Fields Developments Ltd*, supra); see further para **87.4**. The result is that it is still possible for a beneficiary under a settlement to be treated as controlling a company, and thus to be treated as a settlor in relation to funds provided by the company, even if he personally owns no shares in it.

Fortunately this defect has been recognised by HMRC, for ESC D40 provides that for these purposes a beneficiary under a trust is not treated as a participator solely because of his status as a beneficiary. In 2015 HMRC consulted on draft legislation to put ESC D40 on a statutory footing. A statutory instrument was expected to be passed at some point in 2016, but at the time of writing (early October 2016) has not yet appeared.

Corporate beneficiary

76.23 The term 'defined person' includes any company controlled by any one or more of the individual defined persons listed in para 76.4 above and any other company associated with such a company. The rules for determining whether a company is controlled by one or more individual defined persons are the same as those applicable in determining who is settlor, save that ESC D40 does not apply. As under those rules, the term 'associated' is also defined with reference to the close company legislation (TCGA 1992, Sch 5 para 5(9)). Two companies are thus associated if one controls the other or both are under common control (CTA 2010, s 449).

In determining whether a pre-1998 grandchildren's settlement attracts the transitional exemption described in para 76.5, the companies which must be excluded from benefit are restricted to those controlled by the settlor, his spouse, or their children and companies associated with any such company. However, this is of little practical significance, for as described above, under CTA 2010, s 448, a person's associates include his descendants (see para 87.8).

The practical importance of defined persons including companies is that even if all individual defined persons are excluded, the settlor will still have an interest in the settlement if companies are, or are being capable of being added as, beneficiaries under the settlement and such companies do not exclude those which fall within the definition of defined person. The problem may be more widespread than at first appears, for most powers of addition are expressed in terms of persons and the term 'person' normally includes companies. In English law, such is implied by Interpretation Act 1978, Sch 1.

Can a company be a settlor?

76.24 Apart from these rules treating participators as settlors, no rule exists to prevent s 86 or Sch 5 from applying to a corporate settlor, although the only categories of defined person would be the settlor company and controlled or associated companies. As a result, if an open company creates a settlement s 86 could apply to it unless it and connected and associated companies are wholly excluded. The language of the Sch 5 para 8(4) is, it may be suggested, wide enough to prevent any close company from being taxed as settlor. These issues arise particularly with employee benefit trusts (see para 25.5).

TREATY ISSUES

Dual resident trusts

76.25 Schedule 5, para 1(4) makes special provision for any trust which is within s 86 where the following conditions are met:

(1)   The trust is resident in the UK during all or part of a tax year.
(2)   At the same time it is resident in a foreign territory under the domestic laws of that territory.
(3)   There is a double taxation treaty between the UK and the foreign territory.
(4)   Under the tie-breaker clause in the treaty, the trust is treated as resident in the foreign territory. In practice, any such determination is likely to be on the basis that the place of effective management of the trust is in the foreign territory (see para **100.6**).

In any such case, s 86 applies to the net gains realised by the trust in the tax year concerned (TCGA 1992, s 86(4)). The general rule is that in computing the net gains attributed to the settlor, only disposals of treaty protected assets are taken into account. However, the trust's total net gains are attributed if less (Sch 5, para 1(4)).

Trustees non-UK resident and treaty resident elsewhere

76.26 A separate issue is whether a charge to tax for a settlor under s 86 may be precluded by a treaty where:

(1)   The trust is non-UK resident (so that Sch 5, para 1(4) is not in point).
(2)   It is resident in a foreign territory under the domestic laws of that territory.
(3)   There is a treaty between the UK and the foreign territory, under which the trust is treated as resident in that territory, and which gives that territory the exclusive right to tax gains of the trust.

This difficult issue is discussed at para **104.17**. The conclusion reached there is that in this situation a s 86 charge cannot be precluded by a treaty.

Settlor dual resident and treaty resident elsewhere

76.27 A further issue is whether a s 86 charge may be precluded by a treaty where the settlor is dual resident, and is resident for the purposes of the treaty in the other contracting state.

One would expect the answer to be yes. However, the question is one of some difficulty. The reason is that the general rule under a treaty which follows the OECD Model Treaty is that gains from the alienation of property are only taxable where the 'alienator' is resident. The issue with this where s 86 is concerned is that the gains attributed to and taxed on the settlor are considered to be generic deemed gains (see para **104.17**). They are not the same gains as those realised by the trustees, and on one view, at least, do not result from an alienation of property. It is, in any event, difficult to see the settlor as an 'alienator' of property in respect of which the s 86 gains have arisen.

Thus, for treaty protection to be available in this situation a court would need to adopt a purposive construction of the treaty. In principle, a double taxation treaty should be interpreted purposively so that it provides effective relief (see para **99.10**), but where anti-avoidance provisions are concerned the courts have tended to take a narrow approach which denies treaty protection (see CHAPTER 104). It would be incautious therefore to assume that a settlor who is treaty resident in another country is necessarily protected from liability under s 86.

Chapter 77

SECTION 87

INTRODUCTION

77.1 TCGA 1992, ss 87–97 tax UK resident beneficiaries on the gains of non-resident trusts. They require a computation for each tax year of the s 2(2) amount, ie net chargeable gains of the trust. That amount is treated as chargeable gains accruing to beneficiaries if and to the extent that the beneficiaries receive capital payments. Tax is charged if the recipient beneficiary is resident and domiciled in the UK and, in some cases, if he is UK resident but non-domiciled.

Sections 87–97 were extensively amended in 2008 (FA 2008, Sch 7 paras 108–114). This chapter explains the law as it now stands. HMRC have published guidance, which includes many worked examples. This guidance may be found in the Capital Gains Manual at CG 382000BC and following paragraphs.

APPLICATION

77.2 Section 87 applies to a settlement for any tax year in which the trustees are non-UK resident throughout the year. It so applies regardless of the residence or domicile status of the settlor or the beneficiaries, although if the settlor is both resident and domiciled in the UK, gains treated as accruing to him under TCGA 1992, s 86 are left out of account in the s 87 computations (see para **77.13** below).

In certain contexts where a trust immigrates or emigrates, s 87 can apply to a settlement with UK resident trustees. This is covered in paras **77.33** to **77.38**.

Section 87 applies separately to each settlement. The term 'settlement' has the same meaning as given in the anti-avoidance rules attributing income to the settlor (TCGA 1992, s 97(7); see ITTOIA 2005, s 620 and para **75.14**). It thus means not merely settlements in a true sense but also includes arrangements. The implications of this are discussed in para **77.52**.

SECTION 2(2) AMOUNTS

77.3 The section 2(2) amount has to be determined for each tax year in which s 87 applies to the settlement. It means simply the amount upon which the trustees would have been chargeable to CGT under TCGA 1992, s 2(2) if they had in fact been UK resident in the tax year in question (s 87(4)(a)). In other words what is required is a straightforward CGT computation on a year by year basis.

Where the settlor was both resident and domiciled in the UK, the trustees will often have computed their s 2(2) amounts on a year by year basis. But in other cases no computations may have done until UK residents receive capital payments and in such cases a historic exercise may be required, computing s 2(2) amounts back to the inception of the settlement.

It is not wholly clear from the wording of the legislation whether s 2(2) amounts are calculated according to the law of the year when they accrued or according to the law obtaining in the year of matching. However, the overall structure of the legislation indicates that the former must be correct, as otherwise the s 2(2) amounts of old years would fluctuate according to future changes in CGT rules, and would indeed revive after being wholly matched insofar as relieving provisions were abolished. HMRC's guidance indicates that they share this conclusion (CG 38610).

The practical result of this is that knowledge of old law is required where historic s 2(2) amounts are being computed. The constant changes that successive governments have made to CGT mean acquiring or reviving such knowledge can be a challenging exercise.

Losses

77.4 The charge under s 2(2) is on the aggregate gains of the year, less allowable losses realised in the year and brought forward losses of the trustees. The allowability of losses is thus brought into the computation of the s 2(2) amount, the rule that losses accruing to non-residents are not allowable being specifically disapplied (TCGA 1992, s 97(6)).

Annual exemption

77.5 Section 2(2) amounts are computed without any annual exemption, as that operates on the amount otherwise chargeable under TCGA 1992, s 2 (TCGA 1992, s 3(5) and Sch 1 para 2).

Rebasing on death

77.6 One relief which is potentially available is the automatic rebasing which applies on death. This is in point in the event of the death of a beneficiary with a qualifying interest in possession (TCGA 1992, s 72(1)). The relief applies even if the beneficiary is the settlor. Qualifying interests in possession are considered in CHAPTER 61 and in practice are now normally only encountered under long-standing settlements created by settlors both resident and domiciled in the UK (see further CHAPTER 5 and especially para 5.15). But the point is one to look out for when computing historic s 2(2) amounts, for until 2006 all interests in possession resulted in an updated base cost on the death of the life tenant (TCGA 1992, ss 72 and 73 as in force prior to 22 March 2006).

Absolute entitlement

77.7 The s 2(2) amount includes any gains accruing should a person become absolutely entitled to trust property in the year in question (TCGA 1992, s 71).

The normal case where a person becomes absolutely entitled to trust property is where an individual beneficiary becomes absolutely entitled either automatically or under an appointment by the trustees. But absolute entitlement also occurs when funds pass from one settlement to another or when a sub-fund election is made (see *Roome v Edwards* [1981] STC 96 and TCGA 1992, Sch 4ZA, para 19). In all such cases the assets concerned are disposed of at market value and the resultant gains or losses go into the transferor settlement's s 2(2) amount.

Where an individual beneficiary becomes absolutely entitled, absolute entitlement also results in a capital payment to the beneficiary equal to the value of the property to which the person becomes absolutely entitled (see para **78.2**). The result is that the same event can generate both gains included in the s 2(2) amount and a capital payment. As LIFO applies in matching (see paras **77.20** to **77.22**) the capital payment and the s 2(2) amount are ipso facto matched.

The gain is not included in the s 2(2) amount if a holdover election is able to be made and is in fact made (TCGA 1992, s 260(2)(a) and Sch 7, paras 2 and 3). Holdover elections are only competent if the person becoming absolutely entitled is UK resident (TCGA 1992, ss 166 and 261). A claim is required, and, as with all claims, the general rule is that the claim is only competent if made within four years of the end of the tax year in which absolute entitlement occurs (TMA 1970, s 43).

The effect of a holdover election is that the trust's gain is deducted from the recipient's base cost. Superficially this is attractive as the gain is then excluded from the trust's s 2(2) amount. But this attraction is only likely to be real if the trust neither has existing s 2(2) amounts nor is likely to have further s 2(2) amounts in the future. Should it have such s 2(2) amounts, those past or prospective s 2(2) amounts render the capital payment constituted by the absolute entitlement taxable in any event. A holdover election merely results in further tax on the deferred trust gains when the recipient eventually disposes of the asset.

Entrepreneurs' relief

77.8 As a result of changes made in 2010, Entrepreneurs' relief is not material in computing s 2(2) amounts. This is because it is effected as a reduction in the rate of CGT rather than as a reduction in the chargeable gain (TCGA 1992, s 169N as amended by FA 2010, Sch 1, paras 1 and 5). The entrepreneurs 10% rate cannot apply to s 87 gains accruing to beneficiaries as the relief operates on the gain accruing to the party making the disposal that qualifies for the relief.

Foreign currency

77.9 In computing gains and losses the comparison is between the sterling cost of the asset when acquired, using exchange rates then prevailing, and the sterling value of the proceeds of disposal, using exchange rates prevailing at the time of disposal (*Capcount Trading v Evans* [1993] STC 11). As a result s 2(2) amounts can and do include gains or losses on fixed interest assets whose value has remained constant in the currency of issue.

Up to 5 April 2012 the general rule was that a bank account denominated in a foreign currency was a chargeable asset. As a result, withdrawals from an account were disposals for CGT purposes. There was an exception from charge for individuals for money held for personal or family expenditure outside the UK.

There is no doubt that in computing s 2(2) amounts for 2011–12 and earlier tax years, disposals occasioned by withdrawals from trust bank accounts up to 5 April 2012 must be included. This is extremely tiresome in practice and often has the result of making s 2(2) computations much more expensive than they would otherwise be. It is generally accepted that bank accounts do not come within the pooling and identification rules applicable to securities (see TCGA 1992, s 104(3), and HMRC Notice 10 December 2009 (reproduced SWTI [2010] p 45).

In one respect the law, as respects 2011–12 and earlier tax years, was tempered. SP 10/84 allowed taxpayers to treat all bank accounts in the same currency as a single asset. This means that movements between the accounts can be disregarded.

In computing s 2(2) amounts for 2012–13 and later tax years, the practical difficulties posed by foreign currency bank accounts no longer arise. This is because from 6 April 2012 no chargeable gain (or allowable loss) arises on withdrawals from a bank account denominated in a foreign currency (TCGA 1992, s 252 as substituted by FA 2012, s 35). This applies as much to non-resident trusts as it does to resident trusts.

It should be noted that the 2012 relief applies only to bank accounts and thus does not protect money market funds or other similar investments designed to replicate cash. The relief operates only where the trust holding the account is the original creditor of the bank or where it has become absolutely entitled to the account as against another trust (TCGA 1992, s 251(1) and (5)). Thus the relief would not be in point on any account assigned to the trust by the settlor although, obviously, it does apply to an account opened by the trust and credited with receipts which the settlor pays in by transfer from his own account.

Offshore income gains

77.10 Offshore income gains are excluded from the computation of s 2(2) amounts as these are subject to special rules (see CHAPTER 82). But should the disposal of an interest in a non-reporting fund generate a loss, that loss is allowable for CGT purposes and so reduces the s 2(2) amount of the current or a future year (see para **82.3**).

UK residential property

77.11 The s 2(2) amount of 2015–16 and subsequent years excludes gains on UK residential property charged to NR CGT (see Chapter **65** and especially para **65.11**). In such a case, the gain included in the s 2(2) amount is the pre-5 April 2015 gain plus (or minus) any part of the post-6 April 2015 gain (or loss) not charged to NR CGT (TCGA 1992, Sch 4ZZB, para 7). Where straight line apportionment has been elected for, the gain included in the s 2(2) amount is the part not apportioned to NR CGT (Ibid para 8).

Unless straight line apportionment is elected for, the rules can result in the gain included in the s 2(2) being greater than the total gain. This is the position if the value of the property when sold is less than its value on 5 April 2015. NR CGT losses are computed in the same way as gains (see para **65.12**) and so the above rules apply to exclude losses from s 2(2) amounts in the same way as gains.

Private residence relief may be claimed if the UK residential property was the only or main residence of a beneficiary (TCGA 1992, s 225). But it only applies if claimed by the trustees, so a claim should be made even if there is no immediate prospect of tax being charged by reference to capital payments. The claim must be made within four years of the end of the tax year in which the house is sold (TMA 1970, s 43).

Assuming the disposal is after 6 April 2015, a notice specifying which of two or more residences is the beneficiary's main residence must be given in accordance with NR CGT rules, ie in the NR CGT return filed when the residence is disposed of (TCGA 1992, s 222A; see para **65.14**). Although this is a NR CGT rule, on the wording of the legislation it applies also to the part of the gain that accrued before NR CGT and is thus within s 87. As part of such a gain is a NR CGT gain, the non-qualifying tax year rules in TCGA 1992, s 222B (see para **65.14**) apply to the part of the gain within s 87. They thus deny relief for any tax year in which the occupying beneficiary was non-UK resident, unless he or his spouse spent 90 or more midnights in the property or in another UK property in the year concerned.

Should the disposal have been before 6 April 2015, normal CGT rules apply in determining availability of private residence relief. A claim is required by the trustees within four years of the tax year of the disposal and any election as between two or more residences is only competent if made within two years of the date on which the particular combination of residences started (TCGA 1992, s 222(5)). The non-qualifying tax year rules are not in point.

Non-UK residential property

77.12 It is open to the trustees to claim private residence relief as respects a non-UK residence. Here the disposal is by definition not within NR CGT, so the pre-2015 rules just described apply, including those as to the timing of elections.

Gains attributed to the settlor

77.13 The s 2(2) amount of any given year excludes any gain of the trustees which is attributed to a settlor under TCGA 1992, s 86 (s 87(4)(b)). Thus gains realised during a settlor's lifetime will generally not give rise to a s 2(2) amount if he is both resident and domiciled in the UK (see CHAPTER 76). But a s 2(2) amount will be generated if gains are realised by non-resident trustees and the settlor is non-resident, non-UK domiciled or dead (see para 76.20).

Sch 4B gains

77.14 As explained in para 81.4 the effect of a Sch 4B transfer is to move the s 2(2) amounts of years up to and including the year of the transfer to Sch 4C pool. Gains thereafter are computed on the basis that the Sch 4B transfer has wholly or, as the case may be, partially rebased the trust assets (see para 80.25).

GAINS IN UNDERLYING COMPANIES

77.15 The rules in TCGA 1992, s 13 attributing the gains of non-resident close companies to UK participators apply also to non-resident trusts (s 13(10)). So too do the rules attributing treaty protected gains to trusts, including the rule which requires attribution through UK resident close companies (TCGA 1992, s 79B). Section 13 is explained in CHAPTER 88, and the rules about treaty protected gains in para 104.15.

In their application to trusts, these various rules are subject to the reliefs described in CHAPTER 88. The most important are those introduced in 2013 to the effect that a gain cannot be attributed to participators under s 13 unless either the disposal giving rise to the gain, or the acquisition or holding of the asset concerned, formed part of a scheme of arrangements, one of whose purposes was the avoidance of capital gains tax or corporation tax (s 13(5)(cb)).

The implications of this significant relief are considered in paras 88.37 to 88.39. It precludes the majority of corporate gains from being in s 2(2) amounts, particularly as avoidance of other taxes other than capital gains tax or corporation tax does not preclude the relief. However a number of points do need to be noted.

2011–12 and prior

77.16 The restrictions on s 13 only came into effect on 6 April 2012 (or 6 April 2013 if the trustees so elect before 5 April 2017: see para 88.40). As a result s 13 in its pre-2013 form must be applied in computing s 2(2) amounts for earlier years, with the result, in general, that gains are attributed up.

Nonetheless there is one important qualification which is that currency gains and gains on debt instruments are excluded. This important point is explained in para **88.8** and it means the calculation of the s 13 element in s 2(2) amounts is simpler than might be supposed. The qualification applies also in computing s 2(2) amounts of 2012–13 and post in cases where s 13 is not excluded by the 2013 changes.

A second qualification, which also applies post-2013 as well, is that in computing the corporate gains included in s 2(2) amounts, indexation is allowed. This is explained in para **88.7**.

2012–13 and post

77.17 In applying s 13 in s 2(2) computations for 2012–13 and post, the relief introduced in 2013 applies automatically without need for a claim (see para **88.39**). However the onus is on the taxpayer to show the conditions for the relief are met, so it is important that trustees relying on it collate and retain the evidence. Some of the common scenarios where the applicability or otherwise of the relief falls to be considered are discussed in para **88.38**.

Unfairness in s 13

77.18 Where s 13 does apply it can result in a doubling up of gains, for it means the trust s 2(2) amounts include both the gains realised by the company on its investments and any gains realised by the trustees when the company is sold or liquidated. The credit which is otherwise available under s 13(7) on a sale or liquidation of the company does not apply to non-resident trusts, for the trustees do not themselves pay the s 13 tax. So too the credit relief for distributions made within three or more years of the gain being realised will rarely if ever apply. This subject is discussed further in para **88.32**.

As described in para **88.19**, the general rule is that losses in s 13 companies are not apportionable and do not offset the gains in the company. The one exception is that s 13 losses can be apportioned on a current-year basis and set against (and set only against) s 13 gains apportioned to the settlement in the same tax year. The practical result is that in a trust and company structure there may be significant unrelieved losses.

CAPITAL PAYMENTS

77.19 The meaning of the term 'capital payment' is explained in CHAPTER 78. A capital payment is only taken into account for the purposes of s 87 if it is not allocated to offshore income gains under TCGA 1992, s 762 or to Sch 4C gains (see paras **82.4** and **81.30**). The term also excludes any receipt taxed as a benefit under the transfer of assets code (see para **78.5**). The order of priority in the application of different anti-avoidance rules to capital payments is explained in CHAPTER 9.

Although s 87 is expressed in terms of beneficiaries receiving a capital payment it in fact applies whenever any person receives a capital payment from the settlement (TCGA 1992, s 97(8); see further para **78.9**). It thus applies not merely on distributions of capital to individuals but also on distributions to companies. However, where the company is close and non-resident the payment may be treated as made to UK resident participators (see para **78.18**). A payment made to a non-resident close company which is not attributable to a UK resident participator is disregarded (TCGA 1992, s 87C; FA 2008, Sch 7 para 119; see further para **78.18**).

MATCHING

77.20 In the form re-enacted by FA 2008, s 87 treats gains as accruing to beneficiaries if in the tax year concerned s 2(2) amounts are matched with capital payments. It contains express matching rules, set out in TCGA 1992, s 87A. Matching for the purposes of s 87 is required regardless of the residence status of the beneficiary.

The rules in s 87A operate on a last in first out, or LIFO, basis. They are best analysed separately, according as to whether the starting point is a capital payment or a s 2(2) amount.

Capital payments

77.21 A capital payment is in the first instance matched with the s 2(2) amount of the year in which the payment is made. If the s 2(2) amount is less than the payment, or nil, the payment is carried back and set against the s 2(2) amounts of previous tax years. Previous tax years are taken in reverse date order, so the surplus payment is first set against the s 2(2) amount (if any) of the immediately preceding tax year before any less recent year is looked at. Self-evidently the s 2(2) amount of any earlier tax year is net of any capital payments previously matched with it.

If after this process is completed some or all of a capital payment is still unmatched, the surplus is carried forward. It is matched against s 2(2) amounts of subsequent years. But it is only matched against the s 2(2) amount of a future year to the extent that the s 2(2) amount is not offset by capital payments made in that year or any intervening year.

Should more than one capital payment be made in a tax year, all are matched with the s 2(2) amount of the year. Should the aggregate payments be more than the s 2(2) amount a pro rata proportion of each payment is matched and the balance of each payment is carried back and set against the s 2(2) amount of the prior year. Should the aggregate of the balances be greater than the prior year s 2(2) amount, the process is repeated until the capital payments are all matched or the prior year s 2(2) amounts are exhausted. In the latter event the proportion of each capital payment which is still unmatched is carried forward and set against s 2(2) amounts of future years insofar as those s 2(2) amounts are not matched to younger payments.

Assuming the capital payments of a year are matched with current year and past year s 2(2) amounts, they are treated as chargeable gains accruing to the recipient beneficiaries in the year in question. If the payments exceed the current year and brought-forward s 2(2) amounts, the matched proportion of each capital payment is treated as chargeable gains for that year. The surplus capital payments are treated as chargeable gains accruing to the beneficiaries only when and to the extent matched with future s 2(2) amounts.

Section 2(2) amounts

77.22 In accordance with the rules described above, a section 2(2) amount in a tax year results in chargeable gains accruing to beneficiaries if and to the extent that those beneficiaries receive capital payments in that tax year. If it exceeds those payments it is carried back and matched with unutilised capital payments of earlier tax years, taking later years before earlier years. To the extent that there are no such payments the s 2(2) amount is carried forward. Once carried forward it is matched against capital payments of future years, but only if those payments are not matched to s 2(2) amounts of the current year and any intervening years.

Practical result

77.23 The practical result is that chargeable gains accrue to beneficiaries in a tax year if and to the extent that there are either:

(a)   both current year capital payments and a current year s 2(2) amount;
(b)   current year capital payments and brought forward s 2(2) amounts; or
(c)   a current year s 2(2) amount and brought forward capital payments.

Dead beneficiaries

77.24 It is sometimes suggested that if on his death a beneficiary has surplus capital payments, matching carries on even after the tax year of his death. The argument is not that this imposes a tax charge on his estate, but that future s 2(2) amounts are washed out. In reality such a suggestion is not right, as the basic charging provision, s 87(2), requires the individual to be a beneficiary of the settlement in the year of matching, a status a dead person cannot enjoy. This is accepted by HMRC (CG 38605). Matching can occur in the tax year of death even if the matched gains are realised after the beneficiary has died.

EVENTS BEFORE 6 APRIL 2008

77.25 Section 87 in the form recast in 2008 takes account of events before 6 April 2008. The relevant transitional provisions are in FA 2008, Sch 7 para 120.

Section 2(2) amounts of 2007–08 and prior

77.26 The s 2(2) amounts of 2007–08 and earlier tax years are matched with capital payments under the current regime if the latter exceed the s 2(2) amounts of the current year and any prior year since 6 April 2008. Should this happen the s 2(2) amount of the settlement has to be calculated for 2007–08 and each prior year during which s 87 applied to the settlement (FA 2008, Sch 7 para 120). A calculation has also to be made of the total chargeable gains treated as having accrued to beneficiaries in 2007–08 and prior years under the old s 87 rules. This total is referred to as the total deemed gains (para 120(2), step 2). It is deducted from the pre-6 April 2008 s 2(2) amounts, taking the amounts of earlier years before later years. Only the s 2(2) amounts left after this process, ie the younger s 2(2) amounts of 2007–08 and prior, are available to carry forward and match with capital payments of 2008–09 and post.

As explained in para 77.3, each s 2(2) amount is calculated according to the law of the tax year in which it accrued. This means indexation and taper have to be considered in computing the s 2(2) amounts of 2007–08 and prior.

At trust level, indexation was only allowed for RPI increases up to April 1998 (TCGA 1992, s 53(1A)). Such indexation is plainly preserved in pre-6 April 2008 s 2(2) amounts, as the abolition of indexation affected only disposals on or after 6 April 2008 (FA 2008, Sch 2 para 83).

Taper relief was allowed only at trust level. Its continuing application to the s 2(2) amounts of 2007–08 and prior is not entirely clear, for the abolition of taper has effect in relation to chargeable gains accruing or treated as accruing in 2008–09 and subsequently (FA 2008, Sch 2 para 56(3)). On one view such abolition impacts on s 2(2) amounts of 2007–08 and earlier tax years, for if matched to post-6 April 2008 capital payments, the ensuing chargeable gains accruing to beneficiaries are of 2008–09 or a subsequent year. But the reality is that, under old s 87, the chargeable gains in relation to which taper relief applied were the gains at trust level, it being expressly provided that the gains treated as accruing to beneficiaries by virtue of s 87 were untapered (see s 87(6A) as originally enacted). It follows that the gains in relation to which the abolition of taper has effect are the gains used in computing s 2(2) amounts and so, as that amount is governed by the law in the year of accrual, the s 2(2) amounts carried forward into 2008–09 remain tapered.

Any other conclusion would be absurd, as if pre-6 April 2008 s 2(2) amounts were detapered, all would have to be recomputed, as far back as the introduction of taper in 1998. As indicated above, HMRC's guidance confirms that they share the conclusion (CG 38610).

Capital payments

77.27 Capital payments made before 6 April 2008 are available for set off against surplus s 2(2) amounts of 2008–09 and subsequent years. But this is only so insofar as the capital payments were not matched with trust gains under the old rules which obtained until 5 April 2008 (FA 2008, Sch 7 para 122). Where some but not all of the pre-6 April 2008 capital payments were matched with pre-6 April 2008 trust gains, the earlier rather than the later capital payments are treated as having been so matched (para 122(3)).

A brought-forward capital payment is not available for matching in 2008–09 and subsequent years if it was made to a non-domiciliary between 12 March and 5 April 2008 and, in the year when it would otherwise be matched, the recipient is resident but not domiciled in the UK (FA 2008, Sch 7 para 125).

This rule does not prevent the capital payment from being set against trust gains of 2007–08 and prior years under old s 87, and was designed to forestall avoidance of the new s 87 by non-domiciliaries (see para **79.19**). Should the recipient become UK domiciled or non-UK resident, the availability of the capital payment to match with s 2(2) amounts is reinstated from the time of the change in domicile.

Commencement rules

77.28 The computation of s 2(2) amounts has to go back to the inception of the settlement or, if later, 1981–82. A s 2(2) amount can never be computed for 1980–81 and prior tax years as s 87 only came into force in 1981–82 (see FA 2008, Sch 7 para 120(2), step 1; TCGA 1992, s 87(1) as originally enacted; and ibid Sch 11 para 29 and ibid s 87(5)).

Capital payments must be taken into account if made at any time during the life of the settlement, save that those made before 10 March 1981 are ignored (FA 2008, Sch 7 para 116). Capital payments made between 10 March 1981 and 6 April 1984 are ignored insofar as treated under the law then obtaining as representing a trust gain of 1980–81 or prior.

A later cut-off date of 17 March 1998 applies to both capital payments and s 2(2) amounts if the settlor was either non-resident or non-domiciled (or both) when he made the settlement and has remained so or is dead. In the case of multiple settlors, all must satisfy these conditions for the cut off to apply. The effect of this rule is that the s 2(2) amount of 1997–98 includes only gains or losses realised after 17 March 1998, and there is no s 2(2) amount for 1996–97 and prior tax years. So too capital payments made before 17 March 1998 do not go to reduce the subsequent s 2(2) amounts up to 2007–08 and cannot be matched with s 2(2) amounts of 2008–09 and post.

This rule, enacted by Sch 7 para 118, has its origins in FA 1998, s 130, which extended s 87 to settlements made by non-resident and non-domiciled settlors. Before that date s 87 did not apply to such settlements (s 87(1) as originally enacted).

An important practical point is whether events now can cause the cut-off to be lost. This issue arises should the settlor, or one of the settlors, become both resident and domiciled in the UK, or if some other party with that status adds funds to the settlement and so becomes a settlor. Under the terms of para 118 any such event causes the cut-off to be lost, effective as from the beginning of the tax year when the settlor's status changes or the addition is made, the cut-off being restored in the former case should the settlor die or lose his UK residence or domicile.

However the reality in these circumstances is that the cut-off is not in fact lost. The reason for this somewhat odd conclusion as respects s 2(2) amounts is that a s 2(2) amount is deemed to be nil in any year in which s 87 did not apply to the settlement (FA 2008, Sch 7 para 120(2), step 1). Until 17 March 1998 s 87 did not apply at all unless the settlor was both resident and domiciled in the UK, either when he put funds into the settlement or when the trust gains accrued. The reason as respects capital payments is similar and is that a capital payment is disregarded if made in a period when s 87 did not apply to the settlement (TCGA 1992, s 89(1)).

TRANSFER BETWEEN SETTLEMENTS

77.29 When the trustees of one settlement transfer all the settled property to another settlement the s 2(2) amounts of the transferor settlement are similarly transferred across (TCGA 1992, s 90). The s 2(2) amounts are net of any capital payments made by the transferor settlement in the year of the transfer. The s 2(2) amounts are treated as leaving the transferor settlement at the end of the tax year of the transfer, but as arriving in the transferee settlement at the beginning of that year (s 90(7), (8)). This means that in that year they can be matched with capital payments from the transferee settlement as well as with capital payments from the transferor settlement.

Should the trustees of the transferor settlement transfer only part of the settled property, only a proportion of the s 2(2) amounts is carried across. The proportion is the proportion that the value of what is transferred bears to the total value of the settlement (s 90(4)).

These rules as to transfers do not apply if the transfer is linked with trustee borrowing and so caught by TCGA 1992, Sch 4B (see s 90(10)(a) and CHAPTER 80). They do not apply to any s 2(2) amounts which are in a Sch 4C pool, for Sch 4C has its own rules dealing with transfers between settlements (see paras **81.14** and **81.15**).

It is generally accepted that s 90 is engaged where the trustees of one settlement become absolutely entitled as against those of another. Such can happen for CGT purpose when the trustees resettle or advance funds where the transferee trusts are exhaustive (see further para **77.53**). This is so even if both sets of trustees are the same.

Capital payments

77.30 A transfer between settlements does not carry across capital payments. A curious point arises if the transferee settlement has surplus capital payments and the transferor settlement surplus s 2(2) amounts. It is fairly clear that such payments made in the year of the transfer are matched with the s 2(2) amounts transferred across, whether of the current or past years. Brought forward capital payments of past years are more difficult. However it is provided that the increase in s 2(2) amounts resulting from the transfer has effect for the year of the transfer and subsequent years (s 90(7)). This suggests that the old year surplus capital payments of the transferee settlement cannot be matched against the old year s 2(2) amounts of the transferor settlement and that both must continue to be carried forward in the transferee settlement.

The contrary view is that old year surplus capital payments of the transferee settlement are, in the year of the transfer, matched with the old year s 2(2) amounts carried across from the transferee settlement. Were this view right it would offer scope for avoidance, as where the surplus payments were to non-residents. It would also be a trap for the unwary, as where the recipients of the surplus payments were UK resident and domiciled. Such anomalies are a further argument that the construction suggested in the preceding paragraph is right; and it is that construction which is adopted by HMRC in their guidance (see CG 38810).

Meaning of 'transfer'

77.31 The term 'transfer' is not defined. However the rules described above do not apply to a transfer which satisfies the following two conditions (s 90A):

(a)   It is for consideration in money or money's worth, and
(b)   The amount or value of the consideration equals or exceeds the market value of the property transferred.

Should the consideration be less than the value of the property, the undervalue only is treated as transferred (s 90A(3)).

This exclusion of commercial transfers indicates that of itself the term 'transfer' is not confined to gratuitous transfers of trust assets from one settlement to another. Instead the term must be regarded as having its normal meaning, namely the transfer of property from one settlement to another, whether gratuitously or for consideration.

A difficult issue is whether the term includes loans. In logic it should, for on a loan, the lent property is transferred from lender to borrower, and the lender receives in return the borrower's obligation to repay. On this analysis loans are, therefore, transfers but they fall to be disregarded if the obligations assumed by the borrower constitute consideration equal in value to what is lent. This they do if the loan is on commercial terms or, it may be suggested, if the loan is repayable on demand. Where an interest-free term loan is made, the actuarial value of the lender's right to repayment of the principal is reduced by the delay in receiving repayment and the lack of interest as compensation for that delay. There is therefore an undervalue element to the transfer, which will be caught by s 90.

Another issue is whether the concept of 'transfer' extends to the distribution of income by one settlement to another. On a literal reading such a transaction could be seen as a transfer of settled property, for undistributed income is an asset of the settlement. But the overall scheme of s 90 makes it unlikely this construction is right. Section 90 appears to focus on trust capital and what proportion stays in the transferor settlement and what proportion goes into the transferee settlement.

Transfers before 6 April 2008

77.32 In 2007–08 transfers between settlements were governed by TCGA 1992, s 90 in the form originally enacted. Special rules apply, from 6 April 2008, to determine the s 2(2) amounts of the transferor and transferee settlement for 2007–08 and earlier years (FA 2008, Sch 7 para 121).

The essence of these rules is to require a two-stage calculation. The first is to determine the s 2(2) amounts of the transferor settlement for the year of the transfer and earlier years, and those of the transferee for the years prior to that of the transfer. The total deemed gains (see para 77.26) for the years in question are then deducted from the s 2(2) amounts of the respective settlements in date order. Once this first stage has been completed the additions and reductions to s 2(2) amounts required by s 90 are made. The s 2(2) amounts of both settlements are then calculated for the tax years from the transfer until 2007–08. The deemed gains are deducted save insofar as already deducted on the transfer. In accordance with the general 'first in, first out' rule under para 120, these deemed gains are deducted first from the s 2(2) amounts of years before the transfer insofar as the latter are still available.

UK RESIDENT SETTLEMENTS

77.33 The general rule is that s 87 does not apply to settlements resident in the UK. This is because residence outside the UK is a basic precondition for the section. As a result there is no s 2(2) amount for any tax year when the settlement is UK resident. But there are three respects in which s 87 does have to be taken into account when dealing with resident settlements.

Emigration

77.34 A capital payment made by a resident settlement before emigrating from the UK can count as a capital payment for the purposes of s 87. But this is only so if it is made in anticipation of a disposal by the trustees when non-resident (TCGA 1992, s 89(1)). It will be noted that it is not sufficient to engage this rule if the capital payment is merely in anticipation of emigration: a disposal must be in prospect as well.

Immigration

77.35 Although s 2(2) amounts cannot accrue once the settlement has become UK resident, unmatched s 2(2) amounts of the non-resident period are carried forward. They are matched with capital payments made when the settlement is UK resident, and the matching continues until the s 2(2) amounts are exhausted (TCGA 1992, s 89(2)). As generally under the matching rules, 'last in, first out' applies, so the unmatched s 2(2) amounts of later years are taken before those of earlier years.

Transfers between settlements

77.36 Where a non-resident settlement transfers all or part of the trust fund to a resident settlement, the rules in TCGA 1992, s 90 (para 77.29) operate to transfer all or a proportion of the s 2(2) amounts of the transferor settlement to the transferee settlement (s 90(6)). The result is that the transferee settlement, although UK resident, comes to have s 2(2) amounts for such of the year of the transfer and prior year insofar as the transferor settlement had such amounts and those amounts were not matched with capital payments in and before the year of the transfer.

Such s 2(2) amounts can be matched with capital payments from the UK-resident transferee settlement in the year of the transfer and subsequent tax years. For the reasons given in para 77.29, they cannot be carried back and set against capital payments of the transferee settlement in tax years prior to the transfer.

Losses

77.37 Where a trust emigrates from the UK it may be found that, in the year of emigration, the trust has unrelieved carry-forward losses. These may be deducted in computing s 2(2) amounts post emigration. That result follows because the s 2(2) amount is the amount upon which the trustees would have been chargeable if still UK resident (s 87(4)(a)).

The converse situation is the trust with carry-forward losses on immigration. The general CGT rule is that losses accruing to a non-resident are non-allowable (TCGA 1992, s 16(3)). But as noted above (para 77.4) this rule is disapplied in relation to s 87 (TCGA 1992, s 97(6)). The language of that disapplication is wide enough to allow surplus losses to be carried forward and set against gains of the year of immigration and subsequent years.

Dual resident settlements

77.38 A dual resident settlement is one which is UK resident under UK domestic law but falls to be treated as resident in a territory with which the UK has concluded a double tax treaty under the tie breaker clause under the relevant treaty. Sections 87–97 apply to dual resident settlements on the basis that the s 2(2) amount for each treaty-protected year comprises only gains and losses on treaty-protected assets (TCGA 1992, s 88). No account can be taken of s 2(2) amounts or capital payments made before 6 April 1991 (TCGA 1992, s 88(1); FA 2008, Sch 7 para 117).

THE CHARGE TO TAX

77.39 Gains accruing to a beneficiary under s 87 are personal gains for the year in which the matching occurs. This inter alia means that if the capital payment is brought forward and it is a current year s 2(2) amount which results in matching, the personal gain accrues in the year of matching rather than when the payment was made.

Rate of tax

77.40 The rate of tax is governed by the rates applicable in the year of matching and not (if different) by that applicable when any brought forward capital payment or s 2(2) amount was made or accrued. Currently the rate is normally 20% (TCGA 1992, s 4(4)). But this is subject to two qualifications.

The first is that the rate is 10% if and insofar as the recipient beneficiary has not, in the tax year concerned, utilised, or fully utilised, his income tax basic rate band (TCGA 1992, s 4(2)). However, once the s 87 gains (and any other personal gains) absorb the basic rate band, or what is left of it, the rate on the balance is 20%.

The second is that in many cases the 10% or 20% rate is not in fact the rate charged on s 87 gains. If the conditions of TCGA 1992, s 91 are otherwise met, it is inflated by supplemental tax, with the result, at its highest, that the 10% rate becomes 10% and the 20% rate 32%. Supplemental tax is explained in paras 77.48 to 77.51.

From 2010–11 to 2015–16, the rates were 28% and 18%. Those rates still obtain on certain categories of gain, known as upper rate gains (TCGA 1992, s 4(2A)). Gains treated as accruing under s 87 cannot be upper rate gains as that term is defined by reference to specific kinds of transaction on which the gain accrues. Section 87 gains, by contrast, accrue not on the transactions which give rise to the s 2(2) amount, but as a result of the matching.

Annual exemption

77.41 Section 87 gains qualify for the basic annual exemption in the same way as other personal gains (TCGA 1992, s 3). Where s 87 gains fall within the exemption, supplemental tax is not in issue. Because the rate of tax on the exempt amount is nil, there is nothing for the supplemental tax to bite on.

Personal losses

77.42 Section 87 gains cannot be offset by personal losses (TCGA 1992, s 2(4)). This ungenerous rule was first introduced with the former taper relief and survived the abolition of taper in 2008. In this respect, s 87 gains contrast with gains accruing under TCGA 1992, Sch 4C for, as explained in para **81.26**, those gains can be offset by personal losses. The non-deductibility of personal losses was at issue in an unsuccessful *Hastings-Bass* application in *Futter v Futter* [2011] STC 809.

Allocation to the settlor

77.43 Should a capital payment be made to the settlor, s 2(2) amounts are matched with it in the same way as on payments to any other beneficiary. It might be thought that if the trust is settlor-interested there are no s 2(2) amounts as all trust gains will be attributed to the settlor on an arising basis under s 86. But many pre-1991 settlor-interested settlements have s 2(2) amounts and the same applies to settlor-interested settlements where the settlor is (or has previously been) non-resident or is non-domiciled.

Charitable beneficiaries

77.44 In HMRC's view, s 2(2) amounts may be matched to capital payments to charitable beneficiaries. They are exempt if the general conditions for charitable relief are met (TCGA 1992, s 256). This subject is discussed further in para **78.10**.

TERRITORIAL LIMITS

77.45 As will be apparent from the earlier part of this chapter, TCGA 1992, s 87 applies only if the trust is non UK-resident, and s 89 only if the trust, while resident, either has been or is contemplating non-residence (see paras **77.34** to **77.35**). But in addition to these territorial limits by reference to the trust, there are further limits applicable to the beneficiaries.

Non-resident beneficiaries

77.46 The machinery under which matching results in a personal gain accruing to the beneficiary applies whether the beneficiary is resident or non-resident. But this aspect of the machinery operates to relieve rather than charge, for the normal territorial limits of CGT then apply, to the effect that a non-resident beneficiary is not charged on his s 87 gain. Nonetheless the fact of non-chargeability does not prevent the s 87 machinery from operating, with the result that capital payments to non-resident beneficiaries carry s 2(2) amounts out of the trust without tax charge. This has considerable planning potential, as discussed in CHAPTER 10.

There are four important qualifications to the tax advantages of capital payments to non-residents. The first is that capital payments to non-resident beneficiaries are disregarded in matching s 2(2) amounts in a Sch 4C pool, which has been created by a 'transfer of value' coupled with 'trustee borrowing' (see CHAPTERS 80 and 81).

The second is that even under s 87 a capital payment to a non-resident beneficiary is chargeable if there are no or insufficient s 2(2) amounts when it is made and, by the time a s 2(2) amount is available, the beneficiary has become resident in the UK. This result follows because s 87 gains accrue at the time of matching and not (if different) at the time of the capital payment. This can represent a significant trap for the unwary where a beneficiary is moving to the UK and has previously received capital payments which have not yet been fully matched.

The third qualification arises from the fact that an individual generally remains in charge to CGT if he is non-resident for five years or less (TCGA 1992, s 10A; see para **29.6**). In such a case gains accruing during his absence are assessed in the year of return. This applies to gains treated as accruing under s 87 as much as to gains resulting from actual disposals. Prior to 16 March 2005 it could be argued that a beneficiary was protected from this charge if during his absence he resided in a country with which the UK had concluded a treaty giving that country sole rights over capital gains. Such argument is now precluded by s 10A(9C).

The fourth qualification applies to an individual who has previously been non-resident at all times (or has been temporarily non-resident for a period exceeding five years), and who moves to the UK part way through a tax year and qualifies for split year treatment under one of the cases set out in FA 2013,

Sch 45. In such circumstances, any capital payment(s) which he receives in that tax year or which are carried forward from a previous tax year will be matched with the s 2(2) amount on a time-apportioned basis. This will be the case even if the capital payment was made to the individual during the 'overseas part' of the tax year and similarly the s 2(2) amount will be calculated on the basis of the whole tax year. Therefore, if the individual is treated under the split year rules as resident for 50% of the tax year in question, 50% of the gains matched in the tax year will be chargeable if remitted to the UK.

Non-UK domiciliaries

77.47 Should the recipient beneficiary be UK resident but non-UK domiciled, the charge on s 87 gains is tempered by a variety of reliefs. Some of these, most notably rebasing and matching with s 2(2) amounts or capital payments of 2007–08 and earlier years, apply regardless of whether the non-UK domiciliary is a remittance basis user. The remaining relief, the remittance basis, applies only to non-UK domiciliaries actually claiming the remittance basis. These various reliefs are the subject of a separate chapter, CHAPTER 79. Where they have the effect of rendering a s 87 gain non-chargeable they still mean the matched s 2(2) amount is removed from the trust and so in planning terms have the same impact as payments to non-residents.

SUPPLEMENTAL TAX

77.48 The tax charged on UK-resident beneficiaries under s 87 may in certain circumstances be increased by supplemental tax representing notional interest. The rules are laid down in TCGA 1992, s 91. The most important point to make is that these rules cannot come into operation unless CGT is charged in respect of the payment, and only impose notional interest on whatever tax is in fact charged. Section 91 does not therefore extend the basic territorial scope of s 87, so capital payments are free of both CGT and the supplemental tax if the recipient beneficiary is non-resident or, in the circumstances described in CHAPTER 79, non-UK domiciled.

Matching

77.49 The supplemental tax can only be charged if a capital payment is matched with the s 2(2) amount of the settlement for the last but one or an earlier year of assessment (TCGA 1992, s 91(1)(c)). The general rules as to matching in s 87A apply (see para **77.20**).

Supplemental tax

77.50 Assuming that the capital payment is matched with the s 2(2) amount for the last but one tax year or an earlier year any CGT otherwise due is increased by an amount equal to interest at 10% on the tax (TCGA 1992, s 91(2), (3)). The tax is computed on the basis that the capital payment is the first slice of the beneficiary's gains for the year (*Tax Bulletin 16* (April 1995) p 205).

This notional interest runs for the chargeable period. That period ends on 30 November following the tax year in which the payment is made. It begins six years earlier or (if later) on 1 December following the tax year in which the s 2(2) amount matched with the capital payment accrued (TCGA 1992, s 91(4), (5)). The rate of interest may be varied by the Treasury but to date the rate has never in fact been varied (TCGA 1992, s 91(6)). At current rates of interest the maximum supplemental tax on a higher-rate taxpayer is 12%, which gives total tax of 32%.

As supplemental tax cannot be charged unless the capital payment is matched with a s 2(2) amount of the last but one tax year, the rate of supplemental tax effectively jumps from nil where the matching is with the immediately prior year, to two years' worth where the matching is with the year before that. At current rates, this means supplemental tax for a higher rate taxpayer jumps from nil to 4%.

Changes in 2008

77.51 In 2007–08 and earlier years there were no general rules as to matching, so specific rules applied for the purposes of the supplemental charge (TCGA 1992, ss 92–95 as originally enacted). Those rules differed from the matching rules which are now contained in s 87A, in that they required identification on a first-in first-out basis. They thus discouraged trustees from distributing current-year gains to UK residents, particularly as, with the then CGT rate of 40%, the supplemental charge could often result in a 64% tax rate. The present rules provide an incentive to make current-year distributions, as the last-in first-out rule in s 87A means supplemental tax is avoided.

MEANING OF 'SETTLEMENT'

77.52 As noted above (para 77.2) the term 'settlement' bears the income tax anti-avoidance definition given in ITTOIA 2005, s 620. That definition is explained in paras 75.14 to 75.17. It includes bounteous arrangements and outright dispositions.

The definition of settlement has applied to s 87 and its predecessor legislation since the latter was first enacted in 1981. It also applied to the legislation replaced in 1981: FA 1965, s 42. Under s 42, gains arising to an offshore settlement could be apportioned on a just and reasonable basis to the beneficiaries, including discretionary beneficiaries (*Leedale (Inspector of Taxes) v Lewis* [1982] 3 All ER 808, [1982] STC 835, HL).

The extended definition of 'settlement' proved important in defeating schemes to counter s 42. Thus in *Chinn v Collins (Inspector of Taxes)* [1981] AC 533, [1981] STC 1, Jersey trustees appointed shares to UK resident beneficiaries absolutely, contingently on them surviving three days. During those three days the beneficiaries sold the contingent interests to a Jersey company, but had the right to buy the shares back once they were absolutely vested in the company. The House of Lords held that the contingent appointment and the repurchase of the shares was an arrangement and that it was bounteous as bounty had clearly been conferred on the UK resident beneficiaries.

Ewart v Taylor (Inspector of Taxes) [1983] STC 721, 57 TC 401 was another case on s 42. Here an English settlement had been made on 18 March 1965. On 12 March 1969 that settlement was exported to Jersey, and on the same day the Jersey trustees appointed assets to a newly created Jersey settlement. The taxpayer argued that the English and the Jersey settlements were a single arrangement and thus a single settlement for the purposes of s 42, with the result that relieving provisions could apply as the making of the English settlement predated the commencement of CGT on 6 April 1965. Vinelott J was inclined to accept the argument that the two settlements were a single arrangement, but held that even if they were, the arrangement was not made until the Jersey phase of the exercise in March 1969.

When what is now s 87 was first enacted its compass was clearly trusts, for it referred to acts of the trustees and capital payments received by beneficiaries. But these implicit limitations now no longer apply. In relation to 'trustees' the term includes, where the settlement has no actual trustees, any person in whom the settled property or its management is vested (TCGA 1992, s 97(7A)). As respects beneficiaries, the position is as described in para **78.9**, namely that if someone who is not a beneficiary receives a capital payment he is deemed to be a beneficiary (TCGA 1992, s 97(8)).

Where all this leaves bounteous arrangements which are not trusts in any sense of the term is unclear. All that can be said is that no decided case on s 87 has ever concerned arrangements which were not trusts. It is believed HMRC accepts that s 87 does not extend beyond trusts, and foreign entities equivalent to trusts, such as certain foundations (as to which see further CHAPTER **33**).

One corollary of the incorporation of the income tax definition works in favour of taxpayers, namely the fact that the income tax definition is subject to the bounty requirement. It has long been accepted that genuine commercial arrangements by an employer to attract, retain, and motivate good quality staff are protected by the bounty test (*Tax Bulletin 16* (April 1995) p 204; CG 38580). As a result, employee benefit trusts are generally outside s 87, a point recently confirmed by HMRC (see 'EBT Settlement Opportunity FAQ's', August 2012 para 3.8).

SUB-TRUSTS AND SEPARATE SETTLEMENTS

77.53 It is common for trustees to appoint sub-trusts for different groups of beneficiaries. In some cases the various sub-trusts may be operated entirely separately, in accordance with the wishes of the different groups of beneficiaries.

Section 87 poses problems for such trusts. Essentially the problems are two-fold:

(1)   s 2(2) amounts at the time the separate funds are appointed are not allocated to the funds pro rata but remain a single pool, allocated to capital payments according to the tax year in which made, regardless of the fund from which such are made.

(2) Gains realised after the appointment of the sub-funds also go into the global s 2(2) amounts, regardless of which fund the gain is realised in. In an extreme case, this can mean a capital gain in one fund is allocated in full to a capital payment from another.

Sometimes this capriciousness can work in favour of the beneficiaries, as where the beneficiaries in receipt of the capital payments are non-resident. In other cases the reverse is true, particularly where, for example, the beneficiaries of the fund realising the gain are non-resident and the beneficiaries of the fund making the capital payment are not.

The conventional solution to this problem is for the trustees to appoint not sub-trusts or sub-funds but to create entirely new settlements for the various groups of beneficiaries. If this is done, the rules in TCGA 1992, s 90 described in para **77.29** above come into play and the s 2(2) amounts of the original settlement are split proportionately. Further each successor settlement has its s 2(2) amounts allocated only to capital payments it makes.

This solution is not however without difficulties:

(1) It is not effective if the original settlement has outstanding trustee borrowing, for then the transfer to the new trusts creates a Sch 4C pool able to be allocated to any of the new settlements (see CHAPTER 81).

(2) Insofar as any of the assets are showing latent gains, such are triggered, thereby increasing the s 2(2) amount for the year of the transfer.

(3) It is necessary to be certain that the new settlements really are separate settlements.

This last point is of some interest. For CGT purposes generally, funds pass out of one settlement and into another if the trusts of the new settlement are exhaustive with no possibility of the funds reverting to the old one (see *Roome v Edwards* [1981] STC 96; *Bond v Pickford* [1983] STC 517; *Swires v Renton* [1991] STC 490; and SP 7/84). But for s 87 purposes the definition of settlement is, as noted above (para **77.2**), not the CGT definition but the income tax anti-avoidance definition (as to which see para **75.14**). Two notes of warning may be sounded.

The first arises out of the case of *Elibeck v Rawling* [1980] STC 192. Here in the Court of Appeal Buckley LJ had to consider whether a reversionary interest under a transferee settlement arose under the transferor settlement, with the result it was within the exemption for beneficial interests under TCGA 1992, s 76 (cf para **10.0**). He held it did so arise, as the transfer to the transferee settlement was made in exercise of a special power. But he expressly said that the issue of whether the two settlements would be treated as separate for the purposes of charging gains realised by the trustees had no bearing on the point at issue in the case. It follows that *Eilbeck v Rawling* is not directly relevant to the issues being discussed here.

The second point arises from the fact that the term 'settlement' is, for the purposes of s 87, defined as including any arrangement. As described above (para **77.52**), the transferor and transferee settlement can on one view be described as a single arrangement. But this point too should be immaterial for, as described above, where two settlements constitute an arrangement it is made at the time of the last. It follows that even on the arrangement scenario there is a transfer, from the transferor settlement on its own to the composite arrangement represented by transferor and transferee.

Such a conclusion is entirely in line with the overall structure of the capital payments code, for s 90 expressly deals with transfers between settlements. It would have little point if all the settlements concerned were liable to be treated as one.

As regards case law, it is noteworthy that HMRC did not argue that the transferor and transferee settlement should be viewed as one in *Herman v HMRC* [2007] STC (SCD) 571, *Burton v HMRC* [2009] UKFTT 203 (TC), [2009] SFTD 682, or in *Bowring v Revenue and Customs Comrs* [2016] STC 816. These cases are discussed in CHAPTER 78.

On any view such risks as there are, will be less if the transferee settlement is a long-standing separate settlement rather than one created specifically for the purpose of effecting the transfer. Other factors than can help to differentiate the settlements are if the terms of the trusts are different; they are governed by the laws of different countries; the body of trustees of each is resident in a different country. The House of Lords decision in *West v Trennery* [2005] UKHL 5, [2005] STC 214 does not bear on these problems as it turned on the definition of property comprised in the settlement for the purposes of the former TCGA 1992, s 77. This definition finds no equivalent in s 87.

In theory, the sub-fund legislation in TCGA 1992, Sch 4ZA could be used as an alternative to creating new settlements. That legislation is not restricted to onshore settlements. But the conditions for its use are highly restrictive. The biggest difficulty is that an election cannot be made if the sub-funds have any beneficiary in common (Sch 4ZA paras 8 and 9).

Chapter 78

CAPITAL PAYMENTS

INTRODUCTION

78.1 As explained in Chapters **77**, **81**, and **82**, capital gains and offshore income gains are treated as accruing to a beneficiary if he receives a capital payment. This chapter considers what is meant by payment, when it is capital, and the circumstances in which it is treated as received by a beneficiary from the trustees. The relevant terms are defined in TCGA 1992 s 97, which applies to s 87, to Sch 4C and to offshore income gains (TCGA 1992, s 97; The Offshore Funds (Tax) Regulations (SI 2009/3001), reg 20(3)).

PAYMENT

78.2 The term 'payment' excludes any payment made by the trustees under a transaction entered into at arm's length (s 97(1)(b)). However the term includes the following (s 97(2)):

(a)   the transfer of an asset;
(b)   the conferring of any other benefit; and
(c)   any occasion on which settled property becomes nominee property.

Settled property becomes nominee property when one or more persons become absolutely entitled to it (TCGA 1992, ss 60(1) and 71(1)). Absolute entitlement connotes the ability to direct the trustee as to how to deal with the property subject only to the trustee's lien for costs etc (s 60(2)). Absolute entitlement can either arise by express act of the trustee in appointing property to the beneficiary absolutely or automatically under the terms of the trust, as where the reversion to a life interest vests absolutely on the death of the life tenant.

In general, the various methods by which a payment is made require a positive and voluntary decision by the trustees in that cash or other assets cannot be distributed or benefits conferred without a decision by the trustee to do so. But the position is otherwise with absolute entitlement under the terms of the trust and, while this problem normally arises only with old fashioned fixed-interest trusts, the resultant involuntary capital payment can be most unfortunate.

Amount of the capital payment

78.3 The figure brought into account in determining whether gains accrue to a beneficiary under s 87 is the total amount of the capital payments received by the beneficiary in the tax year concerned (TCGA 1992, s 87A(2), Step 2). It is expressly provided that the value of any capital payment which is not an outright payment of money is the value of the benefit conferred by it. This rule is specifically applied to loans (TCGA 1992, s 97(4)).

The reference to the value of the benefit conferred indicates that what is looked at is the value of the benefit to the beneficiary. Such an analysis was adopted by the First-tier Tribunal in *Burton v HMRC* [2009] SFTD 682. The Tribunal in Burton also decided that the reference in s 97(4) to an outright payment of money refers only to outright receipt by the beneficiary. The fact that in conferring the benefit the trustee has wholly parted with the money is immaterial.

Assuming that it is right to quantify the benefit as its value to the beneficiary, there is one important qualification. This arises where the beneficiary has a pre-existing interest in the settlement and here, the rule is that that interest is ignored (*Billingham v Cooper* [2001] STC 1177 at para 39). Thus the fact that the beneficiary has a vested reversion does not preclude a capital payment equal to the full value of the trust fund when the reversion falls in (*Billingham v Cooper* [2000] STC 122, 135).

CAPITAL

78.4 If the recipient is resident or ordinarily resident in the UK a payment is capital unless it is chargeable to tax as his income (s 97(1)(a)). Should the recipient be non-resident, a payment is capital if it is received otherwise than as income. In other words for UK residents the test is liability to income tax, whereas for non-residents the test is whether as a matter of trust law the distribution is income or capital in the hands of the beneficiary. The trust law distinction between income and capital distributions is discussed in CHAPTER 8.

Overlap with ITA 2007, ss 731–735

78.5 A capital distribution from an offshore trust is frequently both a benefit under ss 731–735 (see para 71.4) and a capital payment. However the benefit is not itself chargeable to income tax: as is explained in CHAPTER 71, strictly it is merely one of the elements used in ITA 2007, s 733 in calculating whether and if so what income is treated as arising to the recipient under s 732.

On this strict analysis, double taxation under both s 732 and s 87 would not be avoided. But in reality it is inconceivable that this strict approach would ever be adopted. On a purposive construction a benefit under ss 732 and 733 plainly is charged to income tax when matched to relevant income, and in that connection it is noteworthy that step 6 in s 733(1) states that the amount of s 732 income is the benefits where these are less than the relevant income. In these circumstances there can be little doubt that the general rule in TCGA

1992, s 97(1)(a) does preclude simultaneous tax charges on the same distribution under s 732 and s 87. This is accepted by HMRC (CG 38625).

On the basis this is right that there are three points to note. The first is that a capital distribution or benefit conferred on a non-resident is always a capital payment rather than a benefit brought into account under ss 731–735. This result follows because a benefit is brought into account under ss 731–735 only if the recipient is UK resident in the tax year of receipt (see para **70.14**). Such a capital payment or benefit cannot have gains in a Sch 4C pool matched to it (see para **81.7**), but otherwise s 2(2) amounts and OIG amounts are matched under s 87. Although tax results should the recipient be only temporarily non-UK resident (see para **77.46**), the OIG or s 2(2) amounts matched with the capital payment are otherwise washed out without tax charge (see para **77.46**).

The second point arises if in the year in which a capital distribution is made to a UK resident beneficiary there is no or insufficient available relevant income. In this scenario the distribution is treated as a capital payment to the extent that in the year of the distribution it is matched with current or past year s 2(2) or OIG amounts and, to the extent it is so matched it cannot result in tax under ss 731–735 when relevant income arises in the future (see para **71.4**). If it is not matched with s 2(2) or OIG amounts in the year of receipt the surplus is carried forward and is taxed under ss 731–735 to the extent that relevant income arises in the following year, as a capital payment to the extent that there is no such income but there are trust gains in that year, and carried forward again to the extent that there is neither. This subject is discussed further in CHAPTER 9.

The third point arises where the capital distribution or benefit to a UK resident beneficiary is not taxed under ss 731–735 on account of the motive defence described in CHAPTER 73 or the EU defence described in CHAPTER 74. Here the distribution does count as a capital payment for, even though it is brought into account in the computation under ss 731–735, it is not charged to income tax.

The fourth point is similar and arises if the recipient of the distribution or benefit is a remittance basis user, with the result tax is not charged under ss 731–735 unless and until the notional income is treated as remitted (see CHAPTER 72). Here it is reasonably plain that the benefit or distribution is not a capital payment, for the notional income is still chargeable to income tax, albeit the measure of liability is the remittance basis.

RECEIVED

78.6 The word 'received' is given an extended definition. A capital payment is regarded as received by a beneficiary from the trustees in any of the following circumstances (s 97(5)):

(i)   he receives it from them directly or indirectly;
(ii)   it is directly or indirectly applied by them in payment of any debt of his;
(iii)   it is otherwise paid or applied for his benefit;
(iv)   it is received by a third party at his direction.

Indirect receipt

78.7 In *Bowring v HMRC* [2016] STC 816, the Upper Tribunal considered that the concept of the beneficiary receiving the capital payment from the trustees is the same as that of the trustees making the payment. The Upper Tribunal also held that indirect receipt occurs only if the direct recipient is on the facts a mere intermediary.

The facts of *Bowring* arose from defective drafting of the original trustee borrowing rules, to the effect that s 90 did not operate to transfer outstanding trust gains to a transferee settlement if the transfer was linked to trustee borrowing. As explained in para 81.2, this loophole was blocked in 2003. However the scheme in *Bowring* was implemented before the blocking.

The offshore trust in *Bowring* was set up in 1969 and had substantial s 2(2) amounts which, as the law then stood, would have attracted tax at 64% if distributed to UK resident beneficiaries. In March 2002 the principal beneficiary set up a UK settlement, of which he was one of the trustees. On 2 April 2002, the 1969 trustees borrowed money and transferred £3.8m to the 2002 trust. Starting on 28 April 2002, the 2002 trustees distributed some but not all of this money. These distributions would only have resulted in tax under s 87 if, as HMRC contended, they were indirectly received from the 1969 settlement.

The First-tier Tribunal, following the earlier Special Commissioners decision in *Herman v HMRC* [2007] STC (SCD) 571, held that in law the same capital payment could be received directly from one settlement and indirectly from another, and found that on the facts there had been indirect receipt from the 1969 settlement. The Upper Tribunal, by contrast, held that receipt can only be from one settlement. If the 2002 settlement was a mere intermediary there would have been indirect receipt from the 1969 settlement and no receipt from the 2002 settlement. Otherwise receipt was from the 2002 settlement.

The Upper Tribunal decided that the mere existence of a plan to make tax-free distributions did not make the 2002 settlement an intermediary, even though the 1969 trustees knowingly played their part in the plan. Intermediary status was negatived by the absence of an agreement between the two sets of trustees as to what distributions the 2002 trustees would make and by the fact that the 1969 trustees had no input in the decision-making of the 2002 trustees. The conclusion was reinforced by the fact that, contrary to the original plan, not all the funds that came into the 2002 settlement were in fact distributed.

HMRC now consider it would be exceptional to argue a payment received from one settlement was indirectly received from another (CG 38670).

Onward gifts

78.8 The issue of indirect receipt also arises where one person receives the capital payment from the trustees and then immediately passes it on to someone else. Can the second person be said to have received the payment indirectly? Typically this issue arises where the first recipient is non-UK resident and the second is not, so that the capital payment does not result in tax unless the second person can be said to have received it indirectly.

Bowring indicates that the capital payment will be treated as received by the second person if and only if the first person is an intermediary. The facts of *Bowring* indicate that a recipient of a distribution is not an intermediary provided there is no contractual or equitable obligation on him to make an onward gift and provided the decision to make the onward gift is his alone.

This issue arose as a subsidiary point in *Bowring* in the First-tier Tribunal. One of the distributions from the 2002 trust to the principal beneficiary was made with a view to him passing the money on to his cousins. The First-tier Tribunal held this distribution was received by the principal beneficiary. It could not be regarded as received by the cousins indirectly because the principal beneficiary was not, in law, bound to pay it on to them and it was no longer imprinted with a trust.

The issue of onward gifts also arises with the transfer of assets benefits charge and is discussed in para **70.29**. The relevant legislation is not the same, for the benefits code does not comprehend indirect receipt and the issue is associated operations. Nonetheless the eventual analysis is not dissimilar.

BENEFICIARY

78.9 Even the term 'beneficiary' has an extended meaning. Should a person who is not a beneficiary receive a capital payment he is deemed to be a beneficiary (TCGA 1992, s 97(8)). This does not however apply where an actual beneficiary can be treated as receiving the payment and nor does it apply so as to treat the trustees of another settlement as a beneficiary (s 97(10)(a)). This latter exclusion is necessary because where one trust distributes or advances capital to another, special rules regulate the transfer of s 2(2) and OIG amounts between the trusts (see paras **77.29** and **82.5**).

Charities

78.10 HMRC treat payments by non-resident trusts to UK charities as capital payments. This means that s 2(2) amounts are allocated to them. But the general relief for charitable gains (TCGA 1992, s 256) is regarded as conferring exemption from tax provided that the payment is applicable and applied for charitable purposes including where the payment is used to acquire investments for the charity.

This practice was published in 1998 by reference to TCGA 1992, s 87 (*Tax Bulletin 36* (August 1998) p 573). Its reasoning appears to apply equally to Sch 4C and offshore income gains, the former being omitted because Sch 4C had not been enacted when the practice was published.

In reality the practice is a little curious. Should the charity be a trust, it is unclear why the payment to the charity is not a transfer between trusts and so should be dealt with under the rules in TCGA 1992, s 90 governing transfers between trusts (see paras **77.29** and **82.5**). This point is not germane to incorporated charities, and so on any view the practice described above should apply to payments to them. But there would then be a distinction between corporate and unincorporated charities, which is arguably illogical.

TRANSFERS TO ANOTHER SETTLEMENT

78.11 Difficult issues arise when the trustees transfer all or part of the settled property to another settlement or resettle it. As explained in CHAPTER 77, TCGA 1992, s 90 operates in relation to such a transfer unless the transfer is linked with trustee borrowing (as to which see CHAPTER 80). Absent any trustee borrowing, s 90 provides that all or a proportion of the s 2(2) and OIG amounts are carried forward to the transferee settlement (see paras **77.29** and **82.5**). Should the transfer be linked with trustee borrowing, or should Sch 4C otherwise be in point, the transferee settlement becomes a relevant settlement (para **81.14**).

The question which s 90 and Sch 4C do not address is whether the transfer can constitute a capital payment to any beneficiary of the transferee settlement. On one view it cannot, for s 90 and Sch 4C clearly envisage that transfers between settlements will occasion the carry forward of gains rather than a capital payment. Moreover, even if the benefit a beneficiary takes under the transferee settlement were a capital payment the amount would be nil if the beneficiary's interest is discretionary or terminable by the trustees, for then it is valueless.

A contrary argument focuses on the wording of TCGA 1992, ss 97(2) and 97(5)(b). As noted above s 97(2) proves that the term 'payment' includes the conferring of any benefit, and s 97(5)(b) states that a payment is received by the beneficiary if it is paid or applied for his benefit. Reference is then made to the fact that a resettlement or a transfer to a new settlement can be made in exercise of the statutory power of advancement in s 32 of the Trustee Act 1925 or under some similar power, and the fact that such power only authorises the exercise if it is for the benefit of the particular beneficiary being advanced. In those circumstances it can be said that the resettlement falls squarely within the words of s 97(5)(b) and so is a capital payment to the beneficiary.

At one time HMRC were thought to adopt this analysis both in relation to advances under s 32 and in relation to similar express powers exercisable for the benefit of a specific beneficiary. Whether the analysis is right given the s 90 and Sch 4C regimes for the transfer of trust gains is debatable. If it is right, the capital payment represented by the advance reduces or eliminates the outstanding trust gains carried forward to the new settlement. On the basis of the Tribunal's analysis in *Burton v HMRC* [2009] SFTD 682, the quantum if there were a capital payment would be the value of the beneficiary's interest under the transferee settlement rather than the amount or value of the cash or other assets transferred to it.

In practice, most transfers between settlements are effected not in exercise of the statutory power of advancement or some similar power, but in exercise of an express power authorising the trustees to transfer all or part of the trust fund to another trust. Such powers require some at least of the beneficiaries of the transferor trust to be beneficiaries of the transferee trust, but the trustees in exercising the power are benefiting those beneficiaries collectively rather than any particular beneficiary. In these circumstances it is difficult to see the exercise as a payment or application for the benefit of a particular beneficiary within s 97(5)(b), and even if it was it would be such a payment or application for the benefit of all the beneficiaries common to the two settlements. On that scenario the value of the benefit to each, and thus the amount of any capital payment, would be impossible to determine.

In recent years there have been several avoidance cases involving the transfer of funds from one settlement to another (*Herman v HMRC* [2007] STC (SCD) 571; *Burton v HMRC* [2016] STC 816). In none was it either argued by HMRC or suggested by the Tribunal that the transfer was a capital payment to the beneficiary or beneficiaries of the recipient settlement. In the light of this there can be some confidence the point is bad.

The case which comes nearest to the issue is *Burton*. Here the settlor was a beneficiary of the recipient trust and the transfer was pursuant to the flip-flop scheme designed to avoid him being taxed under TCGA 1992, s 86 on gains in the transferor settlement (see CHAPTER 76 and para 80.2). HMRC's argument was that the transfer was a capital payment to the settlor, but on the basis not that he received a benefit as beneficiary of the transferee trust but that he received a benefit by being relieved of the s 86 charge. The tribunal was divided over whether this point was good in principle, but was at one concluding that even if there were a capital payment it had nil value.

An issue separate from whether the transfer between settlements is itself a capital payment is the issue of whether, if the transferee settlement confers benefit, any ensuing capital payment can be treated as indirectly received from the transferor settlement. As discussed above (para **78.6**) such treatment is only possible if on the facts the transferee settlement is an intermediary. *Bowring v HMRC* [2016] STC 816 indicates it is not an intermediary unless there is an agreement as to distributions between the two sets of trustees or the transferor trustees input into the decision-making process of the transferee trustees.

FREE USE OF PROPERTY

78.12 Trustees frequently allow beneficiaries to borrow from the trust at a low or nil rate of interest. So too, a beneficiary may be given a licence to occupy trust property at a low or nil rent. The question of whether such transactions occasion a capital payment, and if so when and in what amount, have occasioned controversy and difficulty.

Fixed-term loan or licence

78.13 In the case of a fixed term loan or licence, the matter is covered by s 97(4). Unless the loan or licence is on commercial terms, there is a benefit, conferred when the loan is made or licence granted, and equal to the then value of the loan or licence. It is suggested that the benefit will be equal to the net present value of the interest payments or rental payments which would be made over the term of the loan or licence if it were a loan or lease on commercial terms.

Demand loan or licence

78.14 If demand loans and revocable licences were looked at in the same way as fixed-term loans and licenses, there would be a benefit, but its value would be nil, for at any time after the loan was made or licence granted it could be called in or revoked. On this basis there would be nothing to tax.

In *Billingham v Cooper* [2001] STC 1177, the Court of Appeal decided that this is not the correct approach. The right approach is to focus on the trustees' continuing decision to not call in the loan or revoke the licence. This benefit is valued retrospectively each year according as to how long the loan or licence remains outstanding. If it needs to be determined when the benefit is conferred, time apportionment on a daily basis is the fairest course. This is relevant to the matching exercise necessary to determine if supplementary tax is payable (see para 77.49).

In *Billingham v Cooper*, the trust was a fixed-interest trust where a demand loan had been made to the life-tenant. As a subsidiary argument, the taxpayer contended there was no benefit, for the taxpayer would have been entitled to the interest had it been charged. The Court of Appeal rejected this argument also.

Valuation issues

78.15 *Billingham v Cooper* did not determine the amount of the capital payment – ie how the value of the benefit conferred should be determined. In logic the benefit in each tax year should be the difference between a commercial rate of interest or open market rent on the one hand and the interest or rent actually charged (if any) on the other.

In practice HMRC use the official rate provided the loan is denominated in sterling, Swiss Francs or Japanese Yen (CG 38645). The official rate is the rate prescribed for taxing beneficial loans to employees (see para 93.16). Should the loan be denominated in other currencies commercial rates are used.

The issues that can arise if interest is rolled up are the same as apply with the benefits code and are discussed at para 70.20. So also is the possibility of HMRC arguing that an apparent loan is not really a loan at all but should be taxed as an out-and-out payment. Interest agreed retrospectively does not obviate a benefit charge; instead the benefit charge is still made and the interest paid is an addition to the settlement by the beneficiary (CG 28645).

The valuation issues that arise with the rent-free use of land and chattels are also the same as arise under the benefits charge. They are discussed at para 70.19.

PAYMENTS BY AND TO COMPANIES

78.16 Express rules deal with payments involving companies. They apply both to capital gains and offshore income gains.

Payments by close companies

78.17 A payment received from a qualifying company controlled by the trustees counts as received from the trustees (s 96(1)). 'Control' bears its close company definition (CTA 2010, ss 450 and 451; see CHAPTER 87), but no rights or powers of an associate are attributed to a person unless he is himself a participator in the company concerned (TCGA 1992, s 96(10)). A company counts as controlled by the trustees if they control it or if they and the settlor or a person connected with him control it (s 96(7), (8)). A company is a qualifying company if it is close or would be close were it United Kingdom resident (s 96(6)).

Payments to non-resident close companies

78.18 A payment to a non-resident close company is not taken into account as a capital payment. But this proposition is subject to special rules treating the payment as a payment to UK resident participators. These rules are set out in TCGA 1992, s 96(3)–(5) and have been in force since 19 March 1991 (s 96(11)).

The requirement that payment to non-resident companies are not taken into account as capital payments was expressly enacted in 2008 (TCGA 1992, s 87C and Sch 4C para 9(4); Offshore Funds (Tax) Regulations 2009 (SI 2009/3001), reg 20(3)). But it may be argued that express enactment was declaratory of the law, for such a result is the inevitable implication of the rules in s 96 attributing the payments to the participators. HMRC however allow capital payments made to non-resident close companies made in 2007–08 and prior to have s 2(2) amounts matched to them even where s 96 does not apply (CG 38685).

Where the company is controlled by a single UK resident a capital payment to the company counts as received by him. If two or more persons each control the company separately, it counts as received by such of them as are UK resident, divided equally between them if more than one. If it is controlled by two or more persons only if they are taken together, the payment is apportioned among the participators, but excluding any to whom 5% or less would be apportioned (s 96(3)–(5)).

For these purposes control has the same meaning as in the close company provisions (ie CTA 2010, ss 450 and 451; see paras **87.2**, **87.9** and **87.10**), although rights and powers are not attributed to a person unless he is himself a participator (TCGA 1992, s 96(10)). A point overlooked in the legislation is that a beneficiary may count as a participator by virtue of trust holdings in a company (CTA 2010, s 454(2)(c); see paras **87.4** and **87.5**). This means, in law, that a capital payment by trustees to an offshore company they own, or between two such companies, could count as a capital payment to the beneficiaries of the trust. The absurdity of this is, however, relieved by concession, in that a beneficiary is not in practice treated as a participator solely by virtue of his status as a beneficiary (ESC D40). HMRC are currently consulting on draft legislation to put ESC D40 on a statutory footing. Legislation is expected to be laid before Parliament at some point in 2015.

78.18 *Capital payments*

Real difficulties, however, arise if the settlor or a beneficiary own a personal stake in a non-resident company in which the offshore trust, or an intermediate holding company, also own shares. In this event the trustees are associates of the settlor and are likely also to be associates of the beneficiaries either because the beneficiaries are close relatives of the settlor or because as beneficiaries they are interested in the shares (see para 87.8). The result is that if the combined holdings give control, any capital payment made by the trustees to the company or between the companies, may be treated as a capital payment to the settlor or beneficiaries.

In practice, HMRC accept that a payment between companies is not a capital payment if it is made under a transaction at arm's length, is subject to income tax, or is a repayment of capital in a winding up (SP 5/92, paras 38–40).

Payments to other companies

78.19 An interesting issue arises as to whether a payment to a resident company or a non-resident open company counts as a capital payment regardless of s 96. The answer is that it does, for s 97(8) operates where any person who is not a beneficiary receives a payment and deems that person to be a beneficiary. Section 97(8) is displaced if the payment is treated as received by an actual beneficiary (s 97(9)) and as a result a company would only be treated as receiving the payment if outside s 96. As the previous discussion has indicated, a resident company is outside s 96, and so also is a non-resident open company.

In relation to resident close companies, HMRC have confirmed it is their view that a resident close company in receipt of a capital payment counts as a beneficiary and so is taxable under s 87 (*Tax Bulletin* 16 (April 1995)).

Chapter 79

CAPITAL PAYMENTS AND NON-UK DOMICILIARIES

INTRODUCTION

79.1 Until 6 April 2008, beneficiaries who were resident but not domiciled in the UK were not taxed under either TCGA 1992, s 87 or TCGA 1992, Sch 4C. The reforms to the remittance basis enacted by FA 2008 changed this. But the impact of the change was softened by generous transitional reliefs in the form of rebasing and exemption of pre-6 April 2008 capital payments and s 2(2) amounts. Even where those reliefs are not in point, the remittance basis is available to remittance basis users.

This chapter details the rules applicable where s 87 or Sch 4C is in point. The position where a capital payment to a non-UK domiciliary is matched to an OIG amount is discussed in Chapter 82.

THE REMITTANCE BASIS

79.2 The remittance basis applicable to s 87 is set out in s 87B. Section 87B also applies where capital payments are matched with s 2(2) amounts in Sch 4C pools (TCGA 1992 Sch 4C para 8AA).

Foreign chargeable gains

79.3 The remittance basis is delivered by treating the gains which accrue under s 87 or Sch 4C as foreign chargeable gains (s 87B(2)). This is so whether the s 2(2) amounts matched with the capital payments accrued on foreign or on UK situs assets.

The effect of the s 87 or Sch 4C gains being foreign is that TCGA 1992, s 12 applies. As is explained in para 49.1 that section applies only to non-UK domiciliaries who are remittance basis users, ie those who have made a claim under ITA 2007, s 809B (see para 46.1) or are otherwise entitled to the remittance basis under ss 809D or 809E (see para 46.10). Assuming that the non-UK domiciliary is a remittance basis user, the effect of s 12 is that the gain is not treated as accruing until remitted to the UK (s 12(2)).

In the context of s 87B and Sch 4C, the tax year in which the individual must be both non-UK domiciled and a remittance basis user is the tax year in which

913

s 87 or Sch 4C gain accrues. In other words, it is the tax year in which matching under TCGA 1992, s 87A occurs. Save in certain cases under Sch 4C involving relevant settlements (para **81.21**) this is the tax year of the later of the capital payment and the s 2(2) amount matched with it or, if both occur in the same tax year, that tax year. Being a remittance basis user when a capital payment is made is irrelevant if the capital payment has to be carried forward and the individual is not a remittance basis user when matching eventually does occur.

Meaning of 'remittance'

79.4 TCGA 1992, s 12 imports the general law as to the meaning of 'remittance' as set out in ITA 2007 s 809L and subsequent sections (as to which see CHAPTERS 51 to 57). This general law is difficult to apply to s 87B, for under Condition A of s 809L remittance does not in general occur unless money or other property is brought to the UK or used in the UK. In the case of s 87B gains there is no money or other property which can satisfy these conditions. There is merely an arithmetical construct, namely the matching of the capital payment with the s 2(2) amount.

Section 87B tackles this problem by deeming what it calls relevant property or benefits to be derived from the s 87 or Sch 4C gain. It then states that property is relevant if the capital payment is either the payment or transfer of the property, or the vesting of the property in a beneficiary when he becomes absolutely entitled to it. A benefit is relevant if the capital payment is the conferring of the benefit (s 87B(4)).

It is clear that s 87B focuses solely on the capital payment in determining whether the s 87 or Sch 4C gain is remitted. It follows that if the capital payment is not remitted, the s 87 or Sch 4C gain is not remitted. This is so even if the matched s 2(2) amount is remitted by the trustees or underlying company. Where the capital payment is made and remitted before matching, remittance of the s 87 gain is deemed to occur in the year of matching (ITA 2007, s 809U).

But although this basic point is clear, there are problems in applying the general law of remittance to s 87B. One is the general one, common to all deemed derivation (see para **52.16**), namely whether the derivation can be taken any further than the actual asset comprised in the capital payment. The other is how s 87B works in relation to a capital payment which is not the outright transfer or vesting of an asset, but merely the conferring of a benefit in specie, for example a loan or a licence to use property.

Outright capital payments

79.5 As just indicated, it is the relevant property which is treated as derived from the s 87 gain where the capital payment is the payment or transfer of the property or vesting absolutely. The relevant property is thus defined as the property transferred to the beneficiary or to which he becomes absolutely entitled. This appears, therefore, to be an instance of deemed derivation which treats a specific asset as derived from the gain, as s 87B(4)(a) uses the definite article, and thus appears to connote the particular asset vested. As such the general analysis of deemed derivation (see para 52.16 above) represents an argument that the derivation may go no further than the particular asset transferred or vested.

However, this would be a surprising limitation, for inter alia it would mean that once the beneficiary had sold any property vested in him, a remittance would be incapable of occurring. This conclusion must be incorrect, on the grounds that 'property' as used in s 87B is wide enough to comprehend both the property vested and any assets representing it.

Furthermore, where the capital payment is not the transfer or vesting of an asset in specie but a payment of money, ie a payment proper, the gains must surely trace through to any asset acquired with such money. By analogy with the case law on the extended meaning of income (see para 51.10), the character of payment must be retained even if the cash is invested.

Benefit

79.6 The difficulties where the capital payment is the conferring of a benefit in specie are greater. They stem from the fact that Conditions A and B in s 809L require the money or other property used in the UK to be or be derived from the chargeable gain. Where a capital payment is the use of an asset in specie, the asset is indubitably used for the benefit of the beneficiary in the UK. But s 87B deems the benefit constituted by the use of the asset to be derived from the s 87 or Sch 4B gain, not the asset itself.

On the face of it, this means capital payments constituted by the use of an asset in specie in the UK cannot be taxed. But this prima facie impression may not be right as there are two possible analyses by which a remittance charge may be secured.

One is to regard the use of the property as giving rights to the beneficiary and thus constituting a form of property in his hands. If this were the correct analysis, the property would indubitably be used in the UK for his benefit, and so satisfy Condition A in s 809L. But Condition B would not be satisfied as s 87B itself says that where the capital payment is the conferring of a benefit, it is the benefit, not any proprietary interest constituted by the benefit, which is derived from the s 87 or Sch 4C gain.

The second analysis is to focus on the extension of Conditions A and B to services (see CHAPTER 55). It appears that HMRC regard a capital payment constituted by the conferral of a benefit as a service provided by the trustee to the beneficiary (see CG 25341, example 3). On this basis remittance occurs should the benefit be provided in the UK, for then there is, as Condition A of s 809L requires, a service provided in the UK. A purposive construction may deliver this result, albeit that the concept of a trustee delivering a service when he benefits a beneficiary is curious.

HMRC make the point that if the benefit is the use of an asset, the assets must be in the UK for remittance to occur (CG 38810). This is plainly right and works well enough where the asset is real estate or chattels physically in the UK. But HMRC also instance a loan and here it is not clear whether the focus is on where the money is lent or whether account can be taken of where the beneficiary subsequently takes the money which has been lent. If the legislation is read naturally, rather than being contorted so as to do what HMRC might wish it to do, it appears that the focus must be on where the money is lent, and on that alone. The reason is that if a benefit from a trust is deemed to be a service, such service can only result in a remittance of the related s 87 gain if the service is provided in the UK (ITA 2007, s 809L(2)(b)). Thus it is reasonably clear that, on a fair reading of legislation, a loan from a non-resident trust that is made outside the UK does not result in a remittance of the related s 87 gain if the taxpayer then brings the borrowed money into the UK.

In practice

79.7 It is clear from the foregoing that s 87B is open to diverse constructions. Taxpayers minded to take the view it is ineffective to catch a payment brought to the UK or benefit enjoyed there should bear in mind that such does not represent HMRC's view and that the purpose of s 87B is plainly to catch such payments or benefits. Decided cases on the s 87 code have adopted a distinctly purposive construction and, while on different points, are indicative of the likely judicial approach (see especially *Billingham v Cooper* [2001] STC 1177 and para 78.14). Given this context, a taxpayer who takes the position that a payment or benefit enjoyed in the UK is not taxable should, at the very least, include full disclosure with his tax return.

Supplemental tax

79.8 Supplemental tax ceases to run when the s 87 gain accrues rather than when the capital payment is remitted. This follows because the period for which supplemental tax is computed ends on 30 November following the tax year when the capital payment is made (TCGA 1992, s 91(4)(b); see para 77.50). The legislation is silent as to the position where a capital payment is only partially remitted and it has been matched with the s 2(2) amounts of more than one year. In these circumstances the taxpayer may be entitled to adopt the position most favourable to him and treat the part remitted as matched with the younger s 2(2) amounts. Such a conclusion is adopted by HMRC (CG 38830) and is consistent with the 'Last in, first out' rule that applies both to matching under TCGA 1992, s 87A (see para 77.21) and to the remittance basis mixed-fund rule (see ITA 2007, s 809Q and para 53.14).

REBASING

79.9 The term 'rebasing' is something of a misnomer. What is entailed is not a deemed disposal and reacquisition by the trustees but merely a relief conferred on individuals who are resident but not domiciled in the UK. The relief is in point if a s 87 or Sch 4C gain accrues to such an individual, and the matched s 2(2) amount(s) are derived from disposals occurring in 2008–09 or later, of assets that were held as at 5 April 2008. The effect of the relief is that a proportion of the individual's gain may be exempt, the extent of the exemption depending on the extent to which pre-6 April growth in value is reflected in the matched s 2(2) amount(s). Rebasing is thus a rule for computing a relief to non-UK domiciled beneficiaries, and has no impact at trust level.

Rebasing applies whether or not the non-UK domiciliary is a remittance basis user.

Conditions which must be satisfied

79.10 Rebasing is available if the following conditions are met (FA 2008, Sch 7 para 126):

(a) a capital payment is made in 2008–09 or a later year;
(b) it is matched with a s 2(2) amount of 2008–09 or a later year;
(c) a s 87 or Sch 4C gain in consequence accrues to the recipient of the capital payment;
(d) the recipient of the payment is resident but not domiciled in the UK in the tax year of the matching – whether or not the recipient is a remittance basis user;
(e) the trustees were non-resident in 2008–09;
(f) the trustees have made a rebasing election.

If those conditions are met, the s 2(2) amount matched with the capital payment has to be recomputed on the basis that each asset whose disposal is reflected in the s 2(2) amount and has been owned by the trustees since before 5 April 2008 was acquired at its market value on that date. Only a fraction of the s 87 gain is then chargeable, the numerator being the recomputed s 2(2) amount and the denominator the actual s 2(2) amount.

The election

79.11 The general rule is that the election was only valid if made before 31 January 2010 (para 126(2)). This is so even if the first s 87 gain to which it is relevant accrues many years later.

However, a later election is possible if the trustees have at no time in 2008–09 or any later year made a capital payment to a UK resident beneficiary or a s 90 transfer to another settlement. If these conditions are both met, the election is valid if made before 31 January following the tax year in which one or other of them is first breached.

The legislation contains no provision allowing HMRC to accept an election outside these time limits. Such an election could therefore only be accepted by HMRC in exercise of its collection and management discretion. In general this means there must be a reason beyond the trustee's control, and not simply lack of awareness on the part of the trustee or its advisers of the need for an election (see CG 38845, 13800, 13810 and SACM 10040).

The election is made on Form RBE 1. Most trusts with any sort of UK connection elected before 31 January 2010. Inevitably this has had the result of bringing the settlement to the attention of HMRC. For some trustees the prospect of this proved unacceptable, although concerns about onerous reporting obligations being imposed on trusts which have made elections have, to date, proved unfounded.

An election has no impact on UK domiciled beneficiaries, as it works not by preventing s 2(2) amounts from being matched but by exempting part of any gain treated as accruing to a non-UK domiciled beneficiary. An election is appropriate even if the aggregate base cost of the trust's assets acquired in 2007–08 or prior is more than their aggregate net value as at 5 April 2008 as its impact on a given s 2(2) amount turns on which assets are disposed of in the tax year in question. The election has no downside as it cannot operate to increase the s 87 gain (para 126(8)).

Trustees who did not elect before 31 January 2010 need to consider whether it is still open to them to do so. In this connection it should be noted that under s 90 the term 'transfer' is not defined, but includes any transaction between trusts which is not for full consideration (see para **77.31**). The term 'capital payment' is very broad (see CHAPTER 78) and includes benefits such as the rent free occupation of property in specie. Further, where Sch 4C is in point, capital payments also count if made by a relevant settlement (see para **81.13**). Taken together these points mean the right to elect may have expired on 31 January 2010 in more cases than might be supposed, although as noted above there may be scope to make an election out of time.

An interesting issue is whether a payment or benefit is left out of account if it attracts income tax under ITA 2007, s 731. It seems reasonably plain that it should, at least insofar as fully matched and taxed under s 733, for then it does not count as a capital payment for CGT purposes at all (TCGA 1992, s 97(1)(a); see para **78.5**). Benefits to non-residents are not, of course within ss 731–733, but these are immaterial to the election for, as noted above, only capital payments to UK residents count.

Underlying companies

79.12 The election extends to the gains apportioned to the trust from non-resident close companies under TCGA 1992, s 13 (see CHAPTER 88). An asset is covered by the election provided it has been owned by the company making the disposal or a fellow group member since 5 April 2008 (para 126(11), (12) and (14).

A difficulty with underlying companies is that the percentage participation of the trust in the company may have changed, particularly where the company has loan creditors. This problem is addressed in that the election only operates on the minimum proportion of each of the company's assets (paras 126(16)). The minimum proportion is the lowest percentage participation the trust has had in the company at any time in the period between 6 April 2008 and the date on which the asset is disposed of (para 126(17)).

Assets derived from assets

79.13 A general CGT rule, in TCGA 1992, s 43, allows an appropriate proportion of the consideration given for one asset to be allowed as a deduction in computing the gain on the disposal of another asset. This relief applies if the value of the second asset is in some way derived from the first. Where this relief is in point, rebasing applies to the extent that the first asset was held on 5 April 2008 and the second asset not (para 126(13)).

Transfers between trusts

79.14 As explained in para 77.29 a transfer between trusts which is not caught by Sch 4B causes all or a proportion of the transferor trust's s 2(2) amounts outstanding at the end of the tax year of the transfer to move across to the transferee trust. The s 2(2) amount of the year of the transfer is increased by any gains occasioned by the transfer itself.

The availability of rebasing as respects transferred s 2(2) amounts of 2008–09 and later is governed by the election or non-election of the transferor trust. This analysis is shared by HMRC (CG 38890) and follows from FA 2008, Sch 7 para 126(7)(a), which refers to any capital payment and not just to those by the trust which made the election. The election or non-election of the transferee trust is irrelevant as that trust does not satisfy the basic precondition of having owned the transferred assets on 6 April 2008.

Where the transfer is of assets in specie, any latent gain is crystallised by the transfer and thus is included in the s 2(2) amount of the transferor trust for the year of the transfer, all or part of which is transferred across by the transfer. But where the transferred assets include the transferor trust's participation in a non-resident close company this crystallisation does not extend to any latent gains in the company. In such cases the availability of rebasing to subsequent gains of the company included in the transferee trust's s 2(2) amounts is also governed by the election or non-election of the transferor trust (FA 2008, Sch 7 para 127). If both the transferor and the transferee trust have made the election, rebasing after the transfer operates in the normal way in relation to both the transferee trust's direct assets and those of the transferred company. But should the transferee trust not have elected, rebasing operates only on the company assets.

What this latter point means is that rebasing is in point if a capital payment from the transferee trust is matched with a s 2(2) amount which includes gains realised by the transferred company on the disposal of assets held since 5 April 2008. The proportion of the capital payment which is chargeable is arrived at by a fraction of which the denominator is the transferee trust's actual s 2(2) amount for the year and the numerator what the s 2(2) amount would be if the company's assets comprised in the s 2(2) amount had been acquired at market value on 5 April 2008.

Remittance and rebasing

79.15 Should the non-UK domiciled beneficiary benefiting from the rebasing election be a remittance basis user, the part of the s 87 gain relieved by rebasing is not taxed even if the capital payment is remitted. Should part only of the capital payment be remitted, the issue which arises is how rebasing relief applies to the part remitted. There are three possibilities:

(a)   The position is unclear, with the result the taxpayer can adopt the solution most favourable to him and treat the exempt part of the s 87 gain as remitted first.

(b)   The mixed fund rules discussed in CHAPTER 53 treat foreign income and gains of year as remitted before other income and capital (ITA 2007, s 809Q(4)). By analogy, therefore the taxable part of the s 87 gain should be treated as remitted first.

(c)   The rebasing formula is applied to the s 87 gain after remittance, with the result that a proportion of the remitted gain is exempt and a proportion taxable.

It is suggested this third possibility is right, for rebasing is expressed in terms of the chargeable gains which accrue to the non-domiciliary and on which he is charged to tax (para 126(8)). The analogy with the mixed fund rules is false, for these are expressed in terms of foreign chargeable gains simpliciter and do not distinguish such gains on which tax is in fact charged, from such gains on which tax is not charged.

EXEMPTION

79.16 A gain treated as accruing to a non-domiciliary under s 87 is not taxable at all if and to the extent the matched capital payment was made before 6 April 2008 or the matched s 2(2) amount accrued in 2007–08 or an earlier tax year (FA 2008, Sch 7 para 124). This relief applies to all non-domiciliaries, not just remittance basis users. It applies also to Sch 4C gains (FA 2008, Sch 7 para 150).

Capital payment in 2008–09 or later

79.17 The relief is in point if a capital payment is made to a non-UK domiciliary in 2008–09 or a later year. Under the 'last in, first out' rule,, this payment is set first against the s 2(2) amount of the year of payment and any prior years back to 2008–09. To the extent it is so set, it is taxable, albeit subject to rebasing and, if the beneficiary is a remittance basis user, the s 87B remittance basis. But if there are no such s 2(2) amounts, or the payment exceeds them, the matching is with any s 2(2) amounts of 2007–08 or earlier years, and the ensuing gain is tax-free. If, of course, the capital payment exceeds all current and prior year s 2(2) amounts it is carried forward and taxable when there are s 2(2) amounts in the future, again subject to rebasing and the remittance basis.

It may be that a capital payment received by a non-UK domiciliary is matched partly with s 2(2) amounts of 2007–08 and prior and partly with s 2(2) amounts of 2008–09 and post. In these circumstances, on a partial remittance of the payment, the same issue arises as is discussed in para 79.8 in relation to supplemental tax, namely whether the remitted part of the payment is identified with the exempt or the taxable part of the s 87 gain. Here the position favourable to the taxpayer is the opposite to that indicated in para 79.8, in that 'first in, first out' is more attractive, ie identifying the remitted payment with the older, pre-2008, s 2(2) amounts. But this is not consistent with the 'last in, first out' approach generally applicable to s 87 and so may be more difficult to argue for.

Section 2(2) amounts in 2008–09 or later

79.18 Relief is also in point if the trust has s 2(2) amounts in 2008–09 or a subsequent year. These are in the first instance matched with capital payments of the current year and earlier years back to 2008–09. To the extent not so matched they are carried back to payments in 2007–08 and prior years and, if the recipient of those payments is non-UK domiciled in the tax year in which the s 2(2) amounts accrue, the exemption is in point.

12 March to 5 April 2008

79.19 A capital payment made between 12 March and 5 April 2008 is disregarded for these purposes if two conditions are met (FA 2008, Sch 7 para 125):

(a)   The recipient was non-UK domiciled in 2007–08.
(b)   The recipient is non-UK domiciled when the payment would otherwise fall to be matched with a s 2(2) amount.

The effect of this disregard is that s 2(2) amounts of 2008–09 and post are not matched with the capital payment. The result is that those s 2(2) amounts are carried forward insofar as they exceed:

(a)   current year capital payments;
(b)   available prior year capital payments back to 2008–09;
(c)   brought forward capital payments from prior to 12 March 2008; and
(d)   brought forward capital payments made between 12 March and 5 April 2008 which were made either to resident and domiciled beneficiaries or to non-resident beneficiaries.

The result is loss of exemption for the carried forward s 2(2) amount for, being matched with future payments, it loses the exemption which would have applied had it been matched with the payment between 12 March and 5 April 2008.

The reason for the rule was to prevent forestalling, for the transitional reliefs were announced on 12 March 2008. The disregard affects all beneficiaries rather than just the recipient of the payment between 12 March and 5 April 2008 for, by ignoring that payment, it increases s 2(2) amounts of 2008–09 and post available for carry forward.

The disregard contains one particular trap. This is that in its terms it only applies so long as the recipient of the capital payment between 12 March and 5 April 2008 retains the status of being resident and non-UK domiciled. Should he become either UK domiciled, or non-resident, the disregard of the capital payment ceases. This means it is then available to be matched with s 2(2) amounts of the tax year in which the individual's status changes, and later years. Such matching leads to tax if the individual is then UK resident and domiciled.

The rule also applies to Sch 4C (FA 2008, Sch 7 para 151). It might be thought it is irrelevant to Sch 4C, for under old Sch 4C capital payments to non-domiciliaries were disregarded (see para **81.28**). But so to conclude ignores the fact that under the present Sch 4C, capital payments made in the tax year prior to the Sch 4B transfer can be matched (see para **81.8**). Accordingly the rule prevented capital payments made between 12 March and 5 April 2008 from being matched against Sch 4B gains in 2008–09.

1998 cut-off

79.20 The capital payments and s 2(2) amounts of many settlements must be ignored if they pre-date 17 March 1998. This happens if the settlor was either non-resident or non-UK domiciled when he made the settlement or all the settlors were in the case of multiple settlors. The effect of this rule is that the surplus s 2(2) amounts or capital payments of 2007–08 and prior may be less than might be supposed. The precise extent of this rule raises issues of some difficulty, discussed in para **77.28**.

In the context of non-UK domiciliaries this rule operates not as a relieving provision but increases CGT exposure. Such a result follows because any reduction in s 2(2) amounts or capital payments of 2007–08 and prior reduces the availability of the transitional reliefs described above.

Interaction of s 87 and Sch 4C

79.21 As will be apparent from the above, the effect of the 'last in, first out' rule is that the transitional exemption is not enjoyed if and to the extent there are both s 2(2) amounts and capital payments in 2008–09 and later years. To this there is one exception. A capital payment in 2008–09 or post is matched with s 2(2) amounts in a Sch 4C pool before being matched under s 87 with later s 2(2) amounts. If therefore the s 2(2) amounts in the Sch 4C pool accrued in 2007–08 or a prior year, these are matched with a capital payment to a UK resident (whether domiciled or non-domiciled) before the s 2(2) amounts of tax years after the Sch 4B transfer.

Schedule 4C pools as at 5 April 2008

79.22 There is no express transitional exemption for old Sch 4C pools. This is because gains in such pools can never be attributed to non-domiciliaries

(TCGA 1992, Sch 4C para 8(3) as enacted in 2003). This is so whether the non-domiciliary is a remittance basis user or not (see further para **81.29**).

Chapter 80

TRUSTEE BORROWING

INTRODUCTION

80.1 Finance Act 2000 inserted important rules into the CGT treatment of offshore trusts, namely TCGA 1992, Schs 4B and 4C. These schedules give rise to a complete or deemed partial disposal of all the trust assets in certain circumstances where the trustees have outstanding borrowing. Schedule 4B is the principal schedule. Sch 4C was recast in 2003 and again in 2008. It provides for a 'floating' pool of Sch 4B gains, except where such gains are attributed to the settlor on an arising basis under TCGA 1992, s 86. The details of Sch 4C are discussed in CHAPTER 81.

HMRC gave some guidance on Sch 4B in *Tax Bulletin* 66 (August 2003). The issue of whether Schs 4B and 4C are compatible with European law is discussed in para 107.20.

Flip-flop schemes

80.2 Schs 4B and 4C were introduced to counteract a scheme known as the 'flip-flop' scheme. This scheme avoided both the charge on the settlor under TCGA 1992, s 86 and the liability of beneficiaries on capital payments under TCGA 1992, s 87 (see CHAPTERS 76 and 77).

In essence the scheme involved the following steps:

(a)   in year 1 the trustees borrowed money against the security of the trust assets and advanced the cash to a new settlement;

(b)   in year 2 the trustees of the original settlement realised gains;

(c)   distributions to the beneficiaries were made from the new settlement.

In the case of TCGA 1992, s 86, the scheme was thought to work because the settlor and his children and grandchildren and their respective spouses were all excluded from the original settlement before the start of year 2 when the gains were realised (cf para 76.4). In the case of TCGA 1992, s 87, capital distributions from the new trust were thought not to be taxable by reference to gains realised in the old trust in year 2, because capital gains only carry forward from one trust to another if realised in the same year as the transfer between the trusts or an earlier year (TCGA 1992, s 90; cf para 77.32).

Regrettably, the drafting of Schs 4B and 4C means that their impact is far, far, wider than flip-flop schemes. They undoubtedly impose a deemed disposal in many situations where no attempt has been made to avoid CGT. Moreover, the language of the schedules is riddled with uncertainty. Only some of this has been clarified by HMRC (*Tax Bulletin* 66 (August 2003)).

Flip-flop schemes were also used to avoid the former charge on the settlor on gains on resident settlor-interested trusts (TCGA 1992, s 77). In relation to these trusts the scheme has been held in the House of Lords to have failed (*West v Trennery* [2005] STC 214). The reasoning behind this decision turned on the inclusion of 'derived property' in the definition of when the settlor had an interest in a resident settlement, for the purposes of s 77. Equivalent words are not found in s 86 and, reflecting this, the First-tier Tribunal has upheld the effectiveness of flip-flop schemes to avoid the s 86 charge (*Burton v HMRC* [2009] SFTD 682).

PRECONDITIONS

80.3 Schedule 4B para 1 sets out three conditions for the operation of Sch 4B:

(1)   The trustees make what is termed a transfer of value.
(2)   In the tax year of the transfer the settlement is within TCGA 1992, s 86, s 87 or s 89(2). By this is meant either that any net gains in that year are assessable on the settlor on an arising basis or that the settlement is within s 87 (Sch 4B para 3). As will be apparent from CHAPTERS 76 and 77 this language brings any trust which is not resident in the UK within the scope of Sch 4B, regardless of whether it has any connection with the UK.
(3)   The transfer of value is linked with trustee borrowing. By 'linked' is meant simply that at the time of the transfer there is what is called outstanding trustee borrowing (Sch 4B para 5(1)). This is the key concept in the schedule and requires consideration first.

Schedule 4B does not include any express definition of settlement. It follows that in Sch 4B the term 'settlement' bears its normal CGT meaning, which is itself the meaning of the term under general law (cf para 42.1).

OUTSTANDING TRUSTEE BORROWING

80.4 Determination of whether there is outstanding trustee borrowing requires two questions to be asked:

(a)   has there been trustee borrowing?
(b)   is it still outstanding?

As explained below, the latter question is not simply a matter of asking whether a debt is still due from the trustees at the relevant time.

Trustee borrowing

80.5 Trustees are treated as borrowing if:

•   money or any other asset is lent to them (para 4(1)(a)), or

- an asset is transferred to them on terms that it or another asset must be transferred back to the transferor or to another person (para 4(1)(b)).

Trustee borrowing thus includes loans in the normal sense of the word, and the extension of the term to transfers with the obligation to transfer back is anti-avoidance.

Amount borrowed

80.6 Where the trustees have borrowed, the amount of the loan is taken to be 'the market value of the asset' (para 4(2)(a)). In the simple case of a cash loan, this must be construed as meaning that the trustees are treated as having borrowed the principal amount received by them. Para 4(3) indicates that 'the asset' is to be valued immediately before, or in some cases, immediately after, the loan. This valuation provision means that where a loan has been made and interest has accrued on the loan, such accrued interest is ignored for Sch 4B purposes if a transfer of value occurs. Only the principal amount borrowed is taken into account.

In the case where trustee borrowing has arisen due to the transfer of an asset to the trustees, the amount of the deemed trustee borrowing is 'the market value of the asset reduced by the amount or value of any consideration received for it' (para 4(2)(b)). This formulation is believed to mean that any consideration passing from the trustees on the acquisition of the asset reduces the amount of deemed trustee borrowing, but there is no reduction to take account of the obligation to transfer the asset back to the transferor, or to transfer it to any other person.

Scope of borrowing concept

80.7 It is to be noted that the trustee borrowing can be from anybody. Loans from underlying companies, other trusts, or beneficiaries are caught just as much as commercial borrowing. The language is potentially wide enough to cover drawing down on an informal overdraft as well as structured borrowing.

The transaction does however have to involve money or another asset being lent to the trustees or transferred to them with an obligation to transfer it back. What is meant by 'lent' is not defined and so this term must bear its general meaning. There is authority in connection with the transfer of assets code that unpaid purchase money is not of itself a loan (*Ramsden v IRC* (1957) 37 TC 619, 625–626; see para 69.22). It may be suggested this is applicable to Sch 4B, unless the creditor expressly agrees to convert the debt into a loan. In Tax Bulletin 66 it is said that bona fide delay in payment of an invoice does not convert the amount invoiced into trustee borrowing. However, it is open to question whether a court would accept that there is no trustee borrowing where trustees have purchased an asset for a purchase price which the vendor is leaving outstanding indefinitely.

Taking of a lease

80.8 A particular issue raised by the definition is whether a lease comes within the definition of borrowing. If it did, any lease taken by the trustees would result in trustee borrowing.

It might be suggested that, as a matter of ordinary construction, the grant of a lease is not a transfer, because the transfer of an asset to someone requires the asset to exist before the transfer. That is clearly not the case where a lease is granted. As a matter of law, the tenant acquires a new asset, which is separate from the asset held by the lessor (*Ingram v IRC* [1999] STC 37). However, there are indications in Sch 4B that 'transfer' is intended to be construed in a wider manner than this. In particular, para 4(3) states where an asset did not exist immediately before it was transferred, its value shall be taken to be its market value immediately after the transfer. This indicates that the draftsperson thought of the creation of a new asset as a form of transfer.

However, there are other arguments that the grant of a lease is not a transfer:

- Para 13(3) states that references in Sch 4B to a transfer of an asset do not include a transfer of an asset created by a part disposal of another asset. The grant of a lease of land is treated as a part disposal of the land held by the lessor (TCGA 1992, s 240 and Sch 8). The same treatment generally applies to the lease of any other asset (Sch 8, para 9(1)).
- There is no transfer of any asset back to the lessor on the expiry of a lease.
- The grant of a lease is not apt to be described as the lending of an asset.

These arguments should apply to leases of both land and chattels. But it is possible that a court may treat the lease of a chattel as the 'lending' of a chattel.

In the event that a pre-existing leasehold interest is assigned to trustees subject to a contractual obligation to assign the interest back before the expiry of the term, there will be 'trustee borrowing'.

Borrowing by underlying companies

80.9 Para 4(1) is couched in terms of loans or transfers to the trustees. Taking the legislation at face value, it does not encompass a loan or transfer to a company whose shares are held by the trustees. There is no provision in Sch 4B (or elsewhere in TCGA 1992) to the effect that a loan or transfer to an underlying company shall be deemed to be a loan or transfer to the trustees. The logical conclusion is that any borrowing by an underlying company should be ignored when determining whether Sch 4B is engaged.

But ~~re~~ 80.21: a court may ~~disagree~~!

When is trustee borrowing outstanding? 80.30: GC ~~seems happy that~~ ~~this is safe~~

80.10 The basic rule is that where trustee borrowing has been incurred, it remains 'outstanding' until it is repaid.

However, borrowing which has been applied for what are called 'normal trust purposes' is excluded from the ambit of outstanding trustee borrowing (Sch 4B para 5(2)). 'Normal trust purposes' is tightly defined (Sch 4B para 6), having a much narrower meaning than might be supposed. Borrowing is treated as having been applied for normal trust purposes if (and only if):

(a)   it has been used to make payments in respect of 'ordinary trust assets'. The latter expression is itself closely defined (see below);

(b)   it has been used in discharging an existing loan obligation of the trustees, where such loan was itself applied for normal trust purposes (Sch 4B para 6(3)); or

(c)   it has been used to meet bona fide current expenses incurred by the trustees in administering the settlement or any of the settled property (Sch 4B para 6(4)). This is discussed in para **80.13** below.

In addition, trustee borrowing ceases to be 'outstanding' if it has been taken into account under Sch 4B. This concept is discussed below (para **80.26**).

Ordinary trust assets

80.11 The following, and only the following, are ordinary trust assets (Sch 4B para 7):

(a)   shares or securities. The term 'security' bears the definition given in TCGA 1992, s 132 and thus means loan stock or similar;

(b)   tangible property, whether movable or immovable;

(c)   property used in a business carried on by the trustees or by a beneficiary who has an interest in possession in the property;

(d)   rights in or interests over such tangible or business property.

Interests in mutual funds are not specifically referred to in the definition of ordinary trust assets. But shares in open-ended investment companies are shares within the general meaning of the term, and units or interests in other types of offshore fund are deemed to be shares (TCGA 1992, ss 99 and 103A; see paras **3.3** and **3.4**).

Expenditure on ordinary trust assets does not qualify as normal trust purposes unless the asset is held by the trustees immediately after the transfer of value. If the asset is not so held, for example, if it has been sold, the expenditure can only qualify if (para 8):

(a)   the asset is then represented by one or more other ordinary trust assets; or

(b)   the asset was destroyed or became of negligible value so that TCGA 1992, s 24 applied.

A further point is that expenditure on ordinary trust assets does not count unless it is on arm's length terms or is less than what would have been paid at arm's length. It must also constitute allowable expenditure within TCGA 1992, s 38 on the disposal of the asset (Sch 4B para 6(2)). Expenditure which is disallowed for CGT purposes solely because it is an income tax deduction counts, however.

Issues regarding ordinary trust assets

80.12 This definition of 'ordinary trust assets' is fraught with problems. The first is that not all assets are included, specifically intangibles. Obvious exclusions are insurance policies, intellectual property and futures contracts (*Tax Bulletin 66*, para B6). But potentially more serious is the exclusion of simple debts. A debt is an asset of the creditor for CGT purposes (TCGA 1992, s 21(1)(a)) and perhaps the most common category of simple debt is a bank deposit. The practical result is that trustees who borrow money and pay it into the bank are not applying the trustee borrowing for normal trust purposes.

This leads on to a second problem, namely the question of when the expenditure on ordinary trust assets must occur. Must it occur when the borrowing is incurred, as a direct application of the proceeds, or are the proceeds allowed to be represented by another asset first? To take a specific example, can the trustees put borrowed money in the bank, thereby acquiring a debt, and then spend it on ordinary trust assets, or must the money move directly from the lender to the assets? Common sense indicates that the borrowing need not be spent on ordinary trust assets when incurred. This issue is not clarified by *Tax Bulletin* 66 although it is said that putting money in the bank is not regarded as a transfer of value (para **80.15** below). The fact that the issue arises at all shows how ill thought-out Sch 4B is.

A third problem is that particular items of expenditure on ordinary trust assets may not qualify. Thus under TCGA 1992, s 38, enhancement expenditure has to be reflected in the state or nature of the asset at the time of the disposal. Much expenditure, for example, routine maintenance or improvements subsequently obviated, is not so reflected. However such expenditure may still qualify as normal trust purposes under Sch 4B, for in HMRC's view Sch 4B merely requires it to be reflected in the state or nature of the asset at the time it is incurred (*Tax Bulletin 66*, para B5).

Fourth, the fact that simple debts are not ordinary trust assets means any simple loan or capital contribution to any company owned by the trustees is not an application for normal trust purposes. The only way such expenditure can count is if the trustees subscribe for shares or securities in the company. As House of Lords decisions have affirmed, the term 'security' means something akin to loan stock and should involve an appropriate document (cf *Aberdeen Construction Group Ltd v IRC* [1978] STC 127; *WT Ramsay Ltd v IRC* [1981] STC 174).

Fifth and last is the requirement that the asset must be held by the trustees immediately after the transfer of value. As noted above, this requirement is displaced if the asset has been destroyed or if immediately after the transfer of value one or more ordinary trust assets 'directly or indirectly represent' it. Direct and indirect representation is not defined, but on any view should cover the position where the ordinary trust asset is shares and the new asset is shares or debentures acquired on a reconstruction or take-over. Less clear is the position where the original ordinary trust asset is sold and the proceeds applied in the purchase of a new ordinary trust asset. But here it may be suggested that even if the new asset does not represent the old asset it is itself an application of the proceeds of the borrowing, provided that its purchase price is demonstrably funded out of the proceeds of sale of the old asset.

The prime significance of the requirement that the ordinary trust asset or assets representing it be held immediately after the transfer is that the exemption for ordinary trust assets is not in point if the ordinary trust asset is itself the subject of the transfer.

Schedule 4B provides that if there has been a part disposal of the original ordinary trust asset, the part retained and any asset which represents the part disposed of may be looked at in combination to see if the ordinary trust asset condition is met (Sch 4B, para 8(2)). In HMRC's view this has significance in relation to leases, as described below (para **80.19**).

Bona fide current expenses

80.13 Sch 4B para 6(4) requires the expenses to be current, bona fide, and incurred in administering the settlement or the trust property. There is no restriction to income expenses. HMRC accept that capital expenditure is included, and cite as examples capital taxes and costs incurred in reorganising the settlement (*Tax Bulletin* 66, para B5). The term does not however cover the mere making of a reserve in respect of future expenditure. In relation to real property para 6(4) allows borrowing used to fund repairs to count as normal trust purposes and the same applies to payments made under the terms of a lease into a common sinking fund (*Tax Bulletin* 66, para B5).

Somewhat more controversially, HMRC doubt whether the concept of current expenses extends to borrowing taken out to pay off old unpaid debts. The correct analysis is surely that if such expenditure is no longer current it is only so by having become a loan from the creditor. If the original expenditure was bona fide current expenses, borrowing to pay off this loan is borrowing applied in paying off a loan incurred for normal trust purposes and so relieved under para 6(3).

The expenditure must be incurred by the trustees in administering the settlement or on the settled property. This plainly excludes expenditure incurred in administering any underlying holding company. However, HMRC regard the costs of maintaining a nominee company as included in the concept of trustee expenses.

Regulations

80.14 As will be apparent, the rules defining 'normal trust purposes' are a mess and give every impression of being drafted by people with little knowledge of how trusts operate in practice. One potential redeeming feature is that the Treasury has taken power to amend the rules by regulation (Sch 4B para 9). But to date this power has not been exercised.

TRANSFERS OF VALUE

80.15 The term 'transfer of value' does not bear the IHT meaning with which practitioners are familiar. Instead trustees are treated as making a transfer of value in any of the following circumstances (Sch 4B para 2):

(1) they transfer an asset to any person either for no consideration or for consideration less than market value;

(2) they lend money or any other asset to a person;

(3) they issue a security either for no consideration or for consideration less than market value.

The term 'asset' includes sterling (para 13(1)).

Value transferred

80.16 Schedule 4B includes express rules determining the amount of value transferred. In the case of a loan the amount is equal to the 'market value of the asset' (para 2(3)). This is to be determined immediately before or after the making of the loan (para 2(6)). This must mean that only the principal amount lent is taken into account – the subsequent accrual of interest on a loan made by the trustees is not, in itself, a transfer of value.

The amount represented by a security is the value of the security less any amount received by the trustees for it (para 2(5)). HMRC are understood to consider that the amount received excludes the promise to pay of the other party to the security and in the context of Sch 4B this is surely right.

In the case of a transfer, the basic rule is that the amount of value transferred is equal to the value of the cash or other asset transferred (para 2(4)). But if the trustees receive consideration for the transfer, the amount of value transferred is reduced by such consideration unless any part of the value of the asset is attributable to trustee borrowing (para 2(4)).

Scope of transfer concept

80.17 Subject to para 13(3), the term 'transfer' includes any act which constitutes a disposal for CGT purposes (para 13(2)). But it is to be emphasised that such a transaction is only caught if it is for no consideration or for less than market value.

As noted above, para 13(3) says that there is no transfer of an asset for Sch 4B purposes if the asset was created by a part disposal of another asset. It seems to follow that there is no transfer in any situation where TCGA 1992, s 21(2)(b) (part disposals) applies. However, as discussed below (para **80.19**), HMRC seem to disagree about the effect of para 13(3).

The definition of 'transfer of value' plainly covers the ostensible target of Sch 4B, namely flip-flop schemes, for those schemes involved the gratuitous transfer of cash to another trust. But as with Sch 4B generally, the ambit of the definition is far wider. In particular, taking the legislation at face value, it includes any distribution to a beneficiary. However, as discussed below (para

80.20), HMRC practice is to treat certain distributions as excluded from the 'transfer of value' concept.

Loans

80.18 There is no arm's length exclusion for loans. And indeed, as with trustee borrowing (para 80.5), there is no definition of 'lend'.

A number of issues are raised by loans. The first is that a loan can be made in one instance where the expenditure is for normal trust purposes. This is when the trustees subscribe for a debt security, and the issue which arises is whether that transaction is a transfer of value, attracting a deemed disposal under Sch 4B, or expenditure for normal trust purposes. Common sense indicates the latter.

A second point is more basic. Unless the loan is a subscription for a security, any loan to a beneficiary, another trust, or an underlying company is caught. Informal loans to underlying companies are particularly common in practice, but if one is made when there is outstanding trustee borrowing the result is a deemed disposal, inter alia of the trust's shares in the company.

Third, as noted above (para 80.11), the technical legal analysis of a bank deposit is that it is a loan by the depositor to the bank. Accordingly, on a literal reading, whenever the trustees place money in the bank they are making a transfer of value. In fact as *Tax Bulletin* 66 (para B7) affirms this cannot be right, for if it were almost every trustee borrowing of cash would immediately be followed by a transfer of value, regardless of what the ultimate use of the borrowed money was intended to be.

Leases

80.19 As discussed in para 80.8 it is clear that the granting of a lease is not the 'transfer' of an asset, and there is a very good argument that it is not a 'lending' of an asset. However the position is perhaps less certain with leases of chattels than leases of land.

HMRC's *Tax Bulletin* 66 muddies the waters greatly where the granting of leases is concerned. In the bulletin (para B8), it is contended that the grant of a commercial lease by trustees is a transfer of land. The bulletin acknowledges the existence of para 13(3) but asserts that 'The grant of a lease is a part disposal of the freehold interest and therefore the grant of a lease is a transfer of the freehold interest for the purposes of paragraph 2(1)(b) and is not regarded as the transfer simply of the lease.' It is suggested that this makes no sense whatsoever. It is impossible to see how the trustees, granting a lease, could be regarded as thereby transferring the freehold to anyone.

On the basis that the grant of a commercial lease is (in their view) a transfer, HMRC escape the consequences of it triggering a Sch 4B disposal if the trustees incurred borrowing to buy the land. They do so by saying there are two assets, namely the reversion and the lease, and that the lease is represented by the rental stream. As such they say the ordinary trust asset exception applies on the basis of a combination of the freehold being part of the original trust assets and the right to rent representing the rest.

This is plainly gibberish. The implication of it is that in the event that trustees grant a commercial lease, having incurred borrowing to acquire an asset other than the land which is subject to the lease, the HMRC view is that a Sch 4B deemed disposal will be triggered. But any such assertion should be resisted strongly. Para 13(3) makes it clear that the grant of a lease is not a transfer for Sch 4B purposes. Even if, for some reason, this is wrong, the grant of a commercial lease will by definition entail the receipt by the trustees of consideration at least equal to the market value of the leasehold interest acquired by the tenant, and this takes the grant of the lease out of Sch 2(1)(b).

Less clear is the position if the trustees grant a lease for no consideration, or on preferential terms; or if they grant a licence, assuming that a licence can correctly be characterised as a part disposal for CGT purposes. Here the full consideration point is not in issue, but the argument that the lease/licence is not a transfer on account of para 13(3) is still at large.

HMRC practice re trust distributions

80.20 Para B1 in *Tax Bulletin* 66 is potentially more useful. This is headed 'Paragraph 2(1)(b): cash distributions which are income'. The main body of the paragraph reads: 'Where trustees of a discretionary trust make a distribution which is income of the recipient for UK tax purposes, this is not a "transfer of value" within paragraph 2, which is concerned with capital transactions.'

It is to be noted that on its terms, this statement is quite narrow. It applies to distributions which are 'income of the recipient for UK tax purposes'. Clearly, this includes income distributions. However, it is suggested that the wording also catches capital distributions from discretionary trusts which are treated as comprising income of the recipient, or as giving rise to income of the recipient, under the transfer of assets legislation (see CHAPTERS 68 to 74).

Plainly, the statement at para B1 has been included in an attempt to bring the 'transfer of value' and 'capital payment' concepts into some kind of partial alignment. However, it is difficult to see any justification for it in Sch 4B, which is not obviously limited to 'capital transactions'. It seems best to view the statement at para B1 as an extra-statutory concession.

If this is right, it has a number of implications. One is that it could be withdrawn. Another is that there is no legal requirement for a particular taxpayer to treat income distributions, or distributions which are treated as giving rise to income, as falling outside the 'transfer of value' concept for Sch 4B purposes. Occasionally it may, somewhat perversely, be advantageous to take the position that a Sch 4C pool has arisen, or arose earlier than would otherwise be the case; eg where the resultant CGT liabilities would be statute-barred due to the passage of time since the matching of Sch 4C gains. The position taken would of course need to be noted in the individual's tax return or associated correspondence with HMRC.

Transfers by underlying companies

80.21 Like para 4(1), para 2(1) is couched in terms of acts by the trustees. Taken at face value, the paragraph is not engaged if a company whose shares are held by the trustees lends money, transfers an asset or issues a security. There is nothing in Sch 4B which expressly imputes a loan, transfer or issuance of a security by an underlying company to the trustee shareholders. TCGA 1992, s 96 includes provisions which impute capital payments by underlying companies to the trustee shareholders, but such provisions apply only for the purposes of ss 87–90 and Sch 4C, not to Sch 4B.

There is, perhaps, an argument that the statute should be construed broadly and purposively. There may, for example, be some risk of a court taking the position that if an underlying company makes a payment by way of gift to a beneficiary or to another trust, that is in substance a transfer of an asset by the trustees. Depending on the relevant governing law, it may be that the company in question would only be capable, constitutionally, of making such a payment if the trustees resolved that the payment should be made. The procurement of a transfer by the trustees might be seen as equivalent, in substance, to a transfer by the trustees themselves. However, the same would not necessarily apply to a loan by an underlying company. It is suggested that, absent special circumstances, such a loan is clearly outside the definition of a transfer of value.

THE DEEMED DISPOSAL

80.22 The transfer of value occasions a deemed disposal under Sch 4B if the trustee borrowing is outstanding at the material time. The term 'material time' is defined by reference to the transfer of value, as follows (Sch 4B para 2(2)):

(1) if the transfer of value is a loan or security, when the trustees make the loan or issue the security;
(2) if the transfer of value is the transfer of an asset when the transfer is 'effectively completed'.

The term 'effectively completed' means the point at which the transferee becomes for practical purposes unconditionally entitled to the whole of the subject matter of the transfer (para 2(2)).

The deemed disposal is of all the chargeable assets that are held in trust immediately after the material time. The deemed disposal therefore does not apply to assets held by underlying companies, although it will affect the shares in any such company.

Either there is a complete disposal of all assets held by the trustees, or each asset is subject to a proportionate disposal. For these purposes the term 'chargeable asset' means any asset on which a gain would be chargeable (para 10(3)). The term thus excludes, for example, sterling and qualifying corporate bonds. The deemed disposal is deemed to be on arm's length terms at market value (para 10(2)).

The deemed disposal is of the whole of each retained chargeable asset if the amount of value transferred is more than the effective value of the retained chargeable assets (para 11(4)). In other cases, a proportion of each asset is deemed to be disposed of. The proportion is determined by a fraction, of which the denominator is the effective value of the retained chargeable assets, and the numerator is the lesser of the amount of value transferred and the amount of the outstanding trustee borrowing (para 11(2), (3)).

Effective value

80.23 For these purposes the effective value of a chargeable asset is its value less such of that value as is attributable to any trustee borrowing attributable to the asset (para 11(5)). Trustee borrowing is attributable to an asset if either (Sch 4B para 12):

(a)   the asset itself was borrowed and has not been applied for normal trust purposes;

(b)   the proceeds of the trustee borrowing were applied in acquiring or enhancing the value of the asset, or another asset which it represents. This only applies to the extent that the borrowing is still outstanding at the material time.

Trustee borrowing is attributable to the asset under the latter head if the borrowing was outstanding when the expenditure was incurred (para 12(5)). It appears the borrowing remains attributable even if it was repaid after the expenditure was incurred but before the transfer engaging Sch 4B. An interesting point arises where the asset in question had appreciated in value. Is the value attributable to the borrowing the amount of the outstanding borrowing or a pro rata proportion of the enhanced value of the asset? It is thought the former is more consistent with the legislative context.

Linkage with trustee borrowing

80.24 A point to emphasise is that the deemed disposal is triggered regardless of whether the transfer of value is funded by or in any way related to the trustee borrowing. All that is necessary is that at the material time there is trustee borrowing which is outstanding. Moreover, even if the borrowing has ceased to be outstanding because the proceeds have been expended on an ordinary trust asset, if that asset is comprised in the transfer of value, the borrowing reverts to being outstanding in relation to that and subsequent transfers of value. As noted above, this is because expenditure on an ordinary trust asset is not an application for normal trust purposes unless the asset or an asset representing it is held by the trust immediately after the material time (see para 80.11).

Proportion of the chargeable assets deemed to be disposed of

80.25 As should be apparent from the above, if the transfer of value is small, only a small proportion of each chargeable asset is deemed to be disposed of. This is because the amount of value transferred is the numerator of the fraction referred to above unless it is more than the outstanding trustee borrowing.

This point means that on a series of small capital distributions only modest proportions of each chargeable asset are disposed of. But even if the ensuing gains are small there may still be formidable computation and compliance costs.

In one scenario, the proportion of the chargeable assets disposed of will be greater than might be expected. This will be the position where the value of any such asset is attributable to trustee borrowing, for then that part of the value is excluded in determining the denominator in the above fraction. Accordingly the proportion disposed of is correspondingly greater. Thus in an extreme case where the sole retained asset was borrowed by the trustees by way of outstanding trustee borrowing, the whole of that asset would be deemed to be disposed of, regardless of how small the transfer of value is.

Following a Sch 4B disposal, the base cost of the trust assets on future disposals is uplifted. If under Sch 4B only a proportion of each asset is disposed of, the asset has a blended base cost going forward (*Tax Bulletin* 66, para B10).

Exclusion of trustee borrowing on future transfers

80.26 Once trustee borrowing has been taken into account in relation to one transfer of value, it ceases to be outstanding for the future (Sch 4B para 5(2)(b)(ii)). The amount which falls out of account is the amount of the value transferred or, if less, the total borrowing then outstanding (Sch 4B para 5(3)).

SECTION 86 CASES: THE CHARGE TO TAX

80.27 The effect of the deemed disposal if the trust is within s 86 is that the net gain or loss is brought into account in determining whether for the year as a whole the trust has net gains. If it has such net gains, they are attributed to the settlor. At first sight s 85A(3) and (4) appear to prohibit the cross allowance of:

- Ordinary trust capital losses against Sch 4B gains, and
- Sch 4B losses against ordinary trust gains.

But that is not the case. These sub-sections only prevent this cross allowance of losses in the computation of a Sch 4B gain, or a section 2(2) amount for s 87 purposes. They do not prevent the cross allowance of losses under the normal rules of s 2(2) that s 86(1)(e) uses to arrive at the net gain the settlor is chargeable on.

Where s 86 does not apply, the gain goes into the Sch 4C pool and may be attributed to capital payments received by resident beneficiaries. Sch 4C applies in place of the normal capital payment rules in TCGA 1992, s 87 and is discussed in CHAPTER 81.

Offshore funds

80.28 Should the trust hold material interests in non-qualifying funds, those interests are subject to the deemed disposal, for a disposal takes place under the offshore fund legislation when it takes place for CGT purposes (TA 1988, s 757(2); see para **95.13**).

The effect of the deemed disposal is to create a Sch 4C pool of offshore income gains, and the better view is that this pool includes any offshore income gains realised on the deemed disposal itself (see para **82.10**). Even if s 86 is otherwise applicable to the trust, Sch 4B offshore income gains are not taxed on the settlor under that section, as it does not apply to offshore income gains (see para **95.27**).

Should the Sch 4B disposal result in an interest in a non-qualifying fund being disposed of at a loss, the loss is not brought into account in charging offshore income gains (cf para **95.18**). It follows it is available for offsetting ordinary gains on the Sch 4B disposal brought into account under s 86 or Sch 4C.

SETTLEMENTS PREVIOUSLY NON-UK RESIDENT

80.29 Sch 4B applies to one category of resident settlement, namely settlements which have previously been non-UK resident. This follows because Sch 4B applies to settlements within s 87 (para 1(1)) and being within s 87 is defined as including cases where chargeable gains would be treated as accruing under s 89(2) to any beneficiary in receipt of a capital payment (para 3(4)(b)). Section 89(2) is the provision which carries the s 87 pool forward when a settlement immigrates to the UK.

Sch 4B applies to a settlement which was previously non-UK resident only for so long as it has outstanding s 2(2) or OIG amounts, for if it has no such amounts capital payments cannot be treated as accruing to beneficiaries. But if Sch 4B does apply to such a settlement, there is an odd result, for the trustees, being UK resident, suffer tax on the Sch 4B deemed disposal. As explained in para **81.5**, the outstanding s 2(2) or OIG amounts of the trust go into or constitute a Sch 4C pool but the pool does not include any gain realised on the Sch 4B disposal itself.

PRACTICAL STEPS

80.30 Most practitioners would agree that, generally, a Sch 4B transfer is an outcome to be avoided. This is for two reasons:

(1)   If the settlement is within s 86 there is likely to be an immediate tax charge on the settlor.

(2)   In s 87 cases, Sch 4C pools of ordinary gains and offshore income gains are created. This is so whether or not the deemed disposal triggered by the Sch 4B transfer results in a gain or loss. These gains cannot be washed out by payments to non-residents, and can be allocated to beneficiaries of any relevant settlement (see CHAPTER 76 and para **82.10**).

However, there may be situations in which the creation of a Sch 4C pool is not obviously disadvantageous. For example, this may be the case where the trust has no beneficiaries who are non-UK resident and it is unlikely that in future there will be any, and nor is there any likelihood of any other relevant settlements being created. In such a case, the only potential future disadvantage lies in the possibility, which may be felt to be remote, that at some point in future there may be UK resident beneficiaries. If that risk transpired, the Sch 4C pool could be prejudicial to those beneficiaries, and/or could generate additional compliance/administrative costs for the trust.

A Sch 4B transfer can of course be avoided by ensuring that there is no trustee borrowing or, if there is, by clearing such borrowing prior to the occurrence of any transfer of value. On the whole, trustees ought to be able to recognise when they are incurring or have incurred trustee borrowing, but the following points should be noted:

(1)   It should always be remembered that 'upstream' loans from an underlying company, or loans from the settlor, any beneficiary or another trust are borrowing.

(2)   Borrowing to invest is borrowing and only ceases to be outstanding so long as the investment falls within the definition of ordinary trust asset and is retained.

(3)   Any strategy for managing investment portfolios which could involve margin dealing or other short-term loans may give rise to borrowing, at least where the portfolio is a trust level rather than at the level of an underlying company.

(4)   As described above, outstanding invoices are unlikely to be borrowing, but the position of old invoices needs to be watched.

As noted above, borrowing by an underlying holding company does not count as trustee borrowing. Accordingly, if trustees wish to borrow to fund the acquisition of investments, such may safely be done via an underlying company. However, money must not then be lent up to the trust. The company will have to make the investment, a course which may have drawbacks, as described in CHAPTER 6.

A perhaps obvious point is that regardless of what they think the borrowing position is, trustees should make a careful check before making any loan (even to a wholly owned company) or distribution. If in fact there is outstanding borrowing, such loan or distribution will automatically trigger a Sch 4B transfer.

For trustees who have triggered what appears to be a Sch 4B liability, two final thoughts may be offered. One is to consider whether the charge could be obviated by European law (see para **107.20**). The other is to consider whether the transaction in question is voidable either for mistake or under statutory provisions in the relevant offshore jurisdiction to enshrine what is known as the *Hastings-Bass* principle (see CHAPTER 36).

Chapter 81

SCHEDULE 4C POOLS

INTRODUCTION

81.1 Schedule 4C of TCGA 1992 comes into operation when as a result of the rules in TCGA 1992, Sch 4B non-resident trustees make a transfer of value linked with trustee borrowing (see CHAPTER 80). This may be referred to as the Sch 4B transfer, and any gains then realised as Sch 4B gains.

The function of Sch 4C is to create a pool of gains, the Sch 4C pool, which comprises both gains triggered on the Sch 4B transfer and also any s 2(2) amounts in the settlement at the end of the tax year of the Sch 4B transfer. Sch 4C then allocates this pool to UK resident beneficiaries in receipt of capital payments.

HISTORY

81.2 Sch 4C was first enacted when the rules regarding trustee borrowing were introduced in 2000. The initial enactment of those rules introduced TCGA 1992, s 90(5)(a) in its original form, which inadvertently provided a mechanism, the new style flip-flop scheme, for avoiding the charge under TCGA 1992, s 87. Section 90(5)(a) provided that on a transfer between settlements, gains in the s 87 pool of the transferor settlement did not pass into the transferee settlement in accordance with TCGA 1992, s 90 to the extent that the transfer was linked with trustee borrowing. Accordingly, the incurring of a large borrowing in the transferor settlement prior to the transfer enabled s 87 gains to be left behind.

Potentially this rendered distributions from the transferee settlement free of tax under s 87. Indeed, in *Bowring v HMRC* [2015] UKUT 550 (TCC), the Upper Tribunal confirmed the effectiveness of this scheme, at least in that particular case.

In 2003 the government saw fit to block the above scheme. It did so not by admitting that the 2000 legislation was flawed (as of course it was), but by radical amendment to Sch 4C. This amendment not merely blocked the scheme but introduced other significant changes as well. The basic concept is that the Sch 4C pool of gains is a floating pool which can be allocated to any UK resident beneficiary who receives a capital payment either from the settlement which effected the Sch 4B transfer or from any other settlement which has directly or indirectly received funds from it. The commencement date of Sch 4C was 21 March 2000, but transitional provisions limited its impact as respects events prior to 9 April 2003.

In 2008, the recasting of the remittance basis led to further changes to Sch 4C. In the case of trusts which pre-dated these changes, there is scope for two different regimes to co-exist, as such trusts may have Sch 4C pools created before 6 April 2008, and also may have post-5 April 2008, Sch 4C pools. Pre-6 April 2008, Sch 4C pools continue to be governed by the 2003 rules, subject to minor modifications. But Sch 4C pools which have arisen since 6 April 2008 are subject to newer provisions enacted by FA 2008. Save as respects non-UK domiciliaries, the newer provisions mainly follow what was there before, but the language and concepts have been simplified and are thus clearer.

The present chapter primarily focuses on Sch 4C as it exists following FA 2008, ie Sch 4C as it applies to Sch 4C pools arising in 2008–09 and later years. But in paras **81.28** to **81.31**, the salient points applicable to Sch 4C pools existing as at 5 April 2008 are summarised.

WHEN IS A SCH 4C POOL CREATED?

81.3 A Sch 4C pool comes into existence whenever the trustees of a settlement make a Sch 4B transfer (Sch 4C para 1(1)). A point to emphasise is that the Sch 4C pool is created even if no gain results from the transfer or if any such gain is attributed to the settlor on an arising basis under TCGA 1992, s 86 (Sch 4C para 1(5)). Sometimes the transfer of value may be very small, as on a modest capital distribution, and the ensuing Sch 4B gain will be modest or non-existent. But all such cases have the draconian result of bringing a Sch 4C pool into existence.

WHAT GAINS ARE IN THE SCH 4C POOL?

81.4 The contents of the Sch 4C pool are defined by reference to TCGA 1992, s 87 and subsequent sections (as to which see CHAPTER 77). The core concept under s 87 is imported into Sch 4C, as the Sch 4C pool comprises all outstanding s 2(2) amounts of the settlement making the Sch 4B transfer as at the end of the tax year of the transfer.

The outstanding s 2(2) amount of any given year is the s 2(2) amount of that year less any capital payment which has been matched with it under s 87A rules in any year up to and including the year of the transfer (Sch 4C para 1A). But one category of capital payment is disregarded and thus added back into the s 2(2) amounts. This category comprises any capital payment which is made in the same tax year as the Sch 4B transfer and is made to a non-resident beneficiary (Sch 4C para 1A(3)).

The s 2(2) amount of that tax year may also be increased. This happens if the Sch 4B transfer itself results in a net gain (Sch 4C para 1(3A)). This net gain is included in the s 2(2) amount if it is not taxed as the settlor's under TCGA

1992, s 86 (see Sch 4C paras 3 and 6 and para 80.27). It may also be reduced by some brought forward or current year losses.

Brought forward or current year losses on other Sch 4B transfers can only be offset against Sch 4B gains (s 85A(3)). Any unused Sch 4B loss can be carried forward to set against future Sch 4B gains only (Sch 4C para 7(3)).

Whether brought forward or current year ordinary trust capital losses can be set against Sch 4B gains depends on the interpretation of s 85A(4). At first sight it appears to disallow this. But it can also be read as a provision which only prevents the allowance of ordinary trust losses twice – once against ordinary trust gains and once against Sch 4B gains. This latter interpretation would allow ordinary trust losses to be set against Sch 4B gains via the 'chargeable amount' calculated under Sch 4C para 4(2). This latter interpretation is also consistent with the treatment of Sch 4B gains in a s 86 case (see para 80.27).

Should the trustees make another Sch 4B transfer in the same tax year as the original one, any ensuing Sch 4B gain is added to the pool, reduced by any applicable Sch 4B loss (Sch 4C para 1(3A)(b)). The same applies to further Sch 4B transfers in subsequent tax years if the Sch 4C pool is then still outstanding – in other words if part at least has not been allocated to beneficiaries (para 7B(3)). If all the gains in the original pool have been so allocated before the beginning of the tax year in which the further transfer occurs, the latter causes a new Sch 4C pool to come into existence in that year.

An important point to note is that the only Sch 4B gains which go into the pool are those realised by the settlement that made the original Sch 4B transfer. Gains accruing on transfers made by other relevant settlements (para **81.13** below) are not so included.

Gains realised in a subsequent tax year by the settlement which made the Sch 4B transfer are not included in the Sch 4C pool. They therefore are dealt with under ordinary s 87 rules and thus constitute s 2(2) amounts under s 87. However should the settlement make a subsequent Sch 4B transfer these s 2(2) amounts are sucked into Sch 4C, into the original pool if it then still exists and otherwise into a new pool (Sch 4C para 7B(3)).

Settlements which have become UK resident

81.5 As explained in para 80.29 a resident settlement which was previously non-resident can suffer a deemed disposal under Sch 4B. This is the position if in the year of the Sch 4B transfer it has unmatched s 2(2) amounts brought forward from its non-resident period (Sch 4C para 3(4)(b)). In such a case those s 2(2) amounts move across into a Sch 4C pool.

However, it appears that any gain triggered by the Sch 4B disposal does not pass into a Sch 4C pool, as what goes into the pool is the Sch 4B gains as defined in Sch 4C para 3. That definition only includes Sch 4B gains realised while the trustees are non-resident or dual resident. That the Sch 4B gains of a resident trust stay out of the Sch 4C pool is not surprising. Since the trustees are resident, such gains are taxed on the trustees on an arising basis when they accrue (see para 80.29).

HOW ARE SCH 4C GAINS ATTRIBUTED?

81.6 Chargeable gains in a Sch 4C pool are treated as accruing to a beneficiary if two conditions are met (para 8 (1)):

(1)   the trustees make a capital payment to the beneficiary; and
(2)   section 2(2) amounts in the Sch 4C pool are matched with the payment.

As with s 87, gains can also be treated as accruing to an individual who is not a beneficiary of the trust. This follows because the rule deeming a non-beneficiary to be a beneficiary applies to Sch 4C (TCGA 1992, s 97(8)).

Capital payment

81.7 The term 'capital payment' bears the same meaning under Sch 4C as it does for the purposes of s 87 (TCGA 1992, s 97(1); see CHAPTER 78. The rules in TCGA 1992, s 96 treating payments to non-resident close companies as payments to participators are inter alia included (s 96(2)).

However, two categories of capital payment are disregarded for the purposes of Sch 4C:

(1)   Capital payments made before the beginning of the tax year preceding that in which the Sch 4B transfer is made (Sch 4C para 9(2)).
(2)   Capital payments made to a beneficiary who is not resident in the UK. (See Sch 4C paras 1A(3) and 8(3)(b), which have the combined effect that a capital payment is disregarded for Sch 4C purposes if it is made to a beneficiary who is not 'chargeable to tax'.)

The second of these exclusions contrasts with s 87 and means that, unlike s 2(2) amounts in a s 87 pool, s 2(2) amounts in a Sch 4C pool cannot be washed out by distributions to non-residents.

In a case in which there is a mismatch between the tax year of the capital payment and the matching of Sch 4C gains (eg because the capital payment is 'unmatched' in the tax year of receipt, and Sch 4C gains arise in the following tax year), the legislation is ambiguous about whether the residence status of the beneficiary is tested in the tax year of the payment or the tax year of matching. Paragraph 8(3)(b) refers to 'a beneficiary who is chargeable to tax for that year'; this can be read as referring back to the tax year to which s 87A applies (as mentioned at the beginning of para 8(3)), ie the tax year of matching. However, 'chargeable to tax for that year' in para 8(3)(b) can also be read as meaning resident in the tax year of the payment. It is suggested that the former reading is probably correct, as it is more consistent with the testing of the status of beneficiaries who receive capital payments that may qualify for the remittance basis (see para **79.3**).

The legislation excludes two other categories of capital payment, but both these exclusions are largely otiose. The first concerns payments made if and at such time the trust was UK resident: such payments are excluded unless made in contemplation of both the Sch 4B transfer and the trust becoming non-resident (para 9(3)). This is largely otiose because a capital payment is in any event disregarded if made before the tax year preceding that in which the Sch 4B transfer is made.

The second exclusion (para 9(4)) is that payments to non-resident companies are disregarded (save insofar as attributed to a beneficiary under TCGA 1992, s 96). This is also largely otiose as Sch 4C disregards all payments to non-residents: it comes into point if the company was non-resident at the time of payment and is resident in the year of matching.

Matching

81.8 The rules in TCGA 1992, s 87A apply to determine which s 2(2) amounts in a Sch 4C pool are matched with the capital payment (Sch 4C para 8(3)). Matching within the Sch 4C pool is thus conducted on a 'last in, first out' basis: ie the s 2(2) amount of the year of the Sch 4B transfer is matched before any prior year s 2(2) amount. But inherent in the Sch 4C system is an important exception to the 'last in, first out' principle. This is that all s 2(2) amounts in a Sch 4C pool must be matched before any within s 87 (para 8(4)). As by definition the s 87 s 2(2) amounts will post-date the tax year of the Sch 4B transfer (see para **81.4**), the effect is that those s 2(2) amounts are postponed to the earlier amounts in the Sch 4C pool.

An exception to the priority of the Sch 4C pool applies in the event that the settlement has OIG amounts. These are matched in priority to the s 2(2) amounts in the Sch 4C pool, whether or not in a Sch 4C OIG pool (Sch 4C para 8(5)).

As a general rule, matching with the Sch 4C pool occurs when the capital payment is made. This is because Sch 4C pools cannot, save where there is a later Sch 4B transfer, include s 2(2) amounts for tax years subsequent to that of the Sch 4B transfer. But there is one exception, namely where the capital payment is made in the tax year prior to the Sch 4B transfer and is not in that tax year matched under s 87 with current or prior year s 2(2) amounts. On that scenario it is carried forward and matched against the Sch 4B gain and other gains in the s 2(2) amount of that year.

Amount attributed

81.9 The normal rule is that the amount of Sch 4C gains attributed to the recipient beneficiary equals the amount of the payment (para 8(2)). But if the payment exceeds the pool, or it and other payments in the tax year exceed the pool, the beneficiary's gain equals the pool or, in the case of multiple payments, the part of the pool attributed to the beneficiary in question (para 8(2); s 87A(2) step 3). The balance of the payment is then available for matching with s 87 gains.

Payment to non-residents

81.10 As indicated above, a capital payment is disregarded under Sch 4C if made to a non-resident. However, it is not disregarded for the purposes of s 87, and so if there are s 87 and s 2(2) amounts which have arisen since the creation of the Sch 4C pool, these are matched with the payment to the non-resident. They are so matched despite the continuing existence of the Sch 4C pool.

Temporary non-residence

81.11 Schedule 4C, para 12A addresses the position in the event that a formerly UK resident beneficiary receives a capital payment from a settlement while he is non-UK resident, and he subsequently becomes UK resident again, in circumstances such that the temporary non-residence rule in s 10A is engaged (see para **41.40**). In the year of return, there may be a deemed capital payment for the purposes of Sch 4C only. The quantum of the deemed capital payment is equal to the amount of the capital payment that was received while non-UK resident, less any amount of such payment which has had (non-Sch 4C) gains matched to it under s 87 (para 12A(2, 3)). The effect is to allow the matching of Sch 4C gains to the capital payment received while non-UK resident, insofar as it has not been taxed (in the year of return) by reference to ordinary gains of the settlement.

Payment to charity

81.12 There appears no reason why a payment to a UK resident charity should not be matched with Sch 4C gains, despite the fact a charity is not chargeable to tax. This result follows because the exclusion from Sch 4C is defined only in terms of residence status (para 1A(3)). The issues raised by capital payments to charities are discussed further in para **78.10**.

RELEVANT SETTLEMENTS

81.13 A fundamental distinction between Sch 4C and s 87 is that under Sch 4C, capital payments can be taken into account, and can therefore cause Sch 4C gains to be matched if made by a settlement other than that containing the Sch 4C pool. With s 87, matching is only possible if the payment is made by the same settlement as contains the s 2(2) amounts. A settlement can for these purposes be taken into account under Sch 4C if it is what is termed a relevant settlement. There are three categories of relevant settlement.

Transferee settlement

81.14 The first and most obvious category of relevant settlement is in point if the Sch 4B transfer was to another settlement (as distinct to a beneficiary outright). In such a case the transferee settlement is a relevant settlement (para 8A(2)). As indicated above (para **80.15**) a Sch 4B transfer can either be a loan or a transfer for no consideration or at less than market value.

Other transfers

81.15 The second category of relevant settlement arises if after the Sch 4B transfer the which made such transfer settlement either makes a further Sch 4B transfer to a different trust or makes a s 90 transfer to another trust. In such a case, the transferee becomes a relevant settlement on the making of a transfer (para 8A(3)).

As discussed above (para 77.29), TCGA 1992, s 90 applies on any transfer between settlements which is gratuitous or at less than market value. It follows that such a transfer makes the transferee settlement a relevant settlement if the transferor settlement has a Sch 4C pool. The better view is that s 90 does not catch loans between trusts (para 77.31) and if so a loan between the trusts only makes the borrower a relevant settlement should the loan be itself a further Sch 4B transfer – in other words if at that time the transferor settlement still has outstanding trustee borrowing.

A particularly menacing aspect to the relevant settlement concept is that it embraces a transferee settlement not merely if the transferor settlement is the settlement which itself has the Sch 4C pool, but also if it is any other settlement which has become a relevant settlement by reason of an earlier Sch 4B or s 90 transfer. There seems no reason why the chain of relevant settlements cannot be extended indefinitely. The whole apparatus does however come to an end once the Sch 4C pool is exhausted, for then there is nothing further for Sch 4C to bite on.

A further menacing feature is that a settlement becomes a relevant settlement no matter how small the Sch 4B or s 90 transfer. Given that a transfer for consideration comes within these provisions if the consideration is less than market value, the risk of trust-to-trust transactions creating relevant settlements is significant.

Further Sch 4B transfer

81.16 The final category of relevant settlement is in point should a settlement which is already a relevant settlement in relation to one Sch 4C pool itself make a Sch 4B transfer. In such a case, that Sch 4B transfer gives rise to a Sch 4C pool in relation to the relevant settlement in its own right. Under para 8A(4) of Sch 4C, the relevant settlements in relation to that second Sch 4C pool include the transferor and all other relevant settlements of the original Sch 4C pool. The logic behind this is difficult to discern.

Residence status

81.17 A settlement can become a relevant settlement even if it is UK resident. The preconditions for becoming a relevant settlement are the same, regardless of residence status.

RELEVANT SETTLEMENTS: SOME IMPLICATIONS

81.18 The breadth of the definition of relevant settlements has important practical implications.

Capital payments from more than one settlement

81.19 The relevant settlement concept means that in matching Sch 4C pools, capital payments from more than one settlement may well have to be looked at. Should there be capital payments from more than one relevant settlement in the same tax year, the s 2(2) amounts in the Sch 4C pool are shared pro rata (s 87A(2) step 3; Sch 4C para 8(3)(c)).

More than one Sch 4C pool

81.20 The breadth of the definition of relevant settlement, and particularly the last rule (para **81.16**), means that a capital payment may be potentially matchable against the Sch 4C pool of more than one settlement. The legislation gives no guidance as to how the capital payment is to be allocated between the pools, for the matching rules s 87A are predicated on there just being s 2(2) amounts of a single settlement. It is a reasonable inference that as between years, a 'last in, first out' rule should apply across all the pools. The logical approach within years where the capital payment is less than the combined s 2(2) amounts in the pools would be pro rata allocation. But this is not stated in the legislation.

Earlier capital payments

81.21 When a settlement becomes a relevant settlement it is likely to have either brought forward s 2(2) amounts or brought forward capital payments. Brought forward s 2(2) amounts do not raise issues of difficulty: the result of the settlement becoming a relevant settlement is that its future capital payments are matched against the Sch 4C pool of the original Sch 4B settlement in priority to its own s 2(2) amounts.

But should the new relevant settlement have brought forward capital payments, the issue which arises is whether these can be set against s 2(2) amounts in the Sch 4B settlement's Sch 4C pool. Here one point which is clear is that brought forward capital payments are definitely not available for matching if made before the start of the tax year preceding that of the Sch 4B transfer. This is because that is the general start date for capital payments taken into account (para **81.7** above).

With that established, two situations have to be distinguished. The first is where the settlement becomes a relevant settlement in the year of the Sch 4B transfer, as it would if it is the transferee settlement under the Sch 4B transfer. Here there seems no reason why the s 2(2) amount of that year should not be set against capital payments of any settlement which in that year becomes a relevant settlement, whether those payments are made in the same year as the Sch 4B transfer or the preceding year.

The second situation arises if the settlement only becomes a relevant settlement in a tax year after that of the Sch 4B transfer. In that situation, the Sch 4C pool has no current year s 2(2) amount and, absent a further Sch 4B transfer, will never have a current year s 2(2) amount in future years. This scenario does not pose any conceptual difficulty if the relevant settlement makes a capital payment in or after the year in which it becomes a relevant settlement, for then that capital payment is matched in the same way as capital payments from the Sch 4B settlement itself. But what if there is no capital payment in a given year, so that in that year there is neither a current-year s 2(2) amount nor a current-year capital payment? Does s 87A work in that situation to match the past capital payments of the relevant settlements with the past s 2(2) amounts in the Sch 4C pool? Although s 87A is clearly not designed with this situation in mind, it does appear to allow such matching. In particular there seems to be no reason why both limbs in step 5 in s 87A(2) should not operate simultaneously.

Practical ramifications

81.22 Assuming this last point is right, the potentially unfortunate results may be illustrated by the following example. A beneficiary of one settlement, the C Settlement, in good faith receives a capital payment which is tax-free as there are no s 2(2) amounts in that settlement. The same year another settlement, the A Settlement, makes a Sch 4B transfer and a Sch 4C pool is created. A few years later it makes a transfer to another settlement, the B Settlement, and a few years after that the B Settlement makes a transfer to the C Settlement. At this time the C Settlement still has no s 2(2) amounts and the A Settlement's Sch 4C pool still exists. Accordingly, under the rules described above, the gains in the Sch 4C pool are allocated to the beneficiary of the C Settlement and he is taxable. However neither he nor the trustees of the A Settlement know this, and shortly afterwards the A Settlement makes a capital distribution to one of its beneficiaries. The Sch 4C gains are, in the minds of the beneficiary and the trustees of the A Settlement, allocated to that payment and returns made accordingly.

The result of the above sequence of events is that tax is charged on the wrong person. It is for conjecture whether, if that person later discovers the true position, he could make an overpayment relief claim, and whether, assuming that claim was upheld, HMRC could make a discovery assessment on the beneficiary of the C Settlement, given that he had at all times acted in good faith.

Another point to emphasise is that the rules apply even if the capital payment is made from a UK resident settlement which has never been non-resident. The only requirement is that it becomes a relevant settlement. As described above, the payment may be ignored if made earlier than the tax year before the Sch 4B transfer but not, it should be noted, if made between then and the UK settlement becoming a relevant settlement.

THE CHARGE TO TAX

81.23 As with TCGA 1992, s 87, the gain accruing to a beneficiary as a result of matching is charged as his personal gain. The tax year in which such gain accrues is the tax year of matching.

81.23 *Schedule 4C pools*

Normally this is the year in which the capital payment is made. However, this is not so in two scenarios. One is if a capital payment from the year prior to the Sch 4B transfer is brought forward (see para **81.7**). The other is if a capital payment of a relevant settlement is brought forward from a year before it became a relevant settlement (para **81.21**).

Rate of tax

81.24 The rules governing the rate of tax are the same as under s 87 (for which see para **77.40**). The applicable rules include those dealing with gains accruing in 2010–11 (F(No 2)A 2010, Sch 1, para 22(1)(C)).

Supplemental tax

81.25 Supplemental tax applies to Sch 4C gains in the same way as to s 87 gains (Sch 4C para 13; see paras **77.48** to **77.51**). There is, however, one difference, namely that one year's supplemental tax is levied if the capital payment is just one year after the matched s 2(2) amount. In contrast to s 87 (para **77.50**), supplemental tax is not precluded in such cases.

As indicated above (para **81.21**), in some instances Sch 4C gains can accrue in a tax year subsequent to both the capital payment and the s 2(2) amount. In such cases, supplemental tax runs only in respect of the years (if any) by which the s 2(2) amount precedes the capital payment (para 13(4)(b)). The further deferment resulting from the delay in matching is not reflected in supplemental tax.

Losses

81.26 In contrast to s 87, Sch 4C gains can be offset against personal losses. The reason for this is that the provision restricting loss relief is in its terms confined to TCGA 1992, ss 87 and 89 (ibid, s 2(4)). The difference in treatment is, of course, entirely illogical.

Non-UK domiciliaries

81.27 Should the recipient beneficiary be a remittance basis user, the same remittance rules apply as apply to s 87 (Sch 4C para 8AA). In other words, the issue is whether the matched capital payment is or has been remitted (see further paras **79.2** to **79.7**). The s 87 transitional reliefs for non-UK domiciliaries also apply to Sch 4C (FA 2008, Sch 7 paras 126(7)(a) and 150; see further CHAPTER 79).

SCH 4C POOLS AS AT 5 APRIL 2008

81.28 As indicated at the beginning of this chapter, Sch 4C pools in existence on 5 April 2008 remain subject to Sch 4C in the form resulting from the

2003 amendments (FA 2008, Sch 7 para 152). But no such Sch 4C pool can be increased by a Sch 4B transfer in 2008–09 or a later tax year: any such transfer triggers the creation of a new Sch 4C pool governed by the law as amended in 2008 (Sch 7 para 152). The concept of relevant settlement is common to both old and new Sch 4C pools, so a capital payment from any relevant settlement engages old Sch 4C.

Non-UK domiciliaries

81.29 Capital payments to non-UK domiciliaries as well as non-residents are disregarded under old Sch 4C. By this means, old Sch 4C can never result in a tax charge on a non-UK domiciliary and this is so even if the individual is not a remittance basis user. However, in reality the exclusion of non-UK domiciliaries is more likely to increase rather than diminish the overall tax burden, as it precludes washing out of Sch 4C pools by capital payments to them.

Priorities

81.30 A capital payment in 2008–09 or a subsequent tax year is matched to s 2(2) amounts in any available new Sch 4C pool before being set against gains in any old Sch 4C pool (FA 2008, Sch 7 para 155(a)). Where the capital payment is to a resident domiciliary, gains in any available old Sch 4C pool must be exhausted before it is matched with any s 2(2) amount under s 87 (FA 2008, Sch 7 para 155(b)).

Once a capital payment has been matched with an old Sch 4C pool, it is no longer available to be matched in the future under new Sch 4C or s 87 (FA 2008, Sch 7 para 154).

Supplemental tax

81.31 Supplemental tax applies to chargeable gains treated as accruing under old Sch 4C. However in contrast to new Sch 4C and s 87, a 'first in, first out' rule applies to determine which gains are matched with the capital payment for the purposes of computing supplemental tax. This was the original rule under Sch 4C, and, in relation to Sch 4C pools as at 5 April 2008, has not been altered.

Commencement

81.32 Although old Sch 4C resulted from the 2003 amendments, the basic rule was that it applied in any case where the Sch 4B transfer was made on or after the original introduction date of Sch 4B, namely 21 March 2000 (FA 2003, s 163(4)(a)). Where the Sch 4B transfer was made before the 2003 amendments were announced (9 April 2003) the pool was treated as having come into existence on 8 April 2003.

81.32 *Schedule 4C pools*

When Sch 4C was first enacted in 2000, there was no inclusion in the Sch 4C pool of the s 87 pool and so where the Sch 4B transfer took place before 8 April 2003, the s 87 gains which went into the Sch 4C pool were those in the s 87 pool as at 8 April 2003 (FA 2003, s 163(4)(b)). It followed that the s 87 pool had to be computed as at that date under s 87 rules, including inter alia the rule that distributions to non-residents or non-domiciliaries reduced the pool.

The 2003 transitional provisions nullified new style flip-flop schemes (para 81.2) in any case where the transferee settlement did not distribute the funds transferred to it before 9 April 2003. In such case, the s 87 pool by definition remained with the transferor settlement, whence as at 8 April 2003 it passed into the Sch 4C pool. Nothing in the transitional rules prevented gains in this pool being allocated to distributions after 9 April 2003 from the transferee settlement.

Chapter 82

TRUST OFFSHORE INCOME GAINS

INTRODUCTION

82.1 Offshore income gains, or OIGs, are an important tax issue for offshore trusts with UK resident settlors and/or beneficiaries. This is because interests in entities which for UK tax purposes are non-reporting offshore funds form a significant if not dominant part of the portfolios of many trusts.

The general UK tax code applicable to non-reporting funds is explained in CHAPTER 95. This chapter focuses on one particular feature of the code, namely the rules applicable to OIGs realised by non-resident trusts or by non-resident companies in which non-resident trusts are participators.

The relevant rules are contained in regulations 20 and 21 of The Offshore Funds (Tax) Regulations 2009 (SI 2009/3001). These regulations took effect on 1 December 2009 but regulations 20 and 21 to a large extent replicate the previous law, TA 1988, ss 762 and 762ZA. That law was itself a mixture of provisions originally enacted when the offshore fund legislation was first introduced in 1984 and amendments made in 2008 when the tax regime for non-domiciliaries was recast. References in this chapter to regulations are to the 2009 regulations.

As explained in para **95.16**, the general rule is that OIGs are treated as the income of the person to whom they accrue (Reg 18(1)). It might be thought in the light of this that the OIGs of settlor-interested non-resident trusts would be taxed as the income of the settlor under the settlement code (see CHAPTER 75) and that the income tax benefits code in ITA 2007, ss 731–735 would apply to other trusts (see CHAPTER 70). In reality this is not the position. The settlement code is disapplied in its entirety in relation to OIGs of non-resident trusts (Reg 20(1)) and the transfer of assets code, while applicable, occupies a secondary rather than a primary position.

THE PRIMARY RULE

82.2 The primary rule is that the CGT capital payments code in TCGA 1992, ss 87–97 is applied to the OIGs of non-resident trusts (Reg 20(2), (3)).

OIG amounts

82.3 The section 87 rules are applied by replacing references to s 2(2) amounts with references to OIG amounts (cf paras 77.3 to 77.14). The OIG amount for a tax year is the amount of the OIGs arising to the trustees in the year (Reg 20(2)).

The OIG amount of any given tax year is not reduced by losses. This is because of the general rule that losses on non-reporting funds are not deductible from OIGs but are relieved as capital losses against ordinary capital gains (Reg 42; see para **95.18**). Accordingly such losses go to reduce s 2(2) amounts rather than OIG amounts.

OIG amounts are not reduced by attribution to the settlor under TCGA 1992, s 86. This is because TCGA 1992, s 86 does not apply to OIGs. OIGs can be attributed to the settlor under the transfer of assets code by virtue of the secondary rule described below (para **82.12**) but in this event the overlap is governed by the rules described later in this chapter.

Transitional provisions in FA 2008 require OIG amounts of 2007–08 and prior years to be calculated in the same way as s 2(2) amounts of those years (FA 2008, Sch 7 para 99). In other words, the OIG amount of each year in which the settlement existed is calculated. Amounts treated in 2007–08 or prior years as OIGs accruing to beneficiaries under the law as was then in force are deducted from the OIG amounts in chronological order (FIFO).

Matching

82.4 TCGA 1992, s 87A operates to match OIG amounts with capital payments in the same way as described in paras **77.20** to **77.23** in relation to s 2(2) amounts (LIFO). OIG amounts are thus matched to capital payments regardless of the residence and domicile status of the recipient. The rules in TCGA 1992, ss 87C and 96 as to capital payments to companies are also in point (as to which see paras **78.16** to **78.19**).

Should a settlement have both OIG amounts and s 2(2) amounts, OIG amounts are matched before s 2(2) amounts (Reg 20(4)). This is so whether the s 2(2) amounts are within s 87 or are within a separate pool governed by TCGA 1992, Sch 4C, due to the occurrence of a transfer of value at a time when the trust had outstanding trustee borrowing (see CHAPTERS 80 and 81). The priority of allocation is not just within years but across the board, with the result that the OIG amounts of the current and all past years have to be matched before any current year s 2(2) amount can be looked at. If in the absence of OIG amounts, a capital payment is matched with current year or past s 2(2) amounts, it drops out of account and so cannot be matched against future OIG amounts (TCGA 1992, s 87A(4)).

Transfers between settlements

82.5 The CGT rules in TCGA 1992, s 90 as to transfers between settlements apply (Reg 20(3)). As a result a transfer between settlements transfers to the transferee settlement all or a proportion of the transferor settlement's unallocated OIG amounts of the current and past years (see further para 77.29).

Migrating settlements

82.6 The CGT rules concerning settlements emigrating from or immigrating to the UK apply (Reg 20(3)). As a result capital payments from a resident settlement are matched with OIG amounts to the extent that the latter were unmatched in the last year of non-residence (see para 77.35).

Dual resident settlements

82.7 Matching applies also to OIGs realised in dual resident settlements (as to which see para 77.38). However in contrast to CGT, all OIGs are able to be matched to capital payments and not just treaty-protected OIGs. This follows because the rule restricting the s 2(2) amounts of dual resident settlements to the assumed chargeable amount is disapplied for the purposes of OIGs (Reg 20(3)(d)).

Companies

82.8 OIGs realised in underlying companies may be included in the trust's s 2(2) amount for the tax year concerned. This result follows because of the general rule, described in para 95.27, that TCGA 1992, s 13 applies to OIGs (Reg 24). However, as with s 13 generally, inclusion of corporate OIGs in the trust's s 2(2) amount is precluded if one of the defences to s 13 enacted in 2013 is in point. These defences are described in para 88.4 and 88.5. The one which is in practice material to OIGs is the motive defence. This precludes s 13, and thus apportionment of OIGs, where it can be shown that neither the acquisition, holding nor disposal of the interest in the offshore fund formed part of a scheme or arrangements, one of whose purposes was the avoidance of CGT or corporation tax.

The motive defence applies automatically from 6 April 2013 if the conditions for its application are otherwise met. It applies to disposals in 2012–13 unless an election is made to the contrary (FA 2013, s 62(7)). Any such election must be made before 5 April 2017 by the person to whom the OIG would otherwise be treated as accruing.

The charge to tax

82.9 If as a result of matching, OIGs are treated as arising to a beneficiary, he is treated as making the disposal (Reg 20(5)). The point of this rather odd provision is to engage the basic charging rule in Reg 18, which treats OIGs as income arising to the person who makes the disposal. The result is that Reg 18 applies, and treats OIGs resulting from the matching as miscellaneous income (Reg 18(3)).

The income tax so charged is not inflated by supplemental tax, because TCGA 1992, s 91 is not one of the provisions applied to OIGs (Reg 20(3)). But despite the lack of supplemental tax, OIGs taxed under s 87 are normally taxed at a higher rate than ordinary gains. This is because the maximum supplemental tax is 12%, giving a maximum CGT rate of 32%. This is less than the higher and top rates of income tax suffered by OIGs.

Should the beneficiary to whom OIGs are treated as accruing be non-resident, he is not taxed. This is because of the basic territorial limit to the OIG charge (Reg 22; see para **95.16**). But as with OIGs generally, OIGs are charged in the year of return if the beneficiary is non-resident for five or fewer years (Reg 23).

SCH 4C AND OIGS

82.10 A Sch 4B transfer can result in a Sch 4C pool of OIGs (Reg 20(3)). It has this effect if the settlement making the Sch 4B transfer has unmatched OIG amounts for the tax year of the transfer or any prior year. The pool comprises all the unmatched OIG amounts in question. As with s 2(2) amounts, a capital payment to a non-resident beneficiary in the year of the Sch 4B transfer does not reduce OIG amounts.

Reg 20 is contradictory as to whether the Sch 4C OIG pool includes OIGs realised as a result of the Sch 4B transfer itself. The specific Sch 4C rule (Sch 4C para 1(3A)) requiring gains realised on the transfer to be included in the pool is expressly disapplied in relation to OIGs (Reg 20(3)(d)). But equally the rule in TCGA 1992, s 85A(3) preventing gains realised on the transfer from being included in the s 2(2) amount of the year in question is not applied to OIGs. One is left to infer that the Sch 4B OIGs do pass into the OIG amount of the year of the transfer and so, by that back door, into the Sch 4C OIG pool. Were this not so, the Sch 4B OIGs would not be dealt with under either Sch 4C or s 87 rules at all, and the result would then be that they would be transfer of assets income under the secondary rule described below. This would be an eccentric result.

The Sch 4C OIG pool is matched with capital payments by relevant settlements in the same way as the Sch 4C pool of s 2(2) amounts (see paras **81.6** to **81.22**). As with s 2(2) amounts capital payments to non-residents are disregarded. OIGs in the Sch 4C OIG pool are matched before any available OIG amounts which are not in the Sch 4C pool (TCGA 1992, Sch 4C para 8(4) as applied by Reg 20(3)).

Sch 4C and OIGs in 2007–08 and earlier tax years

82.11 Prior to the amendment of the former TA 1988, s 762 made in 2008, the treatment of OIGs on a Sch 4B transfer was obscure. It was however reasonably plain that a Sch 4B transfer did trigger the realisation of OIGs, as a disposal triggering OIGs took place whenever there was a disposal for CGT purposes (TA 1988, s 757(2)).

It is also reasonably clear that a Sch 4B transfer prior to 6 April 2008 did not result in the creation of a Sch 4C pool of OIGs. This is because Sch 4C was not included in the provisions applied to OIGs (TA 1988, s 762(2); FA 2008, Sch

7, paras 101 and 102). The result is that OIGs realised in 2007–08 and prior remain in the OIG amounts dealt with under ordinary s 87 rules, as do OIGs realised on the Sch 4B transfer itself.

The conclusion, therefore, is that there are no pre-6 April 2008 OIG Sch 4C pools. But if there was a Sch 4B deemed disposal in 2007–08 or an earlier tax year, the OIG amount for the year of that deemed disposal is increased by any OIGs realised on the disposal. As now, the rule in TCGA 1992, s 85A(3) preventing Sch 4B amounts from being included in trust gains was not applied to OIGs (TA 1988, s 762(2) as originally enacted).

THE SECONDARY RULE

82.12 The secondary rule is that OIGs realised by a non-UK resident person are deemed to be income payable to that person for the purposes of the transfer of assets code. This rule, which is enacted by Reg 21, applies to all non-residents, and so embraces non-resident trusts and their underlying companies equally. Moreover it is quite separate from the CGT concepts applicable to the primary rule, and so is unaffected, where underlying companies are concerned, by the s 13 motive defence.

The result of the secondary rule is that OIGs are treated as the settlor's transfer of assets income if he is UK resident and either has power to enjoy the trust income or is within capital sum charge (see CHAPTER 69). Otherwise the OIGs are relevant income for the purposes of the non-transferor charge, resulting in notional s 732 income insofar as matched to a benefit received by a UK resident (see CHAPTER 70). But both the settlor and any non-transferor escape tax on the income attributed to them if the motive or EU defences described in CHAPTERS 73 and 74 are in point. In addition, remittance basis users enjoy a form of remittance basis described in CHAPTER 72.

INTERACTION OF THE TWO RULES

82.13 In the absence of provision to the contrary the primary and secondary rules would result in many OIGs being taxed twice. Indeed, strictly that was often the position before the rules were amended in 2008.

The current law avoids overlap as follows:

(1)　An OIG matched with a capital payment under the primary rule cannot be income under the secondary rule in and after the year of matching, provided that the recipient of the capital payment is UK resident in the year of matching. This is the effect of Reg 21(5).

(2)　Where Reg 21(5) is not in point, the OIG amount that may be matched to capital payments under s 87 is reduced by any amount of income treated as arising under the transfer of assets code. Such reduction in the OIG amount is made by Reg 21(6) and takes effect in and after the following tax year.

(3)　An OIG treated under TCGA 1992, s 13 as accruing to a UK resident cannot also be transfer of assets income (Reg 24(7)).

These complex provisions, and the difficult interaction of the primary and secondary rules, are best understood by considering separately the position of transferor and non-transferor trusts.

Transferor trusts

82.14 By transferor trust is meant a trust where the settlor is UK resident and either has power to enjoy the income of the trust, or is within the capital sum charge. In such a case, income of the trust and any underlying company is treated as the settlor's under the transfer of assets code insofar as it is not taxed as his under the settlement code. In practice the settlement code does not apply to OIGs arising to non-resident trusts, as it is disapplied in relation to such gains (Reg 20(1)).

The effect of the overlap rules is that the OIGs are treated as the transferor's income under the transfer of assets code unless two conditions are met:

(1)   The OIGs are matched under s 87, in the year in which they arise, with current year or brought forward capital payments; and

(2)   The recipient(s) of those payment(s) are resident in the UK.

As will be apparent from the above, where both these conditions are met, the primary rule treats the matched OIGs as income of the recipient of the capital payment(s). This treatment, and the preclusion of the secondary rule, applies both where the recipient is the settlor himself and where he is some other beneficiary. It is immaterial whether or not the recipient is UK domiciled or a remittance basis user, but he must be UK resident.

If the above conditions are not met, the way is open for the secondary rule, with the result that the OIGs then form part of the settlor's transfer of assets income and are removed from the trust's OIG amount. This is so even if the settlor is not in fact taxed, for example because the transfer of assets motive defence is in point, or the remittance basis is available.

It might be thought to be a matter of indifference whether the trust OIGs are taxed by reason of matching under s 87 or by reason of the transfer of assets code, as in both cases the result is income tax. But in reality there are two important points of distinction:

(1)   If the motive defence described in Chapter 73 is in point, securing transfer of assets treatment takes the OIGs out of charge. This result follows because:

    (a)   OIGs are removed from the OIG amount for s 87 purposes if they are treated as transfer of assets income; and

    (b)   the motive defence operates as an exemption from tax on income treated as arising under the transfer of assets code and not as a rule preventing the income from arising under the code (see ITA 2007, ss 721(1) and 720(7) and ss 728(1) and 727(5)).

(2)   Should the transferor be non-UK domiciled, securing s 87 treatment enables him to access the transitional reliefs described below (para 82.18).

Should an OIG treated as the transferor's income escape tax because the transferor is a remittance basis user, the issue arises of whether the OIG can count as relevant income in taxing non-transferors. This is the same issue as arises with actual income. As described in para **71.26** it is arguable that such income cannot be relevant income insofar as it has arisen since 6 April 2013. But HMRC have historically taken the contrary position, and, as described in para **71.26** this represents the correct construction of the form the legislation took before 6 April 2013.

The 2013 changes to s 13 mean that rather more OIGs than previously are now caught by the secondary rule rather than being dealt with under the s 87 matching rules. This is because corporate OIGs only come into the trust's OIG amount if unprotected by the s 13 motive defence referred to above. By being kept outside the OIG amount they are fully exposed to the rigours of Reg 21 and the transfer of assets code. This is because, as noted above, Reg 21 is not precluded in relation to corporate OIGs unless the OIG is treated under s 13 as accruing to a UK resident (Reg 24(7)).

Other trusts

82.15 As noted above, a trust is not a transferor trust unless the transferor is alive and UK resident and either has power to enjoy the income or is within the capital sum charge. Should a trust not satisfy these conditions, the transfer of assets code is only in point should a UK resident beneficiary receive a benefit within ITA 2007, ss 731–735. Here the interaction of the primary and secondary rules raises points of complexity and uncertainty.

As will be apparent from CHAPTERS 70 and 88, the term 'benefit' within ss 731–735 has much the same meaning as 'capital payment' for the purposes of s 87. It follows that if a UK resident beneficiary of a trust which is not a transferor trust receives a benefit or capital payment, any OIG amounts in the trust are matched under the primary rule, with the result that there is no scope for the secondary rule. It might be objected that the primary role cannot operate at all, on the grounds that a payment is not a capital payment if it is subject to income tax (see para **78.5**), and the secondary rule has the effect of subjecting it to income tax. But this point is disposed of by Reg 20(3)(e) which disapplies Reg 21 in relation to the definition of 'capital payment' in TCGA 1992, s 97.

Problems come with the exception to the exclusion of the secondary rule where the recipient of the benefit or capital payment is non-UK resident. Here the matching under s 87 removes the OIGs so matched from the trust OIG amounts, but the precondition for the disapplication of the secondary rule, namely accrual to a UK resident, is not met. It follows that the matched OIGs remain within the secondary rule and are thus relevant income.

This works well enough where the capital payment to the non-resident is in one tax year and any capital distributions or benefits to UK residents are in a following year. Here the effect of the capital payment to the non-resident is that the relevant income which is available to be allocated to the later distributions is increased by the OIGs matched to the non-resident under s 87. The exposure to income tax under ss 731–735 is thus increased.

Where difficulty arises is if there are current year or brought forward capital payments to both residents and non-residents. Here s 87 rules match the OIG amounts to both categories of beneficiary, pro rata if the OIG amounts are less than the total capital payments. The OIGs matched with the payments to non-residents remain relevant income and in logic ought to be dealt with under ss 731–735 by being allocated to any payments to UK residents that are not matched under the primary rule and otherwise carried forward as relevant income. Although regs 20 and 21 can on one view be read as not supporting this view, it clearly reflects the underlying purpose of the regulations.

A further anomaly may arise when a capital payment to a non-resident leaves the trust OIGs to be treated as available relevant income. The anomaly is that, read literally, Reg 21(6) requires a further reduction in the OIG amount if and when a s 731 benefit is conferred on a UK resident so that income is treated as arising under s 732. A possible answer to this is that Reg 21(6) should be confined to transferor cases.

Another point which is not immediately clear is whether the disapplication of the secondary rule, ie Reg 21(5), operates where a given OIG amount results from OIGs apportioned from an underlying company under TCGA 1992, s 13 (see para **95.27**). The point arises because Reg 21(5) is expressed as applying where OIGs are treated as accruing to a UK resident by virtue of Reg 20, whereas underlying company gains accrue as a result of Reg 20 combined with Reg 24 (which applies s 13). It may be doubted, however, whether there is anything in this point, for even if an OIG is included in the OIG amount by virtue of s 13, Reg 20 remains the reason why it results in OIGs arising to the beneficiary.

A point which is clear as respects underlying companies is that some OIGs will always be relevant income and can never form part of OIG amounts. As under the transferor charge, this is the position for OIGs protected by the s 13 motive defence. As these OIGs are not and cannot be treated as accruing to a UK resident under s 87 rules, potentially they are relevant income and thus allocated to benefits to UK residents under ss 731–735 before any matching of trust OIG amounts. This priority in allocation follows because a capital payment is not matched under s 87 if it is taxed as income (see further paras **78.4** and **78.5**).

NON-UK DOMICILIARIES

82.16 The reliefs available where the settlor or beneficiaries are non-UK domiciled differ, depending on whether the primary rule or the secondary rule is in point.

Primary rule: remittance basis

82.17 The remittance basis applicable to gains arising as a result of matching under s 87 or Sch 4C is that applicable to CGT, ie that under TCGA 1992, s 87B. This is explained in paras **79.2** to **79.7**. Taxability of the matched OIGs for the remittance basis user depends on whether the capital payment is remitted. Prior to 1 December 2009, s 762(3) did not incorporate s 87B but this defect was remedied by Reg 20(3).

Primary rule: transitional exemptions

82.18 OIGs attract the same transitional exemptions as ordinary capital gains (FA 2008, Sch 7 para 100). As with ordinary gains, these exemptions apply to non-UK domiciliaries generally and not just to remittance basis users. As explained in paras **79.16** to **79.18**, the effect of the exemptions is that OIGs treated as accruing under s 87 or Sch 4C are not taxed if either the OIG amount, or the capital payment, accrued or was made in 2007–08 or earlier.

In contrast to ordinary gains (see para **79.19**) no exception is made for capital payments made to non-UK domiciliaries between 12 March and 5 April 2008. As OIG amounts are allocated to capital payments before s 2(2) amounts, a capital payment made in 2008–09 or later is matched with OIG amounts of 2007–08 and prior before being matched with current year ordinary gains.

Should the trustees have made a 2008 rebasing election (para **79.11**), it applies as much to OIGs as to ordinary capital gains (FA 2008, Sch 7 paras 101 and 102). There is no separate right of election for ordinary gains and OIGs: the election or non-election is indivisible and covers both.

Secondary rule

82.19 Should the secondary rule be in point, none of the transitional reliefs described above apply and the remittance basis available is that applicable to the transfer of assets code, described in CHAPTER 72.

In transferor cases, the applicable remittance basis focuses on the OIG itself, the proceeds of the disposal generating it inevitably being a mixed fund. Remittance occurs if the OIG is brought to the UK by the transferor himself or by the trust or a related entity. The latter follows because the trust and related entities are relevant persons (see paras **54.6** to **54.15**) and is therefore not in point if the OIG was realised in 2007–08 or before.

In non-transferor cases, the matching rules in ITA 2007, s 735A have to be operated. As with relevant income generally these involve relating both the OIG and the benefit to the non-transferor's s 732 deemed income on the first in first out basis described in para **72.5**. Remittance occurs if either is remitted.

In general, non-UK domiciliaries are in a less favourable position under the secondary rule than under the primary rule. However, this is not the case where the motive defence applies. There are other situations, also, in which the secondary rule may be preferable. This includes the situation where the OIGs have not been remitted within the trust, and where it is possible to identify assets of the trust that do not derive from disposals that gave rise to OIGs (or from unremitted income) and such assets are distributed to the non-UK domiciled settlor, for expenditure in the UK. In that scenario, the secondary rule will be preferable to liability under the primary rule, if it is the case that the OIGs that would be matched under the rule do not qualify for the transitional exemption for pre-6 April 2008 gains.

Underlying companies

82.20 As explained above, OIGs realised in underlying companies are within the secondary rule and not the primary rule if the s 13 motive defence is in point. For non-domiciliaries that defence will thus create a less favourable outcome save in the cases described in the previous paragraph. For 2012–13, and only 2012–13, there is the right to elect out of the s 13 motive defence and this should be considered in appropriate cases. The election has to be made by 5 April 2017 (FA 2013, s 62(7)).

Section III

Inheritance tax anti-avoidance legislation

Chapter 83

RESERVATION OF BENEFIT RULES

INTRODUCTION

83.1 The gift with reservation legislation impacts on offshore tax planning in that it can leave an individual's assets exposed to IHT even after he has given them away to an offshore trust or other entity. For non-UK domiciliaries care is needed to ensure the legislation does not result in expensive and often avoidable IHT exposure as respects UK assets. For these reasons an understanding of the legislation is important to offshore tax planning.

The great difficulty with the rules is that their language is obscure and replicates nineteenth century legislation (*Ingram v IRC* [1999] STC 37, 41 per Lord Hoffmann). Until 5 April 2005, this obscurity caused less trouble than one might have expected. But since that date, the pre-owned asset rules described in CHAPTER 86 have meant that it is often as important for UK residents to be certain that facts come within the GWR rules as that they do not, and for that reason the many obscurities and quirks in the legislation have latterly assumed greater importance. Moreover, the proposed extension of IHT to indirect interests in UK residential property, discussed in CHAPTER 27, means that the GWR rules now have relevance in relation to arrangements for the ownership of UK homes of individuals who are non-UK resident and non-UK domiciled, who up to now have essentially been unaffected by this legislation.

This chapter briefly outlines the rules and the many exemptions. It then reviews in rather more detail their application to non-UK domiciliaries.

THE CHARGE TO TAX

83.2 The GWR rules are in issue if at any time in the relevant period, property is subject to a reservation. The relevant period ends on the individual's death and starts seven years before then (FA 1986, s 102(1)). It thus falls to be ascertained retrospectively.

The rules principally come into issue when an individual dies. If on an individual's death, property is subject to a reservation he is treated as beneficially entitled to that property immediately before his death (s 102(3)). It is thus included in his estate for IHT purposes (IHTA 1984, ss 4 and 5).

The rules also come into issue if during the relevant period – ie within seven years of death – the property ceases to be subject to a reservation. In this event the individual is treated as having made a disposition of that property by potentially exempt transfer (s 102(4)). That notional transfer is then brought into account on the individual's death in accordance with the general rules relating to such transfers (IHTA 1984, s 3A). Subject to the nil-rate band and other reliefs the rate of tax is thus 40% if death occurs in the first three years, 32% in year 4, 24% in year 5, 16% in year 6, and 8% in year 7 (IHTA 1984, s 7(4)).

WHEN IS PROPERTY SUBJECT TO A RESERVATION?

The gift

83.3 The first prerequisite for property to be treated as subject to a reservation is that the individual must have disposed of it by way of gift (s 102(1)). The term gift is not defined and sits uneasily with the transfer of value concept, by reference to which IHT is otherwise charged. HMRC consider that the term includes sales at an undervalue, the gift being the undervalue (IHT Manual IHTM14316). Gifts before 18 March 1986 are excluded (s 102(1)).

A loan is not a gift. This inter alia is indicated by the provisions discussed in para **83.9** deeming property lent by the settlor to be comprised in his original gift into settlement for the purposes of the GWR rules (Sch 20 para 5(4)). HMRC accept the correctness of this, but contend that if the loan is not commercial the interest forgone is a gift (IHT Manual IHTM14317). It is difficult, however, to see any basis in the legislation for construing a forbearance to charge interest as a gift. Such forbearance, it may be suggested, would only be a gift if the loan is fixed term and a nil or low rate of interest is agreed at the outset. But even then no property passes from the lender to the borrower, the gift being merely forbearance. If no property passes it is difficult to see what property in the donee's hands the GWR rules can fasten on.

The reservation

83.4 The second prerequisite is that one of two further conditions must be met:

(a)   the donee must not have assumed possession and enjoyment of the property, or

(b)   the property must not have been enjoyed to the entire exclusion, or virtually the entire exclusion, of the donor, and of any benefit to him, by contract or otherwise.

It has long been recognised that the second condition has two limbs. The first focuses on whether there has been any actual enjoyment of the gifted property by the donor, and the second on whether there has been any benefit to him. These two limbs are quite distinct, so, if there is actual enjoyment by the donor it is irrelevant whether or not it is beneficial to him (*Chick v Stamp Duties Comr of New South Wales* [1958] AC 435, [1958] 2 All ER 623, PC, as explained in *Buzzoni v HMRC* [2013] EWCA Civ 1684 paras 45–48).

966

, *Buzzoni v HMRC* [2013] EWCA Civ 1684 has clarified the meaning and scope of the second limb. In that case, the Court of Appeal stated that the first question is whether the alleged benefit to the donor is derived from the gifted property or from some other property. If the benefit is derived from other property the second limb is only engaged if it impacts on the donee's enjoyment of the gift (para 49, explaining *AG v Worrall* [1895] 1 QB 99). If the benefit is derived from the gifted property, prima facie the second limb is engaged. But this is not so if the benefit makes no difference or virtually no difference to the donee's enjoyment of the property, for the legislation itself focuses on the donee's enjoyment being exclusive (paras 50–55).

This last point is illustrated by the facts of *Buzzoni* itself. A head lessee of a flat in London had given an underlease of the flat to a trust from which he was excluded. The gift took place in 1997, but the underlease did not come into possession until 2007. In order to grant the underlease the consent of the head landlord has to be obtained and as a term of that consent the underlessee covenanted directly with the head landlord to perform all the tenant's covenants in the headlease. These covenants were then repeated as between the head tenant and the underlessee in the underlease and it was the covenants as therein expressed which HMRC argued were benefits bringing the second limb into play. The Court of Appeal accepted they were benefits, for having someone else discharge the covenants was not something the head tenant had before the underlease was granted. But in view of the covenants the underlessee trustees had already had to give to the head landlord it neither added to nor subtracted from their enjoyment of the underlease and so did not engage the second limb.

The second limb is subject to one statutory extension, in that a benefit which the donor obtains by virtue of any associated operations is deemed to be by contract or otherwise if the gift is one of the operations (FA 1986, Sch 20 para 6(1)(c)). To date there has been no case law on this provision and, as is discussed in para **83.10**, it may be of limited impact.

Typical cases where the gift with reservation rules apply are where the donor gives a house away and goes on living there, or where he gives a chattel away and continues to use it. A transfer to a joint account is a gift with reservation if there is no restriction on withdrawals by the account-holder making that transfer (*Sillars v Revenue and Customs Comrs* [2004] STC (SCD) 180; *Taylor v Revenue and Customs Comrs* [2008] STC (SCD) 1159).

Trusts

83.5 Property in trust is subject to a reservation if the settlor is a discretionary object. This is so whether the settlement is fully discretionary, or whether it is subject to an interest in possession with overriding powers over capital (*IRC v Eversden (exors of Greenstock, decd)* [2003] EWCA Civ 668, [2003] STC 822; *Lyon (personal representatives of Lyon, decd) v Revenue and Customs Comrs* [2007] STC (SCD) 675).

It is unclear whether trust property is subject to a reservation if the settlor is not a beneficiary but could be made so by the trustees or some other party in exercise of a power of addition. There is much to be said for the view that there is no reservation until he is added, as until then the trust property cannot be used to benefit him with the result that it is enjoyed to his exclusion. The contrary view would be that this takes an excessively literal view of powers of addition, it often being the intention at the outset that such a power will in due course be exercised to add the settlor. HMRC subscribe to this contrary view, stating that a GWR is only avoided if the settlement irrevocably excludes the settlor (IHTM 14393).

The position where the settlor is an initial life tenant is discussed in para **83.17**.

Real estate

83.6 Special rules apply in determining whether a gift of land is a gift with reservation (FA 1986, ss 102A–102C). They are not restricted to land in the UK.

The first rule is in s 102C and applies to gifts of an undivided share in land. Such a gift is a gift with reservation unless either:

(a)   the donor does not occupy the land; or
(b)   he occupies the land for full consideration; or
(c)   the donor and the donee both occupy the land and the donor does not receive collateral benefit.

The second rule is that any other gift of land is tested in the first instance against the general rules described above to determine if it is a gift with reservation (s 102C(6)). If it is not caught by those rules it is still a gift with reservation if it falls foul of s 102A (s 102C(7)).

Section 102A operates if the donor or his spouse is able to occupy all or part of the land or if either of them enjoys some right in relation to the land. Rights or entitlement are disregarded if only exercisable for full consideration. They are also disregarded if they cannot prevent enjoyment of the land to the exclusion, or virtually the exclusion, of the donor.

An interesting point about the first rule is that it does not specify the size of the undivided share given away. It can thus apply where the donor retains less than 50%, although in all such cases avoidance of collateral benefit is essential.

The special rules apply only if the gift of land took place after 9 March 1999. For that reason they were not material to *Buzzoni v HMRC* (supra).

Termination of an interest in possession

83.7 Until 22 March 2006, the termination of an interest in possession did not constitute a gift of the trust property by the life tenant, at least insofar as the termination was by act of the trustees rather than disposition by the life tenant. But now the termination is treated for the purposes of the GWR rules as a gift of the underlying settled property by the life tenant, with the result that the exercise is a gift with reservation if the terms of the settlement allow benefit to be conferred on the former life tenant (FA 1986, s 102ZA). This only applies if the interest terminated is a qualifying interest in possession (see CHAPTER 61). It does not apply if on the termination the life tenant becomes absolutely entitled to the property.

Exempt transfers

83.8 The GWR rules do not apply to certain kinds of exempt transfer (FA 1986, ss 102(5) and 102C(2)). The principal examples are gifts to charities and gifts to spouses. But as the disapplication of the GWR rules operates only where the transfer is exempt, the maximum value that can be transferred to a non-UK domiciled spouse where the transferor is UK domiciled or deemed domiciled without the GWR rules applying, is £325,000. But this is only in point where the non-UK domiciled transferee does not elect to be treated as UK domiciled.

Prior to 22 March 2006 the relief for gifts to spouses also applied to gifts into a trust if the spouse had an interest in possession. But if the gift in such a case was after 20 June 2003, any termination of the spouse's interest in possession causes the gift to be treated as made at the time of the termination (FA 1986, s 102(5A)).

TRACING

83.9 One of the quirks of the legislation, perhaps reflecting its antiquity, is that it presupposes that the item of property given away is the self-same item of property as is subject to the reservation. Thus in the paradigm case, a house is given away, and the donor goes on living there. If the donee has sold the property given to him and bought some other property, the latter is not prima facie capable of being subject to a reservation.

In fact, the GWR legislation does incorporate tracing rules. There are two sets of rules, contained in FA 1986, Sch 20; one set for gifts to persons other than trustees (para 2) and the other set for gifts to settlements (para 5). The provisions regarding gifts to persons other than trustees are subject to some quite bizarre limitations.

Gifts to individuals

83.10 On the face of it, the tracing rules for gifts to persons other than trustees (FA 1986, Sch 20, para 2) do cover the position where the property received by the donee has later been substituted for other property. The rules provide that s 102 shall apply as if the substituted property were the property that had been comprised in the original gift (para 2(1)). So in the case of a sale of the property that was originally given away, it would seem (at first sight) that one must trace into any property purchased using the proceeds of sale of the original property, to assess whether such replacement property is subject to a reservation.

However, it is generally accepted that these rules do not, in reality, have this result. This is for two reasons.

The first is that the tracing rules in para 2 are expressly disapplied where the gifted property is a sum of money in sterling or any other currency (para 2(2)(b)). The second is that the rules expressly state that the whole GWR legislation applies on a sale as if the proceeds were the property comprised in the original gift (para 2(1)). As such, they come within the rule that tracing is disapplied on cash gifts. The result is that it is unusual for tracing to apply in relation to a gift to an individual; one example of where it does being where the donee has received a non-cash asset from the donor (used by the donor) and he has subsequently disposed of that asset in consideration of another non-cash asset (likewise used by the donor).

Associated operations

83.11 The correctness of the above as a general proposition is accepted by HMRC (IHT Manual IHTM14372; Capital Taxes and Estate Planning Quarterly [1992] No 2, 26). However, HMRC consider that if cash is given away and then used by the donee to acquire other property which the donor uses, the GWR rules may be engaged if the acquisition can be considered an associated operation in relation to the gift. The example given in the IHT Manual suggests a restricted application, namely where a gift of cash is followed by the donee using the cash to purchase the donor's house, which the donor then continues to live in (IHTM14372). The manual states that 'This may be a GWR of the residence', and the example is prefaced by the comment that HMRC staff 'must watch out for a gift which initially seems to be of cash that may in reality be a GWR, by associated operations, of other property'.

This position seems to be based on a misunderstanding about the (very limited) scope of the associated operation rules. Although the definition of associated operations (IHTA 1984, s 268(1)) is very wide, the provision applying it (s 268(3)) substantially restricts its practical application, and the two provisions must be considered together. Under s 268(3), an associated operation essentially affects the timing of a transfer of value; it does not allow a re-characterisation of the transferred assets. Moreover, case law has established that the wide definition of associated operations must be subject to some implied limit, and that associated operations can only be taken into account where they are 'relevant': 'in order to be a relevant associated operation it must form part of the scheme reducing the value of the person's estate' (emphasis added) (*Reynaud and others v Inland Revenue Commissioners* [1999] STC (SCD) 185 para 17). If the transfer of value has already occurred when a step takes place, the step may fit the definition of an associated operation, but it is irrelevant to the transfer, and the associated operation provisions need not be considered (*Rysaffe Trustee Co (CI) Ltd v IRC* [2003] EWCA Civ 356, [2003] STC 536, 5 ITELR 706, para 23 per Mummery LJ). Earlier in the same case Park J warned against ignoring the limitations of s 268: 'It is not some sort of catch-all anti-avoidance provision which can be invoked to nullify the effectiveness of any scheme or structure which can be said to have involved more than one operation and which was intended to avoid or reduce inheritance tax' ([2002] STC 872, para 27).

If one construes the associated operations provisions correctly, in light of *Reynaud* and *Rysaffe*, it is clear that these provisions have no part to play in the example given at IHTM14372, and that the GWR rules have no application to the donor's occupation of the house.

Gifts to settlements

83.12 A different set of tracing rules applies where the gift is into settlement (FA 1986, Sch 20, para 5). Here the legislation *does* allow tracing from a cash gift, and through transactions which result in cash being substituted for the property previously held by the trustees. The property to which the rules are applied is the property comprised in settlement when the individual dies or his reservation ends (Sch 20 para 5(1)). But property which neither represents nor is derived from the gift is excluded. Should the settlor make a loan to the settlement, the property caught by the rules includes property derived from the loan. This rule applies whether or not the loan is commercial. But in HMRC's view any amount still outstanding of the loan is deducted for that is in the taxpayer's free estate in any event (IHTM14401).

If property is distributed from the settlement it is then treated as comprised in the gift (para 5(2)). The implication of this is that it is treated, in the form it is when distributed, as then gifted by the donor to the donee. Accordingly, it is thereafter subject to the tracing rules that apply to gifts to individuals (discussed above).

Termination of an interest in possession

83.13 Where the gift with reservation is occasioned by the termination of a qualifying interest in possession the property in the settlement when the life tenant's reservation ends or he dies is treated as the property comprised in the gift. Property derived from any loans he has made to the trust is included (Sch 20 para 4A).

EXCEPTIONS

Full consideration

83.14 Land or chattels are not property subject to a reservation if the donor is paying full consideration for his occupation or use. The basic rule achieving this is FA 1986, Sch 20 para 6(1)(a) and, as indicated above (para 83.4), provision to like effect is included in ss 102A and 102B. Consideration which is rent should be reviewed to market rent at regular intervals.

Change of circumstances

83.15 In the case of land, there is a limited exception where the donor is a relative of the donee and his occupation results from a change in circumstances (FA 1986, Sch 20 para 6(1)(b) and s 102C(3)).

Carve-out

83.16 It is well settled that in applying the original GWR legislation in s 102 it is necessary to look precisely at what is gifted. It is possible to divide property by interest as well as physically, and if on the facts only one interest is given, the GWR rules are not brought into play simply because the donor retains another interest (*Ingram v IRC* [1999] STC 37).

Perhaps the clearest exposition of this principle was given by Lord Radcliffe in *St Aubyn v A-G* [1952] AC 15, [1951] 2 All ER 473. His words were as follows:

'A man may have an arrangement which gives him contractual benefits that affect an estate and may subsequently make a gift of his interest in that estate. If he does, the donee has possession and enjoyment of what is given to the entire exclusion of the donor or of any benefit to him. That is the *Munro* case. Shares may be made the subject of a trust for another person, the maker of the trust having the right under it to be one of the trustees, to retain in his control the voting power in respects of the shares and to take an ultimate resulting interest, yet that benefit does not bring the property within the mischief of a similar provision. That is the *Perpetual Trustee Co.* case. No more is possession and enjoyment of a gift comprised if a man vests property in trustees on trust to provide out of in certain limited benefits for a donee, but subject thereto on a trust for himself. That is the *Cochrane* case. All these decisions proceed on a common principle, namely, that it is the possession and enjoyment of the actual property given that that has to be taken account of, and that if that property is, as it may be, a limited equitable interest or an equitable interest distinct from another such interest which is not given or an interest in property subject to an interest that is retained, it is of no consequence for this purpose that the retained interest remains in the beneficial enjoyment of the person who provides the gift.'

The carve-out principle applied to gifts of land made before 27 July 1999. Now the effect of ss 102A and 102B is to largely preclude it in relation to land, that indeed being the purpose of the enactment of those sections.

Carve-out and settlements

83.17 The application of the carve-out principle to settlements is a matter of difficulty. The starting point is *Commissioner for Stamp Duties of the State of New South Wales v Perpetual Trustee Co Ltd* [1943] 1 All ER 525. Here the settlor had settled shares on trust for his son contingent on the son attaining 21. Had the son failed to attain 21, the shares would have reverted to the settlor. It was held this did not make the gift subject to a reservation as what the settlor had given away was the contingent interest in the shares from which he had received no subsequent benefit. As a result of this case, it is accepted by HMRC that a gift to a children's trust is not a GWR just because it fails to exhaust the beneficial interest or the property reverts to the donor if the children fail to attain a specified age (IHTM 14392). The position is, of course, otherwise if the settlor is a discretionary object under the antecedent trusts.

The converse to the settlor retaining a reversion is where he retains an initial interest in possession, but is otherwise excluded from benefiting from the trust. Many advisers are of the view that, in such a case, all he has given away is the reversion and that, if he is wholly excluded from that, the gift into settlement is not subject to a reservation. This issue was academic when the GWR rules were enacted in 1986 for, until 22 March 2006, the settled property was in any event in the settlor's estate under IHTA 1984, s 49 (see para **61.3**). But now this is only so if the initial interest in possession is qualifying (para **61.2**).

The view that a settlement where all that the settlor retains is an initial interest in possession is not a gift with reservation gains some support from Lord Hoffmann's speech in *Ingram v IRC* [1999] STC 37. Arguments against are furnished by the Court of Appeal's analysis of FA 1986, s 102(5) in *IRC v Eversden* [2003] STC 822. There the proposition that a gift into settlement should be viewed as multiple gifts of the individual beneficial interests was specifically rejected. But neither case is conclusive.

In reality it may be regarded as most unlikely that a modern court would accept that a settlement is not a gift with reservation where the settlor retains an initial interest in possession. In such a case he retains the fullest possible enjoyment of the settled property and, were the gift not subject to a reservation, the absurd position would be reached that if he is merely a discretionary object he does have a reservation whereas if he is entitled to the income as of right he does not. The correct analysis, it may be argued, is suggested by FA 1986, Sch 20 para 5, which requires the property comprised in a settled gift to be taken as the property from time to time comprised in the settlement. Although this operates to counter the tracing rule in relation to settlements (para **83.9**), there appears to be no reason why it should not have wider application. Assuming this analysis is indeed correct it is not inconsistent with the *Perpetual Trustee* case, for that case was premised on the point that the settlor was in fact totally excluded unless and until the reversion fell in.

The issue of whether an initial life interest gives the settlor a reservation is not just relevant to IHT. If there is no reservation of benefit, the settlor may be exposed to income tax under the pre-owned assets legislation.

TERRITORIAL LIMITS

Non-settled property: death of donor

83.18 If property is subject to a reservation on death, the donor is treated as beneficially entitled to it regardless of his domicile. Territorial limits are therefore imposed by general IHT principles.

Common sense indicates that excluded property status is determined by the domicile or deemed domicile of the donor at the time of his death. However, it does have to be observed that IHTA 1984, s 6(1) provides that property is excluded if the person beneficially entitled to it is non-UK domiciled; in the case of an absolute GWR the person in fact beneficially entitled is the donee. There is therefore an argument that property comprised in a GWR can only be excluded property if the donee has neither an actual or deemed UK domicile. This argument is almost certainly wrong, for the effect of the GWR legislation is that there are competing beneficial entitlements – the deemed one of the donor and the actual one of the donee. In such a case IHTA 1984, ss 5(1) and

6(1) do, when read together, indicate that the status of property as excluded is determined by the domicile of the person whom it is sought to charge, ie that of the donee in the case of the donee's death, and that of donor in the case of the donor's death.

Non-settled property: cessation of reservation

83.19 Where the reservation ends inter vivos, the rule that the notional disposition is a PET in theory leaves no room for the excluded property concept. Before a disposition can be a PET it must be a transfer of value, and once it is a transfer of value it is by definition not a disposition of excluded property (IHTA 1984, s 3(2)). On this view, the inter vivos ending of a reservation is a PET, and so subject to IHT if the donor fails to survive seven years, regardless of the situs of the asset and where the donor is domiciled, and indeed regardless of whether he has any connection whatever with the UK.

It is most unlikely that such a view would find favour in the courts if the matter was litigated. As is described in CHAPTER 37, UK tax legislation is subject to territorial limits. However, it can be a matter of some difficulty to identify what those limits are if they are not precisely defined by legislation.

In the case of the GWR legislation the solution is to fasten on to the fact that s 102(4) deems the cessation of the reservation to be a PET. The value of the notional PET has to be determined by normal IHT rules, ie by IHTA 1984, ss 3 and 3A. Section 3A presupposes a PET is a transfer of value, and s 3 provides that in determining the amount of a transfer of value, no account is taken of excluded property. Although the point is not as clear as it should be, a purposive construction would infer from this that excluded property should be omitted in valuing the deemed PET on termination of the reservation and thus that the latter does not extend to excluded property. This point is now accepted by HMRC (IHTM14396).

As on death, the further issue arises of whether excluded property status is governed by the domicile or deemed domicile of the donor or that of donee. For the reasons given above, the former is to be preferred.

Settled property

83.20 In the common situation of a reservation of benefit with respect to assets of a trust, eg on the basis that the settlor is a discretionary beneficiary (see para 83.5 above), the question arises whether the applicable territorial limits are those which apply to settled property, or those which apply to assets in personal ownership as discussed above.

Should the reservation subsist until the settlor's death, the natural reading of the IHT legislation is that the settled property rules apply to determine whether the trust assets are excluded property in relation to him. This result follows because once property is settled, those rules prevail over the free estate rules (IHTA 1984, s 48(3)). Accordingly, provided the donor was non-UK domiciled and not deemed domiciled when he made the settlement, the question of whether the property to which he is treated as beneficially entitled under the GWR rules is excluded is determined regardless of whether he has subsequently acquired an actual or a deemed UK domicile. This point, also, is accepted by HMRC (IHTM14396).

If the settlor's reservation ends inter vivos, the same issue arises as with free estate as to whether the excluded property concept has any place at all. Assuming for the reasons given in para **83.19** that it does, the issue then arises of whether the test should be whether the property is excluded property under the settled property rules, or whether, in applying the excluded property concept, it should be treated as in the donor's free estate. Parity of reasoning with the position on death suggests the former is correct and this is accepted by HMRC (IHTM14396).

Strictly, the application of the settlement excluded property test in IHTA 1984, s 48(3) is probably dependent on the settlor's reservation being over the directly-held assets of the settlement, rather than it being over assets of a holding company. The reservation is normally over the directly-held assets. However, there may be a reservation with respect to an asset of a holding company if the settlor has made a non-cash gift to the company and has then given the company's shares to the trust. In that scenario, there may be reservations at two levels: over the company shares (if the settlor is a beneficiary) and over the asset held by the company (if there is actual enjoyment of that asset by the settlor). With respect to the asset held by the company, the applicable excluded property test is probably the test in IHTA 1984, s 6 (applied by reference to the settlor's tax status), not the settled property test in s 48(3); and if that is right, the acquisition by the settlor of an actual or deemed domicile in the UK will remove any protection from the GWR liability.

Where the reservation is triggered by the termination of a qualifying interest in possession (para **83.3** above), excluded property status on the death of the former life tenant is determined in accordance with whether or not, under the settled property rules, the trust property is excluded. This is because FA 1986, s 102ZA applies only for the purposes of the GWR rules. An ending of the reservation inter vivos raises the issue of whether, in determining whether the property is excluded, the test is the status of the settlement or the domicile or deemed domicile of the life tenant. For the reasons given above, the former should be correct.

PRACTICAL APPLICATION

UK domiciliaries

83.21 For UK domiciliaries, the gift with reservation rules apply in foreign contexts in the same way as they do domestically. Particular points to notice are that they treat the settlor as beneficially entitled to settled property on his death if he is a discretionary beneficiary, and that use by the settlor of foreign property previously given away, for example a house, may trigger the rules.

Non-UK domiciliaries

83.22 Under current law, there are two principal danger areas for non-UK domiciliaries.

The first is where the non-UK domiciliary has made a gift in specie and either the gifted asset is in the UK or the donor has become deemed domiciled. If the donor uses or enjoys the property, the rules are in point. This issue would arise with a chattel if the donor gave the chattel away, whether in the UK or abroad, and the chattel was then put into the donor's hands, as bailee or licensee. The issue can also arise with UK houses if the non-domiciliary gives the house, or a share in it, away and continues using it. But what is unlikely to be caught is a cash gift abroad which the donee then applies in buying a UK house that is later used by the donor (see para **83.11**).

The second risk area is settlements. Should a settlement of which the settlor is a beneficiary hold UK investments directly, those investments are exposed under the GWR rules. Subject to the nil-rate band, those investments attract IHT in the event of the settlor's death. This is so even if the settlor is not resident in the UK. Authorised funds would not, however, be caught for they are excluded property in the hands of a non-UK domiciliary or a settlement created by a non-UK domiciliary (see para **37.11**).

An offshore holding company to hold UK assets may avoid the non-UK domiciliary being exposed under GWR rules, including in a trust context. In general, there is no GWR exposure for a non-UK domiciled settlor with respect to a trust which holds shares in an offshore company, even if that company in turn holds UK assets which are enjoyed by the settlor. Absent any gift by the settlor to the company, the excluded property status of the trust fund ousts the GWR rules. Provided, therefore, that the settlor was non-UK domiciled and not deemed domiciled when the trust was created and funded, there is protection from liability under the GWR rules on his death.

However, as noted above, the analysis is different if the non-UK domiciliary has given non-cash assets to the offshore company, and has given the company shares to the trust (and regardless of which of these steps occurred first). In that scenario, the GWR rules apply to the assets given to the company, as well as to the company shares, and if the assets given to the company (or assets derived from them) are enjoyed by the settlor, there is exposure under the GWR rules unless (a) the company's assets are non-UK situated and (b) the settlor is non-UK domiciled and not deemed domiciled at the time of death.

Moreover, the analysis in relation to non-UK domiciliaries will shortly be modified by legislation that will deem interests in offshore companies and other non-UK entities to be non-excluded property, to the extent that such interests derive their value from UK residential property (see CHAPTER 27). In many cases, this legislation will entirely strip away the IHT benefit hitherto provided by offshore companies as vehicles for the ownership of UK residential property, thanks in part to the GWR rules.

However, the oddities and intricacies of the GWR rules may mean that, in some scenarios, exposure under these rules is avoided. For example, it is possible that the rules will not be in a point if an individual has funded an offshore company by cash gift, or by subscription for shares, and the cash has been used by the company to acquire a UK home, and the company shares have been given to other family members. From 6 April 2017 the shares will be non-excluded property, and will accordingly be within the taxable estates of the individual donees. However, for as long as the company is retained, arguably there is no GWR even if, with the permission of the shareholders, the individual uses the home. The only assets on which the GWR rules can bite are the shares, but arguably possession of the shares has been fully assumed by the donees, and the shares are enjoyed to the entire exclusion of the donor.

Spouse exemption

83.23 Normally the spouse exemption does not prevent a GWR charge on settled property, for that exemption requires property to become comprised in the spouse's estate or the value of the spouse's estate otherwise to be increased (IHTA 1984, s 18). The spouse exemption should however apply if the spouse becomes absolutely entitled to the property on the cessation of the reservation, or if it is then held on trusts subject to a qualifying interest in possession in her favour. But absent one or other of these conditions, the settled property is in the relevant property regime and so the spouse exemption cannot be in point.

Chapter 84

THE IHT TREATMENT OF LIABILITIES DUE FROM INDIVIDUALS

INTRODUCTION

84.1 In recent decades, planning involving loans has become increasingly prevalent. In particular, indebtedness has been used as a means of avoiding or reducing exposure to IHT, in reliance on the general rule that liabilities to IHT are calculated by reference to the net value of the taxpayer's assets, ie the value of the assets after deduction of the taxpayer's debts and other liabilities.

As explained below, this continues to be the general rule, but there are now numerous exceptions, and the IHT treatment of liabilities has become a subject of some intricacy. There is, moreover, the prospect of further change to these already very complicated rules. A consultation document issued by HM Treasury in August 2016 suggested that the Government was considering the introduction, with effect from 6 April 2017, of a rule that would cause any liability to be disregarded for IHT purposes if due to a person connected with the debtor. There was no indication of how connectedness would be defined for these purposes. The context was a discussion of the IHT treatment of interests in UK residential properties, and it is conceivable that if such a rule is introduced, it will be limited in scope to liabilities that would otherwise reduce the value for IHT purposes of UK residential properties or interests in entities that hold such properties (see CHAPTER 19).

Absent any further information on this point, this and the following chapter ignore the possibility of any such further change, and address the rules in force at the time of writing (early October 2016). The discussion in these chapters focuses on those aspects of the subject which are most likely to arise where there is an international element.

In this chapter we address liabilities of individuals, considering the principles which determine whether such liabilities are deductible on death, and if so, which assets such liabilities are 'matched against', ie which assets have their value reduced by the liabilities. The question of which assets liabilities are matched against is academic in some cases (where all assets are fully subject to IHT), but of great importance in others (where some assets are outside the scope of IHT, or qualify for IHT relief). In particular, where an individual is domiciled outside the UK for IHT purposes (see CHAPTER 45), the usual objective is to arrange matters so that his liabilities reduce the value of UK property, rather than being wastefully matched against excluded property which is outside the reach of IHT.

In a couple of places, the chapter identifies possible gaps in the thicket of IHT anti-avoidance legislation which has sprung up in relation to liabilities. Anyone thinking of exploiting such gaps should consider not only the strength of the technical arguments but also the possibility of IHT advantages being counteracted by the GAAR (see CHAPTER 82).

A couple of special topics in relation to the IHT treatment of liabilities, namely the deductibility of trustee liabilities and the deductibility of liabilities when valuing property that is subject to a reservation of benefit, have been addressed in a separate chapter, CHAPTER 85.

DEDUCTIBILITY: BASIC PRINCIPLES

84.2 The general rule that liabilities are deducted from an individual's gross assets is in IHTA 1984, s 5(3). This states that in determining the value of a person's estate, liabilities shall be taken into account, except as otherwise provided by the IHTA 1984.

Requirement for valuable consideration or imposition by law

84.3 IHTA 1984, s 5(5) raises the first of many qualifications to this principle. It provides that, except in the case of a liability imposed by law, a liability incurred by a transferor shall be taken into account only to the extent that it was incurred for a consideration in money or money's worth. The reference to a transferor here includes an individual making a deemed transfer of value on death (see IHTA 1984, s 4). The consideration referred to in s 5(5) must be the consideration provided by the other party to the transaction.

One can compare three situations here:

(1)   A liability incurred for full consideration. For example, the individual may have received a loan equal to the debt incurred, or have acquired an asset for its market value with the purchase price left outstanding. In either case, the debt is taken into account in full, if it is still outstanding on the debtor's death (subject to the various anti-avoidance provisions discussed in this chapter).

(2)   A liability incurred gratuitously. For example, the individual may have entered into a deed of covenant, to pay a particular sum to a relative or a charity, without receiving anything in return for the promise. In this scenario it is clear that no consideration in money or money's worth has been provided. The resultant liability, although legally binding, will be disregarded for IHT purposes – although a payment to a charity by the individual's personal representatives, pursuant to such a promise, will qualify for the exemption in IHTA 1984, s 23.

(3)   A liability incurred for inadequate consideration. For example, the individual may have acquired an asset from a relative for a deliberate overvalue, with the purchase price being left outstanding. This is more contentious.

HMRC's view is that, in this third situation, the debt may be taken into account to the extent that it is attributable to the market value of the asset that was acquired, but no further. For example, a debt of £20,000 incurred to purchase an asset worth £12,000 would be treated as a debt of £12,000, and the balance would be ignored for IHT (IHTM28382).

However, it is arguable that this is a misconstruction. Section 5(5) refers to 'a consideration in money or money's worth'; not full consideration. In the example above, the individual clearly has received consideration in money's worth, in the form of the asset sold to him, notwithstanding that both parties to the transaction were aware that the price exceeded the asset's market value. The law of contract does not generally enquire into the adequacy of consideration or its value to the promisee (see *Chappell v Nestle* [1960] AC 87), and the requirement here for the consideration to be in money or money's worth does not imply a requirement for the consideration to be full (see *Midland Bank v Green* [1981] 1 All ER 583, in which the House of Lords confirmed that a purchaser of a £40,000 house for £500 was a purchaser for value in money or money's worth). It is arguable, therefore, that a £20,000 debt incurred to purchase a £12,000 asset is, subject to the other statutory provisions discussed in this chapter, deductible in full.

HMRC would no doubt point out that s 5(5) states that a liability shall be taken into account 'to the extent that' consideration in money or money's worth has been received, which at first sight seems to support the HMRC view. However, arguably, the correct interpretation of s 5(5) is that, in the event that a liability has been incurred under several transactions, then each of those transactions must be analysed to determine whether the part of the liability which arose under it was incurred for consideration in money or money's worth or not; in the event that any part of the liability was not so incurred, that part is to be disregarded for IHT purposes. But where there was consideration in money or money's worth, s 5(5) does not look at the adequacy of such consideration.

Section 5(5) also allows the deduction of a liability imposed by law. Such liabilities include liabilities to pay lifetime taxes such as income tax and CGT. HMRC assert (IHTM28100) that liabilities to non-UK taxes are generally only deductible from the value of property in the jurisdiction which is seeking to levy such taxes – the justification for this being the principle expressed in *Government of India v Taylor* [1955] AC 491 that no state will assist in the collection of another state's taxes. However, this is now more the exception than the rule, thanks to the the EU Mutual Assistance Directive, the Council of Europe/OECD Mutual Assistance Treaty of 1988, and various other agreements for mutual assistance in tax enforcement. Where such an agreement operates, the foreign tax liability should be considered enforceable in the UK and (subject to the various anti-avoidance provisions discussed in this chapter) deductible from the value of UK situs assets.

Rights to reimbursement and long-dated liabilities

84.4 There are additional rules regarding liabilities in IHTA 1984, s 162. Some of these, discussed below, are concerned with the matching of liabilities to assets. But it is also worth noting, for completeness, the following:

(1)   Section 162(1) provides that a liability shall only be taken into account to the extent that reimbursement of it cannot reasonably be expected to be obtained. Thus a debt will be disregarded for IHT purposes if the debtor had a right of indemnity against a third party, who is capable of meeting his obligation under that indemnity, and there is no obstacle to the right of indemnity being exercised by the debtor's personal representatives.

(2)   Section 162(2) provides that where a liability falls to be discharged after the time at which it is to be taken into account, it shall be valued at the time at which it is to be taken into account. Thus, as one would expect, a long-dated liability will be discounted to reflect its net present value at the time of death.

MATCHING RULES

84.5 More important in practice are s 162(4) and s 162(5). These are both concerned with the question of which asset, or assets, a liability is to be matched against. This is often of considerable importance where an individual who is non-UK domiciled for IHT purposes has property both within and outside the UK.

Section 162(4) states that a liability which is an incumbrance on any property shall, so far as possible, be taken to reduce the value of that property. 'Incumbrance' is thought to have its usual, wide meaning here, including any form of security interest.

Section 162(5) provides that, in certain scenarios, a liability shall, so far as possible, be taken to reduce the value of property outside the UK (which is, of course, an unhelpful result if the debtor is non-UK domiciled for IHT). The subsection does *not* apply if:

(1)   the liability is to a UK resident; or
(2)   the liability 'falls to be discharged' in the UK; or
(3)   the liability is an incumbrance on UK property.

However, if the liability is to a non-UK resident, and does not 'fall to be discharged' in the UK, and is not secured on UK property, s 162(5) requires matching of the liability against non-UK assets, in priority to UK assets.

Where these conditions are met, s 162(5) applies 'so far as possible'. It must be the case that if the individual has a liability secured on non-UK assets, another liability which is affected by s 162(5) will only be matched against those non-UK assets to the extent of any equity in them, after the first liability has been taken into account. Where there are multiple liabilities, s 162(4) must take priority over s 162(5).

It is suggested that a debt 'falls to be discharged' in the UK if the loan agreement requires payment to be made in the UK, ie to a UK account of the lender. HMRC seem to agree: IHTM28394. Liability to a UK resident and a requirement for payment to be made in the UK will normally go hand in hand.

Problems caused by supplementary security

84.6 A situation which quite frequently arises is that an individual who is non-UK domiciled for IHT purposes wishes to borrow from a bank to fund the acquisition of a UK asset, eg a house, and to grant security over that asset, but the lender wishes to take security over non-UK assets as well. Such additional security may also arise under a bank's general terms and conditions; these often provide for a charge or lien over all assets booked with the bank. In principle, this is problematic for IHT, as it is likely to dilute the IHT deduction from the value of the UK asset. There is no authority on how s 162(4) applies in this situation, but it seems likely that (if the value of the secured assets exceeds the amount of the debt) a share of the debt will be matched to each of the secured assets, on a pro rata basis. Clearly, this effect is unwanted if the borrower's exposure to IHT is limited to UK assets.

A solution that is sometimes adopted here is for a 'primary' charge to be granted over the UK assets, with a 'secondary' charge over non-UK assets, the latter being expressed to be exercisable by the lender only if and to the extent that the 'primary' charge proves insufficient for recovery of the debt. There is no authority on whether this is effective as a matter of law, and no indication in the IHT Manual as to whether this approach is accepted by HMRC. However, treating the primary security as the sole incumbrance for the purpose of s 162, unless and until it proves insufficient for recovery of the debt, seems entirely reasonable, and consistent with the rationale for the decision in *St Barbe Green* (discussed in the following chapter, para 85.2).

Matching questions unanswered by statute

84.7 Section 162 does not answer the question of which assets a liability should be matched against in the event that an unsecured liability is due to a UK resident or is required to be discharged by payment to a UK account. It might be assumed that such a liability would be set against UK assets, in priority to non-UK assets. However, it is also possible that a share of the liability should be matched to all assets, irrespective of their situs, on a pro rata basis. It is best to avoid the issue by ensuring that, where a deduction from the value of UK assets is desired, this is achieved by means of an incumbrance on such assets.

LIABILITIES DUE TO DONEES

84.8 A debt or incumbrance which would otherwise be taken into account in valuing an individual's estate may be abated or disregarded for IHT purposes if it is caught by FA 1986, s 103. This is an anti-avoidance section which was introduced at the same time as the rules on gifts subject to a reservation of benefit. Like those rules, s 103 is poorly drafted and suffers from obscurities and uncertainties.

The general intention behind s 103 is tolerably clear, and it is perhaps easiest to explain the section by reference to the sort of arrangement it is designed to prevent. This is where an individual gives an asset to another person, eg his child, on the understanding that the donee will convert the asset to cash and lend the cash to the individual, in such a way as to avoid the application of the GWR rules. For example, the donee might charge the asset as security for a loan, and lend the borrowed money to the individual. Were it not for s 103, the individual would have the use of the cash derived from the value of the asset that he had given away, but for IHT purposes he would have succeeded in depleting his estate; the addition of the cash to his estate on the receipt of the loan would of course be balanced by the liability to the donee. This is the kind of 'having your cake and eating it' scenario that the IHT provisions in the FA 1986 were intended to prevent.

Property derived from the deceased

84.9 Section 103 aims to prevent tax advantages arising from such arrangements through the abatement of an individual debtor's liability, if the creditor has received what the section calls 'property derived from the deceased'. This concept is defined in s 103(3), as any property which was the subject matter of a disposition made by the deceased, or any other property which represents the subject matter of such a disposition, whether directly or indirectly and including via intermediate dispositions.

A liability may be abated if the consideration for the liability is (ie can be traced back to) 'property derived from the deceased'. This is sufficient to catch the hypothetical arrangement outlined above. There may also be an abatement of a liability if the consideration for the liability cannot be traced back to 'property derived from the deceased', but the person who gave the consideration (ie the creditor) was at any time entitled to any such property, or if his or her resources included such property at any time. Thus the sum loaned to the individual need not derive from the subject matter of his gift for there to be an abatement of the liability under s 103; it is sufficient for the creditor to have received property under a disposition made by the individual 'at any time' (s 103(1)). It is clear from s 103(1) that the disposition by the individual can post-date, and need not be in any way connected to, the transaction whereby the individual's liability is incurred.

The definition of 'property derived from the deceased' raises many questions. One uncertainty is what happens if the original asset is sold or exchanged for other property. For example, what is the position if the donee transfers the asset that was the subject matter of the individual's gift to a company, by way of subscription for shares in that company?

It seems clear in such a case that the shares held by the donee are 'property derived from the deceased', on the basis that they represent the original asset in the donee's hands. However, it might be argued that the original asset, now held by the company, has ceased to be 'property derived from the deceased'. Arguably, such property cannot be in two places at once, with double the value that it had originally. HMRC would no doubt wish to argue the contrary, as the interpretation proposed above would allow the individual to borrow from the company and the resultant debt to the company would not be caught by s 103 (although any resultant tax advantage might in any event be annulled by the GAAR).

The exclusion in s 103(4)

84.10 As outlined above, the definition of 'property derived from the deceased' fastens on property which was the subject matter of a 'disposition' by the deceased. 'Disposition' is a broad term, generally considered to be synonymous with 'disposal'. It is not in itself confined to gifts or transactions with any donative intent. Prima facie, therefore, the concept of 'property derived from the deceased' includes not only property given away by the individual but also property sold by the individual on arm's length terms.

In recognition of this, section 103(4) aims to reduce the scope of 'property derived from the deceased'. It directs that a disposition shall be left out of account if it is was not a transfer of value. Dispositions which are not transfers of value include an arm's length transaction not intended to confer gratuitous benefit (IHTA 1984, s 10) and a gift which causes no diminution of the individual's estate, such as a gift to a wholly-owned company.

The exclusion in s 103(4) is, however, severely hedged. The exclusion does not operate if the disposition was part of associated operations which included either:

(a)   a disposition by the individual, except a disposition for full consideration in money or money's worth paid to the individual; or

(b)   a disposition by another party which reduced the value of the individual's estate.

If the disposition *was* part of such associated operations, the subject matter of the disposition is deemed, after all, to be 'property derived from the deceased'.

If the legislation is taken at face value, the reference to associated operations here means that the exclusion in s 103(4) rarely applies. If we take the example of a gift to a wholly-owned company (which, as noted above, is not a transfer of value), it might be assumed that the company would not have 'property derived from the deceased', so it would be possible for the individual to borrow from the company and s 103 would not apply to the debt. However, the loan from the company might be regarded as an associated operation in relation to the gift to the company. If that view is taken, the gift to the company and the loan from the company together form associated operations in relation to each other, which arguably include a disposition by the individual which was not for full consideration in money or money's worth (viz, the gift to the company – which obviously gave no consideration, even though the disposition involved no transfer of value).

A possible counter-argument would be that here, as elsewhere in the IHT legislation, the term 'associated operations' does not have the breadth of meaning that IHTA 1984, s 268(1) appears to give to it. As discussed at para 83.10, a number of cases have pointed to the implied limits of the 'associated operations' concept – the essential point being that where one step in relation to an item of property is followed by another, the second step cannot be an associated operation in relation to the first unless the second step is 'relevant' to, or has a part to play in the achievement of, the IHT effect of the first step. Neither a loose connection between the steps, nor the mere fact that they both affect the same item of property, is sufficient to make one an associated operation in relation to the other. However, it has to be said that this 'relevance' doctrine is more difficult to apply in relation to s 103(4) than in other IHT contexts.

In any event, it can be argued that the reference to 'a disposition by the deceased' in s 103(4)(a) must, as a matter of logic, mean a disposition other than the original disposition referred to in s 103(3). However, in the current environment, it is difficult to be confident that a court would agree. Unfortunately, the intended width of the exclusion provided by s 103(4) is too uncertain for much weight to be given to a purposive construction.

The reference in s 103(4)(a) to 'money or money's worth paid to the deceased' compounds the uncertainty in relation to the s 103(4) exclusion. On one reading, there is a requirement for a cash payment to the individual, so that (for example) a sale of an asset by the individual for a purchase price left outstanding by way of debt would be the wrong sort of disposition to form part of associated operations, notwithstanding that it involves no transfer of value; nothing would have been 'paid' to the individual. But strictly, it is questionable whether 'money's worth' (valuable non-cash consideration) can ever be 'paid'. There is a good argument that 'paid to the deceased' needs to be construed broadly, to include 'received by the deceased', to prevent the reference to 'money's worth' from being otiose.

Loan from excluded property trust to its settlor

84.11 The doubt surrounding the correct interpretation of s 103(4) also creates difficulties where it is proposed that an individual should borrow from an excluded property settlement of which he is the settlor.

It is clear that a gift of excluded property is not a transfer of value. The reason is that a transfer of value is defined as a disposition which causes a reduction in the value of the individual's estate (IHTA 1984, s 3(1)), but for these purposes no account is to be taken of the value of any excluded property which ceases to form part of the estate (s 3(2)).

Accordingly, if excluded property is given to trustees, that property does not qualify as 'property derived from the deceased' – unless it is brought back within the concept of 'property derived from the deceased' by the provisos in FA 1986, s 103(4). This turns on (a) whether a loan made by the trustees to the individual should be considered an associated operation in relation to the gift of excluded property to the trustees, and (b) whether, assuming that the answer to the first question is yes, the reference to 'a disposition by the deceased' in s 103(4)(a) must mean a disposition other than the original disposition referred to in s 103(3). As noted above, this is very uncertain territory. If a settlor is to borrow from a trust that he originally funded using excluded property, he should only do so in the knowledge that the resultant debts may be non-deductible for IHT.

Discharge of liabilities within s 103

84.12 Section 103(5) provides that if money or money's worth is paid or applied by the individual in discharging or reducing the amount of a liability which, on his death, would otherwise be subject to abatement pursuant to s 103, the individual shall be treated for the purposes of the IHTA as having made a potentially exempt transfer (or PET) equal to the money or money's worth so paid or applied.

This is a parallel provision to s 102(4), which applies where property ceases to be subject to a reservation of benefit, and which likewise deems the individual to have made a PET. Both provisions suffer from a lack of any express territorial limit. Taken at face value, they create scope for a charge to IHT even where the individual is non-UK domiciled and has no UK assets or other UK connections. This cannot be right, and an implied territorial limit must be found to prevent these provisions from being unworkable and absurd.

In the case of s 102(4), HMRC's approach is as follows. Although the statute says that the individual is to be treated as having made a disposition of the former GWR property, and that such deemed disposition is a PET, HMRC refer to the direction in IHTA 1984, s 3(2) that, when determining the value transferred by a disposition, no account is to be taken of excluded property which ceases to form part of the individual's estate (IHTM14396). If the former GWR property is excluded property, the value of the property that is subject to a deemed PET which can be taken into account under s 102(4) is zero. Accordingly, in this scenario, no IHT can result from the release of the reservation.

It is suggested that the same approach must be taken to s 103(5), where the money or money's worth used to repay the liability is excluded property in the hands of the individual. The excluded property which ceases to form part of the individual's estate (because it has been used to repay the debt) should, by virtue of IHTA 1984, s 3(2), be disregarded for the purposes of determining the value of the deemed PET which is taken into account under s 103(5). Logically, this argument ought to be accepted by HMRC, as it mirrors HMRC's own argument at IHTM14396.

Limitations on scope of the section

84.13 Section 103 has a wider scope than may at first appear, and needs to be watched for carefully, wherever an individual will be incurring a liability, or granting an incumbrance, to a person who may have received, or may at a later date receive, a disposition by way of gift from the individual. In some cases dispositions by way of gift may, despite a lack of evidence, be assumed from the relationship between the parties and other circumstances (see *Phizackerley v Revenue and Customs Comrs* [2007] STC (SCD) 328).

However, there are some limitations. In particular, it is clear that s 103 can only cause the abatement of a liability consisting of a debt incurred by the individual, or an incumbrance created by a disposition made by the individual (s 103(1)). Liabilities of other persons cannot be abated under this section. It follows that, in principle, there may be opportunities to avoid the impact of s 103 by arranging matters so that the borrower is not the individual himself but a trust or company from which he can benefit.

In principle, a company wholly owned by an individual may borrow from the recipient of a gift made by the individual, without the company's debt being abated under s 103. Such a company could be nominally funded by the individual and could then purchase property, eg an investment portfolio, from the donee, in consideration of an 'on demand' debt due from the company, equal to the portfolio's market value. Section 103 would not prevent the company's debt from being taken into account in valuing its shares, which would have a nil value in the individual's estate, subject to increases in the value of the portfolio.

It is debatable whether the inapplicability of s 103 to liabilities due from persons other than the deceased individual could be considered a 'shortcoming of the legislation' for the purposes of the GAAR. Arguably, it is a deliberate limitation of the provision rather than an inadvertent 'loophole'.

FINANCE ACT 2013 CHANGES

84.14 Until Finance Act 2013, IHT provisions in relation to liabilities were essentially limited to those discussed above. Unfortunately for practitioners, the position now is even more complicated. FA 2013, Sch 36 added new sections to IHTA 1984, which are concerned with:

- liabilities incurred to acquire, maintain or enhance the value of excluded property (s 162A):
- liabilities incurred to acquire, maintain or enhance the value of 'relievable property', ie business property, agricultural property or woodland (s 162B);
- partial repayments of liabilities where s 162A or s 162B are in point (s 162C); and
- liabilities left unpaid after death (s 175A).

The focus here is on s 162A and s 175A. Section 162B works in a broadly similar way to s 162A (as discussed below). Section 162C is a fairly 'niche' provision, which is only relevant where a particular liability (eg a bank debt) has been incurred to fund the acquisition, maintenance or enhancement of assets of different types, one or more of which was excluded property and/or relievable property, and that liability has been partly repaid. It sets out priority rules to determine the extent to which, following such partial repayment, the remaining liability is still affected by s 162A or s 162B.

LIABILITIES INCURRED TO ACQUIRE EXCLUDED PROPERTY

84.15 The aim of s 162A is very easy to understand. It is designed to negate tax advantages from the practice, which was formerly quite widespread among non-UK domiciliaries, of borrowing commercially on the security of UK assets (particularly residential property) and using the borrowed money to invest in non-UK assets. This practice formerly allowed non-UK domiciliaries to unlock value in their UK houses, reduce the value of such houses for IHT purposes (by virtue of the borrowing secured on them) and invest the proceeds in assets which would be outside the ambit of IHT on their death, subject of course to any acquisition of an actual or deemed UK domicile.

The general thrust of s 162A is that any debt resulting from such borrowing is disregarded for IHT purposes. Subject to certain exclusions discussed below, a liability will be left out of account for the purposes of IHT if it is 'attributable to financing (directly or indirectly) (a) the acquisition of any excluded property, or (b) the maintenance, or an enhancement of the value of any such property' (s 162A(1)). It is thought that the 'directly or indirectly' wording means that s 162A is in point where borrowing has been used initially to acquire non-excluded property, but such property has been disposed of and the proceeds have been used to acquire excluded property.

It might, conceivably, be argued that s 162A(1) does not catch a liability resulting from borrowing which was used to acquire an asset which was not excluded property at the outset, but has subsequently become such property (for example, if the debtor was UK domiciled when the borrowing was taken out, and has since become non-UK domiciled); although it might also be argued, with some force, that the 'directly or indirectly' wording in s 162A(1) is sufficient to address this scenario. Any risk of such liabilities falling through the net is in any event eliminated by s 162A(5).

Although s 162B, regarding liabilities incurred to acquire 'relieved property', is only applicable to liabilities incurred on or after 6 April 2013 (FA 2013, Sch 36, para 5(2)), there is no such 'grandfathering' of liabilities incurred to acquire excluded property. Section 162A will therefore affect the IHT treatment of many longstanding arrangements which were put in place in reliance on the law as it then stood.

Sections 162A and 162B are irrelevant where a liability has been incurred to acquire property which was neither excluded property nor 'relieved property'. It follows that an IHT deduction can in principle be obtained by a non-UK domiciliary who has significant living expenses by (a) borrowing on the security of UK assets and (b) keeping the borrowed money in the UK for use to meet such expenses, taking care not to use it to acquire any excluded property. A significant IHT advantage may be achieved if, by the time of death, the stock of borrowed money has been exhausted or severely depleted but the liability remains.

The exclusion in s 162A(2)

84.16 There is an exclusion from s 162A for the situation where a liability has been incurred to acquire excluded property, but:

(a)   such property has been disposed of for full consideration in money or money's worth,

(b)   the consideration is not itself excluded property, and

(c)   the consideration has not subsequently been used to acquire other excluded property (s 162A(2)).

Where these conditions are met, the debt may be taken into account, subject to the various other anti-avoidance provisions discussed in this chapter.

Care must be taken with this subsection. Consider the following scenarios, each involving a non-UK domiciled, and non-deemed domiciled, individual:

(1)   The individual has borrowed and used the borrowed money to subscribe for shares in a non-UK company, of which he is the sole owner. The shares are excluded property, so the liability is caught by s 162A. What happens if the individual puts the company into liquidation and receives the liquidation distribution in a UK bank account? Will this bring the liability within the exclusion in s 162A(2)? Strictly, the exclusion may not apply. The individual has disposed of the excluded property, at least once the shares have been cancelled, but it is questionable whether the disposal could be said to be for consideration. The distribution of property by the liquidator of a company to its shareholders occurs pursuant to company law, not pursuant to any form of bargain between the company and the shareholders. (See *IRC v Laird Group plc* [2003] UKHL 54, [2003] 4 All ER 669, [2003] 1 WLR 2476 at para 37: when a company in liquidation makes a distribution to its shareholders 'they receive only what is already theirs'.) But HMRC do not take the point (IHTM28015, Examples 2 and 3).

(2)   The individual has borrowed to fund the purchase of a chattel, kept outside the UK. The liability is caught by s 162A. He agrees to sell the chattel to a family member, for three-quarters of its market value, and receives the purchase price in his UK account. Logically, the exclusion in s 162A(2) should apply with respect to three-quarters of the debt (with the balance of a quarter being non-deductible). However, the requirement for full consideration means that the liability remains non-deductible in its entirety.

(3)   The individual has borrowed to fund the purchase of non-UK investments, booked at a non-UK bank. The liability is caught by s 162A. The individual instructs the bank to sell all of the investments and to remit the proceeds of sale to his UK bank account. Will this bring the liability within the exclusion in s 162A(2)? The consideration for the sale of the investments will have initially taken the form of a non-UK cash balance – ie excluded property. At first sight, this appears to be a problem. However, there is a good argument that the exclusion does apply in this third scenario. Section 162A(2) refers to consideration which 'is' excluded property (in the present tense). Arguably, the legislation requires the reader to look at the status of the assets representing the consideration at the time at which the deductibility of the debt is in question (ie on death, in the case of a debt due from an individual), not at the time of receipt. Therefore it can be argued that the exclusion

applies if the excluded property has been disposed of and, at the time of death, the assets then representing the proceeds of the disposal are UK assets. HMRC seem to agree (IHTM28015, Example 1).

The exclusion in s 162A(3)

84.17 There is a further exclusion in s 162A(3), which allows deduction of a liability (subject to the other anti-avoidance provisions discussed in this chapter) if and to the extent that the excluded property which was acquired using the borrowed funds has not been disposed of, but has ceased to be excluded property. This will prevent s 162A from causing a liability to be disregarded in two main scenarios:

(1) where there has been a change of situs (eg where chattels, formerly situate outside the UK, have been brought into the UK; or more unusually where the share register of a non-UK incorporated company has been brought into the UK); and

(2) where there has been a change of domicile (ie where the individual has acquired a UK domicile or has become deemed domiciled in the UK).

Acquisition of excluded property by another party

84.18 Where the conditions set out in s 162A are met, ie there is a debt which is attributable to financing the acquisition of any excluded property (and neither of the exclusions apply), the debt is required to be left out of account. The section does not, in so many words, require the person who has acquired the excluded property to be the debtor. The section talks about the acquisition, maintenance, enhancement and disposal of excluded property, but is unspecific about who is doing the acquisition, maintenance, enhancement or disposal. This raises the question of whether an individual's liability may be disregarded for IHT purposes if he has borrowed from a bank, used the borrowed funds to make a gift to another party, and the other party has used the funds to acquire excluded property.

It is difficult to be confident that s 162A does not operate in this scenario. Arguably, the use of the words 'directly or indirectly' in s 162A(1) permits a wide interpretation of the section. The counter-argument would be that, given the punitive effect of s 162A applying, any ambiguity concerning the ambit of the section should be construed in favour of the taxpayer. It might be suggested that the legislation cannot be meant to render the IHT treatment of a liability due from an individual dependent on acts of third parties, eg relatives or trustees, over which the individual may have no control. However, the possibility of an individual's tax position being affected by acts of third parties is far from unprecedented (see, for example, para 12.18).

If it is correct that s 162A can apply to liabilities incurred to make gifts, such liabilities may be disregarded in two main scenarios:

(1)   where an individual (whether UK or non-UK domiciled) has borrowed to make a gift to a non-UK domiciled (and non-deemed domiciled) spouse or other relative, who has used the gift to acquire excluded property; and

(2)   where a non-UK domiciled (and non-deemed domiciled) individual has borrowed to make a gift to the trustees of a settlement that he has established, and the trustees have used the gift to acquire excluded property.

However, the point could arise in other scenarios as well.

Non-residents' foreign currency bank accounts

84.19 On the death of an individual who is neither resident in the UK nor domiciled in the UK for the purposes of IHT, any UK bank account which is not denominated in sterling is disregarded when determining the value of the individual's estate (IHTA 1984, s 157). However, such an account is not (strictly) excluded property. Accordingly, following the FA 2013 changes to the IHT code, there remained theoretical scope for avoidance of IHTA 1984, s 162A by non-UK resident non-UK domiciliaries. Such individuals could, in theory, borrow on the security of UK assets and deposit the borrowed money in a UK account denominated in a currency other than sterling. However, this potential avoidance strategy has been blocked by FA 2014, which has inserted a further section, s 162AA, into IHTA 1984. This broadly replicates s 162A, but in relation to debts incurred to finance the acquisition of foreign currency bank accounts which, on the individual's death, are disregarded by virtue of s 157.

LIABILITIES LEFT UNPAID AFTER DEATH

84.20 IHTA 1984, s 175A imposes a further, and significant, restriction on the ability of personal representatives to claim an IHT deduction in respect of liabilities of the deceased. The general rule under s 175A(1) is that a liability of a deceased individual shall not be taken into account when calculating the value of his or her estate, except to the extent that the liability has been discharged on or after death, out of the estate (or out of excluded property owned by the deceased immediately before death), in money or money's worth.

The clear aim of s 175A is to curtail the practice of using loans, in particular from trusts, as a way of transferring cash to individuals without adding to their estates for IHT purposes. It has become common for beneficiaries of trusts to receive loans, typically without any fixed date for repayment, to be used for personal expenditure, as an alternative to cash being transferred by way of distribution. Before the introduction of s 175A, such loans did not add to the beneficiary's estate, as the debt was deductible (subject to FA 1986, s 103, as discussed above, if the beneficiary was the settlor). Such loans would typically be left outstanding until the death of the beneficiary but would then, not infrequently, be written off by the trustees. However, the IHT deduction in respect of the debt could not be challenged by HMRC, unless there was strong evidence that the transfer of cash to the beneficiary was in reality a distribution 'dressed up' as a loan, ie it was a sham.

In general, such loans will now be disregarded for IHT purposes, unless repaid by the deceased's personal representatives. Repayment of such a loan will have positive IHT consequences (the deductibility of the debt will be restored) but may have negative income tax consequences, in the common scenario that the loan was interest-bearing but interest was allowed to roll up throughout the duration of the loan (the trust will receive a substantial amount of income, which will typically be UK source and therefore immediately taxable for the trustees, even if the trust is non-UK resident). As the rate of income tax applicable to a trust (45%) exceeds the rate of IHT on death (40%), there may be merit in this scenario in the trustees waiving the accrued interest but requiring repayment of the principal.

Section 175A applies in relation to any transfer of value, or deemed transfer of value, after the passing of the Finance Act 2013 (in July 2013). Again, there is no 'grandfathering' with respect to arrangements put in place in reliance on the old rules.

Discharge out of the estate in money or money's worth

84.21 As noted above, for a liability to be allowed under s 175A(1), it must be discharged out of the deceased's estate, or out of excluded property owned by the deceased immediately before death (such property does not, of course, form part of a deceased person's estate for IHT purposes: IHTA 1984, s 5(1)). The term 'estate' here has its normal IHT meaning, which is extended by the treatment of pre-March 2006 interest in possession settlements (discussed in the next chapter, at para **85.2**) and by the GWR rules (also considered in the next chapter, at para **85.8**). Thus the repayment need not always be made out of property that was personally owned by the deceased on his or her death. However, in the case of a repayment out of excluded property, it is essential that the property in question was the deceased's personal property.

The reference in s 175A(1) to a liability being 'discharged out of' property 'in money or money's worth' is, perhaps, slightly odd. The language used clearly covers any situation in which a liability is extinguished by a cash payment equal to the liability, but in addition seems to include the scenario in which a liability is released in consideration of the transfer of a valuable asset to the creditor, whether or not the value of that asset matches the amount of the liability. As discussed above (para **84.3**), 'money's worth' means valuable consideration, but not necessarily full consideration.

HMRC accept that where personal representatives of a deceased individual borrow, in their capacity as such, to raise funds to repay a liability of the deceased, that counts as a discharge of the liability out of the deceased's estate, regardless of the source of the new loan (IHTM28027). Thus, rather counter-intuitively, where the deceased owed money to a trust, there is no obstacle to the personal representatives borrowing from the same trust to facilitate repayment of the original debt, and in principle the trustees can then write off the new debt, without that affecting the deductibility of the original debt when valuing the deceased's estate. However, as noted above, repayment of the original debt may have income tax consequences, depending on whether interest has accrued on it, and on whether such interest is paid or waived.

Liability not repaid after death

84.22 Generally, a liability not repaid during the administration of the estate must be disregarded, pursuant to s 175A(1). However, there is an exception in s 175A(2), which allows a liability to be taken into account (subject to the various other anti-avoidance provisions discussed in this chapter), notwithstanding that it has not been discharged, if:

(a) there is a 'real commercial reason' for the liability not being discharged; and

(b) securing a tax advantage is not the main purpose, or one of the main purposes, of leaving the liability undischarged.

'Tax advantage' here is defined (in s 175A(5)–(6)) so that it includes an advantage in relation to IHT, income tax and CGT, but not in relation to any other tax.

There is a very fair discussion of this exception in the IHT Manual, at IHTM28028. HMRC accept that there may be a 'real commercial reason' for a debt being left unpaid, and being assumed by a legatee of the deceased, even where the creditor is not a commercial lender and the making of the loan may have been made as part of wider arrangements which were aimed at securing a tax advantage. What is critical is the rationale for leaving the debt outstanding after death, not the rationale for the loan when it was originally made.

Chapter 85

THE IHT TREATMENT OF LIABILITIES: TRUSTS AND RESERVATIONS OF BENEFIT

INTRODUCTION

85.1 This chapter considers a couple of special topics in relation to the IHT treatment of liabilities, namely the deductibility of debts due from trustees, and the deductibility of debts in respect of property which is subject to a reservation of benefit. For detailed discussion of the IHT provisions that govern the deductibility of liabilities and how liabilities are matched to particular assets for IHT purposes, reference should be made to the preceding chapter.

As noted in that chapter, there is a possibility of further change to the law regarding the deductibility of liabilities for IHT purposes. The discussion below is concerned with the position as at the time of writing (early October 2016).

QUALIFYING INTEREST IN POSSESSION SETTLEMENTS

Extent of the deeming in s 49(1)

85.2 Liabilities of the trustees of pre-March 2006 interest in possession settlements (and other qualifying interest in possession settlements, such as settlements in which there is an immediate post-death interest) require particular consideration, because of the tax fiction that the property of such a trust is part of the estate of the life tenant (IHTA 1984, s 49(1)). To some extent, there is an aggregation of the life tenant's personal property with the trust property, for IHT purposes. This raises the issue of whether, on the death of the life tenant, a liability of the trustees can be deducted from the value of personal property; or conversely whether a liability of the life tenant can be deducted from the value of trust property.

This issue was considered in *St Barbe Green v IRC* , [2005] EWHC 14 (Ch), [2005] STC 288, [2005] All ER (D) 17 (Jan). The case concerned an individual with a life interest in a number of trusts. The individual had died with liabilities exceeding his personal assets. The trusts, however, had no indebtedness, and the trustees had not guaranteed the deceased's debts. The question in *St Barbe Green* was whether, in determining the aggregate value of the estate for IHT purposes, the deceased's personal liabilities (insofar as they exceeded the gross value of his personal assets) could be deducted from the trust assets.

It was held that they could not. The reasoning was that, for IHT purposes, liabilities can only be deducted from the value of assets 'which are liable to bear them'. The trustees had no liability to pay the debts of the deceased, so those debts could not be deducted from the gross value of the trust assets, notwithstanding the deeming provision in s 49(1).

Impact of anti-avoidance provisions

85.3 All of the anti-avoidance provisions introduced by FA 2013, Sch 36 are potentially applicable to a liability due from the trustees of a QIIP settlement.

IHTA 1984, s 162A (see para **84.15**) will apply in relation to such a trust on the death of the life tenant, in the event that the trust was settled by an individual who was domiciled outside the UK (and not deemed domiciled in the UK), and the trustees hold some UK situs assets, but have borrowed to acquire excluded property. This scenario will be relatively unusual, as generally the trustees of such a trust will have incorporated a non-UK company to hold any UK assets.

In addition, s 175A (see para **84.20**) will apply on the death of the life tenant, on the basis that the trust property is deemed to be included in the life tenant's estate. A liability of the trustees will be deductible if it is paid by the trustees out of trust property, or if there is a 'real commercial reason' for the liability being left outstanding, and the main purpose of the non-payment of the liability is not to secure a relevant tax advantage (see para **84.22**).

What if the liability is *not* paid not by the trustees, but is instead paid by the life tenant's personal representatives? There is likewise a discharge of the liability out of the estate, so again the liability should be allowed in valuing the property of the trust. Section 175A does not, in terms, require the payment of the liability to be made using property which is liable to bear the liability, and there is no reason to impute such a requirement.

It is sometimes suggested by HMRC, for example in the context of trust-based home ownership structures, that a liability due from trustees may in certain circumstances be subject to abatement under FA 1986, s 103 (see para **84.8**). It is abundantly clear that this is wrong, as s 103 affects the deductibility of 'a liability consisting of a debt incurred by [the deceased] or an incumbrance created by a disposition made by [the deceased]' (s 103(1)). A debt incurred by trustees or a charge granted by trustees clearly fall outside the ambit of the section.

Debt due from life tenant to trust

85.4 Occasionally, the situation arises that the life tenant of a QIIP settlement has borrowed from the trust. Where the life tenant is not also the settlor, this arrangement is generally IHT-neutral on the life tenant's death. The life tenant's debt to the trust will be deductible in valuing the property in his or her personal estate, provided that the debt is repaid after death, or the non-payment of the debt is for commercial reasons, so that s 175A(2) applies (see para **84.22**). This IHT deduction will be balanced by additional trust property, in the form of the benefit of the debt, which will be included in the estate pursuant to s 49(1).

However, in some scenarios the debt is not IHT-neutral. A particular trap is where the life tenant is also the settlor. In this scenario, the debt may be subject to full abatement under FA 1986, s 103 (see para **84.8**), so may not be deductible when valuing the life tenant's personal estate, but the benefit of the debt held by the trustees still has to be taken into account in valuing the trust property which is included in the estate under IHTA 1984, s 49(1). This creates scope for double taxation, which would not be mitigated by the IHT (Double Charges Relief) Regulations 1987 (SI 1987/1130).

RELEVANT PROPERTY SETTLEMENTS

Whether liabilities deductible in principle

85.5 There is little or no case law concerning the deductibility of liabilities from the property of a relevant property settlement, for the purposes of determining the charge to IHT on a tenth anniversary of the commencement of the settlement (IHTA 1984, s 64), or when capital exits the settlement (s 65). It is universally accepted, though, that a debt due from the trustees is deductible from the trust property for these purposes, subject to the various anti-avoidance provisions considered in Chapter **84**. References in IHTA, Chapter III, Part III to the value of the relevant property comprised in the settlement must be taken as references to the net value of such property.

Requirement for valuable consideration?

85.6 One point of interesting detail here is the question of whether the requirement in IHTA 1984, s 5(5) (see para **84.3**) for a liability to have been incurred for a consideration in money or money's worth has any application in relation to IHT charges under the relevant property regime. Section 5(5) applies to 'a liability incurred by a transferor'. The trustees of a relevant property settlement on a decennial charge date do not make, and are not deemed to make, any transfer of value. Tax is charged by reference to a hypothetical transfer of value made by a hypothetical transferor, but that is not the same thing.

The title of s 5, 'Meaning of estate', arguably lends support to the view that s 5(5) relates only to the valuation of the estates of individuals, and has no application to the liabilities of trustees under the relevant property regime. If this is correct, a liability due from the trustees of a relevant property settlement may be deductible, when computing a 10-year charge or exit charge, even if the liability was incurred entirely gratuitously, eg under a deed of covenant.

Impact of anti-avoidance provisions

85.7 As discussed in the preceding chapter (para **84.13**), FA 1986, s 103 cannot apply to liabilities of trustees. IHTA 1984, s 175A also has no bearing on IHT charges under the relevant property regime, being solely concerned with the valuation of an individual's estate on his or her death. However, s 162A has a wider ambit and will affect the deductibility of a debt for the purposes of the relevant property regime, where the debt was incurred to acquire, maintain or enhance the value of excluded property (see para **84.15**).

PROPERTY SUBJECT TO A RESERVATION OF BENEFIT

Whether liabilities deductible in principle

85.8 The interaction between the IHT rules on liabilities and the reservation of benefit rules (see CHAPTER 83) is a subject of some difficulty. If an individual gives away property and reserves a benefit over it, 'that property' is treated as included in his estate on his death (FA 1986, s 102(3)). Can a liability of the owner of the property be deducted in determining the property's value, for the purpose of calculating the IHT charge on the donor's estate?

The reference to 'that property' might suggest that the answer is no, and that the gross value of the property must be used in all cases. However, it is generally considered by practitioners that a liability of the owner of the GWR property may, in certain circumstances, be deducted for the purpose of calculating the IHT charge on the estate.

The case for deductibility is, it is suggested, clearest where the reservation of benefit is over the property of a settlement (where the settlor is also a beneficiary). It seems logical that, in line with the principles that apply in valuing trust property for the purposes of the relevant property regime (see para **85.5** above), it is the net value of the trust property which is deemed to be included in the settlor's estate (subject to all the anti-avoidance provisions discussed in the preceding chapter). It is, after all, only the net value which the trustees would be able to distribute to him. HMRC seem to accept this (IHTM14401).

However, the case for deductibility is less obvious where the GWR property is property of another individual. If, for example, an individual has gifted a house to a child, and has then continued to occupy the house, and the child has borrowed on the security of the house, it is not obvious that the child's borrowings affect the value of the GWR property which is deemed to be included in the donor's estate on his death.

One possible analysis here (based on an extension of the reasoning in *St Barbe Green*; see para **85.2** above) is that a debt in respect of GWR property is (in principle) taken into account if the property in question is 'liable to bear' the debt. According to this analysis, a debt charged on the house should be taken into account in valuing the house for the purposes of IHT on the death of the donor, subject to the anti-avoidance provisions which have already been discussed.

Impact of anti-avoidance provisions

85.9 Again, the anti-avoidance provisions introduced by FA 2013, Sch 36 need to be considered to determine whether an IHT deduction can, in fact, be claimed, where a liability has been incurred in respect of GWR property.

Where IHTA 1984, s 175A is concerned, it is suggested that, on the whole, it should be possible to take advantage of the exception in s 175A(2) (see para **84.22**). HMRC should generally accept that there is no commercial reason why the liability should be repaid following the death of the individual who had reserved a benefit. Usually, that individual's death will be irrelevant to the debtor/creditor relationship, and it will not trigger repayment.

However, one situation in which it might be more difficult to utilise the exception in s 175A(2) would be if the liability due from the owner of the GWR property was an 'on demand' debt due to the deceased. Such a debt could be expected to be 'called in' by the deceased's personal representatives. An omission to do so could give rise to double taxation, as the benefit of the debt would be included in the deceased's estate (unless it was excluded property), and so too (if the s 175A(2) exception was unavailable) would be the gross value of the GWR property.

Chapter 86

PRE-OWNED ASSETS

INTRODUCTION

86.1 Finance Act 2004, Schedule 15 imposes an income tax charge on certain individuals in respect of what are called pre-owned assets. It came into effect on 6 April 2005 (s 84(2)).

The rationale behind this legislation was summarised as follows at para 4 of the 2004 Budget Press Release 'Tax treatment of pre-owned assets' (REVBN 40):

> 'The Government is aware that various schemes designed to avoid inheritance tax have been marketed in recent years. These use artificial structures to avoid the existing rules about gifts made with reservation. As a result, people have been removing assets from their taxable estate but continuing to enjoy all the benefits of ownership. The Government is determined to block this sort of avoidance and announced in the Pre-Budget report that people who benefit from these sorts of schemes would be subject to an income tax charge from April 2005, to reflect their additional taxable capacity from receiving these benefits at low or no cost.'

Although the legislation has been in force since 6 April 2005, the arrangements which give rise to it can have been put into place many years previously. The general rule is that only transactions effected before 18 March 1986 are excluded. 18 March 1986 was the date on which the IHT gift with reservation ('GWR') rules took effect.

The legislation has been supplemented by regulations, namely the Charge to Income Tax by Reference to Enjoyment of Property Previously Owned Regulations 2005 (SI 2005/724). HMRC has published guidance on its website. Clarification of many technical points has been given to professional bodies by HMRC under Code of Practice 10 ('COP 10 Questions').

The drafting of the legislation is appalling. The meaning is frequently unclear and on one view certain provisions go far wider than merely countering IHT schemes. However, their purpose is self-evidently to counter arrangements whereby the taxpayer enjoys assets which are no longer in his estate for IHT purposes. This is inter alia indicated by the exemptions discussed in paras **86.19** to **86.26** and by the election provisions explained in para **86.29**. Points of ambiguity should, it may be suggested, be construed with that purpose in mind.

At first sight the pre-owned assets rules have little to do with offshore tax planning, as they were enacted to counter domestic UK tax avoidance. However, they do affect UK resident non-UK domiciliaries, to the extent that they enjoy use of UK situated assets which were once part of their taxable estate for IHT purposes, or which derive from such assets. As a result, for foreign domiciliaries, the pre-owned asset rules are particularly relevant to structures holding UK homes or UK situated intangibles.

It should be remembered that the pre-owned assets rules do not apply to an individual in any tax year during which he is not UK resident.

BASIC STRUCTURE

86.2 Schedule 15 imposes three distinct charges, one on land, one on chattels and one on what are called intangibles but is, in fact, a charge on all kinds of settled property other than land or chattels. Schedule 15 then introduces a series of exceptions and exemptions, including those applicable to non-UK residents and non-UK domiciliaries.

This chapter follows the form of the schedule. It is to be emphasised that the exceptions and exemptions (discussed from para **86.14** below onwards) greatly cut down the ambit of the three charges.

LAND

86.3 The charging provision dealing with land imposes a charge in any year of assessment in which the conditions set out in Sch 15 para 3 are met. Those conditions require the taxpayer to occupy the land. In addition, either the 'disposal condition' or the 'contribution condition' must be satisfied (Sch 15, para 3).

Occupies

86.4 The term 'occupies' is not defined. HMRC construe it as it including not merely residence but also use of the land for storage and occasional use coupled with sole possession of the means of access (Guidance para 4.6). Holiday homes and second homes are thus included.

There is no requirement that occupation be for the entire tax year concerned. However, if occupation is for part only of the year, the charge is based only on the period of occupation (Sch 15 para 4(3)).

The disposal condition

86.5 The 'disposal condition' is satisfied if:

(a)   the taxpayer owned an interest in the land at any time after 17 March 1986;

(b)   at some time after 17 March 1986 he disposed of that interest or of part of it; and

(c)   that disposal was not by an excluded transaction (as to which see para 86.14 below).

The disposal condition is also satisfied if:

(a)   the taxpayer owned an interest in other property at any time after 17 March 1986;

(b)   at some time after 17 March 1986 he disposed of all or part of that interest otherwise than by an excluded transaction; and

(c)   the proceeds of a disposal of the other property were applied directly or indirectly by another person in acquiring an interest in the land now occupied by the taxpayer.

The term 'property' bears its IHT meaning (Sch 15 para 1). The IHT definition is inclusive rather than definitive, but it is provided that the term includes rights and interests of any description (IHTA 1984, s 272). In an IHT context the term plainly comprehends not just tangible property but also intangibles and even money.

The term 'owned' is not defined. Sch 15 is not part of the IHT legislation, so the various instances in IHTA 1984 of deemed beneficial entitlement, most notably interests in possession, are not incorporated. However, a question still arises of whether an individual could ever be said to satisfy the disposal condition if the land he occupies was formerly owned by a trust of which he is a beneficiary, as distinct from being owned by himself personally. This is not inconceivable, at least if he held an interest in possession, as there is authority in other contexts indicating that fixed interest beneficiaries own interests in the settled property (see *R v IRC, ex p Newfields Developments Ltd* [2001] UKHL 27, [2001] STC 901, 906).

The contribution condition

86.6 The 'contribution condition' is satisfied if:

(a)   another person acquired an interest in the land now occupied by the taxpayer;

(b)   the taxpayer directly or indirectly provided all or any of the consideration given by that other person for the acquisition;

(c)   that provision was made after 17 March 1986; and

(d)   the provision was not by way of an excluded transaction (see para 86.14).

The condition is also satisfied if:

(a)   the other person acquired an interest in other property;

(b)   the taxpayer directly or indirectly provided all or any of the consideration for that acquisition otherwise then by way of an excluded transaction;

(c)   the other person has disposed of that property; and

(d)   the other person has applied the proceeds of that disposal, directly or indirectly, towards the acquisition of an interest in the land now occupied by the taxpayer.

Provided

86.7 'Provided' is the key term in the contribution condition. It is not used in the disposal condition, since all that is required under that condition is a disposal.

As is explained in para **86.15**, most commercial transactions are excluded from the disposal condition. There is no similar exclusion in relation to the contribution condition. This raises the issue of and the issue therefore raised is whether the term 'provided' itself connotes bounty. It might be expected that an element of bounty would be required for consideration to have been 'provided', since the term 'provided' has been construed in that manner for the purposes of the income tax settlements legislation (see para **75.20**).

However, in this context, a construction of 'provided' which requires an element of bounty creates certain difficulties. For example, one would expect the contribution condition to be satisfied if a taxpayer has lent money to a trust, which has used the money to acquire a property occupied by the taxpayer, and has subsequently written that loan off. In commercial substance that is of course equivalent to the taxpayer having funded the trust by way of gift. However, if the loan was made on commercial terms, arguably there would be no element of bounty when the loan was made and thus no 'provision' at that stage. The waiver of the debt would of course be bounteous but at that point the consideration would already have been paid. If, therefore, there is a requirement for 'provision' to be bounteous, the contribution condition might not be met in this scenario.

One would also expect the contribution condition to be satisfied (and it is understood that HMRC consider that it is) if a taxpayer has lent money to a trust, which has used the money to acquire a property for occupation by the taxpayer (as in the above example), and the taxpayer has subsequently given the benefit of the debt to a second trust. Prior to FA 2004 such arrangements were quite common as a means of circumventing the gift with reservation of benefit rules, and it is widely understood that it was arrangements of this nature which the pre-owned assets rules were devised to prevent. It is even more difficult in this case to see how bounty has been conferred on the first trust, at least if the loan was made on commercial terms. Bounty has of course been conferred on the second trust, but that trust has not paid the consideration for the property.

It is suggested on the basis of these examples that, although the position is unclear and there is no consensus among advisers, the better view is that there can be 'provision' for the purposes of the contribution condition without that provision being bounteous. It seems likely that a taxpayer would be regarded as having 'provided' the consideration for the purchase of land or a chattel if he has lent funds to the purchaser for that purpose, regardless of the commerciality or otherwise of the loan. However, it is hard to see how there could be provision if the taxpayer has sold or purchased an asset for cash at market value.

HMRC's view on whether 'provision' need be bounteous is not clear. The point is raised in question 32 of the COP 10 Questions but HMRC's answer is inconclusive. In para 1.2.1 of the Guidance HMRC say they do not regard the contribution condition as met where the occupier has lent money to the owner of the property, even if the loan is interest-free, at least where the occupier has retained the benefit of the loan. The stated rationale is that the loan is in the occupier's estate with the result that it would not be 'reasonable' to regard it as within the contribution condition.

It is suggested that this answer reaches the correct result (ie that a tax charge under the pre-owned assets rules cannot arise in the situation described above) but by the wrong route. Arguably the better view is that the contribution condition is satisfied in this scenario, but a tax charge under Schedule 15 is precluded on the basis that the benefit of the debt, which derives its value from the property, is included in the occupier's estate. Accordingly the exemption in para 11(1) applies (see para **86.25** below).

Directly or indirectly

86.8 The term 'directly or indirectly' is important to the contribution condition. It may be suggested that the taxpayer directly provides the consideration given by the other person if he makes a direct gift to that person. Indirect provision would perhaps cover routing through a third party, but here case law in other contexts indicates the third party must be accountable to the other person or that at the very least there must be an expectation he will pass the gift on (see for example *Yuill v Wilson* [1979] STC 486 per Buckley LJ and *Pott's Executors v IRC* [1950] 32 TC 211).

The term 'directly or indirectly' is also used in another context, in that under both the disposal condition and the contribution condition the application of the proceeds of other property in acquiring the interest in the land can be direct or indirect. Here the use of the word 'indirect' raises the issue of whether the proceeds of the other property can first be invested in some other asset, and then the proceeds of sale of that asset be used to buy the land.

It may be suggested that in all these contexts a tracing exercise is required. If on the facts the money used to buy an interest in the land occupied by the taxpayer cannot be traced back to him, neither the disposal condition nor the contribution condition is met. This is so even if within the buyer's overall estate is money or value gifted by the taxpayer, provided it can be shown that money or value has not directly or indirectly gone towards acquiring the interest in the land.

Interest

86.9 Although the taxpayer has to be in occupation of the land as a physical entity, the disposal condition and the contribution condition both focus on interests in the land. Thus to trigger the disposal condition the taxpayer has to have disposed of an interest in the land and to trigger the contribution condition the present owner has to have acquired an interest in the land.

Overlap between the disposal condition and the contribution condition

86.10 It is clear that as a matter of construction there is overlap between the disposal condition and the contribution condition. Indeed on one view the only scenario on which there is not an overlap is where the disposal condition is met by the interest in the land having been disposed of by the taxpayer, ie the first head of the disposal condition in para 86.5 above.

HMRC now accept that if what the taxpayer parted with was cash, the contribution condition alone is met, for it is not natural to refer to cash being disposed of (see COP 10 Questions, answer 31). But both conditions are met where the taxpayer gives assets in specie to the third party, and the third party then sells the assets and uses the proceeds to acquire his interest in the occupied land.

The charge to tax

86.11 When the conditions in para 3 are met (para 86.3) and none of the exemptions described below are in point, the chargeable amount is subject to income tax. The chargeable amount is what is called the 'appropriate rental value' less any payments made by the taxpayer to the owner of the land in pursuance of a legal obligation (para 4(1)). Such payments plainly include rent, a point which means a charge is precluded if the taxpayer pays an arm's length rent.

The starting point in determining the appropriate rental value is the rental value of the occupied land. This is its annual value, ie the amount reasonably obtainable on a yearly tenancy if the landlord repairs and insures (paras 4(3) and 5). A fraction is then applied to that figure to arrive at the appropriate rental value. The denominator is the value of the occupied land as a whole. In the case of the disposal condition, the numerator is the value of the interest in the land previously disposed of by the taxpayer or (as the case may be) such part of the land's value as can reasonably be attributed to the taxpayer's previous disposal of his interest in other property. In the case of the contribution condition the numerator is such part of the value of the land as can reasonably be attributed to the taxpayer's contribution.

The rental value is determined every five years (SI 2005/724 regs 2 and 4). The initial determination looks at the rental value when para 3 first applied, this date being 6 April 2005 where the conditions for the application of para 3 were met before then. Thereafter a revaluation is carried out five years after the start of the first tax year in which para 3 first applied, ie a revaluation was required on 6 April 2010 where the conditions were first met before 6 April 2005. HMRC expect the taxpayer to take all reasonable steps to ascertain rental values, in the same way as if he were letting the property on the open market (Guidance para 2.1).

The rental value is proportionately reduced if the disposal condition is met and the taxpayer received consideration in money for the disposal. Such a disposal is referred to as a non-exempt sale and must have been of the whole of the taxpayer's interest in the land. (Sch 15 para 4(4)). Self-evidently the point is only in issue if the disposal was non-commercial, as if it was at arm's length it would have been an excluded transaction and Sch 15 is then precluded (see para **86.15**).

CHATTELS

86.12 Schedule 15 para 6 enacts the second charging provision of Sch 15, namely that applicable to chattels. It applies where the taxpayer is in possession of or has the use of a chattel and either the disposal condition or the contribution condition is met. In all material respects these conditions are in the same terms as their equivalents relating to land, and para 6 is subject to the same exemptions as land. As with land, where the exemptions are not in point, an amount equal to the chargeable amount is subject to income tax.

The chargeable amount is not related to any assumed rental value. Instead the appropriate amount equates to interest on the value of the chattel as at the valuation date, reduced where appropriate by the same fractions as are applied to the rental value of land (para 7(2)). The rate of interest is the official rate (SI 2005/724, reg 3), currently 3.25% (see para **93.18**). As with land, actual payments made pursuant to a legal obligation are deducted. But because the appropriate amount is based on a rate of interest, payment of a commercial rent for the use of the chattel does not preclude a charge under this head, although it is likely to do so under the GWR exemption (see para **86.23** below).

SETTLED INTANGIBLES

86.13 Schedule 15 para 8 enacts the third and final charging provision, namely that dealing with property other than land or chattels. It is expressed as applying to intangible property, but that term is defined as any property which is not land or chattels (Sch 15, para 1). The paragraph is of more limited compass than its equivalents relating to land and chattels, as it applies only where the intangibles are comprised in a settlement and either are or represent property settled by the taxpayer after 17 March 1986. Further, to come within the paragraph, the settlement must be one whose income is assessable on the taxpayer under ITTOIA 2005, s 624, ie a settlement in which the settlor has an interest (see CHAPTER 69). But for these purposes any interest of his spouse is disregarded (para 8(1)(b)).

This paragraph is subject to the exemptions described in para **86.19** to **86.23** below. In particular it does not apply insofar as the taxpayer is treated as beneficially entitled to the property under the GWR rules.

The quantum of charge where settled property is caught by para 8 is interest at the prescribed rate on such of the settled property as represents the value settled by the taxpayer after 17 March 1986. As with land and chattels, both the rate of interest and the valuation date are prescribed by the regulations, the rate of interest currently being the official rate (SI 2005/724, reg 3).

A bizarre point about the para 8 charge is that the income of the intangibles will already be taxable under s 624, as by definition the taxpayer is within

ITTOIA 2005, Pt 5, Chapter 5 (see Chapter 75). This is acknowledged by para 9 in that the chargeable amount is reduced by any tax in fact paid by the taxpayer under ITTOIA 2005, s 461 (taxation of gains arising from life policies) or s 624, under TCGA 1992, s 86, or under ITA 2007, ss 720–730. But this relief is a deduction of tax from the chargeable amount, not a deduction of tax from tax.

EXCLUDED TRANSACTIONS

86.14 A disposal or contribution by the taxpayer is disregarded if it occurred under an excluded transaction, although only in relation to land or a chattel enjoyed by the taxpayer. The excluded transactions concept has no application to settled intangibles. Schedule 15 para 10 explains what is meant by an excluded transaction.

Commercial transactions

86.15 The main category of excluded transaction arises in relation to the disposal condition, and embraces what may be termed commercial transactions (para 10(1)(a)). A transaction is excluded if it is:

(a)   a disposal of the whole of the taxpayer's interest in the property concerned; and
(b)   the transaction is at arm's length with an unconnected person.

There is one qualification to the requirement that the whole of the taxpayer's interest must be disposed of. This is that he can expressly reserve a right over the property. HMRC construe this as allowing a lease to be reserved (Guidance para 1.3.1).

The taxpayer's disposal of his whole interest in the property may also be an excluded transaction even if it is to a party connected with him. However, for this to apply the transaction must be 'such as might be expected to be made at arm's length between persons not connected with each other'. This language implies not merely that the terms of the transaction must be commercial but also that it must be a type of transaction which is commercial.

There are three circumstances in which the disposal by the taxpayer of part of his interest in the property is an excluded transaction (SI 2005/724, reg 5). They are as follows:

(1)   The disposal was on arm's length terms to an unconnected person.
(2)   It was to a connected person and made before 7 March 2005 on commercial terms.
(3)   It was made to a connected person after 7 March 2005 on commercial terms and for a consideration not comprising cash or readily convertible assets.

In the third of these conditions, the term 'readily convertible asset' bears the meaning used in taxing employment income. This third condition is curious as if the consideration is not cash or readily convertible assets the disposal is unlikely to be commercial. The 'not' in this condition looks like a drafting error.

Spouses

86.16 A transfer by the taxpayer to his spouse or to a settlement in which she has an interest in possession is an excluded transaction for the purposes of both the disposal condition and the contribution condition (Sch 15, paras 10(1)(b) and (c) and 10(2)(a) and (b)). The same applies to transfers in favour of a former spouse if under a court order. However, a settled gift in favour of a spouse or former spouse ceases to be excluded if the spouse's interest terminates (para 10(3)). The exemption where the spouse has an interest in possession applies whether or not the interest is qualifying (cf CHAPTER 61).

IHT exemptions

86.17 A disposal or contribution is an excluded transaction if it comes within IHTA 1984, s 11, the section which prevents certain dispositions for the maintenance of the family from being a transfer of value. The same applies to dispositions which are wholly exempt transfers by virtue of either the IHT annual £3,000 exemption or the £250 small gifts relief (IHTA 1984, ss 19 and 20).

Outright gifts of money

86.18 An outright gift of money is an excluded transaction in relation to the contribution condition if it was made at least seven years before the taxpayer first occupied the land or, as the case may be, used the chattel (para 10(2)(c)). This exclusion applies whether the money is sterling or some other currency, but does not extend to gifts of other assets, even though the donee may have converted them to cash before buying the land or chattels. As a matter of law, the seven years runs from the first use or occupation even if that preceded the enactment of Sch 15. However in practice HMRC accept, by way of concession, that any outright gift of cash made before 6 April 1998 is an excluded transaction (Guidance para 1.3.1).

EXEMPTIONS: PROPERTY SUBJECT TO A RESERVATION

86.19 All three charging provisions are disapplied if the relevant property, or property which derives its value from that property is, in relation to the taxpayer, property subject to a reservation of benefit. This is provided for by Sch 15 para 11. The rules which determine when property is subject to a reservation are those in FA 1986, ss 102–102C.

In the following, the shorthand expression 'derived property' has been used to denote property which derives its value from the relevant property, and property which is subject to a reservation is called 'GWR property'.

Meaning of relevant property

86.20 In relation to the charge on settled intangibles, the relevant property is simply the property from time to time in the settlement (para 11(9)(b)).

In relation to land and chattels the term 'relevant property' has a rather different meaning (para 11(9)(a)), depending on whether the contribution condition or the disposal condition is engaged, as discussed below.

If the contribution condition is satisfied, the relevant property is the property representing the consideration directly or indirectly provided. In the case of chattels, the relevant property is normally the chattel itself. In the case of land, the relevant property is the interest in the land which the recipient of the contribution acquired with the contribution. The reference to consideration 'directly or indirectly' provided suggests that if that property has been sold, the relevant property is the interest in the land or the chattels now owned by the recipient of the contribution, rather than the original property.

Where the recipient of the contribution provided by the taxpayer has borrowed part of the purchase price of the interest in the land or chattels from a third party, the relevant property is the equity in the property. This point has been accepted by HMRC, and while this acceptance was in relation to excluded liabilities (see para 86.26) and interest in possession trusts, there is no reason to suppose it should not be of general application (COP 10 Questions, question 13).

An interesting issue is what happens if a house or chattel is purchased with the aid of commercial borrowing and the house or chattel increases in value. Is all the increase allocated to the taxpayer's contribution or is it divided pro rata between the contribution and the borrowing? It may be argued that the latter is more consistent with the fact that the relevant property is the property that represents the consideration provided by the taxpayer.

If the disposal condition is satisfied, the relevant property is the property disposed of. This is the normally the interest in the land or chattel which the taxpayer occupies or uses. Where the taxpayer disposed of other property and the recipient has since sold that property and used the proceeds to acquire the present interest in the land, the relevant property is not the interest in that land but the original property which has been sold. However, such a disposal is effectively a contribution in specie and so engages the contribution condition (see para 86.10), and in relation to that condition, the interest in the property now occupied or enjoyed is the relevant property. HMRC appear to accept this (COP 10 Questions, reply to question 31(4)).

Derived property

86.21 In some situations, the GWR property is not the relevant property but derived property.

The paradigm example of derived property is shares in a company which owns a house. The house is the relevant property and the shares derive their value from the house.

In practice, such companies are largely capitalised by shareholder loan. Here it is reasonably plain that the shares and the loan are together the derived property, for if the company did not own the property the shares and the loan would be valueless.

Inexplicably, HMRC have indicated that they do not accept this (COP 10 Questions, question 33). However, as explained in para **86.7**, they do not consider the loan to be a contribution at all, where it is retained by the taxpayer. This means, according to the HMRC analysis, that the part of the property representing the loan is excluded in calculating the appropriate rental value or amount charged. The balance is attributable to the shares and should be left out under the reasonability test in para 11(4).

It should be noted that the exemption for property subject to a reservation of benefit does not apply where the value of the derived property is substantially less than that of the relevant property. 'Substantial' is not defined in the legislation, but HMRC take it to mean 20% or more (Guidance para 4.7). Where the test is failed all is not lost, as a reduction by such proportion as is reasonable is made under para 11(4) in the appropriate rental value or (in the case of chattels) in the amount charged. It may be suggested that shares in a company are still derived property where the company owns other assets, provided that such of the value of the shares as is attributable to the relevant property is still not substantially less than that of the property.

Excluded liabilities

86.22 As discussed at para **86.26** below, the existence of an excluded liability can affect the quantification of tax charges under the pre-owned assets rules. However, the excluded liability provisions do not apply to the property subject to a reservation exemption under para 11(3).

Deemed GWR property

86.23 The exemption for GWR property is extended to include property which would be GWR property but for certain exemptions from the GWR rules (para 11(5)). The exemptions concerned include those for gifts to political parties, charities, employee trusts and the like. In the case of land they also include the exemption for a donor's change of circumstances and the exemption that applies where the gifted property is an undivided share in land occupied by the donor and the donee together (FA 1986, s 102B(4)).

In the case of chattels, the para 11 exemption is extended to cases where the donor pays the donee full consideration (para 11(5)(d)). This prevents GWR treatment (FA 1986, Sch 20 para 6(1)(a)) and the extension of the GWR exemption means that, in the case of chattels, payment of an arm's length rent precludes Sch 15. With land, the same result is achieved by the quantification rules (see para **86.11**).

Cash gifts

86.24 The exemption for GWR property does not, in general, apply where GWR treatment is precluded by the inability of the GWR rules to trace through cash. Significantly, this inability applies only to outright gifts, not to settled gifts. But it means that an outright gift sheltered from GWR treatment

1011

by the cash tracing rule is not protected from the Sch 15 charge by para 11. It appears from para 4.2 of the Guidance that HMRC do read the legislation in this way.

In one respect the impact of this rule is tempered: as described in para **86.18** above, a cash gift is an excluded transaction if made before 6 April 1998 or more than seven years before the taxpayer first occupies or uses the land or chattels acquired with the contribution.

EXEMPTIONS: PROPERTY IN THE TAXPAYER'S ESTATE

86.25 Under the terms of para 11(1), all three charging provisions are also disapplied where the relevant property or the derived property are treated for IHT purposes as being in the taxpayer's estate.

This exemption therefore applies where the taxpayer owns the property beneficially and where it is settled property in which he has a qualifying interest in possession (as to which see CHAPTER **61**). The definition of relevant property and the rules as to derived property discussed in paras **86.20** and **86.21** apply equally to this exemption.

In the context of non-UK domiciliaries, it should be noted that the relevant property or derived property is treated for IHT purposes as forming part of the taxpayer's estate, even where that property is excluded property within the meaning of IHTA 1984, s 48. This is because excluded property is treated as being within the non-UK domiciliary's estate until immediately before death, by virtue of IHTA 1984, s 5(1).

Excluded liabilities

86.26 Where the value of the taxpayer's estate is reduced by an excluded liability and that liability affects the value of the relevant property or (as the case may be) the derived property, the relevant or derived property is only treated as comprised in the taxpayer's estate to the extent that its value exceeds the liability. The consequence is that the balance of its value may give rise to income tax under Sch 15.

A liability is an excluded liability if the creation of the liability was an operation associated with either the transaction whereby the relevant property or the derived property came into the taxpayer's estate, or the operation by which the value of the derived property came to be derived from the relevant property. Associated operations for these purposes bear their normal IHT meaning (IHTA 1984, s 268).

In the view of the breadth of the term 'associated operation', a key issue is when it can be said that a liability 'affects' relevant or derived property. Does the property need to be charged as security for the liability for that liability to 'affect' the value of the property? It is suggested that a liability 'affects' relevant or derived property, whether or not there is any security, if it cannot be discharged other than by the property in question. The paradigm case where HMRC are thought to consider that the excluded liability rule is in point is where a pre-23 March 2006 interest in possession trust, which holds a residential property, owes a debt to a second trust. Before the introduction of the pre-owned assets rules, such arrangements were quite commonly put in place as an IHT-avoidance strategy, usually on the basis that the debt due to the second trust was unsecured. Regardless of whether the debt is secured, it reduces the net value of the property that is subject to a qualifying interest in possession and it may be suggested that HMRC are correct to regard the debt as an excluded liability.

Where the contribution condition is in point, commercial borrowing cannot give rise to an excluded liability. As is explained above (para **86.20**) this result follows because only the net value of the property can reasonably be attributed to the taxpayer's contribution. In such a case the relevant property is the equity of redemption.

BENEFITS IN KIND

86.27 Should the owner of a house or chattels be a company, a charge could arise both under Sch 15 and under the benefits-in-kind code (described in CHAPTER 93). In such case the charge under Sch 15 arises only to the extent that the chargeable amount under Sch 15 exceeds the amount treated as earnings (Sch 15 para 19). This provision is in point both where the occupier is an actual director or employee of the company and where HMRC are successful in contending that he is a shadow director.

DE MINIMIS EXEMPTION

86.28 Schedule 15 para 13 confers a *de minimis* exemption. It requires examination of amounts otherwise chargeable under all three heads of Sch 15 in the tax year concerned. If the aggregate of those amounts is £5,000 or less, a charge is not made. However, the limit of £5,000 is not an exempt band, so once it is reached the full amount is taxable.

THE ELECTION

86.29 Under all three charging provisions there is a right to elect out of Sch 15, so that the relevant property will become GWR property and thus within the ambit of IHT on the taxpayer's death. Separate provision is made for land and chattels on the one hand and settled intangibles on the other.

Land and chattels

86.30 Here the rules on elections apply in terms of 'relevant property' which has yet another different meaning. In this context it is the land or chattels which the taxpayer is enjoying (Sch 15 para 21(1)(a)). The taxpayer is allowed, under para 21, to elect that he is not charged under Sch 15 in respect of his enjoyment of the relevant property. Instead, the relevant property or any asset substituted for it is treated in relation to him as property subject to a reservation. This notional reservation subsists so long as he occupies or enjoys the land or chattel or any substituted property.

The election must generally be made by 31 January following the first tax year in which the taxpayer would otherwise be chargeable under Sch 15 by reference to the land or chattels (although see para **86.34** below, regarding late elections). In the case of land or chattels which came within Sch 15 when it came into force on 6 April 2005, 2005–06 was the first year in which the taxpayer was otherwise chargeable. The election was therefore needed by 31 January 2007.

The relief under para 21 was generally thought of as a transitional relief as it enabled taxpayers to unscramble arrangements pre-dating Sch 15. But it is available whenever a taxpayer comes within Sch 15, provided that an election is made before 31 January following the end of the first tax year in which he first does so.

Settled intangibles

86.31 The right of election applicable to settled property defines the settled property as the relevant property. As with land or chattels, it permits the taxpayer to elect that Sch 15 shall be disapplied, at the price of the property being treated as GWR property as long as it remains settled and within ITTOIA 2005, s 624. The time limits are the same.

Interest in possession property

86.32 A special rule applies if the taxpayer making the election is entitled to an interest in possession in the relevant property. This rule applies both to land and chattels and to settled intangibles. In such a case the election still disapplies Sch 15, but the relevant property is not treated as included in the taxpayer's estate for IHT purposes (Sch 15 para 21(2)(b)(ii) and 22(2)(b)(ii)). This provision was enacted by FA 2006, s 80 in conjunction with Sch 15 para 11(12) (see para **86.37** below) and, consonant with the intention of para 11(12), the effect of the election is merely to disapply the revertor to settlor rules in IHTA 1984, ss 53 and 54. On account of the poor drafting of FA 2006, s 80 most cases to which para 11(12) applies are not revertor to settlor cases in the sense of ss 53 and 54 at all, and so the election is without cost.

There is however one trap. The disapplication of the general rule of inclusion in the taxpayer's estate applies, in the case of land and chattels, only where the interest in possession subsists in the relevant property, ie in the land or chattels. It does not apply where the land or chattels are owned by a company and the interest in possession is in the shares in the company. In such a case, the election operates to bring the land or chattels into the taxpayer's estate for IHT purposes in the normal way. This can have unfortunate consequences, particularly where the land or chattels are in the UK and the taxpayer is not UK domiciled.

Form of election

86.33 The election must be made in Form IHT 500 (Income Tax (Benefits received by former owner of property) (Election for Inheritance Tax Treatment) Regulations 2007 (SI 2007/3000)).

Late elections

86.34 Under the original legislation, late elections could only be made if the taxpayer could show reasonable excuse (Sch 15 para 23(3)(4) as originally enacted). This was changed by FA 2007, s 65, and now a late election may be accepted at the discretion of HMRC. HMRC have published guidance as to how they will exercise this discretion (HMRC Technical note, 'Income tax and pre-owned assets guidance section 3', 26 October 2007 (reproduced SWTI [2007] 2446). It has been made clear that s 65 will allow elections which should have been made before 31 January 2007, despite the fact that on that date the changes made by s 66 were not in force (see BN 28, reproduced [2007] STI 914).

TREATMENT OF TRUSTS

Discretionary and post-22 March 2006 interest in possession settlements

86.35 Settled property of a discretionary trust in respect of which the taxpayer is the settlor and a beneficiary will be GWR property in relation to him (FA 1986, s 102) and so exempt from charge under Sch 15 by virtue of the exemption for property subject to a reservation of benefit (para 11(3)).

Similarly, where the taxpayer has a post-22 March 2006 interest in possession in settled property, of which he is the settlor, and is also a potential beneficiary of capital, he will also be exempt from charge under Sch 15 by virtue of the exemption for property subject to a reservation of benefit.

Where a trust is funded by way of an initial gift and a subsequent loan of the funds to acquire the property, the settlor will be treated as having a GWR in the whole property (FA 1986, Sch 20, para 5(4)).

Where the taxpayer has a post-22 March 2006 interest in possession in settled property of which he is the settlor, but cannot otherwise benefit from the trust, the GWR position is less clear and there may be scope for a Sch 15 charge. However, where the relevant property is land, a charge will be precluded as his rent-free occupation of the land will give rise to a GWR in the land (under FA 1986, s 102A) and accordingly the para 11(3) exemption will apply.

Settlor with initial qualifying interest in possession

86.36 Where the taxpayer is the settlor and has an initial pre-22 March 2006 interest in possession in settled property, he will be exempt from charge under

Sch 15 by virtue of the exemption that applies where the relevant property is in the taxpayer's estate (para 11(1)).

Settlor with later qualifying interest in possession (FA 2006, s 80)

86.37 Where the settlor has a qualifying interest in possession in settled property and did not have the interest initially but was appointed it subsequently, the exemption for property within the taxpayer's estate does not apply (Sch 15 para 11(12)). Nor does the exemption for property subject to a reservation, for so long as the qualifying interest in possession subsists (Sch 15 para 11(12)(b)).

The latter restriction has applied since 5 December 2005 and was enacted by FA 2006, s 80. The restriction was intended to counter schemes involving revertor to settlor trusts, which are discussed at the end of section 5 of the Guidance. However, defective drafting means it catches any case where the contribution condition is met by a provision into settlement and the settlor was not entitled to an interest in possession initially but has been appointed one subsequently. HMRC have confirmed it does not catch cases where the settlor's interest has existed since the inception of the settlement (CIOT press release 12 January 2007 reproduced [2007] SWTI 164). The restriction is also precluded where the interest is appointed after 22 March 2006 unless it is a TSI. This is because the restriction does not apply unless the settled property is treated as comprised in the taxpayer's estate (para 11(11)).

Where this problem arises the solution is normally to make an election if the case is one where a late election is allowed (see para **86.32**). But such a course should not be taken if the house is owned by a company (see para **86.32**) and here consideration should be given to terminating the qualifying interest in possession. On the basis that the settlement is an excluded property settlement, this should be without IHT consequences, provided that the non-domiciliary has not in the interim acquired an actual or deemed domicile in the UK, as that would trigger a domicile retest (under IHTA 1984, s 80) with the result that the settlement would lose its excluded property status.

Settlor's spouse with initial qualifying interest in possession

86.38 Where the settlor's spouse took an initial qualifying interest in possession, the settlor will not have a GWR in the settled property, even if he is also a potential beneficiary of the settlement (by virtue of FA 1986, s 102(5)), so the exemption for property subject to a reservation will not apply. However, a Sch 15 charge will still be precluded in relation to land or chattels while the interest in possession subsists, as gifts to a spouse or to a trust in which she has an interest in possession are excluded transactions (see para **86.16**).

Excluded transaction status will be lost if the interest in possession terminates inter vivos (para 10(3)). At that stage, the settled property may then come within the scope of Sch 15, as the settled property will continue to fall outside the GWR rules even if the qualifying interest in possession is subsequently terminated (assuming the settlor is still a beneficiary). However, this is subject to one exception, namely, where the gift into settlement was made after 19 June 2003, as then the termination of the spouse's interest will be treated as though the settlor is making a gift at that time and so the settled property will become GWR property (FA 1986, s 102(5A–5B)) and so will be exempt from charge under Sch 15.

The 2006 changes to IHT mean that this point is not an issue with inter vivos settlements created after 22 March 2006 as even if the settlor's spouse is given an initial interest in possession it is not qualifying and so the settlor will have a GWR from the outset.

IMPACT ON UK RESIDENT NON-UK DOMICILIARIES

86.39 As noted above, a taxpayer is only caught by Sch 15 if he is resident in the UK in the tax year concerned (Sch 15, para 12).

In addition, there are limits on the scope of Sch 15 in relation to foreign domiciliaries. Where the individual is non-UK domiciled, the Schedule only applies to property situated in the UK (unless the individual has acquired an actual or deemed domicile in the UK, in which case it applies regardless of the location of the assets (para 12(2)). In broad terms this equates with the IHT excluded property concept, as it applies to assets outside of trusts. However, there is one important difference. Para 12(2) of Sch 15 focuses on the asset to which Sch 15 would otherwise apply, rather than on the asset held by the donee. Thus in the classic structure of a house or chattels owned by an offshore company, the asset to focus on is the house or chattels rather than the shares in the company and so the exemption under para 12(2) does not apply if the house or chattels are in the UK. Instead, protection from charge will be available under para 11(1) on the basis that the house or chattels are treated as within the non-UK domiciliary's estate for IHT purposes.

A further relief is to be found in para 12(3). This states that if a person was at any time domiciled outside the UK, no regard is had to any property which in relation to him is excluded property under IHTA 1984, s 48(3)(a). That is the subsection which makes foreign property excluded property if it is comprised in a settlement settled by an individual who at the time of making the settlement was not UK domiciled (cf para 62.2). Paragraph 12(3) carries this concept into Sch 15. Again, however, it is necessary to consider assets held at different levels separately. Thus, where the settlement holds shares in an offshore company which in turn holds UK land or chattels, para 12(3) protects the company shares and para 11(1) or 11(3) protects the land or chattels.

For these purposes, a person is to be treated as UK domiciled if he would be so treated for the purpose of IHTA 1984. Thus an individual counts as UK domiciled if he in fact has a UK domicile or if he has an IHT deemed domicile (as to which see CHAPTERS 44 and 45). It is immaterial whether or not he is a remittance basis user.

HOUSE STRUCTURES ESTABLISHED BY NON-UK DOMICILIARIES

86.40 The pre-owned assets rules require careful consideration in relation to structures put in place (typically before the tax charges in 2008) by foreign domiciliaries to own UK houses. In most cases tax charges do not arise, but the analysis is far from simple and there are traps. As Sch 15 does not apply to non-residents, the discussion below applies only to UK resident non-UK domiciliaries.

Companies holding UK houses

86.41 The simplest structure is where the house is owned by an offshore company in which the non-UK domiciliary owns all the shares personally. Such a company may have been capitalised by way of share subscription or by way of loan.

It is unclear whether a share subscription constitutes the 'provision' of consideration to the company. If it does, so that the contribution condition is met, a tax charge under Sch 15 will be precluded if one of the exemptions in paras 11 and 12 are met. The exemption for non-UK domiciliaries (para 12(2)) does not apply as the house is UK situs. But Sch 15 is still precluded, as the shares are derived property and, being owned by the taxpayer beneficially, are in his estate (see para **86.25**). Should the company have borrowed money to buy the property from a third party lender, the shares are still derived property for, assuming what the taxpayer has contributed is a provision at all, it is represented by the equity of redemption (see para **86.20**).

The position may be more complicated if the taxpayer has capitalised the company by shareholder loan. Assuming such a loan is within the contribution condition, it may strongly be argued that the loan and the shares are together derived property. Although HMRC do not accept this (para **86.21**), it is unlikely in the extreme that their view would prevail if the matter was litigated, for both the loan and the shares are in the taxpayer's estate and so outside the mischief of Sch 15.

But even if HMRC's view is right, a charge under Sch 15 would not be in point. This is because the loan would not be seen as a contribution at all (para **86.7**) and so such part of the property's value as is attributable to it would be left out of account in calculating the notional rent. The value attributable to the shares would then be addressed by regarding the relevant property as its value net of the loan (see para **86.20**), on which basis the value of the shares would not be substantially less than that of the relevant property. An alternative analysis would be that it would be reasonable under para 11(4) to reduce the appropriate rental value to nil.

Interesting issues arise if, instead of capitalising the company, the taxpayer buys it when it already owns the property. Here Sch 15 is not in point at all as, in relation to the property, neither the disposal condition nor the contribution condition is met.

Trusts holding UK houses

86.42 A foreign domiciliary's UK house may be owned by an offshore trust of which he is the settlor and a beneficiary. In such a case, there is usually no doubt that the contribution condition is met, for the individual will have funded the trust. So too the disposal condition will be in point if the individual settled assets in specie.

As discussed at para **86.35** above, where the trust is a discretionary trust or a post-22 March 2006 interest in possession trust under which the settlor can also benefit from capital, the exemption for property subject to a reservation is in point. Should commercial borrowing have been incurred, the exemption is still in point as the relevant property is the value of the property net of the borrowing (see para **86.20**).

Where the settlor has a qualifying interest in possession (which may have arisen under the terms of the trust or, at least on HMRC's view, by virtue of his occupation (see para **61.11**)), the house is deemed to be in the taxpayer's estate for IHT purposes and so the exemption for property in the taxpayer's estate is in point (see para **86.25**). This is not affected by any commercial borrowing as the analysis, accepted by HMRC, is that the value of the relevant property is net of the borrowing (see para **86.25**).

Trusts holding UK houses via an underlying company

86.43 Should the trust own the house through a company, the first issue is whether Sch 15 is engaged at all, for the taxpayer's provision will have been to the trust. The trustees will then have capitalised the company by shares or loan, arguably for full consideration (see para **86.41**). It is however difficult to see it being successfully argued that in such a case the taxpayer has not made indirect provision.

Assuming that Sch 15 is in point, the GWR exemption applies if the company is entirely funded by share capital as then the shares are derived property. Should the company be capitalised by shareholder loan, the same issues arise as with directly owned companies. It may be suggested that the answers are the same, particularly as the loan capital held by the trustees is GWR property and thus within the settlor's estate for IHT purposes. The analysis is also the same as for directly owned companies if the company incurs commercial borrowing, for here the value of the relevant property is net of that borrowing and as such not substantially more than the value of the shares.

As regards the shares in the company themselves, these are settled intangibles and so within Sch 15 as the settlor is a beneficiary (see para **86.13**). However, the shares are exempt from charge provided they are excluded property.

Section IV

Other Anti-avoidance Legislation

Chapter 87

CLOSE COMPANIES

INTRODUCTION

87.1 Between 1922 and 1989, the UK had in force rules requiring the undistributed income of closely held companies to be apportioned among the participators. The final iteration of these rules was TA 1988 ss 423–430. The policy objective of the rules was to ensure that the undistributed profits attracted higher rate tax which, at the time those rules were in force, was at penal rates. Thus the primary charging rule was that the income of the company had to be apportioned among the participators according to their respective interests in the company (originally FA 1922, s 21(1), Sch 1 para 8, most recently TA 1988 ss 423(1) and 425(1)).

These rules were abolished in 1989 (FA 1989, s 103). However, their effect lingers on. The reason is that the term 'close company' is used in a wide variety of totally different charging provisions, using the definition that was originally enacted for the now defunct apportionment rules. Similarly the definition of 'control' in those rules is now widely used in other contexts, as is the term 'participator'.

Many of the contexts in which these terms appear are legislation concerned with offshore issues, most notably:

- Apportionment of gains of non-resident close companies (TCGA 1992, s 13; see CHAPTER 88);
- Definition of relevant person for remittance purposes (ITA 2007, s 809M; see CHAPTER 54);
- Capital payments to and from companies (TGGA 1992, s 96; see paras 78.16 to 78.19);
- Corporate settlors and beneficiaries for the purposes of the rules attributing gains to settlors (TCGA 1992, s 86; see paras 76.21 to 76.23); and
- The definitions used in the qualifying criteria for the various reliefs from the 15% penal rate of SDLT and ATED (see CHAPTERS 67 and 66).

For this reason, a discussion of the meaning of 'close company' and related terms is relevant to this book. Currently the definitions are included in the corporation tax code, ie CTA 2010, ss 439–454.

At the outset, one preliminary point needs to be made. The definition of close company *simpliciter* has always been subject to the prerequisite that the company be UK resident (CTA 2010, s 442(a)). In legislative contexts relevant to this book, that prerequisite is disapplied, in that the statutory provisions are almost invariably expressed as applying to close companies but also to non-resident companies which would be close if they were UK resident. In what follows, therefore, the term 'close company' is so used.

CORE MEANING

87.2 The core meaning of the term 'close company' is that the company is under the control of five or fewer participators (CTA 2010, s 439(2)(a)). By 'control' is meant the ability or entitlement to exercise direct or indirect control over the company's affairs (CTA 2010, s 450(2)). What is connoted by such control is the ability to exercise the majority of votes able to be cast in general meeting (*Steele (Inspector of Taxes) v EVC International NV (formerly European Vinyls Corpn (Holdings) BV)* [1996] STC 785, [1996] 69 TC 88, CA; *Kellogg Brown & Root Holdings (UK) Ltd v Revenue and Customs Comrs* [2009] EWHC 584 (Ch), [2009] STC 1359, para 39; *UBS AG v HMRC* [2013] STC 68 para 124; *DB Group Services (UK) Ltd v Revenue and Customs Comrs* [2014] EWCA Civ 452, [2014] STC 2278).

On this basis the exercise required is normally simple. If a majority of the shares in the company are held by five or fewer people the company is close. If they are not, it is not. With the great majority of companies encountered in offshore tax planning this produces the answer that the company *is* close. But where it does not, and the matter has to be looked at further, complexity is encountered.

The reasons for the complexity are threefold:

(1)   The term 'participator' has an extended definition.
(2)   Account has to be taken of what are termed 'associates'.
(3)   The term 'control' also has an extended definition.

Even if not under the control of five or fewer participators a company is also close if either

(a)   It is under the control of participators who are directors; or
(b)   Five or fewer participators, or participators who are directors, would be entitled to the greater part of the company's assets in the event of the company's liquidation.

Control by directors is not constrained by the five or fewer requirements but this situation is not often encountered in an offshore context. The liquidation test is considered further in para **87.10** below.

PARTICIPATOR

87.3 The term 'participator' is defined as any person having a share or interest in the income or capital of the company (CTA 2010, s 454(1)). The following are included in particular:

(a)   Persons who possess share capital or voting rights.
(b)   Loan creditors.

(c)   Persons who possess or are entitled to acquire the right to participate in distributions.
(d)   Persons who are entitled to secure that income or assets of the company are applied for their benefit.

Fixed interest trusts

87.4 The reference to entitlement to participate in distributions means that a life tenant under a fixed interest trust is a participator in any company in which the trust holds shares (*R v IRC ex parte Newfields Developments* [2001] STC 901, para 12). The holder of a vested reversion is also a participator, as entitlement under the extended definition of participator includes anything the person will be entitled to at a future date (s 454(3)). It may be suggested that the position is otherwise where the reversion can be defeated by the exercise of overriding powers of appointment, as in such a case it cannot be said the reversioner will be entitled in the future.

Discretionary trusts

87.5 A difficult issue is whether a discretionary beneficiary is a participator in a company in which the trust holds shares. It is reasonably plain that a discretionary beneficiary does not come within the inclusive meanings of participator given above, as those meanings all look to entitlement or possession. But the question may still be raised of whether a discretionary beneficiary can be said to have an 'interest' in the capital or income of the company in the general sense of the term. In a strict sense he certainly does not, for he has an interest not in the company's assets or income, but merely in the shares issued by the company. But this is too simplistic and the definition requires the company to be looked through (*Alexander Drew and Sons Ltd v HMRC* (1932) 17 TC 140).

On the basis that is right, case-law shows that the term 'interest' can, in certain circumstances, extend to a discretionary beneficiary, his interest being the right to be considered as a potential recipient of benefit by the trustees and have his interest protected by the Court (*Leedale (Inspector of Taxes) v Lewis* [1982] 3 All ER 808, [1982] STC 835, 839, HL, applying Lord Wilberforce's dictum in *Gartside v IRC* [1968] AC 553, 612, [1968] 1 All ER 121, HL). But whether it in fact does so depends on the context, and the context may indicate the term refers only to such interests as can be assigned a value (*Leedale v Lewis* at p 843, per Lord Wilberforce). Such a context would be where the statute necessarily requires ascertainment of the quantum of the interest, as was the case in *Gartside*. It may be suggested the definition of participator falls into this latter category, given that the main purpose of the close company legislation was to provide for the apportionment of close company income to participators. As noted above, that apportionment had to be according to 'the respective interests in the company in question of the participators' and there was no provision for apportionment on a just and reasonable basis.

Such an analysis gains support from *Willingale (Inspector of Taxes) v Islington Green Investment Co* [1972] 3 All ER 849, (1972) 48 TC 547, CA. Here the issue was whether executors of an unadministered estate were persons interested in shares comprised in the estate. The Court of Appeal held they were and made the following important comment as respects the beneficiaries of the estate:

> 'The beneficiaries under the will had no interest at all. They only had the right to have the estate property administered.'

Assuming this analysis is right, a discretionary beneficiary is not a participator. Whether or not that is so, a person who is not a beneficiary, but could be added in exercise of a power of addition, cannot on any view be regarded as a participator, for it is difficult to see how such a person could be said to have an 'interest' in trust assets in even the widest sense. The technical analysis is that unless and until such a person is in fact added as a beneficiary, he is not someone the trustees have to consider as a potential recipient of benefit.

Common trustee

87.6 A further issue arises with trusts, this one focusing on the identity of the trustee. Early case law indicated that in ascertaining whether an individual controlled a company, the capacity in which he held shares was ignored. Thus his personal shares could be aggregated with those held by trusts of which he was trustee (*IRC v J Bibby & Sons Ltd* [1945] 1 All ER 667, [1945] 29 TC 167, HL). This rule, however, ceased to apply in 2006. Now it is provided that 'the trustees of a settlement are together treated as if they were a single person (distinct from the persons who are the trustees of the settlement from time to time)' (ITA 2007, s 474 as applied to corporation tax by CTA 2010, s 1169). It follows that each trust which is a separate settlement in the general sense of the term is treated as a separate person for the purposes of the close company rules.

The relevant legislation, ITA 2007, s 474, is subject to one qualification, in that it operates 'except where the context otherwise requires'. But this means no more than that the definition in s 474 applies unless the context compels the adoption of another interpretation (*Melville v IRC* [2001] STC 628 para 16 per Lightman J as approved [2002] STC 1271 para 32). Here it is plain that s 474, far from being disapplied in determining control, is meant to apply. Such is indicated by CTA 2010, s 30, which disapplies the rule that companies are associated if they are controlled by a common trustee. This disapplication is expressed as applying only where both companies are held in trust and not where one is held beneficially and as such predicates s 474 applies. That such was intended is indicated by the Explanatory Notes to CTA 2010, specifically change 3.

It follows from the above that, regardless of the status of the beneficiaries, the trustees of a trust who hold shares in a company are participators in their own right, as a separate person.

HMRC Practice

87.7 HMRC state in the corporation tax manual that the word 'interested' has a wide meaning and that the trustees, the beneficiaries and the remainderman (if any) of the trust are all interested in trust shareholdings. The authorities cited, however, all concerned fixed interest trusts, not discretionary trusts. Moreover, the principal authority given appears to have turned more on the rule just discussed, requiring aggregation of trust shares with personal shares of the trustees (*IRC v Park Investments Ltd* [1966] Ch 701, 43, [1966] 43 TC 200, CA). Overall, what is said in the manual thus bears little on the position of discretionary beneficiaries.

ASSOCIATES

87.8 The relevance of the 'associate' concept is that in determining whether five or fewer participators control a company, the rights and powers of their associates are attributed to them (Corporation Tax Act 2010 (CTA 2010), s 451(1)(c)). However, if a person is not a participator in the sense discussed above, he is not made such by the fact that his associates are. Associates are only relevant once a person is a participator in his own right.

The term 'associate' is principally defined by reference to an individual. The following are his associates (s 448):

- relatives;
- partners;
- any settlement of which the individual is settlor;
- any settlement of which a living or dead relative is settlor; and
- any settlement owning shares in which he 'has an interest'.

The relatives of an individual comprise:

(a)   his parents or more remote ancestors;
(b)   his children or more remote issue;
(c)   his siblings (but not his nephews and nieces); and
(d)   his spouse (but not the spouses of any of the other above categories).

The inclusion of settlements of which a living or dead relative is settlor is significant and in most cases it brings within the term 'associate' settlements of which the individual is a beneficiary. Where the settlor has the requisite connection with the individual, the settlement is an associate in relation to the individual, even if the individual is excluded from benefit. However, a settlement of which he is a beneficiary is not an associate if the settlor is not his relative, unless the individual 'has an interest' in the shares held by the trustees.

This last limb of the 'associate' definition is the most difficult. However, it is plain that it should be read with the definition of 'participator' discussed above, and thus is the mechanism by which the trust shares are attributed to a life tenant or holder of an absolutely vested reversion.

The effect of the 'associate' concept is inter alia that aggregation is required of shares held by members of the same family as the participators, together with such shares held in any trust of which any of them is or was a settlor, or is a life tenant or vested reversioner.

CONTROL

87.9 The core definition of control in CTA 2010, s 450 treats a person as having control of a company if he exercises direct or indirect control over the company's affairs. The same applies if he is able to exercise such control or is entitled to acquire it (s 450(2)). As indicated in para **87.2**, the control connoted by this definition is control at shareholder level – ie control over a majority of votes able to be cast in general meeting.

The shareholder control can be direct or indirect, and as a result a controlling shareholder in a parent company has control of its direct and indirect subsidiaries (*Kellogg Brown & Root Holdings (UK) Ltd v HMRC* [2009] STC 1359, para 42).

As ability to exercise control is a question of fact, it is possible for a shareholder who does not own a majority of the voting shares to be found to have control. However it appears that cases where such a finding will be justified will be rare. It is not sufficient that an actual shareholder and the alleged controlling party are combining together to implement some pre-planned scheme, for then each party is acting in his own interest, albeit in concert. There must be some additional element which, while not compulsion, is akin to it. What that element is, and whether in a given case it is present, is a question of fact (*DB Group Services (UK) Ltd v Revenue and Customs Comrs* [2014] EWCA Civ 452, [2014] STC 2278).

Deemed control

87.10 In addition to the general definition, there are four situations in which five or fewer participators are deemed to control a company. These are if they possess or are entitled to acquire one or more of the following:

(a)   The greater part of the share capital.
(b)   The greater part of the voting power.
(c)   Such of the share capital as would entitle them to receive the greater part of any distribution of the company's income.
(d)   Such rights as would entitle them to a greater part of the assets available on a winding up.

The third and fourth of these tests focus on the net assets of the company and on its income. The term 'income' is defined in a limited sense, in that it includes anything to which the charge to corporation tax on income applies (CTA 2010, s 1119). It is plain that it excludes capital gains taxed as capital gain, but it does, in view of the inclusive definition, take in capital receipts such as offshore income gains which are deemed to be income.

A difficult issue is what the measure of the income is, but in view of the inclusive definition it is presumably whatever would be computed as being the taxable income of the company if it were UK resident. This (it may be suggested) allows the deduction of expenses of management, and requires loan relationship credits and debits to be brought into account. The reference to corporation tax in theory raises the issue of whether dividends should be excluded, as in most cases dividends are exempt from corporation tax (CTA 2009, ss 931A–931W). Clearly they should not be, as the definition of income is inclusive only, and dividends are income in the general sense of the term.

In applying these rules as to deemed control, rights and powers held by associates of a participator are treated as held by the participator (s 451(4)(c) and (d)). So too are the following:

• Rights and powers held by nominees (s 451(3)).
• Rights and powers held by companies controlled by the participator alone, or by the participator and his associates (s 451(4)(a) and (b)).

Section 451(4) uses the word 'may' in relation to the attribution of rights and powers, but it has been held that this does not give HMRC a discretion. Instead it should be read with s 451(6), which requires attributions to be made under s 451(4) if the result is that the company is then treated as controlled by five or fewer participators (*R v IRC ex parte Newfields Developments Ltd* [2001] STC 901).

The definition of 'control' in other contexts

87.11 The close company definition of control in ss 450 and 451 is widely used as the definition of 'control' when that term is used in other contexts. Perhaps the prime example is in the definition of 'connected persons' (TCGA 1992, s 286; ITA 2007, s 993; CTA 2010, s 1122). Here a person is connected with a company if he controls it, or if he and others are acting together to secure or exercise control of it.

However, in such cases, the courts have held that it is not every provision in the close company definition which is carried across. In particular, s 451(6) applies only for the purposes of determining whether the company is close. Where the definitions in ss 450 and 451 are used in other contexts, for example for the purpose of the definition of connected persons, a person can be treated as controlling a company even if he is not a participator. This is what happened in *R v IRC ex parte Newfields Developments Ltd*, where the 100% participator in the company was a discretionary trust. The taxpayer was still treated as controlling the company, as the settlor was a deceased relative of hers, namely her husband. It is to be stressed, however, that this case is not relevant to the definition of a close company, as the party deemed to control the company was not in fact a participator.

SECONDARY DEFINITION

87.12 As noted in para **87.2**, there is a secondary definition of 'close company', which focuses on the entitlement of the company's participators in a liquidation of the company (CTA 2010, s 439 (3)). Regardless of voting rights, a company is close if five or fewer participators would be entitled to the greater part of the assets were the company liquidated, or would be so entitled were loan creditors disregarded.

In large measure this rule replicates one aspect of the extended definition of control. But no account is taken of associates, and regard is had to group structures in that a participator in the top company is treated as a participator in companies lower down the chain. Such a person is treated as entitled to an appropriate share of whatever the top company would be entitled to in the liquidation of the subsidiaries (ss 440 and 441).

GROUP AND QUOTED COMPANIES

87.13 In group structures, most companies would in the absence of special provision be close, as each is under the control of whichever group member is immediately above it. However, in reality a company is not close if it is controlled by a non-close company. Nor is a company close if it is controlled by several companies, provided none is close (CTA 2010, s 444).

There is no exception for quoted or listed companies as such. However, a company is not close if (CTA 2010, s 446):

(a)   Shares carrying at least 35% of the voting power are beneficially held by the public, and

(b)   Such shares have been dealt in and listed on a recognised stock exchange, and

(c)   the voting power of the company's principal members is less than 85%.

By 'principal member' is meant a shareholder who owns more than 5% of the voting power in the company, or with his associates owns more than 5% of such voting power. Shares do not count as held beneficially by the public if held by directors or associates of directors or by companies under their control (s 447).

Chapter 88

CORPORATE GAINS: SECTION 13

INTRODUCTION

88.1 Gains realised by non-resident companies are in certain circumstances attributed to participators. The relevant rules are set out in TCGA 1992, s 13. The origins of this section go back to the first enactment of CGT in 1965 but over the years s 13 has been much modified, most recently in 2013 (FA 2013, s 62).

PRECONDITIONS

88.2 Although s 13 is not expressed in such terms, it is convenient to see it as subject to three preconditions.

Close company

88.3 The first precondition is that the non-resident company be close. The term 'close company' is widely used in tax legislation and its meaning is set out in CTA 2010, ss 439–454 (TCGA 1992, s 288(1)). That meaning is explained in CHAPTER 87. In practical terms the effect is that a company is normally close unless it, or its ultimate parent, is quoted. Certainly virtually all companies encountered in the tax planning which forms the subject matter of this book are close.

Motive defence

88.4 The second precondition is that the motive defence does not apply. This was the principal change made in 2013 and is set out in TCGA 1992, s 13(5)(cb). The effect of the change is that under the current law, s 13 cannot apply unless a scheme or arrangements can be identified and one of the main purposes of the scheme or arrangements was the avoidance of CGT or corporation tax.

Section 13(5)(cb) requires an investigation of the reasons why the company acquired, held and disposed of the relevant asset. It then has to be asked whether one at least of those reasons involved CGT or corporation tax and, if it did, whether the reason amounted to avoidance. The use of the term 'avoidance' in s 13(5)(cb) must be presumed to be deliberate, and thus is focusing on avoidance as distinct from mitigation (as to which see para **73.21**). Section 13(5)(cb) is considered further at the end of this chapter.

Activities test

88.5 The third precondition is an activities test. Its effect is to disapply s 13 if the company has used the relevant asset in a trade or in economically significant activities carried on outside the UK. Originally this precondition applied only to trades but it was extended to economically significant activities in 2013 (s 13(5)(b) and (ca)).

The term 'trade' bears its normal income tax meaning (TCGA 1992, s 288(1). The concept of economically significant activities covers much the same ground as trade, as it means the provision of goods or services to others on a commercial basis (s 13A(4)). Such provision must involve staff, premises and equipment commensurate with the size and nature of the activities and the company must also add commensurate economic value.

One distinction between trades and economically significant activities is that the exemption for assets used in such activities precludes s 13 only if the activities are carried on wholly or mainly outside the UK. A trade, by contrast, can be carried on partly within and partly outside the UK, provided the asset is used in the non-UK part of the trade. Section 13 is also precluded in relation to assets used in a UK permanent establishment, for gains on such assets are charged to corporation tax in any event (TCGA 1992, ss 12(5)(d) and 10B).

It is unclear whether use in the trade or in the economically significant activities has to have been throughout the company's ownership of the asset, or merely at the time of the disposal. The phrase 'used only' suggests the former is the correct reading.

As is the case elsewhere in UK tax legislation, the commercial letting of furnished holiday accommodation is deemed to be a trade and thus here too s 13 is disapplied (s 13A(1)–(3)). However for some reason this applies only if the holiday accommodation is outside the UK, and the furnished holiday accommodation rules have to have been met throughout the company's ownership.

THE GAIN

88.6 Assuming the preconditions for s 13 are met, it then has to be determined whether a given disposal has resulted in a chargeable gain. In computing the gain, the rules are those applicable to corporation tax (s 13(11A)). This application of the corporation tax rules is anomalous, for that tax is only in fact charged on resident companies and on the permanent establishments of non-resident companies. The anomaly was introduced into s 13 when, for non-corporate taxpayers, taper relief replaced indexation in 1998. The anomaly was not reversed when taper relief was abolished in 2008. The anomaly works to the favour of taxpayers for it brings in a number of disapplications and restrictions to s 13.

Indexation

88.7 The general rule is that CGT rules apply in computing gains for the purposes of corporation tax (TCGA 1992, s 8). However this is subject to one very important exception, namely that indexation, which was phased out for non-corporate taxpayers in 1998 and 2008, continues to apply. In computing s 13 gains, therefore, an indexation allowance is deducted (TCGA 1992, ss 52A and 53).

The indexation allowance is applied to each item of allowable expenditure, and represents the increase in the UK Retail Price Index between the month in which the expenditure was incurred and the month of the disposal. The earliest month that can be taken into account is March 1982 (TCGA 1992, s 54). Indexation relief is of great value, and in the case of long held assets exceeds the actual expenditure. HMRC publish for each month the indexation factor to be used for disposals in that month.

Loan relationships

88.8 The term 'loan relationship' is a corporation tax concept. A company has a loan relationship if it stands in the position of creditor or debtor as respects any money debt, and the debt arose from a transaction for the lending of money (CTA 2009, s 302). In addition certain matters are deemed to be loan relationships (s 302(4)).

It might be thought that loan relationships are of little consequence in a CGT context, in that money and debts are not in general assets which grow in value. However this ignores the fact that loan relationship gains and losses normally include exchange gains and losses (CTA 2009, s 328; CFM para 61000–61180). It follows that if an asset falls within the concept of a loan relationship, exchange gains resulting from a depreciation of sterling are outside s 13.

The technical analysis supporting the exclusion of loan relationship currency gains from s 13 may be summarised as follows:

- For corporation tax purpose, debts and credits arising from the lending of money are taxed as income under the loan relationship rules (CTA 2009, s 295).
- Such debits and credits include exchange gains and losses (CTA 2009, s 328).
- Loan relationship debits and credits may not otherwise be brought into account for corporation tax purposes (CTA 2009, s 464).
- For CGT purposes any gain taken into account in computing the income or profits of the person making a disposal is left out of account in determining the chargeable gain realised by that disposal (TCGA 1992, s 37(1)).
- This rule is applied to corporation tax by TCGA 1992, s 8(4).

It should be noted, in relation to bank accounts, that the exclusion of currency gains is separate from the relief for such gains introduced in 2012 (TCGA 1992, s 252). That relief applies to individuals and trustees and took effect only from 6 April 2012. The exclusion of currency gains from s 13, by contrast, dates back to the application of corporation tax rules to s 13 in 1998. Moreover, the loan relationship concept extends beyond bank accounts and thus includes corporate and government bonds.

Group relief

88.9 The general corporation tax rule is that disposals between UK resident members of a group are no gain/no loss disposals (TCGA 1992, s 171). For these purposes a group is the parent company and those of its subsidiaries that are both 75% subsidiaries and effective 51% subsidiaries (TCGA 1992, s 170). The term 'effective 51% subsidiary' requires the parent to be beneficially entitled to more than 50% of the subsidiary's profits available for distribution and more than 50% of its assets on a winding up (s 171(7)). Entitlement can be either direct or through another subsidiary (CTA 2010, s 167).

Of itself, group relief has no application to s 13, for its only application to non-resident companies is to the assets of UK permanent establishments. However TCGA 1992, s 14 extends group relief to disposals between members of non-resident groups.

The term 'non-resident group of companies' is defined as:

(1)   In the case of a group with no members resident in the United Kingdom, that group (TCGA 1992, s 14(4)(a)(i)).
(2)   In the case of a group two or more members of which are not resident in the United Kingdom, the members which are not resident in the United Kingdom (s 14(4)(a)(ii)).

For corporation tax purposes a company leaving a group is treated as having disposed of and reacquired any asset it acquired from a fellow group member at market value (TCGA 1992, s 179). This charge is not made unless the departure from the group is within six years of the intra-group acquisition (s 179(1)(c)). The time of the deemed disposal and reacquisition is the time of the actual intra group transfer, but any gain or loss resulting from the deemed disposal accrues at the beginning of the accounting period in which the transferee leaves the group (s 179(4)).

Section 14 applies these rules also to s 13. This means that the gain which would have been apportioned to the participators on an intra-group transfer is apportioned to the participators in the event that the recipient company leaves the group within six years of that transfer. As the gain is treated as accruing to that company at the beginning of the accounting period in which it leaves the group, the apportionment under s 13 is to those persons who are participators at that time. It is unclear what the position on timing is if the non-resident company has no accounting period, but presumably the fall back provision in s 179(4)(b) would apply, namely that the gain is treated as accruing at the time of the company's departure from the group.

Should a member of the non-resident group become UK resident, the degrouping charge applies insofar as the immigrating company had made intra-group acquisitions within the last six years, for that company would then cease to be a member of the non-resident group. The same applies if both it and the transferor group member become UK resident, for they would not thereafter be a group of non-resident companies if viewed alone (cf s 179(2) and *Dunlop v Pardoe* [1999] STC 909).

The group rules in TCGA 1992, s 14 provided the basis for the scheme at issue in *Wood v Holden* [2006] STC 443 (see CHAPTER 43). They enabled assets to be transferred by a BVI company administered in Geneva to its subsidiary resident in the Netherlands. The case emphasises that s 14 is not in point if the transferee group member is UK resident, as then it is not a member of the non-resident group.

Substantial shareholdings

88.10 The substantial shareholding exemption (SSE) in TCGA 1992, Sch 7AC applies when one company disposes of shares in another company. The provisions of Sch 7AC are involved, and poorly drafted, and a full discussion of them is beyond the scope of this book. However, some discussion here is merited, as where the SSE applies to a gain realised by a company, such gain is a non-chargeable gain. Where the gain is realised by a closely held non-resident company, the result is to preclude any apportionment of the gain under s 13.

There are, in fact, not one but three exemptions that are collectively referred to as the SSE. One of these (the second 'subsidiary' exemption in Sch 7AC, para 3) is only available where the company making the disposal is UK resident, and is therefore irrelevant here. However, the 'main' exemption is not limited to UK resident companies, and is therefore potentially relevant where a non-UK resident, closely held company makes a disposal, realising a gain that might otherwise be apportioned to UK resident participators (or non-UK resident trustee participators) under s 13.

The essential requirements for the SSE to apply are:

- The company making the disposal (which the legislation, slightly confusingly, calls the 'investing company') has owned a 'substantial shareholding' (broadly speaking, 10% or more of the ordinary share capital) in the 'investee company' (ie the company whose shares are being disposed of) for at least 12 continuous months within the 24-month period leading up to the disposal; and
- The investing company has been a member of a trading group throughout that 12-month period, and also is such a member immediately after the disposal; and
- The investee company has been a trading company throughout that 12-month period, and also is such a company immediately after the disposal.

For these purposes, a trading group is a group, one or more of whose members carry on trading activities and the activities of whose members, taken together (disregarding intra-group activities), 'do not include to a substantial extent activities other than trading activities' (Sch 7AC, para 21). References to a group or to membership of a group are construed in accordance with the provisions of TCGA 1992, s 170, read as if 51% were substituted for 75%. For SSE purposes, a group is therefore a principal company and its (direct or indirect) 51% subsidiaries.

CG53116 (and following pages of the Capital Gains Manual) discuss the requirements imposed by paragraph 21. HMRC take 'substantial' to mean 'more than 20%'. Thus the SSE may be precluded if the aggregate turnover of the trading group derives as to more than 20% from investment, rather than trading, activities; or if the value of non-trading assets held by companies within the trading group is more than 20% of the total value of assets held by such companies; or if the expenditure incurred or time spent by officers and employees on non-trading activities is more than 20% of the total expenditure or time spent across all companies within the trading group. However, the vague nature of the paragraph 21 requirement means that there may be doubt, in a given case, as to whether it is satisfied or not, and some latitude to take a position one way or the other.

THE APPORTIONMENT

88.11 Should a gain be within s 13 it becomes subject to the rules requiring apportionment. These rules are not entirely simple.

UK resident persons

88.12 The core rule is that every UK resident participator in the company is treated as if part of the company's gain had accrued to him (s 13(2)). The term participator bears the same meaning as in the corporation tax close company legislation (s 13(12)). It thus means any person having a share or interest in the capital or income of the company and includes loan creditors and anybody possessing voting rights (CTA 2010, s 454; see further 87.3).

A point to note is that the UK participators to whom apportionment can be made can be individuals, companies or trusts. The term 'participator' connotes a direct interest in the subject company, so where the direct shareholder in a closely-held non-resident company is a UK resident company, the apportionment is to the UK company, and not to the shareholders or parent of that UK company. There is only one limited exception to this which applies where the s 13 gain is treaty protected and the UK company has trustee shareholders.

A particular difficulty with the definition of 'participator' is that where a trust holds an interest in a company, the term extends to fixed interest beneficiaries (see para 87.4). There are thus two persons who count as participators by reference to same interest. In relation to s 13, however, the role of the beneficiary as participator is ignored: only the trust is a participator as respects the trust's interest in the company (s 13(14)).

Amount apportioned

88.13 Subject to the *de minimis* rule discussed below, the amount of the company's gain apportioned to each UK resident participator is the proportion which corresponds to the extent of his interest as a participator (s 13(3)). For these purposes, a person's interest as a participator is the amalgam of all the factors rendering him a participator (s 13(13)(a)). To determine its extent, the interests of all the participators in the company have to be identified, and the extent of the subject interest is then the proportion of the whole which, on a just and reasonable basis, it represents.

In effect this formula requires the gain to be apportioned, on a just and reasonable basis, between all the participators in the company. Its language precludes what would otherwise be possible if the term 'participator' stood alone, namely apportionment of the same gain or part of the gain to several participators simultaneously. In other words it prevents the total amount apportioned from being more than 100% of the gain.

But even with that established, the apportionment formula is not without difficulties. Take, for example, the position of loan creditors, who fall within the term 'participator'. Their debt interests may be much more valuable than the shareholder interests, but is it right that gains should be apportioned to them given that, economically, gains enure to the benefit of shareholders? HMRC appear to think not, stating that the apportionment should be restricted to those participators who have a real economic interest in the gain (CG 57260). If this is right, it excludes normal commercial lenders, but not creditors whose loan is worth less than face value and who thus have an interest in the enhancement of the value of the company's assets.

Another problem area is cell companies. By this term is meant companies with different classes of share, each class of share being exclusively interested in particular funds or assets of the company. Is a gain in one fund apportioned between the shareholders as a whole or merely to the class of shares interested in that fund? As a matter of construction there is much to be said for the view that the former is correct, for s 13(14)(b) requires the interests of all the participators to be looked at. But such an outcome is neither just nor reasonable and, on a purposive approach, is difficult to sustain.

De minimis

88.14 Relief applies where the amount of the gain apportioned to the UK resident participator would be 25% or less (s 13(4)). In that event the gain which would be apportioned is not treated as accruing to the participator and so is not charged. Until 2011–12, the *de minimis* limit was 10%, but for disposals on or after 6 April 2012 it is 25%.

This relief is not as valuable as appears, as participations of connected persons, whether resident or non-resident, have to be taken into account in applying the 25% threshold. 'Connected' bears its normal CGT meaning and thus, in relation to individuals, includes close family members, companies controlled by the individual or his close relatives, and trusts of which the individual or a member of his close family is a settlor (TCGA 1992, s 286).

A particular issue with the connected person concept is that partners are, by the mere fact of being in partnership, connected with each other and with their respective close relatives (s 286(4)). This can deny the *de minimis* exemption where a non-resident company is in genuine diverse ownership, but the owners happen to be in partnership.

Snapshot approach

88.15 A point to stress about s 13 is that it does not apportion by tax years. The apportionment is at the moment the gain accrues and is to those persons who are participators at that moment. It follows that if participations change during a tax year, so also do s 13 outcomes.

Reimbursement

88.16 The participators have no statutory right to require the company to reimburse any tax paid under s 13. But if the company in fact pays the tax, that payment is not treated as a distribution for any tax purpose (s 13(11)).

Non-resident trustees

88.17 Any s 13 gain apportioned to a non-UK resident trust is treated as accruing to the trust in the same way as it would were the trust UK resident (s 13(10)). The rules are the same as for UK resident participators which inter alia means the 25% *de minimis* relief is in point. The position of non-resident trusts is considered further in para **88.31** below.

Non-resident companies

88.18 As noted above, a participator in one company is not, by virtue of that participation, a participator in any other company which that company controls or is otherwise a participator in. In the absence of special provision s 13 would thus have no mechanism for apportioning the gains of subsidiaries of non-resident companies. In fact there is such mechanism, for s 13(9) provides for the apportionment of gains through non-resident companies if and to the extent that one is a participator in another.

LOSSES

Company losses

88.19 As already noted, s 13 apportions each gain realised by the company separately to participators. It does not apportion the company's aggregate net gains of a given tax year or period of account. This is a logical approach to take, as participations can change during the tax year. The approach s 13 takes means it is necessary only to look at participations at the time a given gain is realised.

A result of this is that there is no mechanism for taking account of the company's allowable losses. Section 13 recognises this defect, but only to a limited extent. It does so by allowing a loss on a disposal to be apportioned to the participators, in the same circumstances as a gain would be if the disposal had resulted in a gain (s 13(8)). But the use the participator may make of the apportioned loss is restricted. He may not set it against his general gains and nor may he carry it forward or back. Instead he may set it only against other gains apportioned to him under s 13 in the same tax year. These gains may be in the company which realised the loss or in any other non-resident company in which he is participator (s 13(8)). But insofar as the apportioned loss exceeds such current year apportioned gains, it cannot be used.

Personal losses

88.20 The restrictive treatment of losses described above does not affect the treatment of the participator's personal losses (ie his non s 13 losses). These may be set against apportioned s 13 gains insofar as the latter are not offset by s 13 losses.

DOUBLE CHARGE

88.21 It is inherent in s 13, that the same economic gain may be taxed twice, once when the company realises the gain on a disposal of the underlying asset, and subsequently when the profit represented by the gain is distributed to the participator by way of dividend, or realised on the sale or liquidation of the company. In the case of non-resident group structures the gain could in fact be taxed more than twice, for example where a gain is realised by a subsidiary, the subsidiary is sold or liquidated, and the parent is then sold or liquidated.

Section 13 does not address this problem in any satisfactory manner. Instead it gives two limited reliefs, one for distributions and one a deduction of tax from gain.

Distribution relief

88.22 The distribution relief applies only if the following conditions are satisfied (s 13(5A)):

(a)   a person pays tax in respect of the company gain apportioned under s 13;

(b)   the company does not reimburse the participator;

(c)   the company distributes an amount in respect of the gain by dividend or in liquidation; and

(d)   the distribution takes place within a specified period of the gain accruing.

Where these conditions are satisfied the person who paid the s 13 tax may deduct that tax from any CGT or income tax chargeable on him in respect of the distribution. The distribution is treated for these purposes as the top slice of his income (TCGA 1992, s 13(7A)).

The specified period begins on the date when the gain is realised and ends on the fourth anniversary of that date or, if earlier, three years after the end of the accounting period in which that date falls (s 13(5B)).

There are many reasons why this relief is of limited value:

(a)   It only applies if the second tax charge occurs on a distribution and not, for example, if it is triggered on a sale of the participation.

(b)   It is limited in time, in that the second tax charge must be triggered within the specified period of between three and four years.

(c)   It is limited in scope, in that the second tax charge must be incurred by the same person as is liable for the s 13 charge. Thus it does not apply if he has given away his participation in the meantime and it is only of limited application in respect of non-resident trusts (see para **88.32**).

(d)   The relief is of no use if either the s 13 gain or the second tax charge is relieved by some relief such as loss relief.

The legislation is unclear as to the position where the company pays a dividend funded out of many receipts, of which the disposal generating the gain is just one. On one view, the dividend would fall to be treated as gain only in the same proportion as the gain bears to the total funds from which the distribution is made. But it may be suggested that, with disclosure, a s 13 participator is entitled to take the position that a dividend from a mixed fund is, for the purposes of these rules, gain insofar as the fund contains gains. The problem is avoided if the company carries the proceeds of disposals generating a gain directly to a separate account, and pays the dividend from that account.

Tax deducted from gain

88.23   This second form of relief applies without time limit (s 13(7)). It allows any CGT paid by the participator on the apportioned gain as a deduction in computing any gain when he disposes of whatever interest caused him to be a participator. This relief is not available insofar as the company reimburses the tax. This relief is capable of applying within the specified period under s 13(5A), and indeed is the only relief from a double charge available where the participator sells his interest in the company. Strictly s 13(7) relief only applies if the s 13 tax has been paid, but in practice HMRC do not insist on this (Capital Gains Manual para 57362).

This relief, too, is far from comprehensive:

(a)   It is a deduction of tax from gain, not of tax from tax.

(b)   It applies only on the disposal of the participation. It does not apply if the participator receives an income dividend (which is unrelieved unless within the time limits for distribution relief).

(c)   As described below (para **88.32**) it is of no application to non-resident trusts, for it applies only if the person realising the gain is the same as the person who paid the s 13 tax.

DTT RELIEF

88.24 Section 13 is not confined to companies resident in offshore jurisdictions. It applies regardless of where the company resides, so long as it is not resident in the UK. Relief under a double taxation treaty (DTT) may however be in point.

The interaction between s 13 and DTTs is discussed at para **104.13**. Where the participator in a non-resident closely-held company is an individual, the conclusions can be summarised as follows:

- A CGT charge under s 13 on the individual can be prevented by a DTT. This requires the DTT between the UK and the country in which the company is resident to oust the UK's taxing rights with respect to the company's gain. A considerable number of DTTs entered into by the UK in recent years preserve the UK's right to charge a UK resident to tax even in respect of a gain realised by a resident of the other country, and such DTTs do not prevent a tax charge under s 13.
- Where the DTT does *not* preclude a tax charge on an individual participator under s 13 (ie where the DTT preserves the UK's right to tax the gains), credit relief under the DTT is available.

NON-UK DOMICILED PARTICIPATORS

88.25 Individual participators who are resident but not domiciled in the UK are subject to s 13. Originally, non-UK domiciliaries were exempt from s 13, but this exemption was abolished with effect from 6 April 2008 (FA 2008, Sch 7 paras 103 and 105).

UK situs assets

88.26 Where the asset disposed of by the company is situated in the UK, the gain apportioned to the non-UK domiciled participator is fully charged. The remittance basis does not apply. As s 13 is part of TCGA 1992, the CGT situs rules apply in determining where the asset disposed of is situated (see CHAPTER 37).

Foreign situs assets

88.27 The gain apportioned to a non-UK domiciled participator is treated as a foreign chargeable gain where the asset disposed of by the company is situated outside the UK (TCGA 1992, s 14A(2)). This means that if the non-domiciliary is a remittance basis user in the tax year in which the gain accrues, the remittance basis applies. As a result, the remittance basis user is charged only if remittance occurs.

The remittance rules described in CHAPTERS 51 to 57 operate by treating the consideration obtained by the company on the actual disposal as being derived from the participator's deemed foreign chargeable gain (s 14A(3)(a)). The asset disposed of is itself also treated as so derived if the disposal is at less than market value (s 14A(3)(b)).

The effect of this deeming is that a remittance by the company of all or part of the proceeds of disposal results in a tax charge on the participator. This follows because, by virtue of the participation, the company is a relevant person in relation to him (see para 54.12). The proceeds of disposal are by their nature a mixed fund, and so any partial remittance is of gain before base cost. The rules are unclear where the non-UK domiciled participator is not a 100% participator and so has only proportionate interest in what the company remits. Strictly, however, the rules may require all the company's remittance to be allocated to his gain, save where it can be apportioned to other non-UK domiciled participators.

Generally, a remittance by the company results in tax even if the remittance is effected for investment or to pay for UK services. But if any UK services are paid for abroad and relate to foreign assets, the exemption for services described in paras 55.13 to 55.16 may be in point. And business investment relief may apply if the remittance takes the form of a qualifying investment in an unlisted company (ITA 2007, ss 809VA–809VO; see CHAPTER 58).

As with all instances of deemed derivation in the remittance code, the issue arises of how far the deeming is traced. This issue is discussed in para 52.16. For the reason there given, the derivation into the asset itself which occurs on a non-market value disposal does on one view stop once the asset is sold. But the derivation into the consideration is likely to continue into investment of the consideration and the proceeds of any such investment (see para 51.10).

A remittance is taxable even if effected by the parent or 51% subsidiary of the company which realised the s 13 gain. This follows because those companies are also relevant persons in relation to the participator.

Losses

88.28 Non-resident close company losses are apportioned to non-UK domiciliaries as well as to other participators. As with other participators they are offsettable against, and only against, s 13 gains of the same tax year. There is no restriction on the offsetting of foreign situs losses and so, for example, an apportioned loss which arose on the disposal of a foreign asset can offset a same-year apportioned gain on a UK asset. This is so even if the proceeds of the foreign disposal are not remitted.

In one respect loss relief is restricted for non-UK domiciliaries. This applies if the individual is a remittance basis user in the tax year in which a foreign s 13 gain is realised. In such a case the gain cannot be offset by s 13 losses unless remitted in the same tax year as realised (TCGA 1992, s 14A(4)).

Motive defence

88.29 Many non-UK domiciliaries owning non-UK companies may now find they are protected from s 13 by the motive defence described above (para 88.4). This could be the position if the reasons for forming the company were unconnected with UK tax or if the only tax considered was inheritance tax. If in such a case the motive defence is or could be in point, care should be taken to ensure tax planning activity now does not undermine it.

Trusts

88.30 Should the non-UK domiciliary transfer his participation in the non-resident company to a non-resident trust before the gain is realised, the gain is not apportionable to him and simply goes into the trust's s 2(2) amount. This is so whether the gain is UK or foreign. Remittance of the gain by the company or trust does not result in tax by reference to s 2(2) amounts as tax only arises if a matched capital payment is remitted (see para **79.3**).

Transferring a participation into trust may have IHT and other tax implications which should be considered. It does not secure 2008 rebasing as that requires the trust to have held the participation on 5 April 2008 (see para **79.10**).

Somewhat paradoxically, a non-UK domiciliary who in the past transferred a company to a trust to secure these CGT advantages may find the company has lost the motive defence, which could otherwise have applied to it had he done nothing. Whether the transfer in fact has this result depends on whether it and the acquisition, holding or disposal of a given asset are part of the same scheme or arrangement (as to which see further para **88.35**).

NON-RESIDENT TRUSTS

88.31 As noted at the beginning of this chapter, gains in a non-resident close company are also apportionable to any participator which is a non-resident trust (TCGA 1992, s 13(10)). The apportionment does not result in the trustees being charged to tax for, being non-resident, they are exempt. But if the trust is within TCGA 1992, s 86, any apportioned gains may be assessed as the settlor's and otherwise the apportioned gains are included in the trust's s 2(2) amount for the tax year in question. These rules are described in para **76.16**.

Application of reliefs

88.32 In one respect s 13 bears more heavily on settlors and beneficiaries of non-resident trusts than on direct participators, for the reliefs from double tax described in **88.21** to **88.23** are of limited application. The deduction of tax from gain under s 13(7) is not available, for that relief applies only if the person disposing of the participation is the same as the person who paid the tax (see para **88.23**). That condition is not satisfied with non-resident trusts, for the trustees dispose of the participation and yet tax in respect of the apportioned gain is paid by the settlor in the case of s 86 and by the beneficiary in the case of s 87.

The application of the relief for distributions within the specified period (para **88.22**) is a matter of difficulty. The key point to remember is that the person paying the s 13 tax must be the same person as is taxed on the distribution. With this established, it is clear that s 13(5A) does give relief to the settlor if he is assessed under s 86 on the company's gain and then assessed either to income tax or under s 86 on the distribution.

With s 87 the position is much more complicated. As described in para **88.22**, the conditions for the relief are:

(a) An amount of tax is paid by a person in pursuance of s 13.
(b) An amount in respect of the gain is distributed within the specified period.
(c) The person who paid the s 13 tax is liable to income tax or CGT in respect of the distribution.

On the basis of these conditions it may be argued s 13(5A) could apply if:

(1) The company in fact distributes an amount in respect of the gain to the trust within the specified period; and
(2) The trust makes a capital distribution to the beneficiary, part of which is matched with the s 13 gain and part with the company distribution. The matching with the company distribution would be under s 87 if the distribution by the company was capital but if the company distribution was income, the matching would be allocation under ITA 2007, ss 731–735.

If these conditions are met it would seem that the tax on the part of the trust distribution matched with the company distribution can be offset by the tax resulting from matching with the company gain. Provided that the company distribution is within the specified period, it would not seem to matter that the capital payment or benefit from the trust is later.

It is however far from clear that this argument would be upheld as a matter of strict construction of s 13(5A). It is also clear that it would be much more difficult to run the argument if capital distributions are made to several beneficiaries, so that it is not possible to show that the same beneficiary bears the s 87 tax attributable to the company gain as bears the s 87 or ss 731–735 tax attributable to the company distribution.

Subsidiaries

88.33 The wording of s 13(10) makes it clear that the gains of non-resident subsidiaries of a non-resident close company can also be attributed to a non-resident trust that is a participator in the non-resident close company.

(i.e. attribution of gains goes right up a chain of companies)

Effects of DTTs

88.34 The interaction between s 13 and DTTs is discussed at para **104.15**. Where the participator is a non-resident trust the analysis is somewhat complex, but the conclusions are relatively simple:

- A DTT cannot affect the quantum of CGT payable by a UK resident and domiciled settlor under TCGA 1992, s 86. Nor, where the settlor is dead or he is not chargeable to tax under s 86, can a DTT affect the amount of CGT payable by UK resident beneficiaries under TCGA 1992, s 87.

- Any foreign tax payable by the underlying company on the disposal will be creditable against any CGT on that disposal which is payable by the settlor under s 86. However, the availability of DTT credit relief against tax under s 87 is more debatable.

IMPLICATIONS OF THE 2013 CHANGES

88.35 The changes made to s 13 in 2013 represent one of the most significant legislative interventions in offshore tax planning in recent years.

Economically significant activities

88.36 As HMRC state in the Capital Gains Manual, s 13(5)(ca) is designed to reflect case law on the EU freedom of establishment (see CG57314). However a point to stress is that s 13(5)(ca) applies to companies established in any part of the world and not just to those in the EU.

HMRC at one point state (at CG57314) that s 13(5)(ca):

'seeks to differentiate between companies carrying on legitimate economic activities (which reflect economic reality), and those operating wholly artificial arrangements'

However it would be wrong to take the term 'wholly artificial arrangements' too literally. Due account must be taken of all the various indicia listed in s 13A(4). As is explained in para 88.5, these indicia, or rather the lack of them, are what constitute activities wholly artificial.

It is clear that the passive holding of investments is not an economically significant activity. HMRC (at para CG57315) draw a distinction between using an asset within a business of asset management and 'merely seeking to benefit from the actual or anticipated increase in the value of the asset'. Since the latter is what most offshore companies of the kind discussed in this book do, it follows that most are outside s 13(5)(ca).

Motive test

88.37 The motive test is of much greater relevance. Here the fundamental issue is what is encompassed in a given scheme or arrangements. As is explained above, it is not just a question of identifying the scheme or arrangements whose purposes included the avoidance of CGT or corporation tax. It is also necessary for the acquisition, holding, or disposal of the asset to have formed part of the scheme.

Similar language to s 13(5)(cb) is found in TCGA 1992, s 137, the legislation which makes the CGT relief for share exchanges subject to a purpose test. That language was at issue in two cases discussed in para 29.12, namely *Snell v HMRC* [2007] STC 1279 and *Coll v HMRC* [2010] STC 1849. In both these cases the taxpayer, in selling his company, took loan notes rather than cash. In both cases it was found that at the date of contract he had the intention to emigrate, and realise the loan notes once he was non-resident. It was held that the contract was part of a scheme, which also included the disposal of the loan notes when non-UK resident.

In both cases, the judges relied on dictionary definitions in construing the words 'scheme' and 'arrangement'. The cited definition of scheme was 'a plan of action devised in order to obtain some end'. That of arrangement was 'a structure or combination of things for a purpose'. The common thread in these definitions is that there must be some purpose or end in what is done, and that purpose must exist when the first step is taken.

In the light of this analysis, it is clear that the acquisition, holding or disposal of the assets must have been part of the plan when the scheme or arrangements were entered into. In the case of the future acquisitions it is not, it may be suggested, necessary that specific assets to be acquired should be identified, but merely that assets of some kind would in due course be acquired and sheltered from CGT by the structure.

Examples

88.38 The point may be illustrated by some examples. Suppose, first, that in the 1980s an individual who was resident and domiciled in the UK formed a settlor-interested trust and holding company to hold shares in a newly formed trading company. The avowed purpose of this structure was to shelter any gains realised on the future disposal of the trading company, as was possible as the law then stood (see para 5.5). Suppose that the trading company was duly disposed of in the mid-1990s and, as the law then stood, the gain was taxable only insofar as matched with capital payments (see para 76.13). Suppose further that the offshore company kept the proceeds in cash for a while, the beneficiaries having no immediate need of cash funds. At some point after 1998 the trustees decided, for purely investment reasons, that the offshore company should invest the proceeds in a discretionary portfolio, and this duly happened, gains being realised as when portfolio disposals were made. By this stage the structure delivered no CGT advantage, as all the gains were assessed on the settlor under TCGA 1992, s 86 (see para 5.12).

On the analysis suggested above, the portfolio gains would not be protected by the motive test if, on the facts, use of the proceeds of the trading company to acquire the portfolio had been the intention when the structure was set up, as then CGT avoidance was clearly intended. But if, for example, the intention had been that the settlor would emigrate and have all the proceeds distributed to him, a subsequent change of plan resulting in the retention and investment of the proceeds would mean the portfolio was protected by the motive test.

A slight variation of the facts further illustrates the point. Suppose the trading company had been directly held by and disposed of by the trustees. Suppose the intention had always been that the proceeds should be kept in trust on account of the CGT advantages which were then available. Suppose that, before acquiring the portfolio, the trustees decided for commercial reasons to form a company to hold it.

In this instance it may be suggested that the applicability or otherwise of s 13 depends on when the company was formed. If it was formed before 1998 the structure was still a CGT shelter, and it could well be argued that the formation of the company, and the holding of the investments within it, were part of a scheme to avoid CGT, for CGT was in fact avoided. But the position if the company was formed after 1998 is different. By that time, CGT avoidance was no longer possible, for settlor-interested trusts no longer operated as a shelter (see para 5.6). In this latter scenario s 13(5)(cb) would prevent s 13 applying unless the formation of the company to hold the proceeds of the trading company had been envisaged when the structure was first set up.

A third example concerns the use by non-domiciliaries of offshore holding companies to protect UK investments from IHT (see para 16.7). Here the motive test will be available if IHT was the sole reason for setting up the company. This is very likely to be the position if the company is directly owned by an individual and he was non-UK resident when the company was set up. The same would be the position if the company is owned by a trust, and at the time the company was formed the trust was not seen as for the benefit of UK residents. In both cases, CGT avoidance is inherently unlikely to have been in issue, as the individual or, as the case may be, the beneficiaries, were not exposed to CGT. But the position might well be otherwise if the individual or, as the case may be, the settlor and beneficiaries, were UK resident when the structure was set up, for then it would have delivered CGT advantages, particularly pre-2008, when non-domiciliaries were outside both TCGA 1992, s 13 and TCGA 1992, s 87 (see paras 88.25 and 79.1).

No requirement for a claim

88.39 It is generally accepted that, where its conditions are met, the motive defence in s 13(5)(cb) applies without any formal claim or statement being made in the participator's tax return for the relevant tax year. In this respect the defence in s 13(5)(cb) differs from the motive defence from the transfer of assets rules (see CHAPTER 73).

The two provisions are differently couched. The transfer of assets motive defence requires the taxpayer to 'satisfy' an officer of HMRC that its conditions are met, so there is an express requirement for HMRC agreement; whereas the s 13 motive defence is available 'where it is shown' that its conditions are met. It may be argued that 'where it is shown' means 'where there is evidence', whether or not such evidence has been provided to and accepted by an officer of HMRC.

There is a second, more pragmatic reason why no claim seems to be needed here, whereas a claim is needed (at least in HMRC's view) if the transfer of assets motive defence is to be relied on. This is that the tax return form, which is prescribed by statutory instrument, specifically asks whether the transfer of assets motive defence is being claimed. At present there is no such question regarding the defence in s 13(5)(cb).

TRANSITIONAL PROVISIONS

88.40 Although enacted in 2013, s 13(5)(cb) and the other changes made in 2013 also apply for 2012–13. However an individual to whom a s 13 gain in 2012–13 would otherwise be apportioned can elect to disapply the changes. In the case of individuals and trusts the election must be made by 5 April 2017 (FA 20013, s 62(7)). Such an election is only possible in relation to gains realised in 2012–13.

It might be thought nobody would want to make an election, but in reality there are at least two cases where this is not so. One is where a trust is within s 87 and under the matching rules described in para 77.20 a capital payment in 2012–13 would, absent the election, be matched with past s 2(2) amounts and attract supplemental tax (see para 77.48).

The other case concerns offshore income gains, which are within s 13 rules (see para 95.27). Here there can be advantages, particularly where non-domiciliaries are involved, in having OIGs dealt with under ss 13 and 87, for in the absence of such treatment, they are transfer of assets income where the rules may be less advantageous. Here an election can keep 2012–13 OIGs within ss 13 and 87 (see further CHAPTER 82).

Chapter 89

TRANSACTIONS IN SECURITIES

INTRODUCTION

89.1 In 1960 the then government introduced far reaching anti-avoidance legislation designed to counter schemes to extract profits from companies in tax-free capital form. This legislation was rewritten in 2007 as ITA 2007, ss 682–713. Although its genesis was artificial schemes involving dividend stripping and the like, it was repeatedly affirmed that its ambit went far beyond such schemes (*IRC v Laird Group plc* [2003] UKHL 54, [2003] 4 All ER 669, [2003] 1 WLR 2476 at para 25 per Lord Millett).

In 2010, the previous legislation was replaced by more precisely targeted rules (ss 682–713 as amended by FA 2010, s 38). However these rules draw on many of the concepts used in the earlier version of the legislation, with the result that much of the case law decided on that legislation is of continuing effect. Further amendments were made in 2016 (FA 2016, ss 33 and 34).

For much of the period between 1988 and 2016 the legislation was of limited impact as the rate of capital gains tax was not dissimilar to the income tax rates on dividends. But this changed in 2016, for the CGT rate fell to 20% and the upper and top dividend rates rose to 32.5% and 38.1% respectively.

The legislation is material to offshore tax planning because the companies to which it applies comprise both close companies and companies which would be close if UK resident (ITA 2007, s 713). It is also relevant in another sense, for the original legislation contained a motive defence or escape clause and the present legislation applies only if a purpose test is satisfied (ITA 2007, s 684(1)(c)). The original escape clause generated a significant amount of case law, much of which is also relevant to the purpose defences to the transfer of assets code and TCGA 1992, s 13 (see CHAPTERS 71 and 88).

PROCEDURE

89.2 In contrast to other anti-avoidance legislation, the transactions in securities code applies only if invoked by HMRC. As a result of the changes made in 2016, the trigger is a notice of enquiry issued by HMRC. Such a notice may be issued if HMRC believe the code applies to one or more transactions in securities. The notice must be issued within six years of the tax year in which the tax advantage to which it relates occurred and the person to whom it is issued must be a party to the transaction or transactions in securities (ITA 2007, s 695).

The notice of enquiry leads to one of two consequences. One is that HMRC determine the code applies and issue a counteraction notice specifying the income tax advantages said to have been achieved by the transactions and the adjustments which must be made to counteract them (ITA 2007, s 698). The other outcome is a no counteraction notice which results in no adjustment being made (ITA 2007, s 698A). The taxpayer in receipt of an enquiry notice can force the issue in that he can apply to the First-tier Tribunal for a direction that HMRC issue a no counteraction notice. The Tribunal must give such a direction unless they are satisfied there are reasonable grounds not to do so (ITA 2007,s 698A(4)).

Where the result of the enquiry is a counteraction notice the adjustments required must take one of the following forms:

(a)   As assessment.
(b)   Nullifying a repayment.
(c)   Calculation or recalculation of profits or gains or liability to income tax.

The legislation is also subject to another important filter. It is open to the taxpayer to apply to HMRC for advance clearance of a proposed transaction or transactions (ITA 2007, s 701). Should HMRC give clearance they are precluded from subsequently issuing a counteraction notice (s 702). The time limit for HMRC's response is 30 days, but this is extended if they request further information.

In applying for clearance it is important to fully and accurately disclose all material facts. If this is not done any ensuing clearance is void (s 702(4)).

TECHNICAL PRECONDITIONS

89.3 A notice of enquiry and counteraction notice are not competent unless three technical preconditions are met. These are as follows (ITA 2007, s 684(1)):

(1)   The recipient of the notice is a party to a transaction or transactions in securities.
(2)   One or both of two conditions, referred to as Conditions A and B, are met.
(3)   Either the party on whom the notice is served or some other person has obtained an income tax advantage.

Transaction in securities

89.4 The term 'transaction in securities' is widely defined as a transaction of any description relating to securities (s 684(2)). The phrase was defined in the same terms in the pre-2010 legislation and there it was held the phrase must be given the widest meaning (*IRC v Laird Group plc* [2003] UKHL 54, [2003] 4 All ER 669, [2003] 1 WLR 2476 at para 26).

It is provided specifically that the phrase includes the following (s 684(2)):

- The purchase sale or exchange of securities.
- Issuing or securing the issue of new securities.
- Applying or subscribing for new securities.
- Altering the rights attached to securities.
- Repayment of share capital or share premium.
- Distribution in a winding up.

The word 'securities' also has an extended definition in that the term embraces shares and stock, and also any interests of members of a company that do not take the form of shares (ITA 2007, s 713).

Case law in relation to pre-2010 legislation indicates that the term includes both debentures and unsecured loan notes (*IRC v Laird Group plc*, para 29).

Conditions A and B

89.5 The pre-2010 law enumerated five circumstances, one of which had to be met before the code was engaged (ITA 2007, ss 686–694). Conditions A and B are in essence the old circumstances D and E. They focus on the close company whose profits the transaction(s) in securities access.

Condition A is expressed in terms of relevant consideration. The term 'consideration' is defined as including money or money's worth (s 685(8)) and consideration as so defined is relevant if it represents value available for distribution by the company or value which would be available but for anything done by the company. Since 6 April 2016 it has been possible to take account of value available in subsidiaries (s 685(7B)). But value representing the capital subscribed for the shares in the company is ignored (s 685(7A)). Consideration is also relevant if it represents trading stock in the company or is received in respect of future receipts of the company (s 685(4)).

Condition A is engaged if the party to the transaction in securities receives relevant consideration and does not bear income tax on it. Condition A is also engaged if the receipt is by some other person, if that person obtains an income tax advantage. In either event it is necessary for the receipt of the consideration to be:

(1) as a result of the transaction in securities; and
(2) in connection with the distribution, transfer or realisation of the assets of the company or the application of its assets in discharge of liabilities.

Condition B is expressed in terms of relevant consideration as well, but here the term means shares or securities issued by a close company which represent either value available for distribution or trading stock. Condition B is engaged if the shares or securities are so issued in connection with the transactions in securities, or if two or more close companies are concerned in the transactions.

Where the issue is of non-redeemable shares, Condition B does not operate unless and until the share capital is repaid (s 685(7)). The same applies to Condition A if the consideration is the issue of non-redeemable shares, but only insofar as there is a transfer of assets from one close company to another (s 685(2)(c) and (5).

One important limitation on Conditions A and B is that neither applies where as a result of the transactions in securities there is a fundamental change in the ownership of the company (ITA 2007, s 686). A change is fundamental if after the transactions in securities the original shareholders own less than 25% of the company. For this purpose account is taken of ownership by associates or through other companies.

Income tax advantage

89.6 Identifying whether there is an income tax advantage requires focus on the relevant consideration and the income tax that the person in receipt of the consideration would pay if it were a distribution. The default rule is that such hypothetical tax is the tax advantage. But if the consideration is subject to capital gains tax, the tax advantage is the difference between that capital gains tax and the hypothetical income tax (ITA 2007, s 687). It is to be noted that this definition of tax advantage is much more precisely drawn than its predecessor in the pre-2010 legislation.

Until 5 April 2016, the tax advantage had to have been obtained by somebody who was a party to the transaction(s) in securities. But now it is sufficient if some other person obtains the tax advantage. But whoever obtains the advantage must so obtain it in consequence of the transaction or transactions in securities (s 684(1)(d)).

APPLICATION OF THE TECHNICAL PRECONDITIONS

Parker

89.7 The leading case on the pre-2010 law was *IRC v Parker* [1966] AC 141, [1966] 1 All ER 399, [1966] 2 WLR 486. Here the company redeemed unsecured debentures. The House of Lords held this fell foul of the transactions in securities legislation because:

(a)   The debentures were securities.
(b)   The redemption was a transaction.
(c)   The redemption proceeds represented assets which would have been available to distribute by way of dividend.
(d)   The redemption was not (as the law then stood) otherwise taxable.

Cleary

89.8 *Cleary v IRC* [1968] AC 766, [1967] 2 All ER 48, [1967] 2 WLR 1271, sub nom *IRC v Cleary* 44 TC 399, HL was a disturbing case. Here two sisters owned two companies and caused one to buy the other. The House of Lords held this engaged the pre-2010 legislation as follows:

(a)   The sale of the shares in the target company was the transaction in securities.
(b)   The purchase price paid by the buying company represented profits otherwise available in that company for payment of a dividend.
(c)   The sale proceeds were (as the law then stood) not otherwise taxable.

It will be noted the reasoning in *Cleary* would not have applied had the purchaser company bought some asset other than shares or securities, for then there would have been no transaction in securities. Equally the profits otherwise available for distribution were those of the purchaser company, not those of the company being sold.

In *IRC v Wiggins* [1979] 2 All ER 245, [1979] 1 WLR 325, [1979] STC 244 a company with valuable trading stock was sold to independent purchasers and this was held to engage the former Circumstance D. But this case would not be caught by the present Condition A unless the buyer was connected.

Joiner

89.9 In *IRC v Joiner* [1975] 3 All ER 1050, [1975] 1 WLR 1701, [1975] STC 657, HL, the taxpayer and family trustees owned a successful trading company. A liquidation agreement was entered into whereby that company was to sell its business to a successor company, it was then to be wound up, and its cash and other assets divided in an agreed manner between the taxpayer and the trustees. The House of Lords held these facts engaged the code as follows:

(1)   The liquidation agreement was the transaction in securities.
(2)   The liquidation was something done by the company as it required a resolution of the company.
(3)   Accordingly the liquidation distribution would have been available for payment in dividend but for something done by the company.
(4)   The tax-free consideration received by the taxpayer in the winding up was in consequence of the liquidation agreement and the winding up.

Williams

89.10 *Williams v IRC* [1980] 3 All ER 321, [1980] STC 535, 54 TC 257, HL, was a case of exceptional complexity and a degree of artificiality which could never form part of a tax planning exercise in the current era of purposive construction. It concerned a land dealing company with substantial profits which it was desired to access in tax-free form.

As a first step the shareholders exchanged their shares for shares in a holding company, following which the dealing company paid the profits to the holding company as dividend under a group income election. Subsequently the scheme promoters formed a new company, newco, which borrowed and then on lent funds to the taxpayers on the security of government securities which they had bought for the purpose. The holding company then acquired newco and subscribed the cash it was holding into newco, thereby enabling newco to discharge its debt. The result was the taxpayers ended up with the cash, albeit owing it to newco which by then they controlled.

The House of Lords held that the first stage of this exercise fell within what is now Condition B, in that the holding company shares represented non-taxable consideration received in connection with the distribution of the dealing company's profits. But a tax charge was not possible under this head as the shares were ordinary shares that had not been sold. Faced with this HMRC argued what is now Condition A applied to the loans. This argument was accepted by the House of Lords on the following basis:

(1)   The loans represented profits which would have been available for distribution by the dealing company but for steps taken by that company.

(2)   The recipients of the loans enjoyed a tax advantage as they did not pay tax on the loans.

(3)   That tax advantage was in consequence of one or more transactions in securities.

On this latter point, the House of Lords held that there were many transactions in securities prior to the making of the loans and that as a result the tax advantage represented by the loans was in consequence of them. Lord Dilhorne said (at p 542):

'The transaction in securities] were all necessary ingredients of [the scheme] intended to secure tax free gains to the taxpayers and those gains do not cease to be in consequence of these transactions if one or more links in the chain of operations does not come within the definition.'

It will be noted there was no suggestion the loans were themselves transactions in securities. However as they were secured on government securities they were transactions that related to securities.

Bamberg

89.11 *Bamberg v Revenue and Customs Comrs* [2010] UKFTT 333 (TC), [2010] SFTD 1231, [2010] SWTI 2644 is a recent case. Here the taxpayer had purchased the entire share capital of an insolvent UK resident Guernsey company, together with virtually worthless loan notes issued by the company. He sold the shares to a profitable trading company he controlled and then caused that company to make loans to the Guernsey company. The latter used the borrowed money to repay loan notes held by the taxpayer. The First-tier Tribunal held the pre-2010 legislation was engaged as follows:

(1)   There were on any view transactions in securities and on any view the repayments to the taxpayer were otherwise free of income tax.

(2)   The sums used by the trading company to make the loans to the Guernsey company were otherwise available to the trading company to distribute as dividend.

The present law

89.12 All the above cases were decided on the pre-2010 law. However they turned on Circumstance D in that law, which corresponds to the present Condition A. It may therefore be suggested they remain good law.

THE PURPOSE REQUIREMENT

89.13 As noted above a counteraction notice is not competent unless, in addition to the technical requirements, a purpose test is satisfied (ITA 2007, s 684(1)(c)). Under this test, one of the main purposes of the transaction securities must be the obtaining of an income tax advantage. That latter term has the meaning discussed above (para **89.6**). Where there are multiple transactions in securities, the test is satisfied if one of them had, as one of its main purposes, the obtaining of an income tax advantage.

Prior to 2010, the purpose requirement was expressed as an escape clause rather than as a precondition (ITA 2007, s 685 as originally enacted). This required not merely that income tax advantages were not one of the objects of the transaction(s) but also that the transaction(s) were effected either for genuine commercial reasons or in the ordinary course of making or managing investments. The escape clause generated a remarkable body of case law and operated as a powerful filter to HMRC's use of the legislation. This case law is, it may be suggested, of continuing relevance, albeit that the filter was less robust under the escape clause than under the present purpose requirement, given that the latter focuses only on whether obtaining an income tax advantage was one of the purposes.

IRC v Brebner

89.14 The leading case is *IRC v Brebner* (1967) 43 TC 705. Here a group of directors with a substantial interest in a quoted trading company were faced with an unwanted takeover bid. They borrowed money from the bank to take the company private and then had to repay the bank. They raised the funds to do this by causing the company to reduce its capital and so release cash which, as the law then stood, was taxable as capital. The reduction occurred two years after the company went private, but funding the privatisation out of the company's reserves had always been envisaged. The company could simply have declared a dividend but this was never considered as the tax cost would have been prohibitive.

It was admitted the technical conditions for the transactions in securities legislation were all met. As a result the sole issue was the escape clause. Here the Special Commissioners found that the reduction was effected for bona fide commercial reasons. They recognised there was a tax advantage, but considered this to have been an ancillary result of the main commercial object. As a result the transactions did not have, as one of their main objects, the obtaining of tax advantages.

The House of Lords held that such findings were open to the Special Commissioners. It specifically stated it was open to the Commissioners to view the taking private and the reduction together and that the issue was what subjectively the taxpayers intended when effecting the combined transactions. Lord Upjohn then concluded with the following much quoted passage:

> 'My Lords, I would only conclude my speech by saying, when the question of carrying out a genuine commercial transaction, as this was, is reviewed, the fact that there are two ways of carrying it out – one by paying the maximum amount of tax, the other by paying no, or much less, tax – would be quite wrong, as a necessary consequence, to draw the inference that, in adopting the latter course, one of the main objects is, for the purposes of this section, avoidance of tax. No commercial man in his sense is going to carry out a commercial transaction except upon the footing of paying the smallest amount of tax that he can. The question whether in fact one of the main objects was to avoid tax is one for the Special Commissioners to decide upon a consideration of all the relevant evidence before them and the proper inferences to be drawn from that evidence.'

IRC v Brown

89.15 *IRC v Brown* (1971) 47 TC 217 is a contrasting case. The facts were similar to *Cleary* (para **89.8** above) in that the taxpayer and his wife caused one company they owned to buy the shares they owned in five other companies. The taxpayer and the companies had a history of sophisticated tax planning and the purchasing company had to borrow money from the bank. The only reasons given for the sale were that the taxpayer wished to generate security for his old age and raise funds to buy property in Jersey.

The Tribunal found the escape clause was not satisfied. The Court of Appeal decided this finding was open to the Tribunal. Russell LJ said:

> 'I observe that most of the . . . evidence amounts really to no more than saying that the taxpayer and his wife wanted some money and entered into the transaction in order to get it. Now it seems to me that you do not show that a transaction of sale of securities for full consideration to a company already owned by yourself is a transaction entered into for bona fide commercial reasons merely by saying that it is such a sale transaction and that you wanted the money.'

Clark v IRC

89.16 *Clark v IRC* [1978] STC 614 is the third of a trilogy of early cases which established the parameters of the escape clause. This was another *Cleary* type case, where the company sold was owned 50:50 by two brothers. One brother was a farmer and wanted to sell his shares in order to buy an adjoining farm and the other brother decided to join the sale as he did not want to be left with a deadlock holding. The sale was to another company in family ownership as the wider family wanted to retain ownership of the company being sold.

The Special Commissioners found as a fact that neither brother intended to avoid tax. But they considered the farmer brother had not sold for bona fide commercial reasons or in the ordinary course of managing investments. Their reasoning was that, for the escape clause to apply, the commercial reason had to be connected with the taxpayer's interest in the company sold. Fox J, however, rejected this distinction and held the escape clause applied to both brothers. The sale of the shares was 'merely part of a whole' which was dominated by the farmer brother's wish to acquire the neighbouring farm.

Grogan

89.17 *Grogan v HMRC* [2011] STC 1 is the most modern case on the escape clause. Here the taxpayer owned a majority interest in a car dealing company which was replete with undistributed profits, having sold most of its business. It implemented the following scheme:

(1)   The company established a qualifying share ownership trust or QUEST and paid £633,150 to it.

(2)   This payment gave rise to a corporation tax deduction.

(3)   The QUEST used the money to buy from the taxpayer a proportion of the shares he owned.

(4)   The taxpayer paid CGT in respect of this transaction at the then applicable rate of 10%.

(5)   At the time of the sale the company's remaining dealership was in the course of being sold and it was left with just one employee.

(6)   The scheme was recommended by accountants whose fee was entirely contingent on the tax saved.

The Tribunal decided the escape clause did not on these facts apply. In the Upper Tribunal the taxpayer's main argument was based on *IRC v Willoughby* [1997] STC 995 (see para **73.22**), to the effect that the taxpayer could not have been engaged in avoidance as he was merely availing himself of an express statutory relief, namely the QUEST scheme. This the Upper Tribunal rejected. It stated (at para 112):

'a circular flow of funds where a company contributes cash to a QUEST, where the facts and circumstances are such that there is no desire to incentivise employees, in order to manufacture a capital (rather than an income) receipt for the company's shareholders is very firmly with the scope of the [transactions in securities] code'.

Conclusion

89.18 On the basis of the above cases on the former escape clause, the following conclusions may be drawn as respects the present purpose condition:

(1)   The condition is subjective – ie it is a matter of evidence as to why those entering into the transactions in fact effected them.

(2)   It is open to the Tribunal to look at the totality of what was done, ie both the transaction generating the need for cash and the transaction in securities.

(3)   The fact that cash is extracted from the company in a tax efficient manner may preclude the code if the use of the money is commercial and not tax driven.

(4)   The mere fact the taxpayer needs money does not preclude the code, particularly if he has a history of tax avoidance.

LIQUIDATIONS

89.19 Prior to 5 April 2016, a liquidation did not fall within the term 'transaction in securities' (*IRC v Joiner* [1975] STC 657; *IRC v Laird Group plc* [2003] UKHL 54, [2003] 4 All ER 669, [2003] 1 WLR 2476, para 18). This has now been reversed by statute, in that a distribution in a winding up is a transaction in securities (ITA 2007, s 684(2)(f) as inserted by FA 2016, s 33(3)).

In addition, the 2016 Finance Act inserted a TAAR countering one specific form of abuse. This TAAR may be referred to as the phoenix code. It applies both to UK close companies and to non-resident close companies (ITTOIA 2005, ss 396B and 404A). In contrast to the transactions in securities code, it is within self-assessment and so must be applied in filing regardless of whether HMRC invoke it.

The phoenix code applies only to individuals. It treats the liquidation distribution as a dividend and so subject to income tax if the following conditions are met:

(a)   Prior to the liquidation, the individual must have owned 5% or more of the company.
(b)   A trade or activity similar to that of the company must be carried on after the liquidation.
(c)   A purpose test must be met.
(d)   There must be a gain.

Similar trade or activity

89.20 There is no definition of when a trade or activity is regarded as similar to that of the company being liquidated. However a trade or activity can be caught if it is similar to that carried on by one of the company's 51% subsidiaries.

A similar trade or activity is not caught unless it is carried on within two years of the distribution. But there is no requirement it be started within that period. As a result, cases where the shareholder is already engaged in a similar activity to that of the company being wound up are potentially within the purview of the TAAR. Such a scenario may not be that common with trading companies, but it is by no means abnormal with property and investment businesses.

A similar trade or activity is caught both if it is carried on by the individual shareholder alone, and if it is carried on by a partnership in which he is a partner or a company in which he is a participator. Activities carried on by other connected persons are caught, but only if the shareholder himself is involved in the trade or activity.

The purpose test

89.21 The phoenix code does not apply unless a purpose test is met. The purpose test requires both the winding up on its own and any scheme or arrangements of which it is part to be looked at. The test is met and the code applies if either has as a main purpose the avoidance or reduction of a charge to income tax.

The gain

89.22 The legislation only applies to the extent the liquidation would otherwise result in a gain for CGT purposes. The focus here is on the particular shareholder with the result he may be protected if he has acquired his shares recently and has a high base cost. It makes no difference whether his base cost results from the issue of shares to him by the company or an acquisition of pre-existing shares from another shareholder.

Taxpayers caught

89.23 On its terms the phoenix code applies only to individuals. Trusts and companies are thus outside its scope. Non-resident individuals could be within the TAAR, but no tax results as the effect of the TAAR is to treat the liquidation as a dividend. As such it is disregarded income (ITTOIA 2005, s 825(1); see further para **64.6**).

With individuals it is a little difficult to see when the phoenix code will operate. It is plainly not enough for there to be a similar trade or activity, for the TAAR requires the purpose test to be met as well. It follows that individuals who happen to be carrying on the same trade or activity as the liquidated company are not per se caught. So the mere fact of liquidation and more favourable tax rates is not enough. Some additional element needs to be present: presumably, it may be suggested, a tax driven rationale to the exercise as a whole.

APPLICATION TO DIRECTLY OWNED OFFSHORE COMPANIES

89.24 As the term close company includes non-resident companies, both the transaction in securities code and the phoenix code are of potential application to offshore companies in the direct ownership of UK resident individuals.

Liquidations

89.25 The first and most important point is that both codes should be considered if the liquidation of an offshore company is in prospect. The main concern is undoubtedly the phoenix code, and this needs to be watched wherever the similar trade or activity condition is or may be met. However, as explained above, the code is subject to a purpose test, so a liquidation for genuine commercial reasons should be safe. Such reasons might include the genuine end of the business carried on in the company, or a genuine desire of the owner to reduce his business activities.

Of its nature the transactions in securities legislation is unlikely to be in issue where the phoenix code is precluded by the purpose test. But it would require consideration if the base cost of the shares is high or there is no similar trade or activity. Here a liquidation does satisfy the technical preconditions of the transactions in security code, for a distribution in a winding up is now a transaction in securities and the liquidation surplus is value that but for the liquidation would have been available for distribution by way of dividend.

Nonetheless in the bulk of cases, the purpose test should preclude the code. If, commercially, shareholders no longer wish to retain the company, there is no reason why they have to take the company's retained surplus profits in dividend rather than on a liquidation. The reasoning in *Brebner* (para **89.14** above) is directly in point. However the position could be otherwise if the same business is going to be carried on by some other company and the real reason for the liquidation is to take profits in capital form while still carrying on the business. In other words, the area of vulnerability is much the same as under the phoenix code.

Buy-backs

89.26 As explained in para **32.12**, a share redemption or buy-back by a non-UK resident company is capital. Such a transaction is plainly a transaction in securities and, as with the redemption of debentures in *IRC v Parker* (para **89.7** above), represents the receipt in capital form of profits otherwise available for distribution in dividend. Accordingly a counteraction notice under the transactions in securities code could potentially be competent. But this would not be so unless the purpose test is met and here, on the authority of *Brebner* and *Clark*, a counteraction notice would be precluded if the monies were being raised for a genuine commercial purpose. The same it may be suggested would apply if there is a genuine non-commercial reason, for example funding a divorce, for the present purpose test no longer requires there to be a commercial reason for the transaction.

Sales

89.27 As explained in para **89.5**, sales of shares to third parties are outside the transactions in securities code. But connected party sales are not, and so here to the issue as respects whether a counteraction notice could be served is whether the purpose test is met. On the authority of *Brown* (para **89.15**) a mere desire to raise money may not satisfy the test.

Shareholder loans

89.28 Shareholders often capitalise a company by shareholder loan. The issue such loans raise is whether it would be open to HMRC to serve a counteraction notice when the company repays the loan.

It is reasonably plain that repayment engages Condition A, for the shareholder receives in capital form what could otherwise have been paid in dividend. *Parker v IRC* (para **89.7** above) is directly in point. But in reality there are two compelling reasons why a counteraction notice should not be competent.

One is that it is difficult to see how repayment of a loan as distinct from payment of a dividend could be said to have as a purpose the obtaining of a tax advantage. In general, it is always prudent for a company to use surplus funds to reduce debt rather than pay dividend.

The second argument is that a simple shareholder loan is not a security at all, and so its repayment cannot be a transaction in securities. As explained in para **89.4** above, the term 'securities' is not defined beyond including shares, but the term would not normally be taken as encompassing informal loans. Indeed in *IRC v Laird Group plc* [2003] STC Lord Millett said (at para 29):

'The word "securities" includes not only stocks and shares of every description, including preference shares, but also debentures and unsecured loan notes.'

That the term goes no further than unsecured loan notes is confirmed by *IRC v Parker* itself. Here what was at issue was a debenture secured only by the personal covenant of the company and, unsurprisingly this was held to be a security. The analysis of the term 'security' is in the first instance judgment of Ungoed-Thomas J, and there is no suggestion the term goes beyond what was later said by Lord Millett in *Laird*.

Reference may also be made to the CGT cases on the term 'debt on a security' where the distinction drawn is between a simple unsecured debt and a debt of the nature of an investment (*Ramsay (WT) v IRC* [1981] STC 174; *Taylor Clark International Ltd v Lewis (Inspector of Taxes)* [1998] STC 1259, 71 TC 226, [1999] 01 LS Gaz R 24). Albeit recognising the term 'security' always takes its meaning from the context, the distinction points in the same direction as Lord Millett's words set out above.

Loans to the shareholder

89.29 *Williams v IRC* [1980] 3 All ER 321, [1980] STC 535, 54 TC 257, HL is clear authority that a loan to the shareholder is not, without more, a transaction in securities. As is described above (para **89.10**), the receipt of tax-free consideration in that case was a loan by one of the companies in the scheme to the taxpayers. The issue of whether that tax advantage was in consequence of a transaction in securities was addressed in one of two ways namely:

(1)   the scheme involved antecedent transactions, many of which were undoubtedly transactions in securities; or
(2)   the loan was secured on government stock and as such related to securities.

Given the wide construction of the legislation adopted in Williams and earlier cases, it is inconceivable that the above two analyses would have been ventilated so fully had the mere making of the loan been a transaction in securities.

TRUST STRUCTURES

89.30 As will be apparent from elsewhere in this book, the great majority of companies used in offshore tax planning are offshore companies owned by offshore trusts. The trustees of such trusts are not subject to income tax or CGT as respects the shares in such companies and so it is impossible for them to have a tax advantage in the sense contemplated by the transactions in securities legislation. So too, the phoenix code cannot apply, as that extends only to individuals.

But in relation to the transactions in securities legislation, the issue arises of whether the code could be engaged if a tax advantage is enjoyed by the settlor or a beneficiary. In dealing with this issue, three points must be made at the outset:

(1)   The party to the transaction in securities is the trustees, and it is therefore on them that any counteraction notice must be served (s 695(1)).

(2)   As a result of the 2016 changes, the tax advantage can be obtained by someone other than the party to the transaction in securities.

(3)   Also as a result of the 2016 changes, the tax-free consideration required under Conditions A and B can be received by persons other than the party to the transaction in securities.

On the face of it, these latter two changes do mean offshore trust structures can be within the code. For the sake of illustration, two scenarios can be postulated.

The first concerns a settlor-interested trust with a remittance-basis user settlor. Here the settlor needs funds in the UK, such as would result in income tax if the trustees procured a dividend from an underlying company and distributed the money to the settlor. Assuming proper segregation of capital and income is in place, such income tax is avoided if the distribution is funded by repayment of shareholder loan, by a buy back or following a liquidation of the company.

The second scenario concerns a trust that is not settlor-interested where distributions need to be made to UK beneficiaries. Here a dividend paid by the company to fund the distribution would result in the beneficiary being liable to income tax. But assuming there is no available relevant income, capital treatment is secured if the company effects a buy back, or is liquidated.

To bring these two scenarios within the transactions in securities code would require HMRC to establish at least five points:

(1)   The tax advantage enjoyed by the settlor or beneficiary was in consequence of the corporate transaction (s 684(1)(d)).

(2)   The tax free consideration represented by the distribution is, as Condition A requires, received as a result of the corporate transaction (s 685(2)).

(3)   The distribution represents funds which, apart from what was done by the company, would have been available for payment of a dividend.

(4)   The adjustments made by the counteraction notice can result in tax not on the party on whom the notice is served but on some other person, ie the settlor or beneficiary.

(5)   The purpose test does not provide a defence.

It may be suggested that *Williams v IRC* could be adduced by HMRC in support of the first three points. It is reinforced by *Grogan v HMRC* [2011] STC 1 where Warren J said (at para 31):

> 'It is enough if the tax advantage is obtained as the result of an overall series of transactions which are linked together to form a scheme and where the relevant transaction in securities is part of that scheme.'

But even if the first three points are established, the two remaining ones remain.

As respects the fourth, a key issue is the nature of the adjustment allowed in the notice. One such adjustment is an assessment, but could a counteraction notice on the trustees specify an assessment on the settlor or a beneficiary? Another permitted adjustment is the recalculation of profits or gains or liability to income tax. Would a recalculation of the trust's income, or its relevant income, amount to a recalculation of profits or gains? And if it did, could the counteraction notice adjust the tax liability of another party, namely the settlor or a beneficiary?

These are plainly difficult issues and in addition to them is the fifth point, namely the purpose test, which is fundamental. If the trustees' reason for procuring the corporate transactions is to raise money to fund a distribution, can it be said there is a tax avoidance purpose? Cases such as *Brebner* and *Clark* may be point, particularly as now it is not necessary to show positively the transactions in securities were effected for investment reasons. It could be said that *Brown* (para **89.15** above) means the mere need for money does not enable the purpose test to operate as a bar. But this reasoning may not apply to trustees, given their whole *raison d'etre* is to provide for beneficiaries. And *Brown* would on no view be in point if the beneficiary genuinely needed the money for non-tax avoidance reasons.

The prudent course, undoubtedly is to accept the code could apply and plan accordingly. But in many cases it may be concluded the above points would represent significant difficulties for HMRC were they to open an enquiry. In such cases the risk of being within the technical terms of the code may be one that should be accepted.

Chapter 90

TRANSACTIONS IN UK LAND

INTRODUCTION

90.1 The 2016 Finance Act enacted provisions to counter the use of offshore structures to shelter profits generated by dealing in or developing UK land. The original anti-avoidance legislation directed at artificial transactions in land dated back to 1969 (FA 1969, s 32) and was rewritten as ITA 2007, ss 752–772 and CTA 2010, ss 815–833. This legislation, however, was increasingly circumvented by schemes involving offshore structures and treaties and as a result FA 2016 introduced a more comprehensive code (FA 2016, ss 77 and 79). Much of the language of this code is that of the former legislation, but the new code is free-standing and the old legislation is repealed. The present legislation is twice as long as it needs to be, as it is separately enacted for income tax and corporation tax (ITA 2007, ss 517A–517U; CTA 2010, ss 356OA and 356OT).

CONTEXT

90.2 The new legislation has to be seen in the context of rules, also introduced in FA 2016, which extend the territorial scope of trading in UK land and modify double tax relief.

Territorial scope

90.3 As is discussed in para **26.6**, a non-resident company is within the charge to corporation tax if and insofar as it carries on the trade of dealing in or developing UK land (CTA 2009, s 5(2)(a)). If it is carrying on such a trade, it is charged to corporation tax even if the trade would otherwise be regarded as carried on outside the UK, and, it is chargeable whether or not the trade is carried on through a permanent establishment. Developing UK land is caught only if the development is for the purposes of disposing of the land (CTA 2007, s 5B(2)(b)).

Targeted anti-avoidance rule

90.4 HMRC have power to counteract schemes or arrangements which would other deliver a tax advantage in relation to this charge to corporation tax (CTA

2009, s 5A). Such an adjustment may be made by assessment or modification of an assessment and may be made by the taxpayer company when self-assessing as well as by HMRC.

A tax advantage can only be countered if it relates to the income tax or corporation tax which would otherwise be chargeable on the dealing or development profits. However it is not just avoidance in the strict sense that can be countered, for the term advantage inter alia includes a simple reduction in tax (ITA 2007, s 6A(6); CTA 2009, s 6A(6), incorporating CTA 2010, s 1139).

The tax advantages that may be countered include those obtained by exploiting the provisions of a double tax treaty (s 5A(2)). But this only applies if the advantage is contrary to 'the object and purpose' of the treaty. It is unclear what this mysterious provision means, and in particular what materials may be used in determining the object and purpose. However it is a reasonable inference that the exercise should be in accordance with the law as to interpretation of treaties (see para **99.10** to **99.15**) and thus include preparatory materials and the OECD commentary. What is not clear is whether the present provision goes further than normal treaty interpretation and would enable HMRC to counter structures with little underlying connection with the relevant treaty jurisdiction.

Income tax

90.5 Comparable provisions are made in relation to income tax and non-corporate persons (ITTOIA 2005, ss 6(1A), 6A and 6B). A non-resident individual or trust is thus charged to income tax on profits realised in dealing in or developing UK land, developing being caught only if it is for the purposes of disposing of the land. As corporation tax rates are now much lower than income tax rates, this is a significantly more onerous burden than that placed on non-resident companies. The targeted anti-avoidance rule also applies (s 6A).

Amendment of treaties

90.6 The Crown Dependency treaties were widely used to circumvent the tax charge on dealing and development profits. It was never wholly clear whether such schemes were effective. With effect from 16 March 2016, these schemes are countered by an amendment to the treaties giving the UK taxing rights over gains derived from the alienation of immovable property. The amendments also give the UK taxing rights over gains on unquoted shares insofar as over 50% of their value is derived from UK immovable property. The protocols effecting these amendments are attached to HMRC's Technical Note of 16 March 2016 'Profits from Trading in and Developing UK Land'.

DISPOSALS OF LAND

90.7 Under the 2016 anti-avoidance legislation, the profit or gain realised on a disposal of UK land is deemed to be a trading profit if any one of three conditions is met (CTA 2010, s 3560B; ITA 2007, s 517B). These conditions are the same as applied under the old artificial transactions in land rules and are as follows:

(1)   one of the main purposes of acquiring the land was to realise a profit from disposing of it;
(2)   the land is held as trading stock; or
(3)   the land has been developed, and one of the main purposes of the development was to realise a profit from disposing of the land.

What is odd about these three conditions is that, in logic they would in any event have the result the gain was a trading profit (see para **90.3** above and para **26.7**). This is acknowledged to a limited extent, by a provision excluding any gain from these rules that is otherwise taxed as a trading gain (ss 3560C(3) and 517C(3)). But the question then remains whether these rules can catch transactions which are not trading, on the grounds that those acquiring or developing investment property normally have as one of their purposes the hope of eventual capital gain. With the old artificial transactions in land rules there was an explicit statement that the legislation was enacted to counter tax avoidance and a reasonable inference from that was that simple transactions were not caught (*Yuill v Wilson* [1980] STC 460, 465F, approving [1979] STC 486, 491B). But that implied limitation, if such it was, is not present with the present legislation, as there is no express statement that its purpose is to counter tax avoidance. So the possibility is raised that gains realised on investment property could be turned into income by this legislation.

In reality the issue raised by the question may be more apparent than real, for a distinction needs to be drawn between buying or developing property in the hope it will grow in value and buying or developing property with a view to selling it. The former does not engage the present provision, for even though there may be a purpose of generating enhanced value, there is no purpose of realising that potential gain by selling the property.

As with the former artificial transactions in land rules, the present legislation is also engaged if property deriving its value from the land was acquired and one of the purposes of that acquisition was to realise a profit from disposing of the land (ss 3560B(5), 517B(5)). This provision too was in the old law, and it is only engaged if the basic precondition of ss 3560B and 517B is met, namely that the disposal occasioning the profit is of the land itself.

Property deriving its value from land is defined as including (ss 3560R and 517S):

(a)   A shareholding or partnership interest deriving its value from the land.
(b)   Any interest in settled property deriving its value from land.
(c)   Any option, consent or embargo affecting the land.

The general rule is that the profit or gain realised on the disposal of the land must be realised by the person who acquired, held or developed the land. But a profit or gain is also caught if it is realised by somebody associated with that person. More significantly a profit or gain realised by some unconnected person can be caught if such unconnected person is a party to an arrangement effected with respect to the land which enables the gain to be realised by an indirect method or by a series of transactions (ss 3560B(3) and 517B(3)). A provision in similar terms was in the former legislation and meant that trustees who sold development land on long lease were subject to income tax on the part of the premium representing overage paid as and when completed houses were sold (*Page v Lowther* [1983] 799). There is no requirement that the arrangement have a tax avoidance purpose.

The charge under ss 3560B and 517B applies whether the person concerned is resident or non-resident (ss 3560C and 517C). In either event the profit is treated as a trading profit, the trading profit being allocated to the trade referred to in paras **90.3** and **90.5** above in the case of a non-resident.

Computational rules

90.8 Where the rules are engaged the principles used in computing trading profits apply to determine what the profit is (ss 35601 and 517I). A special rule applies where the rules are engaged because the land has been developed. Here any part of the gain that is fairly attributable to a period before the intention to develop was formed is excluded from the charge (ss 3560L and 517L).

Anti-fragmentation

90.9 One form of deduction is specifically disallowed in computing the gain. This disallowance goes under the generic name of anti-fragmentation and is in point if an associate of the person disposing of the land has made what is called a relevant contribution. Should this condition be met, the disallowance is effected by treating the disponor and the contributor as the same person (ss 3560H and 517H).

A contribution is relevant if it is made to the development of the land or to any activities directed at realising a gain on its disposal. It is specifically provided that the term includes the assumption of risk or any financial contribution and also professional services. There is a de minimis exclusion of this rule, but the exclusion is in point only if the contributor's profit is insignificant by comparison with the overall size of the project.

The term 'associate' is widely defined to include connected persons in relation to individuals and trusts, and related parties in the case of companies (ss 3560H(9) and 517H(9)). Companies are related if their accounts are or should be consolidated. They are also related if one is a direct or indirect participant in the other or one has a 25% investment in the other, or if a third company satisfies one or other of these conditions in relation to both (ss 3560T and 517U). In the case of direct and indirect participants, these terms draw on the transfer pricing concepts discussed in paras **91.6** to **91.10**.

The rule excluding from ss 3560B and 517B amounts otherwise brought into account in computing trading profits would appear to apply. It thus follows that a UK associate is not caught by these rules if whatever he earns forms part of his trading profits. But this would not apply to an overseas service provider outside the scope of UK tax, and such are the target of the anti-fragmentation rule.

PROPERTY DERIVING ITS VALUE FROM LAND

90.10 As noted above (para 90.7), property deriving its value from UK land includes shares or interests in companies or partnerships owning the land, beneficial interests in trusts owning the land, and options, consent rights or embargoes affecting the land. A special rule can apply on the disposal of such derivative property if certain conditions are met (ss 3560D and 517D). The conditions are as follows:

(1)   At least 50% of the value of the derivative property must be derived from land in the UK. This 50% test is applied as at the time of the disposal.

(2)   The disponor of the derivative property is a party to or concerned in an arrangement.

(3)   One of the main purposes of the arrangement is to deal in or develop the land and realise a gain by disposing of the derivative property.

Where these conditions are met, the profit on the disposal of the derivative property is treated as profits of a trade in dealing in or developing UK land. But where the value of the derivative property is not all attributable to the UK land only the proportion so attributable is so treated.

This provision applies even if some of the land owned by the entity concerned is long-term investment land, for the provision is engaged if the arrangement to deal or develop concerns just some of the entity's land. In that event the gain included as trading profit on the derivative disposal reflects all the UK land owned by the entity.

In contrast to the former artificial transactions in land legislation, there is no relief where the entity itself is trading and the land is trading stock. But in such a case the sections are not engaged if the disposal of the derivative property takes place after the offending land has been sold, for it is a prerequisite of the derivative disposal that it derives at least 50% of its value from the land as at the time of disposal.

It is expressly provided that value may be traced through any number of companies, partnership or trusts (ss 3560M and 517M). It follows that in a complex corporate structure owned by an offshore trust or individual, the sections could be engaged either on a disposal of shares in the top company by the non-corporate owner or on a disposal by the top company of any intermediate holding company. In the latter case the charge would be at corporation tax rates and in the former at the much more severe income tax rates.

There is no requirement for the operation of the sections that the arrangement have tax avoidance as a purpose. However in practice the requirement that one of the main purposes of the arrangement include the disposal of the derived property is an important limitation. It means the sections are not engaged just because what is envisaged is disposal of the land itself at a profit.

PROVISIONS OF VALUE OR OPPORTUNITY

90.11 One of the most difficult aspects of the legislation is represented by ss 3560G and 517G. These sections apply if the profit realised by one person is derived from value provided by another person. More generally they also apply if the profit is derived from an opportunity of realising it provided by another person. Should either of these conditions be satisfied, the profit is treated as accruing to the provider rather than the person to whom the gain or profit in fact accrues. In many cases where this provision is in point the practical result is to substitute an income tax liability on the provider for a corporation tax liability on a company realising the gain. The provision of the value or opportunity can be direct or indirect.

In all material respects these sections reproduce provisions in the former artificial transactions in land code (ITA 2007, s 759; CTA 2010 s 821). The provider charge had been upheld in two cases where land was sold to offshore entities who subsequently realised gains. In one case the provider was the seller (*Sugarwhite v Budd (Inspector of Taxes)* [1988] STC 533, 60 TC 679) and in the other the land was sold by UK companies owned by the provider, members of his family, and family trusts (*Yuill v Wilson* [1980] STC 460).

In relation to the comparable provisions in the former code, HMRC recognised the provider charge was a charge on a third party who was not a party to the actual transaction in land. As a result clear and convincing evidence was said to be required to show that the third party really was the provider of the value or opportunity (BIM 60328). The emphasis on the issue being one of fact is supported by the following words of Lord Dilhorne in *Yuill v Wilson* (at p 466d):

> '[The commissioners] found as a fact that [the taxpayer] obtained the gains for these companies. He can hardly have done that without providing them with the opportunity of realising the gains.'

It is noteworthy that *Yuill v Wilson* involved sales by UK companies of land without planning permission to offshore companies and then sales back to the UK companies once planning permission had been obtained. The individual taxpayer was a director of the UK companies. He had no shares in one of the selling UK companies and controlled the others only when account was taken of trust shareholdings. The case thus shows there can be indirect provision of an opportunity even if as a matter of law the taxpayer does not have the ability to procure the provision.

A point that is not immediately clear from the legislation is how the provider charge applies where the gain is realised by a company and the provider is non-corporate. ITA 2007, s 3560G does not cover the position, as on its terms it applies only where the provider is a company. If in these circumstances the provider charge applies at all it is under ITA 2007, s 517G. But if it is to so apply, it is necessary to read the income tax provisions as operating where the actual person realising the gain is a company subject to corporation tax, with the provider provisions then impliedly displacing the corporation tax charge on the company.

The rule for providers applies not merely where the disposal is of the land, but also where the disposal is of derivative property (ss 3560G(1) and 517G(1)).

ANTI-AVOIDANCE

90.12 Although the new legislation is itself anti-avoidance, it is buttressed by a targeted anti-avoidance rule (ss 3090K and 517K). This is in the same terms as the rule described above (para **90.4**) applicable to trading profits. It applies if arrangements have been put in place and one of their main purposes is to generate a tax advantage in relation to the rules described in this chapter. The counteracted advantage can flow from a double tax treaty if the advantage is contrary to the object and purposes of the treaty.

Chapter 91

TRANSFER PRICING

The authors would like to give special thanks to Robert Birchall and Helen Coward of Charles Russell Speechlys LLP for their help with this chapter

INTRODUCTION

91.1 Transfer pricing is principally thought of as relevant in relation to transactions between companies which are members of a multi-national group. In fact it is in point wherever parties in common ownership or under common control do business with each other. Its operation therefore needs to be considered in joint ventures as well as intra-group or related party transactions, and also with regard to transactions with partnerships.

Where transactions take place between related parties, there may be no commercial significance in prices agreed between the parties and so, if one has a more favourable tax position than the other, there may be scope to structure a transaction to secure an overall tax advantage. This practice is known as transfer pricing.

Until 1999 HMRC had two principal weapons to counter transfer pricing, namely a direction challenging related party prices under TA 1988, s 770 and, where the other party to a transaction was based in a treaty jurisdiction, the Associated Enterprises clause in the relevant double tax treaty.

In 1998 s 770 was repealed and the present code, now contained in TIOPA 2010, ss 146–217, was introduced. This makes transfer pricing adjustments a mandatory part of a taxpayer's self assessment procedure.

When originally enacted the present rules did not apply if the party disadvantaged by the non-commercial price was resident and taxed in the UK. This was on the basis that there was no tax lost to the UK exchequer as both the tax advantage and disadvantage were occurring within the UK. In 2004, in response to case law in the European Court (see CHAPTER 106) requiring intra Member State transactions to be treated the same as intra EU transactions, this territorial limit was removed. Consequently, transfer pricing is now applicable to UK-to-UK transactions. At the same time a limited exemption for small and medium-sized enterprises was introduced and the thin capitalisation rules formerly in TA 1988, s 208(2)(da) were brought within the code.

This chapter is concerned with the law as it now exists. A point to stress is that the provisions do not just apply in computing trading profits. As noted below they apply generally in computing income and deductions. Therefore the situations and persons within the code are very wide.

In the aftermath of the financial crisis, there has been increasing global focus on the activities of multinational companies and the extent to which they have taken advantage of national transfer pricing rules to allocate profits to low-tax jurisdictions. The G20 requested that the OECD review how national tax laws may be changed in order to address these concerns and protect the member countries' tax base. The OECD published a 15-point action plan entitled 'Action Plan on Base Erosion and Profit Shifting' on 19 July 2013 and on 16 September 2014 released a set of reports and recommendations. The final reports were published in 2015, with a separate in-depth report for each Action Point. The OECD Transfer Pricing Guidelines have also been updated in response to the work on BEPS. Although the implementation of any recommendations will not take place for a number of years and will be primarily aimed at large multinational companies, it is nevertheless likely that there will be a number of significant changes made to the existing domestic transfer pricing rules as a result of the OECD's ongoing work in this area. Although the UK government stated in early 2015 that it is still committed to the multilateral approach that is integral to the OECD's work in this area, the UK government nevertheless unilaterally introduced the 'Diverted Profits Tax' in the Finance Act 2015 to target some of the perceived abuses the OECD are also attempting to address.

Action 13 is the guidance on transfer pricing documentation and country-by-country reporting. The final report sets out a three-tiered standardised approach to transfer pricing documentation by large multi-national enterprises. Broadly, the recommendation is to require multinational enterprises to provide (i) all relevant tax administrations with high-level information regarding their global operations and transfer pricing, (ii) detailed, country-specific transfer pricing documentation to each relevant tax administration and (iii) a country-by-country report annually. Legislation enacting the country-by-country reporting recommendation was introduced in Finance Act 2015 with effect for accounting periods beginning on or after 1 January 2016. The rules only apply to groups with a consolidated turnover of €750 million or more.

In addition, the recommendations of the final report on Action 4, which is aimed at limiting the deductibility of interest, will be implemented in the UK from 1 April 2017. HMRC is currently consulting on the technical detail of the rules, which will apply after the application of the transfer pricing rules. The key points are that there will be a group-wide restriction of 30% of 'tax EBITDA' for financing deductions and a de minimis allowance of £2m net UK interest expense per annum.

THE BASIC RULE

Preconditions

91.2 The transfer pricing code applies if the following conditions are satisfied (para 1):

(1) 'Provision' has been made or imposed as between any two persons. This provision is referred to as 'the actual provision' and the two persons are referred to as 'the affected persons'.

(2) The actual provision has been made or imposed by means of a transaction or series of transactions.

(3) The actual provision differs from what is called the arm's length provision. This is the provision which would have been made had the affected persons been independent enterprises.

(4) The actual provision confers a potential advantage in relation to UK taxation on one or both of the affected persons. A person so advantaged is referred to as 'the potentially advantaged person'.

(5) One of the affected persons participates directly or indirectly in the management control or capital of the other or a common third party so participates in both.

The adjustment

91.3 Where the above preconditions are satisfied, the adjustment required is that the arm's length provision must be substituted for the actual provision in computing the taxable profits or losses of the potentially advantaged person (s 147(3), (5)). The substitution is mandatory and must be effected by the taxpayer in preparing his self-assessment return.

The potential tax advantage

91.4 An actual provision is treated as conferring a potential tax advantage if, by comparison with the arm's length provision, the advantaged person's profits are less than they should be, or his deductible expenditure and losses are greater (s 155). It is expressly provided that 'profits' includes income (s 156(2)). Deductions and losses includes general expenditure, as well as other explicit deductions including pre-trading expenses, non-trading deficits on loan relationships, excess of management charges and payments for group relief (s 156(1)).

There is an exception to the income to which the regime applies, when looking at a non-resident advantaged person (s 155(5)). The regime does not apply to disregarded income as defined in ITA 2007, ss 813 and 816. Such disregarded income is, broadly, UK source income in respect of which the tax liability of non-residents is restricted to tax deducted at source (see para **64.13**). The principal categories of disregarded income are dividends and interest payments.

The code requires that the actual provision be compared with the arm's length provision. The use of the term 'provision' means that the comparison which must be made is not simply one of price. All the terms of the transactions in question must be looked at, and those which are non-commercial must be adjusted. In *DSG Retail Ltd v Revenue and Customs Comrs* [2009] STC (SCD) 397, 11 ITLR 869 the Special Commissioners stated (at para 76):

> 'para 1 of Sch 28AA requires the identification of a provision between relevantly connected persons and the determination of what provision would have been made between independent persons. That notional provision could be different, not only in price, but in its terms from the actual provision made.'

Meaning of transaction

91.5 The term 'transaction' has an extended meaning. It includes arrangements, understandings and mutual practices, whether or not legally enforceable (s 150). The term 'series of transactions' includes any number of transactions entered into under the same arrangement. It is not necessary for either of the affected persons to be party to such an arrangement, nor that there be any transaction in the series to which they are both parties.

COMMON PARTICIPATION

91.6 The fundamental prerequisite for the transfer pricing regime to apply is common participation of the parties to the transaction (or series of transactions) in the management, control, or capital of each other or in a common third party. The test is satisfied where participation is direct or indirect (s 148).

Direct participation

91.7 One person participates directly in the management, control or capital of another if he controls the other person and that person is a body corporate or partnership (s 157).

Control does not bear its extended close company definition but the narrower meaning given by CTA 2010, s 1124. This applies to partnerships as well as companies.

A person has control of a company under s 1124 if (1) he can secure that its affairs are conducted in accordance with his wishes; and (2) he is able to secure that result by one of two methods. The first method is by the possession of share or voting rights and the second is by powers conferred by the articles.

Under s 1124 a person controls a partnership if he is entitled to more than half its assets or more than half the income. Hence the transfer pricing code can apply to transactions between an individual and a partnership in which his share is greater than half, or between two partnerships in each of which one individual enjoys more than a half share. It also applies to transactions between such partnerships and a company which an individual controls.

Indirect participation

91.8 Indirect participation is a much wider concept (TIOPA 2010, s 159). A person participates indirectly in the management, control, or capital of a company or partnership if either:

(a)   he would be a direct participant if specified rights or powers were attributed to him; or

(b)   he is a 'major participant' in the enterprise of the company or partnership.

Attributed rights and powers

91.9 The rights and powers which may be attributed to a person in determining whether he is an indirect participant in a company or partnership are (s 159(3)):

(1)   Rights or powers which he is entitled to acquire in the future or will become entitled to acquire.

(2)   Rights or powers which are or may be required to be exercised on his behalf, under his direction, and for his benefit.

(3)   Rights or powers exercisable by any person with whom he is connected, or by any person connected with such a connected person.

For the purposes of (3) persons are connected with each other if they are relatives or if one is the trustee of a settlement and the other is a settlor or a person connected with him (TIOPA 2010, s 163). Relatives include children, grandchildren, parents, grandparents and spouses (s 163(4)).

There are two particularly menacing features of these definitions:

(a)   The chain of connection at (3) can go on indefinitely (s 159(6)). Thus if X is the son of Y, Y is the brother of Z, and A is the son of Z, X and A are connected. So too X is connected with any settlement of which A is settlor, and vice versa. Such connections would only cease if Y or Z died.

(b)   It is unclear what is meant at (2) by rights which are, or may be, required to be exercised on behalf of a person or for his benefit. In particular does it mean that shares or voting rights held in trust must be attributed to a beneficiary? The argument that it does is that all powers vested in trustees have to be exercised for the benefit of the beneficiaries. The argument that it does not is that such powers have to be exercised for the benefit of the beneficiaries collectively rather than for the benefit of any one of them to the exclusion of the others.

Major participants

91.10 To determine whether a person is a major participant it is necessary to show that he and one other person control the company or partnership (TIOPA 2010, s 160(3)(b)). It must then be established that each of those persons has at least 40% of those interests rights and powers which give them control (s 160(4)). Transfer pricing can therefore apply to transactions between a taxpayer and a joint venture entity if the taxpayer has 40% or more control of it and there is another participant in the joint venture that also has 40% or more control. In applying these tests, all rights and powers which can be attributed to a person under the tests referred to above are so attributed. It should also be noted that any rights or powers that can only be exercised jointly with one or more persons are considered to be exercisable by the affected person.

The test is therefore extremely broad and situations where the parties regard themselves as independent can be caught.

Financing arrangements

91.11 A special rule exists in relation to financing arrangements (TIOPA 2010, ss 161 and 162). Here control is additionally determined by combining the rights and powers of any persons that have acted together in relation to those financing arrangements. This attribution may be made in determining whether he has control of the company for whom the arrangements are being made or whether he controls any other company which is an affected person in relation to those arrangements.

Most commonly financing arrangements will mean loans, but it can also include equity, guarantees and other financial instruments. The rules are largely aimed at preventing private equity funds from thinly capitalising their acquisitions (see para **91.18**).

THE ARM'S LENGTH PROVISION

91.12 The transfer pricing code does not define what it means by arm's length provision. Instead it requires that the legislation be construed so as to secure consistency with the OECD guidelines applicable to the Associated Enterprises article in Double Tax Treaties (TIOPA 2010, s 164). The OECD guidelines are published in looseleaf form under the title, 'Transfer Pricing Guidelines for Multinational Enterprises and Tax Administrations'. The effect is that these guidelines must be followed in determining what the arm's length provision of a transaction should be.

Such a rule is admirable in securing international consistency. The difficulty is that the language of the OECD guidelines is often elusive and academic, with the result that clear rules can be difficult to identify. However, there is one overriding principle; if it is possible to identify similar transactions between unconnected parties, the price at which those transactions are carried out is the arm's length price which is then compared to the actual price. The aim of any transfer pricing exercise is therefore to identify this price, being the comparable uncontrolled price, known as the CUP.

It is not always possible to find similar transactions from which the CUP can be discerned. Often this is because the related party transaction is not one which independent parties would be likely to enter into; for example, one party buying the whole output of the other. When this is the case other methods may be used, most notably 'cost plus' (where costs of the transaction are ascertained and an appropriate mark up added to remunerate); 'resale minus' (where the price at which an asset is resold to an independent entity is used with an appropriate reduction for the reseller expenses); or some formula for dividing overall profit relative to contribution. All these are variants of CUP in identifying the kind of margin or division that would be agreed at arm's length. Often two of these secondary methods are used to provide a cross-check and justification for a stated arm's length price.

DSG Retail

91.13 To date *DSG Retail Ltd v Revenue and Customs Comrs* [2009] STC (SCD) 397, 11 ITLR 869 is the most significant decision on the present transfer pricing code. In that case Dixons, the electrical group, owned an Isle of Man subsidiary which insured service obligations under service contracts issued when electrical goods were sold. The service contractor was in independent ownership. The arrangements were complex but the overall effect was that the Isle of Man subsidiary's profits could not exceed more than 15% of the premiums paid, the mechanism imposing this cap being a profit commission payable by the subsidiary.

The Special Commissioners decided that there was provision between Dixons group in the UK and its Isle of Man subsidiary, even though there was no direct contractual link, the contracts being between Dixons and the service contractor on the one hand, and the service contractor and the Isle of Man company on the other. They then described the task required in the following terms (at para 73):

> '(a)   We have to identify whether in relation to any appellant there was any provision made or imposed between it and DISL; (b) if so, we have to determine whether the same provision would have been made had that appellant and DISL been independent; (c) if not, then we must determine the provision which would have been made; and (d) we must then determine for each relevant year after 1 July 1999 what effect the making of the different provision would have had on the taxable profits of that appellant.'

In undertaking this task the Special Commissioners examined possible comparables, as OECD methodology required them to do. They found none appropriate and on that basis approached the case as one of profit split. On this basis they found the arrangements to be non-commercial, as the Isle of Man subsidiary's profits were greater than commensurate with the respective bargaining power of it and Dixons group in the UK. As a result an adjustment was required, in the form of a further profit commission payable by the Isle of Man subsidiary.

DSG Retail is a difficult and complicated case. It illustrates the arcane and often highly theoretical nature of transfer pricing methodology.

SMALL AND MEDIUM-SIZED ENTERPRISES

91.14 There is an exclusion from the transfer pricing code where the advantaged party is a small enterprise (TIOPA 2010, s 166). The exclusion also applies where the advantaged party is a medium-sized enterprise unless HMRC give a transfer pricing notice. A small or medium-sized enterprise can irrevocably elect to disapply the exemption. A transfer pricing notice can only be given if HMRC open an enquiry into the enterprise's tax return for the period to which the return relates (TIOPA 2010, ss 168–169).

Definition of small and medium-sized enterprises

91.15 The terms small and medium-sized enterprise bear their EU definitions (TIOPA 2010, s 172). A medium-sized enterprise is one which employs fewer than 250 persons and either has a turnover of €50m or less or has a balance sheet total of €43m or less. A small enterprise employs fewer than 50 people and has a turnover or balance sheet total of €10m or less. These definitions are economist's definitions and thus are not easy to apply to tax law. A particular difficulty is that account must be taken of linked and partner enterprises. That difficulty is discussed in relation to diverted profits tax at para **92.10**.

Exclusion of offshore jurisdictions

91.16 The exemption for small and medium-sized enterprises does not apply where the other party to the transaction, ie the party not enjoying the tax advantage, is resident in a non-qualifying territory (TIOPA 2010, s 167). This exclusion, bringing transactions back within the transfer pricing code, applies if any of the multiple parties to a transaction is resident in a non-qualifying territory.

A territory is non-qualifying unless there is a double tax treaty between it and the UK which includes a non-discrimination provision (s 173). However there is power for the Treasury to designate a territory with such a treaty as non-qualifying. The Treasury also has power to designate other territories as qualifying, but only if there is a Double Tax Treaty of some kind between the UK and the territory concerned. To date these designation powers have not been exercised.

The term 'non discrimination provision' is defined in terms similar to that of the non-discrimination article in the OECD Model Treaty (s 173(4)). It means a provision which prevents the treaty partners from imposing on each other's nationals more burdensome tax requirements than are imposed on their own nationals.

The term 'resident' is also defined (s 167(5)). It means that the person with whom the UK party is entering into the relevant transfer pricing transaction must be liable to tax in the non-qualifying territory by reason of domicile, residence or place of management. Liability in respect of only local-source income or capital is disregarded. Somewhat curiously there is no provision deeming an entity which is not liable to tax anywhere as being ipso facto resident in a non-qualifying territory, such as is found in the CFC legislation.

It follows that the small or medium-sized exemption is potentially in point if the counterpart entity is not taxable anywhere.

Application

91.17 It is most unsatisfactory that a feature of the code as fundamental as the exemption for small and medium enterprises is defined in the way it is. There are two reasons why this is the case:

(1)   The drafting of the Annex to 2003/36/EC is sloppy and imprecise, with the result that it is often difficult to interpret.

(2)   The Annex is expressed in terms of enterprises, ie businesses, whereas transfer pricing is not solely concerned with taxes on business.

In an offshore context these deficiencies may work to the advantage of taxpayers, as is indicated by the definition of residence above. Another issue is how far a trust or a passive asset-holding company may be said to be an enterprise at all. In view of the definition in Article 1 of the Annex, this turns on whether the mere holding of assets is an economic activity. It is suggested that it is, at least insofar as the assets produce income rather than being enjoyed by the owners or beneficiaries in specie.

THIN CAPITALISATION

91.18 The term 'thin capitalisation' normally refers to the funding of a company with debt rather than equity. This may be attractive as dividends are not deductible in calculating taxable income whereas interest is. Within multinational groups there can be little commercial differentiation between financing a group by way of debt or equity. Therefore the ability to reduce the tax liability of a group company may make it desirable to fund that company entirely by debt. Where there is lower equity compared to debt participation the debt company is described as being thinly capitalised.

TIOPA 2010, s 152 renders payment of such interest subject to transfer pricing rules. In determining whether too much interest is being paid by the UK company, account can be taken not merely of whether the rate of interest would have been lower at arm's length, but of whether the loan would have been made either at all or if made, in a lesser amount. The same principles are applied where the offshore owner does not itself make the loan but guarantees some commercial lender who does (s 153). These rules are expressed as applying only where both the parties to the transaction are companies.

DOUBLE COUNTING

91.19 One problem where a transfer pricing adjustment is made is that the other party may already have paid tax on the basis of having enjoyed enhanced profits or unduly modest losses or other deductions. Without a corresponding adjustment to amend the reported profit or deduction by the other party, tax will be paid twice on the same amount. To prevent this, TIOPA 2010, s 174 allows an adjustment to be claimed where both parties are within charge to UK tax in respect of the transactions concerned. This puts the parties back into the position they would be if transfer pricing did not apply. In addition, balancing payments may be made between the parties without tax cost (ss 195 and 196). Clauses requiring such adjustment and payments are usually included in joint venture documentation to which transfer pricing will, or may, apply.

FA 2014 introduced an exception to the general rule that an adjustment may be claimed by both parties within the charge to UK tax in circumstances where the 'disadvantaged person' is within the charge to income tax and the 'advantaged person' is a company (TIOPA 2010, s 174A). This exception has effect from 25 October 2013 and was introduced to prevent what HMRC viewed as abusive arrangements enabling individuals to extract profit from connected companies whilst paying tax only at corporation tax rates.

HMRC are clear that the availability of elections and balancing payments does not authorise taxpayers to ignore transfer pricing even if there will be no net benefit to the exchequer. However they state that they adopt a risk-based approach in deciding which transactions to examine.

Most of this is only likely to be relevant where both parties to the offending transaction are UK based. It also applies, however, where both parties are subject to UK tax on the transaction. For example, where thin capitalisation disallows some of the interest on a loan from a non-resident shareholder, a claim for adjustment may extend to a claim that the excess interest is not chargeable as UK source income with the result that deduction at source does not apply to that excess interest (see s 187).

In most cases where a transfer pricing adjustment is made, double counting results from the other party to the offending transaction being subject to foreign tax. Of itself, UK legislation cannot address such foreign tax.

However, for intra-EU transactions, the EU Arbitration Convention establishes a procedure to resolve disputes where double taxation occurs between enterprises in different member states as a result of an upward adjustment of profits of an enterprise of one member state. It provides for the elimination of double tax by agreement between contracting states including, if necessary, by reference to the opinion of an independent advisory body. In addition, if a double tax treaty is available between the contracting states, it should be possible to claim adjustment under the Associated Enterprises article. Each article provides for a corresponding downward adjustment of profits of the associated enterprise concerned. They do not however generally enforce a binding obligation on the contracting state to eliminate the double tax.

COMPLIANCE

91.20 A fundamental element of the transfer pricing code is that tax computations must be based on arm's length prices where the taxpayer has been a party to transactions within the regime.

This results in one of two requirements:

(1)   the taxpayer must be able to show that the connected party transactions were carried out as they would have been had the same transaction been carried out between wholly unconnected entities; or

(2)   insofar as this cannot be shown, an adjustment must be made in the taxpayer's self-assessment return to report and pay the tax as would have been payable if the transaction had been carried out on that basis.

An equally important point is that transfer pricing is part of the self-assessment regime. This has two important implications:

(1)   If the taxpayer's self-assessment return is not correct, interest and penalties may be charged on any understated tax.

(2)   The taxpayer must create and keep appropriate records to substantiate the entries in the return.

These requirements mean not merely that a taxpayer must be satisfied that he reports or pays his connected party prices on an arm's length basis, but that he must adduce and keep sufficient evidence to prove this. In the case of a company, board consideration with suitable documentation is required.

HMRC state at Manual page INTM483030 that they do not want 'businesses to suffer disproportionate compliance costs so customers should prepare and retain such documentation as is reasonable given the nature, size and complexity (or otherwise) of their business or of the relevant transaction (or series of transactions) but which adequately demonstrates that their transfer pricing meets the arm's length standard'.

In practice the sort of principles the taxpayer should adopt are as follows:

(1)   identify connected party transactions or groups of such transactions as are within the transfer pricing regime;

(2)   identify how the prices and other terms of the transactions were arrived at;

(3)   satisfy himself that the prices accord with arm's length prices, ideally by comparison with comparable transactions with independent parties;

(4)   if he is not so satisfied, ensure tax computations reflect an appropriate adjustment;

(5)   ensure all the above is properly documented with full reasons.

In the case of a company a good method of achieving the above objectives is a full report to the board from a suitably qualified person, followed by properly minuted board consideration and approval.

Should a return not comply with transfer pricing requirements, it may be adjusted with interest on any enquiry. Should fraud or carelessness be involved, the issue of penalties will arise. HMRC set out a number of examples of when they might seek to impose penalties at INTM483120.

Increasingly HMRC are recognising that in many cases requiring a transfer pricing adjustment the potential tax loss is not great. Typically this is the position where both parties to the transaction are taxed at broadly similar rates, a scenario now all too common under the code. Here HMRC have said the business concerned is not expected to do elaborate research or incur significant costs. In these circumstances, in any event, the likelihood of HMRC enquiry is low (see Revenue Press Release, 'Corporation Tax Reform – the next Steps' 10 December 2003 para 1.27).

Risk assessment

91.21 A transfer pricing enquiry into an enterprise's fundamental pricing structure for cross-border transactions with associated enterprises is not undertaken by HMRC without a prior risk assessment being carried out by them. This reflects the fact that a full transfer pricing investigation can be time consuming and expensive both for them and for the taxpayer. Details of the risk assessment procedure are given in HMRC's International Manual at pages INTM482130 to INTM482160.

Advance pricing agreements

91.22 Sections 218–230 of TIOPA 2010 enable taxpayers and HMRC to enter into advance pricing agreements in relation to transfer pricing. Such an agreement allows the taxpayer to be sure that, to the extent that the agreement provides, transfer prices will be acceptable to HMRC. HMRC guidance as to the making and operation of advance pricing arrangements ('APAs') is set out in SP 02/10.

Financing arrangements may be subject to an advance thin capitalisation agreement. Practice and procedure are set out in SP 01/12.

Information

91.23 Should HMRC initiate an enquiry into a UK company's transfer pricing, they have their normal powers to require the company to produce information or documents if the information or documents are reasonably required for the purpose of checking the taxpayer's tax position (FA 2008, Sch 36, para 1). In *Meditor Capital Management v Feighan* [2004] STC (SCD) 273, the taxpayer company was owned by a Bermudian parent which was itself owned by an offshore trust. The Bermudian company was a fund management company and the taxpayer company provided it with investment management services. As part of a transfer pricing enquiry, HMRC inter alia demanded from the taxpayer company information about the employees of the Bermudian company and information about its interests in the funds under management. On the facts of the case, a Special Commissioner held that such documents were within the power and control of the taxpayer company.

UK PROPERTY INVESTMENT

91.24 Transfer pricing issues can arise when offshore investors acquire UK property. HMRC gave some guidance in *Tax Bulletin* 46 (April 2000) p 740 and at Manual page INTM518060.

Non-resident landlord scheme

91.25 *Tax Bulletin* 46 confirms that the transfer pricing code does apply to non-resident landlords.

Loan finance

91.26 Non-resident landlords normally use loan finance to fund their acquisition of UK investment property as the loan interest will be deductible in computing taxable profits on rents or income received. This is so even if the borrowing is abroad and outside the obligation to deduct tax.

Although *Tax Bulletin* 46 was published before the enactment of the present rules as to thin capitalisation, it adopts the same approach as property financing. It takes the position that interest is non-allowable to the extent that the loan exceeds what a commercial lender would lend. It indicates that normally commercial lenders advance 65–80% of the value of the property.

Tax Bulletin 46 does not confine itself to cases where the offshore connected party lending or guaranteeing the loan is a company. In that sense it expresses itself in terms wider than the express provisions dealing with thin capitalisation now in TIOPA 2010, ss 152 and 153 (para **91.18** above). However consideration needs to be given as to whether transfer pricing is in fact in point where the offshore party is a trust or an individual. This, no doubt, turns on how far ss 152 and 153 duplicate the general language of the transfer pricing code.

A widely-debated issue arises where loan or guarantee finance is in excess of the 65–80% guideline but would have been available commercially albeit at a higher interest rate than that in fact being charged. Here *Tax Bulletin* 46 appears to accept a transfer pricing adjustment is not required, save where on the facts the commercial interest would have been more than the investment could stand, implying that at arm's length the loan would not have been made at all. At Manual page INTM518060, HMRC state that in their experience, the market in providing additional finance is relatively small in relation to the market as a whole, and that third-party loans in these circumstances are limited.

Another debated issue is where the actual loan to the property investor is unsecured. Here it is sometimes said that there is no commercial comparable at all, on the grounds that a commercial lender would have required security. But as explained above (para **91.2**) the transfer pricing regime requires all terms of the transaction to be adjusted, and does not look only at price. On this basis security should be assumed if not given, a point implicitly accepted by HMRC in *Tax Bulletin 46*. The *Tax Bulletin* article points out that the assumption of security does not also include an assumption that the interest has a UK source for withholding purposes.

Rent-free residential accommodation

91.27 *Tax Bulletin* 46 also addresses a rather different issue. This is where an offshore company provides rent-free accommodation to an individual who is a participant in it. On a literal reading of the transfer pricing code it could be argued that rent should be imputed to the company as that is what would be charged were the participant and the company dealing at arm's length. In fact it is very doubtful whether the code would bear this construction. Whatever the correctness of that, HMRC confirmed in *Tax Bulletin* 46 they would not take the point.

Chapter 92

DIVERTED PROFITS TAX

The authors would like to give special thanks to Robert Birchall and Helen Coward of Charles Russell Speechlys LLP for their help with this chapter.

INTRODUCTION

92.1 Diverted Profits Tax, or DPT, was introduced from 1 April 2015 for accounting periods beginning on or after that time (and on an apportioned basis for accounting periods straddling that date). In the main it is confined to large companies, but the companies to which it applies are defined by reference to EU law and as a result its scope may be wider than expected. Its focus is on UK resident companies which circumvent transfer pricing rules and on overseas companies which operate in the UK but avoid doing so through a permanent establishment. The rate of tax is 25%, higher than the normal rate of corporation tax. The aim of the legislation is to counter 'profit shifting'.

DPT was announced in December 2014 and enacted in FA 2015, the Finance Bill that passed through Parliament in just three days. As a result the period of consultation and consideration was much less than is normal with radical legislation of this sort. HMRC have published extensive guidance (on 1 November 2015) but much of this is only a little less opaque than the legislation.

What follows is a brief outline of the main points of DPT, focusing on points potentially relevant to this book. For more detailed study, the guidance should be referred to.

UK RESIDENT COMPANIES

92.2 The first head of DPT applies to UK companies and UK permanent establishments of non-UK resident companies (FA 2015, ss 80–85). Before the tax can apply a long list of conditions has to be satisfied, of which the most important for present purposes is that DPT is precluded if all the companies concerned are small or medium-sized enterprises. This is explained in paras **92.9** to **92.13**below. The other conditions are considered here, for clarity the discussion being expressed in terms of UK resident companies alone. Many of the conditions echo transfer pricing rules (see as to which see CHAPTER 91).

The material provision

92.3 DPT requires a material provision to be identified. This is simply a provision between the UK company and another person (FA 2015, s 80(1)) which has been made or imposed by a transaction or series of transactions. The other person is referred to as P and the company as C. P can be either resident or non-resident.

Transactions are caught even if they are arrangements or understandings rather than contractual (FA 2015, s 110). Neither C nor P need be a party to the transactions.

Effective Tax mismatch

92.4 DPT is not in issue unless the material provision results in an effective tax mismatch outcome (s 80(1)(d)). This term is defined in FA 2015, ss 107 and 108 and requires two conditions to be met. The first is that it leads either to deductible expenses of C or a reduction in C's taxable income. The second is that there is no corresponding increase in tax payable by P, or, if there is such an increase it is less than 80% of the reduction enjoyed by C. For this purpose, the tax payable by P which is taken into account includes both corporation tax and income tax and also any foreign tax on income (s 107(8)).

Participation

92.5 Even where there is an effective tax mismatch outcome, DPT is not engaged unless C and P meet a participation condition. The participation condition is met if C or P is participating in the management control or capital of the other, or if a third party is participating in the management control or capital of both (FA 2015, s 106). Participation can be direct or indirect.

Transfer pricing definitions apply to determine what is meant by direct and indirect participation (s 106(7)). These are explained in paras **91.7** to **91.11** and as there explained the basic concept is that either C or P controls the other or both are under common control. But in determining whether control is present account is taken of shares or rights held by connected parties. Also the common participation condition can be met if two participators together have control and each has more than 40% of that controlling interest.

Insufficient economic substance

92.6 The final condition, the insufficient economic substance condition, is at the heart of what DPT is aimed at. It can be met in one of two ways (FA 2015, s 110). The first is that the tax benefits of the material provision exceed the other financial benefits of the transaction or transactions concerned. The second is that at least one person's involvement in the material provision was designed to secure a tax reduction. But there is a staff related exception to this latter condition. This exception is in point if the income generated by P's staff exceeds the other income attributable to the transaction(s) or if the non-tax benefits attributable to P's staff exceed the benefit of the tax reduction (s 110(7)).

Quantum

92.7 Should the conditions for a tax charge be met, a calculation has to be made of whether there are diverted profits and if so what their amount is (FA 2015, ss 82–85). This calculation focuses on two key concepts.

The first is the relevant alternative provision. This is the provision that would have been made had tax on income not been a relevant consideration (s 82(5)). Such hypothetical provision could be not merely between C and P but between C and any company connected with it. It is expressly provided the hypothetical provision can be no provision at all – ie the material transaction is treated as never having taken place.

The second is the actual provision condition. This is in point if both the actual provision and the relevant alternative provision result or would result in expenses which, absent transfer pricing rules, would be deductible in C's corporation tax computation. The condition is met if the relevant alternative provision, ie the hypothetical deductible expenses, would not have resulted in income arising to a company connected with C which is subject to corporation tax.

With these two concepts established the quantum of charge can be arrived at. There are two rules.

The first is in point if the actual provision condition is met, ie if the relevant alternative provision would have resulted in deductible expenses for C but would not have generated corporation tax income of a connected company. It operates by reference to transfer pricing rules and equates the diverted profits to the extra profits that C should have brought into account by virtue of those rules (FA 2015, s 84). If in fact C correctly operates transfer pricing rules, the diverted profits are obviated.

The second rule is in point if the actual provision condition is not met (FA 2015, s 85). Here the diverted profits are what C's profits would have been had the relevant alternative provision been in place rather than the actual provision. Thus, in cases where the relevant alternative provision would have been no transaction the diverted profits are all the profits that would have accrued to C. If the relevant alternative provision would have resulted in a deduction for C and taxable income in a company connected with C, the diverted profit is whatever the income in the connected company would have been plus any adjustment C would have had to make in its own corporation tax return had it been operating transfer pricing rules correctly.

AVOIDANCE OF PERMANENT ESTABLISHMENT

92.8 The permanent establishment head of DPT (FA 2015, s 86) requires the identification of a non-UK resident company that is trading, this company being referred to as the Foreign Company. It also requires the identification of the avoided PE, ie a person who is carrying on activity in the UK in connection with the supply of goods services or other property by the Foreign Company.

In order for this head of charge to apply, it must be reasonable to assume that any of the activity of either the Foreign Company or the avoided PE is designed so as to ensure that the Foreign Company does not carry on a trade in the UK for the purposes of corporation tax.

In addition, one of the main purposes of the arrangement must be the avoidance or a reduction of a charge to corporation tax or, if that condition is not met, the mismatch condition must be satisfied. The mismatch condition is the same concept as is described above in relation to UK companies but here the focus is on transactions between the Foreign Company and another person, A, who satisfies the participation condition. The mismatch condition is satisfied if the transaction results in reduction in the foreign or UK tax on income paid by the Foreign Company and less than an 80% increase in such tax payable by A.

Even when one or other of these conditions is met, DPT is still not in point if the avoided PE is not connected with the Foreign Company and would, if it were in fact a permanent establishment, be within the exceptions for agents of independent status acting in the ordinary course of business (Corporation Tax Act 2010, s 1142; see para 64.2). DPT is also precluded where the UK related sales revenue of the Foreign Company is less than £10m or its UK related expenses are less than £1m (FA 2015, s 87). But in applying these limits connected companies are taken into account.

Assuming a charge to DPT does arise, the quantum of profits caught is simple if the mismatch condition is not met. It is the profits that would have been attributable to the avoided PE had it in fact been a permanent establishment (FA 2015, s 89). The position is more complicated if the mismatch condition is met. Here, as with UK companies, the relevant alternative provision has to be identified and it has to be asked if such would have resulted in income of a connected UK company subject to corporation tax. If such notional income would have arisen, it is included in the profits subject to DPT. The DPT profits also include whatever profits would have been chargeable to corporation tax had the avoided PE in fact been a permanent establishment.

THE THRESHOLD

92.9 Far and away the most important limitation to DPT is the threshold. The charge on UK companies does not apply if both C, ie the UK company, and P, ie the other party to the transaction, are small or medium-sized enterprises (s 80(1)(g)). So too the avoided PE charge does not apply unless both the Foreign Company and the avoided PE are small or medium-sized enterprises (s 86(1)(h)).

Basic definition

92.10 The applicable definition of small and medium-sized enterprise is the EU definition in the Annex to the Commission Recommendation of 6 May 2003 concerning the Definition of Micro Small and Medium-sized

Enterprises (2003/361/EC (FA 2015, s 114(1))). Under this definition an enterprise is small or medium sized if it employs fewer than 250 people and either has an annual turnover of less than €50m or has an annual balance sheet total of less than €43m.

There are two difficulties with this definition. One problem is that it is not specifically a tax definition and thus falls to be construed against the wider economic objectives of the Recommendation (see recital (1) to the Recommendation and *HaTeFo GmbH v Finanzamt Haldensleben*: C-110/13 [2014] All ER (D) 218 (Mar), ECJ). The other is that the definition does not focus only on the head count and financial data of the subject enterprise but instead requires aggregation with what are called linked and partner enterprises.

Linked enterprises

92.11 Two enterprises are linked if one controls a majority of voting rights in the other or has control by virtue of a shareholders agreement. Once two enterprises are linked each must take account of the head counts and financial data of the other, in each case taking account of any other enterprises with which the other is itself linked. In broad terms what is being looked at is groups of companies which are required to prepare consolidated accounts (Recommendation Recital (11)). But consolidation is not the sole criterion and so if one enterprise in fact controls another they are linked.

The term 'enterprise' is defined as any entity engaged in an economic activity. The term is capable of including individuals, for self-employed persons are specifically included in the definition. However in general, enterprises are not linked if in the common ownership of one or more individuals (Recommendation Recital (12)), unless they engage in activity in the same relevant market for competition law purposes or in markets directly upstream or downstream of each other.

More generally it appears that enterprises owned by individuals count as linked if on the facts they constitute a single economic unit (*HaTeFo GmbH v Finanzamt Haldensleben*, supra).

Partner enterprises

92.12 The headcount and financial limits must include the pro rata figures of partner enterprises. The requirement to be a partner enterprise is that one enterprise must hold 25% or more of the capital or voting rights in the other. As with linked enterprises, the issue arises of whether two enterprises are partner enterprises where an individual owns 25% or more of each. It would appear not as such an individual, if merely an investor, is not an enterprise. However clearly the activities of individuals could go beyond investment and become an enterprise: this is recognised by a special-carve out for low-value business angels. There is also a carve out for investment by venture capital companies, ie companies whose interest is in maximising the financial return on their investment in new business rather than being concerned with day-to-day executive management of the investee companies (*Pyreos Ltd v HMRC* [2015] SFTD S17).

Implications

92.13 In the great majority of cases relevant to this book the exclusion of small and medium-sized enterprises disapplies DPT. But the aggregation represented by linked and partner enterprises requires particular attention to detail. A specific challenge is where common ownership is not through an individual but through a trust, the issue being whether the trust would be regarded as an entity and as an enterprise engaged in economic activity. The case of *Olsen v Norwegian State* [2014] Cases E-3/13 and E-20/13, which applied the establishment freedom to a trust, indicates that in an EU context a trust might well be seen as an entity carry out economic activity (see para 107.16). If so, any company owned by the trust has to be aggregated with any other company directly or indirectly owned or controlled by the trust in applying the head count and financial limits.

ADMINISTRATION

92.14 DPT has its own separate administration regime. There is a duty to notify where a company is potentially within the scope of the regime in relation to an accounting period (s 92). That notification must be in writing and be made within three months of the end of the accounting period to which it relates. The triggers for notification are wider than the conditions for the tax to apply.

A charge under DPT does not arise unless HMRC give the company concerned a charging notice (FA 2015, s 95). Before HMRC can issue a charging notice, it must have given the company a preliminary notice under s 93. A preliminary notice must be given if a HMRC officer has reason to believe that one or more of the charging sections of DPT applies and as a result taxable diverted profits arise to the company. HMRC must take account of representations by the taxpayer in relation to the preliminary notice before issuing the charging notice (ss 94 and 95). If the issue is a deduction, the charging notice can simply charge 30% of the claimed deduction, thereby giving the taxpayer entity an incentive to agree the transfer pricing position (s 96(5)).

The taxable profits are estimated in the charging notice and the resultant DPT must be paid within 30 days of the notice (ss 96–98). There is then a review period lasting 12 months during which HMRC must review the charging notice and either issue an amending notice reducing the DPT or a notice imposing an additional charge (s 101).

RELIEF FOR OTHER TAXES

92.15 It is expressly provided that credit is allowed for any corporation tax or corresponding foreign tax that the diverted profits suffer. Such credit is computed on a just and reasonable basis (s 100).

What is not allowed, at least expressly, is credit for income tax. Such would arise, for example, with an avoided PE if the foreign company was trading in the UK, albeit not through a permanent establishment. So too income tax could be at issue under the transfer of assets code as respects both heads of DPT. Given the exclusion of small and medium-sized companies cases of the latter kind may be rare. But they will not be non-existent, particularly in cases where trust ownership may require enterprises to be aggregated in applying the head count and financial limits.

Chapter 93
BENEFITS IN KIND

INTRODUCTION

93.1 The benefits in kind sections of the Income Tax (Earnings and Pensions) Act 2003 (ITEPA 2003) apply to company directors and most other company employees, and operate where a benefit in kind is provided to the director or employee by the company, or indeed by another person where the provision of the benefit is attributable to the directorship or employment, or is deemed to be so attributable. In broad terms the value of any such benefit is treated as employment earnings and taxed accordingly. The primary legislation concerned with benefits in kind (commonly termed the 'benefits code') is contained in Part 3 of the Act, whereas benefits awarded in the form of employment related securities are dealt with under Part 7 of the Act.

EXTENSION TO SHADOW DIRECTORS

93.2 At first sight it may not be obvious what the benefits code has to do with offshore tax planning. It is rare for an individual who has established an offshore structure to be an employee of any entity within that structure, and such an individual can, in principle, avoid being a director of any company which provides any form of benefit to him. However, this initial impression of irrelevance is incorrect, for the benefits code applies to de facto and shadow directors as well as to actual directors. This is because the term 'director' in the benefits code means any of the following (ITEPA 2003, s 67(1)):

- Where the affairs of the company are managed by a board of directors or similar body, any member of that body.
- Where the affairs of the company are managed by a single director or similar person, that person.
- Where the affairs of the company are managed by the members, any member.
- Any person in accordance with whose directions or instructions any of the above are accustomed to act.

The last head brings in shadow directors. An exception is made for those advising in a professional capacity (s 67(2)). The scope of the term 'shadow director' is considered below.

For a long time it was commonly considered that the definition in s 67 did not bring any shadow director who was not an actual employee into the benefits in kind code. The basis for this view was that the code applies to employees and employment and, while s 67 treats certain non-directors as directors, it does not also deem them to have an employment. This view was, however, rejected by the House of Lords in *R v Allen* [2001] UKHL 45, [2001] STC 1537 on the grounds that it was the intention of Parliament in enacting what is now s 67 that accommodation and other benefits in kind received by a shadow director should be taxed in the same way as those received by a director. Accordingly the position now is that if a person falls within the definition of shadow director in s 67 he is caught by the code.

What is a shadow director?

93.3 Before answering the above question it is worth touching on the related, but distinct, concept of de facto directorship. A de facto director is an individual who purports to act as a director, although not validly appointed as such (*Re Paycheck Services 3 Ltd* [2009] EWCA Civ 625, [2010] Bus LR 259, [2009] STC 1639 at para 55; upheld in *Revenue and Customs Comrs v Holland* [2010] UKSC 51, [2011] 1 All ER 430, [2011] STC 269).

A shadow director, by contrast, does not purport to act as director. The term 'shadow director' does not, strictly, apply to someone who participates in board meetings as if he were a director, but rather to someone 'behind the scenes' who, broadly, directs or controls the action taken by the company, typically (although not exclusively) on the basis that he is a sole or majority shareholder in the company, or a beneficiary of a trust which is such a shareholder. In practice, shadow directorship is much more significant in an offshore tax planning context than de facto directorship.

Ensuring that a person is not a shadow director is rendered difficult by the Court of Appeal decision in *Secretary of State for Trade and Industry v Deverell* [2001] Ch 340, [2000] 2 All ER 365, CA. This was not a tax case but turned on the company law definition of 'shadow director' in the Company Directors Disqualification Act 1986, s 22(5). This defines a shadow director as:

'a person in accordance with whose directions or instructions the directors of the company are accustomed to act.'

This definition is essentially in the same terms as the final limb of ITEPA 2003, s 67, cited above; and like s 67 it excludes professional advisers.

In *Deverell*, the trial judge had asserted two important limitations to the definition, as follows:

' . . . advice on its own will not do. Only if such advice is so given and so accepted as to amount to a direction or instruction (coupled with a pattern of the board being accustomed to act on it) is it relevant.'

'Directions or instructions are both words with a mandatory effect. Coupled with the word "accustomed" they . . . contemplate a situation where the board has cast itself in a subservient role to the "shadow", i.e. it does what it is told or to borrow an expression from trust law it "surrenders its discretion" to the shadow. Being accustomed to follow what somebody says does not of itself make what is said a direction/instruction . . . what the court has to find, whether on direct evidence or inference is that the board does what [the shadow] tells it and exercises no (or at least no substantial) independent judgement.'

These limitations were based on *obita dicta* in earlier cases and were widely regarded as correct by advisers. However, they were rejected by the Court of Appeal, which in substance accepted the Secretary of State's formulation as follows:

'It is suggested that the definition is concerned to identify those with real influence in the corporate affairs of the company whatever the label given to the communications from the shadow to the board. Thus, it is argued, all that is required is that what is said by the shadow to the board is not by way of professional advice but is usually followed over a wide enough area and for long enough. In other words frequent non-professional advice usually acted on is sufficient.'

The Court also held that the shadow director's influence did not have to be over the whole field of the company's activities. Instead it adopted the words of an Australian judge (Finn J) in *Australia Securities Commission v AS Nominees Ltd* (1995) 133 ALR 1:

'The reference in the section to a person in accordance with whose directions or instructions the directors are "accustomed to act" does not in my opinion require that there be directions or instructions embracing all matters involving the board. Rather it only requires that, as and when the directors are directed or instructed, they are accustomed to act as the section requires.'

The Court in *Deverell* held that the two individuals under attack were shadow directors. The facts were complex and are not altogether easy to follow in the reported case. However, the following words effectively summarise the factual basis for the decision:

'[The judge's findings] make it plain that Mr Deverell was concerned at the most senior level and with most aspects of the direction of the company's affairs. This could only be achieved by an ostensible consultant if those who were directors acted upon his directions or instructions conveyed by words or conduct. The judge held in terms that Mr Deverell "bossed everyone around from the directors downwards". It is immaterial that, as the judge observed, he was the sort of man who would boss anyone around. The facts, as found, show that he bossed the directors around and, because what he achieved was within the province of the directors, the directors were accustomed to submit to his requirements.'

Implications of Deverell

93.4 Prior to *Deverell*, most advisers in an offshore context approached the question of whether a person was a shadow director on the lines taken by the trial judge. In other words, danger was avoided provided the board gave genuine consideration to matters put before it, and the alleged shadow gave what could fairly be said to be advice. This approach may well not be valid now, and the position may well be that if the board of an offshore company consistently comply with a non-board member's wishes, that individual is at risk of being categorised as a shadow director, save insofar as his advice is given in a professional capacity.

Prior to *Deverell*, the view generally taken was that an offshore company was unlikely to have a shadow director resident in the UK unless the involvement of the alleged shadow was such that the company was in any event resident in the UK under the central management and control test. This follows from the fact that genuine consideration by the board negatives residence in the UK (para **43.10**) and was thought to negative shadow directorship. Comparison between *Deverell* and the cases on company residence referred to in CHAPTER 43 indicate this is no longer so, for it is clear that advice, if regularly followed, may make a person a shadow director under *Deverell*.

Also prior to *Deverell* a commonly-held view was that an individual was much more likely to be a shadow director if he directly owned the company, as distinct from being settlor of or beneficiary under a trust which owned it. The rationale of this view was first that a controlling shareholder is legally able to remove the board and so in practice can give instructions, and second that in any event the shareholder could count as a shadow director as being a member managing the company. These points are still good in relation to directly owned companies and, especially after *Deverell*, make it difficult for a controlling shareholder in an offshore company who is not a director to avoid being a shadow director.

But what may have changed as a result of *Deverell* is the position where the offshore company is owned by an offshore trust. Here the trustees are entitled to take account of the wishes of the settlor, and may after due consideration cause the company to follow them. So too even after the settlor is dead the trustees may at the behest of the settlor be entitled to and in fact follow the wishes of someone designated by him, normally a beneficiary or the protector. The issue raised by *Deverell* is how far the fact that the trustees cause the company to follow the wishes of such a person is sufficient to make him a shadow director.

Strictly, he is not a shadow director if the directors of the company are indeed genuinely managing it and the trustees are properly discharging their duties as trustees. This conclusion follows because in such a case the person who communicates wishes to the board is the trustee shareholder. Any wishes the settlor or beneficiaries have are expressed by them not to the board but to the trustees.

But in reality, the facts on the ground may muddy the waters and lead to a contrary conclusion. Three factors in particular may have this result. The first is that the person's wishes may be communicated directly to the directors of the company. Second, the trustees may so conduct themselves that they are doing no more than to indirectly communicate to the company the wishes of the settlor or other person. Third and last, the same individuals acting on behalf of the trustee in relation to the trust may also be directors of the company. In such a case it may be unclear to whom the settlor or other person is in reality addressing his wishes or advice.

The following paragraphs consider the position where an individual is, or may be alleged by HMRC to be, a shadow director, and he receives a benefit from the company in question, so that the benefits code is or may be engaged.

HEADS OF CHARGE

93.5 The heads of charge under the benefits code are as follows (ITEPA 2003, s 63):

- Expenses payments;
- Vouchers and credit tokens;
- Living accommodation;
- Cars, vans and related benefits;
- Loans; and
- Benefits not otherwise charged.

Of these heads, the one most commonly encountered in the context of offshore tax planning is living accommodation. However note also needs to be taken of the charge on loans, and the residual liability provisions which tax benefits not covered by the other heads of charge.

LIVING ACCOMMODATION

93.6 Living accommodation is brought within the benefits code by ITEPA 2003, ss 97–113. These sections apply to living accommodation provided for an employee or his family or household by reason of his employment (s 97). Where they apply, the cash equivalent of the benefit is treated as earnings from the employment for the tax year concerned (s 102).

By reason of employment

93.7 Any accommodation provided by the employer is regarded as provided by reason of employment (s 97(2)). This deeming provision is not an exclusive definition, and so if accommodation provided by somebody else is in fact provided by reason of employment it is caught.

The extension of this charge to shadow directors is illustrated by *R v Allen* [2001] STC 1537. Here an offshore company in the direct ownership of the taxpayer provided the family home. The taxpayer was found on the facts to be a shadow director and thus the house was provided by reason of his notional employment.

Family or household

93.8 The following comprise the employee's family or household (ITEPA 2003, s 721):

- His spouse or civil partner.
- His parents.
- His children and their spouses or civil partners.
- His dependants.
- His domestic staff.
- His guests.

Cash equivalent

93.9 In law there are two separate rules for computing the cash equivalent. The first applies if the cost of providing the accommodation is less than £75,000. In this case, according to ITEPA 2003, the cash equivalent is the annual value of the accommodation (s 105). This is defined as the difference between the rent obtainable for the property on a yearly letting (with the tenant bearing rates and charges normally borne by the tenant and the landlord repairs and insurance (s 110)) and any sum made good by the employee (s 105(2)(b)).

The second rule applies if the cost of the accommodation is over £75,000. In this case in law the cash equivalent is the sum of two elements:

(a) the annual value of the accommodation; plus
(b) interest at the official rate on the amount by which the cost of providing accommodation exceeds £75,000 (s 106).

Interest at the official rate is interest at the rate prescribed for taxing beneficial loans and is currently (early October 2016) 3% (see para **93.18**).

Cost of providing the accommodation

93.10 The cost of providing the accommodation is the total cost incurred in acquiring or improving the property (s 104). This is brought into account if incurred by any person involved in providing the accommodation. This latter term is defined as the person in fact providing the accommodation, the employer, and any person connected with either of those two parties (s 112). 'Connected' bears the standard meaning given in ITA 2007, s 993 (ITEPA 2003, s 718).

In one situation the actual cost is displaced by market value. This applies where the property was owned by a person involved in providing the accommodation for more than six years before the employee first went into occupation. In such case the cost of providing the accommodation is its market value when the employee first went into occupation plus improvements thereafter (ITEPA 2003, s 107). This rule does not apply in determining whether the £75,000 threshold is exceeded but only in determining the figure to which interest at the official rate is applied if it is.

Reimbursement

93.11 The cost of providing the accommodation may be reduced by payments made by the employee (s 104). To qualify for this treatment the payment must be made to a person involved in providing the accommodation. It must either be reimbursement of expenditure incurred on the acquisition of or improvements to the property or consideration for the grant of a tenancy of the property.

In an offshore context, the exception for reimbursement may prove significant. In most cases the reality is that if the occupier of the property owned by the company is a shadow director, he will, whether directly or otherwise, have provided the funds for the purchase of the property. Economically therefore he ought to be in the same position as the employee of an arm's length company who reimburses accommodation costs. The issue is whether and in what circumstances what he pays may count as reimbursement.

It may be suggested that there is a reimbursement if the individual lends to the company to enable it to purchase the property and then writes the loan off, so that the cost of the purchase is defrayed. In economic substance the position is the same if the individual simply makes a gift to the company to enable it to purchase the property. It may be arguable that in this situation, also, there is a reimbursement of the cost of the purchase. On a narrow view, the concept of reimbursement involves the payment of money to another person to defray a cost already borne by that person, and if that were the correct construction, there would be no reimbursement in this second scenario. However, there may be an argument that 'reimbursement' should be construed broadly, to include the situation where a cost is defrayed prospectively, ie before it has actually been incurred by the other person. The most doubtful case is where the individual provides funding to the company, either to enable it to make the purchase or to repay a commercial loan taken out for that purpose, but the provision of funding is by way of share subscription rather than gift. In that case there is consideration for the transfer of funds to the company and that may well take the payment outside the concept of reimbursement.

The same arguments would apply if a trust owns the company, for, as a person connected with the company, the trust is a person involved in providing the accommodation. The trust could therefore fund the acquisition by the company and then, later, be reimbursed by the shadow director.

Quantum of charge in practice

93.12 As will be apparent from para **93.9** above there is potentially a double charge on properties costing in excess of £75,000. This is because the cash equivalent includes both (a) the annual rental value, and (b) notional interest on the cost over £75,000.

In practice this absurdity is avoided in a more than usually blatant example of untaxing by concession. The position is as follows:

(1)   Ever since the inception of the accommodation charge annual value has been treated as meaning not the market rental value but the gross rateable value under the old rating system abolished in 1990 (IR Press Release 19 April 1990). Values under that system were last fixed in 1973 so in practice the annual value is very low. For UK properties which did not then exist an estimate of what the gross rateable value would have been is made based on comparables. It has been confirmed that this treatment continues to apply under ITEPA 2003 (Employment Income Manual para 11432).

(2)   The use of gross annual value is recognised as inappropriate for properties outside the UK and here annual value is taken as meaning what it says – ie annual market rental value (Employment Income

Manual para 11441). But in such case, by concession, the annual rental value is then the sole measure of cash equivalent – in other words notional interest on the price in excess of £75,000 is not included (ESC A91).

Payment of rent

93.13 As will be apparent from the above, payment of an arm's length rent in practice obviates a charge in respect of foreign property. But in relation to UK property, this is not necessarily the position. It is only so if, on the facts, the rent exceeds the quantum of benefit as calculated under the rules described above – in other words in the normal case if it exceeds interest at the official rate on the cost.

Exceptions

93.14 Exceptions are made to the accommodation charge, notably for representative occupation and for accommodation provided by individuals in the normal course of personal relationships (ITEPA 2003, ss 97(2) and 98–101). None are normally relevant in an offshore context.

Homes outside the UK

93.15 The accommodation charge does not apply to living accommodation outside the UK if certain conditions are met (ITEPA 2003, ss 100A and 100B). The conditions are as follows:

(1)   The property must be the sole or main asset of the company.
(2)   The only activities undertaken by the company must be incidental to ownership of the house or flat.
(3)   The company must be owned by the occupier or by the occupier and other individuals. Ownership through an intermediate holding company is also allowed.
(4)   The company must not have acquired the property from a connected company at an undervalue and nor must any connected company have incurred any expenditure on the property.

In general these conditions must be met throughout the company's ownership of the property. But an exception is made if the occupier acquired the company from an unconnected third party – ie if he acquired the house or flat by buying the company.

This relief is designed for those who acquire holiday homes outside the UK and effect the acquisition through a corporate entity for local tax or succession reasons. It does not apply to houses or flats in the UK and nor does it apply to companies owned in trust.

Despite only being enacted in 2008, the relief is deemed always to have had effect (FA 2008, s 45(2), (3)). HMRC guidance was published in August 2008

(HMRC Notice 28 August 2008 'Holiday homes abroad purchased through a company', reproduced [2008] SWTI 2009).

SUBSIDISED LOANS

93.16 Subsidised loans are brought within the benefits in kind code by ITEPA 2003, ss 173–191. These sections apply insofar as the loan is an employment-related loan and a taxable cheap loan. Where they apply the charge is on the cash equivalent.

Employment-related loans

93.17 A loan can be employment-related if it is made to the employee or a relative of the employee (ITEPA 2003, s 174(1)). Relatives are spouses, civil partners, siblings, parents and children (ITEPA 2003, s 174(6)).

Not surprisingly, any loan made by the employer is employment-related. But in addition, ITEPA 2003, s 174(2) specifies a whole series of other loans which are deemed to be employment-related.

The principal categories of loan so treated are as follows:

(1)   The lender is a company (or partnership) which controls or is controlled by the employer.

(2)   The lender is a company (or partnership) controlled by a person who also controls the employer.

(3)   The lender has a material interest in a UK close company which is either the employer or has control of or is controlled by another company which is the employer.

(4)   The lender has a material interest in a company (or partnership) (whether UK or non-UK) which itself controls a UK close company which is the employer or has control of or is controlled by another company which is the employer.

Control for these purposes means voting control (ITEPA 2003, ss 69 and 719; ITA 2007, s 995). The term 'material interest', however, is much wider. It means beneficial ownership of or control over more than 5% of the ordinary share capital of the company (ITEPA 2003, s 68(2)). If the company is a UK close company it also means entitlement to more than 5% of the assets on a winding up (ITEPA 2003, s 68(3)).

In an offshore context, an important issue is how far loans are caught where, on the facts, the beneficiary of an offshore trust is found to be shadow director of an offshore company owned by the trust. In such a case a loan is caught if made by the company. It is not caught if it is made by the trust because the offshore company is not a UK company and so not within the applicable definition of a close company (see ITEPA 2003, Sch 1 Part 2, ITA 2007, s 989 and CTA 2010, s 442). A loan is, however, caught if made by another company controlled by the trust, even if the borrower was not a shadow director of that company.

A point for offshore trustees to watch is interests in UK close companies. If any such interest is greater than 5%, a loan by the trust to a beneficiary is, on a literal reading of the ITEPA provisions, employment-related if the borrower is an employee of the UK company. This is so even if the reason for making the loan has nothing whatever to do with the employment. Care should also be taken that any loan made by an offshore company or trust does not trigger a tax charge under the 'disguised remuneration rules' (ITEPA 2003, Part 7A Employment Income Provided Through Third Parties). Under these very widely-drawn anti-avoidance provisions, which are discussed in Chapter 91, a liability to income tax (and National Insurance contributions if applicable) could arise on the full value of the loan at the point at which the loan amount is 'earmarked' by a third party (ie a non-group company) for an individual in an employment context.

It may be that the definition of employment-related loans should not be given a wide construction of this sort. A purposive construction would restrict the term to loans funded by the employer or made for reasons connected with the employment. However, the point has not been at issue in any decided case and there is no indication that HMRC subscribe to it.

A loan is caught if, when it is made, the employment is prospective (ITEPA 2003, s 174(3)). But where the employment is not in existence or in prospect when the loan is made, subsequent employment is immaterial.

Taxable cheap loan

93.18 The loan is a taxable cheap loan in any tax year if the employee holds the employment during that year and no interest is payable on the loan or the interest is less than the official rate (s 178). The official rate is the rate specified by the Treasury in accordance with FA 1989, s 175 (ITEPA 2003, s 181). Currently it is 3% (Taxes (Interest Rate) Regulations 1989 (SI 1989/1297) reg 5; Taxes (Interest Rate) (Amendment) Regulations 2015 (SI 2015/411) reg 2).

Certain loans are excepted from being cheap loans by ITEPA 2003, ss 176–180. The main exceptions are certain loans made in the ordinary course of business, loans at a fixed rate of interest equal to the official rate of interest when made, loans where actual interest would qualify for tax relief, and loans of less than £10,000 (in aggregate).

Interest must be paid for each relevant tax year (or part thereof) if the loan is to avoid being treated as a cheap loan. Should the interest be paid after the loan has been taxed as a cheap loan, the tax is repaid (ITEPA 2003, s 191).

The cash equivalent

93.19 Where an employment related loan is a taxable cheap loan, the cash equivalent is interest at the official rate for the tax year concerned, or part of the year during which the loan is outstanding. Where any actual interest is paid, the cash equivalent is reduced by such interest. Should the official rate change during the tax year, the different rates are applied pro rata (ss 182 and 183).

Loan released

93.20 Should the loan be released, its amount is treated as earnings (s 188). This applies whether the employment still subsists at the time of the release or has previously terminated. A charge is not however made if the release is on or after the death of the employee (s 190), subject to the application of the disguised remuneration rules (ITEPA 2003, Part 7A).

It is particularly important to keep these provisions in mind as a charge can arise long after the employment or shadow employment has ceased. It can be a particular trap for offshore trustees if the wide literal meaning of employment-related loan discussed above is right, for it would catch any release of a loan in favour of a beneficiary if when the loan was made that beneficiary had happened to be an employee of a UK company in which the trust had more than a 5% interest.

It is unclear whether the charge applies if at the time of the release the employee is non-resident. ITEPA 2003, s 188(2) provides that if the employment has terminated, the charge on release of the loan is made as if the employment had not terminated. However, there is no deeming of the employee to be UK resident. It would appear to follow that if at the time of release the borrower is non-resident or non-domiciled, the territorial limits described in para **93.24** below are in point.

RESIDUAL BENEFITS

93.21 Benefits not taxed under the specific heads in ITEPA 2003, Part 3 are caught by a residual charge in ss 201–210. This head of charge extends to benefits or facilities of any kind which are provided to the employee or a member of his family or household by reason of the employment (s 201). As with accommodation anything provided by the employer is deemed to be provided by reason of employment (s 201(3)). Any benefit within the specific heads is excluded from this head of charge, with the result that double taxation is avoided and the measure of charge on such specific benefits is that laid down by the specific head of charge in question (s 202).

The residual charge can catch cash sums if for some reason they are not taxable as earnings in the general sense of the term. Payments resulting from a fair bargain are excluded and the employment must subsist at some point in the tax year in which the benefit is conferred (see ITEPA 2003, s 201(4) and *Wilson v Clayton* [2004] EWHC 898 (Ch), [2004] STC 1022).

Cash equivalent

93.22 Where the residual head of charge applies, the cash equivalent of the benefit is included as earnings. The cash equivalent is normally the expense incurred in or in connection with the benefit, less any sum made good by the employee (ss 203(2), 204, and 205(1)). But where the benefit is the transfer of an asset which has already been used, the then value of the asset is used (s 206). Where the benefit is an asset placed at the disposal of the employee without

1105

being transferred to him, the cost of the benefit in any given year is taken as 20% of the value of asset or, if the asset does not belong to the employer, rental or hire charges paid by him (s 205).

R v Allen

93.23 There is no longer any doubt that the residual benefits head applies to shadow directors. It was successfully invoked in *R v Allen* [2001] UKHL 45, [2001] STC 1537 in relation to the provision of premium bonds to the shadow director and his family, the provision of credit cards for their use, and the payment of school fees (see [1999] STC, 846, 858). This case also demonstrates that in the context of shadow directors, the residual benefits head catches what would otherwise be ordinary earnings if there were an actual employment.

TERRITORIAL LIMITS OF THE BENEFITS CODE

93.24 The starting point in establishing the territorial limits of the benefits code is that anything treated as earnings under the code constitutes, together with any actual earnings, the general earnings of the individual (ITEPA 2003, s 7(3), (5)). General earnings are charged to tax insofar as they are taxable earnings (s 9(2), (3)).

The taxable earnings of an individual who is resident and domiciled in the UK are the full amount of the general earnings for the tax year concerned – ie actual earnings plus the cash equivalent of benefits (ITEPA 2003, s 15). By contrast the taxable earnings of an individual who is not resident in the UK are the general earnings – ie actual earnings and benefits – in respect of duties performed in the UK (ITEPA 2003, s 27). This preserves the rule under the old Schedule E that the emoluments of non-residents were taxed only insofar as paid in respect of UK duties. *R v Allen* [2001] UKHL 45, [2001] STC 1537 affirmed that under the old law that limitation applied also to benefits, and this decision is now expressly recognised in ITEPA 2003.

The practical result is that a non-resident who is a shadow director is only taxed on benefits insofar as he can be said to perform duties for the company of which he is a shadow director in the UK. This is probably the case even if the company is UK resident.

The taxable earnings of a non-domiciliary resident in the UK (to whom the remittance basis applies) are his chargeable overseas earnings remitted to the UK plus the full amount of such of his other general earnings as are not chargeable overseas earnings (ITEPA 2003, s 22). Chargeable overseas earnings are defined in the same terms as the former foreign emoluments – ie earnings of the non-domiciliary with a foreign employer in respect of an employment whose duties are performed wholly outside the UK (s 23; see para 50.5).

The practical result is that a UK resident but non-UK domiciled shadow director in receipt of benefits escapes charge under the code if the company of which he is a notional employee is non-UK resident, all the duties of his notional employment can be said to be performed abroad and no part of the benefit is remitted to the UK. It may be suggested this would apply if the non-UK company owns a foreign property and use of that property is the benefit. This may be relevant if the rather restrictive considerations of the relief in relation to homes outside the UK (see para **93.15** above) are not met.

SHARES

93.25 Shares given to employees or transferred to them at an undervalue are treated as earnings in the general sense of the term if the gift or undervalue is in return for services (*Weight v Salmon* (1935) 19 TC 174). Insofar as this is not so, special anti-avoidance rules apply. Until 2003 these rules formed part of the benefits code (ITEPA 2003, ss 192–197). Now they are included in the rules dealing with employment-related securities (ITEPA 2003, Part 7 Chapter 3C).

The effect of those rules is that the gift or undervalue is treated in the same way as a loan under the benefits code insofar as it is not earnings in the general sense of the term. This means that each year notional interest on the undervalue is treated as earnings, and, when the shares are sold, the full amount of the undervalue is taxed as earnings (ITEPA 2003, s 446U). As with loans, that charge is avoided if the shares are retained until the employee's death. But if tax avoidance is one of the purposes of the arrangements under which the shares are acquired, the notional interest regime does not apply and instead the undervalue or gift is treated as earnings when the shares are acquired (ITEPA 2003, s 446UA).

These rules apply to shares or securities insofar as they are employment-related securities. Shares or securities are employment-related if the right to acquire them is made available by the employer or a person connected with the employer (ITEPA 2003, s 421B(3)). 'Connected' bears its normal tax definition and thus, in the case of a corporate employer, means any person controlling the company (ITEPA 2003, s 718; ITA 2007, s 993). 'Control', in this context, does not bear the narrow definition discussed in para **93.17** above in relation to loans but the wide anti-avoidance definition in CTA 2010, ss 450 and 451 (ITA 2007, s 994(1); see further para **87.9**).

In contrast to the benefits code there is no provision deeming shadow directors to be directors or employees. Unless, therefore, the contrary can be inferred as a matter of general interpretation, shadow directors are not caught.

But even assuming that is right, the rules relating to employment-related securities need to be watched by offshore trustees wherever a beneficiary is employed by a company connected with the trust. Any distribution of shares or securities to the beneficiary in specie may be caught, even though an equivalent distribution of cash would not be. The fact that connected persons are taken into account in determining whether the trust controls the employing company means the ambit of these rules can be unexpectedly wide. A further point is that the rules apply even if the shares are not those of the employing company. The potential effect of the disguised remuneration rules should also be considered (ITEPA 2003, Part 7A).

It could be argued that, as and when the relevant provisions in ITEPA are litigated, some limitation will be placed on the apparent breadth of the term 'employment-related securities', requiring there to be some connection with the employment. But at present there is no authority to this effect. A form of remittance basis can apply where the date of acquisition is in 2008–09 or a subsequent tax year (ITEPA 2003, ss 41A–41E), replaced by ss 41F–41L by FA 2014, with effect from 6 April 2015 in relation to employment-related securities and employment-related securities options granted to internationally mobile employees (irrespective of the date of acquisition). This and the territorial limits of the charge are discussed in paras **50.12** to **50.16**.

EARNINGS LESS THAN £8,500

93.26 Prior to 6 April 2016, there was an exemption for lower-paid employees that applied to certain heads of charge under the benefits code. However, this was of limited practical relevance, as (a) the exemption could only be used if the employee's earnings, including earnings that would be attributed to him under the benefits code, were less than £8,500; (b) the exemption did not apply to directors (and, by extension, nor did it apply to shadow directors) unless they worked for the company full-time and had no material interest in it; and (c) the exemption did not apply to the living accommodation charge.

As part of a package aimed at simplifying the administration of employee benefits and expenses announced in Budget 2014, legislation was introduced in the Finance Act 2015 to amend ITEPA 2003 to abolish the £8,500 threshold so that all employees (other than lower-paid ministers of religion and certain carers) will be treated in the same way when it comes to benefits in kind, irrespective of their earnings. The changes took effect on 6 April 2016 (FA 2015, s 13 and Sch 1).

Chapter 94

EMPLOYMENT INCOME PROVIDED THROUGH THIRD PARTIES

INTRODUCTION

94.1 Throughout the 1997–2010 Labour government, a perception grew that employers could protect high-earning employees from income tax, and themselves from NICs, by means of employee benefit trusts (EBTs) and a variety of offshore retirement arrangements. As will be clear from CHAPTER 25, the tax advantages available from EBTs were not as clear cut as some commentators, and indeed some advisers, supposed. But in 2010 the outgoing Labour government was stung into announcing action and this legislative project was brought to fruition by the Conservative/Liberal Democrat coalition government.

The relevant legislation is enacted by Finance Act 2011 (FA 2011), Sch 2, and in the main it comprises a new Part 7A in ITEPA 2003, ss 554A–554Z21. This legislation was initially published in draft on 9 December 2010 and was widely criticised as being impossibly wide and thus catching many wholly commercial arrangements. The government were not prepared to amend the general approach of the legislation to make it more targeted, but did introduce a series of exemptions. As a result, the legislation became even more labyrinthine than the 2010 draft.

The legislation is relevant to offshore tax planning in two respects. First, it counters much of the tax saving potential of EBTs, most of which are offshore. Second, the breadth of its language means it needs to be kept in mind in relation to certain private trusts.

The legislation took effect on 6 April 2011, with limited anti-forestalling provisions backdated to 9 December 2010 (FA 2011, Sch 2 paras 52–59). HMRC published FAQs on 7 July 2011 (HMRC Notice 7 July 2011, reproduced [2011] SWTI 2030). Draft guidance was issued on 18 August 2011. This guidance (including the original FAQs) has now been updated and consolidated into the Employment Income Manual at paragraphs 45000 onwards.

One further preliminary comment must be made. As explained below, the broad purpose of the legislation is to ensure that if payments are made by an employer to an EBT, and a relevant step is taken by the EBT trustees, for example the making of a loan by those trustees to the employee or a member of his family, then the cash or asset that is the subject of that step is treated for tax purposes as earnings of the employee, received when the relevant step is taken. The legislation is premised, in effect, on the employee not being treated as having received earnings when the EBT was funded. However, the judgment of the Court of Session in in the Glasgow Rangers case, *Advocate General for Scotland v Murray Group Holdings Ltd* [2015] CSIH 77, [2016] STC 468, 2015 Scot (D) 2/11, has raised the possibility that, at least in some cases, the employee should be treated as receiving earnings when employer payments are made to the EBT. This on the basis that it may be reasonable to regard such payments as a redirection of the employee's earnings, made with the employee's consent. The discussion which follows assumes that the EBT has been funded without that step in itself giving rise to a tax charge on redirected earnings.

THE TAX CHARGE

94.2 The tax charge is made when what is termed a relevant step occurs, and the amount charged is the value of the relevant step (ITEPA 2003, s 554Z2). Where the relevant step involves a sum of money, its value is simply the amount of the money (s 554Z3(1)). In other cases, the general rule is that the value charged is the market value of the asset involved in the relevant step or, if greater, its cost (s 554Z3(2)).

The general charge on earnings under ITEPA 2003, s 62 takes priority over Part 7A, in that the value of the relevant step is reduced by the amount taxed under s 62 (s 554Z6). But Part 7A displaces the benefits code described in Chapter 93 so that the code does not apply to benefits arising out of the relevant step (see para **94.23**).

In determining what a relevant step is, the key concept is that of the relevant arrangement. The reason for this is that a step can only be relevant if it is taken in pursuance of a relevant arrangement to which Part 7A applies, or if there is a direct or indirect connection between the step and the arrangement. Attention must therefore be turned to the concept of relevant arrangements.

RELEVANT ARRANGEMENT

94.3 The term 'relevant arrangement' requires three questions to be asked, namely (1) whether there is an arrangement; (2) whether, if there is, it is relevant; and (3) whether, if there is a relevant arrangement, Part 7A applies to it.

Arrangement

94.4 The term 'arrangement' includes any of the following (ITEPA 2003, s 554Z(3)):

- Agreement
- Scheme
- Settlement

- Transaction
- Trust
- Understanding

It is expressly provided that understandings are included, even if not legally enforceable. The inclusion of the terms settlement and trust makes it clear that EBTs are caught.

Relevant

94.5 For an arrangement to be 'relevant' an employment has to be identified (s 554A(1)(a)). The employment can be current, former or prospective. The legislation refers to the employer as 'B', and to the employee as 'A'.

The legislation focuses only on actual employments. It does not extend to shadow directors, as the definition of shadow director (in ITEPA 2003, s 67) is not applied.

In determining whether an arrangement is relevant it is also necessary to identify persons which the legislation describes as linked to the employee (s 554A(5)). These persons are listed in s 554Z1 as follows:

(1)   Persons connected with the employee.
(2)   Resident and non-resident close companies in which the employee or a person connected with him is a participator.
(3)   51% subsidiaries of such companies.

The term 'connected' bears its normal tax definition in ITA 2007, s 993 (ITEPA 2003, s 718). It thus includes:

- Spouses
- Siblings
- Parents
- Children and remoter issue
- Trusts of which the employee or any person connected with him is a settlor

The term 'connected' is extended in s 554Z1 to include persons who have formerly been connected with the employee. It is also extended to cohabitees.

With the employment and the linked persons identified, it is possible to approach the term 'relevant arrangement'. An arrangement is relevant if one of two conditions is met (s 554A(1)(b)):

(1)   The employee or another linked person is a party to it, or
(2)   It covers or relates to the employee or another linked person, either in whole or in part.

As will be apparent from this second condition, an arrangement can be relevant if neither the employer nor the employee is a party to it. EBTs and other trusts settled by third parties are thus caught.

Application of the legislation

94.6 However, not all relevant arrangements are caught by Part 7A. Indeed, given that neither the employer nor the employee need be a party, the legislation would be impossibly wide if that were the position.

Instead, the legislation only applies if a further condition is met. This condition is at the heart of the mischief which Part 7A is aimed at and is fundamental in determining whether an arrangement is caught. The condition focuses on rewards, recognition or loans which are connected with the employee's current, past or prospective employment. It requires the relevant arrangement to be either a means of providing such rewards, recognition or loans or to be otherwise concerned with their provision (s 554A(1)(c)).

The key phrase in this condition is that the rewards, recognition or loans be 'in connection with' the employment. If there is no such connection there is no engagement of Part 7A. In determining whether such connection exists, the question which s 554A requires to be asked is whether, in essence, it is reasonable to suppose there is such a connection. In answering that question all relevant circumstances must be taken into account to get to 'the essence of the matter' (s 554A(12)).

The phrase 'the essence of the matter' is an interesting one. It has a distinctly purposive flavour and does, it may be suggested, require an investigation of the real reasons for setting up the arrangement. In this respect it is helpful in private client tax planning, for it gives confidence that family trusts which were not in reality set up to provide remuneration will not risk being caught by Part 7A just because some beneficiaries work for companies owned by the trust. Equally, it will be difficult to structure arrangements which are in substance remuneration to fall outside Part 7A.

THE RELEVANT STEP

94.7 A step is 'relevant' if it falls into one of three categories specified in ss 554B–554D. In summary, s 554C covers payments and transfers of assets, s 554D making assets available, and s 554B earmarking. Each is considered below.

The mere fact a step is relevant does not of itself result in a tax charge. For this to happen two further requirements must be met:

(1)   There must be linkage between the relevant step and the relevant arrangement.
(2)   The person who takes the relevant step must be a relevant third person.

Linkage

94.8 To satisfy the linkage requirement one of two conditions must be satisfied (s 554A(1)(e)):

(1)   The relevant step must be taken in pursuance of the relevant arrangement, or

(2)   There must be some other connection, whether direct or indirect, between the step and the arrangement.

As with determining whether the arrangement is relevant at all, the question to be asked is whether it is reasonable to suppose the relevant step satisfies the above two conditions. In so doing the essence of the matter must be looked at.

Relevant third person

94.9 The general rule is that any person who is neither the employer nor the employee is a relevant third person (s 554A(7)). However either of them counts as a third party if acting as a trustee. Members of the employer's group do not count as third parties unless acting as trustee (s 554A(8)).

PAYMENT OR TRANSFER

94.10 A transaction is a relevant step within s 554C if it is a payment or a transfer of an asset in specie. However s 554C also embraces provision of security, leases in excess of 21 years, and steps relating to securities or interests in securities (s 554C(1)).

The recipient

94.11 It is not necessary for the recipient under the transaction to be the employee. Instead the recipient can be 'any relevant person'. That term means any of the following (s 554C(2)):

- The employee himself.
- Any person linked with the employee, 'linked' bearing the definition discussed in para **94.5** above and thus including connected persons.
- Any person chosen by the employee.
- Any other person insofar as the person taking the step, ie the trustee or other third party, is acting on the employee's direction or request.

As will be apparent, a transfer or payment to some of the above could take place after the employee's death, most notably a payment or transfer to a person who was connected with the employee prior to his death, eg a family member, or was specified in a letter or other expression of the employee's wishes.

Loans

94.12 The term 'payment' is defined as including the making of a loan (s 554Z(7)). This means that where the relevant step is a loan of money, the amount charged is what is lent, not the value (if any) of the loan.

The legislation does not make provision for the tax charge to be reversed if and when the loan is repaid. This has been widely criticised, but the only exception allowed is for loans made between 9 December 2010 and 5 April 2011 which were repaid before 5 April 2012 (FA 2011, Sch 2, para 53(4)). The legislation does however preclude a double charge if the loan is written off, in that the taxable value on the release of the loan is reduced by the value taxed when it was made (s 554Z5). So too, the loan is deemed outside the provisions taxing loans as benefits in kind (s 554Z2(3)).

Consideration

94.13 On their own, the use of the terms 'payment' and 'transfer' in s 554C would mean that payments and transfers for consideration would be caught. This result is avoided by s 554Z8, but only to a limited extent. Where the consideration is the transfer of an asset by the employee, or a person linked with the employee, what would otherwise be the value of the relevant step is reduced by the value of the asset, provided tax avoidance is not involved. So too if the relevant step is a transfer in specie, payment of money by the employee or a linked person is deductible.

In both cases, the transfer or payment must be made before, or at or about the time of the relevant step. What is odd about s 554Z8 is that it does not appear to cover relevant steps at the direction or request of the employee in favour of third parties who are not linked to him.

Distributions

94.14 Section 554C refers to payments and transfers and does not restrict the terms to distributions of capital. It follows that all forms of distribution by an EBT are relevant steps within s 544C.

Some EBTs are long-term vehicles and may adopt a policy of investing for long-term growth, with the result that the funds available for distribution may reflect investment return rather than the contributions by the employer. Section 554C, however, does not draw a distinction between distributions funded by original growth and payments funded by investment return. It follows that all are relevant steps.

It may be thought that under a long-term EBT, particularly one where separate trusts have been appointed for each employee and his family, the connection with the employment would disappear once the employee had retired. In such cases, in logic, it might be thought that s 554C would not be engaged once distributions to date had exceeded the employer's contributions. This would be particularly so after the employee's death when, by definition, he would not be the recipient. In reality however it is difficult to read the legislation in this way, for s 554C is not so restricted and it is almost impossible to say that there is not some connection between such a step and the original formation of the EBT.

MAKING ASSET AVAILABLE

94.15 Section 554D is engaged in two distinct circumstances. The first is in point at any time and the second only when two years have elapsed from the ending of the employment.

The general circumstance in which s 554D is engaged is where an asset is made available in a way that gives the same benefit as if the asset had been transferred outright. As with the transfer charge, s 554D is engaged whether the person to whom the asset is made available is the employee himself or anybody else who falls within the definition of relevant person, discussed in para **94.11** above.

The second circumstance is much wider and is simply that the asset is made available for a relevant person to benefit from. There is no requirement that the extent of the benefit must be tantamount to absolute ownership. Should such a benefit have commenced before two years have elapsed after the end of the employment, it is treated as conferred once the two years are up. This provision would appear to catch benefits in kind, which are not in general caught if the employment no longer exists.

The same provisions apply to benefits conferred after the employee has died as apply to payments and transfers after his death (s 554Z12).

An interesting question is whether the concept of making an asset available for a person to benefit from would, in a trust context, embrace the appointment of an interest in possession over the asset. What certainly would be caught is allowing a beneficiary to use a trust asset in specie, whether such beneficiary had an interest in possession in the asset or was merely discretionary. The sting in s 554D is that it is not simply a charge on the annual benefit but instead it is an upfront charge on the full value of the asset.

It would appear that this up-front charge operates to preclude subsequent income tax charges under other legislation on the annual value of the benefit. This conclusion follows on account of s 554Z13, which provides for a just and reasonable adjustment if a later event results in an income tax charge under other legislation.

EARMARKING

94.16 The most challenging aspect of Part 7A is s 554B, the section which treats earmarking as a relevant step. The particular sting in this section is that it imposes a tax charge at a time when the employee receives neither an asset nor a benefit. In view of its draconian effect, it may be that a court would construe s 554B strictly. At all events, in view of its potential impact, its language repays close attention.

Application

94.17 The primary circumstance in which s 554B is engaged requires the following conditions to be met:

(a)   A sum of money or an asset is held by or on behalf of a person, who is referred to as 'P'.

(b)   That sum of money or asset is 'earmarked' whether formally or informally.

(c)   The earmarking is with a view to a later relevant step being taken, whether by P or some other person.

(d)   That later relevant step will be in relation to the earmarked sum of money or asset, or money or assets derived therefrom.

For s 554B to be comprehensible it needs to be kept in mind that the later relevant step will almost always not be within s 554B, but within ss 554C or 554D. It will thus be either a transfer or payment or an application for benefit. The paradigm case which s 554B covers is a portfolio of investments in an EBT being earmarked for a particular employee and managed in accordance with his advice or instructions.

The reference to the earmarking being formal or informal means s 554B catches not merely formal matters, such as the appointment of a sub-fund by an EBT, but also the informal allocation of assets. This is reinforced by s 554B(2)(c), which expressly states it is immaterial whether or not the employee has any right to have the later relevant step taken. It is also expressly provided that the later relevant step can be subject to conditions which may or may not be met (s 554B(2)(b)).

A somewhat puzzling provision is contained in s 554B(2)(a). This stipulates that it is immaterial if details of the later relevant step have not been worked out at the time of earmarking. It then gives as examples of such details, details of the sum of money or asset which may be the subject of the later relevant step and details of when and by whom and in whose favour the later relevant step will be taken.

Among the issues this raises is whether s 554B covers the appointment of unappropriated shares in a trust fund. It may be suggested that it does not, as the essence of unappropriated shares is precisely that particular assets are not allocated or earmarked. Section 554B(2)(a) could point to a different conclusion in that it could be said any later appropriation is a detail of the assets which will be the subject of the later relevant step. But to do so gives insufficient force to the basic requirement of s 554B, namely the earmarking be of a sum of money or other asset.

A further issue is whether s 554B is engaged if the earmarking is for a class of individuals as distinct from just one. Would it therefore catch an appointment of sub-trusts by an EBT in favour of the employee and members of his family? Assuming the necessary appropriation of assets was made, there would be earmarking, but what would the later relevant step be? Would s 554B apply on the basis that any distribution of income or capital would be a relevant step and that that is enough to engage s 554B? Or would the appointment be seen as an application for the benefit of the beneficiaries in question, in which case the later relevant step would be under s 554D once two years had elapsed after the ending of the employment?

A secondary application of s 554B provides that a relevant step occurs if a sum of money or other asset held by P otherwise starts to be held with a view to the later relevant step (s 554B(1)(b)). Here too the later relevant step has to be in relation to the sum of money or asset or assets derived therefrom. It is difficult to see what this adds to the primary circumstance.

Reliefs

94.18 In contrast to loans under s 554C, relief is given from the earmarking charge if the later relevant step does not in fact happen. This relief is available if a later event (which is not in itself a relevant step) means the earmarked sum or asset cannot suffer any further relevant step. Should this condition be met, the employee (or his estate) has four years from the later event within which to claim repayment of the tax or other relief (s 554Z14). The relief is on a just and reasonable basis and is precluded where tax avoidance is involved.

The paradigm case where this relief is in point is where the earmarked asset is eventually distributed not to the employee or a person who is relevant in relation to him, but to somebody else completely different.

The other context in which relief is given is if the later relevant step occurs. Here the general rule described in para **94.22** is in point, to the effect that the value of the later relevant step is appropriately reduced.

Exclusions

94.19 The provisions imposing a Part 7A charge on relevant steps after the employee's death do not apply to the earmarking charge. It follows that s 554B ceases to be in point insofar as earmarking happens after the employee's death. But it would still be for consideration whether actions after the employee's death would amount to making assets available within s 554D.

Once an asset or sum has suffered the earmarking charge, the income it, or assets representing it, generates is outside the earmarking charge even though the effect of the earmarking is normally that the income will follow the principal (s 554Q). This relief does not however apply to the extent that the income exceeds what would be a commercial return on the assets in question.

The earmarking charge is also excluded in relation to certain tax-favoured or commercial schemes (ss 554E–554O). These are not normally relevant to offshore tax planning.

CHARGING THE TAX

94.20 When a relevant step is taken, its value counts as employment income of the employee (s 554Z2(1)). In the confusing world of ITEPA 2003, the term 'counts as employment income' is a term of art. Items which count as employment income are outside the concept of 'general earnings' (ITEPA 2003, s 7(3)) and thus not subject to the general territorial limits in ITEPA 2003 applicable to actual earnings and benefits in kind (as to which see paras **93.24** and **50.13**). But as is explained in paras **94.24** to **94.26** below, Chapter 7A of ITEPA includes specific territorial limits.

For PAYE purposes, the amount which counts as employment income is treated as a payment of PAYE income of the employee. The amount of such PAYE income is the amount of the relevant step. Liability for the PAYE tax falls on the employer save insofar as the party taking the relevant step deducts the tax and accounts for it to HMRC (ITEPA 2003, ss 687A and 695A). The tax paid by the employer is itself taxed as employment income unless reimbursed by the employee within the period ending 90 days after the tax year in which the relevant step is taken (ITEPA 2003, s 222).

Should the relevant step be taken after the employee has died and the employee is the relevant person (see para **94.11**), the employment income charge will fall on the personal representatives. If the relevant person is not the employee, the notional employment income counts as employment income of the recipient (s 554Z12(4)). But this is displaced if the recipient is not an individual, and here the tax charge is made on the employer or on the person taking the relevant step. The employer is the chargeable person where, as will normally be the case, he or it is still in existence and the person taking the relevant step is non-UK resident (s 554Z12(5)).

Overlap issues

94.21 Given the breadth of Part 7A, the charges that can arise under it potentially overlap both with each other and with other tax liabilities. A number of provisions relieve such double tax.

Later relevant step

94.22 Relief applies insofar as the same asset is subject to two or more relevant steps or where the assets subject to the later relevant step are replacements of those which were the subject of the earlier relevant step. In such a case, the value of the later relevant step is reduced by the value of the earlier step, or, if the overlap is not complete, by a proportion (s 554Z5).

Typically this relief applies where the earlier step is earmarking and the later relevant step is the distribution of the earmarked assets. However in one sense the relief is not complete, for it is only the value of the assets at the time of earmarking which is deducted from the value of the later relevant step. It follows that investment growth is not deducted and so remains in charge under Part 7A on the distribution. This is a somewhat bizarre result, as normally the tax applicable to such investment growth is CGT, not income tax.

A similar point applies in relation to income. As indicated above, the income of the earmarked assets is not itself subject to the earmarking charge. This means that Part 7A applies in full on a distribution of the income, whether as income or as capital following accumulation.

The relief for earlier relevant steps is confined to earlier steps to which Part 7A has applied (s 554Z5(1)(b)).

Income tax charge under other provisions

94.23 As indicated above (para **94.2**), the general charge on earnings takes priority over Part 7A in that the value of the relevant step is reduced by the amount charged as earnings (s 554Z6). The charge on benefits in kind discussed in CHAPTER 93, by contrast, is displaced. This is achieved by s 554Z2(2)(a), which operates where the relevant step gives rise to any amount treated as earnings under the benefits code. The use of the phrase 'gives rise to' signifies that the relief from the code applies both where the taking of the relevant step is the benefit in kind, and where the benefits in kind result from the relevant step, as where the benefit is use of the property comprised in the step.

In many instances, a step may be a payment or distribution which in the absence of Part 7A would be taxable as income under other heads of charge. Such a payment or distribution could be an income distribution from an EBT or a capital distribution or benefit taxed under ITA 2007, ss 731–735. In the case of income distribution, double tax is avoided by the general rules giving employment income charges priority (ITTOIA 2005, ss 366(3) and 575(4)). In the case of ss 731–735, the same result follows on account of the fact that that code applies only to benefits which are not otherwise taxable as income (see para 70.16).

Perhaps more common are cases where the relevant step is followed by a distribution or other payment which is, or is taxed as, income. Here relief applies to the extent that it is just and reasonable (s 554Z13). This relief applies not merely where the later tax is a charge on trust distributions as described above, but also where the later event is earnings in the general sense of the term.

TERRITORIAL LIMITS

94.24 As indicated earlier, Part 7A is not in its terms confined to individuals who are UK resident or UK domiciled. Instead, territorial limits are achieved by specific exemption.

Non-residents

94.25 The exemption for non-residents is applied after the value of the relevant step is determined. Under s 554Z4, the value of the relevant step is reduced if it is for a tax year in which the employee is or was non-UK resident.

Like so much other language in Part 7A, the phrase 'for a tax year' is a term of art and has to be construed in accordance with ITEPA 2003, s 16. This section provides that earnings earned in or otherwise in respect of a period are earnings for that period. A just and reasonable apportionment is made between years if the period is more than one tax year. If earnings are for a year after the employment has ended, they are treated as for the last year of the employment (ITEPA 2003, s 17).

The effect of these rules is that the value of a relevant step is apportioned between all the years of employment to which the EBT or other arrangement relates. If in any of those years the employee was non-resident, the value of the relevant step, and thus the tax charge, is reduced. It follows that if the employee has always been non-resident, the value of the relevant step, and thus the tax charge is nil. By this roundabout route, the vast global population of employees who have no connection with the UK whatever are taken out of Part 7A.

There is one qualification, namely that the reduction in value of the relevant step is not made to the extent the non-resident performed duties in the UK (s 554Z4(4)). The extent to which duties are performed in the UK is determined on a just and reasonable basis.

As will be apparent, these rules mean emigration cannot be used to avoid Part 7A as respects employment prior to emigration. This is because the relevant step will still be related back, at least in part, to the period of UK residence.

It might be thought that immigrants could be sheltered from Part 7A by ensuring a relevant step, for example earmarking, is taken shortly before arrival. The thinking would be that that relevant step would be tax-free and deductible against any later relevant step after immigration. In reality this cannot be done, as earlier relevant steps cannot be deducted insofar as reduced by non-residence.

Non-UK domiciliaries

94.26 The remittance basis is available to non-UK domiciliaries who are remittance basis users (s 554Z9). The term remittance basis user is explained in CHAPTER 46, and connotes those who have made the appropriate claim for the tax year in question or fall within the circumstances where a claim is not required.

The remittance basis applicable to Part 7A requires a determination of which tax years the relevant step is for. The concept of 'for a tax year' is the same as under the rules relating to non-residents, as described above. The remittance basis then potentially applies to such part of the value of the relevant step as is for tax years in which the employee was a remittance-basis user. Each of these years is described as a relevant tax year in the legislation.

For the remittance basis to apply to income which is deemed to arise under Part 7A, two further conditions must be met. The first is that the employer must be foreign, ie not resident in the UK (ITEPA 2003, s 721(1)). The second is that the employee must have performed the duties of the employment wholly outside the UK. These conditions are discussed further in CHAPTER 50.

The remittance basis applies to such of the value of the relevant step which is 'for' tax years where these conditions are met. Such value becomes taxable specific income only when remitted (s 554Z9(2)). In determining whether taxable remittance occurs, the general law of remittance described in CHAPTERS 51 to 57 is applied (s 554Z11(4)). In applying that law, the sum of money or assets involved in the relevant step are deemed derived from the unremitted notional income. This means remittance occurs whether effected by the taxpayer, or any other person who is a relevant person in relation to him for remittance purposes.

The relevant person concept is important in a Part 7A context for the term includes any trust of which the employee is a beneficiary (see paras 54.6 to 54.10). In an EBT case, the EBT is thus a relevant person, so remittance would occur if, following earmarking, the EBT brought the earmarked funds to the

UK. However remittance could not occur if the relevant step was the making of a distribution to an adult who is a linked person but is not either the employee or his spouse or co-habitee. This is because such persons are not relevant persons for remittance purposes. The result is that remittance following such a distribution only occurs if there is benefit to the employee (or his spouse) in the UK or if Conditions C and D are engaged (see CHAPTER 57).

Part 7A envisages that taxable remittance can occur after the death of the employee. Section 554Z12 thus makes provision determining who is liable for tax in such circumstances. It is however confined to cases where the relevant step was within s 554C or s 554D and thus does not extend to earmarking (s 554Z12(1)).

In the most common case, where the employee himself was the recipient under the relevant step, liability for tax on any post-death remittance falls on his personal representatives (s 554Z12(3)). Should the recipient be another individual, the amount remitted counts as employment income of that individual (s 554Z12(4)). In other cases, ie where the recipient is not an individual, the recipient is subject to tax on remittance.

Section 554Z12 matches the general law applicable to remittances of earnings, ITEPA 2003, s 13(4), where liability falls on the deceased's personal representatives. It may be suggested that, at most, taxable remittance could only occur if effected by a person who would have been a relevant person were the deceased still alive. Adult children, and indeed the personal representatives themselves, would thus be excluded, whereas former spouses or cohabitees would not.

3-year period of non-residence

94.27 A remittance basis also applies to those satisfying the 3-year non-residence requirement (s 554Z10). It matches the relief equivalent to that for earnings generally (see para 50.2).

IMPLICATIONS

94.28 The principal impact of Part 7A on the subject-matter of this book is on EBTs, as discussed in CHAPTER 25. It remains to be seen whether Part 7A will be the end of offshore EBTs or whether they will continue to have a role in less aggressive planning.

Part 7A also needs to be watched where offshore trusts own underlying companies and beneficiaries work for those companies. In general such trusts are safe from Part 7A, for it is usually clear on the facts that the trust is not a means of remunerating or rewarding the beneficiaries in connection with their employment. But arguments to the contrary could be raised if a beneficiary's remuneration was less than commercial comparables and his lifestyle was being funded from the trust. A similar argument could be raised even where the remuneration is commercial if it is clear that the employee's retirement will be funded from the trust. In all such cases, care is needed over the possible implications of Part 7A.

The uncertainties of Part 7A are particularly menacing for employers in such cases, for, as described above (para **94.20**) HMRC can in most cases look to the employer for the tax if no other party pays it. At the margins of Part 7A, there will be cases where the employer company does not know what is going on at trust level and may thus have compliance difficulties.

TRANSITIONAL RULES

94.29 As indicated at the beginning of this chapter, the general rule is that Part 7A applies only if the relevant step was taken after 6 April 2011 (FA 2011, Sch 2 para 52). Anti-forestalling provisions applied to payments of sums of money between 9 December 2010 and 5 April 2011, in that such a payment counted as a relevant step taken on 6 April 2012 unless repaid in the meantime (FA 2011, Sch 2 para 53). A similar provision targeted use of readily convertible assets as security (FA 2011, Sch 2 para 54).

The real sting in the transitional rules was that Part 7A applies regardless of when the relevant arrangement was created. Thus EBTs created with the expectation of certain tax advantages have lost those advantages, and lost them moreover at a time when rates of tax on higher levels of income have risen. The legislation offered one limited relief against the impact of higher rates, in that it was possible to agree with HMRC that earmarking before 5 April 2011 gave rise to an employment income tax charge. In such a case, the amount earmarked could be deducted in computing the value of a relevant step taken after 6 April 2011 (FA 2011, Sch 2 para 59). Even where this relief is inapplicable, it may in practice be possible, in light of the Court of Session in the Glasgow Rangers case (discussed at para **94.1** above) for a settlement with HMRC to be reached based on the principle that an employment income tax charge arose when the EBT was funded, due to a redirection of earnings at that time. That may achieve a reduction in the amount of tax that is due, but this will not always be attractive, due to the accrual of interest on the tax in the intervening period. HMRC remain open to the settlement of historic tax liabilities in respect of EBTs, albeit on less favourable terms than was formerly the case (HMRC guidance entitled 'Employee Benefit Trust settlements after 31 July 2015', published online in August 2016).

Chapter 95
OFFSHORE FUNDS

INTRODUCTION

95.1 This chapter explains how investors in offshore funds are taxed. The relevant legislation is now TIOPA 2010, ss 354–363 and The Offshore Fund (Tax) Regulations 2009 (SI 2009/3001). This legislation has been in force since 1 December 2009, ss 354–363 being a re-enactment of FA 2008, ss 40A–42. The legislation replaced earlier law first enacted in 1984 (TA 1988, ss 755AA–764). References in this chapter to regulations and schedules are references to the 2009 regulations

Offshore funds are of great commercial significance for much investment is structured through them. This chapter focuses on the tax treatment of investors as distinct from what a fund has to do to secure reporting status. The latter is a matter for those managing the fund and in the normal case it will be clear from the fund's prospectus or similar whether it has reporting status.

DEFINITION OF OFFSHORE FUND

95.2 The term 'offshore fund' is exclusively and exhaustively defined (TIOPA 2010, s 355). An offshore fund is a mutual fund which is either:

(a)   a company resident outside the UK;

(b)   a unit trust scheme whose trustees are non-resident; or

(c)   other arrangements taking effect under foreign law, which create rights in the nature of co-ownership.

It is expressly provided that partnerships are not offshore funds (s 355(2)).

Mutual fund

95.3 The term 'mutual fund' means arrangements with respect to property which satisfy Conditions A to C (TIOPA 2010, s 356).

Condition A focuses on the purpose or effect of the arrangements. The participants in the arrangements must be enabled to participate in the acquisition, holding, management or disposal of the property. Alternatively they can participate in the profits or income from the property.

Condition B focuses on management. Its effect is that the participants must not have day-to-day control of the management of the property. But they are allowed to have the right to be consulted or give directions.

Condition C is the most important as it focuses on exit value. A reasonable investor participating in the arrangements must have the expectation of realising his investment for a price calculated by reference to the net asset value of the assets of the fund, or by reference to an index.

Generally, a mutual fund will allow an investor to redeem his interest in the fund on the giving of a specified period of notice, at a price calculated by reference to net asset value. However, an arrangement is not a mutual fund if realisation on a net asset value basis is achievable only on the winding up of the fund (TIOPA 2010, s 357), unless the date of winding up is fixed or determinable under the terms of the fund. But even a fixed winding up date is allowed if the fund investments do not produce income or if any such income is taxable on the investors as it arises.

Umbrella arrangements and multiple interests

95.4 Each part of an umbrella arrangement is regarded as a separate fund (TIOPA 2010, s 360). So too are separate classes of interest in the same fund, should the fund offer more than one class to prospective investors (TIOPA 2010, s 361).

Hedge funds and long funds

95.5 Although the term 'offshore fund' is sometimes seen as synonymous with the colloquial phrase 'hedge fund' this is not so. Any non-UK entity which satisfies the conditions described above is an offshore fund, regardless of the investment strategy it pursues. So too, a fund can be an offshore fund even if not resident in or formed under the law of an offshore jurisdiction. All that is required is that it is not UK resident or, if not a company or unit trust, that it takes effect under foreign law. Thus many funds which fall within the definition of offshore fund are in fact funds formed under United States law and resident in the United States.

Contrast with old law

95.6 The present definition of offshore fund differs, at least as a matter of form, from that applicable before 1 December 2009. The latter was expressed not in terms of the mutual fund concept but cross-referred to collective investment schemes as defined in the Financial Services and Markets Act 2000. The cross-reference was unsatisfactory as it introduced regulatory concepts into tax, and meant changes in the regulatory definition had tax implications.

Under the old law, an offshore income gain did not accrue unless a reasonable investor would have had the expectation of realising net asset value within seven years. This was delivered not in the definition of offshore fund but by the concept of material interest, it being provided that an offshore income gain arose only if the interest disposed of was material. This aspect of the rules has now gone.

BASIC TAX TREATMENT

95.7 A UK resident investor in an offshore fund becomes concerned with tax if:

- He receives a distribution, or
- The fund is a reporting fund and income is reported but not distributed (see para **95.12**), or
- He redeems, or otherwise disposes of, his interest.

Distributions

95.8 The tax treatment of distributions depends on the fund's legal form. Should it be a company the general rule is that any distribution is taxed as a dividend. This means it attracts the dividend rates of income tax.

There is one exception to the application of dividend treatment to corporate funds. This is in point should the fund fail to meet what is called the qualifying investments test (ITTOIA 2005, s 378A). In broad terms that test is failed if more than 60% of the fund's assets are cash or securities or other economically similar assets (ITTOIA 2005, s 378A(3); CTA 2009 s 494). Should the test be failed, any distribution by the fund is taxed as interest and thus, in the case of UK resident individuals and trusts, attracts the normal tax rates.

Should a (non-transparent) fund not be a company, distributions are not taxed as either dividends or interest. There is no charging provision specific to such distributions and so the distributions fall to be taxed as either annual payments or miscellaneous income (ITTOIA 2005, ss 683 and 687). The 2009 regulations assume the charge is as miscellaneous income (Reg 96). But whether annual payments or miscellaneous income, the normal income tax rates apply. Bizarrely, therefore, corporate offshore funds confer a tax advantage over non-transparent funds which are not structured as companies.

Redemption or disposal

95.9 The general rule is that the investor's gain or loss on redemption or disposal is computed in accordance with CGT rules. But how a gain is taxed depends on whether or not the fund has been a reporting fund throughout the investor's period of ownership. If it has, the gain is a chargeable gain (Reg 99). In other words, it is within the CGT regime for an individual investor. For a corporate investor, indexation is allowed.

Should the fund not have had reporting status throughout the investor's ownership, any gain is known as an offshore income gain (Reg 38) and is taxed as income (Reg 18). Indexation is not available (Reg 39) and, as is described below, certain other CGT computational rules are modified.

However, whether a fund is a reporting fund or not, any loss realised by the investor on the redemption, or other disposal, of his interest in the fund is a capital loss, offsettable against ordinary gains (including those realised on the disposal of interests in funds with reporting status), but not offsettable against offshore income gains (Reg 42).

REPORTING FUNDS

95.10 A fund has to satisfy a number of conditions before it can be a reporting fund. The principal ones are as follows:

- Accounts must be prepared in accordance with international accounting standards or generally accepted accounting practice (Regs 59–89).
- Reportable income must be calculated for each period of account (Regs 62–72).
- The fund must provide regular reports to participants detailing amounts distributed per unit and amounts of reportable income per unit not distributed (Regs 90–93).
- The fund must provide a report to HMRC for each period of account detailing inter alia reportable income and amounts distributed (Reg 106).

A fund which satisfies these conditions is not in fact a reporting fund unless it makes an application to HMRC for reporting fund status and the application is accepted (Reg 57). Applications may be made by prospective as well as existing funds. For existing funds, an application cannot be effective as respects accounting periods beginning more than three months before the application (Regs 51–56).

Ceasing to be a reporting fund

95.11 A reporting fund can cease to be such voluntarily by notice to HMRC (Reg 116). It ceases to be a reporting fund involuntarily if it is in serious breach of the reporting fund requirements and HMRC give it notice specifying the breach (Reg 114).

Undistributed income

95.12 A key consequence of reporting status is that the undistributed income of the fund is taxed as distributed (Reg 94). This notional distribution is treated as made on the last day of the reporting period in which the income arises or, if the fund issues its report to the investors within six months, on the date when the report is issued. The notional distribution enjoys the same tax treatment in the hands of UK investors as any actual distribution would (Regs 95–98). Thus notional distributions by corporate funds attract the dividend rates unless the qualifying investments test described in para **95.8** is failed (ITTOIA 2005, s 378A(3); CTA 2009, s 493).

Without express provision, the charge on undistributed income could result in double tax, insofar as such income is reflected in the value of the fund when the investor redeems or otherwise disposes of his interest. But in reality such double taxation is avoided, for undistributed income on which the investor has previously been taxed is included in his base cost for CGT purposes (Reg 99).

CGT treatment on disposal does not apply if at any time the fund has been non-reporting. But in such case, any investor can elect for a deemed disposal at market value when the fund's status changes (Reg 48). The same applies should a fund which was a non-distributor fund prior to 1 December 2009 became a reporting fund on that date (Sch 1 para 5). This is discussed further below (para 95.20).

NON-REPORTING FUNDS

Disposals

95.13 As indicated in para 95.9 above, an offshore income gain arises when an interest in a non-reporting fund is disposed of. The computation of the offshore income gain uses the CGT rules in TCGA 1992 (Reg 39) subject to a few alterations. 'Disposal' bears the same meaning as for CGT purposes, but subject to two important modifications (Reg 33).

The first is that when a person dies he is deemed to dispose of any interest he holds in a non-reporting fund at market value (Reg 34). If the interest is standing at a gain, income tax chargeable on the resultant OIG is a deduction for IHT purposes (IHTA 1984, s 174(1)(a)). The second modification is that a disposal is also deemed to occur if the fund is subject to a takeover or reconstruction otherwise relieved from capital gains tax by TCGA 1992, ss 135 and 136. This does not, however, apply if the acquiring entity is itself a non-reporting offshore fund (Regs 35 and 36). The same rules apply if interests of different classes are exchanged in a reorganisation of the fund (Reg 37).

Pooling and identification

95.14 For corporation tax purposes interests in non-reporting funds are relevant securities and so subject to the identification rules in TCGA 1992, s 108. These require shares or units to be identified first with those of the same class acquired within the previous 12 months on a first in first out basis, and then with those of the same class acquired more than 12 months previously on a last in first out basis.

For taxpayers other than UK companies, interests in non-reporting funds are relevant securities for the purposes of TCGA 1992, s 108 and so excluded from the classes of assets subject to pooling (TCGA 1992, s 104(3)). The identification rules for securities in TCGA 1992, s 106A apply (s 106A(10)(c)).

The gain

95.15 The amount of the offshore income gain is the gain as computed for CGT purposes (Regs 38 and 39). Despite the fact that indexation is still available generally to companies, it is not allowed in computing offshore income gains (Reg 39(2)(b)). Holdover relief and the roll-over relief available on incorporation of a business are also not allowed (Reg 41).

It is not wholly clear whether an offshore income gain can accrue on the death of the holder of a qualifying interest in possession (as to the meaning of which see para **61.2**). For CGT purposes the death of the holder of the interest occasions a disposal of the trust assets at market value, but no chargeable gain accrues (TCGA 1992, ss 71(1), 72(1) and 73(1)). As a disposal is treated as occurring, there is a disposal of any non-reporting funds held by the trust, and the better view is that the exclusion of any ordinary gain from chargeability to CGT does not prevent an offshore income gain from accruing. But if this is right, the rule allowing tax on such gains as a deduction for IHT purposes is not in point, as that rule applies only where the OIG crystallised on death is in free estate (IHTA 1984, s 174(1)(a)).

THE CHARGE TO TAX

95.16 An offshore income gain is treated as the income arising to the investor at the time of the disposal (Reg 18). The charge on individuals and trusts is to income tax rather than to CGT. The applicable rates are the normal income tax rates, regardless of the form of the fund. The territorial limits are as follows:

(1)   A person is chargeable if in the tax year of the disposal he is resident in the UK. This is achieved by applying to offshore income gains the territorial limits to capital gains tax (Reg 22).

(2)   A non-resident is only chargeable insofar as he is trading in the UK through a branch, agency, or permanent establishment and the interest disposed of was used or held for the purposes of such trade. The restriction of the charge to UK assets does not apply (Reg 22).

(3)   Should the non-resident be an individual the offshore income gain is treating as arising in the tax year of his return should he be non-resident for a period of five years or less (Reg 23); see further para **41.42**.

Should the offshore income gain accrue to a resident trust, the charge to tax is at the rate for trusts regardless of the form of the trust. If a resident trust is settlor-interested, the gain is assessable as the settlor's under ITTOIA 2005, s 624 (see Chapter 75). This is not expressly provided for but follows from the basic deeming of the gain to be income and is assumed to be so elsewhere in the legislation (see for example Reg 20(1)). Where a child would be absolutely entitled as against the trustee but for being a minor, the gain is also assessed as the settlor's (ITTOIA 2005, s 632).

Avoidance of double charge

95.17 As noted above most disposals of interests in offshore funds are disposals for CGT purposes. Double taxation is avoided by requiring the offshore income gain to be deducted from what is otherwise the consideration for CGT purposes (Reg 45). Where an offshore income gain accrues on a takeover or reconstruction of the fund, it forms part of the acquisition cost of the new holding for CGT purposes (Reg 47).

Losses

95.18 Should the computation result in a loss rather than a gain, the loss is not available for set-off against offshore income gains (Reg 42). For the purposes of the offshore fund legislation such disposal is treated as resulting in a gain of nil. As noted in para **95.9**, it follows that the loss is an allowable loss for CGT purposes. It is not allowable for income tax purposes (ITA 2007, s 152).

EXEMPTIONS FROM CHARGE

95.19 Certain kinds of offshore income gain are exempted from charge (Regs 25–31). Three of the more important are transparent funds, funds which are treated as loan relationships, and certain funds investing in unlisted trading companies.

A transparent fund is a unit trust or contractual arrangement where the fund income is taxable as that of the investors as it arises (Reg 11; see further para **40.16**). An interest in such a fund is exempt provided two conditions are met. One is that the fund gives UK investors sufficient information to discharge their tax obligations. The second is that the fund must not at any time during the investor's ownership have had interests in other non-reporting funds. A de minimis exemption of up to 5% in total is allowed.

A fund is treated as a loan relationship for corporation tax purposes if it fails the qualifying investments test described above (para **95.8**), ie if more than 60% of its investments by value are what are called qualifying investments (CTA 2009, s 490). Should the fund fall to be treated as a loan relationship, corporate investors are charged under the loan relationship rules, and so a charge under the offshore fund rules is not in point (Reg 25). This exemption applies only to companies. Similar exemption applies to funds treated as derivative contracts.

An offshore income gain is also exempt if the purpose of the fund is to invest in unlisted trading companies and 90% of the value of the fund comprises holdings in such companies (Regs 31A and 31B). Should an investee company become listed, the fund must intend to dispose of its holding as soon as reasonably practical.

These exemptions are expressed as exemption from liability to income tax under Reg 17. The gains remain offshore income gains, and as such deductible in computing any gain for the purposes of CGT (Reg 45). The exemptions thus appear to give relief form CGT as well as income tax.

CHANGE OF STATUS

95.20 As indicated above, the investor's gain is an offshore income gain unless the fund has had reporting status throughout his time as an investor. Should its status have changed, he may end up having the worst of both worlds, in that for part of his period of ownership undistributed income will have been attributed to him, and yet on realisation the eventual gain is still taxed as income. A point not explicitly covered in the regulations is whether, in computing that offshore income gain, any undistributed income from the reporting phase is allowed in base cost. It is, however, reasonably plain that such income is so allowed, as the general rule is that offshore income gains are computed in the same way as ordinary gains.

There is one scenario on which a change of status is ignored. This is in point should a non-reporting fund become a reporting fund. If at the time of the change of status, the investor's investment is showing a loss, the fund is treated on any subsequent disposal as having been a reporting fund throughout (Reg 17(3)(d)). But self-evidently this does not apply if before the eventual disposal the fund reverts to non-reporting status.

Elections

95.21 The adverse consequences resulting from a change in the fund's status can be tempered by election (Regs 48 and 100). The investor may make such election in his tax return for the tax year or accounting period which includes the fund's last day under its old status. The effect of the election is that the investor is treated as disposing of his interest at market value, the gain then accruing being taxed accordingly. Any gain on subsequent realisation is then taxed in accordance with its new status (assuming the fund retains its new status).

An election is not effective on a change to reporting status if the deemed disposal would result in a loss for then, as described above, the fund is treated as having had reporting status throughout. To some extent the decision as to whether to elect is a choice between two unattractive alternates, in that an election triggers a tax liability without the advantage of actual proceeds and failure to elect means that at some point there may be or have been undistributed income taxed on a current-year basis without the advantage of ultimate CGT treatment.

Transitional provisions

95.22 Provisions in Sch 1 to the 2009 regulations dealt with the transition from the old offshore fund rules (which distinguished between distributing and non-distributing funds) and the current rules (with their different classification of offshore funds as either reporting or non-reporting). These provisions were discussed in the nineteenth and earlier editions of this book.

REMITTANCE BASIS USERS

95.23 The remittance basis is available to investors in offshore funds who are remittance basis users.

Distributions

95.24 Distributions attract the remittance basis as all the categories of income into which they fall are relevant foreign income (ITTOIA 2005, ss 829 and 830).

Notional distributions

95.25 The remittance basis also applies to the notional distributions imputed where a reporting fund does not distribute all its income. This result follows because such notional distributions are taxed as actual income (Reg 94).

No specific rules explain how the remittance basis works in relation to notional distributions. In particular it is not stated that the proceeds of any disposal are deemed to be derived from the notional income, although it is a fair inference that this is in fact the position. On this basis the proceeds of any disposal are a mixed fund (see para 53.8), comprising notional income, gain proper, and whatever the original capital was derived from. The mixed fund rules treat the capital gain as remitted before the notional income of years prior to the disposal (see para 53.14).

As a matter of literal construction an issue arises as to whether the notional income of remittance basis users is deductible in computing the gain on disposal. This point arises because what is deducted is the accumulated undistributed income (Reg 99(2)). That term is defined as amounts on which the investor has been charged to tax (Reg 99(3)), a condition not satisfied in relation to remittance basis users until remittance occurs. But normally there is nothing in the point, for once a remittance by the investor exceeds both the final year's undistributed income and the gain, net of accumulated undistributed income, what is then treated as remitted is the prior year undistributed income, which by definition is then charged. The point is however material if the investor is no longer a remittance basis user when he realises his interest in the fund, for then the gain is taxed on an arising basis and yet the accumulated undistributed income is not taxed unless the proceeds of the disposal are remitted.

Offshore income gains

95.26 Offshore income gains are deemed to be relevant foreign income, which means the remittance basis applies (Reg 19). The remittance basis operates by treating the actual offshore income gain as derived from the relevant foreign income it is deemed to be (Reg 19(3)). Should the disposal of the material interest be at less than market value, the material interest itself is deemed to be derived from the gain (Reg 19 (b)). The practical result of the latter rule is that, in the case of a disposal by way of gift, remittance by a transferee results in the donor's gain being taxed if that the transferee acquired the interest at an undervalue and he is a relevant person in relation to the non-domiciled disponor. As is explained in CHAPTER 54, this is normally the position if the transferee is a trust or company.

As with all cases of deemed derivation, the issue arises of how far the derivation goes. This issue is discussed in para 52.30. The better view is that derivation extends into any investment of the proceeds of the disposal generating the gain or into the proceeds of such investment.

The proceeds of any disposal are a mixed fund. This means that a partial remittance is of offshore income gain before base cost (see CHAPTER 53).

OFFSHORE INCOME GAINS AND NON-RESIDENTS

95.27 As indicated above (para **95.16**), non-residents are not as such taxed on offshore income gains, save where trading in the UK through a branch, agency, or permanent establishment.

A further point is that offshore income gains arising to a non-UK resident settlement cannot be taxed on the settlor under the income tax settlements code (SI 2009/3001 reg 20(1)).

The manner in which anti-avoidance rules operate in relation to offshore income gains is governed by two other codes, namely the transfer of assets code described in CHAPTERS **68** to **74** and the CGT rules in TCGA 1992, ss 13 and 87. The impact of and the overlap between these two codes is complicated. Their operation in relation to non-resident trusts and to non-resident companies owned by such trusts is described in CHAPTER **82**.

Where a non-resident close company is directly owned by UK residents, the primary rule is that TCGA 1992, s 13 operates to apportion offshore income gains realised by the company to UK participators in the same way as applies to ordinary gains (SI 2009/3001 reg 24). But if s 13 is not in point, the offshore income gain is foreign income for the purposes of the transfer of assets code and taxed as such if the conditions for the application of that code are otherwise met (reg 21 and reg 24(7)). As is explained in CHAPTER **88**, there are now many circumstances where s 13 is disapplied, most notably where the s 13 motive defence is in point, and in these circumstances the charge is under the transfer of assets code.

Where an offshore income gain is apportioned under s 13 it is taxed as income. The participator is treated as having made the disposal generating the gain (Reg 24(6)) and so is charged under Reg 17, the basic charging provision for offshore income gains.

In s 13 cases there is obvious scope for double taxation if, after the offshore income gain is apportioned to a UK participator, the company pays the gain in dividend or is sold or wound up. But the relief described in para **88.22** allowing the deduction of tax from tax where the gain is distributed within the specified period applies, for that relief is expressed in terms of tax generally. The relief in s 13(7) (para **88.23**) also applies, ie if the participator disposes of his shares in the company he can deduct from that gain any income tax paid by him on the offshore income gain.

Originally, s 13 did not apply to non-UK domiciliaries, but since 6 April 2008 it has applied to all UK residents, including individuals who are domiciled outside the UK (see para **88.25**). This applies also to offshore income gains. Where the individual is a remittance basis user, the applicable remittance rules are not those applicable to s 13, but those described earlier in this chapter (para **95.26**). As there indicated, the effect is that the offshore income gain is relevant foreign income. Because the participator is treated as having made the disposal, the proceeds of the disposal, albeit in the hands of the company, are treated as derived from the apportioned gain. Taxable remittance accordingly occurs if those proceeds are remitted by the company.

The capital gains, and thus the offshore income gains, of non-resident close companies are computed as if the company were in charge to corporation tax. It is unclear whether this means funds qualifying as loan relationships fall outside s 13. If they do the result is that gains on such funds are taxable (if at all) only under the transfer of assets code.

The rules in TCGA 1992, s 79B apportioning treaty-protected gains to trustee shareholders are not applied to offshore income gains. Treaty protected offshore income gains are thus potentially also within the transfer of assets code.

Chapter 96

THE REGIME APPLICABLE TO LIFE POLICIES

The authors would like to give special thanks to Lisa-Jane Dupernex of Charles Russell Speechlys LLP for her help with this chapter.

96.1 The UK has a special code for taxing life policies, now comprised in Income Tax (Trading and Other Income) Act 2005 (ITTOIA 2005), Part 4, Chapter 9. When first enacted this was principally concerned with onshore policies, but amendments made in 1984 countered the tax-saving potential of offshore policies.

The legislation was further amended in 1998 inter alia to introduce a special regime for policies that qualify as 'personal portfolio bonds'. In this chapter the general legislation is considered first, and then the rules targeted specifically at personal portfolio bonds.

The general legislation distinguishes qualifying from non-qualifying policies and treats the former more generously than the latter. However, offshore policies are by definition non-qualifying. This is because a policy issued by a non-UK life insurance company after 17 November 1983 is non-qualifying unless the premiums are paid to a UK permanent establishment (TA 1988, Sch 15 para 24).

Since 2008, the regime applicable to life policies which is described in this chapter has not applied to policies owned by companies (FA 2008, Sch 13). Instead, where a company is party to an investment life insurance contract, it is taxable under the loan relationship rules.

The life policies tax legislation is byzantine, poorly drafted and verges on the unreadable. As discussed below, it can also produce results that are surprising, and in some scenarios shocking in their unfairness to policyholders. However, there are reasons to hope that some of the defects of the legislation will soon be remedied.

CHARGEABLE EVENTS

96.2 A life policy has the potential to generate an income tax charge whenever what the legislation calls a 'chargeable event' occurs. Whether such a tax charge is, in fact, generated depends on whether the event in question gives rise to, or is deemed to give rise to, a gain.

The various forms of chargeable event are listed in ITTOIA 2005, s 484. They include:

(1)   a complete surrender of the policy;

(2)   an assignment of all rights under the policy for money or money's worth;

(3)   the falling due of a payment on the maturity of the policy; and

(4)   a partial surrender of the policy, or partial assignment of the policy for money or money's worth, if (in either case) a deemed gain is produced by the event in question. This depends on the outcome of a 'periodic calculation' or 'transaction-related calculation' (see paras **96.3** and **96.6** below).

In addition, in the case of a policy that qualifies as a personal portfolio bond, a chargeable event is deemed to occur on an annual basis. This annual chargeable event can only be avoided by terminating the policy or varying it so that it ceases to qualify as a personal portfolio bond (see para **96.30** ff below).

The forms of chargeable event referred to at (4) above are collectively termed 'calculation events'.

A loan from the insurance company to the policyholder is typically treated as a partial surrender (ITTOIA 2005, ss 500(c) and 501), so such a loan is also capable of being a calculation event.

Timing of chargeable events

96.3 Chargeable events within (1) to (3) above occur at the same time as the actions or circumstances which give rise to them. By contrast, a chargeable event within (4) above is generally deemed to occur not when the partial surrender or partial assignment occurs, but at the end of the relevant insurance year.

An insurance year starts when the policy is first issued, and thereafter a new insurance year starts on each anniversary of that date (ITTOIA 2005, s 499). The final year ends with the maturity or complete surrender of the policy. If that event is in the same tax year as what would otherwise be the end of the previous insurance year, the previous insurance year is extended to the date of the maturity or surrender, to form an extended final year.

There are two exceptions to the general rule that a chargeable event within (4) above is deemed to be deferred until the end of the relevant insurance year. These are the cases in which a 'transaction-related calculation' is required under ITTOIA 2005, s 510, namely:

(a)   where there has been a partial assignment of the policy for money or money's worth at some point in the insurance year; or

(b)   where there has been a partial surrender followed, in the same insurance year, by an assignment otherwise than for money or money's worth (ITTOIA 2005, s 509).

If either of these exceptions is in point, the partial assignment or partial surrender constitutes a chargeable event at the time of the assignment or surrender (ITTOIA 2005, s 514).

HMRC comment that this latter rule 'is designed to ensure that the gain in cases of earlier assignment is charged on the correct person – the assignor – not the person otherwise liable as owner of the rights at the end of the "insurance year". It applies whether or not the earlier assignment gave rise to a chargeable event gain.' (IPTM 3500).

Assignments

96.4 An assignment that is not for money or money's worth is not a chargeable event. A policy can be assigned gratuitously without any income tax charge for the assignor, even if the policy is standing at a gain. There is therefore a marked difference between the treatment of a gratuitous assign-ment of a life policy and a gift of a chargeable asset, which is of course a disposal for CGT purposes, and gives rise to a chargeable gain if the market value of the asset exceeds the donor's base cost.

The explanation for the disparity in treatment is that if there is a chargeable event after the assignment, the calculation of the gain realised by that event takes no account of the extent to which any growth in the value of the policy, and any partial surrenders of the policy, occurred before the policy was acquired by the assignee. Thus if a UK resident assignee surrenders the policy, he is essentially in the same tax position as the assignor would have been, had he retained the policy and himself effected the surrender. An assignment in favour of a UK resident individual creates no scope for income tax to be avoided (although it may be mitigated if the assignee has a lower marginal rate).

However, there is scope for income tax to be avoided if a UK resident individual makes a gratuitous assignment to a non-UK resident individual. In that situation, any latent gain on the policy passes out of the UK tax net.

The question of whether an assignment is for money or money's worth is not always straightforward. Where a shareholder in a company assigns a policy to that company, HMRC take the view (IPTM 7385) that this is an assignment for money or money's worth, because the company's shares will be worth more after the assignment. However, there is a strong argument that an assignment is only for money or money's worth if value is provided by the assignee, and clearly that is not the case where a gratuitous assignment is made to a company, notwithstanding any increase in the value of the shares held by the assignor.

Where an assignment for money or money's worth takes place between persons who are connected with each other (under Income Tax Act 2007 (ITA 2007), s 993) a deemed market value rule applies (ITTOIA 2005, s 493(6)). This rule is of fairly limited compass. It does not cause a gratuitous assignment between connected persons to be treated as having been made for money or money's worth. However, where the assignment is for consideration that is less than the market value of the policy, the market value is substituted for the actual value of the consideration, for the purposes of the calculation of the gain resulting from the event.

An assignment between spouses or civil partners living together is disregarded even if for money or money's worth (ITTOIA 2005, s 487(c)).

Fundamental reconstructions

96.5 HMRC take the view that changes to the terms of a policy may be so fundamental as to terminate the existing contract and bring into existence a new policy in substitution for it (HMRC Insurance Policy Taxation Manual 8110). According to this view, the termination of the original policy will be a full surrender with chargeable event consequences. Less fundamental changes which are mere variation of the policy's terms do not have chargeable event consequences.

Examples of changes that HMRC regard as fundamental include a change to the life assured, changing a contingency (first death or last survivor) on a joint policy, adding or removing critical illness cover that would bring the policy to an end if paid, and converting a whole of life or term policy to an endowment policy or vice versa. A fundamental reconstruction can also occur, in HMRC's view, if a number of simultaneous changes are made which are not fundamental when viewed in isolation but which make a substantial difference to the contract when taken together.

It is not clear that HMRC's position is correct: as a matter of contract law, a new contract is not necessarily created as a result of the parties agreeing a change to a contractual term. As a practical matter, policy terms and conditions will typically prohibit changes which HMRC view as amounting to fundamental reconstructions.

Calculation events

96.6 As noted above, a 'calculation event' may occur if there is a partial surrender of the policy, or a partial assignment of the policy for money or money's worth.

Most commonly, the situation which gives rise to the calculation event is a partial surrender of the policy, which has not been followed in the same insurance year by an assignment of the policy for money or money's worth. In such cases, the tax position is principally governed by the following provisions:

- ITTOIA 2005, s 498, which imposes a requirement to carry out a 'periodic calculation' in accordance with s 507 to determine whether a gain has arisen, and if so its amount;
- ITTOIA 2005, s 507, which sets out the methodology for the periodic calculation; and
- ITTOIA 2005, s 509, which deems a chargeable event to have occurred at the end of the insurance year if the 'periodic calculation' produces a gain.

In the scenario described above, the calculation is carried out at the end of the insurance year, and takes account of all partial surrenders effected in the course of that year (ITTOIA 2005, s 498(2)). The net total value of rights surrendered and/or assigned for money or money's worth up to the end of the relevant insurance year has to be compared with the net total of allowable payments for that year. The concept of 'allowable payments' is discussed below. If the net total value of rights surrendered and/or assigned exceeds the net total of allowable payments, the excess is treated as a gain (ITTOIA 2005, s 507(2)).

Partial assignments which were made gratuitously are generally ignored in carrying out this calculation. However, an exception is made for gratuitous partial assignments made in an insurance year beginning before 6 April 2001 (s 507(4)(b)).

For the purpose of the periodic calculation, the allowable payments are 5% of the premium paid for the first insurance year, plus 5% for each subsequent year up to and including the current year, or (if the policy has been held for more than 20 years) the 20th year (ITTOIA 2005, s 507(5)).

Should the above calculation produce a gain, so that there is a calculation event for the insurance year, the net total of allowable payments and the net total value brought into account are deducted in carrying out the calculation in future insurance years.

Although the periodic calculation rules are complicated, the practical effect is simple. In practice there is a tax-free withdrawal allowance, of 5% of the premium, for each insurance year up to the 20th (so that over the course of 20 years, 100% of the premium can in principle be returned to the policyholder without tax). If in a particular insurance year the 5% allowance is not used, either wholly or in part, the 5% allowance or the unused part of it is carried forward, and is available to be used in subsequent insurance years.

On a partial surrender, there can be no excess if the amount withdrawn is covered by the current insurance year's 5% allowance (if not already used), and/or by 5% allowances carried forward from previous years. But if the amount withdrawn on a partial surrender is greater than any available 5% allowances, there is an excess, which is taxable. That is the case regardless of whether the underlying assets are standing at a gain, because the gain/loss on the underlying investments is not a component in the periodic calculation formula.

Termination

96.7 On a termination of the policy, eg on the occurrence of a surrender of all rights or on the death of the last life assured, the chargeable event gain is the difference between (a) the total benefit value of the policy and (b) the total of the premiums paid, plus any gains treated as accruing on prior calculation events under the rules described above (ITTOIA 2005, ss 491–494).

The total benefit value of the policy is, in general, the sum payable on the termination of the policy, plus any capital sums previously paid under the policy, eg in respect of previous partial surrenders (ITTOIA 2005, ss 492(1) and 493(1)). However, in the case of a termination on the death of the last life assured, the sum payable on termination is not used and instead the surrender value immediately prior to death is used in the calculation (ITTOIA 2005, s 493(7)).

The reason that gains previously treated as accruing on calculation events are netted off in calculating the gain on the termination of the policy is that the tax paid in respect of a calculation event is in effect an accelerated payment of tax on the economic gain which (it is assumed) will in due course be realised when the policy is terminated.

Practical effect

96.8 Certain points should be noted about the rules described above:

(1)   Where a policy terminates on the death of the last life assured, the proceeds payable on death are not used in the calculation of the resultant gain. What matters is the surrender value immediately before death. This may be somewhat less than the payment received.

(2)   Although partial surrenders are not taxed if the proceeds fall within the available 5% allowances, the tax is deferred rather than avoided. This is because a partial surrender constitutes a capital sum paid under the policy for the purposes of ITTOIA 2005, s 492(1). Accordingly, the proceeds of the partial surrender contribute to the total benefit value of the policy, when it matures or is fully surrendered.

(3)   As partial surrenders are taxed by reference to the excess of withdrawals over the available 5% allowances, and not by reference to the value of the underlying assets, a charge to tax can arise even if the underlying assets are not standing at a gain. Indeed, the tax charged on a partial surrender can represent a large proportion of the capital that is extracted from the policy. As discussed below (at para **96.20**), deficiency relief is intended to mitigate the excessive taxation that can result from partial surrenders. However, (a) the relief is postponed until the termination of the policy, and (b) the relief is useless unless, in the tax year in which the policy is terminated, the policyholder has income from other sources which is taxable at the higher rate.

Policies denominated in foreign currency

96.9 It is very well established that when calculating a chargeable gain, proceeds in a foreign currency are to be converted into sterling at the exchange rate applicable on the date of the disposal, and acquisition costs in a foreign currency are to be converted into sterling at the exchange rate applicable on the date(s) on which the costs were incurred (*Bentley v Pike* [1981] STC 360, 53 TC 590). The result is that for CGT purposes, it is sterling values which determine whether tax is payable on the disposal of an asset denominated in a foreign currency, and if so, how much. Due to currency movements, the disposal of such an asset is capable of giving rise to a gain in the reference currency but a loss in sterling, or vice versa.

It might be expected that the same principles would apply to the calculation of chargeable event gains, where the policy is denominated in a foreign currency. However, HMRC's position is that in such cases, the chargeable event gain calculation should be carried out in the reference currency, and then the gain (if any) resulting from that calculation should be converted into sterling using the exchange rate applicable on the date of the chargeable event (IPTM 2700). This means that the selection of the reference currency of the bond can have a significant effect on the tax treatment of the product.

HMRC's practice entails that if an individual proposes to acquire assets denominated in a foreign currency, in the expectation that such currency will appreciate against sterling, there may be a valuable tax advantage in acquiring exposure to such assets via a life insurance bond, denominated in the relevant currency, rather than through direct investment.

NON-LIFE POLICIES

Capital redemption policies

96.10 The code for taxing life policies also applies to capital redemption policies. The term 'capital redemption policy' is defined in ITTOIA 2005, s 473(2) as a contract made in the course of a capital redemption business, within the meaning of Finance Act 2012, s 56(3) (FA 2012). The latter provides that business is capital redemption business if it consists of the effecting on the basis of actuarial calculations, and the carrying out, of contracts under which, in return for one or more fixed payments, a sum of a specified amount (or a series of sums of a specified amount) become payable at a future time or over a period.

One difference between a capital redemption policy and a life insurance policy is that the payment of the sum under a capital redemption policy is independent of any contingency and in particular it is not dependent on a death or survival of a life. Examples include a leasehold redemption policy which builds up a fund to be used on expiration of a lease.

Insurance policies and contracts for deferred annuities are taken outside the scope of CGT except in unusual circumstances. However, the provision which ensures that there is normally no CGT in respect of these contracts (Taxation of Chargeable Gains Act 1992, s 210) does not expressly apply to capital redemption policies. This creates theoretical, and perhaps actual, scope for CGT charges, in some situations on top of income tax charges under the life policy code, when capital redemption policies are subject to disposals. Such disposals include surrenders or assignments, whether complete or partial, and whether or not value is received by the individual.

However, HMRC state in the Capital Gains Manual at CG69004 that capital redemption policies are not within the charge to Capital Gains Tax. It is uncertain on what basis HMRC say this. The statement appears to be incorrect, although taxpayers can probably rely on it as a statement of HMRC's understanding of the law, up to the point at which any change is made to this part of the Manual.

In the event that the Manual is changed, or HMRC refuse to be bound by the statement in their own Manual, it seems most likely that a chargeable gain generated by a surrender or assignment in respect of a capital redemption policy issued by a non-UK resident insurer, and governed by the law of a country outside the UK, would be considered a foreign chargeable gain. If that is correct, the remittance basis would apply, if the policyholder was non-UK domiciled and was a remittance basis user in the tax year of the disposal.

Capitalisation contracts

96.11 It is not uncommon for individuals resident in civil law countries, such as France, to take out policies which involve no life insurance element and provide for an investment-linked payment on redemption. These are sometimes called capitalisation contracts. It is questionable whether such policies are issued in the course of a capital redemption business, as defined in FA 2012, s 56(3) (and discussed above), as actuarial calculations do not appear to be involved. It would seem that if such policies are not life insurance, and are not capital redemption policies, they are outside the life policy tax code and are likely to be subject to the CGT regime as excluded indexed securities.

SEGMENTATION

96.12 In practice, insurance bonds often consist of a large number of individually numbered life policies, known as segments (or sometimes as 'sub-policies'). If a taxpayer wishes to make a partial surrender of more than the available 5% allowances, this can be arranged by a complete surrender of a number of segments (known as vertical surrender) rather than a partial surrender of each segment (known as horizontal surrender). This avoids the disadvantageous consequences which arise where partial surrenders in excess of the available 5% allowances are made.

Where an insurance bond is segmented, it is essential that the taxpayer's election to make a withdrawal by vertical surrender is unambiguous. The First-tier Tribunal considered in *Rogers v HMRC* [2011] UKFTT 791 (TC) that where there is a partial surrender of a segmented policy, the default position is that horizontal rather than vertical surrender occurs. However, where a taxpayer has chosen horizontal surrender in ignorance of the adverse tax consequences of doing so, there is likely to be scope to bring proceedings for rectification of the form by which the surrender was communicated to the insurance company, on the basis of a unilateral mistake (see para **96.28**).

There are anti-avoidance provisions in the life policy tax code regarding 'connected policies', which can cause such policies to be treated as a single policy for the purposes of the calculation of charges in respect of chargeable events (ITTOIA 2005, s 473A). These provisions can only apply where, viewed in isolation, one of those policies is not on commercial terms (s 473A(2)(b)). This is not normally the case in relation to life policy 'segments'. Generally, each 'segment' is on commercial terms.

LIABILITY TO TAX: INDIVIDUALS

UK resident settlors

96.13 Where a policy is held by a non-charitable trust, whether UK resident or not, and the 'creator' of the trust is a living UK resident individual, any chargeable event gain of the trust is attributed for tax purposes to that individual (ITTOIA 2005, s 465(3)).

There is a strong argument that a trust is 'created' by the person who is its settlor for trust law purposes, and that where a trust is settled by person A but person B assigns a policy to the trust, the 'creator' for the purposes of this provision is person A, not person B.

Charge on death

96.14 A chargeable event gain on a policy is taxed as income of an individual if immediately before the chargeable event he (or a trust 'created' by him) owns the policy (ITTOIA 2005, s 465). Since the ownership test is applied immediately before the chargeable event, any gain on the termination of a policy triggered by the individual's own death is treated as the individual's income for the tax year of death. If he dies early in the tax year, it may therefore attract tax at a lower rate than if he dies later on.

Non-UK domiciliaries

96.15 Chargeable event gains derived from a foreign life insurance policy are not deemed to be relevant foreign income. Nor does the chargeable event code enact any bespoke remittance basis. The result is that the remittance basis does not extend to the chargeable event gains of remittance basis users.

It is also worth noting that the ability of a remittance basis user to use withdrawals from a policy falling within the available 5% allowances for experience in the UK, without tax being charged on the remittance of such sums, depends on whether the premium for the policy represented clean capital. If the premium represented foreign income or gains, withdrawals will be taxed if remitted to the UK.

Non-UK residents

96.16 Subject to the rules applicable to temporary non-residents (see below), an individual is not taxed on a policy gain unless he is resident in the UK in the tax year in which the chargeable event occurs (ITTOIA 2005, s 465(1)). The charge where the policy is held in trust applies regardless of whether the trust is resident or non-resident.

Temporary non-residence

96.17 Until 5 April 2013 there was no five-year temporary non-residence rule such as applies to chargeable gains (see para **29.6**). Accordingly, short-term absence from the UK was effective to avoid liability under the chargeable event regime, provided that the gain accrued in a complete year of non-residence.

However, FA 2013 introduced a five-year rule, effective for years of departure from 6 April 2013 (ITTOIA 2005, s 465B). Individuals who are temporarily non-resident (as defined in FA 2013, Part 4, Sch 43) are liable to tax on a chargeable event gain accruing in respect of a policy which was issued prior to the period of non-residence. The tax charge occurs in the year of return to the UK.

Previous non-residence

96.18 Where a chargeable event gain accrues to an individual who has previously been non-UK resident, the gain will be reduced by 'time apportionment relief', under ITTOIA 2005, s 528–528A.

For policies issued before 6 April 2013 and not varied or assigned since that date, the relief applies if the owner of the policy is an individual who has been non-UK resident at any time during the existence of the policy (even if the policy was assigned to him after the commencement of his UK residence). Broadly, the chargeable gain is reduced by A/B, where B is the period in which the policy has been in force and A is the period in which the current policyholder has been non-UK resident.

For policies issued since 6 April 2013, or varied or assigned since then, these rules apply in modified form. Broadly, the chargeable gain is reduced by A/B, where B is the period in which the policy has been held by the individual who is chargeable to tax on the relevant chargeable event, and A is the period in which that individual has been non-UK resident.

Chargeable event certificates (see para **96.42** below) do not factor in time apportionment relief; it is up to any policyholder who is entitled to the relief to recalculate the chargeable event gain and claim the relief in his tax return (see IPTM 3730).

Top-slicing relief

96.19 Top-slicing relief is governed by ITTOIA 2005, ss 535–538. The purpose of the relief, which is only available to individuals, is to mitigate the excess taxation which can result from an individual who would otherwise be a basic rate taxpayer being treated as receiving income in respect of a chargeable event, which in the relevant tax year causes him to be subject to tax at the higher rate. The existence of the relief is in recognition of the fact that the insurance policy tax regime may cause income in respect of policy gains, or deemed policy gains, to be concentrated in a single tax year or a few tax years, causing the applicable income tax rate to be inflated artificially.

The relief does not extend to deemed income under the personal portfolio bond regime which is discussed towards the end of this chapter.

The calculation of the relief is complex. There is an explanation in the Insurance Policy Taxation Manual (IPTM 3830–3850).

Deficiency relief

96.20 Deficiency relief likewise applies only to individuals. Its purpose is to provide a measure of relief if, when a policy terminates, it transpires that the deemed gains which have been charged to tax in respect of previous calculation events have together exceeded the actual gain in the value of the policy. However, as explained below, it is often ineffective in meeting this objective.

The relief applies on the final surrender of the policy, the maturity of the policy or the termination of the policy on the death of the last life assured. Should the computations which are then required give rise to a loss rather than a gain, the individual is given relief against his higher rate tax on general income in that year. The relief is given by way of a tax reduction (ITTOIA 2005, ss 539–541). As with top-slicing relief, the calculation of deficiency relief is complex, but is explained in the Insurance Policy Taxation Manual (IPTM 3860–3880).

Deficiency relief only succeeds in mitigating the disadvantageous tax consequences of large partial surrenders if, in the tax year of termination, the policyholder has other income subject to higher rate tax against which the tax reduction can be used. In many cases, the policyholder does not. If there is insufficient other income in the tax year of termination, there is no statutory ability to carry the relief forward to future tax years or back to previous tax years so that it can be used.

The budget in March 2010 announced proposals to extend corresponding deficiency relief to additional rate tax (see HMRC Technical Note 25 March 2010, [2010] SWT1 1210) but these proposals were abandoned in the June 2010 budget and, at the time of writing, have not been resurrected.

LIABILITY TO TAX: OTHER CASES

UK resident trusts

96.21 Where a policy is held by a UK resident trust, which does not have a living UK resident 'creator', any gain on the policy is chargeable at the trust rate, and assessed on the trustees (ITTOIA 2005, s 467).

This does not apply to policies held in trust since before 17 March 1998 if the 'creator' had died before that date and the policy has not since been varied (FA 1998, Sch 14 para 7).

Non-resident trust or institution

96.22 ITTOIA 2005, s 468 applies if immediately before the chargeable event the policy is held in a non-resident trust in circumstances where the settlor is not liable. It also applies if a foreign institution beneficially owns a share in the rights or if the rights are held for the purposes of a foreign institution. In such case, ITA 2007, ss 720–730 and 731–735 apply on the basis that the gain is income payable to the trustees or institution.

The term 'foreign institution' means a company or other institution resident or domiciled outside the UK (s 468(5)). On the face of it, s 468 draws a distinction between rights owned by the foreign institution beneficially and rights held for its purposes. In the former case s 468 applies only where a share in the rights is so owned, but in the latter case s 468 applies where either a share or all the rights are held (s 468(5)). 'Rights' presumably means rights under the policy. The distinction is not found in the predecessor legislation (TA 1988, s 547) and is curious.

Since the charge is under ITA 2007, ss 720–730 and 731–735, tax liability only arises insofar as the motive defence described in CHAPTER 73 is not in point. Until 5 December 2005, ss 731–735, but not ss 720–730, applied to policy gains, with the result that policy gains accruing to non-resident companies were not taxable on the transferor on an arising basis. The loophole was blocked by FA 2006, Sch 7 para 7.

UK companies

96.23 As noted above, UK resident companies are not within the chargeable event legislation, as life insurance bonds are treated as creditor relationships under the loan relationship rules (CTA 2009, s 562).

JUDICIAL CONSIDERATION

96.24 In recent years there has been a flurry of cases concerning the tax treatment of life insurance bonds, the main emphasis of such cases being on the counter-intuitive and often blatantly unfair outcomes for policyholders who have made large partial surrenders. These cases repay study, not only in terms of what lines of argument may be viable where a policyholder has fallen foul of the regime, but also as a reflection of the growing pressure on the government to reform the life policy tax code. Such pressure comes from a number of sources including the Chartered Institute of Taxation, which has made submissions to the Treasury and HMRC with a view to securing a change of law.

Shanthiratnam

96.25 In *Shanthiratnam v Revenue and Customs Comrs* [2011] UKFTT 360 (TC), the taxpayer held a policy that was divided into segments. He made a partial surrender of all segments in the first insurance year, when the policy was standing at a loss. He was nonetheless deemed to have realised a chargeable event gain equal to about 85% of the proceeds of the surrender.

Acting without legal representation, the taxpayer sought to overturn the assessment of such deemed gain to income tax. His argument was essentially that the chargeable event certificate issued by the life insurance company could not possibly be correct, given that the policy had not increased in value.

Unsurprisingly, that argument was dismissed. The First-tier Tribunal acknowledged the 'extraordinary' and indeed 'frankly ludicrous' tax treatment produced by the legislation and expressed its sympathy with the taxpayer for having fallen into a 'trap' laid by the life policy code. It was noted that the taxpayer could easily, with the benefit of advice, have avoided that trap by making a total surrender of certain of the segments, rather than a partial surrender of all of them. However, that was not what happened.

Downward

96.26 In *Downward v Revenue and Customs Comrs* [2013] UKFTT 517 (TC), the situation was again that the taxpayer held a segmented policy and made a substantial withdrawal in the first insurance year. In ignorance of the implications of doing so, he selected the option of structuring the withdrawal as a partial surrender of all segments, rather than as a full surrender of the required number of segments. He was assessed to tax on a deemed gain representing more than 90% of the proceeds received by him.

In his appeal, he accepted that the assessment was correctly made in accordance with the legislation, but submitted that he had made a mistake in the manner in which he had effected the withdrawal, and that such mistake ought to be capable of correction by the First-tier Tribunal.

The Tribunal concluded that it had no power to re-characterise the partial surrender effected by the taxpayer on the basis of a mistake. This decision was in line with, and based on the reasoning in, the first instance judgment in *Lobler*, discussed below. (However, it would appear from the Upper Tribunal judgment in *Lobler* that *Downward* was wrongly decided.)

Anderson

96.27 In *Anderson v Revenue and Customs Comrs* [2013] UKFTT 126 (TC), [2013] STI 1812, the situation was very like those discussed above. The taxpayer held a number of segmented policies. He elected, apparently in reliance on poor tax advice, to make substantial withdrawals by way of partial surrender of all segments, rather than by full surrender of some. He was subject to income tax on large deemed gains on such partial surrenders, but when the policies were eventually surrendered in full there was little or no overall gain on them. Deficiency relief was claimed, but because the taxpayer had little other income in the tax years in which the policies terminated, the value of that relief was minimal.

The taxpayer's position in the proceedings was that, although he had been correctly assessed to tax in accordance with the letter of the life policy tax code, the result of the application of that code in his case was so contrary to justice and reasonable expectation that the code infringed the Convention for the Protection of Human Rights. Accordingly, it was argued, the life policy code had to be 'interpreted' in a manner which avoided such infringement.

The First-tier Tribunal noted the 'wide margin of appreciation' enjoyed by the State in taxation matters, and the fact that legislative decisions with respect to the exercise of taxing rights generally fall within that margin unless they are 'manifestly without reasonable foundation'. Its view was that the life policy tax code did not violate the taxpayer's human rights. This was primarily on the basis that there was no obligation on the taxpayer to invest in life insurance bonds, and although the life policy tax code may have made such bonds an unsuitable investment in his case, they can be attractive investments for other taxpayers or in other situations. Accordingly, the taxpayer's appeal was dismissed.

However, the Tribunal readily conceded that the tax treatment of partial surrenders represents 'a major fault in the system', 'which penalises the unwary or ill-advised, often with quite disproportionate consequences', and that deficiency relief is in most cases 'a wholly inadequate remedy for the disproportionate consequences of a large part surrender'.

It also noted a further possible ground for challenge to the life policy tax code, which it did not consider further because it had not been raised by the taxpayer. It was suggested that the deficiency relief rules might be incompatible with the EU Treaty right to free movement of capital, on the basis that by failing to give relief at the basic rate, those rules appear to discriminate against the holders of policies issued by non-UK insurers, compared to those who take policies issued by insurers resident in the UK.

Lobler

96.28 By contrast with the rather depressing cases above, *Lobler v Revenue and Customs Comrs* [2013] UKFTT 141 (TC), [2013] SWTI 1777 seems to be cause for optimism about the position for individuals who may in future fall into the large partial surrender trap.

Like the individuals discussed above, Mr Lobler held a segmented policy. He invested around US$1.4 million into the policy and then, over the course of the first few insurance years, withdrew nearly the entire value of the policy, although the withdrawals fell short of a complete surrender. In ignorance of the tax consequences of doing so, he chose to effect the withdrawals by way of partial surrenders of all of the segments. As a result he was assessed to tax on around US$560,000 on the withdrawals, despite having realised no commercial gain. As in other cases discussed above, deficiency relief became available when the policy was subsequently surrendered in full, but the relief was useless to Mr Lobler as he had little income against which the tax reduction could be set.

Facing bankruptcy by reason of the above assessment, he appealed on the basis of mistake and a violation of his human rights.

The First-tier Tribunal described the assessment on Mr Lobler as an 'outrageously unfair result'. It considered whether the document whereby Mr Lobler had elected to make 'horizontal' partial surrenders could be rectified, but concluded that it could not. This conclusion was based on the principle that rectification for bilateral mistake is only available where two parties have entered into an instrument with a common intention as to its content, but the actual content differed from what was intended. In this case no intention at all could be ascribed to the insurance company.

The human rights argument, also, was dismissed, on various bases. These included the fact that, if it was found that the life policy tax code did contravene the Convention for the Protection of Human Rights, the Tribunal's duty would be to construe the legislation in accordance with the Convention 'so far as it is possible to do so'. The Tribunal's view was that the life policy tax code is so prescriptive that a conforming construction would simply not be possible.

Mr Lobler appealed. In the Upper Tribunal, it was argued on behalf of Mr Lobler that the First-tier Tribunal had erred in law in determining that the remedy of rectification for mistake was unavailable. It was argued, and accepted by the Upper Tribunal, that this was not a case which required a finding of a mutual mistake on the part of the policyholder and the insurer. The instructions to the insurer to effect partial surrenders were unilateral acts by Mr Lobler. As such, rectification was available provided that there was a mistake by Mr Lobler, and its gravity was such that it would be unconscionable to leave the mistaken act uncorrected (applying *Pitt v Holt* [2013] STC 1148; see CHAPTER 36).

As rectification was awarded, it was not strictly necessary for the Tribunal to consider the human rights arguments, but it did so in recognition of the public interest in the issue. As in *Anderson*, it was held that the question of whether the legislation violated human rights turns on whether that legislation can be said to be 'devoid of reasonable foundation'. Proudman J considered that 'the scales tip, only just, in favour of reasonable foundation'. Her reasoning was that although the calculations required in relation to partial surrenders produce results which can seem very unfair, the amount of tax payable on such surrenders is, with knowledge of how the rules work, predictable. There is no scope for 'arbitrary interference by the public authorities' in determination of the tax liability, such as would clearly engage the Convention.

PROPOSED REFORM

96.29 In light of the series of controversial cases mentioned above, at Budget 2016 the government announced its intention to change the tax rules applicable to excess events, ie part surrenders or assignments in excess of the 5% allowance. The intention is to introduce a regime which avoids charges which are disproportionate to the policy's underlying economic gains. A consultation was released in April 2016 and closed in July 2016.

The consultation suggested three options for reforming the regime:

(i) Taxing the economic gain – the current 5% tax-deferred allowance would be retained but the regime would bring into charge a proportionate fraction of any underlying economic gain whenever an amount in excess of 5% was withdrawn.

(ii) 100% allowance – the current cumulative annual 5% allowances would be converted into a lifetime 100% tax-deferred allowance. Under this option no gain would arise until all of the premium(s) paid have been withdrawn, after which all withdrawals would be taxed in full.

(iii) Deferral of excessive gains – this would maintain the current method for calculating gains. If the gain exceeds a predetermined amount of the premium (the consultation suggests a cumulative 3% for each year since the policy started) the excess would not be immediately charged to tax. Instead it would be deferred until the next part surrender or part assignment. The gain arising from the next part surrender or part assignment would be increased by the amount of the deferred gain from the earlier event. If this total gain exceeded the predetermined amount, then the excess part of it would be deferred again (and so on). On maturity or full surrender the policy gain would be calculated by deducting premiums and gains (whether deferred or not) from total policy withdrawals. Any deferred gains would be charged to tax. However if the calculation on maturity did not result in a gain, the deferred gains would be reduced by the amount by which premiums and earlier gains exceed withdrawals (a policy deficiency).

At the time of writing, there has been no indication from the government regarding the approach it is minded to take.

PERSONAL PORTFOLIO BONDS

96.30 The tax charge on personal portfolio bonds is set out in ITTOIA 2005, ss 515–527. The legislation uses the concept of the insurance year as defined in ITTOIA 2005, s 499, ie the year starting on the issuance of the policy and each subsequent year starting on the anniversary thereof.

HMRC issued guidance notes giving their view on practical issues shortly after the legislation was first enacted. These guidance notes are now contained within the Insurance Policyholder Taxation Manual (IPTM), at paras 7700–7835.

Definition

96.31 ITTOIA 2005, s 516 defines a personal portfolio bond as one where the following conditions are met:

(i) The benefits under the policy are determined in whole or in part by reference to the value of some form of property, or by reference to an index; and

(ii)   The property or index may be selected by or on behalf of the policyholder or a person connected with him or by a person acting on behalf of either or both of them.

Permitted self-selection

96.32 ITTOIA 2005, ss 517–521 make exceptions for certain types of self-selection.

An index to which policy benefits are linked may be self-selected if it is the RPI or some similar UK or foreign index or if it is a published index of share prices listed on a recognised stock exchange.

Investments may also be self-selected if they comprise any of the following:

- Authorised unit trusts;
- Investment trusts;
- Open-ended investment companies;
- Foreign collective investment schemes, the term collective investment scheme bearing the same meaning as in the Financial Services and Markets Act 2000 (s 235);
- Cash, unless acquired with the purpose of realising a gain on its disposal; and
- Property which the insurance company has appropriated to an 'internal linked fund' (see below).

Self-selection of an index or investments does however have to satisfy one other condition. The index or investment must be available for all policyholders of the life insurance company or, if its availability is limited to a class of policyholders, the terms of membership of the class must be published by the company and the class must not be limited to connected persons (ITTOIA 2005, s 519).

At Budget 2016, the government announced that it would review the property categories listed above and released a consultation paper suggesting that three additional types of investment vehicle may be included in the permitted property categories: real estate investment trusts (UK or foreign equivalents), overseas equivalents of UK approved investment trusts and authorised contractual schemes.

Internal linked funds

96.33 The fact that a policyholder may select investments if appropriated to an 'internal linked fund' significantly reduces the ambit of the rules on personal portfolio bonds. 'Internal linked fund' has the same meaning here as it does in rules for insurers made by the Financial Conduct Authority (ITTOIA 2005, s 520(4)). In essence, such a 'fund' is an account to which assets of the life insurance company have been appropriated, and which are identified in the company's books as assets whose value determines the surrender value of a policy which is linked to the account (see IPTM 7740). Accordingly, whether investments fall within the 'internal linked fund' exemption is fundamentally a book-keeping question.

Typically, the life insurance company's terms will require a certain minimum investment into the bond for assets to be appropriated to an 'internal linked fund', and it is common for the kinds of asset that can be selected within the account to be rather restricted for policyholders who have made only this minimum investment. It is common for the investment restrictions to fall away progressively as greater amounts are invested. As noted above, for self-selection rights to be restricted to a narrow class of policyholders is permitted, provided that the conditions for eligibility to the right to self-select (eg in terms of amounts that must be invested into the bond) are published by the life insurance company, and the members of the class are unconnected.

Self-selection

96.34 Even if the exceptions listed above do not apply, it is to be stressed that a policy is not a personal portfolio bond unless the policyholder has the power to select the underlying investments. As noted above, a power of selection vested in a person connected to the policyholder counts as exercisable by the policyholder, as does a power exercisable by a person acting on behalf of the policyholder (ITTOIA 2005, s 516(4)).

In general HMRC accept that broker managed funds do not give the policyholder power to select, for in managing the investments the broker is acting on behalf of the life insurance company. For the same reason, management of a linked portfolio by an investment adviser does not amount to self-selection. This is so even if the adviser is selected by the policyholder, provided the selection is from a menu of advisers offered by the life insurance company. However, the broker or adviser must not be a mere 'conduit' for the policyholder (see IPTM paras 7725 and 7730).

A point to be stressed is that it is the *ability* to select which is crucial. A policy is thus potentially caught if the policyholder is entitled to self-select but has so far not availed himself of the opportunity.

Timing

96.35 The test of whether a policy is a personal portfolio bond is applied in each insurance year. A policy is caught if it is within the definition at the end of the year (ITTOIA 2005, s 515(1)). The charge can therefore be avoided by means of a variation of the policy terms before the end of the insurance year.

The gain

96.36 If a policy is a personal portfolio bond, a gain is treated as accruing in each insurance year. In the first year the gain is 15% of the premium. In the second year the gain is 15% of the premium plus 15% of the gain charged in the previous year, ie 15% of 115% of the premium (17.25% of the premium).

In subsequent years the gain is 15% of the premium plus 15% of the amount of the gain charged in each previous year since the inception of the policy. In each case the amount to which the 15% is applied is reduced by any excess in the prior insurance year or any earlier year (ITTOIA 2005, ss 522–524).

This formula is draconian in its effect, in that the deemed gain is cumulatively rolled up, and has no relationship whatsoever to the performance of the investments 'wrapped' in the policy. In computing the gain in previous years for policies existing at the start of the regime, it is necessary to go back to the inception of the policy rather than simply to the first insurance year ending after 6 April 2000, the date when the regime started.

The charge to tax

96.37 The gain is treated as a chargeable event occurring at the end of the insurance year (ITTOIA 2005, s 525).

No such chargeable event can occur in the final insurance year of the policy. Because of the rule which can cause the final insurance year to be extended where it would otherwise begin and end in the same tax year (see para 96.3 above), a surrender of a policy in full can achieve avoidance of two separate tax charges under s 525.

All gains charged under s 525 are deductible as calculation event gains in computing any gain when the policy matures or is subject to a complete surrender or assignment for money or money's worth (ITTOIA 2005, s 491(2)). However, such gains are not deducted in determining whether there is an excess on the occurrence of a calculation event, eg a partial surrender or partial assignment for money or money's worth (ITTOIA 2005, s 507(4)).

The practical result of these rules is to give personal portfolio bonds an unacceptable tax cost if held by a UK resident individual or by an offshore trust with a living, UK resident settlor. Such bonds held by other offshore trusts or in a foreign company or other institution do not suffer the immediate tax cost, but the relevant income under ITA 2007, ss 731–735 is disproportionately inflated.

Transitional provisions

96.38 The definition of a personal portfolio bond is narrowed in the case of any policy which was issued before 17 March 1998 and has not been varied since 16 July 1998 so as to increase the benefits or extend the term. In such a case, the policy is not a personal portfolio bond if in addition to the range permitted generally it allows self-selection within quoted shares or securities (Personal Portfolio Bonds (Tax) Regulations 1999 (SI 1999/1029), reg 3). A policy which does not meet even this wider rule could be varied so as to come within it before the end of the first insurance year beginning after 6 April 1999. But such a variation was only effective if since the inception of the policy or if later since 6 April 1994, the self-selection had in fact been within the investments thereby permitted.

Immigrants

96.39 The personal portfolio bond regime is a hazard for any individual who has invested in a single-premium life insurance policy while resident outside the UK, and has subsequently become UK resident. The reason is that unless the policy has been designed with the UK tax legislation in mind, it is highly unlikely that it will constrain the policyholder's rights to select investments to the extent which is sufficient to avoid personal portfolio bond status. The problem for immigrants holding personal portfolio bonds is compounded by the fact that policy gains do not attract the remittance basis.

A measure of relief is given in that if a variation would have been effective under the transitional rule described above, the variation may be made at any time during the first insurance year after immigration (SI 1999/1029 reg 3(5)). This applies provided the policyholder was not UK resident on 17 March 1998 and has not been so between then and immigration.

Scope for challenge: human rights law

96.40 In imposing tax liabilities on policyholders which are completely unrelated to any economic gains, the personal portfolio bond regime is confiscatory in its effect. It may well be arguable that the regime violates the right to peaceful enjoyment of possessions.

However, as noted above in relation to the treatment of partial surrenders (see para 96.28), there are significant difficulties in arguing that the regime is overridden by human rights law. One is that the regime must be found to be 'devoid of reasonable foundation' for the Convention for the Protection of Human Rights to be engaged. It appears that a major consideration (although perhaps not the only one) in determining that issue is whether the regime is certain, or conversely allows scope for 'arbitrary interference by the public authorities'. Here the regime is entirely certain and gives no discretion to the tax authority. A further possible obstacle is that it may, in practice, not be possible to construe the personal portfolio bond regime in a manner that is consistent with the Convention, due to the highly prescriptive nature of the regime.

Scope for challenge: EU law

96.41 For the reasons noted above, the force of the personal portfolio bond regime falls, in practice, almost exclusively on individuals who have taken out policies while resident overseas; particularly in continental Europe where the use of such policies is very widespread. A UK resident individual taking out a single-premium insurance policy is likely to avoid the regime, because provided that the life insurance company is aware of his UK resident status, he is likely to be offered a policy tailored to UK resident policyholders. That policy may in practice give him investment selection rights that are very similar to the rights held by a policyholder under a personal portfolio bond, eg by virtue of the 'internal linked fund' exemption. In substance, there may be little difference between a policy that qualifies as a personal portfolio bond and a policy that does not.

The fact that the regime chiefly penalises individuals who have taken out policies while resident abroad raises obvious questions regarding its compatibility with EU law. It is possible that the regime contravenes Article 21 of the EU Treaty, concerning the free movement of citizens (see para **106.35**). However, it is not clear that this is so, as a well-advised or well-informed immigrant to the UK who holds a bond that will qualify as a personal portfolio bond under the UK tax rules can avoid penal taxation under the regime, by surrendering it shortly after the commencement of residence in the UK (relying on time apportionment relief) and, if desired, investing the proceeds in a bond which has been tailored for UK residents. The law does, therefore, allow nationals of other countries to avoid any discrimination. Nevertheless, the broad effect of the legislation is undoubtedly discriminatory.

Whatever the position may be under the Convention and the EU Treaty, there is a clear need for the current rules to be replaced by a more rational and proportionate regime.

CHARGEABLE EVENT REPORTING

96.42 Generally any non-UK resident life insurance company which derives a more than minimal amount of its revenue from UK resident policyholders is required to report the occurrence of chargeable events, and the amounts of resultant chargeable event gains, not only to the relevant policyholders but also to HMRC, under the Overseas Insurers (Tax Representatives) Regulations 1999, SI 1999/881. The default position is that the insurer must appoint a 'tax representative' in the UK which will then issue chargeable event certificates on the insurer's behalf.

The insurer may be released from the requirement to appoint a 'tax representative' if it undertakes to issue chargeable event certificates to policyholders and HMRC itself. A release may also be obtained if the insurer is resident in an EEA member state in which there existed on 17 March 1998 a criminal sanction for the release of information about policyholders to a foreign tax authority, and such sanction remains in force. This exemption is currently relied on by certain Luxembourg resident insurers. Luxembourg's banking secrecy law is expected to remain in force until 2017.

Section V:

Compliance

Chapter 97

PENALTIES AND THE REQUIREMENT TO CORRECT

INTRODUCTION

97.1 Ever since the first edition in 1986, this book has always been premised on full disclosure to HMRC. Tax planning ceases to be tax planning and becomes evasion if its efficacy relies on non-disclosure or misinformation. Given that premise, it has been unnecessary to include discussion of compliance issues and the sanctions represented by penalties and the criminal law. But now a number of factors mean this forbearance is no longer justified, of which four may be mentioned.

Purposive construction

97.2 The first factor is what many perceive to be a significant shifting of the goalposts by the judiciary. The shift goes under the generic name of purposive construction and, to many eyes at least, crossed a significant threshold in *UBS AG v HMRC* [2016] STC 934. Here the Supreme Court delivered purposive construction by inserting words in the legislation at issue. If this approach is taken in other cases, past tax planning arrangements that were thought when entered into to be lawful and effective may now turn out not to be so. A further point is that purposive construction results in uncertainty, as views can and do differ as to the purpose of legislation.

Complexity

97.3 A second factor is the sheer complexity and, in some cases, downright obscurity, of legislation directed at offshore structures. As chapters elsewhere in this book show, certainty of meaning is difficult to achieve. Quite apart from that, even the best overseas trust and company providers find it difficult to avoid inadvertent mistakes. The Liechtenstein Disclosure Facility and other recent disclosure facilities have brought many past mistakes to light and enabled many matters to be resolved. But some did not avail themselves of these generous opportunities.

Differential penalty regimes

97.4 The third factor is that, as explained below (para **97.16**) the current penalty regime is one of sheep and goats insofar as jurisdictions are concerned. Errors involving the sheep are mostly treated in the same way as those involving purely domestic matters. But the goats are more harshly treated, in some cases much more so. Given the risk of error, any tax planning strategy should factor in the penalty implications of using a particular jurisdiction if something goes wrong.

Extra territoriality

97.5 The fourth and final factor is the growing extra territoriality of UK tax. It has always been the case that liability can attach to the UK source income and UK situs assets of offshore structures and no reputable overseas provider now seeks to ignore such liabilities in the manner that was commonplace as little as twenty years ago. But recently non-residents have been subjected to ATED and non-resident CGT (see CHAPTERS **64** and **66**) and in 2017 there is the prospect of corporate structures being looked through for IHT purposes as respects UK residential properties. All these provisions have compliance implications, and scope for error and uncertainty.

THE COMPLIANCE FRAMEWORK

97.6 The penalty rules interlock with the UK's basic compliance framework. This differs as between income tax and capital gains tax on the one hand and IHT on the other.

Income tax and CGT

97.7 Taxpayers are under three principal obligations as respects income tax and CGT:

(1)   To complete a self-assessment return for each tax year if required by HMRC to do so (TMA 1970, ss 8 (individuals) and 8A (trustees)).
(2)   To notify HMRC of chargeability if HMRC have not required completion of a return (TMA 1970, s 7).
(3)   To file the return and ensure it is correct and complete to the best of the taxpayer's knowledge (TMA 1970, ss 8(2) and 8A(2)).

The return has to be filed before 31 January following the end of the tax year. The taxpayer has a year within which he can amend the return and HMRC have an enquiry window of one year within which they can initiate an enquiry. In general this enquiry window starts on the date on which the return is filed.

Should the enquiry window have closed, HMRC can only claim additional tax if the conditions for a discovery assessment within TMA 1970 s 29 are made out. These conditions are stringent, at least in theory, in that a discovery assessment cannot be made if the taxpayer's original assessment was made in accordance with practice then generally prevailing (s 29(2)). More generally a discovery assessment is also precluded unless what has been called a conduct condition or an officer condition is met (s 29(3); *Hargreaves v Revenue and Customs Comrs* [2016] EWCA Civ 174, [2016] 1 WLR 2981, [2016] STC 1652, para 14). The conduct condition is that the error in the original self-assessment was careless or deliberate. The officer condition is that a hypothetical HMRC officer, having regard to the information made available to him, could not reasonably be expected to have been aware of the error in the return when the enquiry window closed (s 29(5)).

There is much case-law on the officer condition and its details are beyond the scope of this book (see for example *Langham v Veltema* [2004] STC 544 and *Hargreaves v Revenue and Customs Comrs* [2016] EWCA Civ 174, [2016] 1 WLR 2981, [2016] STC 1652). Where a return does not follow HMRC's published view of the law, HMRC consider a simple comment so stating, which clearly identifies the point at issue, precludes the officer condition. (SP 2/06 paras 18 and 19).

Assuming the conditions for a discovery assessment are made out, strict time limits apply, in that normally such an assessment has to be raised within four years of the end of the tax year to which it relates (TMA 1970, s 34). This limit is extended to six years if the taxpayer has been careless and to 20 years if the loss of tax was brought about deliberately. The 20-year limit also applies where the taxpayer has failed to notify chargeability under s 7 or where what is charged should have been notified under DOTAS (TMA 1970, s 36).

Inheritance tax

97.8 Inheritance tax is subject to different procedural rules, a key difference being that the obligations to file and report are governed by events rather than tax years. In general IHT accounts have to be filed within one year of the end of the month in which the reported event took place. But in some instances, most notably the relevant property regime, the time limit is six months (IHTA 1984, s 216).

Should the chargeable party fail to file IHT accounts in respect of a given event, HMRC cannot recover any tax due if more than twenty years have elapsed (IHTA 1984, s 240(7)). But this cut-off does not apply if the failure to report the event was deliberate. Provided an account has been filed, HMRC cannot in general claim further tax once four years have elapsed. But as with income tax and CGT, this is extended to six years in cases of carelessness, and twenty years where loss of tax has been brought about deliberately (IHTA 1984, s 240(3)–(5)).

Careless and deliberate conduct

97.9 As will be apparent, careless and deliberate conduct are key concepts in determining whether extended time limits apply. They are also key concepts in the penalty regime discussed below.

Carelessness is defined as failure to take reasonable care (TMA 1970, s 118(5); IHTA 1984, s 240A(2)). The concept also extends to failure to bring an inaccuracy to HMRC's attention as and when it is discovered (ss 118(6) and 240A(3)).

What constitutes deliberate behaviour is not defined. But a loss of tax brought about by a deliberate inaccuracy in a document supplied to HMRC is expressly included (ss 118(7) and 240A(4)). A particular example of deliberate behaviour is not telling HMRC about an innocent or careless error if and when that error is identified. This is not expressly provided for in the legislation but follows by necessary implication.

REQUIREMENT TO CORRECT

97.10 It is likely that FA 2017 will see the imposition on taxpayers of obligations to positively look for and identify past non-compliance. At the time of writing this proposal is being consulted on and goes under the generic name Requirement to Correct (HMRC consultation document 'Tackling offshore tax evasion: A requirement to correct'). If enacted, it will require taxpayers to identify and correct past tax errors relating to offshore matters. The corrective action will have to be taken in a period which will start on 6 April 2017 and end on 30 September 2018. 30 September 2018 is the date by which the first reports from late adopting territories under the Common Reporting Standard will be received by HMRC.

The Requirement to Correct is being accompanied by a new Worldwide Disclosure Facility which opened on 5 September 2016 (see HMRC guidance 'Worldwide Disclosure Facility: make a disclosure' issued on 5 September 2016). Another aspect of the same thrust towards transparency is the obligation on professional advisers to notify clients of HMRC's impending receipt of information under the Common Reporting Standard and the availability of worldwide disclosure facility (the International Tax Compliance (Client Notification) Regulations 2016 (SI 2016/899). The notifications must be made before 31 August 2017.

INTEREST AND LATE PAYMENT PENALTIES

97.11 The penalties discussed later in this chapter must be distinguished from interest on tax paid late and penalties for failing to pay tax on time.

Interest

97.12 The general rule is that income tax and CGT carry late payment interest from the date on which the tax is due and payable (FA 2009, s 101). But this rule is qualified where the tax results from an amendment to the taxpayer's self-assessment or a discovery assessment. In such cases the interest runs from when the tax would have been due and payable had the taxpayer self-assessed it correctly (FA 2009, Sch 53, para 3). The interest is simple interest, not compounded.

Interest on outstanding IHT normally starts to run six months after the end of the month in which the event occasioning the charge occurred (IHTA 1984, s 233). It should be kept in mind that the time limits for recovering unpaid IHT are more extended than those applicable to income tax and CGT (see para 97.8 above). In such cases the interest element of any payment can be significant, particularly if the liability dates back to before 2009 when interest rates were higher. Interest on tax runs regardless of whether the taxpayer was at fault.

Penalties for late payment

97.13 Penalties for failure to pay income tax or CGT on time become payable if the tax is not paid within thirty days of the date when it should be paid (FA 2009, Sch 56, para 1). The penalty is initially 5%, increasing by a further 5% after five months and another 5% after eleven months (Sch 56, para 3).

In contrast to interest, the date on which the tax should have been paid is when it is in fact due and payable and not when it should have been self-assessed. Thus a late payment penalty only arises under a discovery assessment if the tax is unpaid more than 60 days after the notice of assessment is issued (FA 2009, Sch 56, para 1, table, entry 19).

Currently the late payment regime does not apply to IHT.

PENALTIES FOR ERROR

97.14 The principal penalty regime for misconduct is that imposed by FA 2007, Sch 24. It applies to errors in tax returns, IHT accounts and other documents supplied to HMRC (Sch 24, para 1). It also applies where the taxpayer becomes aware HMRC have made a mistake and does not disclose the mistake (Sch 24, para 2).

Culpability

97.15 The penalty is a percentage of the tax that would have been lost, but for discovery of the error. The primary determinant of what the percentage is turns on the level of taxpayer culpability (Sch 24 para 3), there being three levels, namely careless conduct, deliberate conduct without concealment, and deliberate conduct with the aggravating factor of concealment. Concealment connotes arrangements to conceal the inaccuracy such as submitting false evidence.

There is no level of culpability representing error which is neither deliberate nor careless. This is because a penalty cannot be charged unless the inaccuracy at issue was careless or deliberate (Sch 24, paras 1(3) and 2(1)(b)).

Penalties are recovered by assessment and there is a right of appeal to the First-tier tribunal (Sch 24, para 15).

Territorial categories

97.16 Since 6 April 2011 there has been a further determinant of the level of penalty. This turns on what territorial category the inaccuracy falls into. Currently there are three categories, but changes made by FA 2015 introduce a fourth category, category 0 (FA 2015, Sch 20). At the time of writing this is not yet in force.

Once the FA 2015 change is in force the territorial categories are as follows:

0   Domestic matters plus offshore matters and offshore transfers involving a category 0 territory.
1   Offshore matters and transfers involving a category 1 territory.
2   Offshore matters and transfers involving a category 2 territory.
3   Offshore matters and transfers involving a category 3 territory.

Until the 2015 changes are in force, there is no category 0, domestic matters are in category 1 and no account is taken of offshore transfers. The penalties for carelessness are 30% of the tax in category 0, 37.5% in category 1 (30% until the 2015 changes are in force) 45% in category 2 and 60% in category 3. The equivalents for deliberate and unconcealed error are 70% category 0, 87.5% category 1, 105% category 2 and 140% category 3. It will be noted that the penalties for deliberate error can exceed the tax, and this is still more so where there is concealment.

Offshore matters and transfers

97.17 The term 'offshore' is something of a misnomer as it refers to anywhere outside the UK, regardless of whether or not offshore in the strict sense of the term. A matter is 'offshore' if the potentially lost tax is charged on or by reference to any of the following (Sch 24, para 4A(4)):

(1)   income arising from a source outside the UK;
(2)   assets situate or held outside the UK; or
(3)   activities wholly or mainly carried on outside the UK.

The reference to where assets are held as well as their situs means UK situs assets are caught if owned in a non-UK structure.

Once the 2015 changes are in force, offshore transfers will be viewed in the same way as offshore matters (Sch 24, para 4AA). To determine whether there has been an offshore transfer of income or gains it is necessary to focus on under-declared UK income or gains. Such income or gains count as comprised in offshore transfer if the income or the proceeds of the disposal are received or subsequently transferred outside the UK before the incorrect return or other document is filed. So too with IHT, there is an offshore transfer if assets which have been subject to an IHT disposition are removed outside the UK.

In practice multiple territories may be involved in offshore matters or transfers. In such a case, the level of penalty is governed by that in the highest category (Sch 24, paras 4A(6) and 4AA(6)).

The categories of territory

97.18 The categories of territory are designated by statutory instrument (Sch 24, para 21A). Currently categories 1 and 3 are listed, and every territory not mentioned in either list is in category 2. Once the 2015 changes are in force, category 0 territories will be listed as well.

In deciding which category a territory goes into, the Treasury must have regard to whether the UK has information exchange arrangements with the territory and, assuming there are such arrangements, their nature. Currently category 1 territories include those which exchange information under the EU Savings Directive and thus include Guernsey, the Isle of Man, Liechtenstein and the Cayman Islands (Penalties Offshore Income etc (Designation of Territories) Order 2011, SI 2011/976 as amended by SI 2013/1618). Once the 2015 changes are in force category 0 will comprise territories signed up to the Common Reporting Standard (Budget Press Release 'Strengthening Penalties for Offshore Compliance', 18 March 2015, reproduced [2015] SWTI 1170). Category 0 will thus include all three Crown Dependencies, Bermuda and the Cayman Islands.

The question of which category a given offshore jurisdiction is in is important, for the most favourable ranking, category 0 once the 2015 changes are in force, will be treated in the same way as the UK itself so far as careless errors are concerned. In other words the penalty regime will not in this respect discriminate against offshore jurisdictions per se, but merely those that do not deliver the appropriate level of information exchange. But for deliberate errors the maximum permissible reduction for category 0 territories will be less than for purely domestic matters (Sch 24, para 10A as inserted by FA 2016, Sch 21, para 4).

Reduction of penalty for disclosure

97.19 Where the taxpayer discloses the irregularity the penalty otherwise payable must be reduced (Sch 24, para 10). In general the reduction cannot be by more than half the percentage penalty otherwise applicable, but where the disclosure is unprompted the reduction is greater and in the case of careless rather than deliberate error, the reduction can be to nil.

A disclosure only counts as unprompted where the taxpayer approaches HMRC before he has reason to suppose HMRC are investigating the matter (Sch 24, para 9(2)). But even if the disclosure is prompted it counts as a disclosure providing HMRC are given full details of the irregularities and access to records (Sch 24, para 9(1)).

The quality of the disclosure governs how extensive the reduction is (Sch 24, para 9(3)). The term 'quality' includes the timing, nature and extent of the disclosure (Sch 24, para 9(3)). The reference to timing means, at least in HMRC's view, that an unprompted careless disclosure must always carry a 10% penalty if the matter is more than three years old (HMRC guidance 'Dealing with HMRC – offshore disclosure facilities' as updated 5 September 2016).

In addition to the mandatory percentage reductions, HMRC is given a general discretion to reduce penalties should special circumstances obtain (Sch 24, para 11). This discretion is exercisable by the tribunal should the taxpayer appeal (Sch 24, para 17(3)).

OTHER MISCONDUCT

97.20 Penalties may also be levied if a taxpayer fails to file a return when required or if he fails to notify chargeability should he be liable to tax and not have been sent a return.

Failure to file

97.21 The penalties for failure to file are governed by the penalty date, which is the day after the deadline for filing the return (FA 2009, Sch 55, para 1(4)). The basic penalty is £100 (Sch 55, para 3). But the penalty can be increased to £300 if more than three months elapse from the penalty date and after six months it is 5% of any tax due under the missing return (FA 2009, Sch 55, para 5).

If the failure lasts for more than 12 months after the penalty date, a further penalty of 5% of the tax can be levied. But should the non-compliance be deliberate, much greater percentage penalties are charged, the percentage being governed by the same territory-based categories as apply to errors. Thus in a category 3 offshore matter, the maximum penalty is 200% of the tax if the failure is concealed as well as deliberate, or 140% if it is not concealed. Even in category 0, the percentages are 100% and 70% respectively. There are the same reductions for disclosure, greater if the disclosure is unprompted rather than prompted (FA 2000, Sch 55, para 15).

Failure to notify

97.22 The failure to notify penalties are significant for offshore trustees, for often there can be inadvertent failures to identify UK tax exposure, such as can occur where a trust with UK beneficiaries is in receipt of UK source income (see para **64.8**).

Failure to notify penalties arise if the taxpayer should have notified HMRC of liability to income tax or CGT, but has failed to do so. Under TMA 1970, s 7, the notification must be given during the notification period, which ends six months after the end of the tax year concerned.

Should there be failure to notify the penalty is a percentage of the tax due, the percentages being the same as apply to errors in the return, and thus being governed by whether the failure is deliberate and/or concealed and by the territory categories. In contrast to error, the failure to notify penalties apply even if the failure is innocent, ie not tainted by careless or deliberate conduct. But in such a case, the taxpayer is exonerated from the penalty if he can show reasonable excuse for his failure (Sch 41, para 20).

As with error penalties, disclosure reduces the level of penalty (Sch 41, para 13). But a reduction to zero is achieved only if the failure is regularised within 12 months of whenever the applicable tax should have been paid.

IHT has a different regime for failure to notify. Here the maximum penalty is £3,000 (IHTA 1984, s 245).

SPECIFIC OFFSHORE PENALTIES

97.23 The 2015 and 2016 Finance Acts have seen more severe penalty regimes targeted on offshore matters and transfers, albeit that many of the relevant changes are not yet in force. One of the changes relates to enablers and is described in para **97.29** below, and another reduces the discount given on deliberate penalties where there is disclosure (see para **97.18**). Two further changes have brought in asset-related penalties and penalties for offshore asset moves. The latter, but not the former, is not yet in force and a further still more draconian regime may be brought in under the Requirement to Correct proposal.

As with the penalty regime generally, the use of the term 'offshore' is a misnomer. In essence the regimes are xenophobic rather than targeted on traditional offshore jurisdictions.

Offshore asset moves

97.24 The legislation targeting offshore asset moves is in FA 2015, Sch 21 and came into force on 26 March 2015 (Sch 21, para 9(1)). It comes into play if a penalty is levied under the rules described above in paras **97.14** to **97.22** (Sch 21, para 1(2)) and the error or misconduct giving rise to the penalty was deliberate. If that condition is met, Sch 21 is engaged if there is a relevant offshore asset move and a purpose test is satisfied.

The purpose test requires HMRC to establish two points (para 1(4)):

(a)   one of the main purposes of the asset move was to prevent or delay HMRC's discovery of a potential loss of tax; and
(b)   the deliberate misconduct penalty relates to the same loss of tax.

The key concept is that of the relevant offshore asset move. This concept divides the world into two classes of territory, namely specified territories which are 'good' and non-specified territories which are 'bad'. The specified territories are listed in the Offshore Asset Moves Penalty (Specified Territories) Regulations 2015 (SI 2015/866). They comprise all the territories normally seen as 'good' in tax terms, including EU Member States and, more significantly, the British Overseas Territories, the Crown Dependencies and Liechtenstein.

A relevant offshore asset move occurs should the person subject to the original deliberate error penalty be the beneficial owner of an asset. There are three categories of asset move.

The first two entail a move from a specified territory to a non-specified territory, one type of move being a move of the asset itself and the other a change in the residence of the person who holds the asset (Sch 21, para 4(1)(a)(b)). The third type of asset move is more general and does not, on the face of it, entail a move to a specified territory at all (Sch 21, para 4(1)(c)). This head catches situations in which there is merely a change in the arrangements for the ownership of the asset.

An asset move is potentially caught if it occurs in the tax year to which the original deliberate misconduct penalty relates or at any subsequent time (Sch

21, para 5). The asset move penalty is equal to 50% of the original misconduct penalty, and so is less if that penalty is reduced. There are no separate rules enabling the asset move penalty itself to be reduced.

The curious feature about Sch 21 is that it only operates if the person in receipt of the deliberate misconduct penalty is the beneficial owner of the asset in question (Sch 21, para 4(1)). Further, he or it has to be beneficial owner after the asset move as well as before it. The term 'beneficial ownership' is not defined and so might be expected to bear its normal legal meaning of equitable ownership rather than mere legal or nominee ownership. If so, Sch 21 is of limited ambit and does not catch assets held through trusts and companies unless the trust or company is itself the person subject to the original deliberate misconduct penalty.

Schedule 21 applies only if the offshore asset move is after 26 March 2015, but the original liability can have accrued before then (Sch 21, para 9).

Asset-based penalties

97.25 The legislation providing for asset-based penalties is in FA 2016, Sch 22. The date on which it comes into force has yet to be appointed (FA 2016, s 165(2)).

As with offshore asset moves, the trigger is a deliberate misconduct penalty (Sch 22, para 2). Such penalty must be one imposed in respect of an offshore matter or an offshore transfer and must relate to IHT, CGT or asset-based income tax. Asset-based income tax is defined by reference to a list of provisions (Sch 22, para 13) but is essentially tax on investment income.

Should these conditions be met an additional asset-based penalty is exigible. The amount of this penalty cannot be more than 10% of the value of the asset being penalised (Sch 22, para 7) and in many circumstances it is less. In particular there is reduction where the person being penalised discloses and cooperates (Sch 22, para 8). The extent of such reduction is to be governed by regulations.

Rules determine which asset is used in determining the asset-based penalty. If the misconduct being penalised relates to CGT, the asset is the asset disposed of, and if the tax is IHT it is the asset subject to the IHT disposition (Sch 22, paras 11 and 12). With income tax the general rule is that the asset is the asset giving rise to the asset-based income (Sch 22, para 13).

An asset-based penalty cannot be charged unless the tax loss penalised by the original deliberate misconduct penalty exceeds £25,000 (Sch 22, para 4). The asset-based penalty itself cannot exceed more than ten times that tax loss (Sch 22, para 7(1)(b)).

Requirement to Correct

97.26 A special penalty regime will apply if and when the Requirement to Correct is enacted by FA 2017. Should offshore errors be identified and disclosed in the manner envisaged by the Requirement the penalty regime will be as described earlier in this chapter, with the result the disclosure will need to include the appropriate penalty as well as the tax and interest. But should the taxpayer fail to act before 30 September 2018 a special and more severe penalty regime will apply to errors that are thereafter disclosed or discovered. The nature of this penalty regime is still being consulted on, but one model would mean all penalties fall in a range of 100% to 200% of the unpaid tax, with no reduction below 100% unless the taxpayer can show a reasonable excuse (HMRC consultation document 'Tackling offshore tax evasion: A Requirement to Correct', 24 August 2016, CHAPTER 5).

FIXED GAAR PENALTIES

97.27 Alongside these existing and prospective penalty regimes, there is a fixed-penalty regime for arrangements that are caught by the GAAR (see CHAPTER 98). This applies to arrangements entered into on or after 15 September 2016 (which was the date of Royal Assent to the Finance Act 2016). A fixed penalty is due where:

(a)   a tax document, such as a return, has been submitted on the basis that a particular tax advantage results from the arrangements;

(b)   if the tax document was submitted by a third party, the taxpayer knew, or ought to have known, that the tax document was submitted on the basis referred to above; and

(c)   the tax advantage has been counteracted under the GAAR (FA 2013, s 212A as inserted by FA 2016, s 158(2)).

The penalty is 60% of the value of the counteracted tax advantage. The value of the counteracted tax advantage is the tax saving that would have been achieved, had the tax advantage not been counteracted, making the assumption that the arrangements would have been technically capable of securing that advantage were it not for the counteraction (FA 2013, Sch 43C).

By contrast with the provisions that apply to careless and deliberate conduct, there is no statutory adjustment of the penalty by reference to the degree of culpability on the part of the taxpayer. However, there is a discretion for HMRC to mitigate the penalty prior to any judgment on the matter and, after judgment, to further mitigate or entirely remit the penalty (FA 2013, Sch 43C, para 10).

A fixed penalty for a tax advantage which is counteracted under the GAAR and penalties under certain of the other regimes described in this chapter (for example the regime for inaccuracies resulting from careless or deliberate conduct) can be levied in respect of the same arrangements. However, where this is the case, the aggregate penalty is subject to a cap. The cap varies between 200% and 100% of the tax that is payable by reason of the counteraction/assessment (FA 2013, Sch 43C, para 8).

CRIMINAL SANCTIONS

97.28 This is not the place for a discussion of criminal offences applicable to tax, for the subject of this book is lawful and transparent tax planning, not

criminal evasion. Nonetheless one aspect of the criminal law does require
mention, for this aspect does not require a deliberate intention to break the
law. The offences in question are confined to offshore income, assets, and
activities and were enacted in 2016 as TMA 1970, ss 106B–106H. At the time
of writing the offences are not yet in force and are to be brought into force by
statutory instrument (FA 2016, s 166(2)). They will not apply to tax years
before that in which they come into force (FA 2016, s 166(4)).

Sections 106B–106H enact three offences, defined by reference to the procedural requirements applicable to income tax and CGT. Each of them predicates
offshore income, assets, or activity. As in the penalty regimes discussed above
'offshore' is a misnomer and simply means outside the UK. Thus income is
offshore if it arises from a non-UK source and assets are offshore if situate or
held outside the UK. Activities are offshore if mainly carried on outside the UK
(s 10F(4)). As respects assets it is to be noted UK assets can be caught if the
ownership structure is offshore, as on that scenario the assets are held outside
the UK.

The three offences are as follows:

(1)   Failure to deliver a tax return when required to do so (s 106C).
(2)   Inaccuracy in a return (s 106D).
(3)   Failure to notify chargeability under (TMA 1970, s 7 (s 106B)).

None of these errors amount to a criminal offence unless the unreported tax is
chargeable by reference to offshore income, assets, or activities. Further the
unreported tax must exceed a threshold amount, which is to be designated by
statutory instrument but must exceed £25,000 (s 106F). The penalty on
conviction will be fine or up to six months in prison.

The offences are strict liability offences, which means they are committed even
if there is no deliberate intent to evade tax. However all are subject to a
reasonability defence in that failure to deliver a return or notify chargeability
is not an offence if the taxpayer has a reasonable excuse. So too reasonable
care excludes criminal liability for inaccuracy in a return. But with all these
defences the burden of proving reasonability is on the taxpayer. The offences
will be precluded in other circumstances, these to be prescribed by statutory
instrument (s 106E). One such exclusion will be for income and assets
reportable under the Common Reporting Standard and similar agreements
(TIIN 16 March 2016, reproduced [2016] SWTI 987).

The criminal offences do not apply to trustees acting as such or to personal
representatives (s 106E(1)). For individuals they will render it even more
essential than is currently the case that proper advice is taken on the basis of
full disclosure of all relevant facts to the adviser.

ENABLERS

97.29 The 2016 Finance Act is moving the penalty regime in another direction
not hitherto taken, namely imposing penalties on those to whom it refers as
enablers. Penalties against enablers are enacted by FA 2016, Sch 20, which is
to be brought into force on a date or dates prescribed by statutory instrument
(FA 2016, s 162(2)).

The term 'enabler' means a person who has encouraged, assisted or facilitated offshore tax evasion or non-compliance (Sch 20, para 1(2)(b)). The terms offshore evasion and non-compliance are widely defined and comprehend not merely acts or omissions which result in a criminal conviction, but also acts or omission which attract certain types of penalty (Sch 20, para 1(2)(a)). The types of penalty concerned are the misconduct penalties described earlier in this chapter, namely those levied for failure to notify chargeability, failure to file a return, and for error in a return (Sch 20, para 1(4)). Penalties levied in connection with offshore asset moves are also comprehended.

The enabler is only vulnerable to a penalty if he in fact knew that his actions enabled or were likely to enable the taxpayer to carry out offshore tax evasion or non-compliance. However if there is non-compliance, it is not necessary the taxpayer's actions are deliberate. This result follows because the kinds of taxpayer penalty that can trigger the enabler provisions are only restricted to deliberate acts where the taxpayer penalty is for an offshore transfer (Sch 20, para 2(5)(b); see para **97.17** above).

In the case of non-compliance it is not immediately clear when such non-compliance is carried out and thus when the enabler's knowledge of the effect of his actions is tested. However taxpayer penalties for non-compliance that trigger the enabler provisions are generally only triggered by failure to file or by incorrect filing. It follows that an enabler is only caught if he is involved in the non-filing or incorrect filing. But this does not follow where the taxpayer is being penalised for an offshore transfer or an offshore asset move. Here the enabler is within the enabler provisions if he facilitated and encouraged the transfer or move.

Should a person fall foul of the enabler provisions, the penalty is equal to the tax put at risk by the taxpayer's default. But where the conduct enabled is an offshore asset move, the enabler's penalty is 50% of the tax put at risk (Sch 20, para 3).

The penalty charged on the enabler is reduced if the enabler cooperates with HMRC, either by disclosing what the taxpayer has done or otherwise assisting in the investigation of the taxpayer (Sch 20, para 7). The maximum possible reduction is to 10% of the tax put at risk, applicable where the enabler's disclosure is unprompted. As with penalties generally, the enabler has a right of appeal to the First-tier Tribunal, and there is also provision for a reduction in the penalty in special circumstances (Sch 20, paras 9 and 12–14).

As with other penalty provisions, Sch 20 is expressed in terms of offshore matters and transfers. But those terms are defined in terms of income, assets or activities outside the UK. As a result Sch 20 can apply even if there is no connection with an offshore jurisdiction as that term would normally be understood.

Criminal sanctions

97.30 The regime just described will, when in force, be one of civil penalties. There is also a proposal to extend the criminal law otherwise applicable in this area. The proposed new offence will, if enacted, apply to companies and partnerships and will be in point if a person acting for the company or partnership facilitates tax evasion by a client of the business and that facilitation is itself criminal. Should this happen the company or partnership will be at risk of prosecution unless it can show it had procedures in place to prevent the facilitation. The proposed offence will apply both to UK tax and to foreign tax. At the time of writing the most recent consultation is a document issued by HMRC on 17 April 2016.

Defeated tax avoidance

97.31 The penalty regime and criminal sanctions described above will only be in point where the taxpayer has engaged in tax evasion or non-disclosure. Currently the government is consulting on a significant widening of the enabler penalty regime, whereby it would apply to those who enable tax avoidance that is defeated, (HMRC 'Strengthening Tax Avoidance Sanctions and Deterrents: A discussion document', 17 August 2016). Enablers will include both tax advisers who advised on the defeated arrangements and those who marketed or implemented them. It is unclear what forms of avoidance will be comprehended and how far it will be confirmed to marketed schemes. If enacted this proposed regime will apply to both offshore and domestic matters.

PRACTICAL CONSIDERATIONS

97.32 As indicated at the beginning of this chapter none of the matters described here should be relevant to the subject matter of this book, for the planning described in this book presupposes proper analysis of the law and full disclosure to HMRC. Nonetheless three practical points may be made.

The past

97.33 The first point is that the Requirement to Correct proposal makes it more important than ever that taxpayers with complex arrangements ensure the past is reviewed and any outstanding issues addressed and disclosed. In many cases much the better view may be that there is nil liability, but there may be room for disagreement and in such a situation disclosure is prudent. The appropriate forum may well be the worldwide disclosure facility, particularly as this provides a mechanism for complex disclosures to be reviewed in draft and discussed with HMRC before formal submission.

A particularly important point in the worldwide disclosure facility deals with situations where legal advice is to the effect there is not a liability or the liability is less than might be supposed. Here the facility requires disclosure of the advice and its factual basis. This is a welcome recognition of the fact that in offshore matters many issues are grey and provides a means of achieving certainty that past tax treatment has been correct.

A point that should also be kept in mind both with the facility and with Requirement to Correct is that in general normal time limits apply. Thus innocent error over income tax and CGT is out of charge after four years and careless error after six years (see para **97.7**). There is no suggestion that matters out of time as at 5 April 2017 should require correction. But there is a suggestion that matters naturally open in April 2017 should be subject to a one off-extension of time limits so as to allow failure to operate the Requirement to Correct procedures to be counteracted.

Overseas trusts and companies

97.34 There is no doubt that overseas trusts and companies are as much within the purview of Requirement to Correct as settlors, beneficiaries or participators who are UK resident. For that reason offshore trust and company administrators may need to undertake careful review of trust and companies which have not hitherto participated in a disclosure facility. A particular issue is Inheritance Tax, given the longer time limits that apply to that tax (see para 97.8).

The future

97.35 A third and final point concerns the future. It is simply that while correctly structured offshore tax planning is still effective and necessary, proper legal analysis is essential. Further all matters requiring disclosure to HMRC should be disclosed when filing the annual tax return and, given the increasingly onerous compliance regime, 'white space' or other comparable disclosures should be much more widely used than hitherto. Particular care should be taken over the form of these disclosures, so as to ensure they are sufficient to prevent a discovery assessment, should the enquiry window close without HMRC initiating an enquiry into the return (see para 97.7 above).

Chapter 98

THE GENERAL ANTI-ABUSE RULE

INTRODUCTION

98.1 2013 saw the introduction of a general anti-abuse rule, or GAAR, to the UK tax code. It has effect in relation to arrangements entered into on or after 17 July 2013 (FA 2013, s 215(1)).

The broad effect of the GAAR is to eliminate tax advantages which, absent the GAAR, would be secured under the applicable UK tax rules, as correctly construed. Such advantages are only eliminated if the arrangements are considered 'abusive' – a key concept that is discussed below.

This is not the place for a full discussion of the GAAR. However, some analysis of the legislation is essential, because it is plain from HMRC's guidance that offshore arrangements which are intended to generate a tax advantage are very much within the sights of the GAAR.

The GAAR was developed in 2010–11 by a study group chaired by Graham Aaronson QC. This group of seven individuals comprised judges, academics and corporate tax practitioners. There was no private client practitioner, still less one specialising in offshore tax issues. Many are of the view that this absence is reflected in the GAAR, and makes it particularly difficult to apply in relation to private client and offshore matters.

The framework and the concepts of the GAAR owe much to the transactions in securities legislation (ITA 2007, ss 682–713). This was first enacted some 50 years ago to counter dividend stripping and similar devices. Prior to the GAAR, it was the nearest the UK had to general anti-avoidance legislation, albeit that it was confined to transactions involving shares and securities.

The GAAR legislation is set out in FA 2013, ss 206–215. As discussed below, the legislation is supplemented by detailed guidance written by HMRC but approved by the GAAR advisory panel (referred to below as 'the Guidance').

TAXES WITHIN SCOPE

98.2 As originally enacted, the GAAR permitted the counteraction of advantages in respect of income tax, corporation tax, CGT, petroleum revenue tax, IHT, SDLT and ATED (FA 2013, s 206(3)). Since 13 March 2014, NIC advantages have also been within its scope (NICs Act 2014, s 10(2)).

PRECONDITIONS

98.3 There are three preconditions for the GAAR to apply (s 206(1)):

(1)   Arrangements must be identified;
(2)   Those arrangements must be tax arrangements; and
(3)   Such tax arrangements must be abusive.

Arrangements

98.4 The term 'arrangements' includes any agreement, understanding, scheme, transaction or series of transactions (s 214). It is immaterial whether the component parts of any arrangements are legally enforceable.

Tax arrangements

98.5 Arrangements are 'tax arrangements' if, having regard to all the circumstances, it would be reasonable to conclude that the obtaining of a tax advantage was their main purpose, or one of their main purposes (s 207(1)).

An evidenced subjective intention to generate a tax advantage causes arrangements to be tax arrangements, but such evidence is not a prerequisite. Arrangements also qualify, absent such evidence, if a reasonable outsider, without knowledge of the state of mind of the participants, would conclude that the arrangements must have been tax-driven.

The term 'tax advantage' is defined as including (s 208):

• Relief from tax;
• Repayment of tax;
• Avoidance of tax or of a possible assessment to tax;
• Deferral of tax; and
• Avoidance of an obligation to account for tax.

This definition is derived from the original transactions in securities legislation, still preserved in the current corporation tax code (CTA 2010, ss 731–751). The fundamental concept behind it is encapsulated in a much-cited dictum of Lord Wilberforce (*IRC v Parker* (1966) 43 TC 396, 441):

> 'there must be a contrast as regards the "receipts" between the actual case where these accrue in a non-taxable way with a possible accruer in a taxable way, and unless that contrast exists the existence of the advantage is not established.'

There is no definition of 'tax' for the purposes of the 'tax advantage' definition in the GAAR. Common sense suggests that in this context the word 'tax' must be limited, by implication, to the taxes to which the GAAR applies (as set out in s 206(3); see above). This is HMRC's view (para C2.3 of the Guidance).

Abusive

98.6 Tax arrangements are abusive if they fail what is known as the 'double reasonableness' test, ie if they cannot reasonably be regarded as a reasonable course of action (s 207(1)). Reasonableness is assessed in relation to the relevant tax provisions and having regard to all the circumstances.

The core concept behind the 'double reasonableness' test is this: it is not purely a question of whether a judge or tribunal considers a given set of tax arrangements to be a reasonable course of action; the issue is whether a reasonable person could so regard them. In other words, it is recognised that there can be a wide spectrum of reasonably-held views as to whether particular arrangements are reasonable, and, provided that the tax arrangements fall within that spectrum, they are not abusive.

The Guidance discusses this point and sets out HMRC's perspective, as approved by the GAAR advisory panel, on the question of what constitutes a reasonable body of opinion. Unsurprisingly, HMRC do not consider the view that any taxation is state-sponsored theft to be reasonable (para C5.10.5).

More controversially, HMRC also regard as unreasonable those who consider that it is the job of Parliament and HMRC to get tax legislation right and who take the position that if they fail to do so, it is open to taxpayers to exploit the resultant shortcomings. HMRC say that such a position cannot be regarded as reasonable, because one of the main purposes of the GAAR is to deter and counteract arrangements which exploit such shortcomings (para C5.10.6). The line taken in the Guidance is that the GAAR represents a rejection by Parliament of the approach taken by the courts in cases such as *IRC v Duke of Westminster* [1936] AC 1, 104 LJKB 383, to the effect that taxpayers are free to use their ingenuity to reduce their tax bills by any lawful means, however contrived those means might be and however far the tax consequences might diverge from the real economic position (para B2.1). Any such view must therefore (according to the Guidance) be excluded from the spectrum of reasonable views, for the purposes of the GAAR, even if it is widely-held.

Factors taken into account

98.7 The issue of whether tax arrangements can reasonably be regarded as a reasonable course of action is not left to the bare meaning of the term 'reasonable'. Instead, the legislation prescribes certain factors which must be taken into account in determining reasonableness, and gives examples of other factors which might indicate abusiveness.

The factors specified in determining reasonableness are (s 207(2)):

- whether the substantive result of the arrangements is consistent with any principles on which the relevant tax legislation is based, whether such principles are express or implied;
- whether the arrangements involve contrived or artificial steps; and
- whether the arrangements are intended to exploit shortcomings in the relevant tax legislation.

The factors which might indicate abusiveness include (s 207(4)):

- that the arrangements result in the amount of income, profits or gains for tax purposes being significantly less than the economic amount; and

- that the arrangements result in deductions or losses for tax purposes being of an amount which is significantly greater than the economic equivalent.

The common thread behind these latter two factors is a divergence of the tax consequences of the arrangements from the economic consequences. This echoes a key element in the distinction between avoidance and mitigation, particularly Lord Templeman's analysis in *IRC v Challenge Corporation Ltd* [1987] AC 155, [1986] STC 548, PC (see para **73.23**).

Established practice

98.8 Just one factor is specified as an indicator that tax arrangements are not unreasonable, namely that they are in accordance with established practice, and at the time of the arrangements, HMRC had indicated its acceptance of that practice (s 207(5)).

It is generally thought that failure to legislate following defeat in litigation is tantamount to acceptance, and this seems to be acknowledged by HMRC. The Guidance states (at para D26.5.3) that HMRC 'must be taken to have accepted the practice' of creating pilot trusts on separate days to create an IHT advantage, in view of HMRC's omission (at the time of publication of the Guidance) to amend the relevant property code following the *Rysaffe Trustee Co (CI) Ltd v IRC* [2002] EWHC 1114 (Ch), [2002] STC 872, 5 ITELR 53 case (see para **60.11**). However, the scope of this principle is far from clear, not least because it may take time after HMRC have lost a case for amending legislation to be drawn up.

There is a discussion of what may or may not be taken as acceptance of established practice at paras C5.12.5–C5.12.8 of the Guidance. The point is made that a 'grudging acceptance' by HMRC that the tax rules as drafted could not prevent a tax advantage from being obtained, through arrangements which were not in line with the policy of the legislation, would carry little or no weight in determining whether the arrangements in question should now be considered abusive.

COUNTERACTION

98.9 A counteraction must be made should tax arrangements be abusive (s 209).

The counteraction may be made by assessment or modification of an assessment and may be effected by either the taxpayer or HMRC. It is thus clear that the GAAR is within self-assessment, with the result that if a counteraction is made by HMRC following an enquiry, there may be a liability to interest and penalties. Whether penalties are in fact due will depend on whether the taxpayer took reasonable care in completing the tax return or otherwise disclosing the arrangements to HMRC. In being within self-assessment, the GAAR is in contrast to the transactions in securities legislation, which operates only if HMRC invoke it (ITA 2007, ss 695–698).

Consequential adjustments may be made should a counteraction become final (s 210). Such adjustments may be to the tax liability of the subject taxpayer or that of other taxpayers. A claim is required and this is only valid if made within 12 months of the counteraction becoming final.

It might be thought that all counteraction adjustments will be initiated by HMRC. However, this is not so: a taxpayer is under a duty to make adjustments in respect of advantages deriving from tax arrangements, if they do not pass the double reasonableness test. This duty would for example arise where a tax adviser takes on a new client and concludes that the GAAR should apply for past tax years for which he is preparing returns. But in such cases, it does have to be kept in mind that the GAAR cannot be applied to arrangements pre-dating 17 July 2013.

A point also to keep in mind is that the GAAR is, as HMRC have acknowledged, subject to the self-assessment time limits. Thus, assuming a taxpayer files his return on time, HMRC must initiate any enquiry within 12 months of the filing date (TMA 1970, s 9A). A discovery assessment cannot be made after that time unless the taxpayer has made a deliberately incorrect return or careless mistake or the facts are not fully disclosed (TMA 1970, s 29). Absent deliberate non-compliance, carelessness or non-disclosure, the general rule is that a discovery assessment is time barred after four years from the end of the tax year to which it relates, but this is extended to six years where the taxpayer has been careless and to 20 where he has been deliberate (TMA 1970, ss 34 and 36).

PROCEDURE

98.10 Despite the points made above, it is likely that it will be HMRC who initiate a counteraction in the great majority of cases where the GAAR is in point. But before a counteraction by HMRC can be effective, a series of important procedural safeguards have to be complied with.

The initial notice

98.11 The first requirement is that HMRC must designate an officer, and that officer must give the taxpayer a written notice. This notice must specify what the arrangements are that the officer regards as abusive and the counteraction which he considers ought to be made (FA 2013, Sch 43 para 3).

The taxpayer must be given 45 days within which to make representations to the designated officer (Sch 43 para 4). Should the taxpayer avail himself of this opportunity, the designated officer must consider the representations (Sch 43 para 6).

The advisory panel

98.12 Should the designated officer wish to take the matter further, he must refer it to the GAAR advisory panel (Sch 43 paras 5 and 6(2)). The taxpayer must be notified of the reference and has 21 days from the giving of such notice within which to send representations to the panel (Sch 43 para 9).

The GAAR advisory panel is a panel established by HMRC for the purposes of assessing whether arrangements may be caught by the GAAR (Sch 43 para 1). Currently none of its members is from HMRC, recruitment being by open advertisement.

Any matter referred to the GAAR advisory panel must be considered by a sub-panel of three or more members (Sch 43 para 10). Their job is to produce an opinion as to whether the tax arrangements under review issue are reasonable. In so doing they must have regard to the various indicia of reasonableness and abusiveness described above (see para **98.7**). If the three members of the panel cannot agree they produce separate opinions.

Having received the opinion, the designated officer must consider it. He then has to give the taxpayer notice of whether or not he remains of the view that the GAAR is in point, specifying the adjustments required to give effect to any counteraction. It is to be noted that, in determining whether to give the notice, the designated officer is not bound by the opinion of the panel. Effect is given to the adjustments by assessment, modification of an assessment or amendment or disallowance of a claim (s 209(5)).

Appeal

98.13 The taxpayer has the right to appeal to the First-tier Tribunal (TMA 1970, s 31). On any such appeal, the onus is on HMRC to prove that the tax arrangements are abusive and that the proposed adjustments are just and reasonable (s 211(1)).

In determining these matters, the tribunal (or any subsequent court on appeal) must take account of the opinion of the advisory panel on the particular case in question. It must also take account of the Guidance, but only insofar as such was approved by the GAAR panel at the time the arrangements were entered into (s 211(2)). But the weight which must be given to the Guidance is unspecified.

The tribunal may, but is not obliged to, take account of any other HMRC guidance which had been issued at the time arrangements were entered into. It may also take account of other HMRC or government material in the public domain and may consider evidence regarding established practice.

THE GUIDANCE

98.14 At the time of writing, the Guidance is that approved by the advisory panel with effect from 30 January 2015. This includes more than 130 pages of examples. These are designed to illustrate the frontier between what is and is not abusive. Some of the examples have direct bearing on the subject matter of this book and therefore are worthy of consideration.

Capital payments examples

98.15 Examples D20 and D21 in the Guidance concern the CGT rules matching trust s 2(2) amounts with capital payments (as to which see CHAPTER 77).

Example D20 postulates a trust holding assets worth £4m with aggregate s 2(2) amounts of £2.5m. Two of the beneficiaries are resident and domiciled in the UK and the other two have no connection with the UK. Normal planning, were the trust to be wound up by equal distributions to all four beneficiaries, would be to distribute £2m to the foreign beneficiaries in one tax year and the balance to the UK beneficiaries in the next (see para 10.3).

The effect of this would be to restrict the taxable s 87 gains to £0.5m, rather than £1.25m which would be the position had all of the fund been distributed in the same tax year. The Guidance confirms that this is non-abusive.

Example D21 postulates a trust settled by a non-UK resident non-UK domiciliary. Its sole asset is a company owning a house occupied by a UK resident but non-domiciled beneficiary. The latent gains (after allowing for 2008 rebasing) are £4m and these would be visited on the occupying beneficiary should the company and then the trust be wound up and the house distributed to him.

The scheme entails the settlor adding £4m to the trust. The company is then wound up, and, in the same tax year, the sum of £4m is distributed back to the settlor, thereby carrying out the entire s 2(2) amount under the s 87A matching rules. In the following tax year the house is distributed tax-free to the UK resident beneficiary. This, it is considered, could potentially be counteracted by the GAAR.

House scheme examples

98.16 Example D31 in the Guidance postulates a variety of different structures through which non-UK domiciliaries might own a house in the UK without exposing it to the risk of the IHT charges that are the normal consequence of owning UK situs assets.

Examples 4 and 6 involve a purchase by a settlor-interested trust. In example 4 the settlor settles 30% of the price, leaving the trust to borrow the balance commercially, even though the settlor had the resources to settle the full amount. In example 6 the settlor settles just 5% of the funds required and enables the trust to borrow the remaining 95% by providing a guarantee to the lending bank. In both cases the commercial borrowing is secured on the property and so reduces its value for IHT purposes (see CHAPTER 84).

In example 9 the planning is taken further, in that an individual, X, settles the entire purchase price into one trust, which injects the cash into an underlying company. That company then lends the cash to a second trust, settled by a relative of X. This trust owns the house which in due course X occupies.

The Guidance considers that this latter example is abusive and could be countered, as X is effectively lending his own money to himself. Examples 4 and 6, by contrast, are regarded as commercial and so outside the GAAR.

10-yearly charge example

98.17 Example D28 in the Guidance concerns an excluded property settlement owning UK assets directly (see CHAPTER 63). Just before a 10-year anniversary the trustees borrow funds from the bank, charge the loan on the property and distribute the money to the settlor. Shortly after the 10-year anniversary the settlor resettles the money and the trustees repay the debt.

The Guidance considers that the GAAR could counteract the deductibility of the debt. However the example is not satisfactory, as a major factor leading to that conclusion is the 2013 legislation on the deductibility of debts (as to which see CHAPTER 84). It is unclear what the analysis would be absent that legislation.

IMPLICATIONS OF THE GAAR

98.18 At the time of writing there have been no reported cases on the GAAR. Any comment as to its implications are therefore somewhat tentative.

Lack of certainty

98.19 The double reasonableness test is central to the GAAR. HMRC's view has been noted above (para **98.6**) and it is also worth remembering what Graham Aaronson QC said in his report. He described the following as an overarching principle:

> '[The GAAR] should target those highly abusive contrived and artificial schemes which are widely regarded as intolerable but . . . it should not affect the large centre ground of responsible tax planning.'

Most taxpayers and advisers would agree with these sentiments. The difficulty, in practice, is in identifying where particular arrangements fall in the spectrum between responsible tax planning and contrived and artificial schemes. The reality is that between the extremes of the obviously reasonable and the obviously unreasonable, there is a substantial grey area in which there is scope for debate and doubt about whether the planning in question is, or might reasonably be regarded as, reasonable.

The practical problem with the GAAR, therefore, is the uncertainty it generates. It can be criticised on the grounds that, where this large grey area is encountered, it makes it exceptionally difficult for taxpayers to plan their affairs with confidence and ensure that their self-assessment is accurate.

In one sense the examples in the Guidance are helpful. But a few of the conclusions, and the reasoning behind them, are questionable. And even if one accepts all of the conclusions, the real difficulty comes in extrapolating to other tax contexts and factual situations.

It may be suggested that the difficulties are particularly acute regarding non-UK residents and non-UK domiciliaries, in relation to whom the tax legislation quite often operates in a binary, 'all or nothing' manner, due to territorial limits. Where a small change of facts (for example, whether an asset has a UK or non-UK situs) can produce a dramatic change of tax treatment, it can be hard to determine whether a proposed arrangement is consistent with the policy of the legislation, or indeed what that policy is. Arguably, it should not be considered abusive for a non-UK resident or non-UK domiciliary to take advantage of territorial limitations, which are a form of exemption offered to those who have a less substantial connection to the UK than those who are resident and domiciled there. Nor should it be considered abusive, per se, to put arrangements in place which, compared to possible alternative arrangements, minimise the amount of tax that is paid, even if that result might be regarded as anomalous. There are statements in the Guidance which support this (for example at para D20.6).

Deterrent effect

98.20 When the GAAR was first introduced, it was arguable that its power as a deterrent to aggressive tax planning was limited, as there were no specific penalties or downsides associated with the counteraction of a tax advantage. Taxpayers might have reasoned, at least in some scenarios, that they had little to lose by attempting to secure a tax advantage through proposed arrangements. If the arrangements were technically successful in securing the desired tax advantage, and that advantage was not counteracted under the GAAR, the taxpayer would benefit; whereas if the advantage was counteracted, the taxpayer might not be any worse off than if no planning had been undertaken.

However, this line of thought no longer holds good. HMRC now have a power to demand an upfront payment of tax from the taxpayer, equal to the tax that would be due if the advantage was counteracted, where (a) a counteraction notice has been issued under the GAAR and (b) at least two members of the GAAR advisory panel have opined that the arrangements in question were not a reasonable course of action (FA 2014, s 219(4)). Clearly, any such demand creates a significant cashflow disadvantage for the taxpayer and puts the onus on him to dispute the counteraction notice and incur legal costs in doing so.

Perhaps even more significantly, in relation to arrangements entered into since 15 September 2016, HMRC have had the ability, and indeed the obligation, to impose a fixed penalty in respect of any counteracted tax advantage, of 60% of the tax saving that would have been achieved but for the counteraction. This is discussed in para **97.27**.

These sanctions may be regarded as a justifiable step in the battle against aggressive tax avoidance, or as a grave infringement of taxpayer rights. The truth may be somewhere between these two viewpoints. In any event there is no doubt that the balance of power has shifted and there are now very good reasons for taxpayers to think twice before embarking on planning which is potentially within the ambit of the GAAR.

Part D

INTERNATIONAL AGREEMENTS

Section I:

Double taxation treaties

Chapter 99

INTRODUCTION TO DTTS

99.1 This section deals with double taxation treaties (DTTs), primarily in the context of the taxation of UK resident individuals and offshore structures. The main focus of the section is DTTs which provide relief from income tax, tax on capital gains and corporation tax.

However, the UK also has a limited number of treaties which are concerned with the taxation of gifts and inheritances, and which in certain circumstances prevent the UK from imposing IHT which would otherwise be due under domestic law. These treaties are considered at the end of the section, in CHAPTER 105.

This first chapter is intended to provide an introduction to DTTs. It includes discussion of the typical anatomy of an income/gains/profits DTT, the legal status of DTTs, how they are interpreted, and the time limits for making claims to DTT relief.

For completeness, this chapter also addresses the related subject of the unilateral relief from double taxation which is available under the UK tax code where another country has levied tax on income, a gain or a profit which is also taxable in the UK, there is no DTT with that country.

WHAT IS A DTT?

99.2 DTTs are contracts between pairs of states, which are intended to prevent individuals, companies or other persons from being subject to taxation in both of the contracting states on the same income, gains or profits. Absent relief under a DTT, double taxation may occur in a number of circumstances, most commonly (a) where a country taxes by source, regardless of the residence of the person to whom the income or gain in question has accrued, and (b) in cases of dual residence.

Under a DTT, the prevention of double taxation is typically achieved through a combination of so-called 'distributive' articles, which allocate or restrict taxing rights, and a 'credit' article. In some situations, a distributive article may confer exclusive taxing rights on one of the contracting states with respect to income, gains or profits (ie it will prevent the other contracting state from levying tax which, under its domestic law, is due). In other situations both contracting states have taxing rights, but a distributive article will impose a cap on the rate of tax that can be levied by one of the contracting states. This latter approach is common in relation to dividends. In yet other cases, the distributive articles will leave both contracting states with unlimited taxing rights.

Where both states have unlimited taxing rights under the distributive articles, the credit article should nevertheless avoid double taxation. This article will require one of the contracting states to give credit for tax levied by the other contracting state, where such tax is calculated by reference to the same income, gain or profit as has been taxed by the first contracting state. The result should be that the taxpayer's overall liability in respect of the income, gain or profit is limited to the higher of the tax charges imposed by the two contracting states.

However, this is not always the case. Credit relief may be restricted or denied by one contracting state if the taxpayer has acquiesced in the other contracting state levying tax otherwise than in accordance with the DTT (see para **102.9**). There can also be challenges in securing a credit in the UK in respect of foreign taxation where tax is payable in the UK under anti-avoidance provisions on deemed income/gains, in cases where there is an indirect relationship between those deemed income/gains and the actual income/gains on which foreign tax has been paid (see CHAPTER **104**).

Relevance of DTTs

99.3 One of the unwelcome side effects of the increase in global mobility in recent decades has been an increase in the risk of being found to be tax resident in two jurisdictions at once. This is a hazard whenever an individual changes his country of residence, and particularly so where an individual moves from or to the UK, due to the non-alignment of the UK's tax year with the calendar year used in almost all other systems. This issue arises more frequently now that the UK has a statutory test of residence, which imposes restrictive conditions on split-year treatment (see CHAPTER **41**).

DTTs can also have relevance in relation to foreign domiciled UK residents, particularly those from other parts of Europe, who have investment holding structures in 'onshore' EU jurisdictions rather than traditional 'tax havens'. Such structures may be exposed to local taxation, and in addition there may be scope for UK taxation in respect of the income and gains of the structure, under anti-avoidance provisions in the UK tax code. In this scenario, the taxing rights of the two jurisdictions and the interaction of their respective tax regimes must be considered. As discussed in CHAPTER **104**, difficult issues may arise.

Tax avoidance and DTTs

99.4 It is possible for a DTT to cause 'double non-taxation', ie a situation in which income, gains or profits are not taxed in either contracting state, because the DTT gives exclusive taxing rights to a contracting state whose domestic law exempts the receipt in question from tax.

However, this result is relatively unusual. Opportunities to exploit this phenomenon to avoid taxation tend to be blocked, once they have come to the attention of the relevant tax authority, by an amendment to the DTT, or an amendment of domestic law to override the DTT (see para **99.8**). Moreover, some modern DTTs include 'anti-treaty shopping' provisions which may preclude use of the DTT for tax avoidance of this kind (see para **102.4**).

Governmental efforts to ensure that treaties are not 'abused' mean, in practice, that there is limited scope to use DTTs to avoid tax. They are best regarded as a means to avoid double taxation or what might be considered excessive taxation, particularly in situations where, due to quirks of tax legislation, the same economic income or gains may otherwise be subject to multiple tax levies. In this context, the UK's extensive DTT network is useful.

TYPICAL ANATOMY

99.5 The UK has over a hundred income/gains/profits DTTs. Fortunately, most such DTTs follow the same format, with variations reflecting the outcome of negotiations between the two contracting states. The standard format is that of the Model Treaty published by the Organization for Economic Co-operation and Development (OECD), which was first issued in draft in 1963, then formally issued in 1977 and subsequently updated on numerous occasions, most recently in 2010. However, some of the UK's older treaties, eg those with the Crown Dependencies, follow a different model.

A DTT following the Model Treaty will be laid out as follows:

- Articles setting out the scope of the DTT, in terms of the taxes covered and the persons to whom the DTT applies.
- Definitions of terms, including the expression 'resident of a contracting state'. The latter will incorporate tie-breaker provisions which apply to determine a person's residence for the purpose of applying the treaty, where the person is liable to taxation in both countries.
- 'Distributive' articles, ie those allocating taxing rights between the contracting states, relating to income/profits of various characters (eg income from immovable property, business profits, interest, dividends, royalties, employment income), capital gains, and lastly 'other income' (ie income not dealt with by the preceding distributive articles). As explained above, such articles may preclude taxation by one of the contracting states entirely, or permit that state to levy tax but subject to a cap on the rate of tax.
- An article providing for credit to prevent double taxation, where the distributive articles allow both contracting states to levy tax in respect of the income, gain or profits in question. This article will typically give one of the contracting states the primary taxing right, and will require the other state to give credit for tax levied by the first state, against the tax which the other state levies on the income, gain or profits in question. The credit cannot usually be set against tax on any other item of income, gain or profits.
- Miscellaneous provisions, which may cover non-discrimination, mutual agreement procedures, exchange of information and anti-avoidance.

LEGAL STATUS

Requirement for incorporation

99.6 As explained by Park J in *Boake Allen Ltd v Revenue and Customs Comrs* [2006] BTC 266, [2006] STC 606, [2006] EWCA Civ 25, treaties entered into by the UK are not 'self-executing', ie they are not directly effective as part of the law of the UK. They must be incorporated by statute or statutory instrument into the UK's domestic law in order to modify that law and give rise to rights that can be enforced by UK resident persons or British citizens (a process that is sometimes termed 'domestication'). In the case of a DTT, incorporation is required in order for treaty relief to be enforceable by persons who are, or would otherwise be, subject to UK taxation.

The UK's income/gains/profits DTTs are currently incorporated into UK law by Taxation (International and Other Provisions) Act 2010 (TIOPA 2010), s 6. Prior to the enactment of TIOPA 2010, the relevant provisions were Income and Corporation Taxes Act 1988 (ICTA 1988), s 788 (which allowed relief from income tax and corporation tax), and TCGA 1992, s 277 (which allowed relief from capital gains tax). Inheritance Tax Act 1984, s 158 continues to be the operative provision in relation to IHT.

Scope and effect

99.7 Income/gains/profits DTTs to which the UK is a party typically apply to income tax, CGT and corporation tax in the UK, and in the other contracting state to the equivalent taxes levied by that country, plus any 'substantially similar' taxes which may be introduced by either country after the signing of the treaty. There is variation between DTTs entered into by federal countries regarding the question of whether taxes levied at state or municipal level are affected by the DTT. For example, the UK's DTT with Russia extends to 'taxes on income and on capital gains imposed on behalf of a Contracting State or of its political subdivisions or local authorities' (art 2(1)). By contrast, the UK's income/gains/profits DTT with the USA is expressly limited (where US taxes are concerned) to taxes levied at federal level.

Where the DTT does not cover foreign state/municipal taxation, obviously the DTT cannot be invoked to exempt the taxpayer from such foreign taxes. Nor can credit from UK tax be claimed under the DTT in respect of a foreign state/municipal tax in a situation where the receipt in question has given rise to tax in both contracting states. However, in this situation, relief by way of credit may nevertheless be available under the UK's unilateral credit provisions (see paras **99.16** to **99.17** below).

Priority issues

99.8 Generally, a DTT provision which has been incorporated by statute into the law of the UK will override a provision of domestic tax law. Clearly, DTTs would be futile if they were routinely overridden by domestic tax legislation. Taxation (International and Other Provisions) Act 2010, s 6(1) provides that double taxation arrangements have effect 'despite anything in any enactment'. This might suggest that a DTT provision will always have priority over a domestic charging provision.

However, it is in fact well-established that domestic tax legislation may trump a DTT. An anti-avoidance provision was held to have priority over the UK/Irish DTT in the case of *Collco Dealings Ltd v IRC* [1962] AC 1, [1961] 1 All ER 762, HL. The anti-avoidance provision post-dated the provision by which the DTT was incorporated into UK law. The latter did not include any wording such as 'despite anything in any enactment'. It was therefore relatively easy for the court to conclude that Parliament had intended the subsequent anti-avoidance provision to override the treaty, and that such was the effect of the provision. It was acknowledged by the court that the result was a breach by the UK of its obligations to the Republic of Ireland.

There was a similar result in *MK Padmore (No 2) v Comrs of Inland Revenue* 2001 WL 98070, which concerned a DTT incorporated into UK law by virtue of ICTA 1988, s 788. The relevant provision of UK tax law (now Income Tax (Trading and Other Income) Act 2005 (ITTOIA 2005), s 858) referred to arrangements having effect under ICTA 1988, s 788 and was obviously intended to allow a UK tax charge to arise notwithstanding any relief that might otherwise be available under a DTT. It was held that the provision must override the DTT, as otherwise it would have no effect at all.

There are a number of provisions on the statute book relating to trusts that are intended to defeat DTT planning. Some of these flagrantly override any DTT that might otherwise provide relief from a particular charge to UK tax. Clearly, there is a conflict between such provisions and TIOPA 2010, s 6, but a court would undoubtedly conclude that Parliament intended to derogate from the general principle that a DTT has priority over domestic tax law, in circumstances where tax avoidance would otherwise occur.

Other provisions have the economic effect of overriding a DTT, although they rely on different mechanics. One example is TCGA 1992, s 83. This triggers a deemed disposal at market value of the assets of UK resident trustees if, while remaining UK resident as a matter of domestic law, they become treaty resident in another country, and under the terms of the relevant DTT are exempt from UK tax on gains of the settlement. The deemed disposal occurs immediately before the acquisition of treaty residence in the other territory, so that any resultant gain will fall into the UK tax net before DTT protection kicks in. Clearly, this provision has the economic effect of denying treaty benefits, without (technically) overriding or derogating from the treaty.

It seems clear also that a DTT can, in principle, be overridden not only by a provision of domestic law which has the specific object of preventing treaty relief from being claimed, but also by more general anti-avoidance provisions. In a case of conflict, it is a question of statutory construction whether the treaty or the anti-avoidance provision should be regarded as taking precedence.

The GAAR

99.9 The most obvious example of general anti-avoidance legislation which is capable of trumping a DTT is the GAAR (discussed in Chapter 98). Finance Act 2013, s 212 provides that any 'priority rules' in the UK tax code are to take effect subject to the GAAR, and cites as an example TIOPA 2010, s 6(1), which provides that effect is to be given to double taxation arrangements 'despite anything in any enactment'. In principle, therefore, the GAAR could be invoked by HMRC in respect of arrangements which would otherwise give rise to treaty benefits and which 'cannot reasonably be regarded as a reasonable course of action' and are therefore deemed to be 'abusive'.

In the published GAAR guidance, HMRC make the obvious point (at para B5) that the mere fact that arrangements give rise to DTT relief does not mean that the arrangements amount to abuse. However, it is stated that where there are abusive arrangements which 'try to exploit particular provisions in a DTT, or the way in which such provisions interact with other provisions of UK tax law', then the GAAR can be applied to counteract them. It is a point of some difficulty whether choosing to locate an investment-holding entity in a country which has a favourable DTT with the UK could in any circumstances be regarded as abusive for these purposes. It is suggested that the risk of HMRC taking this point must be low if there are commercial (non-tax) reasons for choosing to establish the entity in the relevant country.

INTERPRETATION

Commerzbank/Memec principles

99.10 DTTs tend to be interpreted differently from UK tax legislation. The judgments in *IRC v Commerzbank AG* [1990] STC 285, 63 TC 218 and *Memec plc v IRC* [1996] STC 1336, 71 TC 77 provide useful guidance on how a DTT should be construed. The main points are:

- The approach to interpreting a DTT should be purposive (rather than literal). Where possible, a DTT provision must be construed so as to give effect to its purpose, where that purpose can be discerned.
- DTTs are the product of negotiations between contracting parties, typically starting from a precedent drafted by an international committee, over which the UK had little influence. Often the UK and the other contracting state have very different tax systems, linguistic usages and approaches to the interpretation of statutes and contracts. These factors tend to generate difficulties of construction and, as a result, DTTs often need to be interpreted creatively.
- The approach should be 'international' rather than domestic. It should not be assumed that rules of construction applicable to English legislation can be applied to a DTT. Nor should it be assumed that a term which has a specific meaning in English law must have the same meaning in a DTT to which the UK is a party. However, see below regarding the incorporation into DTTs, by reference, of specific meanings of terms used in UK tax law.

- Regard should be had to the Vienna Convention on the Law of Treaties, which includes provisions governing the interpretation of treaties. However, strictly, this is only relevant to DTTs concluded after January 1980, when the Vienna Convention came into force.

- Recourse may be had to *travaux preparatoires* (ie 'preparatory works'; in other words, the various documents, including reports of discussions, hearings and floor debates, that were produced during the drafting of the DTT), international case law, writings of jurists, subsequent commentaries, and other supplementary aids to interpretation. However, there is no obligation on a court to consider these and they are, at most, persuasive.

The Vienna Convention

99.11 Article 31(1) of the Vienna Convention on the Law of Treaties stipulates that terms used in an international treaty shall be interpreted in accordance with their 'ordinary meaning [. . .] in their context and in the light of [the treaty's] object and purpose', although art 31(4) provides that a term used in a DTT shall have a 'special meaning [. . .] if it is established that the parties so intended'.

The 'context' and 'object and purpose' will include any preamble to the DTT (as well as any supplementary agreement or instrument made by the parties regarding the interpretation of the DTT, such as an 'exchange of notes'). DTTs entered into by the UK commonly have a preamble referring not only to 'the avoidance of double taxation' but also 'the prevention of fiscal evasion'. It is hard to see how any DTT could prevent 'evasion' in the modern sense of that word, and the meaning must be avoidance. Where a DTT provision is ambiguous, and capable of being read so as to produce so-called double non-taxation, this form of preamble may lend extra weight to the argument that some other construction of it, which does not produce such result, is the right one.

The OECD commentary

99.12 All income/gains/profits DTTs entered into by the UK since the publication of the Model Treaty have been based on that model, with appropriate variations to take into account of the differing economic considerations, tax and legal systems of the two contracting states. Consequently, HMRC approve of the use of the OECD commentary as an aid to interpretation of DTTs.

However, the Model Treaty is a fluid document, being subject to regular amendments, and the same is increasingly true of the commentary. There is a strong argument that it is only permissible to use a particular version of the OECD commentary as an aid to the construction of a DTT if that version had been published at the time of negotiation of the treaty, although this point is not always heeded by the courts.

Case law

99.13 A UK court, required to construe a provision of a DTT, may take into account a judgment regarding the same or a similar provision in the context of another treaty. This includes decisions of foreign courts.

However, there is debate about how much weight can, or should, be given to foreign decisions concerning treaties to which the UK is not a party. Some judges and commentators tend to the view that there is a developing international consensus regarding the interpretation of DTTs (so a foreign decision should, absent special circumstances, be highly persuasive), whereas others subscribe to the view that the interpretation of a DTT is necessarily coloured by the legal and tax systems of the two contracting states (and therefore that the UK courts, interpreting DTTs to which the UK is a party, should be free to diverge from foreign decisions regarding treaties between other countries). The former viewpoint seems to be in the ascendency.

Indofood International Finance Ltd v JP Morgan Chase Bank NA [2006] EWCA Civ 158, [2006] STC 1195, 8 ITLR 653 provides a striking example of the uncertain nature of the 'precedent' set by DTT cases. This was a judgment of the English Court of Appeal, but it was not, strictly, a tax case. The court's decision was reached without representations being made by any tax authority, and related to a non-UK DTT. The litigation concerned the position of a hypothetical Dutch company under the DTT between the Netherlands and Indonesia, the question being whether this hypothetical company would have been the 'beneficial owner' (for the purposes of the Dutch/Indonesian DTT) of interest. Had the company qualified as the 'beneficial owner' of such income, an early repayment of certain bonds would have been avoided (which would have been financially advantageous to one party to the litigation, and disadvantageous to the other).

The evidence was that, had the Dutch company been incorporated, all of the interest receivable by the company would immediately have been paid on to its creditor, under a loan arrangement which would have existed between them. The Court of Appeal found that, on these facts, the Dutch company would *not* have been the 'beneficial owner' of the interest. The court's approach to the matter is discussed below (para **102.2**). Controversy persists about whether the *Indofood* judgment should be regarded as being confined to its particular facts, or has wider relevance for the interpretation of DTTs to which the UK is a party and which make treaty benefits conditional on 'beneficial owner-ship'.

Recourse to domestic meanings

99.14 All DTTs based on the Model Treaty include an article (usually art 3(2)) which states that any expression not defined in the DTT shall, 'unless the context otherwise requires', have the meaning that it has at that time under the law of the relevant contracting state for the purposes of the taxes to which the DTT applies.

This creates an important derogation from the principle that terms should be accorded their 'ordinary meanings' and should be interpreted 'internationally'. It allows expressions to have the technical meaning accorded to them by UK tax statutes, or indeed under common law, where they are used in relation to UK tax and they are not otherwise defined in the treaty. This principle was applied in *Pirelli Cable Holding NV v Revenue and Customs Comrs* [2006] UKHL 4, [2006] 1 WLR 400, (2006) Times, 13 February; the expression 'tax credit' (which was undefined in the UK's DTTs with the relevant contracting states) was accorded a specific meaning that it had in the UK tax code, relating to advance corporation tax.

Bilingual treaties

99.15 Finally, it should be noted that it is common for a DTT to exist in two languages, each with equal authority, in which case there may be a need for comparative analysis. Article 33 of the Vienna Treaty states that dual language treaties are to have equal authority unless otherwise provided; this is almost always stated in a bilingual DTT, or its preamble, in any case. There is no straightforward answer to how a bilingual DTT shall be applied in the event that the different versions of it appear to say conflicting things, or an overtone present in one version is absent from the other. It is possible that, in the case of a bilingual DTT to which the UK is a party, a UK court would give greater weight to the English language version insofar as it is concerned with UK taxation.

UNILATERAL RELIEF

Credit relief

99.16 The UK's treaty network is extensive. Generally, if another country actually levies tax, the UK has a DTT with it. Nevertheless, the UK tax code does include provisions which allow a credit against UK tax, on a unilateral basis, for foreign tax where:

(a)   no relief by way of credit is available under a DTT; and
(b)   if there is a DTT in force between the UK and the country which has levied the foreign tax, that DTT does not expressly prohibit relief by way of credit (TIOPA 2010, s 11).

In practice, this unilateral credit relief is most commonly relevant in relation to foreign taxes levied at state or municipal level, in the (not infrequent) case that there is a DTT with the relevant country, but such DTT excludes non-federal taxes from its scope. However, clearly, such relief may also be relevant where there is no DTT with the other country.

The unilateral credit relief provision is TIOPA 2010, s 9. This permits credit against UK tax in respect of tax paid under a foreign territory, including at state or municipal level (s 9(6)), if such tax is calculated by reference to income arising or a capital gain accruing in the foreign territory, and provided that the UK tax in question is calculated by reference to the same income or gain (s 9(1)–(2)). Where gains are concerned, HMRC acknowledge that 'in determining whether UK tax is computed by reference to the same gain on which the foreign tax is charged, there is no necessity that the respective tax liabilities should arise at the same time or that they should be charged on the same person' (INTM 169040). Logically, it should also be accepted that credit relief is, in principle, allowable in respect of foreign tax on income where there is a mismatch in terms of the timing of tax liabilities or in terms of the persons subject to the UK and foreign tax charges.

There are elaborate provisions regarding dividends (TIOPA 2010, ss 12–17) which sometimes prevent relief being claimed for foreign tax under s 9. However, the most common result is that relief for foreign tax on a dividend arising in the other territory is allowed, on the basis that the foreign tax is charged directly on the dividend (whether it is suffered by the company or by the recipient) and neither the company nor the recipient would have borne such tax unless the dividend had been paid (s 13).

It should be noted that unilateral credit relief under s 9 is limited to foreign tax on income or gains arising/accruing in the other territory, ie primarily, where the other territory is taxing by source or situs. It may not assist where the foreign territory is exerting taxing rights on some other basis. In particular, s 9 provides no credit in the event that the taxpayer is considered to be resident in the foreign territory as well as the UK, and the foreign territory is taxing income from a source in a third country, or gains accruing on the disposal of an asset situated in a third country.

Deduction relief

99.17 The Taxation (International and Other Provisions) Act 2010 provides for an alternative form of unilateral relief in respect of foreign taxation, at ss 112–113. These sections are subordinate to s 9, ie can only apply if credit relief under s 9 is not claimed. Very broadly:

- section 112 permits UK tax on a sum of income to be calculated as if the amount of the income were reduced by any foreign tax paid in respect of that income in the territory in which the income arose; whereas
- section 113 allows UK tax on a gain to be calculated as if the amount of the gain were reduced by any tax payable in a foreign territory on the disposal of the asset which is paid by the person making the disposal.

Both of these sections provide partial relief, in that the foreign tax reduces the income/gain for UK tax purposes, rather than generating a full credit. It is hard to see why relief under s 112 would ever be chosen over credit relief. Section 113, however, is potentially more useful, as the relief is not limited to the situation where a foreign territory has levied tax on a gain arising on the disposal of an asset situated in that territory. Unlike s 9, therefore, it is potentially useable in a dual residence situation, where the UK and the other country of residence both have taxing rights with respect to the disposal of an asset situated in a third country.

TIME LIMITS FOR RELIEF

99.18 The Taxation (International and Other Provisions) Act 2010 also includes time limits for the making of claims for a credit in respect of foreign taxation. For income tax and CGT purposes the deadline for a credit relief claim is the fourth anniversary of the end of the tax year in which the income or gain in question has been charged to income tax or CGT, or if later, the 31 January following the tax year in which the foreign tax is paid (TIOPA 2010, s 19(2)). These limits apply for the purpose of both DTT credit relief claims and unilateral relief claims.

Curiously, the Act does not include any parallel provisions regarding the time limits for claims to other forms of DTT relief, ie relief by way of a full exemption from UK tax or a cap on the rate of UK tax. By implication, where income tax and CGT are concerned the position is governed by the normal Taxes Management Act 1970 (TMA 1970) provisions regarding the time limits for claims to relief. These provide a general deadline of the fourth anniversary of the end of the tax year to which the relief claim relates (TMA 1970, s 43(1)), with a later deadline of the end of the tax year following that in which the assessment to tax has been made, where the claim to relief could not have been made but for the making of the assessment (s 43(2)).

In a discovery assessment case, the taxpayer should in principle be allowed to claim unilateral relief or DTT relief even if the normal deadline for such a claim has passed, by virtue of TMA 1970, s 36(3). However, it is unclear from HMRC's International Manual whether this point is accepted. The Manual refers to HMRC's ability to make an assessment up to six years or 20 years of the end of the tax year to which it relates, where the taxpayer has carelessly or deliberately misreported, but oddly does not comment on the taxpayer's right to claim unilateral relief or relief under a treaty (INTM 330830).

In some cases, the avoidance of double taxation requires timely relief claims both in the UK and abroad, with respect to the same income. This may be so where under the terms of a DTT, another country is permitted to tax income at a capped rate, and the UK also has taxing rights with respect to the income. If the taxpayer allows the other country to tax the income at the full, uncapped rate, and later seeks credit relief against UK tax, HMRC will disallow credit for that part of the foreign tax which exceeded the cap, unless the taxpayer is in time to make a relief claim in the other country, to give retrospective effect to the capped rate (see para **102.9**). The time limits for such claims vary significantly from country to country.

Remittance basis users

99.19 Common sense dictates that where a remittance basis user has become taxable on foreign income or a foreign gain dating from a prior tax year, due to a subsequent remittance of the same, the time limits referred to above run from the tax year of the remittance, not the tax year in which the income or gain arose.

The wording of the claim provisions discussed above supports this conclusion. The position is entirely clear where credit relief is concerned, as TIOPA 2010, s 19(2) applies by reference to the tax year in which the income or gain has been charged to tax. Clearly, there is no charge to tax on foreign income or gains of a remittance basis user until there is a remittance.

It is perhaps rather less obvious in the case of other DTT relief, as the operation of TMA 1970, s 43(1) depends on which tax year the claim 'relates' to. However, it seems natural and reasonable to say that the claim relates to the tax year of the remittance, not any earlier tax year in which the income or gain may have arisen.

Chapter 100

TREATY RESIDENCE

100.1 Correct analysis of the application of an income/gains/profits DTT in a particular situation depends on correct analysis of where the taxpayer will be considered to be resident for the purposes of the DTT (ie where he is 'treaty resident'). This is a fundamental first step when advising on a treaty.

As explained below, in the case of a DTT which follows the Model Treaty, treaty residence in a particular contracting state is only possible if the taxpayer qualifies as 'liable to tax' in that state. However, a person may be 'liable to tax' in both contracting states. In that case, so-called 'tie-breaker' provisions will determine the contracting state in which the taxpayer is treaty resident.

DTTS FOLLOWING THE MODEL TREATY

Why treaty residence matters

100.2 Under a DTT based on the Model Treaty, relief under a distributive article is invariably conditional on income, gains or profits accruing to a person who, for the purposes of the treaty, is a resident of one of the contracting states.

The reason is that the distributive articles concerned with income are only engaged, on their terms, where income is 'paid to', 'derived by' and/or 'beneficially owned' by a resident of a contracting state. Similarly, the effect of the capital gains article of a DTT depends on which contracting state the 'alienator' (ie the person making the disposal which gives rise to the gain) is resident in. Likewise, in the case of business profits, the relevant treaty provisions require identification of the contracting state in which the 'enterprise' in question is resident.

Requirement for 'liability to tax'

100.3 The term 'resident of a contracting state' is usually defined in art 4(1). The usual definition is a 'person who, under the laws of that State, is liable to tax therein by reason of his domicile, residence, place of management or any other criterion of a similar nature', expressly excluding however a person who is liable to tax solely in respect of income from sources in the relevant country.

For obvious reasons, the DTT with the USA includes citizenship among the criteria mentioned in this article.

This provision must be read in conjunction with the definition of 'person', usually in art 3(1). This typically states that 'person' includes any individual, company, or body of persons. However, there is some variance in the drafting of this definition across the UK's DTTs, with some expressly including in the concept of a 'person' any other entity with or without legal personality.

Dual residence situations

100.4 Where, under domestic law, a person is simultaneously taxable in two countries which are parties to a DTT, in each case as a resident or by reason of any other criterion falling within art 4(1), that person will be 'liable to tax' in both countries, within the meaning of art 4(1). In that situation, there is a need to determine which of the countries the person is more closely connected to, by means of 'tie-breaker' provisions.

Such dual residence can be of extended duration. This is most commonly encountered with UK resident US nationals, who are simultaneously taxable in the UK as residents and in the US by reason of their citizenship. In the case of individuals who are not US nationals, protracted dual residence is unusual. With non-US nationals, it is most common for dual residence to arise in an 'overlap period' of transition between residence in the UK and residence elsewhere, or vice versa, due to the non-alignment of the UK's tax year and the calendar tax year commonly used in other countries.

Periods of dual residence can occur even where, in reality, there is a sharp dividing line between the UK resident period and the period of residence abroad. Where individuals are concerned, this situation may be the result of split-year treatment being unavailable under the statutory residence test (see para **41.34** ff).

There was a period of deemed dual residence for the trust in *Smallwood v Revenue and Customs Comrs* [2009] EWHC 777 (Ch), [2009] STC 1222, 11 ITLR 943, which concerned a so-called 'round the world' scheme, intended to avoid CGT on a disposal of assets by the trust. In the course of a single UK tax year, the trust was consecutively resident, by reason of the residence of its trustees, in Jersey, Mauritius and then the UK. The fact that there was a small part of the tax year in which UK resident persons were the trustees caused the trust to be within the charge to CGT (subject to treaty relief) throughout the UK tax year. For art 4(1) purposes, therefore, the trust was considered to be 'liable to tax' in the UK, and therefore a resident of the UK, throughout the UK tax year. The case concerned the availability of treaty relief in respect of a disposal made by the trust when it was factually resident in Mauritius, so (as discussed below) the question was whether the 'tie-breaker' provisions of the DTT between the UK and Mauritius gave taxing rights to the UK or Mauritius.

Tie-breakers for dual-resident individuals

100.5 Under a DTT based on the Model Treaty, the treaty residence of a dual-resident individual is determined (under art 4(2)) by a succession of 'tie-breaker' provisions, which look at:

(1) whether the individual has a permanent home available to him in one of the contracting states only (in which case, he will be treaty resident in such state);

(2) whether the individual has an identifiable 'centre of vital interests' in one of the contracting states (in which case, he will be treaty resident in such state);

(3) whether the individual has a 'habitual abode' in one of the contracting states only (in which case, he will be treaty resident in such state); and

(4) whether the individual is a national of one of the contracting states only (in which case, he will be treaty resident in such state).

Generally these questions must be addressed sequentially, so if one of the tests does not resolve the individual's treaty residence, one must move down to the next test in the sequence. So, for example, if the individual has permanent homes available to him in both contracting states, the 'centre of vital interests' test is applied next.

However, as an exception to this general principle, the Model Treaty wording provides that if an individual does not have permanent homes available to him in either contracting state, one must apply the habitual abode test – skipping the 'centre of vital interests' test. The rationale for this is unclear. Certain DTTs, eg that between the UK and Canada, deviate from the Model Treaty and require the 'centre of vital interests' test to be applied not only where the individual has a permanent home in both states but also where he has a permanent home in neither.

If none of the above tests determines the individual's treaty residence, it must be determined by mutual agreement between the tax authorities of the two contracting states. Clearly, that is a highly unsatisfactory position for a taxpayer to find himself in.

Some of the above tests are conceptually difficult, or may be difficult to apply in practice. The following comments may be made:

- **Permanent home:** The fact that the permanent home test refers to such home being available to the individual indicates that it need not be owned by him. A home held by a trust, for example, may qualify as a permanent home. However, the OECD commentary notes (at para 14 of the guidance on art 4(2)) that 'the permanence of the home is essential; this means that the individual has arranged to have the dwelling available to him at all times continuously, and not occasionally for the purpose of a stay which, owing to the reasons for it, is necessarily of short duration'.

- **Centre of vital interests:** The OECD view is that, when determining where an individual has the centre of his 'vital interests', regard must be had to 'his family and social relations, his occupations, his political, cultural or other activities, his place of business, the place from which he administers his property, etc. The circumstances must be examined as a whole, but it is nevertheless obvious that considerations based on the personal acts of the individual must receive special attention. If a person who has a home in one State sets up a second in the other State while retaining the first, the fact that he retains the first in the environment where he has always lived, where he has worked, and where he has his family and possessions, can, together with other elements, go to demonstrate that he has retained his centre of vital interests in the first State' (para 15 of the guidance on art 4(2)).

• **Habitual abode:** The OECD commentary makes no real attempt to explain the concept of 'habitual abode', which is commonly used to determine taxability in civil law countries, but has no meaning in English law or UK tax law. HMRC comment (in Helpsheet 302) that the test 'applied to each state is whether you live in that state regularly, normally or customarily. The number of visits and the duration of the visits are taken into account and this test is applied over a sufficient period as is necessary depending on the facts of each case'. In a decision of the Tax Court of Canada, *Lingle v Canada*, [2010] FCA 152, [2010] 3 FCR D-5, it was held that the concept of 'habitual abode' 'involves notions of frequency, duration and regularity of stays of a quality which are more than transient' (para 6). The court rejected the view that the frequency of stays or the number of stays is a determining or sole factor to be considered (para 22). According to the court, the correct question is whether the individual has substantial stays in one of the contracting states, or the other, as a matter of habit, leading to the conclusion that such state is a place where the individual 'regularly, customarily or normally' lives (para 30). Self-evidently, given the structure of the 'tie-breaker' provisions, it is possible for the facts to point to the conclusion that an individual has such stays in both contracting states in the period that is being tested, in one of them, or in neither.

Tie-breaker for other persons: the POEM test

100.6 By contrast with the multi-layered 'tie-breaker' tests that are used to determine the treaty residence of a dual-resident individual, the treaty residence of any other dual-resident person is typically decided (under art 4(3)) by a single test, which looks at where the 'effective management' of the person in question is situated. This test applies not only to dual-resident companies, but also to dual-resident trusts. At least from a UK tax perspective, a trust is a 'person' by virtue of the treatment of trustees as a body of persons under UK tax law (see para **103.7**).

The meaning of 'place of effective management' (or POEM) is not immediately clear. The OECD commentary states that 'the place of effective management is the place where key management and commercial decisions that are necessary for the conduct of the entity's business are in substance made', which 'will ordinarily be the place where the most senior person or group of persons (for example a board of directors) makes its decisions . . . ' (para 24 in the discussion of Model Treaty Art 4). On the basis of this passage, it is difficult to discern any real difference between the DTT concept of 'effective management' and the UK law concept of 'central management and control', and indeed the conclusion reached in *Wood v Holden (Inspector of Taxes)* [2006] EWCA Civ 26, [2006] 1 WLR 1393, [2006] STC 443 was that these are different expressions to denote the same thing.

However, a couple of cases in relation to trusts suggest that there could, in fact, be subtle differences between these tests. In both cases the court was required to determine whether the trust in question had its POEM in the UK or overseas. A factor common to the cases was that the trusts had foreign resident trustees but actions were taken by those trustees to give effect to an arrangement proposed by advisers based in the UK.

In *Wensleydale's Settlement Trustees v IRC* [1996] STC (SCD) 241, the Special Commissioner expressed the view that 'effective management' implies 'realistic, positive management' and stated that 'the place of effective management is where the shots are called'. He found that, although trustee decisions were taken in the other country (Ireland), in substance the Irish trustees acquiesced unquestioningly in the plan that had been proposed by a UK adviser; 'there was no "input" from the Republic of Ireland'. Accordingly the POEM was the UK.

Somewhat similarly, in *Smallwood v Revenue and Customs Comrs* [2009] EWHC 777 (Ch), [2009] STC 1222, 11 ITLR 943, the Special Commissioners found that the POEM of the trust was in the UK. This was on the basis that although the trustees in the other country (Mauritius) played a key role in implementing a tax avoidance arrangement, that arrangement was devised and coordinated by UK-based accountants. By a narrow majority, the Court of Appeal upheld that finding, with Hughes LJ commenting that 'The steps taken in the scheme were carefully orchestrated from the United Kingdom . . . There was a scheme of management of this trust which went above and beyond the day to day management exercised by the trustees [in Mauritius] and the control of it was located in the United Kingdom.' But Patten LJ, who delivered the bulk of the judgment, disagreed on this point, noting that:

> 'The findings made do not go beyond saying that [the Mauritian trustees] accepted the advice of [the UK accountants] to proceed with and implement the scheme . . . They retained their rights and duties as trustees to consider the matter . . . and did not . . . agree merely to act on the instructions which they received from [the accountants]. The function of the directors was not therefore usurped . . . ' ([2010] STC 2045).

It is suggested that Patten LJ was right, and that, in reality, the taxpayers in *Smallwood* lost the case not because the trust was managed from the UK in any real sense, but because it was unattractive to the courts that the tax avoidance scheme should be effective. However, it might be concluded from *Wensleydale* and *Smallwood* that, for a trust to have a POEM in the other contracting state, it is necessary to show not only that trustee decision-making genuinely takes place in that other state, but also that there is no 'scheme of management' in the UK or 'orchestration' of steps from the UK, even if that takes the form of professional advice which is properly considered by the overseas trustees. In such cases it may therefore be desirable for UK tax advice to be provided to the overseas trustees by advisers who are themselves outside the UK.

Mutual agreement

100.7 A certain number of DTTs in the Model Treaty format deviate from the model by providing that where a person other than an individual is liable to tax in both contracting states, that person's residence for the purpose of the treaty shall be determined by agreement of the competent authorities (instead of a POEM test). This deeply unhelpful provision is a feature of, among others, the DTT with the USA.

DTTS WITH THE CROWN DEPENDENCIES

100.8 Under the DTTs with Jersey, Guernsey and the Isle of Man, relief under a distributive article typically depends on income or profits having accrued to an individual resident in one of the contracting states, or an 'enterprise' resident in one of those states.

The concept of residence for the purposes of these three treaties is different from that in treaties which follow the Model Treaty. Under the DTTs with the Crown Dependencies, a person is resident in the relevant Crown Dependency (CD) if he/it is resident in the CD for the purposes of the CD's tax, and not resident in the UK for the purposes of UK tax; and symmetrically, a person is resident in the UK for treaty purposes if resident in the UK for the purposes of UK tax, and not resident in the CD for the purposes of the CD's tax. This formulation precludes exemption from tax under a distributive article of one of these treaties where income or profits have accrued to a dual-resident.

Chapter 101
OVERVIEW OF
DISTRIBUTIVE ARTICLES

101.1 As explained in the preceding chapter, the logical first step in applying an income/gains/profits DTT to determine a person's taxability is to establish where the person will be considered treaty resident. Once this has been done, the distributive articles of the DTT can be considered, to establish whether they give exclusive taxing rights to one of the contracting states, or (if not) whether they impose a cap on the rate of tax that can be imposed by one of the contracting states.

Even if its scope were restricted to DTTs based on the Model Treaty, a survey of the UK's income/gains/profits DTTs would reveal considerable variation in their provisions. No two DTTs are precisely the same, and when advising there is no substitute for careful analysis of the relevant DTT. It is dangerous to assume that the provisions of the Model Treaty will necessarily be replicated in a given article of a particular DTT which has been negotiated between the UK and another country, as the DTT may include bespoke provisions reflecting the contracting states' respective tax systems and driven by objectives of their respective tax authorities to block particular avoidance opportunities. In some cases, and in particular that of the UK/USA DTT, such bespoke provisions may transform the effect of the DTT (see paras **102.5** to **102.7**).

In general, though, the process of negotiation and amendment which precedes the signing of a DTT is less transformative in its effect, and generally the distributive articles of the UK's DTTs are broadly in line with the Model Treaty articles from which they are derived. It is useful therefore to have an overview of how these articles typically operate, provided that at all times it is remembered that there is always a need to review the exact wording of the DTT which is in point.

The table below is intended to provide such an overview. A UK tax adviser looking at a DTT is more commonly seeking to determine whether the treaty excludes or limits the UK's taxing rights than whether it affects the taxing rights of the other country. Accordingly, the table sets out the typical effect of a Model Treaty-based DTT's distributive articles, making the assumption that the person to whom income, gains or profits is accruing is treaty resident in the other contracting state – either on the basis that the person is 'liable to tax' in that country and not 'liable to tax' in the UK, or on the basis that the person is 'liable to tax' in both but is considered to be treaty resident in the other country by application of the 'tie-breaker' provisions (as discussed in the preceding chapter). Some comments have been included, regarding frequently encountered variations on the Model Treaty wording and some areas of uncertainty about how the articles interact with aspects of the UK tax code.

For brevity, 'the other contracting state' has been abbreviated in the table to 'OCS'. References to a third country are to a country which is neither the UK nor the OCS, ie a non-party to the DTT which is under consideration. The table does not attempt to deal with all persons or classes of income which are commonly covered by an income/gains/profits DTT – for example, there tend to be distributive articles concerned with entertainers and athletes, government officials and students, but these 'niche' provisions are not covered below.

SCOPE OF 'OTHER INCOME' ARTICLE

101.2 It is worth commenting here on art 21 of a Model Treaty-based DTT, headed 'Other income', as this article is more important in allocating taxing rights between contracting states than is immediately obvious. In the Model Treaty, art 21(1) is worded as follows:

> 'Items of income of a resident of a Contracting State, wherever arising, not dealt with in the foregoing Articles of this Convention shall be taxable only in that State.'

A common variation on this is for art 21(1) to refer to items of income 'not mentioned' in the foregoing articles. In either form, it is not immediately clear that the article is intended to apply not only to classes of income not mentioned in the preceding articles, but also income of a class covered by one of the preceding articles where the article in question has not addressed the position if such income is received in particular circumstances or from a particular source. The OECD commentary notes succinctly that 'the income concerned is not only income of a class not expressly dealt with but also income from sources not expressly mentioned' (para 1 of the discussion of art 21). In some of the UK's DTTs, the ambiguous drafting of the Model Treaty has been rectified by a modification of art 21, so that it makes express reference to items of income of a type not dealt with, or from a source not dealt with, in the preceding articles.

However, even where this modification has not been made, art 21 is invariably construed as determining taxing rights with respect to income from sources that have not been addressed by the preceding articles. This typically includes various classes of investment income where the source is the other contracting state or a third country. As the article confers exclusive taxing rights on the country of which the recipient is a treaty resident (possibly subject to exceptions, eg for income received from trusts and estates) art 21 is, in practice, an important provision.

Type of income or gain (of a person treaty resident in OCS)	Source/situs/ circumstances	Countries with taxing rights	Applicable Model Treaty provision(s)	Comments
Income from immovable property, eg rental income	UK	UK and OCS	Article 6(1)	
	OCS	OCS	Article 21(1)	
	Third country	OCS	Article 21(1)	
Business profits	UK PE	UK (insofar as profits are attributable to the UK PE) and OCS	Article 7(1)	
	OCS (no UK PE)	OCS	Article 7(1)	
	Third country (no UK PE)	OCS	Article 7(1)	
Dividends	UK	UK (subject to cap) and OCS	Article 10(1), 10(2)	Where tax can be levied subject to a cap, the capped rate may be affected by size of shareholding and whether shareholder is a company.
	OCS	OCS	Article 10(2)	
	Third country	OCS	Article 21(1)	
Interest	UK	UK (subject to cap) and OCS	Article 11(1), 11(2)	'Interest' is usually defined as 'income from debt claims of every kind . . .'. It is debatable whether this includes deemed interest; eg whether a distribution from an offshore fund that fails the qualifying investments test (see para **95.8**) is interest for DTT purposes or a dividend.
	OCS	OCS	Article 11(2)	
	Third country	OCS	Article 21(1)	

Type of income or gain (of a person treaty resident in OCS)	Source/situs/circumstances	Countries with taxing rights	Applicable Model Treaty provision(s)	Comments
Royalties	UK	OCS	Article 12(1)	Some UK DTTs are different and allow the UK to tax UK source royalties, subject to a cap (as with interest).
	OCS or third country	OCS	Article 21(1)	
Capital gains	UK	OCS and (if the asset is UK land or all/part of a UK PE) UK	Article 13(1), 13(2), 13(5)	Article 13 is sometimes modified to allow the UK to tax a gain on a person who is a resident of the UK at any time in the tax year in which alienation occurs. See para 104.13.
	OCS or third country	OCS	Article 13(5)	There is debate about whether taxing rights in respect of offshore income gains (see CHAPTER 95) are governed by art 13 or art 21. However, these provisions usually have the same effect.
Employment income	Employment exercised in UK	OCS and (if certain conditions are met) UK	Article 15(1)	Article 15 typically covers 'salaries, wages and other similar remuneration'. There is debate about whether art 15 is engaged in relation to benefits in kind.
	Employment exercised in OCS or third country	OCS	Article 15(1)	

Type of income or gain (of a person treaty resident in OCS)	Source/situs/ circumstances	Countries with taxing rights	Applicable Model Treaty provision(s)	Comments
Directors' fees	Company resident in UK	OCS and UK	Article 16	Where the director is treaty resident in the OCS, the UK has no taxing rights with respect to fees for a directorship with a non-UK resident company, even if director's duties are performed in the UK.
	Company resident in OCS or third country	OCS	Article 21(1)	
Pension income	Any	OCS	Article 18	
Other income, eg income distributions from trusts and estates	Any	OCS	Article 21(1)	Art 21 is sometimes modified to preserve the UK's right to tax income distributions from trusts and estates.

Chapter 102

AVAILABILITY OF RELIEF

102.1 As noted in the preceding chapters, for relief to be claimed under a distributive article of a DTT in respect of income or a capital gain, the person to whom the income or gain has accrued is generally required to be resident for treaty purposes in one of the states which are party to that DTT. For relief to be available from UK tax under a DTT to which the UK is a party, the recipient of the income or the person realising the gain must normally be treaty resident in the other contracting state.

However, treaty residence in the 'correct' contracting state is not always the only requirement for relief under a distributive article. In the case of income, it may also be necessary to show that the recipient is the 'beneficial owner' of the income or is 'subject to tax' in respect of the income. The DTT may also incorporate other 'limitation of benefits', or anti-avoidance, provisions which are capable of precluding a claim to relief under a distributive article. Claiming relief by way of credit under a DTT tends to be more straightforward, but even here there may be restrictions on the credit that is available. These issues are considered below.

BENEFICIAL OWNERSHIP

102.2 DTTs based on the Model Treaty often use a variety of expressions to denote receipt. Perhaps the most commonly used term is 'derive'; a DTT may refer to income of a particular kind being 'derived by' a person resident in one of the contracting states. However, not infrequently, distributive articles of DTTs refer to income 'derived and beneficially owned' by such a person.

This formulation raises several questions. First, is the addition of the words 'and beneficially owned' meaningful? Does it impose some further requirement, which goes to the nature or quality of the person's 'derivation' of the income in question; or is it mere verbiage? And second, if these words are *not* mere verbiage, what precisely does 'beneficially owned' mean in the context of a DTT to which the UK is a party? If, under a DTT, relief from UK tax on income requires the income to be 'beneficially owned' by a resident of the other contracting state, is that issue to be determined applying the English law concept of beneficial ownership, or does this term have a distinct, internationally recognised meaning for the purpose of DTTs, which ousts the English law meaning?

Reference to the OECD commentary indicates that, globally, 'beneficial ownership' for treaty purposes differs from the meaning that an English lawyer or UK tax adviser would instinctively give to the term. For example, in para 12 of the discussion of art 10 of the Model Treaty, regarding dividends, the OECD commentary states that 'The term "beneficial owner" is not used in a narrow, technical sense, rather, it should be understood in its context and in light of the object and purposes of the Convention, including avoiding double taxation and the prevention of fiscal evasion and avoidance.'

International case law suggests that for DTT purposes a person is a 'beneficial owner' of income if the person is not an agent or nominee for a third party (which obviously accords with the English law meaning) but that there is a further requirement, namely that there are no circumstances or arrangements which have the effect that the income is inevitably or automatically paid to a third party. In other words, international practice is to require what might be termed substantive beneficial ownership, which implies some degree of discretion as to what is done with the income once it has been received.

The Court of Appeal judgment in *Indofood* (see para **99.13**) provides support for this latter approach. The Court accepted that the expression 'beneficially owned' should be given an 'international fiscal meaning' in line with the OECD commentary. Since 1986, the OECD's stated position has been that for treaty purposes a person cannot be regarded as a 'beneficial owner' of income if that person is an agent or nominee for another person, or where otherwise than through an agency or nominee relationship, the recipient of the income acts as a 'conduit' for another person 'who in fact receives the benefit of the income concerned'.

As discussed above, the precedential status of the *Indofood* decision, in relation to the UK's DTTs, is questionable. However, it must be correct to treat the case as persuasive, and an indicator of the approach which would be taken by the English courts if the interpretation of 'beneficial ownership' for treaty purposes was a live issue in a dispute regarding a UK DTT.

'SUBJECT TO TAX' REQUIREMENTS

102.3 Certain DTTs impose a further or alternative requirement for income or gains to be exempt from taxation in one of the contracting states – namely that the income or gains must have been received or realised by a resident of the other contracting state who is 'subject to tax' on them. For example the UK/Luxembourg DTT states that interest paid by a resident of one contracting state shall be taxable in the other contracting state only, provided that it is paid to a resident of that other state who is subject to tax in respect of such income (art XI).

As explained above (see para **100.3**), a person is only considered a resident of a contracting state if he is 'liable to tax' in that state. 'Subject to tax' cannot, therefore, be synonymous with 'liable to tax', as if it were, the additional requirement that income/gains be 'subject to tax' would be otiose.

There is, in fact, widespread international agreement that these two similar-sounding expressions have distinct meanings. As a person is considered to be 'liable to tax' if he or it is within the scope of the relevant country's taxing power, 'by reason of [the person's] domicile, residence, place of management or any other criterion of a similar nature' (and irrespective of whether the country actually does impose tax). By contrast 'subject to tax' means actually subjected to taxation. This distinction has been approved and applied in a UK context in *Weiser v Revenue and Customs Comrs* [2012] UKFTT 501 (TC), [2012] SFTD 1381, 15 ITLR 157, in which the First-tier Tribunal considered the meaning of 'subject to tax' in the UK/Israel DTT.

HMRC's view in the International Manual is consistent with this. HMRC state that:

> 'The expression "subject to tax" usually means that the person must actually pay tax on the income in their country of residence. However, a person is still regarded as "subject to tax" if, for example, he or she does not pay tax because their income is sufficiently small that it is covered by personal allowances that are available to set against liability to tax in the other country. [However,] a person is not regarded as "subject to tax" if the income in question is exempted from tax because the law of the other country provides for a statutory exemption from tax. For example [this is the case if] the income is that of a charity . . . ' (INTM 332210).

Tax-exempt entities are considered in the following chapter.

OTHER ANTI-AVOIDANCE PROVISIONS

102.4 Not infrequently, DTTs to which the UK is a party include anti-avoidance provisions, sometimes referred to in this context as 'limitation of benefits' provisions. These may preclude or restrict relief under the terms of the treaty.

Such provisions may be specific to particular forms of income, and if so will typically be incorporated into the relevant distributive articles. For example, it is not uncommon for the article of a DTT dealing with interest payments (typically art 11) to include a paragraph which is capable of limiting relief under that article where the amount of interest paid exceeds what would be paid under an arm's length arrangement, due to a 'special relationship' between the payer and recipient. Where this is the case, only the proportion of the interest which would have been paid under an arm's length arrangement is capable of being relieved under the interest article.

It is also common in the UK's DTTs for there to be a more general anti-avoidance provision, included in the miscellaneous rules article of the DTT (typically art 27) which is directed at remittance basis users. The effect of such a provision, where it applies, is to limit the amount of relief that is available from tax imposed by the other contracting state. Under provisions of this kind, income qualifying for relief from tax in the other state is restricted to the amount, if any, 'which is remitted to or received in the United Kingdom'. Such provisions tend to be limited in scope to income. Generally there is no restriction of relief from foreign tax on capital gains, where the individual concerned is treaty resident in the UK but also resident, as a matter of domestic law, in the other contracting state, and the gains in question have not been remitted to the UK.

Lastly, a DTT may incorporate provisions which are designed to combat 'treaty shopping'. 'Treaty shopping' is a somewhat ill-defined concept, but broadly it is the practice of creating an entity in a particular contracting state with the purpose of obtaining treaty benefits which would not otherwise be available, in a manner which is judged to go beyond what is acceptable tax planning. To discourage this practice, certain modern DTTs include motive-based provisions which preclude treaty benefits where the entity which would otherwise be eligible for them was put in place with the sole or main purpose of securing such benefits. These provisions tend to be somewhat similar to the motive defence against the domestic transfer of assets code (see CHAPTER 73).

THE UK/USA DTT

102.5 Where the availability of treaty relief is concerned, two points must be made regarding the current UK/USA DTT. This treaty is elaborately drafted and far removed, in its effect, from the Model Treaty from which it is derived.

Art 23 – qualified persons restriction

102.6 Article 23 of the UK/USA DTT, headed 'Limitation on benefits', significantly restricts the persons who are capable of taking the benefit of the DTT, where they are treaty resident in one of the contracting states and derive income, gains or profits from the other. Treaty benefits are generally only available to what the article calls 'qualified persons', although other persons may claim relief in certain circumstances, including in the event that the person in question is accepted as having been established without the main purpose of securing benefits under the DTT. The details of the article are baroque, but the broad thrust of the 'qualified persons' definition is that (a) a natural person can take the benefit of the treaty in all cases but (b) for an entity such as a company or trust to be capable of taking the benefit of the treaty, the entity must be a listed company, or otherwise the entity or its capital must be beneficially owned as to at least 50% by 'qualified persons'.

Art 1(4) – saving provision

102.7 Even more drastic in its consequences, although easy for the uninitiated to overlook, is the so-called saving provision in art 1(4) of the UK/USA DTT. This states that, notwithstanding any provision of the DTT, but subject to certain exceptions, 'a Contracting State may tax its residents (as determined under art 4 (Residence)), and by reason of citizenship may tax its citizens, as if [the DTT] had not come into effect'. The remarkably one-sided result of this provision is that, in general, the US retains full taxing rights with respect to US citizens even where they are UK resident and, under the 'tie-breaker', are treaty resident in the UK rather than in the US. By contrast, the UK's taxing rights are, in the normal way, essentially limited to income, gains and profits of UK treaty residents and certain classes of UK source income and UK gains. The exceptions referred to above include the effect of art 24, regarding relief from double taxation, which is of course crucial for the credit relief provisions of the treaty to have effect.

LIMITATIONS ON CREDIT RELIEF

102.8 There are also limits on the amount of credit relief that can be claimed in respect of foreign taxation, under the terms of DTTs and under domestic legislation.

Tax deducted in accordance with treaty

102.9 Where credit relief is being claimed under a DTT based on the Model Treaty, the 'elimination of double taxation' article of the DTT will normally be expressed as providing credit in one country for tax which is payable under the laws of the other country in accordance with the DTT in question. Where a credit against UK tax is sought, the formulation above means that the foreign tax that is creditable is limited to foreign tax from which there was no exemption under the DTT. In a case where the DTT imposes a cap on the amount of foreign tax that may be charged, for example on dividends, the credit against UK tax is limited to the amount of foreign tax that would have been charged at that capped rate. Obviously the same limitations apply, *mutatis mutandis*, where relief from foreign tax is sought by way of a credit in respect of UK tax.

Clearly, this principle puts the onus on the taxpayer to ensure that, in a double taxation situation, the two countries which are levying tax do in fact have the right to do so, and that any cap on the tax rate, under the DTT, is given effect to by means of a claim for relief.

Reasonable steps to mitigate foreign tax

102.10 Domestic law goes further in seeking to restrict credit relief. TIOPA 2010, s 33 applies to credit relief under a DTT and also to unilateral credit relief (see para **99.16**). It limits the amount of foreign tax that may be taken into account for such purposes to the amount which would have been charged 'had all reasonable steps been taken' under the law of the other country, or under any arrangements made between the UK and that country, to minimise the amount of foreign tax. Section 33 specifically provides that such steps may include claiming reliefs, deductions or allowances or making elections. The issue of what steps are to be considered reasonable is to be determined by considering 'what might reasonably be expected to have been done' in the absence of double taxation relief (s 33(3)).

HMRC's views as to what steps will be considered reasonable for these purposes are set out at INTM 164140. Interestingly, HMRC do not consider that there is a requirement for a company to take advantage of a so-called 'designer rate' regime where such regime is available.

The extent of the foreign tax mitigation requirement in TIOPA 2010, s 33 was considered in *Bayfine UK Products v Revenue & Customs* (2008) Sp C 719. In the High Court, Peter Smith J dismissed HMRC's contention that the reasonable steps referred to in s 33 might extend to not doing the transaction which had given rise to foreign tax at all; or that there should be a disregard of foreign tax which would not have arisen if other persons, not under the taxpayer's control, had taken certain steps, such as making tax elections. He commented that ' . . . it is not open to HMRC in my view to say that other parties which are not compellable by the taxpayer could serve notices or do other things which would reduce the foreign tax bill. I do not see how it can be reasonable to take into account something which is beyond the control of the taxpayer in question' (*Bayfine UK v Revenue and Customs Comrs* [2010] EWHC 609 (Ch), [2010] STC 1379, 12 ITLR 935). In the Court of Appeal, Arden J agreed, observing that no regard can be had to tax mitigation steps that could have been taken third parties which the taxpayer had no ability to control, even where those third parties are within the same corporate group and there is a common interest in such steps being taken (*Bayfine UK v Revenue and Customs Comrs* [2011] EWCA Civ 304, [2012] 1 WLR 1630, [2012] Bus LR 796, at para 76).

Chapter 103

PROBLEM ENTITIES

103.1 Entities which are exempt from taxation or which are treated as transparent for tax purposes can create particular difficulties in applying a DTT.

TAX-EXEMPT ENTITIES

103.2 The OECD commentary (at paras **8.6** to **8.7** in its discussion of Model Treaty art 4) notes that:

> 'In many States, a person is considered liable to comprehensive taxation even if the Contracting State does not in fact impose tax. For example, pension funds, charities and other organisations may be exempted from tax, but they are exempt only if they meet all of the requirements for exemption specified in the tax laws. They are, thus, subject to the tax laws of a Contracting State. Furthermore, if they do not meet the standards specified, they are also required to pay tax. Most States would view such entities as residents for purposes of the Convention. [. . .] In some States, however, these entities are not considered liable to tax if they are exempt from tax under domestic tax laws. These States may not regard such entities as residents for the purposes of a convention . . . '

This passage focuses on entities that are conditionally exempted from taxation, and leaves open the question of whether an entity is capable of being treaty resident where it is established or managed if it is unconditionally exempt from tax under domestic legislation. It is arguable that such an entity should still be considered 'liable to tax', since the country in question could, if it saw fit, amend its tax laws to remove the exemption, asserting taxing rights over the entity in accordance with international norms. In fact, there seems to be widespread international support for the proposition that an entity should be regarded as 'liable to tax' in a country if its connecting characteristics with the country are the same as for other persons who are fully subject to tax in that country, even if in practice no tax is levied. In *Weiser v Revenue and Customs Comrs* [2012] UKFTT 501 (TC), [2012] SFTD 1381, 15 ITLR 157 at para 28, the court noted a conclusion to this effect reached in a seminar of the International Fiscal Association.

A minority of the UK's DTTs expressly prevent specified classes of tax-exempt entity from claiming treaty benefits, either in all cases or with respect to particular kinds of income. These include the treaties with the Crown Dependencies, various islands in the Caribbean, Cyprus, Malta and certain CIS states. Such limitation of benefits articles support the view that, as a matter of principle, tax-exempt entities qualify as 'liable to tax' on the basis discussed above.

It is suggested that, in any event, most entities involved in offshore tax planning can be regarded as conditionally tax-exempt. The conditions in question typically relate to the status of the owner, settlor or beneficiaries of the entity as foreign resident(s).

There has been little discussion of this issue in reported cases concerning DTTs to which the UK is a party. In the *Smallwood* tax litigation, which concerned a trust with a Mauritian resident corporate trustee, it appears to have been common ground between the parties that the treaty residence of the trustee turned on the application of the POEM 'tie-breaker' article. This indicates acceptance by HMRC that the trust was 'liable to tax' in Mauritius. In the Court of Appeal, Patten LJ stated that 'PMIL as trustee was clearly resident in Mauritius' (*Smallwood v Revenue and Customs Comrs* [2009] EWHC 777 (Ch), [2009] STC 1222, 11 ITLR 943, para 12). It is possible that this conclusion was so lightly reached because there was evidence that the trust was actually taxed in Mauritius. The authors' understanding is that under the Mauritian tax regime, the default position for a trust with a non-Mauritian resident settlor and non-Mauritian resident beneficiaries is complete exemption from tax. However, the trustee of such a trust can make an election to have the trust treated as a 'resident trust', in which case there is a modest level of Mauritian tax on income received by the trust. It may be that a 'resident trust' election was made by the trustee of the Smallwood trust, but this detail does not emerge from the judgments.

TRANSPARENT ENTITIES

103.3 By contrast with tax-exempt entities, it is generally accepted that an entity which is treated as tax-transparent under the law of a contracting state cannot be 'liable to tax' in that state, and on that basis cannot be resident there for the purposes of a DTT in the OECD form.

The obvious example of this is a partnership – partnerships being commonly, although not universally, transparent under national tax laws. However, the laws of many countries also make provision for corporate bodies which, although not partnerships, are (or may be) treated analogously for the purposes of domestic legislation (and which may, for convenience, be called 'deemed partnerships'). Examples include LLPs in many countries, various forms of company in Luxembourg, and S-corporations and LLCs in the US (except LLCs which have elected to be tax-opaque). As discussed below, the domestic treatment of such entities as tax-transparent does not always coincide with their treatment under other tax systems.

Partnerships

103.4 Where a partnership is managed and controlled in a country whose tax rules treat it as transparent, this generally rules out any exemptive relief under the terms of a DTT between that country and the country in which the partners are resident, assuming that the DTT is based on the Model Treaty. This is because, as explained above, the partnership will not be 'liable to tax' where it is managed and will not, therefore, qualify as a resident of that state.

In the OECD commentary it is stated that where a partnership is fiscally transparent and therefore incapable of qualifying as a resident of the country in which it is managed and controlled, 'the partners should be entitled, with respect to their share of the income of the partnership, to the benefits provided by the Conventions entered into by the States of which they are residents to the extent that the partnership's income is allocated to them for the purposes of taxation in their state of residence' (para 5 of the discussion of Model Treaty, art 1). In other words, the partnership is looked through when applying the DTT, and the income is treated as if it had been received directly by the partners, according to their respective shares of partnership profits.

However, there was a different result in *Padmore v IRC* [1987] STC 36, 62 TC 352, CA, where the relevant treaty was the UK's DTT with Jersey. The case concerned business profits of a partnership which was managed and controlled in Jersey, although the majority of its partners were UK resident individuals. The point at issue was whether those UK resident partners could claim an exemption from income tax on the partnership profits. This turned on whether, within the meaning of the UK/Jersey DTT, the partnership was a 'Jersey enterprise', defined as 'an industrial or commercial enterprise or undertaking carried on by a resident of Jersey'. The UK/Jersey DTT defines 'resident of Jersey' as a person resident in Jersey for the purposes of Jersey tax, and not resident in the UK. The DTT does not use the 'liable to tax' formulation which is standard in DTTs based on the Model Treaty.

The Court of Appeal concluded ('with some hesitation') that the partnership should be considered a resident of Jersey if its central management and control was in Jersey (which, on the facts, it was). It appears that, in reaching this decision, the Court was influenced by provisions of Jersey tax law which impute a place of residence to a partnership and allow partners to be assessed to tax in the name of their partnership, and also the fact that such assessment to tax had indeed been made by the Jersey Comptroller of Income Tax. Presumably the tax so assessed was in respect of the Jersey resident partners only, but this is not clear from the judgment. It is widely considered that the determination that the partnership was a resident of Jersey would not have been reached had the UK/Jersey DTT been based on the Model Treaty.

It is worth noting that following the *Padmore* decision, the UK introduced what is now ITTOIA 2005, s 858, to block possible tax avoidance by UK residents through the use of partnerships managed and controlled in the Crown Dependencies. It was this anti-avoidance provision that was the subject of *Padmore No 2* (see para **99.8**).

Deemed partnerships

103.5 Deemed partnerships can be attractive, as they typically have legal personality, but avoid multiple layers of taxation and help to minimise tax filings. However, where several tax systems are involved, these entities should be treated with caution.

In the event that all relevant countries regard the deemed partnership as transparent, this does not generate any particular difficulties, as each of the contracting states should uphold the convention that income/gains of the deemed partnership accrue to the participators in it, who will be 'liable to tax' in respect of such income/gains in their respective countries of residence. In that situation, the participators can, in principle, qualify for relief under the terms of the DTT between their country of residence and the country in which income/gains are accruing.

However, difficulties can arise in the common situation where one contracting state 'sees' the entity as transparent but the other 'sees' it as a taxable person. A prime example of the issues that this can generate is provided by the *Swift/Anson* litigation, which concerned an LLC established under Delaware law. The LLC was deemed transparent for US tax purposes, but was not accepted by HMRC as being similarly transparent in the UK (see also para 32.8).

Mr Anson, a UK resident member of the LLC, sought relief by way of credit against UK income tax that had been assessed on payments received by him from the LLC, under art 24(4)(a) of the UK/USA DTT. The claimed credit was in respect of US income tax that had been paid on US trading profits of the LLC, which for US tax purposes had been treated as Mr Anson's own profits and had been taxed accordingly. The difficulty was that there was a perceived mismatch between the receipts on which tax was payable in the two countries. Although the US analysis was that Mr Anson had received and had been taxed on a share of the LLC's trading profits, HMRC took the position that, because the LLC was a body corporate that was not a partnership, he was taxable in the UK not on the trading profits as such, but on distributions by the LLC of sums deriving from those profits. In HMRC's view, those distributions could not be characterised as trading profits, but were (in essence) dividends paid by the LLC. Credit relief under art 24(4)(a) was only available if the US tax had been paid on income/profits and the UK tax had been computed by reference to the same income/profits. HMRC's contention was that the mismatch between the US and UK tax analyses of the situation precluded any claim to credit under art 24(4)(a).

In the First-tier Tribunal, John Avery-Jones and Ian Menzies-Conacher accepted expert evidence to the effect that the members' agreement governing the LLC, combined with provisions of the Delaware LLC Act, caused the members to be entitled to payments of profits from the LLC's business as and when such profits arose. The Tribunal found that there was no discretion on the part of the LLC's managers whether or not to make payments of such profits to the members, and no step analogous to the declaration of a dividend was required to make the members' entitlement to the profits enforceable. Accordingly, the Tribunal's assessment was that Mr Anson was taxable in the UK on a share of the LLC's profits, as if the LLC were a partnership, and therefore credit relief was available in respect of the relevant proportion of the US tax levied on such profits (*Swift v Revenue and Customs Comrs* [2010] UKFTT 88 (TC), [2010] SFTD 553).

However, such view was not shared by the Upper Tribunal or the Court of Appeal. Both of these courts considered that, because the members could not be said to have a proprietary interest in the LLC's assets, Mr Anson should not be regarded as having an entitlement to a share of its profits, and was therefore not taxable in the UK on any share of the profits. He should instead be treated, as HMRC had argued, as taxable on dividends from the company. Accordingly there was no juridical double taxation, and art 24(4)(a) was not engaged, even though the result of this was economic double taxation, entailing an overall effective tax rate approaching 70%.

Fortunately for Mr Anson, the Supreme Court disagreed with this analysis. Essentially it reached its decision on the basis that a finding of fact had been made by the First-tier Tribunal, based on expert evidence heard by it, and it was incorrect for the appellate courts to have disturbed that finding. The Upper Tribunal/Court of Appeal judgments had been based on an assumption that the absence of a proprietary interest in assets held by an entity necessarily negates any entitlement to the profits of that entity. The Supreme Court considered that to be a *non-sequitur*. The final result, therefore, was that the credit for US tax was allowed (*Revenue and Customs Comrs v Anson* [2015] UKSC 44, [2015] STC 1777, 17 ITLR 1007).

Following the Supreme Court judgment, HMRC published Revenue and Customs Brief 15 (2015), by way of a response to the judgment. It states that 'HMRC has after careful consideration concluded that the decision is specific to the facts in the case', but adds that 'individuals claiming double tax relief and relying on the *Anson v HMRC* decision will be considered on a case by case basis'. This response is perhaps more helpful to taxpayers than first appears, as it avoids upsetting the treatment of LLCs as non-transparent entities for UK tax purposes where such treatment is desired, but creates scope for transparent treatment where it can be demonstrated that the governing documents of the LLC and the applicable state legislation result in the LLC's members having an entitlement to its profits.

However, notwithstanding the final result in *Swift/Anson*, and Brief 15 (2015), it should be evident that extreme caution is required regarding the use of deemed partnerships where UK taxation is in point. The outcome of the *Swift/Anson* litigation turned on findings of fact as to the provisions of the members' agreement and Delaware law, and an LLC with a differently drafted members' agreement, and/or established under the law of a different state, could be characterised differently. Certainly, the case provides no authority or guidance on whether credit relief can be claimed in respect of foreign tax paid by any other form of deemed partnership, where the taxpayer is a participator in such entity.

TRUSTS

103.6 DTTs generally make limited reference to trusts. The only reference to trusts which is regularly encountered is in art 21, regarding 'other income'. This article gives exclusive taxing rights over income not dealt with in the preceding articles to the contracting state in which the recipient is resident, but an exception is commonly made for income from trusts, which both contracting states are, by implication, permitted to tax. Apart from this, most DTTs are silent regarding trusts.

The application of DTTs to income/gains of trusts is often fraught with difficulty. This goes beyond the uncertainty, touched on above, about whether a trust in a 'tax haven' which is exempted from local taxation can nevertheless be considered 'liable to tax' in the relevant country.

Identifying the recipient of income/gains

103.7 As explained above, it is generally the case that for income or a gain to be relieved from taxation in a contracting state under a distributive article of a DTT, it must accrue to a person who is resident for the purposes of the treaty in the other contracting state – in other words, a person who, under the laws of that contracting state, is liable to tax in that state by reason of his domicile, residence, place of management or any other criterion of a similar nature.

Uncertainty is sometimes expressed as to how this test applies in the case of income or gains of a trust. The requirement for the income or gain to have accrued to a 'person' might seem problematic where trusts are concerned, given that under common law systems a trust lacks legal personality, and is generally thought of as a bundle of rights and obligations, not as a juridical person. However, this misses the point that in a DTT which follows the Model Treaty, 'person' is almost invariably defined so as to include a body of persons. Under UK tax legislation the trustees of a settlement are deemed to be a single body of persons. Many other tax systems also treat the trustees of a settlement, or the settlement itself, as a body which is capable of being taxed, even though under some tax systems a trust may be tax-transparent in particular circumstances.

Such tax-transparency may be complete or partial. A prominent example of complete transparency is what the US tax system calls a grantor trust, the income and gains of which are deemed to be those of the settlor. Whether the income and gains of such a trust are subject to US taxation depends not on the residence of the trust but on the residence and nationality of the settlor.

It is also possible for a trust to be transparent vis-à-vis its settlor for certain domestic tax purposes and not others. For example, under the UK tax legislation, it may be that trust income is taxable on the settlor, whereas gains of the trust are taxable on its trustees or on beneficiaries when benefits are received by them. Or there can be partial transparency vis-à-vis another individual, eg a life tenant. Other tax systems may have similarly schismatic treatments of certain trusts.

Trust transparency can create analytical difficulties where DTTs are concerned. As discussed below, there are some apparent inconsistencies in international jurisprudence, or at least tensions between approaches taken in different countries, where the treatment of trusts is concerned.

Trust subject to UK settlements code

103.8 Suppose that a trust is resident in a country with which the UK has a Model Treaty-based DTT. The trust receives income or dividends from a third country. The trust has a UK resident settlor who has an interest in the settlement for the purposes of ITTOIA 2005, s 624 (see CHAPTER 75). The settlor wishes to secure exemption from UK income tax which would otherwise have to be paid by him on the trust's income. The issue is whether, for DTT purposes, the income is regarded as accruing to the trust or to the settlor. The latter analysis would preserve the UK's taxing rights with respect to the income. Conversely, the former analysis would exclude such rights.

Section 624 provides that, where a trust is settlor-interested, the trust's income is to be treated for income tax purposes 'as the income of the settlor and of the settlor alone'. It is not immediately obvious whether, in this situation, the s 624 deeming should be applied before the DTT, or whether the DTT should be applied by reference to the actual recipient of the income (the non-UK resident trust), disregarding the deeming in s 624.

Strathalmond (Lord) v IRC [1972] 3 All ER 715, [1972] 1 WLR 1511 suggests the latter. The case concerned US source investment income received by a US citizen (Lady Strathalmond) who was married to a UK resident who was not a US citizen (Lord Strathalmond). Under the UK tax code as it then stood, a wife's income was imputed for tax purposes to her husband and taxed accordingly. The relevant provision stated that the wife's income was 'deemed for income tax purposes to be [the husband's] income and not to be her income'.

The UK/USA income/gains/profits DTT in force at that time provided that dividends and interest paid by a US corporation were exempt from UK tax unless the recipient was a UK citizen, resident or corporation. The definition in the DTT of a UK resident excluded a US citizen. It was thus argued, successfully, that by virtue of the DTT, no UK tax was payable by Lord Strathalmond on Lady Strathalmond's US source income.

The court's acceptance of the correctness of this argument implies acceptance of two separate propositions, neither of which is really discussed in the judgment. The first is that when determining the application of a DTT provision which depends on the tax status of the recipient of income, one looks at the *actual* recipient of the income, and ignores any provision of UK tax law which attributes the income to another person. (If the DTT had been applied on the basis that the income had been received by Lord Strathalmond, as per the deeming rule, there would have been no exemption from UK tax.)

The second proposition is that an exemption from tax under a DTT which can be claimed by person A is capable of enuring for the benefit of person B, if, under a provision of UK tax law, person A's income is attributed to person B. This principle that treaty relief can be enjoyed vicariously in this situation is discussed in the following chapter.

The first proposition above is, at first sight, not altogether easy to reconcile with the generally accepted treatment of partnerships for DTT purposes, ie the fact (discussed above) that the income and gains of a partnership are treated as income and gains of the partners, and the partners cannot claim DTT relief by reference to where the partnership is established or managed. One possible response to this tension is that a trust is more an 'entity' than a partnership. The income and gains of a trust accrue to persons (its trustees) who are clearly separate from the settlor, whereas it is harder to draw a distinction between a partnership and the persons who are its partners. Perhaps a more analytical response is that a trust is capable of being a resident of a contracting state under a Model Treaty-based DTT, whereas a partnership is not.

Foreign tax systems

103.9 It appears that the kind of analysis discussed above in relation to the UK settlements code is not limited to imputational provisions in the UK tax legislation. For example, the Federal Court of Appeal of Canada has determined that where a gain is realised by a non-Canadian resident trust, and such gain is treated as accruing to its settlor under the Canadian tax legislation, any exemption from Canadian tax under a DTT between Canada and the country in which the trust is resident will enure for the benefit of the settlor, and will preclude any liability to Canadian tax on the gain (*R v Sommerer* [2012] FCA 207, 15 ITLR 61, paras 60–68). It appears that under the relevant provision of Canadian Income Tax Act, namely s 75(2), the imputation to the settlor applies not only to gains but also to income. Accordingly, this seems to be a case of complete transparency vis-à-vis the settlor, but nevertheless the Canadian view is that treaty relief can be claimed by reference to the residence of the trust. The trust is not ignored for DTT purposes as if it were a partnership.

By contrast, the authors' understanding is that the total transparency of a grantor trust vis-à-vis its settlor under the US tax system gives rise to a different analysis. For US tax purposes, income of a grantor trust is regarded as received by the settlor, bypassing the trust entirely. This eliminates any scope for treaty relief to be claimed under a DTT between the country in which the trust is resident and the country which is the source of the income. However, where the settlor is a US resident or national, such relief could potentially be claimed under the treaty between the US and the source country.

The apparent tension between the approach taken by the Federal Court of Appeal of Canada in *Sommerer* and the US approach to grantor trusts can perhaps be explained by considering the nature of the trusts in question. The entity in *Sommerer* was actually an Austrian foundation. The court doubted that it held its assets in trust, but it was unnecessary to determine that particular issue. Notwithstanding the doubt about that point, the foundation was considered to be trust-like; at least, sufficiently so for it to be treated as a trust for the purposes of the Canadian deeming provision mentioned above. It was clear that, in a broad sense, the foundation was a 'discretionary entity' and that its founder did not have a right to its assets or the power to direct what happened to those assets.

By contrast, the most common form of US grantor trust (a so-called 'living trust') is, in the lifetime of the grantor and while he is mentally capable, essentially a nominee for him. Commonly, the trust agreement and the provisions of the trust law of the relevant US state give the grantor such extensive powers, and so completely deprive other beneficiaries of rights, that it is difficult to see it as a trust at all. It seems natural and appropriate for a 'trust' which is actually, in substance, a nomineeship to be ignored when determining the availability of treaty relief. However, not all trusts that are grantor trusts for US tax purposes are so like a nomineeship, so the nominee-like nature of a US 'living trust' may not fully explain the contrast between the Canadian and US approaches.

Chapter 104

DTTS AND ANTI-AVOIDANCE LEGISLATION

104.1 This chapter discusses the difficult subject of the interaction of DTT provisions with the UK's anti-avoidance legislation. It focuses on provisions of domestic law which attribute income or gains of offshore structures to UK resident individuals.

CONTEXT

104.2 Classical offshore tax planning involves arrangements which cause income or gains which would otherwise have accrued to a resident of a high tax jurisdiction to accrue, instead, to an entity established outside that jurisdiction, and beyond the territorial limits of its tax laws. Most commonly, the entity is a trust or company. There will be a means for the person who created the entity, or related persons, to benefit from the income or gains accruing to it, whether by means of ownership of the entity or as a beneficiary. The aim is to secure an overall tax advantage in the high tax jurisdiction, through the avoidance of tax or tax deferral.

In a UK context, this kind of planning has typically involved entities established in 'tax havens', which have encouraged such arrangements by developing tax regimes under which there is little or no local taxation of entities established or held by non-residents. Some such jurisdictions have a DTT with the UK, but many do not. The Crown Dependencies do, of course, have DTTs with the UK, but these do not follow the OECD Model Treaty and do not, as a rule, provide an exemption from UK tax in respect of investment income or gains.

In recent years there has been slightly greater use of European 'onshore' alternatives to these offshore jurisdictions, eg Luxembourg and Malta. These countries have highly developed DTT networks, which (in combination with their domestic laws) often permit income or gains to be received or distributed with relatively little local taxation. As a seat for holding companies, these jurisdictions are popular with individuals who have come from, and expect to return to, continental Europe.

The particular issue here is the extent to which DTT relief, if available to the non-UK resident entity, may also be claimed to relieve a UK resident individual's liability to UK taxes which are chargeable, under the UK's anti-avoidance legislation, by reference to the income or gains of the foreign entity. For example, if an entity resident in another country (with which the UK has a DTT) realises a gain, and the DTT provides that the gain is taxable only in the other country, can a UK resident participator in, settlor of or beneficiary of the entity use the treaty as a shield against UK tax which would otherwise be charged on him, by reference to the gain of the foreign entity? In certain circumstances the exemption of the foreign entity from UK tax *does* follow through into an exemption from UK tax of the UK resident. This might be termed vicarious exemption from UK taxation.

More often though, for the reasons explained below, the UK resident cannot use the DTT to block UK tax. Where this is the case, there may nevertheless be scope for the UK resident to claim credit relief under the DTT between the UK and the country in which the entity is treaty resident.

THE STATUTORY PROCESS

104.3 What makes the interaction between DTTs and anti-avoidance legislation difficult is that the availability of vicarious exemption is acutely sensitive to the wording of the relevant anti-avoidance provision. Such provisions can, at least theoretically, be divided into two classes.

In one class are anti-avoidance provisions under which the UK resident's liability to tax is regarded as arising in respect of the *same* income or gains as are received or realised by the entity which is resident in the other country. In the other class are anti-avoidance provisions under which the UK resident is taxed on what might be termed *generic* income or gains: deemed income or gains which have a different 'character' from the income or gains of the foreign entity. This difficult taxonomy derives from *Bricom Holdings Ltd v IRC* [1997] STC 1179, 70 TC 272.

Bricom

104.4 *Bricom* concerned a charge to tax on a UK resident company under the controlled foreign company (CFC) rules, in relation to interest received by a Dutch resident subsidiary. The UK/Netherlands DTT provided that the interest was taxable only in the Netherlands; ie the DTT exempted the interest from UK tax. The question to be answered by the court was whether the tax charge on the UK resident parent under the CFC rules was, in fact, tax in respect of the interest received by the subsidiary (in which case vicarious exemption would apply). The Revenue's position was that the tax charge under the CFC rules was in respect of generic deemed profits of the parent, rather than the actual interest received by the subsidiary, so no vicarious exemption was available.

The tax liability of the UK resident company arose in respect of what the CFC legislation termed the 'chargeable profits' of its Dutch subsidiary. These were defined as the amount which would be the company's total profits for the purposes of UK corporation tax if the company were assumed, counterfactually, to be UK resident.

It was held that such 'chargeable profits' were not the same as the interest received by the Dutch subsidiary. In the Court of Appeal, Millett LJ stated that 'the question [of whether vicarious exemption applies] turns on the nature of the statutory process [whereby income or gains of a non-UK resident person give rise to tax for a UK resident.] . . . The interest received by [the subsidiary] is not included in the sum apportioned to the taxpayer on which tax is chargeable. It merely provides a measure by which an element in a conventional or notional sum is calculated, and it is that conventional or notional sum which is apportioned to the taxpayer and on which tax is charged'. As the court's finding was that the UK tax charge was imposed on this 'conventional or notional sum', rather than on the interest received by the Dutch subsidiary, DTT relief was denied.

Subsequent commentary regarding *Bricom* has tended to focus on the element of calculation involved in arriving at 'chargeable profits' for the purpose of the CFC rules. Arguably, though, the true point of the case is that, for vicarious exemption to apply, the taxing provision has to be one which apportions to the UK resident the income/gains of the non-UK resident entity, in a manner which preserves their original character. The problem for the taxpayer in *Bricom* was that, in the court's analysis, the interest received by the subsidiary lost its character in the notional profits on which the CFC charge arose; those notional profits were calculated by reference to the interest received by the subsidiary but they could not be said to be, or have the character of, the interest.

It is, in fact, debatable whether the court reached the right conclusion regarding this issue. It might be argued that the 'chargeable profits' on which the UK resident parent was taxable did represent, and did retain the character of, the interest received by the non-UK resident subsidiary. Certainly, the emphasis in the judgment on the 'chargeable profits' being the product of a mathematical calculation seems ill-conceived, since in the case of *any* company mathematical calculation is required to determine the profits that are taxable. This computational process does not in itself affect the company's ability to take advantage of exemptive relief under a DTT.

In this respect, at least, the *Bricom* judgment is questionable. However, the aspect of the judgment which is much more widely accepted is that for a UK taxpayer to be entitled to exemptive relief under a DTT, from an anti-avoidance provision which would otherwise give rise to tax by reference to income or gains of a non-UK resident entity, the taxpayer's deemed income or gains must be the same as, or have the same character as, the income or gains of the non-resident entity – an issue which turns on the correct construction of the anti-avoidance provision in question.

Strathalmond

104.5 *Bricom* can be contrasted with the earlier case of *Strathalmond (Lord) v IRC* [1972] 3 All ER 715, [1972] 1 WLR 1511. As noted above (para 103.8), Strathalmond concerned the income of a married woman, which under the law at that time was deemed for UK income tax purposes to accrue to her husband. The married woman was a US citizen. The US/UK DTT provided that the income was taxable only in the United States. It was clear that, absent the attribution of the income to her husband, there would have been no UK tax on the income. The question was whether the exemption from UK tax under the DTT enured for the husband.

It was held that it did, as the relevant legislation simply imputed all the wife's income to the husband. The husband was taxable on that income, not (for example) on generic deemed income of an amount determined by reference to the quantum of the wife's income.

It follows from *Strathalmond* that, where income or gains of person A (qualifying for an exemption from UK tax under a distributive article) are 'deemed' to be income or gains of person B, or are 'treated' as person B's, or are 'imputed' to person B (these expressions are generally considered to be synonymous), and the original character of the income/gains is preserved, then in principle person B may be able to claim vicarious exemption from tax, on the basis that there is a fiction that the income or gains are his.

Drawing the line

104.6 The line between *Bricom* and *Strathalmond (Lord) v IRC* [1972] 3 All ER 715, [1972] 1 WLR 1511 situations can be indistinct. The question of the nature of the 'statutory process' which gives rise to tax under a particular provision, and whether the deemed income/gains have the same character as those accruing to the non-UK resident entity, can seem esoteric. And the precise wording of the relevant UK statutory provision can have a drastic and arbitrary effect on whether exemptive relief is available.

It should be remembered that, while a finding that the anti-avoidance provision in question falls into the *Bricom* category will preclude an exemption from UK tax under a distributive article, it will not necessarily preclude a claim for relief by way of credit, under a 'relief from double taxation' article (though this is, of course, less useful). The reason is that, under such articles, credit relief is typically available provided that the UK tax charge is 'computed by reference to' income/gains on which foreign tax has been charged, which is a less demanding test.

This chapter considers the scope to claim DTT relief in respect of anti-avoidance provisions dealing with (1) income and then (2) gains. It should be borne in mind that this area is rife with complexity and uncertainty. Where some provisions are concerned, the most that can be expressed is a tentative view as to the most likely outcome of any litigation on the point.

INCOME TAX PROVISIONS

Charge on settlor under ITTOIA 2005, s 624

Exemption

104.7 As explained in CHAPTER 75, income of a settlement under which a UK resident settlor retains an interest is typically taxable on the settlor under Income Tax (Trading and Other Income) Act 2005 (ITTOIA 2005), s 624.

Section 624(1) states that 'income which arises under a [settlor-interested] settlement is treated for income tax purposes as the income of the settlor and of the settlor alone . . . '.

This is clearly analogous to the situation in *Strathalmond (Lord) v IRC* [1972] 3 All ER 715, [1972] 1 WLR 1511. The settlement income is deemed to be the settlor's own income. The deeming extends to the character of the income as well as its amount. As a result, there is scope for vicarious exemption of the settlor from the s 624 charge.

For such exemption to be available, it will of course be necessary to establish that the trust is 'liable to tax' in, and accordingly treaty resident in, the other contracting state. As discussed in CHAPTER 103, there is an element of uncertainty about whether this requirement can be met if, under the law applicable in the relevant country, the trust is exempted from tax, although it is likely that it can.

Where the DTT requires the interest to be 'beneficially owned' by the trust, it is likely that the exclusion of the UK's taxing rights only applies if the trust is discretionary, ie if its terms do not give any person an interest in possession. See para 102.2.

Credit relief

104.8 Where the relevant DTT does not provide an exemption from UK tax, for example because the trust is treaty resident in the UK rather than the other contracting state, there is no difficulty in credit relief from being claimed under the 'relief from double taxation' article. Foreign tax paid by the trustees can be credited against the settlor's UK tax liability on the settlement income.

Alternatively, in the event that there is no DTT in force between the UK and the country which has levied tax on the trust income, unilateral credit relief will be available under Taxation (International and Other Provisions) Act 2010 (TIOPA 2010), s 9, provided that the income arose in that country (see para 99.16).

This is clear as a matter of general principle, but is confirmed by ITTOIA 2005, s 623, which provides that for the purposes of calculating liability under s 624, a settlor shall be permitted the same deductions and reliefs as if he had actually received the trust income.

Charge on transferor under ITA 2007, s 720

Exemption

104.9 As explained in CHAPTER 69, income arising to a person abroad as a result of a transfer of assets by another person, known as the transferor, is in principle taxable on the transferor under Income Tax Act 2007 (ITA 2007), s 720 if he is a UK resident and has the power to enjoy such income (subject to certain exemptions). Where the person abroad is resident in a state which is party to a DTT with the UK, the primary question is whether DTT relief can be claimed by the transferor as a shield against his s 720 liability, in the event that the DTT confers exclusive taxing rights on the other state.

Under s 720's predecessor, Income and Corporation Taxes Act 1988 (ICTA 1988), s 739, the income of the person abroad was deemed for all purposes to be that of the transferor. There was little doubt that this was a *Strathalmond (Lord) v IRC* [1972] 3 All ER 715, [1972] 1 WLR 1511 case and therefore that, in principle, a DTT could exempt such income from UK tax. Indeed, notes exchanged by the UK and the USA in relation to the UK/USA DTT supported the view that s 739 income had the same character as the income of the person abroad.

Unfortunately, the reformulation of s 739 in the ITA 2007 muddied these waters. The rewritten legislation was somewhat ambiguous, or confused, about whether the actual income of the person abroad was apportioned to the taxpayer, with some sections seemingly pointing to this view but others suggesting that the tax charge for the transferor arose on generic income which did not have the same character as the income of the non-resident entity.

The legislation was amended by Finance Act 2013. Changes were made to ITA 2007, ss 721, 726 and 746 (inter alia), which had the effect of distinguishing the income of the person abroad more clearly from the income of the transferor on which tax is charged – suggesting that the taxed income is fictional and generic, of an amount computed by reference to the amount of income received by the person abroad, but lacking the character of such income.

HMRC have stated that the 2013 changes were intended to 'clarify' that s 720 income is in the *Bricom* category and therefore that treaty protection is precluded. (See 'Reform of two anti-avoidance provisions . . . ', a consultation document published on 30 July 2012, paras 3.35–3.38; and also the explanatory notes which accompanied the 2013 Finance Bill.) It is questionable whether this was a 'clarification' or a change of law. But either way, there does now seem to be significant disassociation of the income of the person abroad from the income which is deemed to accrue to the transferor. The most likely analysis in relation to the amended provisions, applying *Bricom*, is that the deemed income would be considered by a court to be distinct from, and to have a different character from, the income of the non-resident entity, preventing vicarious treaty relief.

This is not universally accepted. It might be argued, *in extremis*, that there is still some ambiguity about whether s 720 income has the same character as the income of the non-resident entity, and furthermore that any such ambiguity should be construed in a manner which is consistent with the UK's treaty obligations. However, the same argument could have been advanced in relation to the CFC legislation in *Bricom*.

Perhaps the most that can be said about this is that HMRC's stance is clear. A taxpayer seeking to rely on a DTT for vicarious exemption from liability under s 720 would very probably need to litigate the point, and given the 2013 changes, the *Bricom* decision and prevailing judicial attitudes, litigation about this would be risky.

The controversy about whether vicarious exemption from s 720 can be claimed is generally moot where it is the business profits article in a DTT which is in point – ie where protection is sought from tax under s 720 on trading/business income of the person abroad. This is because TIOPA 2010, s 130 typically overrides a business profits article in a DTT if that article would otherwise prevent the 'income of a UK resident' from being charged to income tax.

Credit relief

104.10 In principle, where a non-resident entity has paid foreign tax on income which is within the scope of s 720, the transferor can claim credit relief under a DTT between the UK and the country in which the person abroad is resident. This is the case whether or not s 720 is a *Bricom* type provision, because irrespective of that controversy, the s 720 charge is 'computed by reference to' the amount of income on which the person abroad has been taxed, which is the (less stringent) test for credit relief.

On the same basis, in the absence of any DTT between the UK and the country levying tax on the income of the person abroad, credit relief can be claimed by the transferor under TIOPA 2010, s 9, provided that the foreign tax has been levied on income arising in the other country (see para **99.16**).

Income Tax Act 2007, s 746 confirms the availability of credit relief from s 720, by providing that the transferor is to be treated for the purposes of determining applicable deductions and reliefs as if he had personally received the income of the non-resident entity. This is accepted by HMRC (Helpsheet 262).

Charge on non-transferor under ITA 2007, s 731

Exemption

104.11 As explained in CHAPTER 70, under ITA 2007, s 731 a UK resident non-transferor is typically liable to income tax on any benefit not otherwise subject to income tax which is received from a person abroad, where income has accrued to the non-resident entity and such income has, very broadly, been accumulated (giving rise to what the legislation terms 'relevant income'). The amount of the tax charge is calculated using a formula set out in ITA 2007, s 733. Essentially, the tax is on the lower of the value of the benefit received and the amount of the relevant income.

As above, where the person abroad is resident in a state which has a DTT with the UK, the primary question is whether vicarious exemption under a distributive article can be claimed by the UK resident non-transferor in respect of his s 731 liability, if the DTT gives exclusive taxing rights to the other country with respect to the income that has been received and accumulated.

The widely accepted answer is that no exemption is available. Although the accumulated income of the non-resident entity and the deemed income of the non-transferor are connected, they are not the same. There is no direct linkage between the amount of income received by the non-resident entity and the amount of deemed income on which tax is charged under s 731. Nor does the non-transferor's deemed income have the same character as the income of the non-resident (although where the non-transferor is a remittance basis user, the source of the non-resident's income affects whether the deemed income is treated as foreign: ITA 2007, s 735). The result is that s 731 is a *Bricom* type provision, under which tax is charged on a 'conventional or notional sum' which exists only as a product of a calculation. In fact, s 731 is far more clearly in this category than the CFC legislation which was the subject of the *Bricom* litigation.

Credit relief

104.12 In practice, where the person abroad has paid foreign tax on income that has been taken into account in calculating the UK tax charge on the non-transferor under s 731, HMRC tend to resist claims to DTT credit relief.

One possible argument against such relief is the fact that liability under s 731 is not computed solely by reference to the amount of the income of the person abroad which has borne foreign tax, but also takes account of other variables: the amount of that income which has been accumulated, and the value of benefits that have been received by the non-transferor. However, 'relief from double taxation' articles in DTTs do not stipulate that the UK tax must be computed *exclusively* by reference to the amount of income on which foreign tax has been paid. Arguably, if UK tax is paid under s 731 with respect to income of a person abroad on which foreign tax has been paid, applying the matching rules in ITA 2007, s 733, that is enough for credit relief to be available.

A more cogent argument against DTT credit relief in this context is that it is not always possible to identify when a s 731 liability results from the matching of income of the person abroad that has borne foreign tax, as distinct from other income which has not. This is particularly so where the taxpayers in question are not remittance basis users, with the result that the more elaborate matching rules in s 735A are not engaged. However, there will be many situations in which this is a 'non-point'; for example where all income that has been received has been taxed in the hands of a US resident trust, or a US resident/citizen 'grantor'. In that kind of scenario DTT credit relief should, it is suggested, be granted.

The same issues arise in relation to unilateral credit relief under TIOPA 2010, s 9. There is the usual additional requirement for unilateral credit relief that the income must have arisen in the country which taxed it (see para **99.16**).

In default of DTT or unilateral credit, partial relief in respect of foreign tax is available if the foreign tax is paid out of the income received by the non-resident. If so, the income used to pay this tax is not available for the provision of benefits, and therefore falls out of the calculation of 'relevant income' (see para **69.12**).

CGT ANTI-AVOIDANCE PROVISIONS

Charge on corporate gains under TCGA 1992, s 13

Exemption – individual participators

104.13 As explained in Chapter 88, Taxation of Chargeable Gains Act 1992 (TCGA 1992), s 13 provides that, subject to certain exceptions, a UK resident participator in a closely held non-UK resident company to which a chargeable gain has accrued 'shall be treated for the purposes of [the TCGA] as if a part of the chargeable gain had accrued to him'.

It is *the* gain realised by the non-UK resident company (or a part of it) that is attributed to the UK resident participator under s 13. This is analogous to the situation that was at hand in *Strathalmond (Lord) v IRC* [1972] 3 All ER 715, [1972] 1 WLR 1511. It follows that the participator can typically claim exemption from CGT under s 13 if there is a DTT between the UK and the country in which the company is resident, which confers exclusive taxing rights with respect to gains on that country. If there were any doubt about this, the existence of TCGA 1992, s 79B (discussed below) would resolve it. However, the point is accepted by HMRC (CG 57380).

The UK's older DTTs which follow the Model Treaty tend to provide that if the alienator (the person making the disposal of property which has given rise to a gain) is resident in the other contracting state, that other state has exclusive taxing rights, unless the property in question is (a) UK situated land or (b) movable property which forms part of a UK permanent establishment held by an enterprise which is resident in the other state (in which case the UK has taxing rights). Unless either of these exceptions applies, the UK has no right to tax the gain, and where the alienator is a closely held non-UK resident company the DTT typically blocks s 13. For example, this is the case where the alienator is a closely held company resident in Luxembourg.

By contrast, DTTs that have been entered into by the UK more recently have tended to include a saving provision which allows the UK to levy tax in respect of gains on 'a person' who is resident in the UK in the tax year in which the alienation occurs, irrespective of whether that person is the alienator. This wording precludes a claim to exemption from tax under s 13. The UK's DTTs which include this kind of saving provision include those with France, the Netherlands, Switzerland, the United States, Canada, Australia, New Zealand and Mauritius.

Credit relief – individual participators

104.14 In cases where the relevant DTT does not allow the UK resident participator to claim exemption from s 13, there is clearly no obstacle to DTT credit relief being claimed in respect of foreign tax paid on the company's gain (or the appropriate share of that tax, where the UK resident is not the only participator). There is no doubt that the UK tax is computed by reference to the gain on which foreign tax has been paid.

SP D23 acknowledges this. It also notes the alternative possibility of treating the foreign tax paid by the company (or the appropriate share of it) as a deductible expense in determining the gain apportioned under s 13, by virtue of what is now TIOPA 2010, s 113 (see para **99.17**). But clearly, DTT credit relief is likely to be preferable, where it is available.

A further option in the absence of a DTT is unilateral credit relief under TIOPA 2010, s 9. However, s 9 only allows the foreign tax on a gain to be credited where the country levying tax and the country in which the gain has arisen are the same (see para **99.16**).

Exemption – trustee participators

104.15 The analysis is different from the above where the participator in the non-UK resident company is a UK resident trust. Taxation of Chargeable Gains Act 1992, s 79B(1)–(2) provides that, where the trustees of a settlement are participators in a non-UK resident company which would be a close company if it were UK resident, nothing in any DTT shall be read as preventing a charge to tax arising by virtue of the attribution to the trustees of corporate gains under s 13. Thus, for example, where a UK resident trust holds all of the shares in a non-UK resident company, and under a DTT such company is exempt from UK tax on its gains, the exemption does not enure for the benefit of the trustees, who are nevertheless taxable under s 13 on any gains realised by the company.

Section 79B is expressed as applying if the trustees are participators in a non-UK resident company which would be a close company if it were UK resident, or in an actual close company (s 79(1)). The reference to participation in an actual close company is initially puzzling, as gains of such a company (which is by definition of UK resident) cannot be attributed under s 13. However, s 79B is also intended to catch a further situation. This is where the trustees are participators in a (UK resident) close company which is exempt from UK tax on gains by virtue of DTT relief (on the basis that it is dual resident and is treaty resident in the other contracting state), and the close company is a participator in a non-UK resident company which would be a close company if it were UK resident. In that scenario, gains of the non-UK resident company bypass the parent company and are treated as accruing to the trustees (s 79B(3)). Absent s 79B, such gains would be attributed to the parent company but corporation tax on them would be avoided by virtue of the DTT.

Section 79B was first enacted in 2000 and was widely criticised as unsatisfactory and vindictive. Although there may be cases where trustees deliberately cause non-resident companies to reside in treaty jurisdictions so as to avoid CGT, there are also cases where trustees own companies in treaty jurisdictions for genuine trading or investment reasons. In such cases it is wrong for trustee participators to be penalised by anti-avoidance legislation of this sort.

Equally irrational is the way in which s 79B targets trustee shareholders rather than individual or company participators. In particular, this means that trustees holding only a minority interest in a company could be penalised if controlling individual or corporate shareholders cause an offshore company to move to a treaty jurisdiction, although the controlling shareholders will not themselves be within s 79B.

To some extent these concerns have been addressed by the motive defence introduced in 2013. Section 13 now no longer applies unless the acquisition, holding, or disposal of the asset by the non-resident company formed part of arrangements intended to avoid CGT or corporation tax (see para **88.4**). In the majority of treaty cases, the company in the treaty jurisdiction is established for entirely commercial reasons and s 13, and thus s 79B, are not in point. Where these sections do continue to bite is where a s 13 company is moved to or incorporated in a treaty country specifically in order to secure treaty protection for gains. Such schemes, exemplified by *Wood v Holden (Inspector of Taxes)* [2006] EWCA Civ 26, [2006] 1 WLR 1393, [2006] STC 443, continue to be caught by ss 13 and 79B.

Credit relief – trustee participators

104.16 Section 79B(2) states that nothing in any DTT 'shall be read as preventing a charge to tax' on trustee participators. This seems to be directed at DTT provisions which would otherwise exempt the trustees from tax on gains, and not at credit relief provisions. Any foreign tax paid by the non-UK resident close company in a s 79B situation should therefore be creditable against the trustees' CGT on the gains attributed under s 13.

Charge on settlor under TCGA 1992, s 86

Exemption

104.17 As discussed in CHAPTER 76, TCGA 1992, s 86 provides that a UK resident and domiciled settlor of a non-UK resident settlement (or a settlement which is UK resident but resident for the purposes of a DTT in another state) is typically liable to CGT in respect of chargeable gains, which are treated as accruing to the settlor in the relevant tax year. The amount of such deemed gains is equal to the amount on which the trustees of the settlement would be chargeable to tax under TCGA 1992, s 2(2) if they were UK resident in the year or, in the case of a settlement which is UK resident but resident for the purposes of a DTT in another country, if no DTT was applicable (s 86(3)).

HMRC's position is that, in cases where the trustees would, hypothetically, themselves be able to claim exemption from UK tax under a DTT, such exemption cannot be claimed vicariously by the settlor. This is on the grounds that the gains attributed to the settlor are generic deemed gains, not the same gains as realised by the trustees (CG 38545).

On balance, applying the *Bricom* decision, this is probably right. It might be argued that in substance, the attributed gains are the same as those realised by the trustees, but that argument seems difficult in view of *Bricom*; it might be said that in *Bricom*, the profits attributed to the UK resident company were in substance the interest received by the foreign subsidiary, but the court was heavily swayed by the wording of the CFC provisions, which suggested that the UK tax charge was levied on a 'conventional or notional sum'. There is similarity between s 86 and the former CFC legislation as considered in *Bricom*, in that in both cases the tax charge is on deemed receipts which the wording of the statute indicates are separate from the actual receipts of the non-UK resident person, although the linkage between the actual and deemed receipts is pretty direct.

In the case of s 86, there is a secondary argument in HMRC's favour. It can be argued that s 86(3), which determines the amount of the deemed gains that are attributed to the settlor, is intended to override any DTT exemption, as it requires the deemed gains to be quantified as if the settlement were UK resident and not resident in another country for the purposes of a treaty. The result of this counterfactual deeming seems to be that any DTT exemption which may otherwise be available is to be disregarded when gains are attributed to the settlor.

In this respect s 86 differs from the repealed TCGA 1992, s 77, which (until its repeal) attributed gains to the settlor of a UK resident settlement in which the settlor had an interest, of an amount equal to the gains on which the trustees would, apart from s 77, have been taxable. Under the former s 77, there was the same degree of disassociation of the actual gains of the settlement from the deemed gains attributed to the settlor as there is under s 86. However, a key difference between the provisions is that s 77 did not deem the trustees to be treaty resident in the UK. It is possible that this meant that if a settlement was a UK resident as a matter of domestic law, in any part of the tax year, but was a resident for the purposes of a DTT in another country at the time of disposal of trust assets, and the relevant DTT deprived the UK of its right to tax the resultant gains, that exemption from UK tax could be claimed by the settlor. The argument was that, by virtue of the DTT, the amount on which the trustees would, apart from s 77, have been taxable was nil. If s 77 did indeed apply in this situation, the amount of gains attributed under s 77 in this situation was also nil.

This point seems to have been behind the immigration to the UK of the trust in the *Smallwood v Revenue and Customs Comrs* [2009] EWHC 777 (Ch), [2009] STC 1222, 11 ITLR 943 case (see paras **100.6** and **103.2**). This was a non-UK resident trust which was within the scope of s 86. Matters were arranged so that the trust realised a substantial gain while resident in Mauritius and then, before the end of the UK tax year, the Mauritian resident trustee retired in favour of UK resident trustees. The argument was that this immigration of the trust brought it within the ambit of s 77 with respect to gains realised throughout that tax year (and switched off s 86 for that tax year). The immigration was almost certainly effected because it was considered that s 86(3) would prevent the settlor from claiming vicarious exemption under the UK/Mauritius DTT, whereas the wording of s 77 would allow such exemption to be claimed. However, in the event, the planning failed, as it was held that at the time of the disposal of its assets by the Mauritian resident trustee, the trust was treaty resident in the UK rather than Mauritius, so the DTT exemption was not available.

It is interesting to note that in an earlier case relating to a somewhat similar tax avoidance scheme, *Davies (Inspector of Taxes) v Hicks* [2005] EWHC 847

(Ch), [2005] STC 850, 78 TC 95, HMRC apparently accepted that vicarious exemption was available from CGT under s 86. HMRC challenged the scheme, unsuccessfully, on other grounds.

Credit relief

104.18 Where s 86 is concerned, HMRC accept the availability of credit relief under a DTT, where foreign tax has been paid on a gain realised by non-UK resident trustees which is taken into account in quantifying the CGT charge on the settlor (CG 38545). This is correct, because the s 86 charge is computed by reference to the gain on which foreign tax has been levied.

By the same token, unilateral credit relief may be available where there is no DTT between the UK and the other country in which tax has been levied, although this requires the gain to have arisen in that country (TIOPA 2010, s 9; see para **99.16**). Where this relief is unavailable, recourse may be had to deduction relief under TIOPA 2010, s 113 (see para **99.17**). Such relief will reduce the amount on which the trustees of the settlement would be chargeable to tax under TCGA 1992, s 2(2) if they were UK resident in the year (s 86(3), and will therefore indirectly reduce the s 86 tax charge).

Charge on beneficiaries under TCGA 1992, s 87

Exemption

104.19 As explained in Chapter 77, TCGA 1992, s 87 provides that a UK resident beneficiary of a non-UK resident trust is liable to CGT in respect of chargeable gains realised within the settlement which are treated as accruing in the relevant tax year to him, up to the value of capital payments received by him from the settlement.

Section 87 is similar to ITA 2007, s 731, in that the attributed gains are calculated by reference to, but are different from, the gains which are realised within the settlement. They are generic deemed gains. This is therefore a *Bricom* case, so even if a DTT between the UK and the country in which the trustees are resident provides that the trust gains are not taxable in the UK, the exemption is not available to the beneficiary.

The only possible argument against this is on the basis that the gains which are deemed to accrue to the beneficiary under s 87 are calculated by reference to (inter alia) 'the amount upon which the trustees of the settlement would be chargeable to tax under section 2(2) [. . .] if they were resident in the United Kingdom' (s 87(4)). Conceivably, a similar argument might be run here as was apparently attempted in the *Smallwood v Revenue and Customs Comrs* [2009] EWHC 777 (Ch), [2009] STC 1222, 11 ITLR 943, case in relation to s 77 (see para **104.17**) – ie it might be argued that the gains should be computed as if the trustees were UK resident but also, simultaneously, resident in the other contracting state, and were treaty resident in that other state. This is arguable, at a stretch, because s 87(4) does not state expressly that the trustees are to be treated as treaty resident in the UK or as if there were no applicable DTT. However, it seems likely that a court would construe s 87(4) as containing an implicit instruction to ignore any DTT provisions when calculating the amount on which the trustees would be taxed if they were UK resident, on the basis that if the trustees are to be assumed, counterfactually, to be UK resident, they should also be assumed to be treaty resident in the UK. A similar issue of construction arose in *Bricom* (see para **104.4**), and the Court of Appeal considered it to be 'self-evident' that in calculating the 'chargeable profits' of the Dutch company on which its UK resident parent should be taxed, the assumption required by the CFC legislation that the Dutch subsidiary was UK resident entailed, by implication, that the 'chargeable profits' had to be calculated without regard to DTT relief (*Bricom v IRC* 70 TC 272 at p 289). It seems improbable that a court would take a different line in relation to s 87.

Credit relief

104.20 HMRC's Capital Gains Manual states (at CG 38790) that:

> 'It is very unlikely that a beneficiary will be able to claim tax credit relief against the Capital Gains Tax due on a section 87 gain. This is because relief is given for foreign tax charged on the same gain. [. . .] Because of the pooling of trustees' section 2(2) amounts and the matching and possible apportionment of capital payments it is not possible to identify the gain assessable on the beneficiary with the gain that accrued to the beneficiary.'

The third sentence quoted above represents a rather technical objection to credit relief being available in respect of s 87 liabilities. Notwithstanding the matching rules in s 87A, there may be certain situations where capital payments have been received by multiple beneficiaries, in which the legislation will not answer the question of which beneficiary's s 87 liability is specifically attributable to a gain that has given rise to foreign taxation. However, it is suggested that the matching rules will, in practice, answer this question in the majority of cases, and that where they do not, credit relief should be allowed on the basis of a reasonable, pro rata apportionment of the credit among the beneficiaries who have received capital payments.

In the absence of a DTT between the UK and the country which has taxed the trustees' gain, unilateral credit relief will only be available if the gain arose in that country (TIOPA 2010, s 9; see para **99.16**). The Manual notes that 'if tax credit relief is not due foreign tax paid by the trustees may be deducted in calculating the trustees' section 2(2) amount, [under] TIOPA10/S113' (CG 38790).

Chapter 105

IHT TREATIES

The authors would like to give special thanks to Sangna Chauhan of Charles Russell Speechlys LLP for her help with this chapter

INTRODUCTION

105.1 In principle, the inheritance tax (IHT) system, and similar systems that operate in other countries, create considerable scope for double tax charges on the same assets, where there is an international element. In the case of IHT, this is primarily an issue because the tax applies on a global basis to assets of an individual who is domiciled or deemed domiciled in the UK. Double taxation is in principle rather likely to arise, given that under many countries' tax systems, there is a charge to estate tax or similar on assets of a deceased person that are situated in the relevant country.

There is even scope, in principle, for assets to be subject to triple or, in extreme cases, quadruple taxation. For example, the latter can occur where the UK is seeking to tax an individual's estate due to his actual or deemed domicile in the UK; a second country is seeking to tax the estate on the basis that the individual died resident there; a third country, such as the USA, is seeking to tax the estate on the basis that the deceased was a national of that country; and lastly one or more other countries are seeking to tax assets on the basis of their situs. And in theory, the situation can get even more complicated than this, as different countries may have different principles for determining the situs of assets, which creates scope for two countries to claim estate tax or similar on the same asset, both regarding it as situated within their borders.

In recognition of these potential issues, the IHT legislation includes rules to provide unilateral relief from double taxation (IHTA 1984, s 159) and the UK has also entered into a limited number of IHT treaties which will provide bilateral relief in certain circumstances. Where both the unilateral provisions and one of these IHT treaties are potentially applicable, relief will be provided under whichever of these is more beneficial (IHTA 1984, s 159(7)).

This chapter sets out the conditions for unilateral relief and then goes on to review specific aspects of the IHT treaties. The UK has entered into ten IHT treaties: commonly divided into the four 'old' treaties and the six 'new' ones. The four 'old' treaties, namely those made with France, India, Italy and Pakistan, were made in the pre-1974 era of estate duty (although IHTA 1984, s 158(6) ensures that they are carried over into the IHT regime) and they work in a rather different way to the treaties which were negotiated after the introduction of capital transfer tax/IHT.

UNILATERAL RELIEF

105.2 IHTA 1984, s 159 sets out the following conditions for the UK to give unilateral relief against IHT charged on property situated overseas:

- The overseas tax must be of a similar character to IHT or be chargeable on or by reference to death or inter vivos gifts.
- The overseas tax and the IHT must be chargeable by reference to the same disposition or event, and on the same property.
- The person liable for the overseas tax must have paid it.

If these conditions are met, the UK will allow a credit for the overseas tax. Where overseas tax has become payable in the same country as the property on which it has been charged is situated, the credit is equal to the amount of the overseas tax (s 159(2)). Where, on the other hand, overseas tax has become payable with respect to property situated in a third country (ie property which is neither situated in the UK nor in the country which has imposed the overseas tax), a fraction of the overseas tax, determined by the application of a formula, is creditable (s 159(3)). Fractional credit relief is similarly available in the situation in which two or more other countries have imposed tax charges on property situated in third countries (s 159(4)).

THE 'OLD' IHT TREATIES

105.3 In principle, if an individual is deemed domiciled in the UK for IHT, his or her worldwide estate is within the scope of IHT (see CHAPTER 45).

However, this domestic law position may be modified by the effect of a treaty. Many of the IHT treaties override the deemed domicile rules in certain circumstances. As noted above, there are ten such treaties. It makes sense to consider the four 'old' IHT treaties first, namely those made with France, India, Italy and Pakistan.

Although these treaties were entered into by the UK, they refer to estate duty imposed in Great Britain (not the UK). They differentiate between assets within or outside Great Britain (not within or outside the UK), and in certain circumstances the application of these treaties depends on whether or not assets pass under the law of any part of Great Britain (not any part of the UK). 'Great Britain' excludes Northern Ireland, which is of course part of the UK. The reason for the references to Great Britain is that, prior to the introduction of capital transfer tax in 1975, Northern Ireland had a different estate tax regime from the rest of the UK.

Charge to IHT on death

105.4 The 'old' IHT treaties are incorporated into the IHT regime by IHTA 1984, s 158(6). This subsection specifically refers to the charge to IHT that occurs by virtue of IHTA 1984, s 4. This does not include every transfer of value but only, broadly, those that occur on death.

Section 4 applies, on an individual's death, to all property to which he is beneficially entitled, or is deemed to be beneficially entitled under the IHT legislation. This includes assets actually passing on death, property in which he has reserved a benefit (by virtue of FA 1986, s 102(3)) and property in which he has a qualifying interest in possession (IHTA 1984, s 49).

A 'failed' potentially exempt transfer (ie one made within seven years of death) also gives rise to a charge to IHT on death. However, that IHT charge is imposed by a different section, namely IHTA 1984, s 3A. Thus the 'old' IHT treaties offer no protection from tax charges on 'failed' potentially exempt transfers.

Domicile in the other contracting state

105.5 The override will only apply if the individual is domiciled in the other contracting state. The four 'old' IHT treaties direct the reader to apply local law to determine this issue, so that (for example) the question of whether an individual is domiciled in France for the purposes of the UK/French treaty must be answered applying French, not English, law. The concept of 'domicile' in France is essentially that of residence, rather than domicile in an English law sense, so the UK/French treaty will only provide protection from IHT with respect to non-British assets if the individual is French resident. The position is the same under the UK/Italian treaty.

The concept of 'domicile' in India and Pakistan is understood to be much closer to the English meaning, so an individual may be domiciled in India or Pakistan, for the purpose of the relevant treaties, whilst being resident in the UK. However, there are risks in assuming that an individual is domiciled in India or Pakistan for the purposes of the relevant treaty on the basis that, as a matter of English law, he is domiciled there. Local law advice is required for certainty regarding the availability of treaty relief. Old common law concepts, such as the domicile of dependency of a married woman that have since been abolished in English law may remain in force in India.

The treaties with India and Pakistan only provide protection against IHT on non-British assets if, at the time of death, (a) the individual is not domiciled in a part of Great Britain under English common law and, in addition, (b) the individual is domiciled in a part of India or Pakistan, as the case may be. An actual domicile within Great Britain, as a matter of English law, will preclude such protection (even in the event that the individual is simultaneously domiciled in India or Pakistan as a matter of local law). Section 267(2) ensures that the reference in the four 'old' IHT treaties to domicile within Great Britain only catches actual domicile; deemed domicile in some part of Great Britain under s 267(1) does not count.

By contrast, the treaties with France and Italy can in principle apply to limit the scope of IHT even in the case of an individual who is domiciled within Great Britain under English common law, provided that he is domiciled for the purposes of French or Italian law, as the case may be, in the relevant contracting state. In such a case a 'tiebreaker' clause will determine the individual's domicile for the purposes of the treaty. The deciding factors, in order of priority, are: (a) permanent home, (b) centre of vital interests, (c) habitual abode, (d) nationality, and (e) mutual agreement between the relevant taxing authorities.

Situation of assets

105.6 For the override in each treaty to apply, the property in question must be situated outside Great Britain. There is a quirk in the wording of the Pakistan treaty, which appears to say that for the override to apply, the property in question must be situated outside Pakistan (rather than outside Great Britain). This is clearly a clerical error and the respective tax authorities will, presumably, seek to apply the treaty on the basis of what it should say, rather than what it actually does say.

For the purpose of determining whether property is situated outside Great Britain, in the first instance the English common law situs rules are applied (see CHAPTER 38). This is the effect of the provision, common to the four 'old' IHT treaties, that a term which is not otherwise defined shall, where such term is to be applied by one of the contracting states, have the meaning which it has under the law of that state, in relation to the relevant tax. Thus, where the issue is whether HMRC has taxing rights in relation to assets which, it is claimed, are situated outside Great Britain, 'situated' has the meaning given to that expression for the purposes of IHT, so the situs of such assets must be determined applying English common law principles. Conversely, to determine whether a foreign tax authority has taxing rights in respect of assets outside of the other contracting state, 'situated' is to be construed in accordance with the law of that state, as it applies in relation to the relevant foreign duty.

However, there may be a mismatch between the English common law situs rules and the equivalent rules applied in the other contracting state. That mismatch may result in an asset being regarded as situated in the UK for the purposes of IHT but simultaneously situated in the other contracting state for the purposes of the foreign duty. To address this possibility, each of the four 'old' IHT treaties includes contractual situs rules which apply, in substitution for the English common law situs rules and equivalent foreign situs rules, in the event that:

(a) the deceased was domiciled at the date of his death in one of the contracting states; and

(b) the asset in question would otherwise be subject to duty in both contracting states, or would be so subject but for a specific exemption in the law of one of the contracting states.

Both India and Pakistan have now abolished estate duty (or its equivalent). Thus, where these treaties are concerned, there is no scope for the contractual situs rules to come into effect and consideration need only be given to the English common law of situs.

Italy and France, on the other hand, do currently have a succession charge on death. The contractual situs rules may therefore be relevant where these treaties are in point.

Care must be taken, because at times the contractual situs rules (in particular those in the treaty with France) depart significantly from the English rules. Examples include:

- various forms of intellectual property, which are treated as situated where the deceased was domiciled (and not where they are registered);
- company stocks and shares, which are deemed to be situated where the company was incorporated (and not where the shares are registered); and
- various forms of debts, which are treated as situated where the deceased was domiciled (and not where the debtor resides or, in the case of specialties, where the deed is located).

Non-British governing law

105.7 Each of the treaties with India, Pakistan and France specify that for the override to apply, the property in question must not pass 'under a disposition or devolution regulated by the law of some part of Great Britain'. As noted above, Great Britain for these purposes means England, Wales and Scotland.

Viscount Simonds in the old estate duty case *Philipson-Stow v IRC* [1961] AC 727, [1960] 3 All ER 814, HL stated that 'devolution and disposition are mutually exclusive and are exhaustive of the ways in which property can pass on death'. He seems to have considered that assets are subject to a 'disposition' by a will whereas they 'devolve' under the law of intestacy or where they pass by co-ownership. It is suggested that assets 'devolve' where they are held in trust and death triggers a change in the terms of the trust (for example the replacement of one life interest by another), but are subject to a 'disposition' where the deceased exercises a testamentary power of appointment (for example under a trust).

The key issue here is whether the disposition or devolution in question is 'regulated by the law of some part of Great Britain'. Again, turning to Viscount Simonds for guidance, it is the nature of an asset that holds the key to determining the governing law of a particular disposition or devolution, at least with respect to assets comprised within the deceased's free estate: 'the law which regulates [the deceased's] disposition of moveables must be the law of [the deceased's] domicile and the law which regulates his disposition of immoveables must be the lex rei situs'. However, as Michael Parkinson concludes in his article '*A disposition or devolution regulated by the law of some part of Great Britain': the proviso to the limitation of taxing rights in the inheritance tax treaties with France, India and Pakistan*, PCB 2011, 3, 126–130, the position may be different in relation to settled property, where the law governing the devolution of any assets, whether moveable or immoveable, is probably the chosen governing law of the settlement.

The governing law requirements in the treaty with Italy are much narrower in scope than that of the other treaties; it is only property passing under a settlement governed by the law of some part of Great Britain which is excluded from the override. So, an English domiciliary who is domiciled in Italy for the purposes of the treaty (ie resident there), and who is leaving non-British assets under his English law will, may still be free to rely on the treaty. He need only be concerned with the law which governs the devolution of the types of settled property which trigger an IHT charge on death. Such settled property will include the following:

- A qualifying (pre-22 March 2006) interest in possession. The override can be secured provided that the interest in possession subsists under a trust document governed by non-British law.
- A non-qualifying (post-21 March 2006) interest in possession where the gift with reservation of benefit rules apply. It is suggested that the override can again be secured if the trust instrument is governed by non-British law.
- Property of a discretionary trust where the gift with reservation of benefit rules apply. The position is not so straightforward here. The relevant provision of the UK/Italy treaty provides that the override will 'not apply to duty imposed in the territory of the Contracting Party on property passing under a settlement made by its governing law'. On a narrow view, settled property of a discretionary trust does not 'pass' on death and so the override will be available, regardless of the governing law of the settlement. However this narrow view is unlikely to be right, as if it were, it would deprive this provision of any effect. A purposive construction might lead a reader to conclude that the exclusion to the override will apply to any property that is held in a settlement governed by the law of some part of Great Britain. The conservative view, therefore, is that the trust needs to be governed by non-British law for protection from IHT to be available.

Implications

105.8 Where the conditions outlined above are met, a death charge to IHT on assets situated outside Great Britain will be prevented by the relevant treaty. As explained above, the treaties with India and Pakistan can be considered more useful, in terms of blocking IHT liabilities on non-British assets, as they are capable of applying even in relation to an individual resident in a part of Great Britain; whereas the treaties with France and Italy are only of relevance to an individual who has died, or can be expected to die, resident in the relevant contracting state.

By contrast, the treaties with France and Italy are capable of blocking IHT charges on non-British assets even in the case of UK domiciliaries; whereas the treaties with India and Pakistan require the individual to be domiciled in the relevant contracting state, so are irrelevant to UK domiciliaries, but can eliminate the effect of being deemed domiciled in the UK for IHT purposes.

Borrowing arrangements

105.9 As discussed in Chapter **84**, before April 2013 it was common practice for non-UK domiciled individuals (who were not deemed domiciled in the UK for IHT purposes) to secure an IHT advantage by borrowing against the security of UK situated assets and using the borrowed money to invest in non-UK assets, qualifying as excluded property. Generally, such planning has now been blocked by IHTA 1984, s 162A (introduced by FA 2013). However, in certain circumstances the four 'old' IHT treaties preserve the ability to use borrowing for IHT mitigation. A debt incurred to acquire non-British assets of an individual who is, or who has since become, UK domiciled for IHT purposes is not caught by s 162A (either because the proceeds of the borrowing were never excluded property, or because they have ceased to be excluded property; see para **84.17**). It follows that where such an individual is able to take the benefit of one of the 'old' IHT treaties, he can use borrowing on the security of British assets to secure an IHT deduction from their value, whilst keeping the proceeds of such borrowing outside the IHT net on death. One curious result of the interaction between these treaties and s 162A is that, where there is such borrowing, the acquisition of a deemed UK domicile may cause a reduction of, rather than the expected increase to, the value of assets that are within the IHT net on death.

The EU Succession Regulation

105.10 Regulation (EU) No 650/2012 (also known as the EU Succession Regulation, or more colloquially as 'Brussels IV') has applied to estates of individuals who have died since 17 August 2015. The Regulation aims to simplify estate planning in cross-border situations by providing a framework for determining which country will have jurisdiction over an estate and which country's succession laws will apply to the assets. One of the ways in which this is done is by allowing testators to choose the law of their nationality as the law applicable to succession (Article 22).

Any such election should be considered carefully, especially where the intention is to take advantage of one of the 'old' IHT treaties. As noted above, it is possible to eliminate the effect of being deemed domiciled in the UK for IHT purposes under these treaties, but in the case of the treaties with India, Pakistan and France, this is dependent on assets not passing under a 'disposition or devolution regulated by the law of some part of Great Britain'. Consequently an election under the Regulation for the succession law of some part of Great Britain to apply may upset any treaty-based IHT planning, insofar as the Regulation has effect in relation to the assets within the estate.

In this context, it should be noted that under transitional provisions in the Regulation, a 'disposition of property upon death' made prior to 17 August 2015 may be treated for the purposes of the Regulation as an election that the succession law of the individual's nationality shall apply to the assets in his estate. This is the case where the 'disposition', eg a will, was made 'in accordance with' the law of the deceased's nationality (Article 83(4)). A will is likely to be considered to have been made 'in accordance with' a particular country's law if it complies with that country's formal validity requirements and refers to or clearly relies on provisions of that country's law.

It seems very likely therefore that a large proportion of British nationals will be treated as having made an election for the law of some part of Great Britain to apply, by virtue of having made wills governed by the law of England or Scotland. In certain circumstances, this could frustrate planning relying on one of the 'old' estate duty treaties, which may have been put in place before the Regulation came into force.

For example, an Indian domiciled individual with British nationality may have made an Indian law will in relation to his non-UK (including EU) assets and an English law will in relation to his UK assets. Although the law in this area is new and therefore untested, there is a real risk that, due to the transitional provisions, the individual's EU-situated assets would be treated as passing in accordance with the law of some part of Great Britain. If so, they would ineligible for relief from IHT under the treaty with India.

Domicile elections

105.11 A domicile election under IHTA 1984, s 267ZA is to be ignored when applying these treaties (s 267ZA(6)(a)). The result, where the individual is actually non-UK domiciled and is resident or otherwise 'fiscally domiciled' in the other contracting state under its domestic law, is that the UK's taxing rights are, broadly, limited to UK assets. However, where the individual is not resident in or otherwise 'fiscally domiciled' in the other state, for the purposes of its law, the result of the disregard of s 267ZA is that for treaty purposes the individual is domiciled in neither contracting state. The treaty is therefore inapplicable and provides no IHT relief.

THE 'NEW' IHT TREATIES

105.12 As noted above, the UK has entered into six IHT treaties since the introduction of capital transfer tax/IHT. These six 'new' treaties are those with the Netherlands, the Republic of Ireland, South Africa, Sweden, Switzerland and the USA. Each is different, but there are certain common themes.

As with the 'old' IHT treaties, the 'new' IHT treaties are applied without regard to the effect of an election under IHTA 1984, s 267ZA (due to s 267ZA(6)(b)).

Determining treaty domicile

105.13 For the purpose of these treaties, the basic principle is that an individual is to be regarded as a domiciliary of the UK if domiciled there for the purposes of IHT, and is to be regarded as a domiciliary of the other contracting state if domiciled/resident there for the purposes of that state's domestic law (and also, in the case of the treaty with the USA, if a national of the USA). An individual may of course be domiciled in both contracting states under these tests, and 'tie-breaker' provisions are therefore needed to determine which of the contracting states the individual has a stronger connection with. These 'tie-breaker' provisions are based on those in the OECD Model Double Taxation Convention on Estates and Inheritances and Gifts (most recently updated in 1982), which sets out essentially the same test as is applied for determining residence in the OECD Model Treaty for income tax and CGT (see para **100.5**).

However, certain of the treaties impose more specific tests for determining treaty domicile. The treaties with each of the Netherlands, South Africa and the USA, for example, provide that an individual who is domiciled in the UK for IHT purposes and also the other contracting state under its domestic law shall be treaty domiciled in the UK (and not in the other contracting state) if the individual is a UK national (and not a national of the other contracting state) and has not been resident in the other contracting state in seven or more of the previous ten years.

Overriding deemed domicile

105.14 Of the 'new' IHT treaties, four in particular have the effect of overriding the IHT deemed domicile rules in certain circumstances. In each of the treaties with the Netherlands, Sweden, Switzerland and the USA, the tests for treaty domicile operate so that, broadly speaking, an individual who is resident in and/or a national of the other state but no longer UK resident or a UK national will not continue to be treated as domiciled in the UK under either the '17 years rule' or the '3 years rule'. Certain conditions need to be met in order to take advantage of these IHT treaty provisions.

Extension of spouse exemption

105.15 Several of the 'new' IHT treaties expressly address the issue of domicile mismatches (see CHAPTER **45** for a discussion of this issue).

Where a non-UK domiciled spouse leaves assets to a UK domiciled spouse, the UK domestic rules allow for a limited spouse exemption of an amount equal to the prevailing nil-rate band (IHTA 1984, s 18(2A)), but this limited spouse exemption may be enlarged by certain of the UK's IHT treaties. For example, Article 8(3) of the IHT treaty with the USA provides that 50% of the value transferred from a UK domiciliary to a non-UK domiciled spouse will be exempt from IHT if the UK domiciled transferor is also a US national and/or domiciled in the US under US domestic law.

This modification of the limited spouse exemption is broadly replicated in the IHT treaties with Switzerland (Article 10(2)), Sweden (Article 11(1)) and the Netherlands (Article 12(1)). In the Dutch treaty however, the limited spouse exemption is varied in this way only in relation to non-community property and only where the transferor is domiciled in the Netherlands under Dutch law. Dutch nationality does not suffice.

Taxing rights

105.16 As is commonly the case with tax treaties, the 'new' treaties typically use a combination of two approaches to prevent double taxation. The first of these is to give one of the two contracting states exclusive taxing rights. The basic principle is that property of an individual who is treaty domiciled in one of the contracting states shall be taxed by that state only. However, there are invariably exceptions to this. These treaties always reserve a contracting state's right to tax immovable property or certain business assets situated within that state. The UK also reserves a right to tax UK situated shares under the treaty with Switzerland. As certain assets may be taxed by both contracting states, the treaty must then provide credit relief.

By contrast to the above, the treaty with the Republic of Ireland does not give sole taxing rights in any circumstances to the country in which the individual is domiciled. Instead, the treaty simply specifies that the jurisdiction in which the asset is situated will have primary taxing rights with a credit available against the tax due in the other jurisdiction. Where assets are located in a third state, the tax due will be apportioned between the UK and Ireland.

Settled property

105.17 In very limited circumstances, certain of the treaties will prevent tax charges under the relevant property regime or other IHT charges associated with settlements. Notably, the treaties with the Netherlands, South Africa and Sweden prevent most settled property (other than assets such as immoveable property or business assets situated in the UK) from being taxable in the UK provided that, at the time of making the settlement, the settlor was both treaty-domiciled in the other state and had not been treaty-domiciled in the UK within the preceding ten years. The Swedish and Dutch treaties have the additional qualification that the settlor must not have been a UK national at the time of making the settlement.

The US treaty provisions relating to settlements are even more generous. A settlement made by a non-UK national who is treaty domiciled in the US will not be subject to any of the usual IHT charges, unless it holds UK immoveable property or property of a UK permanent establishment.

Section II

EU Law

Section II

EU Law

Chapter 106

THE FUNDAMENTAL FREEDOMS

INTRODUCTION

106.1 Member States of the European Union have consistently reserved for themselves competence over direct taxation. For this reason neither the rates of tax nor the rules for determining the tax base are harmonised in the Union. Nonetheless, the Court of Justice of the European Union ('CJEU') has applied Community law to direct tax, founding its jurisdiction on the freedoms conferred by the Treaty on the Functioning of the European Union ('TFEU' or 'the Treaty'). This Treaty has gone through many iterations, its origin being the treaty of Rome which founded the EEC. The TFEU, which reflects amendments made by the Treaty of Lisbon, came into force on 1 December 2009.

Limited areas of direct tax are covered by directives, most notably the mergers directive of 23 July 1990, the parent and subsidiary directive of 23 July 1990, the directive of 3 June 2003 dealing with interest and royalty payments between associated companies, and the savings income directive also of 3 June 2003. All save the last concern relationships between EU companies. The savings directive impacts on the offshore world in that the UK's Overseas Territories and Crown Dependencies operate its provisions in relation to interest payments.

Nonetheless the principal area where EU law is material for the subject-matter of this book remains the CJEU's interpretation of the freedoms. A point which should be emphasised is that, in the UK, European law has primacy. The matter was put thus by Lord Nicholls in *Re Claimants under Loss Relief GLO* [2005] UKHL 54, [2005] STC 1357 at para 16:

> 'The second basic principle concerns the interpretation and application of a provision of United Kingdom legislation which is inconsistent with a directly applicable provision of Community law. Where such an inconsistency exists the statutory provision is to be read and take effect as though the statute had enacted that the offending provision was to be without prejudice to the directly enforceable Community rights of persons having the benefit of such rights. That is the effect of section 2 of the European Communities Act 1972, as explained by your Lordships' House in *R v Secretary of State for Transport, Ex p Factortame Ltd* [1990] 2 AC 85, 140, and *ICI plc v Colmer (Inspector of Taxes)* [1999] 1 WLR 2035, 2041.'

Leaving the EU

106.2 This chapter, and Chapter 107, have not been updated since the previous (2015) edition of this book, and in particular take no account of the United Kingdom's decision to leave the European Union. At the time of writing it is quite unclear what form the departure will take and how far EU law will remain part of UK law.

OVERVIEW

106.3 The freedoms principally relevant to the subject matter of this book are the right of establishment, conferred by Articles 49–55 of the Treaty, and the freedom relating to capital and payments, conferred by Articles 63–66. There is also the overarching right for citizens of the EU to move freely within the Union, conferred by Article 21, but this is invoked only if other more specific freedoms are not in point. Its implications are considered in para **106.35**.

Prior to the amendments made by the Treaty of Lisbon, the numbering of articles was different. Thus the articles dealing with establishment were Articles 43–48 and those dealing with capital movements Articles 56–60.

As a general rule the freedoms may be invoked only in relation to transactions or movements within the European Union. As such they may in practice have little impact on offshore tax planning. But the freedoms also extend to EFTA countries in the European Economic Area and one freedom, capital, extends to movements involving third countries. This subject is explored further in paras **106.22** to **106.34**.

In relation to tax, the freedoms have been the subject of many and sometimes conflicting decisions of the CJEU. A particular area of difficulty is that national legislation which restricts a freedom is not per se in breach of EU law. The legislation is valid if it pursues a legitimate objective compatible with the Treaty and is justified by overriding reasons of public interest. This, the defence of justification, involves many limbs and frequently enables national governments to save legislation which otherwise restricts a freedom. But the position is complicated still further by the fact that even if the objective is justifiable the national legislation is only valid if and insofar as it is proportionate.

In the result analysis of the freedoms involves four distinct topics:

(1) What is meant by establishment and movement of capital.
(2) What, in national legislation, amounts to a restriction of these freedoms.
(3) What justifications are available to national governments.
(4) How is it decided whether legislation is proportionate.

A fifth issue arises if, having gone through this process, it is found that the national legislation is not compatible with one or other of the freedoms. This issue, discussed in **106.21**, is whether the national legislation is disapplied in its entirety or construed in conformity.

THE APPLICABLE FREEDOMS

Establishment

106.4 Establishment includes the taking up and pursuit of activities as a self-employed person and the setting up and management of companies or firms (Article 49). The term 'company or firm' comprehends any legal person governed by private or public law, save for those which are not profit making (Article 54).

A person is exercising the right of establishment if he owns shares in a company established in another Member State which gives him definite influence over the company's decisions and allows him to determine its activities (*Test Claimants in the Thin Cap Group Litigation v IRC* [2007] STC 906 para 27). Thus 100% owned companies are undoubtedly included and so too are companies over which the person has voting control or those in which he has a 50% or even a 25% holding (*Finanzamt Hamburg-Am Tierpark v Burda GmbH* C-284/06 [2008] STC 2996, para 70; *Scheunemann v Finanzamt Bremerhaven* [2012] Case C-31/11 SWTI 2358, ECJ). The concept of establishment also extends to setting up a permanent establishment in another Member State (*Lidl Belgium GmbH & Co KG v Finanzamt Heilbronn*: C-414/06 [2008] 3 CMLR 31, [2008] STC 3229, para 20).

Capital movements

106.5 The original EU legislation dealing with capital movements required Member States to abolish progressively all restrictions on the movement of capital. In 1988, Directive EC/361/EEC gave effect to that requirement and Article 1 of the Directive required capital movements to be classified in accordance with Nomenclature in Annex 1. Although the Directive has been superseded by what are now Articles 63–66, the CJEU has repeatedly stated that the Nomenclature has indicative value in defining what is meant by movement of capital (*Test Claimants in the FII Group Litigation v IRC* C-446/04 [2007] STC 326, para 179). It is not, however, regarded as exhaustive.

Annex 1 has 13 main headings, each with several sub-headings. For present purposes the most important heads are the following:

I   Direct Investment
II   Investments in Real Estate
III Acquisition of securities
IV   Acquisition of units in collective investment schemes
XI   Personal Capital Movements, the sub-heads of which include gifts and endowments and inheritances and legacies
XII Other capital movements

Investment in shares is a movement of capital provided that the investor and the shares are not in the same country. So too gifts or inheritances are capital movements provided the constituent elements are not all in the same country (*Mattner v Finanzamt Velbert* (2010) C-510/08, para 20; *Fernandez v Finanzamt Stuttgart-Körperschaften* (2009) C-35/08 para 18). A gift is a movement of capital whether in cash or in kind, and it is irrelevant whether the gift is made for altruistic purposes rather than for the purposes of economic activity (*Persche v Finanzamt Lüdenscheid* [2009] STC 586, paras 20–29, C-318/07 [2009] ECR I-359, [2009] All ER (EC) 673, [2009] 2 CMLR 819, ECJ).

An investment in land or the transfer of land to a company or a foundation can also be a capital movement (*Heirs of Barbier v Inspecteur van de Belastingdienst Particulieren/Ondernemingen buitenland te Heerlen* C-364/01 [2003] ECR I-15013; *Ospelt v Schlossle Weissenberg Familien Stiftung* C-452/01, [2003] ECR I-9743). But for capital to be the applicable freedom, the property must not be actively managed, as otherwise the investment in the land is establishment (*Centro di Musicologia Walter Stauffer v Finanzamt München* C-386/04 [2008] STC 1439).

A usufruct or a gift subject to an annuity is a movement of capital, being regarded by the ECJ as a means of anticipated succession inter vivos (*Schröder v Finanzamt Hameln*: C-450/09, [2011] STC 1248, [2011] All ER (D) 18 (Apr), ECJ). So too, a gift to a foundation is a capital movement as is a distribution by a foundation (*Ospelt, supra; F E Familienprivatstiftung Eisenstadt*, Re: C-589/13 (2015) ECLI:EU:C:2015:612, [2015] SWTI 2756, ECJ).

Overlap between freedoms

106.6 The facts of many cases potentially engage more than one freedom. Where this is so the CJEU looks at the purpose of national legislation and considers one only of the freedoms if it is clear that the others are secondary to that purpose (*Glaxo Wellcome GmbH & Co KG v Finanzamt München II*: C-182/08, [2010] STC 244).

As between capital and establishment, legislation which is targeted only at relations within groups of companies engages the freedom of establishment alone, any breach of Article 63 being seen as no more than an unavoidable consequence (*Test Claimants in the Thin Cap Group Litigation*, paras 33 and 34). The same applies to any other legislation which is intended to apply only to shareholdings which enable the shareholder to have definite influence on a company's decisions and determine its activities (*Holböck v Finanzamt Salzburg-Land* C-157/05, [2008] STC 92, para 23; *Test Claimants in the FII Group Litigation v HMRC* C-35/11, [2013] STC 612, para 91).

By contrast is the position where legislation applies to portfolio holdings, ie shareholdings acquired solely with the intention of making a financial investment, without any intention of influencing management and control of the company. Here the applicable freedom is capital (*Haribo v Finanzamt Linz* [2011] STC 917, 961, para 35). Where legislation applies both to shareholdings giving definite influence and to portfolio holdings, the facts of the case govern whether the applicable freedom is capital or establishment (*Test Claimants in the FII Group Litigation v HMRC* C-35/11, [2013] STC 612, para 94).

The boundary between portfolio shares and a holding enabling the shareholder to have definite influence is unclear. However important guidance may be obtained from *Scheunemann*. Here shareholdings comprising more than 25% of the company enjoyed inheritance tax advantages if the company was a German or EU company but not if it was not. Evidence was given that, under German law, a 25% shareholding gives the shareholder a blocking minority in the context of important decisions determining the company's continued existence. The CJEU held that this meant holdings of more than 25% were on the definite influence side of the line and thus that establishment was the only freedom applicable to the inheritance tax rule at issue.

Nationality and residence

106.7 The establishment freedom is expressed in terms of nationals of a Member State and thus nationality, rather than residence, determines its availability. Companies or firms formed under the laws of a Member State are treated as nationals of that Member State provided the registered office, principal place of business or central administration is somewhere in the European Union (Article 54).

The materiality of nationality is illustrated in *Fisher v Revenue and Customs Comrs* [2014] UK FTT 804 (TC), 17 ITLR 141. Here the First-tier Tribunal disapplied the transferor charge as respects a UK resident Irish national on the basis that the transfer at issue was establishment in Gibraltar. The disapplication did not extend to UK national transferors as the tribunal considered the UK and Gibraltar to be the same Member State for the purpose of the freedoms (see para 106.33).

The capital freedom, by contrast, is not expressed in terms of nationality. Instead the applicable connecting factor is residence. Thus the freedom may be invoked by a company incorporated outside the European Union if on the facts it is resident in a Member State (*Kronos International Inc v Finanzamt Leverkusen* Case C-47/12 [2015] STC 351).

Trusts

106.8 The EFTA Court has decided that trusts engage the freedoms (*Olsen v Norwegian State* [2014] Cases E-3/13 and E-20/13). Of itself this conclusion is not surprising given the earlier case law that a transfer to a foundation is a movement of capital (*Ospelt*; see para 106.5). But what is surprising about the decision of the EFTA court, at least to English eyes, is that the freedom engaged can be establishment as well as capital. This is discussed further in para 107.13.

RESTRICTIONS

106.9 Domestic legislation is a restriction if it is either a host country restriction or a restriction in the country of origin.

Host country restrictions

106.10 The host country is the country in which the taxpayer wants to establish or to which his capital is moved. Legislation in the host country constitutes a restriction if it discriminates in favour of its own nationals or residents and against nationals or residents of other EU countries wishing to establish or move capital there.

A well known UK instance is *Metallgesellschaft v IRC* [2001] STC 452 where the ability to pay dividends under a group income election under the former ACT regime was at issue. The election could be made if the parent was resident in the UK and not if it was not. As a result, groups with a UK parent enjoyed a cash-flow advantage in that payment of corporate tax by the subsidiary was delayed. The CJEU held that this restricted the freedom of EU parent companies to establish in the UK and thus breached Article 49. As a result UK subsidiaries of EU groups who paid ACT on group dividends have a right to restitution against HMRC equal to the time cost represented by the accelerated payment (*Sempra Metals Ltd v IRC* [2005] EWCA Civ 389, [2005] STC 687).

The CJEU defines discrimination as treating differently situations which are identical or treating in the same way situations which are different (*Test Claimants in Class IV of the ACT Group Litigation v IRC* [2007] STC 404, para 46). But although this test is simple to express, applying it gives rise to subtle distinctions.

These distinctions are seen in cases involving company distributions where some shareholders are resident in the same Member State as the distributing company and some are not. The issue such distributions raise, which lies at the heart of many CJEU cases, is that of economic double taxation, ie that profit may be taxed twice, once in the hands of the company which earns it and again in the hands of the shareholders when it is distributed. The CJEU's approach is that the position of resident and non-resident shareholders is not comparable if the country where the distributing company is based does not tax non-resident shareholders at all. But if it does the position of the two categories of shareholder is comparable and the non-resident shareholders must not receive less favourable tax treatment than the residents (*Denkavit International BV v Ministre de l'Economie* [2007] STC 452; see also *Test Claimants in the Thin Cap Group Litigation* at paras 89–90 and *Santander Asset Management SGIIC SA (on behalf of FIM Santander Top 25 Euro Fi) v Directeur des résidents à l'étranger et des services généraux*: Joined Cases C-338/11 to C-347/11, [2012] 3 CMLR 291, [2012] STC 1785, para 44, ECJ; *EC v Belgium* C-387/11 [2013] STC 587)).

Restrictions in the country of origin

106.11 The country of origin is the country where the taxpayer establishing or moving capital is based. Legislation in the country of origin constitutes a restriction if it hinders its nationals or residents from establishing in or moving capital to other Member States (*Lidl Belgium GmbH & Co KG* para 19).

In a UK context, *ICI v Colmer* [1998] STC 874 first illustrated the potential for domestic legislation to be a country of origin restriction. Here ICI was a 49% consortium partner, the consortium asset being a holding company with 23 subsidiaries, 4 resident in the UK, 6 in other Member States and 13, a majority, in non-EU countries. Under the then UK domestic law, ICI could have claimed loss relief in respect of its share of the losses of the UK subsidiaries, but only if a majority of the subsidiaries were UK resident. The ECJ held that this restricted the freedom of the consortium members to establish, through the holding company, in other Member States and so potentially infringed Article 49.

Baars v Inspecteur der Belastingdienst Particulieren/Onderneminge Gorinchem [2000] 2 ITELR 660 is another illustration of country of origin restrictions. There the Dutch wealth tax gave an exemption for substantial holdings in trading undertakings established in The Netherlands. The taxpayer owned a substantial holding in an Irish undertaking. This did not qualify for the wealth tax relief as the undertaking was not Dutch. The CJEU held that this difference in treatment breached Article 49.

Despite the fact that legislation is expressed to be a restriction if it is a hindrance, the concept of hindrance requires discrimination or differential treatment. The contrast is between the tax treatment of the activity or capital movement if made in the home country and the tax treatment if it is elsewhere in the EU. Thus the former CFC legislation in the UK was held to be a restriction because it attributed the profits of foreign subsidiaries to the parent whereas the profits of domestic subsidiaries could not be so attributed (*Cadbury Schweppes plc v HMRC*: C-196/04; [2006] STC 1908, at paras 43 and 44).

It is however clear that legislation is not a hindrance and thus not a restriction if it reflects normal principles of fiscal territoriality. Under those principles, a state taxes its residents on worldwide profits and non-residents only on profits sourced in the state (*Marks and Spencer plc v Halsey* [2006] STC 237, para 39). If, therefore, the more burdensome tax on foreign income or assets is the result of unrelieved double tax such is not a hindrance which engages the freedoms, for in such a scenario, the country of origin is treating domestic and foreign investments in the same way. The extra tax burden results from inability of the country of source and the country of residence to properly relieve double taxation. That, the CJEU has repeatedly held, is not a matter for the freedoms, but an issue to be negotiated by the Member States concerned (*CIBA v APEH* [2010] STC 1680 paras 27–29).

This last point is illustrated by *Block v Finanzamt Kaufbeuren* (2009) Case C-67/08, where German estate tax did not allow the deduction of foreign estate tax charged on foreign bank accounts. But the rate of German estate tax was the same for both domestic and foreign bank accounts and this, the CJEU held, meant the freedoms were not engaged. The point also arose in *Haribo Lakritzen Hans Riegel BetriebsgmbH v Finanzamt Linz*: C-436/08 [2011] 2 CMLR 921, [2011] STC 917, ECJ, in that one of the issues in the case was whether Austria was obliged to give credit in taxing foreign dividends for withholding tax levied by the country of origin. The ECJ held it was not.

Countervailing tax advantage

106.12 The fact that the party whose freedom is allegedly infringed may enjoy some countervailing tax advantage is disregarded (*Amurta SGPS v Inspecteur van de Belastingdienst/Amsterdam*: C-379/05 [2008] STC 2851, para 75). Thus, in a case originating in Germany, certain reliefs enjoyed by German registered companies were denied to the permanent establishments of foreign companies (*Compagnie de Saint-Gobain v Finanzamt* [2000] STC 854). Conversely, permanent establishments could remit profits to their foreign head office without suffering withholding tax, whereas withholding tax was chargeable on dividends paid by German subsidiaries to foreign parents. The CJEU held that this latter advantage did not prevent the non-application of the reliefs to permanent establishments from infringing Article 49.

Freedom of movement of capital

106.13 The treaty provisions dealing with capital movements do allow Member States certain flexibility, in that the prohibition of restrictions in Article 63 is subject to Article 65. Article 65(1)(a) reserves the right of Member States to differentiate between taxpayers who are not in the same situation as respects residence or where their capital is invested, and Article 65(1)(b) allows Member States to take all requisite measures to prevent infringement of national law, in particular in the field of taxation. Article 65(2) states that the provisions as to movement of capital are also without prejudice to restrictions on the right of establishment which are compatible with the Treaty. But both Article 65(1) and Article 65(2) are curtailed by Article 65(3), which provides that measures and procedures adopted under Article 65(1) and 65(2) must not constitute arbitrary discrimination or disguised restrictions on the free movement of capital.

In *Manninen* C-319/02 [2004] STC 1444, the CJEU provided a reconciliation of Articles 65(1)(a) and 65(3). Article 65(1)(a) allows unequal treatment, but Article 65(3) prohibits arbitrary discrimination. It follows that if there is difference in treatment, it must concern situations which are not objectively comparable or can be justified by overriding public interest grounds (*EC Commission v Belgium* C-387/11, [2013] STC 587 para 45). But in any case, the difference in treatment must be proportionate (*Manninen*, para 29). In effect, therefore, Article 65(1)(a) does no more than import justifications in any event available as a matter of general principle, as described in paras **106.14** to **106.18** below. This point was implicit in earlier cases such as *X and Y v Riksskatteverket* C-436/00, [2004] STC 1271, 1293, para 72 and *Staatssecretaris van Financien v Verkooijen* C-35/98, [2002] STC 654, 694, para 53. It has been consistently taken as settled in subsequent cases (see eg *Glaxo Wellcome GmbH & Co KG*, para 68).

JUSTIFICATIONS

106.14 As indicated in para **106.3**, the fact that the national legislation constitutes a restriction does not per se mean it breaches EU law. The CJEU will uphold it as permissible if it pursues a legitimate objective compatible with the Treaty and is justified by what are called 'overriding or imperative reasons of public interest' (*Cadbury Schweppes; Marks & Spencer*, para 35).

Abusive practices

106.15 The CJEU regards it as well settled that Community law cannot be relied on for abusive ends (*Halifax plc v Revenue and Customs Comrs* C-255/02, [2006] STC 919, 962, para 62). Accordingly a measure restricting the freedoms is capable of being upheld where it specifically relates to wholly artificial arrangements aimed at circumventing a Member State's legislation (*Test Claimants in the Thin Cap Group Litigation*, para 72). For this reason the UK's former CFC legislation was a restriction capable of being justified (*Cadbury Schweppes*, para 59).

But for a restriction to be justified on these grounds, its specific objective must be to prevent conduct involving the creation of wholly artificial arrangements. Such arrangements must not reflect economic reality and must be made with a view to escaping the tax normally due on the profits generated by activities carried out on the national territory (ibid para 74). The legislation in question must also enable the national court to carry out a case by case examination, based on objective elements in order to assess the abusive conduct of the persons concerned (*Glaxo Wellcome GmbH & Co KG*, para 99).

The key concept in this justification is that of 'wholly artificial arrangements'. This is considered further in para **106.20** below.

Cohesion of the tax system

106.16 The concept of cohesion of the tax system is illustrated by *Bachmann v Belgium* [1994] STC 855. Here Belgian tax law allowed a deduction for pension and life assurance contributions provided the life insurer was Belgian. Foreigners working in Belgium with life and pension arrangements elsewhere challenged the restriction to Belgian providers. The Belgian defence was that the exemption was part of a single regime under which benefits were taxed when paid, the regime thus operating as a deferral. The CJEU accepted the tax on benefits could not readily be enforced if the insurer was foreign and held that that factor, coherence of the tax system, meant Article 49 was not breached.

Subsequent cases, however, have established that cohesion of the tax system is a narrow concept. There must be a tax advantage on the one hand and the offsetting of that advantage by a tax charge on the other. Both the taxpayer and the taxes concerned must be the same (*Bosal Holding BV v Staatssecretaris van Financiën* [2003] STC 1483, 1503, paras 29 and 30).

The cohesion justification has been applied to uphold a German rule applicable to permanent establishments in treaty countries. Under the applicable treaty, profits of the permanent establishment were taxable solely by the treaty partner. German law allowed the German company relief for losses made by the permanent establishment but required the losses to be brought back into account insofar as the permanent establishment subsequently made profits. This, the CJEU held, was a restriction, but could be justified as ensuring coherence to the German tax system (*Finanzamt für Körperschaften III in Berlin v Krankenheim Ruhesitz am Wannsee-Seniorenheimstatt GmbH*: C-157/07, [2009] All ER (EC) 513, [2009] STC 138).

Balanced allocation of taxing rights

106.17 A restriction can be justified if it protects a Member State's right to tax activities carried on within its jurisdiction and ensures a balanced allocation of taxing rights as between Member States (*Glaxo Wellcome GmbH & Co KG*, para 82). This is an application of the territoriality principle, discussed in para **106.11**.

In decided cases, most illustrations of this principle have concerned losses, specifically legislation which prevents companies from electing to have their losses relieved either in their home Member State or in another country. Such legislation has in general been upheld (see for example *X Holding v Staatssecretaris* [2010] STC 941). Another illustration is legislation preventing profits being transferred between companies in different Member States by unusual or gratuitous transactions (*SGI v Belgium* [2010] C-311/08 para 63).

In *Marks and Spencer*, the balanced allocation of taxing rights and two arguments relating to tax avoidance were together held to justify in principle the restriction of group loss relief to losses incurred in UK subsidiaries. The first of the two tax avoidance arguments was that the losses could otherwise potentially be used twice, once in the country of the loss-making subsidiary and once in the country of the profitable group member. The second argument was that the free transfer of losses round a group regardless of territorial limitation would mean that the losses would end up being transferred to group members in the most highly taxed Member States.

In *Marks and Spencer* it was the presence of the three factors together which led the CJEU to find the restriction on loss relief justified. In subsequent cases what has emerged as important is the combination of the balanced allocation of taxing rights with the need to prevent avoidance. Thus in both *Oy AA* and *SGI v Belgium*, the transactions at issue would effectively have transferred profits out of the Member State where they arose and into a Member State where the regime was more favourable. The ECJ held legislation to counter this kind of activity could be justified (see further the analysis in *Thin Cap Claimants v HMRC* [2011] STC 738).

Cadbury Schweppes is another illustration of the principle. The CJEU specifically stated that the creation of wholly artificial arrangements which do not reflect economic reality undermines the right of Member States to exercise their tax jurisdiction in relation to activities carried on in their territory. It thus jeopardises a balanced allocation between Member States of the power to impose taxes (ibid, 1941, para 56).

Reduction in tax revenue

106.18 It is well settled that the protection of a Member State's tax revenue does not of itself justify a restriction (*Cadbury Schweppes*, para 49; *Haribo*, para 126). The German government argued in one case that the restriction of the tax avoidance justification to wholly artificial arrangements is too narrow, it being essential for Member States to be able to enact general measures of principle to counteract tax avoidance. The CJEU, however, declined to adopt this approach (*Rewe Zentralfinanz eG v Finanzamt Köln-Mitte* [2008] STC 2785).

In a broader context, however, the need to prevent tax avoidance may be taken into account. This is apparent from the discussion above, in that the combination of tax avoidance and the need to balance the allocation of taxing rights can together be a valid justification.

It was established as long ago as 1997, that a Member State is allowed to put in place measures to secure effective fiscal supervision (*Futura Participations SA v Administrations des Contributions* [1997] STC 1301). However arguments based on this justification have been rejected, on the grounds that the Mutual Assistance Directive of 19 December 1977 (Directive 77/799/EEC) allows for exchange of information and that a Member State can simply ask a company in its jurisdiction for any information it needs (*Rewe Zentralfinanz eG* at paras 56–58). The Mutual Assistance Directive of 1977 has been replaced by the more extensive Directive on Administrative Cooperation in the Field of Taxation (2011/16/EU) and is discussed further in para **106.25** below. The existence of these Directives does not prevent tax authorities from requiring taxpayers claiming a relief to provide proper documentary evidence demonstrating the conditions for the relief are met (*Meilicke v Finanzamt Bonn-Innenstadt*, C-262/09, [2013] STC 1494 para 53).

Not surprisingly the need to counter evasion is a justification. Thus in *X Passenheim* (Cases C-155/08 and C-157/08) [2009] STC 2441, the Dutch limitation period for the recovery of tax was 5 years in the case of bank accounts or other assets in the Netherlands and 12 years in the case of foreign assets and bank accounts. This, the CJEU held, was inter alia justified by the need to prevent evasion.

PROPORTIONALITY

106.19 Even if national legislation pursues an objective which may be justified, it must still be appropriate to the attainment of the objective and not go beyond what is necessary. In many cases national governments have failed at this hurdle even though the legislation at issue could on a more focussed basis have been justified.

ELISA v Directeur général des impôts and Ministère public C-451/05 [2008] STC 1762 is an example. This case concerned the French 3% tax on French real estate held by companies and other non-natural persons. This tax did not apply to companies established in France. Nor did it apply to companies established in countries with which France had concluded an appropriate convention but in such cases the company had to supply details of its underlying ownership. The CJEU held that the tax was justified as a measure to combat evasion of French wealth tax by use of foreign companies. But it went beyond what was necessary as it did not give companies in non-convention countries the opportunity to demonstrate their underlying beneficial ownership.

Marks and Spencer is another example. Even though the restriction of loss relief in that case was in principle justified, it still had to be proportionate. On the facts, the CJEU held it went further than was permissible insofar as it prevented the offset of a non-resident group member's losses if that group member had exhausted all possibility of utilising them in its home country and there was no possibility of it or a third party doing so in the future (*Marks and Spencer*, para 53).

Cadbury Schweppes is a third example. Here the UK's former CFC legislation was held to be proportionate only insofar as confined to wholly artificial arrangements intended to escape the United Kingdom tax normally payable. The CJEU considered the issue of whether the former CFC legislation satisfied this test turned on the construction of the UK's domestic legislation, and in particular on the motive defence in the former TA 1988, s 748(3) (see para 107.3). It therefore remitted the case back to the UK for final decision.

A fourth illustration of the proportionality principle is represented by a Belgian case, *Société d'investissement pour l'agriculture tropicale SA (SIAT) v État belge* C-318/10, [2012] SWTI 2460, ECJ. Here deductions were disallowed if paid to an entity whose tax regime was 'appreciably more advantageous' than the regime in Belgium unless the taxpayer proved the payments related to genuine and proper transactions and did not 'exceed the normal limits'. The CJEU held that such a rule was disproportionate, both because it was insufficiently certain and because it applied regardless of whether there was in fact tax avoidance or evasion.

Wholly artificial arrangements

106.20 A key concept both in the justifications and in proportionality is that of wholly artificial arrangements. The epithet 'wholly' suggests the concept is narrow and such a conclusion is supported by examples given by the ECJ in *Cadbury Schweppes* (at para 68) in the following terms:

> 'If checking those factors leads to the finding that the [subsidiary] is a fictitious establishment not carrying out any genuine economic activity in the territory of the host member state, the creation of that [subsidiary] must be regarded as having the characteristics of a wholly artificial arrangement. That could be so in particular in the case of a "letterbox" or "front" subsidiary.'

However, the concept may not be as narrow as these last examples might indicate. Earlier in its judgment in *Cadbury Schweppes* (at para 53) the CJEU emphasised that the purpose of the establishment freedom was to 'assist economic and social interpenetration within the EU'. It thus presupposes:

'actual establishment of the company concerned in the host member state and the pursuit of genuine economic activity there.'

Ascertainment of whether these conditions are met:

'must be based on objective factors which are ascertainable by third parties with regard, in particular, to the extent to which the [company] physically exists in terms of premises, staff and equipment.'

The Advocate General in *Cadbury Schweppes* considered three criteria submitted inter alia by the UK to be relevant (at paras 111–114). One, physical presence, was clearly referred to by the CJEU in the passage cited above. The other two, however, are not referred to in the CJEU judgment. One of these latter criteria is whether the services provided by the subsidiary are genuine – ie do the subsidiary's staff have the necessary competence and decision making powers. The other is whether the subsidiary adds value. Here the Advocate General took a more restrictive view than the UK, stating the point could only be relevant insofar as what the subsidiary does is so modest as to mean that in reality it is not giving consideration for the payments it receives.

In the UK, it has been accepted in subsequent litigation that the criteria in determining whether a company is a wholly artificial arrangement is whether it is 'actually established in' the host member state and carries on genuine economic activity there (*Vodafone 2 v HMRC* [2009] STC 1480 at para 24). In policy terms, however, HMRC appear to consider the correct position to be that encapsulated in their three submissions in *Cadbury Schweppes*, disregarding both the watering down of the third by the Advocate General and the fact that only the first was specifically endorsed by the CJEU. That this is HMRC's position was initially implicit in amendments made to the former CFC code (TA 1988, ss 751A and 751B). Their position was reaffirmed in the 2013 legislation purporting to make the transfer of assets code and TCGA 1992, s 13 EU compliant and in the consultative documents preceding that legislation (see paras 107.9 and 107.13, and CHAPTERS 74 and 88).

The conclusion that may be drawn is that HMRC's view of what a wholly artificial arrangement is may be considerably wider than the present state of the authorities would warrant. And there is an even more fundamental point. *Cadbury Schweppes*, and the analysis above, are all based on the underlying purpose of the establishment freedom. That purpose has no relevance to the capital movement freedom and yet the ECJ uses the wholly artificial arrangement concept there also. Here a guide to what is meant by the concept comes from *Glaxo Welcome GmbH & Co KG* at para 89 the CJEU emphasised simply the lack of economic reality referring to:

'wholly artificial arrangements which do not reflect economic reality and whose only purpose is to obtain a tax advantage.'

In the later case brought by the European Commission on TCGA 1992, s 13 (*European Commission v United Kingdom*: C-112/14 (2014) ECLI:EU:C:2014:2369, [2015] 1 CMLR 1515, [2015] STC 591, ECJ) the CJEU elaborated the concept in relation to the capital movement freedom as follows (at para 27):

'Where rules are predicated on an assessment of objective and verifiable elements making it possible to identify the existence of a wholly artificial arrangement entered into for tax reasons alone, they may be regarded as not going beyond what is necessary to prevent tax evasion and avoidance if, on each occasion on which the existence of such an arrangement cannot be ruled out, those rules give the taxpayer an opportunity, without subjecting him to undue administrative constraints, to provide evidence of any commercial justification that there may have been for that transaction.'

DISAPPLICATION OR CONSTRUCTION IN CONFORMITY

106.21 The effect of the freedoms on UK law was expressed in the following terms by Lord Nicholls in *Re Claimants under Loss Relief GLO* at para 17:

'When deciding an appeal . . . the appeal commissioners are obliged to give effect to all directly enforceable Community rights notwithstanding the terms of [the relevant UK legislation]. Accordingly, if an inconsistency with directly enforceable Community law exists, formal statutory requirements must where necessary be disapplied or moulded to the extent needed to enable those requirements to be applied in a manner consistent with Community law.'

The consequence of national legislation breaching EU law is thus either that it must be disapplied in its entirety or that it must be moulded so as to conform with the applicable EU law. It follows that there are two distinct outcomes, one of which is simple disapplication, and the other is construction so as to conform with EU law.

Conforming construction is to be preferred even if it departs from the strict and literal interpretation of the legislation or implies additional words. The only constraints are that the construction must go with the grain of the legislation and be compatible with its underlying thrust. Nor can the courts be required to make decisions for which they are not equipped or which give rise to practical repercussions which they cannot evaluate (*Vodafone 2, supra,* para 38).

In general the UK courts have adopted the conforming construction approach. Thus the result of *Cadbury Schweppes* was that the UK's former CFC legislation must be read subject to an additional exception for companies established in another Member State of the EU and carrying on genuine economic activities there *(Vodafone 2,* supra).

Should disapplication be required, such must neither go beyond what is required under EU law nor operate in situations falling outside the scope of EU law (*Vodafone 2*, supra, at para 61). If the legislation in question can in principle be justified, but is disproportionate, it is unlikely any disapplication will extend beyond cases where it is disproportionate (*Vodafone 2*, supra, para 66).

CAPITAL AND THIRD COUNTRIES

106.22 As indicated in para 106.3 above, the general rule is that the freedoms are breached only if they restrict movement within the EU. Thus in *ICI v Colmer* [1998] STC 874, ICI could not rely on Article 49 to claim the losses as, even with the EU subsidiaries counted as subsidiaries, a majority were still outside the UK (see *ICI v Colmer* [1999] STC 1089).

To the general rule there are a number of exceptions, of which the most important concerns capital movements. Article 63 prohibits restrictions on the movement of capital not only within the EU, but also as between Member States and third countries as well. In view of the wide meaning of movement of capital given in the 1988 directive (see para **106.5** above), Article 63 is important to the subject matter of this book.

The CJEU has made it clear that Article 63 must be interpreted in the same manner in relation to capital movements involving third countries as in relation to movements within the EU (*Skatteverket v A*: C-101/05, [2007] ECR I-11531, [2008] All ER (EC) 638, ECJ, [2009] STC 405, 438, para 38). But despite this, Article 63 is subject to important limitations in relation to third countries, some imposed by the Treaty itself and some by the CJEU.

The standstill

106.23 Currently the most important limitation in the Treaty is the standstill in Article 64(1). This prevents Article 63 from applying to third country movements insofar as the restriction at issue existed on 31 December 1993. However it is not all such restrictions which are preserved. It is only those which relate to the following types of capital movement:

- direct investment, including real estate;
- establishment;
- the provision of financial services; and
- the admission of securities to capital markets.

In cases decided to date, two issues have emerged with respect to the standstill. The first is what is comprehended in the types of capital movement caught. The second is what the position is if legislation which existed in 1993 has been amended since then, or been repealed and renacted.

On the first issue, two instructive cases are *Haribo* and *Finanzamt Ulm v Wagner-Raith* (Case C-560/13, 21 May 2015), *Haribo* raised many issues, among them the rule that in Austria dividends from shareholdings of less than 10% were exempt from tax if the paying company was Austrian, but taxable if it was not. The CJEU pointed out (at para 137) that a shareholding is a direct investment only if it satisfies two conditions:

(1) it is acquired with a view to the establishment or maintenance of lasting and direct economic links between the shareholder and the company;
(2) it allows the shareholder to participate effectively in the management of the company or in its control.

On the basis of this definition the CJEU concluded the shareholdings of less than 10% were not direct investment. As a result the standstill did not apply, even though the Austrian legislation had been in existence since before 1993.

Wagner-Raith concerned the German rules taxing investment funds, specifically a rule imposing flat rate taxation where the fund did not comply with certain notification requirements. This rule had existed since before 1993 and the CJEU held the standstill applied. The basis for the decision was that the acquisition of units in investment funds and the receipt of dividends therefrom involve financial services provided by the fund to the investors.

On the second question, *Haribo* affirmed (at para 136) that the standstill applies not merely to legislation existing since 1993 but also to legislation meeting one of two other conditions. These are as follows:

(1)   the post-1993 legislation is essentially identical to the pre-1993 legislation; or

(2)   the post-1993 legislation does no more than restrict or abolish an obstacle to the freedoms that existed under the previous legislation.

In applying these conditions matters must be looked at from the perspective of the taxpayer. Thus if the legislation at issue has been in place since before 31 December 1993, Article 64(1) applies, even if for part of the period since then the restriction has not been discriminatory. This is illustrated by *Skatteverket v A*: C-101/05, [2008] All ER (EC) 638, [2009] STC 405, where Swedish taxpayers had always been taxed on distributions in specie from, inter alia, Swiss companies. As at 31 December 1993 such distributions were exempt if made by a Swedish company. This exemption was abolished in 1994 but reintroduced in 1995 and extended to companies based in the EEA or in any other country with which Sweden had concluded a double tax treaty providing for exchange of information. As distributions in specie from Swiss companies had at all times remained taxed, Article 64(1) was in point (see further *Test Claimants in the FII Group Litigation v HMRC* [2009] STC 254, 307, para 93 et seq per Henderson J).

Step backwards

106.24 Article 64(3) is potentially a second limitation in the Treaty on the application of Article 63 to third country capital movements. It gives the European Council power to adopt measures which constitute a step backwards as regards the liberalisation of capital movements. But this power has so far not been exercised and is confined to capital movements of the kinds within the standstill.

A similar power is given to the Council or the Commission by Article 65(4). This allows them to declare that a restriction applicable to third countries is to be regarded as compatible with the Treaty. This power too has not so far been exercised and is exercisable only insofar as the restriction is justified by one of the objectives of the European Union.

The CJEU

106.25 In some ways the most significant limitations on the application of Article 63 to capital movements involving third countries have come from the CJEU. This is because the CJEU considers that capital movements between Member States and non-Member States take place in a different legal context than that which obtains on movements within the EU (*Haribo* at para 119). The consequence of this is that when it comes to asking whether a restriction is justified, the answer in relation to non-Member States is not necessarily the same as within the EU.

The distinction in legal framework between EU and non-EU countries which has so far been emphasised by the CJEU is the Mutual Assistance Directive of 19 December 1977 (77/799EEC), replaced from 1 January 2013 by the Directive on Administrative Cooperation in the Field of Taxation (2011/16/EU). The 2011 directive provides for information to be exchanged between Member States as follows:

- Information on request under Article 5 (other than that precluded by the requested state's own law).
- Automatic exchange of certain categories of information under Article 8.
- Spontaneous exchange of certain types of information under Article 9, most notably where tax loss is suspected.

The CJEU relied on the 1977directive to uphold legislation confining reliefs from tax to residents of Member States or of other countries with which arrangements comparable to the directive have been concluded (*Établissements Rimbaud SA v Directeur général des impôts and Directeur des services fiscaux d'Aix-en-Provence*: C-72/09, [2011] 1 CMLR 1433, [2010] STC 2757, 2778, para 33). The rationale has been that the directive or the comparable arrangements allow information to be obtained with which to police the reliefs and ensure that those claiming are in fact entitled. The justifications adduced by the CJEU are the combination of preventing tax evasion and ensuring fiscal supervision.

A good illustration is furnished by *Skatteverket v A* [2009] STC 405. Here the distributions in specie to which the exemption described in para **106.23** applied were those comprising shares in other companies. Certain conditions had to be met, most notably that all the distributing company's shares in the company concerned had to be distributed and both companies had to be trading companies. The CJEU held that the Swedish authorities were entitled to insist on verification of those conditions, and that this was not possible in relation to Swiss companies as the treaty with Switzerland contained no exchange of information provision. On this basis, the restrictions to the relief in the Swedish legislation could be justified.

The point is also illustrated by *Rimbaud*. Like *ELISA*, discussed in para **106.19**, *Rimbaud* concerned the French 3% tax on real estate held by companies and other non-natural persons. In *Rimbaud*, the owning company was a Liechtenstein company and, as no treaty or convention existed between France and Liechtenstein, the legislation was upheld. The basis of the decision was that no mechanism existed by which the French authorities were entitled to obtain from Liechtenstein information to verify what was said by the company about its underlying ownership.

However, the mere fact there is no convention providing for mutual assistance does not of itself justify a third country restriction. The government seeking to uphold the restriction in relation to third countries must produce evidence that the restriction is in fact needed (*Santander Asset Management SGIIC SA*: para 44). A further point is that a double tax treaty with the third country where the affected party is based may provide a mechanism for obtaining the necessary information. Should that be found to be so, the justification may fall away (*Emerging Markets Series of DFA Investment Trust Co v Dyrektor Izby Skarbowej w Bydgoszczy* Case C-190/12, [2014] STC 1660). The Upper Tribunal in the UK has held this is certainly so where the treaty provides for exchange of any information for any purpose of the tax legislation of the contracting states. But it is not so where information is exchanged only for the purposes of preventing fraud and tax avoidance (*Trustees of the BT Pension Scheme v HMRC* [2013] UKUT 0105).

It is also plain that, as with all justifications, any restriction based on the absence of information exchange must be proportionate. Thus in *Haribo*, the tax credit was available on portfolio dividends from companies in EEA countries provided comprehensive procedures for information and enforcement existed between the EEA country concerned and Austria. This, the CJEU held, went further than was necessary, for all that was needed was procedures on information exchange not enforcement (see ibid, 967, para 73). So too the complete lack of a tax credit on portfolio dividends from companies outside both the EU and the EEA could not be justified, as it was not restricted to countries with which Austria had not concluded appropriate information exchange procedures (ibid 976, paras 131 and 132).

The focus in *Rimbaud* and *Haribo* is thus on the ability of the Member State to obtain information – in other words the effective fiscal supervision justification. An important issue is how far the tax evasion justification alone might lead to a more broad-brush approach.

Haribo, however, is clear authority that the need to counter tax evasion does not on its own justify blanket restrictions as respects third countries. Two points in the long and important judgment confirm this:

(1) as indicated above, the blanket refusal of the tax credit on third country portfolio dividends could not be justified; and
(2) it was explicitly stated in relation to the third country dividend issue that reduction in a Member State's tax revenue is not an overriding reason in the public interest and so not a justification ([2011] STC 917, 976, para 126).

Such a conclusion is confirmed by *Rimbaud* where, at para 34, the CJEU said:

'Thus a justification based on the fight against tax evasion is permissible only if it targets purely artificial contrivances, the aim of which is to circumvent tax law, and in consequence any general presumption of evasion is excluded.'

It may cogently be argued that the Tax Information Exchange Agreements which most offshore jurisdictions have concluded with the UK (and other EU countries) satisfy the need to be able to obtain information as of right, for they provide for information to be given on request. They thus meet the substance of the ECJ's concern and, if so, much of the rationale underlying *Skatteverket v A* and *Rimbaud* may now have fallen away. But the position is not clear cut for, in the cases referred to above, the CJEU placed emphasis on the whole of Directive 77/799/EEC, which included spontaneous and automatic exchange.

It has also referred to the EU harmonisation measures on company accounts as another respect in which the legal framework is different (see *Skatteverket v A* [2009] STC 405, 442, para 62).

Overlap with establishment

106.26 A further limitation imposed by the CJEU arises out of the overlap with establishment. As described in para **106.6**, if legislation is directed solely at groups of companies or other situations of shareholder control, the freedom engaged is that of establishment alone. This means that such legislation cannot be challenged under Article 63 in relation to third countries (*Test Claimants in the FII Group Litigation v Revenue and Customs Comrs* C-35/11, [2013] STC 612 para 98; *Scheunemann*). In *Boake Allen Ltd v Revenue and Customs Comrs* [2007] UKHL 25, [2007] 3 All ER 605, [2007] STC 1265, Lord Hoffmann suggested (at para 25) that this limitation applies not merely to the legislation targeted solely at groups of companies but also to other legislation if the facts of any particular case at issue involve a group. It would appear from two later ECJ decisions that this is wrong (*Test Claimants in the FII Group Litigation* C-446/04, [2007] STC 326, para 165; ibid [2010] STC 1251 para 69; *Holbock v Finanzamt Salzburg-Land*: C-157/05, [2008] STC 92, para 24).

It is clear from the FII litigation that legislation directed both at groups of companies or other situations giving the shareholder definite influence and at portfolio investment engages Article 63 in relation to third countries even if the facts at issue involve a group. However, whilst this applies to dividends from third country subsidiaries, it would not apply to restrictions involving market access (*Test Claimants in the FII Group Litigation*, C-35/11, [2013] STC 612 para 100.

EUROPEAN ECONOMIC AREA

106.27 The European Economic Area ('EEA') is constituted by the Agreement on the European Area which first came into force on 1 January 1993. The parties are the Member States of the EU and three member countries of the European Free Trade Area, or EFTA, namely Iceland, Liechtenstein and Norway.

The significance of the EEA is that the Agreement confers the fundamental freedoms in the same terms as the EU Treaty. Thus Article 31 of the Agreement provides that there shall be no restrictions on the freedom of establishment of nationals of any EEA state in any other EEA state. So too Article 40 provides that there shall be no restrictions on the movement of capital belonging to persons resident in EEA states and no discrimination based on nationality or on the place of residence of the parties or on the place where the capital is invested. It is well settled that the rules of the EEA Agreement and those of the EU Treaty must be given uniform interpretation (*Krankenheim Ruhesitz am Wannsee-Seniorenheimstatt GmbH* [2009] STC 138, para 24; *Rimbaud*, para 20).

Article 40 was applied by the CJEU in *Ospelt* where the transaction at issue was a transfer of land to a Liechtenstein foundation. The judgment makes it clear that Liechtenstein's adherence to the EEA agreement renders inapplicable the standstill discussed above in relation to third country capital movements (see para **106.23**). Articles 31 and 40 were both applied in relation to a Liechtenstein trust in *Olsen*. As the taxpayers were Norwegian, the deciding court was the EFTA court. *Olsen* is considered further in para **107.5**.

It might have been thought in the light of this case law that the outcome in cases involving Iceland, Liechtenstein and Norway would be the same as where EU countries are involved. But in one respect this is not so. The CJEU treats the EEA states in the same way as other third countries outside the EU, with the result that justifications which are not apposite within the EU may be upheld. The principal justifications to which this has so far been applied are tax evasion and effective fiscal supervision (*Commission of the European Communities v Italian Republic* [2009] Case C-540/07, [2009] ECR I-10983, [2010] 2 CMLR 243, ECJ).

It may however be doubted whether it is valid for the UK to use these justifications as a basis for treating EEA countries differently from Member States. This is because the UK has concluded full double tax treaties with the three countries concerned.

OFFSHORE JURISDICTIONS

106.28 The application of the Treaty to offshore jurisdictions is a matter of complexity and, in some cases, uncertainty. The reason why this is so is that the Treaty applies differently to different categories of country or territory, and offshore jurisdictions are spread across virtually all the categories.

Member States

106.29 It is perhaps not a natural use of language to describe any Member State as an offshore jurisdiction. But many would regard Cyprus, for example, as having at least some characteristics of an offshore jurisdiction, and to a lesser extent the same may be true of countries such as Luxembourg or Ireland. Indeed Ireland was where the offshore subsidiaries were located in *Cadbury Schweppes* (see further para **107.3**).

There can be little doubt that so far as the freedoms are concerned all Member States are treated in the same way, regardless of how competitive or favourable their direct tax regimes may be. It follows that establishment and capital movement to or from Cyprus or other tax favourable Member States enjoy the freedoms in full and that anti-avoidance legislation avails only to the extent permitted by the justifications described in paras **106.14** to **106.19** above.

EFTA States

106.30 One leading offshore jurisdiction is an EFTA state, namely Liechtenstein. As described in para **106.27**, the EEA Agreement of 1 January 1993 confers the same freedoms as the Treaty and it follows that establishment in or movements of capital to or from Liechtenstein should enjoy the same freedoms as within the EU. The one qualification is the point made in para **106.27**, namely the fact that Liechtenstein is outside the EU legal framework. This means anti-avoidance legislation may be more readily justified. But the rationale of this qualification, inability to obtain information, has now gone, for the full double tax treaty between the UK and Liechtenstein came into force in April 2013 (HMRC Notice 14 January 2013 reproduced [2013] SWTI 226).

The potential application of the freedoms to Liechtenstein is illustrated by the decision of the EFTA Court in *Olsen* (see further para **107.5**). At issue here was a Liechtenstein trust, whose beneficiaries were Norwegian. Norwegian legislation both taxed the trust income on the beneficiaries and subjected them to wealth tax on the trust capital. The EFTA Court held that both the establishment and the capital freedoms were potentially engaged (see further para **107.5**).

Sovereign third countries

106.31 The position as respects offshore jurisdictions which are sovereign third countries is as described in paras **106.22** to **106.26**. In other words the only freedom available is capital and its applicability is curtailed both by the standstill protecting legislation existing on 31 December 1993 and by the greater readiness of the ECJ to uphold restrictions as justified. It might be thought few if any sovereign states are established offshore jurisdictions, but in reality this is not so, and the Bahamas and Mauritius may be mentioned in particular. Further, some at least, for example Mauritius, have full treaties with the UK.

Associated territories

106.32 Annex II to the Treaty lists a number of non-European territories which are dependent on or associated with EU members. They include the Netherlands Antilles and some, but not all, of the British Overseas Territories. Those listed include the Cayman Islands, the Turks and Caicos Islands, the British Virgin Islands, and Bermuda.

The significance of the associated territories is that Article 198 of the Treaty provides for association between them and the EU. Among the objects of such association are freedom of establishment (Article 199(5)). The EU Council is required to lay down detailed rules and procedures (Article 203).

The Overseas Association Decision (most recently Council Decision 2013/755/EU), gives effect to this requirement. Articles 44–46 of that Decision are inter alia headed rules of establishment, but do not add to what the Treaty says. Article 59 of the Decision refers to capital movements but in terms which on the face of it are much more restricted than Article 63 of the Treaty.

It appears the Decision gives the governments of Annex II territories standing in the ECJ. This is apparent from *Government of the Cayman Islands v Commission of the European Communities* ([2002] CILR 91; *Spitz and*

Clarke: Offshore Service, Cases vol 4, p 167). Here the Cayman Islands sought unsuccessfully to delay promulgation of the EU Savings Directive.

The CJEU held in *Prunus v Directeur des services* [2011] STC 1392 that the non-European territories listed in Annex II count as third countries for the purposes of the freedom of movement of capital. This means restrictions on capital movements to or from those territories which breach Article 63 are prohibited. Equally it also means that the standstill for pre-1993 legislation is in point as respects the categories of movement within Article 64.

Prunus was another case concerning the French 3% tax imposed on real estate owned by non-resident companies. The facts were that the property was ultimately owned by two BVI companies. The CJEU held that Article 63 was engaged but also found that the French tax had come into force before 1 December 1993. On that basis, it upheld the application of the tax.

As will be apparent from these facts, *Prunus* concerned a capital movement between a Member State, France and an associated territory of another Member State, the UK. The logic of the decision is that it should equally apply between a Member State and its own associated territory but it is now clear this is not so. In *X BV v Staatssecretaris van Financiën* (Case C-24/12, [2014] STC 2394) withholding tax on dividends paid by Dutch companies was at issue. Dividends paid to a Dutch corporate shareholder were tax free whereas dividends paid to a corporate shareholder based in the Netherlands Antilles suffered withholding tax at 8.3%. The Dutch company, following *Prunus*, argued Article 63 was engaged, but the CJEU rejected this, holding that relations between a Member State and its own associated territories are governed not by the freedoms in the Treaty but by the Overseas Association Decision. It noted that Article 66.2 of the Decision expressly carves out measures aimed at preventing tax avoidance and on that basis upheld the levying of withholding tax on dividends to the Antilles.

On the face of it, *X BV* precludes the freedoms as between the UK and the British Overseas Territories. But in reality matters may not be as simple as this for the CJEU expressed itself in the following terms:

> 'A tax measure such as that at issue in the main proceedings, which is, according to the referring court's description of its history and purpose, intended to prevent excessive capital flow towards the Netherlands Antilles and to counter the appeal of that [territory] as a tax haven, comes under [article 66.2] . . . . . . provided it pursues that objective in an effective and proportionate manner, which is a matter for the referring court to assess.'

In other words, one may be back to the familiar proposition, namely that anti-avoidance legislation cannot be upheld unless it is proportionate.

There are also two further points that need to be made. The first is that the language of Article 59 of the Decision is restrictive, being confined to payments and direct investment. Thus on its terms it does not embrace portfolio investment or personal capital movements. But it is not clear whether it should in fact be read as restricted in this way as in *X BV*, the CJEU commented Article 59 had:

> 'A particularly wide scope, close to the scope of Article [63] in the relations between Member States and third countries.'

The second point is that under Article 199.5 of the Treaty there is a right of establishment as between Member States and associated territories. It is however unclear how far this goes, as it is noteworthy that Article 51 of the Decision uses relations between third countries as a comparator.

Gibraltar

106.33 Gibraltar is not part of the United Kingdom and so does not fall within the term 'Member State' (see Treaty on European Union, Article 52). However Article 355.1 of the Treaty provide that the Treaty provisions, and thus the freedoms, apply to European territories for whose external relations a Member State is responsible. Gibraltar is such a territory and the freedoms therefore apply to it. It follows that a national of a Member State other than the UK can rely on the establishment freedom if establishing in Gibraltar (*Fisher*).

An issue of acute controversy is whether the freedoms can be relied on as between the UK and Gibraltar. This issue turns on whether Article 355.2 means Gibraltar is, for the purposes of the freedoms, the same Member State as the UK or a different Member State. The point is currently being litigated in *Fisher* where UK nationals had set up a trading company in Gibraltar and were taxable under ITA 2007, s 720 on its profits (see further para 69.51). The First-tier Tribunal has held that Gibraltar and the UK are a single Member State for the purposes of the freedoms, with the result that the freedom of establishment is not engaged. But it did not regard the point as sufficiently certain to be *acte claire* albeit deferring any reference to the CJEU to a higher court.

The Crown Dependencies

106.34 The Crown Dependencies are also European territories for whose external relations a Member State, ie the UK, is responsible. But in contrast to Gibraltar, the Treaties apply only to the extent set out in Protocol No 3 to the Accession Treaty of 22 January 1972 between the EEC and the UK. Protocol 3 mainly concerns customs matters and agricultural products and it has been held that for those purposes the UK and the Crown Dependencies are treated as a single Member State (*Jersey Produce Marketing Organisation Ltd v Jersey, intervening* [2005] Case C-293/02, [2005] ECR I-9543, [2006] All ER (EC) 1126, ECJ).

But so far as the subject matter of this book is concerned, none of the matters in Protocol 3 touch either the capital or the establishment freedoms. In other contexts, the CJEU has affirmed that provisions of EU law not covered by Protocol 3 do not apply in the Crown Dependencies (*Roque v Lieutenant Governor of Jersey* [1998] Case C-171/96, [1998] ECR I-4607, [1998] 3 CMLR 143, ECJ). It is noteworthy that in *Prunus*, the CJEU pointed out that associated territories benefit from EU law in a manner similar to Member States only when the Treaty so provides and that otherwise they count as third countries. In logic this reasoning, if applied to Crown

Dependencies, means they are third countries so far as the freedoms are concerned and thus enjoy the capital movement but not the other freedoms. Whether logic will prevail should the matter ever reach the CJEU is a matter of speculation, but it is noteworthy that in *Fisher* the First-tier Tribunal appears to have assumed the capital movement freedom would apply as between the UK and the Crown Dependencies (see para 836).

FREEDOM OF MOVEMENT OF CITIZENS

106.35 Article 21 of the Treaty confers the right on citizens of the EU to move and reside feely within the territory of Member States. National rules which preclude or deter a national of a Member State infringe that freedom. This applies to tax rules as much as any other. Article 21 is thus breached by a rule which allows the gain on the sale of a taxpayer's residence to be rolled into a new residence if the latter is in the same Member State but not if it is elsewhere (*Commission v Sweden* C-104/06, [2007] 2 CMLR 153, [2007] SWTI 194).

Article 21 is only in point in relation to persons who are not economically active (ibid, para 30; *Turpeinen* (2006) C-520/40, [2007] 1 CMLR 783, [2006] SWTI 2458, [2006] All ER (D) 106 (Nov), ECJ). Where the taxpayer is economically active, the applicable freedoms are those of establishment or movement of workers. Their effect is however the same.

This was dramatically illustrated by *De Lasteyrie du Saillant v Ministère de l'Économie* [2004] 6 ITLR 666, a French case concerning capital gains. Under French law, unrealised capital gains on shares were charged to tax on the emigration of the owner insofar as the shares represented (in broad terms) a holding of more than 25% in the company. The charge was postponed if the taxpayer deposited funds to secure the tax and if, in such case, five years elapsed without the asset being sold, the tax ceased to be chargeable. The taxpayer emigrated to Belgium, which has a generally favourable regime for taxing gains.

The CJEU held that the exit charge breached Article 49. It emphasised that a restriction on freedom of establishment is prohibited even if of limited scope or minor importance. It then concluded that the recognition of unrealised gains on emigration would, at the very least, have a dissuasive effect on French residents wishing to establish themselves in another Member State. The CJEU was pressed with the mechanism for deferring and ultimately avoiding the tax if the shares were retained but concluded that the procedure itself constituted a restriction.

However it has subsequently become clear that *de Lasteyrie* is not as far-reaching as was first supposed. In *N v Inspecteur van de Belastingdienst Oost/kantoor Almelo* C-470/4, [2006] All ER (D) 26 (Sep) Dutch legislation treated emigration as the occasion of a deemed disposal by the emigrant of any shares he owned which constituted more than 5% of the company's capital. The tax was deferred and did not become payable if the taxpayer remained abroad for more than ten years. In the meantime the taxpayer had to provide security for the tax.

The taxpayer emigrated from the Netherlands to the UK and owned interests in excess of 5% in several Dutch companies. The CJEU held that those holdings represented establishment by him in the Netherlands from the UK and so engaged Article 49. But the CJEU then found that the restriction was capable of being justified under the territoriality principle as being a balanced allocation of taxing rights (see para **106.17**). It is thus reasonable in principle for a Member State to tax capital appreciation which has accrued during an individual's period of residence, providing payment of the tax is deferred until the asset is in fact sold. However the Dutch rules went further than was justified, both because security was required and because no allowance was made for any fall in value after the taxpayer emigrated.

Another device national governments use to counter emigration is to treat the emigrant as remaining resident or domiciled in his former country for the purposes of estate tax. This was at issue in *Van Hilten – van der Heijden v Inspecteur van de Belastingdienst/Particulieren/Ondernemingen buitenland te Heerlen* C-513/03, [2008] STC 1245. Here Dutch law imposed inheritance tax both on those residing in the Netherlands at the time of death and on those who had ceased to do so within the previous ten years. The CJEU affirmed that an inheritance is a movement of capital, provided its constituent elements extend to more than one state. But the Dutch rule imposing tax on those who had emigrated did not infringe the freedom as it neither deterred non-residents from investing in the Netherlands nor Dutch people from investing abroad.

The applicable freedom in *Van Hilten* was capital as the deceased had moved to Switzerland. It is unclear whether establishment could have been relied on had she moved to a country within the EU. But it is noteworthy that the CJEU cited, as additional support for its decision, that the extension of deemed residence was reasonable exercise of fiscal sovereignty provided it did not exceed ten years (at para 48).

Chapter 107

IMPACT OF THE FREEDOMS ON ANTI-AVOIDANCE LEGISLATION

INTRODUCTION

107.1 This chapter reviews the potential impact of the fundamental freedoms on anti-avoidance legislation relevant to offshore tax planning. It also deals with issues of procedure and limitation. Inevitably this chapter is tentative, for many of the relevant principles are still being developed by the CJEU and by the UK's own domestic courts. As in the previous chapter, no account is taken of the United Kingdom's referendum on 23 July 2016 or of other developments since the last edition of this book.

LEGISLATION ATTRIBUTING INCOME AND GAINS

107.2 The principal type of anti-avoidance legislation to consider here is legislation which, for tax purposes, treats the income or gains of an overseas entity as the income or gains of a UK resident. On the face of it such legislation ought not to be vulnerable to the freedoms, for the tax resulting from the attribution is no greater than if the UK taxpayer had kept the assets or activities in his personal name. But in 2006 the seminal case of *Cadbury Schweppes v HMRC* [2006] STC 1908 showed this is not so. More recently the CJEU has taken the same approach in relation to TCGA 1992, s 13 (*European Commission v United Kingdom:* C-112/14 (2014) ECLI:EU:C:2014:2369, [2015] 1 CMLR 1515, [2015] STC 591, ECJ) as has the EFTA Court in relation to trusts (*Olsen v Norwegian State* [2014] Cases E-3/13 and E-20/13).

Cadbury Schweppes has been extensively referred to in the previous chapter, but each of these three cases requires specific analysis here. It is noteworthy that of all the ECJ cases cited in the previous chapter, they are virtually alone in concerning legislation attributing the income or gains of an overseas entity to a resident person.

Cadbury Schweppes

107.3 *Cadbury Schweppes* concerned two Irish subsidiaries of a UK group performing treasury functions. The legislation at issue was the UK's former controlled foreign company or CFC legislation, which was first enacted in

1984 and most recently constituted TA 1988 ss, 747–756. It was repealed in 2012 with effect for accounting periods beginning on or after 1 January 2013 and replaced by much more limited legislation enacted as TIOPA 2010, ss 371AA–371VJ (FA 2012, Sch 20, paras 1, 14 and 49; see further para **24.18**).

The former UK legislation applied to non-resident companies which were controlled by persons resident in the UK and were subject to a lower level of taxation where resident. It charged UK corporate shareholders in the CFC to corporation tax on the CFC's profits. It was subject to important exemptions, inter alia because it did not apply to companies carrying on exempt activities and was subject to a motive defence. The latter required two conditions to be satisfied namely:

(a)   the diversion of profits from the UK was not one of the main purposes of the company's existence; and

(b)   reduction of tax was not one of the main purposes of transactions in the accounting period under review.

HMRC invoked the CFC legislation in relation to the Irish subsidiaries and sought to tax Cadbury Schweppes on their profits. Cadbury Schweppes countered by arguing that the CFC legislation breached the freedom of establishment and so was inoperative. The Special Commissioners referred this issue to the ECJ and, as explained in paras **106.19** and **106.20**, the ECJ held that the legislation did breach the freedom, but could be justified insofar as it was restricted to companies intended to secure a tax advantage and not established and carrying on genuine economic activities in a Member State. The ECJ remitted the question of whether the Irish subsidiaries satisfied this condition to the Special Commissioners and at the time of writing their decision is still pending.

The s 13 case

107.4   The s 13 case was brought by the European Commission and concerned TCGA 1992, s 13 in the form that section took prior to the amendments enacted in 2013 (as to which see paras **88.4, 88.5** and **88.14**). The Commission relied on the capital movement freedom, and the CJEU found this freedom was engaged, as s 13 has never applied to UK resident companies. The CJEU then held s 13 could potentially be justified by the need to prevent tax avoidance and evasion, but was disproportionate as it was not specifically targeted on wholly artificial arrangements which do not reflect economic reality and are carried out for tax purposes alone.

Olsen

107.5   *Olsen* concerned a Liechtenstein trust, the Ptarmigan Trust, whose beneficiaries were resident in Norway. Both Norway and Liechtenstein are EFTA states, so the adjudicating court was the EFTA court, and the freedoms set out in the EEA Agreement were these in point. But as explained in para

106.27, these freedoms are in essentially the same terms as those of the EU Treaty.

At issue in *Olsen* were two provisions in the Norwegian tax code, namely its CFC rules and its wealth tax. Under Norwegian law, the CFC rules applied to foreign trusts, and their effect was to subject Norwegian beneficiaries to tax on the trust's income at the same rate as the trust would have paid had it been a Norwegian company. The beneficiaries were subject to wealth tax on the trust's assets at the same rate (1.1%) as applied to their personal assets. But this rate was significantly higher than the rate (0.3%) applicable to Norwegian family foundations.

The EFTA court decided that the differential wealth tax was a restriction and thus infringed the freedoms provided that the national court found as a fact a Norwegian family foundation was objectively comparable to a Liechtenstein trust. Of more significance in the present context is the CFC point. Here, as in *Cadbury Schweppes*, the court expressly dismissed as irrelevant the fact that the Norwegian beneficiaries 'do not pay more tax on the profit of a CFC under the Tax Act than would be due were the trust or legal entity established in Norway'. The fact remained that the Norwegian taxpayers were taxed on the profits of another legal person, which would not have been the case had that legal person been a Norwegian company. On this basis, the EFTA court held the freedoms were engaged.

Olsen is significant in another respect. The taxpayer invoking the freedoms was not the settlor, who would have been the person effecting the original establishment or capital movement. Instead the taxpayers were beneficiaries of the Ptarmigan Trust. The court expressly affirmed that the rights under the freedoms were available to the trustees and the beneficiaries as well as to the settlor. Although the express reference to this point was to the freedom of establishment (at paras 102 and 103) the whole tenor of the judgment indicates it applies also to capital.

UK LEGISLATION ATTRIBUTING INCOME AND GAINS

107.6 Even though the former CFC legislation in the UK has now been repealed, there remains on the UK statute book extensive legislation attributing income or gains of non-UK entities to UK taxpayers on an arising basis. Thus the income of non-UK companies can be attributed to individual transferors under ITA 2007, ss 720 and 727 (see CHAPTER 69) and gains can in certain circumstances still be attributed to participators under TCGA 1992, s 13 (see CHAPTER 88).

In addition further anti-avoidance legislation attributes the income and gains of non-resident trusts to UK resident settlors, most notably the income tax settlement code and the rules in TCGA 1992, s 86 attributing gains to the settlor. These rules are discussed in CHAPTERS 69, 75, 76 and 88 respectively. In contrast to the former CFC rules these various rules apply principally to non-corporate taxpayers, exclusively so save for s 13.

The impact of the freedoms on each of these sets of rules is discussed separately below. In the case of transfer of assets and s 13, there is now recognition of EU law in the UK legislation and the discussion below takes account of that also.

TRANSFER OF ASSETS

107.7 As described in CHAPTER 69, the transferor charges under the transfer of assets code apply regardless of the form the non-resident entity to which the income accrues takes. However in relation to trust income the charges generally yield to the settlement code (see para 69.30) so the discussion here is couched in terms of companies and similar entities.

Corporate entities in the EU

107.8 It is clear that the rationale of *Cadbury Schweppes* applies to the transferor charges under the transfer of assets code. Indeed, the point is accepted by the UK government as ITA 2007, s 742A, enacted in 2013, acknowledges that the freedoms can disapply the charges (see CHAPTER 74).

The transfer of assets code potentially engages both the establishment and capital freedoms. Arguably the capital freedom has primacy as the very phrase 'transfer of assets' connotes or even is a synonym for 'movement of capital'. Certainly if the freedom of establishment is engaged at all it is on no view exclusive, as the transfer of assets code is not confined to companies.

Prior to the decision in *Cadbury Schweppes* it might well have been concluded the transferor charges were unaffected by the freedoms. The basis of such conclusion would have been that anti-avoidance legislation such as ss 720–730 does not, in general, result in more tax than would have been payable had the assets been retained by the transferor. But, as noted above, it is clear that this fact is not relevant. In *Cadbury Schweppes*, the ECJ expressly disallowed the argument that the tax Cadbury Schweppes was required to pay under the CFC legislation was no greater than the tax its subsidiary would have suffered if UK resident.

The motive defence explained in CHAPTER 73 might also have been adduced to reject the conclusion that ss 720–730 breach EU law. As described in CHAPTER 73, that defence was reformulated with effect from 5 December 2005. But under both the original legislation and the reformulation, there is nothing which per se precludes s 720–730 where genuine economic activities are being carried on. The first limb of the defence is failed if just one of the purposes of the transfer or associated operations was tax avoidance, and while the second limb does refer to genuine or bona fide commercial transactions, it then focuses on whether the transactions were designed for tax avoidance. Further, such compatibility as the second limb might have had with *Cadbury Schweppes* before 5 December 2005 has gone as the present law requires any tax avoidance purpose to be incidental, and excludes many types of transaction which are in fact commercial (see para 73.16).

The application of the freedoms to ss 720–730 is demonstrated by the tribunal decision in *Fisher v Revenue and Customs Comrs* [2014] UK FTT 804 (TC), 17 ITLR 141. Here UK residents had caused the telebetting business carried on by their UK company to be transferred to, and thereafter carried on by, a Gibraltar company. The avowed purpose of the exercise was to avoid UK betting duty, but the Gibraltar company genuinely carried on the business and employed the requisite staff to do so. The tribunal held that both the establishment freedom and the capital freedom disapplied the transferor charge as respects a UK resident Irish national (see further para **106.33**).

Section 742A

107.9 On the face of it s 742A ought to bring the transfer of assets code into conformity with EU Law, as Condition A disapplies the transferor charges in any case where to apply them would constitute an unjustified and disproportionate restriction on a freedom. But as explained in CHAPTER 74, in reality s 742A does not render the charges compliant. There are three reasons:

(1)   Section 742A only applies to transactions effected after 6 April 2012.
(2)   A transaction is only deemed to be genuine and so within s 742A if it is on arm's length commercial terms or falls within a limited exception made for transactions for personal reasons.
(3)   Where the income abroad is generated by activities involving the provision of goods and services, all the indicia submitted by HMRC in *Cadbury Schweppes* in relation to establishment (para **106.20** above) have to be present.

It may be suggested that the second and third of the above points would, in the event of litigation, be cured by the principle of conforming construction (see para **106.21**). In other words, despite what s 742A says its protection would extend to income arising from any transactions which in an EU sense have economic reality (see para **106.20**). But even assuming that is right, it is difficult to see conforming construction as extending s 742A to pre-2012 transactions and, to that extent at least, the transferor charges remain in breach.

Corporate entities outside the EU

107.10 As noted in para **106.22** above, the freedom of establishment does not extend to companies which are not resident in either the EU or EFTA countries. The freedom of movement of capital in Article 63, however, does, and the issue is what in practice this means to ss 720–730.

The first point to make is that capital, and thus third country movements, would not be an issue at all if ss 720–730 were confined to shareholdings giving the shareholder definite influence over the company's affairs, for then establishment would be the sole relevant freedom (see para **106.6**). But as noted above, ss 720–730 are not expressed in terms of companies at all, and if either freedom has primacy it is likely to be capital. For this reason, capital is clearly in issue.

A more substantial point is that ss 720–730 represent legislation in existence on 31 December 1993, albeit rewritten. On the face of it, this means that the standstill discussed in para **106.23** is in point. But in reality the position may not be as simple as this.

The reason is that the standstill is applicable only to certain types of capital movement, most notably direct investment and establishment (see para **106.23**). The transfer of assets code is not confined to either of these things. A further point is that referred to above, namely that important changes were made to the motive defence in 2006. The effect of those changes is to remove protection from certain commercial structures and deprive an innocent transaction protected by the motive defence of such protection if a subsequent tax driven associated operation takes place. It may be concluded that this extension of ss 720–730 would not on any view be protected by the standstill or, possibly, that ss 720–730 has lost any pre-1993 protection entirely.

For these reasons, the fact that ss 720–730 were enacted well before 1993 may not be a bar to Article 63. But at this point a third issue arises, namely whether ss 720–730 will be found to be restrictions which can be justified in relation to third countries and are proportionate.

Here the important point is that the different legal context which obtains with third countries can cause anti-avoidance legislation to be upheld as justified in circumstances where it would not be so upheld in a purely EU context. As explained in para **106.25**, the tax evasion and fiscal supervision justifications have both been expanded in this way. But even in third country contexts, anti-avoidance legislation still has to be proportionate to the objectives by which it is justified and, as explained in para **106.25**, the existence of a full double tax treaty between the UK and the country in question may preclude any such expansion of the justifications. In the present state of the jurisprudence, it is difficult to predict whether, in relation to third countries, ss 720–730 will be upheld as proportionate and, if so, whether generally or only in specific respects.

The UK government clearly considers that the capital movement freedom can in appropriate circumstances disapply ss 720–730 in cases where third countries are involved. This is apparent from ITA 2007, s 742A itself, which despite spelling out elaborate purported limitations by reference to genuine transactions, nowhere limits s 742A to income arising within the EU. It follows that s 742A is fully applicable in third country contexts, and to the extent that it either expressly or by conforming construction applies, it renders ss 720–730 EU compliant, albeit by doing what EU law would in any event do, namely disapplying the charges. But as indicated above, income rising from pre-2012 transactions is not covered by s 742A and so, to the extent not protected by justifications and the standstill, the code remains non-compliant here also.

It is perhaps apposite to add one point on the justifications, namely that it is very difficult to see the charge by reference to capital sums, ITA 2007, s 727, as being proportionate (see para **69.21**). The position could thus be reached that, in relation to third countries, s 727 is invalid (and where appropriate countered by s 742A), whereas s 720 is not.

European Economic Area

107.11 As noted in para 106.27, all the freedoms apply to the EFTA countries, namely Norway, Iceland and Liechtenstein. Further the standstill which operates in relation to capital movements involving third countries is not in point. For this reason, ss 720–730 may be precluded in relation to corporate entities established in EFTA countries. But as explained in para 106.27, the same approach to justifications is taken as with third country capital movements, which means the issues discussed in the previous paragraph are material here also.

Offshore jurisdictions

107.12 It would be tempting to conclude that all offshore jurisdictions are third countries and thus that the disapplication or otherwise of ss 720–730 as respect companies established in offshore jurisdictions turns on the scope of the capital movement freedom and the considerations set out in para 107.10. But in reality matters are not as simple as this.

On the one hand, this is because certain offshore jurisdictions are in a better position under EU law than third countries, most notably Liechtenstein, which is an EFTA member and jurisdictions such as Cyprus which are EU members. Companies formed in these jurisdictions may therefore be protected from ss 720–730 by both the establishment freedom and the capital freedom. As explained above it may be that the justifications would be more rigorously applied in relation to Liechtenstein, but even this may be precluded by the full double tax treaty between the UK and Liechtenstein (see para 106.30).

The converse position is in point as respects the British Overseas Territories and the Crown Dependencies. Here the relevant considerations are as outlined in paras 106.32 to 106.34, and it is far from clear that the capital freedom does operate in relation to companies in those jurisdictions and if it does, how far it would disapply ss 720–730. Gibraltar is in perhaps the least favourable position, as the decision in *Fisher* indicates that it counts as part of the UK. On this basis the First-tier Tribunal held UK nationals could not rely on the freedoms to disapply s 720 as respects a Gibraltar company.

SECTION 13

107.13 As explained above (para 107.4) s 13 in the form in which it existed prior to 2013 breached the capital movement freedom, and, by implication, the establishment freedom as well. The decision turned on companies in other Member States, and may not be applicable to third countries given that s 13 pre-dated 1993, albeit much amended since then. However in all probability such debate is academic as it may be suggested s 13 is now, in the main, compliant with EU Law.

The first and most important point is that the de minimis under s 13 is now 25% (see para 88.14). On the authority of *Scheunemann v Finanzamt Bremerhaven* [2012] Case C-31/11 SWTI 2358, ECJ (para 106.6 above) this restricts s 13 to situations where the participator has definite influence over the company and so renders establishment the only freedom at issue. On the basis that is right, EU law is relevant only where the company is established in the EU or an EFTA country.

The second point is that s 13 is disapplied where the asset disposed of is used in economically significant activities (para **88.5**). The definition of such activities incorporates the UK's submissions in *Cadbury Schweppes* (see para **106.20**) and to that extent may be too narrow. But it may be argued that any defect could be cured by conforming construction (see para **106.21**) and if so s 13 is, but for one point, compliant.

The one point is that under s 13, the economically significant activities defence is not in point unless the activities are carried on wholly or mainly outside the UK. There does not appear to be any support in EU law for such a limitation and to that extent, in relation to EU and EFTA entities, s 13 may still be non-compliant. It is unlikely to be saved by the s 13 motive defence (see para **88.4**) as that defence does not, as *Cadbury Schweppes* would require, restrict s 13 to wholly artificial arrangements (see para **106.15**).

Section 79B

107.14 Section 79B does two things, namely disapplying exemption relief where a treaty-protected gain is apportioned under s 13 to a trust participator and, second, requiring treaty-protected gains apportioned to a UK resident company to be further apportioned to any trustee participators in the UK company. Now that the freedom engaged by s 13 is exclusively that of establishment, EU issues with s 79B will arise only where the non-resident close company is resident in the EU or EFTA. As with s 13 generally, many if not most such cases will be protected by the motive defence or the defence for genuine economic activity and of those that are not, some at least will be deliberate and artificial attempts to secure treaty protection, as exemplified by *Wood v Holden* [2006] STC 443 (see CHAPTER 43).

But as with s 13 itself, it is possible to envisage cases where the various exemptions from s 13 are not in point and where, even if tax avoidance was intended, the wholly artificial test in *Cadbury Schweppes* is not met. As indicated above, the prime example is UK activities tainted by CGT avoidance. In such a case, justifications may be hard for the government to adduce, for s 79B was a response to schemes exploiting treaty relief and yet is disproportionate in that it applies in other contexts, and is not limited to counteraction of these schemes. If therefore an EU or EFTA company falls outside the various s 13 exemptions, the freedom of establishment may be a more compelling argument for disapplication of s 79B than with s 13 simpliciter.

TRUSTS

107.15 The income tax settlement code and TCGA 1992, s 86 both apply to trusts as distinct from corporate entities.

Characterisation of trusts

107.16 As explained in para **106.7**, the EFTA court has applied the freedoms to a trust (*Olsen v Norwegian State* [2014] Cases E-3/13 and E-20/13). To English eyes it might be thought that the freedom engaged in creating a trust must be the freedom to move capital, for a trust falls within one of the constituent elements of personal capital movements, namely a gift or endowment (see para **106.5**). But the EFTA court held that the freedom of establishment can be engaged as well.

It appears that the freedom of establishment is engaged if the trust pursues economic activities that are real and genuine. In a trust context it is difficult to see what exactly this means, but instances given by the EFTA court were involvement in the management of underlying companies or managing a pool of resources (para 99).

In the view of the EFTA court, both the establishment freedom and the capital freedom can be invoked by the trustees or the beneficiaries as well as by the settlor. Indeed it was to the beneficiaries that the freedoms were applied in *Olsen* itself. As under EU law generally, the mere fact that a trust is set up as a tax shelter is not a bar to the freedoms being applied: for the freedoms to be precluded, the trust must be a wholly artificial arrangement (para 181). It may be suggested that a trust is not such an arrangement so long as the trustees are genuinely exercising their fiduciary function of managing the investments and considering the interests of the beneficiaries.

The conclusion that trusts are within the freedoms is supported by the fact that they are in many respects comparable to foundations (see further CHAPTER 33). In *Ospelt v Schlossle Weissenberg Familienstiftung* C-452/01 [2003] ECR I-9743 (para **106.5** above) the transfer of assets to a foundation was a movement of capital as was a distribution by a foundation in *F E Familienprivatstiftung Eisenstadt, Re*: C-589/13 (2015) ECLI:EU:C:2015:612, [2015] SWTI 2756, ECJ). So too, in *Schröder v Finanzamt Hameln* [2011] STC 1248, the ECJ held that a transfer of property reserving an annuity was a movement of capital. In the light of these authorities, there can be reasonable confidence that a gift to a trust is at the very least a movement of capital.

Settlor-interested trusts within the EU

107.17 It seems unlikely that the settlements code, which attributes the income of a trust to the settlor if he is a beneficiary, infringes the freedoms. This is because ITTOIA 2005, s 624 applies as much to resident as to non-resident trusts.

A further point has also to be faced, namely the fact that the settlor of a settlor-interested trust is usually regarded as the principal beneficiary and in many cases is the person whose wishes are listened to, and who receives distributions should he ask for them. In these circumstances would the trust be regarded as a genuine gift or endowment? Or, looking at the matter another way, would there be much greater risk of it being seen as wholly artificial?

The last point may mean that TCGA 1992, s 86, the legislation attributing trust gains to the settlor, does not infringe Article 63 where the trust is settlor-interested. But the position is not clear, for TCGA 1992, s 77, the legislation attributing the gains of settlor-interested resident trusts to the settlor, ceased to be in force on 6 April 2008. This means that s 86 is like the CFC legislation in one important respect, namely that although the tax payable by the settlor in respect of a non-resident trust is no greater than that payable by a resident trust, it is payable by the settlor rather than the trust. As was decided in both *Cadbury Schweppes* and *Olsen*, such a point does not prevent anti-avoidance legislation from being a restriction.

Other trusts within the EU

107.18 Assuming the settlor and his spouse are excluded, no UK anti-avoidance legislation attributes the income of a trust to a UK resident on an arising basis. But the position is otherwise with gains, for TCGA 1992 s 86 applies where the beneficiaries of a non-resident trust include the settlor's children or grandchildren (see CHAPTER 76). There are clearly good grounds for supposing that here s 86 is a restriction, for, in its application to children's and grandchildren's settlements, s 86 has no equivalent as respects UK trusts.

The present case law indicates that it would not be a defence to the freedoms that the tax payable by the settlor under s 86 is now normally the same as the trust would pay if UK resident. As just noted, that point has been concluded by *Cadbury Schweppes* and *Olsen*. But the issue of whether a trust could be seen as wholly artificial would still be at large. Such arguments would plainly be easier for HMRC to run if all the beneficiaries were UK resident and the whole exercise was tax driven. But these points would be weaker if the beneficiaries were spread around the world and if, on the facts, the chosen jurisdiction had expertise in trust administration and suitable trust laws. Cyprus and Ireland within the EU could be cited here.

Assuming s 86 were held to be justified in principle, it could be difficult for the UK government to justify it as proportionate. In part this is because it lacks a motive defence, and in part because it visits the tax not on the persons who benefit from the gain (ie the beneficiaries) but on the settlor. This point is particularly compelling in the present context given that in the circumstances postulated here the settlor is excluded from benefit and so could not benefit from the trust gains.

Trusts outside the EU

107.19 As Article 63 applies also to movements of capital between EU and third countries, it should, if it disapplies s 86 in relation to the EU, also disapply elsewhere. It is no defence that s 86 was enacted before 1993, as gifts and endowments are not one of the kinds of capital movement to which the standstill for pre-1993 restrictions applies (see para 106.23).

But the issue would still arise of whether the different legal context applicable to third country movements would enable s 86 to be justified in relation to trusts outside the EU and, in relation to offshore jurisdictions, the various issues discussed in paras **106.28** to **106.34** are in point. The issues are the same as are discussed in relation to ss 720–730 above. Self-evidently, the chances of a justification being in point would be greater where the trust is settlor-interested than where it is not.

Trustee borrowing

107.20 It can cogently be argued that the rules as to trustee borrowing in TCGA 1992, Sch 4B (see CHAPTER 80) are without justification or, if they can be justified, that the legislation is wholly disproportionate. It may therefore be argued that Article 63 disapplies Sch 4B. Now that Sch 4B no longer applies to UK resident settlor-interested trusts this may be so both where the settlor is excluded and where he is a beneficiary.

As Sch 4B was first enacted in 2000, it would not on any view be saved in relation to non-EU countries by the standstill. It may be that Sch 4B could be justified as a response to flip-flop schemes (see para **80.2**). But even if able to be so justified it is totally disportionate, for, as explained in CHAPTER 80, its ambit is far wider. Of all anti-avoidance legislation directed at trusts, Sch 4B is most vulnerable to EU law.

Official response

107.21 As of the time of writing, neither the EU Commission nor the UK government has opined on what impact, if any, EU law may have on anti-avoidance legislation targeted on trusts.

OTHER APPLICATIONS

107.22 Although the most significant impact of EU law is on legislation which deems income or gains of overseas entities to be those of UK taxpayers, other kinds of anti avoidance legislation require consideration as well.

Hold-over relief

107.23 The UK currently has two forms of hold-over relief, namely gifts of business assets and gifts involving discretionary trusts (TCGA 1992, ss 165 and 260). Both are precluded if the recipient is non-resident. This restriction is vulnerable in the ECJ as being in breach of both the freedom of establishment and the freedom of movement of capital (see for example *X and Y, Riksskatteverket* C-436/00 [2004] STC 1271). The issue may also come to be raised of whether the vulnerability extends to all transfers to non-residents, and not just to transfers to EU or EEA residents. In that context it does have to be recognised that ss 165 and 260 were both first enacted well before 1993. But the transaction involved where hold-over relief is claimed, namely a gift, is not one of those caught by the standstill (see para **106.23**).

Trust distributions

107.24 The UK has two codes taxing capital distributions from trusts, namely the non-transferor charge in ITA 2007, ss 731–735 and the capital payments code in TCGA 1992, s 87 (see CHAPTERS 70 and 77). As discussed in para **107.16**, a distribution by a foundation has been held to be a capital movement, and it seems reasonable to assume that a distribution from a trust is a capital movement too. Assuming that it is right, there is clearly a strong argument that both codes are restrictions on capital movements in that neither income tax nor CGT attaches to capital distributions from UK trusts which have never been either or non-resident nor funded by non-resident trusts. Further, although both codes predate the standstill, they do not fall within the categories of movement caught by the standstill. It follows that capital distributions from third countries as well as from EU trusts fall to be considered.

It may be regarded as likely that ss 731–735 and s 87, by imposing the charge in respect of trust income or gains on beneficiaries in receipt of capital, would be seen as capable of being justified by one or more overriding reasons of public interest, particularly as respects trusts based outside the EU. If so, the issue will then arise of whether they are proportionate and here, as a general proposition, it might be argued that the basic concept of taxing beneficiaries by reference to receipts is. However, against this it may be said that the real issue is not whether the taxing of distributions is proportionate but whether the trust itself is a wholly artificial arrangement, with the result that if it is not the charge on distributions is per se disproportionate.

In any event, regardless of that point it can strongly be argued that particular features of the codes may not be proportionate and are thus open to EU challenge, particularly where the trust is based in the EU or an EFTA country. The following instances may be given:

(1)   Tax under ss 731–735 is at the normal income tax rates of 20%, 40% and 45%. No credit is given for foreign or UK tax suffered by the relevant income (see para **71.11**) and nor is there any acknowledgement of the fact that some or all of that income may be dividends, which would have attracted the dividend rates and tax credit if received by the beneficiary directly.

(2)   Sections 731–735 do not allocate relevant income to non-resident beneficiaries. This has the result that UK beneficiaries may be taxed by reference to all the trust income whereas in reality only a proportion of the fund is earmarked for them. This point would be particularly compelling if capitalised income remains relevant income even if genuinely paid away to a non-resident (see para **71.28**).

(3)   Should the transferor be non-UK resident all the income is relevant income despite the fact it would not have been taxable at all had he not made the transfer and retained the assets himself.

(4)   As respects s 87, supplemental tax can increase the rate of CGT to 44.8% (see para **77.48**). There may be nothing wrong with the principle of interest to compensate for deferral but the 10% rate of supplemental tax is way above market rates.

(5)   Although generally s 87 allows trust gains to be matched to distributions to non-residents, this is not true of gains in a Sch 4C pool (see para 81.7). In this regard, Sch 4C is open to the same objections as ss 731–735 (point (2) above).

It may be that the first three of the above points are covered by ITA 2007, s 742A (see CHAPTER 74). But even if that is right s 742A only applies where the relevant transaction post dates 6 April 2012 and is thus irrelevant to most existing settlements.

Foreign dividends

107.25 The case of *Manninen* [2004] STC 1444 established that it was contrary to Article 63 to attach a tax credit to dividends from companies established in the same country as the recipient of the dividend, while not giving credit to dividends paid by companies established in other Member States. The principle was extended to third country dividends in *Test Claimants in the FII Group Litigation v IRC* C-446/04 [2007] STC 326.

UK legislation has largely given effect to this line of cases. The abolition of the tax credit from 6 April 2016 does not breach the freedoms as the abolition applies equally to UK and non-UK dividends.

Emigration and exit charges

107.26 Currently the UK imposes an exit charge on companies and trusts which cease to be UK resident (see CHAPTERS 30 and 31). Individuals are not subject to an exit charge save as respects held-over gains. However, individuals becoming UK resident again after a period of non-UK residence may be taxed on their return on gains realised in the interim (see para 29.6).

It may well be that the charges on individuals would be upheld as justified by the need to protect tax revenues and be regarded as proportionate. As explained in para 106.35, in *de Lasteyrie* the ECJ indicated that taxing individuals on return after a brief stay abroad may be acceptable. So too, in *X and Y*, the CJEU indicated an exit charge on deferred gains could be an appropriate method of preventing exploitation of the deferral relief at issue in that case. *N v Inspecteur* (7 September 2006, Case C-470/04) indicates that were the UK to tax any gain accrued at the time of emigration, such would be lawful provided the tax is delayed until the assets in question are sold and allowance is made for any fall in the value of the asset between emigration and sale (*N v Inspecteur* (supra) as explained in *National Grid Indus BV v Inspecteur van de Belastingdienst Rijnmond/kantoor Rotterdam* [2012] STC 114 paras 53–56). So too the tax on emigration can be paid in instalments over a period of five years *DMC Beteiligungsgesellschaft mbH v Finanzamt Hamburg-Mitte* C-164/12 [2014] 2 CMLR 1391, [2014] STC 1345, ECJ).

A point which should be stressed is that *de Lasteyrie* and *N v Inspecteur* both turned on the freedom of establishment and thus are only in point on emigration to a Member State of the EU. *Van Hilten v Inspecteur van de Belastingdienst/Particulieren/Ondernemingen   buitenland   te   Heerlen*

C-513/03, [2008] STC 1245, discussed in para **106.35**, indicates that the emigration does not of itself engage the freedom of movement of capital. If so, exit charges on emigration to countries outside the EU (and EEA) are permissible.

The position in relation to company emigration is complicated by *R v HM Treasury, ex p Daily Mail and General Trust plc* [1988] STC 787. This was decided under the old law whereby UK registered companies could become non-resident but had to apply for Treasury Consent before doing so. The CJEU held this did not breach the freedom of establishment. Subsequently the CJEU rationalised that decision as being in point only where the company's right to retain legal personality was subject to restrictions on the transfer of effective management abroad. Accordingly exit charges levied on the migration of a company which leave its legal personality unimpaired are a restriction (*National Grid Indus BV* [2012] STC 114, para 28). But an exit charge can still be upheld if delayed until realisation of the asset and, in contrast to the position with individuals, account need not be taken of post emigration falls in value ([2012] STC 114, para 58).

The European Commission opined that the UK's exit charges on companies breached the freedom of establishment and formally requested the UK to amend the legislation (EC press release 23 March 2012, reproduced [2012] SWTI 1325). In response, the UK introduced measures allowing the exit charges to be deferred where a company becomes resident and carries on business in the EU or the EEA (TMA 1970, Sch 3ZB as inserted by FA 2013, Sch 49). In such a case the exit charge can be paid in a lump sum by six annual instalments. Alternatively each asset can be treated separately and the charge paid when the asset is disposed of, or, if it is retained, at the end of ten years.

Trust emigration does not normally involve any legal person moving abroad, but instead the retirement of UK trustees in favour of foreign trustees and the transfer of the trust assets to them. As such, in a literal sense, a movement of capital is involved. If indeed the exercise is a movement of capital, the immediate and blanket charge on emigration is, on the face of it vulnerable. Moreover, the transfer to foreign trustees does not, on the face of it, come within the standstill for pre-1993 restrictions (cf para **106.23**).

Offshore Funds

107.27 Two cases originating in Germany raise the possibility that the offshore fund legislation described in CHAPTER **95** engages the freedoms (*Finanzamt Ulm v Wagner-Raith* Case C-560/13 21 May 2015; *Van Caster v Finanzamt Essen-Süd* Case C-326/12 [2015] STC 538). Both these cases concerned legislation which required investment funds to produce to investors and publish in German certain information about distributions. In default of such information the legislation imposed flat rate taxation based on movement in the redemption price of units over the year. The ECJ held that these cases concerned the capital movement freedom, the restriction resulting from the fact that non-German funds would be unlikely to comply with the information obligations.

On the face of it, the reporting fund regime is difficult to distinguish from these German rules, and if so the imposing of income tax on offshore income gains, ie on gains on funds which choose not to report, is a restriction. It is also difficult to see what justification there might be as respects funds resident in other Member States. With third country funds different issues may arise. The standstill however is unlikely to be in point as the offshore fund rules were recast in 2009 (see para **95.1**). In this regard the UK position is potentially in contrast to that in Germany as established in *Wagner Raith* (see para **106.23**).

ENFORCING EUROPEAN LAW

107.28 The issue of how in practice to secure the benefit of a freedom is potentially of critical importance. But in some respects the law is not settled.

Filing

107.29 TMA 1970 provides a statutory procedure for claims and determining liability in the event of dispute with HMRC. That procedure involves appeals to the First-tier Tribunal and, if appropriate, to the Upper Tribunal and beyond. It should therefore be used in all cases where it is available to the taxpayer. It follows that a taxpayer wishing to displace a tax liability by reliance on a freedom should take the point when filing his return. The correct course, it may be suggested, is to complete the return on the basis the freedom applies, but make express disclosure that this has been done and indicate the income or gains which would be taxable were the freedom not in point.

The above rests on clear House of Lords authority, *Re Claimants under Loss Relief Group Litigation Order* [2005] STC 1357. It plainly covers the simple case where, at the time of filing, the taxpayer considers a freedom is in issue.

Reopening past years

107.30 The position where the taxpayer has in past years filed in disregard of the freedoms and now wishes to reopen matters is more difficult. Such reopening has been characteristic of most of the corporate cases on the freedoms, and led to the combining of claims in Group Litigation Orders, or GLOs. At the heart of the issue is whether statutory procedures should be used or whether taxpayers seeking to reopen matters have a restitutionary cause of action in the High Court.

TMA 1970 procedures

107.31 The statutory procedures for recovering overpaid tax are in TMA 1970. The House of Lords has made it clear that if the taxpayer is still within time limits to make a claim for repayment of the wrongly paid tax he should do so and, in the event of HMRC refusal, appeal (*Re Claimants under Loss Relief Group Litigation Order*, para 43). The issue of a restitutionary claim in the High Court arises only if the statutory time limits in TMA 1970 have expired or if for some other reason the TMA procedure is not in point.

Thus by way of example, in *The Trustees of the BT Pension Scheme v HMRC* [2015] EWCA Civ 713 restitution claims in the High Court were stayed pending litigation of the TMA 1970 procedures.

Until 31 Match 2010, TMA 1970, s 33 provided relief for tax paid by reason of an error or mistake in the return. It required the claim to be filed not later than five years after the 31 January next following the year of assessment to which the return related. For claims made from 1 April 2010, whichever year they relate to, a more general code entitling the taxpayer to recover tax he believes was not due (including error or mistake relief claims) applies (TMA 1970, Sch 1AB). This entitles the taxpayer to claim a repayment of tax if he considers the tax was not due. Such a claim must be made no later than four years after the end of the tax year to which it relates (Sch 1AB para 3). This code was enacted by FA 2009 and, as already indicated, took effect on 1 April 2010. It follows that if a claim can be brought within the four-year limit it can and must be so brought. It is expressly provided that a claim under Sch 1AB is the only means by which HMRC can be required to repay overpaid tax (Sch 1AB para 1(6)).

Potential causes of action in the High Court

107.32 The High Court causes of action open generally to individuals claiming redress for breaches of European law are twofold (*FII Claimants v HMRC* [2010] STC 1251, para 132, per Arden LJ). The first is a claim in damages for a serious breach of EU law. This, however, rarely arises in practice in a tax context, for the paradigm case of entitlement to damages is where the national government has disregarded settled European law (see the discussion in ibid paras 199–201). Damages cannot be recovered just because emerging CJEU jurisprudence shows with the benefit of hindsight that national legislation is in breach.

It is, therefore, the second cause of action that is normally relevant. Claims under this head are referred to in the English Courts as *San Giorgio* claims and their essence is that 'Member States are required to provide persons with an effective restitutionary remedy for repayment of charges levied in breach of Community law' (ibid para 132).

The claim is thus a claim in restitution. But the CJEU has not defined the detail of how such claims should be brought. Instead it is left to the domestic legal systems of Member States to designate which courts or tribunals have jurisdiction and to lay down the detailed procedural rules (*Metallgesellschaft v IRC* [2001] STC 452, 492, para 85). In exercising such discretion Member States are required to ensure first that the rules are no less favourable than those governing equivalent domestic actions, and second that they do not make the exercise of EU rights practically impossible or excessively difficult. These two principles are known respectively as the principle of equivalence and the principle of effectiveness (*Test Claimants in the FII Group Litigation v HMRC* Case C-446/04 [2006] ECR I-11753, [2007] STC 326 para 203, ECJ as cited by Lord Walker SCJ in *Test Claimants in the FII Group Litigation v Revenue and Customs Comrs* [2012] UKSC 19, [2012] 3 All ER 909, [2012] STC 1362).

Restitutionary remedies

107.33 In England, two kinds of restitutionary remedy are germane, namely the *Woolwich* remedy for tax unlawfully demanded and the remedy for money paid under mistake of law (see *FII Test Claimants v HMRC*, supra, para 152). The *Woolwich* remedy arose not out of an CJEU case, but because HMRC had unlawfully demanded composite-rate tax from building societies, the demand being unlawful because it was made under ultra vires regulations (*Woolwich Equitable Building Society v IRC* [1993] AC 70, [1992] 3 All ER 737, HL). The mistake of law remedy did arise out of EU law, namely the cases where the ECJ decided that ACT paid by UK subsidiaries to parent companies resident in another Member State breached EU law (see para **106.10**). The House of Lords held that ACT so paid was paid under mistake of law and that such mistake gave entitlement to restitution (*Deutsche Morgan v HMRC* [2007] STC 1).

Time limits

107.34 Under UK domestic law, these two forms of restitution are not mutually exclusive, a point of some importance, for the time-limits for a *Woolwich* claim run from when the unlawful tax is paid, whereas s 32(1)(c) of the Limitation Act 1980 applies to tax paid under mistake of law (*FII Test Claimants v HMRC*, supra, paras 230–245; *Deutsche Morgan v HMRC* [2007] STC, 1). Section 32(1)(c) prevents time from running until the claimant could with reasonable diligence have discovered the mistake.

At this point it is necessary to refer to FA 2004, s 320 and FA 2007, s 107. Section 320 disapplied the extended limitation period in relation to actions brought after 8 September 2003 and s 107 did so in relation to actions brought before then save insofar as the House of Lords had given judgment before 6 December 2006. Both sections could have been valid under EU law had they allowed an appropriate transitional period within which those affected could take up their rights under EU law. But by not doing so they potentially infringed the principle of effectiveness and also the legitimate expectation of taxpayers. Both are therefore invalid (*Test Claimants in the FII Group Litigation v HMRC* [2012] STC 1362); *Test Claimants FII Group v HMRC* Case C-362/12, [2014] STC 638; *United Kingdom v European Commission*: C-640/13 (2014) ECLI:EU:C:2014:2457, [2015] Ch 476, [2015] 2 WLR 1555, ECJ). However what is also clear is that the *Woolwich* claim on its own would have been a sufficient remedy had the mistake of law remedy not also existed, and that the latter could therefore be curtailed provided that such curtailment is neither without notice nor retroactive.

In the Court of Appeal in the *FII Group Litigation* it was held that restitutionary remedies are precluded where the statutory claims procedure under TMA 1970, s 33 could have been used had the claim been brought in time. The Supreme Court, however, decided unanimously this is not so on the basis that s 33 was not exclusive (*Test Claimants in the FII Group Litigation v HMRC* [2012] STC 1362, para 119).

The end result

107.35 The present state of the law is that the Sch 1AB claims procedure should be used wherever the claim is within the statutory four-year time limit. Should the claim be outside that time limit, the taxpayer's only possible remedy will be restitutionary remedies in the High Court, described above. Whether such remedies are in fact available will turn on whether, under EU law, the time limits now in force under Sch 1AB para 3 fall to be disapplied under the principles of equivalence and effectiveness described above. In contrast to s 33, Sch 1AB is expressed to be exclusive (para 1(6)).

IN PRACTICE

107.36 It is extremely difficult to gauge whether European law points should be taken in practice. Over the last 15 years or so, the development of CJEU jurisprudence has furnished the basis for arguments which would have at one time seemed unimaginable. There is a distinct risk of further developments opening up still more avenues, which in particular cases could be time-barred by the time any CJEU judgment is handed down. Equally many of the points which may look like possible arguments now could be closed off by future decisions. In such cases the result of taking a point on European law may simply be an expensive argument with HMRC plus (if tax has not been paid) interest and, possibly, penalties.

Any decision as to how far European law points should be taken in filing is therefore a matter of judgement. But as indicated above, what is clear is that if an item of income or gains is omitted in reliance on European law, full disclosure must be made of the facts and reasons for the omission.

Index

[all references are to paragraph number]

A

Abusive practices
freedom of establishment, and, 106.15
Accrued income profits
transfer of assets abroad, and, 68.20
Accumulation and maintenance trusts
generally, 61.16
trust immigration, and, 11.3
Advance pricing agreements
transfer pricing, and, 91.22
Agency
emigration, and, 29.8
residence of trusts, and
carrying on business, 42.15
generally, 42.16
introduction, 42.13
key issues, 42.14
meaning, 42.18
practical steps, 42.20
trusts becoming UK resident, 42.19
Agents
tax mistakes, and, 36.10
Aggregation
annual tax on enveloped dwellings,
and, 66.13
Allocation of income
non-transferors, and
allocated income, 71.21
construction issues, 71.20
HMRC discretion, 71.23–71.24
introduction, 71.18
remittance basis users, 71.26
'taken into account', 71.19
transferor cases, 71.25
unallocated income, 71.22
non-domiciliaries, and
introduction, 72.10
non-transferors, 72.12
reallocation, 72.13
transferors, 72.11
transferors, and, 69.31
American Depository Receipts (ADRs)
CGT situs rules, and, 39.9

American Depository Receipts (ADRs) – *cont.*
situs of assets, and, 38.15
source of income, and, 40.18
Annual exemption
section 87 pools, and, 77.5
Annual payments
non-residents, and, 64.13
Annual tax on enveloped dwellings (ATED)
And see **ATED-related CGT**
aggregation, 66.13
amount, 66.16
associated dwellings, 66.7
bands, 66.16
charge to tax
amount, 66.16
filing, 66.17
introduction, 66.15
payment, 66.17
chargeable interests, 66.4
collective investment schemes, 66.2
companies, 66.2
connected persons, 66.14
dwelling, 66.5
filing, 66.17
GAAR, and, 98.2
introduction, 66.1
liable persons, 66.2
liable properties
associated dwellings, 66.7
dwelling, 66.5
introduction, 66.3
linked dwellings, 66.8
single dwelling interest, 66.4
time of acquisition or disposal, 66.8
unavailability for use, 66.6
non-qualifying individual, 66.20
partnerships, 66.2
payment, 66.17
persons liable, 66.2
property development, 66.22
property rental business, 66.19
property trading, 66.22
rates and bands, 66.16

Index

Index

Index

Index

Index

Index

Index

Index

Index

Index

Index

Index

Index

Index

Index

Index